Securities Law in Canada

Cases and Commentary

THIRD EDITION

MARY G. CONDON
York University

ANITA I. ANAND
University of Toronto

JANIS P. SARRA
University of British Columbia

SARAH P. BRADLEY
Dalhousie University

emond

Toronto, Canada
2017

Emond Montgomery Publications Limited
60 Shaftesbury Avenue
Toronto ON M4T 1A3
http://www.emond.ca/lawschool

Printed in Canada.

We acknowledge the financial support of the Government of Canada. Canada

Vice president, publishing: Anthony Rezek
Publisher: Danann Hawes
Managing editor, development: Kelly Dickson
Senior editor, production: Jim Lyons
Copy editor: Boris Roginsky
Production editors: David Handelsman and Laura Bast
Permissions editor: Lisa Brant
Proofreader: Nancy Ennis
Typesetter: Tara Agnerian

Library and Archives Canada Cataloguing in Publication

Condon, M. G. (Mary Geraldine), author
Securities law in Canada : cases and commentary / Mary G. Condon, Anita I. Anand, Janis P. Sarra, Sarah P. Bradley. — Third edition.

Includes bibliographical references.
ISBN 978-1-77255-067-2 (hardback)

1. Securities—Canada—Cases. 2. Securities—Canada—Textbooks. I. Anand, Anita, author II. Sarra, Janis Pearl, author III. Bradley, Sarah P., author IV. Title.

KE1065.C65 2017 346.71'092 C2016-906326-7
KF1070.C65 2017

This book is dedicated with love to our families

Nora, Alana, David

Anand, Sonia, Monica, Kashia

Samantha, Danielle, Alexander, and the grandchildren—
Amadea, Jolie, and Carmen

Clarence

Preface to the Third Edition

As in the earlier editions, the objective of the third edition of *Securities Law in Canada: Cases and Commentary* is to give students a solid grounding in the basic principles and practical operation of securities law. It also aims to locate legal developments in this area within broader debates about the role played by securities markets, and regulation of those markets, in the economy and, more generally, in society. The book responds to the rapid pace of change in the securities law field by providing a timely, accurate, and comprehensive account of the current governing principles therein and proposals for reform. It makes a significant contribution by providing contemporary commentary on emerging legal issues not yet canvassed in detail in the academic literature in Canada. A further important goal is to introduce students to the rich language of securities regulation, and to give them an appreciation of the possibilities for contesting the objectives and implementation of the law. We have also drawn from a broad range of secondary literature relevant to securities law in order to give students a flavour of multiple perspectives on the evolution and operation of the law.

Five major themes of the casebook are (1) an assessment of the level of harmonization or divergence of provincial securities law across Canada and an account of developments to date concerning the cooperative regulator initiative; (2) a reflection on the increasing significance of norms and rules of securities regulation to the governance of both public and private firms in Canada; (3) an assessment of the increasing scope for investors' civil remedies in Canada; (4) a discussion of the broad scope of the regulatory power to administer law in this area; and (5) an analysis of securities regulators' responses to the global financial crisis in a number of substantive areas of law. The casebook will be of interest to students of securities law, advanced corporate law, and, indeed, administrative law.

The pace and complexity of change in securities law in Canada has continued since the first and second editions were published, and we have tried to provide students with a guide through the maze of recent actual and potential legal developments, emphasizing those that we think are particularly important to have a good understanding of the scope of the field. We have endeavoured to state the law as of September 1, 2016; responsibility for any errors remains ours.

One of the most rewarding aspects of undertaking this casebook has been the opportunity for us to work together as co-authors on the project, and we think that the finished product is much richer as a result of our mutual collaboration. In this edition, we are delighted to welcome a fourth co-author, Sarah P. Bradley, formerly a professor of corporate and securities law at Dalhousie Schulich School of Law and currently serving as the Canadian Ombudsman for Banking Services and Investments. We would like to express our gratitude to Paul Emond for affording us the opportunity to engage in this fruitful collaboration. We also thank his colleagues Jim Lyons, David Handelsman, and Laura Bast at Emond Publishing for their patience and support. Once again we owe ongoing gratitude to Nancy Ennis for carefully and diligently shepherding this edition through the final stages of publication.

Each of us has additional people we would like to acknowledge for their assistance. In previous editions, Mary Condon benefited greatly from the excellent and efficient research assistance of Sumbul Ali, Zara Merali, and Virginia Torrie as well as the secretarial help of Lynne Fonseca. In the preparation of this edition, she was ably assisted by Marah Smith, Senior Legal Counsel at the Ontario Securities Commission, Colin Lyon, JD student at Osgoode Hall Law School, and Nadia Azizi. Anita Anand would like to express deep thanks to Ryan Sheahan for his dedication to the preparation of the first edition of the casebook, to Amanda Melvin and Emily Bala for invaluable research during the preparation of the second edition, and to Alexander Buckley for his commitment to assisting with the revisions in this edition. Janis Sarra acknowledges with sincere appreciation the assistance of Andrew Burton, Nathalie Golay, Jason Fisher, Bernard Lau, and Jeremy Feist in the first two editions, and Jeremy Bally and Ty Dergousoff for their research assistance with this edition, and expresses heartfelt thanks to Ronald Davis for critiquing a draft of the book.

M.C.
A.A.
J.S.
S.B.

Acknowledgments

A book of this nature borrows heavily from other published material. We have attempted to request permission from, and to acknowledge in the text, all sources of such material. We wish to make specific references here to the authors, publishers, journals, and institutions that have generously given permission to reproduce in this text works already in print. If we have inadvertently overlooked an acknowledgment or failed to secure a permission, we offer our sincere apologies and undertake to rectify the omission in the next edition.

Alberta Law Review Adam Pritchard & Janis P Sarra, "Securities Class Actions Move North: A Doctrinal and Empirical Analysis of Securities Class Actions in Canada" (2009) 47:4 Alta L Rev. Reprinted with permission.

American Bar Association Homer Kripke, "The Myth of the Informed Layman" (1973) 28 Bus Lawyer 631. Reprinted with permission.

Anita Anand Anita Anand, "Regulating Systemic Risk in Canadian Financial Markets" (16 May 2016) 18 One Issue, Two Voices, online: <https://www.wilsoncenter.org/publication/one-issue-two-voices-systemic-financial-risk>. Reprinted with permission.

Anita Anand Anita Anand & Vijay Jog, "Diversity on Boards" (2014) Canadian Law and Economics Association Working Paper. Reprinted with permission.

Brad M. Barber & Terrance Odean Brad M Barber & Terrance Odean, "The Behavior of Individual Investors" (2011). Reprinted with permission.

Canadian Public Policy William J McNally & Brian F Smith, "Do Insiders Play by the Rules?" (2003) 29:2 Can Pub Pol'y 125. Reprinted with permission.

Department of Finance Expert Panel on Securities Regulation, *Creating an Advantage in Global Capital Markets: Final Report and Recommendations* (Ottawa: Department of Finance, January 2009), online: <http://www.expertpanel.ca/eng/reports/final-report/index.html>. Reproduced with the permission of the Department of Finance, 2016.

Department of Finance Expert Panel on Securities Regulation, *Draft Securities Act: Commentary* (January 2009), online: <http://www.expertpanel.ca/eng/reports/final-report/index.html>. Reproduced with the permission of the Department of Finance, 2016.

Department of Finance Mary Condon, "The Use of Public Interest Enforcement Orders by Securities Regulators in Canada" in A Douglas Harris, ed, *WPC—Committee to Review the Structure of Securities Regulation in Canada: Research Studies* (Ottawa: Department of Finance, 2003), online: <http://www.wise-averties.ca/report_en.html>. Reproduced with the permission of the Department of Finance, 2016.

Department of Finance The Cooperative Capital Markets Regulatory System Governance and Legislative Framework (September 2014), online: <http://ccmr-ocrmc.ca/wp-content/uploads/Commentary-English1.pdf>. Reproduced with the permission of the Department of Finance, 2016.

Department of Finance Poonam Puri, "The Role of Local and Regional Interests in the Design of Optimal Securities Regulatory Structure for Canada" (Ottawa: Department of Finance, 2003). Commissioned Reports and Studies. Paper No 118. Reprinted with permission of the Department of Finance, 2016.

Department of Finance Janis Sarra, *Proportionate Securities Regulation: The Potential for Scaled Treatment of Junior Issuers*. Research Study for the Expert Panel on Securities Regulation (September 2008), online: <http://www.expertpanel.ca/eng/reports/final-report/index.html>. Reproduced with the permission of the Department of Finance, 2016.

Department of Finance The Wise Persons' Committee to Review the Structure of Securities Regulation in Canada (WPC), *It's Time* (Ottawa: Department of Finance, December 2003). Reprinted with permission of the Department of Finance, 2016.

Mark DesLauriers Mark DesLauriers, "Commentary on the Evolving Role of Stock Exchanges in Canada" in Anita I Anand & William F Flanagan, eds, *Responding to Globalization: Papers Presented at the 8th Queen's Annual Business Law Symposium 2001* (Kingston, Ont: Faculty of Law, Queen's University, 2002).

Foundation Press William A Klein, John C Coffee Jr & Frank Partnoy, *Business Organization and* Finance, 11th ed (New York: Foundation Press, 2010). Reprinted by permission of West Academic.

Georgia Law Review Faith Stevelman Kahn, "Fiduciary Duty, Limited Liability, and the Law of Delaware: Transparency and Accountability—Rethinking Corporate Fiduciary Law's Relevance to Corporate Disclosure" (2000) 34 Ga L Rev 505.

The Globe and Mail Anita Anand, "One Case, Two Commissions, Several Novel Securities Issues," *The Globe and Mail* (22 July 2016). Reprinted with permission.

Harvard University Press Frank H Easterbrook & Daniel R Fischer, *The Economic Structure of Corporate Law* (Cambridge, Mass: Harvard University Press, 1991). Copyright 1991 by the President and Fellows of Harvard College.

Harvard University Press Richard A Posner, *A Failure of Capitalism: The Crisis of '08 and the Descent into Depression* (Cambridge, Mass: Harvard University Press, 2009). Copyright 2009 by the President and Fellows of Harvard College.

Harvard University Press Michael J Trebilcock, *The Limits of Freedom of Contract* (Cambridge, Mass: Harvard University Press, 1993). Copyright 1993 by the President and Fellows of Harvard College.

Robb C. Heintzmann, Michael D. Schafler, and Solomon Lam Robb C Heintzmann, Michael D Schafler & Solomon Lam, "Secondary Market Liability in Canada: Securities Class Actions" Fraser Milner Casgrain LLP, March 2012. Reprinted with permission.

International Organization of Securities Commissions Board of the International Organization of Securities Commissions, *Strategic Framework for Investor Education and Financial Literacy: Final Report* (Madrid: IOSCO, October 2014), online: <http://www.iosco.org/library/pubdocs/pdf/IOSCOPD462.pdf>. Reprinted with permission.

International Organization of Securities Commissions "Fact Sheet" (October 2016), online: <http://www.iosco.org/about/pdf/IOSCO-Fact-Sheet.pdf>. Reprinted with permission.

Investment Industry Regulatory Organization of Canada Investment Investment Industry Regulatory Organization of Canada, *Our Role & Mandate*, online: <http://www.iiroc.ca/about/ourroleandmandate/Pages/default.aspx>. Reprinted with permission.

Irwin Law Jeffrey G MacIntosh & Christopher C Nicholls, *Securities Law* (Toronto: Irwin, 2002). Reprinted with permission.

John Wiley and Sons Mary Condon, "Technologies of Risk? Regulating Online Investing in Canada" (2004) 26:3-4 Law & Pol'y 411. Reprinted with permission.

Marcel Kahan and Edward Rock Marcel Kahan & Edward Rock, "The Hanging Chads of Corporate Voting" (2008), online: <http://ssrn.com/abstract=1007065>. Reprinted with permission.

LexisNexis Canada David Johnston, Kathleen Doyle Rockwell & Cristie Ford, *Canadian Securities Regulation*, 5th ed (Markham, Ont: LexisNexis Canada, 2014). © LexisNexis Canada Inc., 2014. Reprinted with permission.

T.E. Lynch TE Lynch, "Derivatives: A Twenty-First Century Understanding" (2011) 43:187 Loy U Chicago LJ 5. Reprinted with permission.

McGill Law Journal Anita Anand, "The Future of Poison Pills in Canada: Are Takeover Bid Reforms Needed?" (2015) 61:1 McGill LJ 1. Reprinted with permission.

National Post Anita Anand, "Break Fees: Loathed but Legal," *National Post* (5 March 2002) FP11. Reprinted with permission.

Ontario Securities Commission Gordon Coleman, Garfield Emerson, & David Jackson, *Report of the Committee to Review the Provisions of the Securities Act (Ontario) Relating to Take-Over Bids and Issuer Bids* (Toronto: Ontario Securities Commission, 1983). Reprinted with permission.

Ontario Securities Commission *The Fair Dealing Model: Concept Paper of the Ontario Securities Commission* (January 2004). Reprinted with permission.

Ontario Securities Commission Insider Trading Task Force, *Illegal Insider Trading in Canada: Recommendations on Prevention, Detection and Deterrence* (November 2003).

Ontario Securities Commission Ontario Securities Commission, Office of the Chief Economist, *One Step Forward: A Study of the Economic Impact of OSC Rule 45-501, Exempt Distributions* (Toronto: Ontario Securities Commission, 2003). Reprinted with permission.

Osgoode Hall Law Journal Anita Anand & Mary Condon, "Weather, Leather, and the Obligation to Disclose: *Kerr v Danier Leather Inc*" (2006) 44 Osgoode Hall LJ 727. Reprinted with permission.

Adam Pritchard Adam Pritchard, "Well-Known Seasoned Issuers in Canada" Research Report for the IDA Task Force to Modernize Securities Legislation in Canada, *Canada Steps Up* (4 October 2006), vol 5. Reprinted with permission.

Publications Ontario *Five Year Review Committee Final Report—Reviewing the Securities Act (Ontario)* (21 March 2003). © Queen's Printer for Ontario, 2003. Reproduced with permission.

Thomson Reuters Canada Ltd. Borden Ladner Gervais [BLG], *Securities Law and Practice*, 3rd ed (Toronto: Thomson Canada) (looseleaf). Reproduced by permission of Thomson Reuters Canada Limited.

Thomson Reuters Canada Ltd. Mark R Gillen, *Securities Regulation in Canada* (Toronto: Thomson Carswell, 2007). Reproduced by permission of Thomson Reuters Canada Limited.

Thomson Reuters Canada Ltd. Christopher C Nicholls, *Corporate Finance and Canadian Law*, 2nd ed (Toronto: Carswell, 2013). Reprinted with permission.

TMX Group The Montréal Exchange, *Overview*, online: <http://www.m-x.ca/qui_bref_en.php>. Reprinted with permission.

TMX Group TMX Group, *Connecting Global Capital Markets to Canada*, formerly available online: <http://www.tsx.com/en/about_tsx/corporate_information>. Reprinted with permission.

UBC Law Review Stuart Morrow, "Proxy Contests and Shareholder Meetings" (2003) 36 UBC L Rev 483. Reprinted with permission.

UBC Law Review Janis Sarra, "The Corporation as Symphony: Are Shareholders First Violin or Second Fiddle?" (2003) 36 UBC L Rev 403. Reprinted with permission.

University of Michigan Journal of Law Reform RJ Herron, "Regulating Viatical Settlements: Is the Invisible Hand Picking the Pockets of the Terminally Ill?" (1995) 28:4 U Mich JL Ref 931. Reprinted with permission.

University of Toronto Press Mary G Condon, *Making Disclosure: Ideas and Interests in Ontario Securities Regulation* (Toronto: University of Toronto Press, 1998). Reprinted with permission.

University of Toronto Press J Peter Williamson, *Securities Regulation in Canada* (Toronto: University of Toronto Press, 1960). Reprinted with permission.

Virginia Law Review Frank Easterbrook & Daniel Fischel, "Mandatory Disclosure and the Protection of Investors" (1984) 70 Va L Rev 669. Reprinted with permission.

Martin Wheatley Martin Wheatley, "Human Face of Regulation" (Speech delivered at the London School of Economics, 10 April 2013), online: Financial Conduct Authority <http://www.fca.org.uk/news/speeches/human-face-of-regulation>.

Summary Table of Contents

Detailed Table of Contents

Table of Cases

A page number in boldface type indicates that the text of the case or a portion thereof is reproduced. A page number in lightface type indicates that the case is quoted briefly or discussed by the author. Cases mentioned within excerpts are not listed.

Introduction

In the six years that have passed since we prepared the last edition of this text, changes to securities regulation at the global, national, and local levels—some of them quite fundamental—have continued unabated. At the global level, the International Organization of Securities Commissions (IOSCO) has continued to assert itself as a standard setter of securities law norms for adoption in domestic jurisdictions. In particular, IOSCO developed a new urgency to accommodate the concerns of retail investors in the markets in a variety of ways. Relatedly, provincial securities regulators in Canada began to implement the undertakings made by G20 finance ministers to address some of the causes of the global financial crisis (GFC). This includes initiatives related to the regulation of derivatives trading and systemic risk. At the national level in Canada, the Supreme Court ruled in 2011 on the question of whether the federal government had jurisdiction to regulate securities markets. From a securities policy perspective, attention to retail investor issues has resulted in significant debates about the legal framework governing the provision of financial services. In addition, the economic downturn in the wake of the GFC has prompted a focus on new mechanisms for businesses to raise capital, including a crowdfunding regime. Most recently there has also been fundamental change to the takeover bid rules governing changes of control in Canadian public companies. Meanwhile, jurisprudence has finally begun to accumulate on the interpretation of some of the secondary market civil liability provisions in provincial securities acts. All of nts will be addressed in the chapters to follow. Having said that, the same hat we expressed last time round still stands, which is that we do not aim ovide a complete description of the current state of securities regulation in inces and territories, but it is an important goal of this casebook to convey a flavour of both the attempts to harmonize substantive provisions of provincial securities regulation across the country and the important differences that remain.

In this introduction, we hope to accomplish three things. The first is to provide students coming to securities law for the first time with a brief overview of the scope of the subject and the topics to be canvassed in the chapters that follow. The second is to identify a number of possible intellectual frameworks that could be or have been used to explain, critique, or suggest reform to the current iteration of securities law rules in various provinces. The third is to help students navigate the initially confusing layers of "law" in this area by describing the various sources of relevant legal and regulatory pronouncements.

I. WHAT IS SECURITIES REGULATION ABOUT?

As we will see when cataloguing the sources of securities law, securities regulation is largely statutory law, or law derived from various forms of delegated legislation. In that sense, it requires greater attention to issues of statutory interpretation than many other "common law" subjects. Substantively, securities law is the law relating to the issuing of various types of financial instruments or claims, known as securities, by business or financial organizations to purchasers, with a view to raising capital for enterprises. The classic example of a security is a company share, but we will canvass in Chapter 1 some more challenging examples of financial instruments where the boundary line between what is and what is not a security is blurred. Both of these forms of security are described in Chapter 1. One of the roles of securities law is to govern the capital-raising process. The basic assumption is that an efficient capital-raising process for business enterprises is central to a healthy economy. To achieve this objective, it is thought necessary for prospective investors to have well-founded confidence in the ability of securities markets to act as intermediary between investors and business enterprises. A set of legal rules is supposed to enhance that confidence. In general terms, then, securities regulation is the ongoing attempt to draw a balance between an efficient capital-raising process and the operation of efficient securities markets, and an acceptable comfort level for investors that business enterprises of one kind or another are a good place to invest their savings. The objectives of Ontario securities law, for example, are expressed in s 1.1 of the Ontario *Securities Act*, RSO 1990, c S.5, as amended (OSA) as being "(a) to provide protection to investors from unfair, improper or fraudulent practices; and (b) to foster fair and efficient capital markets and confidence in capital markets." Of course, not all of those subject to regulation believe that the government or the regulators get this balance right. We will see many examples of contestation about this issue in the pages to follow. Some current examples include the very definition of a "security" itself, as well as the ways that exemptions from the foundational prospectus requirement in securities regulation are formulated. The latter, in particular, as we shall see in Chapter 5, has been the subject of vigorous debate since the asset-backed commercial paper (ABCP) crisis occurred in Canada, since the market for ABCP grew significantly because of the existence of a specific prospectus exemption available for the issuance of short-term debt. It is clear, however, that the ideas of fairness and confidence expressed in the goals of securitie ambiguity and require regulators to exercise judgment in a variety

How does securities law assist in regulating economic activity? security is, it establishes the legal requirements to be fulfilled by iss to validly sell the securities to purchasers. Even more important fror view, it creates exceptions to those rules. Securities law also clarifies ities of issuers to purchasers and repurchasers of their securities in the secondary trading markets (where already-issued securities trade). This body of law also deals with legal requirements imposed on those in a special position in the issuer (including those in effective control of it) who wish to sell their securities. It establishes other requirements for more general changes in control of the issuer by way of the sale of issuer securities. Importantly, securities law also provides both civil and criminal remedies for breaches of the substantive requirements of the law, the most notorious of which is the prohibition against insider trading.

One might also argue that the picture painted above of the core of securities law is rather outdated and that while historically securities regulation might have developed to facilitate capital raising, its more important role today is to regulate the sale to investors of a wide variety of investment products that are intended to diversify risk for those investors and allow them to be exposed to the market as a whole by investing modest amounts of savings. This view is bolstered by the reality that the amount of money invested in asset classes such as mutual funds in Canada is broadly equivalent to half of the market capitalization of the TSX. Yet the regulation of investment products and the intermediaries who sell them in the markets, such as brokers, advisers, and mutual fund sales personnel, remains largely unaddressed in basic law school courses (see Mary Condon, "A Discipline in Search of Itself? Contemporary Challenges for Securities Law in Canada" (2014) 65 UNBLJ 340). It is assumed that investors, while they may benefit from the expertise provided by these intermediaries, also need to be protected from the risk that these professionals will be tempted by the possibilities for advancing their own personal interests at the expense of their clients. The regulation of financial market intermediaries begins from the legal proposition that all trading in, or advising about, securities transactions requires the trader to be registered. (See e.g. OSA, s 25.) Over time, a large variety of categories of registration developed in Canadian securities regulation. In fall 2009, a major harmonization effort was accomplished in the registration area with the introduction of NI 31-103, *Registration Requirements and Exemptions*, which recast those categories of registration, streamlined substantive registration requirements, and clarified the role of self-regulatory organizations in this area. In sum, securities law is often described as being composed of three main strategies of regulation: (1) disclosure of information, (2) registration requirements, and (3) after-the-fact enforcement by regulators or investors themselves. (See OSA, s 2.1 and David Johnston, Kathleen Doyle Rockwell & Cristie Ford, *Canadian Securities Regulation*, 5th ed (Toronto: Butterworths, 2014).) The chapters to follow canvass all of these issues in detail.

In the preceding description of the main contours of many provincial securities acts in Canada, it is worth noting that securities law governs only some aspects of the relationship between a business organization and its investors. Provincial and federal corporate law also deals with this relationship, as does commercial law. Indeed, one ongoing theme in academic commentary on securities law is the plausibility or otherwise of a clear dividing line between what constitutes corporate law and what is securities law. This issue is addressed in [illegible]7. (See Anita Anand, "OSC's Power Warrants Close Scrutiny," *Financial Post* (27 June [illegible]) FP11.) Of course, business enterprises that do not issue securities to the "public" may [illegible]t have to worry about the dictates of securities law, but many enterprises are subject to both sets of enactments. Furthermore, business organizations have legal relationships and responsibilities to constituencies other than their investors, such as their employees, consumers, and creditors. These relationships are outside the purview of securities law per se. We will see, however, that, in accordance with the expressed goals of securities legislation, securities regulators focus a great deal of effort on maintaining confidence in securities markets generally, as well as legal relations between individual issuers and their investors. This task is becoming ever more significant as the financial markets become an increasingly vital source of wealth in the economy generally, and may explain why the deployment of regulatory resources in the area of securities law has remained robust. The role played by financial markets is evidenced both by the numbers of people who work in the financial services sector and, more significantly, as described in Chapter 3, by the increasing numbers of Canadians who depend for their retirement financial well-being on returns from investments in securities markets. (See also Mary Condon, "Privatizing Pension Risk: Gender, Law and Financial Markets" in B Cossman & J Fudge, eds, *Privatization, Law, and the Challenge to Feminism* (Toronto: University of Toronto Press, 2002) 128.)

Reference to the role played by the financial markets in securing the financial well-being of "ordinary Canadians" should not obscure the fact that there is more than one kind of investor in securities markets. The scholarship in this area, and, in some instances, securities legislation as well, often makes a distinction between the needs of retail investors and those of institutional investors. The latter category includes various types of financial organizations such as banks, insurance companies, mutual funds, hedge funds, and pension funds, for whom investment in securities markets is a professional activity. The supposed tension between the respective regulatory needs of these constituencies is reflected in a variety of ways in substantive securities regulation. Examples include the exemption of issuers from information disclosure requirements when dealing with so-called accredited investors (see Chapter 5) and the existence of exemptions from the takeover bid regulatory regime for "private agreement" or "control block" takeovers (see Chapter 9). (See also Donald C Langevoort, "Selling Hope, Selling Risk: Some Lessons for Law from Behavioral Economics about Stockbrockers and Sophisticated Customers" (1996) 84 Cal L Rev 627.)

II. INTELLECTUAL PERSPECTIVES ON SECURITIES LAW

Like any other body of law, securities law can be analyzed in either normative or descriptive terms. Normatively, the analyst can assess the values or goals that are or should be achieved by various aspects of the law under consideration. Descriptively, the analyst can examine the operation of the body of law with a view to understanding why it operates the way it does, or why it came into being as it has. There is obviously scope for overlap between these two approaches to analyzing law, with some approaches—for example, a neoclassical economic approach—purporting to be both normative and descriptive. We consider it useful at the outset to canvass some salient frameworks for analysis that could be used to evaluate specific aspects of the substance of securities law. We start with arguably the most widely employed intellectual perspective on securities law, that of neoclassical economic analysis. We will see, however, that this approach has been found wanting by some commentators in the wake of the financial crisis. One argument, deployed by behavioural economists, is that neoclassical economics is flawed because it proceeds from an inadequate understanding of how individuals actually interact with markets. The implication is that regulators of markets should use the insights about how individuals actually conduct themselves in markets to inform their policy-making efforts. Other forms of critical analysis subject the activity of regulation to close analysis in order to understand how policy and rules governing markets actually come to exist.

A. Neoclassical Economic Analysis

The underlying premise of this approach is that individuals should be free as far as possible to make their own choices, because individuals are capable of acting rationally so as to maximize their own welfare. Overall welfare is maximized when the bargains that individuals enter into make them better off, and no one is thereby made worse off. As the excerpt below explains, this notion of Pareto efficiency is enhanced by the Kaldor-Hicks version of efficiency, which is said to result when the winners, in any particular bargaining situation, could compensate the losers and still come out ahead. Further, markets are typically the best organizing device for facilitating the making of individual bargains. Thus, legal rules or government intervention should replace or frame private bargaining in markets only in limited situations. One situation would be the case of "market failure." In the securities law context, market failure would occur when efficient transactions do not result because the market fails to voluntarily provide sufficient information on which to base an investment decision. Disclosure rules in securities law are often analyzed and/or critiqued in these terms. Another legitimate role for securities laws might be that of "gap filling." This is the idea that securities regulation can supply the terms of individual bargains that contractors would have required had they addressed their minds to these issues. A related economic rationale for having a legal rule in any particular instance is that the effect of having the rule lowers the transaction costs that would otherwise be incurred in the making of individual bargains. The excerpt below explains some of these issues at greater length. As you read it, consider how it might apply to securities regulation specifically.

Michael J Trebilcock, *The Limits of Freedom of Contract*
(Cambridge, Mass: Harvard University Press, 1993) ch 1 (footnotes omitted)

The central preoccupation of economics is the question of choice under conditions of scarcity. Given scarcity, economics assumes that individuals and communities will (or should) attempt to maximize their desired ends (which may be of infinite variety) by doing the best they can with the limited resources (means) at their disposal. To the extent that means (or resources) can be made relatively less scarce, or stretched further, more ends or goals of individuals or communities can be realized. Obviously the legal system, in important ways, structures the choices available to individuals and groups in a broad range of settings. In analyzing issues of choice under conditions of scarcity and subject to other constraints, including those imposed by the legal system, neo-classical economics employs two conceptually different kinds of analysis. The first is conventionally referred to as positive analysis, meaning descriptive or predictive analysis. The second is normative analysis, meaning prescriptive or judgmental analysis. The first kind of analysis tends to be much less controversial than the second.

Positive Economics

An analyst adopting a positive economic perspective tends to ask the following kind of question: If this (legal) policy is adopted, what predictions can we make as to the probable economic impacts, allocative (the pattern of economic activities) and distributive (winners and losers), of the policy, given the ways in which people are likely to respond to the particular incentives or disincentives created by the policy? In predicting these behavioural responses, the positive analyst will assume that most individuals are motivated by rational self-interest, in the sense of maximizing their individual utilities, subject to whatever constraints are imposed on the choices open to them. Utility functions may be infinitely varied. Mother Teresa may be motivated out of pure altruism to buy rice on the best possible terms from rice dealers to feed starving children in the streets of Calcutta. Another person may be motivated out of a desire to sustain a decadent lifestyle to buy narcotics for dealing to drug addicts, causing enormous human suffering as a result. In conventional supply and demand analysis, it is assumed that in most contexts more goods or services will be supplied at higher than lower prices and that fewer goods or services will be demanded at higher prices than lower prices—supply curves slope up to the right, demand curves slope down to the right. Even the supply of altruism is likely to be inversely related to its cost; for example, more blood (a renewable resource) is likely to be supplied altruistically than are steak and potatoes. Thus, positive economic analysis is individualistic and subjective in its behavioural premises. A positive analyst of legal issues back in the 1920s might have asked, what behavioural responses on both the supply and demand sides can be predicted in reaction to Prohibition laws? Similar questions might be asked today about various features of the war on drugs. Or the analyst might ask, what kind of first- and second-order behavioural responses might one predict to rent control laws, or agricultural supply management regimes that impose price floors and production quotas on producers, or minimum wage laws, or cost-plus regulation of public utilities, or exclusive dealing contracts, or the adoption of strict products liability over negligence? and so on. Understanding the incentives effects of these various regimes is a necessary prelude to formulating normative judgments as to the merits of the regime under analysis relative to different policies that might be employed to pursue the same or alternative social goals.

• • •

Normative Economics

The orientation of normative economic analysis, like positive analysis, is individualistic and subjective. This style of analysis—conventionally referred to as welfare economics—would tend to ask the question, is it likely that this particular transaction, or this particular proposed policy or legal change, will make individuals affected by it better off in terms of how they perceive their own welfare (not how some external party might judge individuals' welfare)? In this context, two concepts of efficiency are of central importance: Pareto efficiency and Kaldor-Hicks efficiency. Pareto efficiency would ask of any transaction or policy or legal change, will this transaction or change make somebody better off while making no one worse off? Kaldor-Hicks efficiency, in contrast, would ask the question, would this collective decision (for example, a change in legal rules) generate sufficient gains to the beneficiaries of the change that they could, hypothetically, compensate the losers from the change so as to render the latter fully indifferent to it but still have gains left over for themselves? This second approach is effectively a form of cost-benefit analysis. Let me elaborate a little on these two concepts of efficiency.

Neo-classical economists in general attach strong normative value to regimes of private exchange and private ordering and often bring some degree of scepticism to bear on the capacity of collective decision-makers, including legislatures, regulators, bureaucrats, or indeed courts, to adopt policies or laws that will unambiguously increase net social welfare. This predilection for private ordering over collective decision-making is based on a simple (perhaps simple-minded) premise: if two parties are to be observed entering into a voluntary private exchange, the presumption must be that both feel the exchange is likely to make them better off, otherwise they would not have entered into it. Thus, in most exchanges, the economic presumption is that they make all the parties thereto better off, that is, they are Pareto superior. This presumption is rebuttable by reference to a fairly conventional list of forms of market failure or, in a transaction-specific context, contracting failure, which neo-classical economists recognize as inconsistent with this presumption, for example, monopoly, externalities, information failures. Or, as Milton Friedman puts the presumption in *Capitalism and Freedom*: "The possibility of coordination through voluntary cooperation rests on the elementary—yet frequently denied—proposition that both parties to an economic transaction benefit from it, provided the transaction is bilaterally voluntary and informed."

Collective decisions which are not the result of voluntary agreement among all affected parties may technically be able to satisfy the Pareto criterion (making some better off and none worse off), but typically such decisions will generate both winners and losers. The question for the economist then becomes whether the net effect of these decisions is an increase in social welfare as judged by all affected individuals in terms of the impact of such decisions on their levels of present or prospective utility. The central difficulty here is that these impacts on individuals' utility functions are not directly observable by collective decision-makers and there is no ready way of ensuring accurate revelation by individuals of their evaluation of these impacts, thus rendering the utilities and disutilities associated with such a decision largely unmeasurable and incommensurable. For example, suppose that it were proposed that a major new multi-lane highway be constructed through an urban area, generating gains in utility for commuters from more distant areas but losses in utility to inner-city residents immediately adjacent to the throughway. How can decision-makers be confident that the net effect on social welfare of a decision to proceed with construction of the throughway will be positive? Similar questions arise with respect to changes in legal regimes which are imposed on affected parties by collective decision and which make some individuals better off and others worse off. How does one go about determining whether the gains in utility to one group exceed the losses in utility to the other? Thus, economists feel much more confident making welfare judgements about the impact of private exchanges on the parties thereto than the impact of collective decisions on all parties affected by them.

. . .

Reducing Transaction Costs

A second economic function of the law of contracts is to supply parties to given categories of exchanges with standard sets of implied terms, which in most cases save the parties the transaction costs entailed in fully specifying a complete contingent claims contract, but typically leave them free to contract out of these rules if they find them inappropriate to their particular transaction. In addition to various aspects of the common law of contracts, many statutes dealing with sales law and partnership law, and perhaps certain aspects of corporation statutes, can be thought of in these terms.

Filling Gaps in Incomplete Contracts

A related function of the law of contracts is to provide a set of default or background rules where the explicit terms of a contract are incomplete, not because the parties consciously adverted to the default or background rules and accepted them as appropriate to their transaction, but typically because particular contingencies were not consciously adverted to by one or the other party (or both) at all. Here, an economic framework of analysis would tend to ask, what rule would maximize the parties' joint welfare, on the assumption that this rule would generally be the rule that rational parties would have agreed to ex ante?

Thus, from an economic perspective, one could analyze various securities law rules in terms of whether they work to reduce transaction costs, thereby contributing to the efficiency of securities markets. Similarly, disclosure of information is said to contribute to the informational efficiency of these markets, as well as to the level of investor protection provided therein. The question for analysts of securities law is whether mandatory disclosure rules are more efficient than private bargaining about information provision. From a normative point of view, economists also debate the extent to which investor protection should be a predominant policy goal with respect to the operation of securities markets. Easterbrook and Fischel are two scholars that have attempted to address these questions in the US securities regulatory context, as the excerpt below demonstrates.

Frank H Easterbrook & Daniel R Fischel,
The Economic Structure of Corporate Law
(Cambridge, Mass: Harvard University Press, 1991)
276-79, 286-90 (footnotes omitted)

We turn to the principal federal component of corporate law: the need to disclose information before selling securities or collecting proxies from investors. Fitting these mandatory rules into the contractual framework poses something of a challenge. Why are the securities laws mandatory rather than enabling? Why do they govern disclosure rather than the price or contents of securities? Why are they federal? On the normative side, do the securities laws offer benefits for investors? ...

The securities laws have had, since their enactment in 1933 and 1934, two basic components: a prohibition against fraud, and requirements of disclosure when securities are issued and periodically thereafter. The notorious complexities of securities practice arise from defining the details of disclosure and ascertaining which transactions are covered by the disclosure requirements. There is very little substantive regulation of investments. …

Why have the laws survived when other regulatory schemes of that vintage have been transformed or eliminated? Those who enacted these statutes asserted that they were necessary to eliminate fraud from the market and ensure that investors would receive the returns they expected; otherwise, the argument ran, people would withdraw their capital and the economy would stagnate. This explanation seemed especially pressing in 1933, for there had been frauds preceding the Depression and much disinvestment during it. On this public interest story, the interests served by the laws are the same now as they were then, and so the laws have the same beneficial structure.

No one should be comfortable with this simple tale. Fraud was unlawful in every state in 1933, and every state except Nevada then had an administrative apparatus for investigating and preventing securities fraud. Fraud in the sale of houses and education is more important to most people of moderate means (the supposed beneficiaries of the securities acts) than fraud in the sale of securities; these people have a much greater portion of their wealth invested in real estate and human capital than in the stock market. Yet there are no federal laws addressing these other assets. There were many securities frauds before 1933, and there have been many since. …

The recognition that much legislation is the outcome of the interplay of pressure groups—and that only by accident will interest group laws serve the broader public interest—suggests another hypothesis. The securities laws may be designed to protect special interests at the expense of investors. They possess many of the characteristics of interest-group legislation. Existing rules give larger issuers an edge, because many of the costs of disclosure are the same regardless of the size of the firm or the offering. Thus larger or older firms face lower flotation costs per dollar than do small issuers. The rules also help existing investment banks and auditing firms obtain an advantage because they acquire expertise and because rivals cannot compete by offering differentiated products. The securities laws' routinization of disclosure reduces the number of paths to the market and insists that all firms give investors "the best," stifling lower cost alternatives with higher risks.

Some parts of the securities laws had obvious interest-group support … . It is harder to find private interests behind the principal features of regulation, though. Lawyers specialize in corporate and securities work, and other market professionals depend on the intricacies of the law for much revenue. These favored groups (larger issuers, investment banks, the securities bar) have too many members to permit monopoly prices. Delaware's bar has thousands of corporate lawyers, with lawyers in other states practicing its law too; the securities bar is much larger; in both cases, competition prevents monopoly returns. Yet these lawyers, investment bankers, and others have human capital at stake. Thus they have every reason to oppose the abolition of the regulatory system. And if the losses from existing laws are spread across a large number of people (individual investors), each of whom would benefit only slightly from abolition, regulation could survive even if it reduces social welfare.

Unfortunately, no one knows why some pieces of legislation are enacted and survive while others do not. The interest-group explanation that might account for securities litigation also could explain airline and trucking regulation, yet these systems have been almost obliterated. The survival of securities regulation could be attributed to "stronger interest-group support," but this smacks of tautology. Perhaps the laws endured because they are not predominantly interest-group legislation. We think it appropriate, therefore, to search for the "public interest" justifications of the securities laws.

• • •

What does a mandatory disclosure system add to the prohibition of fraud? The implicit public interest justification for disclosure rules is that markets produce "too little" information about securities when the only rule is one against fraud. One often hears the assertion that information is a "public good," meaning that it can be used without being "used up" and that the producer of information cannot exclude others from receiving the benefits. If the producer of information cannot obtain all of its value, too little will be produced. It seems to follow that there are gains in a rule requiring production of all information that would be forthcoming were gains fully appropriable.

This rationale gets us only so far. For one thing, it proves too much. No one can fully appropriate the value of information about toothpaste, but there is no federal rule about disclosing the efficacy of toothpaste in preventing cavities. Why are securities different? We leave other products to competitive markets because we believe that people who make or use a product (or test it, as Consumers' Union does) will obtain enough of the gains from information to make the markets reasonably efficient.

Similarly, those who learn about a security may profit from their information. They cannot obtain all of the benefits, because others in the market will infer the news, and the price of the securities will adjust. The new price will "contain" the news, preventing the person who first learned it from taking further gains. This also means, however, that the value of news decays quickly in securities markets; the information is "used up," and other people then have their own incentives to go out and find more information. Information is far from free even when given away for free. Those who receive the information must spend time digesting it, and this time is lost to other uses. Investors' time is costly. So it is inaccurate to treat information as enduring, cheap to disseminate, and cheap to use.

The more sophisticated version of the public goods explanation is that although investors produce information, they produce both too much and too little of it. They produce too little because the benefits are imperfectly appropriable. If information is worth $100 to investors as a group, but no one can capture more than $10 of gains, then no one will obtain more than $10 worth of information. Investors produce too much information, though, if several create the same $10 bit of information (redundant production). Mandatory disclosure will prevent redundant production of information, the argument concludes.

The other source of excessive production is the gain available from forecasting the future. Some information, such as the quarterly earnings of a firm, offers opportunities for trading gains; the person who learns the news first can make great profits. In one important sense, though, the information is worthless. Trading on news that is bound to come out anyway does not change the future or lead to better investment in new securities. The price will ultimately change to reflect the true earnings. That it changes a day or so quicker is not of much moment for allocative efficiency. The lure of trading profits may induce people to spend a lot of effort and other resources "beating the market"; this is wasteful because the profit opportunity is much larger than the efficiency gains from expediting the transition of prices. The argument concludes by observing that the prompt disclosure of information by the affected firm will extinguish the trading opportunity. When everyone knows the truth, no one can speculate on it. Investors as a group would pay to have these trading gains (and the costly search for information) eliminated. What better way to do this than disclosure by the firm that knows the truth?

These arguments share a problem, because they leap from the benefit of disclosure to the benefit of mandatory disclosure. If disclosure is worthwhile to investors, the firm can profit by providing it. The firm is in privity with its investors, and they should be able to strike a mutually beneficial bargain. A decision by the firm effectively "coordinates" the acts of many investors who could not bargain directly. As we have emphasized from the beginning, managers who omit cost-justified steps for the protection of investors will receive less money for the securities the firm issues; the entrepreneurs and managers, not the investors, pay the price.

Take a firm that wants to issue new securities. It has a project (say, the manufacture of a new computer) that it expects to be profitable. If the firm simply asked for money without disclosing the project and managers involved, however, it would get nothing. Investors would assume the worst because, they would reason, if the firm had anything good to say for itself it would do so. Silence is bad news. A firm with a good project, seeking to distinguish itself from a firm with a mediocre project (or no project at all), would disclose more and more as long as the cost of disclosure (both direct costs of dissemination and indirect costs of giving information to rivals) was worthwhile to its investors. It might even disclose too much from society's perspective, because it would know that time investors devoted to studying its disclosures would be unavailable to study its rivals'. Self-induced disclosure occurs in the secondary market too. The firm's investors want to be able to sell their stock in the aftermarket for the highest price. Their ability to do so depends on a flow of believable information (otherwise potential buyers reduce their offers), which firms must supply if they hope to obtain the best price for their stock on issuance.

The process works for bad news as well as good. Once the firm starts disclosing it cannot stop short of making any critical revelation, because investors assume the worst. It must disclose the bad with the good, else investors will assume that the bad is even worse than it is. And the firm's word is not sufficient. Mere disclosure would be enough if the rule against fraud were perfectly enforced, but it is not. Thus the firm uses the many verification and certification devices we have described. Given these devices, a rule compelling disclosure seems redundant. If the fraud penalty and verification devices do not work, a rule compelling disclosure is not apt to be enforceable either.

Firms have been disclosing important facts about themselves and certifying these facts through third parties-as long as there have been firms. It is possible to trace the use of auditors back to the beginning of the corporation. By 1934, when Congress first required annual disclosure by some companies, every firm traded on the national markets made voluminous public disclosures certified by independent auditors. Between 1934 and 1964, annual disclosure was required only of those firms traded on national exchanges. (In 1964 the statute was amended to cover all firms with more than a specified number of investors.) Firms could avoid disclosure by de-listing or not listing initially. Nonetheless, firms eagerly listed themselves on exchanges and disclosed; firms that were not listed also disclosed substantial amounts of data, following the pattern set by those covered by the statute. Even today, although the securities of state and local governments are exempt from the mandatory disclosure rules, these issuers routinely supply extensive information to purchasers.

Disclosure for the purpose of stilling investors' doubts also reduces investors' incentives to search too much for trading information. The problem, as we have mentioned, is that knowing the future creates profit opportunities without making investors as a group better off. Because searching out such information is costly, investors as a group gain if firms disclose so as to minimize the opportunities for these gains and thus the incentives to search. The net return on a security is its gross return (dividends plus any liquidating distribution) less the costs of information and transactions in holding the security. A firm can increase this net return as easily by reducing the cost of holding the stock as by increasing its business profits. Firms that promise to make disclosures for this purpose will prosper relative to others, because their investors incur relatively lower costs and can be more passive with safety. The more convincing the promise, the more investors will pay for the stock.

However, the advent of the global financial crisis in 2008-9 caused considerable soul-searching among economists and their critics as to the adequacy of their premises about self-correcting markets and voluntary compliance by market participants with legal norms. An example of such soul-searching is provided in the excerpt below.

Richard A Posner, *A Failure of Capitalism: The Crisis of '08 and the Descent into Depression*
(Cambridge, Mass: Harvard University Press, 2009)
at 252-53, 255, 257-60, 266, 289-90

The Economics Profession Asleep at the Switch

One of the biggest puzzles about the failure to anticipate the financial crisis is the lack of foresight of so many academic economists … .

Macroeconomics and financial economics are highly prestigious fields of economics, and the leading macroeconomists and finance theorists are brilliant people. Yet although the housing bubble started to leak air in 2005 and burst in 2006 and the economy was in recession from the end of 2007 at the latest and the drumbeat of signals warning of an impending crash became deafening by the spring of 2008, not enough economists, whether in academia, the government, or business, sounded the alarm in time to have a significant impact on the government or the banking industry. Securitization of mortgages and other debts was taken at face value as protecting us against the kind of housing-credit bubbles that had ravished East Asian countries in the 1990s. …

I attribute such errors of prediction not to obtuseness but to disbelief that the country could be sliding into anything worse than another of the mild recessions that we had had intermittently since the end of World War II. Many other leading macroeconomists, and prominent finance theorists as well, were simply silent as the storm gathered and broke; perhaps that was the prudent course. Even now, the profession seems adrift in uncertainty and irresolution, as if it cannot believe what has happened. No consensus has emerged with regard to how best to respond to the depression. Most economists seem willing to try virtually anything in an effort to dig the economy out of the hole into which it's fallen.

• • •

Not enough economists noticed (or at the least remarked) the relation between executive compensation practices and risky lending, or appreciated the riskiness of mortgage-backed securities, other collateralized-debt obligations, and credit-default swaps, or connected the decline in personal savings to the danger that such lending posed to the economy. Not enough seem to have realized that the crisis of the banking industry, when it hit, was a crisis not of (or at least not mainly of) illiquidity but of insolvency. Not only were warning signs ignored until too late, but when the economics profession finally woke up we learned that neither government economists like Bernanke nor private economists had prepared any contingency plans for dealing with a depression. It should have been reasonably clear that a 20 percent or more drop in housing prices would endanger bank solvency; that such a decline in housing prices against the background of a probable housing bubble was not out of the question; and therefore that measures to strengthen the banks' balance sheets, as by increasing reserve requirements, would be prudent. Greenspan and Rubin have now apologized for their lack of foresight and preparedness, which is to their credit but does not enhance public confidence in the government's management of the economy; and lack of confidence is one of the things that cause people to hunker down in periods of economic distress by reining in their spending.

• • •

Insofar as the depression can be attributed to mistakes by Greenspan, Bernanke, Summers, Rubin, Paulson, and Cox (the last three not economists, however), the mistakes may be due in part to an overinvestment by economists, policymaker, and business leaders in a free-market ideology that opposes aggressive governmental interventions in the operations of the economy. Not all the economists who believe strongly in the robustness of markets and are skeptical about regulation are "conservative" across the board—economists can be liberal in the sense of being egalitarian and favouring redistributive policies without wanting to regulate corporate practices. How to make the economic pie as large as possible is a different question from whether to slice it differently. The point is only that excessive deregulation of the financial industry was a government failure abetted by the political and ideological commitments of mainstream economists, who overlooked the possibility that the financial markets seemed robust because regulation had prevented previous financial crises. The depression is a failure of capitalism, or more precisely of a certain kind of capitalism ("laissez-faire" in a loose sense, "American" versus "European" in a popular sense), and of capitalism's biggest boosters.

• • •

Economic understanding of the causes and cures of depressions has not progressed to the point at which ideology no longer influences analysis. When good arguments, and some evidence, are presented on both sides of an economic debate that engages the political passions that economists share with other people, but the debate cannot be resolved by empirical testing, preconceptions shaped by ideology will exert a mesmerizing influence on the debaters. Still, this depression, like the last, is likely to stimulate fresh thinking by economists, as well as to provide new data for empirical analysis. …

There were three big prevention failures this time: excessive deregulation, neglect of warning signs, and insouciance about the decline in the rate of personal savings and the safety of such savings. These are corrigible, at least to a degree. The first two are related. The existence of multiple federal financial regulatory bodies—including the Federal Reserve, the Federal Deposit Insurance Corporation, the Securities Investor Protection

Corporation, the Securities and Exchange Commission, the Federal Housing Administration, the Federal Housing and Finance Administration, the Office of Housing Enterprise Oversight, the National Credit Union Administration, the Treasury Department and its agencies, such as the Comptroller of the Currency and the Office of Thrift Supervision—and fifty state banking and insurance commissioners—has led to a fragmentation of regulatory authority, a lack of coordination, turf wars, yawning regulatory gaps with respect to hedge funds, bank substitutes, and novel financial instruments, and an inability to aggregate and analyze information about emerging problems in the financial markets.

. . .

B. Behavioural Finance

A more recent innovation in response to the normative approach that elevates rational individual decision-making to paramountcy is the behavioural perspective. This approach attempts to import insights from psychology into an empirical exploration of how individuals actually behave in making decisions, and the factors that influence that decision-making. The claim that individuals act emotionally or with overconfidence, or that "loss aversion" or complicated forms of "mental accounting" frame their investment decision-making, obviously raises the issue of the extent to which the legal rules governing securities trading do or should respond to these empirical claims. This question has assumed considerably more importance in the eyes of regulators since the financial crisis. The excerpt below canvasses some of the insights of this framework for analysis.

Brad M Barber & Terrance Odean, "The Behavior of Individual Investors"
(2011), online: <http://ssrn.com/abstract=1872211> (footnotes omitted)

Introduction

The bulk of research in modern economics has been built on the notion that human beings are rational agents who attempt to maximize wealth while minimising risk. These agents carefully assess the risk and return of all possible investment options to arrive at an investment portfolio that suits their level of risk aversion. Models based on these assumptions yield powerful insights into how markets work. For example, in the Capital Asset Pricing Model—the reigning workhorse of asset pricing models—investors hold well-diversified portfolios consisting of the market portfolio and risk-free investments. In Grossman and Stiglitz's (1980) rational expectations model, some investors choose to acquire costly information and others choose to invest passively. Informed, active, investors earn higher pre-cost returns, but, in equilibrium, all investors have the same expected utility. And in Kyle (1985), an informed insider profits at the expense of noise traders who buy and sell randomly.

A large body of empirical research indicates that real individual investors behave differently from investors in these models. Most individual investors hold under-diversified portfolios. Many apparently uninformed investors trade actively, speculatively, and to their detriment. And, as a group, individual investors make systemic, not random, buying and selling decisions.

Transaction costs are an unambiguous drag on the returns earned by individual investors. More surprisingly, many studies document that individual investors earn poor returns even before costs. Put another way, many individual investors seem to have a desire to trade actively coupled with perverse security selection ability!

Unlike those in models, real investors tend to sell winning investments while holding on to their losing investments—a behavior dubbed the "disposition effect." The disposition effect is among the most widely replicated observations regarding the behavior of individual investors. While taxes clearly affect the trading of individual investors, the disposition effect tends to increase, rather than decrease an investor's tax bill since in many markets selling winners generates a tax liability that might be deferred simply by selling a losing, rather an winning, investment.

Real investors are influenced by where they live and work. They tend to hold stocks of companies close to where they live and invest heavily in the stock of their employer. These behaviors lead to an investment portfolio far from the market portfolio proscribed by the CAPM and arguably expose investors to unnecessarily high levels of idiosyncratic risk.

Real investors are influenced by the media. They tend to buy, rather than sell, stocks when those stocks are in the news. This attention-based buying can lead investors to trade too speculatively and has the potential to influence the pricing of stocks.

As we can see, this approach suggests a number of questions for analysts of securities law. For example, can or should securities law rules take account of the "disposition effect," whereby people tend to avoid regret by not selling losers? Should the takeover bid rules respond in any way to the claims of behavioural researchers about "endowment effects," which suggest that people demand more to sell something than they would be willing to pay to buy it? How might the evidence that investors engage in "mental accounting" have an impact on the investment advice given by intermediaries to investors? As noted above, global regulators have begun to pay specific attention to these issues. A couple of examples are excerpted below, one from a report by the IOSCO and the other from a speech given by the CEO of the Financial Conduct Authority (FCA) in the United Kingdom in 2013.

Board of the International Organization of Securities Commissions, *Strategic Framework for Investor Education and Financial Literacy: Final Report*
(Madrid: IOSCO, 2014) 22-26, online: <http://www.iosco.org/library/pubdocs/pdf/IOSCOPD462.pdf> (footnotes omitted)

Appendix 2—Behavioural Economics and Other Findings Related to Financial Decision-Making

Behavioural economics studies psychology and microeconomic decision-making from the perspective that the efficient market hypothesis is a flawed or incomplete construct. The research indicates that individuals often act irrationally due to cognitive processes and environmental conditions. In the saving and investing environment, there is evidence that people make poor financial decisions due to various biases, for example, inertia, loss aversion, procrastination, perceived lack of knowledge, cultural sensitivities, and a variety of environmental stimuli.

Behavioural economics analysis generally measures the outcomes of participant behaviour in controlled experiments that attempt to model realistic scenarios faced by the investing public. Behavioural responses to investment decision-making have been documented through academic research in recent years. A catalogue of behavioural economics research is annotated in Appendix 3.

The research highlights a number of behavioural responses in financial decision-making that have important implications for the design of investor education and financial literacy strategies. The most significant of these responses are noted below, followed by other biases and effects that can have an impact on financial decision-making.

Key Behavioural Responses in Financial Decision-Making

- *Anchoring and adjustment*—an initial value or starting point influences the final decision. The anchoring effect decreases but does not vanish with higher cognitive ability.
- *Choice preference*—too many options inhibit or overwhelm selection decision-making.
- *Confirmation bias*—people use data selectively to agree or confirm their existing views. Investors with a stronger confirmation bias also exhibit greater overconfidence.
- *Conflict disclosure*—disclosing a conflict of interest may make it more likely that the conflict will actually occur as it increases levels of trust.
- *Inertia*—the default option becomes the de facto selection even if it is not the optimal choice.
- *Loss aversion*—people more strongly prefer to avoid small losses than acquire larger gains. Loss aversion is not invoked when spending money that is within an intended budget for purchases, but only when operating outside the intended budget. Loss aversion can actually be a motivation to invest to the extent that when people perceive a loss, they become risk-seeking as opposed to risk averse. When assessing a situation from the perspective of a potential loss, "loss framing" will occur. An investor on a losing streak, for example, may well decide that greater risk is necessary to achieve their target. See also "framing effect" in Other biases and effects related to financial decision-making.
- *Myopic loss aversion*—combination of loss aversion and a tendency to evaluate outcomes frequently. This leads investors to be more willing to invest a greater proportion of their portfolio in risky assets if they evaluate their investments less frequently.
- *Overconfidence*—people tend to trade frequently and hurt their own investment performance. Investors are more likely to be overconfident when they are less experienced as they learn about their true ability through experience. Investors with biased information-processing behaviour in virtual communities are likely to trade more actively and realise worse performance due to their overconfidence. Overconfident investors, who show a better than average bias, trade more frequently.
- *Temporal framing*—people too heavily discount future benefits in lieu of present consumption.

Other Biases and Effects Related to Financial Decision-Making

- *Ambiguity aversion*—the desire to avoid unclear circumstances, even when this will not increase the expected utility.
- *Availability heuristic*—people judge the frequency or probability of some events on the basis of how easily examples or instances can be recalled or remembered.
- *Disposition effect*—the propensity of an investor to sell winners too early and hold losers too long.
- *Endowment effect*—people demand a higher price to sell something they own than they are willing to pay for acquiring it. This effect may occur for goods whose possession is merely desired. The effect is reduced if a negative mood is induced before the good is acquired.
- *Framing effect*—a decision is influenced by the phrasing or frame in which the problem is presented.
- *Fund-level inattention*—the propensity to trade mutual funds around macroeconomic news events.
- *Herding*—a phenomenon where many people take the same action. Information concerning the number of previous transactions in the market is particularly relevant to explain herding propensity among investors.
- *Illusion of control*—the expectancy of personal success is inappropriately higher than the objective probability would warrant.
- *Inattention to earnings news*—degree to which an investor does not trade a particular individual stock around earnings news.
- *Inattention to macroeconomic news*—degree to which an investor does not trade any individual stocks around macroeconomic news events.
- *January effect*—the tendency for excess share returns in the first few days of January.
- *Local bias*—the propensity to select funds or stocks with headquarters close to the investor's geographical location.
- *Lottery stock preference*—the propensity to select stocks with lottery-like features (low price, volatile returns and skewed returns).
- *Narrow framing*—the propensity to select investments individually, instead of considering the broad impact on the portfolio.
- *Present bias*—the inordinate weight people place on costs and benefits that are immediate.
- *Regret*—a human emotion that can influence decisions.
- *Representativeness*—evaluation of the degree of correspondence between a sample and a population, an instance and a category, or more generally, an outcome and a model.
- *Risk aversion*—when individuals have the same level of financial education, there is no gender difference in the level of risk aversion.
- *Small-firms effect*—the shares of smaller firms have outperformed those of larger firms over a period of several decades.
- *Weekend effect*—there appear to be abnormal returns on Fridays and relative falls on Mondays.

Martin Wheatley, "Human Face of Regulation"
(Speech delivered at the London School of Economics, 10 April 2013), online: Financial Conduct Authority <http://www.fca.org.uk/news/speeches/human-face-of-regulation>

The Reach of Behavioural Economics

The creation of the FCA—the new financial conduct regulator—is a direct response to what hasn't worked. Time and again over the last 20 years we have had major scandals—pensions, endowments, insurance, savings—every one is a blow to confidence in finance and every time there is a big clean-up bill for the industry.

The traditional response to a mis-selling scandal (and not just in the UK) was to require more disclosure of information. The assumption was that if you give rational people more information, they would be better able to take rational decisions.

We got this wrong. We all can, and indeed do, make rational decisions when we can get our head around all the different moving parts. Financial decisions usually however, have too many moving parts—multi-year scenarios, unknown interest rates, deferred consumption and the joys of compound interest—that's too many for the average person. And that's where behavioural economics fits in. …

Freedom of choice is one of the characteristics of a market economy that we most often take for granted.

We would like to think we have the ability to select and pay for products according to cool and calculated judgement; that we can analyse risk proficiently and assess reward proactively.

But experience tells a different story, that the vast majority of us aren't always level-headed risk assessors or careful selectors of products. We don't always choose the right mobile phone tariff or the most appropriate credit card.

• • •

But the problem with financial decisions is that they generally do matter a great deal—and we do not always understand them well. Faced with all the moving parts of a financial decision we find it hard to employ the rational mode so we revert. We react to them instinctively and automatically. Faced with the inability to apply our rational model—we revert to what is easier: the intuitive.

- If a box is ticked at the bottom of a contract, we're likely to leave it ticked.
- If the person dresses smartly and works for a well known brand name—we trust them.
- If we see a framed professional qualification on an office wall we're more likely to believe the person we're talking to.
- If we're given the right nudges, we're more prone to miss the particular weaknesses of various products.

• • •

Historical Approach to Regulation

One of the most significant challenges for modern financial regulators and financial services alike is to recognise that we operate within this very human environment. A fallible world governed and directed by psychology:

> - temptations that lead people to overstretch their finances;
> - mental shortcuts that don't always work and can lead us astray;
> - anchors that lead us towards particular outcomes;
> - and frames that change our perception of a given choice. None of us is immune from these influences.
>
> Yet one of the features of regulation historically was that it was all about compliance. It was almost robotic. Were a particular set of rules followed and boxes ticked? Could a firm demonstrate and document that it had followed those rules to the letter? Did firms disclose the full, un-redacted detail of their products to customers?
>
> . . .
>
> But the new FCA won't be afraid to shine a light on the murkier psychological enticements and entrapments that exist in financial services. The dark arts of behavioural economics. The pushes and pulls, the frames and biases that we sometimes see used to entice customers to buy financial products they may not need, or that might be wholly unsuitable for them.
>
> In other words, we will be looking across markets to see where and how behavioural economics might support our regulatory activity. Looking at areas like auto-enrolment, auto-renewal, information disclosure and product complexity.
>
> So, for example, could we use behavioural economics to understand why some consumers do not switch from one savings product to another after a teaser rate expires?
>
> . . .
>
> Looking forward, the FCA wants to empower customers; to switch to the new best rates or move between suppliers.
>
> We want the regulatory system to use behavioural economics to ascertain whether people are being put off switching products through inertia, inattention or even the simple fear of regret from making a wrong decision.

QUESTION

Do you think that the insights of behavioural economics are or should be limited to how investors act in markets? What about how other market participants act, such as issuers or financial advisers?

C. Socio-Legal Approaches

The socio-legal perspective on the operation of securities markets embraces a diverse set of normative and empirical approaches. One very broad generalization might be that analysts operating from a socio-legal perspective are interested in considering markets as embedded in a set of social and cultural relations. They are concerned to explore the ways in which markets both influence and are influenced by those social and cultural relations. Scholarship that investigates the conjuncture of political, economic, and historical factors that influence the terms of legislation and rule-making is one example of this approach. Another subset of literature that might fall under this rubric is devoted to examining the influence of powerful interest groups in shaping the substance of legislation or rules. Examples of such groups in the context of securities markets include the Toronto Stock Exchange (TSX), the Investment Industry Regulatory Organization of Canada (IIROC) (the group that represents and self-regulates the major investment dealers and brokerage firms operating in the securities markets), major Canadian corporations, and the securities regulators themselves. Assuming that the influence of powerful interests can in fact be descriptively catalogued, whether it is considered to be normatively problematic is a separate issue. Public choice theory in neoclassical economics would argue for the normative appropriateness of this outcome, on the basis of efficiency, whereas a proponent of a critical or social justice perspective would point to the possibility of oppression of some constituencies by others. A related issue here is the extent to which rules that were designed to address specific historical and economic problems when they were introduced, and to meet the needs of a specific constituency such as retail investors, are still appropriate for modern-day markets and modern-day economies.

Mary G Condon, *Making Disclosure: Ideas and Interests in Ontario Securities Regulation*
(Toronto: University of Toronto Press, 1998) 4-7 (footnotes omitted)

The second major concern of regulation scholars is that of constructing explanations for the behaviour of regulatory agencies. This task is obviously closely linked to the project of ascertaining and judging regulatory goals. Regulatory behaviour is thought to need explanation because of a perceived pathology with respect to the identified goals. The behavioural explanations available are many and varied. In accordance with the personification implied by the notion of behaviour, several versions of the "life cycle" theory have been mooted. In the United States in the 1950s the view was popular that as agencies grew older, they matured and became less aggressive in their dealings with their regulatory clients. On the other hand, arguments have been propounded that agencies are engaged in a constant effort to broaden the scope of their activities and expand their ambit of authority.

Some accounts focus on the prescience and philosophies of key actors—usually chairs—within agencies, to explain their behaviour. For example, T.K. McCraw examines the careers, biographies, and personalities of four noted American regulators to argue that each became an "independent social force determining the structure of agency regulation." J. Seligman adopts a similar perspective on the history of the Securities and Exchange Commission in the United States (SEC), according considerable importance to the philosophies and policy preferences of the agency's leadership over the years.

Other explanations for regulatory behaviour emanate from variants of economic public choice theory, which propose that resources are allocated by regulators to those recipients who seek them most forcefully, usually "relatively small and well-organized groups that have a high per capita stake in the regulations," rather than poorly organized groups. For example, G.J. Stigler argues that the "central tasks of the theory of economic regulation are to explain who will receive the benefits or burdens of regulation, what form regulation will take, and the effects of regulation upon the allocation of resources." He received a Nobel Prize in economics in part for his development of "capture" theory, which predicted that a regulatory agency would tend to be captured by the interest groups with which it was most closely associated. A similar analysis was developed by G. Kolko in his study of early American railroad regulation. He argues that regulation was sought by those who ran the railroads to protect their own interests against those of consumers and workers.

As a Marxist historian, Kolko would come to different conclusions about the appropriateness of this result. More recently, I. Ayres and J. Braithwaite have posited the idea of a "continuum" of capture, in order to model varying relationships between regulators and the regulated in different regulatory arenas. As a policy prescription, they argue for "tripartite" practice of regulation, to take place among regulators, the regulated, and PIGs (Public Interest Groups) in order to produce more "responsive" regulation.

The obvious point of convergence of these various explanatory models is a focus on the role of interests—of regulators, of the regulated and of the more diffuse public interest. The assumption is that knowing the configuration of interests will allow reliable prediction of the outcome to regulatory decision-making and therefore an assessment of the "success" or "failure" of an agency. Agency behaviour is thought to result from the rational assessment of the constraints or opportunities afforded by the desires of specific interests.

As an account of what happens in regulatory agencies, this approach seems deficient for a number of reasons. In the first place, "interest" tends to be treated in these analyses as an unproblematic concept and, empirically, as easily discoverable. With respect to so-called "private" interests, it tends to be assumed that autonomous social actors adopt interest positions that are coherent, specifiable in advance, and unchanging over the course of a particular debate. Little attention is typically paid to the formulation of interest positions in the first place. For example, E. Meidinger argues that "self-interest is not a given; it must be constructed and can be reconstructed. How self-interest will be played out institutionally, and moreover, what sway it will be given, are also choices." Indeed, the social locations of actors are often assumed to produce specific interest positions. In other words, the interest group is conflated with the objective desired. Second, a number of commentators have made the point that exponents of "private interest" theories of regulation tend to confuse regulatory effects with causation. Once it is discovered that a new regulatory practice benefits some identifiable constituents, a leap is then made to the assumption that the practice was put in place so as to benefit those constituents. This leap can be made with respect to both inside and outside interests, that is, where the practice affords benefits to regulated entities (or other intermediaries) in the regulatory relationship or to the agency itself.

Third, the analytical distinction usually drawn between public interest and private interest theories of regulation is somewhat problematic. For one thing, one understanding of the public interest is that it consists precisely of the sum of individual private interests and so is indistinguishable from those prior interests. For another, the distinction is intellectually a product of the public/private divide at the core of liberal political theory, whereby the private sphere of action is separate from the public sphere and should be inviolate. This distinction may be increasingly empirically invalid. Thus, L. Hancher and M. Moran argue that the "capture" debate obscures perhaps the single most important feature of economic regulation under advanced capitalism: that the most important actors in the process are organizations, and organizations which, regardless of their formal status, have acquired important attributes of public status. Of the formally "private" organizations with public status, none is more important than the large firm. ... Economic regulation of markets under advanced capitalism can thus be portrayed as an activity shaped by the interdependence of powerful organizations who share major public characteristics. In the economic sphere no clear dividing line can be drawn between organizations of a private nature and those entitled to the exclusive exercise of public authority. The persistence of self-regulatory organizations in the practice of Ontario securities regulation bears witness to this point.

At the least, the focus on outcomes required by interest group theorizing obscures the question of *how* it is that actors may have their interests met by regulation. As one way of achieving greater understanding of the regulatory process and beginning to answer the question of how outcomes occur, Meidinger proposes a concentration on the notion of a "regulatory culture." Thus "a cultural perspective focuses on the understandings that are negotiated and enacted by actors in regulatory arenas. It tends to presume that those understandings are important in their own right and are not simply reducible to other factors, such as pregiven material interests or power." He argues that this focus on negotiated understandings and "shared ideas" as a vital component of regulatory culture "may support an intermediate analytical position which avoids the rigid overdetermination of structural models and the mushy underdetermination of individualistic models of social life."

QUESTION

As an example of the application of these various critical perspectives on securities law rules, consider one of the most basic rules of securities law, the prospectus requirement. This requires that issuers provide to prospective investors a detailed prospectus that includes information about the securities to be offered, the financial position of the issuer as reflected in its financial statements, the risks associated with investing in these securities, and aspects of the internal governance of the issuer. How would the existence of this rule be analyzed under the various perspectives described above?

III. SOURCES OF SECURITIES LAW

The legal regulation of securities markets and securities trading is accomplished by way of statute, regulations, rules, policy statements, and, of course, judicial decisions. Securities law in Canada is typically administered by an expert tribunal, such as the various provincial securities commissions, though self-regulatory organizations also play a key role in the delivery and implementation of regulation. We will see that significant power and autonomy is typically granted to regulators to interpret, elaborate on, and apply the statute, rules, and regulations. As discussed in Chapters 3 and 11, the Supreme Court decisions in *Pezim*, *Asbestos*, and *Cartaway* are illustrative in this regard. A key issue is that the scope of securities law does not end with the statute; various kinds of delegated legislation are crucial to understanding the nature and extent of the law. Thus, sources of securities law could be described in terms of the texts that are used to find and apply the law, or in terms of the various institutions and organizations that apply it.

The authoritative texts of securities law comprise the following sources.

A. Provincial Securities Statutes

All of the provinces and territories have legislation governing the issuance of securities and the operation of securities markets. Although Ontario's *Securities Act* has been amended a number of times over the past few years, the basic structure of the underlying principles (to do with matters such as the disclosure of information to investors, the creation of the so-called exempt market, the prohibition on insider trading, and the regulation of takeovers) has remained unchanged since the last major overhaul of the statute in 1978. One more recent innovation, in 1994, has been the elaboration of specific objectives that securities regulators are required to achieve, along with a number of principles that elaborate on those objectives. See OSA, ss 1.1 and 2.1. A number of provinces have followed the Ontario model very closely (especially Saskatchewan and Alberta in the west and Newfoundland and Labrador and Nova Scotia in the east). In 2004, British Columbia was planning to enact a new statute that would have shifted the philosophy of its securities legislation more toward a principles-based approach. That reform was not pursued at that time, although since then a number of substantive provisions of the BC Act have been removed or recast in more plain language as a result of the promulgation of various National Instruments (see e.g. *Securities Act*, RSBC 1996, c 418, parts 10 and 12). Meanwhile, there continues to be a great deal of interest in moving securities regulation in Canada more toward an outcomes-based, as opposed to a process-based model. (See e.g. Cristie Ford, "Principles-Based Securities Regulation" (Research study prepared for the Expert Panel on Securities Regulation, January 2009), online: <http://www.expertpanel.ca/documents/research-studies/Principles%20Based%20Securities%20Regulation%20-%20Ford.English.pdf>). Yet, whether the approach taken in the statute is rule-oriented or principle-oriented, it is important to emphasize that a clear appreciation of the scope and content of securities law cannot be obtained without a thorough familiarity with the provisions of the statute. It should also be noted here that in response to the Supreme Court's ruling in 2011, a number of provinces and the federal government have agreed in principle to regulate their securities markets cooperatively. These issues will be canvassed in more detail in the chapters to follow, but for now it should be noted that those provinces and the federal government have released for comment two draft pieces of legislation, one entitled *Capital Markets Act* (CMA) and the other *Capital Markets Stability Act* (Canada) (CMSA). As these pieces of legislation are still in draft form and subject to change, they cannot be considered authoritative sources of law, though they may be generally referenced in the chapters to follow.

B. Regulations and Rules

Provincial securities acts typically include the power to make *regulations* under their authority. In Ontario, for example, this authority is exercised by the lieutenant governor in council. However, this form of delegated legislation is of decreasing importance in some of the bigger provinces, which have provided a *rule-making* power to the regulator itself, subject to a "notice and comment" procedure and the approval of the provincial minister responsible for overseeing the activities of the regulator. The power to make rules, which has been very significant for the securities regulators who have it, was first granted in Ontario in the mid-1990s. The power was granted as a result of a set of events that began with a legal claim by a market participant that the Ontario Securities Commission (OSC) was engaging in an unauthorized practice of promulgating policy statements elaborating on statutory provisions, and was enforcing those policies as though they were mandatory. Following the decision of the Ontario Court (General Division) in *Ainsley* (subsequently confirmed by the Court of Appeal) (*Ainsley Financial Corp v Ontario (Securities Commission)* (1994), 21 OR (3d) 104, 28 Admin LR (2d) 1, 18 OSCB 43 (CA)), the provincial government acted quickly to establish a task force to examine the situation, since it threatened to affect the power of the regulators to effectively respond to emerging regulatory problems. In accordance with the recommendations of the task force, the legislature expanded the powers of the regulators to include the power to make binding rules. (See Mary Condon, "Power Without Responsibility or Responsibility Without Power?" (1995) 10:2 BFLR 221.) Now, much of the detail of disclosure requirements, availability of prospectus exemptions, and corporate governance requirements among other matters, is to be found in these binding rules.

In Ontario, s 143 of the OSA enumerates the scope of the rule-making power in the province. This section itemizes over 60 areas of securities law in respect of which the OSC is authorized to make rules. While this is an expansive list, from time to time the regulator is required to seek a legislative amendment in order to engage in rule-making on an issue that is not specifically identified in s 143. Other provinces, such as Alberta and British Columbia, accord a power to their regulator to make rules on matters not already contemplated in their governing legislation by way of a "basket provision" authorizing rules governing any other matters related to the carrying out of securities law. The Five Year Review Committee, *Reviewing the Securities Act (Ontario)—Final Report* (Toronto: Queen's Printer for Ontario, 2003), recommended in 2003 that the OSC receive such basket rule-making authority, identical to that conferred on the lieutenant governor in council in relation to regulations.

Since the power to make binding rules confers considerable power on the regulator, it is accompanied by a detailed set of procedures that must be followed. These procedures are designed to ensure transparency and consultation in the process of making rules. There is some inconsistency among the provinces with rule-making power in terms of both the length of time required for a comment period on a proposed rule and whether ministerial approval is required before the adoption of a rule. In Ontario, the OSC is required to publish all proposed rules, along with specified accompanying material (including a description of the anticipated costs and benefits of the rule), and to provide at least a 90-day comment period for interested parties. If the regulator makes "material changes" to the proposed rule following submissions, it is required to republish the rule and give a further opportunity for comment. Once the rule is finalized, the regulator must deliver it to the minister, who has 60 days to either approve or reject it or to return it to the regulator for further consideration. As we have noted above, however, some provinces do not have this power at all. They are therefore dependent on the promulgation of policy to guide the behaviour of market participants in their province, or they must rely on the provincial legislature to enact amendments to legislation in a timely manner. This inconsistency in regulatory powers across the country is one of many arguments made by those who favour a coordinated national approach to securities regulation in Canada.

C. National and Multilateral Instruments

Meanwhile, in an attempt to promote harmonization across the country, the Canadian Securities Administrators (CSA), an umbrella organization of provincial and territorial securities regulators, has begun the practice of promulgating *national or multilateral instruments*. These are an attempt to reduce the amount of duplication required of market participants in matters where the regulation of more than one province would apply (such as where an issuer wants to sell securities in more than one province). They also represent joint responses to problems in securities markets, with a view to making securities regulation more compatible from province to province. A national instrument (NI) is one that has been agreed to by all provinces and territories. As the name implies, a multilateral instrument (MI) has been agreed to by some but not all of the provinces, which again results in a lack of consistency in regulation across the country. These instruments are intended by the CSA to be binding on market participants in provinces or territories that have implemented them. But, because these CSA instruments do not themselves have legal force, they must be implemented by rule or policy in each participating province. As we will see in Chapter 5, it is also possible that some provisions of a National Instrument are not in fact enacted in all provinces.

D. National and Local Policies

National and local policies typically provide additional information about how regulators interpret the provisions of legislation or rules, or are intended to provide guidance to market participants concerning the exercise of regulatory discretion. National policy (NP) statements are joint policy statements agreed to by the CSA (such as National Policy 62-202 on defensive tactics in takeover bids). As we have noted, the making of local policy statements has been the subject of controversy in the past, based on a lack of explicit power to make them granted in statutes such as the OSA. (See *Ainsley*, above.) Now, such a power is provided in Ontario's legislation at s 143.8(11). Provincial rules or CSA instruments often contain a "companion policy" (CP) that elaborates on the meaning of the accompanying rule or instrument, or provides examples of its application for the guidance of those subject to it. The notice below describes the attempt to systematize the numbering system applied to a proliferating number and type of regulatory instrument.

CSA Staff Notice 11-312 (Revised), *National Numbering System* (19 February 2010)[1]

The Canadian Securities Administrators (CSA) follows a system in which securities regulatory instruments are assigned numbers that indicate the type and subject matter of the instrument.

The numbering system was designed so as to:

(i) convey as much information as possible about the particular instrument so that a user knows what type of instrument it is, whether the instrument is national or local and what subject matter it relates to;

(ii) permit all National Instruments, National Policies and CSA Notices to have the same numbers in all jurisdictions (as is currently the case); and

(iii) be flexible enough to permit Local Rules, Policies, Notices and implementing instruments of all jurisdictions to be numbered in accordance with the numbering system without affecting the numbering of National Instruments, National Policies and CSA Notices.

1 This Notice contains minor revisions to CSA Staff Notice 11-312, as published on 6 February 2009. The publishing of this staff notice coincided with the withdrawal of OSC Staff Notice 11-724, *Numbering System for Policy Reformulation Project* (19 OSCB 4258).

Under the numbering system, each instrument is assigned a five digit number, with a hyphen appearing between the second and third digit. There are four components to the number assigned to a document:

- The first digit represents the broad subject area.
- The second digit represents a sub-category of the broad subject area.
- The third digit represents the type of the document.
- The last two digits represent the number of the document within its document type in its sub-category (in sequential order starting at 01).

More specifically, these four components may be described as follows:

- The *first* digit relates to the subject matter category into which the instrument has been classified. The nine subject matter categories are:

    1. Procedures and Related Matters
    2. Certain Capital Market Participants (Self-Regulatory Organizations, Exchanges and Market Operations)
    3. Registration Requirements and Related Matters (Dealers, Advisers and other Registrants)
    4. Distribution Requirements (Prospectus Requirements and Prospectus Exemptions)
    5. Ongoing Requirements for Issuers and Insiders (Continuous Disclosure)
    6. Take-over Bids and Special Transactions
    7. Securities Transactions Outside the Jurisdiction
    8. Investment Funds
    9. Derivatives

    For example, in the context of 54-101, the number "5" indicates that the instrument relates to Ongoing Requirements for Issuers and Insiders.

- The *second* digit relates to the sub-category of the subject matter category into which the instrument has been classified (see the "sub-category" column of the table below).

    Using the 54-101 example, within the Ongoing Requirements for Issuers and Insiders category, a sub-category for instruments dealing with Proxy Solicitation is denoted by the number "4." Accordingly, all instruments dealing with this matter commence with the numbers "54."

- The *third* digit classifies the document as one of nine types of documents:

    1. National[2] Instrument/Multilateral Instrument and any related Companion Policy or Form(s)
    2. National Policy/Multilateral Policy
    3. CSA Notice

2 A National Instrument or Policy is an instrument or policy that has been adopted by all CSA jurisdictions, whereas a Multilateral Instrument or Policy is an instrument or policy that has not been adopted by one or more CSA jurisdictions.

4. CSA Concept Proposal or Discussion Paper
5. Local Rule, Regulation or Blanket Order or Ruling and any related Companion Policy or Form(s), except an Implementing Instrument described below.
6. Local Policy
7. Local Notice
8. Implementing Instrument[3]
9. Miscellaneous

Using the same example, the third digit in 54-101 indicates that the type of instrument is a National Instrument or Multilateral Instrument (or a related Companion Policy or Form).

- The *fourth* and *fifth* digits represent a number assigned to instruments of the same type in consecutive order from 01 to 99 within a particular sub-category.

  Again, using the example 54-101, the number "01" indicates that the instrument is the first document of its type in the sub-category "Proxy Solicitation."

A Companion Policy or Form that is related to an Instrument or Local Rule will have the same number as the Instrument or Local Rule to which it relates, followed by "CP" in the case of a Companion Policy or "F" in the case of a Form. If there is more than one Form related to a particular instrument, the Forms will be numbered consecutively (F1, F2, F3, etc.).

3 For this purpose, an Implementing Instrument is a local rule making consequential changes relating to the implementation of a National Instrument/Multilateral Instrument.

Category, Sub-Category and Document Type Numbers

<table>
<tr><th>Category (1st digit)</th><th>Sub-Category (2nd digit)</th><th>Document Type (3rd digit)</th></tr>
<tr><td>1 Procedure and Related Matters</td><td>1 General
2 Applications
3 Filings with Securities Regulatory Authority
4 Definitions
5 Hearings and Enforcement</td><td rowspan="4">1 National or Multilateral Instrument (Rule) and any related Companion Policy and Form

2 National or Multilateral Policy

3 CSA Notice or CSA Staff Notice

4 CSA Concept Proposal or Discussion Paper

5 Local Rule, Regulation or Blanket Order or Ruling and any related Companion Policy or Form

6 Local Policy

7 Local Notice

8 Implementing Instrument (Local Rule that gives effect to a National or Multilateral Instrument)

9 Miscellaneous item (e.g., a Form that does not relate to another Instrument or Policy)</td></tr>
<tr><td>2 Certain Capital Market Participants</td><td>1 Stock Exchanges
2 Other Markets
3 Trading Rules
4 Clearing and Settlement
5 Other Participants</td></tr>
<tr><td>3 Registration and Related Matters</td><td>1 Registration Requirements
2 Registration Exemptions
3 Ongoing Requirements Affecting Registrants
4 Fitness for Registration
5 Non-Resident Registrants</td></tr>
<tr><td>4 Distribution Requirements</td><td>1 Prospectus Contents—Non-Financial Matters
2 Prospectus Contents—Financial Matters
3 Prospectus Filing Matters
4 Alternative Forms of Prospectus
5 Prospectus Exempt Distributions
6 Requirements Affecting Distributions by Certain Issuers
7 Advertising and Marketing
8 Distribution Restrictions</td></tr>
<tr><td>5 Ongoing Requirements for Issuers and Insiders</td><td>1 Disclosure—General
2 Financial Disclosure
3 Timely Disclosure
4 Proxy Solicitation
5 Insider Reporting
6 Restricted Shares
7 Cease Trading Orders
8 Corporate Governance</td><td></td></tr>
<tr><td>6 Take-Over Bids and Special Transactions</td><td>1 Special Transactions
2 Take-over Bids</td><td></td></tr>
<tr><td>7 Securities Transactions Outside the Jurisdictions</td><td>1 International Issuers
2 Distributions Outside the Jurisdiction</td><td></td></tr>
<tr><td>8 Investment Funds</td><td>1 Investment Fund Distributions</td><td></td></tr>
<tr><td>9 Derivatives[4]</td><td>1 Trades in Derivatives</td><td></td></tr>
</table>

4 Please note that in Québec, derivatives regulations will be made under the *Derivatives Act* (Québec) and not the *Securities Act* (Québec).

E. Staff Notices

Staff notices are a mechanism for the CSA or provincial regulatory staff to communicate with market participants in a less formal manner, often in relation to emerging regulatory problems that have not yet become the subject of a policy or a rule. Notices are also used to convey to the market the results of staff investigations into how specific issues are handled by market actors, such as executive compensation disclosure or specific accounting issues.

F. Self-Regulatory Organization Rules or Policies

The day-to-day regulation of the capital markets in Canada relies heavily on the activities of self-regulatory organizations (SROs). In particular, SROs such as IIROC or the Mutual Fund Dealers Association (MFDA) have power to discipline their members for breaches of securities law, including the SRO's own rules or policies. IIROC is also responsible for the self-regulation of the securities markets themselves, by way of the application of a set of universal market integrity rules (UMIRs). UMIRs deal with issues such as prohibitions on deceptive or manipulative trading, short selling, and the requirement for the "best execution" of a customer's trade. Finally, stock exchanges such as the TSX also play a rôle in establishing and maintaining listing standards for issuers.

G. Appellate Court Decisions

Decisions of appellate courts reviewing the decision-making or regulatory activities of provincial securities commissions are an authoritative and increasingly important source of law in this area. Most of the Supreme Court's jurisprudence in the area of securities law will be discussed in various chapters of this book. The most prominent of these decisions include *Pacific Coast Coin Exchange of Canada v Ontario Securities Commission*, [1978] 2 SCR 112, 80 DLR (3d) 529 [*Pacific Coast*]; *Pezim v British Columbia (Superintendent of Brokers)*, [1994] 2 SCR 557, 114 DLR (4th) 385 [*Pezim*]; *Committee for the Equal Treatment of Asbestos Minority Shareholders v Ontario (Securities Commission)*, 2001 SCC 37, [2001] 2 SCR 132 [*Asbestos*]; *Cartaway Resources Corp (Re)*, 2004 SCC 26, [2004] 1 SCR 672 [*Cartaway*]; *Global Securities Corp v British Columbia (Securities Commission)*, 2000 SCC 21, [2000] 1 SCR 494 [*Global Securities*]; *Kerr v Danier Leather Inc*, 2007 SCC 44, [2007] 2 SCR 331 [*Kerr*]; *Theratechnologies Inc v 121851 Canada Inc*, 2015 SCC 18, [2015] 2 SCR 106 [*Theratechnologies*]. It should also be noted that there are some areas where the judicial oversight of corporate law principles intersects with the concerns of securities regulators. An important area where this occurs is in relation to takeover bids, discussed in Chapter 9.

H. Regulatory Decisions, Orders, and Rulings

Most provincial securities legislation grants to the provincial commission the power to hold hearings to review decisions made by regulatory staff. Most provincial acts also require a hearing to be held before various types of enforcement orders may be made by regulators. Accordingly, decisions rendered by commissions in these circumstances are a useful source of information about how the regulators interpret provisions of the legislation or rules, and the factors influencing their application of these rules to specific factual circumstances. Many examples of such administrative decision making will be found throughout this book. (See

Mary G Condon, "The Use of Public Interest Enforcement Powers by Securities Regulators in Canada" in A Douglas Harris, ed, *WPC—Committee to Review the Structure of Securities Regulation in Canada: Research Studies* (Ottawa: Department of Finance, 2003).)

I. International Organization of Securities Commissions

An increasingly important source of justification for domestic regulatory activity is conformity with principles promulgated by the International Organization of Securities Commissions (IOSCO). The goals of IOSCO, in which Alberta, British Columbia, Ontario, and Québec are members or associate members, are to cooperate in developing and promoting adherence to internationally recognized standards of regulation, oversight, and enforcement in order to protect investors, maintain fair, efficient, and transparent markets, and seek to address systemic risks, as well as to exchange information with respect to market developments and enforcement (online: <http://www.iosco.org/about/?subsection=about_iosco>). Much of IOSCO's business is done through subcommittees, which engage in standard setting in specific areas such as regulation of secondary markets or multinational disclosure rules. In 1998, IOSCO promulgated a comprehensive set of principles of securities regulation. IOSCO has been particularly engaged in providing an international regulatory response to the global financial crisis, examining issues such as the regulation of credit rating agencies, disclosure requirements related to the sale of asset-backed securities, the deployment of behavioural economics as an aid to rule-making for retail investors and the meaning of systemic risk.

A final note on sources of useful information about securities regulation in Canada is that several major task forces recommending changes to various aspects of Canadian securities regulation have reported within the past few years. Although not, of course, authoritative sources of "law" as described above, these task forces and the detailed research reports that have accompanied them contain invaluable information about the economic and social context of securities law as well as a multiplicity of recommendations for legal change. The most important of these endeavours are the Final Report of the Wise Persons Committee (2003) (<http://www.wise-averties.ca/main_en.html>), the report of the Task Force to Modernize Securities Legislation in Canada (2006) (<http://www.tfmsl.ca>), and the Expert Panel on Securities Regulation (2009) (<http://www.expertpanel.ca/eng/>), all of which were prepared in conjunction with the commissioning of detailed research studies.

FURTHER READING

Barber, Brad M & Terrance Odean. "Boys Will Be Boys: Gender, Overconfidence, and Common Stock Investment" (2001) 116 QJ Econ 261.

Baldwin, Robert & Martin Cave. *Understanding Regulation* (New York: Oxford University Press, 1999).

Black, Julia. "Empirical Legal Studies in Financial Markets: What Have We Learned?" LSE Law, Society and Economy Working Papers 4/2010, LSE Law Department, online: <http://www.lse.ac.uk/collections/law/wps/>.

Easterbrook, Frank H & Daniel R Fischel. *The Economic Structure of Corporate Law* (Cambridge, Mass: Harvard University Press, 1991).

Erta, Kristine, Stefan Hunt, Zanna Iscenko & Will Brambley. "Applying Behavioural Economics at the Financial Conduct Authority," Financial Conduct Authority Occasional Paper No 1 (April 2013), online: <http://www.fca.org.uk/static/documents/occasional-papers/occasional-paper-1.pdf>.

Gilson, Ronald J & Reiner Kraakman. "The Mechanisms of Market Efficiency Twenty Years Later" (2003) 28:4 J Corp Law 715.

Granovetter, Mark S & Richard Swedberg, eds. *The Sociology of Economic Life* (Boulder, Colo: Westview Press, 2001).

Malloy, Robin Paul. *Law in a Market Context: An Introduction to Legal Concepts in Market Reasoning* (New York: Cambridge University Press, 2004).

Nofsinger, John R. *The Psychology of Investing*, 2nd ed (Upper Saddle River, NJ: Pearson Prentice Hall, 2005).

Posner, Richard A. *Economic Analysis of Law*, 6th ed (New York: Aspen, 2003).

Schiller, Robert J. *Irrational Exuberance* (Princeton, NJ: Princeton University Press, 2000).

Sunstein, Cass R, ed. *Behavioral Law and Economics* (New York: Cambridge University Press, 2000).

CHAPTER ONE

Foundational Concepts

I. INTRODUCTION: KEY DEFINITIONS

Securities legislation imposes considerable substantive obligations on those subject to its ambit. Accordingly, it is important to have as clear an understanding as possible of when the legislation and accompanying rules and policies apply. As we will see in this chapter, the basic building blocks of securities law are characterized by significant ambiguity and open-endedness. In most provinces, the three most significant of these basic statutory concepts are "security," "trade," and "distribution." However, while the Québec *Securities Act*, CQLR c V-1.1 (QSA), employs the term "security," s 1 notes that the Act applies to "the following forms of investment." The QSA does not contain a definition of "trade." A tiered form of analysis is usually used to determine whether and to what extent securities law applies. Thus, if the item being bought or sold is not a security, the law in this area does not apply. If a security is not being traded, there are no registration or disclosure requirements. If the trade does not amount to a distribution or an offering of securities, there is no question of a prospectus requirement or an exemption to this requirement. This progressive definitional approach is useful to begin the analysis of when and how substantive securities law applies, though regulators have rendered it more complicated through their decision making. See the Ontario Securities Commission's (OSC's) decision in *Re Albino* (1991), 14 OSCB 365, below.

A further objective of this chapter is to introduce several other basic concepts that will be referred to in the chapters to follow. These concepts are necessary to understand the interaction between legal and finance or economic principles in this area. One of these is the concept of "efficiency." Another is the finance concept of "valuation." And a third is the notion of "materiality," which, as we will see, triggers the disclosure requirements imposed by the legislation. Finally, we also introduce the concept of "systemic risk," which has become the subject of much debate since the financial crisis.

II. WHAT IS A SECURITY?

Many people think of company shares or bonds as quintessential examples of securities. Indeed, these types of financial instruments are specified as securities by clause (e) of the definition of security in the Ontario *Securities Act*, RSO 1990, c S.5 (OSA), s 1(1), which refers to, for example, "a bond, debenture … share, stock, unit." We will examine the language of the definition of security in provincial statutes below. Before doing so, however, let us look at some examples of more specialized financial transactions engaged in by business entities, financial institutions, or entrepreneurs. They are, admittedly, rather complex, but provide real-world examples of transactions where the analyst has to consider the application of securities regulation principles. The issue is, therefore, how would we decide whether securities law, requiring disclosure of information and the possibility of sanctions, should apply to these transactions? Keep in mind that you are considering whether the legislative definition of a security, as interpreted by the courts and discussed below, helps us to decide. Let us look first at a type of financial instrument that has recently grown in popularity and in which various regulators have been interested.

A. Principal Protected Notes

A principal protected note (PPN) is described by Canadian securities regulators as "an investment product that offers an investor potential returns based on the performance of an underlying investment and a guarantee that the investor will receive, on maturity of the PPN, not less than the principal amount invested" (Canadian Securities Administrators (CSA) Notice 46-303, Principal Protected Notes (29 OSCB 5538)). During the last several years, the size of the market for PPNs grew significantly, from less than $10 billion at the end of 1999 to over $30 billion by mid-2006, with much of the growth coming from the retail sector. Securities regulators voiced concern about various aspects of the disclosure being provided to those who invested in these products. Public concern reached greater intensity in 2005 with the collapse of a portfolio manager named Portus Alternative Asset Management (PAAM) that was alleged to have solicited some $800 million in funds from consumers and placed it in financial products that involved the purchase of PPNs. (See Wes Voorheis, "Collapse of Portus Alternative Asset Management Inc and Norshield Asset Management (Canada) Ltd" (Research study submitted to the Task Force to Modernize Securities Legislation), *Canada Steps Up*, vol 3.) In March 2007, the federal Department of Finance announced that it proposed to develop regulations pertaining to the issue of PPNs by federally regulated financial institutions. These regulations came into force on July 1, 2008 (SOR/2008-180, s 1). In them, a PPN is defined as follows:

Principal Protected Notes Regulations

SOR/2008-180, s 1

principal protected note means a financial instrument that is issued in Canada by an institution to an investor and that

(a) provides for one or more payments to be made by the institution that is determined, in whole or in part, by reference to an index or reference point, including,

(i) the market price of a security, commodity, investment find or other financial instrument, and

(ii) the exchange rate between any two currencies; and

(b) provides that the principal amount that the institution is obligated to repay at or before the note's maturity is equal to or more than the total paid by the investor for the note.

The "regulatory impact analysis statement" that accompanies the promulgation of these regulations indicates that the regulations "specify the content, manner, and timing of disclosure that federally-regulated deposit-taking institutions are required to provide for various sales channels (in-person, telephone and online). They also specify that institutions make available, and provide on request, information to aid consumers in monitoring their investment." Compliance with these regulations is monitored by the Financial Consumer Agency of Canada (FCAC). Meanwhile, the CSA issued Multilateral Staff Notice 46-306 (2012) 35 OSCB 8064 that "sets out our expectation that banks and other federal and provincial deposit-taking institutions will use registered dealers (and registered individuals acting on behalf of those dealers) to distribute PPNs that do not fall within a limited class." It also noted that the CSA would continue to monitor the distribution of PPNs.

B. Segregated Funds

A second form of investment that is popular in Canada is an investment in an individual variable insurance contract (IVIC), also known as a segregated fund. This product is sold by insurance agents in Canada, and sales are overseen by insurance regulators, who enforce guidelines promulgated by the Canadian Life and Health Insurance Association (CLHIA). According to a news article citing figures from Investor Economics, $113.1 billion has been invested in IVICs in Canada as of March 31, 2015. (See Rob Carrick, *Globe and Mail*, 29 May

2015.) An IVIC is defined in CLHIA guidelines (incorporated by reference into Ontario Regulation 132/97 (*Variable Insurance Contracts*)) as follows: "'individual variable insurance contract' means an individual contract of life insurance, including an annuity, or an undertaking to provide an annuity, as defined by provincial and territorial insurance statutes and by the Civil Code of Québec, under which the liabilities vary in amount depending upon the market value of a specified group of assets in a segregated fund, and includes a provision in an individual contract of life insurance under which policy dividends are deposited in a segregated fund." A brochure for consumers issued by CLHIA provides further detail about the benefits of investing in segregated funds. These include the facts that guaranteed death benefits and potential creditor protection are included. The brochure notes that "in addition to these special contractual features" segregated funds offer diversification through a selection of growth, income and balanced funds, flexibility to switch between funds offered within the same contract, and liquidity allowing the investor to "promptly redeem all or part of your investment." Ontario Regulation 132/97 prescribes material that is required to be filed by insurers with the Superintendent of the Financial Services Commission of Ontario (FSCO) and defines what constitutes unfair or deceptive practices with respect to the sales or marketing of IVICS or the treatment of segregated fund assets.

Finally, we introduce another genre of investment opportunity that, as we shall see, has recently been considered by the OSC.

C. Viatical Settlements

RJ Herron, "Regulating Viatical Settlements: Is the Invisible Hand Picking the Pockets of the Terminally Ill?"
(1995) 28:4 U Mich JL Ref 931 (footnotes omitted)

One such technique, the "viatical settlement," was developed in the late 1980s as a response to the financial needs of PWAs [people with AIDS] and other terminally ill people. In a viatical settlement, a terminally ill policyholder (the viator) assigns the death benefit of his policy to a viatical settlement provider (the company), in exchange for an immediate payment of less than the expected death benefit of the policy. By the terms of the agreement, the entire death benefit is paid to the viatical settlement provider upon the viator's death. Although viatical settlements theoretically could be available to anyone with a dramatically shortened life expectancy, the vast majority of viatical settlements have been undertaken by PWAs, with terminal cancer patients comprising much of the remainder.

From the viator's perspective, the viatical transaction itself is fairly simple. The applicant contacts as many viatical settlement providers as he wishes and fills out detailed application forms, typically consisting of a questionnaire, an authorization to release medical records, and an authorization to release insurance policy information. Once the viatical provider has received all of the information, its panel of physicians evaluates the applicant's records and renders an opinion to the provider as to the applicant's prognosis. If the provider finds that the applicant has a sound insurance policy and, in consultation with its physicians, finds that the applicant has a qualifying condition that results in a life expectancy of less than two years, the provider then calculates a purchase price and makes an offer to the applicant. The offer typically amounts to between fifty and eighty percent of the policy's face value. If the applicant accepts the offer, the provider and applicant (now a viator) sign the purchase documents, which include a purchase agreement for the policy, a change of ownership form, and a change of beneficiary form. The latter two forms then are forwarded to the viator's life insurance company, which records the information, files the documents, and sends a confirmation to the viator. Once the viatical provider receives confirmation of the changes, it pays the viator, in a lump sum, the full amount of the viatical settlement, either by cashier's check or wire transfer. The entire process can be completed in three to six weeks.

D. Legislative Definition of a Security

Turning now to typical statutory definitions of security, OSA, s 1(1) sets forth a long list of items that fall within the scope of the term. These are that

"security" includes,

(a) any document, instrument or writing commonly known as a security,

(b) any document constituting evidence of title to or interest in the capital, assets, property, profits, earnings or royalties of any person or company,

(c) any document constituting evidence of an interest in an association of legatees or heirs,

(d) any document constituting evidence of an option, subscription or other interest in or to a security,

(e) a bond, debenture, note or other evidence of indebtedness or a share, stock, unit, unit certificate, participation certificate, certificate of share or interest, preorganization certificate or subscription other than,

(i) A contract of insurance issued by an insurance company licensed under the *Insurance Act*, and

(ii) evidence of a deposit issued by a bank listed in Schedule I, II or III to the *Bank Act* (Canada), by a credit union or league to which the *Credit Unions and Caisses Populaires Act, 1994* applies, by a loan corporation or trust corporation registered under the *Loan and Trust Corporations Act* or by an association to which the *Cooperative Credit Associations Act* (Canada) applies,

(f) any agreement under which the interest of the purchaser is valued for purposes of conversion or surrender by reference to the value of a proportionate interest in a specified portfolio of assets, except a contract issued by an insurance company licensed under the *Insurance Act* which provides for payment at maturity of an amount not less than three quarters of the premiums paid by the purchaser for a benefit payable at maturity,

(g) any agreement providing that money received will be repaid or treated as a subscription to shares, stock, units or interests at the option of the recipient or of any person or company,

(h) any certificate of share or interest in a trust, estate or association,

(i) any profit-sharing agreement or certificate,

(j) any certificate of interest in an oil, natural gas or mining lease, claim or royalty voting trust certificate,

(k) any oil or natural gas royalties or leases or fractional or other interest therein,

(l) any collateral trust certificate,

(m) any income or annuity contract not issued by an insurance company,

(n) any investment contract,

(o) any document constituting evidence of an interest in a scholarship or educational plan or trust, and

(p) any commodity futures contract or any commodity futures option that is not traded on a commodity futures exchange registered with or recognized by the Commission under the *Commodity Futures Act* or the form of which is not accepted by the Director under that Act, whether any of the foregoing relate to an issuer or proposed issuer.

For purposes of comparison, it is interesting to note that the QSA relies on somewhat more broadly based wording.

Securities Act
CQLR c V-1.1, s 1

Applicability

1. This Act applies to the following forms of investment:

(1) any security recognized as such in the trade, more particularly, a share, bond, capital stock of an entity constituted as a legal person, or a subscription right or warrant;

(2) an instrument, other than a bond, evidencing a loan of money;

(3) a deposit of money, whether or not evidenced by a certificate except a deposit received by the Gouvernement du Québec, the Government of Canada, or one of their departments or agencies;

(4) (Repealed)

(5) (Repealed)

(6) a share in an investment club;

(7) an investment contract;

(8) (Repealed)

(8.1) an option or other non-traded derivative whose value is derived from, referenced to or based on the value or market price of a security, granted as compensaton or as payment for a good or service;

(9) any other form of investment determined by regulation of the Government.

Investment contract

An investment contract is a contract whereby a person, having been led to expect profits, undertakes to participate in the risk of a venture by a contribution of capital or loan, without having the required knowledge to carry on the venture or without obtaining the right to participate directly in decisions concerning the carrying on of the venture.

The text of the Ontario version contains definitions that are both broadly and specifically defined. However, both the Ontario and Québec definitions are open ended so as to be inclusive rather than definitive.

1. Specific Definitions of Security

In Ontario, the most traditional and frequently encountered clause of the definition is (e), above, which covers shares and debt instruments such as bonds and debentures. Meanwhile, the Québec definition considers that common forms of securities, such as corporate shares or bonds, are examples of a more generic category of "any security recognized as such in the trade." Equally specific, though more complicated, definitions in the OSA are found in clauses (d) and (p), which refer to options and commodity futures contracts, respectively. Chapter 3 will return to the question of how options, futures, and derivatives work. Additional information is provided in the following excerpt.

Jeffrey G MacIntosh & Christopher C Nicholls, *Securities Law*
(Toronto: Irwin, 2002) at 18-22 (footnotes omitted)

Options

a) Options Are Securities

An option is an instrument that gives the holder the right to buy or sell an underlying interest in respect of a named issuer at an agreed price, on or before an agreed date, but does not obligate the holder to do so. The underlying interest is often common shares of the named issuer. Options are "securities" within the meaning of Canadian securities legislation.

b) Options Issued by a Corporation

A corporation may issue options that entitle holders to buy the issuer's own securities. A "right" is a common example of such an option. A right gives the holder the option to buy an additional share, or a fraction of an additional share, of a stated issuer at a stated price, on or before a stated date. For example, a right issued on 1 January 2001 might give the holder the right to buy one share of the corporation, on or before 15 February 2002 at a price of $50. In this case, the underlying interest of the option is the corporation's common shares, and the "exercise price" is $50.

• • •

A "warrant" is essentially the same kind of option, although it may give the holder the right to exercise it over a longer period of time. Further, it will often be attached to the issuance of some other type of security, such as a bond.

• • •

d) Options Issued by Persons Other Than the Corporation

Share options need not be issued by the corporation that is the issuer of the underlying shares. Other persons frequently issue options whose underlying interest is a security issued by a publicly traded corporation. The most common examples are put and call options.

A call option on a corporation's shares may be created by an option "writer" (i.e., a seller). The option writer sells the option to a purchaser for a price known as the option premium. The call option entitles the purchaser, if it so wishes, to force the writer to sell an outstanding share of a third-party corporation at a specified price (the exercise price) on or before a specified date. The corporation that originally issued this optioned share takes no part whatsoever in this transaction. Suppose, for example, that the price of an ABC Corp. common share is $25 on 1 March 2001. The writer (perhaps an investment banking firm) may create a call option with an exercise price of $30 to be exercised by the holder (if the holder so wishes) on or before 1 June 2001. The purchaser of the call option hopes that the price of ABC Corp.'s common shares will rise to more than $30 before 1 June. If it does not, the option will expire and be worthless. Obviously, the writer of the option hopes that the price of ABC's common shares will not rise to more than $30 on or before 1 June. In a sense, the writer and the purchaser of the option are making contrary "bets" on the future value of ABC stock. Once issued, call options may be traded in the secondary market.

A put option on corporate shares also may be created by an option writer; however, the purchaser of the option acquires the right to require the writer to purchase a corporate share from her at a stated price on or before a certain date. Using the example of ABC Corp. again, where the share price on 1 March is $25, the writer of a put option might sell the purchaser a put option, entitling the option purchaser to force the writer, on or before 1 June 2001, to buy from the purchaser a share of ABC Corp. at a price of $20. Note that at the time of issuance, the put option is "out of the money." If it expired on the date of issuance, its value would be zero. The purchaser hopes that the price of ABC will drop to an amount below $20 on or before 1 June. If it drops to $15, for example, the purchaser can enter the market, buy a share of ABC at $15, immediately exercise the put option, and resell that same share to the writer for $20, for a $5 profit.

e) Options May Have a Variety of Underlying Interests

An option can be written against virtually any underlying interest, financial or otherwise, whose price is subject to variation.

. . .

f) Options Issued as a Compensation Device

Corporations frequently issue call options or other similar types of options as compensation for the services of senior executives and/or directors (referred to collectively below as "managers"). Options are a useful compensation device because, among other things, they give the managers more "leverage" than simply holding shares. In order to hold shares in the corporation, the manager must invest money. When options are granted, no investment takes place. The manager eventually profits to the extent that the share price rises above the exercise price of the options. Such options are thought to provide managers with a potent incentive to increase the value of the companies they manage, although critics sometimes see such options as little more than a subterfuge for transferring corporate value from shareholders to managers.

Futures

Futures (exchange-traded) and forwards (over-the-counter, or OTC) are contracts to sell a specified asset on a stated date in the future at a stated price. Like option contracts, futures contracts are written against a wide variety of underlying interests, the most common of which are currencies, commodities, indexes, and interest rates.

A hypothetical future example is a contract struck on 1 March 2001, in which the underlying interest is four litres of milk, the sale price is $10, and the settlement date is 1 June 2001. In this contract, the purchaser agrees to buy, and the seller agrees to sell, four litres of milk on 1 June for $10. Although the sale will not take place until 1 June, both parties are contractually committed to complete the transaction when that date arrives.

Futures contracts have long been used as a risk management tool. Farmers, for example, often sell futures contracts to purchasers of the commodities they produce, even before the crop or the animals have been raised. This transfers the risk of price fluctuations in the underlying interest to the purchasers.

Futures contracts are "securities" within the meaning of Canadian securities legislation and thus fall within the domain of securities regulators. However, commodity futures contracts that are publicly traded on a commodity futures exchange are excluded from the definition of "security" because they are separately regulated under special legislation dealing with commodities futures. This legislation is nonetheless administered by the securities regulators.

Derivative Securities

The value of a "derivative security" depends on (or "derives" from) the value of another security, financial asset, or other reference value, which (as noted above) is referred to as the underlying interest. Rights and warrants, as discussed above, are, thus, types of derivative securities, as are put and call options.

The term "derivative security" is also used to refer to futures and forward contracts. In fact, every derivative security, no matter how complex, can be characterized as either an option contract, a futures (or forward) contract, or a (frequently elaborate) combination of the two. The term derivative security is an umbrella term used to refer to a vast range of different types of financial instruments whose values vary with the underlying interests.

Derivative securities have exploded in popularity in the last decade, mainly as a result of an increased demand to hedge risk in volatile currency, interest rate, commodity, and stock markets. Although not all derivative instruments are "securities" within the meaning of provincial securities legislation, the securities legislation of some provinces nonetheless gives the regulators the power to regulate such instruments.

As the excerpt above explains, the term "derivative" is not actually included in the definition of a "security" under the OSA though the most common forms of derivatives—options and futures—are so included. However, since the GFC, Canada's securities regulators, along with their counterparts in other countries, have been developing a regulatory framework for the trading of derivatives. We provide a description of this framework below.

Clauses (j), (k), and (o) of the definition also refer to specific types of investment in natural resources and scholarship plans, respectively, and their inclusion is consistent with the protective goals of securities legislation. Indeed, some clauses represent specific legislative responses to attempts to defraud investors, such as clause (c), referring to documents "constituting evidence of an interest in an association of legatees or heirs."

2. *Open-Ended Definitions of Security*

Clauses (a), (b), (i), and (n) of the Ontario definition are much broader. They require detailed consideration because these clauses are often where the new definitional developments take place and where reference to the underlying policy of the legislation becomes pivotal. In this connection, it should be remembered that the issue of whether what was being sold was a security or not will likely arise from attempts to design schemes that will escape the requirements of the Act, or from attempts by purchasers to recoup on schemes that "went bad." See e.g. the *Howey* and *Pacific Coast Coin Exchange* cases, excerpted below.

With respect to the "commonly known" definition, it is clear that this requirement means that the instrument is commonly known as a security, not by the uninformed person on the street but rather by sophisticated analysts or securities lawyers. An example of this interpretation of the "commonly known" wording is found in the Québec Securities Commission decision of *Geldermann*, [1972] 3 QSCWS No 65. This regulatory decision in turn relied on the decision of *Securities & Exchange Commission v CM Joiner Leasing Corp*, 320 US 344 at 352 (1943) that "the test rather is what character the instrument is given in commerce by the terms of the offer, the plan of distribution, and the economic inducements held out to the prospect." In that case, the claims being sold were leasehold interests in property that Joiner Leasing hoped would contain oil. In soliciting the interest of the purchasers of the leasehold interests, Joiner Leasing undertook to drill test wells to confirm this potential. In *Geldermann*, the Commission des valeurs mobilières du Québec (CVMQ) concluded that "proof of common knowledge must be based on an overwhelming set of facts and conclusive evidence."

Clause (b) of the Ontario Act is also extremely broad, because "evidence of title to … property" could mean any commodity you can buy. Here courts and regulators are likely to engage in policy-oriented analysis, using as a reference point the goals of securities regulation, to restrict the application of this otherwise all-encompassing wording. Often a key issue is whether the person acquiring the interest was *making an investment* as opposed to *buying a commodity*. *Re Ontario Securities Commission and Brigadoon Scotch Distributors (Canada) Ltd* ([1970] 3 OR 714 (H Ct J)) involved Scotch whisky warehouse receipts. They were held to be a security because the whisky was stored and then sold, on behalf of investors', to blenders who used it to produce a final whisky product. The contracts featured the performance of service by others that was meant to increase the value of the product. The issue was whether the purchaser wanted the whisky itself or the profit that could be obtained from reselling it. Obviously, this leaves some room for definitional flexibility where the motives of the purchaser are mixed, as they often are. More generally, one might argue that the distinction between an investment and a commodity becomes blurred in the context of products like units of mutual funds, which are by some measures clearly investments but by others are marketed in ways similar to other consumer products.[1]

The definition of a security as an "investment contract" is where much of the jurisprudential consideration of the concept has been concentrated. As we shall see shortly, the Supreme Court of Canada (SCC), in *Pacific Coast Coin Exchange v Ontario Securities Commission*, [1978] 2 SCR 112 at 127, adopted the idea drawn from US commentators that these categories are meant to be "catchalls" that cover "arrangements that do not permit the customers to know exactly the value of the investment they are making." In dealing with this more open-ended wording, courts and regulators have tended to take a "purposive" approach, looking through the form of the transaction in question to its substance. Here, it is assumed that the purpose in question is to protect purchasers of financial claims from

1 See e.g. Glorianne Stromberg, *Investment Funds in Canada and Consumer Protection* (Ottawa: Office of Consumer Affairs, 1998).

those who would seek to take advantage of them. This was the case even before securities legislation began to specify the goals that regulators should achieve in administering the Act. Now what may happen is that certain of the legislative objectives of the Act become key to making the decision about whether the Act applies at all. We will see how the SCC has operationalized this approach in the leading case of *Pacific Coast*. However, the SCC's decision in *Pacific Coast* built upon jurisprudence from the United States some years before. As you read the following two US decisions, consider how the test established in *Hawaii* differs from the US Supreme Court's decision in *Howey*. Note also the different levels of court involved in these cases. Both the *Howey* and the Canadian *Pacific Coast Coin Exchange* cases featured strong dissenting judgments, which are also included in the excerpts from the respective cases.

3. *Case Law on the Definition of Investment Contract*

Securities and Exchange Commission v WJ Howey Co et al
328 US 293 (1946)

Suit by the Securities and Exchange Commission against W.J. Howey Company and Howey-in-the-Hills Service, Inc., to restrain alleged violations of the Securities Act.

MURPHY J (delivering the opinion of the court) (Frankfurter J dissenting): This case involves the application of s. 2(1) of the *Securities Act of 1933* to an offering of units of a citrus grove development coupled with a contract for cultivating, marketing and remitting the net proceeds to the investor. The Securities and Exchange Commission instituted this action to restrain the respondents from using the mails and instrumentalities of interstate commerce in the offer and sale of unregistered and nonexempt securities in violation of s. 5(a) of the Act .... The District Court denied the injunction ... , and the Fifth Circuit Court of Appeals affirmed the judgment ....

... The respondents, W.J. Howey Company and Howey-in-the-Hills Service Inc., are Florida corporations under direct common control and management. The Howey Company owns large tracts of citrus acreage in Lake County, Florida. During the past several years it has planted about 500 acres annually, keeping half of the groves itself and offering the other half to the public "to help us finance additional development." Howey-in-the-Hills Service, Inc., is a service company engaged in cultivating and developing many of these groves, including the harvesting and marketing of the crops.

Each prospective customer is offered both a land sales contract and a service contract, after having been told that it is not feasible to invest in a grove unless service arrangements are made. While the purchaser is free to make arrangements with other service companies, the superiority of Howey-in-the-Hills Service, Inc., is stressed. Indeed, 85% of the acreage sold during the 3-year period ending May 31, 1943, was covered by service contracts with Howey-in-the-Hills Service, Inc.

The land sales contract with the Howey Company provides for a uniform purchase price per acre or fraction thereof, varying in amount only in accordance with the number of years the particular plot has been planted with citrus trees. Upon full payment of the purchase price the land is conveyed to the purchaser by warranty deed. Purchases are usually made in narrow strips of land arranged so that an acre consists of a row of 48 trees. During the period between February 1, 1941, and May 31, 1943, 31 of the 42 persons making purchases bought less than 5 acres each. The average holding of these 31 persons was 1.33 acres and sales of as little as 0.65, 0.7 and 0.73 of an acre were made. These tracts are not separately fenced and the sole indication of several ownership is found in small land marks intelligible only through a plat book record.

The service contract, generally of a 10-year duration without option of cancellation, gives Howey-in-the-Hills Service, Inc., a leasehold interest and "full and complete" possession of the acreage. For a specified fee plus the cost of labor and materials, the company is given full discretion and authority over the cultivation of the groves and the harvest and marketing of the crops. The company is well established in the citrus business and maintains a large force of skilled personnel and a great deal of equipment, including 75 tractors, sprayer wagons, fertilizer trucks and the like. Without the consent of the company, the land owner or purchaser has no right of entry to market the crop; thus there is ordinarily no right to specific fruit. The company is accountable only for an allocation of the net profits based upon a check made at the time of picking. All the produce is pooled by the respondent companies, which do business under their own names.

The purchasers for the most part are non-residents of Florida. They are predominantly business and professional people who lack the knowledge, skill and equipment necessary for the care and cultivation of citrus trees. They are attracted by the expectation of substantial profits. It was represented, for example, that profits during the 1943–1944 season amounted to 20% and that even greater profits might be expected during the 1944–1945 season, although only a 10% annual return was to be expected over a 10-year period. Many of these purchasers are patrons of a resort hotel owned and operated by the Howey Company in a scenic section adjacent to the groves. The hotel's advertising mentions the fine groves in the vicinity and the attention of the patrons is drawn to the groves as they are being escorted about the surrounding countryside. They are told that the groves are for sale; if they indicate an interest in the matter they are then given a sales talk.

It is admitted that the mails and instrumentalities of interstate commerce are used in the sale of the land and service contracts and that no registration statement or letter of notification has ever been filed with the Commission in accordance with the *Securities Act of 1933* and the rules and regulations thereunder.

Section 2(1) of the Act defines the term "security" to include the commonly known documents traded for speculation or investment. This definition also includes "securities" of a more variable character, designated by such descriptive terms as "certificate of interest or participation in any profit-sharing agreement," "investment contract" and "in general, any interest or instrument commonly known as a 'security.'" The legal issue in this case turns upon a determination of whether, under the circumstances, the land sales contract, the warranty deed and the service contract together constitute an "investment contract" within the meaning of s. 2(1). An affirmative answer brings into operation the registration requirements of s. 5(a) unless the security is granted an exemption under s. 3(b) … . The lower courts, in reaching a negative answer to this problem, treated the contracts and deeds as separate transactions involving no more than an ordinary real estate sale and an agreement by the seller to manage the property for the buyer.

The term "investment contract" is undefined by the *Securities Act* or by relevant legislative reports. But the term was common in many state "blue sky" laws in existence prior to the adoption of the federal statute and, although the term was also undefined by the state laws, it had been broadly construed by state courts so as to afford the investing public a full measure of protection. Form was disregarded for substance and emphasis was placed upon economic reality. An investment contract thus came to mean a contract or scheme for "the placing of capital or laying out of money in a way intended to secure income or profit from its employment." This definition was uniformly applied by state courts to a variety of situations where individuals were led to invest money in a common enterprise with the expectation that they would earn a profit solely through the efforts of the promoter or of someone other than themselves.

By including an investment contract within the scope of s. 2(1) of the *Securities Act*, Congress was using a term the meaning of which had been crystallized by this prior judicial interpretation. It is therefore reasonable to attach that meaning to the term as used by Congress, especially since such a definition is consistent with the statutory aims. In other words, an investment contract for purposes of the *Securities Act* means a contract, transaction or scheme whereby a person invests his money in a common enterprise and is led to expect profits solely from the efforts of the promoter or a third party, it being immaterial whether the shares in the enterprise are evidenced by formal certificates or by nominal interests in the physical assets employed in the enterprise. Such a definition necessarily underlies this Court's decision in *Securities Exch. Commission v. C.M. Joiner Leasing Corp.*, 320 US 344 … , and has been enunciated and applied many times by lower federal courts. It permits the fulfillment of the statutory purpose of compelling full and fair disclosure relative to the issuance of "the many types of instruments that in our commercial world fall within the ordinary concept of a security." H. Rep. No. 85, 73rd Cong., 1st Sess., p. 11. It embodies a flexible rather than a static principle, one that is capable of adaptation to meet the countless and variable schemes devised by those who seek the use of the money of others on the promise of profits.

The transactions in this case clearly involve investment contracts as so defined. The respondent companies are offering something more than fee simple interests in land, something different from a farm or orchard coupled with management services. They are offering an opportunity to contribute money and to share in the profits of a large citrus fruit enterprise managed and partly owned by respondents. They are offering this opportunity to persons who reside in distant localities and who lack the equipment and experience requisite to the cultivation, harvesting and marketing of the citrus products. Such persons have no desire to occupy the land or to develop it themselves; they are attracted solely by the prospects of a return on their investment. Indeed, individual development of the plots of land that are offered and sold would seldom be economically feasible due to their small size. Such tracts gain utility as citrus groves only when cultivated and developed as component parts of a larger area. A common enterprise managed by respondents or third parties with adequate personnel and equipment is therefore essential if the investors are to achieve their paramount aim of a return on their investments. Their respective shares in this enterprise are evidenced by land sales contracts and warranty deeds, which serve as a convenient method of determining the investors' allocable shares of the profits. The resulting transfer of rights in land is purely incidental.

Thus all the elements of a profit-seeking business venture are present here. The investors provide the capital and share in the earnings and profits; the promoters manage, control and operate the enterprise. It follows that the arrangements whereby the investors' interests are made manifest involve investment contracts, regardless of the legal terminology in which such contracts are clothed. The investment contracts in this instance take the form of land sales contracts, warranty deeds and service contracts which respondents offer to prospective investors. And respondents' failure to abide by the statutory and administrative rules in making such offerings, even though the failure resulted from a bona fide mistake as to the law, cannot be sanctioned under the Act.

This conclusion is unaffected by the fact that some purchasers choose not to accept the full offer of an investment contract by declining to enter into a service contract with the respondents. The *Securities Act* prohibits the offer as well as the sale of unregistered, non-exempt securities. Hence it is enough that the respondents merely offer the essential ingredients of an investment contract.

We reject the suggestion of the Circuit Court of Appeals ... that an investment contract is necessarily missing where the enterprise is not speculative or promotional in character and where the tangible interest which is sold has intrinsic value independent of the success of the enterprise as a whole. The test is whether the scheme involves an investment of money in a common enterprise with profits to come solely from the efforts of others. If that test be satisfied, it is immaterial whether the enterprise is speculative or non-speculative or whether there is a sale of property with or without intrinsic value. See *S.E.C. v. C.M. Joiner Leasing Corp., supra* ... . The statutory policy of affording broad protection to investors is not to be thwarted by unrealistic and irrelevant formulae.

FRANKFURTER J (dissenting): "Investment contract" is not a term of art; it is a conception dependent upon the circumstances of a particular situation.

• • •

For the crucial issue in this case turns on whether the contracts for the land and the contracts for the management of the property were in reality separate agreements or merely parts of a single transaction. It is clear from its opinion that the District Court was warranted in its conclusion that the record does not establish the existence of an investment contract: the record in this case shows that not a single sale of citrus grove property was made by the Howey Company during the period involved in this suit, except to purchasers who actually inspected the property before purchasing the same. The record further discloses that no purchaser is required to engage the Service Company to care for his property and that of the fifty-one purchasers acquiring property during this period, only forty-two entered into contract with the Service Company for the care of the property.

Simply because other arrangements may have the appearances of this transaction but are employed as an evasion of the *Securities Act* does not mean that the present contracts were evasive. I find nothing in the *Securities Act* to indicate that Congress meant to bring every innocent transaction within the scope of the Act simply because a perversion of them is covered by the Act.

Let us turn now to consider the subsequent unanimous Supreme Court of Hawaii decision, which offers a somewhat different focus for the determination of whether the transactions in question involved the distribution of a security.

State of Hawaii v Hawaii Market Center, Inc et al
52 Haw 642 (Sup Ct 1971)

Action by State to enjoin further promotion and execution of "founder-member purchasing contract agreements" allegedly constituting unregistered securities.

LEVINSON J: The legal issue presented by this case is whether the "Founder-Member Purchasing Contract Agreements" issued by Hawaii Market Center, Inc., one of the appellants, constitute securities within the meaning of the Hawaii Uniform Securities Act (Modified). An affirmative answer to this question would bring into operation the registration requirements of HRS s. 485-8. Before determining the nature of these agreements it is first necessary to delineate clearly the economic relationship existing between Hawaii Market Center, Inc. and persons who have contracted with it pursuant to these agreements.

Hawaii Market Center, Inc. (hereinafter referred to as HMC) is a Hawaii corporation with a capitalization of $1000.00. The corporation's expressed purpose was to open a retail store which would sell merchandise only to persons possessing purchase authorization cards. In order to raise capital for the financing of this enterprise HMC recruited founder-members. The maximum number of such members was set at five thousand.

Prospective founder members were asked to attend recruitment meetings. At these meetings a speaker explained how members would be eligible to earn (1) immediate income before the store became operational, and (2) future income after the store became operational. In order to earn such income an invitee was required to become either a founder-member distributor or a founder-member supervisor.

A person became a founder-member distributor by purchasing from HMC either a sewing machine or a cookware set (each with a wholesale value of $70.00) for $320.00. The purchaser also executed a "Founder-Member Purchasing Contract Agreement" with the corporation. This agreement states that a distributor is able to earn money in five ways. He may: (1) distribute the 50 authorized buyer's cards, which have been issued to him and thereafter earn a 10% commission on each sale resulting from the use of one of these cards in the HMC store; (2) earn a $50.00 fee each time a person he refers becomes a founder-member distributor; (3) receive a $300.00 fee as compensation for establishing a new member as a supervisor or upgrading an old member from distributor to supervisor. The fourth and fifth sources of income relate to the earning of credits which are applied to a $900.00 fee paid by a distributor to his supervisor if the distributor wishes to be upgraded.

A person became a supervisor by executing a founder-member contract and purchasing both a sewing machine and a cookware set for a total price of $820.00. A supervisor earns higher fees and commissions than a distributor. In addition, a supervisor receives an override commission if his distributor enlists a new member. He also receives override commissions on all sales made to holders of purchase authorization cards distributed by any founder-member whose entry into the organization can be traced back to the supervisor.

. . .

I. The Essential Characteristics of an Investment Contract Under the Hawaii Uniform Securities Act (Modified)

A. The Test Embodied in the Howey Case Is Too Mechanical to Protect the Investing Public Adequately

In arguing whether the interests represented by HMC's founder-member contracts constitute investment contract securities within the meaning of HRS s. 485-1(12) both the appellant and the appellee rely for guidance principally upon the Supreme Court decision in *Securities & Exchange Commission v. W.J. Howey Co.*, 328 US 293 … (1946). That case sought to formulate a test for the existence of an "investment contract," such a contract being included within the definition of "security" under the *Federal Securities Act*. The Court concluded that an investment contract exists whenever "a person invests his money in a common enterprise and is led to expect profits solely from the efforts of the promoter or a third party." *Securities & Exchange Commission v. W.J. Howey, Co.*, supra at 299 … .

The appellants urge us to adopt the *Howey* formula as the test to be applied in the present case. It is contended that under the *Howey* test the contracts in question are not investment contracts because founder-members in the HMC plan are expected to recruit new members and distribute purchase authorization cards in order to earn income; they do not, therefore, "expect profits solely from the efforts" of others.

The State also relies upon the *Howey* case but contends that the test enunciated therein is not to be taken literally. It argues that the efforts expected of the founder-members are minimal in nature and, as a practical matter, the founders are substantially dependent upon the management of the corporation for a successful return on their investment. Thus the State asserts, under the real meaning of the *Howey* rule, the disputed agreements are investment contracts. We agree that the present agreements constitute "securities" within the coverage of the *Hawaii Uniform Securities Act (Modified)*. We do not choose, however, to base this decision on the restrictive formula laid down by the Supreme Court in the *Howey* case.

The primary weakness of the *Howey* formula is that it has led courts to analyse investment projects mechanically, based on a narrow concept of investor participation. Thus courts become entrapped in polemics over the meaning of the word "solely" and fail to consider the more fundamental question whether the statutory policy of affording broad protection to investors should be applied even to those situations where an investor is not inactive, but participates to a limited degree in the operation of the business. In fulfilling the remedial purposes of our state act, we believe a sounder approach to securities regulation requires that courts focus their attention on the economic realities of security transactions: that is, "(t)he placing of capital or laying out of money in a way intended to secure income or profit from its employment" in an enterprise.

B. The Risk Capital Approach to Defining an Investment Contract

The salient feature of securities sales is the public solicitation of venture capital to be used in a business enterprise. This subjection of the investor's money to the risks of an enterprise over which he exercises no managerial control is the basic economic reality of a security transaction. Any formula which purports to guide courts in determining whether a security exists should recognize this essential reality and be broad enough to fulfill the remedial purposes of the *Securities Act*. Those purposes are (1) to prevent fraud, and (2) to protect the public against the imposition of unsubstantial schemes by regulating the transactions by which promoters go to the public for risk capital. HRS s. 485-10(e). Therefore, we hold that for the purposes of the *Hawaii Uniform Securities Act (Modified)* an investment contract is created whenever:

(1) An offeree furnishes initial value to an offeror, and
(2) a portion of this initial value is subjected to the risks of the enterprise, and
(3) the furnishing of the initial value is induced by the offeror's promises or representations which give rise to a reasonable understanding that a valuable benefit of some kind, over and above the initial value, will accrue to the offeree as a result of the operation of the enterprise, and
(4) the offeree does not receive the right to exercise practical and actual control over the managerial decisions of the enterprise.

The above test provides, we believe, the necessary broad coverage to protect the public from the novel as well as the conventional forms of financing enterprises. Its utility is best demonstrated by its application to the facts in the instant case.

II. The Contracts in Question Constitute Investment Contracts Within the Meaning of HRS, s 485-1(12)

A. The Initial Value Subjected to the Risks of the Enterprise

Each person who executes a "Founder-Member Purchasing Contract Agreement" is required by Hawaii Market Center, Inc. to make a "one-time retail purchase" of $320.00 in order to become a distributor and $820.00 in order to become a supervisor. The record indicates that the total wholesale cost to HMC of the purchased merchandise is $70.00 and $140.00 respectively. The appellants have made no attempt to characterize these transactions as the simple purchase of merchandise, nor do we deem them such. The terms of the offer and the inducements held out to the prospects clearly indicate that the substantial premiums paid by founder-members to HMC are given in consideration for the right to receive future income from the corporation. These overcharges constitute the offerees' investments or contributions of initial value, such value being subjected to the risks of the enterprise.

It is uncontested that the recruitment of founder-members was motivated by the need to raise capital to finance the opening of the proposed Hawaii Market Center store. Inextricably bound to the success of this enterprise is the ability of the founder-members to recoup their initial investment and earn income. The recruitment fee paid to distributors and supervisors, during the pre-operational phase of the plan, rests upon the promoters' ability to sell the success of the plan to prospective members. In addition, those members who choose to rely solely on the second method of earning income, the payment of commissions based on sales, receive no return at all on their investment unless the store functions successfully. This latter point is particularly important because recruitment of members increases geometrically. Therefore, since membership is limited to five thousand, a very large percentage of founder-members will be totally dependent on sales commissions to recover their initial investment plus income. It is thus apparent that the security of the founder-members' investments is inseparable from the risks of the enterprise. The success of the plan is the common "thread on which everybody's beads (are) strung." *Securities & Exchange Commission v. C.M. Joiner Leasing Corp.*, 320 US 344 … (1943).

B. The Promise of a Valuable Return on the Offeree's Investment

The appellants contend that because of the nature of the receipts promised to founder-members the trial court erred in finding the existence of a security. They stress that founder-members do not participate in the profits of the enterprise. They are promised fixed fees and commissions, which are payable regardless of the existence of profits. Therefore, it is argued, the essential profits sharing element of a security is lacking. Once again, this argument ignores the economic realities underlying securities regulation.

It should be irrelevant to the protective policies of the securities laws that the inducements leading an investor to risk his initial investment are founded on promises of fixed returns rather than a share of profits. The reference point should be the offeree's expectations, not the balance sheet of the offeror corporation. The unwary investor lured by promises of fixed fees deserves the same protection as a participant in a profit sharing plan. For this reason courts have avoided a narrow definition of "profits." They have recognized securities sales even where the promised benefits to the offeree were indirect, arising from an anticipated increase in the value of the property received, rather than direct payments from the offeror. *Securities & Exchange Commission v. C.M. Joiner Leasing Corp.*, supra, 320 US at 348-349; … *Roe v. United States*, 287 F.2d 435, 439 (5th Cir.), cert. denied, 368 US 824 … (1961). Thus, the fact that in the instant case HMC guaranteed the offerees amounts of money independent of enterprise profits does not undermine the investment nature of the transactions.

C. The Lack of Managerial Control Over the Enterprise

Finally, as previously stated, it is irrelevant to the remedial purposes of the *Securities Act* that an investor participates in a minor way in the operations of the enterprise. Courts should focus on the quality of the participation. In order to negate the finding of a security the offeree should have practical and actual control over the managerial decisions of the enterprise. For it is this control which gives the offeree the opportunity to safeguard his own investment, thus obviating the need for state intervention. Coffey, "The Economic Realities of a 'Security': Is There a More Significant Formula?," supra at 396-398.

In the present case the founder-members possess none of the incidents of managerial control which would preclude the finding of a security. The members have no power to influence the utilization of the accumulated capital. Nor will they have any authority over those decisions which will affect the operation of the store, if it is successfully established. Judged by an ability to protect their original investment, the offerees in this case are powerless. Thus, under the economic realities approach presently advocated, they properly belong to the class of investors falling within the remedial purposes of the *Securities Act*. Therefore we hold that the present agreements are investment contracts within the meaning of the *Hawaii Uniform Securities Act (Modified)* and must be registered with the Commission of Securities prior to distribution.

The court in *Howey* concluded that the transfer of property was merely an incident of a larger scheme involving an investment contract and refused to be bound by the technical legal structure of the transaction as a purchase of land. In focusing on the individual motivations of the purchasers, the court found that they were attracted by the "expectation of substantial profits." The court also emphasized the fact that the purchasers intended their profits to accrue "solely" from the efforts of others. This emphasis suggests a level of judicial acceptance of the Marxist definition of capitalism as the exploitation of the labour of others.[2] Meanwhile the *Hawaii* case glossed both the "expectations of profits" issue and the requirement imposed by *Howey* that profits are made "solely" through others' efforts. Anticipating by some years the findings of behavioural psychologists about the phenomenon of loss aversion (that individuals act more cautiously in connection with the risk of losing what they already possess than in connection with possible additional gains), *Hawaii* is generally known as the "risk capital" case because it emphasizes the risk of loss to the investor and the lack of control of the investor over the success of her investment.

The Canadian version of these decisions is *Pacific Coast Coin Exchange* (PCCE). In this case, PCCE operated a scheme whereby it offered bags of silver coins for sale to members of the public that could be bought either for cash or on margin. Most of the relevant purchases of bags of coins were on margin. The promotional literature for the scheme described the bags of coins as an "investment" that operated as a protection against inflation. Once the purchasers paid their deposits, the transactions could be completed either by paying the rest of the purchase price by a particular time and receiving the bags of silver or by selling the bags of coins again at the then purchase price, through PCCE. The purchaser would then make as profit or loss the difference between the price for which she had contracted to buy the bags and the price for which they were later sold. PCCE was not obliged under the contract to repurchase the bags of coins, though its literature asserted that "it had never failed to make a market for its customers in the past." Specific bags were not allocated to any purchaser until such time as the purchaser paid the balance of the price if they ever did so. PCCE kept very few bags of silver in inventory to pay off these contracts, but it made its own futures contracts in bags of coins to offset its obligations to deliver them to purchasers. PCCE also earned commission on all contracts to purchase and sell. The OSC issued a cease trade order with respect to these transactions, and PCCE appealed to the courts. The dissenting and majority judgments, respectively, are excerpted below.

Pacific Coast Coin Exchange of Canada v Ontario (Securities Commission)
[1978] 2 SCR 112

LASKIN CJ (dissenting): … We are concerned here with giving meaning and application to the term "investment contract," which is one of the many kinds of "security" included within the *Securities Act*, RSO 1970, c. 426, as amended and hence brought within its regulatory authority. The term, it is conceded, cannot be given a literal meaning because to do so would bring within the scope of *The Securities Act* innumerable transactions

2 Personal communication from Osgoode Hall Law School Professor Emeritus Harry Glasbeek.

which have no public aspect. Even with respect to that, it is common ground that commodity futures contracts are not per se within the regulatory regime of the Act.

My brother de Grandpré has noted in his reasons that securities legislation in the United States has similarly left the term "investment contract" undefined, so that it fell to the Courts in various proceedings to isolate or extract a meaning consistent with the purpose of securities legislation, namely, to ensure that investors in public offerings are supplied with full information to enable them to appreciate (if they are minded to examine it) the risks involved in making an investment. The more extensive judicial experience in the United States has been regarded as useful for Canadian courts called upon to wrestle with similar problems of interpretation and application, and so it is that in the present case the so-called *Howey* test (laid down in *Securities and Exchange Commission v. Howey*, [328 US 293 (1946)]) and the *Hawaii* test (laid down in *Hawaii Commissioner of Securities v. Hawaii Market Centre Inc.* [485 P (2d) 105 (1971)]) were considered and utilized by the Courts below in determining that the appellants were dealing in securities through their commodity account agreements with their customers.

It is easy, in a case like the present one, when faced with a widely-approved regulatory statute embodying a policy of protection of the investing public against fraudulent or beguilingly misleading investment schemes, attractively packaged, to give broad undefined terms a broad meaning so as to bring doubtful schemes within the regulatory authority. Yet if the Legislature, in an area as managed and controlled as security trading has deliberately chosen not to define a term which, admittedly, embraces different kinds of transactions, of which some are innocent, and prefers to rest on generality, I see no reason of policy why Courts should be oversolicitous in resolving doubt in enlargement of the scope of the statutory control.

Although there was evidence of spot purchases of silver coins, that is purchases for cash, the issue before this Court concerns margin purchases under the terms of the appellants' standard commodity account agreements. Spot purchases are clearly outside of *The Securities Act*. The commodity account agreement is a terminable agreement under which purchasers on margin contract for some desired number of bags of silver coins and pay by way of deposit thirty five per cent of the purchase price. Delivery in specie may be had on 48 hours' notice after paying up the balance of the purchase price plus commission, and interest and storage charges as applicable. The appellants, to honour the contracts, must either have bags of silver coins on hand or go into the market to buy futures, and they would do so to cover outstanding obligations to their customers rather than trade in silver on their own account.

The result of investment of money under the commodity account agreements was to give the appellants a pool of money—which became its money—and tied the customers to the appellants in the consummation of their purchases, either by taking delivery of bags of coins (which was rarely done) or by closing out their accounts by selling at the market price through the appellants, paying a commission on selling as well as on buying. The commodity account agreements were not assignable by the customers without the appellants' consent but, of course, the appellants could use them as bank collateral.

The appellants controlled the so-called base price; that is, the price at which investors bought bags of silver coins for future delivery was fixed by the appellants in relation to the then market price. The appellants did not, however, control the market price but were themselves subject to it, nor did they control the cost of money which would enter into a customer's calculation, along with the market price, on whether to close out his account.

It was in respect of these features of the transactions with their customers that counsel for the appellants took objection to the emphasis placed by the Courts below on hedging, calling it a non-issue.

Counsel contended that it was immaterial to the customers whether the appellants hedged or not on their future obligations to them. If they did not hedge, they simply took the risk of a larger loss or a larger profit when called upon by a customer to deliver the bags of coins which he purchased or when the customer closed out his account by instructions to sell. If they did hedge, it was still for the customer to decide, irrespective of the hedging, whether to call for delivery or whether to sell out if the market price of silver made it advantageous to do so. Hedging concerned only the financial position of the appellants and, indeed, it seems to me that it was only their solvency which created any risk to the customer. Yet it was the view of the Ontario Court of Appeal, speaking through Dubin JA, that the solvency issue was not enough to bring the commodity account agreements within the scope of *The Securities Act*. I can understand the reluctance to find that solvency or insolvency is a determining factor in this case. It is equally a factor in the realization of future benefits under any commercial contracts providing for them, but there has been no suggestion that, even if there be a network of such contracts, they should be recognized by the Courts as investment contracts for security regulation purposes.

I see no more than three factors which can be said to enter into consideration of the question whether the commodity account agreement is an "investment contract" as that term is included in the definition of "security" under the Ontario *Securities Act*. There is the fixing of the base price at which customers make their purchases; there is the consequent gathering up of a pool of money by the appellants representing the required deposits under the commodity account agreements; and there is the question of the solvency of the appellants. The same factors under a similar scheme were present in *Jenson v. Continental Financial Corporation* [404 F Supp 792 (1975)], a judgment of the United States District Court, District of Minnesota, upon which counsel for the respondents in this case placed heavy reliance. The Court in the *Jenson* case faced the same question that the Courts in this case faced, namely, whether a gamble on the behaviour of the silver market is anything more than a commodity futures transaction and hence not a security subject to regulatory legislation.

In coming to a conclusion on the *Howey* test that the commodity account agreement was within the regulatory statute, the Court laid emphasis on the pooling of investors' money in a common enterprise in which the risk of profit or loss depended solely (or perhaps substantially) on the promoters' ability to gauge the market and hence to assure its own solvency to meet its obligations to its customers. I do not see in this view of the matter anything more than solvency, because it would be the market that would determine whether and when the customer would have a profit, and he was free to close out his account or to ask for delivery in specie at his instance and not when the promoter chose to permit him to do so. Certainly, I do not see any controlling factor in managerial effort, to which the Court in *Jenson* alluded, when it is the market that determines profitability and not the promoter. The notion of managerial effort obviously came from the *Howey* case where, on the facts, the citrus grove enterprise promoted by the respondents there was managed and serviced by them. Here there is no parallel, any more than there is a parallel with a manufacturing company whose shares are purchasable in the open market.

I am not persuaded that a test stemming from a particular set of facts such as those in *Howey*, or the broader risk capital approach based on another set of facts as in *Hawaii*, can or should be generalized to fix the conclusion in yet the different set of facts present here. In *Howey* and in *Hawaii*, the Courts were concerned with schemes relating to land management and to merchandise selling respectively, under which managerial control rested in the promoters. There was no such substantial reliance on the market, outside of the promoter's control, as existed in the present case. I think it apt to refer to the dissent of Frankfurter J in the *Howey* case, at p. 302, where he objected to bringing every innocent transaction within the scope of securities legislation simply because a perversion of them is covered by it.

I would allow the appeal, set aside the judgments below and quash the prohibitory order of the Ontario Securities Commission, with costs to the appellants throughout.

DE GRANDPRÉ J (Martland, Judson, Ritchie, Spence, Pigeon, Dickson, and Beetz JJ concurring): By notice given pursuant to the provisions of sub. 1 of s. 144 of *The Securities Act*, RSO 1970, c. 426, respondent informed appellant that a hearing would be held on the 24th of July 1974 "to determine whether the Commission should act in the public interest to order that all trading in the securities of Pacific Coast Coin Exchange of Canada Limited should cease forthwith pending the filing and acceptance of a prospectus and compliance with the registration provisions of *The Securities Act*." Appellant was also informed that it would be urged that such order should issue because the plan or manner of business of appellant "involves the offer and sale … of securities to the public" in that

> 1) it constitutes "an investment contract" within the meaning of s. 1(1)22xiii of the Act; in the alternative, it constitutes "evidence of title to or interest in the capital, assets, property, profits, earnings or royalties" of the appellant within the meaning of s. 1(1)22ii of the Act.

On October 11, 1974, following the hearing, respondent did issue a prohibitory order; its reasons indicate that it relied principally on s. 1(1)22ii of the Act although it added that s. 1(1)22xiii is also applicable. The Divisional Court agreed with the conclusion reached by respondent although it did so only on the basis that the transactions entered into between appellant and its clients are investment contracts; the Divisional Court felt that these agreements did not constitute evidence of title within the meaning of s. 1(1)22ii of the Act. (1975) 7 OR (2d) 395; also (1975) 55 DLR (3d) 331. An appeal to the Court of Appeal was dismissed, that Court also being of the view that the transactions constitute investment contracts; it found it unnecessary to determine whether they are also securities within the meaning of s. 1(1)22ii of the Act. (1975) 8 OR (2d) 257; also (1975) 57 DLR (3d) 641.

The principal issue in this appeal is to determine whether the agreement between appellant and its customers is an investment contract. Should a negative answer be given to that question, it will be necessary to examine whether or not the agreement constitutes a security under s. 1(1)22ii.

The Facts

…

Appellant Pacific is a Canadian corporation carrying on business in the Province of Ontario and other Canadian provinces; its shares are owned by Mr. Louis Carabini and Dr. Neil Chamberlain. … It might be noted that, at the time of the hearing, Pacific had some 12,000 customers in the United States and 226 in Canada.

Pacific commenced to carry on business in Ontario in the Spring of 1973. …

Pacific solicits its customers primarily through newspaper advertising in which the public is invited to request information by returning a mail slip to the Company. A "literature pack" is sent to potential customers. This pack emphasizes silver coins as an "investment" and presents them as a "reliable" and "almost perfect" protection of the customer's savings and assets against inflation. The price performance of silver is compared favourably with other forms of investments, such as common stocks. The literature predicts continued rampant growth of inflation and suggests a possible return to a depression. Emphasis is placed on an inevitable increase in the price of silver notwithstanding inflation, devaluation of money and depressed stock markets.

Appellant presents two ways to invest in silver coins: the outright purchase of bags of silver coins in specie which are delivered to the investor and the purchase of bags of silver coins on margin. Margin purchases are promoted over outright purchases by means of a comparison which illustrates that a person with $10,000 to invest can purchase seven bags of silver on margin while he can only purchase two bags in specie.

Over 90 per cent of purchases are by the margin contract mode. Whichever method is used, Pacific requires the customer to enter into a "Commodity Account Agreement." As this is the only document evidencing the contract between Pacific and its customers, it must now be examined insofar as it governs the rights and obligations of the margin purchasers:

a) the commodity consists of one or more bags of silver coins;
b) the customer pays a commission of 2 per cent on the purchase price and when he sells, he is also asked to pay a second commission of 2 per cent;
c) the customer puts down a deposit (it was 35 per cent of the purchase price at the time of the hearing) and is required to maintain adequate margin in his account in such amounts as are from time to time required by Pacific;
d) Pacific is under no obligation to make delivery until the customer has paid in full therefore, which means the balance of the purchase price plus all interest (approximately 12 per cent at the time of the hearing), commission and storage charges; the customer agrees to purchase all the commodities ordered by it and pay for them in full before delivery;
e) the Agreement is terminable at the will of either party but in any event will terminate five years from the date of the last purchase under the Agreement;
f) the price at which Pacific sells to its customers is fixed by Pacific several times during the day and published by it and, in total, consists of a base price being the market value quoted by Pacific plus commissions and other charges;
g) the customer may obtain the release of any or all of the commodities credited to his account within forty-eight hours after payment in full for such commodities;
h) Pacific retains no power of attorney nor authority to direct the customer trading and maintains no control over the customer s account subject to certain security provisions to secure outstanding indebtedness by the customer to Pacific;
i) the customer obtains no specific interest in any particular bag of silver under the contract until he makes payment in full therefor and accepts delivery of the bags purchased under the contract;
j) certain events of default are provided for and remedies retained by Pacific in that event to liquidate the customer's account or realize on any commodities

purchased by the customer and credited to his account to off-set any indebtedness in the event of default by the customer to Pacific;

k) the provisions of the Agreement are assignable by Pacific but not by the customer without Pacific's consent.

More than 85 per cent of all margin account purchasers close-out their account without taking delivery. When a margin account buyer closes out his account, he receives or pays the difference between the per unit price at which his position is closed-out and the amount he owes on margin, plus applicable interest, commissions and storage charges.

Although the Agreement spells out that Pacific "may, but need not at all times, make a market in commodities," Pacific in its literature points out that it has never failed to make a market for its customers in the past. Pacific will not repurchase margin contracts acquired from another coin exchange nor will other coin exchanges repurchase Pacific margin contracts.

Pacific's only obligation to margin customers is to deliver the bags of silver covered by the contract if and when the customer pays the outstanding balance. In practice, Pacific covers or hedges its obligation to margin customers:

a) by purchasing futures contracts for silver; approximately 85 per cent of Pacific's obligations to margin account customers is covered by futures contracts;
b) by maintaining a small inventory of silver coins in specie.

Pacific has a policy of covering not less than 95 per cent of its margin obligations.

Pacific obtains title to the funds paid by the margin account investors as a deposit. The pooled monies are distributed in Pacific's general funds. Some of this money is used to secure its own futures contracts and some of it is used for its own investment purposes.

In conducting its hedging operations, Pacific trades for its own account and in its own name; all purchases and sales of futures contracts are made by Pacific as principal and not as agent for a customer. As the silver futures contract comes close to delivery date, the Operations' Department, some 55 persons strong, must decide whether to pay the balance owing on the contract and take delivery of the silver, or roll the contract over by selling it and replacing it with a contract for a more distant month.

In its literature, Pacific cautions against individuals speculating in futures contracts. Such investments are not for the uninitiated or unwary:

> They are primarily for speculators who welcome extremely high-leveraged, short term situations, and for hedgers who use futures to balance their existing long or short commitments with an equal and opposite commitment. If you plan to buy silver futures, you should be prepared to spend a great deal of time studying the silver situation, staying on top of it every day.

Investment Contract

Section 35 of the Act spells out the prohibition for anyone to "trade in a security" in the absence of a prospectus. "Security" is defined in s. 1 as including fourteen categories, the thirteenth one being "any investment contract, other than an investment contract within the meaning of *The Investment Contracts Act*." It is common ground that in the case at bar, the contract is not one covered by this last mentioned statute.

The expression "investment contract" is not defined in the Act. In their search for its meaning, the Courts below have been guided by the leading US authorities and counsel have invited us to follow the same path. I agree. While the statute under consideration here does not read word for word like its US counterpart, the expression "investment contract" is found in both. In addition, the policy behind the legislation in the two countries is exactly the same, so that considering the dearth of Canadian authorities, it is a wise course to look at the decisions reached by the US Courts. This approach has also been adopted by the Court of Appeal of Alberta in *Re Regina Great Way Merchandising Ltd.* [(1971), 20 DLR (3d) 67], as well as by Nemetz JA in the Court of Appeal of British Columbia in *Re Bestline Products of Canada Ltd.* [(1972), 29 DLR (3d) 505].

I have alluded to the policy of the legislation. It is clearly the protection of the public as was said by Hartt J in *Re Ontario Securities Commission* and *Brigadoon Scotch Distributors (Canada) Limited* [[1970] 3 OR 714], at p. 717:

> … the basic aim or purpose of the *Securities Act, 1966*, … is the protection of the investing public through full, true and plain disclosure of all material facts relating to securities being issued.

If any doubt could be entertained as to the intention of the Legislature in the present instance, that doubt should be dispelled by the very wide terms employed in defining the word "security." The fourteen subdivisions of the definition encompass practically all types of transactions to such an extent that this definition had to be narrowed down by a long list of exceptions to be found in s. 19.

At this point, reference should be made to a work by Professor Louis Loss who was called by appellant as an expert witness before the Commission. In the second edition of his *Securities Regulation* ((1961) vol. I at pp. 483, 488-489) and in the 1969 supplement thereto (vol. IV at p. 2501), Prof Loss recognizes that "the various categories in the definition are not mutually exclusive and are meant to be 'catchalls.'" This view of the definition in the United States statute is valid in our case as well.

Such remedial legislation must be construed broadly, and it must be read in the context of the economic realities to which it is addressed. Substance, not form, is the governing factor. …

In the search for the true meaning of the expression "investment contract," another guideline must also be present in the forefront of our thinking. In the words of the Supreme Court of the United States in *SEC v. W.J. Howey Co.* [328 US 293 (1946)], any definition must permit (at p. 299):

> … the fulfillment of the statutory purpose of compelling full and fair disclosure relative to the issuance of "the many types of instruments that in our commercial world fall within the ordinary concept of a security." … It embodies a flexible rather than a static principle, one that is capable of adaptation to meet the countless and variable schemes devised by those who seek the use of the money of others on the promise of profits.

Which does not mean that the legislation is aimed solely at schemes that are actually fraudulent; rather, it relates to arrangements that do not permit the customers to know exactly the value of the investment they are making.

It is with all the foregoing in mind that the Supreme Court of the United States in *Howey* (supra, at pp. 298, 299, 301) laid down the following test:

> Does the scheme involve "an investment of money in a common enterprise, with profits to come solely from the efforts of others"?

…

In the case at bar, it is obvious that an investment of money has been made with an intention of profit. The questions before us are the following: Is there a common enterprise? Are the profits to come solely from the efforts of others? These two questions are so interwoven that I will be endeavouring to answer them together.

The word "solely" in that test has been criticized and toned down by many jurisdictions in the United States. It is sufficient to refer to *SEC v. Koscot Interplanetary, Inc.* [497 F (2d) 473 (1974)], and to *SEC v. Glen W. Turner Enterprises, Inc.* [474 F (2d) 476 (1973)]. As mentioned in the *Turner* case, to give a strict interpretation to the word "solely" (at p. 482) "would not serve the purpose of the legislation. Rather we adopt a more realistic test, whether the efforts made by those other than the investor are the undeniably significant ones, those essential managerial efforts which affect the failure or success of the enterprise." In the same case of *Turner*, the expression "common enterprise" has been defined to mean (p. 482) "one in which the fortunes of the investor are interwoven with and dependent upon the efforts and success of those seeking the investment or of third parties." These refinements of the test, I accept.

Like the Courts below, I hold the view that both these questions must be answered in the affirmative. … I will simply underline the common enterprise aspect and attempt to highlight two facets of the dependence of the customer upon Pacific, namely for the success of the venture and for the existence of a true market.

In my view, the test of common enterprise is met in the case at bar. I accept respondent's submission that such an enterprise exists when it is undertaken for the benefit of the supplier of capital (the investor) and of those who solicit the capital (the promoter). In this relationship, the investor's role is limited to the advancement of money, the managerial control over the success of the enterprise being that of the promoter; therein lies the community. In other words the "commonality" necessary for an investment contract is that between the investor and the promoter. There is no need for the enterprise to be common to the investors between themselves.

As to the dependence of the customer for the success of the enterprise, it should be recalled that appellant in its literature underlines the danger for the ordinary investor to deal in futures; the text of the warning has been quoted earlier in these reasons. This is echoed by Professor Loss in his testimony: "The ordinary fellow isn't equipped to trade in commodity futures." Appellant now attempts to recant from that position and submits that there is nothing mysterious about dealing in commodity futures contracts. The Courts below have refused to accept that submission and have held quite rightly that the end result of the investment made by each customer is dependent upon the quality of the expertise brought to the administration of the funds obtained by appellant from its customers. If Pacific does not properly invest the pooled deposit, the purchaser will obtain no return on his investment regardless of the prevailing value of silver; there is nothing that the customer can do to avoid that result.

This dependence of the investors upon the appellant is also apparent when it is noted that the margin purchaser may only look to Pacific for the performance of his contract. Until the investor has paid the full purchase price, he has no title to any physical property but only a claim against Pacific. Should the price of silver go down, there is no possibility for the investor to finance his balance (except through his own resources) and from that moment, he is at the mercy of Pacific. This is not to say that we are looking at a pure question of solvency. As pointed out by the Court of Appeal (p. 259), the conclusion of the Divisional Court does not rest "on such a narrow basis."

The key to the success of the venture is the efforts of the promoter alone, for a benefit that will accrue to both the investor and the promoter. Thus, the nature of the relationship between Pacific and its margin customers establishes that it satisfies the *Howey* test. It matters not that the relationship was built around an object that is a commodity and which in another context could be the subject matter of transactions in the futures market that would not attract the restrictions of *The Securities Act.*

Another test to determine the economic realities of a security transaction is to be found in the decision of the Supreme Court of Hawaii in *State of Hawaii v. Hawaii Market Center, Inc.* [485 P (2d) 105 (1971)], a decision of 1971. This test is possibly still more favourable to respondent in the present instance and the Divisional Court has examined the facts in that light also and has concluded that the risk capital approach would bring about the same conclusion. I agree.

At the risk of repetition, I will underscore that the question raised by this appeal is not whether or not commodity futures contracts are investment contracts. The parties agree that they are not. What is at issue is the relationship between Pacific and its margin customers examined particularly in the light of the *Howey* and the *Hawaii* tests. …

A last word. At the invitation of the parties, I have examined the facts in the sole light of the *Howey* and *Hawaii* tests. Like the Divisional Court, however, I would be inclined to take a broader approach. It is clearly legislative policy to replace the harshness of caveat emptor in security related transactions and courts should seek to attain that goal even if tests carefully formulated in prior cases prove ineffective and must continually be broadened in scope. It is the policy and not the subsequently formulated judicial test that is decisive.

QUESTIONS

1. How does the test from *Pacific Coast* differ from those in the US cases of *Howey* and *Hawaii*?

2. The key point of contention between the majority and minority in *Pacific Coast* revolves around the nature of the dependency exhibited by the investors on aspects of Pacific Coast's expertise and the implications of the inequality of knowledge between the two parties. Which of the two approaches do you find more convincing and why?

3. Would the analysis engaged in by the majority concerning the "legislative policy" of the Act change now that the Ontario statute specifies a range of goals for regulators to achieve (OSA, s 1.1)? Consider in particular the fact that Justice Iacobucci in the Supreme Court decision in *Asbestos* exhorted regulators to be more cognizant of the policy goal of efficiency. See the discussion of the *Asbestos* decision in Chapter 11.

4. Note that the Québec *Securities Act*, CQLR c V-1.1, explicitly defines an investment contract to mean "a contract whereby a person, having been led to expect profits, undertakes to participate in the risk of a venture by a contribution of capital or loan, without having the required knowledge to carry on the venture or without obtaining the right to participate directly in decisions concerning the carrying on of the venture" (QSA, s 1). Should this definition be incorporated into other provincial statutes or into a potential federal securities statute?

4. *Regulatory Consideration of the Definition of a Security*

Regulators also have occasion to reflect on the meaning of "security." The OSC's decision in *Re Albino* (1991), 14 OSCB 365, demonstrates the importance of regulatory context as an influence on the basic decision about whether an instrument is or is not a security. The context in this instance was a concern about potential insider trading on the part of a senior executive of a Canadian corporation. The decision revolved around the fact that, as part of his compensation, Mr. Albino of Rio Algom (RA) was given an incentive plan whereby he would be paid the difference between the price at which the stock of RA was trading on its award and the price at which it was trading when encashed. An incentive unit was the equivalent of one common share of RA. The gain on the incentive unit was the excess of the "defined" market value of a common share on the exercise date over the "defined" market value on the award date. The executive was not being awarded any stock, just the relevant price difference. Were these "phantom stock options" (PSOs) a security? The specific regulatory issue was that at the time Mr. Albino cashed in his incentive units, he had in his possession material undisclosed information having to do with revisions of a contract between RA and Ontario Hydro for the sale of uranium, which revisions would have had negative consequences for RA.

The OSC's three-person hearing panel all made different decisions on the substance of the issue. One panel member concluded that the PSOs were not securities, another said they were, and the third did not decide that question but agreed that nonetheless the OSC had jurisdiction to sanction. Commissioner Blain, who held that PSOs were not a security, did so because phantom stock options were not "commonly known" in the business world as securities. Rather, this was like any other employment contract where there was an interest in the profits or earnings of the company, and these were generally not securities. There was insufficient nexus with the capital market here (even though their value was determined by the market) to make it different from the debt obligations represented by other employment or other compensation contracts. No money was paid by the executive, no trading or assignment of award units was allowed, and no stock of RA changed hands. For this commissioner, it was significant that the plan defined specific periods when award units could be cashed in and times when executives were prohibited from cashing in their award units. This was a significant restraint on the liquidity of the shares. No shareholders were harmed—that is, the actions were "market neutral" and hurt the company only, not the capital markets.

Commissioner Salter, who held that they were securities, adopted dicta of the SCC in *Pacific Coast* that the legislation must be read broadly and purposively. The relevant context here was the prohibition against illegal insider trading, and the regulation of trading by insiders via disclosure. The PSOs here should be considered the same as other derivative securities, which draw their value from the underlying securities. For this commissioner, the encashment of award units was a "constructive sale" of the securities of RA. Looking at the economic reality of the transaction, sanctions should be applied. Also objectives with respect to prohibiting insider trading would justify finding this to be a security.

The third commissioner (Commissioner Bennett) did not decide the issue whether these PSOs were a security or not. She concluded that there was a sufficient nexus with the capital markets for the OSC to exercise its discretionary power to sanction in the public interest (now OSA, s 127). The behaviour was "seriously prejudicial to public confidence in the capital markets." The "economic reality of action by Albino with respect to the encashment of the award units was exactly that which the insider trading rules work to eliminate—that is, to prevent an insider profiting on the basis of material, non-public information. Further, the encashment of award units generated the same signal to the marketplace as a sale of shares. Both must be reported if the signals on insider trading are to reach the market place" (at 54-55).

See also *R ex rel Swain v Boughner*, [1948] OWN 141 (H Ct J); *Re Sunfour Estates* (1992), 15 OSCB 269; *Beer v Towngate* (1995), 25 OR (3d) 785 (Gen Div); *R v Sisto Finance* (1994), 17 OSCB 2467.

5. Conclusion on PPN, Segregated Fund, and Viatical Settlement Examples

With all of this material in mind, let us return for a moment to the examples of possible securities with which we began this chapter. Based on the definition of "security" in the OSA, do you think that principal protected notes, as defined in the federal regulations, are or are not securities? What about the description of a segregated fund? With respect to viatical settlements a recent example of the OSC's consideration of this issue is the *Universal Settlements* decision, excerpted below.

In *Universal Settlements*, a unanimous panel of the OSC concluded that the instruments being offered for sale constituted securities. Universal Settlements International (USI) was a private Ontario corporation whose business involved finding investors interested in investing in viaticals and American viators interested in selling viaticals. USI had not registered under the OSA, nor had it filed a prospectus under the act for its viatical products. USI sold a viatical product that it called GLS-II, under which an investor would acquire a fractional interest in the death benefit of a specific life insurance policy of a specific viator. The other viatical product sold by USI, GLS, was identical to GLS-II; however, GLS also contained third-party contingency insurance that paid an amount equal to the death benefit if the viator had not died by an agreed-upon date.

When USI had accumulated sufficient funds from investors, it sought out potential viators who wished to sell the amount payable by the insurance company on their life insurance policies upon the viator's death for a price less than the full face amount. USI engaged various entities to select viators pursuant to USI's selection criteria. It matched viators and viaticals with the investment parameters set by each investor. In some cases no match could be found and USI's practice was to return the funds committed by the investor. When a purchase of a viatical was made, the investor acquired a fractional interest in the viatical. USI would then send the investor a closing package, including a copy of assignment of the interest in the death benefit to USI's US trust, a medical review estimating life expectancy, a beneficiary designation, financial ratings of the viator's insurance company, and the contingency policy of insurance where applicable. USI monitored when the contingency policy matured and was responsible for making claims.

In the Matter of Universal Settlements International Inc
(2006), 29 OSCB 7880

. . .

[8] The key issue in this hearing was whether the viatical products USI offers to investors in Ontario are investment contracts under the definition of securities in s. 1(1) of the Act. If they are investment contracts, the prospectus and registration requirements of the Act apply.

[9] Based on the three pronged test for an investment contract set out in the leading American case of *Securities and Exchange Commission v. W.J. Howey Co. et al.*, 328 US 293 (1946) as slightly modified by later cases, the viatical products of USI would constitute investment contracts under s. 1(1) of the Act, if they involve: (i) an investment of funds with a view to profit, (ii) in a common enterprise, (iii) where the profits are derived from the undeniably significant efforts of persons other than the investors.

[10] Staff and the respondent agreed that the viatical products offered by USI involve an investment of funds with a view to profit. Therefore, the issue was whether there is a common enterprise, where the profits are derived from the undeniably significant efforts of persons other than the investors.

. . .

[91] In our case, investors do not participate in the profits of the business enterprise of USI but are promised fixed returns on their investments that, on an annualized basis, will be more or less profitable depending on the period of time funds are deployed in the common enterprise. The investors furnish the capital that is deployed to purchase viaticals in the common enterprise and that is the source of the fees and income of USI and its agents from the common enterprise.

[92] In *Hawaii*, the court stated at p.111 that "to negate the finding of a security the [investor] should have practical and actual control over the managerial decisions of the enterprise. For it is this control which gives the [investor] the opportunity to safeguard his own investment, thus obviating the need for state intervention." Investors in the USI viatical offering cannot exercise any such managerial control over their investment.

[93] In *Securities and Exchange Commission v. Life Partners, Inc.*, 87 F3d 536 (DC Cir. 1996), the United States Court of Appeals for the District of Columbia found that a scheme for the sale of viaticals to investors by Life Partners International (LPI) resulted in sufficient commonality in which there was an investment of funds for profit. However, Justice Ginsburg, speaking for the majority of the court, found that the profits in the investment did not come predominantly from the efforts of persons other than the investors. Justice Wald dissented on this issue.

[94] In *Life Partners*, LPI offered fractional interests in viaticals. LPI performed many of the tasks that USI performs for its investors. However, unlike in our case, viaticals and viators were found and scrutinized by LPI before investors were assembled or paid their funds to LPI. Thus, in *Life Partners*, LPI evaluated the viator's medical condition, reviewed the life insurance policy, negotiated the purchase price and prepared the legal documentation before the investor made his investment decisions.

. . .

[97] LPI structured purchases of viaticals through a trust established for that purpose and investors' funds and payments for investors went through the trust and not LPI itself. Thus the funds from investors were not commingled with the funds of LPI. Justice Ginsburg held at p. 544 that "it is the inter-dependency of the investors that transforms the transaction substantively into a pooled investment" and that "if the investments are inter-dependent it would not matter if LPI scrupulously avoided commingling investors' funds—for example by passing [investor] checks directly to the seller at closing." We concluded that in our case it is not necessary that the capital or assets employed in the common enterprise also become capital and assets of USI, subject to its solvency risk, before we can find an investment contract.

. . .

[102] Justice Ginsburg concluded that the combination of LPI's pre-purchase services as a finder-promoter and its largely ministerial post-purchase services were not enough to establish that the investor's profits flow predominantly from the effort of others. We believe that this conclusion is inconsistent with the finding that the pre-purchase activities were undeniably essential to the overall success of an investor's investment.

[103] In a strong dissent, Justice Wald held that where profits depend on the success of the promoter's activities, there is less access to key information, i.e., that specific to the promoter. The investor needs to know the risk factors attached to the investment and whether there is any reason why the investor should be leery of the promoter's promises. This need for information holds true for investors prior to purchase as much as for investors who have committed their funds. Justice Wald held that an artificial line should not be drawn between pre-purchase and post-purchase activities. To do so, Justice Wald held, elevates a formal element, timing, over the economic reality of the investors' dependence on the promoter, and undercuts the flexibility and ability to adapt to "the countless and variable schemes" that are the hallmarks of the *Howey* test.

[104] In our case, most, if not all, of the pre-purchase activities in *Life Partners*, occur after an investor makes his investment by paying the committed amount and signing the purchase agreement. Those activities in *Life Partners* that occurred before investors were assembled, occur in our case, after they are assembled.

[105] While Justice Ginsburg acknowledged that it is the length of the viator's life that is of overwhelming importance to the value of the viatical settlements marketed by LPI, Justice Wald emphasized that the realization of expected investor profits depended not on the timing of the viator's death per se but rather on whether the death occurred within the period estimated by LPI.

...

[109] The real issue in *Mutual Benefits* was whether the investor's expectation of profits was based solely on the efforts of the promoter or a third party. MBC relied on *Life Partners*. The court, however, specifically declined to adopt the test on this issue set forth in *Life Partners*.

[110] The court agreed with the dissenting opinion of Justice Wald in *Life Partners* that significant pre-purchase managerial activities undertaken to insure the success of the investment may also satisfy the third prong of the *Howey* test.

...

[111] We have two conflicting cases of the US Court of Appeals (*Life Partners* and *Mutual Benefits*) on the third prong of the *Howey* test. While we are not bound to follow US cases, we are of the opinion that *Mutual Benefits* and Justice Wald's dissenting opinion in *Life Partners* are correct and reflect the economic reality and flexible approach endorsed by the Supreme Court of Canada in *Pacific Coast*. Furthermore, we are troubled by the inconsistency in the reasoning of the majority opinion in *Life Partners*. Even so, the facts in our case are sufficiently different from those in *Life Partners*—many of the pre-purchase activities that the majority in *Life Partners* described as "undeniably essential to the overall success of the investment" are post-purchase activities in our case [i.e., they occur after the assembling of investors and after the commitment of funds]—that based on *Life Partners* alone, we could find that USI's viatical products are investment contracts.

...

[115] The court [in *Siporin*] disagreed with the statement in *Life Partners* that investors' profits from viatical settlements "depend entirely upon the mortality of the insured"

and that in such a situation, a potential investor's "need for federal securities regulation is greatly diminished." On the contrary, the court in *Siporin* held, at p. 99:

> The mortality of the viator is merely another factor to be considered when the seller assembles a viatical settlement agreement that will, the parties hope, be profitable for the investor upon the inevitable death of a viator. What truly determines viatical settlement profitability is the realization, over time, of an outcome predicted by the seller through its analyses of the viator's life expectancy, the soundness of the insurer, the actions needed to keep the policy in effect for the original face amount, and the insurer's unconditional liability under the policy's terms.

[116] We agree with this statement.

...

[123] Based on the facts, and consistent with the cases discussed above, we find that USI's relationship with its investors in GLS-II and GLS constitutes a common enterprise and that the profits of the common enterprise are derived from the undeniably significant efforts of USI and its agents. Accordingly, USI's viatical products are investment contracts, and, therefore securities under the Act.

See also *Re Pogachar* (2012), 35 OSCB 3389.

QUESTIONS

1. Do you think that the decision to apply sanctions in *Re Albino* was the right one?
2. When the first draft of a proposed *Provincial Capital Markets Act* (PCMA) was published in August 2014, branch (f) of the proposed definition of a security read as follows:

> (f) any agreement under which the interest of the purchaser is valued for purposes of conversion or surrender by reference to the value of a proportionate interest in a specified portfolio of assets, other than, unless otherwise provided by the regulations, a contract issued by an insurance company governed by the laws of Canada or of a province which provides for payment at maturity of an amount not less than three quarters of the premiums paid by the purchaser for a benefit payable at maturity.

Compare this wording to that contained in the current branch (f) of the definition of security under the OSA. Why do you think that 7 of the 62 commenters on this proposed PCMA were insurance companies or representatives of insurance companies who took issue with this definition?

3. Who are securities regulators protecting in the viatical settlements example?

III. EVOLVING REGULATION OF DERIVATIVES IN CANADA

As noted above, as a result of the GFC, securities regulators around the world began to pay attention to the need to develop a regulatory framework for the trading of derivatives. As a relatively unregulated market, the volume of trading in the derivatives markets had increased steadily in the decade before the crisis. The following extract provides an account of the major features associated with financial instruments grouped under the heading "derivative."

TE Lynch, "Derivatives: A Twenty-First Century Understanding"
(2011) 43:187 Loy U Chicago LJ 5 at 5-14 (footnotes omitted)

Derivatives have been a popular topic of conversation in recent years. And, indeed, they should be. The presence of derivatives in the global financial industry has grown enormously in the last two decades. Many different categories of derivatives have grown enormously too, some of which did not exist twenty years ago.

For example, the notional amount of derivatives contracts outstanding globally in 1990 was approximately $6 trillion, but by the end of 2009, this amount was estimated at $691 trillion, a one-hundredfold increase. The notional amount of outstanding credit default swaps, which were non-existent as of 1990, is estimated to have been as high as $58 trillion in recent years. The notional amount of outstanding interest rate swaps at the end of 1990 was an estimated $2.3 trillion, but by 2009, this figure had increased to an estimated $349 trillion. For foreign exchange derivatives, the figure in 1990 was $578 billion, but by 2010, it had grown to $49 trillion.

The markets for exchange-traded options and futures derivatives have also grown. As of June 2010, the outstanding notional amount of exchange-traded futures contracts was $23 trillion (with a quarterly turnover of $384 trillion), and the figures for options were comparable. More than 10 million oil derivatives contracts are traded each month on derivatives exchanges. In fact, this market is so large that the daily turnover on the International Petroleum Exchange of futures contracts on Brent crude, an oil extracted only from the North Sea, approximates twice the daily global production of oil.

Additionally, derivatives are not necessarily innocuous things. Recent history is rife with examples of firms and municipalities suffering severe and sometimes disastrous economic losses as a result of losing their derivatives bets. For example, Metallgesellschaft, formerly one of Germany's largest industrial conglomerates, lost approximately $1.4 billion in 1993 speculating in oil futures. Barings Bank went bankrupt in 1995 after losing approximately $1.3 billion in speculative derivatives, approximately half of those bets on the level, volatility and direction of the Nikkei 225 stock index. In the mid-nineties, Orange County, California lost $1.7 billion of taxpayer money on speculative derivatives, and the Sumitomo Corporation lost an estimated $2.6 billion on speculative derivatives, many of them copper futures. The hedge fund Long-Term Capital Management lost approximately $1.3 billion in 1998 speculatively selling options, most referencing European stock indices. More recently, IKB Deutsche Industribank lost approximately $4 billion in 2007, much of it speculating in derivatives referencing American subprime mortgages. In 2008, Société Générale reported that it had lost approximately $7 billion in large part due to derivatives trading. And AIG, through its subsidiary AIG Financial Products, speculatively sold hundreds of billions of dollars of credit default swaps insuring its counterparties against, among other things, losses that might be incurred as a result of a collapse in the U.S. housing market and the collapse of their third-party contractual counterparties. AIG found itself on the brink of collapse when the housing market and the economy moved against it.

Furthermore, derivatives, particularly credit default swaps and various "synthetic" securities, have been identified as culprits contributing to the current global financial crisis. Warren Buffet famously referred to derivatives as "time bombs" and "financial weapons of mass destruction."

As a result of their growth and apparent dangers, American and foreign government officials have recently turned their attention to better regulating derivatives. Unfortunately, regulatory, policy, and even legal discussions of derivatives are often muddled and demonstrate persistent misunderstandings of what derivatives are. Many people who probably should be conversant with derivatives shy away from rigorous discussion about them because they are allegedly so "complex" and "exotic."

A derivative is invariably described in words to the following effect: "a financial instrument whose value depends on or is derived from the performance of a secondary source such as an underlying bond, currency, or commodity," or "a financial instrument whose value depends on (or derives from) the value of other, more basic, underlying variables." This is the definition that is almost always used in legal scholarship and in policy discussions. But for legal and policy analysis purposes, this definition is inadequate—it is imprecise, incomplete, and fails to capture the nature and scope of modern derivative transactions. The common definition is both over- and under-inclusive in that it encompasses investments that are obviously not derivatives, such as stocks and bonds, while excluding others that clearly are, such as event derivatives, insurance policies, and Super Bowl bets. As a result, policy makers and legal analysts are often less than fully informed as compared to derivatives industry groups, who often do understand their true nature.

A persistent misunderstanding of derivatives hampers our ability to differentiate between socially useful and socially harmful derivatives. The framework offered in this Article facilitates this valuable differentiation.

A persistent misunderstanding of derivatives also prolongs the use of an outdated derivatives regulatory scheme. Derivatives regulation in the United States involves a multiplicity of state and federal laws, as well as the administrative and regulatory functions of many state and federal agencies. The federal derivative legislative process is overseen by various congressional commissions, primarily (of all things!) the Senate Committee on Agriculture, Nutrition and Forestry and the House Agricultural Committee. This hodge-podge of a regulatory structure reflects the evolution of derivatives over time, appearing first as simple futures and options on agricultural commodities used for hedging purposes by producers and consumers of these commodities but morphing into such truly exotic beasts as synthetic collateral debt obligations that reference sets of credit default swaps, which themselves reference tens or hundreds of thousands of American subprime mortgages. As the scope and scale of derivatives evolved, mere patches and band-aids were placed on the then-existing regulatory scheme, the latest band-aid being the Dodd-Frank Act. At times, extensive deregulation occurred, leading to eras of explosive derivatives evolution, leaving the regulatory apparatus struggling to keep up. As a result, we are left with a derivatives regulatory regime that often appears confusing, incomplete, contradictory, greatly subject to interpretation, incapable of addressing derivatives innovation, and even at times, simply irrational or incomprehensible. The framework presented in this Article will facilitate the process of developing a modern, comprehensive derivatives regulatory regime.

Most pressingly, a persistent misunderstanding of derivatives hampers regulators' attempts to develop rational, desirable, optimal derivatives regulation as required by the recently enacted Dodd-Frank Act. In Dodd-Frank, Congress significantly altered derivatives regulations but was unable to wrestle successfully with many of the difficult issues

> embedded within the modern derivatives industry. Congress, therefore, left much of the difficult regulatory line-drawing to the Commodity Futures Trading Commission ("CFTC"), the Securities and Exchange Commission ("SEC"), and the Treasury Department. Each of these agencies has recently started a prolonged process of addressing these difficult issues. The framework described in this Article will facilitate Dodd-Frank rulemaking.
>
> Furthermore, members of the financial industry have come to appreciate the true nature of derivatives, as well as their flexibility and manipulability, which has enabled them to develop new and innovative derivatives over the course of the last two decades.
>
> . . .
>
> So what exactly is a derivative? At the risk of oversimplifying, all derivatives are contracts between two counterparties in which the payoffs to and from each counterparty depend on the outcome of one or more extrinsic, future, uncertain events or metrics. This means that they are "aleatory contracts" in which each counterparty expects the outcome to be opposite to that expected by the other counterparty. … As an initial step, it is expedient to understand that derivatives provide, in the aggregate, zero-sum payoffs to the counterparties. … There are specific ways, however, that a derivatives contract can create non-monetary value—e.g., by providing one or both counterparties a consumer or producer surplus, hedging value or entertainment value, or by creating certain positive externalities such as improved price discovery. Understanding these value-creating scenarios will help refine our definition.

The International Monetary Fund's (IMF) report on Canada's financial system included some information about derivatives-related activity in Canada. It distinguishes between derivatives that are traded on an exchange and those traded over-the-counter (OTC). In order for a derivative contract to be exchange traded, its terms must be sufficiently standardized that many customers would be interested in buying and selling on those terms. Most derivatives are traded OTC, meaning that the contracts are bilateral and customized to the needs of the participants. The IMF report notes that the Montreal Exchange is Canada's financial derivatives exchange, listing equity, currency, index, and interest rate derivatives. Meanwhile the OTC derivatives market in Canada is concentrated among six Canadian banks, who trade most often with foreign counterparties. In 2012, Canada accounted for US$18 trillion in OTC derivatives, with interest rate swaps and foreign exchange contracts being the dominant products. This volume of trading amounted to 2.8 percent of the global derivatives market. (IMF, *Canada: Financial Sector Assessment Program, IOSCO Objectives and Principles of Securities Regulation-Detailed Assessment of Implementation* (Washington, DC, March 2014) at 12).

In this chapter, we focus on developments with respect to the definition of a derivative that could be subject to regulation under provincial securities acts. In the OSA, the analysis begins with the definition of a derivative in s 1(1). Accordingly,

> "derivative" means an option, swap, futures contract, forward contract or other financial or commodity contract or instrument whose market price, value, delivery obligations, payment obligations or settlement obligations are derived from, referenced to or based on an underlying interest (including a value, price, rate, variable, index, event, probability or thing), but does not include,
>
> (a) a commodity futures contract as defined in subsection 1 (1) of the Commodity Futures Act,
>
> (b) a commodity futures option as defined in subsection 1 (1) of the Commodity Futures Act,

(c) a contract or instrument that, by reason of an order of the Commission under subsection (10), is not a derivative, or

(d) a contract or instrument in a class of contracts or instruments prescribed by the regulations not to be derivatives; ("produit dérivé")

We can see that this definition is quite expansive, since it covers a variety of types of contract or instrument whose key features are "derived from, referenced to or based on an underlying interest." However, the definition allows for discretion to reside in the OSC to order that an instrument not be classified as a derivative, or for the regulations to prescribe a class of contracts or instruments not to be derivatives. Section1(1) also includes a definition of a "designated derivative," which is a derivative that is designated by order of the Commission or that belongs to a class prescribed by the regulations.

OSC Rule 91-506 (Derivatives: Product Determination (2013) 36 OSCB 11015), which came into force on December 31, 2013, clarifies the conditions under which a contract or instrument will not be considered a derivative. These conditions include situations where the contract or instrument is regulated by gaming control legislation, or if it is an insurance or annuity contract regulated by insurance law, if it is a contract for the purchase or sale of currency or commodities with certain features that do not bring it within the scope of a derivative (including that the intention is that the contract be settled by the delivery of the currency or commodity). The Rule also purports to address situations where a contract or instrument could be considered to be both a security and a derivative.

From the perspective of substantive derivatives regulation, Ontario has also passed a trade reporting rule that creates a reporting obligation for derivatives trading where local counterparties are involved (OSC Rule 91-507 Trade Repositories and Derivatives Data Reporting (2014) 37 OSCB 245). The regulatory purpose here is to increase transparency in the market for derivatives and assist in the determination of whether the volume or concentration of derivatives activity could pose a systemic risk to the Canadian financial system. It has also extended the application of some of the substantive rules in the *Securities Act*, such as the registration requirements and certain market conduct requirements such as insider trading requirements or fraud, to include those trading in derivatives.

Much of this legislative and rule-making activity has been based on a series of consultation papers published by the Canadian Securities Administrators between 2010 and 2013.

IV. WHAT IS A TRADE?

The definition of a "trade" is also central to the application of securities law. Several provincial securities acts provide that if there is a trade, the trader has to be registered (British Columbia *Securities Act*, RSBC 1996, c 418 (BCSA), s 34; QSA, s 148). Meanwhile the OSA now provides that those who are engaged in the business of trading are required to be registered (s 25). Several offences created by securities law require a finding that trading took place, including, most notably, insider trading. The relevant definition of "trade" at OSA, s 1(1) says:

"trade" or "trading" includes,

(a) any sale or disposition of a security for valuable consideration, whether the terms of payment be on margin, instalment or otherwise, but does not include a purchase of a security or, except as provided in clause (d), a transfer, pledge or encumbrance of securities for the purpose of giving collateral for a debt made in good faith,

(b) any participation as a trader in any transaction in a security through the facilities of any stock exchange or quotation and trade reporting system,

(b.1) entering into a derivative or making a material amendment to, terminating, assigning, selling or otherwise acquiring or disposing of a derivative, or

(b.2) a novation of a derivative, other than a novation with a clearing agency,

(c) any receipt by a registrant of an order to buy or sell a security,

(d) any transfer, pledge or encumbrancing of securities of an issuer from the holdings of any person or company or combination of persons or companies described in clause (c) of the definition of "distribution" for the purpose of giving collateral for a debt made in good faith, and

(e) any act, advertisement, solicitation, conduct or negotiation directly or indirectly in furtherance of any of the foregoing.

Again, the definitions provided are not exhaustive, and although clause (e) of the definition is broad, there is presumably a residual area of discretion available to the regulators to decide that some other activity outside these parameters is also a trade. Note that the British Columbia *Securities Act* adds, in its clause (b), that a trade includes entering into "an option that is an exchange contract."

A. Sale for Valuable Consideration

The first clause of the Ontario definition of trade includes "any sale or disposition of a security for valuable consideration," and the wording in the BC Act is similar. It raises a series of interpretive questions. Why does the definition not apply to *purchases* of securities? What about takeover bids? Is someone who purchases a security on the basis of material undisclosed information in Ontario engaging in insider trading? Note that most definitions of trade cover both primary and secondary market trades. What about the typical requirement that the sale or disposition be "for valuable consideration"? Why are gifts excluded? What about corporations that declare stock dividends?

B. Trades by Professionals

Clauses (b) and (c) of the Ontario definition of trade are directed toward the regulation of persons involved in carrying out trades on behalf of others, who have to fulfill extensive registration requirements. This definition is arguably necessary to give legal authority to the regulatory strategy of registering professional traders and is consistent with the policy objective of controlling access to the activity of professional trading in the interests of protecting investors in relation to their interactions with such professionals. Note that clauses (b.1) and (b.2) capture the entering into or amending of a derivative contract within the definition of trading.

C. Trades by Control Persons

Various transactions from the holdings of "control persons" "for the purpose of giving collateral for a debt made in good faith" are considered trades by virtue of clause (d) of the definition of trading in Ontario. We will see that sales of securities from the holdings of control persons are considered distributions in many provinces. Why is the pledging of shares as collateral, where the control person might ultimately retain the securities, also singled out for specific mention? Note that such pledging by non-control holders is specifically excluded from the first clause of the definition of trade. Does it have something to do with the assumption that control persons might have superior access to information about the issuer? How are the activities of control persons relevant to other investors?

D. Acts in Furtherance of a Sale

The scope of the definition of "trade" is extended significantly by Ontario's clause (e) (clause (f) in the British Columbia *Securities Act* definition of trade), which incorporates any act in furtherance of a sale of a security. This might include various kinds of presale activities or sales pitches, such as providing a list of names of prospective purchasers, or placing advertisements in widely circulated publications before the incorporation of a company. The regulatory concern is that any sales pitches might include pressure tactics or misrepresentations, which would influence the buyer, but not be caught by the legislation because they take place prior to the actual trade. Thus the inclusion of presale activities in the definition is intended to maintain the integrity of the markets and to protect investors. The provision has been read to exclude an entity that is not involved in the investment decision-making process. One example of this would be a firm that provided bookkeeping and administrative services to investment dealers trading in mutual fund securities. The involvement of this trust company occurred only after the trade in a security had taken place between the broker and the client. See *Re Ontario Securities Commission and CAP Ltd* (1971), 22 DLR (3d) 529 (Ont H Ct J). More recently, the OSC has held that accepting money from investors and depositing investor cheques for the purchase of shares in a bank account constitute acts in furtherance of trades (*Re Limelight Entertainment Inc* (2008), 31 OSCB 1727 at para 133). Mark R Gillen points out that it is not entirely clear whether the acts described under other clauses of the definition need to *eventually* be completed before the notion of a "furtherance" can be said to apply (*Securities Regulation in Canada*, 3rd ed (Toronto: Carswell, 2007)). He concludes that this would be too limited a position to take on the intent of the legislative provision. Such an interpretation might, for example, prevent an injunction being granted to forestall a trade. Thus, a broad reading of the legislation would probably prevail here.

E. Jurisdictional Issues in Relation to Trading

It may sometimes be necessary to determine where a trade is in fact taking place in order to assess whether a particular regulator has jurisdiction over that trading. This issue has become ostensibly more complicated with the advent of Internet-based trading and will be canvassed further in later chapters. A typical example of the sort of issue that can arise is found in the *Limelight Entertainment* decision cited above, where the commission found that it had jurisdiction over the matter because several acts in furtherance of trading took place in Ontario, even though many of the investors solicited were outside the province. More recently, in *Re XI Biofuels Inc* (2009), 108 OR (3d) 410, the Ontario Superior Court of Justice upheld a decision of the OSC that it had jurisdiction to sanction several corporations and their individual officers or de facto officers where acts in furtherance of trading had taken place in Ontario, even though securities of the corporations involved were sold only to offshore investors. Finally, we add here an excerpt from an Alberta Securities Commission (ASC) decision, *World Stock Exchange*, which addressed the issue whether the ASC could sanction the promoters of an "Internet stock exchange." World Stock Exchange (WSE) was incorporated in the Cayman Islands and its website was also located there. It solicited a number of

Albertans and Alberta companies to raise money on WSE despite its not being recognized by the ASC as an exchange and the individuals involved not being registered. The ASC addressed the issue of whether the respondents traded in securities contrary to the Alberta legislation in the following manner.

Re World Stock Exchange
(2000), 9 ASCS 658

The principles expressed in *McKenzie* were applied by the Commission to telephone solicitations in *Re Cromwell Financial Service Inc. et al.* (1996, unreported) and, in our view, these same principles apply to solicitations by any method of communication, including the Internet. The Internet is revolutionary in the way it permits instantaneous communication and interactivity on a global scale, but its function in relation to securities trading remains essentially similar to the mail or the telephone. We agree with the statement in "Securities Activity on the Internet" (a *Report of the Technical Committee of the International Organization of Securities Commissions* published in September 1998), that the "fundamental principles of securities regulation do not change based on the medium."

These principles are also reflected in National Policy 47-201 Distribution of Securities Using the Internet and other Electronic Means ("NP 47-201"), which became effective January 1, 2000. Although its provisions are not authoritative in this proceeding, the following section of NP 47-201 is completely consistent with our view:

2.2 Trading in a Jurisdiction

(1) The securities regulatory authorities generally consider a person or company to be trading in securities in a local jurisdiction if that person or company posts on the Internet a document that offers or solicits trades of securities, and if that document is accessible to persons or companies in that local jurisdiction.

(2) Despite subsection (1), the securities regulatory authorities consider the posting of a document on the Internet that offers or solicits trades of securities not to be a trade or, if applicable, a distribution, in a local jurisdiction if

(a) the document contains a prominently displayed disclaimer that expressly identifies the local jurisdictions and/or foreign jurisdictions in which the offering or solicitation is qualified to be made, and that identification does not include the local jurisdiction; and

(b) reasonable precautions are taken by all persons or companies offering or soliciting trades of securities through the document posted on the Internet not to sell to anyone resident in the local jurisdiction.

(3) Market participants are reminded that the registration requirements of securities legislation apply in connection with the posting of a prospectus or other offering document on the Internet for use in connection with a distribution in a local jurisdiction. The act of posting a prospectus or offering document in those circumstances is an act in furtherance of a trade in that local jurisdiction, and the person or company posting the prospectus or offering document must, in order to comply with the registration requirements

(a) be registered to trade in the local jurisdiction;

(b) have the benefit of an exemption from the registration requirements in connection with the distribution in the local jurisdiction; or

> (c) refer all inquiries concerning the document to a registered dealer in the local jurisdiction.
>
> It is clear that the respondents traded in the securities of the WSE. They similarly traded in the securities of the companies listed on the WSE.

See also *Committee for the Equal Treatment of Asbestos Minority Shareholders v Ontario (Securities Commission)*, 2001 SCC 37, [2001] 2 SCR 132.

V. WHAT IS A DISTRIBUTION?

Once a determination is made that the transaction involves a security and a trade, the next question in many jurisdictions is whether the trade in that security constitutes a distribution. Again, the importance of this determination is that a prospectus (or an exemption from the prospectus requirement) is necessary when securities are being distributed. See e.g. OSA, s 53 or QSA, s 11.

In most provincial jurisdictions, the definition of distribution is likewise broad but rather more straightforward than the definition of a security. OSA, s 1 provides:

> "distribution," where used in relation to trading in securities, means,
>
> (a) a trade in securities of an issuer that have not been previously issued,
>
> (b) a trade by or on behalf of an issuer in previously issued securities of that issuer that have been redeemed or purchased by or donated to that issuer,
>
> (c) a trade in previously issued securities of an issuer from the holdings of any control person,
>
> (d) a trade by or on behalf of an underwriter in securities which were acquired by that underwriter, acting as underwriter, prior to the 15th day of September, 1979 if those securities continued on that date to be owned by or for that underwriter, so acting,
>
> (e) a trade by or on behalf of an underwriter in securities which were acquired by that underwriter, acting as underwriter, within eighteen months after the 15th day of September, 1979, if the trade took place during that eighteen months, and
>
> (f) any trade that is a distribution under the regulations,
>
> and on and after the 15th day of March, 1981, includes a distribution as referred to in subsections 72(4), (5), (6) and (7), and also includes any transaction or series of transactions involving a purchase and sale or a repurchase and resale in the course of or incidental to a distribution and "distribute," "distributed" and "distributing" have a corresponding meaning.

A. Securities Not Previously Issued

The first clause of the Ontario definition of distribution has to do with trades in a security of an issuer "that have not been previously issued." An "issue" here means the offer of securities for sale. An "issuer" simply means "a person or company who has outstanding, issues or proposes to issue, a security" (e.g., OSA, s 1). A person or company offering a security for sale that has not previously been offered for sale is making a distribution in Ontario, and a prospectus will be required unless an exemption is available. Another way of putting this is to say that in many provinces a prospectus is required in all circumstances involving the issuing of new securities other than those outlined in the statutory exemption sections of the Act, Regulations, or Rules, for those provinces that can pass them. We have noted that the QSA does not contain a definition of "trade." Accordingly, the first branch of the QSA's definition of distribution (QSA, s 5) refers to "the endeavour to obtain, or the obtaining, by an issuer, of subscribers, or acquirers of his securities."

B. Reissue of Securities

The second meaning refers to the idea that the reissue by the issuer of securities previously issued is also a distribution. The point is that on reissue, the issuer might have in its possession material information not otherwise available to the public. Gillen points out that this clause of the definition of distribution is moot for many Canadian corporations, because both the *Canada Business Corporations Act*, RSC 1985, c C-44 (CBCA) s 39(6) and the Ontario *Business Corporations Act*, RSO 1990, c B.16 (OBCA) s 35(6) require that shares that are redeemed cannot be held for resale but must instead be cancelled. See Mark R Gillen, *Securities Regulation in Canada*, 3rd ed (Toronto: Carswell, 2007) at 134.

C. Sales of Securities by Control Persons

In many provinces, one aspect of the definition of distribution refers to sales of securities by control persons.

1. *Reasons Why Sales by Control Persons Are Considered to Be Distributions*

1. Despite the fact that sales of securities by control persons involve sales of already issued securities, their regulation in this way is justified by a number of policy concerns. The assumption is that those in control have better knowledge of the issuer and the possibility of influence over internal and board decisions. Regulating control transactions on this basis is justified as an issue of equality of access for all investors.
2. Control persons have a superior ability to alter the value of the issuer. If the sale involves a substantial number of securities, the market price of the security may be affected and the sale itself may therefore be a "material" event.
3. Similarly, the control person herself may be an important factor in the success of the enterprise, and the sale of her shares should therefore be disclosed to other shareholders by way of the imposition of a prospectus requirement.

2. *What Is a Control Block of Shares?*

The OSA contains a specific definition of "control person" as follows:

> (a) a person or company who holds a sufficient number of the voting rights attached to all outstanding voting securities of an issuer to affect materially the control of the issuer, and, if a person or company holds more than 20 per cent of the voting rights attached to all outstanding voting securities of an issuer, the person or company is deemed, in the absence of evidence to the contrary, to hold a sufficient number of the voting rights to affect materially the control of the issuer, or

(b) each person or company in a combination of persons or companies, acting in concert by virtue of an agreement, arrangement, commitment or understanding, which holds in total a sufficient number of the voting rights attached to all outstanding voting securities of an issuer to affect materially the control of the issuer, and, if a combination of persons or companies holds more than 20 per cent of the voting rights attached to all outstanding voting securities of an issuer, the combination of persons or companies is deemed, in the absence of evidence to the contrary, to hold a sufficient number of the voting rights to affect materially the control of the issuer;

The following elements of this definition are relevant:

1. Under the Ontario statute, the meaning of "holdings" refers to the situation where the person is in a position to exercise rights with respect to securities. Thus, it would probably not include nominees who have no right to vote or to receive dividends.
2. The only type of relevant control is that arising from the holding of voting rights attached to outstanding voting securities (that is, not being a director or creditor). The reference to the ability to "affect materially" includes less than actual control. If certain activities can be blocked (such as significant transactions like amalgamations or sales of substantially all the assets) by a holding of securities that is not large enough to actually control the issuer, the effect of the holding on control may nevertheless be material—e.g., a voting agreement between a 15 percent shareholder and a 40 percent shareholder. An ability to control as well as actual exercise of control appears to be contemplated by the Ontario provision.
3. According to the definition of control person, a holding of more than 20 percent of the voting rights attached to all outstanding voting securities is deemed to represent a control block unless there is evidence to the contrary (such as evidence that the holder does not have the ability to control where another person or combination holds the majority of the voting securities or is in a position to control the election of the board of directors). As noted above, it is important to remember that less than 20 percent of the voting securities may still constitute a control block, depending on circumstances such as "the existence of sufficiently large security holdings by others, the pattern of voting behaviour by various holders, the way in which securities are distributed and, possibly, an analysis of the recent history of ownership of the securities in question" (Borden Ladner Gervais, *Securities Law and Practice*, 3rd ed (Toronto: Carswell) (loose-leaf) (BLG) at 17-115).
4. The second branch of the Ontario definition is the identification of a "combination of persons or companies, acting in concert by virtue of an agreement, arrangement, commitment or understanding, which holds in total a sufficient number of the voting rights attached to all outstanding voting securities of an issuer to affect materially the control of the issuer." Some sort of relationship between the persons "is required before they constitute a combination, such as a relationship inferred from family or intercorporate ties, voting agreements, or previous actions undertaken in concert or for a common purpose" (BLG at 17-100). It does not appear to be a requirement that every issuer must have a controlling shareholder or group of shareholders; however, the definition makes clear that each person or company in the combination could be a control person.

D. Resale of Securities

Finally, most, but not all, provincial legislation controls the process of *resale* of securities sold under a prospectus exemption where another exemption is unavailable, by initially deeming the resale to be a distribution, unless the relevant substantive resale rules are satisfied. See Chapter 5 for more on this subject. It should be noted that the Ontario wording at the end of the definition of distribution makes reference to ss 72(4) to (7) of the OSA, even though these sections have been removed from the Act by the legislature.

VI. WHAT IS A REPORTING ISSUER?

The statutory concept of a reporting issuer carries an enormous amount of regulatory weight because it is the mechanism whereby securities law accomplishes the objective of ensuring the obligation to continuously disclose information to investors. As we will see in more detail in Chapter 6, all provinces impose continuous disclosure requirements on reporting issuers. For example, in Québec, s 68 of the QSA says: "A reporting issuer is an issuer that has made a distribution of securities to the public; a reporting issuer is subject to the continuous disclosure requirements of Chapter II of this title."

In Ontario, a

> "reporting issuer" means an issuer,
>
> (a) that has issued voting securities on or after the 1st day of May, 1967 in respect of which a prospectus was filed and a receipt therefor obtained under a predecessor of this Act or in respect of which a securities exchange take-over bid circular was filed under a predecessor of this Act,
>
> (b) that has filed a prospectus and for which the Director has issued a receipt under this Act,
>
> (b.1) that has filed a securities exchange take-over bid circular under this Act before December 14, 1999,
>
> (c) any of whose securities have been at any time since the 15th day of September, 1979 listed and posted for trading on any stock exchange in Ontario recognized by the Commission, regardless of when such listing and posting for trading commenced,
>
> (d) to which the *Business Corporations Act* applies and which, for the purposes of that Act, is offering its securities to the public,
>
> (e) that is the company whose existence continues following the exchange of securities of a company by or for the account of such company with another company or the holders of the securities of that other company in connection with,
>
> (i) a statutory amalgamation or arrangement, or
>
> (ii) a statutory procedure under which one company takes title to the assets of the other company that in turn loses its existence by operation of law, or under which the existing companies merge into a new company,
>
> where one of the amalgamating or merged companies or the continuing company has been a reporting issuer for at least twelve months, or
>
> (f) that is designated as a reporting issuer in an order made under subsection 1(11).

A. Securities Issued Under a Predecessor Act

The first clause of the Ontario definition deals with entities that issued securities prior to the coming into force of the current Act and obtained a prospectus receipt for them. Note that this definition applies only to having issued "voting" securities. It does not include issuers whose securities were issued before 1967 and who have not subsequently qualified a prospectus in Ontario.

B. Obtaining a Receipt for a Prospectus

This is the most widely applicable of the various Ontario definitions because it refers to any issuer that has obtained a receipt for a prospectus from the regulator. Note that the specific requirement is only that a receipt was obtained for the prospectus, rather than that securities were ultimately distributed. One implication of this in Ontario is that it enables issuers who have issued securities under prospectus exemptions to qualify those securities for general resale by obtaining a receipt for a subsequent prospectus. Thus, in order to create or facilitate a broad secondary market for securities issued via exemptions, an issuer may use s 53(2) of the Ontario Act to become a reporting issuer. Clause (b.1) is now of historical interest only in Ontario, because it represents the closing of a significant loophole in the definition of a reporting issuer that formerly allowed issuers to become reporting issuers by filing a takeover bid circular, which involved the exchange of securities as consideration for the bid. This possibility created a form of "reverse takeover" that enabled businesses that were not reporting issuers to become so, with little or no scrutiny by regulators, by taking over an inactive company. However, becoming a reporting issuer by filing a securities exchange takeover bid circular is still a possibility in British Columbia. See clause (f) of the definition of reporting issuer in s 1 of the BCSA.

C. Listing on a Recognized Stock Exchange

For purposes of clause (c) of the Ontario definition of reporting issuer, the Toronto Stock Exchange (TSX), the TSX Venture Exchange, the Canadian Stock Exchange (CSE), and Aequitas Innovations Inc and Aequitas Neo Exchange Inc are recognized by the OSC for the purposes of this definition. However, one of the requirements for listing on CSE in the first place is that an issuer must first be a reporting issuer (or equivalent) in a jurisdiction in Canada. This meaning has been held responsible for allowing the infamous Bre-X corporation to become a reporting issuer in Ontario without ever qualifying a prospectus in that province. At the root of this analysis is the view that the listing standards of the Toronto Stock Exchange (TSE) (as it then was) were insufficiently rigorous, such that Bre-X became listed on the TSE because one of the then acceptable criteria for a listing was "prior trading on another market"—in this case, another provincial exchange in Canada. For a note of caution here, see Jeffrey G MacIntosh, "Lessons of Bre-X (?): Some Comments" (1999) 30:2 Can Bus LJ 223; see also OSC Staff Notice 51-719, Emerging Markets Issuer Review (2012), 35 OSCB 3004.

D. Regulatory Power to Deem Issuers to Be Reporting Issuers

Finally, the OSC relatively recently acquired the power to deem issuers to be reporting issuers. The power to make such an order is now in s 1(11) of the OSA and must be exercised on a public interest standard. This was intended to allow the Ontario regulator to deem reporting issuers in other Canadian jurisdictions to be reporting issuers in Ontario where Ontario residents might access their securities. Issuers might also be deemed to be reporting issuers in Ontario where their securities trade on exchanges not recognized in accordance with clause (c) of the Ontario definition of reporting issuer. See OSC Policy 12-602 (2007), 30 OSCB 2641. See Philip Anisman, "Proposed Amendments to the Ontario Securities Act: An Open Letter to the Ontario Securities Commission" (1998) 31:2 Can Bus LJ 272 for a critique of this expansion of the regulators' discretionary power. See also Alberta *Securities Act*, RSA 2000 c S-4 (ASA), s 145 for a similar power in that province.

Now we will introduce an additional series of concepts that are thematically linked to each other and very much a part of the discourse of regulation, as well as of popular and scholarly understanding of securities markets. They are, respectively, the concepts of "efficiency," "materiality," "valuation," and "systemic risk." Only the concept of "materiality" is defined in any form in Canadian securities statutes.

VII. EFFICIENCY

The term "efficiency" is used in ordinary discourse in a number of different ways to mean a number of different things. Often it is used, by business people and citizens alike, synonymously with cost–benefit analysis. Thus, it is efficient, or cost effective, to engage in projects or activities where the benefits of the activity outweigh the costs. A number of different meanings of efficiency, including allocative efficiency, were canvassed in Professor Trebilcock's excerpt in the introduction to this book. At the rhetorical level, arguments for one or another form of policy change are often justified in efficiency terms. So a prevailing claim is that government regulation produces inefficiency and hampers the operation of the capital markets. In the scholarly literature, an important starting point in the discussion of efficiency in relation to securities trading is that there are a variety of meanings for the term. Furthermore, a very important link is posited between disclosure of information and efficient markets. The idea is that efficient markets are those that absorb information about issuers as quickly as possible and adjust prices accordingly. However, as the excerpt below makes clear, in this case, the meaning of efficiency varies according to the *type* of information (that is, historical, current, insider, etc.) assumed to affect stock prices.

Christopher C Nicholls, *Corporate Finance and Canadian Law*
2nd ed (Toronto: Carswell, 2013) at 169-70, 173-75, 176-77, 178-80, and 184-86 (footnotes omitted)

(i) What Does "Efficiency" Mean?

Capital markets may be "efficient" in a number of ways. They may allocate financial resources efficiently; they may operate efficiently, in the sense that they impose minimal transaction costs on participants and minimize waste; they may be "dynamically efficient," in the sense that they are designed to improve over time in response to changing conditions, technologies and other advances; or they may be efficient in the sense that they operate such that information is rapidly incorporated into asset prices. When modern finance theorists refer to the efficient capital market hypothesis, they generally have in mind the fourth type of efficiency—sometimes called informational efficiency.

Efficient market theory arose from early attempts to answer the question: Is it possible, at any given moment, to predict how the price of a capital asset, such as a share of a publicly-traded corporation, will move within the next short period of time? Studies of stock prices seemed to suggest that it was not possible to make such a prediction with any degree of certainty. It might be possible for a few able professional traders, by careful study, to identify small pricing errors or anomalies and exploit them rapidly; but the amateur investor is not likely to be able to "beat the market" with any degree of consistency. Information relative to stock values is impounded into stock prices so quickly, by the time the ambitious amateur notices any pricing anomaly, it will already have disappeared.

...

The significance of efficient market theory, however, is not simply the answer it attempts to provide to the question of how stock prices move, but also the explanation or the "story" it offers as to *why* the market is so difficult to beat, and the empirical research it has prompted on the actual behaviour of stock prices.

...

(iii) Development of the Efficient Market Hypothesis

Efficient market theory began its ascent to prominence among financial theorists in the 1950s and 1960s, owing to the work of such people as Maurice Kendall, Harry Roberts, and Eugene Fama (who appears to have coined the term "efficient markets"). Research on stock prices appeared to indicate that such prices followed no discernible pattern. Prices appeared, instead, to move randomly. Random movement does not, of course, imply arbitrary movement. In other words, stock prices don't simply move up and down regardless of the performance of the companies that have issued them, or of the economy generally. New relevant information about a stock will, naturally, have an impact on the stock's price. But new information, by definition, is unpredictable. (If it weren't unpredictable, it wouldn't be new.) Thus, although stock prices reflect relevant information about a company at any given moment, there is no way of predicting whether the next piece of relevant information to be revealed will be good or bad, and so no way of predicting whether a stock's price, in future, will move up or down. Stock prices—observed in unpredictable isolation—should not be expected to follow any pattern.

The observed *phenomenon* that the efficient market theory attempts to explain, then, is that stock prices appear to move randomly. The proposed *explanation* for this phenomenon is that relevant information is absorbed by the markets so quickly that, at any given moment, a stock's price, in effect, impounds the market's collective assessment of all available information. The *implication* of the efficient capital markets hypothesis is that we should expect shares traded in actual liquid stock markets to be fairly priced, at any given moment in the sense that their prices accurately impound all available information and so reflect the present value of the issuing firm's expected future cash flow. It should therefore be impossible, at least for the amateur investor, to find "bargains" and so beat the market with any consistency. Investors might deceive themselves into thinking they have superior investment savvy if, for example, they invest in high-risk stocks that outperform the market over the short-term. (The winners of "stock-picking" contests invariably use such high-risk investment strategies.) In fact, overtime, the abnormally high returns such investors might earn in one period will likely be offset by abnormally high losses in other periods, so that, again, on average, they will be unlikely to consistently earn above-market returns.

Many empirical tests have been conducted to attempt to confirm the efficient market hypothesis. The hypothesis has, for testing purposes, been "subdivided" into three forms:

- Weak-form efficiency. A market is weak-form efficient, if current prices reflect all historical price information.
- Semi-strong form efficiency. A market is semi-strong form efficient, if current prices reflect not only all historical price information, but also all publicly-available information.
- Strong-form efficiency. A market is strong-form efficient, if current prices reflect all relevant information about a stock—whether or not publicly-disclosed.

• • •

For some time, the weight of authority seemed to favour the view that markets were certainly weak-form efficient, probably semi-strong form efficient, but almost certainly not strong-form efficient. Recently, however, some scholars have argued that markets are not even weak-form efficient, and that there may even be exploitable share price patterns. And occasional dramatic market reversals, such as the 1987 stock market crash, the more recent turmoil driving the financial crisis or the May 2010 "flash crash" discussed in Chapter 9, are often identified by EMT skeptics as proof that this particular theoretical emperor has no clothes. Modern research, particularly in areas such as behavioural finance, have also highlighted weaknesses in EMT, but have not diminished the importance of the hypothesis as one of the landmark theories in financial economies.

• • •

More broadly, behavioural finance theorists have chronicled many irrational investor attitudes, such as so-called endowment effects, and have documented investors' underreactions and overreactions to information and so-called "momentum effects" that all seem difficult to reconcile with EMT. Defenders of EMT—in particular, Eugene Fama—have responded to behavioural finance researchers by pointing out that merely identifying isolated examples of apparent shortcomings in the EMT falls well short of putting forth a coherent alternative theory with superior explanatory power. Increasingly, however, behavioural finance has gained ground and is now regularly featured in mainstream discussions of corporate finance theory.

(iv) Efficient Market Hypothesis and the Law

(A) Securities Legislation

Because efficient market theory links the dissemination of information about issuing corporations to the market prices at which the shares of such corporations trade in the market, securities regulators have sometimes invoked the theory as a justification for disclosure-based securities laws. So, for example, when it first introduced its short-form Form S-3 Registration Statement (and the 415 shelf-registration regime), the U.S. Securities and Exchange Commission ("SEC") explicitly stated that it was relying upon efficient market theory. In Canada, too, we have seen explicit attempts to link the securities law disclosure regime to the principles of efficient market theory. Indeed, Gilson and Kraakman, writing in 1984, concluded that "the [efficient capital markets hypothesis] is now *the* context in which serious discussion of the regulation of financial markets takes place." What is not altogether clear, however, is whether efficient market theory really does support our current mandatory disclosure regime, or whether, it should, instead be seen as a theory that actually buttresses the case for dismantling that regime. Certainly securities regulators, and many leading legal academics favour the view that efficient market theory strengthens—or at least does not weaken—the case for mandatory disclosure. But some financial economists take a contrary view, arguing, essentially, that information relevant to the pricing of corporate securities would be disclosed in the absence of statutory requirements in any event; thus, securities regulation simply imposes needless costs. Although there are clearly compelling reasons to expect that corporate managers would voluntarily disclose some corporate information, it must be said that there is little in the history of corporate disclosure practices, prior to the introduction of mandatory disclosure regimes, to suggest that firms have been generous in volunteering information, or that they felt in any way compelled to make significant disclosure as a pre-condition to enjoying access to the capital markets. Though it might be argued that any disclosure inadequacies would eventually be rectified as the market disciplined firms that provide sub-optimal disclosure, it is unclear how robustly and how quickly market forces would effect change in the absence of regulation.

. . .

(II) Valuation Issues

It must be said that courts in both Canada and the United States have, in general, maintained a healthy scepticism about the efficient market hypothesis.

Courts have been urged to consider the efficient market hypothesis in cases where disputes arise as to the fair value of the shares of a publicly-traded corporation. If markets are efficient, it is reasoned, then the market price for such shares is the best indication of their fair market value. The courts need to look no further.

Yet, our courts often do look further. Chancellor Allen, of the Delaware Court of Chancery, rather eloquently articulated the judicial attitude toward efficient market theory in the takeover "premium" context, in one of the leading early Delaware hostile takeover bid cases, *Paramount Communications, Inc. v. Time*:

> This view [i.e., that markets are efficient] may be correct. It may be that in a well-developed stock market, there is no discount for long-term profit maximizing behavior except that reflected in the discount for the time value of money … Perhaps wise social policy and sound business decisions ought to be premised upon the assumptions that underlie this view. But just as the Constitution does not enshrine Mr. Herbert Spencer's social statics, neither does the common law of directors' duties elevate the theory of a single, efficient capital market to the dignity of a sacred text.

In a similar context (and apparently in a similar vein), an Ontario judge once endorsed the actions of the directors of a takeover bid target who "found the intrinsic value of the company was not being recognized by *those people* who trade in the stock exchange."

From time to time, other U.S. judges have appeared somewhat more sympathetic to certain modern financial views on securities markets. Yet, particularly in the corporate law dissent and appraisal context, where corporate shareholders have exercised their statutory rights to dissent from certain corporate decisions and demand to be paid fair

> value for their shares, courts in both Canada and the U.S. seem reluctant to rely on the markets as a determinant of the value of such shares. …
>
> All in all, then, although the efficient market hypothesis seems at times to be taken seriously by securities regulators, it is not clear that it enjoys broad support among our judges.

VIII. MATERIALITY

We have seen that for a securities market to achieve efficiency, it must receive information that can be used to adjust trading prices. While the issue whether issuers would voluntarily disclose information in the absence of mandatory requirements is a matter of lively scholarly debate, the fact remains that legislatures currently impose significant reporting requirements on those who issue securities (as well as those with power to influence issuers). The extent of those reporting requirements is discussed in detail in Chapters 4 and 6. However, at this point it is important to note that securities legislation acknowledges that issuers cannot be expected to disclose every piece of information that investors might find interesting or even significant. The threshold that distinguishes information that is legally disclosable and that which is not is expressed in the concept of "materiality." If information is material, it should be disclosed. We will see later that many provincial statutes include concepts such as "material fact" or "material change" as characterizing the nature of information that should be disclosed in specific circumstances. For now, we want to examine more generally the issue when the threshold of materiality will be considered to be met. How do issuers decide what information is material and what is not? Chapter 4 contains a useful excerpt from the final report of Ontario's Five Year Review Committee, which canvasses these issues and makes a proposal for reform. As it indicates, the current statutory standard in many Canadian jurisdictions is what is called a "market impact" test—that is, information that should be disclosed is information that would affect the "price or value" of the issuer's securities. However, the analysis employed under US securities law is the "reasonable investor" test. In the United States, information should be disclosed if there is a substantial likelihood that a "reasonable investor" would consider it important to an investment decision. Some commentators claim that the Canadian test is broader in scope than the American test; some argue the reverse; and some contend that it really makes no difference. Ultimately, as we will see in Chapter 4, the Five Year Review Committee recommended that the Canadian test come into conformity with the US formulation in the interest of harmonization with US regulatory standards. For now, it is sufficient to note that the standards imposed on issuers require them to make an assessment of the "effects" of information on the market generally (or on the reasonable investor, as in the US formulation). It might also be argued that the "market impact" formulation of the standard of materiality appears consistent with the some of the definitions of efficiency that we have noted above.

QUESTION

Does the material on the behavioural finance approach to analyzing investment decision-making canvassed in the introduction to this casebook create any difficulties for a "reasonable investor" standard of disclosable information?

IX. VALUE

It is claimed that information disclosed to the securities market about an issuer and its activities should, in an efficient market, have the effect of moving the price of those securities in an upward or a downward direction. However, a question we have not yet addressed is whether the market price at which a particular security is trading is the same as its value. Analysts frequently talk about securities being undervalued or overvalued. There are a number of diverse purposes for which an analysis of a security's value will be necessary—e.g. pricing a new issue of securities. Another would be where a bidder intends to make an offer for the shares of a target. Still others would include situations where the securities of an enterprise do not trade on an organized securities market, or where investor remedies or regulatory enforcement actions are at issue. It can be readily seen, therefore, that issues of securities' value and techniques of valuation are implicated in the subject matter of almost all of the chapters in this casebook. The following extract discusses the approach that financing experts take to the task of valuing shares. Note the distinction drawn in the extract between the valuation of shares and the market price at which shares may trade.

William A Klein, John C Coffee Jr & Frank Partnoy,
Business Organization and Finance
11th ed (New York: Foundation Press, 2010), 288-91 (footnotes omitted)

a. *Dividends.* Most publicly held corporations pay cash dividends to shareholders. Dividends are often said to be paid "out of" current earnings. In light of the fact that money is fungible, and that the word "earnings" refers to the outcome of a complex process, not to a fund, it is more accurate to say that the amount of the dividend (usually) will depend on or be limited to the amount of the corporation's current earnings. Sometimes corporations will pay dividends in amounts larger than current earnings; the excess will then usually be thought of as coming out of the previously undistributed earnings of earlier years. Typically, corporations over the long haul will pay out less than all their earnings as dividends. A portion of earnings will be retained and reinvested in the business. But all that the shareholders see is the dividend. That is their return. It is now widely accepted in the sophisticated academic financial literature that the value of shares of common stock is best thought of as a function of the dividends (including any final, liquidating dividend paid when the corporation's existence ends) that the corporation can be expected to pay out over its life. Many people consider this to be a peculiar proposition because they think instinctively about capital gain (sale price less cost) as part of the return on common stock.

The fact is, nonetheless, that capital gain must be a function of expectations about future dividends. Imagine a series of shareholders. The first shareholder pays a given amount for the shares, based on an estimate of the amount of cash dividends plus a gain (or loss) at some time in the future. The next shareholder makes the same kind of calculation. That is, the gain, if any, will depend on the next shareholder's expectation as to cash dividends plus capital gain (or loss). And so on. If we think of the entire series of shareholders, some may have greater capital gains or losses than others, depending on the timing of their purchases and sales and on collective expectations, reflected in market prices, at the time of those purchases and sales. But the gains and losses are transfers among all the shareholders who hold the shares over the entire time that they are outstanding. Those gains or losses do not increase or decrease the total return on the shares over that time. The only return that shareholders collectively can expect over the life of the shares in which they invest is the dividends (including, as indicated above, any final or liquidating dividend) paid on those shares. It can be seen, then, that if people are rational the value of the shares at any point in time must be derived solely from the series of expectations about dividends. Any gain in the value of shares must be based on expectations concerning dividends to be paid at some point in the future.

. . .

This does not mean that the shares of a corporation that pays no dividends *currently* are worthless. Many companies have operated for years without paying dividends. Many of these have been successful, growing companies that were retaining all of their earnings in order to take advantage of attractive investment opportunities. People do, rationally, pay money for shares of such companies. They do so because they expect that at some point in the future dividends will be paid.

. . .

b. *Earnings.* If, as we have just seen, dividends alone determine value, what is the relevance of earnings (as they are defined by traditional accounting principles)? If earnings are not paid out as dividends, and assuming that earnings have not been misstated, the amount retained will be "invested" by the corporation. To the extent that earnings are retained, and invested, the value of the firm's assets should increase and its earnings and capacity to pay dividends in the future should increase correspondingly. Thus, the earnings figure is relevant in determining the value of the firm's shares because it provides information about future capacity to pay dividends. Concern with earnings is therefore entirely consistent with the proposition that the value of the shares is solely a function of dividends.

What if the retention of earnings does not produce any improvement in future earnings and dividend-paying capacity? Suppose, for example, that over a period of many years a firm reports yearly earnings of $3 per share and pays yearly dividends of $1 per share. If the earnings remain constant at $3, what is the firm doing with the $2 that it is purportedly retaining and investing each year? One possibility is that it is figuratively pouring the retained earnings down a rathole—making utterly worthless investments. More likely there is something wrong with the $3 figure. If $2 must be reinvested each year just to keep the firm at a steady level then that $2 should be regarded as part of the cost of doing business. The true earnings figure is $1 per share. Thus, by examining a firm's dividends over time, one can often gain insight into the reliability of its reported earnings figures.

c. *Dividends, Earnings, and Share Prices.* Suppose that at the beginning of the year a share of common stock of X Corporation sells for $100 and that during the year X Corp. earns $10 per share. All other variables being held constant, and assuming that the earnings figure is accurate and realistic, the price of the share at the end of the year should be $110. The wealth of shareholders will be $100 per share at the beginning of the year and $110 at the end. If, at year's end, X Corp. retains the $10 per share of earnings, the price of the shares should remain at $110. If, on the other hand, the $10 is paid out as a dividend, the price should fall to $100. The shareholder will now have a share worth $100 plus $10 in cash. His or her wealth will be the same as if the earnings had been retained—a total of $110 consisting of the share worth $100 plus the $10 in cash. If earnings are retained to finance an unwise investment, the value of the share will be less than $110, but that outcome is a result of the unwise investment decision, not of the decision to retain.

QUESTION

Do the principles underlying a "materiality" analysis with respect to disclosure of information seem consistent with the academic theory of valuing shares, excerpted above?

X. SYSTEMIC RISK

While the concept of systemic risk had been familiar to banking regulators before the GFC, it was added to the lexicon of securities regulators in 2008. The global effects of the sale of unregulated financial products and the activities of credit rating agencies prompted securities regulators to consider the extent to which, and how, they should monitor the presence of systemic risk in securities markets. This task is rendered more difficult by the open-ended nature of the concept. Professor Anand discusses the conceptual confusion surrounding the idea of systemic risk in the following excerpt.

Anita Anand, "Regulating Systemic Risk in Canadian Financial Markets"
(16 May 2016) 18 One Issue, Two Voices at 9-12

What Is Systemic Risk?

Most commentators agree that there is no universally accepted definition of systemic risk. It comes as no surprise, then, that a primary criticism lodged against proponents of regulating systemic risk is that the term defies precise definition: "If we cannot define it, how can we regulate it?" An examination of the academic literature, as well as writings and speeches of policy makers during and following the financial market crisis, suggests that the term systemic risk has itself evolved over time. While originally conceived as describing the failure of one financial institution that in turn causes the domino-style failure of others, systemic risk now generally describes a possibility of financial meltdown that affects an entire economic system.

Traditionally, the literature has focused on the concept of systemic risk in the financial sector alone, referring to a triggering event that causes a chain of negative economic consequences. Crockett explains this domino-style effect as follows:

For banks, this effect may occur if Bank A, for whatever reason, defaults on a loan, deposit, or other payment to Bank B, thereby producing a loss greater than B's capital and forcing it to default on payment to Bank C, thereby producing a loss greater than C's capital, and so on down the chain.

Thus, the traditional definition of systemic risk relates specifically to financial institution failure brought on by defaults in contractual relationships between and among institutions. The risk of a domino effect is central to this conception of systemic risk, as is the risk of some triggering event that occasions the fall of the first domino. To give one example, these features are apparent in the definition of systemic risk adopted by the Supreme Court of Canada:

> [R]isks that occasion a "domino effect" whereby the risk of default by one market participant will affect the ability of others to fulfill their legal obligations, setting off a chain of negative economic consequences that pervade an entire financial system.

Unfortunately, this traditional definition has several problematic ambiguities. For example, at what point must the "risk" crystallize in order to be referred to as "systemic"? Is evaluation of the risk possible only after the financial institution has failed (for example, by declaring bankruptcy)? If only one financial institution fails, and others survive because of government intervention, does systemic risk arise? What type of triggering event can cause systemic risk—only the failure of financial institutions to meet their contractual obligations? The traditional definition leaves all of these questions, and others, unanswered.

These ambiguities have led John Taylor, a professor of economics at Stanford University, to develop a more structured definition. He highlights three components of any definition of systemic risk: the risk of a large triggering event; the risk of financial propagation of such an event through the financial sector; and macroeconomic risk that the entire economy will be affected. The triggering event can arise from the failure of a financial institution, as described above; however, as Taylor explains, it may also arise from an exogenous shock—such as a terrorist attack (9/11) or a natural disaster—and the contracting of liquidity in the public sector.

While Taylor's three-part definition of systemic risk leaves room for questions (for example, what is "financial propagation"?), at the very least it suggests that the term can (and should) be interpreted more broadly to include risks that not only occasion the failure of financial institutions but also destabilize an entire economy. Along these lines, Kaufman and Scott explain that the term "refers to the risk or probability of breakdowns in an entire system, as opposed to breakdowns in individual parts or components, and is evidenced by co-movements (correlation) among most or all of the parts." Similarly, Dijkman asserts that "systemic risk usually refers to financial shocks that are likely to be serious enough to damage the real economy." Thus, a link is drawn between the financial markets and the "real economy," that is, the economy concerned with producing and consuming goods and services as opposed to buying and selling financial products.

Policy makers, it appears, have also adopted a more general understanding of systemic risk than merely the domino-style failure of financial institutions. For example, Bank of England governor Mark Carney refers to the "probability that the financial system is unable to support economic activity." Similarly, former Federal Reserve chairman Ben Bernanke writes that the concept of systemic risk should be broadly defined to include "developments that threaten the stability of the financial system as a whole and consequently the broader economy, not just that of one or two institutions."

Even with a broad understanding of "systemic risk," however, the question arises as to whether the existence of systemic risk is discoverable *ex ante* (before the risk arises) or only *ex post* (after a breakdown in the financial system has made the risk evident). The development of policy relating to the mitigation of systemic risk depends on the ability to make predictions and determine whether those predictions are valid. There were moments before the crisis in the United States when regulators could have responded to systemic risk. For example, the former chair of the Commodity Futures and Trade Commission (CFTC), Brooksley Born, is widely acknowledged to have predicted the crisis in over-the-counter (OTC) derivatives before the 2007 financial market crash. Yet the U.S. Congress moved to enact legislation that prevented the CFTC from taking any pre-emptive regulatory action.

If we agree that systemic risk may in fact require regulation, then we move into the sphere of "macroprudential regulation," a term that refers to a definite intention by regulators to respond to systemic risk (above and beyond merely identifying it). The Group of Thirty has declared that "macroprudential policy is concerned not only with systemic risk but also with developing the appropriate responses to those risks in order to strengthen the financial system and avoid similar crises in the future." The focus is on "the interconnectedness of financial institutions and markets, common exposures to economic variables, and procyclical behaviors [that] can create risk." The reforms contemplated below modify this concept by seeking to ensure that any regulatory response to crises takes account of common institutions and markets.

Systemic Risk and the Canadian Financial System

Some commentators may have difficulty discussing systemic risk in the Canadian context—and not only because of the definitional issues associated with the concept. Canadian capital markets fared relatively well during the recent financial crisis, and it could be argued that systemic risk has not been an issue for Canadian regulators, especially given that, historically, the Bank of Canada has regulated at least the clearing and settlement process. However, there are aspects of the Canadian economy that can give rise to systemic instability—as, for example, with the asset-backed commercial paper (ABCP) crisis (discussed below).

Many commentators rightly point to the efficacy of Canada's regulatory framework in safeguarding against financial contagion. Nevertheless, a consensus seems to be emerging regarding certain sources of systemic risk, perhaps applicable in any jurisdiction, which augmented the scale of the financial crisis. These sources include regulatory capital requirements, credit ratings, derivatives trading, registration exemptions, clearing and settlement systems, and lending standards and securitization. Conflicts of interest or other moral hazard problems are also endemic in Canada—particularly those associated with creditors (bank and non-bank), rating agencies, monoline (specialized) insurance policy providers, and distribution agents (dealers and investment advisors)—which may contribute to systemic risk.

See also Anita Anand, ed, *What's Next for Canada? Securities Regulation After the Reference* (Toronto: Irwin Law, 2012).

The International Organization of Securities Commissions has also published a number of papers on the topic of systemic risk, beginning with one titled *Mitigating Systemic Risk: A Role for Securities Regulators* in February 2011. (See M Condon, "Products, Perimeters and Politics: Systemic Risk and Securities Regulation" in C Williams & P Zumbansen, *The Embedded Firm: Corporate Governance, Labor and Finance Capitalism* (Cambridge, UK: Cambridge University Press, 2011).) And as we will see in later chapters, the evolving federal–provincial co-operative regulatory system in Canada provides more explicitly for the monitoring of systemic risk in Canadian securities markets, though it remains to be seen exactly what regulatory tools will be deployed to achieve this.

XI. CHAPTER SUMMARY

In this chapter, we have considered a number of basic conceptual tools to analyze a securities transaction. We have seen that the definitions of "security," "trade," and "distribution" are susceptible to discretionary analysis on the part of courts and regulators as to the scope of the concepts. The analysis is heavily policy-driven, with an emphasis on the investor protection goals of securities law, though it is an open question as to whether concerns of market efficiency may drive the analysis to a greater extent in the future. We have also seen that there may be important differences among investor, common sense, and judicial understandings of terms such as "efficiency" and share "value," and the ways in which those terms are employed in the academic, economic, and finance literature.

CHAPTER TWO

Historical and Constitutional Development of Securities Regulation

Modern securities regulation is a young area of law in Canada relative to other areas of law, such as constitutional and criminal law. The first part of this chapter sets forth a brief history of the development of securities law in Canada. The chapter then focuses on the structure of the securities regulatory regime, as well as developments in the constitutional law relating to securities regulation.

I. HISTORY OF SECURITIES REGULATION IN CANADA

The objectives of securities regulation are to protect investors and to foster fair and efficient capital markets. These objectives are, generally speaking, enshrined in the securities legislation of the various provinces and territories. However, the original purpose of securities law focused only on one of these objectives: investor protection. As the excerpts below suggest, it was thought that unwary investors who were willing to purchase securities in a company should be protected from fraud committed by members of that company. Note the importance of disclosure as the primary means to provide investors with information about the securities that they may purchase and the absence of corresponding enforcement actions apart from provisions in company statutes. (Note also that specific section numbers of the statutes referred to in the judgments may have changed over the years, but the reasoning in these historical judgments remains highly relevant.) The following excerpt sets forth a brief history of the development of securities law in Canada. It traces this history back to England and also highlights the US influence.

J Peter Williamson, *Securities Regulation in Canada*
(Toronto: University of Toronto Press, 1960) 3-14, 20-34

Fraud and lesser improprieties in the sale of securities are no newcomers to the commercial scene. The history of securities regulation in one form or another can be traced back at least as far as a statute of 1285, authorizing the licensing of stock brokers in the City of London. …

But, apart from provisions for the licensing of brokers, securities legislation as we know it today is not much over a century old. Nor has an end yet come to the struggle between the two philosophies underlying securities regulation. The first in time of origin was the principle of full disclosure, conceding freedom to sell anything provided the truth, and the whole truth, is told about it. This is the basis of the prospectus provisions in the English and Canadian (both Dominion and provincial) companies acts, and of the United States *Securities Act of 1933*. The second type of securities regulation, so-called "blue sky" regulation, involves the imposition of standards of conduct on securities issuers, going beyond disclosure, and frequently providing for discretionary licensing of issuers. This interposition of the business or ethical judgment of a government official between the seller and purchaser, requiring some official stamp of approval (or indication of the official's failure to find anything to disapprove), is characteristic of the securities acts of the provinces and of many states. …

1. *Full Disclosure: The English Origin*

Modern securities regulation began in England in 1844. The English *Joint Stock Companies Act of 1844* required, before a company might be incorporated, that the promoters file a return, including a copy of any prospectus and advertisement they intended to use … . There were no disclosure requirements imposed on the raising of new capital by a going corporation. …

It was not until 1867 that a real effort was made to bring "inside" information to the investor. *The Companies Act of 1867* required that every prospectus and notice inviting subscriptions ("prospectus" was not yet solicitations) identify all parties to the company's contracts. Civil liability was spelled out for failure to comply. Here, then, was the first disclosure requirement imposed on the raising of new capital by a going corporation. But the prospectus did not have to be filed.

The next development followed up on the civil liability provision. In 1889 the House of Lords held in a suit against a director, based on untrue statements in a prospectus, that belief, in good faith, in the truth of the statements, however unreasonable, was a sufficient defence. Parliament replied with the *Directors Liability Act*, 1890, imposing upon every director and promoter (and everyone authorizing a prospectus) liability for loss, sustained by reason of an untrue statement in the prospectus, to anyone who subscribed for securities on the faith of the prospectus. …

Disclosure was brought along much further in the *Companies Act*, 1900, and it might be said that the modern prospectus really dates from this Act. The contents were specified now not only for a prospectus issued by a company, but for one issued "by or on behalf of a company, or by or on behalf of any person who has been engaged or interested in the formation of the company." This meant that a promoter's disposition of his own shares to the public was now covered. Prospectus was defined to mean virtually any written offer of shares or debentures to the public.

. . .

2. *The Canadian Companies Acts: Development to 1912*

The first general incorporation statute for the Dominion was the *Canada Joint Stock Companies Letters Patent Act*, 1869. Eight years later, the *Canada Joint Stock Companies Act*, 1877 introduced the requirement that a company's prospectus disclose corporate contracts, copying section 38 from the English Act of 1867. And in 1902 the English inspection provisions were copied.

Nova Scotia introduced incorporation by letters patent in 1883, copying much of the Dominion Act of 1877. New Brunswick followed in 1885 and Prince Edward Island in 1888. All three included the prospectus provisions from the English Act of 1867.... Other provinces soon adopted the same provisions. ...

British Columbia in 1897 adopted the prospectus and inspection provisions of the English Act of 1890, and in 1914 the first Yukon Companies Ordinance was copied from the British Columbia Act. In 1899 Newfoundland (at that time still a British Colony) copied most of the English Act of 1867, including the prospectus provision.

Ontario did not introduce any securities regulation until 1891, but in that year it became the first Canadian jurisdiction to adopt the English *Director's Liability Act*. Six years later Ontario companies were required to furnish financial statements to stockholders, and the English inspection provisions were adopted.

The *Ontario Companies Act*, 1907, drew on the English Act of 1900 for the content of a prospectus (the minimum subscription and inspection provisions were copied, too), but the Ontario Act went much further in its scope than did the English. The definition of "prospectus" was original. To the English coverage of "notices," etc. "offering securities for subscription or purchase," were added notices "published or issued for the purposes of being used to promote or aid in the subscription or purchase of such shares, debentures or securities."

. . .

3. *Blue Sky Laws: The Sale of Shares Act, 1912-1926*

The first securities legislation to go beyond disclosure and introduce a comprehensive licensing requirement—"blue sky" legislation, in the strict sense—was enacted in Kansas in 1911. ...

... The issuer was required to obtain a permit from the Kansas bank commissioner before offering or selling its securities to anyone in Kansas. This required the filing of information, under oath, about its finances, and, if the issuer were a foreign corporation, qualification to do business in Kansas, and the filing of a consent to service of process on the secretary of state, apparently for any kind of legal action. The bank commissioner was to examine the application, and "if advisable," to make a detailed examination of the company. If he was satisfied that the issuer was sound and the offering a fair one ... the commissioner was to grant a permit. Agents of an issuer had to register with the commissioner, who was authorized to revoke registration "for cause appearing to him sufficient." To retain its right to offer securities an issuer was required to file semi-annual reports and maintain various business records, to be available to the commissioner. Insolvency or improper conduct, or a refusal to file required papers, were made the basis for receivership proceedings, to be instituted by the attorney-general. …

The paternalistic blue sky type of securities law was popular: within two years two provinces and seventeen states had adopted acts copying the Kansas statute.

Manitoba was the first province to enter the field with its *Sale of Shares Act* of 1912. Taken almost verbatim from the Kansas Act, this statute did have a few significant differences. For one thing, the Manitoba Act clearly applied to secondary as well as primary offerings; either the selling shareholder or the company whose securities were to be offered was required to obtain a certificate from the Public Utility Commission. And even the printing or publishing in Manitoba of an advertisement for the securities was made unlawful if the certificate had not been issued.

• • •

Saskatchewan was the next province with securities legislation, copying its *Sale of Shares Act* of 1914 almost verbatim from the Manitoba Act, and Alberta followed in 1916. …

New Brunswick joined the three western provinces in 1923, by adopting the Alberta Act.

In 1924 Québec brought in "An Act respecting the issue and sale of shares, bonds and other securities." This was essentially a disclosure act, requiring the filing of documents but not requiring any official consent before the sale of securities commenced. …

5. *The Security Frauds Prevention Acts, 1928-1945*

The basis for a real advance in securities legislation had been laid in the Manitoba *Municipal and Public Utility Board Act*, in 1926, but it was Ontario that adopted the first of the new security frauds prevention acts. …

The *Security Frauds Prevention Act*, 1928 was aimed at controlling traders in securities rather than the issuing of securities. At the same time the disclosure provisions in the *Companies Act* were transferred to the *Companies Information Act*, 1928, and this Act then covered the issuing of new securities.

Having waited until 1928 to proclaim a securities act, Ontario now came up with a really significant one. With a few changes this act became the model for the uniform statute adopted by 1930 in almost every province. Much of its wording can be found in the present acts of every province except Québec.

The Ontario Act combined anti-fraud provisions with a requirement that brokers and salesmen be registered. Disclosure by issuers was left to the *Companies Information Act*, but the issuer was required to register as a broker.

The Act began with a list of what was declared to constitute fraud. This was an innovation. The sale of shares acts had never explicitly banned any conduct as fraudulent. Now such things as intentional omission of material facts, outlandish promises, fictitious trades, the gaining of unconscionable commissions and violation of the Act or Regulations were defined as fraudulent and offences under the Act. There was no attempt to create civil liabilities based on these "fraudulent" acts; they constituted offences and were punishable by fine or imprisonment and they could be the basis for an injunction.

The registration requirement was based on the prohibition against "trading" without registration. Since the definition of "trade" or "trading" covered virtually any offer or sale, a rather comprehensive set of exemptions was required to put the registration provisions in perspective.

There were the usual exemptions for judicially supervised sales, transactions with existing security holders, and sales of government securities and commercial paper. Isolated trades made by or on behalf of the owner of a security and not made in the "course of continued and successive transactions" were also exempted. This left the security holder free to dispose of his own securities as long as he did not make too much of a business of it … . An issuer, of course, was required to register (as a broker) under the 1928 Act, because the isolated trade exemption applied only to sales of a security holder.

No standards for registration were set out in the Act; application was to be "upon forms provided by the Registrar" and accompanied by a fee and a bond. …

Investigation to uncover fraud was left entirely to the discretion of the attorney-general, who was given the power of a Supreme Court judge to subpoena witnesses and documents and compel evidence on oath. No privilege on grounds of self-incrimination was to be recognized. Failure to appear or to give information demanded was, first, an offence under the Act and, second, *prima facie* evidence of fraud, and sufficient basis for a ten-day suspension by the attorney-general, an injunction, or a conviction under the Act. …

The attorney-general's decisions (the principal ones being the grant or denial of registration and the ten-day suspension) were explicitly made not subject to judicial review, and the first privative clause in a Canadian securities act precluded the use of extraordinary remedies.

The Ontario pattern was a popular one. Manitoba actually introduced the same definition of fraud and investigation procedure in its Security Frauds Prevention Act about a month before the Ontario Act became effective. But this Manitoba statute was purely a fraud act—it contained no more than the definition and investigation provisions—and the registration of brokers and securities continued to be governed by the Municipal and Public Utility Board Act until 1929. …

Three other Provinces followed the Ontario pattern, in 1929, with security frauds prevention acts: Prince Edward Island (this was its first securities act), and two of the … three pioneers in securities legislation, Alberta and Saskatchewan.

• • •

7. *The Securities Acts, 1945 to [1960]*

The first Canadian securities act that can really be called a modern one was the *Ontario Securities Act* of 1945. The statute came at a rather critical time. Fraudulent stock promotion was getting out of hand and the government was faced not only with criticism from within the province but with loud complaints from the United States. A Royal Commission on Mining (the Urquhart Commission) had reported in 1944 on the state of mining developments in Ontario and the effect of the *Securities Act*. The Commission concluded that the Act had both restricted prospecting activity and failed to curb fraudulent activity. In recommending provisions for a new act, the Commission hoped to correct both defects by tightening control of broker-dealers and assuring full disclosure in securities offerings, but without any direct restraint on issuers.

• • •

The significant change in 1945, however, was the refining and expanding of disclosure requirements. Building on companies acts provisions, the *Securities Act* forbade any broker or salesman (and "broker" was defined to include an issuer) from trading in any security "in the course of primary distribution to the public" until a "statement" had been filed with the Commission and a receipt obtained and until the broker had notified the Commission of his intention to participate in the distribution. A copy of the statement was to be delivered to every purchaser.

The excerpt from Williamson traces the history of securities regulation to 1945. But what developments occurred thereafter? In the following excerpt, Professor Condon discusses the next major legislative change in Canadian securities regulation: *The Securities Act 1966* (Ontario), RSO 1966, c 142, which formed the basis of securities legislation across Canada. Professor Condon also makes reference to the Kimber Report, which was a very influential report commissioned by the Ontario government, in which substantial changes and additions were proposed for Ontario's securities law. The Kimber Report formed the basis of the 1966 Act. You will see excerpts from the Kimber Report throughout this casebook.

Mary G Condon, *Making Disclosure: Ideas and Interests in Ontario Securities Regulation*
(Toronto: University of Toronto Press, 1998) 89-91

The new *Securities Act* was proclaimed on 23 January 1967. There is no need to rehearse all the details of this legislation, but it is important to identify the key themes of the Act, examined in terms of what is now known of the context from which it emerged. The conventional view and the one held by Ontario regulators—not surprising in view of its authorship—was that "the results [*Securities Act 1966*] represent the faithful conversion of the [Kimber] report's recommendations into legislation."

• • •

J.P. Williamson, a prominent commentator, was clear that disclosure was the key to understanding the new legal regime. He argued that "The ability to evaluate is important in itself. The new legislation seems to recognize the economic value of full disclosure as something apart from traditional investor protection. Confidence in individual companies and in securities markets generally rests on adequate information. And the efficient investment of institutional and individual funds is not possible without a constant flow of information to facilitate continuous evaluation of portfolios." It should be noted that, again, the value of disclosure-based legislation and policy is partly that it is capable of being linked to either or both of economic or legal discourses. For Williamson, the economic function of disclosure as contributing to the efficiency of the market was seen to be superior to its value in preventing unfair advantage for some market participants, which is a distinctively legal preoccupation. …

• • •

The requirement of disclosure was imposed in a wide variety of situations within the statute. This, of course was especially true of Part VII, dealing with trading in the course of primary distribution, where there were already disclosure provisions in existence.

Within this part, s. 35 prohibited trading in the course of primary distribution to the public until both a preliminary prospectus and a prospectus had been filed with the commission and receipts had been obtained. Harry Bray argued that the requirement for the prospective purchaser to have "full, true and plain disclosure" of all material facts at his or her disposal by means of a mandatory preliminary prospectus, before there was any legal obligation to complete the contract, was an adaptation of "SEC experience to Ontario conditions." A preliminary prospectus was therefore introduced in order to enhance the notice and information available to the purchaser on which to base his or her judgment in advance of the sale's completion.

Section 41 outlined the contents of the prospectus itself. Yet one commentator had little faith in the possibility of constructing definitive legal requirements that would be adequate for all eventualities. Describing the preparation of a prospectus as "not a science but an art," which was susceptible to "personal standards of protection," S.E. Nixon asserted that "it is impossible for prospectuses to include all factors properly involved in the assessment of an individual security. Many standards have been established by custom and usage … . Seldom dealt with at length in prospectuses are such important factors as the regulatory practices and political climate affecting a public utility company and the extent and importance of tariff protection to a manufacturing company. …"

On the subject of the financial information to be provided at the time of distribution, s. 46 could be described as a combination of disclosure and opinion requirements: a prospectus had to contain a report on the financial statements by an auditor who was "acceptable to the Director." This was a significant development in that it appeared to recognize that, despite the political rhetoric, disclosures by companies themselves would not serve as an adequate solution to the problems identified, since they would be made in the context of attempts to stimulate interest and investment in the issue. Accordingly, a judgment would be required by an impartial "expert" who would ascertain, in accordance with a professional code, if a "fair" picture of the financial position of the company had been presented.

QUESTIONS

1. What are blue sky laws?
2. Why is it important to ensure that those individuals and entities who deal in securities are registered?
3. Why did the purpose of securities regulation shift from only protecting investors to also fostering fair and efficient markets? Can securities legislation successfully balance these two goals?
4. What are the key themes of the various pieces of legislation described above? Did these themes change or evolve over the years?

II. DIVISION OF POWERS

Although securities regulation is designed to protect investors, the process by which securities regulation is enacted has, historically speaking, not been straightforward. As you will note in the excerpts below, legislators have been constrained by both the *Constitution Act, 1867* (30 & 31 Vict, c 3, as amended) (formerly the *British North America Act*) and the *Charter of Rights and Freedoms* (Part I of the *Constitution Act, 1982*, being Schedule B of the *Canada Act 1982* (UK), 1982, c 11). Furthermore, provincial securities regulatory authorities are limited in the extent of their flexibility and discretion by their enacting legislation. This section examines the division of powers and the influence of the Charter on the development of securities regulation.

Students should note the conflict between the provincial and federal governments with respect to jurisdiction over securities regulation. At the time of the confederation of Canada, the *British North America Act* (BNA Act) divided responsibility for legislation between the provinces and the federal government. Under s 91, the federal government was given responsibilities that included the peace, order, and good government of Canada (the residual power); the regulation of trade and commerce; and the criminal law. Case law developed the residual power to include the ability to create and regulate federal corporations. Under s 92, the provincial governments were given powers that included the regulation of property and civil rights. As case law developed, this power came to include the regulation of securities market transactions. Over time, provincial securities regulation came to be challenged on the basis that it infringed federal powers.

In one of the first division of powers cases, *Manitoba (Attorney General) v Canada (Attorney General)*, [1929] 1 DLR 369 (JCPC) [*Manitoba*], a conflict arose whereby corporations incorporated under the federal residual power were prevented from issuing securities unless they obtained the prior approval of provincial authorities. The Privy Council held that the conflict was not governed by s 92 and that the provincial legislation under consideration interfered with the capacity of a Dominion incorporated company to raise capital.

One of the consequences of the *Manitoba* case was that it contributed to the development of a more complicated system of securities regulation and preceded the development of the doctrine of interjurisdictional immunity, which protects the core of certain powers belonging to one level of government from interference by the other level of government. Prior to the case, it was well settled that provincial legislatures were not competent to legislate so as to impair the status and essential capacities of Dominion companies to a substantial degree. In keeping with the line of cases that gave rise to this rule, the Privy Council in *Manitoba* held that the capacity of a Dominion company to obtain capital by the sale of its shares was essential and, therefore, the provincial legislation was *ultra vires* the province insofar as it applied to Dominion companies. The viability of this approach was tested in the following case in which the Privy Council held that the provincial securities legislation in question did not encroach on the federal legislative power with respect to criminal law.

Mayland and Mercury Oils Limited v Lymburn and Frawley
[1932] 1 WWR 578 (Alta JCPC)

Under the terms of s. 9 of the [*Security Frauds Prevention Act* (Alberta)], the Attorney-General or any delegate appointed by him has power to examine any person or company at any time in order to ascertain whether any fraudulent act as defined by the statute or any offence against the Act or the regulations has been, is being, or is about to be committed.

[The plaintiffs challenged the powers of the attorney general, claiming that the statute or, alternatively, s 9, was *ultra vires* the province.]

LORD ATKIN (delivering the Lordships' judgment): … The plaintiffs, by their statement of claim, claimed a declaration that the statute or, alternatively, s. 9, was *ultra vires* the Province, and an injunction restraining the Attorney-General and Mr. Frawley from proceeding with the examination. They gave notice of motion for an interim injunction which came before Ives J, and with the consent of the defendants was referred by him to the Appellate Division of the Supreme Court. On April 23, 1931, the Appellate Division made an order declaring that s. 9 of the Act had no application to the plaintiff or the three companies mentioned above, and that the defendants had no authority to proceed with the examinations and investigations referred to in the statement of claim. The reasons for the judgment were delivered by Harvey CJ, concurred in by Walsh and Clarke JJA … . The learned Chief Justice reviewed the statute as a whole, but founded his decision on the ground that the provincial Legislature could not delegate to the Attorney-General power to obtain information unlimited in extent inasmuch as that Legislature itself was restricted in its power to obtain from a Dominion company unlimited information, apparently because such a requirement would clash with the Dominion legislation as to companies. It was therefore held that s. 9 was not applicable to Dominion companies; not as would appear as a matter of construction but because it was *ultra vires* in relation to such companies, though it would severably be valid as to other companies.

Before the Board the attack was made on a broader ground. The whole Act was invalid so far as it related to Dominion companies because it destroyed their status by making it impossible for them to issue their share capital. In this respect it was said the case was covered by the decision of this Board in *A-G Man. v. A-G Can.* … It was further contended that apart altogether from Dominion companies the Act was invalid because under the colour of dealing with the prevention of fraud in share transactions it was assuming to legislate as to criminal law a class of subject reserved to the Dominion. Apart from invalidity it was further said that if the terms of the Act were examined the three Dominion companies in question as well as the plaintiff Mayland did not carry on any business as brokers in shares: and it was only to transactions by brokers that the provisions of s. 9 applied. Their Lordships cannot accept any of these contentions.

… [Under] the framework of the Act … [r]egistered persons must enter into a personal bond and may be required to enter into a surety bond each in the sum of $500 conditioned for payment if the registered person, amongst other events, is (in the former bond) "charged with," (in the latter bond) "convicted of" a criminal offence or found to have committed an offence against the Act or the regulations made thereunder. It was contended on behalf of the Attorney-General for the Dominion that to impose a condition making the bond fall due upon conviction for a criminal offence was to encroach upon the sole right of the Dominion to legislate in respect of the criminal law. It indirectly imposed an additional punishment for a criminal offence. Their Lordships do not consider this objection well founded. If the legislation be otherwise *intra vires*, the imposition of such an ordinary condition in a bond taken to secure good conduct does not appear to invade in any degree the field of criminal law.

There is no reason to doubt that the main object sought to be secured in this part of the Act is to secure that persons who carry on the business of dealing in securities shall be honest and of good repute, and in this way to protect the public from being defrauded. Incidentally the net has been drawn so wide as to cover the issue of shares by a public company, with the result that a company cannot issue its shares to the public unless for that purpose it employs a registered broker or salesman, or unless the company itself is registered. It is said that these provisions so far as they affect Dominion companies are *ultra vires* according to the principles adopted by this Board in *John Deere Plow Co. Ltd. v. Wharton* … ; *Gt. West Saddlery Co. v. The King* … ; and *A-G Man. v. A-G Can.* … .

In those cases there was a general prohibition to companies either to trade at all or to issue their capital unless the company was registered. The legislation was held *ultra vires* because the legislative powers of the Province are restricted so that "the status and powers of a Dominion company as such cannot be destroyed" (*John Deere Plow Co.* …) and legislation will be invalid if a Dominion company is "sterilised in all its functions and activities" or "its status and essential capacities are impaired in a substantial degree" (*Great West Saddlery Co.* …). It appears to their Lordships impossible to bring this legislation within such a principle. A Dominion company constituted with powers to carry on a particular business is subject to the competent legislation of the Province as to that business and may find its special activities completely paralysed as by legislation against drink traffic or by the laws as to holding land. If it is formed to trade in securities there appears no reason why it should not be subject to the competent laws of the Province as to the business of all persons who trade in securities. As to the issue of capital there is no complete prohibition as in *A-G Man. v. A-G Can.* in 1929; and no reason to suppose that any honest company would have any difficulty in finding registered persons in the Province through whom it could lawfully issue its capital. There is no material upon which their Lordships could find that the functions and activities of a company were sterilised or its status and essential capacities impaired in a substantial degree.

• • •

Section 9, under which the examination in dispute in these proceedings was ordered, empowers the Attorney-General or any delegate appointed by him to examine any person or company in order to ascertain whether any fraudulent act or any offence against the Act or regulations has been, is being, or is about to be committed. The definition of fraudulent act appears to be very wide, in some cases having no relation to securities or dealing in securities; and it is possible that if the question becomes relevant a limited construction would be put upon the very general terms used. But this has no bearing upon the question of validity. The examination is not confined to questions of registration, nor are the persons or companies to be examined limited to persons or companies who themselves trade in securities. It seems obvious that the object of the section would be defeated unless the powers of examination extended to persons who might have relevant knowledge, including companies and the officials of companies whose securities might be or be about to be the subject of dealings with the public. The provisions of this part of the Act may appear to be far reaching; but if they fall, as their Lordships conceive them to fall, within the scope of legislation dealing with property and civil rights, the legislature of the province, sovereign in this respect, has the sole power and responsibility of determining what degree of protection it will afford to the public. There appears to be no reason for excluding Dominion companies from the inquiries of the Attorney-General under this section; and no inconsistency between this legislation and the powers of inquiry under the *Dominion Companies Act* made on application of members of a company and for a limited purpose viz., the investigation of the affairs of the company. Their Lordships are unable to agree with the view which was adopted by the Appellate Division that in respect of the subject-matter under discussion the Legislature of the Province has only a limited right to require information.

Part III of the Act provides for the appointment of auditors to audit the accounts of brokers and to advise the executive committees of stock exchanges in the province. There appears to be no ground for disputing the validity of these provisions.

Part IV by s. 14 contains a provision making it an offence for a broker in certain transactions for customers to place beyond his control securities he may be carrying for customers, and ss. 15 and 16 provide for the necessary records of such transactions. The penal provisions of s. 14 have been subsequently incorporated into the *Criminal Code* of the Dominion by 1930 (Can.), c. 11, s. 5, which now presumably occupies the field so far as the criminal law is concerned. The substantive provisions of the section avoiding the impugned transaction at the option of the customer and the provisions of the other sections of this part cannot be attacked.

Part V has general provisions which need not be noticed except as to the argument of the respondents founded on the words of s. 20 which provide *inter alia* that any person who does any fraudulent act not punishable under the provisions of the *Criminal Code of Canada* shall be liable to fine and imprisonment.

It is said that this encroaches on the exclusive legislative power of the Dominion as to criminal law. Having regard to the wide definition of fraudulent act above referred to it may well be that this argument is well founded. But so far as the section is invalid it appears to be clearly severable. In any case it appears to their Lordships, after reviewing the whole Act, that there is no ground for holding that the Act is a colourable attempt to encroach upon the exclusive legislative power of the Dominion as to criminal law. They have already given their reasons for holding that the Act cannot be considered invalid as destroying the status of Dominion companies. The provisions therefore of Part II of the Act appear to be competent provincial enactments dealing with Property and Civil Rights and have to be obeyed by persons subject to them.

In the result the order of the Appellate Division must be set aside and the motion must be dismissed. The respondents must pay the costs here and below. In the Court below the appellants agreed that if the Court decided in favour of the plaintiffs the motion should be treated as the hearing of the action and that final judgment should be given accordingly. There appears to be no such agreement by the respondents in the event that has happened. Presumably they will so agree, but in the meantime their Lordships can only say that the judgment for the plaintiffs should be set aside with the consequences already stated, and the action continue in the Supreme Court, and they will humbly advise His Majesty accordingly.

Appeal allowed.

The *Mayland* case shifted the division of powers between the provinces and the federal government. As the court stated,

> If [a Dominion company] is formed to trade in securities there appears no reason why it should not be subject to the competent laws of the Province as to the business of all persons who trade in securities. As to the issue of capital there is no complete prohibition as in *A-G Man. v. A-G Can.*

in 1929; and no reason to suppose that any honest company would have any difficulty in finding registered persons in the Province through whom it could lawfully issue its capital. There is no material upon which their Lordships could find that the functions and activities of a company were sterilised or its status and essential capacities impaired in a substantial degree.

The *Mayland* case also left open the possibility that, depending on the legislation in question, securities regulation enforcement provisions could still infringe on the federal jurisdiction over criminal law. In the words of the court:

Section 9, under which the examination in dispute in these proceedings was ordered, empowers the Attorney-General or any delegate appointed by him to examine any person or company in order to ascertain whether any fraudulent act or any offence against the Act or regulations has been, is being, or is about to be committed. The definition of fraudulent act appears to be very wide, in some cases having no relation to securities or dealing in securities; *and it is possible that if the question becomes relevant a limited construction would be put upon the very general terms used.* [Emphasis added.]

This issue was addressed in a more conclusive manner in the following case decided over 30 years later. At the time, a provision in the *Criminal Code* (s 343, now s 400) (RSC 1985, c C-46, as amended) prohibited the publishing of "a prospectus known to be false in a material particular with intent to induce persons to become shareholders in a company." This provision overlapped with a section in the provincial securities legislation that penalized corporations that incorporated false information in a prospectus. Excerpted below is the judgment of Martland J. Although Martland J's decision in the case was a concurring judgment and not the majority, it came to be relied on in subsequent cases. Martland J held that the matter of the provincial legislation at issue was not so related to a certain provision of the *Criminal Code* as to infringe upon the scope of the criminal law power in s 91 of the BNA Act. Students should note that there was also a dissenting judgment in the case delivered by Locke J but not excerpted here because of space considerations.

Smith v The Queen

[1960] SCR 776 (footnotes omitted)

[Facts: The accused was charged with certain offences under s 63 of *The Securities Act* (Ontario). The trial judge held the pith and substance of the provision of the *Securities Act* as falling under criminal law, and therefore trespassing upon the exclusive jurisdiction of Parliament. He declared the provision *ultra vires* the provincial government and prohibited the magistrate from further proceeding with the charge.

The Court of Appeal reversed the judgment of the trial judge and quashed the order of prohibition. The accused appealed to the Supreme Court of Canada. The court dismissed the appeal (Locke, Cartwright, and Ritchie JJ dissenting).]

[The Legislation]

s. 63. (1) Every person, including any officer, director, official or employee of a company, who is knowingly responsible for,

(a) any fictitious or pretended trade in any security;

(b) any course of conduct or business which is calculated or put forward with intent to deceive the public or the purchaser or the vendor of any security as to the nature of any transaction or as to the value of such security;

(c) the making of any material false statement in any application, information, statement, material or evidence submitted or given to the Commission, its representative, the registrar or any person appointed to make an investigation or audit under this Act, under this Act or the regulations;

(d) the furnishing of false information in any report, statement, return, balance sheet or other document required to be filed or furnished under this Act or the regulations;

(e) the commission of any act or failure to perform any act where such commission or failure constitutes a violation of any provision of this Act or the regulations; or

(f) failure to observe or comply with any order, direction or other requirement made under this Act or the regulations,

shall be guilty of an offence and on summary conviction shall be liable to a penalty of not more than $2,000 or to imprisonment for a term of not more than one year or both.

(2) Subsection 1 shall be deemed to apply, mutatis mutandis, to any company save that the money penalties may be increased in the discretion of the magistrate to a sum of not more than $25,000.

(3) Every person or company is a party to and guilty of an offence under this Act,

(a) that actually commits the offence;

(b) that does or omits an act for the purpose of aiding another person or company in the commission of the offence;

(c) that abets another person or company in the commission of the offence; or

(d) that counsels or procures another person or company to commit the offence.

• • •

s. 343. (1) Every one who makes, circulates or publishes a prospectus, statement or account, whether written or oral, that he knows is false in a material particular, with intent

(a) to induce persons, whether ascertained or not, to become share-holders or partners in a company,

(b) to deceive or defraud the members, shareholders or creditors, whether ascertained or not, of a company,

(c) to induce any person to entrust or advance anything to a company, or

(d) to enter into any security for the benefit of a company, is guilty of an indictable offence and is liable to imprisonment for ten years.

(2) In this section, "company" means a syndicate, body corporate or company, whether existing or proposed to be created.

• • •

MARTLAND J (Abbott and Judson JJ concurring): … The question in issue is as to whether or not it was within the competency of the Legislature of Ontario to create the offences contemplated by the application of s. 63(1)(d) and (e) to the provisions of s. 38(1) and (9) of *The Securities Act*, R.S.O. 1950, c. 351.

There would appear to be unanimity of view that the provisions of s. 38 of that Act are *prima facie* within the powers of the Legislature. The sole issue is as to whether the paragraphs of s. 63 above mentioned are in conflict with the provisions of s. 343 of the *Criminal Code so as* to make them inoperative.

The Securities Act exists to regulate the securities business. This is achieved through two main forms of control, the first of which is directed towards the persons or companies selling the securities and the second of which is directed to the securities being sold.

Trading in securities without registration is prohibited by s. 6 of the Act. The duty to grant registration and the power to refuse, suspend or cancel such registration are imposed upon and vested in the Commission by s. 7 and s. 8 of *The Securities Act*.

Trading in securities in the course of a primary distribution of such securities to the public is prohibited by ss. 38, 39 and 40 of *The Securities Act* unless certain prerequisites, which vary somewhat depending on whether the company whose securities are being offered is a mining, industrial or investment company, are first completed in accordance with the relevant section. Each of the sections requires that a prospectus first be submitted to the Commission making "full, true and plain disclosure" relating to the securities which it is proposed to offer containing the information stipulated in the section. The Commission, under s. 44 of *The Securities Act*, in its discretion, may accept the prospectus submitted to it for filing and direct the Registrar to issue the receipt referred to in ss. 38, 39 and 40, unless it appears that one of the circumstances set out in s. 44 exists. In such a case it is implicit that the Commission is under a duty not to accept the material and forthwith to give the notice provided for by s. 45. The equivalent of s. 8, which provides for suspension or cancellation of existing registrations, is s. 46 which empowers the Commission, where it discovers that any of the circumstances in s. 44 exist following the issuance of a receipt for the prospectus by the Registrar, to order that all trading in the primary distribution to the public of the securities to which the prospectus relates shall cease.

Thus control is exercised through the registration of persons and companies before they are permitted to trade in securities coupled with what is essentially the registration of the securities themselves before the securities may be traded in the course of a primary distribution to the public.

The important feature of ss. 38, 39 and 40 is that, in addition to requiring that a prospectus filed with the Commission shall contain a true, full and plain disclosure relating to the securities proposed to be issued, it is also required that the prospectus shall set forth the specific, detailed information required in each of these sections and shall be accompanied by certain additional material, including financial statements. Unless the material required by these sections is filed with and accepted by the Commission, there can be no lawful trading in the securities in question in the course of a primary distribution.

If the material required to be furnished to the Commission under these sections is accepted by it and a receipt issued, then, and only then, ss. 47 and 47a come into operation and require that a copy of the prospectus and of the financial statements filed with the Commission shall come into the hands of the members of the public who are invited to buy the securities involved. This requirement is not only to compel the furnishing to such persons of a prospectus which is true, but also that it must be one which gives the detailed information regarding the affairs of the company which is required to be furnished to the Commission itself under ss. 38, 39 and 40.

The scheme of these sections of the act is, therefore, to prevent trading in securities in the course of primary distribution until the Commission has received all the information required by the Act and has accepted such material for filing, and then to ensure that persons who are asked to subscribe for such securities shall have all the information which the Commission itself has received.

The purpose of these sections is, of course, defeated if the information is untrue and, in my opinion, the Legislature has the power to require that this information shall be true and to penalize persons who furnish false information, or who fail to comply with the requirements of the Act.

It does not appear to me that there is a conflict between s. 63(1) (d) and (e) and s. 343 of the *Criminal Code*. The latter provision makes it an offence to make, circulate or publish a prospectus known to be false in a material particular with intent to induce persons to become share-holders in a company. This section deals with a false statement in a material particular deliberately made in order to persuade someone to subscribe for shares in a company. The section, of course, has nothing to say as to what the contents of a prospectus must be.

Section 63(1) (d) and (e), on the other hand, is designed to penalize a person who, required as he is, by the provisions of the Act, to furnish full, detailed information about the company whose securities are sought to be sold, is knowingly responsible for the incorporation in that material of information which is false. A good deal of that information might never be incorporated in a prospectus at all unless the Act had required it. Paragraph (d) is not limited to falsity of the prospectus "in a material particular," but applies to any information required to be furnished under the Act. It affects any one who is knowingly responsible for the furnishing of the information, whether he personally is interested in the marketing of the securities or not; for example, the engineer, geologist or prospector who furnishes the report on the property of a mining company under subs. (2) of s. 38, or the auditor who furnishes a report pursuant to subs. (8a) of that section.

The test to be applied in cases of this kind is that which was stated by Duff CJ in *The Provincial Secretary of the Province of Prince Edward Island v. Egan*:

> In every case where a dispute arises, the precise question must be whether or not the matter of the provincial legislation that is challenged is so related to the substance of the Dominion criminal legislation as to be brought within the scope of criminal law in the sense of section 91. If there is repugnancy between the provincial enactment and the Dominion enactment, the provincial enactment is, of course, inoperative.

For the reasons already given, I do not think that the matter of the provincial legislation in question here is so related in substance to s. 343 of the *Criminal Code* as to be brought within the scope of criminal law in the sense of s. 91 of the *British North America Act*. I do not think there is repugnancy between s. 63(1) (d) and (e) of *The Securities Act* and s. 343 of the *Criminal Code*. The fact that both provisions prohibit certain acts with penal consequences does not constitute a conflict. It may happen that some acts might be punishable under both provisions and in this sense that these provisions overlap. However, even in such cases, there is no conflict in the sense that compliance with one law involves breach of the other. It would appear, therefore, that they can operate concurrently.

I do not think that the views expressed by Lord Atkin in *Lymburn v. Mayland* … , with reference to s. 20 of *The Security Frauds Prevention Act*, 1930 (Alta.), c. 8, are adverse to the conclusion which I have reached.

Section 20(1) of that Act provided, in part, as follows:

> 20(1) Every person who violates any provision of this Act or the Regulations designated as an offence, or who does any fraudulent act not punishable under the provisions of *The Criminal Code of Canada*, shall be liable upon summary conviction thereof to a penalty.

Referring to this section, at p. 327 of the report, Lord Atkin said:

> It is said that this encroaches on the exclusive legislative power of the Dominion as to criminal law. Having regard to the wide definition of "fraudulent act" above referred to, it may well be that this argument is well founded. But so far as the section is invalid it appears to be clearly severable.

It will be noted that the portion of s. 20 to which he directed his attention was not that which imposed a penalty for the violation of the Act, or of the Regulations, but the general provision relating to "any fraudulent act not punishable under the provisions of *The Criminal Code of Canada*." This wide provision might, as he indicated, have gone beyond the imposing of a penalty for enforcing a provincial law. The provisions of s. 63(1) (d) and (e) of the Ontario Act do not offend in that way.

In my opinion, therefore, the appeal should be dismissed with costs, but there should be no costs to or against the Attorney General of Canada nor the Attorneys General of any of the provinces.

QUESTIONS

1. Do you agree that *Mayland* shifted the division of powers?
2. Do you think that Martland J was "splitting hairs" when he held that the matter of the provincial legislation at issue was not so related to the *Criminal Code* as to infringe upon the scope of the criminal law power in s 91 of the BNA Act?
3. Can you think of any basis on which to counter the argument that securities regulation is a matter of provincial, rather than federal, jurisdiction?

As the excerpt from Williamson indicated, one of the fundamental tenets of securities regulation is that individuals who complete trades in securities on behalf of others are registered with provincial securities authorities. But a puzzling question arises: What happens when a registered securities dealer in Ontario sells securities by mail and telephone to an investor living in Manitoba? The following case examines this question, focusing on two jurisdictional conflicts. The first conflict arises from the Constitution, particularly the apparent conflict between the provincial power of property and civil rights and the federal power of trade and commerce. The second conflict arises from geographical boundaries, in this case between the securities regulation of Ontario and Manitoba's interest in preserving its legislative sovereignty. The case builds on the principle elaborated in *Mayland*, particularly its holding that the provincial securities legislation did not invade the federal power to regulate trade and commerce. This decision further holds that the securities legislation of one province governs trading initiated and pursued in another.

R v W McKenzie Securities Limited

(1966), 55 WWR 157 (Man CA)

[Facts: The accused individuals were registered under the Ontario *Securities Act*, and operated from their offices in Toronto. However, they dealt with a customer in Shilo, Manitoba, soliciting him by mail and telephone calls to purchase certain securities. The accused were charged and convicted with unlawfully trading in securities in Manitoba. They sought to appeal their conviction on the basis that the *Securities Act* of Manitoba, to the extent that it purports to apply to the activities of the accused, is *ultra vires* the province of Manitoba on the ground that it seeks to regulate interprovincial trading. The Manitoba Court of Appeal dismissed the appeal and maintained the convictions.]

FREEDMAN JA: … Something must be said about the pattern of operations which gave rise to the charges in question. Substantially what was involved here was the promotion and sale of various shares of stock, through the medium of correspondence, supplemented later by long distance telephone calls. W. McKenzie Securities Ltd. carries on business as a broker-dealer from offices situated at 825-37 Eglinton Ave. W. in Toronto, Ontario. It is registered as such broker-dealer with the Ontario Securities Commission, pursuant to the *Securities Act*, RSO 1960, c. 363. It is not and was not similarly registered, however, under the *Securities Act of Manitoba*. The accused Philip West at all material times was president, director, and trading officer of W. McKenzie Securities Ltd. The accused Irwin Dubros at all material times was a salesman for the company and was registered as such with the Ontario Securities Commission. Neither West nor Dubros, however, was in any way registered under the *Securities Act of Manitoba* to enable them to trade in securities in this Province.

The dealings in question here were with one Henry Joseph McCaffrey, a school teacher living at Shilo in Manitoba. The evidence shows that commencing in the late summer of 1962 he began to receive certain literature by mail from W. McKenzie Securities Ltd. inviting him to purchase shares of stock. The first literature pertained to a company called Canadian Gift Sales Limited, whose virtues and potentialities were there extolled and whose shares he was urged to purchase. In specific terms, Mr. Philip West, the president of W. McKenzie Securities Ltd., wrote to Mr. McCaffrey on September 12, 1962, thus: "So on my personal recommendation, I suggest you act now by sending in your order for shares of CANADIAN GIFT SALES LIMITED right away." On or about September 26, 1962, McCaffrey did in fact agree to purchase 300 such shares at the then price of $2.50 per share. His cheque for $750 in payment of these shares was sent by mail from Shilo to the office of W. McKenzie Securities Ltd. in Toronto. The cheque was drawn on the Royal Bank of Canada, Shilo Branch.

Four other purchases of shares were subsequently made by McCaffrey through W. McKenzie Securities Ltd. In May, 1963, he acquired 3,000 shares of Tinex Development Exploration Limited at 28 (CENTS) per share; in January, 1964, a further 3,000 shares of stock of the same company, this time at 30 (CENTS) each; later that same month an additional 2,000 shares of Tinex, at 35 (CENTS) per share; and in February, 1964, he purchased 1,000 shares of Marimac Mines Limited at 30 (CENTS) each. In every case payment was made by McCaffrey by his cheque drawn on the Shilo Branch of the Royal Bank of Canada and mailed by him from Shilo to the office of W. McKenzie Securities Ltd. in Toronto.

Of the five total purchases made by McCaffrey the first two were the result of communications sent to him by mail, and the invoices evidencing these purchases specifically credit the transactions to "Mail." The third and fourth resulted from telephone calls made by the accused Dubros from Toronto to McCaffrey at Shilo, and on the invoices relating to these purchases the name "Dubros" is credited. The final purchase occurred on February 17, 1964. On that date McCaffrey telephoned from Shilo to the company in Toronto. The price of shares of Canadian Gift Sales Ltd. had dropped to about $1.25, and the purpose of his call was to discuss the sale of his holdings in that company. He spoke first to Dubros who, after telling him not to sell, turned him over to West. West also urged McCaffrey not to sell but to hold the shares for another week or two. It was during this telephone conversation that West raised the question of shares in Marimac Mines Ltd., pointing out that if McCaffrey purchased them at that time he could get them at the special shareholders' price of 30 (CENTS), but that in a week or two they would be offered to the general public at 35 (CENTS) each. McCaffrey accordingly bought 1,000 such shares; and it may be noted the name "West" is credited on the invoice arising from this purchase.

Two further matters are of interest in this recital of the facts. W. McKenzie Securities Ltd. mailed to McCaffrey at Shilo several issues of its weekly newsletter called "Spotlight," containing endorsements and promotion of various stocks, including specifically those which he in fact did purchase. Also, not long after the telephone conversation of February 17, 1964, in which McCaffrey was dissuaded from selling his shares in Canadian Gift Sales Ltd., the fortunes of that company declined still further, its shares could not be sold at any price and, in due course, it went into bankruptcy, with a resultant financial loss to McCaffrey. This last circumstance is mentioned not because it has any bearing on the guilt or innocence of the accused but because it led to McCaffrey making a complaint to the authorities in Manitoba, which in turn ultimately resulted in the laying of charges that the accused had unlawfully traded in securities in Manitoba without being registered to do so.

Counsel for the accused has raised a constitutional issue. He contends that the activities of the accused were entirely lawful and constituted solely interprovincial trading, the regulation of which is within the exclusive legislative authority of the Parliament of Canada as coming under the head of s. 91(2) of the *BNA Act*, dealing with regulation of trade and commerce. To the extent that the *Securities Act of Manitoba* can be said to have application to the activities of the accused it should be declared, he says, to be *ultra vires* of the Legislature of Manitoba.

In dealing with the constitutional question, some assistance can be derived from certain cases in which the nature and purpose of statutes parallel to the *Securities Act of Manitoba* were examined and considered. *Lymburn et al. v. Mayland* … , involved the *Security Frauds Prevention Act*, 1930 (Alta.), c. 8. That statute provided, as does its Manitoba counterpart, that no person might trade in securities without being registered as a broker or salesman. The challenge to the constitutional validity of that statute was based on the claim that it was invalid in relation to Dominion companies. That contention was rejected by the Judicial Committee of the Privy Council, which declared that a Dominion company formed to trade in securities was subject to the competent laws of the Province as to the business of all persons who traded in securities. Lord Atkin, for the Committee, defined the purpose of the Act thus … :

> There is no reason to doubt that the main object sought to be secured in this part of the Act is to secure that persons who carry on the business of dealing in securities shall be honest and of good repute, and in this way to protect the public from being defrauded.

As such it constituted valid provincial legislation dealing with property and civil rights.

It is worthy of note that the *Lymburn v. Mayland* case was cited with approval by the Supreme Court of Canada in the case of *Smith v. The Queen*, … . The latter case concerned the *Securities Act of Ontario*. One of the provisions of that Act prohibited trading in securities in the course of a primary distribution to the public unless a true prospectus, containing specified particulars, had been filed with the Commission. The accused was charged in respect of allegedly false information given in such a prospectus. He contended that it was incompetent of the Province to create, as it purported to do, the offence of knowingly furnishing false information in such a prospectus, on the ground that such an offence was within the realm of criminal law and specifically conflicted with s. 343 of the *Criminal Code*. By a majority of six to three the Court held that the legislation was valid as being designed to support the regulatory scheme of the Act to control the trading of securities in the Province.

Even more recently the Supreme Court of Canada again had to consider a similar Act, this time the *Québec Securities Act*, 1954-55 (Que.), c. 11. The case of *Gregory & Co. Inc. v. Québec Securities Commission* … , revealed a state of facts in some respects similar to those in the present appeal but viewed from another vantage point. Gregory & Co. Inc. was engaged in the promotion of four mining companies operating in Québec, and published a weekly bulletin promoting the sale of the shares of these companies, this bulletin being mailed in large numbers exclusively to persons residing outside the Province. The specific issue facing the Court was whether the business activities of the Gregory company were subject to the jurisdiction of the Québec Securities Commission, thereby requiring the company to be licensed. It was the contention of the company that because the securities in which it traded were for the account of customers outside Québec, and because its bulletins were mailed to clients outside Québec, it could not be said to be carrying on the business of trading in securities within that Province. Upon reviewing the nature of the business of the company, including the fact that its weekly bulletins were prepared and printed in Montreal and mailed from that city to clients in other Provinces, the Court concluded that the company must be deemed to be carrying on the business of trading in securities within the Province.

It should be observed that in the *Gregory* case counsel for the company had originally raised certain constitutional points, including the claim that the trade carried on by the company was interprovincial and international, and that any regulation of such trading was outside the legislative competence of the Province and fell within the legislative sphere of Parliament. The notice which is required to be given in constitutional matters by Rule 18 of the *Rules of the Supreme Court of Canada* had not been given. The constitutional question was, accordingly, not argued, and the decision of the Supreme Court of Canada in that case, although relevant for its conclusions as to the general purpose and object of the Act, leaves undecided the question whether the *Québec Securities Act* is valid legislation with regard to activity of the nature there considered.

…

It seems clear that the true nature of the provincial statutes above considered, no less than the *Securities Act* of our own Province, is to provide protection to the public through a system of regulating and supervising the conduct of persons who engage in trading activities in securities within the Province. The *Securities Act of Manitoba* is not designed to reach out beyond provincial borders and to restrain conduct carried on in other parts of Canada or elsewhere. Its operation is effective within Manitoba, and nowhere else. For a person to become subject to its restraint he must trade in securities in Manitoba. This is not to say that a nonresident of Manitoba can never become subject to the controls of the statute. If the activities of such a non-resident can fairly and properly be construed as constituting trading within the Province, then they fall within the purview of the Act.

Thus examined, the Act cannot justly be considered as designed in any way for the regulation of interprovincial trading. It accordingly does not invade the domain of trade and commerce reserved to the Dominion by the provisions of s. 91(2) of the *BNA Act*. I would, accordingly, hold it to be competent provincial legislation.

The issue as to whether the activities of the accused constituted a violation of the *Securities Act of Manitoba* falls to be decided solely on what occurred within this Province. That they were registered to trade in securities in Ontario would only be relevant if they were faced with a charge of violating the corresponding statute of that Province. It is an irrelevant circumstance in the present prosecution. The sole point to be determined is whether the accused Dubros and the accused West, both of whom were unlicenced here, traded in securities in Manitoba. That they did not physically enter the borders of the Province is not conclusive of the matter. A person may, from outside the borders of a Province, do certain acts within the Province so as to make himself liable to the provisions of this statute. Williamson, op. cit., at p. 204 says:

> There seems to be no reason why a person cannot become subject to a licensing statute of a province without ever entering the province, constitutional questions aside.

Although offences are local, the nature of some offences is such that they can properly be described as occurring in more than one place. This is peculiarly the case where a transaction is carried on by mail from one territorial jurisdiction to another, or indeed by telephone from one such jurisdiction to another. This has been recognized by the common law for centuries. Thus, where a threatening letter was written and posted in London, and delivered in Middlesex, it was held by the Court that the writer could properly be tried in Middlesex: *R v. Girdwood* … . Vide also *R v. Esser*. …

It is appropriate to note that one of the acts which is included in the definition of "trade" or "trading" in s. 2(k) of the *Securities Act* is "the solicitation or obtaining of a subscription to the capital stock of any organization, whether incorporated or not." Solicitation of subscriptions to the capital stock of various corporations is precisely what the accused were engaged in doing in the present case. Can it effectively be denied that such solicitation took place, at least in part, in Manitoba? I think not … . I think it completely unrealistic to suggest that when the accused sent their letters by mail from Toronto, Ontario, to Shilo, Manitoba, the act of solicitation there represented took place only in Toronto or at most within the borders of Ontario … . It was in this Province that McCaffrey was solicited by the accused to purchase the shares in question, and it was in this Province that McCaffrey responded favourably to such solicitation. I would agree with the learned Magistrate and the learned County Court Judge that what took place in the present case constituted an act of trading in securities within the definition of the *Securities Act of Manitoba*.

QUESTIONS

1. What is a ratio from the *McKenzie Securities* case?

2. To what extent is a system of provincial securities inefficient for dealers who have clients in various provinces? Later chapters discuss how securities regulators have sought to address these issues.

3. Can a valid argument be made that interprovincial securities transactions are within federal, not provincial, jurisdiction because they involve extraterritorial issues?

One of the primary constitutional conflicts between the federal government and the provinces concerns insider trading. As we will discuss in Chapter 8, insider trading occurs when individuals make trades that are based on material undisclosed information. The conflict in the case below arose because federal corporate laws and provincial securities regulation overlapped with near-identical provisions, which continues to be the case even today in various areas of law such as insider trading and proxy solicitations. The following decision sought to resolve the conflict by interpreting the federal power to incorporate and regulate the management of federal corporations as allowing the federal government to regulate insider trading. Similar provincial regulation was permitted to overlap on the basis that federal and provincial legislation could operate concurrently. Note that Dickson J is careful not to foreclose the possibility of an entire federal securities system that would take into account a national Canadian capital market. The issue of a national regulator is one that we will address at the end of the chapter.

Multiple Access Ltd v McCutcheon
[1982] 2 SCR 161

[Facts: the Ontario Securities Commission was required to bring an action on behalf of a federal company to enforce "insider trading" liability against the defendants because the shareholders of the company secured a court order through s 114(1) of the Ontario *Securities Act*. At first instance, the weekly court judge held the Ontario provisions not suspended by federal paramountcy. The Divisional Court reversed and the Ontario Court of Appeal affirmed this decision.

The appeal to the Supreme Court of Canada revolved around three questions: (1) whether ss 100.4 and 100.5 of the *Canada Corporations Act* are *ultra vires* Parliament; (2) whether ss 113 and 114 of the *Securities Act* are *ultra vires* the Ontario Legislature; and (3) if both are *intra vires*, whether the impugned provisions of the Ontario *Securities Act* are suspended and inoperative because of the doctrine of paramountcy. (Note: Sections 100.4 and 100.5 of the *Canada Corporations Act* concerned insider trading. Section 100.4 focused on the cause of action for insider trading. Section 100.5 allows one to commence an action and to enforce liability created under s 100.4. Sections 113 and 114 of the *Securities Act* of Ontario are concerned with the same, with s 113 being the equivalent to s 100.4 of the *Canada Corporations Act*, and s 114 being the equivalent to s 100.5.) The two provisions stated as follows:

> 113(1) Every insider of a corporation or associate or affiliate of such insider, who, in connection with a transaction relating to the capital securities of the corporation, makes use of any specific confidential information for his own benefit or advantage that, if generally known, might reasonably be expected to affect materially the value of such securities, is liable to compensate any person or company for any direct loss suffered by such person or company as a result of such transaction, unless such information was known or ought reasonably to have been known to such person or company at the time of such transaction, and is also accountable to the corporation for any direct benefit or advantage received or receivable by such insider, associate or affiliate, as the case may be, as a result of such transaction.

(2) An action to enforce any right created by subsection 1 may be commenced only within two years after the date of completion of the transaction that gave rise to the cause of action.

114(1) Upon application by any person or company that was at the time of a transaction referred to in subsection 1 of section 113 or is at the time of the application an owner of capital securities of the corporation, a judge of the High Court designated by the Chief Justice of the High Court may, if satisfied that,

(a) such person or company has reasonable grounds for believing that the corporation has a cause of action under section 113; and

(b) either,

(i) the corporation has refused or failed to commence an action under section 113 within sixty days after receipt of a written request from such person or company so to do; or

(ii) the corporation has failed to prosecute diligently an action commenced by it under section 113,

make an order, upon such terms as to security for costs and otherwise as to the judge seems fit, requiring the Commission to commence or continue an action in the name of and on behalf of the corporation to enforce the liability created by section 113.

(2) The corporation and the Commission shall be given notice of any application under subsection 1 and has the right to appear and be heard thereon.

(3) Every order made under subsection 1 shall provide that the corporation shall co-operate fully with the Commission in the institution and prosecution of such action and shall make available to the Commission all books, records, documents and other material or information known to the corporation or reasonably ascertainable by the corporation relevant to such action.

(4) An appeal lies to the Court of Appeal from an order made under subsection 1.]

DICKSON J (Laskin CJ and Martland, Ritchie, McIntyre, and Lamer JJ concurring): This appeal raises the issue of "insider trading" in securities. Insider trading is the purchase or sale of the securities of a company by a person who, by reason of his position in the company, has access to confidential information not known to other shareholders or the general public. He learns, for example, that the company is going to be the object of a take-over bid at a price per share well above the market. He buys shares. Or, to take a more common occurrence of late, he learns that the company is in dire straits. He sells shares. He thus places personal benefit or advantage in conflict with, and superior to, his relationship with, and duty to, other shareholders and to the company.

...

The argument against the validity of ss. 113 and 114 of the *Ontario Securities Act* is that they are beyond the legislative power of the Province in that they purport to apply to companies incorporated under the laws of Canada; these sections are not in pith and substance enactments regulating the securities business; in actuality they define critical corporate relationships; it is beyond the power of a province to enact laws that regulate the corporate relationships of a federally-incorporated company.

...

Subject to that exception, a federal company empowered to carry on a particular business in a province is subject to the competent legislation of the province as to that business. If it wishes to raise capital through the sale of securities there is no reason why it should not be subject to the laws of the province applicable to all those in the province who wish to raise capital through security sales, and subject thereafter to rules requiring honest dealings in securities, so that the public be not defrauded. Sections 113 and 114 further the provincial object of assuring that persons who carry on the business of dealing in securities shall be honest and of good repute. As Mr. Justice Fauteux, as he then was, stated in *Gregory & Company Inc. v. Québec Securities Commission* … (at p. 588):

> The paramount object of the Act is to ensure that persons who, in the province, carry on the business of trading in securities or acting as investment counsel, shall be honest and of good repute and, in this way, to protect the public, in the province or elsewhere, from being defrauded as a result of certain activities initiated in the province by persons therein carrying on such a business.

In *Smith v. The Queen* Mr. Justice Martland stated (at p. 797):

> The *Securities Act* exists to regulate the securities business. This is achieved through two main forms of control, the first of which is directed towards the persons or companies selling the securities and the second of which is directed to the securities being sold.

And later (at p. 798):

> Thus control is exercised through the registration of persons and companies before they are permitted to trade in securities coupled with what is essentially the registration of the securities themselves before the securities may be traded in the course of a primary distribution to the public.

In my opinion ss. 113 and 114 of *The Securities Act* of Ontario constitute valid legislative provisions in relation to the subject matter of property and civil rights in the province, with respect to trading of the capital securities of a company. These sections do not sterilize the functions and activities of a federal company nor do they impair its status or essential powers (see *Canadian Indemnity Co. v. Attorney-General of British Columbia* …).

Having found ss. 100.4 and 100.5 of the *Canada Corporations Act* to be *intra vires* the Parliament of Canada and ss. 113 and 114 of the Ontario *Securities Act* to be *intra vires* the Legislature of Ontario there remains but to respond to the third and final question. Are sections 113 and 114 of the Ontario Act suspended and rendered inoperative in respect of corporations incorporated under the laws of Canada[?]

…

Morden J [wrote the majority judgment of the Divisional Court, which reversed the judgment of Henry J in Weekly Court. Morden's judgment was affirmed by the Court of Appeal of Ontario, which led to this appeal] adopts the older and more prevalent view of the commentators that "The authorities establish one of the implications of Dominion paramountcy to be that provincial duplicative legislation is suspended and inoperative. Simple duplication by a province is not permitted" (Lederman, "The Concurrent Operation of Federal and Provincial Laws in Canada," *supra*, at p. 195; see also Abel, Laskin's *Canadian Constitutional Law* (1975), at p. 117: "If member and federal measures are substantial duplicates, every situation covered by the one is likewise covered by the other and there is no provincial room left, given full operation of the federal law"). Morden J finds that "Resort to one statute, from a practical point of view, precludes the other from having any application."

The conflict between the reasons of Mr. Justice Henry and the reasons of Mr. Justice Morden lies in large measures upon the opinion of the latter that the paramountcy doctrine became applicable because a plaintiff could resort to one set of provisions only and, having done so, there would be no scope for the other to have operational effect. That is unquestionably an important consideration but it is not, in my view, conclusive. The provincial legislation merely duplicates the federal; it does not contradict it. The fact that a plaintiff may have a choice of remedies does not mean that the provisions of both levels of government cannot "live together" and operate concurrently. In the Smith case the provincial and federal provisions were virtually identical in substance, and the law authorities could prosecute the proscribed conduct as a provincial offence or as a federal offence under the *Criminal Code*.

I agree with the submissions of counsel for Saskatchewan that it would be ironic if a province, by adding elements of differentiation in its legislation (which do not conflict with federal provisions governing the same conduct but which, in effect, go further than the federal) could create valid operative provisions whereas in regard to the same legislative field, it could not merely duplicate the federal provisions; the cases where overlapping provincial legislation has not been rendered inoperative cannot be validly distinguished on the basis that in each of them there were elements of difference between the provincial and the federal legislation; there is no true repugnancy in the case of merely duplicative provisions since it does not matter which statute is applied; the legislative purpose of Parliament will be fulfilled regardless of which statute is invoked by a remedy-seeker; application of the provincial law does not displace the legislative purpose of Parliament.

The respondents strenuously support Mr. Justice Morden's reasons in this Court. Counsel for the respondent McCutcheon argues "Where two actions are brought under the federal and provincial legislation against the insider, either concurrently or *seriatim*, the Court will not permit both to proceed to judgment [...] Both pieces of legislation cannot operate concurrently in that resort to one precludes resort to the other. The legislation under which one action is commenced operates to prevent the application of the other. In such case, the two statutes meet and are in conflict." I am not of that opinion.

With Mr. Justice Henry I would say that duplication is, to borrow Professor Lederman's phrase, "the ultimate in harmony." The resulting "untidiness" or "diseconomy" of duplication is the price we pay for a federal system in which economy "often has to be subordinated to … provincial autonomy" (Hogg, at p. 110). Mere duplication without actual conflict or contradiction is not sufficient to invoke the doctrine of paramountcy and render otherwise valid provincial legislation inoperative.

…

In principle, there would seem to be no good reasons to speak of paramountcy and preclusion except where there is actual conflict in operation as where one enactment says "yes" and the other says "no"; "the same citizens are being told to do inconsistent things"; compliance with one is defiance of the other. The courts are well able to prevent double recovery in the theoretical and unlikely event of plaintiffs trying to obtain relief under both sets of provisions. The fact that a court must authorize proceedings under the Ontario Act provides a safeguard against double recovery if the company has already proceeded under the federal Act. In addition the Court at the final stage of finding and quantifying liability could prevent double recovery if in fact compensation and an accounting had already been made by a defendant. No court would permit double recovery.

I find that ss. 113 and 114 of *The Securities Act* of Ontario are not suspended or rendered inoperative in respect of corporations incorporated under the laws of Canada by ss. 100.4 and 100.5 of the *Canada Corporations Act*.

Students will note that many of the cases that we have discussed in this chapter originate in Ontario because Ontario's markets were more developed and more active than markets in other areas of Canada. In terms of the law thus far discussed, it appears that the principle of provincial extraterritorial incompetence—that is, a rule that can strike down provincial legislation—is limited to situations where the pith and substance of the challenged legislation is in relation to extraprovincial rights. If the pith and substance of the legislation is within the province's competence, then incidental effects on extraprovincial rights will not render the legislation *ultra vires*.

In the following case, the legislation at issue was within provincial competence as concerning property and civil rights in the province. The controversy was whether it was a valid exercise of power for the Ontario Securities Commission to enforce Ontario securities law on the actions of a Crown corporation in another province (Québec). The Ontario Court of Appeal found that the Ontario law was not unconstitutional because of extraterritoriality. The court held that it could hardly be considered fair and reasonable to suggest that only residents of Ontario are subject to Ontario regulatory rules while operating in the province's capital markets.

Québec (Sa Majesté du Chef) v Ontario Securities Commission
(1992), 10 OR (3d) 577 (CA)

McKINLAY JA (Lacourcière and Krever JJA concurring): …

(1) Is the application of Ontario law to the transaction in question unconstitutional by reason of extra-territoriality?

… [T]he appellant argues not that the OSC is without jurisdiction because the legislation under which it would act is beyond the legislative competence of the province of Ontario, but rather, that the application of the Act to the facts of this case would have an extra-territorial effect which should not be tolerated in a federal state.

…

The instant case involves clearly valid provincial legislation which, by its terms, may affect parties outside of Ontario. The appellant in its factum recognizes that valid laws of one province, drafted in general terms, may have tolerable extra-provincial effects "provided that the pith and substance of the legislation in question is in relation to matters which fall within provincial subject-matter jurisdiction, and the extra-provincial effects are necessarily incidental to that proper legislative purpose." It acknowledges *Churchill Falls (Labrador) Corp. v. Newfoundland (AG)* … , as authority. At p. 332 SCR, p. 30 DLR, McIntyre J, speaking for the court, limits the application of *R v. Royal Bank of Canada*, *supra*, to situations where the pith and substance of the legislation in question is in relation to extra-provincial rights. His Lordship then goes on to state:

> Where the pith and substance of the provincial enactment is in relation to matters which fall within the field of provincial legislative competence, incidental or consequential effects on

extra-provincial rights will not render the enactment *ultra vires*. Where, however, the pith and substance of the provincial enactment is the derogation from or elimination of extra-provincial rights then, even if it is cloaked in the proper constitutional form, it will be *ultra vires*. A colourable attempt to preserve the appearance of constitutionality in order to conceal an unconstitutional objective will not save the legislation.

There can be no doubt that the pith and substance of the legislation involved in this case concerns property and civil rights in the Province of Ontario. Although it may have incidental or consequential effects on extra-provincial rights, the legislation is clearly not a "colourable attempt … to conceal an unconstitutional objective." The legislative objective is to regulate the operation of the capital markets in Ontario for the protection of all who use them.

...

The principles advanced by counsel for the appellant are not ones which have been accepted by courts in this country, but are ones which have been gleaned primarily from learned treatises. They are articulated by counsel as follows:

(a) The province with the most significant connection with the transaction and the parties should have jurisdiction;
(b) Less compelling governmental interests of one province should be sacrificed to more compelling governmental interests of another province;
(c) The exercise of jurisdiction must be fair and reasonable; and
(d) The exercise of jurisdiction must be consistent with the needs of a federated system, resulting in interprovincial harmony.

Although other sources were cited, the primary sources of the appellant's thesis were J.-G. Castel, *Canadian Conflict of Laws* (1975); Reese, "Limitations on the Extraterritorial Application of Law" (1978), 4 *Dalhousie LJ* 589; and J. Swan, "The Canadian Constitution, Federalism and The Conflict of Laws" (1985), 63 *Can. Bar Rev.* 271.

… [T]here is no choice of law issue here: only the law of Ontario is involved, and no competing Quebec law was proven or argued before the OSC or before this court. If Ontario tribunals are without jurisdiction in this case because the transactions involved are more closely connected to the Province of Quebec, then in all cases where Ontario wishes to regulate the operation of its capital markets, it must first determine whether the transaction or series of transactions involved are more closely connected to Ontario or to some other province or country. If this is so, individuals and corporations need only structure their transactions in such a way that the test of "closest connection" is met, and then, regardless of whether the transactions involved are detrimental to persons resident in Ontario or are contrary to the trading policies established by the Government of Ontario, they can be carried out with impunity.

On the totality of the facts conceded for the purpose of this appeal, I am not prepared to hold that those facts have a more significant connection to the Province of Québec than to the Province of Ontario. However, even were I prepared to so hold, I do not consider that the jurisdiction of the OSC is ousted by that consideration alone. To hold otherwise would be to severely limit the ability of the Province of Ontario to regulate the operation of capital markets within its borders.

...

The appellants argue a second dimension to the extra-territorial application issue, and that is, quoting from its factum: "The courts in any civilized federation, in deciding what law applies to multi-jurisdictional situations, must protect parties against arbitrary and unreasonable assertions of jurisdiction by a province that violate the reasonable expectations of affected parties with respect to the applicable law." I do not intend to discuss the more sophisticated aspects of this argument, since I am satisfied that there is a simple and inevitable response to it. Quebec would have reasonable expectations that any other province, when entering Quebec's capital markets, would abide by Quebec's regulatory laws. When Quebec enters the capital markets of other provinces, the converse should be true.

The remedies contemplated by the notice of hearing should also be kept in mind. If the OSC were to apply to the court to request a compliance order, the extra-territorial application of Ontario law would be obvious, and its enforcement subject to scrutiny in such an event. However, in the event the OSC were to withdraw from the Québec Government the statutory exemptions it enjoys under the Act, any extra-territorial application of Ontario law would be minimal, and would arise only because an out-of-province user of the Ontario markets wished to avail itself of Ontario market opportunities. It can hardly be considered fair and reasonable to suggest that only Ontario residents are subject to Ontario regulatory rules when operating in Ontario capital markets. The fact that the offending party is the government of another province should not change the perception of fairness and reasonableness.

I see no reason, on the basis of the law as it exists, or on the basis of the untested principles put forward by the appellant, why the application of Ontario law to the facts of this case should be held unconstitutional by reason of extra-territoriality.

Leave to appeal in the case was denied; however, the decision excerpted here was implicitly confirmed by the Supreme Court of Canada (SCC) in *Committee for the Equal Treatment of Asbestos Minority Shareholders v Ontario (Securities Commission)*, 2001 SCC 37, [2001] 2 SCR 132.

A relatively recent and pertinent case relating to division of powers is the *Global Securities* case, excerpted below. In this case, a British Columbia brokerage firm, Global, challenged the authority of the British Columbia Securities Commission to order Global to produce documents that were to be handed over to the United States Securities and Exchange Commission. The BC *Securities Act* at the time allowed the commission to require registered brokers in the province ("registrants") to produce records in their control "to assist in the administration of the securities laws of another jurisdiction." Global claimed that this provision did not fall within the powers granted to the provinces by the *Constitution Act, 1867*. Justice Iacobucci, writing for the SCC, disagreed. He held that Global failed to understand that the pith and substance of the provision in question was the enforcement of British Columbia's securities laws. In his view, this purpose clearly falls within provincial domain under the "property and civil rights" clause in s 92(13) of the *Constitution Act, 1867*.

Global Securities Corp v British Columbia (Securities Commission)
2000 SCC 21, [2000] 1 SCR 494

IACOBUCCI J: …

[34] Given the Commission's legitimate concern with ensuring that domestic registrants are "honest and of good repute," another obvious purpose of s. 141(1)(b) is uncovering violations of foreign law by domestic registrants. The intervener the Attorney General for Quebec aptly summarized the point in its factum as follows (at p. 7):

> [TRANSLATION] … the Securities Commission could take into account violations such persons have committed in carrying on that business outside the province, in order to protect the clients of such persons within the province and with respect to transactions taking place there.

[35] The respondent disagrees, arguing that this purpose explains s. 141(1)(d), not s. 141(1)(b). The former provision authorizes an order for production of documents "in respect of matters in British Columbia relating to trading in securities in another jurisdiction." If British Columbia is interested in foreign violations, the respondent submits, it should conduct its own investigation pursuant to s. 141(1)(d).

[36] With respect, I cannot agree. If British Columbia can legitimately conduct its own investigation of foreign violations, certainly it can choose to have that task carried out by a foreign regulator, which is presumably better positioned to conduct such an investigation. The simple fact that the Commission is itself empowered to investigate under s. 141(1)(d) does not change the purpose of s. 141(1)(b). I therefore conclude that another primary goal of the latter provision is uncovering foreign violations of securities laws by domestic registrants.

(c) The Extra-provincial Aspects of the Law Are Incidental

[37] The respondent puts a great deal of emphasis on the fact that the impugned provision enables the Commission to turn evidence over to a foreign regulatory body. As such, it argues that the purpose must be to assist the enforcement of foreign law. With respect, this argument confuses the purpose of a law with the means chosen to achieve that purpose. As discussed above, the purpose of s. 141(1)(b) is the enforcement of domestic securities law, both by obtaining reciprocal assistance from foreign regulators, and by discovering foreign securities law violations by domestic registrants. Authorizing an order for production of information to assist a foreign regulator under s. 141(1)(b) is merely the means by which the Commission achieves these goals. Indeed, given the overwhelming evidence supporting the appellant's position, I cannot agree with the respondent that British Columbia has passed a law whose dominant purpose is to assist a foreign body. Accordingly, in these circumstances, I would not ascribe such a purpose to s. 141(1)(b).

[38] Moreover, I do not believe the effects of s. 141(1)(b) alter my analysis of its pith and substance. While it does involve relations with a foreign authority, s. 141(1)(b) does not attempt to extend the reach of provincial legislation outside its borders: see *McGuire v. McGuire* … . As several provincial interveners pointed out in their submissions, administrative arrangements between provinces and foreign authorities are quite common. Without commenting on the constitutionality of any of these arrangements, I would note

simply that where, as here, there is a clearly dominant intraprovincial purpose, the mere fact that the province is co-operating with a foreign authority in the pursuit of that purpose will not change the law's pith and substance: see E. Edinger, "Territorial Limitations on Provincial Powers" (1982), 14 *Ottawa L Rev.* 57, at p. 94. In short, the extra-provincial effects of s. 141(1)(b) are clearly incidental to the dominant purposes described above.

2. Assigning the Legislation to a Head of Provincial Jurisdiction

[39] Having characterized the law, I now turn to determining whether the law can be assigned to an enumerated head of provincial authority. In argument, the respondent and several interveners suggested two possible sources: "Property and Civil Rights," and "Administration of Justice." Because of my conclusion that the legislation fits within "Property and Civil Rights," I do not find it necessary to address the "Administration of Justice" issue.

(a) Section 92(13): Property and Civil Rights in the Province

[40] I conclude that the "pith and substance" of s. 141(1)(b), as described above, falls within the scope of s. 92(13) of the *Constitution Act, 1867*, "Property and Civil Rights in the Province." Section 141(1)(b)'s dominant purpose is the effective regulation of domestic securities, a task that has long been recognized to fall within provincial authority: see *Multiple Access Ltd. v. McCutcheon* … , at pp. 183-85; *Smith, supra*; *Lymburn, supra*.

[41] Moreover, it is well established that the provinces' authority over securities regulation is not limited to purely intraprovincial matters. In *Gregory, supra*, the Québec-based broker in question was prosecuted solely for transactions outside the province. This Court nonetheless held that Quebec had a legitimate interest in those transactions. Conversely, in *R v. W. McKenzie Securities Ltd.* … , the Manitoba Court of Appeal held that a province can regulate a broker located outside the province if that broker transacts with clients within the province.

[42] Two different courts of appeal have also acknowledged that provincial regulatory bodies may have jurisdiction to investigate violations of foreign law. In *Re Legault and Law Society of Upper Canada* … the Ontario Court of Appeal upheld the Law Society's authority to entertain a complaint about the conduct of an Ontario lawyer in another jurisdiction. As the court noted at p. 643, "the jurisdiction of the Law Society over its member is a personal one, which extends to the member's conduct without territorial limitation." In *Re Underwood McLellan & Associates Ltd.* … , the court similarly upheld the power of the Association of Professional Engineers to examine conduct outside the province in making its licensing decisions.

[43] Both these cases recognize that provincial regulatory bodies governing professions with a strong interjurisdictional aspect must be able to take into account events occurring abroad. This rationale may not necessarily hold in all circumstances, and each case must be decided on its own facts. However, given the Commission's clear authority over domestic securities regulation, and the clearly interjurisdictional nature of securities regulation in general, I find that it must apply in the present appeal. Assisting in the investigation of possible violations of foreign securities laws falls under the Commission's power under s. 92(13) to regulate British Columbia's securities market.

[44] I therefore conclude that the pith and substance of s. 141(1)(b) falls within British Columbia's authority to regulate securities. Obtaining reciprocal cooperation and uncovering violations abroad are both aspects of the Commission's mandate, which fits easily within s. 92(13).

C. *The Ancillary Doctrine*

[45] Having concluded that s. 141(1)(b) is, in pith and substance, valid provincial legislation, there is no need to discuss the last two steps of the analysis set out by Dickson CJ in *GM Canada*, *supra*, frequently referred to collectively as the "ancillary" doctrine: see Hogg, *supra*, at p. 15-35. Indeed, given that this appeal does not involve an allegation that one level of government is trenching on another's sphere of competence, as *GM Canada* did, it is not even clear that this doctrine is applicable. Nevertheless, I would note that even if s. 141(1)(b) were not in pith and substance provincial, it would clearly be justified under the ancillary doctrine. Section 141(1)(b) is a part of a valid legislative scheme, namely, the *Securities Act*. Moreover, even assuming that the most rigorous version of the ancillary doctrine applies, I believe that s. 141(1)(b) is "necessarily incidental" to the *Securities Act* and would therefore also uphold it under the ancillary doctrine.

[46] The Attorney General of Canada intervened in this appeal to argue that:

> [I]f the provision in question is held to be within provincial jurisdiction, this decision would not preclude overlapping federal jurisdiction over securities matters in respect of international and interprovincial transactions and co-operation, or any other relevant head of federal jurisdiction.

Since the central question presented by this appeal is the power of the province to enact s. 141(1)(b), I decline to comment on the constitutionality of hypothetical overlapping federal legislation. I would note, however, that this Court has already upheld aspects of federal securities regulation, in another context, in *Multiple Access*, *supra*, under the "double aspect" theory. The Court's decision in the present appeal should not be taken in any way to question the holding of that case.

VII. *Conclusion and Disposition*

[47] In summary, I find that s. 141(1)(b) of the British Columbia *Securities Act* is, in pith and substance, aimed at furthering the effective enforcement of domestic securities laws and as such falls within the province's powers under s. 92(13) of the *Constitution Act, 1867*. The appeal is allowed with costs throughout, the judgment of the Court of Appeal for British Columbia is set aside, and the judgment of Macdonald J is restored.

QUESTIONS

1. How easy is it to determine what the "pith and substance" of a legislative provision is?
2. What is the "closest connection" test highlighted in *Asbestos*?
3. Describe the ancillary doctrine. How relevant is it to the holding in *Global Securities*?

We can thus see that the legal discussion of the division of powers with regard to securities law has been a vibrant one. The issue of the federal trade and commerce power was discussed extensively in *Reference re Securities Act*, 2011 SCC 66, [2011] 3 SCR 837, in which the Supreme Court of Canada held that the 2010 draft federal *Securities Act*, set out in Order in Council PC 2010 667, was not valid under the general branch of federal power to regulate trade and commerce of the *Constitution Act, 1867*, s 91(2), and thus did not fall within the legislative authority of the Parliament of Canada.

The 2010 draft *Securities Act* was aimed at creating a single Canadian securities regulator. The purposes of the Act were to provide investor protection; to foster fair, efficient, and competitive capital markets; and to contribute to the integrity and stability of Canada's financial system. The proposed Act included registration requirements for securities dealers, prospectus filing requirements, disclosure requirements, specific duties for market participants, a framework for the regulation of derivatives, civil remedies, and regulatory and criminal offences pertaining to securities. The proposed Act did not unilaterally impose a unified system, but would have permitted provinces and territories to opt in, with the hope of creating an effective unified national securities regulation system. However, the authority of the federal government was highly contested in some provinces. In provincial references, both the Alberta Court of Appeal (2011 ABCA 77, 41 Alta LR (5th) 145) and the Québec Court of Appeal (2011 QCCA 591) concluded that the proposed Act was unconstitutional. In the reference to the Supreme Court of Canada, the federal government, joined by Ontario and other interveners (including the Canadian Foundation for Advancement of Investor Rights, the Canadian Coalition for Good Governance and the Ontario Teachers' Pension Plan Board), argued that the Act, viewed in its entirety, fell within the general branch of Parliament's power to regulate trade and commerce under s 91(2) of the *Constitution Act, 1867*. Alberta, Québec, Manitoba, New Brunswick, and other interveners argued that the scheme fell under the provincial power over property and civil rights under s 92(13) of the *Constitution Act, 1867* and would trench on provincial legislative jurisdiction over matters of a merely local or private nature (s 92(16)).

The Supreme Court of Canada found that the main thrust of the Act was to regulate, on an exclusive basis, all aspects of securities trading in Canada, including the trades and occupations related to securities in each of the provinces. It held that the purpose of the proposed Act was to implement a comprehensive Canadian regime to regulate securities with a view to protect investors; to promote fair, efficient, and competitive capital markets; and to ensure the integrity and stability of the financial system. Its effects would be to duplicate and displace the existing provincial and territorial securities regimes. The court further held that, viewed in its entirety, the Act could not be classified as falling within the general trade and commerce power. Its main thrust did not address a matter of genuine national importance and scope going to trade as a whole in a way that is distinct and different from provincial concerns. While the court acknowledged that the preservation of capital markets is a matter that goes beyond a specific industry and engages trade as a whole, it found that the proposed legislation was chiefly concerned with the day-to-day regulation of all aspects of contracts for securities within the provinces, including all aspects of public protection and professional competences. The court held that these matters remain essentially provincial concerns falling within property and civil rights in the provinces and are not related to trade as a whole. It observed that while the economic importance of the securities market may, in principle, support federal intervention that is qualitatively different from what the provinces can do, it did not justify a wholesale takeover of the regulation of the securities industry. The judgment, excerpted below, also sets out the history of reform efforts in respect of a national securities regulatory system:

Reference re Securities Act
2011 SCC 66, [2011] 3 SCR 837

THE COURT:

I. *Overview of the Court's Opinion*

[1] This reference under s. 53 of the *Supreme Court Act*, R.S.C. 1985, c. S-26, requires the Court to determine whether the proposed Securities Act set out in Order in Council P.C. 2010-667 falls within the legislative authority of the Parliament of Canada.

[2] The proposed *Securities Act* represents a comprehensive foray by Parliament into the realm of securities regulation. If validly adopted, it will create a single scheme governing the trade of securities throughout Canada subject to the oversight of a single national securities regulator.

[3] The government of Canada ("Canada"), supported by the Attorney General of Ontario ("Ontario") and other interveners, argues that the entirety of the Act can be sustained as a proper exercise of the general branch of Parliament's legislative power to regulate trade and commerce, grounded in s. 91(2) of the *Constitution Act, 1867*. The Attorney General of Alberta, the Attorney General of Quebec and other provincial attorneys general and interveners oppose the Act, arguing that securities regulation is a matter falling within s. 92(13) of the *Constitution Act, 1867*, which gives the provinces legislative jurisdiction over property and civil rights within their borders. Certain opponents of the Act also submit that securities regulation relates to provincial jurisdiction over matters of a merely local or private nature, under s. 92(16) of the *Constitution Act, 1867*.

[4] Canada does not challenge the proposition that certain aspects of securities regulation fall within provincial authority in relation to property and civil rights in the provinces. Nor does Canada argue that any provisions of the Act fall within federal legislative authority because they are necessarily incidental to the exercise of federal powers. Canada's contention is simply that the securities market has evolved from a provincial matter to a national matter affecting the country as a whole and that, as a consequence, the federal general trade and commerce power gives Parliament legislative authority over all aspects of securities regulation. This authority, Canada argues, is concurrent with that of the provincial legislatures over all aspects of securities presently regulated by the provinces.

[5] The propriety of such a constitutional realignment cannot simply be assumed. The shift in regulatory authority that the proposed Act seeks to achieve requires justification. Canada asserts that this justification is found under the "general" branch of the trade and commerce power. However, it has failed to show that this power, interpreted as required by the case law, supports the proposed Act.

[6] Canada has shown that aspects of the securities market are national in scope and affect the country as a whole. However, considered in its entirety, the proposed Act is chiefly directed at protecting investors and ensuring the fairness of capital markets

through the day-to-day regulation of issuers and other participants in the securities market. These matters have long been considered local concerns subject to provincial legislative competence over property and civil rights within the province. Canada has not shown that the securities market has so changed that the regulation of all aspects of securities now falls within the general branch of Parliament's power over trade and commerce under s. 91(2). Applying the settled test, we conclude that the proposed Act does not fall within the general trade and commerce power.

[7] It is a fundamental principle of federalism that both federal and provincial powers must be respected, and one power may not be used in a manner that effectively eviscerates another. Rather, federalism demands that a balance be struck, a balance that allows both the federal Parliament and the provincial legislatures to act effectively in their respective spheres. Accepting Canada's interpretation of the general trade and commerce power would disrupt rather than maintain that balance. Parliament cannot regulate the whole of the securities system simply because aspects of it have a national dimension.

[8] We therefore answer the reference question in the negative.

[9] It is open to the federal government and the provinces to exercise their respective powers over securities harmoniously, in the spirit of cooperative federalism. The experience of other federations in the field of securities regulation, while a function of their own constitutional requirements, suggests that a cooperative approach might usefully be explored, should our legislators so choose, to ensure that each level of government properly discharges its responsibility to the public in a coordinated fashion.

[10] At this juncture, it is important to stress that this advisory opinion does not address the question of what constitutes the optimal model for regulating the securities market. While the parties presented evidence and arguments on the relative merits of federal and provincial regulation of securities, the policy question of whether a single national securities scheme is preferable to multiple provincial regimes is not one for the courts to decide. Accordingly, our answer to the reference question is dictated solely by the text of the Constitution, fundamental constitutional principles and the relevant case law.

II. The Proposed Act and the Parties' Positions

A. National Securities Proposals in Canada

[11] Recommendations for national securities regulation in Canada are not new. Over the years, many proposals have been put forward, but none implemented. The various proposals, in different ways, attempted to come to grips with the problem underlying this reference—how to achieve national securities regulation within the constitutional division of powers between Parliament and the provincial legislatures. Not surprisingly, the proposals generally envisaged cooperation between the provinces and the federal government as the route to achieving national standards and regulation.

[12] The first proposal dates to 1935, when the Royal Commission on Price Spreads recommended the formation of an investment securities board to oversee the issuance of securities by companies incorporated under federal legislation (*Report of the Royal Commission on Price Spreads*, at pp. 41-42).

[13] In the 1960s, various recommendations and proposals were mooted. The 1964 Royal Commission on Banking and Finance (the "Porter Commission") accepted the

desirability of uniform legislation and administration of the Canadian securities industry and recommended the creation of an additional regulatory body, based on cooperation between the federal and provincial governments (Report of the Royal Commission on Banking and Finance). The body, to be headed by a federal regulator, would have set uniform standards for securities distributed interprovincially and internationally, while permitting existing provincial regulators to continue to govern "local matters such as the licensing of security dealers and their salesmen and the registration of issues to be offered only within their own province" (p. 348).

[14] The Porter Commission hoped that the establishment of a federal agency would lead to greater agreement and cooperation, eliminating the duplication that the Commission saw as hampering effective securities regulation. In particular, the Commission hoped that the introduction of uniform federal standards would foster the adoption of similar standards in the provinces and free the provinces to focus on purely local matters by automatically clearing federally regulated issues. In its view, a single federal agency would improve cooperation with the United States Securities and Exchange Commission and "would be responsible for and interested in the growth, development and efficiency of the whole Canadian securities industry" (p. 348).

[15] In 1967, just three years after the release of the Porter Commission's report, the Ontario Securities Commission ("OSC") circulated a very different proposal for a single, highly decentralized, national securities regulator. CANSEC—the "Canada Securities Commission"—was to be a three-tiered structure (a council of ministers, CANSEC and administrative staff) designed to achieve uniformity in Canadian securities regulation through cooperation by the federal and provincial governments, rather than by forcing each province to surrender its regulatory activity in the field to a federal body. CANSEC would operate on an opt-in basis: no province would be required to join or remain in CANSEC. Moreover, participation by provinces would not involve a permanent surrender of power: "A government which has passed an amendment in order to bring themselves into the scheme can repeal that amendment" ("CANSEC: Legal and Administrative Concepts" (November 1967), OSCB 61, at p. 66). Provinces would have been able to join CANSEC, then withdraw and regulate independently as before.

[16] The OSC anticipated that CANSEC would be brought into existence through the passage of an organizational statute by the federal government and the subsequent commitment by participating jurisdictions to have the new commission administer their own securities acts. In bringing CANSEC into existence, the OSC did not consider it necessary that the provincial laws themselves be substantively uniform; rather, similar schemes of administration and "some modest degree of uniformity" in securities legislation would suffice (p. 66). The provinces would retain jurisdiction over "nearly all substantive issues," delegating to the commission authority only to deal with federal corporate, international and criminal matters not clearly within provincial jurisdiction (J.L. Howard, "Securities Regulation: Structure and Process," in *Proposals for a Securities Market Law for Canada* (1979), vol. 3, 1607, at p. 1693).

[17] The discussion over securities regulation continued in the 1970s and 1980s. In 1979, the federal Department of Consumer and Corporate Affairs produced a three-volume study entitled Proposals for a Securities Market Law for Canada, which contemplated a national securities commission working in cooperation with the provinces. The study recommended the creation of a federal securities commission and the enactment of

federal securities legislation and envisioned a "nationally coordinated system of regulation that involves cooperation between a federal commission with federal jurisdiction and provincial and foreign commissions" (vol. 2, at p. 5). It contemplated administration either by a federal commission, by a cooperative body developed through negotiations among the federal and provincial governments, or a body lying on the spectrum between that and a single federal agency.

[18] In 1985, the Royal Commission on the Economic Union and Development Prospects for Canada concluded that there was no reason to tamper with the existing system of provincial regulation of stock markets, but noted that "[t]echnological change, the increasing international integration of capital markets, and the desire of provinces, especially Quebec, to regulate markets in pursuit of provincial development goals are all likely to place greater strains on the existing system in the near future" (*Report*, vol. 3, at p. 167).

[19] In 1994, the premiers of the Atlantic provinces asked the federal government to establish a national securities regulator. The proposal ultimately took the form of a draft memorandum of understanding ("MOU") between the federal government and participating provinces, which was circulated among the provinces ((1994), 17 OSCB 4401). The MOU proposed the creation of a "Canadian Securities Commission" and envisioned a "uniform securities regulatory structure which [would] apply comprehensively within and across all participating provinces" (preamble).

[20] Like the proposal to establish CANSEC, the MOU was premised on opting in by the provinces and explicitly stated that no government would give up any jurisdiction by joining. Participating provinces were to have the ability to adopt regulations exempting certain securities from provisions of the federal legislation. The jurisdiction of provincial securities regulatory authorities in provinces which elected not to participate in the uniform securities regulatory structure would not be affected. Canada, however, committed to "developing consultation and coordination mechanisms between the Canadian Securities Commission and the securities commission or equivalent office of any province which is not a Party to [the] agreement to maintain the benefits of harmonization of securities regulation in Canada and to promote further such harmonization in the future" (MOU, at cl. 29).

[21] In the past decade, calls for a national securities regulator have intensified.

[22] The Wise Persons' Committee ("WPC") of 2003 recommended the adoption of a comprehensive scheme of capital markets regulation for Canada, to be accomplished by the passage of comprehensive federal securities legislation, followed by provincial legislation incorporating the federal law by reference and delegating administrative powers to a newly established "Canadian Securities Commission."

[23] The WPC rejected the "dual structure" of securities market regulation recommended by the OSC proposal to establish CANSEC, the 1979 study by the Department of Consumer and Corporate Affairs and the 1994 MOU. In its view, "a dual structure, in which securities matters limited to a single province would be regulated provincially, while interprovincial and international matters would be regulated by a national body," was not appropriate "[g]iven the nationally integrated nature of Canada's capital markets and the history of provincial regulation of securities matters with incidental effect on matters outside the regulating province" (It's Time (2003), at p. 59). In the WPC's view, "efficient capital markets require that the federal legislation extend to all matters related to securities regulation" (p. 60).

[24] The WPC therefore recommended the enactment of a single, comprehensive code for the regulation of Canadian capital markets by the federal government. The single set of rules would cover "all securities regulatory matters in Canada" (p. 59). Provincial participation would be achieved through an obligation on the federal government to consult with the provinces before amending the legislation.

[25] The 2006 Crawford Panel on a Single Canadian Securities Regulator, established by the government of Ontario, endorsed the adoption of Canadian securities legislation (*Blueprint For A Canadian Securities Commission—Final Paper*). The Panel proposed that uniform regulation would be achieved by all jurisdictions incorporating, by reference, legislation enacted by one province as the Canadian Securities Act and establishing a "Canadian Securities Commission." A common body of securities law would then apply across the country. However, like the WPC, the Crawford Panel viewed the participation of all provinces and territories and the federal government as "ideal" but not necessary for the Commission to be established. The key was "that there be an initial core group of Participating Jurisdictions that agrees to enact, or to enact through incorporation by reference, common legislation that establishes the [Commission] and delegates to it authority over capital markets regulation" (p. 16).

[26] Three years after the Crawford Panel presented its "blueprint," the Expert Panel on Securities Regulation (the "Hockin Panel") released a report that informed the Securities Act proposed by Canada in this reference (*Creating an Advantage in Global Capital Markets—Final Report and Recommendations* (2009) (the "Hockin Report")). Like the Crawford Panel, the Hockin Panel recommended the establishment of a "Canadian Securities Commission" to oversee a single "Securities Act" for Canada.

[27] The Hockin Panel envisioned the establishment of a "comprehensive national regime" of securities regulation (p. 60), to be brought into force in participating jurisdictions through the repeal of local legislation. However, the Panel acknowledged that not all provinces (at least initially) might be willing to participate. It therefore recommended that in the absence of unanimity on the part of the provinces, the Act should provide for voluntary provincial participation, limiting its application to participating jurisdictions during the transition to a comprehensive national regime (p. 60). The Panel foresaw that, faced with such circumstances, the federal government might consider a "market participant opt-in feature" (p. 61), and proposed that the Commission consider negotiating memoranda of understanding with non-participating jurisdictions to coordinate securities regulation.

[28] In response to the Hockin Report, the federal government established the Canadian Securities Regulation Regime Transition Office in the *Budget Implementation Act, 2009*, S.C. 2009, c. 2, and prepared a draft Act implementing the Report's proposals. On May 26, 2010, the Governor General in Council referred this draft legislation to the Court for an advisory opinion as to its constitutional validity.

B. The Proposed Act

[29] The preamble of the proposed Act states that its immediate purpose is to create a single Canadian securities regulator. More broadly, s. 9 states that the underlying purposes of the Act are to provide investor protection, to foster fair, efficient and competitive capital markets and to contribute to the integrity and stability of Canada's financial system.

[30] The Act includes registration requirements for securities dealers, prospectus filing requirements, disclosure requirements, specific duties for market participants, a framework for the regulation of derivatives, civil remedies and regulatory and criminal offences pertaining to securities. It provides for the comprehensive regulation of securities in Canada, under the oversight of a single national regulator. It also provides for a single set of laws and rules designed to permit uniform regulation and enforcement on a national basis, thus fostering the integrity and stability of Canada's capital markets at a national level. While various parties emphasize different facets of the scheme, advancing interesting arguments on the implication of words such as "national," "capital markets," "securities industry" and "securities trading," it seems uncontrovertible that what the Act seeks is comprehensive national securities regulation, with the aim of fostering fair and efficient capital markets and contributing to the stability of Canada's financial system.

[31] The Act, as proposed, does not seek to unilaterally impose a unified system of securities regulation for the whole of Canada. Rather, it permits provinces to opt in, if and when they choose to do so. The hope is that, eventually, all or most provinces will opt in, creating an effective unified national securities regulation system for Canada. If this were to occur, it would represent a dramatic realignment in the manner in which securities have been regulated in this country.

...

B. Legislative Competence Over Securities: A Shared Field

[43] Provinces have jurisdiction to regulate securities within their boundaries (intra-provincial jurisdiction) as a matter of property and civil rights, pursuant to s. 92(13) of the Constitution Act, 1867. As Lord Atkin stated in *Lymburn v. Mayland*, [1932] A.C. 318 (P.C.), "If [a company] is formed to trade in securities there appears no reason why it should not be subject to the competent laws of the Province as to the business of all persons who trade in securities" (p. 324).

[44] More recently, this Court, in *Multiple Access Ltd. v. McCutcheon*, [1982] 2 S.C.R. 161, *per* Dickson J. (as he then was), confirmed:

> It is well established that the provinces have the power, as a matter of property and civil rights, to regulate the trade in corporate securities in the province, provided the statute does not single out federal companies for special treatment or discriminate against them in any way. ... Since the decision of the Privy Council in *Lymburn v. Mayland*, [1932] A.C. 318 the provisions of provincial securities acts have been given a wide constitutional recognition. [p. 183]

(See also *Global Securities Corp. v. British Columbia (Securities Commission)*, 2000 SCC 21, [2000] 1 S.C.R. 494, at para. 40.)

[45] The provincial power over securities extends to impacts on market intermediaries or investors outside a particular province (*Global Securities*, at para. 41; *R. v. W. McKenzie Securities Ltd.* (1966), 56 D.L.R. (2d) 56 (Man. C.A.), leave to appeal refused, [1966] S.C.R. ix (*sub nom. West & Dubros v. The Queen*); *Gregory & Co. v. Quebec Securities Commission*, [1961] S.C.R. 584). The case law also recognizes provincial jurisdiction where the province's capital markets are engaged (*Québec (Sa Majesté du Chef) v. Ontario Securities Commission* (1992), 10 O.R. (3d) 577 (C.A.), leave to appeal refused, [1993] 2 S.C.R. x

(*sub nom. R. du chef du Québec v. Ontario Securities Commission*); *Bennett v. British Columbia (Securities Commission)* (1992), 94 D.L.R. (4th) 339 (B.C.C.A.)).

...

[47] Canada bases its argument that the proposed Act is constitutional entirely on the s. 91(2) general trade and commerce power. It does not rely on the s. 91(2) power over interprovincial trade which gives Parliament the power to legislate on interprovincial and international aspects of securities. Nor does it invoke other heads of powers under the Constitution. The only question before us therefore is whether the Act can be supported under the general trade and commerce power.

...

[61] While flexibility and cooperation are important to federalism, they cannot override or modify the separation of powers. The Secession Reference affirmed federalism as an underlying constitutional principle that demands respect for the constitutional division of powers and the maintenance of a constitutional balance between federal and provincial powers.

[62] In summary, notwithstanding the Court's promotion of cooperative and flexible federalism, the constitutional boundaries that underlie the division of powers must be respected. The "dominant tide" of flexible federalism, however strong its pull may be, cannot sweep designated powers out to sea, nor erode the constitutional balance inherent in the Canadian federal state.

B. Pith and Substance and Double Aspect

[63] The "pith and substance" analysis is used by Canadian courts to determine the constitutional validity of legislation from a division of powers perspective. The analysis looks at the purpose and effects of the law to identify its "main thrust" as a first step in determining whether a law falls within a particular head of power (in this case the s. 91(2) general trade and commerce power). … Incidental effects may be discounted; the search is for the main thrust of the law.

[64] Intrinsic evidence, such as purpose clauses and the general structure of the statute, may reveal the purpose of a law. Extrinsic evidence, such as Hansard or other accounts of the legislative process, may also assist in determining a law's purpose. The *effects* of a law include the legal effect of the text as well as practical consequences of the application of the statute (*Lacombe*, at para. 20; *Kitkatla*, at para. 54).

[65] After analyzing the legislation's purpose and its effects to determine its main thrust, the inquiry turns to whether the legislation so characterized falls under the head of power said to support it—the classification stage (*Reference re Firearms Act (Can.)*, 2000 SCC 31, [2000] 1 S.C.R. 783, at para. 15). This may require interpretation of the scope of the power. If the main thrust of the legislation is properly classified as falling under a head of power assigned to the adopting level of government, the legislation is intra vires and valid.

[66] Canadian constitutional law has long recognized that the same subject or "matter" may possess both federal and provincial aspects. This means that a federal law may govern a matter from one perspective and a provincial law from another. The federal law pursues an objective that in pith and substance falls within Parliament's jurisdiction, while the provincial law pursues a different objective that falls within provincial jurisdiction (Canadian Western Bank, at para. 30). This concept, known as the double aspect doctrine, allows for

the concurrent application of both federal and provincial legislation, but it does not create concurrent jurisdiction over a matter (in the way, for example, s. 95 of the Constitution Act, 1867 does for agriculture and immigration).

[67] Canada argues that the main thrust of the proposed Act brings it within the general branch of Parliament's jurisdiction over trade and commerce. It is to this head of power that we now turn.

VI. Section 91(2): The Federal Trade and Commerce Power

[68] Canada contends that securities have evolved in a way that brings the entire field of securities regulation under the general branch of the s. 91(2) trade and commerce power, even if some aspects also fall under provincial competence in relation to property and civil rights in the province. To support this contention, Canada seeks to establish that the main thrust of the Act falls under the s. 91(2) general trade and commerce power. As noted earlier, Canada grounds its submission in support of the Act's constitutionality entirely on this power.

[69] As discussed in the preceding section, as a general rule, determining the validity of a statute proceeds in two steps: (1) identifying the main thrust of the legislation having regard to its purpose and effects; and (2) asking whether the main thrust falls under the head of power said to support it. In this case, the validity of the Act ultimately comes down to the breadth of the general branch of the federal trade and commerce power under s. 91(2) of the *Constitution Act, 1867*. We therefore turn next to the jurisprudence on s. 91(2).

[70] On its face, the general trade and commerce power (as distinguished from the more specific federal power to regulate interprovincial and international trade and commerce) is broad—so broad that it has the potential to permit federal duplication (and, in cases of conflict, evisceration) of the provincial powers over large aspects of property and civil rights and local matters. This would upset the constitutional balance envisaged by ss. 91 and 92 and undermine the federalism principle. To avoid this result, the trade and commerce power has been confined to matters that are genuinely national in scope and qualitatively distinct from those falling under provincial heads of power relating to local matters and property and civil rights. The essence of the general trade and commerce power is its national focus.

[71] In the delineation of the scope of the general trade and commerce power, courts have been guided by fundamental underlying constitutional principles. The Canadian federation rests on the organizing principle that the orders of government are coordinate and not subordinate one to the other. As a consequence, a federal head of power cannot be given a scope that would eviscerate a provincial legislative competence. This is one of the principles that underlies the Constitution (*Secession Reference*, at para. 58, citing *Re the Initiative and Referendum Act*, [1919] A.C. 935 (P.C.), at p. 942).

[72] The jurisprudence on the general trade and commerce power reflects this fundamental principle. An overly expansive interpretation of the federal trade and commerce power under s. 91(2) not only would subsume many more specific federal heads of power (e.g., federal power over banking (s. 91(15)), weights and measures (s. 91(17)), bills of exchange and promissory notes (s. 91(18))), but, more importantly, would have the potential to duplicate and perhaps displace, through the paramountcy doctrine, the clear provincial powers over local matters and property and civil rights which embrace trade and commerce in the province. Duff J. (as he then was) expressed this concern in the

following manner in *Lawson v. Interior Tree Fruit and Vegetable Committee of Direction*, [1931] S.C.R. 357:

> The scope which might be ascribed to head 2, s. 91 (if the natural meaning of the words, divorced from their context, were alone to be considered), has necessarily been limited, in order to preserve from serious curtailment, if not from virtual extinction, the degree of autonomy which … the provinces were intended to possess. [p. 366]

[73] The circumscribed scope of the general trade and commerce power can also be linked to another facet of federalism—the recognition of the diversity and autonomy of provincial governments in developing their societies within their respective spheres of jurisdiction. As stated in the *Secession Reference*, "[t]he federal structure of our country also facilitates democratic participation by distributing power to the government thought to be most suited to achieving the particular societal objective having regard to this diversity" (para. 58).

[74] Thus, the starting point is that the general trade and commerce power under s. 91(2) does not encompass all trade and commerce; the power is necessarily circumscribed. At the same time, failure to give meaningful scope to the general trade and commerce power would violate the notion of balance between the federal and provincial orders of government inherent in the division of powers and impermissibly amend the Constitution.

• • •

[80] In *General Motors*, the issue was the constitutionality of a civil right of action conferred by a provision of the federal *Combines Investigation Act*. Dickson C.J. delivered the opinion of the Court, upholding the right to a civil action and the statute generally under s. 91(2). Adopting his analysis in *Canadian National Transportation*, he emphasized the need to strike a balance between ss. 91(2) and 92(13). He went on to suggest five indicia of federal competence: (1) whether the impugned law is part of a general regulatory scheme; (2) whether the scheme is under the oversight of a regulatory agency; (3) whether the legislation is concerned with trade as a whole rather than with a particular industry; (4) whether it is of such a nature that provinces, acting alone or in concert, would be constitutionally incapable of enacting it; and (5) whether the legislative scheme is such that the failure to include one or more provinces or localities in the scheme would jeopardize its successful operation in other parts of the country (pp. 661-62).

[81] Dickson C.J. explained that where the general trade and commerce power is advanced as a ground of constitutional validity, a "careful case by case analysis remains appropriate" (*General Motors*, at p. 663). He further cautioned that the indicia of validity are not exhaustive, nor is it necessary that they be present in every case (pp. 662-63). He noted that the final three share a common theme—namely "that the scheme of regulation [must be] national in scope and that local regulation would be inadequate" (p. 678). He held that the regulation of competition met the test because it was not an issue of purely local concern but "one of crucial importance for the national economy" (p. 678). If the federal government were not able to legislate, there would be a gap, in practical effect, in the distribution of legislative powers.

[82] This Court confirmed this approach in *Kirkbi AG v. Ritvik Holdings Inc.*, 2005 SCC 65, [2005] 3 S.C.R. 302, holding, *per* LeBel J., that the federal *Trade-marks Act*, R.S.C.

1985, c. T-13, was concerned with trade as a whole rather than trade within a particular industry, since trademarks "apply across and between industries in different provinces" (para. 29).

[83] When *Canadian National Transportation*, *General Motors* and *Kirkbi AG* are read together, a common theme emerges. Provided the law is part of a general regulatory scheme aimed at trade and commerce under oversight of a regulatory agency, it will fall under the general federal trade and commerce power if the matter regulated is genuinely national in importance and scope. To be genuinely national in importance and scope, it is not enough that the matter be replicated in all jurisdictions throughout the country. It must, to use the phrase in *General Motors*, be something that the provinces, acting either individually or in concert, could not effectively achieve. To put it another way, the situation must be such that if the federal government were not able to legislate, there would be a constitutional gap. Such a gap is constitutional anathema in a federation.

[84] The *General Motors* indicia continue to offer an appropriate analytical framework for addressing the question of whether a law is validly adopted under the general trade and commerce power. These indicia are not cast in stone and are interrelated and overlapping. The first two indicia may be viewed as directed at identifying the required formal structure: a federal regulatory scheme under the oversight of a regulator. The final three indicia go to whether federal regulation is constitutionally appropriate. They direct our attention to whether the matter is one of genuine national importance and scope that goes to trade as a whole in a way that is distinct from provincial concerns, thus invoking Parliament's unique ability to effectively deal with economic issues of this category.

[85] The result is a balanced approach that preserves a meaningful role for federal regulation under s. 91(2), without endangering "the very idea of the local" in provincial commercial regulation. The *General Motors* test asks whether the subject of a federal law presents a distinct federal aspect falling within the general branch of the trade and commerce power. Under the double aspect doctrine, federal legislation adopted from this distinct perspective will be constitutional even if the matter, considered from another perspective, also falls within a provincial head of power. In the end, the *General Motors* test is aimed at preserving the balance that lies at the heart of the principle of federalism, which demands that a federal head of power not be given such scope that it would eviscerate a provincial legislative competence.

...

VII. Application: Does the Proposed Act Fall Within Section 91(2)?

[91] Where particular provisions of a statute are challenged, the proper approach is to focus on the constitutionality of those provisions, read in the context of the statute as a whole (*General Motors*, *Kitkatla* and *Kirkbi AG*). Here, the issue, as framed by the reference question, is the constitutionality of a single, integrated regulatory scheme. It stands or falls as a whole. The question is whether the sum of its particular provisions, read together, falls within the general trade and commerce power, on the test set out above.

[92] To answer this question, we must identify the main thrust of the proposed legislation having regard to its purpose and effects, and then ask whether the scheme, thus characterized, meets the indicia set out in *General Motors*.

A. *The Purpose and Effects of the Act*

[93] The first step in the pith and substance analysis is to ascertain the purpose and effects of the Act, viewed as a single, comprehensive scheme.

[94] The task at this stage is not to determine conclusively whether the legislation is provincial or federal in nature—that is the ultimate question of the division of powers analysis—but only to ascertain its main thrust. In some cases, determining the main thrust of a law will be pivotal in terms of its ultimate constitutional validity. In others, validity may depend on close analysis of the constitutional power that is said to support it. As we will see, this case is of the latter sort. While we must ascertain what the Act seeks to do and does, saying at the outset that it is in pith and substance "national" or "federal" simply begs the final question.

[95] Turning first to purpose, the Act's preamble states that Canada intends to create a single Canadian securities regulator. This is consistent with previous proposals for such a body. As discussed earlier, the idea of a single Canadian securities regulator has been percolating for more than 50 years. The Act represents the culmination of sustained efforts towards unification of the provincial securities regulatory regimes. Section 9 of the proposed Act reveals the legislation's broader, underlying purposes: to provide investor protection, to foster fair, efficient and competitive capital markets and to contribute to the integrity and stability of Canada's financial system.

[96] The immediate object of the Act—to create a national securities regulator—does not shed much light on whether the subject matter of the Act is federal or provincial. It is equally consistent with the federal government's contention and with the contention of the opposing provinces that the Act is simply a provincial securities act writ large.

[97] The broader purposes set forth in s. 9 send a mixed message. One goal is investor protection, which, without more, has historically been a provincial responsibility under s. 92(13). Another goal is to foster fair, efficient and competitive capital markets. Opponents of the Act argue that these are properly provincial responsibilities. The federal government, on the other hand, argues that fostering fair, efficient and competitive capital markets, viewed from a pan-Canadian perspective, also falls under the general trade and commerce power. The third stated goal—to contribute to the integrity and stability of Canada's financial system—also has a federal aspect.

[98] This brings us to the effects of the proposed federal scheme. We must look not only at the direct effects of the legislation, but also at the follow-through effects the legislation may be expected to produce (*Kitkatla*).

[99] The direct effect of the proposed Act is to establish a federal securities regulation scheme. If implemented as contemplated, all provinces and territories will eventually join the scheme. This will produce follow-through effects. Once a sufficient number of jurisdictions opt in, the current provincial and territorial securities regulation schemes will be effectively displaced. Indeed, in order to be included in the comprehensive regulatory scheme created by the Act, provinces and territories must suspend their own securities laws. The follow-through effects of the proposed Act will therefore be to subsume the existing provincial and territorial legislative schemes governing securities under the federal regulation scheme.

[100] A detailed look at the provisions of the Act confirms that once in place, it will regulate many matters which Canada concedes also fall within the provincial power over

property and civil rights under s. 92(13). Parts 1 and 2 establish regulatory oversight mechanisms. These are followed by a number of provisions broadly pertaining to the registration of persons. To this end, Part 3 of the Act gives the Chief Regulator the power to recognize a person as a self-regulatory organization, an exchange, a clearing agency and an auditor oversight organization (s. 64). These bodies must in turn regulate standards of practice and business conduct of participants in the securities industry (s. 66). Part 4, in similar vein, provides the Chief Regulator with the authority to designate a person as a credit rating organization, an investor compensation fund, a dispute resolution service, an information processor, a trade repository or another entity that provides a market participant with prescribed services (s. 73). Designation engages information sharing duties (s. 74). Part 5 requires registration of dealers, advisers and investment fund managers (s. 76). Parts 6, 7, 8 and 9 deal with the registration of securities, public information on securities and the monitoring of securities and issuers. Other provisions of the Act set standards for trading. For instance, Part 10 prohibits misrepresentations (s. 114), market manipulation (s. 116), insider trading (s. 117(1)), tipping (s. 117(2)) and other unfair practices. It also contains certain standards of conduct and obligations to avoid conflicts of interest that pertain to registered persons (see, e.g., ss. 109 to 113). Finally, Part 11 locks these routine regulatory provisions in place by establishing a scheme for the administration and enforcement of the Act.

[101] The effect of these provisions is in essence to duplicate legislative schemes enacted by provincial legislators exercising their jurisdiction over property and civil rights under s. 92(13) of the *Constitution Act*, 1867.

[102] Against this, Canada argues that what appears, on superficial inspection, to be duplication of provincial legislation is in fact directed at distinct federal concerns—preserving fair, efficient and competitive capital markets throughout Canada and ensuring the integrity and stability of Canada's financial system. Duplication of provincial provisions, Canada correctly points out, does not mean that there is no federal aspect that can support the Act. Moreover, Canada argues that the Act is not merely duplicative. It includes provisions that go beyond provincial powers. For example, it contains provisions for the control of systemic risk and for data collection on a nationwide basis, something Canada argues cannot be accomplished at the provincial level.

[103] Systemic risks have been defined as "risks that occasion a 'domino effect' whereby the risk of default by one market participant will impact the ability of others to fulfil their legal obligations, setting off a chain of negative economic consequences that pervade an entire financial system" (M.J. Trebilcock, *National Securities Regulator Report* (2010), Reference Record, vol. I, 222, at para. 26). By definition, such risks can be evasive of provincial boundaries and usual methods of control. The proposed legislation is aimed in part at responding to systemic risks threatening the Canadian market viewed as a whole. Without attempting an exhaustive enumeration, the following provisions of the proposed Act would appear to address or authorize the adoption of regulations directed at systemic risk: ss. 89 and 90 relating to derivatives, s. 126(1) on short-selling, s. 73 on credit rating, s. 228(4)(c) relating to urgent regulations and ss. 109 and 224 on data collection and sharing.

[104] The expert evidence adduced by Canada provides support for the view that systemic risk is an emerging reality, ill-suited to local legislation. Prevention of systemic risk may trigger the need for a national regulator empowered to issue orders that are valid

throughout Canada and impose common standards, under which provincial governments can work to ensure that their market will not transmit any disturbance across Canada or elsewhere.

[105] The emphasis in the proposed Act on nationwide data collection may similarly be seen as aimed at anticipating and identifying risks that may transcend the boundaries of a specific province. By analogy with Statistics Canada, it might be argued that broad national data-collecting powers may serve the national interest in a way that finds no counterpart on the provincial plane.

[106] Against this background, we return to the question at hand: What is the main thrust of the proposed *Securities Act*? The purpose of the proposed Act, we have seen, is to implement a comprehensive Canadian regime for the regulation of securities with a view to investor protection, the promotion of fair, efficient and competitive capital markets and ensuring the integrity and stability of the financial system. The effects of the proposed Act would be to duplicate and displace the existing provincial and territorial securities regimes, replacing them with a new federal regulatory scheme. Thus, the main thrust of the Act is to regulate, on an exclusive basis, all aspects of securities trading in Canada, including the trades and occupations related to securities in each of the provinces.

[107] These conclusions do not, however, permit us to connect the Act to a particular head of power, federal or provincial. To do that, we must ask whether, applying the *General Motors* factors, the legislation, viewed as a whole, addresses a matter that is truly national in importance and scope and that transcends provincial competence.

B. Classification: Does the Act Fall Within the General Trade and Commerce Power?

[108] To recap, the General Motors test frames the inquiry into whether a legislative scheme falls within the general trade and commerce power in terms of the following non-exclusive indicia: (1) Is the law part of a general regulatory scheme?; (2) Is the scheme under the oversight of a regulatory agency? (3) Is the law concerned with trade as a whole rather than with a particular industry? (4) Is the scheme of such a nature that the provinces, acting alone or in concert, would be constitutionally incapable of enacting it? (5) Would failure to include one or more provinces or localities in the scheme jeopardize its successful operation in other parts of the country?

[109] The *General Motors* indicia invite the Court to examine the legislative scheme through the lens of five interrelated inquiries to determine whether, viewed in its entirety, it addresses a matter of genuine national importance and scope that goes to trade as a whole in a way that is distinct from provincial concerns. The inquiry focuses on the nature of the proposed scheme and its purpose and effects, intended and actual. It is contextual, grounded in the record and the legislative facts. With this in mind, we turn to the *General Motors* indicia.

[110] The first two *General Motors* indicia need not detain us. Clearly they are met. The Act would institute a national regulatory regime for securities across Canada. The new national regulatory scheme for securities would feature a Council of Ministers; the Canadian Securities Regulatory Authority (composed of a Regulatory Division headed by the Chief Regulator and an independent Canadian Securities Tribunal headed by a Chief Adjudicator); a Regulatory Policy Forum; and an investor advisory panel. Indeed,

all parties agree that the Act would create a federal regulatory scheme under the oversight of a regulator.

[111] This leaves the third, fourth and fifth *General Motors* inquiries. These questions take us to the concern that lies at the heart of this case—whether Canada has shown that the proposed Act, viewed as a whole, addresses a matter of national importance and scope, distinct from provincial concerns. Is the proposed Act concerned with trade as a whole rather than with a particular industry? Do the provinces possess the constitutional capacity, acting alone or in concert, to achieve the objectives of the scheme? Finally, would the failure to include one or more provinces frustrate the success of the scheme? If the answers to these questions support the conclusion that the proposed Act falls within the general branch of the trade and commerce power, the double aspect doctrine applies, the balance between the federal and provincial powers required by the federalism principle is satisfied and the proposed law may be validly enacted by Parliament. We now turn to the final three *General Motors* inquiries.

[112] The third question is whether the proposed Act is directed at trade as a whole rather than at a particular industry. This requires us to look at both the purpose and the effects of the Act. Opponents of the Act argue that it is aimed at a particular industry—the securities industry. From their perspective, economic activity consisting of the trading in securities represents a specific industry. They are correct to state that, on their face, the provisions of the proposed Act aimed at government registration and the day-to-day conduct of brokers or investment advisers are not obviously related to trade as a whole.

[113] Canada argues, however, that the proposed Act goes beyond these matters. It sees the Act as fostering a fair, efficient and competitive national capital market and contributing to the integrity and stability of Canada's financial system. Moreover, Canada points out that the securities market is a mechanism for channelling capital from suppliers to consumers and that the capital transferred is applied throughout the Canadian economy in innumerable areas of activity. The securities market thus has a pervasive and significant impact throughout the national economy. It is a pillar of the economy of immense importance to the country as a whole. Regulating this market, Canada argues, relates to trade as a whole and is not an industry-specific matter.

[114] We accept that preservation of capital markets to fuel Canada's economy and maintain Canada's financial stability is a matter that goes beyond a particular "industry" and engages "trade as a whole" within the general trade and commerce power as contemplated by the *General Motors* test. Legislation aimed at imposing minimum standards applicable throughout the country and preserving the stability and integrity of Canada's financial markets might well relate to trade as a whole. However, the proposed Act reaches beyond such matters and descends into the detailed regulation of all aspects of trading in securities, a matter that has long been viewed as provincial. In justifying the reach of the Act, Canada argues that while securities trading may once have been mainly a local matter, it has evolved to become a matter of transcendent national concern that brings it within the s. 91(2) general trade and commerce power.

[115] No doubt, much of Canada's capital market is interprovincial and indeed international. Trade in securities is not confined to 13 provincial and territorial enclaves. Equally, however, capital markets also exist within provinces that meet the needs of local businesses and investors. While it is obvious that the securities market is of great importance to modern economic activity, we cannot ignore that the provinces have been deeply engaged

in the regulation of this market over the course of many years. To make its case, Canada must present the Court with a factual matrix that supports its assertion of a constitutionally significant transformation such that regulating every aspect of securities trading is no longer an industry-specific matter, but now relates, in its entirety, to trade as a whole.

[116] A long-standing exercise of power does not confer constitutional authority to legislate, nor does the historic presence of the provinces in securities regulation preclude a federal claim to regulatory jurisdiction (see *Ontario Hydro v. Ontario (Labour Relations Board)*, [1993] 3 S.C.R. 327, at p. 357, *per* Lamer C.J.). Nevertheless, the fact remains that Canada must establish that the Act, read as a whole, addresses concerns that transcend local, provincial interests. Canada's argument is that this area of economic activity has been so transformed that it now falls to be regulated under a different head of power. This argument requires not mere conjecture, but evidentiary support. The legislative facts adduced by Canada in this reference do not establish the asserted transformation. On the contrary, the fact that the structure and terms of the proposed Act largely replicate the existing provincial schemes belies the suggestion that the securities market has been wholly transformed over the years. On the basis of the record presented to us, we conclude, as discussed below, that the day-to-day regulation of securities within the provinces, which represents the main thrust of the Act, remains essentially a matter of property and civil rights within the provinces and therefore subject to provincial power.

[117] Aspects of the Act, for example those aimed at management of systemic risk and at national data collection, appear to be directly related to the larger national goals which the Act proclaims are its *raison d'être*. However, important as these elements are, they do not, on the record before us, justify a complete takeover of provincial regulation. Individuals engaged in the securities business are still, for the most part, exercising a trade or occupation within the province. On the record before us, we are unable to accept Canada's assertion that the securities market has been so transformed as to make the day-to-day regulation of all aspects of trading in securities a matter of national concern. For example, the record does not support a necessary link between the national interest in fair, efficient and competitive capital markets and the registration requirements applicable to a securities dealer in Saskatchewan or Quebec. Viewing the Act as a whole, we conclude that it overreaches the proper scope of the general branch of the trade and commerce power descending well into industry-specific regulation. The wholesale displacement of provincial regulation it would effect is not justified by the national concerns that Canada raises.

[118] The fourth *General Motors* consideration addresses the constitutional capacity of the provinces and territories to enact a similar scheme acting in concert. The provinces opposing the Act argue that if there is a national interest in both fair, efficient and competitive capital markets and the need to provide an effective national response to systemic risk, they can meet it by legislating in concert. No doubt the provinces possess constitutional capacity to enact uniform legislation on most of the administrative matters covered by the federal Act, like registration requirements and the regulation of participants' conduct. By way of administrative delegation, they could delegate provincial regulatory powers to a single pan-Canadian regulator.

[119] The difficulty with the provinces' argument, however, is that, as a matter of constitutional principle, neither Parliament nor the legislatures can, by ordinary legislation, fetter themselves against some future legislative action (P.W. Hogg, *Constitutional Law of Canada* (5th ed. Supp.), vol. 1, at pp. 12-8 ff.). Inherently sovereign, the provinces

will always retain the ability to resile from an interprovincial scheme and withdraw an initial delegation to a single regulator. This may not be problematic in many areas. Indeed, it is in the nature of a federation that different provinces adopt their own unique approaches consistent with their unique priorities when addressing social or economic issues.

[120] The provinces' inherent prerogative to resile from an interprovincial scheme aimed for example at managing systemic risk limits their constitutional capacity to achieve the truly national goals of the proposed federal Act. The point is not that the provinces are constitutionally or practically unable to adopt legislation aimed at systemic risk *within* the provinces. Indeed, some provincial securities schemes contain provisions analogous to the ones aimed at systemic risk found in the proposed Act. The point is simply that because provinces could always withdraw from an interprovincial scheme there is no assurance that they could effectively address issues of national systemic risk and competitive national capital markets on a sustained basis.

[121] It follows that the fourth *General Motors* question must be answered, at least partially, in the negative. The provinces, acting in concert, lack the constitutional capacity to sustain a viable national scheme aimed at genuine national goals such as management of systemic risk or Canada-wide data collection. This supports the view that a federal scheme aimed at such matters might well be qualitatively different from what the provinces, acting alone or in concert, could achieve.

[122] However, this only takes Canada so far. Canada's problem is that the proposed Act reflects an attempt that goes well beyond these matters of undoubted national interest and concern and reaches down into the detailed regulation of all aspects of securities. In this respect, the proposed Act is unlike federal competition legislation, which has been held to fall under s. 91(2) of the *Constitution Act, 1867*. It would regulate *all* aspects of contracts for securities within the provinces, including all aspects of public protection and professional competence within the provinces. Competition law, by contrast, regulates only anti-competitive contracts and conduct—a particular aspect of economic activity that falls squarely within the federal domain. In short, the proposed federal Act overreaches the legislative interest of the federal government.

[123] The fifth and final *General Motors* inquiry is whether the absence of a province from the scheme would prevent its effective operation. On lesser regulatory matters the answer might well be no. However, when it comes to genuine national goals, related to fair, efficient and competitive markets and the integrity and stability of Canada's financial system, including national data collection and prevention of and response to systemic risks, the answer must be yes—much for the reasons discussed under the fourth question. On these matters a federal regime would be qualitatively different from a voluntary interprovincial scheme. Viewed as a whole, however, because the main thrust of the proposed Act is concerned with the day-to-day regulation of securities, the proposed Act would not founder if a particular province declined to participate in the federal scheme. Incidentally, we note that the opt-in feature of the scheme, on its face, contemplates the possibility that not all provinces will participate. This weighs against Canada's argument that the success of its proposed legislation requires the participation of all the provinces.

[124] Against the backdrop of these considerations, we come to the ultimate question—whether the Act, viewed in its entirety, addresses a matter of genuine national importance and scope going to trade as a whole in a way that is distinct and different from provincial concerns.

[125] The provisions of the proposed Act, viewed as a whole, compel a negative response. The Act chiefly regulates contracts and property matters within each of the provinces and territories, overlain by some measures directed at the control of the Canadian securities market as a whole that may transcend intraprovincial regulation of property and civil rights. A federal scheme adopted from the latter, distinctly federal, perspective would fall within the circumscribed scope of the general trade and commerce power. But the provisions of the Act that relate to these concerns, although perhaps valid on their own, cannot lend constitutional validity to the full extent of the proposed Act. Based on the record before us, the day-to-day regulation of all aspects of trading in securities and the conduct of those engaged in this field of activity that the Act would sweep into the federal sphere simply cannot be described as a matter that is truly national in importance and scope making it qualitatively different from provincial concerns.

[126] The conclusion that the Act's attempt to take over regulation of the entirety of the securities trade in Canada exceeds the general branch of the trade and commerce power is also supported by the tenor of the case law. While the jurisprudence acknowledges that securities regulation may possess federal aspects, it has generally viewed basic securities regulation within the provinces as a local matter of property and civil rights (*Lymburn*; *Multiple Access*; *Duplain v. Cameron*, [1961] S.C.R. 693; *Smith v. The Queen*; *Ontario Securities Commission*; *Global Securities*).

[127] A review of the expert evidence does not lead to a different conclusion. We do not find it necessary or helpful to set out a detailed analysis of the many reports filed on both sides of the issue. For reasons already discussed, arguments in the reports as to whether securities should be regulated federally or provincially as a matter of policy are irrelevant to the constitutional validity of the legislation. A reasonable reading of the reports suggests that routine securities regulation is mainly concerned with the regulation of securities as an industry. It also confirms the local nature of much of Canada's securities industry. J.-M. Suret and C. Carpentier, for example, point to different focuses and specializations from province to province (*Securities Regulation in Canada: Re-examination of Arguments in Support of a Single Securities Commission* (2010), Reference Record, vol. IX, 8). Mining listings compose approximately two thirds of the securities market in British Columbia. About half of Ontario's securities market is attributable to large financial services companies. Alberta is the dominant national market for oil and gas and roughly a quarter of technology listings emanate from Quebec.

[128] To summarize, we accept that the economic importance and pervasive character of the securities market may, in principle, support federal intervention that is qualitatively different from what the provinces can do. However, as important as the preservation of capital markets and the maintenance of Canada's financial stability are, they do not justify a wholesale takeover of the regulation of the securities industry which is the ultimate consequence of the proposed federal legislation. The need to prevent and respond to systemic risk may support federal legislation pertaining to the national problem raised by this phenomenon, but it does not alter the basic nature of securities regulation which, as shown, remains primarily focused on local concerns of protecting investors and ensuring the fairness of the markets through regulation of participants. Viewing the Act as a whole, as we must, these local concerns remain the main thrust of the legislation—its pith and substance.

[129] This is not a case of a valid federal scheme that incidentally intrudes on provincial powers. It is not the incidental effects of the scheme that are constitutionally suspect; it is rather the main thrust of the legislation that goes beyond the federal power. The federal government properly did not invoke the ancillary powers doctrine. To apply that doctrine, the proposed statute considered as a whole must be valid—which it is not. We further note that we have not been asked for our opinion on the extent of Parliament's legislative authority over securities regulation under other heads of federal power or indeed the interprovincial or international trade branch of s. 91(2).

[130] While the proposed Act must be found ultra vires Parliament's general trade and commerce power, a cooperative approach that permits a scheme that recognizes the essentially provincial nature of securities regulation while allowing Parliament to deal with genuinely national concerns remains available.

[131] The various proposals advanced over the years to develop a new model for regulating securities in Canada suggest that this matter possesses both central and local aspects. The same insight can be gleaned from the experience of other federations, even if each country has its own constitutional history and imperatives. The common ground that emerges is that each level of government has jurisdiction over some aspects of the regulation of securities and each can work in collaboration with the other to carry out its responsibilities.

[132] It is not for the Court to suggest to the governments of Canada and the provinces the way forward by, in effect, conferring in advance an opinion on the constitutionality on this or that alternative scheme. Yet we may appropriately note the growing practice of resolving the complex governance problems that arise in federations, not by the bare logic of either/or, but by seeking cooperative solutions that meet the needs of the country as a whole as well as its constituent parts.

[133] Such an approach is supported by the Canadian constitutional principles and by the practice adopted by the federal and provincial governments in other fields of activities. The backbone of these schemes is the respect that each level of government has for each other's own sphere of jurisdiction. Cooperation is the animating force. The federalism principle upon which Canada's constitutional framework rests demands nothing less.

VIII. Conclusion

[134] The *Securities Act* as presently drafted is not valid under the general branch of the federal power to regulate trade and commerce under s. 91(2) of the *Constitution Act, 1867*.

Judgment accordingly.

QUESTIONS

1. Do you agree with the Supreme Court's reasoning in this judgment? Why didn't the ability of provinces to opt out of the scheme have a more persuasive force in the court's decision?

2. Do you think the federal government would have had more success if it argued the first (rather than the second) branch of the trade and commerce power, given that the court found that much of Canada's capital market is interprovincial and international?

3. The Supreme Court held that the provinces, acting in concert, lack the constitutional capacity to sustain a viable national scheme aimed at genuine national goals such as management of systemic risk or Canada-wide data collection, but held that the proposed Act went well beyond these matters of national interest and reached down into the detailed regulation of all aspects of securities. In your view, how can securities regulators proceed, given these seemingly intractable challenges?

4. Consider the Supreme Court's decision from the perspective of the intellectual frameworks discussed in the introduction to this book. How would this decision be analyzed from the law and economics perspective? How would someone interested in interest group theory consider it?

III. CHARTER ISSUES

There have not been many challenges to securities law under the *Canadian Charter of Rights and Freedoms*. In the few times that securities laws have been challenged under the Charter, the issues revolved around s 7 and s 13 rights being violated by having to testify against one's own interests; s 8 protection from "unreasonable search or seizure"; and s 11 for protections in criminal and penal proceedings.

One of the first securities law cases to deal with the Charter is *Sebastian v Saskatchewan Securities Commission* (1985), 39 Sask R 252 (QB). The case involved whether the right of the plaintiff guaranteed under s 7 of the Charter was violated by the securities commission making a "temporary" and a "permanent" order against the plaintiff, and whether its rights guaranteed under ss 7, 11(c), and 11(d) of the Charter were violated by being compelled to give evidence at the hearing conducted by the securities commission. McIntyre J of the Court of Queen's Bench was satisfied in this case that the procedures of the commission comply with the principles of fundamental justice. McIntyre J further held that the plaintiff was not charged with an offence at the hearing but was compelled to give evidence at a civil hearing; therefore, s 11 had no application.

In the following case, the appellants claimed that a provision of the British Columbia *Securities Act* violated ss 7 and 8 of the Charter. The British Columbia Securities Commission commenced an investigation into a company following a report by the company's auditors that disclosed questionable expenditures. The appellants, two of the officers of the company, were served with summonses compelling their attendance for examination under oath and requiring them to produce all information and records in their possession relating to the company. The summonses were issued pursuant to s 128(1) (now s 144(1)) of the province's *Securities Act*. When the appellants failed to appear, the commission petitioned the British Columbia Supreme Court for an order committing the appellants in contempt. In response, the appellants applied for a declaration to the effect that s 128(1) violates ss 7 and 8 of the *Canadian Charter of Rights and Freedoms*. The application was dismissed. The superior court judge rejected the appellants' claims in respect of the privilege against self-incrimination and of a right to remain silent under s 7. He also concluded that the seizure authorized by s 128(1)(c) of the *Securities Act* is not "unreasonable" within the meaning of s 8. The appellants were ordered to comply with the summonses or, in default, to show cause or be held in contempt. An appeal to the British Columbia Court of Appeal was dismissed.

British Columbia Securities Commission v Branch
[1995] 2 SCR 3

SOPINKA and IACOBUCCI JJ (Lamer CJ and La Forest, Cory, McLachlin, and Major JJ, concurring):

[2] In *S.(R.J.)*, a majority of this Court held that the principle against self-incrimination, one of the principles of fundamental justice protected by s. 7 of the *Canadian Charter of Rights and Freedoms*, requires that persons compelled to testify be provided with subsequent "derivative use immunity" in addition to the "use immunity" guaranteed by s. 13 of the *Charter*. In addition, a majority of the members of the Court (albeit a different majority) were of the view that courts could, in certain circumstances, grant exemptions from compulsion to testify

...

[7] In view of the conclusions reached in *S.(R.J.)*, any test to determine compellability must take into account that if the witness is compelled, he or she will be entitled to claim effective subsequent derivative use immunity with respect to the compelled testimony or other appropriate protection. The common feature of the respective compellability tests proposed in the reasons in *S.(R.J.)* is that the crucial question is whether the predominant purpose for seeking the evidence is to obtain incriminating evidence against the person compelled to testify or rather some legitimate public purpose. This test strikes the appropriate balance between the interests of the state in obtaining the evidence for a valid public purpose on the one hand, and the right to silence of the person compelled to testify on the other.

[8] In applying this test, the Court must first determine the predominant purpose for which the evidence is sought. To qualify as a valid public purpose, compelled testimony in a criminal prosecution or prosecution under a provincial statute must be for the purpose of obtaining evidence in furtherance of that prosecution. In *S.(R.J.)*, Sopinka J suggested some guidelines for determining whether this is the predominant purpose. In other proceedings, discerning the purpose is more complex. Where evidence is sought for the purpose of an inquiry, we must first look to the statute under which the inquiry is authorized. The fact that the purpose of inquiries under the statute may be for legitimate public purposes is not determinative. ...

[9] ... [I]f it is established that the predominant purpose is *not* to obtain the relevant evidence for the purpose of the instant proceeding, but rather to incriminate the witness, the party seeking to compel the witness must justify the potential prejudice to the right of the witness against self-incrimination. If it is shown that the only prejudice is the possible subsequent derivative use of the testimony then the compulsion to testify will occasion no prejudice for that witness. The witness will be protected against such use. ...

...

[30] The following constitutional questions were stated on February 25, 1993:

1. [Does] s. 128(1) of the *Securities Act*, SBC 1985, c. 83, infringe ss. 7 or 8 of the *Canadian Charter of Rights and Freedoms*?
2. If the answer is yes, is the limitation one which is reasonable, prescribed by law, and demonstrably justified pursuant to s. 1 of the *Charter*?

Analysis

1. *Section 7 of the Charter*

[31] This case is unlike *S.(R.J.)* in two respects. First, it is outside the criminal realm, and is within a regulatory regime. Secondly, since Bruce Branch and Pal Arthur Levitt are directors of Terra Nova, it must be discerned whether corporate officers may raise *Charter* violations.

[32] The s. 7 *Charter* challenge against s. 128(1) of the *Securities Act* involves two issues:

(a) testimonial compulsion; and
(b) documentary compulsion

[Only the first issue is examined.]

(a) Testimonial Compulsion

[33] … The liberty interest is engaged at the point of testimonial compulsion. Once it is engaged, the investigation then becomes whether or not there has been a deprivation of this interest in accordance with the principles of fundamental justice.

[34] The portion of s. 128(1) of the *Securities Act* which is relevant to testimonial compulsion reads as follows:

> 128(1) An investigator appointed under section 126 or 131 has the same power …
> (b) to compel witnesses to give evidence on oath or in any other manner. …

We must determine the predominant purpose of such an inquiry at which a witness is compelled to attend. In *Pezim v. British Columbia (Superintendent of Brokers)*, … Iacobucci J, writing for the Court referred to the regulatory nature of the *Securities Act* (at p. 589):

> It is important to note from the outset that the [*Securities Act*] is regulatory in nature. In fact, it is part of a much larger framework which regulates the securities industry throughout Canada. Its primary goal is the *protection of the investor* but other goals include *capital market efficiency* and *ensuring public confidence in the system*: David L. Johnston, *Canadian Securities Regulation* (1977), at p. 1. [Emphasis added.]

The goal of protecting our economy is a goal of paramount importance. In *Pezim*, the preeminence of securities regulation in our economic system was emphasized (at pp. 593 and 595):

> This protective role, common to all securities commissions, gives a special character to such bodies which must be recognized when assessing the way in which their functions are carried out under their Acts.
>
> …
>
> The breadth of the [British Columbia Securities] Commission's expertise and specialisation is reflected in the provisions of the [*Securities Act*]. Section 4 of the Act identifies the Commission as being responsible for the administration of the Act. The Commission also has broad powers with respect to investigations, audits, hearings and orders.
>
> …
>
> In reading these powerful provisions, it is clear that it was the legislature's intention to give the Commission a very broad discretion to determine what is in the public's interest. …

> It must also be noted that the definitions in the [*Securities Act*] exist in a factual or regulatory context. They are part of the larger regulatory framework discussed above. They are not to be analyzed in isolation but rather in their regulatory context.

[35] Clearly, this purpose of the Act justifies inquiries of limited scope. The Act aims to protect the public from unscrupulous trading practices which may result in investors being defrauded. It is designed to ensure that the public may rely on honest traders of good repute able to carry out their business in a manner that does not harm the market or society generally. An inquiry of this kind legitimately compels testimony as the Act is concerned with the furtherance of a goal which is of substantial public importance, namely, obtaining evidence to regulate the securities industry .... Hence, the predominant purpose of the inquiry is to obtain the relevant evidence for the purpose of the instant proceedings, and not to incriminate Branch and Levitt .... Both orders of the Commission and the summonses are in furtherance of the predominant purpose of the inquiry to which we refer above. The proposed testimony thus falls to be governed by the general rule applicable under the Charter, pursuant to which a witness is compelled to testify, yet receives evidentiary immunity in return: *S.(R.J.), supra.*

. . .

[37] Clearly, the individuals Branch and Levitt are entitled to claim the protection of subsequent derivative use. ...

. . .

2. *Section 8 of the Charter*

[49] To reiterate, the issue raised by this portion of the appeal is whether s. 128(1) of the *Securities Act* infringes s. 8 of the *Charter*. The foundation for a s. 8 analysis was laid by Dickson J (as he then was) in *Hunter v. Southam Inc.* .... As Dickson J stated, at pp. 159-60, one of the clear purposes of the *Charter* is the protection of the individual's reasonable expectation of privacy .... .

. . .

[51] ... It is clear that the context within which the alleged violation takes place must be considered, for it is the context which determines the expectation of privacy that is legitimately expected. ...

[52] ... The greater the departure from the realm of criminal law, the more flexible will be the approach to the standard of reasonableness. The application of a less strenuous approach to regulatory or administrative searches and seizures is consistent with a purposive approach to the elaboration of s. 8: *Thomson Newspapers.*

[53] While the expectation of privacy with respect to criminal matters seems certain, the standard of reasonableness to be applied in the regulatory and administrative realm is less well defined. Wilson J found in *McKinlay Transport*, at pp. 645-46, that the point was aptly made by A.D. Reid and A.H. Young in "Administrative Search and Seizure Under the Charter" (1985), 10 *Queen's LJ* 392, at pp. 398-99:

> There are facets of state authority, generically associated with search or seizure, that are so intertwined with the regulated activity as to raise virtually no expectation of privacy whatsoever. ... *Other activities are regulated so routinely that there is virtually no expectation of privacy from state intrusion. Annual filing requirements for banks, corporations, trust companies, loan companies, and the like are inextricably associated with carrying on business under state licence.*

> There are other situations in which government intrusion cannot be as confidently predicted, yet the range of discretion extended to state officials is so wide as to create in the regulatee an expectation that he may be inspected or requested to provide information at some point in the future. This may arise in the form of an inspection carried out either on a "spot check" basis, or on the strength of suspected non-compliance. The search may be in the form of a request for information that is not prescribed as an annual filing requirement, but is required to be produced on a demand basis. For the most part, there is no requirement that these powers be exercised on belief or suspicion of non-compliance.

[54] Thus, it is incumbent that an examination of the nature of the securities context be undertaken. As mentioned above, the primary goal of securities legislation is the protection of the investor, but other goals include capital market efficiency and ensuring public confidence in the system. …

[55] With this in mind, the obvious question becomes what degree of privacy can those subject to investigation under the British Columbia *Securities Act* reasonably expect in respect of activities and matters with which such investigations may be concerned. …

[56] … As we have already mentioned, the primary goal of securities regulation is the protection of the investing public. The importance of this goal, as against the reasonable expectation of privacy of securities traders, is what we are considering here. At this intersection, the words of our colleague, La Forest J, in *Thomson Newspapers*, *supra*, at pp. 506-7, ring particularly true:

> But the degree of privacy the citizen can reasonably expect may vary significantly depending upon the activity that brings him or her into contact with the state. In a modern industrial society, it is generally accepted that many activities in which individuals can engage must nevertheless to a greater or lesser extent be regulated by the state to ensure that the individual's pursuit of his or her self-interest is compatible with the community's interest in the realization of collective goals and aspirations. In many cases, this regulation must necessarily involve the inspection of private premises or documents by agents of the state. The restaurateur's compliance with public health regulations, the employer's compliance with employment standards and safety legislation, and the developer's or homeowner's compliance with building codes or zoning regulations, can only be tested by inspection, and perhaps unannounced inspection, of their premises. Similarly, compliance with minimum wage, employment equity and human rights legislation can often only be assessed by inspection of the employer's files and records.

[57] There are areas of business, for example, that are subject to regulation as a matter of course. Persons who carry on the business of trading in securities realize that the industry is heavily regulated and for good reason. It is a crucial part of our economy that is at stake. …

[58] In our opinion, persons involved in the business of trading securities do not have a high expectation of privacy with respect to regulatory needs that have been generally expressed in securities legislation. It is widely known and accepted that the industry is well regulated. Similarly, it is well known why the industry is so regulated. The appellants in this case were well aware of the dictates of the *Securities Act*. …

[59] … [T]he *Securities Act* is essentially a scheme of economic regulation which is designed to discourage detrimental forms of commercial behaviour. The provisions provided by the legislature are pragmatic sanctions designed to induce compliance with the Act.

After all, the Act is really aimed at regulating certain facets of the economy and business. This has obvious implications for the nation's material prosperity: *Thomson Newspapers*. As such, the effective implementation of securities legislation depends on the willingness of those who choose to engage in the securities trade to comply with the defined standards of conduct. In this respect, we fully agree with Wilson J's comments that "[a]t some point the individual's interest in privacy must give way to the broader state interest in having the information or document disclosed": *Thomson Newspapers*, at p. 495.

• • •

[62] … Documents produced in the course of a business which is regulated have a lesser privacy right attaching to them than do documents that are, strictly speaking, personal. …

[63] Therefore, we conclude that those who are ordered under s. 128(1) of the *Securities Act* "to produce records and things" can claim only a limited expectation of privacy in respect of these materials. The operative question becomes whether s. 128(1) unreasonably infringes on this limited expectation of privacy.

[64] In our view it does not. We have already mentioned that in a highly regulated industry, such as the securities market, the individual is aware, and accepts, justifiable state intrusions. All those who enter into this market know or are deemed to know the rules of the game. As such, an individual engaging in such activity has a low expectation of privacy in business records. …

• • •

[66] We would dismiss the appeal with costs.

In the following case, the Alberta Securities Commission Board issued a notice of hearing, to be held on March 31, 1988, seeking cease-trading orders against the appellants. The hearing proceeded on April 3 and 4, 1989 despite the appellants' absence, though they had notice of the proceedings. The board issued cease-trading orders in two cases for the life of the persons subject to them. On appeal to the Alberta Court of Appeal, the appellants challenged the validity of the cease-trading orders made against them, stating the Alberta Securities Commission violated their ss 11 and 13 Charter rights. The Alberta Court of Appeal held that the Charter did not apply to these proceedings because they were not the sort of "offence" proceedings to which ss 11 and 13 of the Charter were applicable.

Holoboff v Alberta (Securities Commission)
1991 ABCA 133

THE COURT: …

Facts

[4] The appellants have never been registered under s. 54 of the [*Securities Act*, SA 1981, c S-6.1,] or under its predecessors.

[5] On March 22, 1988, pursuant to ss. 165 and 166 of the Act, a notice of hearing to be held on March 31, 1988 was issued by the Alberta Securities Commission (the Commission) and served upon the appellants. The notice sought cease trading orders, a denial of exemptions and s. 21 interim relief.

[6] On March 31, 1988, the appellant, Jane Elizabeth Holoboff (Mrs. Holoboff), appeared before the Commission and applied for an adjournment. The application was not opposed and was granted. Section 21 interim relief although requested was denied.

[7] On April 14, 1988, the appellants were represented before the Commission by counsel who requested a further adjournment. This request was granted. Section 21 interim relief was also granted.

[8] On April 28, 1988, Mrs. Holoboff alone appeared and obtained a further adjournment so that Mr. Holoboff could be present. The Board at that time determined that the hearing had commenced on April 14th.

[9] On June 23, 1988, a further adjournment was granted.

[10] On December 23, 1988, a notice of continuation of hearing was issued for January 18, 1989. The hearing was again adjourned to April 3 and 4, 1989 to accommodate the appellants.

[11] On March 28, 1989, a certificate was issued pursuant to s. 189 of the Act. This certificate was signed by the deputy registrar of the Alberta Securities Commission Agency and stated, *inter alia*, that:

> None of the facts upon which the within proceedings are based came to the knowledge of the Alberta Securities Commission before an application was made for an Interim Order on March 31, 1988 at Calgary, Alberta.

[12] The hearing proceeded on April 3rd and 4th. It is conceded that the appellants and their counsel were served with notice of continuation. Neither the appellants nor anyone on their behalf appeared. We were advised by counsel appearing on behalf of the appellants before this court that the appellants' then counsel had advised them not to appear at the continuation of the hearing.

[13] Evidence was adduced before the Board in the form of taped and sworn telephone conversations, documents, affidavits, examinations for discovery from related civil actions and *viva voce* testimony. In its reasons the Board stated that it relied "primarily on the evidence of the three complainants who testified and on the documents identified by those three complainants."

Grounds of Appeal

[14] …

1. The cease trading orders imposed by the Board are "penal" in nature and thus the use in the hearings before the Board of sworn evidence from other proceedings contravenes s. 13 of the *Canadian Charter of Rights and Freedoms*. This contravention, it is argued, is not saved by s. 1 of the *Charter*. A similar position is taken by appellant's counsel with regard to s. 11 of the *Charter*.

• • •

I. Canadian Charter of Rights and Freedoms

[21] The proceedings before the Board did not expose the appellants to any criminal or quasi-criminal charges. They were not prosecutions and the remedies available did not include incarceration or monetary fines.

[22] The paramount objective of the Act is to protect the public. In *Brosseau v. Alberta Securities Commission* … , L'Heureux-Dubé J said at pp. 253 to 254:

> Securities Acts in general can be said to be aimed at regulating the market and protecting the general public. This role was recognized by this court in *Gregory & Co. Inc. v. Québec Securities Com'n* … , where Fauteux J observed:
>
>> The paramount object of the Act is to ensure that persons who, in the province, carry on the business of trading in securities or acting as investment counsel, shall be honest and of good repute and, in this way, to protect the public, in the Province or elsewhere, from being defrauded as a result of certain activities initiated in the Province by persons therein carrying on such a business.
>
> This protective role, common to all securities commissions, gives a special character to such bodies which must be recognized when assessing the way in which their functions are carried out under their Acts.

[23] In our view, the remedies imposed by the Board fall squarely within the principle enunciated by Wilson J in *R v. Wigglesworth* … , where she said at pp. 560-561:

> There is also a fundamental distinction between proceedings undertaken to promote public order and welfare within a public sphere of activity and proceedings undertaken to determine fitness to obtain or maintain a licence. Where disqualifications are imposed as part of a scheme for regulating an activity in order to protect the public, disqualification proceedings are not the sort of "offence" proceedings to which s. 11 is applicable.

[24] The proceedings before the Board did not violate s. 11 or s. 13 of the Charter.

In sum, unlike the law relating to division of powers, there have been very few cases based on the Charter. While this lacuna may be a function of the Charter's relative youth, it is also because of the types of grievances or wrongs that occur in the capital markets area. For example, s 7 challenges tend to fail because most remedies do not threaten life, liberty, or security of the person.[1] The s 8 Charter cases have focused on the regulators' broad powers to investigate, including to search and seize. We saw in *Branch* that the standard of reasonableness depends on the circumstances of the case. In any event, the search and seizure power is rarely used relative to other methods of investigation.[2] The one area that may be the subject of legal discussion in the years to come is found in ss 11 and 13. As we saw in *Holoboff*, the appellants challenged the validity of cease-trading orders made against them, arguing that the provincial commission violated their ss 11 and 13 rights. The Alberta Court of Appeal held that the Charter did not apply because there were no criminal or quasi-criminal charges, no prosecutions, and no possibility of incarceration. Thus, in terms of future Charter challenges, much will depend on the enforcement route taken by regulators and others. If the proceeding is criminal or quasi-criminal, it may be that ss 11 and 13 will be activated.

1 Kathleen Doyle Rockwell, David Johnston & Cristie Ford, *Canadian Securities Regulation*, 5th ed (Markham, Ont: LexisNexis Canada, 2014) 141.

2 However, for an important decision involving the intersection of investigations, search and seizure, and s 7, see the discussion of *R v Jarvis*, 2002 SCC 73, [2002] 3 SCR 757 in Chapter 11.

QUESTIONS

1. As you have no doubt seen in your other law school courses, Charter litigation is very much interest-group based. Which interests compete in the securities law sphere?
2. Some of the Charter challenges discussed here deal with the property of an individual, not in the sense of land or real estate, but in regard to documents and other records (see *Branch*). Should individuals be entitled to privacy over the types of things that are pertinent to trading in the capital markets?
3. Why do you think most of the constitutional issues that have arisen in securities regulation relate to division of powers as opposed to Charter rights?

The Future of Canadian Securities Regulation

As you have seen in this chapter, the Supreme Court held in the *Securities Reference* that the proposed federal *Securities Act* was not valid under the general branch of the federal power to regulate trade and commerce under s 91(2) of the *Constitution Act, 1867*. The court also gave an extensive summary of the history of legislative reform of securities law in Canada, including a number of setbacks and obstacles to creating a national or integrated securities law regime. Most interestingly, despite the holding in the case, the court suggested that a cooperative approach to securities regulation could pass constitutional muster. Such an approach would recognize the essentially provincial nature of day-to-day securities regulation while allowing Parliament to deal with genuinely national concerns such as minimizing systemic risk and performing national data collection.

Since the *Securities Reference*, Canadian regulators have still been unable to reach a final agreement on a cooperative approach. However, six provincial and territorial regulators, from British Columbia, Ontario, Saskatchewan, New Brunswick, Prince Edward Island, and Yukon, have joined with the federal government to propose a Cooperative Capital Markets Regulatory System. Under this regime, each of the provinces and territories would enact a uniform *Capital Markets Act* (CMA) while the federal government would enact a *Capital Markets Stability Act* (CMSA). The specific provisions of these two draft statutes are discussed in the chapters that follow. Administration of both statutes would be delegated to a common regulator—the Capital Markets Regulatory Authority (CMRA).

Although this approach is promising, and consistent with the Supreme Court's dicta in the *Securities Reference*, numerous obstacles remain. The CMA and CMSA are subject to legislative approval and will not become law unless introduced in, and enacted by, the Parliament of Canada and, in the case of the CMA, the legislatures of the participating provincial and territorial jurisdictions. Drafting these statutes has been a long and careful process with significant opportunity for comment from stakeholders. For example, although the first draft of the CMSA was released in 2014, the federal government has revised it after an extensive period of public comment. The latest draft was released in May 2016. Furthermore, because Alberta and Québec are opposed to the proposed regime, constitutional challenges are likely. In fact, Québec has already referred two questions about the constitutionality of the draft federal statute to the Court of Appeal of Québec. Participating jurisdictions are actively engaged in finalizing proposed legislation to establish jointly the Capital Markets Regulatory Authority, which would administer the CMA, the federal *Capital Markets Stability Act* and the initial regulations. In addition, implementation legislation is being developed to ensure a smooth transition to the new regime and to integrate the new regime into the general laws of each participating province and territory.

IV. CHAPTER SUMMARY

This chapter introduced students to the history of securities regulation in Canada and some of the constitutional issues that are inherent in the regulatory regime. The themes raised in this chapter will appear repeatedly throughout the book. They include the importance of protecting investors in securities regulation; the push of the provinces to retain the jurisdiction over securities transactions; and finally, the tension in Canada over the structure of the regulatory regime and any new structure that may be implemented. Students should note the reappearance of these themes throughout the book and indeed note that transformations in the securities regulatory regime seem to be taking shape.

CHAPTER THREE

Regulators and Types of Markets

I. INTRODUCTION: THE ECONOMICS OF REGULATION

Chapter 2 discussed the historical development of securities regulation and the constitutional issues underpinning the current system. In regulating the activities of issuers, the securities regime sets the framework for how securities are offered and traded, disclosure standards, proxy rules, and protection against insider and other self-dealing transactions. These provisions are aimed at fostering fair and efficient capital markets, creating transparency and confidence in capital markets, and providing protection to investors from unfair, improper, or fraudulent practices. This chapter examines types of markets and securities regulators and discusses recent regulatory reform initiatives. Readers will also learn about Canada's somewhat unique regulatory system in which numerous regulators supervise the capital markets within their constitutionally granted jurisdictions, as well as ways in which the costs of such a system have been controlled by interjurisdictional cooperation. Finally, the chapter provides a comparative view of developments in Canada with two major securities regulators, the United States and the European Union.

Controversy has surrounded the regulation of trading in securities markets since the first national regulation was implemented in the United States as part of the New Deal in the 1930s. The issue is often cast as whether or not the market can achieve maximum "efficiency" with any particular form of regulation. That debate has received renewed vigour with the recent crises in financial markets globally. The policy debate raises the issue of the role of regulators in tempering or preventing market excesses and enhancing efficiency. Efficiency, in this context, must encompass two somewhat contradictory goals. The first is to limit regulatory intervention in order to control transaction costs associated with capital formation and investment. The second is to impose sufficient regulation in order to ensure a certain level of investor protection. The role of disclosure as a primary tool of regulation exemplifies this debate. There has long been a belief that where there is disclosure of all information relevant to the pricing of securities, market participants are able to make informed investment decisions, but increased levels of disclosure are inevitably costly for issuers and may inhibit their ability to participate in regulated markets. The role or purpose of regulation of securities markets continues to be a fundamental source of disagreement. Contrast the views of these legal scholars.

Cynthia A Williams, "The Securities and Exchange Commission and Corporate Social Transparency"
(1999) 112 Harv L Rev 1197 at 1209-11

On examination, Congress adopted mandatory disclosure in the federal securities laws to advance a number of distinct purposes. One of the major purposes of disclosure was to prevent fraud by corporate issuers and underwriters in the initial sale and subsequent trading of securities. Another purpose was to promote market efficiency so that the prices of securities would more accurately reflect the underlying values of the securities. In the case of section 14(a), Congress required disclosure of a broader range of information about management practices and policies to promote informed corporate suffrage, thereby strengthening the position of shareholders in the corporate governance relationship. Significantly, though, Congress also intended disclosure to play an additional role: disclosure was intended to affect corporate conduct. This conclusion is consistent with the intellectual derivation and legislative history of the acts, particularly the legislative history of the *Securities Act*, which most directly uses disclosure as its regulatory method.

Frank Easterbrook & Daniel Fischel, "Mandatory Disclosure and the Protection of Investors"
(1984) 70 Va L Rev 669 at 714-15

A variety of private and public responses to the problem of asymmetric information establish powerful incentives for firms to disclose what investors want to know. Mandatory national disclosure legislation may well improve the incentives, but if it does this, the improvement comes about for reasons other than a need to deal with fraud or any systematic tendency to hide. Intervention is most likely to be useful when sellers lack incentives to disclose information because of third-party effects, holdouts among other firms, and attempts by states to exploit investors who live elsewhere. Sometimes firms simply will not find it in their interest to disclose adequate industry-wide, comparative, or standardized information. Because securities are not homogeneous products, and direct inspection of business prospects by investors is not cost-effective, there may be gains from collective insistence on certain disclosures.

This is a far cry from saying that our existing securities rules are optimal. No satisfactory data suggest that the SEC's rules are beneficial. Perhaps problems in implementation prevent realization of whatever savings are available in principle. There is less reason to regulate securities than, say, the funeral industry, which also lacks standardized transactions and in which shopping by informed traders may not lead to efficient prices. We have not constructed a compelling case for regulation of any sort, let alone for the particular regulations the SEC uses.

There is nonetheless a case for mandatory disclosure, and it is a far different case from that usually advanced by those who endorse the securities laws. Our approach suggests that the telling blows that can be struck against the usual case are not fatal.

What is the appropriate response to this "conclusion," if something so uncertain may be called that? The proponent of change in the legal order bears a substantial burden. Rules of law may be beneficial in ways we do not understand, and if all we can say is that we cannot identify either benefit or detriment from a given set of rules, the injunction to leave well enough alone has great force. At the same time, the study of regulation is sufficiently advanced to support a contrary injunction: Most regulatory regimes reduce aggregate welfare, although they also profit special interest groups. There is no shortage of groups that gain from securities regulation. The impetus that led to the elimination of the CAB and the deregulation of many modes of transportation and communication—and the observable benefits of this deregulation—suggest that the maxim "If it ain't broke, don't fix it" applies only to the outcome of private orderings. Yet the inefficient systems of regulation commonly have entry limits or price controls, which securities laws do not. The final difficulty, as we emphasized at the outset, is that the question for decision is not regulation versus the market but one kind of regulation (disclosure rules enforced by the SEC) versus another (fraud and "material omission" rules, and perhaps disclosure rules, enforced by state courts and agencies). We cannot say that the existing securities laws are beneficial, but we also are not confident that their probable replacements would be better.

John C Coffee Jr & Hillary A Sale, "Redesigning the SEC: Does the Treasury Have a Better Idea?"

(2008), online: <http://papers.ssrn.com/sol3/papers.cfm>

[In 1984], the Efficient Capital Market Hypothesis ("ECMH") was at stage center and the zenith of its acceptance, with a number of authors arguing that it implied that law should play only a secondary and severely constrained role. Others explained that markets worked, less because of law or the threat of liability, but rather because information was produced, collected, verified and disseminated by "reputational intermediaries"—investment banks, auditors, securities analysts, and credit rating agencies—who pledged their reputational capital behind their opinions and judgments. Hence, these intermediaries would have little incentive to misrepresent or distort … . Today, the bloom is clearly off the rose of finance theory. Intellectual paradigms have shifted over the interim, as a new generation of "behavioral economists" have come to view the ECMH more skeptically, emphasizing in particular the limits of arbitrage. Deregulation is no longer the presumptive policy prescription; indeed today, the sense is growing that the current crisis may have been deepened by excessive deregulation, which a process of international regulatory arbitrage arguably enforced. Similarly, the naiveté behind the view that markets are always quickly self-correcting because of the efforts of reputational intermediaries now seems apparent. "Reputational intermediaries" proved to have their own biases and to be highly vulnerable to issuer pressure. Yet, they remain indispensible because there are simply a number of contexts where investors cannot themselves undertake the verification and evaluative tasks that these experts perform.

The excerpts above illustrate the different normative views of disclosure as an instrument to promote market efficiency and the efficacy of regulatory intervention to enhance disclosure by both issuers and intermediaries. The need for regulation, how much regulation, and its justifications are controversial. However, the ability of the markets themselves to be efficient is also the subject of debate. A dominant premise in policy development has been that only regulatory action that facilitates capital formation is appropriate, and any other regulatory activity that adds transaction costs to capital markets is inefficient. Hence from the inception of securities regulation, disclosure formed a major underpinning as the mechanism of least intervention. The US Congress, in enacting the first US securities legislation, discussed the interaction of market forces and regulatory intervention. House reports include the following comments:

> The idea of a free and open public market is built upon the theory that competing judgments of buyers and sellers as to the fair price of a security brings about a situation where the market price reflects as nearly as possible a just price. Just as artificial manipulation tends to upset the true function of an open market, so the hiding and secreting of important information obstructs the operation of the markets as indices of real value (HR Rep. No. 73-1383, at 11 (1934)).
>
> • • •

> The items required to be disclosed [in the prospectus], set forth in detailed form, are items indispensable to any accurate judgment upon the value of the security ... because of their wide dissemination, they determine the market price of the security, which in the last analysis reflects those manifold causes that are the impelling motive of the particular purchase (HR Rep. No. 73-85, at 3, 10 (1933)).

Implicit in the use of disclosure as the main tool to regulate securities is the assumption that market participants will be "rational" when the information is presented to them. Rational in this context means being able to use the information disclosed to act in their own best interests in market transactions. However, scholarship in behavioural economics has questioned whether disclosure of information alone is sufficient to overcome certain human decision-making strategies that inhibit our ability to be rational in market transactions. This scholarship thus raises issues about the use of disclosure as the main tool in securities regulation. Is it sufficient? Is it efficient? These issues were canvassed in the Introduction to this chapter.

A. How Securities Markets Are Structured

Capital markets can be global, national, or regional: issuers access different markets depending on the types of securities they wish to sell, the amount of capital they seek, and the regulatory framework in which they wish to operate. Capital is raised by issuers in primary markets (first offering of securities to the public). Previously issued securities are resold in secondary markets. Different regulatory rules apply depending on the type of market.

1. *Global Trading*

New technologies, declining trade barriers, and new financial products have increased the complexity and pace of capital market transactions and have facilitated sale of securities on a global basis. Global capital markets have generated competition for capital and a need for a regulatory regime that provides investors from around the world with sufficient confidence to make investing in its issuers' securities attractive. Issuers that offer securities in multiple jurisdictions want a regulatory regime that allows them to offer securities in a timely and cost-effective manner.

The international market for Canadian securities is large and growing. In 2006, foreign investment in Canadian securities was $31 billion annually, and by 2015, this investment had reached $96 billion. Canadian investment in foreign securities has remained steadier—$79 billion in 2006 and $60 billion in 2015 (Statistics Canada quarterly report, Canada's international transactions in securities, online: <http://www.statcan.gc.ca/daily-quotidien/160217/cg-a001-eng.htm>). There are 136 Canadian issuers listed on the New York Stock Exchange (NYSE) (as of May 31, 2016 data at nyse.com), up from 78 in 2003; and 183 are traded on the National Association of Securities Dealers Automated Quotation System (NASDAQ) (as of July 2016 data at nasdaq.com), up from 81 in 2003.

Canadian regulators are under pressure from the range of regulatory regimes available to issuers to be competitive in providing both confidence to investors and efficient procedures for approval to issuers. The challenge to regulators is to find an appropriate balance between the two goals, a challenge that is made more difficult by recent market volatility and declines in investor confidence in the integrity of issuers and the system of securities law enforcement.

William Hess, "The Evolving Role of Stock Exchanges in Canada"
in Anita I Anand & William F Flanagan, eds, *Responding to Globalization: Papers Presented at the 8th Queen's Annual Business Law Symposium, 2001*
(Kingston, Ont: Faculty of Law, Queen's University, 2002) 69 at 73

Impact of Technology

It is the advances in technology and changing regulatory environment, however, that has been the catalyst for competition within the securities industry. The role of the Internet in changing the structure of the securities industry cannot be underestimated. It is providing more direct and less expensive access to capital markets, thereby challenging the role of financial intermediaries and exchanges. Technology is also erasing the boundaries of regional and national capital markets. The borderless fluidity of capital threatens the role of regional and even national stock exchanges and technology has enabled 24-7 trading to satisfy the insatiable appetite of investors to move money anywhere, anytime. Consumer behaviour has clearly changed, and as today's children grow older, their preoccupation with technology will further fuel its impact on stock exchanges of the future. A clear example of this can be found in a Forrester Research study, which reported that in 2000, over 50 percent of retail trades in the US were done on-line. It cannot be denied that the role of technology, and especially the Internet, is worthy of consideration by stock exchanges as they contemplate their role in the capital market system.

There has been a global move toward the harmonization of standards at the same time that domestic jurisdictions are grappling with a broader range and more complex and specialized types of securities. The response to that pressure has varied. British Columbia's response was to propose principles- and outcomes-based legislation with streamlined filing and review processes, which was to have come into force in 2005. It delayed implementation in order to work toward greater provincial and territorial cooperation. Other provinces were of the view that there was a need for greater codification, some of it responding to US regulatory initiatives. Over time, there has been some convergence of views, as discussed later in this chapter. The International Organization of Securities Commissions (IOSCO) is an organization with members representing over 115 jurisdictions that actively promotes harmonization of securities regulatory standards to facilitate cross-border trading and promote international cooperation in enforcement.

2. *The National Scope of Securities Trading*

The Wise Persons' Committee to Review the Structure of Securities Regulation in Canada (WPC) reported the following profile of Canadian securities markets:

- Two-thirds of the approximately 7,600 reporting issuers in Canada are reporting issuers in more than one jurisdiction.
- All listed companies, including those that are reporting issuers in only one province, are necessarily interprovincial, because investors from across the country and around the world can buy or sell listed securities over the exchanges.

- Of the approximately 3,800 companies listed on the Toronto Stock Exchange (TSX) and TSX Venture Exchange, almost 1,200 or 31 percent are "national issuers"—that is, reporting issuers in all 10 provincial jurisdictions.
- There are 777 companies with a market capitalization over $75 million—almost all of which are national issuers. They accounted for $1.275 trillion, or 98 percent, of the approximately $1.3 trillion total market capitalization in Canada.
- Canada's debt market is largely national in scope. Of the $4.4 trillion in bond trading activity in 2002, 80 percent was in Government of Canada bonds.
- The vast majority of the 1,956 mutual funds offered for sale in Canada at the end of last year were offered for sale in all provinces and held by investors across the country.

(Wise Persons' Committee to Review the Structure of Securities Regulation in Canada, *It's Time* (Ottawa: Department of Finance, December 2003) (WPC) at 5.)

The 60 companies constituting the Standard and Poor's S&P/TSX 60 index account for more than 74.4 percent of the total market capitalization of the TSX (July 2016, online: <http://www.tsx.com>). In Canada, capital markets provided 88 percent of the long-term financing of Canadian firms in 2002 (WPC at 4).

The WPC also reported that the majority of Canadians have an interest in Canadian capital markets. Forty-six percent of Canadians own publicly traded equities, either directly through their purchase of securities or indirectly through their mutual funds (TSX Group, *Canadian Shareowners Study* (Toronto: TSX, 2003)). This number includes almost all Canadians if one includes pension fund investments and the Canada Pension Plan (WPC at 6). Debt markets are also key components of the capital markets, including the financing of public infrastructure, public–private partnerships, and the financing of workouts for financially distressed issuers.

This profile highlights the importance of Canadian capital markets to the domestic economy. It also reveals that capital in Canada is still relatively concentrated, with 60 companies dominating the overall market and less than 800 companies accounting for 98 percent of all market capitalization. Most of the larger issuers are also listed on US exchanges, emphasizing the need to have a measure of compatibility with US capital markets and to enhance cross-border review, trading, and enforcement activity.

Trading has become increasingly electronic and multijurisdictional with sophisticated trading platforms. The Internet has become a major means for investors to access information about issuers and to undertake investment transactions (TSX Group, *Canadian Shareowners Study* (Toronto: TSX, 2003)). Two national policies were introduced in 1999 to provide guidance to issuers and other market participants regarding electronic disclosure requirements under securities regulation: NP 47-201, *Trading Securities Using the Internet and Other Electronic Means*, amended in 2013, and NP 11-201, *Delivery of Documents by Electronic Means*, amended in 2011. NP 11-201 allows for electronic delivery of documents, including mechanisms for determining delivery, accessibility requirements for the recipient, and the security of electronic documents. For example, the policy notes that an issuer that provides a hyperlink in a document to information outside the document risks incorporating that hyperlinked information into the document and thereby becoming legally responsible for the accuracy of that hyperlinked information; and the existence of hyperlinks in a document delivered by electronic delivery to a separate document raises the question of which documents are being delivered, an issue that may be particularly relevant in the delivery of a prospectus, in terms of ensuring that recipients understand which of the documents being delivered constitute the prospectus (at 3.3). While issuers must continue to meet statutory requirements, NP 47-201 provides guidance on the promotion and distribution of securities on the Internet and explains jurisdictional matters that may arise. "Electronic roadshows," where issuers disseminate information about an offering to a large audience, must meet the same requirements as those promotions conducted in person in terms of disclosure to potential investors.

3. *Regional Markets*

As noted in the above profile, the vast majority of Canadian-based issuers access capital markets nationally. There are, however, some regional markets, particularly in the resource sector. A research study by Professor Poonam Puri for the WPC found that where there is a critical mass of issuers of a certain industry type in a jurisdiction, such as mining in British Columbia and oil and gas in Alberta, centres of regulatory expertise have developed, stimulating local investment markets and attracting capital to the jurisdiction. Although the infrastructure for raising capital in these specialized markets appears local or regional, trading in the relevant securities usually extends beyond the region.

Poonam Puri, "The Role of Local and Regional Interests in the Design of Optimal Securities Regulatory Structure for Canada"
(Ottawa: 2003). *Commissioned Reports and Studies.* Paper No 118 at 209

This study finds that LICRs (local infrastructures for capital raising) exist for certain industries and levels of market capitalization. This study finds that Alberta hosts an LICR for oil and gas, BC hosts an LICR for micro-cap issuers, and Ontario hosts an LICR for financial services. Certain LICRs exist in more than one province: Both BC and Ontario host LICRs for mining; Ontario, Québec and BC for communications and media; Ontario and Québec for life sciences; and BC, Alberta and Ontario each host an LICR for small cap issuers.

However, the existence of LICRs for certain industries does not allow us to conclude that the economic activity associated with these industries is local to host provinces or that host provinces have distinct local interests in the capital markets regulation or general regulation of those industries.

The activities of issuers concentrated within an LICR have an impact outside the geographic boundaries of the province that hosts and regulates the LICR. Other provinces may have an interest equal to that of the regulating province, given investor location and the importance of those industries to the economies of other provinces, as borne out by GDP data.

For private equity financing, which is investing and capital raising that takes place under an exemption from the prospectus requirements as discussed below, there is a continued preference for local and regional investing with the majority of investments involving an investor and an entrepreneur residing in the same province (D Cumming, A Kaul & V Mehrotra, "Provincial Preferences in Private Equity" in A Douglas Harris, ed, *WPC Committee to Review the Structure of Securities Regulation in Canada: Research Studies* (Ottawa: Department of Finance, 2003)).

B. Primary Markets

A securities issuer can be a corporation or other entity that issues securities. A primary market transaction, usually referred to as a "distribution," takes effect where the issuer sells its own securities or sells them through the services of an underwriter. A "private placement" is a sale of securities by the issuer directly to specific investors, frequently institutional investors, using a specific exemption from securities regulatory requirements. Private placements are fundamental to the closed system, discussed in Chapter 5. Unlike private placements that often target specific investors, an "initial public offering" (IPO) occurs when an issuer is first offering securities to the public generally. Since the adoption of the closed system of securities regulation in Canada in the late 1980s, all initial distributions of securities require the development of a prospectus, providing clarity and consistency in the requirements for a public offering, unless the issuer has received an exemption, as discussed in Chapter 5. The primary market also includes follow-on (seasoned) public offerings in which the issuer is raising additional capital and must meet the requirements of a new prospectus, if not otherwise exempted.

C. Secondary Markets

After an issuer has issued securities through a prospectus offering, it becomes a "reporting issuer" under securities legislation and is required to comply with ongoing reporting obligations as a condition of its securities being in the public domain. A reporting issuer is defined in securities legislation. For example, s 1 of the British Columbia *Securities Act*, RSBC 1996, c 418, as amended, defines "reporting issuer" as follows:

> "reporting issuer" means an issuer that
> (a) has issued securities in respect of which
> (i) a prospectus was filed and a receipt was issued,
> (ii) a statement of material facts was filed and accepted, or
> (iii) a securities exchange take over bid circular was filed,
> under a former enactment,
> (b) has filed a prospectus or statement of material facts and the executive director has issued a receipt for it under this Act,
> (c) has any securities that have been at any time listed and posted for trading on any exchange in British Columbia, regardless of when the listing and posting for trading began,
> (d) is an issuer that has exchanged its securities with another issuer or with the holders of the securities of that other issuer in connection with an amalgamation, merger, reorganization, arrangement or similar transaction if one of the parties to the amalgamation, merger, reorganization, arrangement or similar transaction was a reporting issuer at the time of the amalgamation, merger, reorganization, arrangement or similar transaction,
> (e) is designated as a reporting issuer in an order made under section 3.2,
> (e.1) is a person that is within a prescribed class of persons, or
> (f) has filed a securities exchange take over bid circular under this Act for the acquisition of securities of a reporting issuer and has taken up and paid for securities subject to the bid in accordance with the circular,
> unless the commission orders under section 88 that the issuer has ceased to be a reporting issuer;

When the securities of a reporting issuer are sold among investors, these sales are called secondary market transactions. Secondary markets are those in which shares and other securities are traded after being issued by the issuer for the first time. If the securities were issued in a private placement, then a sale can take place only in accordance with the restrictions of the exempt market, discussed in Chapter 5. Where the securities were issued through a public offering, shares are usually traded through stock exchanges or other securities markets. Even where issuers are listed in only one jurisdiction, exchanges facilitate the buying and selling of securities internationally.

In order to facilitate rapid trading, many shares today are held in central depositories that hold inventories of shares and perform clearing services recording the daily exchange of shares. The introduction of central depositories has facilitated capital market activity; however, securities holders are usually beneficial owners of the shares as opposed to registered shareholders, creating challenges for accountability to investors of corporate management, as discussed in Chapters 6 and 7. In Canada, many aspects of secondary market activity are regulated by provincial and territorial securities regulators or by self-regulatory organizations.

D. Marketplace Operation

The term "marketplace" encompasses the different types of trading systems that match buyers and sellers in the secondary market. A marketplace is an exchange, a quotation and trade reporting system (QTRS), or an alternative trading system (ATS) (Companion Policy to NI 21-101, *Marketplace Operation* (2001) (NI 21-101CP), amended 2015). Canadian securities regulators developed two national policy instruments in 2001 to regulate marketplace operation (National Instrument 21-101, *Marketplace Operation* (2001) (NI 21-101), amended effective 1 October 2015, and National Instrument 23-101, *Trading Rules* (2003) (NI 23-101), amended effective 6 July 2016. Their rationale is set out below, along with the definition of exchange-traded securities.

Companion Policy to National Instrument 21-101, *Marketplace Operation*

Effective October 1, 2015

PART 1 Introduction

1.1 Introduction—Exchanges, quotation and trade reporting systems, and ATSs are marketplaces that provide a market facility or venue on which securities can be traded. The areas of interest from a regulatory perspective are in many ways similar for each of these marketplaces, since they may have similar trading activities. The regulatory regime for exchanges and quotation and trade reporting systems arises from the securities legislation of the various jurisdictions. Exchanges and quotation and trade reporting systems are recognized under orders from the Canadian securities regulatory authorities, with various terms and conditions of recognition. ATSs, which are not recognized as exchanges or quotation and trade reporting systems, are regulated under National Instrument 21-101 Marketplace Operation (the Instrument) and National Instrument 23-101 Trading Rules (NI 23-101). The Instrument and NI 23-101, which were adopted at a time when new types of markets were emerging, provide the regulatory framework that allows and regulates the operation of multiple marketplaces.

The purpose of this Companion Policy is to state the views of the Canadian securities regulatory authorities on various matters related to the Instrument, including:

(a) a discussion of the general approach taken by the Canadian securities regulatory authorities in, and the general regulatory purpose for, the Instrument; and
(b) the interpretation of various terms and provisions in the Instrument.

1.2 Definition of Exchange-Traded Security—Section 1.1 of the Instrument defines an "exchange-traded security" as a security that is listed on a recognized exchange or is quoted on a recognized quotation and trade reporting system or is listed on an exchange or quoted on a quotation and trade reporting system that is recognized for the purposes of NI 21-101 and NI 23-101.

. . .

A security that is inter-listed would be considered to be an exchange-traded security. A security that is listed on a foreign exchange or quoted on a foreign quotation and trade reporting system, but is not listed or quoted on a domestic exchange or quotation and trade reporting system, falls within the definition of "foreign exchange-traded security."

1.3 Definition of Foreign Exchange-Traded Security—The definition of foreign exchange-traded security includes a reference to ordinary members of the International Organization of Securities Commissions (IOSCO). To determine the current list of ordinary members, reference should be made to the IOSCO website at <www.iosco.org>.

NI 21-101 regulates all marketplaces operating in Canada and sets out the distinction between different marketplace participants.

National Instrument 21-101, *Marketplace Operation*
Effective October 1, 2015

1.1 Definitions—In this Instrument

. . .

"marketplace,"
(a) in every jurisdiction other than Ontario, means
(i) an exchange,
(ii) a quotation and trade reporting system,
(iii) a person or company not included in clause (i) or (ii) that
(A) constitutes, maintains or provides a market or facility for bringing together buyers and sellers of securities,
(B) brings together the orders for securities of multiple buyers and sellers, and
(C) uses established, non-discretionary methods under which the orders interact with each other, and the buyers and sellers entering the orders agree to the terms of a trade, or
(iv) a dealer that executes a trade of an exchange-traded security outside of a marketplace, but does not include an inter-dealer bond broker, and

(b) in Ontario has the meaning set out in subsection 1(1) of the *Securities Act* (Ontario);

"marketplace participant" means a member of an exchange, a user of a quotation and trade reporting system, or a subscriber of an ATS;

"member" means, for a recognized exchange, a person or company

(a) holding at least one seat on the exchange, or

(b) that has been granted direct trading access rights by the exchange and is subject to regulatory oversight by the exchange,

and the person or company's representatives;

...

"recognized exchange" means

(a) in Ontario, a recognized exchange as defined in subsection 1(1) of the *Securities Act* (Ontario),

(b) in Québec, an exchange recognized by the securities regulatory authority under securities or derivatives legislation as an exchange or a self-regulatory organization, and

(c) in every other jurisdiction, an exchange recognized by the securities regulatory authority as an exchange, self-regulatory organization or self-regulatory body;

"recognized quotation and trade reporting system" means

(a) in every jurisdiction other than British Columbia, Ontario and Québec, a quotation and trade reporting system recognized by the securities regulatory authority under securities legislation to carry on business as a quotation and trade reporting system,

(b) in British Columbia, a quotation and trade reporting system recognized by the securities regulatory authority under securities legislation as a quotation and trade reporting system or as an exchange,

(b.1) in Ontario, a recognized quotation and trade reporting system as defined in subsection 1(1) of the *Securities Act* (Ontario), and

(c) in Québec, a quotation and trade reporting system recognized by the securities regulatory authority under securities or derivatives legislation as an exchange or a self-regulatory organization;

Canadian securities regulators developed National Instrument 23-101, *Trading Rules* in 2001, with an amended instrument effective 6 July 2016, to deal with specific trading practices. Its companion policy (NI 23-101CP, *Trading Rules*) specifies that, a general matter, Canadian securities regulatory authorities expect marketplace participants to transact business openly and fairly, and in accordance with just and equitable principles of trade (NI 23-101CP, s 1.2). NI 23-101 is aimed at setting standards for best execution by dealers on behalf of clients; marketplace establishment of trading hours; regulatory halts; prohibition of manipulation and fraud in trading practices; the monitoring and enforcement of requirements governing conduct of members set by a recognized exchange, a recognized QTRS, or an ATS; audit trail requirements; and agreements between marketplace participants and regulation service providers (NI 23-101, ss 3.1, 4.2, 5.1, 6.6, 7.1, 7.4, 8.2, 11.2).

A recognized exchange and a recognized QTRS can set their own requirements governing the conduct of members. They can monitor and enforce these requirements either directly or indirectly through a regulation services provider (NI 23-101, ss 7.1, 7.3). In contrast, an ATS must enter into an agreement with a regulation services provider, and its subscribers (participants in the ATS) must also enter agreements that form the basis on which a regulation services provider will monitor the trading activities of the ATS and its subscribers (NI 23-101, s 8.2, NI 23-101CP, s 7.2). A regulation services provider is a person or company that provides regulation services and is either a recognized exchange, recognized QTRS, or a recognized self-regulatory entity (NI 23-101CP, s 7.1). The requirements set by a regulation services provider must include requirements that the ATS and its subscribers will conduct trading activities in compliance with the instrument (NI 23-101CP, s 7.2).

A regulation services provider monitors the conduct of the market participant and its members and enforces requirements under national instruments regulating marketplace operation (NI 23-101, ss 7.2, 7.4, 8.3). A regulation services provider is obligated to coordinate monitoring and enforcement of the requirements under the Instrument with other marketplace participants performing the same role (NI 23-101, s 7.5). Hence readers must be careful to consult all of these rules, instruments, and statutory provisions in determining the obligations of marketplace participants.

II. NATIONAL EXCHANGES AND SELF-REGULATORY ORGANIZATIONS

As noted above, exchanges are key marketplace participants and are considered self-regulatory organizations. "Self-regulatory organization" (SRO) is a general term that applies when there has been a delegation of authority from a first-level regulator to a second-level regulator, which is typically done in circumstances where industry expertise and/or national scope are important to the quality and efficiency of regulation in a specific area. Under securities legislation, self-regulatory organization is specifically defined as "a person or company that is organized for the purpose of regulating the operations and the standards of practice and business conduct, in capital markets, of its members and their representatives with a view to promoting the protection of investors and the public interest (see e.g. OSA s 1). An SRO that wishes to operate as a marketplace participant must apply for recognition under securities legislation (NI 21-101 s 3.1; OSC rule 23-501, *Designation as a Market Participant* (2001)). The term SRO also applies to organizations such as the Investment Industry Regulatory Organization of Canada (IIROC), which oversees all investment dealers and trading activity on debt and equity marketplaces through setting and enforcing rules regarding the proficiency, business, and financial conduct of dealer firms and their registered employees, and enforcing market integrity rules regarding trading activity on Canadian equity marketplaces.

Stock exchanges, as one form of SRO, are required to obtain "recognition" from a provincial securities regulator. Recognition is essentially a process whereby the stock exchange makes a formal application to a commission and the commission in turn issues a formal document that grants recognition. Once recognition has been obtained, the entity becomes a market participant and is subject to various provisions of the legislation such as those relating to financial examination orders and compliance reviews. In Canada, because all provincial and territorial securities acts have provisions requiring the recognition and oversight of exchanges, and because it would be administratively burdensome for an exchange to report continuously to more than one regulator, Canadian securities regulators have entered into a memorandum of understanding with one another to establish a "lead regulator model" regarding the oversight of exchanges. Under the lead regulator model, exchanges are recognized in one province, known as the "lead regulator," and formally exempted from the recognition requirements in the other provinces and territories, which are known as the "exempting regulators." Lead regulators are responsible for conducting oversight of the exchanges they recognize and for informing the exempting regulators of these activities.

Securities regulators have express power to make any decision in the public interest regarding the manner in which a recognized stock exchange carries on business and engages in the listing or trading of securities, to ensure that it complies with securities law (see e.g. British Columbia *Securities Act*, s 27; Ontario *Securities Act*, s 21(5)). Once recognized, the stock exchange is self-regulatory in many respects, although provincial securities regulators exercise oversight of their activities.

Canadian stock exchanges date back to the 1800s. The first stock transactions in Montreal took place at the Exchange Coffee House in 1832, and the Montreal Stock Exchange was established in 1874 after more than 40 years of informal trading. Today, the Bourse de Montréal (TMX Montreal Exchange), which evolved out of the Montreal Stock Exchange, is the Canadian derivatives and options exchange. The familiar television image of the trading floor of the stock exchange, filled with traders continuously buying and selling securities, was very much the history of stock exchanges throughout the past century. The process involved floor traders filling orders submitted by their clients by going to the trading post of the floor and buying the securities using the "open outcry" method—a process akin to a mix of auction, negotiation, and exchange. Actual trading floors have for the most part disappeared with the move by exchanges to electronic trading. Modern stock exchanges are characterized by increasingly sophisticated electronic trading platforms that are coordinated globally.

Before 1999, there were five stock exchanges in Canada. Since that time there has been merger of some exchanges, specialization, and the emergence of new and innovative exchanges. Today, the major Canadian exchanges are the Toronto Stock Exchange, which specializes in senior equities; the TSX Venture Exchange and Canadian National Stock Exchange, which specialize in junior equities; the Bourse de Montréal, which controls the derivatives market; and Canada's newest exchanges, the Aequitas NEO Exchange and TMX Alpha Exchange, which provide innovative trading environments intended to reduce the impact of certain forms of high-frequency trading.

The recognizing securities regulator in its oversight capacity is authorized to make decisions relating to a recognized stock exchange. Specifically, the regulator may make decisions in the public interest in respect of how the exchange carries on business or its policies, procedure, and practice; how securities are traded; and decision-making in regard to any security listed or any issuer trading on the exchange. Hence, although the exchange is self-regulating, the authority granted to securities regulators tempers the activities of exchanges. The staff of regulatory authority (often referred to as the "director" in securities legislation) may apply to a panel of the securities commission to review any decisions, direction, or ruling of a stock exchange (see e.g. BCSA, s 28; OSA, s 21.7(1)). While an exchange has the authority to set responsibilities for issuers, its sanctioning power consists of delisting the issuer. The securities commission has broader powers to pursue remedies for violations of securities laws.

A. Toronto Stock Exchange and TSX Venture Exchange

The Toronto Stock Exchange (TSX) is the exchange through which the shares of the largest Canadian issuers, called senior equities, are traded. In 2000, the TSX demutualized, changing from a not-for-profit mutual company to a for-profit corporation, a trend that exchanges are following globally. The rationale for demutualization was that the TSX needed to become more entrepreneurial and customer focused (Toronto Stock Exchange, *A Blueprint for Success* (Toronto: Toronto Stock Exchange, 1998)). While the exchange is still referred to as TSX, the company that owns the TSX changed its name in 2008 to the TMX Group. In 2002, the TSX (now TMX Group) completed its initial public offering, changing it from a company owned by the brokerage firms that used its services, to a publicly owned corporation. In order to meet regulatory concerns regarding the TMX's self-monitoring after demutualization, the recognition order granted by the Ontario Securities Commission required the TMX to delegate market regulation activities to another organization. As a result, Market Regulation Services (RS) was created as a regulation services provider, owned in part by the TMX (*Re Toronto Stock Exchange* (2000), 23 OSCB 2495). RS subsequently merged with the Investment Dealers Association of Canada, as discussed in Section IV of this chapter, as part of a response to calls for more efficient and independent oversight. Today, TMX Group's subsidiaries operate the Toronto Stock Exchange, TSX Venture Exchange, TSX Alpha Exchange, Montreal Exchange, and Natural Gas Exchange (NGX), and other TMX Group companies provide trading markets, clearing facilities, depository services, trust administration services, data products and other services to the global financial community (<https://www.tmx.com/tmx-group>).

There are over 3,200 issuers on the TSX and TSXV, with an average size of $1.5 billion on the senior market and $12.9 million on the junior market (<http://www.tsx.com/listings/listing-with-us>). Canadian-based issuers represent approximately 96 percent of the companies listed on the TSX and TSX Venture Exchange (TSXV) and 92 percent of the aggregate market capital of public companies, while foreign issuers represent a relatively small, but increasing number of total TSX and TSXV listings. The TSX is the largest small-to-medium enterprise (SME) exchange in North America, and second in the world based on the number of issuers listed. Canada's public equities market is a tiered market with 59 percent of companies listed on the TSXV. More than a third of TSX-listed issuers, 1,373, are mining companies. Based on aggregate market capital, the oil and gas industry is the most significant industry in Canada, at 25 percent, followed by financial services at 24.8 percent, and mining at 17 percent. Many issuers on the TSXV are at the development or exploration stage (Rik Parkhill, Interim Co-CEO, TSX Group Inc, Speech to 8th Annual Metals and Mining Conference of The New York Society of Security Analysts, 4 June 2008).

The following passage summarizes the marketplaces in which the TMX Group has activities.

TMX Group, *Connecting Global Capital Markets to Canada*
formerly available online:
<http://www.tsx.com/en/about_tsx/corporate_information>

From its pre-eminent domestic base, TMX Group's reach extends internationally, providing the global financial community with access to Canada's equity capital and energy markets. Each TMX Group operation is connected to and supports the activities of the others; all are focused on providing exceptional customer service from our offices in Vancouver, Calgary, Toronto and Montréal. Toronto Stock Exchange (TSX)—As Canada's senior equities market, TSX provides an efficient, liquid market for a broad cross-section of Canadian issuers. TSX assists about 1,500 issuers through services designed to increase retail and institutional investors. TSX Venture Exchange—Serving the public venture equity market, TSX Venture Exchange provides access to capital for companies at the early stages of their growth while offering investors a well-regulated market for making venture investments. TSX Markets—TSX Markets facilitates trading on TSX and TSX Venture and provides innovative trading products to increase investor participation, particularly across North America. Natural Gas Exchange (NGX)—As a leading North American energy exchange, Natural Gas Exchange connects the buyers and sellers of natural gas and electricity contracts, enabling them to manage the risks inherent in energy trading, and provides the associated clearing and settlement services. TSX Datalinx—To meet growing global demand for financial and capital markets information, data is packaged and sold with more than 118,000 subscriptions worldwide via TSX Datalinx, connecting the Canadian capital markets to investors at home and abroad.

In February 2011, the TMX Group and the London Stock Exchange Group announced that they had reached an agreement to merge and become the second largest stock exchange group in the world. This announcement was the subject of considerable debate in Canada regarding whether such a merger would empower Canada's exchanges to compete on the world stage, or would result in the hollowing out of Canada's capital markets and related industries. By June 2011, a consortium of Canadian banks and large financial institutions had assembled a rival bid for TMX Group. Known as the Maple Group Acquisition Corporation, the consortium made a bid of $3.6 billion for the TMX Group. The Maple bid ultimately succeeded in July 2012, when the takeover bid was approved by over 91 percent of TMX Group's shareholders and the acquisition was completed in September 2012. As a part of this transaction, the TMX Group also acquired control of the Alpha Exchange, discussed below, and Central Depository Services (CDS), Canada's depository, clearing, and settlement business.

Junior equities, the securities of smaller companies that do not yet qualify for listing on the TSX, are often listed on the TSXV. The listing requirements for the TSXV are tailored to the characteristics of junior issuers and are less onerous than those of the TSX. Professor Puri has described the capitalization of the TSXV as follows.

Poonam Puri, "The Rule of Local and Regional Interests in the Design of Optimal Securities Regulatory Structure for Canada"
(Ottawa: 2003). *Commissioned Reports and Studies.* Paper No 118 at 215, 224, 225

Of the 2,041 issuers listed on the TSX Venture Exchange, the greatest portion consists of issuers headquartered in BC (983 issuers at 48 percent). This is followed by Alberta (415 issuers at 22 percent), Ontario (415 issuers at 20 percent), and Québec (142 issuers at 7 percent).

The total market capitalization of all issuers listed on the TSX Venture Exchange is approximately $11.8 billion. Over 40 percent of the TSX Venture Exchange's market

> capitalization is comprised of issuers headquartered in BC. This is followed by Alberta (at 27 percent), Ontario (at 21 percent) and Québec (at 7 percent).
>
> Almost one half of all TSX Venture Exchange issuers are classified as Mining issuers (918 issuers at 45 percent) followed by Technology issuers (324 at 16 percent), Diversified Industry issuers (335 at 16 percent) and Oil and Gas issuers (282 at 14 percent).
>
> The market capitalization analysis reveals similar results. Mining represents 45 percent of the total market capitalization of the TSX Venture Exchange, followed by Oil and Gas at 20 percent, Diversified Industries at 16 percent and Technology at 13 percent.
>
> • • •
>
> Micro cap issuers represent 76 percent of all TSX Venture Exchange listed issuers. Of the 1,705 micro cap issuers listed on the TSX Venture Exchange, over one half (882 at 52 percent) are headquartered in BC and are therefore most likely regulated by the BCSC as the principal regulator...
>
> Small cap issuers represent 23 percent of all TSX Venture Exchange listed issuers. Of the 519 small cap issuers listed on the TSX Venture Exchange, 204 (39 percent) are headquartered in BC and therefore most likely regulated by the BCSC as the principal regulator.

Issuers that are listed on the TSX or TSXV must comply with TSX policies and rules in respect of investor protection, governance, and reporting, bringing some harmonization of standards to issuers on these exchanges. Unlike the New York Stock Exchange, which has prescribed mandatory corporate governance rules, the TSX and TSXV require only disclosure of any governance practices measured against non-mandatory guidelines. This is known as a "comply or explain" system. Although there has been considerable debate as to whether the guidelines should be mandatory, the Canadian Securities Administrators (CSA) have essentially ended this debate by entering the market for corporate governance, promulgating NI 58-101, *Disclosure of Corporate Governance Practices* (effective 17 March 2008, amended 17 November 2015), which sets out a series of "comply or explain" disclosure requirements, including details relating to executive compensation and the representation of women on each issuer's board and senior management. These initiatives are discussed at length in Chapter 7.

The TSXV has very deep roots in Canada's capital markets. The exchange was formerly known as the Canadian Venture Exchange (CDNX), which was created in 1999 following an agreement among Canada's major exchanges to realign and specialize their services in Canada. The CDNX was created through the merger of the Vancouver Stock Exchange, the Alberta Stock Exchange, some small-cap listings from the Bourse de Montréal and the Winnipeg Exchange, and some of the larger members of the Canadian Dealing Network (CDN). CDN was a subsidiary of the TSX that existed to serve the trading needs of smaller companies that were unable to meet the exchange filing standards of the major exchanges. The CDN facilitated exchanges for securities of these smaller companies through a "quoted" segment in which dealers quoted prices at which they were prepared to sell and buy securities and a "reporting" segment in which trades were reported for non-quoted issuers. Several hundred companies were involved in both the quoted and the reporting segments of the CDN.

Since 2003, the TSXV has operated a separate board, known as the NEX which provides a trading forum for listed companies that have fallen below the TSXV's ongoing listing standards. In 2016, there were approximately 390 companies listed on the NEX board (data available online: <http://apps.tmx.com/en/nex/index.html>).

B. Bourse de Montréal

The Montréal Exchange, called Bourse de Montréal in French, evolved out of the original Montréal Stock Exchange. While the former Montréal exchange previously competed in the same market as the TSX, the Bourse de Montréal is now engaged in derivative securities and options trading and is owned by TMX Group. It describes its activities as follows.

The Montréal Exchange, *Overview*
online: <http://www.m-x.ca/qui_bref_en.php>

The Montréal Exchange (MX), Canada oldest exchange, is a fully electronic exchange dedicated to the development of the Canadian derivative markets.

A Complete Line of Integrated Services

As the sole financial derivatives exchange in Canada, MX today exerts its leadership in the following areas of expertise:

- Financial derivatives markets
- Information technology solutions
- Clearing services

Unique Risk Management Products

The market for exchange-traded derivatives is one of the strongest segments of the broader financial risk management industry worldwide. MX offers individual and institutional investors, both in Canada and abroad, a wide range of risk management products for protecting their investments and ensuring growth. MX currently lists:

- Equity options
- Options on ETFs
- Currency options (options on the US dollar)
- Index derivatives
- Interest rate derivatives (bond and money markets)

A Notable Entrance in the American Market

In February 2004, MX took a position in the huge and growing US equity options market through its majority ownership interest in the Boston Options Exchange (BOX). As technology partner in BOX, MX is responsible for the market operations and technological development of the exchange.

Reliable, Flexible and Advanced Trading Technologies

Advanced electronic trading software plays a key role in the development of financial exchanges worldwide. MX and BOX markets are supported by reliable, flexible and advanced trading technologies. As a dynamic institution with a proven capacity to innovate, MX has developed and completed a proprietary "next generation" trading system called SOLA®. Thanks to SOLA®, MX now leads the way in trading software innovations.

Top-Rated Clearing Services

The MX clearing house, the Canadian Derivatives Clearing Corporation (CDCC), provides central counterparty clearing services to participants. The CDCC, who rigorously manages risk exposures, continues to distinguish itself by upholding a top investment rating and a strong reputation. Recently, the CDCC completed regulatory rule changes allowing the clearing house to offer risk management services to partners in the OTC market.

A Growing Number of Market Participants

MX market liquidity is on the rise. This growth is driven by the increased appetite of traders and investors from a growing list of countries for exposure to derivative instruments. More than 90 approved participants from London, New York, Chicago, and Montréal now connect directly to MX electronic trading system.

C. Other Canadian Exchanges

Another of Canada's original exchanges was the Winnipeg Commodity Exchange, which was established in 1887 and was the national agricultural commodities futures and option exchange. It was acquired by Atlanta-based Intercontinental Exchange (ICE) in 2007, which then announced that its Winnipeg Commodity Exchange subsidiary would be renamed ICE Futures Canada, effective January 1, 2008. ICE Futures Canada is designed for effective agricultural hedging with futures and options contracts on canola, milling wheat, durum wheat, and barley (<https://www.theice.com/futures-canada>).

The Canadian Securities Exchange (CSE), formerly known as the Canadian National Stock Exchange (CNSX) and the Canadian Trading and Quotation System Inc (CNQ), was recognized in 2004 as a new Canadian stock exchange for trading the equity securities of emerging companies. The CSE had grown to list more than 200 companies by 2016. CSE also operates a separate platform for the trading of companies listed on other Canadian exchanges (<http://thecse.com/about/our-people>).

The Alpha Exchange was originally created as an ATS in 2008 by a consortium that included six of Canada's biggest banks as well as a number of other large financial institutions as an alternative trading platform to compete with the exchange services of the dominant TMX Group. By 2012, Alpha had received recognition as an exchange and had grown to handle over 20 percent of Canadian trading in TSX listed stocks (<http://www.newswire.ca/news-releases/alpha-market-share-over-20-538218671.html>). In 2012, however, many of the key owners of Alpha launched the Maple bid to acquire the TMX, which resulted in the Alpha Exchange joining the TMX Group as part of the Maple acquisition in September 2012. Since joining the TMX Group, the TSX Alpha Exchange provides specialized trading in securities that are listed on the TSX and TSXV and has introduced "speed bump" technology in certain circumstances which adds very small amounts of time to the processing of each trade and is intended to reduce the impact of high frequency trading.

The Aequitas Neo Exchange (NEO), Canada's newest exchange, received recognition from the OSC in 2014. NEO is backed by a group of Canadian banks and institutions that were not involved in the Maple acquisition of the TMX Group. NEO operates an innovative exchange, which also uses "speed bump" technology, in order to reduce the impact of high frequency trading and "optimize the quality of execution by promoting liquidity striving to reduce order fragmentation and produce larger fill sizes. Market integrity is enhanced through a transparent price discovery process, protected from a variety of predatory trading strategies" (<https://aequitasneoexchange.com/en/trading/trading-solutions/>).

D. Quotation and Trade Reporting System

The discussion of marketplace participants above described how securities regulators define a QTRS. Recall that QTRSs are operating facilities that permit the dissemination of price quotations for the purchase and sale of securities and reports of completed transactions in the securities for use of registered dealers. NI 21-101 also sets out access requirements, public interest rules, and the requirement to have compliance rules.

National Instrument 21-101, *Marketplace Operation*
Effective 1 October 2015

PART 5 Marketplace Requirements

5.1 Access Requirements

(1) A marketplace must not unreasonably prohibit, condition or limit access by a person or company to services offered by it.

(2) A marketplace must

(a) establish written standards for granting access to each of its services, and

(b) keep records of

(i) each grant of access including the reasons for granting access to an applicant, and

(ii) each denial or limitation of access, including the reasons for denying or limiting access to an applicant.

(3) A marketplace must not

(a) permit unreasonable discrimination among clients, issuers and marketplace participants, or

(b) impose any burden on competition that is not reasonably necessary and appropriate.

5.2 No Restrictions on Trading on Another Marketplace—A marketplace must not prohibit, condition, or otherwise limit, directly or indirectly, a marketplace participant from effecting a transaction on any marketplace.

5.3 Public Interest Rules

(1) Rules, policies and other similar instruments adopted by a recognized exchange or a recognized quotation and trade reporting system

(a) must not be contrary to the public interest; and

(b) must be designed to

(i) ensure compliance with securities legislation,

(ii) prevent fraudulent and manipulative acts and practices,

(iii) promote just and equitable principles of trade, and

(iv) foster co-operation and co-ordination with persons or companies engaged in regulating, clearing, settling, processing information with respect to, and facilitating, transactions in securities.

(2) [repealed]

5.4 Compliance Rules—A recognized exchange or a recognized quotation and trade reporting system must have rules or other similar instruments that

(a) require compliance with securities legislation; and

(b) provide appropriate sanctions for violations of the rules or other similar instruments of the exchange or quotation and trade reporting system.

5.5 Filing of Rules—A recognized exchange or a recognized quotation and trade reporting system must file all rules, policies and other similar instruments, and all amendments thereto.

E. Alternative Trading Systems

Alternative trading systems (ATS) is the term used to capture computer-based systems that automate the process of trading in securities. An ATS is defined as any automated matching system that brings together orders from buyers and sellers by using predetermined, established methods or rules. These systems may operate as continuous auction books, dealer markets, call markets, or anonymous matching networks using prices determined in the principal marketplace. National Instrument 21-101, *Marketplace Operation* was promulgated to provide a framework for the operation of ATS (NI 21-101, initially in force 1 December 2001, revised instrument effective 1 October 2015). It defines ATS and places limitations on their trading activities.

National Instrument 21-101, *Marketplace Operation*
Effective 1 October 2015

1.1 Definitions—In this Instrument

. . .

"alternative trading system,"

(a) In every jurisdiction other than Ontario, means a marketplace that

(i) is not a recognized quotation and trade reporting system or a recognized exchange, and

(ii) does not

(A) require an issuer to enter into an agreement to have its securities traded on the marketplace,

(B) provide, directly, or through one or more subscribers, a guarantee of a two-sided market for a security on a continuous or reasonably continuous basis,

(C) set requirements governing the conduct of subscribers, other than conduct in respect of the trading by those subscribers on the marketplace, and

(D) discipline subscribers other than by exclusion from participation in the marketplace, and

(b) in Ontario has the meaning set out in subsection 1(1) of the *Securities Act* (Ontario);

. . .

PART 6 Requirements Applicable Only to ATSs

6.1 Registration—An ATS shall not carry on business as an ATS unless
(a) it is registered as a dealer;
(b) it is a member of a self-regulatory entity; and
(c) it complies with the provisions of this Instrument and NI 23-101.

6.2 Registration Exemption Not Available—Except as provided in this Instrument, the registration exemptions applicable to dealers under securities legislation are not available to an ATS.

6.3 Securities Permitted to be Traded on an ATS—An ATS must not execute trades in securities other than
(a) exchange-traded securities;
(b) corporate debt securities;
(c) government debt securities; or
(d) foreign exchange-traded securities.

NI 21-101 specifies that an ATS that is not recognized as an exchange must register as a dealer in each jurisdiction in which it wants to carry on business (NI 21-101, s 6.1). An ATS is considered to be carrying on business in a jurisdiction if it provides direct access services to subscribers in that jurisdiction. However, where all the subscribers in a jurisdiction are registered dealers, the securities regulatory authority in that jurisdiction may consider granting the ATS an exemption from the requirement to register as a dealer. In determining whether the exemption is in the public interest, a securities regulatory authority will consider a number of factors, including whether the ATS is registered in another jurisdiction and whether the ATS deals only with registered dealers in that jurisdiction (NI 21-101CP, s 3.4(4)). An ATS must also be a member of a self-regulatory organization (NI 21-101, s 6.1(b)). The following passages describe some of the issues raised by the introduction of ATSs into the Canadian marketplace.

Mark DesLauriers, "Commentary on the Evolving Role of Stock Exchanges in Canada"

in Anita I Anand & William F Flanagan, eds, *Responding to Globalization: Papers Presented at the 8th Queen's Annual Business Law Symposium, 2001* (Kingston, Ont: Faculty of Law, Queen's University, 2002) 80 at 83-84

ATSs are markets that operate as alternatives to exchanges and match orders from buyers and sellers of listed securities using predetermined, established methods or rules, typically in an automated computer-based system.

Having advised a number of ATSs currently operating in the US and international markets, my experience with the new rules is that they create significant hurdles for established foreign ATSs that would like to provide Canadian brokerdealers and institutions with access to new markets for foreign securities.

Unfortunately, the new ATS rules do not exempt securities that trade exclusively outside Canada nor do they provide any regulatory relief to foreign ATSs that are regulated as exchanges or broker-dealers in the US. Under the new rules, foreign ATSs that operate in Canada must either become regulated as an exchange in Canada, become a member of an exchange, or become a fully registered investment dealer with IDA membership. However, registration as an investment dealer in Canada is only available to entities that are incorporated or otherwise domiciled in Canada. In addition, members of the IDA are subject to a variety of substantial regulatory requirements, including:

- proficiency exams for officers and sales personnel,
- minimum "free" capital requirements and related filings,
- requirements to maintain a presence in Canada, and
- requirements to make contingency fund contributions.

As a result of the regulatory hurdles mentioned above, I expect the ATS rules to significantly limit the number of foreign ATSs that will register to offer their services to Canadian investors and market participants. This would be an unfortunate result. I appreciate that there is a need to protect the Canadian exchanges against market fragmentation, particularly when the Canadian exchanges carry the burden of regulating listed companies. However, the securities regulators could have limited the full application of the new requirements to ATSs trading securities of companies listed on Canadian exchanges. This would have provided adequate protection to the Canadian exchanges without denying Canadian investors access to foreign ATS markets.

By creating entry barriers for foreign ATSs that trade exclusively in foreign securities, the ATS rules are denying Canadian investors and market participants the opportunity to invest abroad through what may be more cost-effective or more efficient marketplaces. As a result, Canadian investors and market participants must look to Canadian exchanges and any Canadian ATSs that emerge to provide better and cheaper access to securities traded in foreign markets.

The introduction of ATSs also raises questions of market fragmentation and illiquidity, as well as the long-term implications for the survival of an independent capital market in Canada. The excerpt below highlights some of the public policy questions raised by these developments.

Mary Condon, "Technologies of Risk? Regulating Online Investing in Canada"
(2004) 26:3-4 Law & Pol'y 411 at 422-23, 424-25, 426-28

An issue which goes to the core of the growth of online investing is that of the proliferation of markets on which securities can be traded online. The development of trading technology makes it possible for more providers to enter the market for marketplaces. In the Canadian context, again following suit from the US, regulators recently considered the issue of what to do about so-called alternative trading systems (ATS), which provide automated matching systems bringing together orders from multiple buyers and sellers. In accordance with new economy imperatives, the policy debate was conducted using discourses of competition, efficiency, anonymity, choice and cheaper information costs. However, along with these ideas came the peculiarly Canadian concern with market fragmentation and consequent illiquidity. What is different from the suitability example considered above is the somewhat broader cast of characters in relation to ATSs, which include established trading markets and both institutional and retail investors. Canadian imperatives for the regulation of ATSs implicated at least two distinctive features of domestic capital markets, the size of the Canadian market for capital relative to that in the US, and the highly concentrated nature of the domestic financial services sector. In relation to the first issue, regulators articulated a fear that the advent of choices about marketplaces on which to trade securities would result in the development of a "capital market controlled and directed by other countries, in which only premium Canadian companies and major-league Canadian investors will be able to participate" (Brown 1999). Thus the discourse of "the survival of an independent capital market in Canada" and a fear of being swamped by new players with agendas not consistent with Canadian national interests framed the policy debate about how to regulate ATSs. With specific reference to the growth of ATSs in the US, Brown noted that "Alternative trading systems are about choice. If money managers or investors don't have that choice, they will take their business elsewhere."

Regulators presented the survival of Canadian capital markets as necessary to meet the needs of Canadian issuers and investors. However, another relevant aspect of the context here is the economics of the domestic financial services sector. In November 2000, William Hess, then the President and CEO of the Canadian Venture Exchange (CDNX) noted that the trading activities of all five of the bank-owned brokers on the Toronto Stock Exchange account for 53 percent of the TSX's trading volume and ten brokerage firms represent 80 percent of the TSX's volume. The fear articulated by the established exchanges then is as much about losing market share to competing ATSs set up by one or more large Canadian banks or investment dealers as it is about competitors from the US (such as Instinet or Archipelago) entering the Canadian market for marketplaces. Added to this is what Brown describes as a measurable growth in the "upstairs" market, that is the practice of crossing large blocks of shares for institutional customers off the exchange itself. Therefore one hypothesis about stock exchange responses to the introduction of the new rules for the operation of ATSs is that they are concerned to protect their own ongoing economic interests. …

The characteristics of ATSs are established so as to draw a clear distinction between them and organized exchanges with respect to regulation of issuers, disciplining of members/subscribers and a guarantee of a market. The absence of a guarantee of a two-sided market, which is also relevant in connection with the regulation of payments for order flow, imports some uncertainty about liquidity into the very definition of an ATS, despite the fact that increased liquidity is one of the policy goals of allowing ATSs to operate. Thus the regulation introduces a level of fragmentation and complexity into the very idea of a market, which is, as we have seen, one of the core mechanisms of neoliberal policy. It also facilitates a range of options for the manner in which investors may be governed. …

A significant feature of the rules relating to ATSs in Canada is that at present, the types of securities that can be traded on them are restricted to exchange-traded securities, corporate debt securities, government debt securities and foreign exchange-traded securities. …

This ensures that, at least in relation to equity securities, those traded on an ATS are also traded on at least one more senior marketplace. Another way of putting this obviously, is to say that TSX and one or more ATS will compete for orders related to securities listed on the TSX. …

A significant feature of the rule is that, as well as providing for the development of new marketplaces giving investors additional choices, marketplaces themselves also have choice about how they will be regulated. The options they may choose among are to be regulated as (i) a member of an exchange, (ii) as an exchange, (iii) as an ATS. An ATS will not be expected to discipline its subscribers or establish listing requirements for issuers. The approach of allowing choices among forms and intensity of regulation suggests that, as neo-liberal thinking would have it, regulation itself is being increasingly fragmented along with the markets, such that the intensity of regulation will vary among entities performing similar trading functions. …

Meanwhile, as we have seen, ATSs cannot carry on business unless they are registered as dealers, are members of an SRO, and comply with 21-101 and 23-101. ATSs have to keep subscriber's trading information confidential, including the identity of subscribers and their orders unless the subscriber otherwise consents, or the information is required by law to be released (such as, presumably, insider reporting rules). They are required to provide risk disclosure to subscribers who are not dealers, to the effect that they do not ensure best execution for subscribers. Subscribers are required to acknowledge that they have received this disclosure before their first order is traded (NI 21-101, s. 6.11). Significantly, ATSs are required to enter into a contract with a "regulation services provider" which will set requirements for ATS trading, monitor the trading activities of the ATS and its subscribers, and enforce its own rules (NI 23-101, s. 8.2). The regulatory body for ATSs has to be recognized by the OSC before any ATS can start trading. The record keeping requirements for marketplaces are found in Part 11 of 21-101. ATSs also have to enter into agreements with their subscribers that the latter will comply with the requirements of the regulation services provider. This arrangement also appears to be consistent with neoliberal modes of governing through decentralized contractual agreements rather than the content of regulation being centrally imposed by the government regulator. Indeed the very language of "regulation services provider," used for the first time in Canadian securities regulation, turns on its head the notion of regulation as a set of authoritative pronouncements from a centralized power and implies that "regulation services" are themselves another commodity to be bought and sold in the market. Again there is evidence of an increasing fragmentation of regulatory systems as well as of markets. However, the state regulators have retained the power to oversee the activities of regulation services providers, by way of, for example, requiring periodic reporting of its regulatory activities, approval of "significant changes" in the way regulation services are provided, and reporting of market misconduct if investors may suffer "serious damage" or there are grounds to believe fraud may be involved, as well as notification of "material systems failures and changes" (RS Recognition Order, January 29, 2002).

F. Price Reporting System

The companies listed on the CDN that did not join the Canadian Venture Exchange in 1999 became part of the Canadian Unlisted Board Inc (CUB), now a subsidiary of the TMX Group. CUB is a web-based system for dealers to report completed trades in unlisted and unquoted equity securities in Ontario (pursuant to part VI, reg 1015, under the OSA). CUB is a price quotation and reporting system, not a trading system. Trades are reported to the OSC for market surveillance purposes only. The OSC maintains regulatory jurisdiction over those issuers whose shares trade on the CUB, and who still must meet the prospectus and continuing disclosure requirements under securities law (Ontario Securities Commission, "Communication" (27 July 2004)).

With numerous exchanges, QTRSs, and ATSs, the securities market may seem overwhelmingly complex. However, it should be kept in mind that buyers and sellers of securities have to deal with only one marketplace participant depending on the type of securities they want to trade. In addition, securities regulations typically apply to issuers and registrants, not to members of the public who want to buy securities. This framework is acknowledged by way of the imposition of a registration requirement to trade securities, along with a series of exemptions from that requirement discussed below in Chapter 12. A key problem is that although the public is protected by these regulations, their complexity makes the scope and details of the protection offered difficult for the public to determine.

III. THE CURRENT CANADIAN REGULATORY STRUCTURE

With the range of markets discussed above, there has been a range of regulatory responses, including the development of securities commissions and self-regulatory organizations. However, these regulatory institutions do not operate in isolation; they are closely interconnected, both domestically and internationally.

A. Global Securities Regulation

Although securities trading within Canada is regulated domestically, Canada works with regulators internationally in an effort to bring some consistency and certainty to capital markets.

International Organization of Securities Commissions, *Fact Sheet*
(October 2016), online: <http://www.iosco.org/about/pdf/IOSCO-Fact-Sheet.pdf>

The International Organization of Securities Commissions (IOSCO) is the international body that brings together the world's securities regulators and is recognized as the global standard setter for the securities sector. IOSCO develops, implements, and promotes adherence to internationally recognized standards for securities regulation. It works intensively with the G20 and the Financial Stability Board (FSB) on the global regulatory reform agenda.

. . .

Scope of Activities
IOSCO was established in 1983. Its membership regulates more than 95% of the world's securities markets in more than 115 jurisdictions and includes all the major emerging markets.

The IOSCO Objectives and Principles of Securities Regulation have been endorsed by both the G20 and the Financial Stability Board (FSB) as the relevant standards in this area. They are IOSCO's main instrument to develop and implement internationally recognized and consistent standards of regulation, oversight and enforcement. They form the basis for the evaluation of the securities sector for the Financial Sector Assessment Programs (FSAPs) of the International Monetary Fund (IMF) and the World Bank.

Objectives

IOSCO members have resolved:

- to cooperate in developing, implementing and promoting adherence to internationally recognized and consistent standards of regulation, oversight and enforcement in order to protect investors, maintain fair, efficient and transparent markets, and seek to address systemic risks;
- to enhance investor protection and promote investor confidence in the integrity of securities markets, through strengthened information exchange and cooperation in enforcement against misconduct and in supervision of markets and market intermediaries; and
- to exchange information at both global and regional levels on their respective experiences in order to assist the development of markets, strengthen market infrastructure and implement appropriate regulation.

. . .

The 2020 Strategic Direction

At its Annual Conference in June 2015, IOSCO approved its 2020 Strategic Direction, which envisages that its goal for the rest of this decade will be to reinforce its position as the key global reference point for securities regulation. The strategy and the goal will be implemented through 43 initiatives in Action Plans covering six priority areas:

- *Research and Risk Identification*: Identifying risks arising from securities markets, including market activities, technology and product developments, and unintended consequences of changes or proposed changes in laws and regulations;
- *Standard Setting and Developing Guidance*: Improving the international regulatory framework for securities markets by developing standards and guidance that are timely, responsive to market developments, and internationally recognized;
- *Implementation Monitoring*: Promoting implementation of IOSCO standards through monitoring and assessment;
- *Capacity Building*: Addressing capacity building needs of its members, particularly in growth and emerging markets;
- *Co-operation and Information Exchange*: Strengthening the exchange of information and co-operation in the enforcement of markets regulation, and in the supervision of markets and market intermediaries; and
- *Collaboration and Engagement with other International Organizations*: Ensuring effective representation of IOSCO's views in other international organizations and effective collaboration with other standard setters within the international financial regulatory community.

B. Provincial and Territorial Securities Regulation in Canada

Each province and territory has a securities regulator, resulting in 13 separate regulatory authorities for securities law in Canada. The Canadian system is characterized as largely a "closed system" of securities regulation, based on the idea that all distributions of securities must be qualified by a prospectus and its attendant regulatory oversight unless an exemption applies. However, some jurisdictions have "open" aspects under their legislative framework in that they are not undertaking regulatory oversight for some types of distribution (see e.g. NI 45-102, *Resale of Securities*, as amended effective 25 January 2016, discussed in Chapter 5).

The BC Court of Appeal has commented on the issues that arise as a result of lack of harmonization of the provincial and territorial remedies available with respect to distributing securities.

Pearson v Boliden Ltd
2002 BCCA 624

[2] Most of the Acts create a "closed system" of securities trading and thereby regulate initial distributions of shares to the public, takeover bids, insider trading and the disclosure of information relating to publicly-traded shares. …

• • •

[63] In a very real sense, then, the Acts are analogous to consumer protection legislation. The conduct in the province of issuers, brokers and other market intermediaries, wherever they may reside or carry on business, is regulated in order to protect the public, and the integrity of the market, in that province. A dealer or broker may not trade in British Columbia unless it is registered to do so under the British Columbia Act. It matters not where the intermediary (or its customer) resides or carries on business. Similarly, an issuer that wishes to distribute shares in New Brunswick must comply with the prospectus requirements of the New Brunswick Act. This is so regardless of where the document is prepared or where the issuer has its head office. In this way, each province protects the investing public from misconduct in its territory, but at the same time, honours the principle of comity by respecting the legislative authority of other provinces to do likewise.

[64] I also take from the foregoing cases that the *lex loci delicti* choice of law rule is not directly applicable to the question of which provincial Act or Acts may found a statutory cause of action for misrepresentation in a prospectus. As La Forest J observed in *Tolofson*, courts are limited in exercising their powers (as to choice of law issues) to the same extent as the provincial legislatures. Thus, with all due respect to Mr. Klein's argument, I do not agree that it is open to a plaintiff, or a court of law, to choose to apply the Act of one province that will provide a cause of action in misrepresentation for a plaintiff who was solicited in and purchased his or her shares pursuant to a distribution in another province. Once the Act of a province applies to regulate (by means of a prospectus requirement) the "distribution" of securities taking place within the province's boundaries, *the same* Act must surely be looked to for any statutory cause of action for misrepresentation contained in the document. Its form, contents and filing are all mandated by the Act; the creation of a right to civil damages for infringing the Act must also be found in that Act.

[65] This is not to suggest that a provincial *Securities Act* may not have extra-provincial aspects or that activities in one province may not be incidentally affected by legislation in another. (*Gregory* and *McKenzie Securities* are obvious examples; see also *Global Securities Corp. v. British Columbia (Securities Commission)* [2000] 1 SCR 494.) Nor do I suggest that an issuer or market intermediary may not be subject to more than one Act in carrying on its business. The broad definition of "trade" in most of the Acts, extending to advertisements and solicitations, means that an underwriter or investment dealer in Ontario, for example, who mails out a monthly newsletter to all its clients across Canada, and who receives orders from investors in Alberta, is subject to the Acts of both provinces—Alberta because of the solicitation there, and Ontario because of the dealer's preparation of the bulletin, as well as its receipt of the buy order, there. But in respect of a misrepresentation contained in a prospectus circulated in a province and deemed to be relied on by a person in purchasing securities offered thereby, a court would in making a choice of law be bound to follow the constitutional principle that it is the province in whose territory the securities are distributed which has the jurisdiction (in the constitutional sense) to regulate the manner in which the distribution is carried out and to attach civil consequences to non-compliance.

[66] There are also practical reasons that support this choice of law. In an industry in which certainty and predictability are important, it avoids the complexity and uncertainty of rules such as the *lex loci delicti* rule applied to torts and the "most substantial connection" rule applied to contracts. It provides a principled way through the thicket of the many extra-provincial aspects that will be involved in any national securities distribution—the vagaries of where the issuer carries on business or maintains its share register, where the prospectus was prepared, where the issuer's directors reside, where the stock exchange (or now, the securities depository) is located (if electronic records can be said to be located anywhere), or where a particular plaintiff or defendant resided or carried on business at any particular time. (As an example of the difficulty of determining the *lex loci delicti* of a misrepresentation at common law, see *Canadian Commercial Bank v. Carpenter* (1989) 39 BCLR (2d) 312 (BCCA).) As well, it comports with what a reasonable investor would expect—that when he or she purchases shares offered under a distribution taking place in a province, the securities legislation of that province will govern the filing of the prospectus, its contents, and the rights and obligations of the parties thereunder.

QUESTIONS

1. List five distinguishing characteristics of Canadian capital markets.
2. What implications does this choice-of-law rule have for a competitive market for securities regulation?
3. Is competition among securities marketplaces beneficial or detrimental to Canada's capital markets?
4. Do provincial and territorial securities regulators compete with one another in Canada? Is this beneficial or detrimental to Canada's capital markets?

Securities regulators derive their authority from the provincial or territorial securities statute in their jurisdiction, which sets out their authority to regulate trading in securities. For example, the OSC is the regulatory body responsible for the administration of securities legislation in Ontario. It is a Crown corporation without share capital, composed of 9 to 16 members appointed by order in council (OSA, ss 3(2), 3(4), 3(12)). It is self-funded, primarily through fees payable by market participants to the commission under the OSA. Securities commissions interpret their jurisdiction having regard to the objectives of securities statutes. The purposes of the Ontario *Securities Act*, which is similar to securities laws across Canada, are:

> 1.1 The purposes of this Act are,
> (a) to provide protection to investors from unfair, improper or fraudulent practices; and
> (b) to foster fair and efficient capital markets and confidence in capital markets.

In pursuing these objectives, the Ontario *Securities Act* specifies that the commission will have regard to six fundamental principles, specifically:

> 2.1 In pursuing the purposes of this Act, the Commission shall have regard to the following fundamental principles:
> 1. Balancing the importance to be given to each of the purposes of this Act may be required in specific cases.
> 2. The primary means for achieving the purposes of this Act are,
> i. requirements for timely, accurate and efficient disclosure of information,
> ii. restrictions on fraudulent and unfair market practices and procedures, and
> iii. requirements for the maintenance of high standards of fitness and business conduct to ensure honest and responsible conduct by market participants.
> 3. Effective and responsive securities regulation requires timely, open and efficient administration and enforcement of this Act by the Commission.
> 4. The Commission should, subject to an appropriate system of supervision, use the enforcement capability and regulatory expertise of recognized self-regulatory organizations.
> 5. The integration of capital markets is supported and promoted by the sound and responsible harmonization and coordination of securities regulation regimes.
> 6. Business and regulatory costs and other restrictions on the business and investment activities of market participants should be proportionate to the significance of the regulatory objectives sought to be realized.

The Five Year Review commented on these principles and recommended additional principles.

Ontario Ministry of Finance, *Five Year Review Committee Final Report—Reviewing the Securities Act (Ontario)*
(Toronto: Queen's Printer for Ontario, 2003) 67-69 (footnotes omitted)

A) Promoting the Informed Participation of Investors in the Marketplace

Individual Canadians are investing in the capital markets in increasing numbers. With access to on-line research, advice and trading, individuals are becoming more directly involved in managing their own investments. In this environment, investor education has taken on a new importance. Retail investors face a bewildering array of choices. To invest wisely they need to understand the basics of investing and saving, know how to evaluate an investment or salesperson, and know how to protect themselves against possible fraud. We therefore recommend as reflected below that the Act be amended to incorporate in the Principles Clause the principle that effective and responsive securities regulation should promote the informed participation of investors in the marketplace. We note that the Commission has devoted considerable attention and resources to investor education in recent years.

B) Ontario's Place in Global Capital Markets

In Part 1 of this report, we discussed the importance of Canadian capital markets being competitive on a global basis. Globalization of financial services, coupled with advances in information technology, mean investors are no longer geographically bound. Cross-border, 24-hour trading is already commonplace. If our markets are healthy and vibrant, investors will choose Canada. If our markets do not measure up to international standards, investors will bypass Canada and seek quality elsewhere. We therefore recommend as reflected below that the Act be amended to incorporate in the Principles Clause the principle that capital markets are international in character and it is desirable to maintain the competitive position of Ontario's capital markets.

C) Facilitating Innovation

In recent years we have seen the development of new technologies, new financial products, new market participants and new trading methods. Such financial innovations should be encouraged. They reduce costs and enable investors to better manage their money. Regulators should work with the securities industry to facilitate innovation. In particular, participants should be encouraged to discuss new product ideas and new market developments with the regulators at an early stage to ensure that the risks and regulatory implications are properly understood and managed. Similarly, regulators should avoid unreasonable barriers to entry or restrictions on market participants launching new products. We therefore recommend as reflected below that the Act be amended to incorporate in the Principles Clause the principle that innovation in Ontario's capital markets should be facilitated.

D) Competition Among Market Participants

Competition among market participants is the main engine for innovation and in general works to consumers' best interests. The Commission should seek to ensure that its rules and policies do not impede or distort competition. In particular, it is important to maintain a level playing field among all market participants. We therefore recommend as reflected below that the Act be amended to incorporate in the Principles Clause the principle that the administration and enforcement of Ontario's securities law should not unnecessarily impede or distort competition among persons carrying on regulated activities .... Many of the principles complement one another and the Commission should consider them together when exercising its statutory mandate. We recognize that, in practice, there may be tensions between the different principles and that balancing these principles will not always be easy. We believe, however, that it should be left to the Commission to balance and prioritize competing principles as necessary.

The OSC operates under a memorandum of agreement with the Ontario Minister of Finance that sets out the respective roles and responsibilities, the accountability relationship, and the responsibility of the OSC to provide to the minister business plans, operational budgets, and any proposed significant changes in the activities of the commission (OSA, s 3.7). A chart setting out its structure follows on the facing page. The commission may also make bylaws governing the activities of the commission and setting out the powers and duties of commission members (OSA, s 3.2).

Securities law provides for investigation and enforcement, granting the commission authority to investigate and inquire into the affairs of the person or company, including any trades, communications, negotiations, or transactions. The commission has authority to examine the financial affairs of a market participant for the due administration of Ontario securities law or the regulation of the capital markets (OSA, ss 11(1), 11(3), 11(4), 12(1)). The commission can review the books, transaction records, and documents that are required to be kept by market participants and stock exchanges for the purpose of determining whether securities law is being complied with (OSA, s 20(1)). The enforcement powers of securities commissions are discussed in Chapter 11. The OSC is empowered to conduct hearings both within Ontario and outside the jurisdiction on matters arising under the statute. The OSC can also hold hearings in conjunction with other regulatory authorities, and joint hearings have become increasingly common as securities matters touch on multiple jurisdictions (OSA, ss 3.5, 3.6). The commission's mandate includes the review of decisions by the "director," a defined term in the Act that refers to the executive director, a director or deputy director of the commission, or other person employed by the commission and designated by the executive director (OSA, s 1(1)). Where the director has made a decision, any person or company directly affected by the decision may, within 30 days, request and be entitled to a hearing of the commission to review the decision (OSA, ss 8(1) to (4)).

The decisions of securities regulators are subject to review by the superior court of the province or territory. The decision being appealed still takes effect immediately, although the commission and the court both have jurisdiction to grant a stay pending disposition of an appeal. Generally, the courts accord a high level of deference to the decisions of securities regulators. In *British Columbia (Securities Commission) v CWM*, the appellant argued that the BC Securities Commission had not met the requirements of fundamental justice in denying the appellant the right to cross-examine an investigator.

British Columbia (Securities Commission) v CWM
2003 BCCA 244, 226 DLR (4th) 393, leave to appeal to SCC refused, [2003] SCCA No 341

[25] … [A]lthough (as noted in [*British Columbia Securities Commission v Imbeault*, [1998] BCJ No 1544 (QL) (SC)]) the *Securities Act* does not require judicial scrutiny for the issuance of a demand or summons by the Commission, the Court does retain a discretion to set aside an invalid summons or demand in order to prevent abuse of an "exceptional process." However, this does not equate to a right to cross-examine the investigator generally about her case. …

. . .

Ontario Securities Commission: Executive and Senior Management

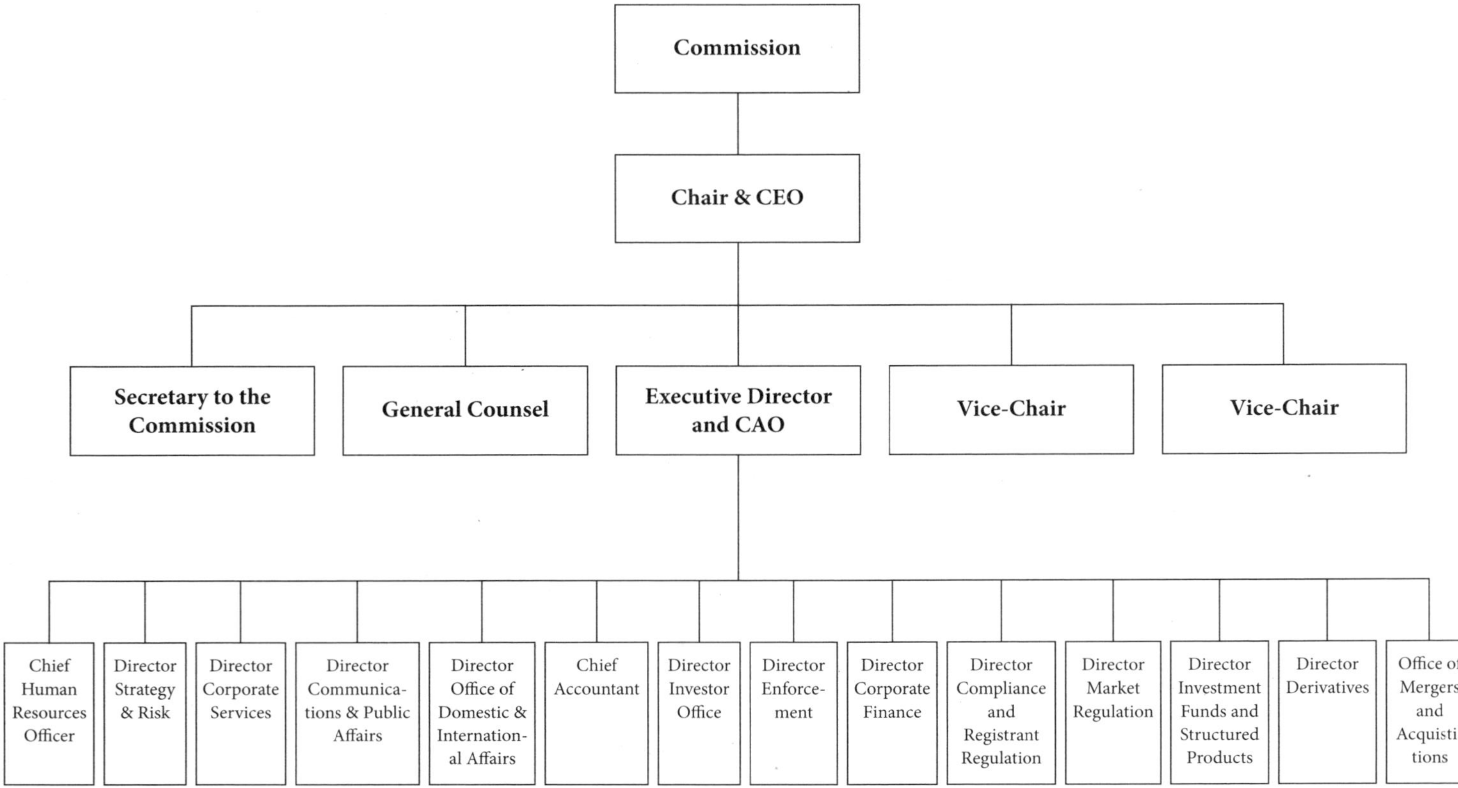

[33] *Branch* leaves no doubt that securities regulation is subject to much less stringent procedural safeguards than criminal law and that the compelling of personal attendance and document production for investigative purposes are generally not constitutionally objectionable. There is simply no basis in law for the notion that a person in [the appellant's] position has a constitutionally-protected right to cross-examine an investigator on an affidavit filed in support of a petition in the circumstances of this case.

In *Committee for the Equal Treatment of Asbestos Minority Shareholders v Ontario (Securities Commission)*, the Supreme Court of Canada discussed the scope and limits of securities regulators' authority. In particular, the Supreme Court examined the power to intervene in the market in the public interest. This discretion is granted to regulators where there is concern regarding protection of investors or public policy concern about the integrity or efficiency of the capital market. As you read the excerpt, consider how the Supreme Court endorses the broad scope of public interest jurisdiction while setting limits on the exercise of this power by securities regulators.

Committee for the Equal Treatment of Asbestos Minority Shareholders v Ontario (Securities Commission)
2001 SCC 37, [2001] 2 SCR 132

[45] In summary, pursuant to s. 127(1), the OSC has the jurisdiction and a broad discretion to intervene in Ontario capital markets if it is in the public interest to do so. However, the discretion to act in the public interest is not unlimited. In exercising its discretion, the OSC should consider the protection of investors and the efficiency of, and public confidence in, capital markets generally. In addition, s. 127(1) is a regulatory provision. The sanctions under the section are preventive in nature and prospective in orientation. Therefore, s. 127 cannot be used merely to remedy *Securities Act* misconduct alleged to have caused harm or damages to private parties or individuals.

• • •

[49] In this case, as in *Pezim*, it cannot be contested that the OSC is a specialized tribunal with a wide discretion to intervene in the public interest and that the protection of the public interest is a matter falling within the core of the OSC's expertise. Therefore, although there is no privative clause shielding the decisions of the OSC from review by the courts, that body's relative expertise in the regulation of the capital markets, the purpose of the Act as a whole and s. 127(1) in particular, and the nature of the problem before the OSC, all militate in favour of a high degree of curial deference. However, as there is a statutory right of appeal from the decision of the OSC to the courts, when this factor is considered with all the other factors, an intermediate standard of review is indicated. Accordingly, the standard of review in this case is one of reasonableness.

• • •

[57] The OSC was cautious in the application of its public interest jurisdiction in this case. This approach was informed by the OSC's previous jurisprudence and by four legitimate considerations inherent in s. 127 itself: (i) the seriousness and severity of the sanction applied for, (ii) the effect of imposing such a sanction on the efficiency of, and public

confidence in Ontario capital markets, (iii) a reluctance to use the open-ended nature of the public interest jurisdiction to police out-of-province activities, and (iv) a recognition that s. 127 powers are preventive in nature, not remedial.

[58] As noted above, in reaching its decision in this case, the OSC relied on its previous jurisprudence in [*Re Canadian Tire Corp* [(1987), 10 OSCB 857] and [*Re HERO Industries Ltd* (1990), 13 OSCB 3775] to identify the relevant factors to be considered. The OSC found that "the actions of the Quebec Government and SNA failed to comply with the spirit underlying the take-over bid rules of the Act …" (para. 71). However, the OSC did not, on the evidence, conclude that the transaction in this case was intentionally structured to avoid Ontario law (at para. 73):

> We were not presented with any evidence that the transaction which finally occurred was structured so as to make an Ontario transaction appear to be a non-Ontario one. This is not the case, like *Canadian Tire*, of "transactions that are clearly designed to avoid the animating principles behind" Ontario's take-over bid legislation and rules. The evidence was clear that the principal (and so far as the evidence went, the sole) purpose for structuring the transaction in its final form was the minimization of taxes on the profit received by GD Canada and GD US. In our view, the structuring of the transaction was not abusive of the integrity of the capital markets of this province, and cannot be relied on to provide the required nexus.

This finding of fact is reasonable and supported by the evidence.

[59] Granted, the OSC did find that "the actions of the Quebec Government and SNA … were abusive of the minority shareholders of Asbestos and were manifestly unfair to them" (para. 71). However, whether a s. 127(1) sanction is warranted depends on a consideration of all of the relevant factors together. In this case, the OSC also found that the capital markets in general, and the minority shareholders of Asbestos in particular, were not materially misled by the statements of Quebec's Minister of Finance respecting the prospect of a follow-up offer. This finding is supported by the evidence, including the several published reports that recommended caution and characterized an investment in Asbestos as speculative. In this case, such a finding can and did properly inform the OSC's discretion under s. 127.

[60] In addition, consistent with the two purposes of the Act described in s. 1.1 and because s. 127(1) sanctions are preventive in nature, it was open to the OSC to give weight to the fact that there has been no abuse of investors or other misconduct by the province of Quebec or SNA in the 13 years since the transaction at issue in this appeal. The OSC was also entitled to give weight to the fact that the removal of the province's exemptions is a very serious response that could have negative repercussions on other investors and the Ontario capital markets in general.

[61] Furthermore, the OSC did not find that there was no transactional connection with Ontario in this case, but that the transactional connection was insufficient to justify its intervening in the public interest. As noted by Chairman Beck in his dissenting opinion in *Re Asbestos Corp.* (1988), 11 OSCB 3419, a review of the OSC decisions on s. 124 (now s. 127) indicates that there has been careful use of the public interest jurisdiction and that in each case there was a clear and direct transactional connection with Ontario, contrary to the facts here: see *H.E.R.O., supra*; *Re Atco Ltd.* (1980), 15 OSCB 412; *Re Electra Investments (Canada) Ltd.* (1983), 6 OSCB 417; *Re Turbo Resources Ltd.* (1982), 4 OSCB 403C; *Re Genstar Corp.* (1982), 4 OSCB 326C.

[62] It is true that the OSC placed significant emphasis on the transactional connection factor. However, it was entitled to do so in order to avoid using the open-ended nature of s. 127 powers as a means to police too broadly out-of-province transactions. Capital markets and securities transactions are becoming increasingly international: see *Global Securities Corp. v. British Columbia (Securities Commission)*, [2000] 1 SCR 494, 2000 SCC 21, at paras. 27-28. There are a myriad of overlapping regulatory jurisdictions governing securities transactions. Under s. 2.1, para. 5 of the Act, one of the fundamental principles that the OSC has to consider is that "[t]he integration of capital markets is supported and promoted by the sound and responsible harmonization and co-ordination of securities regulation regimes." A transaction that is contrary to the policy of the Ontario *Securities Act* may be acceptable under another regulatory regime. Thus, the OSC's insistence on a more clear and direct connection with Ontario in this case reflects a sound and responsible approach to long-arm regulation and the potential for conflict amongst the different regulatory regimes that govern the capital markets in the global economy.

[63] In summary, the reasons of the OSC in this case were informed by the legitimate and relevant considerations inherent in s. 127(1) and in the OSC's previous jurisprudence on public interest jurisdiction. The findings of fact made by the OSC were reasonable and supported by the evidence. I conclude that the decision of the OSC in this case was reasonable and therefore should not be disturbed.

The court in *Committee for the Equal Treatment of Asbestos Minority Shareholders* held that, in exercising their public interest jurisdiction, securities regulators should consider the protection of investors and the efficiency of, and public confidence in, capital markets generally. These notions are further developed in the following case, *Re Cartaway Resources Corp*, where the Supreme Court of Canada considered the deterrent objectives of the sanctions provided in securities regulation.

Cartaway Resources Corp (Re)
2004 SCC 26, [2004] 1 SCR 672

[55] In this appeal we are asked whether it is reasonable to decide that general deterrence has a role to play in the policing of capital markets. The conventional view is that participants in capital markets are rational actors. This is probably more true of market systems than it is of social behaviour. It is therefore reasonable to assume, particularly with reference to the expertise of the Commission in regulating capital markets, that general deterrence has a proper role to play in determining whether to make orders in the public interest and, if they choose to do so, the severity of those orders.

[56] This approach is consonant with United States securities jurisprudence, which accepts that general deterrence may be a consideration in imposing penalties for fraudulent behaviour. The rationale is that the public interest demands appropriate sanctions to secure compliance with the rules, regulations and policies of the Securities and Exchange Commission (SEC) … .

...

[58] "Public interest" is not defined in the Act. This Court considered the scope of a securities commission's public interest jurisdiction in *Asbestos, supra*. At issue in *Asbestos* was the Ontario Securities Commission's jurisdiction to intervene in Ontario's capital markets, for purposes of protection and prevention, if it is in the public interest to do so pursuant to s. 127(1) of the *Securities Act*, RSO 1990, c. S.5. This Court held that the discretion to act in the public interest is not unlimited. In exercising its discretion the Commission should consider "the protection of investors and the efficiency of, and public confidence in, capital markets generally" (*Asbestos*, supra, at para. 45). Because s. 127 is regulatory, its sanctions are not remedial or punitive, but rather are preventative in nature and prospective in application. As a result, this Court held that s. 127 could not be used to redress misconduct alleged to have caused harm to private parties or individuals: *Asbestos, supra*, at paras. 41-45. It should be observed that our Court was not considering the function of general deterrence in the exercise of the jurisdiction of a securities commission to impose fines and administrative penalties nor denying that general deterrence might play a role in this respect.

[59] Braidwood J.A. understood *Asbestos, supra*, to foreclose the imposition of public interest penalties for the purpose of general deterrence. With respect, Braidwood J.A.'s interpretation was mistaken.

[60] In my view, nothing inherent in the Commission's public interest jurisdiction, as it was considered by this Court in *Asbestos, supra*, prevents the Commission from considering general deterrence in making an order. To the contrary, it is reasonable to view general deterrence as an appropriate, and perhaps necessary, consideration in making orders that are both protective and preventative. Ryan J.A. recognized this in her dissent: "The notion of general deterrence is neither punitive nor remedial. A penalty that is meant to generally deter is a penalty designed to discourage or hinder like behaviour in others" (para. 125).

[61] The *Oxford English Dictionary* (2nd ed. 1989), Vol. XII, defines "preventive" as "[t]hat anticipates in order to ward against; precautionary; that keeps from coming or taking place; that acts as a hindrance or obstacle." A penalty that is meant to deter generally is a penalty that is designed to keep an occurrence from happening; it discourages similar wrongdoing in others. In a word, a general deterrent is preventative. It is therefore reasonable to consider general deterrence as a factor, albeit not the only one, in imposing a sanction under s. 162. The respective importance of general deterrence as a factor will vary according to the breach of the Act and the circumstances of the person charged with breaching the Act.

[62] It may well be that the regulation of market behaviour only works effectively when securities commissions impose ex post sanctions that deter forward-looking market participants from engaging in similar wrongdoing. That is a matter that falls squarely within the expertise of securities commissions, which have a special responsibility in protecting the public from being defrauded and preserving confidence in our capital markets.

QUESTIONS

1. In its discussion of market actors, the Supreme Court of Canada refers to them as rational actors. What does the concept of a rational actor in a market have to do with whether general deterrence is appropriate in determining sanctions under securities laws?

2. What are the countervailing arguments as to whether securities regulators' authority to intervene in markets and make decisions "in the public interest" should be interpreted narrowly or broadly?

3. Multi-million dollar penalties can be imposed by securities regulators in Canada. Why is it important that the Supreme Court of Canada has determined that such penalties are not punitive or remedial and that they can be imposed for the purpose of general deterrence?

Most of Canada's larger securities commissions have an advisory committee comprising industry professionals and securities law practitioners to provide advice on legislative and policy initiatives, important capital market trends, and on the legal, regulatory, and market implications of policies. Canadian securities regulators will also usually engage in an open process of public consultation in respect of any significant changes to securities regulation. The purpose of such consultations is to ensure that the effects and implications of any proposed changes are understood and that the public and industry are aware of potential changes well in advance of their implementation.

1. Independence of the Adjudication Function

Most securities regulators in Canada perform both the investigative and adjudicative functions under securities law. This structure of securities enforcement has been criticized because it differs from the notion that only an arm's-length, independent quasi-judicial tribunal should review decisions made by those investigating and enforcing a remedial statute in the first instance.

Ontario Ministry of Finance, *Five Year Review Committee Final Report: Reviewing the Securities Act (Ontario)*
(Toronto: Queen's Printer for Ontario, 2003) 64-65 (footnotes omitted)

The Commission is a multi-functional administrative agency. It discharges a number of different and overlapping roles at the same time, including making policy, conducting investigations and sitting as an administrative tribunal.

We have considered whether the structure of the Commission, which permits it to develop policy, conduct investigations and adjudicate issues which come before it, should be modified. We reviewed the structure of other administrative tribunals in Canada, and of securities regulatory authorities in Canada, the U.S., the U.K. and Australia. We have also considered the case law in Canada concerning the functions of administrative tribunals.

The structure of the Commission, combining both regulatory and adjudicative functions in one administrative agency, is neither unique to the Commission nor contrary to the common law doctrine of reasonable apprehension of bias. The Supreme Court of Canada has considered multi-functional administrative agencies similar to the Commission on several occasions, and has consistently held that if the multiple functions are authorized by statute (as they are in the case of the Commission), the administrative tribunal cannot be attacked on grounds of reasonable apprehension of bias, solely because the structure, albeit statutorily authorized, expressly authorizes and directs it to perform overlapping functions.

The question, then, is not whether the current structure is permissible, but whether it is one which gives rise to perceptions of potential for conflict or abuse. This is a complex issue. There are advantages and disadvantages to both an integrated tribunal with "overlapping functions" as well as a bifurcated model where the investigative and adjudicative functions are performed by separate entities. We make no recommendation on this issue at this time other than to note that because the structure of a multi-functional agency can give rise to perceptions of potential for conflicts or abuse, the current structure of the Commission merits further thought and study on a priority basis.

Recommendation

We recommend that the current structure of the Commission as a multi-functional agency be given further thought and study by the Commission and the Minister on a priority basis.

Subsequent to this recommendation, the OSC initiated an examination of the independence of the adjudicative function. A committee chaired by The Honourable Coulter Osbourne released its final report on March 5, 2004, *Report of the Fairness Committee to the Ontario Securities Commission* (Toronto: Queen's Printer, 2004), recommending bifurcation of the adjudicative function. The report recommended the creation of an adjudicative tribunal that would be separate from the policy-setting, rule-making, and enforcement functions of the OSC. Such a separation would address concerns regarding the perception of fairness and independence in the adjudication of decisions made by securities regulators. The Osbourne report concluded that such bifurcation would allow for better articulation of public interest standards by the adjudicative tribunal, in turn allowing market participants to better govern themselves (*Report of the Fairness Committee* at 15). The report also concluded that separation of the adjudicative function would enhance the current role of securities commissioners, freeing them to take an active role in the establishment of enforcement priorities and practices and ensuring better accountability mechanisms within the commission. The WPC had also recommended a bifurcated structure. The Expert Panel on Securities Regulation in Canada, in its proposal for a common securities regulator, has also proposed an independent adjudicative tribunal, as discussed below.

A report of the Ontario Legislature's Standing Committee on Finance and Economic Affairs followed the Osborne report recommendations and endorsed a bifurcation of the adjudicative function of securities regulation. As a result, in November 2004, the Ontario government announced plans to overhaul the OSC by splitting its roles as prosecutor and adjudicator (K Howlett, "OSC Policing, Judging Roles to Be Split in Major Overhaul," *The Globe and Mail* (2 November 2004) B1).

Philip Anisman offers a different viewpoint on the adjudicative function, suggesting that "Concerns about impartiality in Commission adjudication implicate the commission's accountability. If the commission's decisions were reviewable *de novo* by the courts, concerns over its adjudicative structure, especially in light of its internal separation of functions, might be viewed less seriously. In the current circumstances, the commission's accountability remains an important issue that extends well beyond its adjudicative functions"; Philip Anisman, "The Ontario Securities Commission as Regulators: Adjudication, Fairness, and Accountability" in Anita I Anand & William F Flanagan, eds, *Conflicts of Interest in Capital Market Structures* (Kingston, Ont: Faculty of Law, Queen's University, 2005).

The Expert Panel on Securities Regulation proposed a national independent adjudicative tribunal as part of its draft national securities act in 2009.

Expert Panel on Securities Regulation, *Creating an Advantage in Global Capital Markets*

Final Report and Recommendations (January 2009) at 29-31 (footnotes omitted)

We have reviewed the merits of an independent adjudicative tribunal for Canada. We note that this issue is fundamentally about the perception of fairness in the adjudication of regulatory matters rather than strengthening enforcement.

Most securities commissions in Canada conduct regulatory, enforcement, and adjudicative functions. They develop policies and rules, investigate and prosecute alleged regulatory misconduct, and preside over adjudicative proceedings. The adjudication of regulatory matters is conducted by the commissioners of the securities commission who preside over hearings to review the facts of the case, to hear the arguments, and to render a decision. Numerous commentators suggest that this multifunctional commission structure fosters the perception that the adjudicative process is unfair, lacking independence and impartiality. They recommend that the responsibility for adjudication should be given to an independent adjudicative tribunal.

...

We believe that an independent adjudicative tribunal should be established within a framework of a single securities act administered by a single securities regulator for Canada. A national tribunal, adjudicating matters based on the securities regulations and rules administered by a single securities regulator, would provide greater consistency in decisions and concentrate adjudicative expertise. The adjudicative tribunal would also better support a more principles-based approach to securities regulation, since it would likely provide greater consistency in the interpretation and application of principles in its decisions.

In the absence of a single securities regulator, action should be taken to examine proposals that respond to recent calls to create a pan-Canadian independent adjudicative tribunal within the current system. Such a tribunal could be established unilaterally by the provinces, or in collaboration with the federal government, depending on the desired scope of adjudicative powers to be delegated to the tribunal.

The proposed Cooperative Capital Markets Regulatory System discussed below involves the creation of the Capital Markets Regulatory Authority (CMRA), which will have a regulatory division and a separate adjudicative division. The regulatory division will be responsible for policy, regulatory operations, advisory services, and enforcement functions of the CMRA, and the adjudicative division will adjudicate enforcement and other administrative proceedings through a tribunal of independent expert adjudicators.

The CMRA will also feature a regulatory policy forum for consultation on policy issues, which will include members from both divisions for the purpose of facilitating discussion among the regulators and adjudicators of the CMRA on significant policy issues (Memorandum of Agreement Regarding the Cooperative Capital Markets Regulatory System (23 July 2015), online: <http://ccmr-ocrmc.ca/publications/>.

QUESTIONS

1. Should securities commissions simultaneously perform policy-making, enforcement, and adjudication, or should there be a separate, independent quasi-judicial or judicial process to review the policy and enforcement decisions of securities regulatory authorities? What are the advantages of each model?
2. Is it feasible, in the absence of a national or cooperative regulator, to create a pan-Canadian independent adjudicative tribunal within the current system as the expert panel recommended?

2. Structural Shifts

With the move to global markets, provincial securities regulators are shifting their structure and priorities in an effort to increase enforcement and enhance investor confidence. For example, Québec consolidated its regulatory authority under the Autorité des marchés financiers (AMF), following a global trend toward integration. Established on February 1, 2004, the AMF was created pursuant to the *Act respecting the Autorité des marchés financiers* (CQLR c A-33.2), whose purpose is to better integrate the supervision of all financial sector participants under the government's jurisdiction. The AMF's mission is to enforce the laws governing the regulation of the financial sector, notably in the areas of insurance, securities, deposit-taking institutions other than banks, and the distribution of financial products and services. The AMF reports that almost 15,000 businesses and approximately 48,000 individuals operate in these areas.

When it was established, the AMF brought together the responsibilities and staff of five separate organizations: the Québec Securities Commission; the Québec Deposit Insurance Board; the Financial Services Office; the Financial Services Compensation Fund; and the Inspector General of Financial Institutions. The explicit rationale for this consolidation of the operations of these various financial regulatory entities was to improve consumer protection and consumer confidence; to establish a regulator better able to act responsively, particularly in times of crisis; and to increase regulatory efficiency and reduce the administrative burden on industry by providing a single point of access for all financial regulation in the province. It was also thought that a single regulator would be better able to monitor capital market activity and approach regulatory issues in a more holistic and less fragmented or siloed manner than the five predecessor organizations.

Provincial governments in Saskatchewan, New Brunswick, and Manitoba have also integrated securities regulation with the regulation of other financial services in their respective provinces. In Saskatchewan, the former Saskatchewan Securities Commission is now the

Securities Division of the Financial and Consumer Affairs Authority, which was established in 2011 and has responsibility for regulating securities as well as insurance, pensions, credit unions, trust and loan companies, mortgage brokers, payday lending, and many other financial services. In New Brunswick, the Financial and Consumer Services Commission was established in 2013 and is responsible for the administration and enforcement of provincial legislation relating to securities as well as insurance, pensions, credit unions, trust and loan companies, co-operatives, and a wide range of other consumer legislation. In Manitoba, the Manitoba Securities Commission operates as a division of the Manitoba Financial Services Agency, which was created in 2012 and also administers regulations relating to insurance, trusts, cooperatives and credit unions.

The current system of securities regulation in Canada has been criticized as inefficient. A principal criticism is that registrants and issuers must meet the legal requirements of each province and territory in which they seek to distribute securities, resulting in costly duplicative processes. Although this inefficiency has been mitigated by the passport system described below, and there are advantages in terms of accessibility to regulators on a regional basis, many issuers now trade in multiple jurisdictions and are interested in minimizing any perceived inefficiencies and compliance risks. Moreover, with changes to technology, the need to have a physically accessible commission is not as pressing as it was historically.

Notwithstanding the inefficiency that occurs with the existence of multiple regulators, the cooperation of provincial and territorial securities regulators is growing through a series of national instruments and accompanying national policy statements that are discussed throughout this casebook. The forum for this collaboration is the Canadian Securities Administrators (CSA), an association with representatives of the 13 provincial and territorial regulators and a permanent secretariat that undertakes policy and administrative support for its initiatives. The CSA has been instrumental in the considerable advances made in the past two decades toward the harmonization of Canadian securities laws. It has facilitated the development of national instruments with respect to disclosure, mutual fund regulation, cross-border trading, and other key regulatory areas. Instruments are adopted by provinces through their statutory rule-making power, by policy, or by regulation, depending on the jurisdiction.

An early milestone in the harmonization of Canadian securities regulation was the development of the Mutual Reliance Review System (MRRS) by the CSA in 1999 ((1999), 22 OSCB 7308 (NP 43-201); National Policy 12-201). MRRS allowed a securities regulator to rely on the review and analysis of a regulator from a different provincial or territorial jurisdiction in respect of prospectus review, exemptive relief applications, pre-filing, annual information forms, and waiver applications. MRRS allowed the issuer to ask that one regulator act as principal regulator, which would then provide comments and a decision on behalf of all the other regulators. The MRRS went a long measure toward fostering cooperation and facilitating the distribution of securities. There were, however, disadvantages to the system. Each regulator retained statutory jurisdiction to opt out of this process at any time and impose its own requirements on the market participant seeking approval of the prospectus or application for exemptive relief. This rarely occurred, however, absent a highly unusual issue that engaged the public policy concerns of the particular regulator. While there was some convergence effect as a result of joint MRRS decisions, the system did not explicitly seek to harmonize standards. Issuers had to comply with the securities laws of 13 different jurisdictions if they wished to distribute in all of Canada and were required to pay fees in every jurisdiction in which they wished to register and distribute securities, which maintained a cost barrier in the system.

C. The Passport System

In 2008, the CSA introduced the passport system, replacing the MRRS system. Under the passport system, all Canadian regulators, except Ontario, have agreed that one securities regulatory authority acts as the principal regulator for all materials relating to a filer (Multilateral Instrument 11-102, *Passport System* (MI 11-102) and Companion Policy 11-102CP, *Passport System* (CP 11-102)). National Instrument 41-101, *General Prospectus Requirements*, was amended at the time to expressly recognize the passport system, creating a "passport prospectus" and a "dual prospectus," where issuers are seeking to distribute securities in more than one Canadian jurisdiction. All jurisdictions have agreed to cooperate under National Policy 11-202, *Process for Prospectus Reviews in Multiple Jurisdictions*, effective 17 March 2008 (NP 11-202), which describes the process for filing and review of prospectuses, including investment fund and shelf prospectuses, amendments to prospectuses and related materials in multiple jurisdictions, and sets out the means by which an issuer can enjoy the benefits of coordinated review by the principal regulator and Ontario regulator in filing and receipting of prospectuses. The introduction of the passport system marked a new level of coordination among securities regulators.

The purpose of MI 11-102 and CP 11-102 is to implement, in the main areas of securities regulation, a system that gives a market participant access to the capital markets in multiple jurisdictions by dealing only with its principal regulator and meeting the requirements of one set of harmonized laws. Although the OSC did not adopt MI 11-102, it can be a principal regulator under the instrument, thereby giving market participants in Ontario access to the capital markets in passport jurisdictions by dealing only with the OSC (NP 11-202, National Policy 11-203, *Process for Exemptive Relief Applications in Multiple Jurisdictions,* and National Policy 43-201, *Mutual Reliance Review System for Prospectuses*, effective 18 March 2008). The Instrument gives each market participant a single window of access to the capital markets in multiple jurisdictions. It enables a person or company to deal only with its principal regulator to get deemed receipts in other jurisdictions (except Ontario) for a preliminary prospectus and prospectus, and obtain automatic exemptions in other jurisdictions (except Ontario) equivalent to most types of discretionary exemptions granted by the principal regulator.

One advantage of the passport system is that the process of negotiation among different regulators to develop and maintain the system has allowed for considerable public policy debate on the impact of proposed standards on particular types of issuers, investors, and the market more generally. The disadvantage of the passport system is the inefficiency inherent in building consensus on regulatory changes that may be required. There is also the challenge that different regulators may interpret and enforce nationally negotiated standards differently, although regulators make significant efforts to cooperate in their compliance and enforcement initiatives.

CSA has also developed and maintained a number of vital national information technology systems, including:

- The System for Electronic Document Analysis and Retrieval (SEDAR), a national web-based filing system that facilitates the electronic filing of securities information that is required by securities regulators. SEDAR provides public access to most of the documents filed by issuers as part of the continuous disclosure regime (National Instrument 13-101, *System for Electronic Document Analysis and Retrieval (SEDAR)*, as amended 8 December 2015, online: <http://www.sedar.com>).

- The System for Electronic Disclosure by Insiders (SEDI), which facilitates the filing and public dissemination of insider reports in electronic format via the Internet (<http://www.sedi.ca>). SEDI is discussed in Chapter 8 on insider trading.
- The National Cease Trade Order Database, which provides a publicly searchable database of all cease trade orders issued by CSA members.
- The National Registration Database, which is an integrated database of all persons and companies registered by securities regulators in Canada.
- The National Registration Search, which is a searchable, web-based tool to provide information about individuals and firms registered with securities regulators to the public (<http://www.securities-administrators.ca/nrs/nrsearchprep.aspx>).
- The Disciplined List, which provides a publicly searchable web-based list of names of individuals and companies that have been disciplined by securities regulators in Canada (<https://www.securities-administrators.ca/disciplinedpersons.aspx>).

Many of these systems are based on aging technology. As part of its 2016-2019 business plan, the CSA has initiated a large scale project to replace all of these national systems with a single, intuitive and secure filing system for regulators and market participants to be delivered in phases over a three-year period (<https://www.securities-administrators.ca/uploadedFiles/General/pdfs/CSA_Business_Plan_2016-2019.pdf>).

These initiatives illustrate how technology is being used to increase the transparency, accessibility, and timeliness of disclosures required under securities legislation and other information of importance to the investing public. There are also cross-border initiatives with US securities regulators and the Multijurisdictional Disclosure System (MJDS), as discussed in Chapter 4.

IV. THE OVERSIGHT ROLE OF OTHER SELF-REGULATORY ORGANIZATIONS

As discussed above in relation to markets, self-regulatory organizations (SROs) are non-government organizations that regulate the operations and business conduct of their members in the public interest. These organizations include marketplaces, clearing agencies, and investor protection funds, as well as national organizations that oversee the activities of registered investment dealers and mutual fund dealers. The OSA gives the commission the power to "recognize" SROs and explicitly states that the commission should use the enforcement capability and regulatory expertise of recognized SROs in pursuing the purposes of the act (OSA, s 2.1(4)). A recognized SRO is required to regulate the operations and the standards of practice and business conduct of its members and their representatives in accordance with its bylaws, rules, regulations, policies, procedures, interpretations and practices (OSA, s 21.1(3)). The commission retains the power to oversee the activities of a recognized SRO, however, and can make any decision with respect to any bylaw, rule, regulation, policy, procedure, interpretation or practice of a recognized SRO (OSA, s 21.1(4)).

Securities regulators have the authority to assign specified powers and duties in respect of marketplace regulation to SROs and to require them to undergo independent audits of their activities and to file financial reports. There are also provisions for independent audit of their activities and the filing of financial reports with the commissions. In the case of the TSX in Ontario, there are specified restrictions on the amount of interest in the TSX that any one entity can own—specifically, no entity can beneficially own or control more than 5 percent of any class or series of voting shares without prior approval of the commission (OSA, s 21.11). Securities legislation also specifies that any rules, policies, procedures, or practices implemented by exchanges and QTRS must not contravene securities laws. Securities commissions also retain jurisdiction to review decisions, orders, rules, and policies of the recognized stock exchange, recognized SRO, recognized QTRS, or recognized clearing agency, in the same manner that review and hearing of decisions of the director are heard and determined by the commission.

A. Investment Industry Regulatory Organization of Canada

When the TSX decided to become an issuer itself, there was concern that it would function under a conflict of interest. How could the exchange be a for-profit entity and regulate the conduct of members on the exchange at the same time? Thus a separate entity, Market Regulation Services Inc (RS) was created as part of the self-regulatory system to monitor trading on the TSX exchanges. RS was co-owned by the Investment Dealers Association of Canada (IDA) and the TSX Group. In 2008, IDA and RS merged to create the Investment Industry Regulatory Organization of Canada (IIROC) with a purpose of setting high-quality regulatory and investment industry standards, protecting investors, and strengthening market integrity while maintaining efficient and competitive capital markets. IIROC carries out its regulatory responsibilities through setting and enforcing rules regarding the proficiency, business, and financial conduct of dealer firms and their registered employees and through setting and enforcing market integrity rules regarding trading activity on Canadian equity marketplaces. It received approval from securities regulators in 2008. For example, in Ontario, the Minister of Finance approved the memorandum of understanding (MOU) regarding the oversight of IIROC, in effect on 1 September 2008.

IIROC carries out its regulatory responsibilities under recognition orders from the ten provincial securities regulators in Canada. For administrative ease, these ten securities regulators have entered into a memorandum of understanding regarding the oversight of IIROC, which provides that IIROC's activities will be monitored by an oversight committee made up of staff representatives from each regulator. This committee is the venue for the discussion of issues, concerns, and proposals related to the oversight of IIROC and conducts oversight and regular operational reviews of IIROC's activities. A principal regulator is also designated under the memorandum of understanding to act as a primary regulatory contact for IIROC.

IIROC describes its activities as follows.

Investment Industry Regulatory Organization of Canada,
Our Role & Mandate
online: <http://www.iiroc.ca/about/ourroleandmandate/Pages/default.aspx>

IIROC carries out its regulatory responsibilities through setting and enforcing rules regarding the proficiency, business and financial conduct of dealer firms and their registered employees and through setting and enforcing market integrity rules regarding trading activity on Canadian equity marketplaces. To fulfill our mandate as a national self-regulatory organization, we must act with integrity, transparency and fairness.

What IIROC Does

- Writes rules that set high regulatory and investment industry standards.
- Screens all investment advisors employed by IIROC-regulated firms to ensure they are of good character, are properly trained and have successfully completed all the required educational courses, background checks and programs.
- Conducts financial compliance reviews and sets minimum capital requirements to ensure that firms have enough capital for the specific nature and volume of their business. This reduces the possibility of firms failing by preventing excessive leverage and risky business practices. (IIROC-regulated firms also participate in the Canadian Investor Protection Fund which protects individual investors in the unlikely event that a firm should go bankrupt.)
- Conducts business conduct compliance reviews to check that firms have procedures in place to properly supervise the handling of client accounts and that advice and transactions appropriately reflect the client's needs and instructions. IIROC-approved advisors must follow suitability and "know your client" rules by being familiar with a client's financial situation, investment needs, objectives, investing experience and tolerance for risk.
- Conducts trading conduct compliance reviews to check trading firms' trade-desk procedures. The reviews assess whether trade-desk procedures comply with the Universal Market Integrity Rules (UMIR) and applicable provincial securities law.
- Conducts market surveillance and trading review analysis to ensure that trading is carried out in accordance with UMIR and applicable provincial securities law.
- Investigates possible dealer or marketplace misconduct by its dealer firms, approved persons and other market participants and can bring disciplinary proceedings which may result in penalties including fines, suspensions and permanent bans or terminations for individuals and firms. (Money from fines and settlements is contributed to IIROC's restricted fund, which IIROC uses to fund capital expenditures necessary to address emerging regulatory issues, projects relating to investor and industry education, and other uses authorized under IIROC's Recognition Orders.)

IIROC's ownership structure is one of membership and not shareholders. The members are dealers and marketplace members. For example, the TSX is a marketplace member because it is one of the marketplaces that IIROC regulates. IIROC currently provides regulation services in relation to equity securities trading on a number of Canadian marketplaces. A marketplace that retains IIROC to be its regulation services provider will become a marketplace member. In order to retain IIROC's market regulation services, a marketplace must be recognized by or registered with a member of the Canadian Securities Administrators, in compliance with the applicable securities laws within each jurisdiction. In addition, where the marketplace is an alternative trading system, it must also be an IIROC dealer member in order to qualify as a marketplace member. IIROC's financing comes from member fees.

Previously, because RS was owned in part by one of the exchanges that it monitored, there was some question as to whether it was the appropriate vehicle to monitor TSX and TSXV exchange activity. There was normative disagreement as to whether the TSX, which owned RS, could be adequately monitored by it, as well as debate about the public policy implications of the TSX move to capture the market for regulation. One view suggested that the concern about conflicts of interest had been overstated and that experience was needed before one could assess whether the lack of a competitive market for regulation services would disadvantage Canadian capital markets. Another view has suggested that there are some risks associated with the model of contracting out market regulation services to a market and the regulator being functionally detached from the market, particularly where the market for regulation services has been captured by established interests such that the objectives of creating the market in the first place, including promotion of greater investment choices and broader competition, may not be fully realized. For a discussion of contrasting views on this issue, see Richard Balfour, "Publicly Listed Stock Exchanges and Conflicts of Interest: The Case of TSX," unpublished paper presented at the Queen's Annual Business Law Symposium 2003, and Mary Condon, "Technologies of Risk? Regulating Online Investing in Canada" (2004) 26:3-4 Law & Pol'y 413. Under the new structure, there might still be some potential for conflict of interest because marketplace members also contract with IIROC to provide regulation services to that marketplace.

B. Other Intermediaries in the Regulatory Structure

There are a number of other financial intermediaries and SROs that are involved in monitoring and enforcement of the integrity of capital markets. SROs make rules about the requirements for participation in the markets or professions to which they control access. The Mutual Fund Dealers Association of Canada (MFDA) is the national self-regulatory organization for the distribution side of the Canadian mutual fund industry, and was established in 1998 at the initiative of the CSA. The MFDA regulates the operations, standards of practice, and business conduct of its members and their representatives with a mandate to enhance investor protection and strengthen public confidence in the Canadian mutual fund industry. The MFDA is structured as a not-for-profit corporation and its members are mutual fund dealers that are licensed with provincial securities regulators.

The Canadian Depository for Securities, now a subsidiary of TMX Group, undertakes the clearing, settlement, and payment for trades; one of three depositories along with the Canadian Derivatives Clearing House and the Canadian Payments Association, which operates national clearing and settlement systems that facilitate the flow of funds between institutions and mitigate risk to payment system participants.

The Canadian Investor Protection Fund was established in 1969 as an industry-sponsored trust that is designed to protect investors from the harshest consequences of insolvency of a member firm. CIPF operates under a memorandum of understanding with the CSA that addresses its governance, funding and maintenance as well as its investor protection and reporting responsibilities. All dealer members of IIROC are required to be members of CIPF (<http://www.cipf.ca/Public/AboutUs.aspx>).

Following the fraud and accounting scandal that resulted in the 2002 collapse of Enron and Arthur Anderson, then one of the United States' largest companies and one of the world's largest accounting firms, the accounting industry collaborated with securities regulators and the Office of the Superintendent of Financial Institutions to set up a public accountability board designed to improve investor confidence. The Canadian Public Accountability Board (CPAB) was established in 2003 as a federal not-for-profit corporation. CPAB is recognized formally by Canada's securities regulators through National Instrument 52-108, *Auditor Oversight* (NI 52-108), which requires auditors of reporting issuers to be registered with CPAB. Its mission is "Effective regulation—Proactively identify current and emerging risks to the integrity of financial reporting of public companies in Canada by assessing how auditors effectively respond to those risks, identifying root causes and requiring remediation of any audit firm quality issues, and engaging those charged with governance, regulators and standard setters to develop sustainable solutions to enhance audit quality" (NI 53-108, CPAB, *Backgrounder* (2016), online: <http://www.cpab-ccrc.ca/en/About/Backgrounder/Pages/default.aspx>).

CPAB carries out its mission by conducting inspections of the firms over which it has oversight responsibility, on a schedule that depends on the number of reporting issuers the firm audits. Firms with 100 or more reporting issuer clients are inspected annually, those with between 50 and 99 reporting issuer clients are inspected at least once every two years, and those with less than 50 reporting issuer clients are inspected at least once every three years (<http://www.cpab-ccrc.ca/en/About/Inspections/InspectionProcess/Pages/default.aspx>). To enable audit oversight for foreign audit firms with Canadian clients and to assess the quality of audits involving global issuers, CPAB has entered into protocols and reciprocal sharing agreements with the Public Company Accounting Oversight Board (PCAOB) as well as similar organizations in the United Kingdom, Australia, Japan, the Netherlands, France, and Germany (<http://www.cpab-ccrc.ca/en/About/InternationalActivity/Pages/default.aspx>).

As will become clear in later chapters, accountants who act as auditors of public companies are a crucial component of the disclosure-based regime of securities regulation. Their professional independence in auditing financial reports makes them one of the "gatekeepers" of confidence in capital markets.

V. CRITIQUES OF THE CANADIAN REGULATORY SYSTEM

The current regulatory structure poses a number of problems. All capital market participants face great difficulty in undertaking policy development. Although there have been major advances in collaboration among regulators, there continue to be inconsistencies in standards and enforcement. For investors, there are unequal investment opportunities across Canada because issuers are required to pay various fees and potentially seek regulatory approval in different jurisdictions. Issuers may make distribution determinations that bypass smaller provinces and territories because of the transaction costs involved. This problem has been somewhat remedied by the passport system.

Arguably, the local presence of provincial and territorial regulators has ensured effective investigation and enforcement of securities laws violations because of the proximity of the regulator to the capital market participants in its jurisdiction (WPC at 19). Historically there was merit in having the regulatory authority proximate to where securities were being issued and distributed, because the issuer, investors, and registered dealers and advisers were located in the same region. Today, however, the challenges posed by the need to participate internationally, the need for enhanced enforcement, the availability of online advice channels, and the need to reduce the amount of complexity in regulatory instruments may have overshadowed the benefits of regional regulation. Notwithstanding its regional basis, securities enforcement has been problematic. There have been insufficient resources directed toward monitoring and enforcement, which arguably encourages self-dealing and misconduct because the risk–benefit calculation may encourage parties to distribute without meeting securities law requirements. The WPC made the following observations in 2003.

Wise Persons' Committee to Review the Structure of Securities Regulation in Canada, *It's Time*
(Ottawa: Department of Finance, 2003) at 11, 28-29

The securities regulators are not uniform in either structure or function. Four are self-funded government agencies, five are structured within governmental departments and the rest occupy a spectrum between the two extremes with respect to funding and governance. The largest regulators have significant professional staff, make rules, formulate policy and sit as administrative tribunals. The smallest regulators are thinly staffed and perform only certain of these functions.

Although provincial and territorial securities law statutes are based on similar principles and objectives and, in many areas, are substantively very similar, none of them is the same. There are differences in both the legislation and its administration. Rules, which have supplanted legislation and policies as the primary source of regulation, vary from jurisdiction to jurisdiction. Indeed, some jurisdictions do not have rule making authority.

. . .

Provincial securities regulators generally work well together on enforcement and compliance matters. Regulators' compliance departments share information in connection with reviews of registrants and issuers. However, compliance reviews can be slowed considerably because of co-ordination difficulties.

Investigations and enforcement proceedings may also be impeded if jurisdictions do not cooperate. Under current law an investigating jurisdiction must obtain the assistance of other jurisdictions to utilize their compulsory powers to gather evidence in those other jurisdictions. Provincial regulators also lack the ability to compel the attendance of a witness from another jurisdiction. Capital market participants can exploit these inter-jurisdictional limitations to avoid or delay investigations and proceedings. The OSC notes in its submission that:

> The increasing complexity of financial transactions means that inter-jurisdictional activity is becoming more the rule than the exception. On occasion, businesses with national scope hide behind the fragmented regulatory system as an excuse not to cooperate with commission investigations.

Moreover, when an offender is banned from participating in the capital markets in a jurisdiction, the offender may move to another jurisdiction and attempt to carry on business there. In order for the offender to be banned in additional jurisdictions, separate orders must be issued. This contributes to the perception that wrongdoers too often go unpunished under the current system.

A further weakness of the current system is the potential for multiple investigations and enforcement proceedings by different regulators in respect of the same respondent. The problems are illustrated by the insider trading case relating to trades alleged made in connection with a take-over bid for Doman Industries Limited, which resulted in overlapping proceedings in both British Columbia and Ontario. The Cartaway Resources Corporation and Yorkton Securities cases are two more recent examples where regulators brought multiple proceedings.

The regulators have recently made significant improvements in coordination among themselves and SROs (self-regulatory organizations). Today the number of cases pursued concurrently by more than one regulator is estimated to be less than 5 percent of the total, although overlap is most common in the highest-profile cases. Coordination is typically effected through the appointment of a lead regulator (on an informal and cooperative basis) with primary carriage of the matter, joint investigations or hearings, or partitioning of the investigation. …

A further weakness of the current system is unjustified variation among the provinces and territories in enforcement priorities and statutory protections. As discussed, it is not clear to what extent differences in enforcement priorities across Canada are in response to distinctive local and regional issues. It is safe to assume, however, that while some differences may be justified by different local needs, all differences are not.

Differences in statutory enforcement provisions result in different levels of investor protection across the country. There is inconsistency in the enforcement powers and sanctions among the provinces. Regulators in British Columbia, Saskatchewan and Nova Scotia have the ability to make general compliance orders, whereas regulators in the other jurisdictions can only make orders requiring compliance with a specific portion of securities legislation. Likewise, there are varying powers to order restitution, disgorgement and/or compensation to investors, as well as to impose administrative fees.

There have been important efforts to develop national standards through national policies and instruments that are discussed throughout this textbook. However, there are costs and delays to negotiating national instruments that attempt to align the requirements of multiple securities regulators. As with any consensus process, there are often also compromises in policy development that may meet regional needs or political sensitivities, but risk creating overly complex regulatory instruments. Even where all the regulatory authorities endorse a national instrument, provincial and territorial regulators can pass amendments. It is becoming increasingly difficult for issuers to be satisfied that they are complying with all of the regulatory requirements by complying with a national instrument. In a number of instances, statutory and regulatory change in each provincial and territorial authority is duplicative of other efforts across Canada, yet absent voluntary cooperation to negotiate a national instrument, policy development that meets the changing needs of both capital markets and society in general is slowed down.

The WPC made the following observation in respect of the enforcement component of securities regulation in 2003.

Wise Persons' Committee to Review the Structure of Securities Regulation in Canada, *It's Time*
(Ottawa: Department of Finance, 2003) at 26

The adequacy of Canada's enforcement has been seriously questioned for some time. The criticism intensified following the wave of corporate scandals in the United States involving companies such as Enron, WorldCom and Tyco. In Canada, a number of high-profile corporate scandals have also occurred, including Bre-X and the massive fraud it represented. There is a perception both in Canada and abroad that serious misconduct in Canada too often goes unpunished.

Provincial and federal legislators and regulators have taken steps to address these concerns. Ontario has recently amended its securities legislation to create new offences, increase penalties and provide additional powers to the OSC. The federal government has proposed amendments to the *Criminal Code* creating new offences and increasing the penalties for existing securities fraud offences, and has provided $120 million in new funding over the next five years for the establishment of dedicated investigation teams with capital markets expertise. …

Although these are positive developments, there are structural limitations of the current system that need to be addressed. They are (i) inefficient allocation of resources, (ii) coordination difficulties in multijurisdictional proceedings and (iii) unjustified variation in enforcement priorities and statutory protections for investors.

QUESTIONS

1. In what sense can Canadian capital markets be understood to be inefficient?
2. The excerpts above indicate that securities regulators have considered increased enforcement a priority in recent years. Why is public enforcement needed if capital markets involve primarily private actors?
3. In the *Asbestos Minority Shareholders* case, above, the securities regulators and the courts both agreed not to intervene in a case where minority shareholders were abused and treated unfairly because no one was materially misled and there was no strong transactional link with Ontario. Does this reasoning contribute to a perception that Canada's securities regime is not sufficiently protective of investors?

VI. CURRENT REFORM INITIATIVES

As described by the Supreme Court of Canada in *Reference re Securities Act*, 2011 SCC 66, [2011] 3 SCR 837 [*Securities Reference*], the debate among securities regulators and public policy makers as to whether there should be a single regulatory system in Canada has been ongoing for decades. For many years, Ontario has advocated for the implementation of a national securities regulator, with representation from the provinces. Prior to the CMRA initiatives described below, the British Columbia Securities Commission (BCSC), although not opposed to amalgamation per se, disagreed with the trend of Ontario and other provinces with regard to increased regulatory requirements, instead advocating simplified outcomes-based rules for market participants.

In 2003, the final report of the Five Year Review Committee on the Ontario *Securities Act* recommended that all governments work toward the creation of one national securities regulator responsible for capital markets across Canada. In the same year, the WPC also recommended the establishment of a national securities regulator through the passage of comprehensive federal legislation, which would be incorporated by reference in legislation to be passed by each participating provincial legislature.

The contours of the debate regarding reform are set out in the discussion of regulatory options below. These options raise the question of how to most efficiently regulate capital markets, particularly in the context of increasingly global markets. There is a question of the cost and efficiency of regulatory systems with inconsistent, or in many cases overlapping, requirements.

Part of the debate about creating a national securities regulatory authority is coloured by the unwillingness of some provinces to relinquish control over a regulatory function that generates revenue. Another aspect of the debate raises a more fundamental question of whether there should be a market for securities regulation, much as there is currently for corporate law, with different jurisdictions competing for capital and subject to the incentive to continuously adapt, improve, and innovate their regulatory systems.

A. Uniform Securities Legislation Project

The CSA has long been an advocate for regulatory harmonization and has proposed uniform securities legislation and rules and the possibility of a pan-Canada national regulatory authority; a key initiative advanced in 2003 was called the Uniform Securities Legislation (USL) project. The primary goal of the USL was to develop a uniform securities act and rules with substantively the same content as the then-existing securities laws from across Canada, which could then be adopted by each jurisdiction in Canada. The USL proposed to create "platform" legislation, establishing the core rights, powers, and obligations of the system, with most detailed requirements being set out in the uniform rules. The CSA described the advantages of this structure in the following terms:

> This regulatory framework would facilitate future reforms through the rule making process. Currently, it can take several years to amend all of the securities acts of Canada due to different legislative timetables. The capital markets are on a much faster timetable. We are regularly faced with new products, market structures, enforcement priorities and policy issues that require us to respond in a timely manner if we are to regulate effectively. (CSA, Uniform Securities Legislation Project, *Blueprint for Uniform Securities Laws for Canada* (2003) 26 OSCB 943)

Another reform option was proposed by the WPC and the Expert Panel on Securities Regulation. Both proposals called for the creation of a Canadian securities act and national securities commission, and their recommendations ultimately received the full support of the federal government and resulted in the draft federal *Securities Act* that led to the 2011 *Securities Reference* case discussed in Chapter 2.

B. The Wise Persons' Committee and the Proposal for a National Securities Act

In its final report issued in December 2003, the Wise Persons' Committee to Review the Structure of Securities Regulation in Canada recommended a fundamentally new structure of a single national regulator administering a single securities code. The committee's mandate was to consider an improved regulatory model that would provide increased protection to investors, rigorous enforcement of standards, and encourage accessible and innovative capital markets in Canada. The WPC concluded that Canada was out of step with the needs of capital market participants, particularly as it seeks to participate in global capital markets, and that the regulatory burden was impeding capital formation. The committee found that of more than 100 countries (including 20 with federal political structures) represented at IOSCO, only Canada and Bosnia-Herzegovina lacked a national or supra-national regulator (WPC at 9).

The major recommendations of the WPC included that the federal government enact a new Canadian securities act to provide a comprehensive scheme of capital market regulation in Canada, taking into account both provincial legislative reform proposals and the CSA-driven USL project. The proposal included strong, functionally empowered regional offices that would be responsible for review and enforcement, and would contribute to policy development. The WPC further recommended that amendments to the legislation would not be implemented if a majority of provinces representing a majority of the Canadian population objected. The WPC concluded that there would be a number of comparative advantages to this model, including the efficient allocation of resources, the ability to set consistent standards and have uniformity in investor protection, the elimination of duplicative compliance costs for issuers, the provision of equal access to investment opportunities for all Canadian investors, and the establishment of clear accountability and governance mechanisms. A national securities regulatory system would also bring stability, because there would be no ability for regional interests to opt out. The WPC found that there were relatively few issues distinctively local or regional such that policy-making needed to be undertaken regionally (WPC at 21). This is in contrast to enforcement, which it concluded needed a strong regional presence. The WPC expressly rejected the passport system on the basis that it would not bring sufficient reform to address Canada's international capital market credibility, it would continue the multiplicity of regulators and duplicative fee payments, and policy development would continue to suffer from the need to forge consensus among different regulators (WPC at 67-68).

C. Proposed Canadian Securities Act

The work of the WPC led to the creation of the Expert Panel on Securities Regulation, which issued its final report in January 2009, proposing a draft Canadian *Securities Act* that would establish a common securities regulator, including shifting some priorities to dealing with systemic risk.

Expert Panel on Securities Regulation, *Final Report*
(January 2009)

The core objectives of securities regulation are to:

- protect investors from unfair, improper, or fraudulent practices; and
- foster fair and efficient capital markets and confidence in those markets.

The guiding principles of regulatory conduct include:

- facilitating the reduction of systemic risk, including through monitoring of systemic events or developments and cooperation and coordination with other financial authorities;
- recognizing that the business and regulatory costs and other restrictions on the business and investment activities of market participants should be proportionate to the benefits sought to be realized;
- maintaining the competitive position of Canada's capital markets, which is desirable as capital markets are international in character;
- facilitating innovation in Canada's capital markets;
- promoting the informed participation of investors in the capital markets to support effective and responsive securities regulation; and
- recognizing regional markets and sectors.

a) Systemic Risk

Securities regulators' focus on systemic risk has been primarily concerned with clearing and settlement issues, setting minimum capital requirements, and limiting the contagion from failing securities dealers. Globally, securities regulators have been much less involved in the more comprehensive financial stability mandates of prudential regulators and central banks. This approach was largely based on the conventional wisdom that systemic risk and the prospect of systemic failure are predominantly a banking phenomenon.

Recent developments in the global financial system have highlighted the need for securities regulators to be involved in the management of systemic risk through increased monitoring, coordination, and crisis management. Systemic failures, once largely confined to banking institutions, are increasingly manifesting themselves in capital markets. This transformation has largely been caused by the fact that it has become easier to access capital directly from the capital markets rather than through traditional banking institutions with systemic safeguards.

Along with this shift has come a corresponding concern that systemic risk in capital markets is growing. Financial innovation has led to the introduction of increasingly complex instruments. The impact of these complex instruments on capital markets is not well understood. Hedge funds and private equity funds are growing in importance, but are less-regulated and more opaque. Securities firms are becoming larger and more international, increasingly affiliated with commercial banks or insurance firms, and more involved in global trading activities, particularly in over-the-counter derivatives.

. . .

After careful consideration, we have come to the conclusion that the role of a securities regulator in facilitating the reduction of systemic risk should be explicitly addressed in securities legislation and regulation. Although the prudential regulator and the monetary authority have a more direct role in mitigating systemic risks to the larger financial system, securities regulators should play a significant role in working to help reduce systemic risk. We believe that securities regulators should have the power to take interim measures to deal with market events that might pose systemic risks to Canada's capital markets. As a result, we have suggested language in the draft Securities Act for such a power.

Expert Panel on Securities Regulation, *Draft Securities Act: Commentary*
(January 2009)

Introduction

The Expert Panel on Securities Regulation ("Expert Panel") has recommended in its Final Report that a comprehensive national securities act be adopted to govern Canadian capital markets. The Draft Securities Act ("DSA" or the "Act") has been developed to provide a starting point for such a national securities act, and illustrates how certain of the specific recommendations made by the Expert Panel in respect of such a national securities act might be implemented.

. . .

(b) Overview of DSA and Key Provisions

The general legislative drafting approach reflected in the DSA, consistent with many existing provincial statutes, is to include core, fundamental provisions in the statute while allowing for more detailed and technical requirements to be implemented through rules. This approach is believed to be more conducive to the development of more proportionate, principles-based regulation, which the Expert Panel has addressed in its Final Report. As noted in the study on principles-based securities regulation commissioned by the Expert Panel, in a principles-based system less detail is provided in the statute and more is left to be filled in through the regulator's rule-making powers. This approach is also consistent with recent developments in provincial securities legislation, facilitates greater flexibility by allowing a comprehensive securities regime to be built upon the statute as complimented by the rules, and conforms to the approach taken in the USL.

As a result of this approach, the provisions of the DSA relating to, for example, registration and prospectus requirements, continuous disclosure and takeover bids have been drafted to include the fundamental provisions relating to these matters in the statute, while allowing for the related technical requirements to be implemented through rule-making. For this reason, the rule-making provisions in the Act are intended to provide the regulator with broad-based and comprehensive rule-making ability. It is the recommendation of the Expert Panel that the regulator also strive to take a more principles-based approach with respect to the development of the rules.

The DSA reflects a number of the recommendations that are made in the Final Report of the Expert Panel. Set out below is a description of some of the ways in which the DSA incorporates those recommendations:

1. Taking a more principles-based approach to securities regulation—DSA, Commission (Part 1) and general legislative drafting approach;
2. Inclusion of a core set of objectives of securities regulation—DSA, Section 11;
3. Inclusion of guiding principles to be observed in pursuing the objectives of securities regulation, including facilitating the reduction of systemic risk, implementing a cost-benefit approach to regulation, regulating with regard to the need to facilitate innovation and maintain the competitiveness of Canada's capital markets, promoting international cooperation and informed participation of investors, providing for appropriate avenues of redress for securities law violations and taking into account regional markets and sectors—DSA, Section 14;

4. Providing the regulator with appropriate interim powers in the legislation to deal with market events that might pose significant systemic risks—DSA, Section 30;
5. Timely reporting to the public on advancing statutory objectives—DSA, Section 32;
6. Establishment of an independent reporting issuer panel to represent the views and interests of small reporting issuers in the formulation of securities regulation—DSA, Section 25;
7. Establishment of an independent investor panel to represent the views of investors in the formulation of securities regulation—DSA, Section 25;
8. Establishment of the Canadian Securities Commission (the "Commission" or the "CSC")—DSA, Council of Ministers (Section 12), Nominating Committee (Section 13) and Commission (Part 1). (The DSA includes the establishment of the CSC, the Council of Ministers and the Nominating Committee for purposes of the nomination of Commissioners, but does not otherwise address the institutional aspects of the CSC.);
9. Establishment of an independent adjudicative tribunal—DSA, Canadian Securities Tribunal (Part 2). (Although the DSA contemplates the establishment of a Canadian Securities Tribunal (the "Tribunal"), it does not contain related operative provisions. The Expert Panel has recommended consideration of the Quebec Bureau de décision et de révision en valeurs mobilières for such purposes.);
10. Empowering the securities regulator with the ability to order compensation as a means of redress for investors incurring losses on account of a violation of securities law—DSA, Section 149;
11. Inclusion of the ability to designate a third-party dispute resolution body and to require registrants to participate in its dispute-resolution mechanisms—DSA, Section 58; and
12. Regulation of exchange-traded derivatives through securities legislation—DSA, Trading in Securities and Exchange Contracts (Part 5).

The *Securities Act* drafted by the expert panel proposed multiple reforms including a duty of care on all registrants to deal fairly, honestly, and in good faith with clients, in addition to the duty of care imposed on investment fund managers and new provisions to empower the federal minister responsible to designate a federal dispute resolution body to deal with complaints respecting registrants. The expert panel also recommended that there be a full examination of larger structural reforms, including an assessment of the merits of consolidating administrative and criminal enforcement, and that these be undertaken after the commission had been established. The civil liability provisions of the draft securities act were primarily modelled on existing provincial legislation and attempted to harmonize some of the material differences among the provincial statutes. A separate independent adjudicative tribunal was also recommended, as discussed earlier in the chapter.

The recommendations of the expert panel for a federal securities regulator and the draft securities act were accepted by the federal government, which created the Canadian Securities Transition Office (CSTO) in 2009 to lead and manage the transition to the new federal system.

The proposals were not universally accepted, however, and a number of provinces opposed the initiative. The provinces of Québec and Alberta both launched constitutional challenges before their respective superior courts and both the Québec Court of Appeal and Alberta Court of Appeal concluded that the proposed legislation was unconstitutional (2011 ABCA 77; 2011 QCCA 591). British Columbia, Manitoba, Saskatchewan, and New Brunswick also intervened to oppose the proposed act when its constitutionality was considered by the Supreme Court of Canada in the *Securities Reference* case, discussed in Chapter 2.

In addition to their arguments that the proposed legislation was unconstitutional, the provinces opposed to the federal securities commission proposals also advanced other reasons for their view that the initiative was ill-founded. First, they argued that a national securities regulator was not necessary because Canada's existing system of securities regulation is already highly coordinated and harmonized, in large measure due to the work of the CSA, the national SROs, and national information systems, and that further harmonization remained possible. They noted that Canada's existing system of securities regulation performed well during and after the 2008 financial crisis, is recognized as among the most effective and respected in the world, and is regularly highly ranked in international evaluations. They also expressed the view that the process of negotiation and collaboration required to implement national securities regulations in Canada is beneficial because it requires a process of careful consideration and balancing of regional interests and preserves the ability of local regulators to tailor regulation to specific regional needs. They also observed that despite its status as an umbrella organization, the CSA has worked collaboratively and effectively with the federal Department of Finance and Office of the Superintendent of Financial Institutions to develop and coordinate regulatory efforts relating to systemic risk (see Louis Morisset, "It's Time to Re-emphasize Fundamentals of Canada's Steadfast Securities System, *The Globe and Mail* (26 December 2015).

D. The Cooperative Capital Markets Regulatory System

In the *Securities Reference* case, the Supreme Court of Canada noted that certain aspects of the proposed legislation were national in scope and within the federal jurisdiction to regulate, such as the management of systemic risk and national data collection (para 121), while others, such as the day-to-day regulation of issuers and other securities markets participants, fell under the provincial constitutional power to regulate property and civil rights in the province. In the course of its decision, the court made numerous observations about the importance of cooperative federalism and went so far as to observe that while the proposed legislation was *ultra vires* the federal government's general trade and commerce power, a cooperative approach between federal and provincial governments remained available (at paras 130, 132). The court observed that "[s]uch an approach is supported by the Canadian constitutional principles and by the practice adopted by the federal and provincial governments in other fields of activities. The backbone of these schemes is the respect that each level of government has for each other's own sphere of jurisdiction. Cooperation is the animating force. The federalism principle upon which Canada's constitutional framework rests demands nothing less" (at para 133).

Following the *Securities Reference* decision, efforts to develop a Canadian securities regulator continued on a cooperative basis. In September 2013, the ministers of finance of British Columbia, Ontario, and the government of Canada announced that they had signed an agreement in principle to establish a Cooperative Capital Markets Regulatory System (CCMR) and they invited other provinces to join them in this initiative. In July 2014, New Brunswick and Saskatchewan joined the CCMR initiative, and they were followed by Prince Edward Island in September 2014 and by Yukon in April 2015. Also in 2015, a nominating committee was appointed by the ministers of the participating provinces, an inaugural board chair was appointed, and draft initial legislation and regulations were released for public comment. In July 2015, the government of Québec launched a reference case challenging the constitutionality of the CCMR initiative. A revised draft provincial/territorial *Capital Markets Act*, draft initial regulations, and a draft *Capital Markets Stability Act* (Canada) were subsequently released, and 2016 also saw the appointment of the first board of directors, chief regulator, and chief administrative officer.

An overview of the CCMR initiative is provided in the commentary document accompanying the release of the initial draft *Provincial Capital Markets Act* and the initial draft *Capital Markets Stability Act (Canada).*

The Cooperative Capital Markets Regulatory System Governance and Legislative Framework

(September 2014), online: <http://ccmr-ocrmc.ca/wp-content/uploads/Commentary-English1.pdf>

I. Overview

This document provides an overview of the governance and legislative framework for the cooperative capital markets regulatory system (the Cooperative System). The governance framework is set out in the Memorandum of Agreement signed by the governments of British Columbia, Ontario, Saskatchewan, New Brunswick and Canada. The legislative framework includes the consultation drafts of two key pieces of proposed legislation, which will be administered by the Capital Markets Regulatory Authority (the Authority). The uniform provincial *Capital Markets Act* (PCMA), which will be proposed for enactment by each participating province and territory, modernizes existing provincial securities legislation and harmonizes the regulatory approaches taken by the British Columbia, Ontario, New Brunswick and Saskatchewan securities acts. The complementary federal *Capital Markets Stability Act* (CMSA) empowers the Authority to collect data and manage systemic risk related to capital markets on a national basis and modernizes capital markets-related criminal offences.

Together with the Memorandum of Agreement (MOA), the publication of these consultation drafts marks a significant step forward in establishing the Cooperative System. A key objective of this initiative is to create enhanced oversight and protection of Canada's capital markets, leveraging resources across participating jurisdictions to achieve consistent, cohesive and timely regulation.

The Cooperative System will foster more efficient and globally competitive capital markets in Canada. It will facilitate the raising of capital within participating provinces and territories from both domestic and international investors through more integrated markets governed by innovative, responsive and flexible regulation based on a single set of regulations that are consistently applied. It will provide increased protection for investors through a combination of more consistent compliance activities, more effective enforcement against misconduct and improved coordination with law enforcement and prosecution authorities both within and outside Canada. To address future threats to financial stability, it will strengthen Canada's capacity to identify and manage capital markets systemic risk on a national basis. Finally, the Cooperative System will enable Canada to play a more empowered and influential role in international capital markets regulatory initiatives.

II. Structure, Governance, and Accountability

The MOA sets out the structure, governance and accountability of the Authority and the Cooperative System. It is envisaged that most of these elements will be included in separate legislation, and that the participating jurisdictions will jointly establish the Authority.

Oversight and Governance

The Cooperative System will be overseen by a Council of Ministers (the Council), composed of a Minister from each of the participating provinces and territories and the Minister of Finance of Canada. The Council's responsibilities with respect to appointments, oversight and approvals are set out in s. 4.2 of the MOA. The Council will be co-chaired by the Minister of Finance of Canada and, on a two-year rotational basis, the responsible Minister from each major capital markets jurisdiction (defined in the MOA as a participating province or territory that represents at least 10 percent of the national gross domestic product derived from financial services).

The Authority will be a jointly established and operationally independent regulator supervised by an expert board of independent directors (the "board"). The board will be composed of at least nine and no more than 12 independent directors (the MOA provides for a smaller board of at least five directors during a transition period). The directors will be appointed by the Council on the recommendation of an expert nominating committee. As a group, the board members will collectively possess the requisite capital markets expertise, including international capital market and venture market expertise, and will be broadly representative of the regions of Canada. The board will recommend a chair from among its members for confirmation by the Council, and will be accountable to the Council for the exercise of its responsibilities as set out in s. 7.2 of the MOA, including supervising the management of the Authority's business and affairs and exercising the power to make regulations under the PCMA and the CMSA.

Integrated Structure and Management

The Authority will have a Regulatory Division responsible for the policy, regulatory operations, advisory services and enforcement functions of the Authority and an independent Tribunal which will adjudicate enforcement and other administrative proceedings. The Regulatory Division will be led by the Chief Regulator, who will administer a single set of regulations in accordance with common standards. The Tribunal will be led by the Chief Adjudicator and composed of independent adjudicators with capital markets and adjudicative experience, who will be appointed by the Council on the recommendation of an expert nominating committee. The two divisions will interact through their participation in the Regulatory Policy Forum, which will support the Tribunal's expertise and promote a consistent approach to policy, oversight and adjudication.

Each participating province will have a regulatory office that will continue to provide the services that are provided by securities regulators today with local decision-making authority that is exercised in accordance with common standards. Each regulatory office will have the staff, expertise and resources that are commensurate with the regulatory and enforcement demands of the participating jurisdiction. The regulatory offices will deliver consistent regulation in a way that is responsive to the interests and sensitivities of Canada's regions and market sectors. This office structure is intended to leverage the capital markets regulatory expertise that exists across Canada to enhance efficiencies and reduce costs, while remaining responsive to local needs.

The Regulatory Division will have an Executive Committee that will include the Chief Regulator and the Deputy Chief Regulators. The Executive Committee will serve as the primary executive decision making body for the Regulatory Division, providing input to the Chief Regulator and serving as a forum for the integration of regional and functional perspectives. The Chief Regulator will be accountable to the board for the management of the Regulatory Division's business and operations and will be housed in the Authority's executive head office in Toronto. Deputy Chief Regulators based in a regulatory office in a major capital markets jurisdiction or in a regulatory office in a region will oversee the operations and staff of their office or the offices in their region, contribute to policy development and provide insight into the needs, interests and perspectives of the regulatory office(s), investors, market participants and other stakeholders in their jurisdiction or region.

Both the PCMA and the CMSA confer important powers on the Tribunal. The Authority's establishing legislation will include provisions to establish the Tribunal as a separate division of the Authority that is independent from the Regulatory Division, and will provide for the appointment of Tribunal members. The Tribunal will have sufficient members to conduct hearings (in both English and French) across Canada, and all Tribunal members will be independent. The establishing legislation will also set out the Tribunal's powers. The Tribunal will be organized along the principles of providing expert adjudication, holding hearings across Canada (as well as the capacity to make orders of national application under the CMSA), and fair and efficient decision-making.

. . .

IV. A Modern Regulatory Approach

The PCMA updates and modernizes current provincial securities legislation, retaining key components while introducing new elements to promote flexibility within a robust regulatory framework. One difference from current legislation, particularly the Ontario regime, is the extent to which the PCMA takes a platform approach to capital markets regulation. It sets out the fundamental provisions of capital markets law while leaving detailed requirements, including some requirements that are currently contained in provincial securities legislation, to be addressed in regulations. This approach promotes regulatory flexibility, allowing the Authority to respond to market developments in a timely manner and appropriately tailor its regulatory treatment of various entities and activities.

QUESTIONS

1. What are the differences between Uniform Securities Legislation, the proposed CCMR system, and a passport system?
2. Is harmonization under a passport system necessary in order for the system to work?
3. What are the benefits and challenges associated with the platform-based approach proposed under the CCMR system?
4. Do you think that the proposal for an "opt-in" system to a federal regulator will be successful in ultimately creating a common regulatory framework?

VII. DEVELOPMENTS IN US SECURITIES REGULATION

US securities law has a number of the same components as Canadian securities law in terms of substantive requirements for issuers, although its structure is a federal–state system aimed at creating uniform standards where possible. Securities law is generally governed by federal statutes except for intrastate securities markets. There have been a number of recent initiatives in US securities reform, first, in the wake of Enron and other corporate failures, and more recently, as a result of the 2008 global financial crisis.

The *Securities Act of 1933*, c 38, Title I, § 1, 48 Stat 74, 15 USC, §§ 77a–77z-3, as amended (1933 Act), focuses primarily on registration and initial distribution of securities. It requires that investors receive financial and other significant information concerning securities being offered for public sale and prohibits deceit, misrepresentations, and other fraud in the sale of securities. All companies, both domestic and foreign, must file their registration statements and the accompanying prospectuses electronically and deliver the statement and prospectus to each potential investor, unless their offerings are exempted. Registration statements are subject to examination for compliance with disclosure requirements in terms of their accuracy and completeness. Issuers with more than $10 million in assets whose securities are held by more than 500 owners must file annual and other periodic reports. These reports are available to the public through the Securities and Exchange Commission's (SEC's) EDGAR database. There are potential civil and criminal liabilities for material misstatements or omissions from prospectuses and other disclosure documents. The 1933 Act also requires the SEC to meet with state securities regulators through the North American Securities Administrators Association (NASAA), which also includes Canadian, Mexican, and Puerto Rican securities regulators, for the purpose of engendering cooperation, information sharing, the development and maintenance of uniform securities forms and procedures, and the development of a uniform registration exemption for small issuers (s 19(d)).

Under the 1933 Act, there are exemptions from the registration requirement, including private offerings to a limited number of persons or institutions; offerings of limited size; intrastate offerings; and securities of municipal, state, and federal governments. By exempting small offerings from the registration process, the SEC seeks to foster capital formation by lowering the cost of offering securities to the public (<http://www.sec.gov/about/laws.shtml>).

The *Securities Exchange Act of 1934*, c 404, Title I, § 1, 48 Stat 881, 15 USC, §§ 78a–78mm, as amended, created the Securities and Exchange Commission (SEC) granting broad authority over all aspects of the securities industry, including the power to register, regulate, and oversee brokerage firms, transfer agents, and clearing agencies as well as the nation's securities self-regulatory organizations (SROs), such as the New York Stock Exchange (NYSE),

American Stock Exchange (Amex), and the National Association of Securities Dealers, which operates the NASDAQ system. SROs must create rules that allow for disciplining members for improper conduct and for establishing measures to ensure market integrity and investor protection.

The *Securities Exchange Act* identifies and prohibits certain types of conduct in the markets; provides the SEC with disciplinary powers over regulated entities and associated persons; and empowers the SEC to require periodic reporting of information by companies with publicly traded securities. Registration statements are subject to examination for compliance with disclosure requirements. Companies with more than $10 million in assets whose securities are held by more than 500 owners must file annual and other periodic reports, available to the public through the SEC's EDGAR database. The *Securities Exchange Act* also governs disclosure of proxy materials used to solicit shareholders' votes in annual or special meetings held for the election of directors and the approval of other corporate action, which must be filed with the SEC in advance of any solicitation to ensure compliance with the disclosure rules. Solicitations, whether by management or shareholder groups, must disclose all important facts concerning the issues on which holders are asked to vote (<http://www.sec.gov/about/laws.shtml>).

The *Securities Exchange Act* requires disclosure of important information by anyone seeking to acquire more than 5 percent of a company's securities by direct purchase or tender offer. US securities laws prohibit fraudulent activities in connection with the offer, purchase, or sale of securities, and the SEC takes disciplinary action against fraudulent insider trading. Specified market participants must register with the commission, including exchanges, brokers and dealers, transfer agents, and clearing agencies (<http://www.sec.gov/about/laws.shtml>).

The *Investment Company Act of 1940*, c 686, Title I, § 1, 54 Stat 789, 15 USC, §§ 80a1–80a-64, as amended, regulates the organization of companies, including mutual funds, that engage primarily in investing, reinvesting, and trading in securities, and whose own securities are offered to the investing public, requiring these companies to disclose their financial condition and investment policies to investors when stock is initially sold and, subsequently, on a regular basis. The *Investment Advisers Act of 1940*, as amended in 1996 and 2010, regulates investment advisers, requiring that firms or sole practitioners compensated for advising others about securities investments must register with the SEC and conform to regulations designed to protect investors. With the 1996 amendments, generally only advisers who have at least $25 million of assets under management or advise a registered investment company must register with the SEC (<http://www.sec.gov/about/laws.shtml>).

The *National Securities Markets Improvement Act of 1996*, 15 USC (NSMIA), §§ 77z–80b empowered the SEC to regulate nationally in a number of areas. It restructured federal–state securities regulation, partly pre-empting state law for "covered securities," a defined term that includes securities listed on the NYSE, Amex, and NASDAQ (ss 18(a) and (b), *Securities Act of 1933*, as amended). Since 99.9 percent of the $11.2 trillion in listed stocks in 2001 were listed on one of these exchanges, it covers most of the large issuers (SEC, Ann Rep 178 (2002)) (available at <http://www.sec.gov>). Registration, filing, and disclosure obligations thus come under federal laws for these issuers, pre-empting state authority in specified aspects of registration and periodic reporting. State regulators retain concurrent jurisdiction for intrastate securities distributions and jurisdiction to investigate and enforce unlawful conduct by brokers or dealers in securities transactions (*Securities Act of 1933*, as amended, s 18(c)). Whereas previously, state laws included "merit recognition" in which state regulators could refuse registration on the basis that a business plan, corporate constating documents, or proposed contracts were unfair, inequitable, unjust, or oppressive to investors (known as "blue sky" laws), these provisions were pre-empted by NSMIA. One of the policy objectives of enacting NSMIA was to harmonize registration, disclosure, and proxy solicitation requirements nationally.

Under US securities laws, the SEC can bring enforcement actions either in the federal courts or before an administrative law judge. The commission has an examination and inspection program for registered self-regulatory organizations, broker-dealers, transfer agents, clearing agencies, investment companies, and investment advisers. It conducts inspections to foster compliance with the securities laws, to detect violations of the law, and to keep the commission informed of developments in the regulated community. When the SEC finds deficiencies, it issues a "deficiency letter" identifying the problems that need to be rectified and monitoring the situation until compliance is achieved, providing expeditious and informal correction of compliance problems. Violations that appear too serious for informal correction are referred to the Division of Enforcement.

The US system has thus encouraged convergence of standards with a view to as much uniformity as possible in federal and state regulatory standards. The SEC and NASAA have cooperated to develop uniform securities forms and procedures, share information regarding issuer registration and exemptions, and develop a uniform exemption from registration for small issuers (*Securities Act of 1933*, as amended, s 19(d)3). Joel Seligman has suggested that the federal–state system of US securities regulation has worked well overall, although there are costs associated with multiple fees and some continuing difference in respect of disclosure standards (Joel Seligman, "The United States Federal–State Model of Securities Regulation" in A Douglas Harris, ed, *WPC Committee to Review the Structure of Securities Regulation in Canada: Research Studies* (Ottawa: Department of Finance, 2003), online: <http://www.wise-averties.ca/report_en.html>) (Seligman). State statutes were retained after enactment of federal laws, in part because they were rewritten to reduce compliance obligations for federally registered issuers and because the states have performed a significant enforcement role. Seligman observes that over 40 state jurisdictions authorize securities regulation by coordination, meaning that they unilaterally agree to reduce their securities registration requirements when issuers have filed a registration statement under the *Securities Act of 1933* such that the registration statement automatically becomes effective at the state level at the time the federal registration statement becomes effective (Seligman at 89). He also observes that while NASAA has developed 60 policy statements aimed at uniformity that allow states to adapt to market changes on a uniform basis, there is considerable time and delay in developing these, given the coordination challenge of 50 states with different priorities in respect of securities regulation and enforcement (Seligman at 101).

The United States has faced problems of inadequate incentives to compliance, including inadequate monitoring and enforcement. This problem was a contributing factor to the scandals at Enron, WorldCom, and other large US corporations. Since 2002, various rules have been adopted by the SEC to implement the *Sarbanes-Oxley Act* (SOA), Pub L 107-204, 116 Stat 745 (2002). The *Sarbanes-Oxley Act of 2002* mandated a number of reforms to enhance corporate responsibility, enhance financial disclosures, and combat corporate and accounting fraud. It also resulted in the creation of the Public Company Accounting Oversight Board to oversee the activities of the auditing profession. In 2002, a new *Uniform Securities Act* was approved by the National Conference of Commissioners on Uniform State Laws to facilitate harmonization of state securities legislation.

In the fall of 2006, Congress passed the *Credit Rating Agency Reform Act*, providing the SEC for the first time with authority to supervise rating agencies effective June 2007. The SEC has adopted two major rule-makings, conducted an extensive ten-month examination of three major credit-rating agencies, and in 2009 had several pending proposals to further the Act's purpose of promoting accountability, transparency, and competition in the rating industry (<http://www.sec.gov/news/press/2009/2009-46.htm>).

In the immediate aftermath of the 2008 financial crisis, the SEC considered further reforms. The chair of the SEC, Mary Schapiro, gave the following testimony to Congress in March 2009.

Mary Schapiro, Chair, US Securities and Exchange Commission, *Testimony Concerning Enhancing Investor Protection and Regulation of the Securities Markets*
before the United States Senate Committee on Banking, Housing and Urban Affairs (26 March 2009), online: <http://www.sec.gov/news/testimony/2009/ts032609mls.htm>

A. Regulation of the Integrity of Markets

Investor protection starts with fair and efficient capital markets. In these tumultuous economic times, despite record volumes and enormous volatility, the markets that the SEC oversees have priced, processed, and cleared trillions of dollars in customer orders in an orderly and fair way. The dollar value of average daily trading volume was approximately $251 billion a day in February 2009 in stocks, exchange-traded options and security futures. By comparison, the average daily trading volume for such securities was approximately $87 billion a day in February 1999, and $10 billion a day in February 1989.

...

Innovation has completely transformed our securities markets over the last decade. The shouts on the trading floors of the nation's securities exchanges have largely given way to the whir of computers. Transactions that took minutes to execute now take well under a second. In an instant, traders can search within markets and across markets to locate counterparties willing to pay the very best price. Spreads—that is the price differences in transactions captured by intermediaries rather than investors—have narrowed dramatically over the past decade. This has been due in part to the SEC's rules requiring intermediaries acting for customers to trade at the very best prices as well as rules permitting securities prices to be quoted in pennies. In many instances, spreads in stocks have shrunk from twelve cents to less than a penny. According to a 2005 GAO study, decimalization of stock quotes alone cut trading costs by 30-50 percent. We've achieved similar results in the options markets.

These pro-investor changes have been possible because of a regulatory regime that focuses on competition—one that does not pick winners and losers but instead, one that removes barriers to new entrants. It is a regime that requires a focus on the needs of investors and their welfare, allowing market participants to innovate and compete for their customers' business. While it is a regime that works well, it is one that requires a regulator to keep up with the breakneck pace of change in our ever-evolving markets.

This is not to say that our markets always function perfectly. There are practices that are contrary to fair and orderly markets; abusive short selling, for example, would fall into that category. To target potentially abusive "naked" short selling in certain equity securities, the Commission has tightened up the close-out requirements and adopted a new antifraud rule specifically aimed at abusive short selling when it is part of a scheme to manipulate the price of a stock. And, early next month, the Commission will consider proposals to re-institute the uptick rule, or something much like it.

B. Regulation of the Integrity of Market Information

However well structured, markets fail without timely and reliable information. Accurate information is the lifeblood of the securities market. A big part of the SEC's mission is to safeguard the markets' blood supply.

. . .

Registrants file extensive disclosures about their business performance annually and update them quarterly, and—because today's markets demand immediate information—whenever certain specified events occur. We review these filings on a selective basis, and work closely with reviewed companies to improve the quality of their disclosure. In fiscal year 2008, our staff reviewed the filings of nearly 5000 reporting companies in addition to more than 600 new issuers.

Accurate information, of course, encompasses both words and numbers, and we work to protect the integrity of both. We play a special role in the formation of accounting standards for public companies and other entities that file financial statements with the Commission.

. . .

Our rules, given new vigor by the landmark *Sarbanes Oxley Act* that emerged from this Committee in 2002, promote the independence of those who audit the financial statements of public companies.

Investors need accurate and comprehensive information not only when they trade but also when they vote, whether it is to elect directors, adopt compensation plans, approve transactions, or consider shareholder proposals. And so we have a variety of means to promote fair corporate voting.

. . .

C. Regulation and Oversight of Financial Intermediaries and Market Professionals

For our markets to be fair and efficient and to operate in the best interests of investors, those who control access to our capital markets must be competent, financially capable, and honest. That brings me to a third core function of the SEC: regulation and oversight of financial intermediaries and other market professionals, including approximately 5,500 broker-dealers, over 11,000 investment advisers, stock and option exchanges, clearing agencies, credit rating agencies and others. Exchanges and clearing agencies are an essential part of the plumbing of our financial system.

. . .

Since 2006, with the authority provided by the Congress, we have adopted significant reforms related to credit rating agencies. Given the critical role of ratings in our capital markets, it is essential that we stay active in this area. We have rule proposals outstanding and are convening a public roundtable on possible further reforms to be held next month.

Some of our rules regulating financial intermediaries need to be modernized, and the Commission is considering what, if any, legislation to ask for from the Committee. Among other things, we are considering asking for legislation that would require registration of investment advisers who advise hedge funds, and possibly the hedge funds themselves. We are studying whether to recommend legislation to break down the statutory barriers that require a different regulatory regime for investment advisers and broker-dealers, even though the services they provide often are virtually identical from the investor's perspective. We also are carefully considering whether legislation is needed to fill other gaps in regulatory oversight, including those related to credit default swaps and municipal securities.

. . .

III. A Capital Markets Regulator Devoted to Investor Protection Should Be Independent

As we look to the future of securities regulation, we believe that independence is an essential attribute of a capital markets regulator that protects investors.

. . .

We are a creature of the Congress. The vision of the Congress when it created an independent SEC was to make sure that there was one agency of government focused single-mindedly and without dilution on the well-being of America's investors. That independence has allowed us to build expertise and a culture of investor protection, which benefits the public and the economy. And it has been a tremendous success as US capital markets lead the world.

If there were ever a time when investors need and deserve a strong voice and a forceful advocate in the federal government, that time is now.

. . .

IV. A Strong and Independent Capital Markets Regulator Is Important to Systemic Risk Oversight

An independent, investor-first capital markets regulator is vital to a revamped regulatory structure that pays due attention to overarching systemic risk. Investor protection enhances the mission of controlling systemic risk. More than that, financial services exist to serve investors and our markets, and a focus on investors is absolutely essential to any credible regulatory restructuring. The SEC, as the independent capital markets regulator with unique experience and competencies, must continue to be the primary regulator of important market functions, and would be a critical party in contributing to any systemic risk regulator's evaluation of risks. Appropriate regulation must safeguard both investor protections and important market functions.

In July 2010, the *Dodd-Frank Wall Street Reform and Consumer Protection Act* was signed into law. The long title of the legislation is "an Act to promote the financial stability of the United States by improving accountability and transparency in the financial system, to end 'too big to fail,' to protect the American taxpayer by ending bailouts, to protect consumers from abusive financial services practices, and for other purposes." The legislation was passed during the recession that followed the global financial crisis of 2008 and brought sweeping reforms to the US regulatory system in a number of areas including consumer protection, trading restrictions, credit ratings, regulation of financial products, corporate governance and disclosure, and transparency. The Act included over 85 mandatory rule-making provisions, requiring the SEC to develop and adopt rules relating to private funds, clearing agencies, executive compensation, asset-backed securities, and credit-rating agencies, among other issues. In 2015, on the anniversary of the enactment of Dodd-Frank, SEC chair Mary Jo White issued a statement, reflecting on the magnitude of the changes and the progress made.

Statement on the Anniversary of the Dodd-Frank Act

Securities Exchange Commission Chair Mary Jo White (16 July 2015), online: <https://www.sec.gov/news/statement/statement-on-the-anniversary-of-the-dodd-frank-act.html>

Five years ago, the Dodd-Frank Act was signed into law to address critical issues that triggered the worst financial crisis since the Great Depression. Thousands of Americans had lost their jobs, watched their savings dwindle, and were forced out of their homes. The Commission and our fellow regulators have been working hard to strengthen our nation's financial systems by implementing the rules mandated by the Dodd-Frank Act and by enacting other critical reforms to protect investors and our markets. I especially want to thank the expert, hard-working SEC staff for their dedication to these efforts to build a lasting regulatory regime for a robust financial system that supports the broader U.S. economy.

The Commission has taken action to address virtually all of the mandatory rulemaking provisions of the Dodd-Frank Act, and at the same time we have focused on additional measures to bolster our financial infrastructure. Within a year of the legislation taking effect, the Commission began bringing greater transparency and oversight to hedge fund and other private fund advisers with an extensive series of reforms. The Commission also established stronger standards for the clearinghouses that stand at the center of the global financial system and built an enhanced program for their supervision.

Since I became Chair a little more than two years ago, the agency has continued to advance reforms for stronger, more resilient financial markets. Working with our fellow financial regulators, we finalized the Volcker Rule's restrictions on proprietary trading and investments by banks. To combat the inflated credit ratings that contributed to the crisis, the Commission adopted a comprehensive package of reforms to the governance and management of the credit rating agencies. We put in place the foundational rules for a new regulatory framework for security-based swaps.

The Commission set up new safeguards to protect municipalities and investors in the municipal securities markets from conflicted advice and unregulated advisors. We adopted wide-ranging rules for the asset-backed securities market that increase the accountability of securitizers and better protect investors. And we proposed a suite of mandated rules to improve the transparency of executive compensation and require executives to pay back compensation that they were awarded erroneously.

The overarching objective of these rulemakings is to promote the long-term sustainability of the U.S. financial system. That is also the objective of the other powerful tools that the Dodd-Frank Act gave the SEC, such as the whistleblower award program and other enhancements to the SEC's enforcement authority. The whistleblower program has increased the efficiency of our program by expanding whistleblower protections and remedies for retaliation while creating powerful incentives for whistleblowers to come forward with evidence of financial wrongdoing.

While the worst of the financial crisis is behind us, the Commission intensively continues its critical work beyond the Dodd-Frank Act to fulfill our obligation to protect investors, enhance market stability, and promote capital formation. Doing so today requires a dynamic, persistent assessment of the risks to investors and markets, as well as to the financial system as a whole.

In 2012, the US government passed the *Jumpstart Our Business Startups Act* ("the JOBS Act"). The JOBS Act was intended to help businesses raise funds in public capital markets by minimizing regulatory requirements. A key initiative endorsed by the JOBS Act is the facilitation of equity crowdfunding—allowing companies to raise limited amounts of money from investors without complying with prospectus requirements, usually through online portals. The JOBS Act required the SEC to write rules and issue studies on capital formation, disclosure and registration requirements. The SEC found this mandate challenging, however, taking over 3 years to complete the rule-making process. While waiting for the SEC to develop its rules, many states chose to implement their own intra-state crowdfunding legislation, allowing companies in the state to raise limited amounts of money from investors within the state. This method of capital raising and investing has been less popular in practice than some expected, however (Stacey Cowley, "Tired of Waiting for U.S. to Act, States Pass Crowdfunding Laws and Rules," *New York Times* (2 June 2015), online: <http://www.nytimes.com>). In October 2015, the SEC adopted final rules facilitating equity crowdfunding, which came into effect in May 2016. The new rules allow companies to raise up to $1 million in a 12-month period through a crowdfunding campaign. Companies raising money this way are obliged to provide their investors with audited financial statements, though some first-time issuers and those seeking less than $500,000 can disclose unaudited statements (<https://www.sec.gov/spotlight/jobs-act.shtml>). Canada has implemented similar crowdfunding rules, discussed below in Chapter 5.

QUESTIONS

1. What is a "no action" letter and what policy function does it perform?
2. What is the difference between periodic disclosure under the US system and continuous disclosure under the Canadian system? Do recent US reforms move the US securities system closer to a continuous disclosure regime?

3. Why have state and federal regulators moved ahead so quickly with equity crowdfunding rules? What are the challenges faced by securities regulators in relation to equity crowdfunding?
4. How can systemic risk be managed?

NYSE and NASDAQ

The corporate history of the the New York Stock Exchange (NYSE) is an example of the modern trend toward amalgamation of large securities exchanges into global securities exchange groups. NYSE is currently owned by Intercontinental Exchange (ICE), an American company that owns 11 exchanges around the world, including ICE Futures Canada, the former Winnipeg Commodity Exchange.

Prior to the acquisition of NYSE by ICE, NYSE was a part of NYSE Euronext, a holding company created by the combination of NYSE Group, Inc and Euronext NV that launched in 2007. The amalgamation of NYSE and Euronext brought together six equities exchanges in five countries and six derivatives exchanges. At the time, NYSE Euronext operated the world's largest exchange group. In 2011, NYSE Euronext announced its plans to merge with the Deutsche Böurse to form a new company and create the world's largest exchange operator. While this bid was open, ICE and NASDAQ launched a joint counterbid for NYSE Euronext. The Deutsche Böurse merger proposal was blocked the following year by the competition division of the European Commission, which determined that the amalgamated company would have "a near-monopoly in European financial derivatives worldwide" (<http://www.reuters.com/article/us-nyseeuronext-deutscheboerse-idUSTRE8100QL20120201>), and the ICE-NASDAQ bid was also discontinued when it became apparent that US anti-trust regulators were unlikely to approve the merger. In 2013, ICE made a separate bid for NYSE Euronext, and this time was successful in its acquisition. Following the ICE acquisition of NYSE Euronext, Euronext was separated from ICE, completing an initial public offering and returning to its former status as an independent company.

Companies listed on the NYSE must comply with certain standards regarding corporate governance as codified in s 303A of the NYSE Listed Company Manual. Listed companies that do not have a controlling shareholder must have a majority of independent directors, and non-management directors of each company must meet at regularly scheduled executive sessions without management. Listed companies must have a nominating committee, a compensation committee, and corporate governance committee composed entirely of independent directors, as well as an audit committee that satisfies the requirements of rule 10A-3 under the *Exchange Act*. Listed companies must give shareholders the opportunity to vote on all equity compensation plans and must adopt and disclose corporate governance guidelines; a code of business conduct and ethics for directors, officers, and employees; and promptly disclose any waivers of the code for directors or executive officers. Listed foreign private issuers must disclose any significant ways in which their corporate governance practices differ from those followed by domestic companies under NYSE listing standards. Each listed company CEO must certify to the NYSE each year that he or she is not aware of any violation by the company of NYSE corporate governance listing standards. These rules were originally provisions included in the *Sarbanes-Oxley Act*. However, in order to avoid the constitutional problems of federal legislation containing substantive provisions regarding internal corporate regulation, an area that falls within state jurisdiction, they were included as rules that self-regulating organizations must implement in order to maintain their registration under the *Securities Exchange Act of 1934*, as amended.

Canada's National Instrument 52-110, *Audit Committees*, provisions on audit committee independence are drawn in part from these rules. NASDAQ's corporate governance rules are similar, requiring increased board and audit committee independence, strengthening the role of independent directors, implementing a code of conduct for directors and employees, and expanding the authority of the audit committee.

There has been a large increase in securities litigation and enforcement activity since 2001, including the Enron litigation, as Mary Jo White's speech to the IOSCO annual conference states.

Mary Jo White, Chair, "The Challenge of Coverage, Accountability and Deterrence in Global Enforcement"

Speech delivered at the IOSCO 39th Annual Conference, Rio de Janeiro, 1 October 2014, online: <https://www.sec.gov/News/Speech/Detail/Speech/1370543090864>
(footnotes omitted)

Maintaining a robust enforcement program is always a principal area of focus for the SEC and has, not surprisingly, been one of my top priorities. Much of my career has been spent in enforcement, first as a federal prosecutor and now as Chair of the SEC, the primary agency charged with enforcing the U.S. securities laws, using the wide array of civil remedies the SEC is authorized to deploy.

We have a staff of about 1,300 lawyers, accountants, analysts and other professionals in the SEC's Enforcement Division, who work in our Washington, D.C. headquarters or in one of our 11 offices around the United States. They do outstanding work year after year, despite our need for more resources to increase our coverage and to reach all market participants.

In fiscal year 2013, we brought more than 675 enforcement actions and obtained orders for $3.4 billion in total penalties and disgorgement. We will soon be announcing the results for our 2014 fiscal year, which ended yesterday. It was another very productive year as those numbers will show.

But numbers only tell part of the story. The quality and breadth of actions are really the more meaningful measure of an effective enforcement program. At the SEC, we concentrate on bringing high quality cases, spanning a wide swath of the securities markets, to send very strong messages of deterrence to all market participants.

Our cases include actions against securities exchanges to ensure they operate fairly and in compliance with applicable rules; cases against investment advisers for taking undisclosed fees and for other violations of their clients' trust; cases against broker-dealers for disrupting the markets through failures in their automated trading systems; financial reporting actions against issuers; actions against auditors and others who serve as gatekeepers to our financial system; Foreign Corrupt Practices Act cases against international corporations; and a broad variety of cases involving insider trading and offering frauds.

The SEC also concentrates on bringing new and innovative actions to enlarge our enforcement footprint and to strengthen deterrence of wrongdoing. For example, we recently filed our first set of actions charging violations of our market access rule, which requires firms to have adequate risk controls in place before providing customers with access to the market. This past year, we also filed enforcement actions involving Bitcoin, our first case against an individual for misleading and obstructing a compliance officer of an investment adviser, and our first case applying Dodd-Frank Act whistleblower anti-retaliation authority against a firm that demoted and marginalized an employee after learning of his whistleblower submission to the Commission.

> The SEC also continued to make effective use of some unique and tough investor-protection remedies we have, beyond the disgorgement of ill-gotten gains and civil penalties. One of the key tools in our enforcement program is the ability to bar wrongdoers from the securities industry, and to seek orders barring officers or directors of public companies who commit fraud from serving in those roles again. We also have the authority to bar certain professionals, like lawyers or accountants, from practicing before the SEC. These are important forward-looking remedies that we are increasingly using. Stopping someone from participating in the securities industry has bite and sends a powerful message that market participants watch, notice and remember. We also use asset freezes and trading suspensions, particularly in microcap fraud and insider trading cases, to stop fraud in its tracks and prevent wrongdoers from accessing their ill-gotten gains.
>
> I am very proud of our Enforcement Division's accomplishments. But there is always more to be done and we continuously make changes to enhance our effectiveness in achieving the goals of greater coverage, accountability and deterrence.

The SEC's claims of increased litigation and enforcement activity may be overstated, however. Professor Urska Velikonja analyzed the SEC's case data over a 15-year period and concluded that the agency's reported enforcement statistics were significantly overstated. Her research demonstrated that SEC enforcement activity remained largely steady between 2002 and 2014. She suggests that the systemic overstatement of enforcement statistics is directly related to the US Congress's power to cut agencies' budgets for failing to meet performance targets, and hypothesizes that this threat leads agencies such as the SEC to use methodologies that skew numbers higher so that they can protect their own ability to continue to do their work (Urska Velikonja, "Reporting Agency Performance: Behind the SEC's Enforcement Statistics" (2016) 101 Cornell L Rev 901).

In the wake of the global financial crisis, the US Congress proposed a number of new initiatives to address perceived weaknesses in US securities regulation. Among these was s 21F of the *Dodd-Frank Act*, entitled "Securities Whistleblower Incentives and Protection." This section directed the SEC to make monetary awards available to individuals who voluntarily provide information that leads to successful enforcement actions resulting in monetary sanctions of over $1 million. Such incentive payments are 10-30 percent of the monetary sanction collected, and are paid from a separate investor protection fund. To administer this program, the SEC established the Office of the Whistleblower to evaluate claims and make recommendations as to whether the claimants meet the eligibility requirements. In 2015, the Office of the Whistleblower received nearly 4,000 whistleblower tips, and between 2011 and 2015, the SEC paid more than $54 million to 22 whistleblowers, with $37 million being paid in 2015 alone (SEC, *2015 Annual Report on the Dodd-Frank Whistleblower Program*, online: <http://www.sec.gov/whistleblower/reportspubs/annual-reports/owb-annual-report-2015.pdf>). In 2016, the OSC introduced a similar whistleblower regime in Ontario.

Another initiative of Congress following the global financial crisis was the proposed *Private Fund Investment Advisers Registration Act*, which was adopted through SEC rules in June 2011. These rules require registration with the SEC for advisers of hedge funds and other private pools of capital, including private equity funds and venture capital funds, whose assets under management exceed a specified threshold. Under the 2010 *Dodd-Frank Act*, s 15E of the *Exchange Act* was amended to enhance the regulation, accountability, and transparency of "nationally recognized statistical ratings organizations" (NRSROs) and create the SEC's Office of Credit Ratings (OCR). The OCR is responsible for administering SEC rules relating to the NRSRO practices in determining credit ratings; the protection of users of credit ratings; the promotion of accuracy in credit ratings issued by NRSROs; ensuring that credit ratings are not unduly influenced by conflicts of interest; and helping to ensure that firms provide greater disclosure to investors (<https://www.sec.gov/about/offices/ocr/ocr-about.shtml>).

Congress also created the Consumer Financial Protection Agency for the purpose of protecting consumers across the financial sector from unfair, deceptive, and abusive practices. The Consumer Financial Protection Agency establishes a single point of accountability for enforcing federal consumer financial laws in the United States. Prior to its creation, this responsibility was divided among multiple federal agencies. The *Dodd-Frank Act* also proposed the creation of a Financial Stability Oversight Council (FSOC) of financial regulators to monitor and take actions to address systemic risk. The FSOC's mandate is to provide comprehensive monitoring of the US financial system by identifying risks to the financial stability of the country, promoting market discipline, and responding to emerging risks (<https://www.treasury.gov/initiatives/fsoc/Pages/home.aspx>).

Another initiative of the *Dodd-Frank Act* required the SEC to conduct a study of whether a uniform fiduciary standard should be applied to both broker-dealers and investment advisers. The SEC carried out this work and published its *Study on Investment Advisers and Broker-Dealers* in January 2011, recommending that the agency proceed with rule-making to adopt a uniform fiduciary standard for brokers and investment advisers that provide personalized investment advice to retail consumers. In April 2015, the US Department of Labor proposed a rule requiring fiduciary advice for retirement accounts, held hearings, and received more than 3,000 letters regarding the proposed rule. The final rule was released in April 2016 and made effective June 7, 2016 (<https://www.dol.gov/ebsa/regs/conflictsofinterest.html>).

These initiatives illustrate the United States' commitment to finding appropriate policy responses to the global financial crisis and, in particular, to addressing deficiencies that it has identified in its regulatory oversight of capital markets and all of these developments affect Canadian issuers to the extent that they wish to market their securities in the United States. Even where they are granted exemptions as foreign private issuers, there may be a perception among investors that the protection for investors is inferior to that offered by those issuers who fully comply with US securities regulations.

VIII. DEVELOPMENTS IN EUROPEAN SECURITIES REGULATION

The European Union (EU) has made concerted efforts in recent years to become less dependent on bank lending and to foster liquid capital markets. Although EU capital markets experienced some setbacks by depressed economic conditions, delisting, and the ripple effects of shocks in other capital markets, EU initiatives have made progress toward greater integration of capital markets. The launch of the Euro in 1999, technological innovation, and the expansion of stock and derivatives exchanges across national borders have also facilitated capital market development, including higher trading volumes and increased liquidity. The recent shift in the EU to an increasingly integrated and harmonized set of EU securities law directives reflects a decision to increase the competitiveness of the EU capital market globally.

Historically, the EU sought completely harmonized securities laws, an effort that was unsuccessful because of the time, cost, lack of enforcement of harmonization requirements, and resistance by member states to loss of control of regulatory standards. In the 1980s, the

EU determined that a mutual recognition system would better enhance integration of EU markets, involving minimal harmonization of laws. While progress was made over almost 20 years, the system continued to be plagued by uneven standards, barriers to cross-border transactions, and the inflexibility of the system to adapt to new financial products. This led the EU to engage in a long process of capital markets integration. Initially, efforts were made to improve the mutual recognition system and move toward greater harmonization through European Community directives, member state transposition and implementation, and the development of the EU Financial Services Action Plan (FSAP), an overarching plan for an EU single market in financial services, including various aspects of securities regulation. The FSAP was created in 1999 by the European Commission as a mutual recognition system aimed at harmonizing principles and minimum technical standards at the EU level. Member states were responsible for transposing EU law into national law and for supervising compliance with standards. The FSAP objectives included revising the common legal framework for integrated securities and derivatives markets; enhanced transparency; ensuring the continued stability of European financial markets through a series of directives; moving toward the adoption of uniform international accounting standards; and providing legal security to underpin cross-border securities trades. One of the difficulties identified was the concern as to whether the framework could adapt to ongoing market developments in a timely manner. The FSAP was intended to be fully implemented over a period of six years and a final evaluation of its impact was completed in 2009.

In February 2001, an EU Wise Persons' Committee on the Regulation of European Securities Markets chaired by Baron Alexandre Lamfalussy issued a report advocating a passport system to achieve more integrated capital markets among the EU members (the Lamfalussy report (15 February 2001), online: <http://www.europa.eu>). The report expressed concern that there was no mechanism in place to adopt or update directives in a timely manner; that there was excessive delay in transposing and implementing EU directives by the member states; and that there was a lack of enforcement mechanisms by non-implementing states. It also found that many directives failed to distinguish between core principles and detailed implementing provisions, making them rigid and inefficient. In response, the EU adopted what has been dubbed the Lamfalussy process, based on the report's recommendations. The Lamfalussy process was an approach to the development of financial services law in the EU that set out a four-stage process of legislative and rule development. The first stage of the process was legislative, and involved the European Parliament and Council of the European Union enacting legislation that established the core values of the law and providing guidelines for implementation. The next level of the process engaged specialized committees and regulators from all EU jurisdictions to consider and advise on technical details for the regulation. Once this was complete, the regulation would progress to the national regulator level, where work on harmonizing the new regulation with other nations would take place, and the final stage of the process dealt with the ultimate compliance and enforcement process for the new laws and regulations.

The Lamfalussy process was endorsed by the Stockholm European Council of March 2001 on the basis that the four-level process would make the regulatory process for European Community securities legislation more efficient and transparent. In November 2007, the EC published a Review of the Lamfalussy Process and its four-level regulatory approach for the adoption, implementation and enforcement of legislation and implementing measures across the securities, banking and insurance sectors. The EC observed that although the process has broadly met its overall objectives, some changes were required in order to make it more efficient; in particular, the report called for improvements in the functioning of the Level 3 Committees to enhance supervisory convergence and cooperation.

A. Lamfalussy Process, Committee of European Securities Regulators, and European Securities Committee

The Committee of European Securities Regulators (CESR) and the European Securities Committee (ESC) were independent committees set up under the Lamfalussy process to provide an advisory function and regulatory function, respectively, and they were responsible for the development of a number of important EU Directives between 2001 and 2010.

EU directives were essential instruments in the move toward a single capital market in the EU, because they take precedence over the domestic laws of member states. The directives set the principles, and member states have control over the design and implementation of the law, which must comply with the principles and the stated objectives of the directive.

The Prospectus Directive came into force in July 2005, introducing a "single passport for issuers," making securities available to investors either through a public offer procedure or by admitting their shares to trading. Once approved by the regulatory authority in one member state, a prospectus then has to be accepted everywhere else in the EU. In order to ensure investor protection, that approval is granted only if the prospectus meets common EU standards for what information must be disclosed and how (Directive 2003/71/EC). The EC announced a comprehensive overhaul of the directive on November 30, 2015, proposing changes including higher thresholds for the prospectus exemptions for small offerings, lighter prospectus requirements for small companies, shorter prospectus documents, a simplified offering process for listed companies, a fast-track regime for frequent issuers, and a single access point for all EU prospectuses (European Commission press release, "The Commission proposes to overhaul prospectus rules to improve access to finance for companies and simplify information for investors" (30 November 2015), online: <http://europa.eu/rapid/press-release_IP-15-6196_en.htm?locale=en>).

The Transparency Directive, effective December 2004, amended June 2013, requires all securities issuers to provide annual financial reports within four months after the end of the financial year. Investors in shares will receive more complete half-yearly financial reports. Those issuers who do not publish quarterly reports must provide quarterly management statements. The Transparency Directive is aimed at imposing continuous disclosure obligations, enhancing material change reporting, and improving communication to securities holders in order to encourage greater participation at shareholder general meetings. The directive also simplified the language requirements that issuers must meet. It was a shift from the earlier requirements in some member states that the information be reported in the language of the member state in which securities were distributed, instead giving issuers a new option of publishing the information in a language customary in the international sphere of finance (Transparency Directive, online: <http://ec.europa.eu/finance/company-reporting/transparency-directive/index_en.htm>).

The Market Abuse Directive was originally enacted in 2003 and has been amended extensively in recent years, particularly in the wake of the global financial crisis. The directive set out broad principles covering both insider information in relation to derivatives on commodities, insider trading, notification of managers' transactions, and the notification of suspicious transactions (Market Abuse Directive, online: <http://ec.europa.eu/finance/securities/abuse/index_en.htm>).

The Markets in Financial Instruments Directive (MiFID), 2004/39/EC, as amended), sets out requirements for record-keeping obligations for investment firms, transaction reporting, market transparency, admission of financial instruments to trading, and defined terms for the purposes of that directive. MiFID is aimed at removing obstacles to firms' use of the EU-wide investment "passport," fostering competition and a level playing field between Europe's trading venues, and ensuring a high level of protection for investors across Europe. The directive is intended to give investment firms, banks, and exchanges a "single passport" to operate and provide their services throughout the EU on the basis of their home country authorization. The financial crisis of 2008, however, exposed weaknesses in the system, particularly a lack of transparency in the non-equities market. In response, in October 2011, the European Commission tabled significant revisions to the MiFID, known as MiFID2, dealing primarily with systems and conduct requirements for investment businesses, and regulations, known as the Markets in Financial Instruments Regulation (MiFIR), dealing with transparency, transaction reporting, clearing, and supervision of positions. MiFID2 and MiFIR are expected to come into force in January 2017, and market participants will need to comply with the new regulations by January 2018 (Investment Services and Regulated Markets, online: <http://ec.europa.eu/finance/securities/isd/index_en.htm>).

The work of the CESR and the ESC in establishing these and other directives was vital in the development of EU capital market integration. Although the process represented a significant advance over prior regimes, it was nevertheless criticized as too complex and unwieldy. While the directives worked to create greater consistency across member states and assisted in fostering more coordinated capital markets, there was continued debate about the need for fuller harmonization. There was also tension in respect of the amount of control in securities regulation that should devolve to the EC and how much member states would continue to control. Then there was the added challenge of addressing the 2008 financial crisis, as the excerpt below highlights.

Charlie McCreevy, European Commissioner for Internal Market and Services, *Financial Markets & Economic Recovery*

Horwarth Bastow Charleton Conference—Strategies in a Crisis Forum (20 March 2009)

The scale of irresponsible origination and underwriting, lack of due diligence, toxic securitization, and reckless credit ratings was far greater in the United States than anywhere else in the world. There is no doubt but that it was primarily this that triggered the global crisis on the scale that we are now seeing.

That said European banks bought into these toxic securities and in Europe there is now a broad consensus that our supervisory systems are not and have not been up to the mark or fit for purpose. Not fit for purpose at an EU institutional level. Not fit for purpose at a Member State level. With cross-border banking groups now accounting for 80 per cent of Europe's banking assets the absence of strong co-ordination mechanisms between supervisors as well as effective early warning arrangements was and is an unacceptable gap in our regulatory and supervisory framework.

The Commission's plan for restoring stability to the financial system is based on four priorities:

- Getting the supervision right;
- Getting the regulation right;
- Getting the risk management and pay incentives right;
- Getting the sanctions right.

Let's take *supervision* first, as it's so crucial. A special group we established some time back to look at financial supervisory structures in the EU—known as the de Larosière group—issued its report three weeks ago. It proposed a radical overhaul of the supervisory framework for the EU. In particular, it proposed the creation of a European Systemic Risk Council, chaired by the President of the ECB, to protect the European financial system against systemic risk—what we call macro risk. No such body currently exists. Regarding risk to individual financial institutions—micro risk—it proposes a European System of Financial Supervision, and turning existing supervisory committees into supervisory authorities with real teeth. In our reaction to the de Larosière report, we have committed to making formal proposals by the end of May and to coming forward with concrete legislative proposals in the autumn. We currently have a consultation ongoing on financial supervision, with a deadline of 10 April for comments.

I won't prejudge the outcome today. But I'm on the record as saying that the status quo is not an option. The existing set up in Europe—the Committees of Supervisors—clearly lack teeth. Bold steps are needed but there are very different ideas on how to go about it. Indeed there is a good deal of hypocrisy and double-speak too: while Member State governments are pretty well unanimous that the issue needs to be addressed, the fact is that any time over the past decade when proposals—however modest—have been put forward to address them the consensus breaks down. Member State governments must come to recognise and address the need to stand up to the vested interests of their home supervisors who resist ceding anything with an eye to protecting their own empires. However, never again will the political climate be so favourable for making a meaningful step forward and never before has so much momentum been built up towards a search for meaningful progress in this area.

Regulation: Existing and New Initiatives

I turn now, *regulation*. We have already done a lot in this field in 2008, in particular with the proposed Regulation on Credit Rating Agencies, the Solvency II Directive for insurance companies, which I very much hope will find agreement in Council and Parliament soon, and the proposal for revising the Capital Requirements Directive which regulates the capital requirements for banks.

The subject of the CRD brings me to its basis, Basel 2. In my view, the entire Basel 2 Accord clearly requires some fundamental overhaul. The Commission services have been looking at the areas of weakness in the existing framework: It is now patently obvious that the shortcomings of that framework include the absence of any overall gearing cap on bank balance sheets, wholly inadequate and inappropriate risk weightings for AAA rated structured products, the stupidities of intellectually refined value at risk models, over-reliance on External Credit Rating assessments undertaken by agencies who are paid by the issuer, and the absurdities of some mark to market requirements when markets are totally illiquid. All these regulatory weaknesses must be urgently addressed.

• • •

Pay Incentives and Risk

I turn now to the third of the pillars which I mentioned: risk management and pay incentives. There has been too much short-termism and excessive risk taking in financial institutions, often encouraged by inappropriate bonus structures. We are going to issue a new Recommendation on remuneration in financial services companies, and in the framework of the forthcoming revision of the CRD, we will look at whether capital requirements need to be increased in the case of institutions with inappropriate bonus structures which promote excessive risk-taking. We will also consider possible regulatory action on corporate governance for banks, if we conclude that it is inadequate.

Sanctions

At present, sanctioning regimes in the Member States are diverse and often not strong enough. We need to give investors, consumers and companies confidence that misbehaviour within the financial industry will be dealt with quickly, fairly and effectively. The Commission will therefore conduct a review on sanctions, and on the Market Abuse Directive, and report back this autumn.

Consumers, Investors, and SMEs

We also have to protect consumers, small investors and SMEs. Last month I proposed to lighten the financial reporting burden for micro-enterprises, which could save them up to 1,200 euros per year. For retail investors, we're going to make proposals next month to safeguard customers of retail investment products.

Multilateral Discussions

However, our efforts will not achieve their desired impact if they are limited to Europe. That's why we have to take part actively in the multilateral discussions in the G20 and the Financial Stability Forum in particular, to make sure that global solutions to the present financial market dysfunctioning are found. The Commission is active in the working groups of the G20 which are preparing the Heads of State summit in London on 2 April, and we are also pushing for full membership of the Commission in the FSF. We think that the decisive measures which we are taking in Europe can serve as a good example to other jurisdictions worldwide, although of course each jurisdiction needs to adopt solutions appropriate for its own economy and institutions.

B. European Securities and Markets Authority and Capital Markets Union

In January 2011, the European Commission launched the European System of Financial Supervision framework in response to the financial crisis of 2008. The framework established three independent European regulatory authorities: The European Banking Authority, the European Insurance and Occupational Pensions Authority, and the European Securities and

Markets Authority (ESMA), as well as the European Systemic Risk Board, the Joint Committee of the European Supervisory Authorities. The new ESMA replaced the Committee of European Securities Regulators.

ESMA's mandate is to enhance the protection of investors and promote stable and orderly financial markets. ESMA pursues this mandate through four key activities: promoting supervisory convergence, risk monitoring and analysis, supervision of credit rating agencies and trade repositories, and establishing a "single rulebook" for EU Markets. ESMA's single rulebook for securities markets covers a broad range of areas including asset management; investment firms; derivatives; trading venues; credit rating agencies; and preparatory work for product transparency, derivatives reporting, and the oversight of trade repositories (ESMA Annual Report 2015, online: <https://www.esma.europa.eu>).

The delegation of power to EU agencies, including ESMA, has been a point of some contention among EU member states. In 2014, the UK government challenged ESMA's power to exercise direct powers before the Court of Justice of the European Union (CJEU) in *United Kingdom v European Parliament and Council (ESMA)* (case C-270/12) (22 January 2014). The UK government objected specifically to the operation of article 28 of regulation 236/2012, which gives ESMA emergency powers to prohibit or impose conditions on short sales and similar transactions, or to require notice or publication of such positions. The UK argued that granting ESMA direct power to impose conditions and empowering the agency to pass measures of general application with the force of law breached EU constitutional limits as established in earlier cases. The EU Parliament and Council successfully resisted the UK's application, urging the CJEU to consider the earlier case law in the light of the modernization of EU agency law that occurred under the Lisbon Treaty. They also argued that an appropriate legal basis for ESMA's powers existed because it amounted to a harmonising measure under EU internal market law.

In February 2015, the Directorate-General for Financial Stability, Financial Services and Capital Markets Union of the European Commission launched a public consultation on the basis of the green paper "Building a Capital Markets Union." Following the consultation period, the European Commission adopted an action plan to achieve a "true single capital market for Europe" to be known as the Capital Markets Union (CMU). Below is an excerpt from the announcement of this plan.

Action Plan on Building a Capital Markets Union

Communication from the Commission to the European Parliament, the Council, the European Economic and Social Committee and the Committee of the Regions (30 September 2015), online: <http://eur-lex.europa.eu/legal-content/EN/TXT>

The free flow of capital was one of the fundamental principles on which the EU was built. Despite the progress that has been made over the past 50 years, Europe's capital markets are still relatively underdeveloped and fragmented. The European economy is as big as the American one, but Europe's equity markets are less than half the size, its debt markets less than a third. The gap between Member States is even bigger than that between Europe and the US. More integrated capital markets will lead to efficiency gains and support Europe's ability to fund growth.

Capital Markets Union will reinforce the third pillar of the Investment Plan for Europe. It will offer benefits for all 28 Member States, while also buttressing Economic and Monetary Union by supporting economic convergence and helping to absorb economic shocks in the euro area, as set out in the report of the Five Presidents on Completing Economic and Monetary Union.

Stronger capital markets will complement Europe's strong tradition of bank financing, and will:

- Unlock more investment from the EU and the rest of the world: Capital Markets Union will help to mobilise capital in Europe and channel it to all companies, including SMEs, infrastructure and long term sustainable projects that need it to expand and create jobs. It will provide households with better options to meet their retirement goals.

- Better connect financing to investment projects across the EU: Member States with small markets and high growth potential have a lot to gain from a better channelling of capital and investment into their projects. Member States with more developed capital markets will benefit from greater cross-border investment and saving opportunities.

- Make the financial system more stable: integrated financial and capital markets can help Member States, especially those inside the euro area, share the impact of shocks. By opening up a wider range of funding sources, it will help to share financial risks and mean that EU citizens and companies are less vulnerable to banking contractions. Furthermore, more developed equity markets, as opposed to increased indebtedness, allow for more investment over the long term.

- Deepen financial integration and increase competition: more cross-border risk-sharing, deeper and more liquid markets and diversified sources of funding will deepen financial integration, lower costs and increase European competitiveness.

Put simply, Capital Markets Union will strengthen the link between savings and growth. It will provide more options and better returns for savers and investors. It will offer businesses more choices of funding at different stages of their development.

• • •

There is no single measure that will deliver a Capital Markets Union. Instead there will be a range of steps whose impact will cumulatively be significant. The Commission will take forward measures to remove the barriers which stand between investors' money and investment opportunities, and overcome the obstacles which prevent businesses from reaching investors. The system for channelling those funds will be made as efficient as possible, both nationally and across borders.

As the closer integration of capital markets and gradual removal of remaining national barriers could create new risks to financial stability, we will support actions to increase supervisory convergence, so that capital market regulators act in a unified way and strengthen the available tools to manage systemic risks prudently.

• • •

The successful adoption and implementation of these actions will require a sustained and concerted effort. This is a project for all 28 Member States and the Commission will work closely with them and the European Parliament to take forward these proposals.

To build early momentum, concrete proposals are being announced today and others will soon follow. First actions include a comprehensive package on securitisation with updated calibrations for CRR, the definition of infrastructure and revised calibrations for Solvency II, and a proposal to review the Prospectus Directive. In other areas, further consultation with interested parties may be needed. In parallel, the Commission will facilitate discussions with Member States on items such as tax and insolvency to enable progress to be reached over the medium to long term.

> The success of the CMU will also depend on market participants. Financial intermediaries must play their part in restoring the trust of their clients and building confidence in capital markets in Europe. This Action Plan includes market-led initiatives and the Commission urges the relevant parties to prioritise progress in these areas.
>
> Furthermore, the Commission will continue to work to identify the main inefficiencies and barriers to deeper capital markets in Europe and work out how best to overcome them, whilst retaining a strong focus on investor protection and market supervision.

The announcement regarding the launch of the CMU initiative has generated considerable debate in Europe, where some have questioned whether a true capital markets union is possible in a system where regulation is harmonized among member states but supervision is undertaken nationally. Others have also raised concerns about the pace of legislative change and voiced concerns about the potential for unintended consequences (see Feedback Statement on the Green Paper "Building a Capital Markets Union," online: <http://ec.europa.eu/finance/consultations/2015/capital-markets-union/docs/summary-of-responses_en.pdf>).

QUESTION

Does the establishment of the ESMA and the CMU offer any insights for Canada's efforts at national securities regulation?

IX. THE IMPETUS FOR REFORM

In Canada, as with the other jurisdictions discussed in this chapter, the impetus for reform of fractured and uneven securities regulatory systems derives from increasingly global capital markets and, more recently, from the crisis in those markets. Both investors and issuers will go to the jurisdiction that offers the least costly market (risk-adjusted) in which the price and value of the security are positively correlated. National systems offer "one-stop shopping," but even they can become overly complex and bureaucratic. Recall the various opinions regarding the legitimacy and proper scope for regulation of trading in securities set out at the beginning of the chapter, where Easterbrook & Fischel defended the then current regime on the ground that those who wished to change existing law bore a heavy onus of justifying the change as better than the status quo. Now the impetus for change is coming from governments, regulators, and investors. It opens up the question again of the extent to which regulation is necessary.

This question brings us back to the purpose of securities regulation. In one view, it is designed to produce sufficiently accurate comparable information about a firm's securities so that rational actors in the market will allocate capital to its most productive use. But what if actors in capital markets do not always act rationally, especially in conditions of uncertainty, such as judging the future prospects of an issuer on the basis of historical data and management's optimistic projections? What does the rational actor theory tell us about how we might deal with individually rational actions that collectively result in systemic destabilization?

X. CHAPTER SUMMARY

This chapter has examined types of markets and securities regulators and discussed recent trends in marketplace operation, including the profound impact of technological change. It explored how Canada's markets function and how they have been divided according to the type of security being distributed or traded. It provided an overview of Canada's unique regulatory system in which numerous regulators supervise trading within their constitutionally granted jurisdictions. Although the costs of such a system have been controlled by interjurisdictional cooperation, there continue to be inefficiencies and lack of investor protection associated with the current structure. Hence the regulatory reform options discussed continue to raise pressing public policy issues that need further resolution. The chapter also provided a comparative view of developments in Canada with two major securities regulators, the United States and the European Union, and raised some issues that may be of assistance to Canadian policy-makers in thinking about the future of securities regulation in Canada.

CHAPTER FOUR

The Prospectus Process

I. INTRODUCTION

Securities laws create a statutory scheme governing the issuance of securities. The Supreme Court of Canada in *Committee for the Equal Treatment of Asbestos Minority Shareholders v Ontario (Securities Commission)*, 2001 SCC 37, [2001] 2 SCR 132, held that the statutory and public policy goals of the system include investor protection, capital market efficiency, and public confidence in capital markets. The goals are set out in each provincial and territorial statute. For example, the Nova Scotia *Securities Act* (NSSA) specifies that "[t]he purpose of this Act is to provide investors with protection from practices and activities that tend to undermine investor confidence in the fairness and efficiency of capital markets and, where it would not be inconsistent with an adequate level of investor protection, to foster the process of capital formation" (NSSA, s 1A(1)). The prospectus process has been an integral part of issuing securities under this regime, as it seeks to promote these statutory objectives.

Securities legislation prohibits a person or issuer from distributing a security or trading in a security where the trade would be a distribution unless a prospectus is filed and receipted or the distribution is exempt from the prospectus requirement. A prospectus is essentially a detailed circular setting out information underpinning the issuer's distribution of the securities to the public. Securities legislation defines distribution as including a trade in a security that has not been previously issued, a trade out of a control block and any transaction or series of transactions involving a purchase and sale of or a repurchase and resale in the course of or incidental to a distribution. Securities legislation defines a "trade" in a non-exhaustive manner to include, among other things: any sale or disposition of a security for valuable consideration; any receipt by a registrant of an order to buy or sell a security; and any act, advertisement, solicitation, conduct, or negotiation directly or indirectly in furtherance of any of the foregoing.

The prospectus provides investors with detailed information regarding the issuer in order that they can make informed valuation and investment decisions. The legislation and National Instrument 41-101, *General Prospectus Requirements* (2008), 31 OSCB (Supp-2), effective 17 March 2008 (as amended effective 8 December 2015) (NI 41-101), set rules regulating who gets entry to the market, aimed in part at a balance of private and public distributions. Current securities law requires a prospectus for distribution of new securities, unless the transaction is exempt, a defined term under securities legislation. As will be discussed in Chapter 5, an issuer may be a reporting issuer that is exempted from the prospectus requirements where there is sufficient information in the market and it chooses to distribute securities in the exempt market, or it may not be a reporting issuer. This chapter addresses prospectus requirements for non-exempt issuers.

A market participant seeking to issue securities must prepare a preliminary and final prospectus. Statutory requirements for preparation and filing of prospectuses compel disclosure of information that is relevant to valuing the securities and hence enhancing the quality of information provided to potential purchasers of the securities. The prospectus process allows for scrutiny by a regulator of the documents prior to the public relying on them. Prospectuses reduce information asymmetries faced by market participants and enhance the transparency of market transactions. Although different forms of prospectuses are used for different types of issuers—that is, industrial issuers, mutual fund issuers, etc.—several fundamental aspects of the prospectus process are common to all. These aspects include disclosure through the preliminary and final prospectus; regulatory oversight of the process; the right of withdrawal and rescission for investors under certain circumstances; and statutory liability for misrepresentations and omissions in relation to the prospectus.

All securities legislation in Canada contains a prospectus procedure, and while the language differs across provincial and territorial systems, the requirements are substantially the same. NI 41-101, *General Prospectus Requirements*, as amended effective 8 December 2015, creates a uniform approach to filing of prospectuses, although it is important to continue to check legislation in the jurisdiction in which capital is being raised. Multilateral Instrument 11-102, *Passport System*, and its Companion Policy 11-102CP, *Passport System*, implement a passport system contemplated by the Provincial/Territorial Memorandum of Understanding Regarding Securities Regulation. The passport system allows market participants to distribute across more than one Canadian jurisdiction. The instrument gives each market participant a single window of access to the capital markets in multiple jurisdictions. It enables a person or company to deal only with its principal regulator to get deemed receipts in other jurisdictions (except Ontario) for a preliminary prospectus and prospectus; obtain automatic exemptions in other jurisdictions (except Ontario) equivalent to most types of discretionary exemptions granted by the principal regulator; or register automatically in other jurisdictions (except Ontario). The Instrument also enables a credit rating organization to obtain a deemed designation as a designated rating organization in other jurisdictions (except Ontario) (Companion Policy 11-102CP, *Passport System*, as amended effective 5 May 2015).

National Policy 11-202, *Process for Prospectus Reviews in Multiple Jurisdictions* (NP 11-202); National Policy 11-203, *Process for Exemptive Relief Applications in Multiple Jurisdictions* (NP 11-203); National Policy 11-204, *Process for Registration in Multiple Jurisdictions* [NP 11-204]; and National Policy 11-205, *Process for Designation of Credit Rating Organizations in Multiple Jurisdictions* (NP 11-205) set out the processes for a market participant in any jurisdiction to obtain a deemed prospectus receipt, an automatic exemption, an automatic registration or a deemed designation as a designated rating organization in a passport jurisdiction. These policies also set out processes for a market participant in a passport jurisdiction to get a prospectus receipt or a discretionary exemption from the OSC or to register in Ontario or to obtain designation as a designated rating organization in Ontario.

Earlier chapters have noted that the initially drafted national *Securities Act* was found by the Supreme Court of Canada not to be valid under the general branch of the power to regulate trade and commerce under s 91(2) of the *Constitution Act, 1867* (*Reference re Securities Act*, 2011 SCC 66, [2011] 3 SCR 837). Since then, securities regulators have worked together to try to design a national securities framework that would then be enacted by each provincial and territorial jurisdiction. On December 7, 2015, the ministers responsible for capital markets regulation in British Columbia, Ontario, Saskatchewan, New Brunswick, Prince Edward Island, Yukon, and Canada published a Revised Consultation Draft Provincial/Territorial Capital Markets Act: Summary of Proposed Transition Approach, discussed near the end of this chapter. The CMA and the regulations would together constitute the single set of provincial/territorial laws under the Cooperative Capital Markets Regulatory System (Cooperative System). As you read the national instruments currently in force, consider how capital markets legislation agreed on by six jurisdictions, if enacted, might impact the current prospectus system in Canada.

National Policy 11-202, *Process for Prospectus Reviews in Multiple Jurisdictions*
Effective 28 September 2009

3.2 Passport Prospectus

(1) If the principal regulator is a passport regulator and the prospectus is not filed in Ontario, only the principal regulator will review the prospectus. Under MI 11-102, the issuance of a receipt by the principal regulator will trigger a deemed receipt in each other passport jurisdiction where the prospectus is filed.

(2) If the principal regulator is the OSC and the prospectus is also filed in a passport jurisdiction, only the OSC will review the prospectus. Under MI 11-102, the issuance of the OSC receipt will trigger a deemed receipt in each passport jurisdiction where the prospectus is filed.

3.3 Dual Prospectus

If the principal regulator is a passport regulator and the prospectus is also filed in Ontario, the principal regulator will review the prospectus, and the OSC, as a non-principal regulator, will coordinate its review with the principal regulator. The receipt of the principal regulator will trigger a deemed receipt in each other passport jurisdiction where the prospectus is filed and will evidence the receipt of the OSC, if the OSC has made the same decision as the principal regulator.

The Ontario Securities Commission (OSC) has not adopted the Instrument, but the Instrument provides that Ontario market participants will have access to the passport system when the OSC issues a receipt for a prospectus to an issuer whose principal jurisdiction is Ontario, as a deemed receipt is automatically issued in each passport jurisdiction where the market participant filed the prospectus under the Instrument; and when the OSC grants a discretionary exemption to a market participant whose principal jurisdiction is Ontario, the person obtains an automatic exemption from the equivalent provision of securities legislation of each passport jurisdiction for which the person gives the notice described in the instrument. A firm or individual whose principal jurisdiction is Ontario and who is registered in a category in Ontario is automatically registered in the same category in a passport jurisdiction when the firm or individual makes the required submission under the instrument. Also, when the OSC designates a credit rating organization as a designated rating organization, the credit rating organization obtains a deemed designation in each passport jurisdiction for which the credit rating organization gives the notice under the instrument (Companion Policy 11-102CP, *Passport System*, as amended effective 23 June 2016, s 1.3(6)). This system is colloquially known as "one-way passport." The instrument does not relieve issuers filing in Québec from the linguistic obligations prescribed by Québec law and, thus, where a prospectus is filed in several jurisdictions including Québec, the prospectus must be in French or in French and English (Québec *Securities Act*, s 40.1, 11-102CP, s 1.4).

Section 110 of the Alberta *Securities Act*, RSA 2000, c S-4 (ASA), as amended 2015, and ss 53-57 of the Ontario *Securities Act*, RSO 1990, c S.5 (OSA), as amended 2016, are illustrative of the statutory language requiring a prospectus before trading in a security. Section 110 of the ASA specifies:

> 110(1) No person or company shall trade in a security on the person's or company's own account or on behalf of any other person or company if the trade would be a distribution of the security unless
>
> (a) a preliminary prospectus has been filed and the Executive Director has issued a receipt for it, and
>
> (b) a prospectus has been filed and the Executive Director has issued a receipt for it.
>
> (2) A preliminary prospectus and a prospectus may be filed in accordance with this Part to enable the issuer to become a reporting issuer, notwithstanding the fact that no distribution is contemplated.

Sections 53-57 of the OSA specify:

> *Prospectus Required*
>
> 53(1) No person or company shall trade in a security on his, her or its own account or on behalf of any other person or company if the trade would be a distribution of the security, unless a preliminary prospectus and a prospectus have been filed and receipts have been issued for them by the Director.
>
> *Filing without distribution*
>
> (2) A preliminary prospectus and a prospectus may be filed in accordance with this Part to enable the issuer to become a reporting issuer, despite the fact that no distribution is contemplated.
>
> *Preliminary prospectus*
>
> 54(1) A preliminary prospectus shall substantially comply with the requirements of Ontario securities law respecting the form and content of a prospectus, except that the report or reports of the auditor or accountant required by the regulations need not be included.
>
> *Idem*
>
> (2) A preliminary prospectus may exclude information with respect to the price to the underwriter and offering price of any securities and other matters dependent upon or relating to such prices.
>
> *Receipt for preliminary prospectus*
>
> 55. The Director shall issue a receipt for a preliminary prospectus forthwith upon the filing thereof.
>
> *Full, true and plain disclosure required*
>
> 56(1) A prospectus shall provide full, true and plain disclosure of all material facts relating to the securities issued or proposed to be distributed and shall comply with the requirements of Ontario securities law.
>
> *Supplemental material*
>
> (2) The prospectus shall contain or be accompanied by such financial statements, reports or other documents as are required by this Act or the regulations.
>
> *Amendment to preliminary prospectus on material change*
>
> 57(1) Where a material adverse change occurs after a receipt is obtained for a preliminary prospectus filed in accordance with subsection 53(1) and before the receipt for the prospectus is obtained or, where a material change occurs after the receipt for the prospectus is obtained

but prior to the completion of the distribution under such prospectus, an amendment to such preliminary prospectus or prospectus, as the case may be, shall be filed as soon as practicable and in any event within ten days after the change occurs.

Same, additional securities

(2) If, after a receipt for a prospectus or for an amendment to a prospectus is issued but before the distribution under the prospectus or amendment is completed, securities in addition to those previously disclosed in the prospectus or amendment are to be distributed, the issuer making the distribution shall file an amendment to the prospectus disclosing the additional securities as soon as practicable and, in any event, within 10 days after the decision to increase the number of securities offered is made.

Receipt

(2.1) The Director shall issue a receipt for an amendment to a prospectus that must be filed under subsection (1) or (2) unless the Director refuses in accordance with subsection 61(2) to issue the receipt.

Restriction

(2.2) Unless otherwise permitted by regulation, an issuer shall not proceed with a distribution or an additional distribution until a receipt is issued for an amendment to the prospectus that must be filed under subsection (1) or (2).

Notice of amendment

(3) An amendment to a preliminary prospectus referred to in subsection (1) shall, forthwith after it has been filed, be forwarded to each recipient of the preliminary prospectus according to the record maintained under section 67.

Securities law also allows a preliminary prospectus and a prospectus to be filed to enable the issuer to become a reporting issuer, despite the fact that no distribution is contemplated at that time by the issuer. Prospectus disclosure is also required where there is a sale of securities by persons having a controlling interest in the securities of an issuer. Such persons are likely to have heightened access to information about the issuer, and the disclosure requirements are imposed on their transactions. See the discussion below on prospectus requirements in a secondary offering.

The prospectus system was designed as an instrument to increase public confidence in public offerings. Part of the statutory framework is to provide the appropriate checks and balance in terms of what issuers need to include in the prospectus with the attendant time and cost of preparing materials, and how notice is to be given to potential purchasers in a meaningful and timely manner. There are also national instruments aimed at facilitating prospectus filing across multiple jurisdictions. These instruments and the forms that accompany them are discussed later in this chapter, as well as local rules that provide more detail of what is expected.

The following excerpt summarizes developments in prospectus offerings, the details of which are contained in the remainder of the chapter.

R Yalden, J Sarra, P Paton, M Gillen, R Davis & M Condon,
Business Organizations: Principles, Policies, and Practice
(Toronto: Emond Montgomery, 2007) at 413-14

A. *Contemporary Developments in Prospectus Form*

Historically, the prospectus has been intended to provide information about the security being sold and about the issuer of the security for the purpose of assisting investors in valuing the security. Regulations passed pursuant to securities acts in Canada have typically set out forms for prospectuses of different types of issuers, such as industrial issuers, finance companies, natural resource companies, and mutual funds, with these forms containing lists of items that must be disclosed in the prospectus. The disclosure requirements associated with the so-called long form prospectus for industrial issuers applied both to issuers conducting initial public offerings (IPOs) (that is, issuers raising capital in a non-exempt transaction for the first time) and subsequent offerings of new securities. For at least 40 years, there has been extensive debate among academic economists and securities lawyers as to the ultimate usefulness of the detailed disclosure requirements imposed by long form prospectus content regulations. Perhaps in response to this, Canadian regulators have gradually been diminishing the extent of the disclosure required in a prospectus issued at the time of distributing securities. This process began with the promulgation of several national policies by the CSA, and later the introduction of NI 44-101, *Short Form Prospectus Distributions*, which introduced the possibility of short form prospectus (SFP) distributions for issuers that were able to meet established eligibility requirements. These eligibility requirements revolved around the issuers qualifying as an established "reporting issuer" (an issuer that has previously filed a prospectus) for an appropriate period of time and having a high aggregate market capitalization. Thus, the effect of the short form prospectus rules was to separate the provision of information about the securities to be issued from the provision of information about the issuer itself, and the rule was premised on the existing, timely availability of information about the issuer in the secondary markets.

Recently, in a revision to NI 44-101, the CSA moved to expand the opportunities for issuers to use the SFP process by removing the market capitalization eligibility requirements for reporting issuers. This opens up to several thousand more issuers the possibility of using the SFP process. The significance of the de-emphasis on "point of sale" disclosure is in part an attempt to reduce the regulatory burden on issuers raising capital, especially small and medium-sized businesses. It also acknowledges the reality that over 90 percent of transactions in securities markets take place in the secondary rather than the primary market. The effect of the expansion of NI 44-101 is that the traditional long form prospectus document is retained for IPOs only.

The foundation for the SFP process is the assumption that issuers who are already reporting issuers are abiding by the continuous disclosure obligations of securities law. In particular, they are filing annual information forms (AIFs) that provide extensive information to investors about the history, business lines, and finances of the issuer. With that information backdrop available, reporting issuers may provide to the regulators a much more streamlined prospectus document, which basically describes the characteristics of the securities being offered in the distribution, as well as the use to which the proceeds will be put, at the time the offering takes place.

Cost and Timeliness of the Prospectus Process

For the issuer seeking a wide market in which to raise capital, a public offering through the prospectus process provides the possibility of attracting capital from a much broader source of investors. However, the prospectus process can be both time-consuming and expensive, involving lawyers, underwriters, sector specialists, and accountants. One study by the Toronto Stock Exchange (TSX), *The Costs of Going Public on the Toronto Stock Exchange* (Toronto: TSX, 2003), indicated that the median total costs estimated by issuers for launching an initial public offering (IPO) was $3.9 million for operating companies and almost $11 million for special purpose issuers. While the costs are smaller for smaller issuers, it is nonetheless an expensive and time-consuming process, particularly where there are delays involved in seeking regulatory approval in multiple markets. From the perspective of the issuer seeking to undertake an initial public offering in several jurisdictions, the transaction costs associated with meeting the prospectus requirements of different Canadian securities regulators in the past resulted in more expense than that faced by an issuer in a capital market with a single regulator. In many cases, the requirements were duplicative, likely disadvantaging smaller firms that are less able to bear the costs of compliance across multiple regulatory systems. NI 44-101 addressed some of these issues of cost and timeliness, combined with the national policies discussed above, all aimed at trying to streamline the prospectus process.

The result of the changes in 2008 and subsequently arguably means that some market risks associated with the different timelines and delays in the prospectus approval process of different regulators across Canada have been reduced, although there will still be delays due to the dual process of approval in Ontario for issuers for whom Ontario is not the principal regulator. Generally, public offerings are time-sensitive, and untimely regulatory approval can seriously affect the pricing of securities because there is often an opportune moment or "market window" in which to launch the securities. Failure to meet the market window not only can mean loss in pricing, but also can affect the overall business strategy of the issuer.

In "The Costs of Compliance in Canada's Securities Regulatory Regime," a research study prepared for the Wise Persons' Committee (WPC) (in A Douglas Harris, ed, *WPC Committee to Review the Structure of Securities Regulation in Canada: Research Studies* (Ottawa: Department of Finance, 2003)), professors Anand and Klein made the following observation in respect of opportunity cost risks associated with the regulatory approval process for prospectuses:

> Our case study participants emphasized the importance of timing to the success of their IPOs. A "market window" is identified and milestones required to successfully complete an IPO are determined by working back from that window. One of the risks associated with missing a market window is the deferral or outright cancellation of the IPO. A deferral or cancellation can seriously and adversely affect an issuer insofar as the planned IPO would have featured prominently in the issuer's existing business strategy. Business plans that had been intended to follow the IPO would be completely ruined.
>
> . . .
>
> In each case study, participants incurred a minimum incremental delay of five working days waiting for non-principal regulators to either affirm or opt out of the MRRS process. Where

> progress towards completion of an IPO is smooth, these budgeted incremental days may not cause companies to miss market windows. However, timetables can slip for a variety of reasons, and therefore these incremental days represent a real risk to companies listing their shares on an exchange for the first time.

Notwithstanding opportunity costs, the amount of capital raised will likely exceed the upfront costs of launching the public offering; otherwise, the issuer will not pursue the offering. Hence although investor protection is a key goal of the regulatory system, the question of how to find the appropriate balance between this protection and a streamlined but efficient approach to the prospectus process continues to be a live issue across Canada, as discussed in Chapter 3.

The balance of this chapter explores the prospectus process and requirements, as well as remedies for non-compliance.

II. THE PROSPECTUS PROCESS

The prospectus is the cornerstone of the public offering process under existing legislation. A prospectus is required for an IPO and a primary offering of securities. Recall from Chapter 3 that an IPO is the first offering of securities by an issuer entering the market, and a primary offering is a first offering of a particular set of securities by an issuer already in the market, called a reporting issuer. A prospectus is also required in limited instances of a secondary offer (resale of securities by a control block holder), discussed briefly below. The first step in the prospectus process is usually to secure the services of an underwriter. Then there are four stages to the prospectus process: the development and filing of a preliminary prospectus and issuing of a receipt by the securities regulator; comments and revisions during a waiting period; the filing of a final prospectus and issuing of a receipt; and the distribution of securities once the receipt is issued.

The content of the prospectus varies according to the type of issuer and type of security, but, generally, a prospectus discusses the business plan of the issuer and its current and expected activities; provides financial statements; describes the capital structure of the issuer, the estimated proceeds of the issue, and the planned purpose for utilization of the capital; the underwriting agreement; and a description of factors that could make the security risky. The issuer or selling securityholder is to disclose the estimated net proceeds to be received, or, in the case of a non-fixed price distribution or a distribution to be made on a best-efforts basis, the minimum amount, if any, of net proceeds to be received by the issuer or selling securityholder from the sale of the securities distributed (Form 41-101F1, s 6.1).

A junior issuer must disclose additional information, specifically, the total funds available, and the following breakdown of those funds: the estimated net proceeds from the sale of the securities offered under the prospectus; the estimated consolidated working capital (deficiency) as at the most recent month-end before filing the prospectus; and the total other funds available to be used to achieve the principal purposes identified by the junior issuer (Form 41-101F1, s 6.2). A junior issuer that had negative operating cash flow in its most recently completed financial year for which financial statements have been included in the prospectus must disclose the period of time the proceeds raised under the prospectus are expected to fund operations, the estimated total operating costs necessary for the issuer to achieve its stated business objectives during that period of time, and the estimated amount of other material capital expenditures during that period of time (Form 41-101F1, s 8.7).

If the issuer is a venture issuer or an IPO venture issuer that has not had significant revenue from operations in either of its last two financial years, it must disclose a breakdown of material components of exploration and evaluation assets or expenditures, expensed research and development costs, intangible assets arising from development, general and administrative expenses, and any material costs, whether expenses or recognized as assets, not referred to in this list (Form 41-101F1, s 8.6).

NI 41-101 contains definitions of an IPO venture issuer and a junior issuer.

National Instrument 41-101, *General Prospectus Requirements*
As amended effective 8 December 2015, online: <https://www.bcsc.bc.ca/Securities_Law/Policies/Policy4/PDF/41-101__NI___December_8__2015/>

"IPO venture issuer" means an issuer that

(a) files a long form prospectus,

(b) is not a reporting issuer in any jurisdiction immediately before the date of the final long form prospectus, and

(c) at the date of the long form prospectus, does not have any of its securities listed or quoted, has not applied to list or quote any of its securities, and does not intend to apply to list or quote any of its securities, on

(i) the Toronto Stock Exchange,

(i.1) Aequitas NEO Exchange Inc.,

(ii) a US marketplace, or

(iii) a marketplace outside of Canada and the United States of America, other than the Alternative Investment Market of the London Stock Exchange or the PLUS markets operated by PLUS Markets Group plc;

"junior issuer" means an issuer

(a) that files a preliminary prospectus,

(b) that is not a reporting issuer in any jurisdiction,

(c) whose total consolidated assets as at the date of the most recent statement of financial position of the issuer included in the preliminary prospectus are less than $10,000,000,

(d) whose consolidated revenue as shown in the most recent annual statement of comprehensive income of the issuer included in the preliminary prospectus is less than $10,000,000, and

(e) whose equity as at the date of the most recent statement of financial position of the issuer included in the preliminary prospectus is less than $10,000,000,

taking into account all adjustments to asset, revenue and equity calculations necessary to reflect each significant proposed acquisition of a business or related business by an issuer that has progressed to a state where a reasonable person would believe that the likelihood of the issuer completing the acquisition is high, and each completed significant acquisition of a business or related business that was completed,

(f) for paragraphs (c) and (e), before the date of the preliminary prospectus and after the date of the issuer's most recent statement of financial position included in the preliminary prospectus as if each acquisition had taken place as at the date of the issuer's most recent statement of financial position included in the preliminary prospectus, and

(g) for paragraph (d), after the last day of the most recent annual statement of comprehensive income of the issuer included in the preliminary prospectus as if each acquisition had taken place at the beginning of the issuer's most recently completed financial year for which a statement of comprehensive income is included in the preliminary prospectus;

QUESTIONS

1. Why do you think that securities regulators have made distinctions in the type of disclosure required for junior and IPO venture issuers?
2. There is currently policy debate on whether Canada should move more toward proportionate regulation, setting different requirements for different types of issuers. Does such a policy move make sense in the context of prospectus disclosure?

The overriding principle of prospectus disclosure is that there be full, true and plain disclosure of all material facts (OSA, s 56(1); ASA, s 113(1); British Columbia, *Securities Act*, RSC 1996, c 418 (BCSA), s 63(1); Saskatchewan, *The Securities Act, 1988*, SS 1998-89, c S-42.2 (SSA), s 61(1)(a); Manitoba, *The Securities Act*, CCSM c S50 (MSA), s 41(1); New Brunswick, *Securities Act*, SNB 2004, c S-5.5 (NBSA), s 74; Nova Scotia, *Securities Act*, RSNS 1989, c 418 (NSSA), as amended SNS 2006, c 46, ss 61(1), 63; Newfoundland and Labrador, *Securities Act*, RSNL 1990, c S-13 (Nfld SA), s 57(1)). The New Brunswick statutory language is illustrative:

> 74(1) A prospectus shall provide full, true and plain disclosure of all material facts relating to the securities issued or proposed to be distributed and shall comply with the requirements of New Brunswick securities law.
>
> 74(2) A prospectus shall contain or be accompanied by such financial statements, reports or other documents as are required by this Act or the regulations.

NI 41-101, *General Prospectus Requirements*, as amended effective 8 December 2015, applies to any prospectus filed under securities legislation and any distribution of securities subject to the prospectus requirement, other than a prospectus filed under NI 81-101, *Mutual Fund Prospectus Disclosure*, as amended effective 8 December 2015, or a distribution of securities under such a prospectus. NI 41-101, while being the primary instrument regulating prospectus distributions, is not exhaustive, and issuers must still refer to the securities legislation of the local jurisdiction for additional requirements that may apply to the issuer's prospectus distribution (Companion Policy 41-101CP, *General Prospectus Requirements Supplement to the OSC Bulletin* (8 December 2015)).

Issuers are to apply plain language principles when they prepare a long-form prospectus including: using short sentences; using definite everyday language; using the active voice; avoiding superfluous words; organizing the document into clear, concise sections, paragraphs, and sentences; avoiding jargon; using personal pronouns to speak directly to the reader; avoiding reliance on glossaries and defined terms unless it facilitates understanding of the disclosure; avoiding vague boilerplate wording; avoiding abstract terms by using more concrete terms or examples; avoiding multiple negatives; using technical terms only when necessary and explaining those terms; using charts, tables, and examples where it makes disclosure easier to understand (Companion Policy 41-101CP, part 4).

Typically, the issuer works with an underwriter to develop the offering and to draft the preliminary prospectus. Only at the point that a receipt has been obtained for the preliminary prospectus can the issuer or underwriter test the market in terms of determining the level of interest in the securities among potential purchasers. Undertaking such testing of the market any earlier in the process would leave the issuer vulnerable to a charge of distributing without a prospectus or insider trading because of the strict definitions of trade and distribution under securities legislation. Canadian securities regulators have also specified that persons or companies should be aware that the posting of new information on a website during a period of distribution may be construed as advertising, which is subject to restrictions in certain jurisdictions (NP 47-201, *Trading in Securities Using the Internet and Other Electronic Means* (2013), 2.6). The public policy underlying these restrictions is to ensure that there is no self-dealing or other misconduct in the period leading up to the distribution of securities.

In the United States, regulators have moved to recognize issuers about whom there is more information in the market, creating a streamlined offering process for well-known seasoned issuers (WKSI). The US Securities and Exchange Commission explains how the system works.

US Securities and Exchange Commission, Division of Corporation Finance, "Revised Statement on Well-Known Seasoned Issuer Waivers"
(24 April 2014), online: <http://www.sec.gov/divisions/corpfin/guidance/wksi-waivers-interp-031214.htm> (footnotes omitted)

Background

In 2005's Securities Offering Reform release, the Commission adopted various modifications to the registration, communications and offering processes under the Securities Act, including creating a new category of issuer—the "well-known seasoned issuer" ("WKSI")—for the most widely followed issuers representing the most significant amount of capital raised and traded in the United States. WKSIs benefit to the greatest degree from the communications and registration flexibilities provided in Securities Offering Reform. Most notably, WKSIs can register their securities offerings on shelf registration statements that become effective automatically upon filing. As a result, a WKSI is not required to wait until the Division of Corporation Finance reviews and declares its registration statement effective before it is permitted to make sales.

In order to qualify as a WKSI, an issuer may not be an "ineligible issuer." Rule 405 of the Securities Act defines an "ineligible issuer" to be, among other things, an issuer that has (or whose subsidiary has) been convicted of a felony or misdemeanor specified in four enumerated provisions under Section 15 of the Exchange Act or an issuer that has violated (or whose subsidiary has violated) the anti-fraud provisions of the federal securities laws (or that are the subject of a judicial or administrative decree or order prohibiting certain conduct or activities involving the anti-fraud provisions of the federal securities laws). In determining to exclude certain categories of issuers from WKSI status, the Commission noted that certain issuers have been viewed historically as ineligible for disclosure-related relief.

Under Securities Act Rule 405, the Commission may grant waivers of ineligible issuer status "upon a showing of good cause, that it is not necessary under the circumstances that the issuer be considered an ineligible issuer." Authority to act on applications for waivers from ineligible issuer status has been delegated by the Commission to the Director of the Division of Corporation Finance.

On July 8, 2011, the Division issued a statement on WKSI waivers to provide guidance on what constitutes "a showing of good cause" for purposes of an ineligible issuer waiver request. The purpose of that guidance was to provide transparency into the framework that the Division follows in considering an application for a waiver of ineligible issuer status. Based on our experience with WKSI waivers to date, including the 18 months since the issuance of the original policy, the Division has decided to update and refine its policy. This statement outlines the framework the Division generally will follow in considering whether to grant a waiver of ineligible issuer status.

Framework for Determining Waivers

The Division's assessment in determining whether an issuer has shown good cause that ineligible issuer status is not necessary for the public interest or the protection of investors focuses on how the conduct that gave rise to the ineligibility relates to the reliability of the issuer's current and future disclosure and, if it does, what steps the issuer has taken to remediate any deficiencies.

A waiver, which could include conditions or undertakings, may be granted if a review of all of the facts and circumstances leads the Division to conclude that granting the waiver would be consistent with the public interest and the protection of investors. In making this determination, the Division will consider the nature of the violation or conviction and whether it involved disclosure for which the issuer or any of its subsidiaries was responsible or calls into question the ability of the issuer to produce reliable disclosure currently and in the future. In addition, the Division will review whether the conduct involved a criminal conviction or scienter based violation, as opposed to a civil or administrative non-scienter based violation. Where there is a criminal conviction or a scienter-based violation involving disclosure for which the issuer or any of its subsidiaries was responsible, the issuer's burden to show good cause that a waiver is justified would be significantly greater.

The Division will also consider the factors below when it evaluates the appropriateness of granting a waiver from ineligible issuer status. No single factor is dispositive, and the burden will be on the issuer to demonstrate that the conduct that gave rise to the violation, and the facts and circumstances as they currently exist, do not affect its ability to produce reliable disclosure and that it is not necessary under the circumstances that the issuer be considered an ineligible issuer.

- *Who Was Responsible for and What Was the Duration of the Misconduct?* Specifically, the Division would consider who was responsible for the misconduct and whether it was known by the WKSI parent or whether personnel at the WKSI parent ignored warning signs regarding the misconduct. The concern would be the potential impact of such actor(s) and circumstances upon the issuer's ability to file reliable reports with the Commission. In this regard, the Division would consider whether the individuals responsible for or involved in the misconduct were officers or directors of the WKSI parent, or were lower level employees in the operation of a subsidiary. The Division would also consider whether there were red flags about the conduct and whether more senior officers of the WKSI parent disregarded these warning signs. The Division would also look at the duration of the violative conduct. Did the conduct last over a period of years or was it an isolated instance? If the conduct was an isolated instance conducted at the subsidiary level and not known or disregarded by the WKSI parent, then it would be more likely that this factor would weigh in favor of granting a waiver. However, if the conduct was known or warning signs were disregarded by the WKSI parent, or the conduct lasted over several years, or it reflected a tone at the top that condoned or chose to ignore the conduct, then this factor would weigh against granting a waiver. Greater emphasis will be placed on this factor if individuals involved with, or with influence over, the issuer's disclosure were participants in or knew or should have known about the misconduct resulting in ineligibility, as this may call into question the reliability of the issuer's current and future disclosure.

- *What Remedial Steps Did the Issuer Take?* The Division will consider what remedial measures the issuer has taken to address the violative conduct and whether those actions would likely prevent a recurrence of the misconduct and mitigate the possibility of future unreliable disclosure. The Division will look at whether there were key changes in the personnel involved in the violative or criminal conduct. The Division will also look at whether the issuer has taken steps to improve training or made improvements to internal controls and disclosure controls and procedures. The Division's analysis of the importance of these remedial steps will focus on how they relate to the issuer's ability to produce reliable disclosure. The effectiveness of these actions would help support a conclusion that, despite past violations, the issuer's disclosure to the markets would be more likely to be reliable in the future. On the other hand, if the conduct in question or similar conduct has happened on prior occasions, it may raise questions about the efficacy of the remediation and the adequacy of an issuer's internal controls, which could bear on the issuer's ability to produce reliable disclosure.
- *Impact If the Waiver Request Is Denied.* We will weigh the severity of the impact on the issuer if the waiver request is denied and weigh any such impact against the facts and circumstances relating to the violative or criminal conduct to assess whether the loss of WKSI status would be a disproportionate hardship in light of the nature of the issuer's misconduct. We will also look at any effects that the issuer's loss of WKSI status could have for the markets as a whole and the investing public in considering whether a waiver would be consistent with the public interest and the protection of investors.

Issuers seeking a waiver must submit a request letter that includes appropriate justification, based on the framework outlined above, for why a waiver should be granted and will bear the burden of establishing such justification.

III. UNDERWRITING AN OFFERING

There are three main parties in the offering process: the issuer, the underwriter, and the investor. In this section, we discuss the underwriter's function as a critical link between issuers and investors. We also discuss why issuers employ underwriters.

Underwriting is the process of selling securities in the market. Underwriters offer credibility to issuers, using their reputation as experienced market participants to bolster the claims of the issuer regarding its present profitability and/or future prospects. The due diligence investigation undertaken by an underwriter usually results in enhanced quality of disclosure in the prospectus, and the underwriter can provide valuable advice regarding the pricing and marketing of securities.

Most public offerings are underwritten by investment banking firms. The underwriter usually determines the terms and price of the offering, given the market demand. It also provides some governance advice in terms of changes to the business plan that the issuer should make in order to make the securities more attractive. Although an underwriter is a private market participant in that it assists the issuer, the underwriter has public obligations to ensure that the required assurances and covenants are obtained and that the integrity of the system is maintained. The issuer must provide extensive representations and warranties to the underwriter as to the authorization of the issuance of the securities, as well as agree to complete the prospectus process in a timely manner. The underwriting agreement may also contain a period in which the issuer is prohibited from issuing similar securities as those that the underwriter has agreed to underwrite. The underwriting agreement may also give the underwriter first right of refusal on underwriting a future public offering. Underwriters also perform a number of functions relating to information transfer for investors and are therefore often referred to as "gatekeepers" of the securities law system.

There are several types of underwriting arrangements. A common type is an agency agreement in which the underwriter agrees to use its "best efforts" to sell the securities as an agent of the issuer. The underwriter takes a commission for those securities it is able to sell to purchasers in the market. There is a range of fees, and underwriters can charge up to 7 percent of the offering price. Another form of underwriting is a "firm commitment," in which the underwriter makes an agreement to purchase the securities and resell them. Firm commitment agreements occur where the underwriter is confident that it can make a profit between the issue price from the issuer and the price that it will receive from sale of the securities. The profit between the issue price and the sale price is also known as the underwriter's "spread." One form of firm commitment arrangement is a "bought deal" underwriting agreement, which is discussed below. However, the underwriter can also agree to sell at the issue price and charge an underwriting fee linked to the issue price, a practice that occurs with the sale of equities (Al Anand, "The Efficiency of Direct Public Offerings" (2003) 7:3 J Small & Emerging Bus L 433).

A prospectus must contain a certificate signed by the underwriter(s) in a contractual relationship with the issuer or securityholder whose securities are being offered by the prospectus that to the best of the underwriter's knowledge, information, and belief, the prospectus constitutes full, true, and plain disclosure of all material facts relating to the securities offered by the prospectus (NI 41-101; see also e.g. OSA, s 59(1), amended by SO 2007, c 7, Schedule 38, s 5; NSSA, s 63; NBSA, s 74(3)).

OSA, s 59(1) is illustrative:

> 59(1) Subject to subsection 63(2), where there is an underwriter, a prospectus shall contain a certificate in the prescribed form, signed by the underwriter or underwriters who, with respect to the securities offered by the prospectus, are in a contractual relationship with the issuer or securityholder whose securities are being offered by the prospectus.

This certificate is distinguishable from the issuer's certificate, discussed in Section VIII of this chapter, in that the standard is higher for the issuer as it has direct access to all information. Every prospectus must contain a statement of the rights given to a purchaser (see e.g. OSA, s 60). While such provisions were historically set out in securities legislation, many jurisdictions repealed the provisions when they adopted NI 41-101. Those underwriters that sign the certificate and all of the directors are potentially liable for any misrepresentation in the prospectus.

The following excerpt from the *YBM Magnex International* decision illustrates how securities commissions view the role of the underwriter in terms of disclosure and certification.

YBM Magnex International Inc
(2003), 26 OSCB 5285

Underwriters

[187] An issuer's certificate under subsection 58(1) of the Act must be signed by the CEO, CFO and any other two directors. It must certify that the prospectus contains full, true and plain disclosure of all material facts. The underwriter's certificate under subsection 59(1) of the Act must certify that the prospectus constitutes full, true and plain disclosure of all material facts, but only "to the best of our knowledge, information and belief." In general terms, the certificates are different due to the underwriter's access to information. Directors and officers are generally in a better position to obtain information and data that may be unavailable to the underwriter.

[188] The phrase "to the best of our knowledge, information and belief" carries with it a requirement to obtain information before an underwriter can make that affirmation; *Re A.E. Ames & Co. Ltd.*, [1972] OSCB 98 at 112 (*Ames*). Although that phrase acknowledges that an underwriter may not have the same access to corporate information that the officers and directors have, the underwriter is a gatekeeper of the public interest with professional expertise in the capital markets … An underwriter must go beyond the statements of the issuer's directors, officers and counsel and must avoid automatic reliance. In *Ames*, the Commission noted at 112:

> The underwriter stands between the issuer and the public as an independent, expert party in bringing new securities to the market. In a sense the underwriter and the issuer are joint-venturers, but in another and more important sense they must be adversaries. That is the underwriter must seek out and question all relevant and material facts concerning the issuer and reasonably ensure himself that these facts are fully and truly set before the investing public.

[189] While underwriters may be at an informational disadvantage, the essence of their role was captured in a poignant paragraph in *Feit v. Leasco Data Processing Equipment Corp.*, 332 F. Supp. 544 at 582 (EDNY 1971), where Weinstein J stated:

> [The duty of dealer-managers] to investigate should be considered in light of their more limited access. Nevertheless they are expected to exercise a high degree of care in investigation and independent verification of the company's representations … the underwriters must play devil's advocate.

[190] In this regard, an underwriter must challenge the disclosure the issuer proposes to make to the investing public. Otherwise, the underwriter cannot be said to have met the standard to the best of its knowledge, information and belief.

[191] Lead underwriters must be adversarial and more so in some circumstances. Reliance on counsel cannot be an excuse for failing to make an adequate examination of the facts. While legal advice will be a factor that affects an underwriter's belief that there were no omissions of material facts, if counsel did not make an adequate examination, the underwriter must bear the consequences; *Escott* at 697.

QUESTIONS

1. Can an underwriter be both a joint venturer and a public independent expert party as the *YBM Magnex International* decision suggests?
2. What conflicts are inherent in the role and how can they be addressed?
3. What mechanisms do securities regulators have to control underwriters?

OSC Staff Notice 51-719 *Emerging Markets Issuer Review*
(20 March 2012), online: <http://www.osc.gov.on.ca/documents/en/Securities-Category5/sn_20120320_51-719_emerging-markets.pdf>

[The staff notice noted that the integrity of public disclosure by reporting issuers, including financial reporting, is core to investor information and protection, and depends critically on a number of market players performing their duties responsibly. With respect to underwriters, the staff notice observed at pages 14-15:]

> Underwriters, as gatekeepers to our securities markets, are uniquely situated to verify information about an issuer, its operations and management. In prospectus offerings, underwriters must certify that to the best of their knowledge, information and belief, the prospectus constitutes full, true and plain disclosure of all material facts relating to the offered securities. In the listing process, the underwriters may act as sponsors. In this role, they conduct due diligence and may prepare reports on, among other things, the issuer's business and financial position, the issuer's directors and officers, and the issuer's qualifications for meeting all relevant listing criteria. The role of the sponsor in the listing process is a critical part of the listing review and approval.
>
> Underwriters should participate in the offering process with a healthy amount of scepticism regarding management claims. Their due diligence must be designed to detect if there are material misstatements or omissions in prospectus disclosure. An underwriter must also develop a full understanding of an issuer's finances, management, operations, industry and country of origin, in order to be able to certify the prospectus. They should also document their findings in a clear and concise manner.

A. "Bought Deal" Underwriting Agreements

A variation on the firm commitment arrangement is a "bought deal" underwriting agreement, in which the underwriter makes a firm commitment early in the process, at the preliminary prospectus stage, where a short-form prospectus process is contemplated. Short-form prospectuses are discussed later in this chapter. The advantage of a bought deal is that the underwriter typically provides a firm commitment to purchase a large block of securities, signed before the preliminary prospectus is filed. It must be an enforceable agreement and a preliminary short-form prospectus must be filed within four business days of signing the agreement, accompanied by a media release announcing the transaction, NI 44-101, *Short Form Prospectus Distributions* (2000), as amended 2015. This exception to general prospectus rules is to facilitate the distribution of securities and to reduce the risk of the offering to the underwriter by allowing it to canvass potential purchasers early in the prospectus process.

NI 44-101 was amended in 2008 to allow for solicitations of expressions of interest for over-allotment options.

NI 44-101, *Short Form Prospectus Distributions*
As amended effective 8 December 2015

Part 7 Solicitations of Expressions of Interest

7.1 Definitions and Interpretations

(1) In this Part:

"bought deal agreement" means a written agreement

(a) under which one or more underwriters has agreed to purchase all securities of an issuer that are to be offered in a distribution under a short form prospectus on a firm commitment basis, other than securities issuable on the exercise of an over-allotment option,

(b) that does not have a market-out clause,

(c) that, other than an over-allotment option, does not provide an option for any party to increase the number of securities to be purchased, and

(d) that, other than what is agreed to under a confirmation clause that complies with section 7.4, is not conditional on one or more additional underwriters agreeing to purchase any of the securities offered;

"comparables" means information that compares an issuer to other issuers;

"confirmation clause" means a provision in a bought deal agreement that provides that the agreement is conditional on the lead underwriter confirming that one or more additional underwriters has agreed to purchase certain of the securities offered;

"market-out clause" means a provision in an agreement which permits an underwriter to terminate its commitment, or underwriters to terminate their commitment, to purchase securities in the event that the securities cannot be marketed profitably due to market conditions;

"U.S. cross-border offering" means an offering of securities of an issuer being made contemporaneously in the United States of America and Canada by way of a prospectus filed with a securities regulatory authority in a jurisdiction of Canada and a U.S. prospectus filed with the SEC;

"U.S. prospectus" means a prospectus that has been prepared in accordance with the disclosure and other requirements of U.S. federal securities law for an offering of securities registered under the 1933 Act.

(2) In this Part, for greater certainty, a reference to "provides" includes showing a document to a person without allowing the person to retain or make a copy of the document.

7.2 Solicitations of Expressions of Interest

Subject to subsection 7.4(2), the prospectus requirement does not apply to a solicitation of an expression of interest made before the issuance of a receipt for a preliminary short form prospectus for securities to be qualified for distribution under a short form prospectus pursuant to this Instrument or for securities to be issued or transferred pursuant to an over-allotment option that are qualified for distribution under a short form prospectus pursuant to this Instrument, if

(a) before the solicitation,

(i) the issuer has entered into a bought deal agreement;

(ii) the bought deal agreement has fixed the terms of the distribution, including, for greater certainty, the number and type of securities and the price per security, and requires that the issuer file a preliminary short form prospectus for the securities not more than four business days after the date that the bought deal agreement was entered into; and

(iii) immediately upon entering into the bought deal agreement, the issuer issued and filed a news release announcing the agreement,

(b) the issuer files a preliminary short form prospectus for the securities pursuant to this Instrument within four business days after the date that the bought deal agreement was entered into,

(c) upon issuance of a receipt for the preliminary short form prospectus, a copy of the preliminary short form prospectus is sent to each person or company that, in response to the solicitation, expressed an interest in acquiring the securities, and

(d) except for a bought deal agreement under paragraph (a) or a more extended form of underwriting agreement referred to in subsection 7.3(6), no agreement of purchase and sale for the securities is entered into until the short form prospectus has been filed and a receipt has been issued.

A bought deal arrangement also has implications for purchaser remedies under securities legislation. Unlike agency agreements where the issuer is still the party selling the securities, under a bought deal, the underwriter is selling the securities. In *Kerr v Danier Leather*, below, the Ontario Superior Court held that a bought deal process meant that the purchaser had no remedy of rescission against the issuer for misrepresentations based on the issuer's financial forecasts, although the court held that it was enough to found a claim for damages. While the judgment on damages was subsequently overturned on appeal, the Superior Court's finding in respect of rescission is informative.

Kerr v Danier Leather Inc
(2001), 13 BLR (3d) 248 (Ont Sup Ct J)

CUMMING J: …

[28] The plaintiff's shares were purchased from Nesbitt Burns Inc. ("Nesbitt"), one of the underwriters of Danier's IPO. The plaintiff and his spouse jointly acquired 5,000 shares of Danier at $11.25 per share pursuant to the IPO. They sold 2,000 of the shares September 22, 1998 at the issue price. They then acquired an additional 4,500 shares in October 2000.

[29] Where the purchaser has purchased the shares from an underwriter, s. 130(1) allows the purchaser to "elect to exercise a right of rescission against *such … underwriter*." (emphasis mine)

[30] When the shares are purchased from an underwriter, the right of *rescission* under s. 130(1) is available only against that seller. The record establishes that Nesbitt sold the shares as "principal" to the plaintiff. The Prospectus says (at 1, 46) that Nesbitt was a principal, pursuant to the Underwriting Agreement. That is, it was a so-called "bought deal" on the part of Nesbitt.

[31] The record establishes this was not an agency or "best efforts" offering by Nesbitt. Therefore, the issuer, Danier, was not the actual vendor.

…

[34] The evidentiary record establishes that the proposed representative plaintiff cannot assert a right of rescission for a misrepresentation under s. 130 against the named defendants. …

[35] For the reasons given, the claim for rescission is dismissed.

QUESTIONS

1. An underwriter need only certify according to its best knowledge, information and belief. Does the purchaser in a "bought deal" thus have a more restricted right of rescission against the underwriter than available against the issuer when it is the "seller" of the securities?
2. Does the decision regarding underwriter certification in *YBM Magnex International*, quoted above, provide any comfort for purchasers in a bought deal?

B. Market-Out and Disaster-Out Clauses in Underwriting Agreements

Even with a firm commitment agreement, the underwriting agreement usually contains a market-out clause under which the underwriter can terminate the agreement if it determines, acting reasonably, that the securities cannot be marketed profitably. Similarly, a disaster-out clause allows the underwriter to terminate the agreement if a significant event affects the issuer's business or the capital markets.

In *Retrieve Resources Ltd v Canaccord Capital Corp* (formerly known as *LOM Western Securities Ltd, Canarim Investment Corporation Ltd and CLD Financial Opportunities Limited)*, [1994] BCJ No 1897 (QL) (SC), the British Columbia Supreme Court considered the meaning of a market-out clause in a case where the underwriter terminated the agency agreement, particularly the issue of when an underwriter is able to shed its commitment. The court examined whether or not the phrase "the state of the financial markets" referred to a general market downturn or the market for that issuer's shares. The issuer had entered into an agency agreement with the defendant, CC Ltd, by which the latter agreed to use its best efforts as agent for the plaintiff to secure the private placement of 100,000 common shares of the plaintiff. On the same day, the plaintiff Retrieve entered into a private placement agreement with the defendant CLD to purchase 100,000 shares of the plaintiff at $2.50 per share subject to certain conditions, including the currency of the agency agreement at the time of the closing. The agency agreement provided a market-out clause to the effect that the obligations of the agent may be terminated by the agent at any time in the event that the state of the financial markets became such that the securities could not, in the agent's opinion, be privately placed. By mid-December 1987, before the agreements could close, there had been a significant deterioration in the market for the plaintiff's shares and CC Ltd exercised its right to terminate the agreement under the market-out clause. CLD followed suit, relying on the condition of the private placement agreement requiring the currency of the agency agreement at the time of closing. The action was dismissed, with the court finding at paras 51-53.

Retrieve Resources Ltd v Canaccord Capital Corp
[1994] BCJ No 1897 (QL) (SC)

Although the "market-out" clause refers to "the state of the financial markets" in a general sense, the phrase must, if it is to be given meaning, be interpreted to refer specifically to the market in the specific shares to be placed. If it meant otherwise, there would be the potentially illogical result that a market-out could be made in circumstances where the private placement could be readily made because the company was favourably regarded but the general market conditions were poor. Further, if the "state of the financial markets" indeed refers to all markets, then presumably conditions adversely affecting all markets would have to exist before the market-out clause could be relied upon.

It is also significant that, under clause 10 of the agency agreement, the obligations of the agent could be terminated by Canarim at any time. Both Mr. Brown and Mr. MacFayden testified that, in regards to the market-out clause, it made no sense for CLD to purchase shares at $2.50 in December, 1987, when the market in the shares had dropped to $2.00 per share. As counsel for the defendants asserted in argument, CLD was obviously not in the business of buying shares at a premium.

I conclude that the only sensible interpretation is that the clause is intended to afford protection to the placee in reference to the specific shares to be placed.

C. Conflicts of Interest in Underwriting

As discussed in Chapter 3, the financial services industry in Canada is highly concentrated, giving rise to some risk of conflicts of interest in the underwriting and distribution process. One example of such a situation would be where the underwriter is a subsidiary of a bank and one purpose of the issuer's offering of securities is to enable it to pay down indebtedness to the bank. As a consequence of this risk of conflict of interest, securities regulators developed NI 33-105, *Underwriting Conflicts* (2001), 24 OSCB 7687 (as amended 8 September 2015), which requires that a non-independent underwriter make certain disclosures under a prospectus or other document, including full disclosure of the relationship between the underwriter and issuer or selling securityholder and, in some instances, requires involvement of an independent underwriter. There are exemptions for distributions of securities of a foreign issuer (NI 33-105, s 3.2). The Companion Policy (CP) to NI 33-105 sets out the basic framework and policy rationale, as follows.

Companion Policy 33-105CP to NI 33-105, *Underwriting Conflicts*
As amended effective 28 September 2009

1.2 General Policy Rationale for the Instrument

(1) Two of the basic objectives of securities legislation are to ensure that investors purchasing securities in the course of a distribution purchase those securities at a price determined through a process unaffected by conflicts of interest, and receive full, true and plain disclosure of all material facts regarding the issuer and the securities offered. The Instrument is based upon the premise that those objectives are best achieved if the issuer and the underwriters deal with each other as independent parties, free of any relationship that might negatively affect the performance of their respective roles.

(2) The Instrument seeks to protect the integrity of the underwriting process in circumstances in which there is a direct or indirect relationship between the issuer or selling securityholder and the underwriter that might give rise to a perception that they are not independent of each other in connection with a distribution. The Instrument imposes two basic requirements in those circumstances. First, full disclosure of the relationships giving rise to the potential conflict of interest is required to be given to investors, and second, an independent underwriter is required in certain circumstances to participate in the transaction.

Part 2 General Structure of the Instrument

2.1 Relationships of Concern

(1) The Instrument identifies three types of relationships between a specified firm registrant acting as underwriter on a distribution and the issuer or selling securityholder of securities in the distribution that give rise to concerns over conflicts of interest; each of these relationships may be subject to the requirements of the Instrument.

(a) The specified firm registrant as issuer or selling securityholder. This relationship represents the relationship with the highest degree of conflict of the three recognized by the Instrument.

(b) An issuer or selling securityholder that is a "related issuer" of the specified firm registrant. This relationship is created primarily as the result of cross-ownership between an issuer or selling securityholder and the specified firm registrant. Subsection 1.2(2) of the Instrument provides that an entity is a related issuer to another entity if one of them is an "influential securityholder" of the other, or each of them is a related issuer of the same third party.

(c) An issuer or selling securityholder that is not a related issuer of the specified firm registrant, but that has some other relationship with the specified firm registrant that would cause a reasonable prospective purchaser of the securities being offered to question if the specified firm registrant and the issuer or selling securityholder are independent of each other for the distribution. This type of issuer is a "connected issuer" of the relevant specified firm registrant.

(2) The Instrument recognizes the relative degrees of relationships and the resulting potential for conflict by imposing additional requirements for distributions by specified firm registrants and their related issuers than for distributions by connected issuers.

(3) The term "independent underwriter" is defined in the Instrument to mean a specified firm registrant acting as direct underwriter in a distribution if the specified firm registrant does not have one of the relationships with the issuer or selling securityholder described in this section. The term "non-independent underwriter" is used in this Policy to describe a specified firm registrant acting as direct underwriter that does have one of those relationships.

2.2 General Requirements of the Instrument

The general requirements of the Instrument, contained in section 2.1, provide, in effect, that a specified firm registrant that would be a non-independent underwriter on a distribution may not act as a direct underwriter in the distribution, unless certain requirements are satisfied or an exemption is available. The requirements are the disclosure obligation, required by subsection 2.1(1) of the Instrument and discussed in section 2.3 of this Policy, and, in the case of related issuer distributions, the independent underwriter obligation, required by the combination of subsections 2.1(2) and (3) of the Instrument and discussed in section 2.4 of this Policy. An exemption from the independent underwriter obligation is contained in section 3.2 of the Instrument and discussed in Part 3 of this Policy.

2.3 Disclosure Obligation

(1) The disclosure obligation applicable to a distribution in which a non-independent underwriter participates, contained in subsection 2.1(1) of the Instrument, requires that the distribution be made under a prospectus or other document that contains the information described in Appendix C of the Instrument. This requirement is applicable both to transactions made under a prospectus and to those done by way of a private placement without a prospectus. Appendix C is designed to require full disclosure of the relationship between the underwriter and issuer or selling securityholder.

(2) Market participants are reminded that section 10.1 of National Instrument 71-101 *The Multijurisdictional Disclosure System* exempts distributions under that National Instrument from the disclosure requirements of the Instrument.

2.4 Requirement for Independent Underwriter Involvement

(1) Subsection 2.1(2) of the Instrument provides that, in the case of a distribution of special warrants or a distribution made under a prospectus, a specified firm registrant may not act

(a) as an underwriter if the specified firm registrant is the issuer or selling securityholder in the distribution; or

(b) as a direct underwriter if a related issuer of the specified firm registrant is the issuer or selling securityholder in the distribution.

(2) Subsection 2.1(3) of the Instrument provides that subsection 2.1(2) of the Instrument does not apply to a distribution otherwise caught by that subsection if there is an independent underwriter and if certain disclosure is made in a disclosure document or prospectus. The requirement for independent underwriter involvement is satisfied if at least one independent underwriter participates in the offering to the extent specified in subsection 2.1(3). Subsection 2.1(3) provides alternate threshold criteria for such involvement, depending upon whether the distribution is a "firm commitment" underwriting or a "best efforts agency" offering.

In the case of a firm commitment underwriting, an independent underwriter is required to underwrite not less than the lesser of

(a) 20 percent of the dollar value of the distribution, and

(b) the largest portion of the distribution underwritten by a specified firm registrant that is not an independent underwriter.

In the case of a best efforts agency offering, an independent underwriter must receive a portion of the total agents' fees equal to an amount not less than the lesser of

(a) 20 percent of the total agents' fees for the distribution, and

(b) the largest portion of the agents' fees paid or payable to a specified firm registrant that is not an independent underwriter.

(3) Subsection 2.1(3) of the Instrument requires the relevant disclosure document to disclose what role the independent underwriter played in the structuring, pricing and due diligence activities of the distribution. The Instrument does not specify what functions the independent underwriter must fulfil, because it is recognized that the appropriate role will vary according to the nature of the distribution and the issuer or selling securityholder, and because it is expected that the requirement to disclose the role actually played will impose a measure of market discipline on the process. Subsection 2.1(3) of the Instrument also requires the name of the independent underwriter to be disclosed.

NI 41-101 also sets out the rules for calculating the size of a distribution and the requirements for independent underwriter involvement, particularly where distributions occur in more than one jurisdiction. NI 41-101 restricts the distribution of securities under a prospectus to a person acting as an underwriter to 10 percent, determined as if all convertible or exchangeable securities offered under the prospectus were exercised for the underlying securities (NI 41-101, s 11.2; CP 41-101CP, s 2.5). Except in Ontario, a prospectus must contain a certificate signed by each underwriter who, with respect to the securities offered by the prospectus, is in a contractual relationship with the issuer or a securityholder whose securities are being offered by the prospectus (NI 41-101, s 5.9(1); OSA, s 59(1)).

In *Goldsmith v National Bank of Canada*, 2016 ONCA 22, the Ontario Court of Appeal clarified distinctions in the role of underwriters and "promoters." While the judgment is rendered in the context of a proposed secondary market class action under part XXIII.1 of the Ontario *Securities Act*, it makes reference to the implications for prospectus underwriting. *Goldsmith* was one of 13 class actions commenced in Alberta, Ontario, and Québec following the collapse of Poseidon Concepts Corp, an Alberta-based energy company. The court observed that a "promoter" is defined in s 1 of the OSA as a person who "acting alone or in conjunction with one or more other persons, companies, or a combination thereof, directly or indirectly, takes the initiative in founding, organizing or substantially reorganizing the business of an issuer." The Court of Appeal held that to be a "promoter," one must do more than simply influence the decision-maker's actions, indirectly participate in the initiative, or influence or participate with the decision-makers in the founding, organization or reorganization of an issuer's business. In dismissing the appeal, the court held as follows.

Goldsmith v National Bank of Canada
2016 ONCA 22

[38] First, to reiterate, the *OSA* provides that a person or company is a promoter if they, acting alone or in conjunction with others, "[take] the initiative in founding, organizing or substantially reorganizing the business of an issuer."

[39] When one considers the ordinary meaning of "[taking] the initiative" it is clear that the appellant's interpretation is not plausible. That phrase requires a form of active and autonomous involvement in the organization or reorganization of a company. For instance, the *Canadian Oxford Dictionary*, 2d ed., provides a number of definitions for the term "initiative," including the "ability to initiate things; enterprise, self-motivation" and "[the] power or right to begin something." To initiate something is defined as to "cause something to begin."

[40] In contrast, the appellant submits that the "initiative functionality" can be met simply by "influencing or participating with the decision makers." That interpretation accepts a level of passive involvement that is simply incompatible with "[taking] the initiative."

[41] Second, the relevant legislative context undermines the appellant's interpretation. Part XXIII.1 provides that a promoter may be liable as an "influential person." In addition to promoters, the definition of an influential person includes the following:

- A "control person," meaning a person or company, or combination thereof, which holds voting securities sufficient to "to affect materially the control of the issuer."
- An "insider" which includes a person or company that holds more than ten percent of the voting rights of a reporting issuer.
- An "investment fund manager" which means a person or company that directs the business, operations or affairs of an investment fund.

[42] Section 58(1) obliges the chief executive officer, the chief financial officer, two directors of the issuer, and "any person or company who is a promoter of the issuer" to sign a certificate contained in a prospectus. Section 61(2) provides that a receipt for a prospectus may be refused based on the financial condition or past conduct of "any of the issuer's officers, directors, promoters, or control persons."

[43] In all of these provisions, promoters are listed alongside people and companies who exercise meaningful control over a reporting issuer's business, such as officers, directors, and control persons. It suggests that a promoter is someone who plays a comparable role in a company's business. It does not support the appellant's claim that the provisions should capture people and companies who merely exercise some influence over the actual decision makers.

...

[45] A promoter is not someone who is casually connected with the issuer. It is a person or company that played a driving role in founding an issuer, and who consequently

> wields influence comparable to that of an officer or director. However, the appellant's interpretation can capture people who are far removed from that level of influence. It could render liable as a promoter a lawyer who gave general advice about corporate restructuring to a board like Open Range's or a tax advisor who provides generic advice on restructuring choices. The legislature could not have intended such an outcome when enacting Part XXIII.1.
>
> [46] The text, context, and purpose of the promoter provisions all support the conclusion that a person or company that merely provides advice for or assists during an issuer's organization or reorganization cannot be a promoter. Therefore, because the appellant's interpretation explicitly provides for that possibility it is simply implausible.
>
> . . .
>
> [53] There is a clear theme running through the applicable jurisprudence: a promoter is someone who plays a vital or leading role in the organization or reorganization of an issuer's business. Anything less is insufficient. Merely being involved in organizing or reorganizing a business is not sufficient, even if that involvement involves important services or support. Rather, one must be an "active participant," a "driving force" behind the reorganization, or at the "very heart of the issuer and the organization."

IV. THE PRELIMINARY PROSPECTUS

A preliminary prospectus is the first version of the final document that will accompany a public offering of securities. The supporting documentation for a prospectus filing typically includes a resolution of the board of directors authorizing the filing, the underwriting agreement, financial statements, and certification notes by senior officers. Although called "preliminary," the prospectus is the issuer's near-to-final form that it will use in a distribution to the public once the review process has been completed and any necessary revisions are made, the final prospectus is filed, and a receipt given.

The preliminary prospectus must contain a caution that it is not final, often referred to as a "red herring" because of the requirement to highlight in red ink and in italics at the top of the cover page that: *"[a] copy of this preliminary prospectus has been filed with the securities regulatory authority(ies) in [each of/certain of the provinces/provinces and territories of Canada] but has not yet become final for the purpose of the sale of securities. Information contained in this preliminary prospectus may not be complete and may have to be amended. The securities may not be sold until a receipt for the prospectus is obtained from the securities regulatory authority(ies)"* (Form 41-101F1, *Information Required in a Prospectus,* as amended effective 17 November 2015, s 1.2).

There are specified requirements under securities law for the form and content of a preliminary prospectus (NI 41-101). A preliminary prospectus must substantially comply with the rules governing a final prospectus. However, the preliminary prospectus is not required to disclose information with respect to the price paid to the underwriter or the offering price of any securities and other matters relating to such prices. It is anticipated that the offering price will be set based on the market conditions that exist at the time of filing the final prospectus. However, if the offering price or the number of securities being distributed, or an estimate of the range of the offering price or the number of securities being distributed, has been publicly disclosed in a jurisdiction or a foreign jurisdiction as of the date of a preliminary long-form prospectus, the issuer must disclose that information in the prospectus (Form 41-101F1, s 1.7).

Similarly, the auditor's report does not need to be filed with the preliminary prospectus because the financial information contained in the prospectus must be updated by the final receipt date. Regulators have set out the disclosure requirements for a preliminary (and final prospectus).

Form 41-101F1, *Information Required in a Prospectus*
As amended effective 17 November 2015

Basic Disclosure about the Distribution

1.3 State the following immediately below the disclosure required under sections 1.1 and 1.2 with the bracketed information completed:

[PRELIMINARY] PROSPECTUS [INITIAL PUBLIC OFFERING OR NEW ISSUE AND/OR SECONDARY OFFERING]

[(Date)]

[Name of Issuer]

[number and type of securities qualified for distribution under the prospectus, including any options or warrants, and the price per security]

Distribution

1.4(1) If the securities are being distributed for cash, provide the information called for below, in substantially the following tabular form or in a note to the table:

	Price to Public (a)	**Underwriting discounts or commission (b)**	**Proceeds to issuer or selling securityholders (c)**
Per Security			
Total			

(2) Describe the terms of the over-allotment option or any option to increase the size of the distribution before closing.

(2.1) If there may be an over-allocation position provide the following disclosure:

A purchaser who acquires [*insert type of securities qualified for distribution under the prospectus*] forming part of the underwriters' over-allocation position acquires those securities under this prospectus, regardless of whether the over-allocation position is ultimately filled through the exercise of the over-allotment option or secondary market purchases.

(3) If the distribution of the securities is to be on a best efforts basis, and a minimum offering amount

(a) Is required for the issuer to achieve one or more of the purposes of the offering, provide totals for both the minimum and maximum offering amount, or

(b) Is not required for the issuer to achieve any of the purposes of the offering, State the following in boldface type:

> **No minimum amount of funds must be raised under this offering. This means that the issuer could complete this offering after raising only a small proportion of the offering amount set out above.**

(4) If a minimum subscription amount is required from each subscriber, provide details of the minimum subscription requirements in the table required under subsection (1).

(5) If debt securities are being distributed at a premium or a discount, state in boldface type the effective yield if held to maturity.

(6) Disclose separately those securities that are underwritten, those under option and those to be sold on a best efforts basis, and, in the case of a best efforts distribution, the latest date that the distribution is to remain open.

(7) In column (b) of the table, disclose only commissions paid or payable in cash by the issuer or selling securityholder and discounts granted. Set out in a note to the table

(a) commissions or other consideration paid or payable by persons or companies other than the issuer or selling securityholder,

(b) consideration other than discounts granted and cash paid or payable by the issuer or selling securityholder, including warrants and options, and

(c) any finder's fees or similar required payment.

(8) If a security is being distributed for the account of a selling securityholder, state the name of the securityholder and a cross-reference to the applicable section in the prospectus where further information about the selling securityholder is provided. State the portion of the expenses of the distribution to be borne by the selling securityholder and, if none of the expenses of the distribution are being borne by the selling securityholder, include a statement to that effect and discuss the reason why this is the case.

The issuer must provide additional disclosure that applies to distributions of asset-backed securities, including the nature, performance and servicing of the underlying pool of financial assets; the structure of the securities and dedicated cash flows; and any third-party or internal support arrangements established to protect holders of the asset-backed securities from losses associated with non-performance of the financial assets or disruptions in payment (Form 41-101F1, s 10.3). Additional disclosure is applicable to distributions of derivatives, restricted securities and special warrants (Form 41-101F1, ss 10.4, 10.5, 10.6). A long-form prospectus must also include disclosure about any credit supporters that have provided a guarantee or alternative credit support for all or substantially all of the payments to be made under the securities being distributed (Form 41-101F1). The issuer is required to disclose legal proceedings and regulatory actions (Form 41-101F1, s 23.1) and any probable reverse takeovers (Form 41-101F1, s 36.1).

The issuer must identify the market for the securities. If the issuer is an IPO venture issuer, it must include a statement, in substantially the following form:

> As at the date of this prospectus, [name of issuer] does not have any of its securities listed or quoted, has not applied to list or quote any of its securities, and does not intend to apply to list or quote any of its securities, on the Toronto Stock Exchange, Aequitas NEO Exchange Inc., a US marketplace, or a marketplace outside Canada and the United States of America other than the

Alternative Investment Market of the London Stock Exchange or the PLUS markets operated by PLUS Markets Group plc. (Form 41-101F1, s 1.9(4))

Once a preliminary prospectus is filed, the director of the principal securities commission must forthwith issue a receipt for the preliminary prospectus. Section 65 of the British Columbia *Securities Act* is illustrative:

Receipts for prospectus

65(1) Subject to section 64(1), the executive director must issue a receipt for a preliminary prospectus as soon as practicable after it has been filed under this Part.

(2) Subject to the regulations, the executive director must issue a receipt for a prospectus filed under this Part unless the executive director considers it to be prejudicial to the public interest to do so.

(3) The executive director must not refuse to issue a receipt for a prospectus without giving the person who filed the prospectus an opportunity to be heard.

QUESTIONS

1. As a securities lawyer, what would you tell your client about what information ought to be included in a preliminary prospectus?
2. Why does the legislation stipulate that both a preliminary and a final prospectus be issued?
3. What information would likely not be contained in the preliminary prospectus?
4. What do you think the policy rationale is for requiring addition disclosure for asset-backed securities and derivatives?

NI 41-101 sets out the content of prospectuses, including direction on what is material. Readers should refer to this instrument, along with its companion policy. Section X of this chapter discusses material fact and material change reporting in some detail.

V. THE WAITING PERIOD AND REVIEW PROCESS

A. The Process

With the filing of a preliminary prospectus, there is a mandatory waiting period after the receipt is issued in which the activities of the issuer are restricted in terms of communicating with potential investors. NI 41-101 specifies that "waiting period" means the period of time between the issuance of a receipt by the regulator for a preliminary prospectus and the issuance of a receipt by the regulator for a final prospectus. Pursuant to s 5.4 of NP 11-202, the principal regulator will use its best efforts to review the materials relating to a preliminary long-form prospectus and provide a first comment letter within 10 working days of the date of the preliminary receipt or of receiving the *pro forma* prospectus and related materials in acceptable form. The principal regulator may provide further comments as a result of the filer's responses or the continuing review of the materials (NP 11-202, s 5.4). In the case of a "dual prospectus," which is an application to distribute in Ontario and at least one passport jurisdiction, the OSC will, within five working days of the date of the preliminary receipt or of receiving the *pro forma* prospectus and related materials in acceptable form, use its best efforts to advise the principal regulator of any concerns with the materials that, if left unresolved, would cause the OSC to opt out of the dual review or indicate on SEDAR that it is clear to receive final materials (NP 11-202, s 5.4(2)).

The waiting period allows regulators the opportunity to consider the filed preliminary prospectus and to determine whether it complies with all the statutory and regulatory requirements.

A filer that receives a receipt for a preliminary prospectus or prospectus from the principal regulator will be deemed to have a receipt for the preliminary prospectus or prospectus in a passport jurisdiction if certain conditions are met, including that the filer filed the preliminary prospectus or prospectus in the passport jurisdiction, and the regulator of the passport jurisdiction is not the principal regulator for the prospectus filing (MI 11-102, NP 11-202, s 7.1(1)). The principal regulator lists in its receipt the passport jurisdictions in which it understands the filer has a deemed receipt. In the case of a dual prospectus, the principal regulator's receipt for a preliminary prospectus will also evidence that the OSC has issued a receipt.

The principal regulator will issue a preliminary receipt if it determines that the filer has filed acceptable materials and the filer provides a letter to the principal regulator with the materials confirming the following, to the best of its knowledge and belief: the filer filed the materials, including all required translations, with, and paid the required fees to, the principal regulator and all non-principal regulators; the filer delivered all documents required to be delivered under the securities legislation of each jurisdiction in which the filer filed the materials; and the filer is not subject to a cease-trade order issued by the regulator of any jurisdiction in which the filer filed the materials (NP 11-202 , s 7.2).

Where an underwriter is required to sign a certificate, at least one underwriter that signed the certificate must be registered, or have filed an application for registration or for exemption from registration, in each jurisdiction in which the filer will offer securities to purchasers. Where an underwriter is required to sign a certificate in a jurisdiction in which the filer is making the distribution and none of the underwriters that signed the certificate is registered in that jurisdiction, but one of them has filed an application for registration or for exemption from registration, that underwriter files an undertaking with the principal regulator not to solicit in that jurisdiction until it is registered or exempt from registration. If the filer plans to distribute the securities itself, the filer is registered in each jurisdiction in which the filer will offer securities to purchasers, has filed an application for registration or for exemption from registration, or is not required to be registered (NP 11-202, s 7.2(f)). If the filer has filed an application for registration or exemption from registration in a jurisdiction, the filer must file an undertaking with the principal regulator not to solicit in that jurisdiction until the filer is registered or exempted from registration (NP 11-202, s 7.2(g)).

Regulators engage in selective review of preliminary prospectuses, not a review of all that are filed. There is an initial screening process for determining the scope of review, if any. Prospectuses pursuant to initial public offerings continue to receive a full review, as do those prospectuses in instances where the prospectus appears to raise matters for which a full review would be beneficial. In other cases, regulators conduct an issue-oriented review limited to a specific concern or a specific accounting, legal, or disclosure issue. Alternately, they may determine that no review is required. Examples of issues that have been the subject of targeted reviews in prospectus documents include: disclosure—where the OSC required material disclosure changes to a prospectus, particularly in respect of the description of business and regulatory environment; risk factors relating to the business and/or offering;

MD&A disclosure in a long-form prospectus; and failure to provide comprehensive use of proceeds disclosure (OSC Staff Notice 51-725, *Corporate Finance Branch 2014-2015 Annual Report* at 13-14, online: <http://www.osc.gov.on.ca/documents/en/Securities-Category5/sn_20150714_51-725_cf-rpt-2015.pdf>).

Once the review process is complete, the regulator sends a comment letter to the issuer advising of any required revisions or additional information. The issuer revises accordingly and then submits the final prospectus to the commission, which then generally issues a receipt. The process is a mixture of regulatory control and an information clearing house. Generally, the director or other regulatory official does not interfere with the substance of the prospectus; however, it must be satisfied that the prospectus and other offering documents comply with the legislation and other regulatory requirements. Moreover, there is a public interest aspect to the commission's work in protecting both investors and the integrity of capital markets. Securities legislation provides the regulator with discretion to refuse a receipt for a prospectus where it is not in the public interest to issue the receipt. Securities legislation imposes statutory liability in connection with prospectus disclosure, to provide investors with a remedy if a prospectus does not contain full, true and plain disclosure of all material facts relating to the securities being distributed.

The issuer has an ongoing obligation to amend the prospectus if there is any material change in the business and affairs of the issuer during the waiting period. Material change is discussed at length in Section X of this chapter. See also the recent Supreme Court of Canada judgment in *Kerr v Danier*, excerpted below.

The preliminary prospectus may be distributed during the waiting period. For example, under part XVI of the OSA, it is permissible during the waiting period to distribute a notice, circular, advertisement, or letter or to otherwise communicate with any person identifying the security proposed to be issued. The notice or communication must state the price, if then determined, the name and address of a person or an issuer from whom a preliminary prospectus may be obtained and purchases of the security may be made. The issuer or its underwriter can solicit expressions of interest from a prospective purchaser if, prior to such solicitation or forthwith after the prospective purchaser indicates an interest in purchasing the security, a copy of the preliminary prospectus is forwarded to him, her, or it. However, no distribution of shares to the public can occur until the final prospectus is filed and a receipt issued (see e.g. OSA, s 53(1); NSSA, s 58). The policy rationale for allowing distribution of the preliminary prospectus is that investors are given an opportunity to consider the offering by receiving the information in a timely manner, along with the offering documentation that underpins the expected issue.

Any dealer distributing a security must send a copy of the preliminary prospectus to each prospective purchaser who, without solicitation, indicates an interest in purchasing the security and requests a copy of the preliminary prospectus; however, it must ensure that it sends any amended prospectus to the potential purchasers, in order that they have accurate information during the process of purchasing the securities. These requirements were previously in the statutes, but were repealed in most jurisdictions with the implementation of NI 41-101.

The waiting period for a short-form prospectus, shelf prospectus, post-receipt pricing (PREP) prospectus, or multijurisdictional disclosure system (MJDS) offering (discussed in

Section VII, below) can be shorter than ten days where regulators approve the prospectus. This time frame tends to apply to large issuers that are already established with regulators and well known to market participants. However, for a smaller issuer or one that does not have a history in the market, the waiting period can take up to several months until the securities regulator is satisfied that the prospectus meets the statutory requirements.

B. Restrictions on Activities During the Waiting Period

Where it appears to the director that a preliminary prospectus is defective in that it does not substantially comply with the requirements of securities law as to form and content, the director may, without giving notice, order that any activities to which the preliminary prospectus relates shall cease until a revised preliminary prospectus satisfactory to the director is filed and forwarded to each recipient of the defective preliminary prospectus (see e.g. OSA, s 68; ASA, s 126).

Advertising during the waiting period has some specified restrictions (NI 41-101, parts 13 and 13A). Advertising or marketing activities subject to the prospectus requirement may be oral, written, or electronic and include television or radio advertisements or commentaries; published materials; correspondence; records; videotapes or other similar material; market letters; research reports; circulars; promotional seminar text; telemarketing scripts; and reprints or excerpts of any other sales literature. Communication of factual information concerning the business of the issuer that is released in a manner consistent with the regular past communications practices of the issuer if that communication does not refer to the distribution of securities is not generally considered advertising (CP 41-101). Over the past decade, the rules in respect of advertising have liberalized somewhat, but the underlying public policy objectives remain: although advertising and marketing are allowed to advise the public of the availability of the preliminary prospectus, the information must be clear as to its scope and limits. NI 41-101, *General Prospectus Requirements*, as amended effective 8 December 2015, addresses advertising and marketing in connection with prospectus offerings of issuers other than investment funds in part 13 and advertising and marketing in connection with prospectus offerings of investment funds in part 13A. Marketing is permitted if the information accurately contains the information required in the prospectus. The brief excerpt below is illustrative of requirements regarding advertising during the waiting period, this excerpt addressing advertising a prospectus offering by an investment fund.

National Instrument 41-101, *General Prospectus Requirements*
As amended effective 8 December 2015

Advertising During the Waiting Period

13A.4 If the issuer is an investment fund, an advertisement used in connection with a prospectus offering during the waiting period may state only the following information:

(a) whether the security represents a share in an incorporated entity or an interest in an unincorporated entity;

(b) the name of the issuer;

(c) the price of the security;

(d) the fundamental investment objectives of the investment fund;

(e) the name of the manager of the investment fund;

(f) the name of the portfolio manager of the investment fund;

(g) the name and address of a person or company from whom a preliminary prospectus may be obtained and purchases of securities may be made;

(h) how many securities will be made available;

(i) whether the security is or will be a qualified investment for a registered retirement savings plan, registered retirement income fund, registered education savings plan or tax free savings account or qualifies, or will qualify, the holder for special tax treatment.

QUESTION

Why is advertising and marketing allowed prior to the final receipt for the prospectus being issued? Is there any risk to the investing public?

VI. FINAL PROSPECTUS

The prospectus that is ultimately used in the distribution is frequently called the final prospectus, although the statutory language usually refers to it solely as the prospectus. It is an amended version of the preliminary prospectus, meeting all the requirements discussed above. It also contains the final pricing information and audit reports. Accompanying financial statements include a balance sheet of the issuer's assets and liabilities; a cash flow statement providing information regarding the issuer's cash from operations, investments, and financing activities during the accounting period; and an income statement presenting a firm's revenues, expenses, gains, losses, and earnings over the specified period of time. Once the receipt for the final prospectus is issued, the actual sale can begin. For a dual prospectus, the principal regulator's receipt for a final prospectus will also evidence that the OSC has issued a receipt, if the OSC has indicated on SEDAR that is it "clear for final." (NP 11-202, s 7.1(2)).

An issuer must not file a final prospectus more than 90 days after the date of the receipt for the preliminary prospectus or an amendment to the preliminary prospectus that relates to the final prospectus (NI 41-101, s 2.3(1.1)). Unless an amendment to the final prospectus is filed and the regulator has issued a receipt for the amendment, if securities are being distributed on a best efforts basis, the distribution must cease within 90 days after the date of the receipt for the final prospectus (NI 41-101, s 8.2(1)).

A final prospectus can be amended and the regulator is to issue a receipt unless it concludes that there is a violation of securities law, as set out in NI 41-101.

National Instrument 41-101, *General Prospectus Requirements*
As amended effective 8 December 2015, online: <https://www.bcsc.bc.ca/Securities_Law/Policies/Policy4/PDF/41-101__NI___December_8__2015/>

Amendment to a Final Prospectus

6.6(1) Except in Ontario, if, after a receipt for a final prospectus is issued but before the completion of the distribution under the final prospectus, a material change occurs, an issuer must file an amendment to the final prospectus as soon as practicable, but in any event within 10 days after the day the change occurs.

[Note: In Ontario, subsection 57(1) of the *Securities Act* (Ontario) imposes a similar requirement to file an amendment to a final prospectus where there has been a material change.]

(2) Except in Ontario, if, after a receipt for a final prospectus or an amendment to a final prospectus is issued but before the completion of the distribution under the final prospectus or the amendment to the final prospectus, securities in addition to the securities previously disclosed in the final prospectus or the amendment to the final prospectus are to be distributed, an amendment to the final prospectus disclosing the additional securities must be filed, as soon as practicable, but in any event within 10 days after the decision to increase the number of securities offered.

[Note: In Ontario, subsection 57(2) of the *Securities Act* (Ontario) imposes a similar requirement to file an amendment to a prospectus any time there is a proposed distribution of securities in addition to that disclosed under the prospectus.]

(3) Except in Ontario, the regulator must issue a receipt for an amendment to a final prospectus filed under this section unless the regulator considers that there are grounds set out in securities legislation that would cause the regulator not to issue the receipt for a prospectus.

[Note: In Ontario, subsection 57(2.1) of the *Securities Act* (Ontario) imposes a similar obligation for the Director to issue a receipt for an amendment to a prospectus unless there are proper grounds for refusing the receipt.]

(4) Except in Ontario, the regulator must not refuse to issue a receipt under subsection (3) without giving the issuer who filed the prospectus an opportunity to be heard.

[Note: In Ontario, subsection 57(2.1) and 61(3) of the *Securities Act* (Ontario) impose a similar restriction on the Director to refuse to issue a receipt for a prospectus without first giving an issuer an opportunity to be heard.]

(5) Except in Ontario, an issuer must not proceed with a distribution or additional distribution if an amendment to a final prospectus is required to be filed until a receipt for the amendment to the final prospectus is issued by the regulator.

[Note: In Ontario, subsection 57(2.2) of the *Securities Act* (Ontario) imposes a similar restriction in respect of a distribution or additional distribution before a receipt is issued for an amendment to the final prospectus.]

(6) Subsection (5) does not apply to an investment fund in continuous distribution.

[Note: In Ontario, section 2.2 of OSC Rule 41-801, *Implementing National Instrument 41-101 General Prospectus Requirements and Consequential Amendments* provides a similar exemption for an investment fund in continuous distribution from the requirement to obtain a receipt prior to making a distribution or additional distribution under an amendment to a final prospectus.]

It is an offence to fail to deliver a prospectus or distribute a security without the regulator having issued a receipt for the prospectus, unless the issuer is otherwise exempt. Sanctions for failure to comply with the prospectus requirements can include cease-trading orders or cancellation or restriction of the party's registration (see e.g. MSA, ss 8, 148, as amended SM 2006, c 11, s 30; NBSA, s 87(1); OSA, s 127). In some jurisdictions, the regulator can order that the person in violation of the prospectus requirements resign or be prohibited from acting as director or officer (see e.g. ASA, s 198(1)(d)). There are also remedies for misuse of exemption provisions, as discussed in the *Deacon* case in Chapter 5. There is a time lag between obtaining the final receipt and completing a distribution, which can be significant in terms of disclosure obligations, as is discussed in *Kerr v Danier*, excerpted below.

VII. SHORT-FORM PROSPECTUS, SHELF PROSPECTUS, POST-RECEIPT PRICING PROSPECTUS, AND MULTIJURISDICTIONAL DISCLOSURE SYSTEM

There are a number of alternatives to the traditional long-form prospectus and this part of the chapter discusses four types that are commonly used by issuers: the short-form prospectus, the shelf prospectus, the PREP prospectus, and the MJDS prospectus.

A. Short-Form Prospectus

A short-form prospectus allows issuers who are repeat issuers to make public offerings in a timelier manner. The policy rationale for allowing a shorter prospectus is that there is already considerable information regarding the issuer in the public domain, and thus it is appropriate that the issuer be allowed to build on previously filed and reviewed documents. The availability of the short-form prospectus can expedite the raising of capital and lower the costs of the offering. The investing public is protected both by prior vetting of disclosures—that is, the issuer is eligible from previous securities approval processes to use a short-form prospectus—and by the specific requirements of the short-form prospectus process. The short-form prospectus evolved from an earlier tool, the prompt-offering prospectus (POP), which is no longer used.

There is a national instrument on short-form prospectuses that has encouraged greater harmonization of short-form prospectus requirements across Canada. National Instrument 44-101, *Short Form Prospectus Distributions* is aimed at streamlining the procedure and shortening the time period by which qualified issuers and their selling securityholders can obtain access to the Canadian capital markets through a prospectus offering. It sets out the substantive tests for an issuer to qualify to file a prospectus in the form of a short-form prospectus.

Originally, NI 44-101 required a company to have an aggregate market value of the issuer's equity securities, listed and posted for trading on an exchange in Canada, of $75,000,000 or more on a date within 60 days before the date of the filing of the issuer's preliminary short-form prospectus (NI 44-101, *Short Form Prospectus Distributions* (2000), 23 OSCB (Supp) 421). However, that requirement has changed, allowing thousands more issuers the opportunity to use a short-form prospectus. To satisfy the eligibility criteria, the issuer must fit into one of the following categories:

National Instrument 44-101, *Short Form Prospectus Distributions*
As amended effective 8 December 2015

2.2 Basic Qualification Criteria

An issuer is qualified to file a prospectus in the form of a short form prospectus for a distribution of any of its securities in the local jurisdiction, if the following criteria are satisfied:

(a) the issuer is an electronic filer under NI 13-101;
(b) the issuer is a reporting issuer in at least one jurisdiction of Canada;
(c) the issuer has filed with the securities regulatory authority in each jurisdiction in which it is a reporting issuer all periodic and timely disclosure documents that it is required to have filed in that jurisdiction
(i) under applicable securities legislation,
(ii) pursuant to an order issued by the securities regulatory authority, or
(iii) pursuant to an undertaking to the securities regulatory authority;
(d) the issuer has, in at least one jurisdiction in which it is a reporting issuer,
(i) current annual financial statements, and
(ii) a current AIF;
(e) the issuer's equity securities are listed and posted for trading on a short form eligible exchange and the issuer is not an issuer
(i) whose operations have ceased, or
(ii) whose principal asset is cash, cash equivalents, or its exchange listing.

There are alternative qualification criteria for issuers of approved rating non-convertible securities; for issuers of guarantee non-convertible debt securities, preferred shares and cash settled derivatives; and for issuers of guaranteed convertible debt securities or preferred shares, as set out in NI 44-101.

National Instrument 44-101, *Short Form Prospectus Distributions*
As amended effective 8 December 2015

2.3 Alternative Qualification Criteria for Issuers of Designated Non-Convertible Securities

(1) An issuer is qualified to file a prospectus in the form of a short form prospectus for a distribution of non-convertible securities in the local jurisdiction, if the following criteria are satisfied:

(a) the issuer is an electronic filer under NI 13-101;
(b) the issuer is a reporting issuer in at least one jurisdiction of Canada;
(c) the issuer has filed with the securities regulatory authority in each jurisdiction in which it is a reporting issuer all periodic and timely disclosure documents that it is required to have filed in that jurisdiction
(i) under applicable securities legislation,
(ii) pursuant to an order issued by the securities regulatory authority, or
(iii) pursuant to an undertaking to the securities regulatory authority;

(d) the issuer has, in at least one jurisdiction in which it is a reporting issuer,

(i) current annual financial statements, and

(ii) a current AIF;

(e) the securities to be distributed

(i) have received an approved rating on a provisional basis,

(ii) are not the subject of an announcement by a designated rating organization or its DRO affiliate, of which the issuer is or ought reasonably to be aware, that the designated rating given by the organization may be down-graded to a rating category that would not be a designated rating, and

(iii) have not received a provisional or final rating lower than a designated rating from any designated rating organization or its DRO affiliate

(2) Paragraph (1)(e) does not apply to an issuer filing a short form prospectus that is a base shelf prospectus under NI 44-102.

2.4 Alternative Qualification Criteria for Issuers of Guaranteed Non-Convertible Debt Securities, Preferred Shares, and Cash Settled Derivatives

(1) An issuer is qualified to file a prospectus in the form of a short form prospectus for a distribution of non-convertible debt securities, non-convertible preferred shares or non-convertible cash settled derivatives in the local jurisdiction, if the following criteria are satisfied:

(a) a credit supporter has provided full and unconditional credit support for the securities being distributed,

(b) at least one of the following is true:

(i) the credit supporter satisfies the criteria in paragraphs 2.2(a), (b), (c) and (d) if the word "issuer" is replaced with "credit supporter" wherever it occurs;

(ii) the credit supporter is a US credit supporter and the issuer is incorporated or organized under the laws of Canada or a jurisdiction of Canada;

(c) unless the credit supporter satisfies the criteria in paragraph 2.2(e) if the word "issuer" is replaced with "credit supporter" wherever it occurs, at the time the preliminary short form prospectus is filed

(i) the credit supporter has outstanding non-convertible securities that

(A) have received a designated rating,

(B) have not been the subject of an announcement by a designated rating organization or its DRO affiliate, of which the issuer is or ought reasonably to be aware, that the designated rating given by the organization may be down-graded to a rating category that would not be a designated rating, and

(C) have not received a rating lower than a designated rating from any designated rating organization or its DRO affiliate, and

(ii) the securities to be issued by the issuer

(A) have received a designated rating on a provisional basis,

(B) have not been the subject of an announcement by a designated rating organization or its DRO affiliate, of which the issuer is or ought reasonably to be aware, that the designated rating given by the organization may be down-graded to a rating category that would not be a designated rating, and

(C) have not received a provisional or final rating lower than a designated rating from any designated rating organization or its DRO affiliate.

(2) Subparagraph (1)(c)(ii) does not apply to an issuer filing a short form prospectus that is a base shelf prospectus under NI 44-102.

2.5 Alternative Qualification Criteria for Issuers of Guaranteed Convertible Debt Securities or Preferred Shares

An issuer is qualified to file a prospectus in the form of a short form prospectus for a distribution of convertible debt securities or convertible preferred shares in the local jurisdiction, if the following criteria are satisfied:

(a) the debt securities or the preferred shares are convertible into securities of a credit supporter that has provided full and unconditional credit support for the securities being distributed;

(b) the credit supporter satisfies the criteria in section 2.2 if the word "issuer" is replaced with "credit supporter" wherever it occurs.

2.6 Alternative Qualification Criteria for Issuers of Asset-Backed Securities

(1) An issuer established in connection with a distribution of asset-backed securities is qualified to file a prospectus in the form of a short form prospectus for a distribution of asset-backed securities in the local jurisdiction, if the following criteria are satisfied:

(a) the issuer is an electronic filer under NI 13-101;

(b) the issuer has, in at least one jurisdiction of Canada,

(i) current annual financial statements, and

(ii) a current AIF;

(c) the asset-backed securities to be distributed

(i) have received a designated rating on a provisional basis,

(ii) have not been the subject of an announcement by a designated rating organization or its DRO affiliate, of which the issuer is or ought reasonably to be aware, that the designated rating given by the organization may be down-graded to a rating category that would not be a designated rating, and

(iii) have not received a provisional or final rating lower than a designated rating from any approved rating organization or its DRO affiliate.

(2) Paragraph (1)(c) does not apply to an issuer filing a short form prospectus that is a base shelf prospectus under NI 44-102.

As is evident from the above excerpt from NI 44-101, issuers are granted access to the short-form prospectus process only where key information about them is already widely disseminated in the market. Some of the alternative qualification criteria also recognize particular aspects of a market in which they are distributed. For example, investment-grade debt securities such as bonds or debentures have been graded by credit-rating agencies, and the creditworthiness and interest rates are considered the important information in valuing the securities and making investment decisions. Another example is distribution of asset-backed securities, whereby an issuer is qualified to file a short-form prospectus for a distribution of asset-backed securities in the local jurisdiction if it has current annual financial statements, a current AIF, and the asset-backed securities to be distributed have received an approved rating on a provisional basis, as set out above.

The short-form prospectus provides information on the distribution plan, the intended market, what the proceeds will be used for, rights attaching to the securities, and other information relevant to the distribution. It is premised on previously disclosed materials containing a level of disclosure that is on the same standard as a prospectus, including an AIF (Form 44-101F1).

Form 44-101F1 requires disclosure of each of the principal purposes for which the net proceeds will be used by an issuer. Additional disclosure is required for distributions of asset-backed securities, including the nature, performance, and servicing of the underlying pool of financial assets, the structure of the securities and dedicated cash flows, and any third-party or internal support arrangements established to protect holders of the asset-backed securities from losses associated with non-performance of the financial assets or disruptions in payment (Form 44-101F1, s 7.3). There is also additional disclosure applicable to distributions of derivatives and restricted securities (Form 44-101F1, ss 7.4, 7.7).

The issuer must also disclose any proposed acquisition that has progressed to a state "where a reasonable person would believe that the likelihood of the acquisition being completed is high" and that would, if completed on the date of the short-form prospectus, be a significant acquisition for the purposes of part 8 of NI 51-102 (Form 44-101F1, s 10.2(2)). The issuer is required to include the financial statements or other information relating to proposed acquisitions if the information is necessary for the short-form prospectus to contain full, true and plain disclosure of all material facts relating to the securities being distributed (Form 44-101F1, s 10.2(3)). The issuer must also describe the "risk factors" material to the issuer that a reasonable investor would consider relevant to an investment in the securities being distributed (Form 44-101F1, s 17.1).

Below is a brief excerpt from Form 44-101F1, which many more issuers now use instead of the long-form prospectus. The excerpt shows the particulars required for reporting underwriting. Note how Form 44-101F1 still contains considerable detail in terms of information regulators require before approval of the short-form prospectus.

National Instrument Form 44-101F1, *Short Form Prospectus*
As amended effective 13 August 2013, online: <https://www.bcsc.bc.ca/Securities_Law/Policies/Policy4/PDF/44-101F1__F__August_13__2013/>
(Instruction notes omitted)

1.10 Underwriter(s)

(1) State the name of each underwriter.

(2) If applicable, comply with the requirements of NI 33-105 for front page prospectus disclosure.

(3) If an underwriter has agreed to purchase all of the securities being distributed at a specified price and the underwriter's obligations are subject to conditions, state the following, with the bracketed information completed:

> We, as principals, conditionally offer these securities, subject to prior sale, if, as and when issued by [name of issuer] and accepted by us in accordance with the conditions contained in the underwriting agreement referred to under Plan of Distribution.

(4) If an underwriter has agreed to purchase a specified number or principal amount of the securities at a specified price, state that the securities are to be taken up by the underwriter, if at all, on or before a date not later than 42 days after the date of the receipt for the short form prospectus.

(5) If there is no underwriter involved in the distribution, provide a statement in boldface type to the effect that no underwriter has been involved in the preparation of the short form prospectus or performed any review of the contents of the short form prospectus.

(6) Provide the following tabular information:

Underwriter's position	Maximum size or number of securities available	Exercise period or acquisition date	Exercise price or average acquisition price
Over-allotment option			
Compensation option			
Any other option granted by issuer or insider of issuer to underwriter			
Total securities under option issuable to underwriter			
Other compensation securities issuable to underwriter			

Now most reporting issuers use the short-form prospectus for primary offerings, allowing faster access to the market. This shift in financing has heightened the responsibility of such issuers to ensure accurate and complete continuous disclosure that fairly and comprehensively discloses the material aspects of their business and operations.

QUESTIONS

1. Why is it useful to allow issuers to issue securities using a short-form prospectus?
2. The excerpt above is only the underwriting part of the disclosure requirements under Form 44-101F1. Why do you think this expedited form of prospectus is still so detailed?
3. An issuer is required to disclose whether unallocated funds will be placed in a trust or escrow account as opposed to invested or added to the working capital of the issuer. Why would such disclosure be required?
4. What additional disclosures are necessary for asset-backed securities and directives, and why do you think these additional disclosures are required?

A person or company may file a short-form preliminary prospectus, and any such prospectus that complies with the applicable regulatory requirements is considered to provide sufficient disclosure of all material facts relating to the securities issued or proposed to be distributed under the prospectus. National Policy 11-202, *Process for Prospectus Reviews in*

Multiple Jurisdictions sets out the process for filing and review of prospectuses, including investment fund and shelf prospectuses, amendments to prospectuses and related materials in multiple jurisdictions. Under NP 11-202, one securities regulatory authority acts as the principal regulator for all materials relating to a filer.

There is generally a much shorter review period for a short-form prospectus, as set out below in National Policy 11-202.

National Policy 11-202, *Process for Prospectus Reviews in Multiple Jurisdictions*

As amended effective 28 September 2009, online: <https://www.bcsc.bc.ca/Securities_Law/Policies/Policy1/PDF/11-202_Process_for_Prospectus_Reviews_in_Multiple_Jurisdictions_-_September_2009/>

5.4 Review Period for Preliminary Long Form Prospectuses and Pro Forma Prospectuses

(1) The principal regulator will use its best efforts to review the materials relating to a preliminary long form prospectus or pro forma prospectus and provide a first comment letter within 10 working days of the date of the preliminary receipt or of receiving the pro forma prospectus and related materials in acceptable form. The principal regulator may provide further comments as a result of the filer's responses or the continuing review of the materials.

(2) In the case of a dual prospectus, the OSC will, within five working days of the date of the preliminary receipt or of receiving the pro forma prospectus and related materials in acceptable form, use its best efforts to:

(a) advise the principal regulator of any concerns with the materials that, if left unresolved, would cause the OSC to opt out of the dual review; or

(b) indicate on SEDAR that it is clear to receive final materials.

5.5 Review Period for Preliminary Short Form Prospectuses and Preliminary Shelf Prospectuses

(1) The principal regulator will use its best efforts to review the materials relating to a preliminary short form prospectus or preliminary shelf prospectus and provide a first comment letter within three working days of the date of the preliminary receipt. The principal regulator may provide further comments as a result of the filer's responses or the continuing review of the materials.

Where a security is a relatively new form of security or involves a particularly complex offering, the tight time periods offered generally by the short-form preliminary prospectus process will not be available to the issuer. For examples of a short-form prospectus, see SEDAR (System for Electronic Document Analysis and Retrieval), online: <http://www.sedar.com>).

The issuer can file a summary statement with securities regulators, which will be sent to prospective purchasers. Where a summary statement is filed with a prospectus, the director can decline to issue a receipt for the prospectus if it appears that the summary statement does not comply with the regulations. A summary statement filed with a prospectus for which a receipt has been issued may be sent or delivered by a dealer to a purchaser of securities instead of a prospectus. Where a dealer elects to send a summary statement, the provisions with respect to a prospectus apply with necessary modifications to the summary statement. Every summary statement sent to a purchaser must inform the purchaser that a copy of the prospectus that was filed with the summary statement will be provided to the purchaser on request, and each person or issuer who signs, or causes to be signed, the certificate contained in the prospectus shall ensure compliance with any such request. Any misrepresentation contained in a summary statement filed with a short-form prospectus is deemed to be a misrepresentation contained in the prospectus for purposes of liability under the statute (see e.g. OSA, s 63(8); NSSA, s 68(8); Nfld SA, s 64(8)). The AIF is incorporated by reference into the short-form prospectus, so that a misrepresentation there will ground a liability claim.

B. Shelf Prospectus

For issuers that are eligible for the short-form prospectus process, shelf prospectuses are also available, governed by NI 44-102, *Shelf Distributions* (2000), as amended effective 22 September 2014. A shelf prospectus allows the issuer to file the prospectus, governed by the same disclosure provisions as the short-form prospectus, and then leave it "on the shelf" for up to 25 months. Anytime in that period, the issuer can take the securities "off the shelf" and distribute them. The premise underlying the shelf prospectus is the same as for the short-form prospectus. It is available only to certain classes of issuers for which there is considerable information in the market. Issuers qualified under NI 44-101 to file a short-form prospectus and their securityholders can distribute securities under a short-form prospectus using the shelf distribution procedures under NI 44-102.

The advantage of a shelf prospectus is that in order to distribute the securities, only a supplement updating information is required, which does not require review by the regulator. A distribution under a short-form prospectus using the shelf procedures is subject to all the requirements of NI 44-101, *Short Form Prospectus Distributions*, some of the requirements of NI 41-101, *General Prospectus Requirements*, and other provisions of securities legislation, as supplemented or varied by NI 44-102 and the implementing law of the jurisdiction. Companion Policy 44-102CP to NI 44-102, *Shelf Distributions*, sets out the shelf qualification and the length of time the receipt for a shelf prospectus is effective.

Companion Policy 44-102CP to National Instrument 44-102, *Shelf Distributions*

As amended effective 13 August 2013, online: <https://www.bcsc.bc.ca/Securities_Law/Policies/Policy4/PDF/44-102CP__CP__August_13_2013/>

Part 2 Shelf Procedures

2.1 Shelf Qualification

(1) The principle guiding the qualification provisions of NI 44-102 is that any distribution under a short form prospectus, other than rights offerings, may be effected using the shelf procedures.

(2) A distribution using the shelf procedures is necessarily a distribution under a short form prospectus. Therefore, issuers must be qualified to file a prospectus in the form of

a short form prospectus under NI 44-101 and must satisfy the additional qualification criteria under Part 2 of NI 44-102.

2.2 Period of Receipt Effectiveness

(1) NI 44-102 provides that a receipt for a base shelf prospectus is effective until the earliest of the following three events: (i) the date 25 months from the date of the issuance of a receipt for the base shelf prospectus, (ii) the time immediately before selling the securities, if certain prescribed conditions relating to the issuer's qualification to file a prospectus in the form of a short form prospectus are not satisfied, and (iii) in Ontario, the lapse date of the receipt prescribed by securities legislation, if no relief has been granted to the issuer through a blanket ruling or upon application by the issuer. This receipt expiry mechanism is designed to impose a limit of, essentially, two years on shelf distributions under the same base shelf prospectus and to prevent distributions of securities under a base shelf prospectus if the issuer would no longer be qualified under NI 44-101.

(2) The securities legislation in some jurisdictions provides that a prospectus receipt does not continue to be effective for more than one year absent relief granted by the securities regulatory authority in that jurisdiction. Some of these jurisdictions have provided blanket relief for receipts issued for base shelf prospectuses.

C. Post-Receipt Pricing Prospectus

A post-receipt pricing prospectus (PREP prospectus) is another alternative to a long-form prospectus; the eligibility requirements are set out in NI 44-103, *Post-Receipt Pricing* (2000), as amended 2013. It is available to all issuers and is more directed than a shelf prospectus; it is used for a specific transaction and a single type of security. In contrast, a shelf prospectus can be used for multiple types of securities. A PREP prospectus cannot be used for a rights offering (NI 44-103, s 2.1). The PREP prospectus is reviewed by securities regulators and then can be "on the shelf" for a period of 90 days. Note that this period is a much shorter shelf life than the shelf prospectus discussed above. When the issuer makes the actual distribution, the supplement that it must give to prospective purchasers does not need further regulatory approval. The short shelf life can be extended where a supplemental PREP prospectus is filed within specified times (NI 44-103, s 3.5). Any documents incorporated by reference in the PREP prospectus contain the same liability risks for any misrepresentation as the prospectus itself. NI 44-103CP sets out the availability of, and procedures for, a PREP prospectus.

Companion Policy 44-103CP to National Instrument 44-103, *Post-Receipt Pricing*

As amended effective 13 August 2013, online: <https://www.bcsc.bc.ca/Securities_Law/Policies/Policy4/PDF/44-103CP__CP__August_13__2013/>

Part 1 Introduction

1.1 Implementation of the Instrument

Certain jurisdictions have implemented National Instrument 44-103 *Post-Receipt Pricing* (the "Instrument") by one or more instruments forming part of securities legislation or securities directions in the jurisdiction. As a result, the provisions of the Instrument apply in those jurisdictions to the extent provided by, and except as modified by, the implementing law of the jurisdiction.

1.2 Availability of PREP Procedures

Access to the PREP procedures is not restricted to issuers qualified to file a prospectus in the form of a short form prospectus. Any issuer that wishes to use the PREP procedures, or enable a selling securityholder to use the PREP procedures, to distribute securities may file a prospectus that is a base PREP prospectus.

1.3 Relationship of the Instrument to Securities Legislation

(1) Issuers are reminded that the rules and procedures contained in the Instrument for distributions made using the PREP procedures should be read in conjunction with other provisions of securities legislation in each jurisdiction in which a distribution is being made.

(2) A distribution under a short form prospectus using the PREP procedures is subject to all the requirements of National Instrument 44-101 *Short Form Prospectus Distributions*, some of the requirements of National Instrument 41-101 *General Prospectus Requirements* and other provisions of securities legislation, as supplemented or varied by the Instrument and the implementing law of the jurisdiction. Reference is made to Part 1 of the Companion Policy to NI 44-101 for a discussion of the relationship between NI 44-101 and various other pieces of securities legislation and section 1.2 of the Companion Policy to NI 41-101 for a discussion of the relationship between NI 41-101 and various other pieces of securities legislation.

(3) Similarly, a distribution using the PREP procedures not made under a short form prospectus is subject to securities legislation, as supplemented or varied by the Instrument and the implementing law of the jurisdiction, including NI 41-101.

Part 2 Prospectus Amendments

2.1 Prospectus Amendments

(1) Section 4.4 of the Instrument provides that the size of an offering may be increased or decreased by up to 20% between the filing of the prospectus and the filing of the supplemented PREP prospectus. The section further provides that, in cases where such a change in the size of the offering constitutes a material change, the requirement in Part 6 of NI 41-101 or other securities legislation to file an amendment if a material change occurs may be satisfied by filing the supplemented PREP prospectus. The form of certificates required in the supplemented PREP prospectus are those set out in subsection 4.5(2) of the Instrument. For changes in the size of the offering by more than 20% that constitute a material change, this flexibility in filing of the amendment is not available.

(2) The securities regulatory authorities are of the view that an issuer's ability to use the PREP procedures does not prevent the filing of a prospectus amendment to make some or all of the changes to the prospectus that are permitted to be made by a supplemented PREP prospectus.

Part 3 PREP Procedures

3.1 Firm Commitment Distributions

Paragraph 10 of section 3.3 of the Instrument provides that a base PREP prospectus for securities to be distributed by one or more underwriters that have agreed to purchase the securities at a specified price is not required to indicate that the securities are to be taken up by the underwriters, if at all, on or before a specified date. This subsection provides an exemption from the requirement of securities legislation that this disclosure must be contained in a prospectus. Issuers are reminded that paragraph 1 of subsection 4.5(2) requires all information omitted from a base PREP prospectus to be included in a supplemented PREP prospectus. Therefore, it is necessary to comply with the relevant requirement of securities legislation in a supplemented PREP prospectus relating to specific distributions that are being effected on a firm commitment basis.

3.2 Best Efforts Distributions

Similarly, paragraph 11 of section 3.3 of the Instrument provides that a base PREP prospectus for a distribution of securities underwritten on a best efforts basis for which a minimum amount of funds are required by an issuer is not required to include disclosure required under securities legislation concerning the maximum length of time for which the distribution may continue and concerning the disposition of subscription funds. Issuers are reminded, as in the previous subsection, that paragraph 1 of subsection 4.5(2) requires all information omitted from a base PREP prospectus to be included in a supplemented PREP prospectus. Therefore, it is necessary to comply with the relevant requirement of securities legislation in a supplemented PREP prospectus relating to specific distributions that are being effected on a best efforts basis. Issuers are also reminded that where PREP procedures are used in connection with securities offered on a best efforts basis for which a minimum amount of funds are required, the issuer may not reduce the size of the distribution pursuant to section 4.4 of the Instrument in a supplemented PREP prospectus to a size that would yield less than the minimum amount of funds.

3.3 Rights of Rescission or Withdrawal

The securities regulatory authorities are of the view that statutory rights of rescission or withdrawal commence from the time of the purchaser's receipt of a supplemented PREP prospectus. It is only at this time that the entire prospectus has been delivered.

3.4 Supplemented Prospectus Not an Amendment

The securities regulatory authorities do not consider a supplemented PREP prospectus to constitute an amendment to a prospectus within the meaning of Part 6 of NI 41-101 or other securities legislation.

QUESTIONS

1. What is the difference between a preliminary and final prospectus?
2. What are the differences between the various types of short-form offerings?

A number of alternatives to the current system have been suggested that might recognize those issuers that already have considerable information in the market with respect to their activities. One suggestion has been to move toward greater proportionate regulation, based on the size and experience of the issuer. For example, the excerpt below suggests that Canada could benefit from the relaxed rules for well-known seasoned issuers in the United States.

Adam Pritchard, "Well-Known Seasoned Issuers in Canada"
Research Report for the IDA Task Force to Modernize Securities Legislation in Canada, *Canada Steps Up* (4 October 2006), vol 5 at 7-9

In 2005, the United States Securities and Exchange Commission (SEC) adopted a series of rules relaxing the restrictions imposed on public offerings. The largest US public companies, labelled by the SEC as "well-known seasoned issuers," were the recipients of the greatest regulatory relief. Well-known seasoned issuers (more popularly known as WKSIs) came in for favoured treatment based on the SEC's conclusion that those issuers were most closely followed by analysts and institutional investors.

What benefit do companies get from WKSI status? WKSI eligibility means that a company is eligible for "automatic shelf registration." Automatic shelf registration affords well-known seasoned issuers immediate effectiveness for their registration statements, so there are no delays in going to market. More importantly, a WKSI can effectively register an unlimited amount of securities to be sold for an unlimited period of time (or more precisely, it can add securities to its registration statement as it goes). Finally, well-known seasoned issuers are generally excused from the "gun-jumping" restrictions that would otherwise limit public statements that might be construed as offers prior to the filing and effectiveness of a registration statement. Thus, WKSIs have much less reason for concern that their public statements, such as press releases and media appearances by corporate officials, could run afoul of the offering rules. The bottom line for WKSIs is essentially a system of "company registration," with unrestricted disclosure. WKSIs' affirmative offering disclosure obligations are largely satisfied by the periodic reports that they are required to file as public companies.

...

Canada could adopt a version of WKSI status for the top tier of Toronto Stock Exchange (TSX) issuers as part of a streamlined POP system. Careful consideration must be given, however, as to the appropriate standards for WKSI status in Canada. The standards adopted in the US—US$700 million in market capitalization or US$1 billion in nonconvertible debt issued over the prior three years—might not be appropriate for the Canadian market, where issuers tend to be smaller. While the US WKSI standards bring 30% of listed issuers within the WKSI category, applying the same standards in the Canadian context would only bring regulatory relief to 17% of Canadian companies listed on the TSX, and only 7% of the total companies listed on the TSX and TSX Venture exchanges.

This study analyzes the effect of extending WKSI status to the top 30% of TSX issuers. Broadening the WKSI category in this fashion would reduce the market capitalization cutoff to approximately $330 million and bring in an additional 185 companies. Moreover, it would mean that WKSI status would cover companies representing 93% of Canada's total market capitalization.

Would a broader definition of WKSI status mean less investor protection? Here the critical question is the amount of scrutiny that smaller companies receive from the investment community. In the sample examined here, analyst coverage drops off by about half for companies below the US$700 million/$800 million (Canadian) cutoff, and the incidence of companies with zero analyst coverage increases. The drop-off is not as precipitous, however, for companies making public offerings. Among the Canadian companies in the sample that made an offering, companies with between $345-$800 million in market capitalization had an average of 3.5 analysts per issuer. Only one of the companies in this range in the sample had no analyst coverage at all. This evidence suggests that Canada could adopt a lower market capitalization standard for WKSI status without creating an undue risk of including companies that received little or no market attention.

D. The Multijurisdictional Disclosure System

Since 1990, the SEC and Canada's securities regulators have participated in the Multijurisdictional Disclosure System (MJDS), which permits issuers in the United States and Canada to use the same disclosure forms when selling securities in each other's markets. The MJDS was adopted to facilitate prospectus offerings for distributions in Canada and the United States or distributions by US issuers in Canada where they comply with both US requirements and the requirements of NI 71-101, *Multijurisdictional Disclosure System*, in force 1 November 1998 (1998), 21 OSCB 6919. The MJDS is of significant benefit to Canadian issuers in terms of having timely and cost-effective access to the US capital markets. The MJDS prospectus is similar to a shelf prospectus and based on the same policy considerations as a short-form prospectus—specifically, that considerable information about the issuer is already available in the market. Similar provisions in the United States facilitate distributions by Canadian reporting issuers in the United States. The policy rationale is that Canadian and US regulatory systems are similar and that the framework should facilitate offerings in both jurisdictions.

Companion Policy 71-101CP to National Instrument 71-101,
The Multijurisdictional Disclosure System
Effective 1 November 1998

The purpose of National Instrument 71-101, *Multijurisdictional Disclosure System*, is to reduce duplicative regulation in cross-border offerings, issuer bids, take-over bids, business combinations and continuous disclosure and other filings.

The MJDS is intended to remove unnecessary obstacles to certain offerings of securities of US issuers in Canada, to facilitate take-over and issuer bids and business combinations involving securities of certain US issuers and to facilitate compliance by US issuers with proxy and continuous disclosure requirements, while ensuring that Canadian investors remain adequately protected.

...

The MJDS permits public offerings of securities of US issuers that meet the eligibility criteria to be made in Canada on the basis of disclosure documents prepared in accordance with US federal securities laws, with certain additional Canadian disclosure. A public offering of securities of a US issuer may be made under the MJDS either in Canada and the United States or in Canada only.

The MJDS also reduces disincentives to the extension to Canadian securityholders of rights offerings by US issuers by permitting such rights offerings to be made in Canada on the basis of US disclosure documents. Similarly, it facilitates the extension to Canadian securityholders of US issuers of take-over bids, issuer bids and business combinations in the circumstances contemplated by the National Instrument. The MJDS permits such transactions to be made in Canada generally in the same manner as in the US and on the basis of US disclosure documents.

The MJDS permits US issuers to use US continuous disclosure documents in Canada in lieu of Canadian documents if they are in compliance with US federal securities laws, with certain additional Canadian disclosures (NI 71-101CP, ss 2.1, 2.5, 2.6). It also exempts insiders of US issuers from the requirements to file insider reports provided the required filings are made with the SEC.

NI 71-101 contains general provisions relating to the timing of filing of documents and sets out both the conditions that must be satisfied for an issuer to distribute securities under the national instrument and the general eligibility criteria for US issuers. Under the eligibility criteria, the issuer must have a significant reporting history or be of a size that has attracted considerable review by regulators, self-regulatory organizations (SRO), and investors. These criteria also vary depending on the type of securities being offered. For example, for investment grade debt or preferred shares, issuers must have been reporting issuers under the US *Securities Exchange Act of 1934*, as amended, for a period of 12 months prior to the filing. For a rights offering, issuers must have a 36-month reporting history and must have a class of securities listed on the New York Stock Exchange or the American Stock Exchange, or be quoted on the NASDAQ National Market for a period of 12 months prior to the filing; or the issuer's equity shares must have a public float of US$75 million (NI 71-101, s 3.1).

NI 71-101 (s 3.1) also places restrictions on the types of issuers that can use the instrument to facilitate a distribution. Investment grade debt and preferred shares may also be distributed under an MJDS where the obligations are guaranteed unconditionally by the parent of an issuer that meets specified eligibility criteria (NI 71-101, s 3.2). There are also slightly different process requirements for different Canadian jurisdictions, as set out in NI 71-101CP. Given the detail of the eligibility and approval requirements, readers should consult the national instrument directly for specific requirements.

The MJDS prospectus is subject to review procedures that are similar to those for short form prospectuses. The issuer must file a preliminary prospectus in all jurisdictions in Canada in which it intends to make a distribution and receive a receipt for the preliminary prospectus. The prospectus can be the US prospectus with a supplement that complies with additional filing requirements under NI 71-101 (NI 71-101CP). The issuer selects a principal jurisdiction in Canada to review the material filed (NI 71-101, s 5.1). As with other parts of the Canadian prospectus process, the principal jurisdiction can refuse to issue a receipt where disclosure requirements have not been met. A receipt for the final prospectus will be issued by the principal jurisdiction when the registration statement (the document required in US prospectus filings) is declared effective by the Securities and Exchange Commission (SEC). The issuer can then receive receipts from the other Canadian jurisdictions. There are also certification requirements for the issuer and the underwriter in terms of certifying that the prospectus contains full, true, and plain disclosure of all material facts (NI 71-101, s 4.7).

E. Capital Pool Companies

There are also special arrangements for capital pool companies, which are companies that have no assets other than cash and have not commenced business activity. In 2002, securities regulators from Ontario, British Columbia, Alberta, Saskatchewan, and Manitoba approved a Capital Pool Companies (CPC) Operating Agreement with the TSX Venture Exchange Inc, replacing a series of junior capital pool programs in these different jurisdictions (OSC Policy 41-601, *Capital Pool Companies* (2002), 25 OSCB 3315, in force 15 June 2002). Nova Scotia joined later (Amended and Restated CPC Operating Agreement, 8 April 2005).

Historically, regulators were reluctant to issue a receipt for a prospectus where the prospectus revealed the issuer had no business operations and no assets other than cash. For example, in *Re Loki Resources Inc* (1984), 7 OSCB 583, discussed later in this chapter, the director found that where an issuer has neither assets to appraise nor business activities to evaluate, meaningful information regarding an issuer cannot be provided to market participants, and thus the benefits of reporting issuer status should not be conferred upon the issuer. As a result of *Loki* and other decisions, there continued to be difficulties for businesses in terms of finding early financing. The CPC Operating Agreement is aimed at addressing this issue by allowing a capital pool company to list on the TSX Venture Exchange subject to specific conditions. The following excerpt discusses the operation and policy considerations of the CPC Operating Agreement.

OSC Policy 41-601, *Capital Pool Companies Amended and Restated CPC Operating Agreement*

Effective 8 April 2005, online: <http://www.osc.gov.on.ca/documents/en/Securities-Category4/pol_20020412_41-601_oa.pdf>

1. The CPC Policy establishes a program under which a CPC may conduct an initial public offering by prospectus and obtain a listing on TSX Venture's Tier 2. The program requires the CPC to identify and complete a Qualifying Transaction within a specified period of time after listing. After the CPC obtains the necessary shareholder approval or files the QT Circular on SEDAR, as applicable, it closes the Qualifying Transaction and submits to TSX Venture all required post-meeting and post-closing documents. Provided that the Resulting Issuer meets applicable TSX Venture minimum listing requirements, TSX Venture issues a Final Exchange Bulletin and the Resulting Issuer is no longer considered to be a CPC.

2. TSX Venture administers the CPC program and wishes to review CPC Prospectuses and QT Circulars in order to more effectively administer the CPC program, reduce duplication of review, improve market efficiencies and provide consistent treatment to CPCs among CPC Jurisdictions.

3. In agreeing to accept the CPC program and in determining that the operation of the CPC program is not contrary to the public interest, the Commissions considered that

it was appropriate to enter into this Agreement to set out the standards TSX Venture will apply in review of CPC Prospectuses and QT Circulars.

4. The Commissions, in exercising their discretion under securities legislation, intend to rely primarily on the analysis and review carried out by TSX Venture. However, nothing in this Agreement involves a surrender of jurisdiction by any Commission. Each Commission may conduct a detailed review of a CPC Prospectus and retains its discretion to refuse to issue a Receipt for a CPC Prospectus, whether a preliminary or final or an amendment of either. Nothing in this Agreement is intended to create an obligation on any Commission to review a preliminary CPC Prospectus or draft QT Circular.

The IPO regulator is responsible for issuing the receipt for the preliminary CPC prospectus, the final CPC prospectus and any amendment to a preliminary or final CPC prospectus. A securities commission may elect to conduct a detailed review of a CPC prospectus and, if so, it is to use its reasonable best efforts to advise the TSX Venture of this review in writing, within five business days following the filing of the CPC prospectus.

When reviewing a CPC prospectus or qualifying transaction, the TSX Venture is to exercise its reasonable professional judgment and best efforts, on a timely basis, to apply and enforce the CPC Policy; assess the quality of the disclosure contained in the CPC prospectus to determine whether it appears to comply in all material respects with the CPC prospectus form and contains full, true and plain disclosure of all material facts relating to the securities offered by the CPC prospectus, and identifies material issues; and consider whether there appear to be any receipt refusal concerns (Part IV, OSC Policy 41-601, *Capital Pool Companies, Amended and Restated CPC Operating Agreement*).

F. Special Purpose Acquisition Corporations

An alternative financing vehicle is the special purpose acquisition corporation (SPAC), regulated by the Toronto Stock Exchange (TSX). SPAC bears some similarity to capital pool companies in that both involve the creation of publicly traded shell companies that later acquire an operating business using the initial proceeds raised. However, SPAC is much larger than capital pool companies and has enhanced investor protections. OSA Staff Notice 51-725 reports that the Ontario Securities Commission received, in fiscal 2015, the first initial public offering prospectus filed by an SPAC pursuant to *Part X Special Purpose Acquisition Corporations* of the Toronto Stock Exchange Company Manual (SPAC Rules). The SPAC Rules, adopted in 2008, provide the framework for the initial public offering prospectus and listing of an issuer that has no operating business. This first SPAC obtained relief from certain of the requirements of the SPAC rules from the TSX, including relief that required the concurrence of the OSC. There have been several more applications under the SPAC rules since 2015 (OSC Staff Notice 51-725, *Corporate Finance Branch 2014-2015 Annual Report*, online: <http://www.osc.gov.on.ca/documents/en/Securities-Category5/sn_20150714_51-725_cf-rpt-2015.pdf>).

VIII. CERTIFICATION AS TO ACCURACY OF THE PROSPECTUS

A prospectus must contain a certificate signed by the chief executive officer (CEO), the chief financial officer (CFO), and any two directors of the issuer that the prospectus constitutes full, true and plain disclosure of all material facts relating to the securities offered by the prospectus as required by the statute and regulations (NI 44-101; for an example of statutory provisions, see OSA, s 58). The policy rationale is to encourage director oversight, due diligence and care in the prospectus process. The officers must also certify that there has been full, true and plain disclosure of all material facts relating to the securities previously issued by the issuer. There are provisions for circumstances where the CEO or CFO are not available or where there are fewer directors.

The regulator in each jurisdiction except Ontario has the discretion to require selling securityholders to sign a prospectus certificate (NI 41-101, s 5.13(1)). Under securities legislation, selling securityholders are liable for misrepresentations in a prospectus whether or not they sign a prospectus certificate. There are circumstances, however, where the regulator may determine that it is in the public interest to require the selling securityholder to affirmatively certify the prospectus, usually only sought where the securities being distributed by the selling securityholder represent a substantial portion of the securities being distributed under the prospectus (CP 41-101).

IX. PROMOTERS

There are also provisions under the general prospectus requirements in respect of disclosure of "promoters," who are persons or companies that are, or have been within the two years immediately preceding the date of the prospectus or *pro forma* prospectus, a promoter of an investment fund or its subsidiary (NI 41-101, s 5.11). Securities legislation in some jurisdictions in Canada define "promoter" and require, in certain circumstances, a promoter of an issuer to assume statutory liability for prospectus disclosure. Asset-backed securities are commonly issued by a "special purpose" entity, established for the sole purpose of facilitating one or more asset-backed offerings, and they typically have a promoter because someone has taken the initiative in founding, organizing, or substantially reorganizing the business of the issuer. Regulators interpret the business of such issuers to include the business of issuing asset-backed securities and entering into the supporting contractual arrangements.

Where an entity is determined to be a promoter of an issuer at the time of the issuer's initial public offering, the entity continues to be a promoter of the issuer, in the case of subsequent offerings by the issuer, if the entity's relationship to the issuer and involvement in the offerings remain substantially the same. Thus, regulators require that where an entity establishes a special purpose issuer to act as a dedicated securitization vehicle, and the prospectus filed in connection with a subsequent offering continues to include disclosure relating to the entity's securitization program, the entity must certify the prospectus as a promoter (Companion Policy 41-101CP, *General Prospectus Requirements*, s 2.7).

X. MATERIAL FACT AND MATERIAL CHANGE IN THE PROSPECTUS PROCESS

A. Material Fact

As noted above, the requirement for full, true and plain disclosure of all material facts is an essential requirement of the prospectus process. However, there is no uniform definition of material fact in securities statutes across Canada. Moreover, what is "material" within the meaning of the legislation is sometimes contested. It is important to be aware of the differences among provincial and territorial definitions because securities law creates a liability regime for misrepresentation in a prospectus. Section 1(1) of the Ontario *Securities Act* defines "material fact" as follows:

> "material fact," when used in relation to securities issued or proposed to be issued, means a fact that would reasonably be expected to have a significant effect on the market price or value of the securities.

The Ontario definition of material fact is forward looking and requires disclosure of facts that would reasonably be expected to have a *significant effect* on the market price or value of securities. Alberta and Saskatchewan both have the same definition (ASA, s 1(gg); SSA, s 2(1)(z)), and the Newfoundland and Labrador definitions are similar except that they have both a prospective and retrospective requirement to disclose any "fact that significantly affects, or would reasonably be expected to have a significant effect on, the market price or value of the securities" (Nfld SA, s 2(1)(x)). The Québec *Securities Act* was amended in 2006 to specify that a prospectus "must provide full, true and plain disclosure of all material facts relating to the securities issued or proposed to be distributed" (QSA, s 13, SQ 1982, c 48, as amended SQ 2006, c 50, s 12). British Columbia had proposed a "material information" standard that eliminated the distinction between material fact and material change; however, its new legislation was never proclaimed in force, as discussed in Chapter 3.

Janis Sarra, *Modernizing Disclosure in Canadian Securities Law: An Assessment of Recent Developments in Canada and Selected Jurisdictions*
Research Report for the Task Force to Modernize Securities Legislation in Canada (2006)

I. Is the Line Drawn in the Appropriate Place?

Canadian judgments on the difference between material fact and material change suggest that there is still not a clear or shared understanding by regulators, issuers and other market participants, and the courts regarding the differences between material fact and material change. Has the drawing of a line in terms of disclosure requirements created certainty in the market? Has it unnecessarily deprived investors of relevant information that may affect their decisions to buy, sell or hold securities?

The statutory regime maintains material fact and material change differences, although NI 51-102 suggests a move toward the blurring of these lines for purposes of regulatory compliance. The National Instrument is a move towards a more expansive definition of material information, but here, there is some incongruence with the statutory regime.

In reality, many issuers already disclose to a material information standard. Those listed on the TSX are required to do so. Hence for these issuers, the material fact/change distinction only becomes significant if there is a claim of failure to meet statutory requirements or a civil liability claim. At that point, the issuer and its counsel are trying to slot changes in the material fact category if not disclosed, in order to avoid liability. This seems an inappropriate way to determine statutory compliance. For many issuers, the difficulty is whether and at what point the information is material, not whether it is a fact or a change. The regulatory structure should try to align materiality standards with both industry practice, the TSX standard, and national policy.

The proposed BC continuous market access model would have eliminated the distinction between material fact and material change. The CMA model would require continuous up-to-date disclosure of all material information about issuers, aimed at creating consistency in reporting material information, whether or not issuers raise capital in a given year. The CMA model would eliminate different standards between primary and secondary markets. One question raised by the proposed change is whether adoption of material information will helpfully eliminate bright line distinctions or whether the term is unduly broad such that it might provide issuers too much discretion to determine materiality. However, the experience of TSX listed issuers has not resulted in difficulties discerning the scope of "material information," other than the determination of materiality, as noted above.

The BC material information standard is premised on investor behaviour being based on economic interest; hence the new legislation retained market impact as the benchmark (*New Proposals for Securities Regulation*). With the more comprehensive requirement of disclosure, retention of the market impact test may have provided issuers with a higher comfort level in respect of standards to be met. Some have argued that the market impact test is more objective as a measure than the reasonable investor test. Others suggest that a reasonable investor test would better align Canada with the US and other countries internationally, and can be measured objectively based on a reasonableness assessment. Moreover, there can be time lags in market value, such that the market impact test is not truly reflective of whether the undisclosed information was material. It is possible that it is a distinction without a difference, as discussed in Part 7 in international comparisons, given that market impact is used as one factor in determining what a reasonable investor would believe in the circumstances.

Hence there are several aspects to the material disclosure debate. First, the problems created by line drawing in terms of both investor protection and certainty for issuers. The judgment in *Kerr v. Danier Leather* indicates that investors' expectations in respect of accuracy of prospectus disclosure may be incongruent with the statutory provisions. Second, is the difficulty of issuers knowing when to disclose. Third is the amount of deference that courts should give to issuers' business judgments regarding what is material.

The instructions to Form 41-101F1 are helpful in understanding materiality in the context of material fact and the importance of communicating the information in a manner that is accessible to potential investors.

Form 41-101F1, *Information Required in a Prospectus*

As amended effective 17 November 2015

General Instructions

(1) The objective of the prospectus is to provide information concerning the issuer that an investor needs in order to make an informed investment decision. This Form sets out specific disclosure requirements that are in addition to the general requirement under securities legislation to provide full, true and plain disclosure of all material facts relating to the securities to be distributed. Certain rules of specific application impose prospectus disclosure obligations in addition to those described in this Form.

(2) Terms used and not defined in this Form that are defined or interpreted in the Instrument bear that definition or interpretation. Other definitions are set out in NI 41-101.

(3) In determining the degree of detail required, a standard of materiality must be applied. Materiality is a matter of judgment in the particular circumstance, and is determined in relation to an item's significance to investors, analysts and other users of the information. An item of information, or an aggregate of items, is considered material if it is probable that its omission or misstatement would influence or change an investment decision with respect to the issuer's securities. In determining whether information is material, take into account both quantitative and qualitative factors. The potential significance of items must be considered individually rather than on a net basis, if the items have an offsetting effect.

(4) Unless an item specifically requires disclosure only in the preliminary prospectus, the disclosure requirements set out in this Form apply to both the preliminary prospectus and the prospectus. Details concerning the price and other matters dependent upon or relating to price, such as the number of securities being distributed, may be left out of the preliminary prospectus, along with specifics concerning the plan of distribution, to the extent that these matters have not been decided.

(5) The disclosure must be understandable to readers and presented in an easy-to-read format. The presentation of information should comply with the plain language principles listed in section 4.1 of Companion Policy 41-101CP General Prospectus Requirements. If technical terms are required, clear and concise explanations should be included.

(6) No reference need be made to inapplicable items and, unless otherwise required in this Form, negative answers to items may be omitted.

(7) Where the term "issuer" is used, it may be necessary, in order to meet the requirement for full, true and plain disclosure of all material facts, to also include disclosure with respect to persons or companies that the issuer is required, under the issuer's GAAP, to consolidate, proportionately consolidate or account for using the equity method (for example, including "subsidiaries" as that term is used in Canadian GAAP applicable to publicly accountable enterprises). If it is more likely than not that a person or company will become an entity that the issuer will be required, under the issuer's GAAP, to consolidate, proportionately consolidate or account for using the equity method, it may be necessary to also include disclosure with respect to the person or company.

(8) An issuer that is a special purpose vehicle may have to modify the disclosure items to reflect the special purpose nature of its business.

(9) If disclosure is required as of a specific date and there has been a material change or change that is otherwise significant in the required information subsequent to that date, present the information as of the date of the change or a date subsequent to the change instead.

(10) If an issuer discloses financial information in a preliminary prospectus or prospectus in a currency other than the Canadian dollar, prominently display the presentation currency.

(11) Except as otherwise required or permitted, include information in a narrative form. The issuer may include graphs, photographs, maps, artwork or other forms of illustration, if relevant to the business of the issuer or the distribution and not misleading. Include descriptive headings. Except for information that appears in a summary, information required under more than one Item need not be repeated.

(12) Certain requirements in this Form make reference to requirements in another instrument or form. Unless this Form states otherwise, issuers must also follow the instruction or requirement in the other instrument or form. These references include references to Form 51-102F2. Venture issuers must include such disclosure in a preliminary prospectus or prospectus even if they are not otherwise required to file an annual information form under NI 51-102.

(13) Wherever this Form uses the word "subsidiary," the term includes companies and other types of business organizations such as partnerships, trusts and other unincorporated business entities.

(14) Where requirements in this Form make reference to, or are substantially similar to, requirements in Form 51-102F2, issuers may apply the general provision in subpart 1(d) of Form 51-102F2. However, issuers must supplement this disclosure if the supplemented disclosure is necessary to ensure that the prospectus provides full, true and plain disclosure of all material facts related to the securities to be distributed as required under Item 29 of this Form.

(15) Forward-looking information, as defined in NI 5-102, included in a prospectus must comply with section 4A.2 of NI 51-102 and must include the disclosure described in section 4A.3 of NI 51-102. In addition to the foregoing, FOFI or a financial outlook, each as defined in NI 51-102, included in a prospectus must comply with Part 4B of NI 51-102. If the forward-looking information relates to an issuer or other entity that is not a reporting issuer in any jurisdiction, section 4A.2, section 4A.3 and Part 4B of NI 51-102 apply as if the issuer or other entity were a reporting issuer in at least one jurisdiction.

(16) Marketing materials prepared in accordance with subsections 13.7(1) or 13.8(1) of the Instrument are the only documents that can be incorporated by reference into a long form prospectus.

Note that the instructions in Form 41-101F1 specify that the prospectus must also comply with the FOFI requirements set out in NI 51-102, *Continuous Disclosure Obligations*, which are discussed at length in Chapter 6. Specifically, it must comply with the following provisions.

National Instrument 51-102, *Continuous Disclosure Obligations*
As amended effective 17 November 2015, online: <https://www.bcsc.bc.ca/Securities_Law/Policies/Policy5/PDF/51-102__NI___November_17__2015/>

Part 4A Forward-Looking Information

. . .

4A.2 Reasonable Basis

A reporting issuer must not disclose forward-looking information unless the issuer has a reasonable basis for the forward-looking information.

4A.3 Disclosure

A reporting issuer that discloses material forward-looking information must include disclosure that (a) identifies forward-looking information as such; (b) cautions users of forward-looking information that actual results may vary from the forward-looking information and identifies material risk factors that could cause actual results to differ materially from the forward-looking information; (c) states the material factors or assumptions used to develop forward-looking information; and (d) describes the reporting issuer's policy for updating forward-looking information if it includes procedures in addition to those described in subsection 5.8(2).

Part 4B FOFI and Financial Outlooks

4B.1 Application

(1) Subject to subsection (2), this Part applies to FOFI or a financial outlook that is disclosed by a reporting issuer.

(2) This Part does not apply to disclosure that is (a) subject to requirements in National Instrument 51-101 *Standards of Disclosure for Oil and Gas Activities* or National Instrument 43-101 *Standards of Disclosure for Mineral Projects*; (b) made to comply with the conditions of any exemption from the requirements referred to in paragraph (a) that a reporting issuer received from a regulator or securities regulatory authority unless the regulator or securities regulatory authority orders that this Part applies to disclosure made under the exemption; or (c) contained in an oral statement.

4B.2 Assumptions

(1) A reporting issuer must not disclose FOFI or a financial outlook unless the FOFI or financial outlook is based on assumptions that are reasonable in the circumstances.

(2) FOFI or a financial outlook that is based on assumptions that are reasonable in the circumstances must, without limitation, (a) be limited to a period for which the information in the FOFI or financial outlook can be reasonably estimated; and (b) use the accounting policies the reporting issuer expects to use to prepare its historical financial statements for the period covered by the FOFI or the financial outlook.

4B.3 Disclosure

In addition to the disclosure required by section 4A.3, if a reporting issuer discloses FOFI or a financial outlook, the issuer must include disclosure that (a) states the date management approved the FOFI or financial outlook, if the document containing the FOFI or financial outlook is undated; and (b) explains the purpose of the FOFI or financial outlook and cautions readers that the information may not be appropriate for other purposes.

• • •

5.8 Disclosure Relating to Previously Disclosed Material Forward-Looking Information

(1) **Application**—This section applies to material forward-looking information that is disclosed by a reporting issuer other than

(a) forward-looking information contained in an oral statement; or

(b) disclosure that is

(i) subject to the requirements in National Instrument 51-101 *Standards of Disclosure for Oil and Gas Activities* or National Instrument 43-101 *Standards of Disclosure for Mineral Projects*; or

(ii) made to comply with the conditions of any exemption from the requirements referred to in subparagraph (i) that a reporting issuer received from a regulator or securities regulatory authority unless the regulator or securities regulatory authority orders that this Part applies to disclosure made under the exemption.

(2) **Update**—A reporting issuer must discuss in its MD&A

(a) events and circumstances that occurred during the period to which the MD&A relates that are reasonably likely to cause actual results to differ materially from material forward-looking information for a period that is not yet complete that the reporting issuer previously disclosed to the public; and

(b) the expected differences referred to in paragraph (a).

(3) **Exemption**—Subsection (2) does not apply if the reporting issuer

(a) includes the information required by subsection (2) in a news release issued and filed by the reporting issuer before the filing of the MD&A referred to in subsection (2); and

(b) includes disclosure in the MD&A referred to in subsection (2) that

(i) identifies the news release referred to in paragraph (a);

(ii) states the date of the news release; and

(iii) states that the news release is available on www.sedar.com.

(4) **Comparison to Actual**—A reporting issuer must disclose and discuss in its MD&A material differences between

(a) actual results for the annual or interim period to which the MD&A relates; and

(b) any FOFI or financial outlook for the period referred to in paragraph (a) that the reporting issuer previously disclosed.

(5) **Withdrawal**—If during the period to which its MD&A relates, a reporting issuer decides to withdraw previously disclosed material forward-looking information,

(a) the reporting issuer must disclose in its MD&A the decision and discuss the events and circumstances that led the reporting issuer to that decision, including a discussion of the assumptions underlying the forward-looking information that are no longer valid; and

(b) subsection (4) does not apply to the reporting issuer with respect to the MD&A

(i) if the reporting issuer complies with paragraph (a); and

(ii) the MD&A is filed before the end of the period covered by the forward-looking information.

(6) **Exemption**—Paragraph 5(a) does not apply if the reporting issuer

(a) includes the information required by paragraph (5)(a) in a news release issued and filed by the reporting issuer before the filing of the MD&A referred to in subsection (5); and

(b) includes disclosure in the MD&A referred to in subsection (5) that

(i) identifies the news release referred to in paragraph (a);

(ii) states the date of the news release; and

(iii) states that the news release is available on www.sedar.com.

B. Material Change

The issuer generally has an obligation to disclose any material changes during the prospectus and distribution process.

The terms material change is defined differently in different jurisdictions, but Canadian jurisdictions have moved in recent years to introduce a market impact test. For example, Ontario, British Columbia, and Québec all have a market impact test.

The term "material change" is defined under s 1(1) of the BCSA as follows:

"material change" means,

(a) if used in relation to an issuer other than an investment fund,

(i) a change in the business, operations or capital of the issuer that would reasonably be expected to have a significant effect on the market price or value of a security of the issuer, or

(ii) a decision to implement a change referred to in subparagraph (i) made by

(A) the directors of the issuer, or

(B) senior management of the issuer who believe that confirmation of the decision by the directors is probable, and

(b) if used in relation to an investment fund,

(i) a change in the business, operations or affairs of the investment fund that would be considered important by a reasonable investor in determining whether to purchase or continue to hold a security of the investment fund, or

(ii) a decision to implement a change referred to in subparagraph (i) made

(A) by the directors of the investment fund or the directors of the investment fund manager,

(B) by senior management of the investment fund who believe that confirmation of the decision by the directors is probable, or

(C) by senior management of the investment fund manager who believe that confirmation of the decision by the directors of the manager is probable;

The Québec *Securities Act* also uses a market impact test of materiality, adding a different definition for investment funds in SQ 2006, c 50:

"Material change"

5.3. When used in relation to an issuer other than an investment fund, "material change" means a change in the business, operations or capital of the issuer that would reasonably be expected to have a significant effect on the market price or value of any of the securities of the issuer, or a decision to implement such a change made by the directors or by senior management of the issuer who believe that confirmation of the decision by the directors is probable.

When used in relation to an investment fund, "material change" means a change in the business, operations or affairs of the investment fund that would be considered important by a reasonable investor in determining whether to subscribe for, purchase or continue to hold securities of the investment fund, or a decision to implement such a change made by the directors of the investment fund or its investment fund manager, by senior management of the investment fund who believe that confirmation of the decision by the directors is probable, or by senior management of the investment fund manager who believe that confirmation of the decision by the directors of the investment fund manager is probable.

If there is a material adverse change between filing the preliminary prospectus and the completion of the distribution, the issuer must file an amendment to the prospectus as soon as practicable and within ten days after the change occurs (NI 41-101, ss 6.5, 6.6; OSA, s 57(1)). NI 41-101 specifies the following with respect to an amendment to a prospectus.

National Instrument 41-101, *General Prospectus Requirements*
As amended effective 8 December 2015, online: <https://www.bcsc.bc.ca/Securities_Law/Policies/Policy4/PDF/41-101__NI___December_8__2015/>

Amendment to a Preliminary Prospectus

6.5(1) Except in Ontario, if, after a receipt for a preliminary prospectus is issued but before a receipt for the final prospectus is issued, a material adverse change occurs, an amendment to the preliminary prospectus must be filed as soon as practicable, but in any event within 10 days after the day the change occurs.

[Note: In Ontario, subsection 57(1) of the *Securities Act* (Ontario) imposes a similar requirement to file an amendment to a preliminary prospectus where there has been a material adverse change.]

(2) The regulator must issue a receipt for an amendment to a preliminary prospectus as soon as practicable after the amendment is filed.

Amendment to a Final Prospectus

6.6(1) Except in Ontario, if, after a receipt for a final prospectus is issued but before the completion of the distribution under the final prospectus, a material change occurs, an issuer must file an amendment to the final prospectus as soon as practicable, but in any event within 10 days after the day the change occurs.

[Note: In Ontario, subsection 57(1) of the *Securities Act* (Ontario) imposes a similar requirement to file an amendment to a final prospectus where there has been a material change.]

(2) Except in Ontario, if, after a receipt for a final prospectus or an amendment to the final prospectus is issued but before the completion of the distribution under the final prospectus or the amendment to the final prospectus, securities in addition to the securities previously disclosed in the final prospectus or the amendment to the final prospectus

are to be distributed, an amendment to the final prospectus disclosing the additional securities must be filed, as soon as practicable, but in any event within 10 days after the decision to increase the number of securities offered.

[Note: In Ontario, subsection 57(2) of the *Securities Act* (Ontario) imposes a similar requirement to file an amendment to a prospectus any time there is a proposed distribution of securities in addition to that disclosed under the prospectus.]

(3) Except in Ontario, the regulator must issue a receipt for an amendment to a final prospectus filed under this section unless the regulator considers that there are grounds set out in securities legislation that would cause the regulator not to issue the receipt for a prospectus.

[Note: In Ontario, subsection 57(2.1) of the *Securities Act* (Ontario) imposes a similar obligation for the Director to issue a receipt for an amendment to a prospectus unless there are proper grounds for refusing the receipt.]

(4) Except in Ontario, the regulator must not refuse to issue a receipt under subsection (3) without giving the issuer who filed the prospectus an opportunity to be heard.

[Note: In Ontario, subsections 57(2.1) and 61(3) of the *Securities Act* (Ontario) impose a similar restriction on the Director to refuse to issue a receipt for a prospectus without first giving an issuer an opportunity to be heard.]

(5) Except in Ontario, an issuer must not proceed with a distribution or additional distribution if an amendment to a final prospectus is required to be filed until a receipt for the amendment to the final prospectus is issued by the regulator.

[Note: In Ontario, subsection 57(2.2) of the *Securities Act* (Ontario) imposes a similar restriction in respect of a distribution or additional distribution before a receipt is issued for an amendment to the final prospectus.]

(6) Subsection (5) does not apply to an investment fund in continuous distribution.

[Note: In Ontario, section 2.2 of OSC Rule 41-801, *Implementing National Instrument 41-101 General Prospectus Requirements and Consequential Amendments* provides a similar exemption for an investment fund in continuous distribution from the requirement to obtain a receipt prior to making a distribution or additional distribution under an amendment to a final prospectus.]

C. Confidential Material Change Reports

An issuer cannot meet the standard of "full, true and plain" disclosure while a material change report has been filed but remains undisclosed publicly. Accordingly, an issuer who has filed a confidential material change report may not file a prospectus until the material change that is the subject of the report is generally disclosed or the decision to implement the change has been rejected and the issuer so notified the regulator of each jurisdiction where the confidential material change report was filed (41-101CP, s 3.2). Similarly, an issuer may not file a confidential material change report during a distribution and continue with the distribution. If circumstances arise that cause an issuer to file a confidential material change report during the distribution period of securities under a prospectus, the issuer should cease all activities related to the distribution until the material change is generally disclosed and an amendment to the prospectus is filed, if required, or the decision to implement the material change has been rejected and the issuer has so notified the regulator of each jurisdiction where the confidential material change report was filed (41-101CP, s 3.2).

Issuers must file copies of contracts that can reasonably be regarded as materially affecting the rights of their securityholders generally (NI 41-101, s 9.1(a)). A material contract is defined as a contract that an issuer or any of its subsidiaries is a party to, which is material to the issuer (NI 41-101, s 1.1). There is an exemption from the filing requirement for a material contract entered into in the ordinary course of business. Whether an issuer entered into a material contract in the ordinary course of business is a question of fact that the issuer should consider in the context of its business and industry (NI 41-101, s 9.3(2)). The National Instrument describes specific types of material contracts that are not eligible for the ordinary course of business exemption. For example, a material contract on which the "issuer's business is substantially dependent" is not eligible for the ordinary course of business exemption, such as a financing or credit agreement providing a majority of the issuer's capital requirements for which alternative financing is not readily available at comparable terms, or a contract calling for the acquisition or sale of substantially all of the issuer's assets (NI 41-101, s 9.3(2)).

An issuer may omit or redact a provision of a material contract that is required to be filed if an executive officer of the issuer reasonably believes that disclosure of the omitted or redacted provision would violate a confidentiality provision (NI 41-101, s 9.3(3)). An issuer may omit or redact certain provisions of a material contract that is required to be filed if an executive officer reasonably believes that disclosure would be seriously prejudicial to the interests of the issuer, such as violation of applicable Canadian privacy legislation (NI 41-101, s 9.3(3)). In such cases, the issuer must include a brief description of the type of information that has been omitted or redacted.

British Columbia had previously proposed eliminating the distinction between material fact and material change and using the term "material information," which would mean information relating to the business, operations, or securities of an issuer that would reasonably be expected to significantly affect the value or market price of the issuer or a security of the issuer. However, that legislation, enacted in 2004, was never proclaimed in force. TSX-listed issuers do, however, have a requirement to disclose all material information.

There are also provisions setting out the risk factors that must be disclosed, which are material to reasonable investors. The issuer is to disclose risks in the order of seriousness, from the most serious to the least serious. Hence, while Canadian statutory language imposes a market impact test for reporting material change, arguably the new national instrument shifts Canada toward some consideration of what a reasonable investor would consider relevant.

Form 41-101F1, *Information Required in a Prospectus*
As amended effective 17 November 2015, online: <https://www.bcsc.bc.ca/Securities_Law/Policies/Policy4/PDF/41-101F1__F___November_17__2015/>

Risk factors

21.1(1) Disclose risk factors relating to the issuer and its business, such as cash flow and liquidity problems, if any, experience of management, the general risks inherent in the business carried on by the issuer, environmental and health risks, reliance on key personnel, regulatory constraints, economic or political conditions and financial history and any other matter that would be likely to influence an investor's decision to purchase securities of the issuer.

(2) If there is a risk that securityholders of the issuer may become liable to make an additional contribution beyond the price of the security, disclose that risk.

(3) Describe any risk factors material to the issuer that a reasonable investor would consider relevant to an investment in the securities being distributed and that are not otherwise described under subsection (1) or (2).

The Ontario Five Year Review Committee previously discussed the difference between Canada's pre-NI 41-101 market impact test and the reasonable investor test that is used in the United States.

Ministry of Finance, *Five Year Review Committee Final Report—Reviewing the Securities Act (Ontario)*
(Toronto: Queen's Printer for Ontario, 2003) at 148-50 (footnotes omitted)

13.2 What Is the Appropriate Standard for Materiality?

A) Market Impact vs. Reasonable Investor Test

Under the Act, both "material change" and "material fact" are defined with reference to whether the change or fact "would reasonably be expected to have a significant effect on the market price or value of a security." This "market impact" standard of materiality is common to all CSA jurisdictions other than Québec. In contrast, in the US information is material if there is a substantial likelihood that a reasonable investor would consider it important in making an investment decision. To satisfy the US materiality standard, there must be a substantial likelihood that a fact "would have been viewed by the reasonable investor as having significantly altered the 'total mix' of information made available." This "reasonable investor" test is not a statutory test, but has developed through case law.

In 1997, the CSA considered amending the definitions of "material fact" and "material change" by replacing the Canadian "market impact" test with the US "reasonable investor" test. The CSA received a number of comment letters, some of which were supportive. Some commentators raised a number of concerns, including that the proposed definitions raised too many issues of interpretation, that a single materiality standard was not viable and that such a change would introduce an unacceptable level of subjectivity and uncertainty. The CSA ultimately decided not to pursue the proposed changes. …

The comments we received on this issue reflect the continuing range of views. There are good arguments both to support preserving the status quo and to support a change in the materiality standard. Some proponents of the status quo argue that the current "market impact" test works reasonably well and is a more objective test than the reasonable investor test. Others note that, since US courts tend to consider market impact when applying the reasonable investor test, a change in the definition for Canadian law purposes would not produce a significant difference in result. Still others argue that this would require market participants to adopt a different disclosure standard, while contemporaneously becoming subject, for the first time, to a regime that imposes civil liability for non-compliance with such a standard. Accordingly, they argue that the implementation of any proposed change to the materiality standard should be delayed for some period until Canadian capital markets have adjusted to the implementation of the new liability regime.

Advocates of changing the materiality trigger to conform to the US reasonable investor test argue that the standard of "full, true and plain" disclosure applicable to prospectuses is effectively the reasonable investor standard, and "if we aim to promote credible capital markets, the same standard should be applied to trigger continuous disclosure and to its contents." We note also that this standard has already been imported into Ontario securities law in the context of specific regulatory instruments. Others argue that harmonizing Ontario (and ultimately Canadian) securities law with US securities law will eliminate some of the complexity issuers currently face in fulfilling their disclosure obligations, particularly issuers whose securities are traded in both Canada and the US. Also, some observers have noted that the market impact test may allow issuers to take too formulaic an approach in determining what is material. As a result, in practice, the reasonable investor standard is often relied upon when advising issuers as to whether they have an obligation to disclose a particular change as a material change.

Finally, some make the argument that there is really no difference between the Canadian "market impact" test and the US "reasonable investor" test since a "reasonable investor" will only be concerned with whether a fact or change would affect the price or value of the security. This argument can be used to support a change to the Canadian test because it will in fact result in no practical change at all; it can also be used to support the status quo, since change in this case will not result in any meaningful difference in the disclosure standard. …

The Committee deliberated extensively on this matter. We acknowledge that compelling arguments have been made to support keeping the market impact test and to support replacing it with the reasonable investor test. Throughout this Report, we have emphasized the need for increased regulatory harmonization, except where specific policy objectives preclude it. We believe that requiring issuers to contemplate what would be important to an investor is the appropriate standard and therefore recommend that the definition be changed to be consistent with the US "reasonable investor" test.

QUESTIONS

1. Compare the excerpt above on risk factors in Form 41-101F1 with that from the Five Year Review Committee. What is the current standard in terms of disclosing material facts and material changes?

2. Assume that a significant portion of the issuer's business is the development of oil wells in an emerging African nation, and this fact is disclosed in a prospectus. Also disclosed was the grant of an exploration licence by the ruling government. There is a coup d'état and the new government of the African nation announces that it intends to cancel all existing oil exploration licences.

a. Does the announcement require the issuer to amend the prospectus?
b. What if the issuer's licence is officially cancelled?
c. What if the licence is not cancelled but renewed on the same terms and conditions?
d. Would there be any difference if the reasonable investor test were the test for such disclosure instead of the market impact test?

3. By now it should be clear that without an exemption, an issuer must not sell securities without filing a prospectus. A prospectus is to disclose all "material" facts about the issuer and securities. Does the statutory language on its face give you any help in describing what is material?

The issuer, selling securityholder, underwriter, directors, and signatories to the prospectus are potentially liable to investors who purchase securities pursuant to a prospectus in which there was a misrepresentation (OSA, s 130(1)). In addition to civil remedies for misrepresentation, there are sanctions for failure to include material facts in filed documents. Below is an excerpt from a case in which the issuer failed to disclose in its prospectus some material facts, including that it was being investigated in the United States for money-laundering operations. The Ontario Securities Commission in *YBM Magnex International* describes how materiality is determined. As you read, consider the role of directors, officers, underwriters, and auditors in maintaining the integrity of the prospectus process.

YBM Magnex International Inc
(2003), 26 OSCB 5285

[89] Disclosure in securities markets encourages investing and therefore growth. Disclosure protects investors, aids in ensuring that securities markets operate in a free and open manner and ensures that a security will nearly correspond to its actual value. Too much disclosure or information overload can be counter-productive. The boundaries are identified by the concept of "material facts." The definition appears straightforward but its assessment is nuanced.

[90] Assessments of materiality are not to be judged against the standard of perfection or with the benefit of hindsight. It is not a science and involves the exercise of judgement and common sense; *Core Mark International Inc. v. 162093 Canada Ltd.* (8 June 1989) Toronto 1220/89 at 4-5 (Ont. HC).

[91] The test for materiality in the Act is objective and is one of market impact. An investor wants to know facts that would reasonably be expected to significantly affect the market price or value of the securities. The investor is an economic being and materiality must be viewed from the perspective of the trading markets, that is, the buying, selling or holding of securities. Price in an open market normally reflects all available information.

YBM was not a thinly traded stock. As such, its price more likely reflected the information disclosed to the public market. Full disclosure of adverse information may lower the price but it does not shut out a security from the market.

. . .

[154] In our opinion, YBM's prospectus did not contain full, true, and plain disclosure of all material facts by failing to disclose that YBM was subject to unique risks. When each alleged omission is analyzed in isolation, a technical argument can be made that some of them may not be material. We do not believe that is the appropriate approach to this case. The factual context cannot be ignored.

. . .

[157] At a minimum, we believe some disclosure regarding what YBM knew about the US investigation and less muddled disclosure regarding the purpose of the Special Committee would have better informed investors about the risks facing YBM. To this end, Gatti produced draft disclosure for the AIF that was headed in the right direction.

. . .

[246] Did the directors exercise their judgement reasonably in concluding that the Final Prospectus contained full, true and plain disclosure? Was the Special Committee investigation, bolstered by reliance on legal advice and the D&T audit, consistent with diligence sufficient to ground a reasonable judgement or belief that full, true and plain disclosure had been made?

[247] The directors exerted significant efforts through the creation and work of the Special Committee, including the retention of Fairfax, to ascertain further information regarding the concerns of the US authorities and the company. However, there were serious weaknesses in connection with the Special Committee's investigation. Most notably, it was not independent. We indicated earlier that the degree of care required in ensuring full, true and plain disclosure leaves little room for risk.

[248] We are most concerned about Mitchell's dual role as Special Committee Chair and YBM's underwriter, particularly given that the Special Committee conducted its investigation contemporaneously with the Crucible negotiations and while planning the financing. Mitchell was active in all three of these initiatives. Despite suggestions to the contrary, his loyalties were divided.

[249] As YBM's underwriter, Mitchell's influences were clear. The underwriter's fee exclusive of any over-allotment option was $2,376,000. In addition, YBM paid $600,000 to First Marathon for advisory services on the Crucible acquisition. We further note that First Marathon together with GMP dominated trading in YBM's shares on the secondary market including approximately US $12,000,000 in trades effected by the founding shareholders through an account for which Mitchell was investment advisor.

[250] If the independence of one's mandate is threatened, then the reasonableness of one's judgement becomes questionable. While this case does not engage the business judgement rule, even that rule requires directors to act reasonably, in good faith and without any conflicts of interest. Basically, it was hard to determine who was going to show up during the prospectus review—the director, the Chair of the Special Committee or the underwriter. Moreover, Mitchell provided no reasonable response as to why he did not provide a copy of the Report to staff and D&T.

. . .

[253] Generally speaking, a board is entitled to rely on special committees. However, as indicated above, Mitchell's independence and the non-participation of the other two members were questionable. The absence of Schmidt and Davies from meetings with Fairfax or Mitchell rendered them ill-suited to discharge their role. The failure to participate, particularly given Davies' information, seriously limited the exchange of ideas and prevented the Special Committee from being a committee upon which the Board could fully rely. In addition, we note the serious nature of information conveyed to the Board by the Special Committee. This should have resulted in a call to action in light of the pending acquisition of Crucible and the public financing. Instead, we note some additional weaknesses in the process followed by the board:

1. Relying on US legal advice provided months before regarding potential defamation concerns, the Directors did not even get a copy of the Report. This could have aided the questioning and decision around disclosure. More than a one shot briefing from Mitchell was required.
2. The entire Board should have requested a meeting with Fairfax to discuss Fairfax's unfiltered continuing concerns regarding YBM's end users or money laundering. Fairfax wanted to do more work including interviewing the auditors, reviewing their work papers, conducting a complete investigation of customers and vendors including knocking on doors and checking all invoices, and explaining the actions taken by the Board to the US Government. Fairfax's services were not inexpensive, but, in relative terms, the financing raised $106 million. Fairfax's additional services were not called upon.
3. Wilder was counsel to the Special Committee and YBM. Rossman advised the Board that the Special Committee should retain its own independent counsel. The Board declined this advice based upon Peterson's suggestion that "lawyers were not going to solve this problem." This advice was improvident. Despite Fairfax's expertise, the nature of the issues confronting YBM required independent legal counsel.

[254] The board relied on legal advice throughout. Good faith reliance upon legal advice that is fully informed, ostensibly credible and within the lawyer's area of expertise is consistent with the exercise of reasonable care; *Blair v. Consolidated Enfield Corp.* (1993), 15 OR (3d) 783 at 796-801, aff'd. [1995] 4 SCR 5. The board, however, cannot have it both ways. It relied on legal advice, but on the other hand, minimized the value of retaining inherently independent legal advice. …

…

[559] We have concluded that YBM, Bogatin, Fisherman, Mitchell, Davies, First Marathon and GMP breached the prospectus disclosure provisions of the Act by failing to make full, true and plain disclosure of all material facts. There is no due diligence defence available for YBM. The other respondents have not persuaded us as to the availability of their due diligence defences. Moreover we have found that YBM, Bogatin, Fisherman, Mitchell and Antes have breached the timely disclosure provisions of the Act and that they have no defence to their failure to file forthwith. Normally, if a respondent has breached the Act and has not made out a due diligence defence, an order in the public

> interest is warranted. However, the respondents further submit that even if they have breached the Act, an order in the public interest is unwarranted.

The commission ultimately declared a permanent prohibition on being a director and officer of a reporting issuer for several key corporate officers and a three- to five-year prohibition for some outside directors (*YBM Magnex International, Order* (27 June 2003)). This case will be discussed in greater detail in Chapters 6 and 10, dealing with continuous disclosure and civil liability remedies, respectively.

QUESTIONS

1. How can deciding what is material be both a matter of judgment and common sense and tested by an objective standard?
2. It seems apparent that issues of investigation into money laundering would clearly be material such that disclosure should have been made on the prospectus; why would the directors fail to undertake this disclosure?
3. Is materiality an elusive concept, as the Ontario Securities Commission suggests? If so, why?
4. Directors, underwriters and auditors all perform a gatekeeping role in securities systems. What are the differences in their roles, and how did this gatekeeping function fail in the *YBM Magnex International* case?

The period between issue of the receipt for the preliminary prospectus and the end of the distribution period cannot be more than 12 months and is often a much shorter period. The length of time of this period creates a reasonable possibility of a material change during the period. The courts have distinguished between material facts and material changes in terms of statutory reporting obligations. In *Pezim v British Columbia (Superintendent of Brokers)*, [1994] 2 SCR 557 at 597, Iacobucci J found that the relationship between "material fact" and "material change" was the following:

> Both "material change" and "material fact" are defined in ... the Act. They are defined in terms of the significance of their impact on the market price or value of the securities of an issuer. The definition of "material fact" is broader than that of "material change"; it encompasses any fact that can "reasonably be expected to significantly affect" the market price or value of the securities of an issuer, and not only changes in the "business, operation, assets or ownership of the issuer" that would reasonably be expected to have such an effect.
>
> The use of these two terms in the Act also reflects the differences in their scope. For example, a prospectus relating to a public distribution of securities must disclose all material facts relating to the issuer .... However, the prospectus need be amended only when a material change occurs.

In *Kerr v Danier Leather Inc*, 2007 SCC 44, [2007] 3 SCR 331, the Supreme Court of Canada affirmed the express obligation to amend a prospectus or to publicize and file a report for the modification of material facts:

> [32] ... The Act supplants the "buyer beware" mind set of the common law with compelled disclosure of relevant information. At the same time, in compelling disclosure, the Act recognizes the burden it places on issuers and in Part XV sets the limits on what is required to be disclosed. The problem for the appellants is that when a prospectus is accurate at the time of filing, s. 57(1) of the Act limits the obligation of post-filing disclosure to notice of a "material change," which the Act defines in s. 1 in relevant part as "a change in the business, operations or capital of the issuer that would reasonably be expected to have a significant effect on the market price or value of any of the securities of the issuer ... ." An issuer has no similar express obligation to amend a prospectus or to publicize and file a report for the modification of material *facts* occurring after a receipt for a prospectus is obtained. That is where the legislature has drawn the line.

It is also important to note that the statutory language requiring amendment of the prospectus continues until the end of the distribution period. This date may be different from when the underwriter's distribution process ends. If the underwriter is selling as part of a distribution, the issuer has an obligation to update the prospectus until the completion of the distribution under the prospectus. Where there is any question, securities regulators are authorized to determine when a distribution has concluded (OSA, s 74(2); Nfld SA, s 75(2); MSA, s 59(4); ASA, s 144(3)). This period may also be relevant in terms of insider transactions relating to securities, as discussed in Chapter 8.

In *Sharbern Holding Inc v Vancouver Airport Centre Ltd*, 2011 SCC 23, [2011] 2 SCR 175, the Supreme Court of Canada set out a test for materiality relating to investment disclosure under the (BC) *Real Estate Act*, RSBC 1996, c 397, referencing securities law. The court held that materiality is to be determined objectively; materiality depends on the specific facts, determined in light of all relevant considerations and circumstances forming the total mix of information made available to investors; and there must be a substantial likelihood that the fact in question would have assumed actual significance in a reasonable investor's decision-making. The court expressly noted that it was using the judgment to clarify the common law test of materiality.

Sharbern Holding Inc v Vancouver Airport Centre Ltd

2011 SCC 23, [2011] 2 SCR 175

I. Introduction

[1] When securities are offered to the general public, the rule of *caveat emptor* no longer applies. Securities legislation imposes on issuers a statutory duty of disclosure. That duty may vary in detail from one Act to another or from one jurisdiction to another. However, the common theme is that issuers must disclose to potential investors information affecting their investment decision. Even so, issuers are not subject to an indeterminate obligation, such that an unhappy investor may seize on any trivial or unimportant fact that was not disclosed to render an issuer liable for the investor's losses. Rather than issuers being required to provide unlimited disclosure, disclosure obligations have been enacted to provide a balance between too much and too little disclosure.

[2] The appeal arises from a class action lawsuit in which the appellant, Sharbern Holding Inc. ("Sharbern"), represents a class of investors who purchased strata lots in a Hilton hotel (the "Hilton Owners") from the respondent developer, Vancouver Airport Centre Ltd. ("VAC"). Sharbern claimed that VAC was liable for failing to disclose details

about differences in the financial arrangements given to the Hilton Owners, and those given to purchasers of strata lots in the adjacent Marriott hotel (the "Marriott Owners") that VAC was developing on the same property. Sharbern alleged that the differences resulted in an undisclosed conflict of interest in that they created an incentive for VAC to favour the Marriott over the Hilton in its operation and management of the two hotels.

[3] Two main questions are raised on appeal. The first is whether VAC is liable for alleged misrepresentations contained in the offering memorandum and disclosure statement (the "Hilton Disclosure Statement") that VAC used to sell the Hilton strata lots. The second is whether VAC is liable for breach of fiduciary duty when it acted as manager of the Hilton under an agreement (the "Hotel Asset Management Agreement") entered into between VAC and the Hilton Owners, including Sharbern. In the reasons that follow, I conclude that Sharbern's claims fail on both grounds, and I would dismiss the appeal.

[4] As to the first question, I am of the opinion that the trial judge erred in law in concluding that VAC is liable for misrepresentation, either under the statutory cause of action found in the *Real Estate Act*, R.S.B.C. 1996, c. 397 [now repealed by *Real Estate Services Act*, SBC 2004, c 42, s 146, BC Reg 507/2004] or under the common law of negligent misrepresentation.

[5] Under s. 75 of the *Real Estate Act*, VAC could only be liable if it is found to have made material false statements to Sharbern, and cannot rely on the defence contained in the section. I am of the respectful view that the trial judge erred in law with respect to the materiality of the alleged false statements. The legal errors were: treating the conflict of interest as inherently material; reversing the burden of proof of materiality from the plaintiff to the defendant; and failing to consider all of the evidence relevant to the determination of materiality. She further erred in not considering the statutory defence which would avail to the benefit of VAC.

[6] Although this Court has previously dealt with the issues of materiality and disclosure obligations in the context of securities law, this case represents the first time that the Court has considered the common law test for materiality. Even though the test is not new in Canadian law, this case represents an opportunity to clarify important aspects of the test.

• • •

[61] In sum, the important aspects of the test for materiality are as follows:

i. Materiality is a question of mixed law and fact, determined objectively, from the perspective of a reasonable investor;
ii. An omitted fact is material if there is a substantial likelihood that it would have been considered important by a reasonable investor in making his or her decision, rather than if the fact merely might have been considered important. In other words, an omitted fact is material if there is a substantial likelihood that its disclosure would have been viewed by the reasonable investor as having significantly altered the total mix of information made available;
iii. The proof required is not that the material fact would have changed the decision, but that there was a substantial likelihood it would have assumed actual significance in a reasonable investor's deliberations;
iv. Materiality involves the application of a legal standard to particular facts. It is a fact-specific inquiry, to be determined on a case-by-case basis in light of all of the relevant considerations and from the surrounding circumstances forming the total mix of information made available to investors; and

v. The materiality of a fact, statement or omission must be proven through evidence by the party alleging materiality, except in those cases where common sense inferences are sufficient. A court must first look at the disclosed information and the omitted information. A court may also consider contextual evidence which helps to explain, interpret, or place the omitted information in a broader factual setting, provided it is viewed in the context of the disclosed information. As well, evidence of concurrent or subsequent conduct or events that would shed light on potential or actual behaviour of persons in the same or similar situations is relevant to the materiality assessment. However, the predominant focus must be on a contextual consideration of what information was disclosed, and what facts or information were omitted from the disclosure documents provided by the issuer.

. . .

[91] In sum, the trial judge erred in law by treating this conflict of interest as inherently material, reversing the onus of proof of materiality, and failing to consider all of the evidence relevant to the determination of materiality. It also appears from the record before the trial court that no evidence was adduced by Sharbern which could reasonably have supported a finding that the Compensation Differences and any conflict of interest they created were material. Separating materiality from the conflict of interest analysis, applying the burden of proof appropriately and taking account of all relevant evidence, I am of the opinion that it has not been demonstrated that there was a substantial likelihood that disclosure of the Compensation Differences would have assumed actual significance in a reasonable investor's investment decision.

. . .

[121] I am of the opinion that the trial judge's findings pertaining to the common law of negligent misrepresentation cannot stand because she did not consider all of the elements necessary to establish the tort. As set out in *Queen v. Cognos Inc.*, [1993] 1 S.C.R. 87:

> The decisions of this Court cited above suggest five general requirements: (1) there must be a duty of care based on a "special relationship" between the representor and the representee; (2) the representation in question must be untrue, inaccurate, or misleading; (3) the representor must have acted negligently in making said misrepresentation; (4) the representee must have relied, in a reasonable manner, on said negligent misrepresentation; and (5) the reliance must have been detrimental to the representee in the sense that damages resulted. [p. 110]

[122] The requirements set out in Cognos were not included in the list of common liability issues. Nor was the framework discussed or utilized by the trial judge in her reasons. While she clearly dealt with the duty of care, and it might be inferred that her misrepresentation analysis dealt with whether the Compensation Differences were untrue, inaccurate or misleading (though this was not done so expressly), the trial judge did not consider the third Cognos requirement. She also did not consider the fourth requirement of reasonable reliance and fifth requirement of resulting damages. However, reasonable reliance and damages would likely be dealt with in the class action proceeding through future common or individual trials.

[123] The third Cognos requirement obligated Sharbern to prove that VAC had "acted negligently in making [the] misrepresentation." This requirement is concerned with the standard of care, and was described by Iacobucci J. in *Cognos*:

> The applicable standard of care should be the one used in every negligence case, namely the universally accepted, albeit hypothetical, "reasonable person." The standard of care required by a person making representations is an objective one. It is a duty to *exercise such reasonable care as the circumstances require to ensure that representations made are accurate and not misleading*. … [Emphasis added; p. 121.]

[124] In considering the standard of care, the trial judge would have had to address whether, on an objective basis, VAC had taken such reasonable care as the circumstances required to ensure that the representations made in the Hilton Disclosure Statement were accurate and not misleading. She made no such finding. Instead, she summarily concluded that VAC "negligently misrepresented" the Compensation Differences, without having addressed the standard of care.

[125] Sharbern submits that the trial judge's conclusion that VAC's representations were negligent is "sound" (A.F., at para. 47). In oral argument, counsel for Sharbern conceded that the trial judge's "reasoning is sparse on her conclusion as to negligence" but insisted that her conclusion was "obvious in the circumstances" (transcript, at pp. 8-9).

[126] I am unable to agree. I do not think it appropriate to collapse the Cognos requirement into a bare assertion of obviousness. Failure to demonstrate how VAC breached the standard of care is fatal to Sharbern's common law claim. Sharbern, as plaintiff, bears the burden of proving its allegations. Sharbern does not point to evidence that could support a finding that the standard of care was breached. Nor does it explain how such a conclusion could have been reached based on the trial judge's "sparse" reasoning.

[127] Rather, Sharbern asserts that it was not required to adduce expert evidence as to what a developer ought to disclose. It argues that the case is about an experienced businessman (Mr. Lalji) who, while aware of the undisclosed incentive, defends his failure to disclose it by assuring us he would not put his own interests first. Sharbern contends that VAC's evidence of its reliance upon industry and expert evidence and upon the advice of its solicitors in respect of its disclosure obligations did not establish that VAC did not breach the standard of care.

[128] Nonetheless, in the circumstances of this case, a bare assertion that something is obvious, without more, cannot establish the applicable standard of care. In the face of considerable evidence before the trial court as to why the Compensation Differences or the potential conflict of interest they created would not have been material to the decision of investors, Sharbern did not provide the court with any evidence to counter VAC's position. For this reason, Sharbern's common law claim of negligent misrepresentation must fail.

[129] I would add one observation on the fourth *Cognos* requirement—reasonable reliance. In this case, Sharbern did not adduce evidence of actual reliance. Instead it relied upon the statutory deeming provision in the *Real Estate Act*. While the trial judge appears to have contemplated the necessity of individual trials on the issue of reliance at the outset of this litigation, her failure to differentiate between the common law and statutory claims in her reasons conveys the impression that the statutory deeming provision can establish common law reliance, removing the need for further trials. This approach would be problematic. I do not think a plaintiff may dip into a statutory cause of action for a helpful element in order to establish the "actual reliance" required to maintain a common law claim for negligent misrepresentation.

[130] For these reasons I conclude that VAC cannot be held liable for negligent misrepresentation at common law.

This excerpt illustrates that both statutory definitions and the common law may be important for determining what are material facts and material changes. The Ontario Securities Commission's 2011 judgment in *Coventree*, immediately below, specifically addressed the issue of prospectus disclosure and material change issues in the context of the asset-backed commercial paper (ABCP) market, which was experiencing a crisis in 2007. As you read the judgment, consider what the commission found not to be material in the context of prospectus disclosure. Then take note of its findings that the disclosure in the prospectus was less than full, true and plain disclosure, given that the prospectus did not disclose that 80 percent of Coventree's revenues, or any other proportion of its revenues or conduit assets, were derived from credit arbitrage transactions as of the date of the prospectus.

In the Matter of Coventree Inc, Geoffrey Cornish and Dean Tai
Ontario Securities Commission, Reasons for Decision (28 September 2011)

[2] This proceeding relates to whether Coventree Inc. ("Coventree") complied with its obligations (i) to disclose material facts related to its credit arbitrage business in its final prospectus dated November 15, 2006 offering its common shares for sale to the public (the "Prospectus"), and (ii) to disclose material changes that Staff alleges occurred on January 19, 2007 and August 1, 2007, or thereafter and prior to the market disruption in the asset-backed commercial paper ("ABCP") market that occurred on August 13, 2007. Staff alleges that Geoffrey Cornish ("Cornish") and Dean Tai ("Tai"), both senior officers and directors of Coventree, authorized, permitted or acquiesced in Coventree's non-compliance with the [*Securities Act*, RSO 1990, c S.5 (the "Act")] and are therefore deemed also to have not complied with the Act. Staff also alleges that Coventree breached the Act in April, 2007 by making a misleading statement as to the total U.S. subprime mortgage assets held by Coventree sponsored conduits. Coventree, Cornish and Tai are referred to collectively in these reasons as the "Respondents" and individually as a "Respondent."

...

[164] Staff alleges that Coventree failed to make full, true and plain disclosure of all material facts in its Prospectus by failing to disclose that DBRS had adopted more restrictive credit rating criteria for new credit arbitrage transactions in November 2006. In particular, Staff alleges that Coventree failed to disclose the DBRS November Letter ... .

...

2. Law Related to Prospectus Disclosure

[192] In order for capital markets to function fairly and efficiently, public companies must provide accurate and truthful disclosure to investors about their business and affairs. The importance of public disclosure cannot be underestimated. The Commission has emphasized the importance of disclosure to investors and capital markets in a number of decisions. In *Philip Services Corp.*, the Commission stated that:

> Disclosure is the cornerstone principle of securities regulation. All persons investing in securities should have equal access to information that may affect their investment decisions. (*Philip Services Corp.* … , at para. 7)

[193] Information that is publicly disclosed must be accurate and not misleading or untrue in order to accomplish the goals of Ontario's securities regulatory regime to protect investors from unfair or improper practices and to foster fair and efficient capital markets and confidence in those markets (*Re Rex Diamond* … , at para. 205).

[194] A prospectus is an important means for ensuring that investors receive the information that permits them to make an informed decision when investing in the securities offered.

Full, True and Plain Disclosure

[195] The Act requires that a preliminary prospectus and a final prospectus be filed, and receipts be obtained, where a distribution of securities is made (Act, *supra*, subsection 53(1)).

[196] The Act provides that a prospectus shall contain full, true and plain disclosure of all material facts relating to the securities issued or proposed to be distributed and shall comply with the requirements of Ontario securities law (Act, *supra*, subsection 56(1)).

[197] The Act requires that where a prospectus is filed, the issuer's chief executive officer, chief financial officer and any two of its directors, on behalf of the board of directors, must certify that the prospectus contains full, true and plain disclosure of all material facts relating to the securities offered (Act, *supra*, subsection 58(1) and section 37.2 of Form 41-101F1—*Information Required in a Prospectus* (the "Prospectus Form")). Underwriters in a prospectus distribution are required to certify that, to the best of their knowledge, information and belief, the prospectus constitutes full, true and plain disclosure of all material facts relating to the securities offered (Act, *supra*, subsection 59(1) and section 37.3 of the Prospectus Form).

[198] "Full" disclosure is achieved when disclosure is made of facts sufficient to permit investors to make an informed investment decision. "True" disclosure is achieved if the disclosure is accurate and not misleading and does not omit a fact that is either material itself or is necessary to understand the facts that have been disclosed. "Plain" disclosure must be understandable to investors and in plain language.

[199] Disclosure in the Prospectus is governed by National Instrument 41-101—*General Prospectus Requirements* (2002), 23 OSCB 761. The Prospectus Form provides detailed instructions for the preparation of a prospectus and sets out 37 separate matters or "items" that must be disclosed. Item 29 requires issuers to disclose any other material fact not covered by any of the other items that is "necessary in order for the prospectus to contain full, true and plain disclosure of all material facts." Section 4.1 of Companion Policy 41-101CP provides that "[i]ssuers should apply plain language principles" when preparing a prospectus.

3. Analysis

[200] In considering the allegations of misleading or inadequate disclosure in the Prospectus, we have read the entire Prospectus with some care. We recognise that statements

in the Prospectus can be taken out of context. While we quote selectively from the Prospectus in these reasons, we are mindful of that caution.

. . .

DBRS November Letter Not a Material Fact

[205] On balance, however, we have concluded that the DBRS November Letter did not constitute a material fact with respect to Coventree at the date of the Prospectus. We come to that conclusion for three reasons.

[206] First, it appears that the DBRS November Letter was primarily focused on "managing the future growth of SFA-backed transactions" and ensuring that only high quality transactions were approved.

[207] It is at best unclear exactly what DBRS was saying in the DBRS November Letter and what criteria it would apply in reviewing future SFA transactions. Loke agreed with that assessment in his testimony. He testified that DBRS had not established the criteria it would apply pursuant to the DBRS November Letter. Coventree submits that the only way to determine what the DBRS November Letter really meant was to submit proposed transactions to DBRS to see how DBRS responded. In an e-mail to Toten dated November 30, 2006, Cornish stated "… my vote is that we should submit [to DBRS] every deal that we want to do as per usual in CDOs … it is only once we get into this new process that we will find out how it will really apply to us and others."

[208] Based on Loke's testimony, it appears that other market participants also had concerns as to exactly what the DBRS November Letter meant.

[209] With that uncertainty as to its meaning and application, it was difficult to assess, at the time the Prospectus was filed, the likely impact of the DBRS November Letter on Coventree and its business. To the extent that DBRS was simply saying that it would in the future approve only higher quality SFA transactions, Coventree may well have concluded that the letter was not addressed to the transactions it typically carried out, and that it would have a limited adverse effect on its business.

[210] Secondly, the DBRS November Letter does appear to be a continuation of DBRS's existing "measured approach" to approving SFA transactions. A measured approach is quite different than saying that no future LSS transactions would be approved. Further, the DBRS November Letter seems to be captured by the statement in the Prospectus that "there is no assurance that DBRS will not adopt additional requirements in the future that may adversely affect the Company's ability to carry on business or to execute transactions through its conduits on the same basis as in the past" (Prospectus, at p. 64; see paragraph 182 of these reasons). That disclosure does not relieve Coventree of its legal obligation to disclose material facts in the Prospectus *as they existed on the date of the Prospectus*, but it does alert a reader to the possibility that DBRS could take future action that would adversely affect Coventree's ability to complete future securitization transactions.

[211] Finally, the DBRS November Letter did not affect outstanding transactions or transactions that were then being reviewed by DBRS, although the letter indicates that the latter transactions would be reviewed on a case by case basis.

[212] We note that Loke testified that DBRS did not approve any new CDO related SFA transactions after the DBRS November Letter, other than grandfathered transactions

and transactions that had the benefit of global style liquidity. It also appears that Coventree did not propose any new CDO related transactions to DBRS after the DBRS November Letter. However, if those were consequences of the DBRS November Letter (rather than the DBRS January Release), they were apparent only with the benefit of hindsight. We do not believe that those consequences of the DBRS November Letter were reasonably apparent to Coventree at the date of the Prospectus.

[213] We would add that we do not view the fact that no change was made to the disclosure in the Prospectus in response to the DBRS November Letter as a relevant factor in our analysis of this issue.

4. *Conclusions*

[214] One way of asking whether the DBRS November Letter was a material fact is to ask whether, if disclosure of the DBRS November Letter had been made in the Prospectus, that disclosure would have significantly affected the price investors would have paid to purchase Coventree shares under the Prospectus. We consider that unlikely.

[215] Based on the foregoing, we have concluded, on balance, that the DBRS November Letter would not reasonably be expected to have had a significant effect on the market price or value of Coventree shares. Accordingly, the DBRS November Letter did not constitute a "material fact" at the date of the Prospectus within the meaning of the Act. We therefore find that Coventree did not contravene section 56 of the Act by failing to disclose the DBRS November Letter in the Prospectus.

5. *Other Prospectus Disclosure Issues*

[216] The allegation referred to in paragraph 164 of these reasons is Staff's only allegation that Coventree contravened section 56 of the Act. There are, however, two other issues with respect to the disclosure in the Prospectus that are relevant to other allegations we must address in these reasons.

(a) Importance of Credit Arbitrage to Coventree's Business Staff Allegation

[217] Staff alleges that the Prospectus did not disclose that approximately 80% of Coventree's revenues were derived from credit arbitrage transactions. Staff has conceded, however, that the failure to make that disclosure did not contravene section 56 of the Act. Staff submits that allegation is relevant only in considering whether the DBRS January Release gave rise to a material change in Coventree's business. We discuss that issue later in these reasons.

. . .

Discussion

[231] Coventree does not dispute that, at the time of the Prospectus, approximately 80% of its revenues were derived from credit arbitrage transactions. That conclusion is consistent with the statements in the letter to Staff referred to in paragraph 222 of these reasons (although those statements relate to periods ending subsequent to the date of the Prospectus).

[232] The Prospectus does not disclose the proportion of Coventree's revenues derived from credit arbitrage transactions. Coventree knew that the underwriters involved in the IPO considered that information to be relevant to investors. Two of the underwriters involved in the IPO requested Coventree to disclose that information in the Prospectus, but Tai successfully resisted disclosure on the basis that the information was confidential and proprietary. In an email to Tai dated August 21, 2006, McCloskey stated: "[a]lso surprised that you won't disclose in the prospectus the breakdown of revenue and profit that come from your programs vs. 'Proprietary/arb trading.' The latter will command a lower valuation multiple. I would think that a proposed investor would want to know. Too sensitive from a business perspective?" McCloskey testified that he discussed this disclosure question with his legal counsel and they ultimately concluded that additional disclosure was not required.

[233] We have difficulty seeing how the proportion of Coventree's revenues or business derived from credit arbitrage transactions was commercially sensitive. Child appeared to agree with that in her testimony. It is also clear to us on the evidence that Coventree tracked transactions on a deal by deal basis and characterized those transactions as either funding transactions (traditional securitizations) or investment transactions (credit arbitrage). It does not appear to us that it would have been difficult for Coventree to determine its revenue derived from credit arbitrage transactions and there is nothing preventing the disclosure of that information in the Prospectus. It also appears to us to be information that an investor reading the Prospectus would want to know.

[234] Accordingly, we do not accept the submissions set out in paragraph 221 of these reasons as valid grounds for not making clear in the Prospectus the importance of credit arbitrage transactions to Coventree's business.

Disclosure in the Prospectus

[235] Having said that, it is clear from the Prospectus that Coventree was engaged through its sponsored conduits in both traditional securitization transactions and credit arbitrage transactions. We accept that a reader of the Prospectus could determine, based on a careful reading, that credit arbitrage assets represented approximately 44% of the assets held by Coventree sponsored conduits (see paragraph 225 of these reasons) and that credit arbitrage transactions represented approximately 54% of Coventree's total investments (see paragraph 226 of these reasons).

[236] We also note that the Prospectus discloses that Nereus, Coventree's 75.5% owned subsidiary at the time, "focuses principally on structured credit arbitrage" and that "Nereus has close to $3 billion in fundings outstanding" (Prospectus, at p. 26). The total combined fundings of Coventree and Nereus conduits were $14.9 billion at the time. Accordingly, a reader would know from the Prospectus that Nereus focused principally on credit arbitrage and that it had fundings outstanding of close to $3 billion, representing approximately 20% of Coventree's total fundings.

[237] At the same time, the Prospectus gives much less emphasis to Coventree's direct involvement in the credit arbitrage business. For instance, the Prospectus states that:

> Coventree establishes multi-seller, multi-asset securitization conduits which are funded principally with ABCP, including ECP [extendible commercial paper]. Currently, the fundings outstanding in Coventree sponsored conduits are approximately $12 billion. Coventree

engages in similar activities through its credit arbitrage securitization and asset management activities. (Prospectus, at p. 18) That statement could be read as suggesting that credit arbitrage transactions were not included in the $12 billion of outstanding fundings, but the statement at least suggests that credit arbitrage is a secondary activity.

[238] Coventree also states in the section of the Prospectus describing Nereus that:

Currently, Nereus focuses principally on structured credit arbitrage. Coventree's business is more diversified in nature, but some similarities exist between the business of Coventree and Nereus. (Prospectus, at p. 26) That statement seems misleading when one realizes that approximately 80% of Coventree's revenues at the time were derived from credit arbitrage transactions.

[239] It is not up to investors reading the Prospectus to have to follow the somewhat convoluted and less than clear trail through the disclosure in the Prospectus, and through the disclosure in Coventree's financial statements contained in the Prospectus, to determine what proportion of Coventree's revenues or conduit assets were derived from credit arbitrage transactions. That information was important to investors given the competitive and other pressures that the credit arbitrage business was under (as described in the Prospectus). We also note in this respect that, in connection with the IPO, the underwriters applied different earnings multiples in valuing the credit arbitrage business and the traditional securitization business.

[240] *The Prospectus does not disclose that 80% of Coventree's revenues, or any other proportion of its revenues or conduit assets, were derived from credit arbitrage transactions as of the date of the Prospectus.*

[241] Accordingly, in our view, based on a fair reading of the Prospectus, the disclosure in the Prospectus on this subject was less than full, true and plain disclosure. We believe that a reader of the Prospectus would have been rightly surprised to be told that approximately 80% of Coventree's revenues were derived from credit arbitrage transactions.

[242] Mowat does not appear to have been aware until late June 2007 of the importance of credit arbitrage to Coventree's business. She sent an e-mail on June 27, 2007 to another Board member that stated, in part:

... the Board meeting was awesome. Now the light bulb is going on for me and I wish we could get that into our disclosure ... . I had no idea that over half the profit is from CDOs as opposed to traditional securitization and that the traditional business from an origination side had "dried up so much." David Allan's presence is timely. ... Mowat was Chair of the Coventree Audit Committee and signed the Prospectus on behalf of the Board.

[243] That statement is relevant because it suggests that investors would not have known how important credit arbitrage was to Coventree's business based on a review of the Prospectus. We do not accept Mowat's testimony that her statement related only to her understanding of the nature or structure of CDO transactions.

Conclusion

[244] We have concluded that the disclosure in the Prospectus relating to the proportion of Coventree's business derived from credit arbitrage was less than full, true and plain disclosure. There was less than full disclosure of the proportion of Coventree's revenues

or conduit assets that were derived from credit arbitrage transactions and the information on that topic was not plain to a reader of the Prospectus. However, we have concluded that one would fairly conclude based on a careful reading of the Prospectus that a significant portion of Coventree's business, measured by revenues or conduit assets, was derived from credit arbitrage transactions. One would not know that the proportion of Coventree's revenues derived from credit arbitrage transactions was approximately 80%, but one would know the proportion was substantial.

[245] We have not concluded that the Prospectus failed for this reason to provide full, true and plain disclosure of all *material facts*. Staff did not make that allegation and we have not addressed it.

(b) The Credit Arbitrage Business Was Dying Coventree Submissions

...

[246] Coventree also submits that it was disclosed in the Prospectus that the credit arbitrage business was "dead or dying" and that Coventree expected in the future to do only the occasional, one-off credit arbitrage transaction. Coventree submits, based in part on the disclosure in the Prospectus referred to in paragraphs 247 to 249 of these reasons, that an investor would expect that Coventree's future growth would come from its investment in new businesses such as its efforts as part of the Chapter Two initiatives to establish a U.S. conduit, a Canadian retail bank, and an asset management business. Coventree also submits that an investor would expect that, while Coventree built these new businesses over the ensuing years, its net income could be flat or declining. Coventree submits that is the result of combining the expectation that revenues from the credit arbitrage business were not likely to grow significantly in the future with the expectation that Coventree would be incurring significant costs associated with its planned diversification.

Relevant Disclosure in the Prospectus

[247] The Prospectus discloses that:

> Past accomplishments don't guarantee future successes. At least part of these achievements are derived from fortuitous timing, and many of the more recent years' results are derived from anomalous, one-time events. One-time events include unique up-front structuring fees, sale/termination of transactions fees and the gain on the sale of shares from certain investments. (Prospectus, at p. 32)

[248] The Prospectus discloses that there was increasing competition and a narrowing of spreads in Coventree's credit arbitrage business. The Prospectus states that the expectation of Coventree's leaders is that "potential returns on credit arbitrage [will] become further compressed due in part to competition in that market ..." (page 28 of the Prospectus) and that new entrants into the market puts "additional pressures on margins in the credit arbitrage business where spreads have narrowed dramatically ..." (page 32 of the Prospectus). The Prospectus states that: There has also been a decline in spreads in the credit arbitrage business. If this trend continues or if credit spreads remain tight, the average spread on the credit arbitrage assets will decrease in the future resulting in lower revenue. (Prospectus, at p. 38)

[249] Coventree concludes in the Overview section of Management's Discussion and Analysis of Financial Condition and Results of Operations in the Prospectus that:

> As a result of all the above, the leaders of the Company believe that *net income growth* excluding AcG-15 could be flat if not declining for the next few years and expect volatility in short term quarterly results. [emphasis added] (Prospectus, at p. 33)

[250] Accordingly, the Prospectus alerts investors to the narrowing spreads and increased competition in the credit arbitrage business and the possibility that Coventree would have flat or declining "net income growth" in the future and volatility in short term financial results.

[251] Despite the increased competition in the credit arbitrage business and the fact that credit arbitrage transactions had become less profitable, Coventree continued to enter into credit arbitrage transactions in the two month period leading up to the filing of the Prospectus, generating total revenue backlog of approximately $37 million from four transactions. In addition, Coventree's business plan, developed in May 2006, and updated in September 2006, contemplated new credit arbitrage fundings of over $4 billion. That is approximately 50% of Coventree's projected total fundings for its 2007 financial year of $9.5 billion (excluding Nereus).

Discussion

[252] In our view, while a reader of the Prospectus would conclude that there were significant challenges to the credit arbitrage business going forward, they would also conclude that credit arbitrage would continue to be a substantial portion of Coventree's business. There is no express statement in the Prospectus that Coventree even intends to shift its strategic focus from credit arbitrage to traditional securitization transactions (perhaps because of the failure to clearly disclose the importance of Coventree's credit arbitrage business in the Prospectus).

[253] We would add that the Prospectus indicates that Coventree's

> … expanded corporate objective is to become a financial services company focused on niches. Targeted niches include structured financing using securitization technology, conduit administration outsourcing services for third parties, asset management and private equity investments in synergistic enterprises, as well as eventual entry into certain retail banking activities. (Prospectus, at p. 18) Establishing a U.S. conduit, a Canadian retail bank and an asset management business were Coventree's so-called "Chapter Two" initiatives (see paragraphs 106 to 111 of these reasons). The Prospectus discloses that "[m]any of these initiatives are in the initial or early planning stages, and there is no assurance that all, or any, of Coventree's current growth experiments will be successful" (Prospectus, at p. 18).

. . .

[254] None of the Chapter Two initiatives had been established by the time of the Prospectus and none of them had contributed any revenue to Coventree prior to the occurrence of the market disruption on August 13, 2007. To the contrary, the Chapter Two initiatives were expected to give rise to substantial costs before they were fully implemented.

[255] Coventree submits that one of the reasons why changes in its securitization business were not material to investors is because Coventree had changed its strategic

focus and was moving forward with the Chapter Two initiatives. We do not accept that submission. In our view, based on the disclosure in the Prospectus, investors in Coventree would have been focused on its successful securitization business which had generated the substantial financial results described in the Prospectus. That is confirmed by the Roadshow Presentation that highlighted, among other factors, Coventree's "solid financial performance" and "strong core business to fund growth" (see paragraph 259 of these reasons). The Chapter Two initiatives were acknowledged by Coventree to be "experiments" and, in our view, had not been sufficiently advanced to form a significant reason why investors would purchase shares under the Prospectus.

[256] Coventree was in the securitization business. Its financial results at the time of the Prospectus were primarily derived from the credit arbitrage business, although its focus going forward was shifting to the traditional securitization business, to providing third-party conduit administration and to the Chapter Two initiatives. Allan joined Coventree on January 22, 2007, in part, because of the expected shift in focus to the traditional securitization business. There is no doubt, however, that Coventree's financial success to the date of the Prospectus was based on its securitization business and, in particular, credit arbitrage.

[257] *In our view, a reader of the Prospectus would not have fully understood the significance of credit arbitrage to Coventree's business and financial success and would not have known that Coventree considered that business to be dead or dying or that Coventree expected in the future to carry out only occasional, one-off credit arbitrage transactions. The Prospectus does not say that.*

[258] Further, if that expectation was true, it would mean that Coventree was for all intents and purposes out of the credit arbitrage business. That itself raises a question whether appropriate disclosure was made in the Prospectus.

...

Risk Factor Disclosure

[267] There is no question that the Prospectus contains extensive risk factor disclosure that addresses many of the events that ultimately occurred and are relevant to this proceeding. In particular, the Prospectus discloses the following risks affecting Coventree and Coventree sponsored conduits that are relevant for our purposes:

(a) "liquidity risk (inability to sell financial instruments or other assets in the market in the ordinary course)" (Prospectus, at p. 58);
(b) "market disruption risk (the risk that difficulties affecting one or more other financial institutions causes systemic repercussions to the financial system including the inability to roll funding)" (Prospectus, at p. 58);
(c) the risk that "[i]f the supply of available ABCP exceeds the demand for such securities from investors in Canada, this market will no longer provide a reliable funding source for Coventree sponsored conduits" (Prospectus, at p. 58) and the risk that "[w]ith less investor demand, the Company would have no assurances that the conduits the Company sponsors could raise funds in a timely or economical manner and would be forced to limit their ABCP issuance accordingly" (Prospectus, at p. 59);

(d) the risk of a market disruption that "would not only prevent conduits sponsored by Coventree from issuing new paper necessary to acquire new deals but also could prevent the conduits from rolling their outstanding ABCP" (Prospectus, at p. 59);
(e) the risk that "[a]lthough Coventree has no legal obligation to fund the conduits to buy back ABCP from investors in the event of a disruption, Coventree's reputation in the industry and on going ability to access the capital markets could be severely adversely impacted if it did not or could not do so" (Prospectus, at p. 59);
(f) "[t]he potentially limited size of the ECP [extendible commercial paper] market in Canada," and the fact that the issue of extendible commercial paper "has been a major driver of Coventree's growth to date" (Prospectus, at p. 59);
(g) the risk that "a relatively high percentage of the outstanding ABCP issued by its conduits has been purchased by a small number of ABCP investors," including the fact that, "at certain times, a substantial minority percentage of the securities issued by its conduits has been purchased by one investor, the Caisse" (Prospectus, at p. 60);
(h) the risk that "[i]f the spread between CDOR and the interest rates payable on the ABCP issued by the Company's conduits widens, the Company's revenues can be materially decreased" (Prospectus, at p. 60);
(i) the risk that securitization transactions executed in Coventree sponsored conduits "often involve buying long-term assets that typically pay a fixed interest rate and funding these assets with short-term floating rate ABCP" (Prospectus, at p. 62);
(j) the risk of increased reliance by investors on Coventree because the ABCP market and the assets funded by the conduits are generally opaque to investors (Prospectus, at p. 63); and
(k) the risk of reliance on DBRS as sole provider of rating services to Coventree (Prospectus, at p. 64).

[268] Clearly, the risk factor disclosure in the Prospectus is extensive and comprehensive. As a result, investors in Coventree shares offered under the Prospectus cannot validly take the position that they were unaware of the material risks to which Coventree's business was subject. At the same time, however, disclosure of a risk to which a business is subject is quite different than the actual occurrence of an event reflected in the risk factor. When an event that is material to the business actually occurs and gives rise to a material change, an issuer will have a disclosure obligation regardless of whether the risk giving rise to the material change had been previously identified and disclosed. The previous disclosure of risk factors does not affect or qualify an issuer's obligation to disclose material changes, when they occur, in accordance with section 75 of the Act.

(c) Conclusion

[269] The disclosure deficiencies discussed under "Other Prospectus Disclosure Issues" (commencing at paragraph 216 of these reasons) made it much more difficult for public shareholders and potential investors to fully understand and assess the significance to Coventree's business of the subsequent events and developments discussed in these reasons.

QUESTIONS

1. What are the prospectus disclosure deficiencies identified by the commission in the judgment above?
2. How does the commission distinguish what was or was not material to the prospectus in this case?
3. Does the fact that the judgment relates to the asset-based commercial paper market matter to the reasoning on prospectus disclosure and materials fact?
4. The commission addresses disclosure issues that go beyond the issues raised by OSC staff, finding deficiencies. In your view, does the panel have the authority to determine prospectus disclosure issues where the allegations have not been brought forward by staff? Why or why not?

XI. FUTURE-ORIENTED FINANCIAL INFORMATION

Financial forecasting can be included in the prospectus, with the agreement of the regulator, but can be problematic in terms of both the content and the appropriate cautions provided. Future-oriented financial information (FOFI) should include a cautionary note of the risk that actual performance may vary considerably from the forecast. The issuer must update the forecast where there is a change in either the underlying assumptions or external events such as market changes that cause the issuer to revise its forecast. One difficulty with forecasting is that it may create incentives to inflate projections and leave investors vulnerable to unnecessary losses.

Securities laws provide a remedy for a misrepresentation in a final prospectus. Such remedies are not generally applicable to a preliminary prospectus because it is viewed as a draft only, with the issuer having the opportunity to revise it before the securities are sold. Any right to prior damages could deter issuers from ever circulating a preliminary prospectus. The provisions regarding final prospectuses deem purchasers to have relied on the misrepresentation for purposes of a remedy under the statute, removing the hurdle of having to prove a causal link between the misrepresentation and the investment decision (see e.g. OSA, s 130(1)).

The following judgment deals with the failure to correct a financial forecast during the distribution period. Issuers do not have to include forecasts in their prospectus, but when they do, they are subject to standards aimed at eliciting as full, true, and plain disclosure as possible. This case was the first securities class action ever to go to trial, and the Ontario Superior Court awarded more than $10 million in damages, interest, and costs to holders of 5 million shares; however, the judgment was overturned on appeal.

Kerr v Danier Leather Inc
2007 SCC 44, [2007] 3 SCR 331

BINNIE J (McLachlin CJ and Bastarache, LeBel, Deschamps, Fish, Abella, Charron, and Rothstein JJ concurring):

[1] This appeal raises questions about the continuous disclosure obligations of an issuer seeking to sell its shares to the public by a prospectus governed by the Ontario

Securities Act, RSO 1990, c. S.5. Purchasers under a prospectus are given a statutory right of action if the prospectus or any amendment contains a misrepresentation against the issuer and officers of the issuer who signed the prospectus.

...

[6] The warm days of spring are not a blessing for everyone, it seems. As temperatures rise, the sales of leather clothing can lag even in otherwise prospering leather goods retail stores. The downturn in sales may simply reflect the weather and indicate nothing negative about the strength of the underlying business, as turned out to be the case here. Nevertheless, about two weeks *after* closing, the respondents did issue a revised forecast indicating that Danier would fall short of the sales and net income figures in the original forecast. Danier's share price dropped by about 22 percent. It took until August 2000 for the shares to get back to their issue price. By then, Danier's business had grown substantially.

[7] A number of purchasers had sold their new shares soon after the announcement and lost money. The appellants then initiated a class action against the respondents for failure to disclose material information, i.e., the disappointing intraquarterly results. They argued that the prospectus contained a misrepresentation on the closing date (May 20), because even though the year-end sales forecast was reasonable on the filing date (May 6), lagging sales thereafter rendered it misleading to management's knowledge at the date of closing. The respondents, they argued, "omi[tted] to state a material fact [that is, lagging sales] that is ... necessary to make a statement [that is, the sales forecast in the prospectus] not misleading in the light of the circumstances in which it was made," and this constituted an actionable misrepresentation within the meaning of ss. 1 and 130 of the Act.

...

[10] In 1997, Danier decided to go public. In preparation for its IPO, Danier filed with the Ontario Securities Commission ("OSC"), three preliminary prospectuses, each of which contained a forecast. The forecast in the April 6 preliminary prospectus was dated April 2, 1998, and was included, unchanged, in the (final) prospectus, which was receipted by the OSC on May 6, 1998 (herein "prospectus forecast").

...

[13] During the week before closing, Wortsman asked Tatoff to assemble and analyse the financial results for the first half of the fourth quarter. The underwriters had not requested a due diligence review, but Wortsman thought that this "was the prudent course of action to take" (R.R., at p. 39). Tatoff prepared an analysis as of May 16, and Wortsman admitted that he received the results "certainly before closing" (R.R., at p. 41). These results were worse than the results projected in the store budgets (which were the basis of the sales forecast). In particular, as of May 16, Danier's actual fourth quarter revenue was 24 percent behind projections. Moreover, the company had as of May 16 posted a fourth-quarter net loss of $240,000 instead of the projected (as of May 16) fourth-quarter net earnings of $259,000. Nonetheless, Wortsman and Tatoff testified that, at closing, they still believed that by year end Danier would achieve or exceed the prospectus forecast. As they explained, store budgets are "front-end loaded." Adjusting for that fact, the gross revenue shortfall as of May 16 was really only about $700,000, they said, which put the net earnings disappointment in a better light. With two major sales promotions planned for the second half of the fourth quarter, Wortsman and Tatoff thought that Danier would at least make up this shortfall.

...

[16] Accordingly, on June 4, 1998, Danier announced in a press release and a material change report that it had revised downwards its forecast for the 1998 fiscal year. The company advised that, "[d]ue to unseasonably warm weather in most regions of the country with the exception of Vancouver, the company believes that it will fall short of the previous sales and net income forecast" (A.R., at p. 931). …

• • •

[18] The market quickly demonstrated the "materiality" of this information. Prior to June 4, the company's shares had been trading above their issue price of $11.25, but the share price dropped immediately upon release of this revised forecast. The trial judge found that the market had fully absorbed the revision (and the share price stabilization activities carried out by the underwriters) by June 10, when the shares closed at $8.90. The appellant investors concluded that Danier had sat on the bad news to ensure the success of its IPO, and that those who had purchased in ignorance were entitled to compensation.

[19] However, in the remaining weeks of the fourth quarter, Danier's sales improved significantly. The weather cooled, and the company held a successful 50 percent discount promotion. In the end, the trial judge found that Danier "substantially achieved" the prospectus forecast.

[20] On November 13, 1998, an action for prospectus misrepresentation was commenced under s. 130(1) of the Act, claiming that the results of the May 16 analysis should have been released before the IPO closed. On December 3, 2002, the action was certified as a class proceeding with the "class" defined as:

> (a) Those persons in Canada who purchased shares of Danier Leather Inc. in the distribution under its initial public offering which closed on May 20, 1998, and who continued to hold those shares on June 4, 1998, but not including [the defendants and certain persons associated with the defendants].

James Frederick Durst was appointed as the sole representative plaintiff for this class. …

• • •

[38] … An issuer has no similar express obligation to amend a prospectus or to publicize and file a report for the modification of material *facts* occurring after a receipt for a prospectus is obtained. That is where the legislature has drawn the line … . Imposition of civil liability under s. 130(1) for an omission to do what the legislature as a matter of policy has declined to require in s. 57(1) would simply be to substitute the court's view of policy for that adopted by the legislature. The distinction between "material change" and "material fact" is deliberate and policy-based, as explained by a former chairman of the OSC:

> The term "material fact" is necessary when an issuer is publishing a disclosure document, such as a prospectus or a take-over bid circular, where all material information concerning the issuer *at a point in time* is published in one document which is convenient to the investor. The term "material change" is limited to a change in the business, operations or capital of the issuer. *This is an attempt to relieve reporting issuers of the obligation to continually interpret external political, economic and social developments as they affect the affairs of the issuer*, unless the external change will result in a change in the business, operations or capital of the issuer, in which case, timely disclosure of the change must be made. [Emphasis added.]

(Remarks of Peter J. Dey concerning disclosure under the *Securities Act* made to securities lawyers in Calgary and Toronto on June 7 and 9, 1983.) …

[39] Firstly, if an issuer has fully complied with its regulatory obligations under ss. 56 to 58 of the Act it would be contrary to the scheme of the Act, and to the intent of the Ontario legislature reflected therein, to find civil liability against an issuer under s. 130(1) for failing to disclose post-filing information that does not amount to a material change.

[40] Secondly, the statutory definition of "misrepresentation" uses the past tense in the phrase "in the light of the circumstances in which it was made." The appellants say the past tense "contemplates that a statement may need correction later" (A.F., at para. 51). In my view, however, this past tense simply signals that the relevant date for assessing the accuracy of a statement is the effective date when the statement *was* made, i.e., the date the prospectus (or an amendment) was filed.

[41] Thirdly, the appellants rely on the phrase "if it was a misrepresentation at the time of purchase" but this reliance too, in my view, is misplaced. These are words of limitation designed to ensure that s. 130(1) does not impose civil liability for a representation that had become cured or corrected at the date of purchase. Suppose, for example, that Danier owned an important patent on a process for working leather, and trumpeted this fact in its prospectus, inadvertently failing to disclose that a competitor had mounted a serious court challenge to the patent's validity. The Act gives the purchasers the benefit of "deemed" reliance. The existence of a serious court challenge would be a material fact. Yet if the challenge were settled or discontinued and the patent thus vindicated *before* the time of purchase, why should the omission attract damages or rescission? The answer, according to the language of s. 130(1), is that it does not.

[42] The appellants' reliance on the common law as a guide to the interpretation of s. 130(1) is also unconvincing. The common law does not require a person selling shares to issue a prospectus. It does not define or distinguish between material facts and material changes. It does not create a scheme of compelled disclosure with its own requirements and limits on those requirements. It is the Act and not the common law that settles the policy.

…

[47] It almost goes without saying that poor intra-quarterly results may *reflect* a material change in business operations. A company that has, for example, restructured its operations may experience poor intra-quarterly results because of this restructuring, but it is the restructuring and not the results themselves that would amount to a material change and thus trigger the disclosure obligation. Additionally, poor intra-quarterly results may motivate a company to implement a change in its business, operations or capital in an effort to improve performance. Again, though, the disclosure obligation would be triggered by the change in the business, operations or capital, and not by the results themselves.

[48] In the present case, there is no evidence that Danier made a change in its business, operations or capital during the period of distribution. It is not disputed that the revenue shortfall as of May 16 was caused by the unusually hot weather, a factor external to the issuer. Consequently, Danier experienced no material change that required disclosure and did not breach s. 57(1).

C. Did the Forecast Contain an Implied Representation of Objective Reasonableness?

[49] The trial judge found that the forecast contained an implied representation of objective reasonableness that extended until closing on May 20. The Court of Appeal disagreed, holding that the forecast contained no implied representation of objective reasonableness in fact, and that none is implied as a matter of law. In my view, as a matter of *fact*, the forecast *did* carry an implied representation of objective reasonableness rooted in the language of the prospectus, but this implied representation extended only until the prospectus was receipted on May 6.

[50] The forecast was prepared as of April 2, and in the prospectus it is stated that "[t]he Forecast is based on assumptions that reflect management's best judgment of the most probable set of economic conditions and the Company's planned course of action as of April 2, 1998" (Final Prospectus, at p. 26). Likewise, the Auditors' Report, dated April 6, advises that "the assumptions developed by management are suitably supported and consistent with the plans of the Company, and provide a reasonable basis for the forecast" (*Ibid.*). The prospectus further states that the assumptions were "considered reasonable by the Company at the time of preparation of the forecast" and that "[t]he Forecast has been prepared using generally accepted accounting principles" (*Ibid.*, p. 27). Significant assumptions are then listed. That is enough, it seems to me, for potential investors to infer not just that the forecast represents management's best judgment (as the Court of Appeal held), but also that management's judgment is based on facts and assumptions that reasonable business people in possession of the same information as Danier's management would reasonably regard as reliable for the purpose of a forecast.

[51] The forecast was not, however, put forward as objectively reasonable as of May 20 or, for that matter, as of any date after May 6. The prospectus stated that "[t]he financial reports issued by the Company to its shareholders during the forecast period will contain either a statement that there are no significant changes to be made to the Forecast or a revised forecast accompanied by explanations of significant changes" (Final Prospectus, at p. 26), but no financial reports were issued to shareholders during the period of distribution. The prospectus did *not* promise that the forecast would be updated if and as soon as conditions changed. Potential investors should therefore have recognized that the forecast was just a snapshot of the company's prospects as of May 6. Accordingly, the trial judge, having found the forecast to be objectively reasonable as of May 6, erred in going on to evaluate the objective reasonableness of the forecast at the date of closing, and assessing damages for its perceived deficiencies as of that date. …

[52] The respondents invoke the Business Judgment Rule. The Court of Appeal held that the trial judge had paid insufficient deference to management's expertise in forecasting sales based on years of hands-on retail experience. At para. 165, the Court of Appeal said: The trial judge's point of view is necessarily a retrospective one. By contrast, the point of view of Wortsman and Tatoff was a prospective one, informed by the circumstances as they were on May 20. Their view might have been an optimistic one, but it was not unreasonable in the sense that it was outside a range of reasonable views of Danier's situation at that time. Accordingly, in that court's view, there was no breach of any implied assertion of "objective reasonableness" as of May 20. Thus, even if (which they doubted) there was such an implied assertion, no follow-up disclosure obligation was triggered.

For the reasons already stated, I accept that as of May 6 (the date of receipt) there was an implied assertion by the issuer of objective reasonableness. The trial judge found the assertion to be true as of May 6. End of argument.

[53] However, even if the situation is to be considered as of May 20, as contended for by the appellants (a faulty approach, as already stated), the trial judge still erred in finding that the implied assertion was incorrect as of the closing date. The respondents' expert had testified that the forecast remained objectively reasonable as of May 20, and neither of the appellants' experts testified to the contrary. The trial judge failed to provide any persuasive reasons to reject the unchallenged expert testimony on that point. His finding in that respect "can properly be characterized as 'unreasonable' or 'unsupported by the evidence'": *H.L. v. Canada (Attorney General)*, [2005] 1 SCR 401, 2005 SCC 25, at para. 56.

[54] On the broader legal proposition, however, I agree with the appellants that while forecasting is a matter of business judgment, disclosure is a matter of legal obligation. The Business Judgment Rule is a concept well-developed in the context of *business* decisions but should not be used to qualify or undermine the duty of disclosure. The Business Judgment Rule was well stated by Weiler JA in *Maple Leaf Foods Inc. v. Schneider Corp.* (1998), 42 OR (3d) 177 (CA):

> The court looks to see that the directors made a reasonable decision not a perfect decision. Provided the decision taken is within a range of reasonableness, the court ought not to substitute its opinion for that of the board even though subsequent events may have cast doubt on the board's determination. As long as the directors have selected one of several reasonable alternatives, deference is accorded to the board's decision. … [Emphasis deleted; p. 192.]

[55] I do not agree with the respondents that the Business Judgment Rule, thus formulated, applies here. This is not to say that the expertise of Wortsman and Tatoff was not relevant to an analysis of the events leading up to the May 20 closing. If, contrary to my view, a disclosure obligation had arisen as the appellants contend, management would have been required to disclose the fourth quarter slump in sales but management could have announced with confidence that in its business judgment the forecast would nevertheless be met by the company's financial year end. Potential investors would have the current facts and might accept or not management's business judgment about the future outcome. However, the disclosure requirements under the Act are not to be subordinated to the exercise of business judgment. I do not believe the Court of Appeal intended to say otherwise, although its treatment of the "objective reasonableness" issue arguably had that effect in this case. It is for the legislature and the courts, not business management, to set the legal disclosure requirements.

• • •

[58] The traditional justifications for the rule argue against its application here. It is said, truly enough, that judges are less expert than managers in making business decisions. Moreover, business decisions often involve choosing from amongst a range of alternatives. In order to maximize returns for shareholders, managers should be free to take reasonable risks without having to worry that their business choices will later be second-guessed by judges. These justifications—based on *relative expertise*, and on the need to support *reasonable risk-taking*—do not apply to disclosure decisions. Agreement with the appellants

> on this point, while it is an important point, does not change the outcome of the appeal. The appellants' argument had already suffered two fatal blows before arriving at this point. The appeal on liability must still be dismissed.

Kerr v Danier introduces a number of key issues in the prospectus distribution process, such as whether a forecast is a fact; whether a significant change in financial forecast is always a material change; how assessment of the reasonableness of a forecast is dependent on the forecaster having used reasonable care and skill; and the question of how long the requirement to disclose material facts in a prospectus process remains.

The court's reasoning is further discussed in Chapter 10, Civil Liability. See also the discussion in Chapter 6 on NI 51-102, *Continuous Disclosure Obligations* (as amended effective 17 November 2015) in respect of FOFI.

In *Tucci v Smart Technologies Inc*, 2013 ONSC 802, a certification decision of the Ontario Superior Court of Justice, Justice Perell excluded investors who purchased securities of the defendant on the secondary market from a proposed class of investors pursuing claims for prospectus misrepresentation under s 130(1) of the *Securities Act* (Ontario). The decision discusses why s 130(1) does not apply to secondary market purchasers even if the secondary market purchase was made during the "period of distribution" of the prospectus offering, and the court orders that the proposed class definition be revised to exclude those purchasers. Smart Technologies Inc had made an initial public offering (IPO) of shares in Canada and the United States, and as the shares began trading on the TSX and NASDAQ on the same date, certain secondary market purchases were made during the period of distribution of the IPO. In a proposed class action, the plaintiff, a primary market purchaser, sought damages under s 130 of the Act and equivalent provisions of other Canadian securities legislation, alleging that the prospectus contained misrepresentations that became apparent when corrective disclosure was later made. Justice Perell concluded that existing precedents, including the BC Court of Appeal decision in *Pearson v Boliden Ltd*, 2002 BCCA 624, confirm that the remedies provided under s 130(1) are available exclusively to primary market purchasers.

QUESTIONS

1. Can a financial forecast be a fact that can be misrepresented?
2. Given the uncertainty inherent in FOFI, why would an issuer include such information in its prospectus?
3. How did the Supreme Court of Canada use the business judgment rule in coming to its decision?
4. Why do you think secondary market purchasers have been excluded from class action proceedings for violations of prospectus disclosure requirements?

XII. PROSPECTUS REQUIREMENTS IN A SECONDARY OFFERING

A prospectus is required where there is a sale of previously issued securities by a person distributing within the meaning of securities legislation, where the person has not received an exemption as discussed in Chapter 5. This requirement includes control persons, as illustrated in the following provisions of the OSA (s 1(1)):

"control person" means,

(a) a person or company who holds a sufficient number of the voting rights attached to all outstanding voting securities of an issuer to affect materially the control of the issuer, and, if a person or company holds more than 20 per cent of the voting rights attached to all outstanding voting securities of an issuer, the person or company is deemed, in the absence of evidence to the contrary, to hold a sufficient number of the voting rights to affect materially the control of the issuer, or

(b) each person or company in a combination of persons or companies, acting in concert by virtue of an agreement, arrangement, commitment or understanding, which holds in total a sufficient number of the voting rights attached to all outstanding voting securities of an issuer to affect materially the control of the issuer, and, if a combination of persons or companies holds more than 20 per cent of the voting rights attached to all outstanding voting securities of an issuer, the combination of persons or companies is deemed, in the absence of evidence to the contrary, to hold a sufficient number of the voting rights to affect materially the control of the issuer;

"distribution," where used in relation to trading in securities, means, …

(c) a trade in previously issued securities of an issuer from the holdings of any control person,

• • •

"trade" or "trading" includes,

(a) any sale or disposition of a security for valuable consideration, whether the terms of payment be on margin, instalment or otherwise, but does not include a purchase of a security or, except as provided in clause (d), a transfer, pledge or encumbrance of securities for the purpose of giving collateral for a debt made in good faith,

(b) any participation as a trader in any transaction in a security through the facilities of any exchange or quotation and trade reporting system,

(b.1) entering into a derivative or making a material amendment to, terminating, assigning, selling or otherwise acquiring or disposing of a derivative, or

(b.2) a novation of a derivative, other than a novation with a clearing agency,

(c) any receipt by a registrant of an order to buy or sell a security,

(d) any transfer, pledge or encumbrancing of securities of an issuer from the holdings of any person or company or combination of persons or companies described in clause (c) of the definition of "distribution" for the purpose of giving collateral for a debt made in good faith, and

(e) any act, advertisement, solicitation, conduct or negotiation directly or indirectly in furtherance of any of the foregoing;

In this context, securities legislation requires control persons distributing their securities to file a prospectus. Control person includes the person or group of persons who have sufficient control over voting rights of the issuer to materially affect the control of that issuer. As the definition above indicates, a person or a group of persons acting together, holding more than 20 percent of the voting rights attached to all outstanding voting securities of an issuer is deemed, in the absence of evidence to the contrary, to hold sufficient voting rights to materially affect the control of the issuer. A sale by persons in control is considered a distribution because of the control person or group's ability to influence the issuer, with the resultant potential risk of improper disclosure in order to enhance the value of the security. The control person or group may be selling a large percentage of shares, which can affect market price. Moreover, the exit of a controlling person has a signalling effect in the market in terms of information that might be possessed by the control person or the decision to remove investment or influence from the issuer. Hence enhanced disclosure requirements are aimed at reducing information asymmetries.

When a prospectus is required in a trade of previously issued securities, the issuer and its directors and officers must supply the information and certificates that allow the holder to sell the securities. Where the issuer is not cooperating, the regulator has the authority to require the issuer to provide the required information. Alternatively, the regulator can determine that the securityholder selling the securities need not comply with the statutory requirements, where satisfied such a waiver is not likely to prejudice any person or company (see e.g. OSA, s 64(2); ASA, s 122(2); NSSA, s 69(2)). Similarly, where a person or company proposing to make a distribution of previously issued securities of an issuer is unable to obtain any or all of the signatures to the certificates required by the statute or regulations, the director may, if satisfied that all reasonable efforts have been made to comply and where no person or company is likely to be prejudicially affected by such failure to comply, make an order waiving any of the provisions, subject to such conditions as the director considers proper (OSA, s 64; ASA, s 122; NSSA, s 69).

XIII. REFUSAL TO ISSUE A RECEIPT FOR A PROSPECTUS

When a prospectus is filed, the authorized regulatory decision-maker ("the director") must issue a receipt if the prospectus complies with the statutory requirements, unless it appears to the director that it is not in the public interest to do so, or the director determines that the prospectus contains a statement, promise, estimate, or forecast that is misleading, false, or deceptive; contains a misrepresentation; or an unconscionable consideration has been paid or given for promotional purposes or for the acquisition of property (see e.g. OSA, s 61(1)).

The director can also refuse to issue the receipt if it appears that the proceeds received from the sale of securities to be paid to the treasury of the issuer, together with other resources of the issuer, will be insufficient to accomplish the purposes stated in the prospectus. Resources include financial resources and people. If a sufficient number of the directors and officers of the issuer do not have relevant knowledge and experience, the securities regulator may conclude that the human and other resources are insufficient to accomplish these purposes, unless it is satisfied that the issuer has contracted to obtain the knowledge and experience from others.

A receipt may be refused where the issuer cannot reasonably be expected to be financially responsible in the conduct of its business. A receipt may also be refused where the past conduct of the issuer or an officer, a director, a promoter, or a controlling securityholder affords reasonable grounds for belief that the business of the issuer will not be conducted with integrity and in the best interests of its securityholders. For a full list of instances in which the director may refuse to issue a receipt for a prospectus, see NI 41-101. Securities laws also set out a list of reasons a receipt may be refused; OSA, s 61 is illustrative.

> 61. *Refusal of receipt*
>
> (2) The Director shall not issue a receipt for a prospectus or an amendment to a prospectus if it appears to the Director that,
>
> (a) the prospectus or any document required to be filed with it,
>
> (i) does not comply in any substantial respect with any of the requirements of this Act or the regulations,

(ii) contains any statement, promise, estimate or forward-looking information that is misleading, false or deceptive, or

(iii) contains a misrepresentation;

(b) an unconscionable consideration has been paid or given or is intended to be paid or given for any services or promotional purposes or for the acquisition of property;

(c) the aggregate of,

(i) the proceeds from the sale of the securities under the prospectus that are to be paid into the treasury of the issuer, and

(ii) the other resources of the issuer,

is insufficient to accomplish the purpose of the issue stated in the prospectus;

(d) the issuer cannot reasonably be expected to be financially responsible in the conduct of its business because of the financial condition of,

(i) the issuer,

(ii) any of the issuer's officers, directors, promoters, or control persons, or

(iii) the investment fund manager of the issuer or any of the investment fund manager's officers, directors or control persons;

(e) the business of the issuer may not be conducted with integrity and in the best interests of the securityholders of the issuer because of the past conduct of,

(i) the issuer,

(ii) any of the issuer's officers, directors, promoters, or control persons, or

(iii) the investment fund manager of the issuer or any of the investment fund manager's officers, directors or control persons;

(f) a person or company that has prepared or certified any part of the prospectus, or that is named as having prepared or certified a report or valuation used in connection with the prospectus, is not acceptable;

(g) an escrow or pooling agreement in the form that the Director considers necessary or advisable with respect to the securities has not been entered into; or

(h) adequate arrangements have not been made for the holding in trust of the proceeds payable to the issuer from the sale of the securities pending the distribution of the securities.

Hearing

(3) The Director shall not refuse to issue a receipt under subsection (1) or (2) without giving the person or company who filed the prospectus an opportunity to be heard.

Note that OSA, s 61(3) specifies that the regulator cannot refuse to issue the receipt without engaging in some due process.

In *Re Loki Resources Ltd* (1984), 7 OSCB 583, the Ontario Securities Commission refused to issue a receipt because the proceeds of the issue and the resources of the issuer were insufficient to accomplish the purpose of the issue. The Commission held as follows:

[1] Part XIV of the Act provides in section 52(2) that "(a) preliminary prospectus and a prospectus may be filed in accordance with this Part to enable the issuer to become a reporting issuer, notwithstanding the fact that no distribution is contemplated."

[2] The filings which lead to this hearing raise the question whether it is in the public interest to issue receipts for such prospectuses where the issuer currently has no resources, properties or prospects and has no present intention to acquire any such. That question is answered in the negative.

[3] … [T]he Issuer had been inactive since its incorporation, currently had no resources, properties or prospects and that it had no present intention to acquire any exploration or development resource property.

As noted earlier in this chapter, the concerns raised by the regulator in refusing to issue a receipt in *Loki* have subsequently been addressed by the Capital Pool Companies Operating Agreement.

In *Tricor Holdings* (1988), 11 OSCB 4059, the Ontario Securities Commission upheld the director's right to refuse a receipt where there was evidence that the issuer had previously been controlled by a convicted felon and only circumstantial evidence that the convicted individual continued to control the company. The commission held as follows (at 39-43):

> In our view it is and has always been of first importance to restrict participation in the distribution and trading of securities to persons who are honest and of good repute. Securities laws are intended primarily to protect the public from fraud and the manipulation of markets. The scheme of the Ontario statute and regulations, in item 26 of the prospectus form and the accompanying instructions, clearly places the onus upon an issuer of securities to establish the identity of the persons whose beneficial shareholdings put them in a position of control. If the Director believes the persons so identified to be unacceptable, he must establish reasonable grounds for his belief. Such grounds are to be found in the past conduct of such persons.
>
> Where the issuer is unable to identify the beneficial owners, the Commission has stated the view (Interpretation Note 2—[1983] OSCB 4536) "that generally a receipt should not be issued for a prospectus if the issuer is unable to identify the individual, if any, who controls a principal securityholder of that issuer. Issuers are therefore advised that they should organize themselves in a manner which will enable them to obtain and disclose information concerning principal securityholders. If, however, the issuer has exercised reasonable efforts to obtain the information concerning the principal securityholder and has been unable to do so, the Commission may, in appropriate circumstances, issue a receipt for the prospectus and may exercise its powers to deny access to Ontario capital markets to the principal securityholder which has not disclosed the required information." ... It is our view that resort need not be had to Interpretation Note 2 and would be inappropriate. We have concluded, on the balance of the probabilities, that the identity of the person in control of Tricor has been established and that person is Irving Kott. ...
>
> The other evidence adduced at the hearing—the collateral circumstances connecting Irving Kott with Tricor—supports our conclusion but we did not find it necessary to rely upon it. We do not say that in other cases the Commission would be wrong to base its conclusions on such evidence; given the mechanisms of modern securities markets, the multiplicity of jurisdictions and the shelter of secrecy laws such evidence may be all that can be found and the public interest may compel reliance upon it .... We accordingly confirmed the Director's decision to refuse a receipt for the Tricor prospectus and denied Tricor's application for revocation of the cease trading order.

The statutes contain due process requirements. For example, the director cannot refuse to issue a receipt without giving the person or company who filed the prospectus an opportunity to be heard. It may also refer a matter to the commission for determination where it appears to the director that a prospectus raises a material question involving the public interest or a novel question of interpretation that might result in the director's refusing to issue a receipt (OSA, s 61(4); ASA, ss 30(1), 120(1), 120(3); Nfld SA, ss 62(1), 127(1); NSSA, s 66(4); SSA, ss 134, 135.1). In such a case, the director states the question being referred to in writing, setting out the facts on which the question is based. Then the question, together with any additional material, is lodged by the director with the secretary of the commission, and a copy is served by the secretary on any interested person or company. The commission, after giving the parties an opportunity to be heard, determines the question and refers the matter back to the director for final consideration. The commission's determination is generally binding on the director, subject to any court order (OSA, s 61(8); NSSA, s 66(8); SSA, s 60.1).

The following excerpt from *YBM Magnex International*, discussed earlier in this chapter, provides insights into how regulators exercise their power to issue, or refuse to issue, a receipt for a prospectus.

YBM Magnex International Inc
(2003), 26 OSCB 5285

[71] Numerous meetings and conference calls were held throughout the months of June and July 1997. Staff met with Price Waterhouse and reviewed various matters with them. By the end of June, staff advised the underwriters' and company's counsel that they were not prepared to issue a receipt for a final prospectus until YBM's income statement was confirmed by a "Big Six" accounting firm. Staff were not pursuing the rumours and innuendo surrounding YBM, but wanted to confirm issues of related-party transactions. In early July, staff was insisting on seeing actual customer lists for magnets and oil products, classified by location and type of customer (end user versus distributor).

[72] With some reluctance, on July 23, 1997, YBM advised staff that D&T had been retained and had commenced work on a full audit. Staff met with counsel and D&T the next day to discuss the procedures to be undertaken by D&T and staff's requirement of a clean audit opinion. Staff expressed its concerns as to (a) the existence and identity of customers and end users; (b) the tracing of cash receipts and revenue; and (c) the geographic location of customers, which could not be verified to date.

[73] D&T rendered an unqualified audit opinion on YBM's 1996 financial statements on October 13, 1997. On November 4, D&T, Peterson, Gatti, and YBM's and underwriters' counsel met with senior members of staff to discuss the audit. During a discussion on the timing of the receipt for the Final Prospectus, Wilder informed staff that YBM faced an $8 million penalty pursuant to the subordinate convertible notes in the event that a receipt was not issued by November 17. Staff then asked D&T and Gatti over 70 detailed questions about the audit. Peterson responded to questions about the Board's involvement in the audit process.

[74] On November 12, YBM's Board of Directors approved the final prospectus by written resolution. The next day, YBM filed a material change report in respect of D&T's audit and the restated financial statements, particularly the adjustments to geographic sales information. The underwriters held their "bring down" due diligence session soon thereafter. On November 17, the certificates were signed and the Final Prospectus was filed.

[75] The Commission issued a receipt for the Final Prospectus on November 20, after five months of review by Market Operations. During the course of the prospectus review, Enforcement advised YBM that they had opened an investigation file on YBM. The final prospectus disclosed that as part of its continuing review, staff of the Commission requested certain source documentation underlying YBM's disclosure record in connection with the 1996 financial statements. The final prospectus disclosed most but not all of the recommendations made in the Report of the Special Committee. Apart from the AIF, this was the only additional disclosure relating to the Special Committee.

...

> [600] We do not intend to review the decision to receipt the prospectus. That is not the purpose of this hearing. However, we have some comments with respect to the process.
>
> [601] The fundamental concern was one of fairness. How could the issuer persuade the Commission to make a favourable decision when it would not have access to the confidential information? Subsection 61(4) provides that where a prospectus raises a material question involving the public interest that might result in the director refusing a receipt, the director may refer the question to the Commission for determination. This hearing is *inter partes* and as such can be utilized in appropriate cases. Subsection 61(1) provides for no receipt if it is not in the public interest to issue a receipt.
>
> [602] The denial of a receipt does not invoke the same broad principles as the right to make full answer and defence in a section 127 case. Both require devotion to the principles of fairness, but the statutory framework within which fairness is to operate must be considered, and while rare, a limit must necessarily be implied. What is essential is substantial fairness to the company which may be accomplished by providing as much information as possible without necessarily disclosing the precise information or sources. This balances the requirements to the company of fairness without adversely affecting the scheme of the Act, which has as a paramount objective investor protection.

In March 2012, the CSA issued Staff Notice 41-307, *Corporate Finance Prospectus Guidance, Concerns regarding an issuer's financial condition and the sufficiency of proceeds from a prospectus offering*, which is aimed at alerting issuers and their advisers about potential concerns by CSA staff regarding the financial condition of an issuer and/or the sufficiency of proceeds in the context of a prospectus offering. The staff notice applies to all prospectus reviews, regardless of whether the offering is an IPO, a new issue, or a secondary offering. The notice describes issues that have arisen in past prospectus reviews. The guidance specifically applies to issuers that have short-term liquidity concerns and/or offerings that do not appear to be raising sufficient proceeds. The decision-maker will not issue a receipt for a prospectus where it appears that the prospectus inadequately discloses an issuer's financial condition and going-concern risk, or where there is adequate disclosure about the issuer's financial condition, but it appears that either the sufficiency-of-proceeds receipt refusal provision is applicable or that it is not in the public interest to issue the receipt. The staff notice expressly states that it recognizes the importance of capital formation in Canada, and that the guidance is not intended to inhibit capital raising through a prospectus offering other than where there are significant investor protection concerns.

Staff Notice 41-307 notes that consideration of an issuer's financial condition is a critical part of every prospectus review. A prospectus must contain clear disclosure on how the issuer intends to use the proceeds raised in the offering, as well as disclosure of the issuer's financial condition, including any liquidity concerns. This disclosure is important to investors because it provides warnings about significant risks that the issuer is facing or may face in the short term and may help investors avoid or minimize negative consequences when making investment decisions.

The staff notice specifically addresses five issues that have been of concern in the past and for which comments may be raised: missing information regarding offering amount and pricing; offering structure; use of proceeds disclosure; risk factor disclosure; and representations to support ability to continue operations. Note that the list is not exhaustive, but it gives examples of the types of additional information that may be requested.

QUESTIONS

1. Does the statutory language granting the director discretion to refuse to issue a receipt achieve the appropriate balance between encouraging public offerings through the prospectus process and protecting the public interest?
2. Why would anyone need to be protected from buying the securities offered in *Loki Resources*, above?

XIV. RIGHT TO WITHDRAW OR RESCISSION

Investors that have made an order or subscription for securities have a cooling-off period in which to consider the final prospectus once a receipt is issued for it and the prospectus has been delivered to them. This right is a form of consumer protection that encourages early subscriptions because the investor is automatically given the opportunity to reconsider on the basis of an examination of the information in the final prospectus regarding the offering. The prospectus must advise purchasers of their right to withdraw or rescission.

Form 41-101F1, *Information Required in a Prospectus*
As amended effective 17 November 2015, online: <https://www.bcsc.bc.ca/Securities_Law/Policies/Policy4/PDF/41-101F1__F___November_17__2015/>

Item 30: Rights of Withdrawal and Rescission

General

30.1 [The prospectus must] [i]nclude a statement in substantially the following form, with the bracketed information completed:

> Securities legislation in [certain of the provinces [and territories] of Canada/the Province of [insert name of local jurisdiction, if applicable]] provides purchasers with the right to withdraw from an agreement to purchase securities. This right may be exercised within two business days after receipt or deemed receipt of a prospectus and any amendment. [In several of the provinces/provinces and territories,] [T/t]he securities legislation further provides a purchaser with remedies for rescission [or[, in some jurisdictions,] revisions of the price or damages] if the prospectus and any amendment contains a misrepresentation or is not delivered to the purchaser, provided that the remedies for rescission[, revisions of the price or damages] are exercised by the purchaser within the time limit prescribed by the securities legislation of the purchaser's province [or territory]. The purchaser should refer to any applicable provisions of the securities legislation of the purchaser's province [or territory] for the particulars of these rights or consult with a legal adviser.

There are also rights to an action for rescission for misrepresentation in a prospectus. Where a purchaser has already resold its securities, it may not have a remedy. In *Pearson v Boliden Ltd*, 2002 BCCA 624 at para 92, the BC Court of Appeal relied on the words "depreciation in value" under the BCSA to reject the claims of plaintiffs who sold prior to the date that a misrepresentation was disclosed:

> [92] The final group of persons sought to be excluded from the action are those who purchased in the distribution but sold their shares prior to the date on which the failure of the tailings dam was reported. On this point, I agree with the defendants that s. 131(10) of the British Columbia *Act* and its provincial counterparts preclude such persons from recovering, since it cannot be said that any "depreciation" of their shares "resulted from" the misrepresentation. As the Ontario Divisional Court stated in *Bre-X*, no shareholder's loss before the event could have been caused by any misrepresentation—any loss before then was caused by the sale, not the event. The fact that the failure of the tailings dam was the "catalyst" or "triggering event" for the misrepresentation action seems to me irrelevant to the operation of s. 131(10) and its counterparts. As for the argument enunciated by the Chambers judge that the "early sellers" may have paid too much for their shares, if that is correct then they also *sold* their shares for "too much."
>
> [93] Finally on this point, although Mr. Klein sought to persuade us that such persons suffered some "loss of opportunity," it is clear in my view that this is not the kind of loss referred in s. 131(10) and its counterparts, even if such loss could be quantified. Thus I would exclude the "early sellers" from the class of plaintiffs.

QUESTIONS

1. Clearly, on the "paid too much" theory, the early sellers suffered as a result of the misrepresentation contrary to the securities law. Why should they not get a right to claim damages?
2. Is there some other statutory provision that provides a remedy for failure to disclose?

XV. THE PASSPORT SYSTEM AND THE PROSPECTUS PROCESS

As discussed in Chapter 3, the MRRS was replaced by Multilateral Instrument 11-102, *Passport System* [MI 11-102], as amended effective 9 May 2016, and National Policy 11-202, *Process for Prospectus Reviews in Multiple Jurisdictions* [NP 11-202], effective 28 September 2009. Under MI 11-102 and the interface policies, the principal regulator for a prospectus offering will usually be the regulator in the jurisdiction where the market participant's head office is located.

MI 11-102 gives each market participant a single window of access to the capital markets in multiple Canadian jurisdictions, enabling a person or company to deal only with its principal regulator to get deemed receipts in other jurisdictions (except Ontario) for a preliminary prospectus and prospectus. MI 11-102 and its companion policy implement the passport system contemplated by the Provincial/Territorial Memorandum of Understanding Regarding Securities Regulation. The Ontario Securities Commission has not adopted the Instrument, but the Instrument provides that the OSC can be a principal regulator for purposes of a prospectus filing. Consequently, when the OSC issues a receipt for a prospectus to an issuer whose principal jurisdiction is Ontario, a deemed receipt is automatically issued in each passport jurisdiction where the market participant filed the prospectus. A market participant whose principal jurisdiction is Ontario obtains an automatic exemption from the equivalent provision of securities legislation of each passport jurisdiction for which the person who makes the application gives the notice described in s 4.7(1)(c) of MI 11-102 if the OSC grants the discretionary exemption.

NP 11-202, *Process for Prospectus Reviews in Multiple Jurisdictions*; NP 11-203, *Process for Exemptive Relief Applications in Multiple Jurisdictions*; and NP 11-204, *Process for Registration in Multiple Jurisdictions* set out the processes for a market participant in any jurisdiction to obtain a deemed prospectus receipt or an automatic exemption in a passport jurisdiction. These policies also set out processes for a market participant in a passport jurisdiction to get a prospectus receipt or a discretionary exemption from the OSC.

Multilateral Instrument 11-102, *Passport System*

As amended effective 9 May 2016, online: <https://www.bcsc.bc.ca/Securities_Law/Policies/Policy1/PDF/11-102_Passport_System>

Part 3 Prospectus

3.1 Principal Regulator for Prospectus

(1) For the purposes of this section, the specified jurisdictions are British Columbia, Alberta, Saskatchewan, Manitoba, Ontario, Québec, New Brunswick and Nova Scotia.

(2) Subject to subsection (3) and section 3.2, for the purposes of a prospectus filing subject to this Part the principal regulator is the securities regulatory authority or regulator of the jurisdiction in which

(a) the issuer's head office is located, if the issuer is not an investment fund, or

(b) the investment fund manager's head office is located, if the issuer is an investment fund.

(3) If the jurisdiction identified under paragraph (2)(a) or (b) is not a specified jurisdiction, the principal regulator is the securities regulatory authority or regulator of the specified jurisdiction with which the issuer or, in the case of an investment fund, the investment fund manager, has the most significant connection.

3.2 Discretionary Change of Principal Regulator for Prospectus

If a person or company receives written notice from a securities regulatory authority or regulator that specifies a principal regulator, the securities regulatory authority or regulator specified in the notice is the principal regulator as of the later of (a) the date the person or company receives the notice, and (b) the effective date specified in the notice, if any.

3.3 Deemed Issuance of Receipt

(1) Subject to section 3.5(1), a receipt for a preliminary prospectus is deemed to be issued if

(a) the preliminary prospectus is filed under a provision set out in Appendix B and under a national prospectus instrument,

(b) at the time of filing the preliminary prospectus, the filer indicates on SEDAR that it is filing the preliminary prospectus under this Instrument,

(c) the local jurisdiction is not the principal jurisdiction for the preliminary prospectus, and

(d) the preliminary prospectus is filed with the principal regulator and the principal regulator issues a receipt for it.

(2) A receipt for a prospectus is deemed to be issued if

(a) the prospectus is filed under a provision set out in Appendix B and under a national prospectus instrument,

(b) subject to section 3.5(2), the filer

(i) complied with paragraph (1)(b) at the time of filing the related preliminary prospectus, or

(ii) indicated on SEDAR that it filed the related pro forma prospectus under this Instrument at the time of filing the related pro forma prospectus,

(c) the local jurisdiction is not the principal jurisdiction for the prospectus, and

(d) the prospectus is filed with the principal regulator and the principal regulator issues a receipt for the prospectus.

Hence, the principal regulator must be the securities regulatory authority or regulator in a specified jurisdiction. Section 3.1(1) of the Instrument specifies the following jurisdictions for purposes of that section: British Columbia, Alberta, Saskatchewan, Manitoba, Ontario, Québec, New Brunswick, and Nova Scotia. A receipt is deemed to be issued for a preliminary prospectus or prospectus in the local jurisdiction if certain conditions are met and a deemed receipt has the same legal effect as a receipt issued in the principal jurisdiction. The filer must file on SEDAR the preliminary prospectus or the *pro forma* prospectus, and the prospectus, in both the local jurisdiction and the principal jurisdiction. These filings trigger the obligation to file supporting documents, such as consents and material contracts. The filer must also pay the fees required for the preliminary prospectus, *pro forma* prospectus or prospectus in the local jurisdiction. NP 11-202 sets out the process for making a waiver application for a prospectus filing subject to part 3 of the Instrument.

If the principal regulator refuses to issue a receipt for a prospectus, it will notify the filer and the non-principal regulators by sending a refusal letter through SEDAR. In these circumstances, the Instrument will no longer apply to the filing and the filer may deal separately with the local securities regulatory authority or regulator in any non-principal jurisdiction in which the prospectus was filed to determine whether the local securities regulatory authority or regulator would issue a local receipt (Companion Policy 11-102CP, *Passport System*).

Instead of having to obtain receipts for both a preliminary prospectus and final prospectus from multiple regulators in the jurisdictions in which it intends to make an offering, the passport system allows the issuer to ask that one regulator act as principal regulator. National Policy 11-202 describes procedures for the filing and review of a preliminary prospectus and related materials in more than one Canadian jurisdiction. Where the principal regulator is a passport regulator and the prospectus is not filed in Ontario, the prospectus is referred to a "passport prospectus." Where the principal regulator is the OSC and the prospectus is also filed in a passport jurisdiction, it is also a "passport prospectus." Where the principal regulator is a passport regulator and the prospectus is also filed in Ontario, the prospectus is referred to as a "dual prospectus."

National Policy 11-202 sets out how prospectus review now occurs under the passport system.

National Policy 11-202, *Process for Prospectus Reviews in Multiple Jurisdictions*

Effective 28 September 2009, online: <https://www.bcsc.bc.ca/Securities_Law/Policies/Policy1/PDF/11-202_Process_for_Prospectus_Reviews_in_Multiple_Jurisdictions_-_September_2009/>

3.2 Passport Prospectus

(1) If the principal regulator is a passport regulator and the prospectus is not filed in Ontario, only the principal regulator will review the prospectus. Under MI 11-102, the issuance of a receipt by the principal regulator will trigger a deemed receipt in each other passport jurisdiction where the prospectus is filed.

(2) If the principal regulator is the OSC and the prospectus is also filed in a passport jurisdiction, only the OSC will review the prospectus. Under MI 11-102, the issuance of the OSC receipt will trigger a deemed receipt in each passport jurisdiction where the prospectus is filed.

3.3 Dual Prospectus

If the principal regulator is a passport regulator and the prospectus is also filed in Ontario, the principal regulator will review the prospectus, and the OSC, as a non-principal regulator, will coordinate its review with the principal regulator. The receipt of the principal regulator will trigger a deemed receipt in each other passport jurisdiction where the prospectus is filed and will evidence the receipt of the OSC, if the OSC has made the same decision as the principal regulator.

NP 11-202 specifies that the principal regulator for a prospectus filing under this policy is the regulator of the jurisdiction in which the issuer's head office is located. If the regulator identified under s 3.4(4) is not in a specified jurisdiction (British Columbia, Alberta, Saskatchewan, Manitoba, Ontario, Québec, New Brunswick, or Nova Scotia), the principal regulator is the regulator in the specified jurisdiction with which the issuer has the most significant connection (NP 11-202, s 3.4(5)). The factors that an issuer should consider in identifying the principal regulator based on its most significant connection are, in order of influential weight: (1) location of management; (2) location of assets and operations; (3) location of trading market or quotation system in Canada; and (4) location of securityholders, if the securities are not traded or quoted on a trading market or quotation system in Canada. For issuers not based in Canada, regulators may also consider: location of underwriter, location of legal counsel, and location of transfer agent.

In very limited circumstances, there can be a change in principal regulator. If the principal regulator determines that it is not the appropriate principal regulator, it must first consult with the filer and the appropriate regulator, and then give the filer a written notice of the new principal regulator and the reasons for the change (NP 11-202, s 3.5). Alternatively, a filing issuer may request a discretionary change of principal regulator for a prospectus filing if the filer believes that the principal regulator is not the appropriate principal regulator, likely to be approved by regulators only in exceptional circumstances. The National Policy should be consulted for detailed requirements in respect of the passport system and filing a prospectus, including required materials to be filed and review of materials.

There is a form of decision that is rendered for a passport prospectus and for a dual prospectus. The Passport System has reduced many of the transaction costs and timing problems associated with a national offering.

While it is important to facilitate the prospectus and offering process in order to encourage the economic activity that investment in securities can bring, it is equally important to ensure that a balance is struck between facilitating that activity and protecting consumer investors. It is also important to bear in mind that prospectuses are less important for major investors because they frequently have the information and resources to undertake their own due diligence in the investigation of an offering. For the less sophisticated investor, the prospectus provides the primary, if not sole, source of accurate information on the offering, and hence the gatekeeping role of regulatory authorities in respect of the prospectus process is considered vitally important.

XVI. LAPSE DATES AND REFILING OF PROSPECTUS

In order to ensure that information remains current, securities legislation sets a "lapse date." Previously these dates were set out in the statutes, but most jurisdictions have repealed the statutory provisions, given the introduction of NI 41-101.

NI 41-101 specifies the following in respect of lapse dates and refiling.

National Instrument 41-101, *General Prospectus Requirements*
As amended effective 8 December 2015, online: <https://www.bcsc.bc.ca/Securities_Law/Policies/Policy4/PDF/41-101__NI___December_8__2015/>

Part 17 Lapse Date

Pro Forma Prospectus

17.1(1) In this Part, "pro forma prospectus" means a long form prospectus that complies with the requirements described in subsection (2).

(2) A pro forma prospectus must be prepared in the form of a long form prospectus in accordance with Form 41-101F1, Form 41-101F2 or Form 41-101F3, as applicable, and other securities legislation, except that a pro forma prospectus is not required to contain prospectus certificates or to comply with sections 4.2, 4.3 and 4.4 of this Instrument.

(3) This Part does not apply to a prospectus filed in accordance with NI 44-101, NI 44-102 or NI 44-103.

Refiling of Prospectus

17.2(1) This section does not apply in Ontario.

(2) In this section, "lapse date" means, with reference to the distribution of a security that has been qualified under a prospectus, the date that is 12 months after the date of the most recent final prospectus relating to the security.

(3) An issuer must not continue the distribution of a security to which the prospectus requirement applies after the lapse date unless the issuer files a new prospectus that

complies with securities legislation and a receipt for that new prospectus is issued by the regulator.

(4) Despite subsection (3), a distribution may be continued for a further 12 months after a lapse date if,

(a) the issuer delivers a pro forma prospectus not less than 30 days before the lapse date of the previous prospectus;

(b) the issuer files a new final prospectus not later than 10 days after the lapse date of the previous prospectus; and

(c) a receipt for the new final prospectus is issued by the regulator within 20 days after the lapse date of the previous prospectus.

(5) The continued distribution of securities after the lapse date does not contravene subsection (3) unless and until any of the conditions of subsection (4) are not complied with.

(6) Subject to any extension granted under subsection (7), if a condition in subsection (4) is not complied with, a purchaser may cancel a purchase made in a distribution after the lapse date in reliance on subsection (4) within 90 days after the purchaser first became aware of the failure to comply with the condition.

(7) The regulator may, on an application of a reporting issuer, extend, subject to such terms and conditions as it may impose, the times provided by subsection (4) where in its opinion it would not be prejudicial to the public interest to do so.

[Note: In Ontario, section 62 of the *Securities Act* (Ontario) imposes similar requirements and procedures regarding refiling of prospectuses.]

As the excerpt above indicates, subject to any extension granted, all trades completed in reliance on the prospectus after the lapse date may be cancelled at the option of the purchaser within 90 days of the purchaser's first knowledge of the failure to comply with conditions concerning the continuation of a distribution. The commission may, on application of a reporting issuer, extend the statutory time frame, subject to such terms and conditions as it may impose, where in its opinion it would not be prejudicial to the public interest to do so.

XVII. THE PROPOSED NATIONAL SECURITIES LEGISLATIVE FRAMEWORK

The Expert Panel on Securities Regulation Report in 2009 proposed a draft national securities act that would take a more principles-based approach to securities regulation and include a core set of objectives (Expert Panel on Securities Regulation, *Creating an Advantage in Global Capital Markets, Final Report and Recommendations*, January 2009). However, as noted earlier in the chapter, the draft national *Securities Act* was found by the Supreme Court of Canada not to be valid under the general branch of the power to regulate trade and commerce under s 91(2) of the *Constitution Act, 1867* (*Reference re Securities Act*, 2011 SCC 66, [2011] 3 SCR 837), as discussed in Chapter 2. After several years more of negotiations among provincial ministers and securities regulators, on August 25, 2015, the ministers responsible for capital markets regulation in British Columbia, Ontario, Saskatchewan, New Brunswick,

Prince Edward Island, and Yukon published a Revised Consultation Draft of the provincial and territorial *Capital Markets Act* (CMA) for comment, accompanied by draft Initial Regulations under the CMA, as contemplated by the Memorandum of Agreement Regarding the Cooperative Capital Markets Regulatory System. The CMA is subject to legislative approval and will not become law unless introduced in, and enacted by, the legislatures of the provincial and territorial participating jurisdictions. Participating jurisdictions are actively engaged in finalizing proposed legislation to establish jointly the Capital Markets Regulatory Authority, which would administer the CMA, the federal Capital Markets Stability Act, and the initial regulations. In addition, implementation legislation is being developed to ensure a smooth transition to the new regime and to integrate the new regime into the general laws of each participating province and territory.

A second draft of the CMA was published in December 2015, following receipt of a large number of comments from market participants, investors and academics. Part 5 of the CMA is the relevant part regarding proposed prospectus requirements; its substance does not deviate significantly from the prospectus-related provisions in current provincial acts, including requirements to file a prospectus, preliminary prospectus requirements, the opportunity to be heard, permitted activities under the preliminary prospectus, duties under the process, and potential remedies.

QUESTIONS

1. The draft legislation reflects the language of numerous statutes and instruments discussed throughout this chapter. Do you think it will move securities law toward a more principled approach to the requirements, or do you view the draft as a modified form of the current statutory requirements?
2. The draft legislation still makes a distinction between material facts and material change and does not adopt the notion of a single standard of material information, as discussed earlier in this chapter. Why do you think this distinction has been maintained?
3. Why do you think there is only partial support across Canada for the draft legislation, in terms of cooperating provinces; and do you think any real progress is being made toward the objective of a national securities law framework?

CHAPTER FIVE

Exempt Market Transactions

I. WHAT IS THE EXEMPT MARKET AND WHY IS IT IMPORTANT?

As discussed in Chapter 4, the traditional default rule of securities regulation has been that new securities cannot be issued without an accompanying panoply of disclosure requirements. However, that basic rule is relaxed in the case of exempt transactions, where securities can be issued without the accompanying mandated disclosure. Thus the exempt market is created by the set of rules in securities law concerning the circumstances in which it is permissible to issue securities without issuing a prospectus. This market is obviously important to issuers and investors alike in that it enables capital to be raised on more flexible and cost-effective terms. For regulators, however, it is an area where the protective ethos that undergirds much of their activity cedes to the norms of efficiency in the sense of facilitating transactions.

The regulation of the exempt market in Canada was in a great deal of flux for several years though a significant level of harmonization has now been achieved. Conceptually, the exempt market is considered to consist of two levels of transaction that raise connected regulatory concerns. The first level, broadly speaking, consists of the set of transactions that take place directly between issuers of securities and the investors who buy from them. Here the issue for regulators and legislatures is the extent to which it is feasible to eliminate the default prospectus requirement on an issue of new securities. With respect to the issuer/investor set of transactions, a major step forward was achieved by the introduction in 2005 of NI 45-106, which governs the circumstances in which such transactions could take place without a prospectus. This rule both repeals, in some cases, and adds to, in others, existing legislative requirements in various provinces. Before this harmonization there were three sets of rules operating in Canada: OSC Rule 45-501, MI 45-103 (operating in all provinces except Ontario and Québec), and provisions of the QSA. As we will see, some differences among provinces persist within NI 45-106.

Regulators are also concerned with regulating the process of reselling those securities to other investors, where the initial rationale for an exemption might no longer apply. The classic example would be where subsequent investors are not sufficiently "investment savvy" so as to dispense with the information that a prospectus would provide. With respect to this second level of transaction, legislatures and regulators have promulgated *resale* rules, designed to prevent the phenomenon of "backdoor underwriting"—that is, using the exemptions to avoid the prospectus requirement while disseminating securities broadly into the market. Here there has been consistency across the country, with NI 45-102, *Resale of Securities* (2004), 21 OSCB (Supp-4) 121, as amended 14 January 2016, being implemented in all jurisdictions. This apparent harmonization is, however, somewhat deceptive because significant components of these rules do not apply in Manitoba because this jurisdiction does not attempt to regulate the second level of transaction unless a control distribution is involved. (See Companion Policy (CP) to NI 45-102, s 1.3, above.) Finally, it is crucial to understand that the restrictions governing when issuers can issue securities without a prospectus apply to both non-reporting issuers and reporting issuers (essentially, issuers that have never qualified securities by way of a prospectus and those that have for a previous issue of securities or that have become reporting issuers otherwise).

Another way of summarizing this discussion is to say that the regulation of the process of distributing securities in most provinces is "closed." This means that all possible legal ways of issuing securities are contemplated by the legislation and the accompanying rules. The regulatory options applicable to issuers distributing securities within a closed system are:

1. provide a prospectus;
2. qualify for an exemption such as those in NI 45-106, with resale of those securities being likewise considered a distribution unless resellers qualify for the relevant resale rules;
3. apply for a discretionary exemption from the prospectus requirement from the regulator where applicable (see e.g. Ontario *Securities Act*, RSO 1990, c S.5 (OSA), s 74).

A final terminological point is that, in securities law parlance, some of these exempt transactions are known as "private placements," to distinguish them from prospectus offerings. This is not, however, a defined term in securities legislation. Generally, the term refers to the ability of certain purchasers, usually sophisticated parties, to obtain securities without a prospectus if they qualify for an exemption such as the "accredited investor" exemption discussed below.

II. POLICY OBJECTIVES OF PROSPECTUS EXEMPTIONS

Four primary policy objectives underlie the complex variety of traditional prospectus exemptions.

1. The first is the perceived regulatory need to address the specific problems of start-up, small, or medium-sized issuers by allowing them more flexibility than the prospectus system provides to generate initial amounts of working capital. A large number of recommendations with respect to easing the regulatory burdens on small and medium-sized business enterprises (SMEs) were made by Ontario's Task Force on Small Business Financing in the mid-1990s. (See Ontario Securities Commission, *Task Force on Small Business Financing: Final Report* (Toronto: Queen's Printer for Ontario, October 1996).) The recommendations included liberalizing the rules in relation to future-oriented financial information for SMEs and changes to escrow requirements (that limit how soon after an initial public offering (IPO) significant shareholders of an issuer can sell their shares). The most significant recommendations, however, concerned the creation of new prospectus exemptions for "closely held business issuers" and an expanded category of "accredited investors." The "closely held issuer" exemption in OSC Rule 45-501 was omitted from NI 45-106, but the "private issuer" and "family, friends and business associates" exemptions in NI 45-106 represent efforts to implement those recommendations in an attempt to solve some persistent regulatory problems in the SME sector. More recently, governments in many jurisdictions—inside and outside Canada—have been preoccupied with low rates of economic development in the wake of the GFC. This political concern has led to renewed focus by securities regulators on developing innovative responses to the need to stimulate economic activity. As we will see below, existing exemptions have been expanded in scope in the last several years. A new one, the crowdfunding exemption, has been implemented in provincial and territorial jurisdictions across Canada, as well as in the United States and the United Kingdom. Overall, these exemptions are a response to the concern that established financial institution creditors or sophisticated investors such as pension funds or mutual funds may be unwilling or legally discouraged from investing in start-up or small business enterprises.

2. The second objective is the acknowledgment that some wealthy and/or sophisticated investors are capable of making the decision to bear investment risk without the information that a prospectus provides. It is considered to be unduly paternalistic of regulators to require issuers to provide extensive prospectus disclosure to a class of investors that is composed of sophisticated financial institutions or pension funds with billions of dollars under their administration, as well as "high net worth" individuals. In the interests of market efficiency, prospectus disclosure rules can be relaxed where the buyers of the securities fall into such a category. The assumption here is that such investors are capable of acting rationally in their own economic self-interest and will seek out directly from the issuer or its representatives any information they consider relevant to their investment decision-making. The material provided about the findings of behavioral economics in the Introduction to this book might be relevant to assessing this premise. (See Donald C Langevoort, "Selling Hope, Selling Risk: Some Lessons for Law from Behavioral Economics About Stockbrokers and Sophisticated Customers" (1996) 84:3 Cal L Rev 627.) Note that, in contrast to the policy rationale above, exemptions in this second category are based on the characteristics of the buyer of securities, not the seller.

3. Third, where issuers are issuing securities to those with whom they have a pre-existing relationship, it is considered that the prospectus requirement may be relaxed. The basic assumption here is that in these cases, the investor either has or has access to adequate current information about the issuer and its financial prospects. This justification is at the root of exemptions such as rights offerings, where additional securities are offered to existing securityholders, trades to senior executives, more general employee-related exemptions (NI 45-106, ss 2.22-2.26, 28 OSCB (Supp-4) 3, as amended 21 July 2016), and also the "family, friends and business associates" exemption in NI 45-106. These exemptions may also be justified on the ground of reducing costs to issuers where no countervailing concern about investor protection exists. One issue to consider is whether each of these constituencies is in fact in the same position with respect to an ability to make investment decisions in the absence of the prospectus requirement. See e.g. *SEC v Ralston Purina*, 346 US 119 (1953), which considered whether employees should be regarded as members of the public for purposes of obtaining a prospectus. In 1953, the US Supreme Court answered yes to this question.

4. Finally, some types of securities are so safe that a prospectus is considered to be redundant. Thus, should a government default on payments related to its own bond issues, there is little risk that the investor in the bonds will ultimately not be repaid. The same is considered to be true of a variety of financial institutions (but see *Re Standard Trustco* (1992), 15 OSCB 4322). The list of such securities is contained in NI 45-106, ss 2.34-2.38 and includes bonds, debentures, or other evidence of indebtedness of or guaranteed by the government of Canada, any province or territory of Canada, governments of foreign jurisdictions, Canadian municipal corporations, Ontario school boards, financial institutions governed by other legislation, securities issued by charitable issuers, among others. Some of these exemptions rely on the availability of "a credit rating from a designated rating organisation," an issue that became controversial during the asset-backed commercial paper crisis in fall 2007 (IOSCO Technical Committee, "Consultation Report on Credit Rating Agencies" (March 2008), online: <http://www.iosco.org/library/pubdocs/pdf/IOSCOPD263.pdf>).

In conclusion, it can be seen that each of the policy rationales makes a set of assumptions about the relationship between disclosure and the risk involved in investing in particular securities, as well as the trade-offs that can occur between the two regulatory concerns. Where the risk to the investor is low, disclosure can be dispensed with to some extent, if not entirely. It should be noted, however, that the policy rationales enumerated above refer to a variety of levels or kinds of risk. Thus, the investment risk faced by a sophisticated pension fund is likely different in quality from that faced by a close friend of an entrepreneur. One question to ask yourself, therefore, as you proceed through the section to follow, is whether the nature of the risk assumed by a purchaser in a particular exempt transaction is matched by an appropriate level of information disclosure.

III. NOTE ON REGISTRATION REQUIREMENTS

Since we saw in Chapter 1 that issuing securities involves, by definition, trading in those securities, the question arises as to whether registration is required to so trade. Since 2009, the securities law framework governing registration in most jurisdictions has required registration where a person or company is engaging in or holding himself, herself, or itself out as "engaging in the business of trading in securities." This can raise the issue of whether an issuer issuing securities under a prospectus exemption also needs to be registered under provincial securities law to do so, and thereby required to meet substantive registration requirements. The answer to this question will revolve around the interpretation of the language about "engaging in the business of trading in securities." Some of the prospectus exemptions, as we will see, prohibit issuers from paying intermediaries to find investors for them. Where this is not the case, if an issuer uses an intermediary to find investors, in principle that intermediary must be registered to trade in securities. These issues will be canvassed further in the chapter on registration.

IV. SELECTED PROSPECTUS EXEMPTIONS

While NI 45-106 has consolidated many of the available prospectus exemptions in Canada into one rule, it is not possible in this chapter to canvass all of the exemptions contained therein. In Ontario, some additional prospectus exemptions are also still available in OSC Rule 45-501 (28 OSCB (Supp-4) 95, as amended 6 June 2016), and in one important instance Ontario has moved an exemption out of NI 45-106 and into the OSA. For a more complete treatment, readers should consult Borden Ladner Gervais, *Securities Law and Practice*, 3rd ed (Toronto: Thomson Carswell) (loose-leaf). However, we will introduce the major exemptions contained in NI 45-106 as well as the more recent exemption introduced in NI 45-108, the crowdfunding exemption. Our approach will be to group exemptions according to their underlying policy rationale, though it should be remembered that specific exemptions may be susceptible to more than one policy justification. In the case of each exemption, we will canvass the regulatory criteria imposed in order to qualify to use the relevant exemption. Further, as we have seen above, it is important to note that disclosure requirements here are not an on/off switch. Rather, some substantive disclosure requirements may be retained in order to satisfy the terms of an exemption. We will see that this is especially true of the offering memorandum exemption in NI 45-106, s 2.9. A final word of advice in relation to navigating these highly technical rules is that the companion policies that go along with some of the newer rules are often very helpful to elucidate complicated rule provisions.

A. Exemptions for Small and Medium-Sized Enterprises or Start-Up Issuers

1. Private Issuer Exemption (NI 45-106, Section 2.4)

a. Definition

A private issuer is defined by s 2.4(1) as follows:

> "private issuer" means an issuer
> (a) that is not a reporting issuer or an investment fund,
> (b) the securities of which, other than non-convertible debt securities,
> (i) are subject to restrictions on transfer that are contained in the issuer's constating documents or securityholders' agreements, and
> (ii) are beneficially owned by not more than 50 persons, not including employees and former employees of the issuer or its affiliates, provided that each person is counted as one beneficial owner unless the person is created or used solely to purchase or hold securities of the issuer in which case each beneficial owner or each beneficiary of the person, as the case may be, must be counted as a separate beneficial owner, and
> (c) that
> (i) has distributed its securities only to persons described in subsection (2), or
> (ii) has completed a transaction and immediately following the completion of the transaction, its securities were beneficially owned only by persons described in subsection (2) and since the completion of the transaction has distributed its securities only to persons described in subsection (2).

The noteworthy elements of this definition are first, the limit of not more than 50 persons that may be securityholders of a private issuer, exclusive of employees or former employees of the issuer or its affiliates. The intention is to limit use of the exemption to issuers with a numerically small number of securityholders who might be otherwise deemed to be in need of investor protection, but who will not receive a prospectus because of the more pressing goal of supporting entrepreneurial activity. We will see that although the definition assumes a straightforward numerical calculation of the category of permissible subscribers for securities, quantitative assessments still have to be made about who can qualify as one of the securityholders. The definition also contains an "anti-avoidance" provision similar to tax law, such that regulators look through a device of a corporation, partnership, trust, or other entity to count individually each beneficial owner of an equity interest in the investing entity, if the entity "is created or used solely to purchase or hold securities of the issuer."

Second, the requirement for restriction on share transfer in order to use this exemption is intended to enable the issuer to control, or at least be aware of, any changes or increases in the number of shareholders of the entity. However, the de facto requirement to maintain a list of securityholders to ensure that the issuer is not offside the exemption and, possibly, to amend the articles of the corporation if they are not already in conformity with the requirements of the definition poses practical difficulties for issuers.

b. Substance of Private Issuer Rule

This definition must, however, be read in conjunction with the substance of the exemption, which provides:

2.4 Private Issuer

(2) The prospectus requirement does not apply to a distribution of a security of a private issuer to a person who purchases the security as principal and is

(a) a director, officer, employee, founder or control person of the issuer,

(b) a director, officer or employee of an affiliate of the issuer,

(c) a spouse, parent, grandparent, brother, sister, child or grandchild of a director, executive officer, founder or control person of the issuer,

(d) a parent, grandparent, brother, sister, child or grandchild of the spouse of a director, executive officer, founder or control person of the issuer,

(e) a close personal friend of a director, executive officer, founder or control person of the issuer,

(f) a close business associate of a director, executive officer, founder or control person of the issuer,

(g) a spouse, parent, grandparent, brother, sister, child or grandchild of the selling securityholder or of the selling securityholder's spouse,

(h) a securityholder of the issuer,

(i) an accredited investor,

(j) a person of which a majority of the voting securities are beneficially owned by, or a majority of the directors are, persons described in paragraphs (a) to (i),

(k) a trust or estate of which all of the beneficiaries or a majority of the trustees or executors are persons described in paragraphs (a) to (i), or

(l) a person that is not the public.

It should be noted that, in Ontario, the operative part of the private issuer exemption is now contained in OSA, s 73.4(2), though the terms of the latter are identical to NI 45-106, s 2.4(2).

We see that issuers may use the private issuer exemption to distribute securities to a variety of classes of purchasers, as long as the numerical ceiling is not exceeded. These classes include (1) close personal friends and business associates of management or control persons of the issuer; (2) family members of management or control persons or other selling securityholders; (3) accredited investors; and (4) persons that are "not the public." It does not appear that accredited investors can be excluded from the ceiling of 50 persons or companies, as they could have been in an earlier Ontario version of this rule.

With respect to the "not the public" category, NI 45-106CP, s 3.6 notes:

> Whether or not a person is a member of the public must be determined on the facts of each particular case. The courts have interpreted 'the public' very broadly in the context of securities trading. Whether a person is a part of the public will be determined on the particular facts of each case, based on the tests that have developed under the relevant case law. A person who intends to distribute securities in reliance upon the private issuer prospectus exemption in s. 2.4(2) of NI 45-106 to a person not listed in paragraphs (a) through (j) of that section will have to satisfy itself that the distribution of the security is not to the public.

Two leading decisions cited as elucidating the concept of the public for the purposes of using securities regulation exemptions are the above-mentioned US Supreme Court decision of *Ralston Purina* and the Alberta Court of Appeal decision in *R v Piepgrass* (1959), 23 DLR (2d) 220. The excerpt from Gillen, following, summarizes the uncertainty arising from these decisions.

Mark R Gillen, *Securities Regulation in Canada*
(Toronto: Thomson Carswell, 2007) at 240-41

Although courts did occasionally grapple with the meaning of the words "to the public," they were unable to give them a precise meaning. One of the leading cases addressing the meaning of the words "to the public" was *Securities and Exchange Commission v. Ralston Purina Co.* Ralston Purina instituted an employee share ownership plan under which shares of the company were made available to "key employees." However, shares were offered to any employee who expressed an interest in the shares. Shares were sold to employees in several different states and included such employees as a chuck loading foreman, a clerical assistant, a stock clerk and a production trainee. The United States Supreme Court held that the sales constituted a distribution to the public and thus were subject to the *Securities Act of 1933*. In discussing the meaning of "to the public" the court noted that the security need not be made available to the whole world and that "to the public" applies whether the offer is made to many persons or to only a few persons. The key question, in the view of the court, was whether the persons who are offered the security need to know the kind of information that the prospectus would provide.

In *R v. Piepgrass*, a leading Canadian case, $50,000 worth of capital was sought by soliciting farmers, most of whom were known by the promoter from previous business dealings. The Alberta Court of Appeal upheld the trial decision which held that sales to the persons solicited constituted a distribution to the public. The Court of Appeal noted that the persons sold to "were not in any sense friends or associates of the accused, or persons having common bonds of interest or association." The court did not expand on the reason for this test. However, the concept appears to be that one is not likely to take advantage of friends, associates or persons who have common bonds of interest or association. Also, persons having common bonds of interest or association may have access to the kind of information that would appear in a prospectus. Such persons would thus not need the protection provided by prospectus disclosure accompanied by withdrawal rights and civil liability.

The tests set out in these cases are known respectively as the "need to know" test and the "common bonds" test. Although these two tests provided some guidance as to the meaning of the expression "to the public," there remained considerable ambiguity as to whether a distribution constituted a distribution "to the public." Thus it was often not clear whether a prospectus was required. Cautious solicitors resolved this doubt by seeking an exemption order from the Securities Commission. There were numerous applications to the Commission for clarifying orders.

See, more recently, *Re Future Solar Developments Inc* (2016), 39 OSCB 4495, in which a panel of the OSC considered the meaning of "a person that is not the public." In this case, the respondents argued that when they distributed securities to four investors who did not qualify for the accredited investor exemption (the other seven investors did) they had the private issuer exemption available to them because those four investors were not members of the public. The panel concluded (at paras 80-81):

> In this case, a few of the 11 investors were known to either Qin or to Li. Further, they were investors of significant wealth and with the desire to emigrate to Ontario. We feel that they are not

> "the public" at large. They formed part of a network of people known to the immigration consultants as desirous of investing abroad and emigrating to a foreign country.
>
> When viewed with the seven or eight people who are Accredited Investors, the few individuals known to Qin and/or Li, the Future Solar materials provided to each investor and the questioning by those investors of the investment opportunity, we conclude that the distribution of preference shares to the 11 investors is from a private issuer.

It does not appear that any disclosure obligations accompany the use of this exemption. Finally, NI 45-106CP, part 3 indicates that the use of registrants, finders, or advertising to solicit purchasers under the private issuer exemption "may give rise to a presumption that the relationship required for the use of these exemptions is not present." However, use of a finder by a private issuer to find an accredited investor will not preclude reliance on the private issuer exemption.

2. Family, Friends, and Business Associates Exemption (FFBA) (NI 45-106, Sections 2.5, 2.6, 2.6.1)

> **2.5 Family, Friends and Business Associates**
>
> (1) Subject to section 2.6 [*Family, friends and business associates—Saskatchewan*] and section 2.6.1 [*Family, friends and business associates—Ontario*], the prospectus requirement does not apply to a distribution of a security to a person who purchases the security as principal and is
>
> (a) a director, executive officer or control person of the issuer, or of an affiliate of the issuer,
>
> (b) a spouse, parent, grandparent, brother, sister, child or grandchild of a director, executive officer or control person of the issuer, or of an affiliate of the issuer,
>
> (c) a parent, grandparent, brother, sister, child or grandchild of the spouse of a director, executive officer or control person of the issuer or of an affiliate of the issuer,
>
> (d) a close personal friend of a director, executive officer or control person of the issuer, or of an affiliate of the issuer,
>
> (e) a close business associate of a director, executive officer or control person of the issuer, or of an affiliate of the issuer,
>
> (f) a founder of the issuer or a spouse, parent, grandparent, brother, sister, child, grandchild, close personal friend or close business associate of a founder of the issuer,
>
> (g) a parent, grandparent, brother, sister, child or grandchild of a spouse of a founder of the issuer,
>
> (h) a person of which a majority of the voting securities are beneficially owned by, or a majority of the directors are, persons described in paragraphs (a) to (g), or
>
> (i) a trust or estate of which all of the beneficiaries or a majority of the trustees or executors are persons described in paragraphs (a) to (g).
>
> (2) No commission or finder's fee may be paid to any director, officer, founder, or control person of an issuer or an affiliate of the issuer in connection with a distribution under subsection (1).
>
> (3) Subsection (1) does not apply to a distribution of a short-term securitised product or, in Ontario, a distribution under subsection 73.4(2) of the *Securities Act* (Ontario).

a. Analysis of Exemption

In 2015, Ontario joined other provinces in Canada by implementing the FFBA exemption. It repealed its own made-in-Ontario version, known as the "founder, control person and family" exemption. In so joining other provinces, Ontario took a significant step toward harmonizing the rules related to prospectus exemptions for SMEs. However, Ontario's version of the FFBA exemption does require a risk acknowledgment form to be signed by purchasers, as discussed below. Unlike the private issuer exemption, the use of this exemption does not carry a restriction on the numbers of investors to whom securities may be sold. However, NI 45-106CP notes (at s 3.1) that "[i]f, for example, an issuer advertises or pays a commission or finder's fee to a third party to find purchasers under the family, friends and business associates exemption, it suggests that the precondition of a close relationship between the purchaser and the issuer may not exist and therefore the issuer cannot rely on this exemption." Relatedly, there is no prohibition on "the use of registrants, finders or advertising in any form ... to solicit purchasers under any of the exemptions" (NI 45-106CP, s 3.1). Section 1.10 of the CP clarifies that sellers are responsible for determining whether an exemption is available. It is advised that in relation to the exemption under discussion, issuers obtain signed statements from purchasers describing the purchaser's relationship with, for example, a director of the issuer. On the basis of the factual information, the issuer should determine whether the purchaser qualifies as a close personal friend of that director.

One of the most interesting aspects of this exemption is how regulators purport to define the categories of "close personal friends" and "close business associates." It appears to require a level of qualitative assessment as to the nature of personal relationships that is at odds with some of the more apparently objective standards in securities regulations and rules. Thus, NI 45-106CP, s 2.7, notes that a "'close personal friend' ... is an individual who knows the director, executive officer, founder or control person well enough and has known them for a sufficient period of time to be in a position to assess their capabilities and trustworthiness." Furthermore, an individual is not a close personal friend "solely because the individual is: (a) a relative, (b) a member of the same club, organization, association or religious group, (c) a co-worker, colleague or associate at the same workplace, (d) a client, customer, former client or former customer, (e) a mere acquaintance, or (f) connected through some form of social media, such as Facebook, Twitter or LinkedIn."

b. *Disclosure Requirements*

According to NI 45-106, s 6.1, issuers distributing securities under this exemption are required to file a report in the jurisdiction where the distribution takes place no later than ten days after the distribution. The required form of report is Form 45-106F1, which accompanies NI 45-106. Additionally, in both Ontario and Saskatchewan, sellers are required to obtain "risk acknowledgment forms" (Form 45-106F5), which must be retained by the seller for eight years after the distribution. The Ontario version of this requirement reads as follows.

> 2.6.1(1) In Ontario, section 2.5 [Family, friends and business associates] does not apply to a distribution of a security of an issuer unless all of the following are satisfied:
>
> (b) the person making the distribution obtains a risk acknowledgement signed by all of the following:
>
> (i) the purchaser;
>
> (ii) an executive officer of the issuer other than the purchaser;
>
> (iii) if the purchaser is a person referred to under paragraph 2.5(1)(b), the director, executive officer or control person of the issuer or an affiliate of the issuer who has the specified relationship with the purchaser;
>
> (iv) if the purchaser is a person referred to under paragraph 2.5(1)(c), the director, executive officer or control person of the issuer or an affiliate of the issuer whose spouse has the specified relationship with the purchaser;

(v) if the purchaser is a person referred to under paragraph 2.5(1)(d) or (e), the director, executive officer or control person of the issuer or an affiliate of the issuer who is a close personal friend or a close business associate of the purchaser; and

(vi) the founder of the issuer, if the purchaser is a person referred to in paragraph 2.5(1)(f) or (g) other than the founder of the issuer.

The substantive requirements of the risk acknowledgment form are identified in Form 45-106F12.

3. *The New Crowdfunding Exemptions*

a. Overview

In the notice that accompanied the publication in November 2015 of MI 45-108, *Crowdfunding* (2016), 39 OSCB 278, the CSA noted that the "45-108 crowdfunding regime is intended to leverage the use of the internet and social media to facilitate capital formation primarily for start-ups and SMEs that foster innovation and to provide new investment opportunities for investors." It noted that "selling securities over the internet to a large number of investors … has emerged as a new way for some businesses, particularly start-ups and small and medium-sized enterprises (SMEs), to access capital that would not have otherwise been accessible." Thus, crowdfunding represents a new departure in the regulatory scheme governing prospectus exemptions. Not only does it explicitly harness new technologies, but it also throws the exemption open to retail investors (the crowd) generally who have no previous connection with the issuer. On the other hand, as we will see shortly, there are features of the way the exemption operates that are intended to protect investors from the full rigours of caveat emptor. Kitay explains:

> In a crowdfunding transaction, an individual or a business (referred to as the project initiator) seeks capital by making a pitch for such funds from a community of individuals or businesses (referred to as the crowd). The crowd considers the pitch and decides whether to commit funds to the project. The organization that brings project initiators together with the crowd is known as a funding portal.

Bill Kitay, "Land of Confusion—Crowdfunding Regulations in Canada" (April 2016), online: <https://www.pallettvalo.com/news-centre/newsletters/land-of-confusion-ndash-crowdfunding-regulations-in-canada>.

In terms of regulatory requirements, there is a mosaic of approaches across Canadian provinces. Saskatchewan was the first Canadian province to issue a crowdfunding exemption, in December 2013 (General Order 45-925, *Saskatchewan Equity Crowdfunding Exemption* (2013), revoked 14 May 2015). One set of requirements, MI 45-108, is only currently operative in some provinces of Canada. Those that have adopted this instrument, excerpted below, are Manitoba, Ontario, Québec, New Brunswick, and Nova Scotia. Meanwhile, securities regulators in British Columbia and Saskatchewan (as well as Manitoba, Québec, New Brunswick, and Nova Scotia) issued Multilateral CSA Notice 45-316, *Start-Up Crowdfunding Registration and Prospectus Exemptions* (2015) in May 2015. This latter notice indicates that the participating jurisdictions are adopting a crowdfunding exemption (the start-up crowdfunding exemption) that is more narrowly focused on non-reporting issuers. Compliance with the exemption requires that such issuers cannot raise aggregate funds of more than $250,000 per distribution and are restricted from raising funds in no more than two crowdfunding distributions through a funding portal per calendar year. Investors are prohibited from investing more than $1,500 per distribution. A number of restrictions are placed on the activities of the funding portal, and there is a "sunset clause" of May 2020 for the expiration of the orders that will be made in each participating province that adopts this approach. Specifically, BC Instrument 45-535 (*Start-Up Crowdfunding Registration and Prospectus Exemptions* (2015), as amended 30 June 2016) is an example of this approach. Finally, in July 2016, the Alberta Securities Commission issued a notice requesting comment on two initiatives intended to facilitate capital-raising for SMEs with appropriate accompanying investor protection. One initiative involved Alberta adopting MI 45-108. The other involved the facilitation of "very modest" financings by way of ASC Rule 45-517, *Prospectus Exemption for Start-Up Businesses* (2016).

Meanwhile, MI 45-108 imposes requirements on both "eligible crowdfunding issuers" and on "funding portals." The definition of an "eligible crowdfunding issuer" is provided below.

b. *Definition of "Eligible Crowdfunding Issuer"*

"eligible crowdfunding issuer" means an issuer if all of the following apply:

(a) the issuer and, if applicable, its parent are incorporated or organized under the laws of Canada or any jurisdiction of Canada;

(b) the head office of the issuer is located in Canada;

(c) a majority of the directors of the issuer are resident in Canada;

(d) the principal operating subsidiary of the issuer, if any, is incorporated or organized under

(i) the laws of Canada or any jurisdiction of Canada, or

(ii) the laws of the United States of America or any state or territory of the United States of America or the District of Columbia;

(e) the issuer is not an investment fund;

As we can see from this definition, the focus of this exemption is on ensuring that a crowdfunding issuer has a strong Canadian presence as it accesses the Canadian securities market. These requirements reflect the genesis of this exemption in the concern to stimulate local economic activity in innovative ways.

c. *Substance of MI 45-108 Exemption*

The key components of the MI 45-108 crowdfunding exemption may be found in the following excerpt from the instrument.

5(1) The prospectus requirement does not apply to a distribution by an eligible crowdfunding issuer of an eligible security of its own issue to a person or company that purchases the security as principal if all of the following apply:

(a) the issuer offers the securities during the distribution period and the distribution period ends no later than 90 days after the date the issuer first offers its securities to purchasers;

(b) the total proceeds raised by the issuer group in reliance on the crowdfunding prospectus exemption does not exceed $1,500,000 within the 12-month period ending on the last day of the distribution period;

(c) in Ontario, the acquisition cost of the securities acquired by the purchaser

(i) in the case of a purchaser that is not an accredited investor, does not exceed

(A) $2,500 for the distribution, and

(B) $10,000 for all distributions in reliance on the crowdfunding prospectus exemption in the same calendar year,

(ii) in the case of a purchaser that is an accredited investor that is not a permitted client, does not exceed

(A) $25,000 for the distribution, and

(B) $50,000 for all distributions in reliance on the crowdfunding prospectus exemption in the same calendar year, and

(iii) in the case of a purchaser that is a permitted client, is not limited;

(d) except in Ontario, the acquisition cost of the securities acquired by the purchaser

(i) in the case of a purchaser that is not an accredited investor, does not exceed $2,500 for the distribution, and

(ii) in the case of a purchaser that is an accredited investor, does not exceed $25,000 for the distribution;

(e) the issuer distributes the securities through a single funding portal;

(f) before the purchaser enters into an agreement to purchase the securities, the issuer makes available to the purchaser, through the funding portal, a crowdfunding offering document that is in compliance with

(i) section 7 [Certificates] and section 8 [Right of withdrawal], and

(ii) section 9 [Liability for misrepresentation—reporting issuers] or section 10 [Liability for untrue statement—non-reporting issuers], as applicable.

d. Eligibility Requirements

We can see above that capital-raising limits are imposed on crowdfunding issuers, who may be reporting or non-reporting issuers. All provinces that have adopted this instrument have established a cap of $1,500,000 on the amount of capital that may be raised in a 12-month period. It remains to be seen by experience if this amount of capital is enough to allow a start-up business to develop sufficiently within a year, though it is true that such a business may also be able to access other prospectus exemptions during this period. The distribution period may be no longer than 90 days. The reference to "eligible securities" issued by the crowdfunding issuer should also be noted. This defined term includes basic forms of security, such as a common share, a non-convertible preference share, or a unit of a limited partnership. Interestingly, despite the deployment of technology, via a funding portal, to match investment opportunities with investors, s 11 of MI 45-108 prohibits issuers from advertising for investors.

Meanwhile, the rule also imposes eligibility requirements on purchasers of crowdfunding securities. Here there is some difference between the expectations imposed on Ontario purchasers and those investors resident in Manitoba, Québec, New Brunswick, or Nova Scotia. All of these provinces, including Ontario, prevent non-accredited purchasers from paying more than $2,500 for securities distributed under this exemption and accredited investors from paying more than $25,000. Only Ontario also imposes a $10,000 yearly limit on crowdfunded purchases for non-accredited investors and $50,000 per year for accredited investors. These purchasing limits are clearly meant to reduce investors' exposure to financial loss through equity crowdfunding purchases.

e. Disclosure Requirements

The terms of this exemption impose a number of different disclosure requirements that may be categorized as follows: (1) a crowdfunding offering document required at the time of initial purchase of the securities; (2) a risk acknowledgment form; (3) in Ontario, a confirmation of investment limits form; and (4) ongoing disclosure requirements.

1. Crowdfunding offering document: Section 5(1) of MI 45-108 requires that the issuer must make available to the purchaser, through the funding portal, a crowdfunding offering document before the purchaser enters into an agreement to purchase securities. This document must contain information about purchaser withdrawal rights, certificates executed by the issuer with respect to misrepresentations or untrue statements of material fact (as applicable) and information about issuer liability in this context. Further detailed requirements concerning the contents of a crowdfunding offering document are contained in Form 45-108FI, which covers 11 separate items.
2. Risk acknowledgment form: Section 6 of MI 45-108 prohibits the closing of a crowdfunding distribution unless the issuer has received risk acknowledgment forms from purchasers where the purchaser "positively confirms having read and understood the risk warnings and the information in the crowdfunding document."
3. Confirmation of investment limits form (Ontario): In this province only, Form 45-108F3 specifically requires purchasers to indicate how they qualify to purchase under the crowdfunding exemption—that is, whether they are a "permitted client," an accredited investor (under any or all of the income or asset tests), or a retail investor.
4. Ongoing disclosure requirements: A significant innovation involved in the use of this exemption is that non-reporting issuers have ongoing disclosure obligations after the exempt distribution is completed. Sections 16-17 of MI 45-108 identify the requirements on issuers to provide annual financial statements and annual disclosure of use of proceeds. Additionally, in Ontario, New Brunswick, and Nova Scotia, non-reporting issuers are required to "make reasonably available" to securityholders a notice in Form 45-108F describing each of the following types of events within ten days of their occurrence: (a) a discontinuation of the issuer's business, (b) a change in the issuer's industry, and (c) a change of control of the issuer.

f. Liability Issues

A final distinctive feature of the rules relating to crowdfunded distributions involve the liabilities imposed on issuers, depending on whether they are reporting issuers or not. In the former case, the crowdfunding offering document must make a contractual right of action for rescission or damages in a case of misrepresentation available to purchasers where there is no comparable statutory right of action. Section 9 of MI 45-108 describes how purchasers may enforce this right. In the latter case, where the issuer is not a reporting issuer, a contractual right of action must be provided in the offering document where that document contains "an untrue statement of a material fact."

Finally, part 3 of MI 45-108 contains detailed requirements imposed on funding portals, primarily with respect to registration requirements.

For an analysis of crowdfunding exemptions from an investor protection perspective, see Anita Anand, "Is Crowdfunding Bad for Investors?" (2014) 55:2 Can Bus LJ 215.

B. Wealthy/Sophisticated Investor Exemptions

The previous set of exemptions were clearly designed with an eye to the specific financing needs of SMEs. The exemptions to be considered in this section are not so limited in terms of the characteristics of the issuers that may use them; instead, the focus is on the characteristics of the purchaser of securities. The policy rationale for waiving prospectus requirements where the purchaser of securities meets a certain threshold of wealth or investment sophistication is, as we have seen above, that financings can thereby be conducted on more efficient terms without unduly compromising investor protection. Let us consider first the accredited investor exemption. Until recently, all of the elements of this exemption were to be found in NI 45-106, s 2.3. However, in Ontario, certain features of the exemption have been moved to OSA, s 73.3(2).

1. Accredited Investor Exemption (NI 45-106, Section 2.3)

a. Definition

Under NI 45-106, the definition of an "accredited investor" reads as follows:

> "accredited investor" means
>
> (a) except in Ontario, a Canadian financial institution, or a Schedule III bank,
>
> (b) except in Ontario, the Business Development Bank of Canada incorporated under the *Business Development Bank of Canada Act* (Canada),
>
> (c) except in Ontario, a subsidiary of any person referred to in paragraphs (a) or (b), if the person owns all of the voting securities of the subsidiary, except the voting securities required by law to be owned by directors of that subsidiary,
>
> (d) except in Ontario, a person registered under the securities legislation of a jurisdiction of Canada as an adviser or dealer,
>
> (e) an individual registered under the securities legislation of a jurisdiction of Canada as a representative of a person referred to in paragraph (d),
>
> (e.1) an individual formerly registered under the securities legislation of a jurisdiction of Canada, other than an individual formerly registered solely as a representative of a limited market dealer under one or both of the *Securities Act* (Ontario) or the *Securities Act* (Newfoundland and Labrador),
>
> (f) except in Ontario, the Government of Canada or a jurisdiction of Canada, or any crown corporation, agency or wholly owned entity of the Government of Canada or a jurisdiction of Canada,
>
> (g) except in Ontario, a municipality, public board or commission in Canada and a metropolitan community, school board, the Comité de gestion de la taxe scolaire de l'île de Montréal or an intermunicipal management board in Québec,
>
> (h) except in Ontario, any national, federal, state, provincial, territorial or municipal government of or in any foreign jurisdiction, or any agency of that government,
>
> (i) except in Ontario, a pension fund that is regulated by the Office of the Superintendent of Financial Institutions (Canada), a pension commission or similar regulatory authority of a jurisdiction of Canada,
>
> (j) an individual who, either alone or with a spouse, beneficially owns financial assets having an aggregate realizable value that, before taxes but net of any related liabilities, exceeds $1 000 000,
>
> (j.1) an individual who beneficially owns financial assets having an aggregate realizable value that, before taxes but net of any related liabilities, exceeds $5 000 000,
>
> (k) an individual whose net income before taxes exceeded $200 000 in each of the 2 most recent calendar years or whose net income before taxes combined with that of a spouse exceeded $300 000 in each of the 2 most recent calendar years and who, in either case, reasonably expects to exceed that net income level in the current calendar year,
>
> (l) an individual who, either alone or with a spouse, has net assets of at least $5 000 000,

(m) a person, other than an individual or investment fund, that has net assets of at least $5 000 000 as shown on its most recently prepared financial statements,

(n) an investment fund that distributes or has distributed its securities only to

(i) a person that is or was an accredited investor at the time of the distribution,

(ii) a person that acquires or acquired securities in the circumstances referred to in sections 2.10 [*Minimum amount investment*], or 2.19 [*Additional investment in investment funds*], or

(iii) a person described in paragraph (i) or (ii) that acquires or acquired securities under section 2.18 [*Investment fund reinvestment*],

(o) an investment fund that distributes or has distributed securities under a prospectus in a jurisdiction of Canada for which the regulator or, in Québec, the securities regulatory authority, has issued a receipt,

(p) a trust company or trust corporation registered or authorized to carry on business under the *Trust and Loan Companies Act* (Canada) or under comparable legislation in a jurisdiction of Canada or a foreign jurisdiction, acting on behalf of a fully managed account managed by the trust company or trust corporation, as the case may be,

(q) a person acting on behalf of a fully managed account managed by that person, if that person is registered or authorized to carry on business as an adviser or the equivalent under the securities legislation of a jurisdiction of Canada or a foreign jurisdiction,

(r) a registered charity under the *Income Tax Act* (Canada) that, in regard to the trade, has obtained advice from an eligibility adviser or an adviser registered under the securities legislation of the jurisdiction of the registered charity to give advice on the securities being traded,

(s) an entity organized in a foreign jurisdiction that is analogous to any of the entities referred to in paragraphs (a) to (d) or paragraph (i) in form and function,

(t) a person in respect of which all of the owners of interests, direct, indirect or beneficial, except the voting securities required by law to be owned by directors, are persons that are accredited investors,

(u) an investment fund that is advised by a person registered as an adviser or a person that is exempt from registration as an adviser,

(v) a person that is recognized or designated by the securities regulatory authority or, except in Ontario and Québec, the regulator as an accredited investor, or

(w) a trust established by an accredited investor for the benefit of the accredited investor's family members of which a majority of the trustees are accredited investors and all of the beneficiaries are the accredited investor's spouse, a former spouse of the accredited investor or a parent, grandparent, brother, sister, child or grandchild of that accredited investor, of that accredited investor's spouse or of that accredited investor's former spouse;

With respect to the elements of this definition that do not apply in Ontario, that province has moved these elements to OSA, s 73.3(2); however, no changes have been made to the scope of the entities eligible to use the exemption. Thus, financial institutions such as banks, loan or trust corporations, insurance companies, and credit unions as well as various levels of government are designated as accredited investors. Assuming that they are appropriately regulated, pension funds and investment funds are now specifically recognized as accredited investors; they do not have to request the status of an exempt purchaser on a case-by-case basis.

As we have seen, the rationale for this exemption is the idea that these market participants have investment expertise or financial resources such that they do not need to be given a prospectus in advance of making an investment decision. The trend here is clearly to expand the categories of people and entities that can avail themselves of this exemption. For example, some years ago, individuals could not take advantage of exempt purchaser status.

In this respect, note that NI 45-106 provides several ways in which individuals can qualify for accredited investor status. They can fulfill one of three asset tests (NI 45-106, s 1.1(j), (j.1), or (l)) or an income test (NI 45-106, s 1.1(k)). "Financial assets" (referenced in s 1.1(j)) must have an "aggregate realizable value that before taxes, but net of any related liabilities," exceeds $1 million and are defined to mean "cash, securities, or a contract of insurance, a deposit or an evidence of a deposit that is not a security for the purposes of securities legislation." NI 45-106CP, s 3.5(3) elaborates on factors that are indicative of beneficial ownership of financial assets. They are:

> (a) physical or constructive possession of evidence of ownership of the financial asset;
> (b) entitlement to receipt of any income generated by the financial asset;
> (c) risk of loss of the value of the financial asset; and
> (d) the ability to dispose of the financial asset or otherwise deal with it as the individual sees fit.

Alternatively, individuals may qualify for accredited investor status by virtue of the "net asset" test, which requires a threshold of at least $5 million, which must "reasonably reflect" the "estimated fair value" of the assets (NI 45-106CP, s 3.5(4)). Net assets are calculated by subtracting a purchaser's total liabilities from total assets. Finally, note the income levels required of individuals, either alone or together with their spouses, to fulfill the income test provided in clause (k) of the definition of accredited investor.

QUESTIONS

1. Clearly, the accredited investor exemption is designed to target certain sophisticated investors who are deemed not to require prospectus-level disclosure in connection with their purchases of securities. Think of various ways in which an exemption in favour of sophisticated parties could be framed.
2. In your opinion, are the tests for individuals to qualify for accredited investor status set at the right thresholds to meet the objectives of the exemption?

b. Substance of Rule Governing Trades to Accredited Investors

The substantive rules with respect to trades to accredited investors in NI 45-106, s 2.3 are very simple. Subsection (1) says that "[t]he prospectus requirement does not apply to a distribution of a security if the purchaser purchases the security as principal and is an accredited investor." OSA, s 73.3(2) is substantively identical to s 2.3(1). Note that all that is required is for the *purchaser* to be an accredited investor purchasing as principal. This allows securities to continue to circulate among accredited investors without triggering a prospectus or resale requirement. There is no minimum purchase amount required, unlike NI 45-106, s 2.10 (discussed below).

c. Disclosure Requirements

With respect to accompanying disclosure requirements, s 6.1 requires a report to be made to regulators within ten days of a trade. The report is to be filed in accordance with Form 45-106F1. Since 2015, an important modification to the operation of the accredited investor exemption in Canada is that individual accredited investors who qualify as such under para (j), (k), or (l) of the definition (but not para (j.1)) must sign a risk acknowledgment form on or before signing the agreement to purchase the security. This is an attempt to offer additional protection to individual accredited investors by requiring them to focus on the risks they are assuming.

2. *Minimum Amount Investment Exemption (NI 45-106, Section 2.10)*

The saga of the minimum investment exemption, now found in NI 45-106, s 2.10, provides some interesting insight into the intersection of economic analysis and the compromises required by a harmonization exercise. This exemption, available for a distribution where the purchasers were paying a specific amount of money to acquire the securities (originally $97,000 per transaction and later $150,000), appeared in a number of provincial securities statutes. It was available in Ontario since the last major overhaul of the statute in 1978. The idea was that if an investor was prepared to pay that amount of money to purchase securities in a single transaction, it could safely be assumed that they were sophisticated enough to make that decision without the disclosure provided by a prospectus. However, in 2001, Ontario removed the minimum investment exemption, in favour of a version of the accredited investor exemption contained in its Rule 45-501, which was substantially similar to the current exemption in NI 45-106. Indeed, as the excerpt below demonstrates, the economic benefits of this move were studied by the OSC's Office of Chief Economist in 2003 and found to be positive.

Ontario Securities Commission, Office of the Chief Economist,
One Step Forward: A Study of the Economic Impact of OSC Rule 45-501, Exempt Distributions
(Toronto: Ontario Securities Commission, 2003) at 2

This study examines the impact of the revision of Rule 45-501, coming into force on Nov. 30, 2001. For this analysis, data was collected for a period prior to the revision (1995-1998) and for the period after the revision (2001-2002). The objective of the study was to determine if the revision had facilitated investment via the prospectus-exempt market. …

The rule revision included the replacement of previous investor restrictions with new criteria for accredited investors that would serve as proxies for the "sophistication" of an investor or the means to tolerate the potential risks of investing in a non-prospectus environment.

The goal of the new rule was to have a positive impact on this regime. The magnitude of the post-revision results has been shown to clearly exceed the activity and total value of transactions of the previous period. The results have demonstrated that:

- Total trading activity has increased,
- Average size of transactions has increased,
- The range of transaction sizes have broadened (there are more small and large transactions),
- Almost half of the transactions are valued at $150,000 and below,
- The overall size of the prospectus-exempt market has grown.

The possibility exists that other factors have contributed to the growth in this market. However, given the contraction in overall capital markets' issuance, particularly in areas of higher risk, the results suggest that the rule change was the most significant contributor to performance.

Overall, the value of investment increased from an annual average of $6.2 billion during the 1995-1998 period to $20.97 billion for the eleven months after Rule 45-501 came into force in late 2001. … [S]mall and medium-sized enterprises (SMEs) were a targeted stakeholder in the introduction of this Rule. As a result, the increase of almost $15 billion was desegregated by size and type of deal to arrive at an estimate of the impact on SMEs. Removing investment fund placements and distributions in excess of $100 million generated an estimate of $2.6 billion of investment directed to the small business sector for the eleven months over 2001-2002 relative to the average from 1985-1998.

The Office of the Chief Economist contracted with the Institute for Policy Analysis of the University of Toronto to estimate the impact, based on appropriate assumptions, of an increase in small business financing of $2.6 billion using the Focus-Ontario macro econometric model. The results follow:

> A simulation with the Focus-Ontario model indicates that the initiative added 0.56% to Ontario GDP in 2002, or 2.63 billions of 2002 dollars. In 2003 the impact is slightly smaller, at 0.50% of GDP or 2.42 billions of 2002 dollars … . In terms of other indicators, the simulation indicates that the initiative generated 16,500 jobs in 2002 and will generate about 19,400 in 2003.

Nonetheless, when NI 45-106 appeared in 2005, the minimum amount investment exemption was retained and available for use in all the provinces. However, in 2015 an important modification was made to this exemption in all provinces such that it may no longer be accessed by individuals. The current exemption is crafted as follows:

> **Minimum amount investment**
>
> 2.10(1) The prospectus requirement does not apply to a distribution of a security to a person if all of the following apply:
>
> (a) that person is not an individual;
>
> (b) that person purchases as principal;
>
> (c) the security has an acquisition cost to that person of not less than $150 000 paid in cash at the time of the distribution;
>
> (d) the distribution is of a security of a single issuer.
>
> (2) Subsection (1) does not apply to a distribution of a security to a person if the person was created, or is used, solely to purchase or hold securities in reliance on the exemption from the prospectus requirement set out in subsection (1).

As we can see, the terms of the exemption are quite straightforward. It focuses on the acquisition cost of the securities of a single issuer to the purchaser, and requires full payment in cash at the time of the trade. The Companion Policy to NI 45-106 clarifies at s 3.9 that the issuer is able to issue more than one kind of security in the transaction, provided that the acquisition cost of the transaction in total is not less than $150,000. It also contains an anti-avoidance component to ensure that an entity is not created to amalgamate the contributions of a number of smaller investors so as to defeat the policy underpinnings of the exemption.

Finally, NI 45-106, s 6.1 provides for the filing of a report where the minimum investment exemption is used.

C. Exemptions Based on a Pre-existing Relationship with the Issuer

In this category of exemption, the provisions of NI 45-106 likewise significantly supersede provincial statutory provisions. Several of the exemptions discussed below deal with trades between issuers and existing securityholders.

1. Dividends (NI 45-106, Section 2.31)

NI 45-106, s 2.31 deals with securities issued to existing securityholders as a dividend.

Where a company issues its own securities in payment of a dividend to its securityholders, in principle this would be a distribution, so the exemption allows this to occur without the necessity of a prospectus. Does this scenario involve a trade in the first place? Note that NI 45-106, s 2.2 provides an exemption for trades made under dividend or interest reinvestment plans in respect of publicly traded equity securities of the issuer's own issue (where participants in the plan apply dividends or interest paid on securities to acquire additional securities of an issuer). An optional cash payment under such plans is included in s 2.2, but only under certain conditions, including the condition that the aggregate number of securities issued in a financial year under the optional cash payment plan must not exceed 2 percent of the issued and outstanding securities of the class.

2. Business Combinations and Reorganizations (NI 45-106, Section 2.11)

This prospectus exemption provides as follows:

> **Business combination and reorganization**
>
> 2.11(1) The prospectus requirement does not apply to a distribution of a security in connection with
>
> (a) an amalgamation, merger, reorganization or arrangement that is under a statutory procedure,
>
> (b) an amalgamation, merger, reorganization or arrangement that
>
> (i) is described in an information circular made pursuant to National Instrument 51-102 *Continuous Disclosure Obligations* or in a similar disclosure record and the information circular or similar disclosure record is delivered to each securityholder whose approval of the amalgamation, merger, reorganization or arrangement is required before it can proceed, and
>
> (ii) is approved by the securityholders referred to in subparagraph (i), or
>
> (c) a dissolution or winding-up of the issuer.

Section 2.11 deals with various types of reorganizations of a business entity that involve the issuing of securities. They include amalgamations or arrangements under statutory procedures such as those provided under corporate statutes or under statutes such as the *Companies Creditors' Arrangements Act* that regulate the reorganization of business entities in financial difficulty. In the latter scenario, debt obligations are often exchanged for equity as the business entity tries to rehabilitate itself financially. The rationale for providing a prospectus exemption for the distribution of equity securities is that regulators do not want to add to the difficulties of an issuer in financial distress, as well as the fact that creditors may have other avenues of access to information about the issuer through the terms of their debt agreements. See also NI 45-106CP, s 4.2.

3. *Conversions or Exchanges of Securities (NI 45-106, Section 2.42)*

Issuers will often issue securities that carry with them a conversion or exchange feature whereby the securities initially issued can be converted into or exchanged for other securities, or can carry an option to acquire additional securities. A typical example would be preferred shares that carry the feature that they can be converted into common shares. When executed, the conversion, exchange, or exercise of the right involves the issuing of new securities (the so-called underlying securities). Section 2.42 provides an exemption from the prospectus requirement for the issue of the underlying securities, as long as that issuance is in accordance with the terms and conditions of the previously issued securities. Thus, the section provides:

> **Conversion, exchange, or exercise**
>
> 2.42(1) The prospectus requirement does not apply to a distribution by an issuer if
>
> (a) the issuer distributes a security of its own issue to a securityholder of the issuer in accordance with the terms and conditions of a security previously issued by that issuer, or
>
> (b) subject to subsection (2), the issuer distributes a security of a reporting issuer held by it to a securityholder of the issuer in accordance with the terms and conditions of a security previously issued by that issuer.
>
> (2) Subsection (1)(b) does not apply unless
>
> (a) the issuer has given the regulator or, in Québec, the securities regulatory authority, prior written notice stating the date, amount, nature and conditions of the distribution, and
>
> (b) the regulator or, in Québec, the securities regulatory authority, has not objected in writing to the distribution within 10 days of receipt of the notice referred to in paragraph (a) or, if the regulator or securities regulatory authority objects to the distribution, the issuer must deliver to the regulator or securities regulatory authority information relating to the securities that is satisfactory to and accepted by the regulator or securities regulatory authority.

We will see in discussing the resale rules that regulators tend to be concerned about the possibility of abuse in the use of this exemption—that is, issuers might use convertible securities as a way of issuing equity while circumventing the disclosure rules that would normally be required for that issue.

4. *Rights Offerings (NI 45-106, Section 2.1)*

NI 45-106, s 2.1 addresses the scenario involving the granting of rights by an issuer to its securityholders to acquire additional securities of its own issue and the issue of securities pursuant to the right (both scenarios are exempt). The exemption is designed to allow issuers the opportunity to offer to their existing securityholders the right to buy additional securities based on the number of securities already held by these securityholders (for example, one additional share for each ten shares held) without a prospectus being required. Rights offerings can be a useful alternative financing method for issuers; they involve the issuer approaching a class of potential purchasers that has already expressed interest in the issuer's securities. They often feature a "standby commitment" provided by an investment bank that undertakes to purchase any securities not subscribed for by the existing securityholders.

The CSA recently reconsidered the scope of the rights offering exemption. The current provisions require that the issuer be a reporting issuer in at least one jurisdiction of Canada and that it has filed all the appropriate continuous disclosure requirements expected of it. A separate set of requirements under NI 45-106, s 2.1.2 applies to issuers with a "minimal connection" to Canada. The most significant change to the way this exemption works is that a reporting issuer may now distribute rights such that the number of outstanding securities of the relevant class may increase by up to 100 percent. Previously, a rights offering could not have the effect of increasing the number of outstanding securities by more than 25 percent. The exercise period for the rights must be between 21 and 90 days after a rights offering notice is sent to securityholders. The subscription price for the security must be lower than the "market price" of the security on the day the rights offering notice is filed. Section 2.1.4 of NI 45-106 also makes clear that the secondary market civil liability provisions apply to the acquisition of securities under a rights offering circular.

In terms of disclosure obligations accompanying the use of this exemption, NI 45-106 now prescribes only that the issuer files with regulators and sends to all securityholders of the relevant class, a notice in accordance with Form 45-106F14 that indicates who may participate in the offering and how the rights may be exercised. Meanwhile, the more detailed rights offering circular must fulfill the requirements of Form 45-106F15. This form prescribes some prospectus-like information, such as detailed information about the attributes of the rights, a brief description of the business of the issuer, information about significant ownership of securities of the issuer, and the use to be made of the proceeds of the offering. Item 35 of Form 45-106F15 requires that the circular include information about any resale restrictions associated with the security, disclosing when the rights and their underlying securities will become freely tradeable. However, since this exemption is available only to reporting issuers, the CSA considers the securities "generally freely tradeable." The rights offering circular is filed on SEDAR.

5. Trades to Employees (NI 45-106, Section 2.24)

This prospectus exemption enables an issuer or a control person of an issuer to distribute securities to its employees or employees of its affiliates without providing a prospectus as long as participation is voluntary. Employees, executive officers, directors, and consultants of the issuer are all included within the scope of this exemption. The exemption forms the basis for employee incentive plans such as stock purchase or stock option plans, where employees are given equity participation as part of a remuneration package. The acceptable consideration has to be past services. No disclosure requirements are prescribed in connection with the use of this exemption. However, additional regulatory requirements are imposed on "unlisted reporting issuers" in connection with this exemption. See NI 45-106, s 2.25.

QUESTIONS

1. Is the limiting requirement—that participation in the trade or employee incentive plan be voluntary in order to obtain the prospectus exemption—a reasonable one, in your view?
2. Is the policy rationale—the lack of a "need to know" on the part of employees—reasonable, in your view? Would it matter to your answer whether the issuer was an SME or a large multinational?

D. The Offering Memorandum Exemption (NI 45-106, Section 2.9)

a. Overview and Policy Rationale

A final notable advance in the harmonization of prospectus exemptions across Canada is that the offering memorandum (OM) exemption is now available in Ontario. Prior to 2016, this exemption was available, in one form or another, in all provinces except Ontario and in the Northwest Territories and Nunavut, but in Ontario it was available only as an accompaniment to another exemption. In light of the realities of population density in Ontario, the availability of the OM exemption in Ontario as of January 2016 may significantly increase its use.

One puzzle about the OM exemption as it is currently conceived relates to its underlying policy rationale. As we will see, its use is not limited to the kinds of start-up or SME issuers who are intended to be assisted by the private issuer, crowdfunding, or FFBA exemptions. Nor is access to the OM exemption limited to AI investors, though there are limitations, as we will see, on the amounts that retail investors can invest in an OM offering. The OM itself is often described as a "prospectus-like" document. It is defined in the OSA, s 1 as

> a document . . . purporting to describe the business and affairs of an issuer that has been prepared primarily for delivery to and review by a prospective purchaser so as to assist the prospective purchaser to make an investment decision in respect of securities being sold in a distribution to which section 53 would apply but for the availability of one or more of the exemptions contained in Ontario securities law.

The definition goes on to exclude a "document setting out current information about an issuer for the benefit of a prospective purchaser familiar with the issuer through prior investment or business contacts." This exclusion may allow issuers defending themselves from claims relating to misrepresentations in documents provided to investors under certain exemptions to claim that the document did not fall within the definition of an offering memorandum.

The full text of the current lengthy OM exemption is reproduced below.

> 2.9(1) In British Columbia and Newfoundland and Labrador, the prospectus requirement does not apply to a distribution by an issuer of a security of its own issue to a purchaser if
>
> (a) the purchaser purchases the security as principal, and
>
> (b) at the same time or before the purchaser signs the agreement to purchase the security, the issuer
>
> (i) delivers an offering memorandum to the purchaser in compliance with subsections (5) to (13), and
>
> (ii) obtains a signed risk acknowledgement from the purchaser in compliance with subsection (15).
>
> (2) In Manitoba, Northwest Territories, Nunavut, Prince Edward Island and Yukon, the prospectus requirement does not apply to a distribution by an issuer of a security of its own issue to a purchaser if
>
> (a) the purchaser purchases the security as principal,
>
> (b) the purchaser is an eligible investor or the acquisition cost to the purchaser does not exceed $10 000,
>
> (c) at the same time or before the purchaser signs the agreement to purchase the security, the issuer
>
> (i) delivers an offering memorandum to the purchaser in compliance with subsections (5) to (13), and

(ii) obtains a signed risk acknowledgement from the purchaser in compliance with subsection (15), and

(d) if the issuer is an investment fund, the investment fund is

(i) a non-redeemable investment fund, or

(ii) a mutual fund that is a reporting issuer.

(2.1) In Alberta, New Brunswick, Nova Scotia, Ontario, Québec and Saskatchewan the prospectus requirement does not apply to a distribution by an issuer of a security of its own issue to a purchaser if

(a) the purchaser purchases the security as principal,

(b) the acquisition cost of all securities acquired by a purchaser who is an individual under this section in the preceding 12 months does not exceed the following amounts:

(i) in the case of a purchaser that is not an eligible investor, $10 000;

(ii) in the case of a purchaser that is an eligible investor, $30 000;

(iii) in the case of a purchaser that is an eligible investor and that received advice from a portfolio manager, investment dealer or exempt market dealer that the investment is suitable, $100 000,

(c) at the same time or before the purchaser signs the agreement to purchase the security, the issuer

(i) delivers an offering memorandum to the purchaser in compliance with subsections (5) to (13), and

(ii) obtains a signed risk acknowledgement from the purchaser in compliance with subsection (15), and

(d) the security distributed by the issuer is not either of the following:

(i) a specified derivative;

(ii) a structured finance product.

(2.2) The prospectus exemption described in subsection (2.1) is not available

(a) in Alberta, Nova Scotia and Saskatchewan, to an issuer that is an investment fund, unless the issuer is a non-redeemable investment fund or a mutual fund that is a reporting issuer, or

(b) in New Brunswick, Ontario and Québec, to an issuer that is an investment fund.

(2.3) The investment limits described in subparagraphs (2.1)(b)(ii) and (iii) do not apply if the purchaser is

(a) an accredited investor, or

(b) a person described in subsection 2.5(1) [*Family, friends and business associates*].

(3) In Manitoba, Northwest Territories, Nunavut, Prince Edward Island and Yukon, this section does not apply to a distribution of a security to a person described in paragraph (a) of the definition of "eligible investor" in section 1.1 [*Definitions*] if that person was created, or is used, solely to purchase or hold securities in reliance on the exemption from the prospectus requirement set out in subsection (2).

(3.0.1) In Alberta, New Brunswick, Nova Scotia, Ontario, Québec and Saskatchewan, this section does not apply to a distribution of a security to a person that was created, or is used, solely to purchase or hold securities in reliance on the exemption from the prospectus requirement set out in subsection (2.1).

(3.1) Subsections (1), (2) and (2.1) do not apply to a distribution of a short-term securitized product.

(4) No commission or finder's fee may be paid to any person, other than a registered dealer, in connection with a distribution to a purchaser in the Northwest Territories, Nunavut and Yukon under subsection (2).

(5) An offering memorandum delivered under this section must be in the required form.

(5.1) In Alberta, New Brunswick, Nova Scotia, Ontario, Québec and Saskatchewan, an offering memorandum delivered under subsection (2.1)

(a) must incorporate by reference, by way of a statement in the offering memorandum, OM marketing materials related to each distribution under the offering memorandum and delivered or made reasonably available to a prospective purchaser before the termination of the distribution, and

(b) is deemed to incorporate by reference OM marketing materials related to each distribution under the offering memorandum and delivered or made reasonably available to a prospective purchaser before the termination of the distribution.

(5.2) A portfolio manager, investment dealer or exempt market dealer must not distribute OM marketing materials unless the OM marketing materials have been approved in writing by the issuer.

(6) If the securities legislation where the purchaser is resident does not provide a comparable right, an offering memorandum delivered under this section must provide the purchaser with a contractual right to cancel the agreement to purchase the security by delivering a notice to the issuer not later than midnight on the 2nd business day after the purchaser signs the agreement to purchase the security.

(7) If the securities legislation where the purchaser is resident does not provide statutory rights of action in the event of a misrepresentation in an offering memorandum delivered under this section, the offering memorandum must contain a contractual right of action against the issuer for rescission or damages that

(a) is available to the purchaser if the offering memorandum, or any information or documents incorporated or deemed to be incorporated by reference into the offering memorandum, contains a misrepresentation, without regard to whether the purchaser relied on the misrepresentation,

(b) is enforceable by the purchaser delivering a notice to the issuer

(i) in the case of an action for rescission, within 180 days after the purchaser signs the agreement to purchase the security, or

(ii) in the case of an action for damages, before the earlier of

A) 180 days after the purchaser first has knowledge of the facts giving rise to the cause of action, or

B) 3 years after the date the purchaser signs the agreement to purchase the security,

(c) is subject to the defence that the purchaser had knowledge of the misrepresentation,

(d) in the case of an action for damages, provides that the amount recoverable

(i) must not exceed the price at which the security was offered, and

(ii) does not include all or any part of the damages that the issuer proves does not represent the depreciation in value of the security resulting from the misrepresentation, and

(e) is in addition to, and does not detract from, any other right of the purchaser.

(8) An offering memorandum delivered under this section must contain a certificate that states the following: "This offering memorandum does not contain a misrepresentation."

(9) If the issuer is a company, a certificate under subsection (8) must be signed

(a) by the issuer's chief executive officer and chief financial officer or, if the issuer does not have a chief executive officer or chief financial officer, an individual acting in that capacity,

(b) on behalf of the directors of the issuer, by

(i) any 2 directors who are authorized to sign, other than the persons referred to in paragraph (a), or

(ii) all the directors of the issuer, and

(c) by each promoter of the issuer.

(10) If the issuer is a trust, a certificate under subsection (8) must be signed by

(a) the individuals who perform functions for the issuer similar to those performed by the chief executive officer and the chief financial officer of a company, and

(b) each trustee and the manager of the issuer.

(10.1) If a trustee or the manager that is signing the certificate of the issuer is

(a) an individual, the individual must sign the certificate,

(b) a company, the certificate must be signed

(i) by the chief executive officer and the chief financial officer of the trustee or the manager, and

(ii) on behalf of the board of directors of the trustee or the manager, by

(A) any two directors of the trustee or the manager, other than the persons referred to in subparagraph (i), or

(B) all of the directors of the trustee or the manager,

(c) a limited partnership, the certificate must be signed by each general partner of the limited partnership as described in subsection (11.1) in relation to an issuer that is a limited partnership, or

(d) not referred to in paragraphs (a), (b) or (c), the certificate may be signed by any person or company with authority to act on behalf of the trustee or the manager.

(10.2) Despite subsections (10) and (10.1), if the issuer is an investment fund and the declaration of trust, trust indenture or trust agreement establishing the investment fund delegates the authority to do so, or otherwise authorizes an individual or company to do so, the certificate may be signed by the individual or company to whom the authority is delegated or that is authorized to sign the certificate.

(10.3) Despite subsections (10) and (10.1), if the trustees of an issuer, other than an investment fund, do not perform functions for the issuer similar to those performed by the directors of a company, the trustees are not required to sign the certificate of the issuer if at least two individuals who perform functions for the issuer similar to those performed by the directors of a company sign the certificate.

(11) If the issuer is a limited partnership, a certificate under subsection (8) must be signed by

(a) each individual who performs a function for the issuer similar to any of those performed by the chief executive officer or the chief financial officer of a company, and

(b) each general partner of the issuer.

(11.1) If a general partner of the issuer is

(a) an individual, the individual must sign the certificate,

(b) a company, the certificate must be signed

(i) by the chief executive officer and the chief financial officer of the general partner, and

(ii) on behalf of the board of directors of the general partner, by

(A) any two directors of the general partner, other than the persons referred to in subparagraph (i), or

(B) all of the directors of the general partner,

(c) a limited partnership, the certificate must be signed by each general partner of the limited partnership and, for greater certainty, this subsection applies to each general partner required to sign,

(d) a trust, the certificate must be signed by the trustees of the general partner as described in subsection 10 in relation to an issuer that is a trust, or

(e) not referred to in paragraphs (a) to (d), the certificate may be signed by any person or company with authority to act on behalf of the general partner.

(12) If an issuer is not a company, trust or limited partnership, a certificate under subsection (8) must be signed by the persons that, in relation to the issuer, are in a similar position or

perform a similar function to any of the persons referred to in subsections (9), (10), (10.1), (10.2), (10.3), (11) and (11.1).

(13) A certificate under subsection (8) must be true

(a) at the date the certificate is signed, and

(b) at the date the offering memorandum is delivered to the purchaser.

(14) If a certificate under subsection (8) ceases to be true after it is delivered to the purchaser, the issuer cannot accept an agreement to purchase the security from the purchaser unless

(a) the purchaser receives an update of the offering memorandum,

(b) the update of the offering memorandum contains a newly dated certificate signed in compliance with subsection (9), (10), (10.1), (10.2), (10.3), (11) or (11.1) and

(c) the purchaser re-signs the agreement to purchase the security.

(15) A risk acknowledgement under subsection (1), (2) or (2.1) must be in the required form and an issuer relying on subsection (1), (2) or (2.1) must retain the signed risk acknowledgment for 8 years after the distribution.

(16) The issuer must

(a) hold in trust all consideration received from the purchaser in connection with a distribution of a security under subsection (1), (2) or (2.1) until midnight on the 2nd business day after the purchaser signs the agreement to purchase the security, and

(b) return all consideration to the purchaser promptly if the purchaser exercises the right to cancel the agreement to purchase the security described under subsection (6).

(17) The issuer must file a copy of an offering memorandum delivered under this section and any update of a previously filed offering memorandum with the securities regulatory authority on or before the 10th day after the distribution under the offering memorandum or update of the offering memorandum.

(17.1) In Alberta, New Brunswick, Nova Scotia, Ontario, Québec and Saskatchewan, the issuer must file with the securities regulatory authority a copy of all OM marketing materials required or deemed to be incorporated by reference into an offering memorandum delivered under this section,

(a) if the OM marketing materials are prepared on or before the filing of the offering memorandum, concurrently with the filing of the offering memorandum, or

(b) if the OM marketing materials are prepared after the filing of the offering memorandum, within 10 days of the OM marketing materials being delivered or made reasonably available to a prospective purchaser.

(17.2) OM marketing materials filed under subsection (17.1) must include a cover page clearly identifying the offering memorandum to which they relate.

(17.3) Subsections (17.4) to (17.21) apply to issuers that rely on subsection (2.1) and that are not reporting issuers in any jurisdiction of Canada.

(17.4) In Alberta, an issuer must, within 120 days after the end of each of its financial years, file with the securities regulatory authority annual financial statements and make them reasonably available to each holder of a security acquired under subsection (2.1).

(17.5) In New Brunswick, Ontario, Québec and Saskatchewan, an issuer must, within 120 days after the end of each of its financial years, deliver annual financial statements to the securities regulatory authority and make them reasonably available to each holder of a security acquired under subsection (2.1).

(17.6) In Nova Scotia, an issuer must, within 120 days after the end of each of its financial years, make reasonably available annual financial statements to each holder of a security acquired under subsection (2.1).

(17.7) Despite subsections (17.4), (17.5) and (17.6), as applicable, if an issuer is required to file, deliver or make reasonably available annual financial statements for a financial year that ended before the issuer distributed securities under subsection (2.1) for the first time, those annual financial statements must be filed in Alberta, delivered in New Brunswick, Ontario, Québec and Saskatchewan or made reasonably available in Nova Scotia, as applicable, on or before the later of

(a) the 60th day after the issuer first distributes securities under subsection (2.1), and

(b) the deadline in subsection (17.4), (17.5) or (17.6), as applicable, to file, deliver or make reasonably available the annual financial statements.

(17.8) The annual financial statements of an issuer referred to in subsections (17.4), (17.5) and (17.6) must include

(a) a statement of comprehensive income, a statement of changes in equity, and a statement of cash flows for

(i) the most recently completed financial year, and

(ii) the financial year immediately preceding the most recently completed financial year, if any,

(b) a statement of financial position as at the end of each of the periods referred to in paragraph (a),

(c) in the following circumstances, a statement of financial position as at the beginning of the financial year immediately preceding the most recently completed financial year:

(i) the issuer discloses in its annual financial statements an unreserved statement of compliance with IFRS, and

(ii) the issuer

(A) applies an accounting policy retrospectively in its annual financial statements,

(B) makes a retrospective restatement of items in its annual financial statements, or

(C) reclassifies items in its annual financial statements,

(d) in the case of the issuer's first IFRS financial statements, the opening IFRS statement of financial position at the date of transition to IFRS, and

(e) notes to the annual financial statements.

(17.9) If the annual financial statements referred to in subsection (17.8) present the components of profit or loss in a separate income statement, the separate income statement must be displayed immediately before the statement of comprehensive income referred to in subsection (17.8).

(17.10) The annual financial statements referred to in subsection (17.8) must be audited.

(17.11) Despite subsection (17.10), for the first annual financial statements of an issuer referred to in subsections (17.4), (17.5) and (17.6), comparative information relating to the preceding financial year is not required to be audited if it has not been previously audited.

(17.12) Any period referred to in subsection (17.8) that has not been audited must be clearly labelled as unaudited.

(17.13) In Alberta, New Brunswick, Ontario, Québec and Saskatchewan, if an issuer decides to change its financial year end by more than 14 days, it must deliver to the securities regulatory authority and make reasonably available to each holder of a security acquired under subsection (2.1) a notice containing the information set out in subsection (17.15) as soon as practicable and, in any event, no later than the earlier of

(a) the deadline, based on the issuer's old financial year end, for the next annual financial statements referred to in subsections (17.4) and (17.5), and

(b) the deadline, based on the issuer's new financial year end, for the next annual financial statements referred to in subsections (17.4) and (17.5).

(17.14) In Nova Scotia, if an issuer decides to change its financial year end by more than 14 days, it must make reasonably available to each holder of a security acquired under subsection (2.1) a notice containing the information set out in subsection (17.15) as soon as practicable and, in any event, no later than the earlier of

(a) the deadline, based on the issuer's old financial year end, for the next annual financial statements referred to in subsection (17.6), and

(b) the deadline, based on the issuer's new financial year end, for the next annual financial statements referred to in subsection (17.6).

(17.15) The notice referred to in subsections (17.13) and (17.14) must state

(a) that the issuer has decided to change its financial year end,

(b) the reason for the change,

(c) the issuer's old financial year end,

(d) the issuer's new financial year end,

(e) the length and ending date of the periods, including the comparative periods, of the annual financial statements referred to in subsections (17.4), (17.5) and (17.6) for the issuer's transition year and its new financial year, and

(f) the filing deadline for the annual financial statements for the issuer's transition year.

(17.16) If a transition year is less than 9 months in length, the issuer must include as comparative financial information to its annual financial statements for its new financial year

(a) a statement of financial position, a statement of comprehensive income, a statement of changes in equity, a statement of cash flows, and notes to the financial statements for its transition year,

(b) a statement of financial position, a statement of comprehensive income, a statement of changes in equity, a statement of cash flows, and notes to the financial statements for its old financial year,

(c) in the following circumstances, a statement of financial position as at the beginning of the old financial year:

(i) the issuer discloses in its annual financial statements an unreserved statement of compliance with IFRS, and

(ii) the issuer

(A) applies an accounting policy retrospectively in its annual financial statements,

(B) makes a retrospective restatement of items in its annual financial statements, or

(C) reclassifies items in its annual financial statements, and

(d) in the case of the issuer's first IFRS financial statements, the opening IFRS statement of financial position at the date of transition to IFRS.

(17.17) A transition year must not exceed 15 months.

(17.18) An SEC issuer satisfies subsections (17.13), (17.14) and (17.16) if

(a) it complies with the requirements of U.S. laws relating to a change of fiscal year, and

(b) it delivers a copy of all materials required by U.S. laws relating to a change in fiscal year to the securities regulatory authority at the same time as, or as soon as practicable after, they are filed with or furnished to the SEC and, in any event, no later than 120 days after the end of its most recently completed financial year.

(17.19) The financial statements of an issuer referred to in subsections (17.4), (17.5) and (17.6) must be accompanied by a notice of the issuer disclosing in reasonable detail the use of the aggregate gross proceeds raised by the issuer under section 2.9 in accordance with Form 45-106F16, unless the issuer has previously disclosed the use of the aggregate gross proceeds in accordance with Form 45-106F16.

(17.20) In New Brunswick, Nova Scotia and Ontario, an issuer must make reasonably available to each holder of a security acquired under subsection (2.1) a notice of each of the following events in accordance with Form 45-106F17, within 10 days of the occurrence of the event:

(a) a discontinuation of the issuer's business;

(b) a change in the issuer's industry;

(c) a change of control of the issuer.

(17.21) An issuer is required to make the disclosure required respectively by subsections (17.4), (17.5), (17.6), (17.19) and (17.20) until the earliest of

(a) the date the issuer becomes a reporting issuer in any jurisdiction of Canada, and

(b) the date the issuer ceases to carry on business.

(17.22) In Ontario, an issuer that is not a reporting issuer in Ontario that distributes securities in reliance on the exemption in subsection (2.1) is designated a market participant under the Securities Act (Ontario).

(17.23) In New Brunswick, an issuer that is not a reporting issuer in New Brunswick that distributes securities in reliance on the exemption in subsection (2.1) is designated a market participant under the Securities Act (New Brunswick).

(18) [Repealed].

Let us explore in more detail two aspects of the terms of this exemption: (1) eligibility to purchase under the OM and (2) disclosure requirements imposed pursuant to the exemption.

b. Eligibility Requirements

While the OM exemption is now available in some form in all provinces and territories of Canada, the text of the exemption clearly depicts a significant lack of harmonization about the level of financial investment that can be made by different types of investors and associated requirements. Thus, in British Columbia and Newfoundland and Labrador, any investor can purchase securities under an OM in any amount as long as the purchaser is purchasing as principal and signs a risk acknowledgment form. In all other provinces and territories, there is a limit on the amount of financial investment that can be made if the investor is not an "eligible investor," a defined term in NI 45-106. The asset and income thresholds for "eligible investor" status are significantly lower than those for accredited investors. Provinces such as Alberta, New Brunswick, Nova Scotia, Ontario, Québec, and Saskatchewan impose a limit of $30,000 of investment in a 12-month period on eligible investors, though this limit rises to $100,000 if the eligible investor receives advice from a portfolio manager, investment dealer, or exempt market dealer that the investment is suitable. See Schedules 1 and 2 of Form 45-106F4 for more detail here. A signed risk acknowledgment form is still required for all these purchasers in those jurisdictions.

c. Disclosure Requirements

As can be seen from the text of s 2.9 above, a variety of disclosure requirements accompany the use of the OM exemption, in a manner somewhat similar to the terms of the crowdfunding exemption. They can be sorted into the following four categories: (1) the OM itself, (2) the risk acknowledgment form, (3) OM marketing materials, and (4) ongoing disclosure obligations. Let us consider each of these categories separately.

1. Offering memorandum: It appears that all provinces establish a distinction between the scope of disclosures required in the OM depending on whether the issuer is a "qualifying issuer" or not. One form (Form 45-106F3) may be used by "qualifying issuers"; the other (Form 45-106F2) may be used by all other issuers. See the definition section of NI 45-106 for an explanation of "qualifying issuer," which refers to reporting issuers who are SEDAR filers and have filed an annual information form along with other required disclosure documents. Such qualifying issuers can use material from annual information forms, management discussion and analysis, and other continuous disclosure documents to fulfill the offering memorandum requirements. See Chapter 6 for more detail on these concepts. For the other issuers who must use Form

45-106F2, it is sufficient to note here that the list of some 13 items that need to be included bear a striking resemblance to the type of information required for a prospectus. The items include financial statements; risk factors associated with the investment; information about the compensation and securities held by directors, officers, promoters, and significant shareholders of the issuer; purchaser's rights; and resale restrictions. The document is also required to contain a certificate stating the following: "This offering memorandum does not contain a misrepresentation."

2. Risk acknowledgment form: Form 45-106F4 indicates the risk acknowledgment that the purchaser under the offering memorandum exemption must sign. It reminds investors that they "could lose all of the money" that they invest, as well as the possibility that the investor may never be able to sell the securities, if the issuer is not a reporting issuer.
3. A new feature of the OM exemption is the regulation of so-called offering memorandum marketing materials. This defined term refers to written communications intended for prospective purchasers that contains material facts related to the issuer, securities, or offering. In a number of provinces (Alberta, New Brunswick, Nova Scotia, Ontario, Québec, and Saskatchewan), the OM is required to incorporate OM marketing materials by reference and those materials must also be filed with the regulator. The significance of the incorporation by reference requirement is that the marketing materials will also be subject to the liability for misrepresentation provisions applicable to offering memoranda generally. Further commentary on this issue can be found at NI 45-106CP, s 3.3.1.
4. As can be noted from the text of s 2.9, paras (17.4) to (17.21) contain detailed requirements related to the filing of annual financial statements by non-reporting issuers who have distributed securities in reliance on the OM exemption. These requirements vary across a number of the provinces that have adopted the exemption. This requirement for ongoing financial information is a significant departure from previous formulations of prospectus exemptions for non-reporting issuers, which focused only on requirements at the time of securities issuance. It should also be noted that in New Brunswick, Nova Scotia, and Ontario, NI 45-106, s 2.9(17.20) requires issuers to make "reasonably available" to each holder of a security acquired under s 2.9(2.1) a notice of each of the following events: a discontinuation of the issuer's business, a change in the issuer's industry, or a change of control of the issuer. Presumably it is the view of regulators in each of these three jurisdictions that such events are a sufficiently dramatic change in the affairs of the issuer that they warrant deviating from the long-held view that securities of non-reporting issuers trading in the exempt market were not subject to reporting requirements. The need to disclose the occurrence of one of these events persists until the issuer becomes a reporting issuer or until it ceases to carry on business.

Finally, s 2.9(7) makes a contractual right of action against the issuer for rescission or damages available where the province or territory of residence of the purchaser does not provide a statutory right of action. The right of action for a deficiency in an offering memorandum has now been placed on a statutory footing in Ontario. See OSA, s 130.1 for provisions dealing with grounds of liability (misrepresentation); defences available (knowledge, depreciation not due to misrepresentation, not receiving proceeds); and remedies available. More detail on these provisions is provided in Chapter 10. In conclusion, it should be noted that the OSC's Statement of Priorities for 2016-17 indicated that it will be "vigilant in its oversight" of the exempt markets "as they evolve under the new regulatory framework." This will include risk-based supervision of issuers, registrants, and portals operating in this market, as well as the collection and analysis of data on the use of exemptions.

QUESTIONS

1. Given that offering memoranda typically provide prospectus-like information where they are used and that there is a statutory right of action for a misrepresentation in an offering memorandum, are there any advantages for the issuer in using an offering memorandum as opposed to a prospectus to raise funds?
2. Several of the prospectus exemptions discussed above now require purchasers to sign risk acknowledgment forms. Does what we have studied about the findings of behavioural economics with respect to investor decision-making shed any light on the usefulness of such forms?

E. Discretionary Exemptions

Traditionally, securities practitioners advise their clients that if the financing they want to raise cannot be structured so as to fit the terms of the various prospectus exemption rules, it is possible to apply to securities regulators to obtain a transaction-specific exemption from the prospectus requirement. Many provincial statutes provide for this discretionary power to be exercised by regulators. Examples include OSA, s 74; ASA, s 144; and BCSA, s 76. In most cases, the exercise of this legislative power requires the regulator to determine that it is not prejudicial to the public interest to allow the exemption, which involves the regulators analyzing whether the terms and structure of the proposed transaction undermine the policy objectives of legislation, particularly with respect to investor protection. However, one of the avowed purposes of broadening and rationalizing the available exemptions by way of introducing private issuer and the accredited investor exemptions was to reduce the number of discretionary orders sought and granted. A good example of the OSC's reasoned refusal of an exemption application on public policy grounds can be found in *In the Matter of the University of Guelph and GUARD Limited Partnership* (1995), 18 OSCB 1255. See also the more recent NP 11-203 (2008), 31 OSCB 1066, as amended 7 January 2016, which deals with the process for making exemptive relief applications in multiple provincial jurisdictions.

V. POLICY OBJECTIVES OF RESALE RULES

One of the biggest concerns for regulators about the use of prospectus exemptions is what happens when the original purchaser who qualified for an exempt transaction wants to resell his or her securities, or when, for example, holders of private issuer securities want to resell when the private issuer no longer qualifies for that status. What if the second-round or non-exempt buyers need additional information that the seller is unwilling or unable to supply? For securities of business entities that have only used the exempt market to raise capital, there may be little or no published information about the entity in existence. As well as disclosure issues like this, regulators have historically also been concerned about issuers using the exempt market to distribute their securities for immediate resale so as to avoid the obligations of ongoing information disclosure. This "backdoor underwriting" problem created a need for a mechanism for the orderly transfer of securities from the exempt distribution system to the publicly traded marketplace. These related policy objectives are accomplished by way of the resale rules in securities law. In addition to the policy objectives of preventing backdoor underwriting and promoting disclosure of information, the Five Year Review Committee also noted in its final report that "[h]old periods create an incentive for issuers to complete a public offering by reducing the price the private placee will pay for the securities given that they are not freely tradeable" (*Five Year Review Committee Final Report—Reviewing the Securities Act (Ontario)* (Toronto: Queen's Printer for Ontario, 2003) at 138). The committee is referring to the fact that, as we will see, one mechanism used in the resale rules to address regulatory concerns is to impose a hold or restricted period on some exempt purchasers, delaying the possibility for them to resell their securities. The lack of liquidity that this creates for these exempt purchasers will be reflected in the price they will be willing to pay for securities. Thus, it is hoped that this consideration might encourage issuers to make prospectus offerings. A final, more specific regulatory problem is how to handle sales from the holdings of control persons in issuers. We have seen that sales from control blocks are considered to be distributions in most provinces on the assumption that control block holders have superior access to relevant information about the issuer, which might give them an advantage in a securities transaction with another investor. But it is also recognized by legislators that this concern should be balanced by giving control persons an alternative for selling their securities other than the requirement to prepare a prospectus so as to facilitate the orderly transfer of their securities into the secondary market. This alternative is also provided by the resale rules.

However, the policy objectives underlying resale rules may require some rethinking in light of the expansion of the possibilities for exempt distributions. If sophisticated investors are assumed to be able to make a trade-off between a cheaper acquisition and a lack of liquidity, it is not clear that the same is true of retail investors in general, who can now purchase securities under the crowdfunding or OM exemptions. While the OM exemption is long-standing in some provinces, it may become a more attractive vehicle for capital-raising now that securities can also be distributed in Ontario under this exemption. It should be noted that the CSA Business Plan for 2016-2019 indicates that one of the CSA's priorities over this period is to "study the current resale regime for prospectus-exempt securities under National Instrument 45-102 Resale of Securities to determine whether the resale provisions continue to be relevant in today's markets and to assess the impact of alternative regulatory approaches."

VI. SUBSTANTIVE REQUIREMENTS OF RESALE RULES

MI 45-102 became a national instrument when it was adopted by Québec in 2005. Where pre-existing provincial statutory provisions dealing with resale rules have not been repealed, NI 45-102 removes their effectiveness. (See NI 45-102, s 2.2 and appendix C.) By way of introduction to the rule, it is important to understand that two separate resale rules are created for non-control block resales by NI 45-102. They are found in ss 2.5 and 2.6 of the Instrument, and they are described below. Different exemptions in different provinces require one or the other of these two resale rules to be applied. One of the rules is more stringent than the other.

One underlying rationale for variation in the resale rule that applies to a specific exemption appears to be that the more stringent rule is applicable where there is more chance of a backdoor underwriting taking place. In other words, NI 45-102, s 2.5, the more onerous resale rule, governs those exempt transactions that are considered more susceptible to being abused by issuers or initial purchasers. In these situations, s 2.5 imposes requirements both that the issuer of the securities has become a reporting issuer at the time of resale (the "seasoning" period) *and* that the reseller hold the securities for a period of time before resale (the "restricted" period). Variations of these requirements imposed in order to validly resell securities originally purchased by means of an exemption have been in existence in some provinces since the 1970s. Condon provides an account of some of the twists and turns of legislative reform related to prospectus exemptions in the excerpt below dealing with the various securities bills that were before the Ontario legislature throughout this decade, culminating in the passage of the Ontario *Securities Act* in 1978.

Mary G Condon, *Making Disclosure: Ideas and Interests in Ontario Securities Regulation*

(Toronto: University of Toronto Press, 1998) at 193, 195 (footnotes omitted)

Writing in 1975, Dey describes the successive attempts at establishing a new securities regime in Ontario as a situation where "the overkill of Bill 154 … was replaced by the moderation of Bill 75 … and recently by the harder line of Bill 98" … .

The exemption provisions in Bill 75 are likely to have contributed to Dey's assessment of the bill as "moderate." This is because the bill removed the requirement that exempt purchasers so designated by the OSC as well as private placees would have to demonstrate investment intent. The removal of this requirement was at odds with the OSC's Merger recommendations. Further, a private placee could now be an individual.

Yet if the requirements to make an initial exempt trade had been loosened, the same could not be said of the resale provisions proposed in the bill. These provisions set up a scheme of holding periods, which had to be adhered to in order to prevent a resale becoming a distribution. Neither the Merger Committee nor the TSE had been in favour of a holding period system because of their liquidity implications. Bray states that the differences in time periods here were "intended to discourage the use of these exemptions by persons who are not long-term sophisticated investors." This suggests an attempt by the legislators to influence the routine investment strategies of institutional investors. As well as the disclosure obligations of being a reporting issuer, the varying holding periods were also predicated on the understanding that more information was available to buyers about securities listed on the TSE. On the other hand, Taylor argues, without elaboration, that the abolition of the need for investment intent "through the establishment of fixed holding periods" was "consistent with … the interest" of institutional investors.

A. Which Exemptions Attract Which Resale Rule?

Appendixes D and E to NI 45-102 list the provincial and multilateral exemptions that attract the NI 45-102 resale rules ss 2.5 and 2.6, respectively. Considering the capital-raising exemptions as a group, most of these, including the new crowdfunding exemption, attract the s 2.5

resale rules, though the private issuer exemption attracts the s 2.6 rule. Both the accredited investor exemption and the minimum amount exemption attract s 2.5. Most of the exemptions based on a pre-existing relationship with the issuer attract the less restrictive rule. However, we have noted that the convertible/exchangeable securities exemptions may create the possibility of backdoor underwritings taking place. The resale rules work for convertible securities such that if the original security was acquired under an exemption to which the resale rule in NI 45-102, s 2.5 would apply, then the resale rule in s 2.5 applies to the converted or underlying security (NI 45-102, appendix D). If the convertible security was originally acquired under an exemption to which NI 45-102, s 2.6 would apply, s 2.6 applies to the converted security (NI 45-102, appendix E). However, if the original security was acquired under a prospectus, then NI 45-102, s 2.10 applies. These rather confusing rules are captured in the accompanying table.

Prospectus Exemptions and Their Accompanying Resale Rules

Exemption	Applicable NI 45-102 Resale Rule
Private issuer exemption (NI 45-106, s 2.4)	Section 2.6 (Seasoning)
Family, friends, and business associates (NI 45-106, s 2.5)	Section 2.5 (Restricted)
Crowdfunding exemption (MI 45-108)	Section 2.5
Accredited investor exemption (NI 45-106, s 2.3)	Section 2.5
Minimum amount investment exemption (NI 45-106, s 2.10)	Section 2.5
Stock dividend exemption (NI 45-106, s 2.31)	Section 2.6
Business combinations and reorganization (NI 45-106, s 2.11)	Section 2.6
Convertible or exchangeable securities exemption (NI 45-106, s 2.42)	Section 2.5 applies to the converted or underlying security if the original security was acquired under an exemption to which the resale rule in NI 45-102, s 2.5 would apply Section 2.6 applies to the converted or underlying security if the original security was acquired under an exemption to which the resale rule in NI 45-102, s 2.6 would apply Section 2.10 applies to the converted or underlying security if the original security was acquired under a prospectus
Rights offering exemption (NI 45-106, s 2.1)	Section 2.6
Distribution to employees, etc. (NI 45-106, s 2.24)	Section 2.6
Offering memorandum exemption (NI 45-106, s 2.9)	Section 2.5

B. Note on Securities Originally Issued Under Old Prospectus Exemption Rules

It is possible that initial purchasers may still hold securities that were purchased under the terms of some of the prospectus exemptions in various provinces that have now been removed by rule. One example is the closely held issuer (CHI) prospectus exemption formerly available in Ontario by OSC Rule 45-501 between 2001 and 2005, but now no longer in force. This exemption was similar but not identical to the private issuer exemption. What is the resale position for securities distributed under that exemption? The answer to this is provided by appendixes D and E of NI 45-102. Securities issued under the various former exemptions listed in these appendixes in all the subscribing provinces will attract either new resale rule s 2.5 or new resale rule s 2.6 of NI 45-102. For the CHI example, appendix D's transitional provisions indicate that the new resale rule would be NI 45-102, s 2.5.

C. What Is the Substance of the Resale Rules?

1. *NI 45-102, Section 2.5 Rule*

Let us deal first with the s 2.5 resale rule in NI 45-102. It provides as follows:

2.5 Restricted Period

(1) Unless the conditions in subsection (2) are satisfied, a trade that is specified by section 2.3 or other securities legislation to be subject to this section is a distribution.

(2) Subject to subsection (3), for the purposes of subsection (1) the conditions are:

1. The issuer is and has been a reporting issuer in a jurisdiction of Canada for the four months immediately preceding the trade.
2. At least four months have elapsed from the distribution date.
3. If the distribution date is on or after March 30, 2004, or, in Québec, on or after September 14, 2005, and either of the following apply:
   (i) if the issuer was a reporting issuer on the distribution date, the certificate representing the security, if any, carries a legend stating:

   Unless permitted under securities legislation, the holder of this security must not trade the security before *[insert the date that is 4 months and a day after the distribution date]*; or

   (ii) if the issuer was not a reporting issuer on the distribution date, the certificate representing the security, if any, carries a legend stating:

   Unless permitted under securities legislation, the holder of this security must not trade the security before the date that is 4 months and a day after the later of (i) *[insert the distribution date]*, and (ii) the date the issuer became a reporting issuer in any province or territory.

3.1 If the security is entered into a direct registration or other electronic book-entry system, or if the purchaser did not directly receive a certificate representing the security, the purchaser received written notice containing the legend restriction notation set out in subparagraphs (i) or (ii) of item 3.

4. The trade is not a control distribution.
5. No unusual effort is made to prepare the market or to create a demand for the security that is the subject of the trade.

6. No extraordinary commission or consideration is paid to a person or company in respect of the trade.
7. If the selling securityholder is an insider or officer of the issuer, the selling securityholder has no reasonable grounds to believe that the issuer is in default of securities legislation.

(3) Items 3 and 3.1 of subsection (2) do not apply to a trade of an underlying security if the underlying security is issued at least four months after the later of

(a) the distribution date, and

(b) the date the issuer became a reporting issuer in any jurisdiction of Canada.

As mentioned above, the key aspect of the rule in NI 45-102, s 2.5 is that it imposes conditions on both the issuer and the reseller of the securities. In contrast to this, the rule in NI 45-102, s 2.6 imposes no "restricted period" on the initial purchaser who wants to resell under NI 45-102 in any jurisdiction of Canada. Let us examine the key aspects of this rule in more detail.

a. *The Seasoning Period*

The rationale for condition 1 of the rule that the issuer be a reporting issuer for a four-month "seasoning" period relates to the policy objective of ensuring that subsequent purchasers of securities initially distributed without a prospectus have access to adequate information about that issuer. Note that this four-month requirement represents a much less onerous burden on issuers than previous versions of the resale rules. This is particularly true because this time period is further reduced if the issuer only becomes a reporting issuer by filing a prospectus after the distribution date (see NI 45-102, s 2.7). The "distribution date" refers to the date that the securities were originally distributed by the issuer. The rationale for the reduced burden in terms of time periods appears to be the introduction of more rigorous continuous disclosure requirements for all reporting issuers by way of NI 51-102. If the issuer never becomes a reporting issuer, the seasoning period requirement remains unfulfilled, thus preventing the securities from being resold unless a further exemption is available.

b. *The Restricted Period*

Condition 2 of NI 45-102, s 2.5(2) substitutes the idea of a "restricted period" for the former "hold periods" present in most provincial securities legislation. We have noted above that the definition of "distribution date" in NI 45-102, in the case of non-control distributions, refers to "the date the security that is the subject of the trade was distributed in reliance on an exemption from the prospectus requirement by the issuer." Again, this new rule represents a relaxation of the former time requirements concerning hold periods imposed on resellers. These former provisions, in general terms, varied according to whether the issuer was listed on a recognized stock exchange or not, and in any event imposed time periods that were never less than six months long. CP 45-102CP, s 1.8 provides guidance as to the calculation of the appropriate restricted period where there have been a series of transactions involving more than one exempt purchaser. It says:

1.8 Calculation of Restricted and Seasoning Periods

The restricted period in item 2 of s. 2.5(2) of NI 45-102 is calculated from the distribution date, that is, the date the securities were distributed in reliance on an exemption from the prospectus requirement by the issuer or a control person. For example, if an issuer or control person distributes securities under a private placement exemption to a purchaser in Saskatchewan and the private placee resells the securities during the restricted period to a purchaser in Alberta under a further private placement exemption, upon resale by the Alberta purchaser, that purchaser will determine whether the restricted period has expired by calculating the time period from the date the issuer or control person distributed the securities to the Saskatchewan purchaser.

For the application of restricted and seasoning period rules to underlying securities in connection with provisions like NI 45-106, s 2.42, see CP 45-102CP, s 1.10 and NI 45-102, s 2.5(3).

c. Legending Requirements

The purpose of the requirements in condition 3, that securities certificates or ownership statements carry a legend indicating the date when the securities may be validly resold, is an attempt to provide more transparency to downstream purchasers of securities issued under prospectus exemptions. The reference to ownership statements is intended to deal with the modern reality of much of securities trading, which is that paper security certificates rarely change hands. Rather, ownership changes are accomplished by changes to the information about beneficial ownership of securities held in centralized depository systems.

d. Preparing the Market and Paying Extraordinary Commissions

The following excerpt canvasses the issues arising from conditions 5 and 6 of NI 45-102, s 2.5.

Borden Ladner Gervais, *Securities Law and Practice*
3rd ed (Toronto: Thomson Carswell) (loose-leaf) at § 17.8.7

Two of the conditions of both s. 2.5 and s. 2.6 of NI 45-102 are that (i) no unusual effort may be made to prepare the market or create a demand for the securities, and (ii) no extraordinary commission or consideration may be paid in respect of the trade.

Except in Alberta, there is no elaboration on what these conditions mean although s. 1.9 of Companion Policy 45-102CP refers the reader to s. 3.1 of ASC Rule 45-11 and the *Daon Development Corporation* order.

Section 3.1 of ASC Rule 45-11 provides that an unusual effort to prepare the market or to create a demand for securities takes place if one or more of the following activities is engaged in by or on behalf of the vendor of the securities:

> (a) the dissemination to prospective purchasers of material soliciting orders to purchase, unless the material consists only of a letter or communication (i) identifying the securities being sold, and (ii) advising that they are available, and that letter or communication may comprise or be accompanied by one or more of an annual report, interim report, information circular, take-over bid circular, issuer bid circular, prospectus, offering memorandum or another document or documents prepared pursuant to a statute or a regulation primarily for some other purpose;
>
> (b) the formation of a selling group or any similar arrangement to co-ordinate the efforts of more than one registrant to effect the sale;

(c) the commencement of any transaction or sequence of transactions, plan or other arrangement to manipulate or adjust the market price of the securities, other than price stabilization activities reasonably necessary for the maintenance of an orderly market and not going beyond what is accepted on the market where those activities occur;

(d) any sales effort that is illegal or improper by the standards of the market in which it is made or involves the communication of false or misleading information;

(e) the making of a sale to a purchaser with whom the vendor is not dealing at arm's length, in order to put the purchaser in a position where the purchaser may re-sell the securities free of constraints to which the vendor was subject; and

(f) in the case of control block sales, where there is a market for the securities, the making of a sale other than a sale made in the market in which securities of the particular class are customarily traded and in a manner customary in the market or a sale made under a prospectus exemption.

Section 3.2 of ASC Rule 45-11 provides that an extraordinary commission or consideration is paid in respect of a trade if the trade is effected:

(a) on an agency basis and the aggregate compensation paid to the registrant through whom the securities are sold is greater than that which is customary in agency transactions of similar size involving similar securities in the relevant market;

(b) through a stock exchange or other market in which it is customary for registrants to trade on an agency basis but the securities are instead sold by the vendor to another registrant acting as principal if the sale was prearranged to avoid the operation of clause (a); or

(c) through the sale of the securities by the vendor to a registrant and the excess of the then market value of the particular securities over the price paid is greater than that which is customary in principal transactions of similar size involving similar securities in the relevant market.

The OSC adopted the predecessor of these provisions in *Daon Development Corp.* (1983), 6 O.S.C.B. 2004.

e. *No Reasonable Grounds to Believe Issuer Is in Default*

The terms of condition 7 impose a good faith requirement on insiders or officers of issuers that they are not selling securities acquired in an exempt transaction because of a default in securities regulatory requirements on the part of the issuer. This is a recognition of the assumed information asymmetries that exist as between these classes of investor and "outside" investors.

QUESTIONS

1. What is the rationale for continuing to impose a restricted period on resellers in addition to a seasoning requirement for an issuer? Does it have to do with a persistent information asymmetry between an exempt purchaser and a subsequent non-exempt buyer? Is the rationale more plausible with respect to issuers that only use the exempt market as opposed to reporting issuers who also use it? In other words, does it matter to how one thinks about the backdoor underwriting problem whether the issuer is or is not a reporting issuer at the time of the initial exempt purchase?

2. Is a restricted period of four months likely to be successful at preventing the problem of backdoor underwriting?

3. Given that the seasoning period is reduced if the issuer becomes a reporting issuer after the distribution date (NI 45-102, s 2.7), does the seasoning period requirement add anything of value to the rules relating to when purchasers can resell under NI 45-102, s 2.5?

4. What advice would you give to the CSA about how it might rethink the resale rule requirements?

2. *NI 45-102, Section 2.6 Rule*

NI 45-102, s 2.6 is known as the "seasoning period" rule because a "seasoning" requirement for the issuer is the main regulatory obligation imposed on the resale process. The rule provides as follows:

> **2.6 Seasoning Period**
>
> (1) Unless the conditions in subsection (3) are satisfied, a trade that is specified by section 2.4 or other securities legislation to be subject to this section is a distribution.
>
> (2) The first trade of securities issued by a private company or private issuer made after the issuer has ceased to be a private company or private issuer is a distribution unless the conditions in subsection (3) are satisfied.
>
> (3) For the purposes of subsections (1) and (2), the conditions are:
>
> 1. The issuer is and has been a reporting issuer in a jurisdiction of Canada for the four months immediately preceding the trade.
> 2. The trade is not a control distribution.
> 3. No unusual effort is made to prepare the market or to create a demand for the security that is the subject of the trade.
> 4. No extraordinary commission or consideration is paid to a person or company in respect of the trade.
> 5. If the selling securityholder is an insider or officer of the issuer, the selling securityholder has no reasonable grounds to believe that the issuer is in default of securities legislation.

The conditions to be met in order to satisfy the requirements of the NI 45-102, s 2.6 rule should be familiar from our discussion of NI 45-102, s 2.5. Chief among them is that the issuer must satisfy a seasoning period obligation of four months in order for the purchaser to be able to validly resell the securities to non-exempt purchasers. From a regulatory point of view, there is presumed to be little danger of a backdoor underwriting problem in connection with the type of exemptions that attract the s 2.6 resale rule, such as issuers selling securities to employees or distributing securities by way of a stock dividend. Note also that by NI 45-102, s 2.7(2), there is a similar reduction in the seasoning period where the issuer becomes a reporting issuer by way of a prospectus filed after the distribution date. See NI 45-102, s 2.10 for provisions with respect to underlying securities.

QUESTIONS

1. What if the issuer is already a reporting issuer for several years when the securities are first issued?

2. When do resale rules apply to private issuers? Is the NI 45-102, s 2.6 rule appropriate to control these resales? Consider the following example. Assume that XYZ qualifies to be a

private issuer, according to the definition in NI 45-106. The directors of XYZ are A, B, and C. XYZ has 20 securityholders, including D and E. D is a close personal friend of A. E is a close personal friend of B. Now consider whether there are any securities regulatory issues raised by the following transactions:

a. XYZ issues securities to F, a close personal friend of C.

b. D wants to sell her securities in XYZ to E.

c. B wants to sell her securities in XYZ to G, a fly-fishing instructor she met on a recent vacation trip.

d. XYZ completes an IPO in September 2016. On October 1, 2016, E wants to sell her securities.

VII. RESALE RULES FOR CONTROL PERSONS

Traditionally, securities legislation in Canada has carved out specific, and more onerous, resale rules for control persons who wish to resell their securities to those who do not qualify for a prospectus exemption. The logic here is another example of the general regulatory concern with information asymmetry and the possibility that control persons may be selling into the marketplace on the basis of information not available to investors generally. Let us first review the definition of a control person.

A. What Is a Control Distribution?

We have seen that one typical clause in the statutory definition of distribution refers to sales by control persons from their holdings. (See also appendix A of NI 45-102.) According to this definition, sales by a control person are considered to be distributions even if the control person acquired the securities initially by means of a prospectus. We discussed the characteristics of control persons in Chapter 1. It will be a question of fact whether the control person holds a sufficient number of securities to "affect materially the control of the issuer," though they will be deemed to do so if they hold more than 20 percent of the voting rights attached to all outstanding voting securities of an issuer. The analysis will depend on the characteristics of the shares held, the number and type of shareholders, and the relationships among the shareholders.

B. Alternatives Available to Control Persons Distributing Securities

Given that sales from the holdings of control persons are defined as distributions, such control holders will likely want to avoid, if possible, the obligation to prepare a prospectus in order to sell their securities. The options available to them are as follows:

1. The control person could include his, her, or its shares as a secondary offering with a distribution by an issuer pursuant to a prospectus.
2. He, she, or it could seek a discretionary exemption from the regulator. This is unlikely to be granted absent unusual circumstances, given the policy objectives of regulating these transactions in the first place.
3. A control person could sell to another person who qualifies for an exemption. In this case, such buyers would themselves be subject to resale rules.

4. Control persons could follow the strictures of the resale rule in NI 45-102, s 2.8. There are two advantages of taking this route. One is that it is not necessary to find selected purchasers who meet prospectus exemption requirements so that, for example, the securities could be sold on the TSX. The second is that, as mentioned earlier, the buyer is not subjected to further resale rules.

C. Substance of the NI 45-102, Section 2.8 Rule

The text of the s 2.8 resale rule reads as follows:

2.8 Exemption for a Trade by a Control Person

(1) The prospectus requirement does not apply to a control distribution, or a distribution by a lender, pledgee, mortgagee or other encumbrancer for the purpose of liquidating a debt made in good faith by selling or offering for sale a security pledged, mortgaged or otherwise encumbered in good faith as collateral for the debt if the security was acquired by the lender, pledgee, mortgagee or other encumbrancer in a control distribution, if the conditions in subsection (2) are satisfied.

(2) For the purposes of subsection (1), the conditions are:

1. The issuer is and has been a reporting issuer in a jurisdiction of Canada for the four months immediately preceding the trade.
2. The selling securityholder, or the lender, pledgee, mortgagee or other encumbrancer if the distribution is for the purpose of liquidating a debt, has held the securities for at least four months.
3. No unusual effort is made to prepare the market or to create a demand for the security that is the subject of the trade.
4. No extraordinary commission or consideration is paid to a person or company in respect of the trade.
5. The selling securityholder has no reasonable grounds to believe that the issuer is in default of securities legislation.

(3) The selling securityholder, or the lender, pledgee, mortgagee or other encumbrancer if the distribution is for the purpose of liquidating a debt, under subsection (2) must

(a) complete and sign a Form 45-102F1 no earlier than one business day before the Form 45-102F1 is filed;

(b) file the completed and signed Form 45-102F1 on SEDAR at least seven days before the first trade of the securities that is part of the distribution; and

(c) file, within three days after the completion of any trade, an insider report prepared in accordance with either Form 55-102F2 or Form 55-102F6 under National Instrument 55-102 *System for Electronic Disclosure by Insiders (SEDI)*.

Subsections (4) and (5) of the rule provide time periods for the expiry of Form 45-102F1. Most of these conditions, such as the seasoning period and the prohibition on unusual efforts to prepare the market, familiar from the other resale rule contexts. (Note also a similar reduction in the seasoning period pertaining to NI 45-102, s 2.8 resales where the issuer becomes a reporting issuer after the distribution date: see NI 45-102, s 2.7(3).) Like NI 45-102, s 2.5, this resale rule imposes a restricted period on the control person or the pledgee standing in the place of the control person. The unique aspects of the rule revolve around specific undertakings required of control persons, which are discussed in the next section.

D. Filing Requirements: NI 45-102, Section 2.8(3) Rule

Section 2.8 imposes two types of filing requirements on control persons.

1. Form 45-102F1 must be filed on the System for Electronic Document Analysis and Retrieval (SEDAR) at least seven days before the first trade. This form is to be signed no earlier than one business day before filing. The form represents advance notice of the control person's intention to resell. The terms of the form itself are relatively straightforward and brief. Probably its most significant aspect is the requirement for the control person to certify that he, she, or it has "no knowledge of a material fact or material change with respect to the issuer of the securities that has not been generally disclosed" and that "the information given in this form is true and complete." These provisions are obviously intended to address the issue of potential inequality of information as between control persons and other investors. The form expires 30 days from the date it is filed.
2. Insider reporting requirements (discussed in detail in Chapter 8) must be fulfilled within three days after the completion of any trade.

Finally, it should be noted that there is a separate specific rule for "eligible institutional investors" (such as banks, pension or mutual funds, and investment managers) under NI 45-106, part 4 and NI 62-103 (2005), 28 OSCB (Supp-4) 120, as amended 9 May 2016.

VIII. IMPLICATIONS OF INCORRECT RELIANCE ON PROSPECTUS EXEMPTIONS

The following case from 1986 addresses the forms of redress available to purchasers where sellers inappropriately rely on a prospectus exemption to distribute securities. It involved the use of the former private company exemption to distribute securities. The plaintiff claimed that, as a member of the public, he should have been provided with a prospectus pursuant to the distribution.

Jones v FH Deacon Hodgson Inc
(1986), 56 OR (2d) 540 (H Ct J)

HENRY J:

[1] The issue on this motion is whether a sale of shares in contravention of s. 52 [now s 53] of the *Securities Act*, RSO 1980, c. 466, is void for failure to file a prospectus with the Ontario Securities Commission. That section provides in part:

> 52(1) No person or company shall trade in a security on his own account or on behalf of any other person or company,
>
> (a) before the 15th day of March, 1981, where such trade would be a distribution to the public of such security;
>
> (b) on and after the 15th day of March, 1981, where such trade would be a distribution of such security.

> unless a preliminary prospectus and a prospectus have been filed and receipts therefor obtained from the Director.

[2] The facts as pleaded by the plaintiff in the action are as follows and are not disputed for the purposes of this motion.

[3] The defendant F.H. Deacon Hodgson Inc. (Deacon), is an investment dealer. In December 1980, Deacon caused a private company Bacova Investments Limited to be incorporated for the purpose of investing in Lumax Oil and Gas Limited, an oil exploration company whose shares are traded over the counter. In January 1982, Deacon offered for sales shares in Bacova and solicited subscribers. It is common ground that this constituted a distribution of shares to the public within the meaning of s. 52(1) of the *Securities Act*; it is also common ground that Bacova did not file a prospectus with the Ontario Securities Commission as required by s. 52(1)(a).

[4] The plaintiff purchased shares in Bacova through the defendant Deacon in January 1982. The plaintiff's action, commenced in February 1986, is for a declaration that the contract of purchase and sale of the shares is void; he also claims return of $24,000, the price paid by him to Deacon for the shares together with interest.

[5] The defendant now brings this motion to dismiss the action on the ground that it is statute-barred. The rationale of this position is as follows:

(1) Section 70(1) [now s 71] of the *Securities Act* creates an obligation for a dealer to deliver a prospectus to a purchaser of securities and states as follows:

> 70(1) A dealer not acting as agent of the purchaser who receives an order or subscription for a security offered in a distribution to which subsection 52(1) or section 61 is applicable shall, unless he has previously done so, send by prepaid mail or deliver to the purchaser the latest prospectus and any amendment to the prospectus filed either before entering into an agreement of purchase and sale resulting from the order or subscription or not later than midnight on the second day, exclusive of Saturday, Sundays, and holidays, after entering into such agreement.

(2) Section 130 [now s 133] of the *Securities Act* creates civil liability for a dealer or offeror who fails to deliver a prospectus to a purchaser of securities. That section provides:

> 130. A purchaser of a security to whom a prospectus was required to be sent or delivered but was not sent or delivered in compliance with subsection 70(1) or an offeree to whom a take-over circular or issuer bid circular was required to be communicated but was not communicated in compliance with section 92 has a right of action for rescission or damages against the dealer or offeror who failed to comply with the applicable requirement.

(3) Section 135 [now s 138] of the *Securities Act* provides a maximum three-year limitation period in the following language:

> 135. Unless otherwise provided in this act, no action shall be commenced to enforce a right created by this Part more than,
>
> (a) in the case of an action for rescission, 180 days after the date of the transaction that gave rise to the cause of action; or

(b) in the case of any action, other than an action for rescission, the earlier of,

(i) 180 days after the plaintiff first had knowledge of the facts giving rise to the cause of action, or

(ii) three years after the date of the transaction that gave rise to the cause of action.

To this the plaintiff simply replies that he is not relying on s. 130 which creates a civil remedy for breach of s. 70(1); he relies solely on the breach of s. 52(1) which he submits gives rise to a common law right of action for its breach; it is not a right of action created by Pt. XXII of the Act and the limitation provision in s. 135 does not apply to it.

The defendant counters by saying that by enacting s. 52(1) the Legislature did not intend to provide a civil remedy for its breach but has provided a criminal penalty only. The only civil remedy available to the plaintiff is s. 70 which is "triggered" by the breach of s. 52(1) and s. 130; hence the action, being commenced more than three years after the shares were purchased and sold, is statute-barred.

I have reached the conclusion on the basis of the full and able submissions of counsel, that the plaintiff's cause of action properly lies for breach of s. 52(1) and that the limitation period prescribed by s. 135 does not apply to it.

…

[9] Section 52(1) of the Ontario *Securities Act* in clear terms prohibits any person from trading shares of a company unless a prospectus has been filed with the Ontario Securities Commission and a receipt therefore obtained from the director. By s. 60(1) [now s 61] the director shall issue a receipt for a prospectus filed unless it appears to him that it is not in the public interest to do so; the remainder of the section sets out the grounds on which the director shall not issue the receipt and for a hearing before the Commission where he intends to refuse to issue it. In short, not only must the prospectus be filed but the Commission and the director must be satisfied that the prospectus does not contain any element that is contrary to the public interest. Absent the receipt, no person may trade in the shares of the issuing company.

[10] There can be no question but that the filing of a prospectus and its acceptance by the Commission is fundamental to the protection of the investing public who are contemplating purchase of the shares. The effect of s. 60 is, by the issue of the receipt, to authorize the sale of the company's shares; the effect of s. 52 is to prohibit outright trading in the shares by way of distribution to the public unless the distribution is authorized by the Commission. In the language of Mignault J in *Northwestern Trust*, the purpose of the statute "is to protect the general public against schemes or campaigns to sell shares or securities of doubtful value to unwary investors." That, as the Court said, "deals with a matter of public policy and that anything done in contravention of its prohibitions is void and not merely voidable." The principle as applied to the fundamental as opposed to nonfundamental provisions, in my opinion, is not in any way impaired by the Court's subsequent decision in *Myers*: see per Martland J. …

[11] Breach of that provision without more, gives rise to a common law right in the purchaser (the plaintiff in this case) to have the sale declared a nullity. There are, however, three factors that must also be considered:

(a) the Act by s. 118 [now s 122] in Pt. XXI entitled "Enforcement" provides that any person who contravenes the Act is guilty of an offence and on summary conviction is liable to a fine or in the case of an individual to a fine and imprisonment or both; the penal provisions are applied by the Courts in accordance with the procedure for offences punishable on summary conviction with the consent and under the direction of the Minister (s. 119). Part XXI also provides authority to the Commission, where a person or company has failed to comply with a provision of the Act or regulations, to apply to a High Court Judge for an order directing compliance or restraining further violation (s. 122) [now s 128]. The Commission may, where in its opinion it is in the public interest to do so, order that trading shall cease in the securities affected (s. 123) [now s 127]. Proceedings under this part are subject to periods of limitation in s. 125 [now s 129.1]. No doubt in the case at Bar, it would have been open to the Minister to institute a prosecution for the breach of s. 52(1) or to the Commission to have taken the regulatory action authorized by ss. 122 and 123 had the breach been drawn to the attention of the Commission in the first place; but none of the provisions in Pt. XXI appears to me to assist a purchaser of securities who is already committed to an unlawful transaction such as that before me. Part XXI merely permits the barn door to be locked after the horse has bolted.

(b) the Act by Pt. XXII prescribes civil remedies by creating causes of action for breach of specific provisions of the Act. There is no reference to a civil remedy for breach of s. 52(1). The cause of action is provided only in the case of a purchaser of shares who is not provided with a prospectus as required by s. 70 which does not apply here.

(c) there is no provision in the Act that expressly deprives a person of his common law remedy for breach of s. 52(1).

. . .

[13] The combined effect of the Supreme Court of Canada's decisions in *Northwestern Trust* and *Myers* is that a sale of securities that is prohibited by the statute is void; but that where a penalty is provided the Court must determine whether that penalty is intended merely to deter persons from entering into the contract or is also intended to invalidate the contract of purchase and sale in law. The Court held in *Myers* that the prohibition of sales at a residence, i.e., at a particular place, was not part of the "general pattern" of protecting the public against trading in securities by persons who have not satisfied the regulatory authority of their proper qualifications to do so; its purpose was not to prevent trading of an unauthorized kind but it was to prevent trading at a specified place. The penalty was held to be merely a deterrent and the contract of sale was not invalidated by the breach. That is not the case here; the breach is of a fundamental element of the statutory scheme to protect the public against unauthorized trading.

[14] The statutory scheme in the Ontario *Securities Act* as it relates to this subject is this: first the seller may not trade in the shares unless the company has filed a prospectus and it has been accepted by the Commission. The prohibition is absolute (s. 52(1)) and the provision is fundamental.

[15] Second, Pt. XXII creates several civil remedies. Section 70(1) makes a special provision respecting a purchaser who places an order to purchase shares to which s. 52(1) applies; the dealer is required to deliver to the purchaser the latest prospectus and amendments *filed with the Commission*. He must do so either before entering into the agreement of purchase and sale or within two days after making the agreement. By s. 70(2) the

purchaser may reject the sale within two days after receiving the prospectus. It is therefore open to the purchaser to abort the transaction after receiving the prospectus.

[16] It is important to recognize that the prospectus that s. 70(1) requires to be delivered to the purchaser is the most recent prospectus and amendments thereto filed with the Commission in accordance with s. 52(1). The investing public is protected first by the requirement that the prospectus be filed and accepted and second by ensuring that the purchaser is provided with a copy of it before he is finally committed to the contract of purchase and sale.

[17] It is also noteworthy that s. 70(1) does not make the resulting sale unlawful or prohibited as does s. 52(1). By contrast the contract is one that can be aborted or rescinded at the option of the purchaser; he may avoid being bound once he receives the prospectus or if he does not receive it he may if so advised proceed by way of an action for rescission or damages against the dealer who failed to comply with s. 70(1). That cause of action is created by s. 130, in Pt. XXII; it is one of several created by Pt. XXII of the Act … . By s. 135 no action shall be commenced to enforce the right created by Pt. XXII after the expiry of the limitation period therein prescribed.

[18] In ss. 126 [now s 130] and 127 [now s 131], which create special liability for misrepresentation in a prospectus it is also provided that the right of action for rescission or damages thereby conferred is in addition to and not in derogation of any other right the purchaser may have at law, thereby preserving any common law action he may have for fraud or misrepresentation.

[19] Third, none of the remedies created by Pt. XXII applies to a breach of s. 52(1) by failure to file any prospectus at all. In such a case s. 70 does not avail the purchaser because it assists him only when the dealer fails to provide him with a prospectus filed with the Commission; if none is filed there is no breach as no such prospectus exists. There is a lacuna; the Act neither provides a cause of action for breach of s. 52(1) nor does it expressly or by necessary intendment abolish the purchaser's remedy in common law or equity to have the prohibited transaction declared null and void as in *Northwestern Trust*.

[20] It is therefore not correct to say, as Mr. Steep submits, that breach of s. 52(1) "triggers" the cause of action created by s. 70 so that the purchaser has a remedy created by Pt. XXII, albeit one that is limited by s. 135. Section 70 applies only where a prospectus has been filed; the Act does not contemplate a sale where no prospectus that is required by s. 52(1) has been filed with the Commission. Where none is filed the purchaser is left to such remedy as he may otherwise have in law or equity. …

[21] The rule as applied in *Northwestern Trust* is founded on public policy for the protection of the investing public. The requirement in s. 52(1) is equally to protect the public and it is one of the fundamental components of the scheme of the *Securities Act*. The prohibition is clearly expressed; the result of its breach is that the sale of shares to the plaintiff is void. Having regard to the scheme of the Act and the central place in that scheme of the requirement to file a prospectus, that result in law is not to be taken to be abrogated by the Legislature unless it is abrogated in clear terms or by necessary intendment. The creation of specific causes of action in Pt. XXII, even on the expressio unius rule, does not achieve that result; nor is that result achieved by mere failure to deal with the effect of a breach. The transaction is illegal and void and there is no contract of purchase and sale of the shares. That is the effect in law and I cannot find any ground for holding that the Legislature has altered it.

…

[26] By way of recapitulation:

(a) No prospectus was filed with the Ontario Securities Commission, and the sale by Deacon was in breach of s. 52(1) which is a fundamental element of the statutory scheme of full disclosure and regulation by the Commission for protection of the investing public in cases not exempt by the Act from the prospectus requirements.

(b) Section 70 does not here create a remedy for the plaintiff because that section applies only where a prospectus has been filed and a receipt obtained from the director.

(c) Breach of s. 52(1) does not "trigger" an offence under s. 70(1) where no prospectus is filed; the limitation in s. 135 does not apply because no cause of action is here created by Pt. XXII.

(d) Breach of s. 52(1) stands on its own; it is subject to a quasi-criminal penalty and regulatory action under Pt. XXI. The general rule however, is that the sale is void in common law. That principle requires a clear expression by the Legislature if it was intended to abrogate it—there is none here.

[27] While the Court should be reluctant to interfere with contracts freely made, in this case the overriding consideration is the need to support the fundamental purpose of the statute as a matter of public policy to protect the integrity of the regulatory scheme of the Act; contractual integrity must give way; the penalty alone and the remedies available to the Commission, in my opinion, ought not to be the only deterrent or remedy. Moreover the scheme would be seriously impaired were the Court to preserve the legal transaction and deprive the purchaser of a remedy where no prospectus has been filed at all and to recognize his only civil remedy is that created by s. 70 and other provisions of Pt. XXII all of which are limited to cases where s. 52 has been complied with; that would ignore the fundamental breach and support only the remedies provided in cases in which the prospectus has been filed and accepted as required.

(e) I am aware that while my decision precludes the dealer from enforcing an illegal contract against the purchaser, the purchaser cannot enforce it against the vendor should he prefer to do so; he of course may prefer not to exercise his remedy and continue to hold the shares. It seems to me, however, that the purchaser otherwise may maintain an action for a declaration that the contract is void and that he is entitled to recover the price paid for the shares as a form of unjust enrichment in the hands of the vendor. The Court ought to provide him with that remedy at least as an innocent party (so far as this motion is concerned). On the other hand, I should deem it sound judicial policy for the Court to refuse to entertain an action by the vendor (or allow it a defence), in reliance on the void transaction on the ground that to do so would enable the vendor to profit by his illegal conduct. This latter point I am frank to say is obiter as I am not obliged to decide it.

[28] The defendant's motion is for an order dismissing the action. For the reasons I have outlined the motion must fail.

The significance of *Jones v FH Deacon Hodgson Inc* lies in what it says about the potential consequences for issuers of wrongly relying on an exemption in the statute. The case revolved around the distinction between the absolute failure to file a prospectus, whether or not by virtue of incorrectly interpreting an exemption and the failure to deliver a prospectus which *had* been filed, to the specific purchaser, for which there is an explicit statutory remedy that must be exercised within three years. The court held that the failure to file a prospectus with the regulator rendered the contracts of purchase and sale void, so there was no question of a limitation period for a remedy to be available. This was a contract prohibited by the statute. In other words, the provision of a prospectus is so fundamental to the scheme of securities regulation that a remedy for failure to file it should not be statute-barred.

The result of this decision seems to be that if an issuer relies on an exemption inappropriately, so that it should have provided a prospectus, those who purchased the securities are not time-limited in seeking a remedy. Thus, the consequences of improper reliance on an exemption are potentially significant. Commentators argued that this decision was problematic because there should be a time when an issuer would not have its shortcomings coming back to haunt it. What a decision like this suggests is that issuers or selling securityholders who are unsure about whether an exemption applies to them would be well advised to seek the advice of securities regulators on the matter; otherwise they will always run the risk of being sued.

For a more recent consideration and endorsement of the principles established in *Jones v FH Deacon Hodgson Inc*, see *Singh v Trump*, 2015 ONSC 4461.

QUESTION

Is there a conceptual problem about using the language of unjust enrichment to allow purchasers to get their money back?

IX. CHAPTER SUMMARY

NI 45-106 and NI 45-102 contain the more popular and frequently used rules across Canada that allow issuers and selling securityholders to sell securities without fulfilling a prospectus requirement. These rules are characterized by a high degree of harmonization across the country, though significant differences remain. Recent expansion of the opportunity to raise capital in the exempt market marks a rebalancing of the regulatory goals of efficient markets and investor protection. The position with respect to resale rules is substantially harmonized and was revised some years ago to reduce the burden of these rules on issuers and initial exempt purchasers. However, the question remains as to the continued cogency of these rules in light of the expanded opportunities for retail investors to access the exempt market.

CHAPTER SIX

Continuous Disclosure

I. INTRODUCTION

Once an issuer becomes a reporting issuer, it has ongoing disclosure obligations that must be met if the issuer's securities are to continue to trade in securities markets. This chapter explores the underlying rationale for the continuous disclosure system, as well as the requirements for timely and periodic disclosure, including material change reporting. It canvasses recent changes to the continuous disclosure system and explores current public policy issues in respect of continuous disclosure and the debate among securities regulators as to whether Canada should move to more or less regulation of issuers.

There are two fundamental components of the continuous disclosure regime in Canada: periodic disclosure of interim and annual financial statements and accompanying reports, and timely and accurate disclosure of material changes experienced by the issuer. The requirement to undertake timely disclosure has been facilitated by the move to electronic reporting and trading, yet technological developments present both benefits and challenges for the continuous disclosure system.

This chapter is integrally linked to Chapter 7 on securities regulators and corporate governance. Many of the recent initiatives by securities regulators, such as codifying the role of audit committees and CEO and CFO certification requirements, are directly tied to and integrated with the disclosure requirements set out in this chapter. As you are reading, consider what the role of securities regulators is in terms of the continuous disclosure system and how this role might be relevant to both the governance of a reporting issuer and the protection of investors.

A. The Underlying Rationale for Continuous Disclosure

The continuous disclosure system is a critically important aspect of Canadian capital markets, aimed at providing transparent and efficient access to information about issuers. It is an integral part of the ability of the issuer to cost-effectively raise capital, because without the continuous disclosure system, there would be a disincentive for investors to provide capital. Issuers are required to provide information to the market on a range of governance, financing, and operational issues on a regular basis. About 95 percent of all capital market activity in Canada is in secondary markets (Ontario Ministry of Finance, *Five Year Review Committee Final Report—Reviewing the Securities Act* (2003); Canadian Securities Administrators (CSA) Notice 53-302 (2000), 23 OSCB 7383). Because there is no prospectus involved, the continuous disclosure regime becomes key to ensuring that issuers provide investors with the most accurate and current information possible on which to base their risk and investment choices. An issuer's continuous disclosure record, which includes filings required under securities laws and regulations, as well as other communications, is the mechanism through which existing and potential investors assess the performance and integrity of the issuer and its officers. Disclosure is a critically important factor in investor protection and maintaining confidence in the capital markets.

Continuous disclosure can also facilitate an issuance of new securities, because reporting issuers can use publicly available information about them to gain timely access to additional public financing through the use of short-form, shelf, or post-receipt pricing prospectuses, or multijurisdictional disclosure system (MJDS) prospectuses, as discussed in Chapter 4, or more easily make the use of prospectus exemptions, as discussed in Chapter 5. This approach is often referred to as integrated disclosure.

Full and timely disclosure can also increase financial analyst coverage, ensure an appropriate risk premium, and encourage better capital allocation decisions. The issuer must disclose periodic results, whether they are positive or less positive than the issuer expected due to market fluctuations or unanticipated operational changes. Failure to disclose changes and to explain them to existing and potential investors can lead to seriously impaired confidence in the directors and officers of the issuer, ultimately resulting in a higher cost of capital through lower trading prices and a lower credit rating. Failure to meet statutory disclosure standards can lead to civil liability under the civil liability provisions in a number of provinces.

Disclosure has a corporate governance role as well, a topic that is canvassed more fully in Chapter 7. The board can use it as a monitoring tool in its oversight of corporate managers. It can be a signalling device for corporate directors, as it allows the board to assess both upside and downside changes and adjust its strategic planning accordingly. Disclosure can also act as a signalling device for investors in respect of the quality of director oversight, officer managerial skills and operational efficiency.

Scholar Faith Stevelman has commented on the connection between corporate law, securities law, and the disclosure system in respect of shareholder rights in the context of US securities law.

Faith Stevelman Kahn, "Fiduciary Duty, Limited Liability, and the Law of Delaware: Transparency and Accountability—Rethinking Corporate Fiduciary Law's Relevance to Corporate Disclosure"
(2000) 34 Ga L Rev 505

Shareholders' right to determine on an informed, rational basis whether to keep their capital invested in the firm or to divest it therefrom is a fundamental aspect of the corporation laws and corporate governance system that operate on behalf of shareholders in public companies, despite the fact that it has rarely expressly been discussed as such. From a normative perspective, the affirmation by courts of equity of shareholders' continued autonomy over their investment decision functions to reaffirm shareholders' status as principals within the corporate fiduciary relation, and thus to check the abuse of managerial power. From a positive and market-oriented perspective, shareholders' ability to choose, on the basis of adequate, accurate information, whether to hold or to sell their shares is the operative mechanism by which the capital and takeover markets promote managerial accountability and thus influence corporate governance for the better.

Proxy disclosures relevant to shareholder votes are, thus, only one variable in the informational equation of shareholders' rights and managerial power. Shareholders' decision making regarding whether to retain their investment within the firm also is affected significantly by corporate disclosures publicized through periodic reports (SEC filings on forms 10-K, 10-Q and 8-K), corporate press releases, and the annual report to shareholders mandated by SEC Rule 14a-3. Shareholders rely on the full complement of official public disclosures made by publicly traded firms, and are affected by them, even where they omit a direct review of the relevant documents, since important new information disclosed therein is digested, analyzed and circulated by brokers, analysts and an expanded financial media operating through print, television, radio, and web-based formats.

Put simply, bad news travels fast, but corporate managers' disclosure of erroneous favorable information short-circuits this process. Without such accurate information, shareholders cannot seize the opportunity to exert informal pressure on existing management as a means of addressing their firms' problems. In terms of formal action, shareholders will not be motivated to install a new, potentially more dynamic, creative or competent board if they are being told that the firm's performance and prospects are "on target." And certainly, in many instances, shareholders might elect to sell their shares, in the attempt to minimize their losses, if information about diminished profitability or worsened prospects were disclosed. But even more universally, where managers' presentation of erroneously favorable information has deprived equity holders of their capacity for rational decision making vis-à-vis their invested capital, such injury should be compensable, in at least nominal terms, independent of the attempt to quantify their damages, ex post, in relation to their stock's trading price at some earlier, hypothetical time of sale (at 517-519).

There has been some scholarly debate in respect of whether the degree and type of disclosure required by securities regulators has been appropriately targeted. Homer Kripke offers the following critique of the US disclosure system.

Homer Kripke, "The Myth of the Informed Layman"
(1973) 28 Bus Lawyer 631

If we could get away from the assumption that the lay investor keeps his [or her] mind blank to everything except what is in the document that the Commission permits to be handed to him with its name on it, a serious new effort could be made to make securities disclosures meaningful. The present system does not address itself to the realities by which judgments on securities are formed. While for a new company coming to market for the first time, the prospectus is likely to be the only available written source of information, the situation is entirely different for the regularly reporting company, the one for which the prospects for rational judgment are best. The primary document which communicates information to investors in the established company in the real world is not the prospectus nor the annual report on Form 10K which gets buried in the Commission's files, but the annual report to stockholders. The way to do a real job of disclosure to the investing public is through the improvement of the information in the annual report to stockholders.

• • •

If we explode the myth and are not hampered by the necessity of writing down to the lay[person], what should be the future goals of disclosure? Our discussion must necessarily assume that the market is rational and that market value will fluctuate around enterprise value as the norm. Ultimately enterprise value, which is therefore what the rational investor is searching for, is a subjective thing. Like beauty, it is in the eye of the beholder. The fact that we have 20 million shares traded daily on the New York Stock Exchange means that people differ as to whether any security is a good buy or a good sell. Every analyst forms his [or her] own judgment as to the value of a company and of its securities, not only from judgment factors relating to the particular company and the particular industry, but also from judgment factors as to the appropriate discount rate for future earnings because of the future course of money rates, of the whole economy, of the political situation, and indeed of the international situation. Given all of these variables of the future that affect a company, enterprise value is not a thing or a fact. It is a judgment.

Disclosure should be oriented to disclosing what the informed investor may think is important to that judgment: value estimates, earnings projections, probable and potential minerals—not exclusively what is in the past and not limited to what the lay[person] can handle. The significant items all point to the future, and the uncomfortable reality is that they are all possibilities and probabilities, not certainties. But the Commission should not for that reason suppress the estimates for the future which really make the value of a security. The Commission's function should be to give the information to the people

> straight and let them make their own judgments in their own way. As I have argued elsewhere [Kripke, "The SEC, the Accountants, Some Myths and Some Realities" (1970) 45 NYU L Rev 1151 at 1169-70], those who try to use disclosure rationally are going to use professional help in doing so anyway.
>
> How does this concept affect accounting, the present principal repository for financial information? I think that we may have been on the wrong track in trying to reduce accounting to single numbers whose derivations are found in an Opinion of the Accounting Principles Board, because there are many aspects of financial events on which different people have different judgments. Perhaps accounting should move backwards somewhat in the direction of disclosing more detail, more information, and letting the analyst or the informed investor make his [or her] own decisions as to what is significant.
>
> . . .
>
> Although the SEC in my day as a staff member used to preach the necessity for firm rules to avoid burying the meat of a financial statement in pages of explanatory footnotes, we may have to produce more complete disclosure of the elements that go into the conclusions of financial data. I realize that we could go too far. If you just drown people in information, you can overwhelm even the professional portfolio manager who has a problem of forming a judgment on several hundred companies. But what we need is a new departure, with disclosure oriented towards the sophisticated person able to handle it, through whom suggestions for action will filter down to the lay[person].

As noted in earlier chapters, securities legislation is aimed at fostering fair and efficient capital markets, creating confidence in capital markets and providing protection to investors from unfair, improper or fraudulent practices. Disclosure requirements are aimed at transparency and creating a "level playing field" for investors in their assessment of the risks and benefits of investing in securities of an issuer.

B. Continuing Enhancement of the Disclosure System

The objective of transparency in disclosure has received heightened attention in the wake of fluctuating economic conditions and corporate accounting scandals globally. Investors seek greater assurance about the validity of issuers' financial information. Canadian securities regulators are part of an international move to enhance continuous disclosure and restore public confidence in capital markets. Securities regulators have an ongoing concern as to whether financial statements provide the information they are supposed to provide that will allow investors to make informed investment choices.

In an era in which confidence in capital markets has been shaken, the question is whether Canadian issuers, in complying with financial reporting requirements and in following generally accepted accounting standards in their disclosure practice, are really providing investors with information in a form that allows them to realistically assess the risks and benefits of investing in the firm. There is debate as to whether there is a need for enhanced regulatory protection or better enforcement of existing protection. There is also debate as to whether any improvement should take the form of new rules or a shift toward more principles-based regulation. The Expert Panel on Securities Regulation has recommended a more principles-based approach to continuous disclosure requirements, as discussed in Section III.E of this chapter (Expert Panel on Securities Regulation, *Creating an Advantage in Global Capital Markets, Final Report and Recommendations*, January 2009).

In Canada, there have been numerous initiatives undertaken by securities regulators to respond to problems of investor confidence and to align Canadian securities regulation with initiatives that have been undertaken in the United States. In 2002, Canadian securities regulators issued a new policy of best practices in disclosure (National Policy (NP) 51-201, as amended 31 May 2013) and agreed upon a national instrument aimed at bringing uniformity and transparency to issuer reporting National Instrument (NI) 51-102, *Continuous Disclosure Obligations*, effective 30 March 2004, as amended 17 November 2015. Other national and multilateral instruments also have the same objectives. Companies should now have written disclosure policies and a senior officer or committee must have oversight of the policy. The policy must specify financial, operational and structural data, which companies must release in a fair and careful manner. Material information that must be disclosed includes changes to accounting policies, changes in rating agency decisions, and any exceptions to corporate ethics or practices that are put in place for key employees. All information filed on the System for Electronic Document Analysis and Retrieval (SEDAR) website should also be immediately posted on the corporation's website and any investor should be able to listen to analyst conference calls (<http://www.sedar.ca>). The national policy notes that "best practice" also suggests that issuers should be cautious in circulating analysts' reports to investors because such circulation could be construed as endorsement of the report.

Another important part of the continuous disclosure system is the System for Electronic Disclosure by Insiders (SEDI), discussed in Chapter 8, Insider Trading. SEDI was established by securities regulatory authorities to facilitate the filing and public disclosure of insider reports in electronic format via the Internet (<http://www.sedi.ca>). Issuers filing in SEDAR are required to file in SEDI certain issuer information, including their lists of security designations and corporate event information. Insiders of foreign reporting issuers that are not required to file their disclosure documents in SEDAR are exempt from filing in SEDI, but are still required to file insider reports in paper format with the applicable securities regulator.

C. Materiality

Chapter 4 discussed the notion of materiality—specifically, what constitutes material fact or material change in terms of prospectus requirements. Materiality is also very important to the continuous disclosure system. The statutory definitions of material change differ across jurisdictions; however, there has been increased harmonization of material change reporting with the adoption of NI 51-102, *Continuous Disclosure Obligations*.

In the context of continuing disclosure requirements, NI 51-102 defines material change as follows:

> 1.1 "material change" means
>
> (a) a change in the business, operations or capital of the reporting issuer that would reasonably be expected to have a significant effect on the market price or value of any of the securities of the reporting issuer; or
>
> (b) a decision to implement a change referred to in paragraph (a) made by the board of directors or other persons acting in a similar capacity or by senior management of the reporting issuer who believe that confirmation of the decision by the board of directors or any other persons acting in a similar capacity is probable.

NI 51-102 requires the reporting issuer to describe any plans or proposals for material changes in its business affairs or the affairs of an acquired business that may have a significant effect on the results of operations and financial position.

The material change reporting requirements are explored later in this chapter in several recent judgments. It is important, however, to note that issuers must also comply with a different type of standard if they are listed on the Toronto Stock Exchange (TSX) or the Toronto Venture Exchange (TSXV), that of "material information." While securities legislation sets a standard that distinguishes between material fact and material change, the TSX and the TSXV continuing disclosure requirements eliminate the distinction between material fact and material change, requiring transparency of material information. British Columbia had previously enacted legislation that would have shifted to a material information requirement; however, that legislation was never proclaimed in force. Sections 407 to 411 of the TSX Company Manual describe the material information standard required for TSX listed issuers.

TSX Company Manual

(2016), online: <http://tmx.complinet.com/en/tsx_manual.html>

Material Information

Definition

Section 407

Material information is any information relating to the business and affairs of a company that results in or would reasonably be expected to result in a significant change in the market price or value of any of the company's listed securities.

Material information consists of both material facts and material changes relating to the business and affairs of a listed company. In addition to material information, trading on the Exchange is sometimes affected by the existence of rumours and speculation. Where this is the case, Market Surveillance may require that an announcement be made by the company whether such rumours and speculation are factual or not. The policy of the Exchange with regard to rumours is set out more fully in Section 414.

The timely disclosure policy of the Exchange is designed to supplement the provisions of the OSA, which requires disclosure of any "material change" as defined therein. A report must be filed with the OSC concerning any "material change" as soon as practicable and in any event within ten days of the date on which the change occurs. The Exchange considers that "material information" is a broader term than "material change" since it encompasses material facts that may not entail a "material change" as defined in the Act. It has long been the practice of most listed companies to disclose a broader range of information to the public pursuant to the Exchange's timely disclosure policy than a strict interpretation of the Act might require. Companies subject to securities legislation outside of Ontario should be aware of their disclosure obligations in other jurisdictions.

It is the responsibility of each listed company to determine what information is material according to the above definition in the context of the company's own affairs. The materiality of information varies from one company to another according to the size of its profits, assets and capitalization, the nature of its operations and many other factors. An event that is "significant" or "major" in the context of a smaller company's business and affairs is often not material to a large company. The company itself is in the best position to apply the definition of material information to its own unique circumstances. The Exchange recognizes that decisions on disclosure require careful subjective judgments, and encourages listed companies to consult Market Surveillance when in doubt as to whether disclosure should be made.

NP 51-201 sets out what is meant by materiality in terms of timely disclosure. In making materiality judgments, issuers must take into account a number of factors, including the nature of the information itself, the volatility of the company's securities, and prevailing market conditions. The materiality of a particular fact or change may vary depending on the size of the company and the nature of its operations. NP 51-201 gives examples of potentially material information.

National Policy 51-201, *Disclosure Standards*
12 July 2002 (footnotes omitted)

Part II—Timely Disclosure

2.1 Timely Disclosure

(1) Companies are required by law to immediately disclose a "material change" in their business. For changes that a company initiates, the change occurs once the decision has been made to implement it. This may happen even before a company's directors approve it, if the company thinks it is probable they will do so. A company discloses a material change by issuing and filing a press release describing the change. A company must also file a material change report as soon as practicable, and no later than 10 days after the change occurs. This policy statement does not alter in any way the timely disclosure obligations of companies.

(2) Announcements of material changes should be factual and balanced. Unfavourable news must be disclosed just as promptly and completely as favourable news. Companies that disclose positive news but withhold negative news could find their disclosure practices subject to scrutiny by securities regulators. A company's press release should contain enough detail to enable the media and investors to understand the substance and importance of the change it is disclosing. Avoid including unnecessary details, exaggerated reports or promotional commentary.

2.2 Confidentiality

(2) Securities legislation permits a company to delay disclosure of a material change and to keep it confidential temporarily where immediate release of the information would be unduly detrimental to the company's interests. For example, immediate disclosure might interfere with a company's pursuit of a specific objective or strategy, with ongoing negotiations, or with its ability to complete a transaction. If the harm to a company's business from disclosing outweighs the general benefit to the market of immediate disclosure,

withholding disclosure is justified. In such cases a company may withhold public disclosure, but it must make a confidential filing with the securities commission. Certain jurisdictions also require companies to renew the confidential filing every 10 days should they want to continue to keep the information confidential.

(2) We discourage companies from delaying disclosure for a lengthy period of time as it becomes less likely that confidentiality can be maintained beyond the short term.

2.3 Maintaining Confidentiality

(1) Where disclosure of a material change is delayed, a company must maintain complete confidentiality. During the period before a material change is disclosed, market activity in the company's securities should be carefully monitored. Any unusual market activity may mean that news of the matter has been leaked and that certain persons are taking advantage of it. If the confidential material change, or rumours about it, have leaked or appear to be impacting the share price, a company should take immediate steps to ensure that a full public announcement is made. This would include contacting the relevant exchange and asking that trading be halted pending the issuance of a news release.

(2) Where a material change is being kept confidential, the company is under a duty to make sure that persons with knowledge of the material change have not made use of such information in purchasing or selling its securities. Such information should not be disclosed to any person or company, except in the necessary course of business.

• • •

Part IV—Materiality

4.1 Materiality Standard

(1) The definitions of "material fact" and "material change" under securities legislation are based on a market impact test. The definition of "privileged information" contained in the "tipping" provision of the securities legislation of Québec is based on a reasonable investor test. Despite these differences, the two materiality standards are likely to converge, for practical purposes, in most cases.

(2) The definition of a "material fact" includes a two part materiality test. A fact is material when it (i) significantly affects the market price or value of a security; or (ii) would reasonably be expected to have a significant effect on the market price or value of a security.

4.2 Materiality Determinations

(1) In making materiality judgements, it is necessary to take into account a number of factors that cannot be captured in a simple bright-line standard or test. These include the nature of the information itself, the volatility of the company's securities and prevailing market conditions. The materiality of a particular event or piece of information may vary between companies according to their size, the nature of their operations and many other factors. An event that is "significant" or "major" for a smaller company may not be material to a larger company. Companies should avoid taking an overly technical approach to determining materiality. Under volatile market conditions, apparently insignificant variances between earnings projections and actual results can have a significant impact on

share price once released. For example, information regarding a company's ability to meet consensus earnings published by securities analysts should not be selectively disclosed before general public release.

(2) We encourage companies to monitor the market's reaction to information that is publicly disclosed. Ongoing monitoring and assessment of market reaction to different disclosure will be helpful when making materiality judgements in the future. As a guiding principle, if there is any doubt about whether particular information is material, we encourage companies to err on the side of materiality and release information publicly.

4.3 Examples of Potentially Material Information

The following are examples of the types of events or information which may be material. This list is not exhaustive and is not a substitute for companies exercising their own judgement in making materiality determinations.

Changes in Corporate Structure

- changes in share ownership that may affect control of the company
- major reorganizations, amalgamations, or mergers
- take-over bids, issuer bids, or insider bids

Changes in Capital Structure

- the public or private sale of additional securities
- planned repurchases or redemptions of securities
- planned splits of common shares or offerings of warrants or rights to buy shares
- any share consolidation, share exchange, or stock dividend
- changes in a company's dividend payments or policies
- the possible initiation of a proxy fight
- material modifications to rights of security holders

Changes in Financial Results

- a significant increase or decrease in near-term earnings prospects
- unexpected changes in the financial results for any periods
- shifts in financial circumstances, such as cash flow reductions, major asset write-offs or write-downs
- changes in the value or composition of the company's assets
- any material change in the company's accounting policy

Changes in Business and Operations

- any development that affects the company's resources, technology, products or markets
- a significant change in capital investment plans or corporate objectives
- major labour disputes or disputes with major contractors or suppliers
- significant new contracts, products, patents, or services or significant losses of contracts or business

- significant discoveries by resource companies
- changes to the board of directors or executive management, including the departure of the company's CEO, CFO, COO or president (or persons in equivalent positions)
- the commencement of, or developments in, material legal proceedings or regulatory matters
- waivers of corporate ethics and conduct rules for officers, directors, and other key employees
- any notice that reliance on a prior audit is no longer permissible
- de-listing of the company's securities or their movement from one quotation system or exchange to another

Acquisitions and Dispositions

- significant acquisitions or dispositions of assets, property or joint venture interests
- acquisitions of other companies, including a take-over bid for, or merger with, another company

Changes in Credit Arrangements

- the borrowing or lending of a significant amount of money
- any mortgaging or encumbering of the company's assets
- defaults under debt obligations, agreements to restructure debt, or planned enforcement procedures by a bank or any other creditors
- changes in rating agency decisions
- significant new credit arrangements

The Five Year Review Committee, in considering whether Ontario should move to the standard of "material information," made the following observations.

Ministry of Finance, *Five Year Review Committee Final Report—Reviewing the Securities Act (Ontario)*
(Toronto: Queen's Printer for Ontario, 2003) at 145-47

The proposal to change the current trigger for making timely disclosure from a "material change" to "material information" has some appeal. First, by requiring prompt disclosure of "material information," more information would be available to the marketplace, which in turn would enable investors to make more informed investment decisions. Second, removing the distinction between a "fact," "change" and "information" would also help to bring more clarity to this difficult disclosure area. And third, mandating disclosure of material information under the Act would reduce reliance on exchange requirements that, in practice, have been difficult to enforce. …

There are four reasons why we do not recommend that the disclosure requirement be moved to "material information." First, we believe that when the Civil Liability Amendments are proclaimed in force, issuers will have a strong incentive to take a more principled and less technical view of developments or matters that ought to be disclosed as "material changes," which should contribute to a more robust timely disclosure regime. Second, as one commenter to the Committee noted, the "issue of when to disclose becomes much more problematic and difficult for issuers when material information or facts must be disclosed, such as merger negotiations and financial difficulty, etc., especially when such disclosure can and will be reviewed in hindsight particularly should statutory civil liability be instituted." Phil Anisman's dissenting statement in the Allen Report also notes:

> Canadian securities legislation thus accommodates the fact that the materiality of corporate intentions and business plans develops with their progress and implementation. The legislation requires timely disclosure only after such plans have matured to the point where they are sufficiently firm that they may be characterized as a change in the issuer's business, operations or affairs, while recognizing that they may, if generally known, significantly affect share prices at an earlier stage and precluding those who are aware of them from using their knowledge to trade in the issuer's share before the change, and public disclosure, occurs.

Third, disclosure of all material information would impose a significant burden on issuers to continually monitor matters external to them for the purpose of informing investors. Finally, if there are perceived gaps in information that is being disclosed by reporting companies on a continuous disclosure basis, the Commission has the necessary rulemaking authority to promulgate specific disclosure requirements similar to the SEC's Form 8-K approach noted above, and should be encouraged to do so where appropriate. Periodic reports, like the SEC's Form 8-K, should in our view be used to augment the existing framework of timely disclosure.

The United States has created substantially more codification of disclosure requirements and assurances. Given the amount of capital market activity by Canadian issuers in US markets, the multijurisdictional instruments and exemptions are an invaluable means for issuers to gain access to these markets. Securities regulators are under some pressure to ensure that Canadian securities law aligns with US initiatives or they risk withdrawal by US regulators of the special regulatory status Canada enjoys.

D. National Instruments and Multilateral Instruments

Securities regulators have, through initiatives of their umbrella association, the Canadian Securities Administrators, made an effort in recent years to standardize continuous disclosure requirements. There are now more than 25 national and multilateral instruments that are aimed at enhancing the system; many of these relate to continuous disclosure. For example, NI 51-102, *Continuous Disclosure Obligations*, which is discussed at length in this chapter, is aimed at the harmonization of continuous disclosure obligations. NI 71-101, *The Multijurisdictional Disclosure System*, was a joint initiative of the CSA and the US Securities and Exchange Commission (SEC) to reduce duplicative regulations in cross-border offerings, issuer bids, takeover bids, business combinations, and continuous disclosure requirements (NI 71-101CP). In addition to facilitating prospectus filing of US securities distributed in Canada, it sets out provisions for material change reporting, financial statements, management discussion and analysis (MD&A), and proxy and proxy solicitation rules to facilitate offerings being made to Canadian securityholders on the basis of US disclosure documents (NI 71-101, parts 14, 15, and 16).

There are also sector-specific disclosure instruments, such as instruments for oil and gas activities and mineral projects, which set out requirements and standards for disclosure by reporting issuers engaged in those activities (NI 51-101, *Standards of Disclosure for Oil and Gas Activities* (2002, as amended effective 1 July 2015); NI 43-101, *Standards of Disclosure for Mineral Projects* (2001, as amended effective 9 May 2016)).

There is also NI 55-104, *Insider Reporting Requirements and Exemptions*, effective 30 April 2010. NI 55-104 consolidates the principal insider reporting requirements. For example, it addresses disclosure of "economic exposure," which is the link between a person's economic or financial interests and the economic or financial interests of the reporting issuer of which the person is an insider; and disclosure of "related financial instruments," which includes equity monetization, a variety of sophisticated derivative-based strategies that permit investors to dispose of, in economic terms, an equity position in a public company without attracting certain tax and non-tax consequences associated with conventional disposition. The underlying rationale is that where a reporting insider enters into a monetization transaction and does not disclose the existence or material terms of that transaction, there is potential for harm to investors and the integrity of the insider reporting regime, because an insider in possession of material undisclosed information, although prohibited from trading in securities of the issuer, may be able to profit improperly from such information by entering into derivative-based transactions that mimic trades in securities of the reporting issuer; and since the insider's publicly reported holdings no longer reflect the insider's true economic position in the issuer, the public reporting of such holdings may in fact materially mislead investors (Companion Policy 55-104CP, *Insider Reporting Requirements and Exemptions*). NI 55-104 is discussed in detail in Chapter 8.

Enhanced disclosure requirements are also implicated in other instruments aimed at protecting investors and the integrity of capital markets. See, for example, the discussion of disclosure and corporate governance in Chapter 7.

All these instruments are aimed at enhancing the amount of information that is available to investors and potential investors. They complement provincial and territorial securities regulation, and it is important to consult these requirements in addition to any statutory language and regulations.

II. TIMELY AND PERIODIC DISCLOSURE REQUIREMENTS

The essential elements of the continuous disclosure system are timely and periodic disclosure by reporting issuers. For securities practitioners, timely disclosure usually refers to timely disclosure of material changes; however, periodic reporting requirements also carry with them the obligation to be timely in reporting on the periodic basis. Where the disclosure is periodic, the timing is set out in national instruments and securities legislation and regulations, as discussed throughout this chapter. Where a material change occurs, timely disclosure can mean forthwith, as soon as practicable, or in some instances no later than ten days, depending on the jurisdiction. Here, national instruments, statutory language, and case law have clarified what timeliness means in respect of material change.

Periodic disclosure includes quarterly and annual financial statements, a management discussion and analysis (MD&A) of financial condition and results document, the annual information form (AIF), and information circulars in connection with proxy solicitation prior to annual or special general meetings of shareholders. NI 51-102, *Continuous Disclosure Obligations*, as amended 17 November 2015, is aimed at providing consistency in reporting financial statements, MD&A, and the AIF. Its requirements are discussed in some detail below. Although annual reports are not required in most jurisdictions, many issuers also produce them as a development tool for prospective investors and a reporting tool for existing securities holders, and such reports include much of the mandatory information reporting. Issuers are also increasingly using their own Web pages to provide existing and prospective investors with timely and detailed information. The discussion in this Chapter relates only to the reporting requirements, not the full range and means of information communication that an issuer may engage in.

In *Re Canaco Resources Inc*, 2013 BCSECCOM 310, a three-member panel of the British Columbia Securities Commission dismissed allegations that Canaco Resources Inc and four of its directors contravened the BC *Securities Act* by failing to immediately disclose positive drill results emanating from the company's marquee property. The case turned on whether the drill results were material, and based on detailed evidence from management and two independent experts, the BC Securities Commission panel concluded that the drill results did not significantly change the tonnage, grade, or value of the deposit and were, therefore, not material. The commission held that the materiality test requires issuers to assume that the market is generally efficient, and that all value-relevant information is quickly reflected in the price of the security. It follows that, in assessing whether a fact would reasonably be expected to affect significantly the value of a security, management is simultaneously answering the question of whether that fact would reasonably be expected significantly to affect the security's market price. This ruling suggests that management should focus on whether the undisclosed fact changes the value of the business at the time of the information. The panel also found that a commission review of disclosure decisions is to be made without the benefit of hindsight; actual market movements following disclosure are irrelevant.

A. Who Must Disclose

A reporting issuer is subject to all periodic and timely disclosure obligations. "Reporting issuer" is a defined term, as discussed in Chapter 3. A reporting issuer has securities trading in the public domain through a previously issued prospectus; through a merger, amalgamation, or arrangement of securities; or where a securities commission has deemed that the company has been issuing securities. The concept of reporting issuer was initially adopted from US securities regulation (*Securities Exchange Act of 1934*, 15 USC 78a, as amended; Ontario Securities Commission [OSC], *Report of the OSC on the Problems of Disclosure Raised for Investors by Business Combinations and Private Placements* (Toronto: Queen's Printer for Ontario, 1970)). In exchange for the benefits of distributing and having their securities trading publicly, reporting issuers must provide timely and accurate information.

An issuer can apply and be deemed a reporting issuer where it would not be prejudicial to the public interest to do so. A publicly traded issuer that has completed offerings in other provinces or territorial jurisdictions can become a reporting issuer in another jurisdiction.

Criteria include that the issuer has been a reporting issuer in its home jurisdiction for at least one year (OSC Policy 12-602 (2001), 24 OSCB 1531, as amended and restated effective 16 March 2007). The deeming provisions are aimed at allowing issuers whose securities are publicly traded access to the continuous disclosure system with the concomitant ability of investors to access the information to make their trading decisions. An issuer can also apply to and receive the consent of a securities commission to cease being a reporting issuer, if it is not prejudicial to the public interest (Alberta *Securities Act*, RSA 2000, c S-4 (ASA), s 153; Newfoundland and Labrador, *Securities Act*, RSNL 1990, c S-13 (NLSA), s 84, as amended SNL 2004 c 37, s 62; Nova Scotia, *Securities Act*, RSNS 1989, c 418 (NSSA), s 89, as amended SNS 2006, c 46, s 37; Québec *Securities Act*, CQLR c V-1.1 (QSA), s 69, as amended SQ 2006, c 50, s 29; Saskatchewan, *The Securities Act, 1988*, SS 1988-89, c S-42.2 (SSA), s 92, as amended SS 2015, c 21, s 38).

It is important to note that for continuous disclosure, many specific statutory provisions have been superseded by NI 51-102. It is essential to check both the statutory language and national and multilateral instruments in order to ascertain precise disclosure and filing requirements, because a jurisdiction may have adopted an instrument but may not yet have amended its securities legislation. See e.g. OSC Rule 51-801, which implements NI 51-102 and indicates that certain statutory provisions do not apply to issuers complying with NI 51-102.

B. Periodic Disclosure Requirements: What Must Be Disclosed

The periodic disclosure requirements under Canadian securities legislation and instruments are discussed in turn below, including interim and annual financial statements, MD&A, AIF, and the preparation, delivery, and filing of information circulars. Both NI 51-102 and statutory requirements define timely disclosure: specifically, when each of the reports must be filed and/or made public. NI 51-102 also requires the issuer to send a request form to securityholders that they may use to request a copy of the reporting issuer's interim and/or annual financial statements and MD&A (NI 51-102, s 4.6).

1. *Financial Statements*

Each reporting issuer must prepare and file quarterly and annual financial statements. Generally, annual and quarterly reporting includes a statement of comprehensive income, a statement of changes in equity, a statement of cash flows, a statement of financial position at the end of the most recently completed financial year and the financial year immediately preceding the most recently completed financial year (NI 51-102, s 4.1). Financial statements are, by their nature, mainly historical. They are the record of past transactions and their impact on the issuer's financial position. Both securities laws and national instruments set out the timing requirements for interim financial reports and annual financial statements, including content and filing deadlines. As discussed later in this chapter, there are also officer and director certification requirements, and the audit committee of the issuer must review the financial statements before they are publicly disclosed (NI 52-109, *Certification of Disclosure in Issuers' Annual and Interim Filings*, replacing MI 52-109, effective 15 December 2008 (as amended effective 17 November 2015), and NI 52-110, *Audit Committees*, 28 April 2008 (as amended effective 17 November 2015), replacing MI 52-110 (2003), 26 CSCB 4884).

Securities statutes historically specified that every reporting issuer that is not a mutual fund must file interim reports quarterly within a specified time. The timelines for this disclosure have been amended by NI 51-102 and accompanying provincial and territorial implementation rules, and many provinces have repealed the statutory provisions because they did not align with the new requirements. Where the reporting issuer has completed its first financial year, the interim reports must include a comparative statement to the end of the same quarter in the last financial year, because consistency is important. The reports must be in accordance with International Financial Reporting Standards (IFRS), which replaced Canadian generally accepted accounting principles (GAAP) effective 1 January 2011 (Implementation Plan for Incorporating IFRSs into Canadian GAAP, 23 March 2007), or, in the case of US issuers in Canada, US GAAP, if certain conditions are met. The interim financial reporting requirements for mutual funds generally allow longer periods before reporting (NI 51-102).

IFRS is used in 140 countries, and all publicly traded EU companies have prepared their consolidated accounts using IFRS since 2005. The SEC has changed its rules to remove the reconciliation requirement for foreign issuers that prepare accounts under IFRS, effective 2009 (IASCF, Discussion Paper, Conceptual Framework for Financial Report, July 2006), and the IASB and the US Financial Accounting Standards Board (FASB) have been working to achieve convergence of IFRS and US GAAP through discussion to create a common set of high-quality global standards (IFRS, "Convergence Between IFRS and US GAAP" (August 2015), online: <http://www.ifrs.org/Use-around-the-world/Global-convergence/Convergence-with-US-GAAP/Pages/Convergence-with-US-GAAP.aspx>). IFRS is less prescriptive than US accounting rules, with different rules for revenue recognition. There are costs associated with companies having to comply with the new requirements, although the shift in accounting rules will facilitate greater international convergence in financial reporting.

NI 51-102 specifies that the audited annual financial statements must be filed, for a reporting issuer other than a venture issuer, within 90 days after the end of its most recently completed financial year; and the date of filing, in a foreign jurisdiction, annual financial statements for its most recently completed financial year. Venture issuers have 120 days. Deadlines for filing interim financial reports are 45 days for non-venture issuers and 60 days for venture issuers after the end of the interim period or the date of filing, in a foreign jurisdiction, interim financial reports (NI 51-102, ss 4.2, 4.4).

National Instrument 51-102, *Continuous Disclosure Obligations*
In force 30 March 2004, as amended effective 17 November 2015

Part 4 Financial Statements

4.1 Comparative Annual Financial Statements and Audit

(1) Subject to subsection 4.8(6), a reporting issuer must file annual financial statements that include

(a) a statement of comprehensive income, a statement of changes in equity, and a statement of cash flows for

(i) the most recently completed financial year; and

(ii) the financial year immediately preceding the most recently completed financial year, if any;

(b) a statement of financial position as at the end of each of the periods referred to in paragraph (a);

(c) in the following circumstances, a statement of financial position as at the beginning of the financial year immediately preceding the most recently completed financial year:

(i) the reporting issuer discloses in its annual financial statements an unreserved statement of compliance with IFRS, and

(ii) the reporting issuer

(A) applies an accounting policy retrospectively in its annual financial statements,

(B) makes a retrospective restatement of items in its annual financial statements, or

(C) reclassifies items in its annual financial statements;

(d) in the case of the reporting issuer's first IFRS financial statements, the opening IFRS statement of financial position at the date of transition to IFRS; and

(e) notes to the annual financial statements.

(2) Annual financial statements filed under subsection (1) must be audited.

(3) If a reporting issuer presents the components of profit or loss in a separate income statement, the separate income statement must be displayed immediately before the statement of comprehensive income filed under subsection (1).

4.2 Filing Deadline for Annual Financial Statements

The audited annual financial statements required to be filed under section 4.1 must be filed

(a) in the case of a reporting issuer other than a venture issuer, on or before the earlier of

(i) the 90th day after the end of its most recently completed financial year; and

(ii) the date of filing, in a foreign jurisdiction, annual financial statements for its most recently completed financial year; or

(b) in the case of a venture issuer, on or before the earlier of

(i) the 120th day after the end of its most recently completed financial year; and

(ii) the date of filing, in a foreign jurisdiction, annual financial statements for its most recently completed financial year.

Note that venture issuers have a longer deadline for filing both annual financial statements and interim financial reports. A venture issuer is defined in NI 51-102 as a reporting issuer that, at the applicable time, did not have any of its securities listed or quoted on any of the Toronto Stock Exchange, Aequitas NEO Exchange Inc, a US marketplace, or a marketplace outside Canada and the United States, other than the Alternative Investment Market of the London Stock Exchange or the PLUS markets operated by PLUS Markets Group plc (NI 51-102, s 1.1). The aim is to give junior issuers more flexibility about fulfilling periodic disclosure requirements, NI 51-102 recognizing the different resources available to venture and non-venture reporting issuers.

The board of directors of the reporting issuer must approve the interim financial reports and annual financial statements before the statements are filed (NI 51-102, s 4.5). However, the board of directors can delegate the approval of interim financial reports to its audit committee (NI 51-102, s 4.5(3)).

The following excerpt from a research study for the Expert Panel on Securities Regulation highlights how the different disclosure periods and other substantive requirements for venture issuers are a form of proportionate regulation.

Janis Sarra, *Proportionate Securities Regulation: The Potential for Scaled Treatment of Junior Issuers*
Research Study for the Expert Panel on Securities Regulation
(September 2008) at 30-31

NI 51-102, *Continuous Disclosure Obligations*, is another example of proportionate regulation by type of listing, recognizing different requirements for venture and non-venture reporting issuers. Proportionate requirements include, most notably, different filing deadlines for annual and interim financial statements [Note: now called interim financial reports since this article was written] and specified exemptions from some disclosure requirements for junior and senior reporting issuers. NI 51-102 specifies that non-venture issuers must file audited annual financial statements within 90 days after the end of its most recently completed financial year; venture issuers have 120 days. Deadlines for filing interim financial statements are 45 days for non-venture issuers and 60 days for venture issuers after the end of the interim period [now called interim financial reports].

This modification of regulation through different reporting timelines, as a policy choice, can be compared with the AIM's frequency of disclosure, where small issuers are required to give only annual and semi-annual financial statements. Frequency is an option to consider, in that if investors are not reading quarterly results, it may be that junior issuers could be exempted. However, any exemption can only be effective if the integrity of the issuer and the market were assured. If it appears to investors that junior issuers are being downgraded in terms of oversight or compliance, then such a change will not meet the express goals of the regulatory system. The issue is what periodic disclosure is really relevant to investors and potential investors and how frequently they want an update on that relevant information.

Venture issuers in Canada are exempted from filing an AIF. Venture issuers are also exempted from specified disclosure requirements under NI 51-102, such as filing a report on matters submitted to a vote at a meeting of securityholders. Under liquidity disclosures, issuers are required to discuss balance sheet conditions or income or cash flow items in a summary and tabular form, but venture issuers do not have to provide the summary and table. Venture issuers do not have to provide an analysis of their critical accounting estimates as non-venture issuers do. Pursuant to Form 51-102F6, *Statement of Executive Compensation*, there are also different disclosure requirements in respect of stock appreciation rights (SAR), in that venture issues do not have to make a number of specified disclosures that non-venture issuers do. However, a venture issuer must disclose which grants of options or SARs result from repricing and explain in reasonable detail the basis for the repricing. [Note: Since this article was written, SAR changed to share-based awards and option-based awards, and the form underwent revision: see <https://www.bcsc.bc.ca/Securities_Law/Policies/Policy5/PDF/51-102F6__F___June_30__2015/>.]

. . .

NI 51-102 also imposes increased disclosure requirements on venture issuers in at least one circumstance. Venture issuers, without significant revenue in the prior two financial years, must disclose in their MD&A capitalized or expensed exploration and development costs, expensed research and development costs, and deferred development costs. [Note to reader: since this article was written "capitalized or expensed exploration and development costs" has been replaced with "exploration and evaluation assets or expenditures," and "deferred development costs" now replaced with "intangible assets arising from development" in NI 51-102]. The objective is to focus venture issuers' discussion and analysis of results of operations on expenditures and progress towards achieving business objectives and milestones. Certain venture issuers must provide, in their annual or interim MD&A, a breakdown of material costs whether capitalized, deferred or expensed [now described as "whether expensed or recognized as assets"].

. . .

Hence, this second example illustrates four types of proportionate regulation: exemption from particular disclosure requirements, scaled timing for compliance with periodic disclosure requirements, modified requirements in terms of details to be disclosed, and "tailored" requirements, such as MD&A exploration and development disclosure requirements for venture issuers without significant revenue in the prior two financial years. The delineation by type of listing does not result in less rigorous requirements; rather, they are proportionate to the type of issuer, its capacity to make periodic disclosure on a timely basis, and more focused in terms of being aimed at what the particular investor needs to know to make investment choices. In this respect, disclosure requirements could focus more clearly on junior issuers. Given the fact that many junior issuers do not generate much, if any, revenue, timely information such as drill results, clinical trial results, and approval of mineral licenses can be more important than financial statements in making investment decisions.

Where a reporting issuer has not completed its first financial year, it must file an interim financial report for the interim periods of the reporting issuer's current financial year unless that period is less than three months in length. Where a reporting issuer has completed its first financial year, interim financial reports for the interim periods of the reporting issuer's current financial year must be filed (NI 51-102, s 4.3). The interim financial reports must include a statement of financial position, a statement of comprehensive income, a statement of changes in equity, and statement of cash flows, all for the year-to-date interim period, and comparative financial information and statement of financial position for the corresponding interim period in the immediately preceding financial year, if any; for interim periods other than the first interim period in a reporting issuer's financial year, a statement of comprehensive income for the three-month period ending on the last day of the interim period and comparative financial information for the corresponding period in the immediately preceding financial year, if any, and notes to the financial statements (NI 51-102, ss 4.3(2)(c), (f)). In the case of the reporting issuer's first interim financial report required to be filed in the year of adopting IFRS, the issuer must disclose the opening IFRS statement of financial position at the date of transition to IFRS (NI 51-102, s 4.3(2)(e)). If a reporting issuer presents the components of profit or loss in a separate income statement, the separate income statement must be displayed immediately before the statement of comprehensive income (NI 51-102, s 4.3(2.1), as amended 17 November 2015).

A reporting issuer, including a mutual fund, must file its annual financial statement within a specified period. The annual financial statement must include comparative data from the same time frame for the previous reporting year, or where the reporting issuer is in its first financial year, from the time of its incorporation. Previously, many statutes specified 140 days from the end of a reporting issuer's last financial year; however, NI 51-102 has amended this period and the statutory provisions in most jurisdictions were repealed.

NI 51-102 is also tailored to type of issuer in respect to additional disclosure requirements in its MD&A requirements. For venture issuers without significant revenue in the prior two financial years, NI 51-102 requires disclosure of material components of exploration and evaluation assets or expenditures, expensed research and development costs, and intangible assets arising from development, general and administration expenses; and any material costs, whether expensed or recognized as assets, not referred to in these categories (NI 51-102, s 5.3(1)). If the venture issuer's business primarily involves mining exploration and development, the analysis of exploration and evaluation assets or expenditures must be presented on a property-by-property basis (NI 51-102, s 5.3(1)). The objective is to focus venture issuers' discussion and analysis of financial performance on expenditures and progress toward achieving business objectives and milestones (Form 51-102F1). Venture issuers are excluded from filing an Annual Information Form (AIF) (NI 51-102, s 6.1). A component of cost is generally considered to be a material component if it exceeds the greater of 20 percent of the total amount of the class, and $25,000 (51-102CP, *Continuous Disclosure Obligations*, s 5.2).

Venture issuers are also exempted from specified disclosure requirements, such as filing a report on matters submitted to a vote at a meeting of securityholders (NI 51-102, s 11.3). Under liquidity disclosures, issuers are required to discuss statements of financial position or income or profit or loss attributable to owners of the parent or cash flow items in a summary and tabular form, but venture issuers do not have to provide the summary and table (Form 51-102F1).

NI 51-102 specifies that the annual financial statements must be audited (NI 51-102, s 4.1(2)). NI 51-102 provisions for disclosure of the auditor's review of the financial statements are aimed at enhancing investor confidence in the disclosure and reducing the risk of auditor capture (NI 51-102, s 4.3(3)). Reporting issuers are encouraged to file their annual financial statements as soon as practicable after the date of the auditor's report. Section 4.3 also requires the issuer to disclose whether or not an auditor has reviewed the interim financial reports, including any reason that the review was not completed. Where the auditor has a reservation of opinion, the interim financial reports must be accompanied by a written review report from the auditor.

Section 4.1 of NI 51-102 requires a reporting issuer to file annual financial statements that include comparative information for the immediately preceding financial year and that are audited. The auditor's report must cover both the most recently completed financial year and the comparative period, except if the issuer changed its auditor during the periods presented in the financial statements and the new auditor has not audited the comparative period. In this situation, the auditor's report would normally refer to the predecessor auditor's report unless the predecessor auditor's report on the prior period's annual financial statements is reissued with the financial statements. This requirement is consistent with Canadian Auditing

Standard 710, *Comparative Information—Corresponding Figures and Comparative Financial Statements* (51-102CP, s 3.2).

The board of directors of a reporting issuer, in discharging its responsibilities for ensuring the reliability of an interim financial report, should consider engaging an external auditor to carry out a review of the interim financial reports (51-102CP, s 3.4(1)). The reporting issuer must disclose if an auditor has not performed a review of the interim financial reports; if an auditor was unable to complete a review and why, and file a written report from the auditor if the auditor has performed a review and expressed a reservation in the auditor's interim review report (NI 51-102, s 4.3(3)). An issuer's disclosure of the reasons why the auditor was unable to complete the review would normally include a discussion of inadequate internal control, a limitation on the scope of the auditor's work, or the failure of management to provide the auditor with the written representations the auditor believes are necessary (NI 51-102CP, s 3.4(2)).

The issuer must also disclose any change in auditor, including information on whether there was a difference of opinion between personnel of a reporting issuer responsible for the financial statements and the former auditor responsible for authorizing the issuance of audit reports or communication of the results of the auditor's review of the interim financial reports. This disclosure is mandatory (1) where the difference of opinion resulted in a reservation or would have resulted in a reservation in the former auditor's audit report on the financial statements or (2) resulted in a qualified or adverse communication or denial of assurance in respect of the former auditor's review of the reporting issuer's interim financial reports. The issuer must disclose any decision by the board of directors to propose to securities holders that its auditor be removed before expiry of its term of appointment or that a different person or company be appointed as its auditor on expiry. It must disclose any matter that in the former auditor's opinion has, or could have, a material impact on the financial statements or reports provided by the auditor relating to the financial statements. There are specific disclosure requirements on both the auditor and the successor auditor (NI 51-102, s 4.11). The policy objective is to place all the relevant information regarding the external audit process and results into the hands of investors.

A reporting issuer must annually send a request form to the registered holders and beneficial owners of its securities, other than debt instruments, which the registered holders and beneficial owners may then use to request a copy of the interim financial reports and/or annual financial statements and related MD&A (NI 51-102, s 4.6). The reporting issuer must send the request form to the beneficial owners of its securities who are identified under NI 51-102 as having chosen to receive all securityholder materials sent to beneficial owners of securities. If the reporting issuer sends its annual financial statements to all its securityholders, it does not need to send the request form (NI 51-102, s 4.6(5)).

If a registered holder or beneficial owner requests the annual financial statements or interim financial reports, the reporting issuer must send a copy of the requested financial statements and related MD&A to the person or company that made the request, without charge, by the later of ten calendar days of the request or the filing deadline for the financial statements (NI 51-102, s 4.6(3)). A reporting issuer is not required to send copies of annual financial statements or interim financial reports that were filed more than one year before the issuer receives the request (NI 51-102, s 4.6(4)). The requirement to send financial statements only when requested is an innovation in current regulation, because previous law required the mailing of the financial statements to all securityholders. The premise is that the financial statements are available on SEDAR for securityholders to examine if they choose. Thus, NI 51-102 reduces the duplication that would arise if the issuer sent the financial statement to all holders and those holders have also viewed the financial statement on SEDAR.

NI 51-102 makes special provision for reporting issuers that are filing financial statements in compliance with US SEC requirements and US GAAP, specifying that US GAAP has the same meaning as in NI 52-107, *Acceptable Principles and Auditing Standards*. NI 52-107 defines US GAAP as meaning "generally accepted accounting principles in the United States of America that the SEC has identified as having substantial authoritative support, as supplemented by Regulation S-X under the 1934 Act, as amended from time to time." Generally, the issuer has an obligation to reconcile the reporting and file a restated financial statement. The specifics of s 4.3(4) follow.

National Instrument 51-102, *Continuous Disclosure Obligations*
In force 30 March 2004, as amended effective 17 November 2015

4.3(4) SEC Issuer—Restatement of an Interim Financial Report

If an SEC issuer that is a reporting issuer

(a) has filed an interim financial report prepared in accordance with Canadian GAAP applicable to publicly accountable enterprises for one or more interim periods since its most recently completed financial year for which annual financial statements have been filed; and

(b) prepares its annual financial statements or an interim financial report for the period immediately following the periods referred to in paragraph (a) in accordance with US GAAP,

the SEC issuer must

(c) restate the interim financial report for the periods referred to in paragraph (a) in accordance with US GAAP; and

(d) file the restated interim financial report referred to in paragraph (c) by the filing deadline for the financial statements referred to in paragraph (b).

There are also provisions requiring timely filing of interim financial reports and annual financial statements after becoming a reporting issuer, aimed at ensuring transparency of financial reporting documents both immediately prior to and after becoming a reporting issuer (NI 51-102, s 4.7). An issuer is, however, not required to provide comparative interim financial information for periods that ended before the issuer became a reporting issuer if, to a reasonable person, it is impracticable to present prior-period information on a basis that it could be compared. The issuer is to include what prior information exists and a note to the interim financial reports disclosing the fact that the prior-period information has not been prepared on a basis consistent with the most recent interim financial information (NI 51-102, s 4.7).

Disclosure is also required if there has been a change in year-end or change in corporate structure. Also required is disclosure of any reverse takeover and financial statements for an acquirer.

Additional filing requirements are set out in NI 51-102. A reporting issuer must file a copy of any disclosure material that it sends to its securityholders, or that it files with or furnishes to the SEC, including material filed as exhibits to other documents, if the material contains information that has not been included in disclosure already filed in a jurisdiction by the SEC issuer (NI 51-102, s 11.1). A reporting issuer must also file a notice promptly if it changes its status, such as becoming a venture or non-venture issuer (NI 51-102, s 11.2). An issuer must also report voting results, including a description of the matter voted on, the outcome, and if the vote was conducted by ballot, the number of votes cast for, against, and withheld (NI 51-102, s 11.3). Venture issuers do not have to comply with the voting results disclosure.

A reporting issuer must file a copy of any news release issued by it that discloses information regarding its historical or prospective financial performance or financial condition for a financial year or interim period (NI 51-102, s 11.4). If a reporting issuer decides it will refile a document or restate financial information for comparative periods in financial statements for reasons other than retrospective application of a change in an accounting standard or policy or a new accounting standard and the refiled information differs materially from the information originally filed, the issuer must immediately issue and file a news release authorized by an executive officer disclosing the nature and substance of the changes (NI 51-102, s 11.5).

A reporting issuer must also file a copy of any contract that it or any of its subsidiaries is a party to, other than a contract entered into in the ordinary course of business, that is material to the issuer and was entered into within the last financial year, or before the last financial year but is still in effect (NI 51-102, s 12.2). Where the executive officer has reasonable grounds to believe that disclosure of certain provisions of a contract required to be filed would be seriously prejudicial to the interests of the reporting issuer, or would violate confidentiality provisions, the reporting issuer may file the contract with those specific provisions omitted or marked so as to be unreadable, but must include a description of the type of information that has been omitted (NI 51-102, s 12.2). The securities regulator may grant an exemption from NI 51-102, in whole or in part, subject to conditions (NI 51-102, s 13.1).

These requirements for extensive disclosure err on the side of more, rather than less, information, so that investors can make informed decisions; and issuers are exempt from requirements in some instances where the disclosure burden would be too onerous. The national instrument grants the regulator the ability to relieve against the filing requirements where such relief is not prejudicial to the public interest (NI 51-102).

NI 51-102 also requires that a reporting issuer that has a significant equity investee must disclose, in its MD&A, summarized information of the equity investee, including the aggregated amounts of assets, liabilities, revenue and profit or loss; and the reporting issuer's proportionate interest in the equity investee and any contingent issuance of securities by the equity investee that might significantly affect the reporting issuer's share of profit or loss. "Equity investee" means a business that the issuer has invested in and accounted for using the equity method (NI 51-102, s 1.1).

Form 51-102F6 was amended effective 30 June 2015; specifically, s 1.3(9) was amended to provide flexibility if the company's performance goals and similar conditions disclosed in the Compensation Discussion and Analysis are in a currency different than the currency presented in the prescribed tables, which may be for purposes of consistency with financial reporting. It clarifies that if the company used any benchmarking in determining compensation or any element of compensation, the company should include the benchmark and describe why the benchmark group and selection criteria are considered by the company to be relevant. In terms of compensation governance, the issuer must disclose the name of each committee member and whether the member is independent or not independent. It also requires transparency in terms of disclosing whether or not a consultant or adviser has provided any services to the company, or to its affiliated or subsidiary entities, or to any of its directors or members of management, other than or in addition to compensation services provided for any of the company's directors or executive officers, including describing the nature of the work, whether the board of directors or compensation committee must pre-approve other services the consultant or adviser, or any of its affiliates, provides to the company at the request of management. The forms also require disclosure of pension plan benefits payable to executives.

The executive compensation provisions of NI 51-102 refer to a "named executive officer" (NEO), referring to the most highly compensated executive officers or highly compensated individuals acting in a similar capacity.

National Instrument 51-102, *Continuous Disclosure Obligations*
In force 30 March 2004, as amended effective 17 November 2015

11.6 Executive Compensation Disclosure for Certain Reporting Issuers

(1) A reporting issuer that is not required to send to its securityholders an information circular and does not send an information circular that includes the disclosure required by Item 8 of Form 51-102F5 and that does not file an AIF that includes the executive compensation disclosure required by Item 18 of Form 51-102F2 must

(a) disclose all compensation paid, payable, awarded, granted, given, or otherwise provided, directly or indirectly, by the issuer, or a subsidiary of the issuer, to each NEO and director, in any capacity, including, for greater certainty, all plan and non-plan compensation, direct and indirect pay, remuneration, economic or financial award, reward, benefit, gift or perquisite paid, payable, awarded, granted, given, or otherwise provided to the NEO or director for services provided, directly or indirectly, to the issuer or a subsidiary of the issuer, and

(b) include detail and discussion of the compensation, and the decision-making process relating to compensation, presented in such a way that it provides a reasonable person an understanding of

(i) how decisions about NEO and director compensation are made,

(ii) the compensation paid, made payable, awarded, granted, given or otherwise provided to each NEO and director, and

(iii) how specific NEO and director compensation relates to the overall stewardship and governance of the reporting issuer.

(2) The disclosure required under subsection (1) must be provided for the periods set out in, and in accordance with, Form 51-102F6 *Statement of Executive Compensation*,

(2.1) Despite subsection (2), a reporting issuer that is a venture issuer may provide the disclosure required under subsection (1) for the periods set out in and in accordance with Form 51-102F6V *Statement of Executive Compensation—Venture Issuers*.

(3) The disclosure required under subsection (1) must be filed not later than 140 days after the end of the reporting issuer's most recently completed financial year.

(4) For the purposes of this section, "NEO" and "plan" have the meaning ascribed to those terms in Form 51-102F6 *Statement of Executive Compensation* or, for a venture issuer relying on subsection (2.1), in Form 51-102F6V *Statement of executive Compensation—Venture Issuers.*

(5) This section does not apply to an issuer that satisfies securities legislation requirements relating to information circulars, proxies and proxy solicitation under section 4.6 or 5.7 of National Instrument 71-102 *Continuous Disclosure and Other Exemptions Relating to Foreign Issuers.*

Form 51-102F6, *Statement of Executive Compensation*

Effective 30 June 2015

Item 1 General Provisions

1.1 Objective

All direct and indirect compensation provided to certain executive officers and directors for, or in connection with, services they have provided to the company or a subsidiary of the company must be disclosed in this form.

The objective of this disclosure is to communicate the compensation the company paid, made payable, awarded, granted, gave or otherwise provided to each NEO and director for the financial year, and the decision-making process relating to compensation. This disclosure will provide insight into executive compensation as a key aspect of the overall stewardship and governance of the company and will help investors understand how decisions about executive compensation are made.

A company's executive compensation disclosure under this form must satisfy this objective and subsections 9.3.1(1) or 11.6(1) of the Instrument.

1.2 Definitions

. . .

"equity incentive plan" means an incentive plan, or portion of an incentive plan, under which awards are granted and that falls within the scope of IFRS 2 *Share-based Payment*;

"external management company" includes a subsidiary, affiliate or associate of the external management company;

"grant date" means a date determined for financial statement reporting purposes under IFRS 2 *Share-based Payment*;

"incentive plan" means any plan providing compensation that depends on achieving certain performance goals or similar conditions within a specified period;

"incentive plan award" means compensation awarded, earned, paid, or payable under an incentive plan;

. . .

"NEO" or "named executive officer" means each of the following individuals:

(a) a CEO;

(b) a CFO;

(c) each of the three most highly compensated executive officers of the company, including any of its subsidiaries, or the three most highly compensated individuals acting in a similar capacity, other than the CEO and CFO, at the end of the most recently completed financial year whose total compensation was, individually, more than $150,000, as determined in accordance with subsection 1.3(6), for that financial year; and

(d) each individual who would be an NEO under paragraph (c) but for the fact that the individual was neither an executive officer of the company or its subsidiaries, nor acting in a similar capacity, at the end of that financial year;

. . .

1.3 Preparing the form

(1) All compensation to be included

(a) When completing this form, the company must disclose all compensation paid, payable, awarded, granted, given, or otherwise provided, directly or indirectly, by the company, or a subsidiary of the company, to each NEO and director, in any capacity, including, for greater certainty, all plan and non-plan compensation, direct and indirect pay, remuneration, economic or financial award, reward, benefit, gift or perquisite paid, payable, awarded, granted, given, or otherwise provided to the NEO or director and for services provided and for services to be provided, directly or indirectly, to the company or a subsidiary of the company.

(b) Despite paragraph (a), in respect of the Canada Pension Plan, similar government plans, and group life, health, hospitalization, medical reimbursement and relocation plans that do not discriminate in scope, terms or operation and are generally available to all salaried employees, the company is not required to disclose as compensation

(i) any contributions or premiums paid or payable by the company on behalf of an NEO, or of a director, under these plans, and

(ii) any cash, securities, similar instruments or any other property received by an NEO, or by a director, under these plans.

(c) For greater certainty, the plans described in paragraph (b) include plans that provide for such benefits after retirement.

(d) If an item of compensation is not specifically mentioned or described in this form, it is to be disclosed in column (h) ("All other compensation") of the summary compensation table in section 3.1.

. . .

(4) External management companies

(a) If one or more individuals acting as an NEO of the company are not employees of the company, disclose the names of those individuals.

(b) If an external management company employs or retains one or more individuals acting as NEOs or directors of the company and the company has entered into an understanding, arrangement or agreement with the external management company to provide executive management services to the company directly or indirectly, disclose any compensation that:

(i) the company paid directly to an individual employed, or retained by the external management company, who is acting as an NEO or director of the company; and

(ii) the external management company paid to the individual that is attributable to the services they provided to the company directly or indirectly.

(c) If an external management company provides the company's executive management services and provides executive management services to another company, disclose the entire compensation the external management company paid to the individual acting as an NEO or director, or acting in a similar capacity, in connection with services the external management company provided to the company, or the parent or a subsidiary of the company. If the management company allocates the compensation paid to an NEO or director, disclose the basis or methodology used to allocate this compensation.

(5) Director and NEO compensation

Disclose any compensation awarded to, earned by, paid to, or payable to each director and NEO, in any capacity with respect to the company. Compensation to directors and NEOs must include all compensation from the company and its subsidiaries.

Disclose any compensation awarded to, earned by, paid to, or payable to, an NEO, or director, in any capacity with respect to the company, by another person or company.

(6) Determining if an individual is an NEO

For the purpose of calculating total compensation awarded to, earned by, paid to, or payable to an individual under paragraph (c) of the definition of NEO,

(a) use the total compensation that would be reported under column (i) of the summary compensation table required by section 3.1 for each executive officer, as if that executive officer were an NEO for the company's most recently completed financial year, and

(b) exclude from the calculation,

(i) any compensation that would be reported under column (g) of the summary compensation table required by section 3.1,

(ii) any incremental payments, payables, and benefits to an executive officer that are triggered by, or result from, a scenario listed in section 6.1 that occurred during the most recently completed financial year, and

(iii) any cash compensation that relates to foreign assignments that is specifically intended to offset the impact of a higher cost of living in the foreign location, and is not otherwise related to the duties the executive officer performs for the company.

(7) Compensation to associates

Disclose any awards, earnings, payments, or payables to an associate of an NEO, or of a director, as a result of compensation awarded to, earned by, paid to, or payable to the NEO or the director, in any capacity with respect to the company.

. . .

(10) Plain language

Information required to be disclosed under this form must be clear, concise, and presented in such a way that it provides a reasonable person an understanding of

(a) how decisions about NEO and director compensation are made, and

(b) how specific NEO and director compensation relates to the overall stewardship and governance of the company.

. . .

Item 2 Compensation Discussion and Analysis

2.1 Compensation discussion and analysis

(1) Describe and explain all significant elements of compensation awarded to, earned by, paid to, or payable to NEOs for the most recently completed financial year. Include the following:

(a) the objectives of any compensation program or strategy;

(b) what the compensation program is designed to reward;

(c) each element of compensation;

(d) why the company chooses to pay each element;

(e) how the company determines the amount (and, where applicable, the formula) for each element; and

(f) how each element of compensation and the company's decisions about that element fit into the company's overall compensation objectives and affect decisions about other elements.

(2) If applicable, describe any new actions, decisions or policies that were made after the end of the most recently completed financial year that could affect a reasonable person's understanding of an NEO's compensation for the most recently completed financial year.

(3) If applicable, clearly state the benchmark and explain its components, including the companies included in the benchmark group and the selection criteria.

(4) If applicable, disclose performance goals or similar conditions that are based on objective, identifiable measures, such as the company's share price or earnings per share. If performance goals or similar conditions are subjective, the company may describe the performance goal or similar condition without providing specific measures.

If the company discloses performance goals or similar conditions that are non-GAAP financial measures, explain how the company calculates these performance goals or similar conditions from its financial statements.

Exemption

The company is not required to disclose performance goals or similar conditions in respect of specific quantitative or qualitative performance-related factors if a reasonable person would consider that disclosing them would seriously prejudice the company's interests.

For the purpose of this exemption, a company's interests are not considered to be seriously prejudiced solely by disclosing performance goals or similar conditions if those goals or conditions are based on broad corporate-level financial performance metrics which include earnings per share, revenue growth, and earnings before interest, taxes, depreciation and amortization.

This exemption does not apply if it has publicly disclosed the performance goals or similar conditions.

If the company is relying on this exemption, state this fact and explain why disclosing the performance goals or similar conditions would seriously prejudice the company's interests.

If the company does not disclose specific performance goals or similar conditions, state what percentage of the NEO's total compensation relates to this undisclosed information and how difficult it could be for the NEO, or how likely it will be for the company, to achieve the undisclosed performance goal or similar condition.

(5) Disclose whether or not the board of directors, or a committee of the board, considered the implications of the risks associated with the company's compensation policies and practices. If the implications were considered, disclose the following:

(a) the extent and nature of the board of directors' or committee's role in the risk oversight of the company's compensation policies and practices;

(b) any practices the company uses to identify and mitigate compensation policies and practices that could encourage an NEO or individual at a principal business unit or division to take inappropriate or excessive risks;

(c) any identified risks arising from the company's compensation policies and practices that are reasonably likely to have a material adverse effect on the company.

(6) Disclose whether or not an NEO or director is permitted to purchase financial instruments, including, for greater certainty, prepaid variable forward contracts, equity swaps, collars, or units of exchange funds, that are designed to hedge or offset a decrease in market value of equity securities granted as compensation or held, directly or indirectly, by the NEO or director.

2.2 Performance graph

(a) This section does not apply to (i) venture issuers, (ii) companies that have distributed only debt securities or non-convertible, non-participating preferred securities to the public, and (iii) companies that were not reporting issuers in any jurisdiction in Canada for at least 12 calendar months before the end of their most recently completed financial year, other than companies that became new reporting issuers as a result of a restructuring transaction.

(b) Provide a line graph showing the company's cumulative total shareholder return over the five most recently completed financial years. Assume that $100 was invested on the first day of the five-year period. If the company has been a reporting issuer for less than five years, use the period that the company has been a reporting issuer.

Compare this to the cumulative total return of at least one broad equity market index that, to a reasonable person, would be an appropriate reference point for the company's return. If the company is included in the S&P/TSX Composite Total Return Index, use that index. In all cases, assume that dividends are reinvested.

Discuss how the trend shown by this graph compares to the trend in the company's compensation to executive officers reported under this form over the same period.

2.3 Share-based and option-based awards

Describe the process the company uses to grant share-based or option-based awards to executive officers. Include the role of the compensation committee and executive officers in setting or amending any equity incentive plan under which a share-based or option-based award is granted. State whether previous grants of option-based awards are taken into account when considering new grants … [summary compensation tables omitted].

2.4 Compensation governance

(1) Describe any policies and practices adopted by the board of directors to determine the compensation for the company's directors and executive officers.

(2) If the company has established a compensation committee

(a) disclose the name of each committee member and, in respect of each member, state whether or not the member is independent or not independent;

(b) disclose whether or not one or more of the committee members has any direct experience that is relevant to his or her responsibilities in executive compensation;

(c) describe the skills and experience that enable the committee to make decisions on the suitability of the company's compensation policies and practices; and

(d) describe the responsibilities, powers and operation of the committee.

(3) If a compensation consultant or advisor has, at any time since the company's most recently completed financial year, been retained to assist the board of directors or the compensation committee in determining compensation for any of the company's directors or executive officers

(a) state the name of the consultant or advisor and a summary of the mandate the consultant or advisor has been given,

(b) disclose when the consultant or advisor was originally retained,

(c) if the consultant or advisor has provided any services to the company, or to its affiliated or subsidiary entities, or to any of its directors or members of management, other than or in addition to compensation services provided for any of the company's directors or executive officers,

(i) state this fact and briefly describe the nature of the work, and

(ii) disclose whether the board of directors or compensation committee must pre-approve other services the consultant or advisor, or any of its affiliates, provides to the company at the request of management, and

(d) for each of the two most recently completed financial year, disclose,

(i) under the caption "Executive Compensation-Related Fees," the aggregate fees billed by each consultant or advisor, or any of its affiliates, for services related to determining compensation for any of the company's directors and executive officers, and

(ii) under the caption "All Other Fees," the aggregate fees billed for all other services provided by each consultant or advisor, or any of its affiliates, that are not reported under subparagraph (i) and include a description of the nature of the services comprising the fees disclosed under this category.

The commentary to Form 51-102F6 suggests that the issuer must provide enough analysis to allow a reasonable person to understand the disclosure and the significant principles underlying policies and the decisions relating to compensation provided to an NEO. The information contained should give readers a sense of how compensation is tied to the NEO's performance. Boilerplate language is to be avoided. The commentary provides examples of items that will usually be significant elements of disclosure concerning compensation, including: contractual or non-contractual arrangements, plans, process changes, or any other matters that might cause the amounts disclosed for the most recently completed financial year to be misleading if used as an indicator of expected compensation levels in future periods; the process for determining perquisites and personal benefits; policies and decisions about the adjustment or recovery of earnings, payments, or payables if the performance goal or similar condition on which they are based is restated or adjusted to reduce the earning, payment, or payable; and any waiver or change to any specified performance goal or similar condition to payout for any amount, including whether the waiver or change applied to one or more specified NEOs or to all compensation subject to the performance goal or similar condition (Form 51-102F6, s 2.1 commentary).

a. Do Current Financial Statements Provide Adequate Disclosure?

When combined with prior financial projections or analysts' predictions of the following quarter's financial earnings, financial statements can dramatically affect the price of securities in the secondary market. Even where an issuer's overall financial position is healthy, a failure to meet previously specified targets can lead to a sharp drop in price, while a quarter in which the issuer's performance exceeds the targets is often a source of rapid price increases. These factors serve as an incentive for management to ensure that the financial reports meet or exceed targets, especially where management's compensation is tied to the price of the stock. The use of market-value accounting rather than book value has enabled estimates of future revenue projects and costs to be reflected in the issuer's financial statements before they are actually realized. This practice has made financial statements more vulnerable to subtle but effective manipulation, as many figures are matters of judgment rather than records of completed transactions. The outbreak of major earnings "restatements" at a number of large public issuers following Enron raised important issues about the appropriate role of financial disclosure in securities markets and whether the law provides adequate protection for investors in secondary markets. Nortel is a case in point. Subsequent to financial restatements, it settled actions against it in Canada and the United States for over US$1 billion.

Securities regulators continue to be concerned about the accuracy of disclosure in financial statements. Relatively new civil liability provisions in many Canadian jurisdictions create a statutory right of action in favour of secondary market investors against issuers and key related persons for making public misrepresentations about the issuer or for failing to disclose material changes as required by securities law. The provisions, together with existing authority by securities regulators to take action when issuers breach securities law, seek to encourage directors, officers, and other persons with control to ensure that the issuer meets its continuous disclosure obligations.

As a consequence of these challenges, supplementary documents to financial statements are increasingly common. A significant factor is the existence of any system designed to ensure that the responsible issuer meets its continuous disclosure obligations. Issuers frequently establish written disclosure policies to ensure adequate controls and monitoring of continuous disclosure and for determinations as to when a change is material. This factor aligns with requirements whereby the CEO and CFO, must certify that, among other things, the financial statements and other financial information in the annual filings and interim filings fairly present the financial condition, results of operations, and cash flows of the issuer as discussed in Chapter 7.

Hence NI 51-102 is aimed at uniformity of financial statements across Canada and across size of firm as much as possible; and imposes requirements for accompanying documents as part of periodic reporting requirements.

Securities regulators have taken steps to ensure that the disclosure of executive compensation complies with regulatory requirements. In February 2009, the Ontario Securities Commission issued a notice of hearing and related statement of allegations in respect of Research in Motion Limited (RIM) and its executive officers pertaining to conduct relating to stock options granting practices at RIM that over a ten-year period from December 1996 to July 2006 were inconsistent with the terms of RIM's stock option plan and with RIM's public disclosure. The following is an excerpt from the notice, followed by an excerpt of settlement of the proceedings two days later.

In the Matter of Research in Motion Limited et al

(3 February 2009) (Statement of Allegations of Ontario Securities Commission)

The Stock Option Plan

11. In advance of RIM becoming a reporting issuer in December, 1996, RIM's Board of Directors (the "Board") approved a new stock option plan (the "Plan") to govern the granting of stock options ("Options") for the RIM both before and after it became a reporting issuer. The Plan was subsequently amended by the Board but contained substantially the same requirements during the Material Time.

12. The Respondents should have taken reasonable steps to be and remain aware during the Material Time of the terms of the Plan. In respect of pricing, Options were to be priced "at the money," where the exercise price per share is equal to the closing market price of the shares on the last trading day immediately preceding the date of the grant. The Plan was to be administered by the Board or a Compensation Committee by delegation.

Incorrect Options Dating Practices

13. As described below, Balsillie, Lazaridis, Kavelman and Loberto engaged in the grant of Options, in which option backdating or option repricing occurred. The grant dates selected resulted in more favourable pricing for the Options or "in the money" grants. In many instances, the lowest share price in a period was chosen using hindsight in order to set the grant date and, therefore, the exercise price. These practices are collectively referred to as "Incorrect Dating Practices."

14. Approximately 1,400 of 3,200 Option grants made by RIM during the Material Time were made using Incorrect Dating Practices, many of which gave the recipient an undisclosed benefit that was not authorized or permitted by the Plan or the applicable rules of the TSX (the "TSX Rules").

15. The individual respondents (all the respondents apart from RIM, the "Individual Respondents") personally received an undisclosed benefit from grants of Options that were "in the money" at the time they were made, in breach of the Plan and the TSX Rules. They have, however, all since repaid any "in the money" benefits received, with interest, or have repriced unexercised Options.

16. The total "in the money" benefit resulting from the Incorrect Dating Practices for all employees was approximately $66 million, of which approximately $33 million has not been reimbursed or repaid to RIM or otherwise forfeited or cancelled.

17. The Incorrect Dating Practices at RIM and the Individual Respondents' participation in them were contrary to the public interest.

Misleading Disclosure

18. As a reporting issuer, RIM was obliged to make certain annual and periodic disclosure in accordance with the requirements of Part XVIII of the *Securities Act* (the "*Act*"), particularly sections 77 and 78. From July 1998 to August 2006, RIM repeatedly made statements in many of its filings, including prospectuses, financial statements, annual reports, and management information circulars, that contained the misleading or untrue statement that Options were priced at the fair market value of RIM's common shares at the date of the grant and were granted in accordance with the terms of the Plan. These statements were contrary to Ontario securities law and to the public interest.

19. Balsillie as Chairman of the Board and co-CEO, Lazaridis as President and co-CEO, Kavelman as CFO, and Estill, Cork, Wright and Fregin as directors failed to ensure the statements were accurate.

20. RIM made the above misleading disclosures, and the Individual Respondents authorized, acquiesced in, or permitted those statements to be made contrary to the *Act* and/or the public interest.

CEO and CFO Certificates

21. On March 30, 2004, RIM became subject to the requirement to file CEO and CFO certificates, pursuant to NI 52-109 *Certification of Disclosure in Issuers' Annual and Interim Filings* ("NI 52-109").

22. Balsillie, Lazaridis and Kavelman, in their capacity as the certifying officers for RIM, failed to ensure the underlying Annual Information Forms, financial statements, and Management's Discussion & Analysis concerning RIM's Options granting practices were accurate.

Lack of Diligence by Directors and Senior Officers

23. The directors and officers of RIM owed a duty to RIM to provide proper oversight to ensure that its policies and procedures, and its disclosure obligations under the *Act* were complied with fully, accurately, and in a timely way.

24. The Individual Respondents did not take reasonable steps to provide proper oversight in relation to RIM's Options granting practices or to ensure that RIM's public disclosure reflected those practices during the Material Time, contrary to the *Act* and the public interest.

RIM's Costs

25. RIM has paid about $45 million to investigate and deal with Incorrect Dating Practices at RIM. Balsillie and Lazaridis have paid a total of $15 million ($7.5 million each) towards those costs, leaving $30 million outstanding.

Conduct Contrary to Ontario Securities Law and/or the Public Interest

26. By engaging in the conduct described above, the Respondents have breached Ontario securities law by contravening s 122 of the *Act* and, additionally in respect of the Individual Respondents, pursuant to s 129.2 of the *Act*, or have acted contrary to the public interest.

Re Research in Motion Ltd Settlement Agreement
as approved in *Research in Motion Ltd* (2009), 32 OSCB 4434

AND WHEREAS the Respondents have entered into the following undertakings as part of the Settlement Agreement:

(a) Balsillie undertakes not to act as a director of any reporting issuer until the later of (a) twelve months from the date of this order, and (b) RIM's compliance with paragraphs 17 and 18 of the Governance Assessment document attached as Schedule "C" to the Settlement Agreement;

(b) Balsillie, Lazaridis and Kavelman undertake to contribute $38.3 million (which includes interest of $5.3 million) to RIM in respect of the outstanding benefit arising from incorrectly priced stock options granted to all employees from 1996 to 2006;

(c) Balsillie, Lazaridis and Kavelman undertake to contribute $44.8 million to RIM to defray costs incurred by RIM in the investigation and remediation of stock options granting practices and related governance practices at RIM, which will be reduced by $15 million as credit for amounts already paid by Balsillie and Lazaridis in respect of costs incurred;

(d) As determined by the Board of Directors of RIM, with the Individual Respondents abstaining, to be in the best interests of RIM, the amounts described in recitals (b) and (c) above, may be settled by Balsillie, Lazaridis and Kavelman agreeing not to exercise certain vested RIM stock options that collectively have a fair value equal to the amounts described in recitals (b) and (c) above. The fair value of such RIM stock options is to be determined on a Black-Scholes calculation based on the last trading day prior to the issuance of a Notice of Hearing in this matter;

(e) Lazaridis undertakes to complete a course acceptable to Staff regarding the duties of directors and officers of public companies within twelve months from the date of this order;

(f) Each of Loberto, Cork, Wright, Estill, and Fregin undertakes that he has repaid to RIM any increased benefit he received from the allocation to him of incorrectly priced options;

AND WHEREAS the Commission is of the opinion that it is in the public interest to make this Order;

IT IS HEREBY ORDERED that:

(a) the settlement is approved;

(b) RIM shall submit to a review of its practices and procedures pursuant to s127(1)(4) of the Act by an independent person agreed to by Staff of the Commission and RIM and paid for by RIM, as set out in Schedule "C" to the Settlement Agreement;

(c) James Balsillie:

(i) shall pay an administrative penalty of $5 million to be allocated for the benefit of third parties by the Commission, pursuant to section 3.4(2) of the Act;

(ii) shall pay $700,000 to the Commission towards the costs of its investigation; and

(iii) shall be reprimanded by the Commission;

(d) Mike Lazaridis:

(i) shall pay an administrative penalty of $1.5 million to be allocated for the benefit of third parties by the Commission, pursuant to section 3.4(2) of the Act;

(ii) shall pay $150,000 to the Commission towards the costs of its investigation; and

(iii) shall be reprimanded by the Commission;

(e) Dennis Kavelman:

(i) is prohibited from becoming or acting as a director or officer of any reporting issuer until the later of (a) five years from the date of this order, and (b) the date he completes a course acceptable to Staff of the Commission regarding the duties of directors and officers of public companies;

(ii) shall pay an administrative penalty of $1.5 million to be allocated for the benefit of third parties by the Commission, pursuant to section 3.4(2) of the Act;

(iii) shall pay $150,000 to the Commission towards the costs of its investigation; and

(iv) shall be reprimanded by the Commission;

(f) Angelo Loberto:

(i) is prohibited from becoming or acting as a director or officer of any reporting issuer, until he has completed a course acceptable to Staff regarding the duties of directors and officers of public companies;

(ii) shall pay $50,000 to the Commission towards the costs of its investigation; and

(iii) shall be reprimanded by the Commission;

(g) Kendall Cork:

(i) shall complete a course acceptable to Staff regarding the duties of directors and officers of public companies within twelve months from the date of this order, failing which he will be prohibited from acting as a director pending completion of such course; and (ii) shall be reprimanded by the Commission;

(h) Douglas Wright:

(i) shall complete a course acceptable to Staff regarding the duties of directors and officers of public companies within twelve months from the date of this order, failing which he will be prohibited from acting as a director pending completion of such course; and

(ii) shall be reprimanded by the Commission;

(i) James Estill:

(i) shall complete a course acceptable to Staff regarding the duties of directors and officers of public companies within twelve months from the date of this order, failing which he will be prohibited from acting as a director pending completion of such course; and

(ii) shall be reprimanded by the Commission;

(j) Douglas Fregin shall complete a course acceptable to Staff regarding the duties of directors and officers within twelve months from the date of this order, failing which he will be prohibited from acting as a director of a reporting issuer pending completion of such a course; and

(k) the Individual Respondents will not seek, accept, or be offered indemnification from or through RIM for any of the payments associated with or paid by the Individual Respondents as a result of this settlement and this order.

QUESTIONS

1. What was the improper conduct of the executives of Research in Motion Limited?
2. In your view, do the remedies set out in the settlement agreement respond to the misconduct?
3. What is the role of such remedies and sanctions in preserving the integrity of the securities regulatory regime?

2. *Management Discussion and Analysis*

In Canada, all reporting issuers are required to provide an MD&A of financial condition and results that accompanies the financial statements. The MD&A is a narrative explanation, through the eyes of management, of how the issuer performed during the period covered by the financial statements, and of the issuer's financial condition and future prospects. Management's objective under the MD&A is to improve the company's overall financial disclosure by giving a balanced discussion of the company's financial performance and financial condition including, without limitation, such considerations as liquidity and capital resources—openly reporting bad news as well as good news. The MD&A should help current and prospective investors understand what the financial statements show and do not show; discuss material information that may not be fully reflected in the financial statements, such as contingent liabilities, defaults under debt, off-balance sheet financing arrangements, or other contractual obligations; discuss important trends and risks that have affected the financial statements, and trends and risks that are reasonably likely to affect them in the future; and provide information about the quality, and potential variability, of the company's profit or loss and cash flow, to assist investors in determining if past performance is indicative of future performance (Form 51-102F1, part 1, (a)).

The requirements for MD&A are set out in NI 51-102, part 5. Although MD&As were originally required to be prepared only by larger issuers, NI 51-102 is aimed at a much broader application. MD&A disclosure is particularly important for junior companies that do not have a history of profitable operations that might otherwise give investors assurance about the company's long-term prospects. The MD&A offers an opportunity to provide investors and others that review the information with management's view of how the issuer has performed and how that performance will likely affect future plans. It allows investors and potential investors to assess underlying value in making their decisions about continued or new investments in securities of the issuer.

Introduced in Canada in the late 1980s, the MD&A was originally a supplementary document to a company's financial statements (OSC Policy Statement No 5.10, *AIF and MD&A of Financial Condition and Results of Operation* (1989), 12 OSCB 4275). However, over the years, the MD&A has become an integral part, with financial statements, of continuing disclosure and accountability to investors.

Form 51-102F1, *Management Discussion and Analysis* describes what is material in terms of what should be disclosed in the MD&A. As you read the excerpt below, consider why the form focuses on a reasonable investor standard when securities legislation and national policy (NP 51-201, *Disclosure Standard*, 12 July 2002) have definitions of "material fact" and "material change" based on a market impact test.

> **Part 1**
>
> *(f) What Is Material?*
>
> Would a reasonable investor's decision whether or not to buy, sell or hold securities in your company likely be influenced or changed if the information in question was omitted or misstated? If so, the information is likely material.

This definition of material differs slightly from the statutory formulation of material change, discussed later in this chapter.

A Canadian reporting issuer must file an MD&A. An SEC issuer can complete Form 51-102F1, *Management's Discussion & Analysis*, or use a management's discussion and analysis prepared in accordance with item 303 of Regulation S-K under the 1934 US *Securities Act* (NI 51-102, s 1).

A reporting issuer must disclose, in its MD&A or its interim MD&A, the capital structure of the issuer. This disclosure includes the designation and number or principal amount of each class and series of voting or equity securities of the reporting issuer for which there are securities outstanding; each class and series of securities of the reporting issuer for which there are securities outstanding that are convertible into, or exercisable or exchangeable for, voting or equity securities of the reporting issuer; and each class and series of voting or equity securities of the reporting issuer that are issuable on the conversion, exercise, or exchange of outstanding securities of the reporting issuer (NI 51-102, s 5.4). The annual and interim MD&A that a reporting issuer is required to file must be approved by the board of directors of the issuer before being filed or, in the case of the interim MD&A, by the board's audit committee (NI 51-102, s 5.5). The MD&A must disclose what additional information is available on the issuer's SEDAR web page, in order that investors are alerted to where to find additional information about the issuer (NI 51-102CP, s 1.15 (2003), 26 OSCB (Supp 3)).

Effective 30 June 2015, the companion policy to NI 51-102 specifies that venture issuers are not required to update their MD&A when they release quarterly highlights (NI 51-102CP, s 5.6). These amendments are another example of proportionate regulation in that they impose slightly less onus disclosure requirements for venture issuers. The amendments streamline and tailor disclosure by venture issuers. They are intended to make the disclosure requirements for venture issuers more suitable and manageable for issuers at their stage of development. The CSA reports that the amendments are designed to focus disclosure of venture issuers on information that reflects the needs and expectations of venture issuer investors and eliminate disclosure obligations that may be less valuable to those investors. The amendments are also intended to streamline the disclosure requirements for venture issuers to allow management of those issuers to focus on the growth of their business. In addition, the amendments include enhancements to the governance requirements for venture issuers (CSA Notice of Amendments to National Instrument 51-102, *Continuous Disclosure Obligations*, 9 April 2015).

Companion Policy 51-102CP to National Instrument 51-102,
Continuous Disclosure Obligations
In force 30 March 2004, as amended effective 30 June 2015

5.6 Venture Issuers—Quarterly Highlights

(1) A venture issuer that provides quarterly highlights is not required to update its annual MD&A in the quarterly highlights. However, to meet the requirements of section 2.2.1 of Form 51-102F1, the venture issuer should disclose in its quarterly highlights any change, if material, from plans disclosed in the annual MD&A. For example, if a mining issuer discloses a drill program in its annual MD&A and decides to make a change to that drill program in a subsequent interim period, that change, if material, should be disclosed in the quarterly highlights for that period.

(2) Although all venture issuers have the option of providing quarterly highlights, there are some instances where a venture issuer may want to consider providing full interim MD&A instead of quarterly highlights. We believe the option to use quarterly highlights will likely satisfy the needs of investors in smaller venture issuers. However, investors in larger venture issuers, including those with significant revenue, may want full interim MD&A to assist them in making informed investment decisions. Issuers will likely take the needs of their investors into consideration when determining whether to provide quarterly highlights or full interim MD&A.

(3) For greater certainty, a reference to interim MD&A is a reference to the quarterly highlights a venture issuer has the option of providing in accordance with section 2.2.1 of Form 51-102F1. As such, any requirements in National Instrument 52-109 *Certification of Disclosure in Issuer's Annual and Interim Filings* that apply to interim MD&A will apply to the quarterly highlights.

The Alberta Securities Commission's *Corporate Finance Disclosure Report* (ASC, December 2014) notes that an issue with MD&A is that the commission continues to see deficiencies in the area of updating forward-looking information disclosure, specifically, failing to provide the required updated information when the actual results vary materially from what was disclosed, particularly problematic when the actual results are less favourable than what had been expected, and investors are not provided a clear explanation of the reasons for the variance (<http://www.albertasecurities.com/Publications/CFReport2014.pdf>).

The Québec Autorité des marchés financiers' review of deficiencies in MD&A in 2015 found that the deficiencies were primarily related to non-GAAP measures predominant in MD&A presented by companies, sometimes to the detriment of the financial measures set out in the financial statements (Autorité des marchés financiers, *Activity Report for the Continuous Disclosure Review Program* (September 2015), online: <http://www.lautorite.qc.ca/en/cdr-publications-pro.html>).

British Columbia has stepped up its enforcement initiatives under its review of the continuous disclosure regime, including review of MD&A. Of 1,800 companies that it reviewed in 2000-1, it required over 40 percent to amend and refile their MD&A to meet regulatory requirements (<http://www.bcsc.bc.ca>). Where an issuer's disclosure is seriously lacking, it can be placed on BCSC's issuers in default list without notice. Where the issuer has made a serious misrepresentation or engaged in another serious breach of the statute and regulations, a cease-trading order is issued. In the first six months of 2004, more than 40 cease-trading orders were issued on this basis (<http://www.bcsc.bc.ca>). By 2014, the BCSC reported that only 2 of the 173 cases it commenced in 2014 involved disclosure violations (*BCSC 2014 Enforcement Report*, <http://www.bcsc.bc.ca/Enforcement>). See also OSC Staff Notice 51-713, *Report on Staff's Review of MD&A* (2004), 27 OSCB 715.

3. *Annual Information Forms*

The AIF is similar to a prospectus in that it requires very detailed information about the history, operations and financial affairs of the reporting issuer, including discussion of the issuer's prospects. It is a document that provides a basis for ongoing disclosure because of the extensive nature of the information provided, which can then be updated annually. The AIF was originally conceived for larger issuers, as a means to communicate extensive information in order to qualify for the short-form prospectus process. It is still used for this purpose, as discussed in Chapter 4. An AIF is required for all reporting issuers that are not venture issuers (NI 51-102, s 6.1, Form 51-102F2).

The AIF must be filed within 90 days after the end of the issuer's most recently completed financial year (NI 51-102, s 6.2). In an effort to facilitate cross-border capital market activity, if the reporting issuer is an SEC issuer that files its AIF through required SEC forms (Form 10-K, or Form 20-F), the AIF can be filed within the 90 days or the date that the reporting issuer files with the SEC (NI 51-102, s 6.2(b)). There is no requirement to send an AIF directly to securityholders, although some of the information is frequently included in company annual reports. Moreover, the information is publicly accessible though SEDAR and, hence, both securityholders and other interested parties can readily access the AIF through the Internet.

NI 52-110, *Audit Committees*, sets out disclosure requirements that must be included in the AIF in respect of the audit committee of a reporting issuer, discussed at some length in Chapter 7. NI 52-110, which has been adopted by all securities regulators in Canada, specifies that the AIF must disclose the text of the audit committee's charter, the name of each audit committee member, and whether or not each is independent and financially literate (NI 52-110, *Audit Committees*, as amended effective 17 November 2015; and Form 52-110F1).

The AIF must disclose any oversight issues in relation to auditors. Hence, if a recommendation of the audit committee to nominate or compensate an external auditor was not adopted by the board of directors, the AIF must state that fact and explain why (Form 52-110F1, s 7).

The AIF must also disclose and describe any specific policies and procedures for the engagement of non-audit services. The AIF must disclose, by category, all external auditor services fees in each of the last two fiscal years (Form 52-110F1, s 9). It must disclose, under the caption "Audit Fees," the aggregate fees billed by the issuer's external auditor for audit services and under the caption "Audit-Related Fees," the aggregate fees billed for assurance and related services by the issuer's external auditor that are reasonably related to the performance of the audit or review of the issuer's financial statements, including a description of the nature of the services. Under the caption "Tax Fees," the AIF must disclose the aggregate fees billed for professional services rendered by the issuer's external auditor for tax compliance, tax advice, and tax planning, including a description of the nature of the services. Finally, the AIF must disclose all other fees in the same period and a description of the nature of the services (Form 52-110F1, s 9).

Interestingly, the AIF form under NI 51-102 expands the scope of disclosure from that required in the AIF before 2004. It now expressly includes disclosure of social and environmental policies, as well as risk factors such as environmental and health risks and political considerations. The required standard of disclosure of social or environmental policies is that the policies are fundamental to operations. Where risks are most likely to influence an investor's decision to purchase securities, the standard for risk factors is as follows. Note that this requirement represents an expanded threshold for the inclusion of information.

Form 51-102F2, *Annual Information Form*
Effective 30 June 2015

Item 5 Describe the Business

5.1 General

(1) Describe the business of your company and its operating segments that are reportable segments as those terms are described in the issuer's GAAP. For each reportable segment include:

. . .

(k) Environmental Protection

The financial and operational effects of environmental protection requirements on the capital expenditures, profit or loss and competitive position of your company in the current financial year and the expected effect in future years.

(l) Employees

The number of employees as at the most recent financial year-end or the average number of employees over the year, whichever is more meaningful to understand the business.

. . .

(4) Social or Environmental Policies

If your company has implemented social or environmental policies that are fundamental to your operations, such as policies regarding your company's relationship with the environment or with the communities in which it does business, or human rights policies, describe them and the steps your company has taken to implement them.

5.2 Risk Factors

Disclose risk factors relating to your company and its business, such as cash flow and liquidity problems, if any, experience of management, the general risks inherent in the business carried on by your company, environmental and health risks, reliance on key personnel, regulatory constraints, economic or political conditions and financial history and any other matter that would be most likely to influence an investor's decision to purchase securities of your company. If there is a risk that securityholders of your company may become liable to make an additional contribution beyond the price of the security, disclose that risk.

Instructions

(i) Disclose the risks in order of seriousness from the most serious to the least serious.

(ii) A risk factor must not be de-emphasized by including excessive caveats or conditions.

QUESTIONS

1. What is the significance of requiring disclosure of environmental protection and social policies?

2. Do you think that the required disclosure of risk factors will better alert corporate directors and securityholders to environmental and health risks in such a way that they become concerned about the social effects of the issuer's economic activities?

a. The Impact of National Instrument 51-102

Adequate disclosure has been a major challenge in the securities regulatory system. In continuing its priority in oversight of continuous disclosure requirements, the Alberta Securities Commission undertook 379 continuous disclosure reviews in fiscal year 2015, focusing in particular on the effectiveness of issuers' controls, revenue recognition, restatements, operation in higher risk countries and IFRS compliance (Alberta Securities Commission, 2015 Annual Report).

The Québec Autorité des marchés financiers (AMF) has a Continuous Disclosure Review Program (CDR Program) that forms part of the oversight activities of the AMF. It targets the documents filed by issuers pursuant to their continuous disclosure obligations under the Québec statute and the regulations. These documents constitute the continuous disclosure record, which includes the financial statements, MD&A or the management report of fund performance, the AIF, and the management proxy circular. The CDR Program's goal is to enhance the quality of the continuous disclosure records of companies and investment funds by helping issuers understand the nature and scope of their continuous disclosure obligations, and ensuring compliance with those obligations.

The AMF reports that of 300 companies reviewed last year under its CDR program, 59 underwent a full review and 59 underwent an issue-oriented review. While 81 percent of the companies reviewed were required to make improvements due to the deficiencies identified, only 12 had to refile documents and none of them were subject to a cease trade order. The majority of improvements consisted of prospective changes in future filings. Deficiencies in financial statements were: failure to disclose management's judgments in the process of applying the company's accounting policies that have a significant effect on the amounts recognized in the financial statements; failure to properly describe, without the use of boilerplate language, the accounting policy adopted for the recognition of revenue, including the methods adopted to determine the stage of completion of transactions involving the rendering of services; and failure to disclose the amount of each significant category of revenue recognized during the period, including revenue arising from the sale of goods, the rendering of services, or the receipt of interest. With respect to executive compensation, deficiencies included: incomplete discussion of named executive officer compensation due to failure to adequately describe how each element of compensation is determined, particularly the link between performance goals and reported compensation; and incomplete statement of director compensation, including share-based awards and option-based awards, and other types of compensation granted. In corporate governance practice disclosure, deficiencies included incomplete description of ethical business conduct, in particular, the way in which the board of directors ensures compliance with the code of conduct and ethics, and the measures taken to encourage and promote a culture of ethical business conduct; and incomplete audit committee's written charter, due to failure to include all prescribed responsibilities (AMF, *Activity Report for the Continuous Disclosure Review Program* (September 2014), online: <http://www.lautorite.qc.ca/en/cdr-publications-pro.html>).

In July 2015, the Canadian Securities Administrators (CSA) issued Staff Notice 51-344 (CSA Staff Notice 51-344, *Continuous Disclosure Review Program Activities for the Fiscal Year Ended March 31, 2015*, 16 July 2015), which contained the results of the reviews conducted pursuant to their Continuous Disclosure (CD) Review Program. During fiscal 2015, a total of 1,058 CD reviews (280 full reviews and 778 issue-oriented reviews (IOR)) were conducted. The goal of the program is to improve the completeness, quality and timeliness of continuous disclosure provided by reporting issuers in Canada by assessing the compliance of CD documents and to help issuers understand and comply with their obligations under the CD rules. See also CSA Staff Notice 51-312 (revised), *Harmonized Continuous Disclosure Review Program*.

CSA Staff Notice 51-344 highlights that securities regulators apply both qualitative and quantitative criteria in determining the level of review and type of review required. An IOR focuses on a specific accounting, legal or regulatory issue. IORs may focus on emerging issues, implementation of recent rules or on matters where CSA staff believe there may be a heightened risk of investor harm. A full review covers the selected issuer's most recent annual and interim financial reports and MD&A filed before the start of the review. For all other CD disclosure documents, the review covers a period of approximately 12 to 15 months. In certain cases, the scope of the review may be extended in order to cover prior periods. The issuer's CD documents are monitored until the review is completed. A full review also includes an issuer's technical disclosure (e.g. technical reports for oil and gas and mining issuers), annual information form, annual report, information circulars, news releases, material change reports, business acquisition reports, corporate websites, certifying officers' certifications and material contracts. In fiscal 2015, a total of 26 percent of the CD reviews were full reviews. Of CSA review outcomes, 59 percent required issuers to take action to improve and/or amend their disclosure or resulted in the issuer being referred to enforcement, ceased traded, or placed on the default list. The refilings of issuers' CD records included financial statements, including compliance with recognition, measurement, and disclosure requirements in IFRS; MD&A compliance, including non-GAAP measures, discussion of operations, liquidity, related-party transactions, disclosure controls, and procedures and internal controls over financial reporting (ICFR); and compliance with other regulatory matters, which included, but was not limited to, mining technical reports and investor presentations for content deficiencies, business acquisition reports, certificates, and filing of previously unfiled documents, such as material contracts, or clarifying news releases to address concerns around unbalanced disclosure.

The following notable areas were highlighted by the CSA as being common sources of disclosure deficiencies:

- Certification of disclosure**:** Inconsistencies between the conclusions in certificates about the effectiveness of internal controls over financial reporting (ICFR) and the corresponding disclosure in an issuer's MD&A. CSA staff also found that some issuers identified the same material weakness in the design or operations of ICFR for several consecutive years and during that time period grew their operations significantly.
- Material contracts: Issuers were failing to file material contracts by the time that they file their annual information forms, including financing or credit agreements with terms that relate directly to anticipated cash distributions or contracts on which the issuer's business is substantially dependent.
- Material change reports: Issuers did not always comply with the requirement that a material change report must be filed as soon as practicable after the date of a material change, or within ten days of such date.
- Selective disclosure: The CSA cautioned that selective disclosure, being the provision of material non-public information to some persons and not broadly to the investing public, should be avoided. Specifically, as per National Policy 51-201, *Disclosure Standards*, when issuers hold private meetings with analysts or attend industry conferences, they must ensure that selective disclosure is not provided at these venues. If such disclosure has occurred, issuers must make a public announcement and contact the relevant stock exchange to have trading halted.
- News releases: Certain issuers failed to issue and file a news release on a timely basis after deciding to refile a continuous disclosure document or restate financial information in financial statements. Section 11.5 of National Instrument 51-102, *Continuous Disclosure Obligations*, provides that if an issuer decides to refile a document that differs materially from information originally filed, the issuer must immediately issue and file a news release disclosing the change.

The excerpts from CSA Staff Notice 51-344 below identify a couple of examples of what the CSA calls "hot button" issues identified with continuous disclosure.

CSA Staff Notice 51-344, *Continuous Disclosure Review Program Activities for the Fiscal Year Ended March 31, 2015*

(16 July 2015)

Financial Statement Deficiencies

Hot Buttons

	Observations	Considerations
Financial Statements		
Operating Segments	• We continue to see issuers that fail to disclose certain information about geographic areas, in particular revenues from external customers. • We also see issuers that fail to disclose information about major customers, in particular when revenues from transactions with a single external customer amount to 10% or more of the issuer's revenues.	• Issuers must disclose information about operating segments so that investors are able to evaluate the nature and financial effects of the business activities in which they engage and the economic environments in which they operate. • Disclosure about major customers may assist users in determining if there is economic dependence. *Reference: Paragraph 33 and 34 of IFRS 8 Operating Segments*
Business Combinations	• Upon acquisition of a business, issuers are reporting a significant portion of the purchase price in goodwill without separately identifying and assigning a value to other intangible assets, such as customer lists, intellectual property, etc.	• The allocation to the appropriate identifiable assets is important as it may impact an issuer's accounting for intangibles in its financial statements. For example, definite life intangibles require amortization into the statement of profit or loss and will therefore impact income in subsequent periods. • The measurement period shall not exceed one year from the acquisition date. *Reference: Paragraph 10 to 13 and 45 and Appendix B of IFRS 3 Business Combinations*

Fair Value Measurement	• We continue to see issuers that fail to disclose a description of the valuation technique and inputs used for fair value measurements categorized within Level 3 of the fair value hierarchy.	• For Level 3 fair value measurements, issuers must describe the valuation technique used in the fair value measurement. • Issuers must also describe and provide *quantitative* information about *all* significant unobservable inputs used. • These disclosures will assist users to understand the measurement uncertainty inherent in fair value measurements. *Reference: Paragraph 93(d) to (h) of IFRS 13 Fair Value Measurement*

• • •

MD&A Deficiencies

Hot Buttons

	Observations	Considerations
MD&A		
Liquidity and Capital Resources	• We continue to see issuers that fail to provide sufficient analysis of their liquidity and capital resources. • Issuers often reproduce information in the MD&A that is readily available from the financial statements. For example, repeating the balances of cash flows from operating, investing and financing activities.	• This section of the MD&A should focus on an issuer's ability to generate sufficient liquidity in the short term and long term in order to fund planned growth, development activities or expenditures necessary to maintain capacity. • In addition, the MD&A should provide an analysis of an issuer's capital resources, including the amount, nature and purpose of commitments and the expected source of funds to meet these commitments. • While these disclosures are required for all issuers, they are especially important when issuers have negative cash flows from operations, a negative working capital position or a deteriorating financial condition. • This disclosure enables users to assess how the issuer will meet its obligations and its short and long term objectives. *Reference: Item 1.6 and 1.7 of Form 51-102F1*

All securities regulation relies heavily on continuous disclosure, and NI 51-102 has enhanced disclosure through more systematic and consistent dissemination of financial and operational information about reporting issuers.

4. Information Circulars and Proxy Solicitation Rules

Another aspect of the continuous disclosure system is the obligation of issuers to communicate with investors and to provide them with information and a means of expressing their preferences through proxy voting. While this requirement is another form of periodic disclosure, it differs from the periodic reporting already discussed in that there is an interactive element to the proxy process, and the process implicates both corporate and securities laws for a reporting issuer that is a company. The relationship between the proxy requirements under corporate laws and securities laws is not always clear, and readers must have regard to both in determining rights and obligations of reporting issuers and securities holders in the proxy process. The disclosure aspects of the proxy process are discussed in this chapter; however, note that there are equally important policy considerations regarding proxies and corporate governance that are discussed at some length in Chapter 7.

It is also important to note that reform in one area of the law informs legislative initiatives in the other, as is evident in this excerpt from the Senate Standing Committee on Banking, Trade and Commerce in its discussion of corporate law reform in the mid-1990s.

Canada, Senate, *Report of the Senate Standing Committee on Banking, Trade, and Commerce on Corporate Governance*
(Ottawa: Public Works and Government Services, August 1996)

The CBCA provides that a corporation is required to send shareholders corporate information, such as notices of meetings, proxy-related materials, and audited financial statements. The growth of two kinds of shareholders—beneficial and registered—has made the sending of this material more problematic. Beneficial shareholders are persons who have purchased shares and are entitled to dividends and capital gains but who may not be registered on the corporation's records for the purposes of voting at annual meetings. Often a depository, broker or other intermediary is listed as the registered owner. The Discussion Paper points out that over the past few decades shareholder ownership practices have changed; in the past individual shareholders had possession of their share certificates and had their names recorded on the books of the corporation as shareholders while today shares of publicly traded corporations are registered in the names of nominees, rather than the individuals who have actually bought them. Under the nominee system, intermediaries hold securities in "nominee form," and maintain a list of the beneficial owners they represent. Because the issuing corporation shows the intermediary as the registered shareholder, it does not know the beneficial owner of the shares.

The growth of the depository system increased the distance between the corporation and its beneficial shareholders. In the 1970s, securities depositories were developed to facilitate the trading and settlement of securities by eliminating the need for delivery of share certificates between intermediaries. Most securities are held on deposit with clearing agencies for intermediaries and ownership changes are made through book-entry transfers in the appropriate accounts. An important aspect of the nominee and the depository systems is that when shares are traded, the shareholders' register of the corporation does not have to be changed. National Policy Statement Number 41, instituted in 1987 by the Canadian Securities Administrators, sets out obligations for share issuers, intermediaries and clearing agencies with respect to shareholder communications. It creates a regime whereby issuers forward proxy materials to beneficial shareholders through the offices of intermediaries. NP 41 has been criticized on a number of fronts. Proposals are being examined that would allow corporations to obtain the names of the beneficial owners of its shares from intermediaries.

a. The Process

NI 51-102 now specifies requirements for information circulars and the proxy solicitation process. It is aimed at bringing transparency and continuity to the proxy provisions of securities laws. It specifies to whom proxies and information circulars are to be issued, requires the filing of circulars and proxy-related materials, and specifies the content of proxies. The information circular provides the background information such that investors can exercise their proxy rights on an informed basis. The excerpt below specifies the circumstances in which management is required to send a proxy solicitation and information circular.

National Instrument 51-102, *Continuous Disclosure Obligations*
In force 30 March 2004, as amended effective 17 November 2015

Part 9 Proxy Solicitation and Information Circulars

9.1 Sending of Proxies and Information Circulars

(1) If management of a reporting issuer gives notice of a meeting to its registered holders of voting securities, management must, at the same time as or before giving that notice, send to each registered holder of voting securities who is entitled to notice of the meeting a form of proxy for use at the meeting.

(2) Subject to section 9.2, a person or company that solicits proxies from registered holders of voting securities of a reporting issuer must,

(a) in the case of a solicitation by or on behalf of management of a reporting issuer, send an information circular with the notice of meeting to each registered securityholder whose proxy is solicited; or

(b) in the case of any other solicitation, concurrently with or before the solicitation, send an information circular to each registered securityholder whose proxy is solicited.

There are limited exceptions to the requirement to send information circulars. Section 9.2 of NI 51-102 specifies the circumstances under which an issuer is not required to send an information circular: where there are fewer than 15 securityholders, to beneficial owners where they exist, and where two or more persons or companies who are joint registered owners of one or more securities are considered to be one securityholder (NI 51-102, s 9.2). This exemption from sending an information circular is premised on the notion that where there are only a few securityholders, they will have access to information such that a full proxy circular is not required.

The issuer must promptly file a copy of the information circular, form of proxy, and all other material required to be sent in connection with the meeting to which the information circular or form of proxy relates (NI 51-102, s 9.3). The information must be current and it is an offence to not have timely and accurate information. See also the discussion of *Re Pacifica Papers Inc* in Chapter 7 on the timing of when information circulars must be sent.

b. *The Content*

NI 51-102 also sets out the required contents of the proxy, aimed at ensuring that securityholders have the clearest possible understanding of how they are delegating their voting rights. A proxy is a completed and executed form by which a securityholder has appointed a person or company as the securityholder's nominee to attend and act for the securityholder on the securityholder's behalf at a meeting of securityholders (NI 51-102, s 1.1). As s 9.4, below, indicates, it must clearly specify the meeting that the proxy applies to and must contain a space for the person to designate a proxy nominee, if the securityholder does not agree to the proposed person as the nominee to exercise their proxy rights. It creates the ability to have the securityholder direct how the discretion is to be exercised.

National Instrument 51-102, *Continuous Disclosure Obligations*
In force 30 March 2004, as amended effective 17 November 2015

9.4 Content of Form of Proxy

(1) A form of proxy sent to securityholders of a reporting issuer by a person or company soliciting proxies must indicate in bold-face type whether or not the proxy is solicited by or on behalf of the management of the reporting issuer, provide a specifically designated blank space for dating the form of proxy and specify the meeting in respect of which the proxy is solicited.

(2) An information circular sent to securityholders of a reporting issuer or the form of proxy to which the information circular relates must

(a) indicate in bold-face type that the securityholder has the right to appoint a person or company to represent the securityholder at the meeting other than the person or company if any, designated in the form of proxy; and

(b) contain instructions as to the manner in which the securityholder may exercise the right referred to in paragraph (a).

(3) If a form of proxy sent to securityholders of a reporting issuer contains a designation of a named person or company as nominee, it must provide an option for the securityholder to designate in the form of proxy some other person or company as the securityholder's nominee.

(4) A form of proxy sent to securityholders of a reporting issuer must provide an option for the securityholder to specify that the securities registered in the securityholder's name will be voted for or against each matter or group of related matters identified in the form of proxy, in the notice of meeting or in an information circular, other than the appointment of an auditor and the election of directors.

(5) A form of proxy sent to securityholders of a reporting issuer may confer discretionary authority with respect to each matter referred to in subsection (4) as to which a choice is not specified if the form of proxy or the information circular states in bold-face type how the securities represented by the proxy will be voted in respect of each matter or group of related matters.

(6) A form of proxy sent to securityholders of a reporting issuer must provide an option for the securityholder to specify that the securities registered in the name of the securityholder must be voted or withheld from voting in respect of the appointment of an auditor or the election of directors.

(7) An information circular sent to securityholders of a reporting issuer or the form of proxy to which the information circular relates must state that

(a) the securities represented by the proxy will be voted or withheld from voting in accordance with the instructions of the securityholder on any ballot that may be called for; and

(b) if the securityholder specifies a choice under subsection (4) or (6) with respect to any matter to be acted upon, the securities will be voted accordingly.

(8) A form of proxy sent to securityholders of a reporting issuer may confer discretionary authority with respect to

(a) amendments or variations to matters identified in the notice of meeting; and

(b) other matters which may properly come before the meeting, if,

(c) the person or company by whom or on whose behalf the solicitation is made is not aware within a reasonable time before the time the solicitation is made that any of those amendments, variations or other matters are to be presented for action at the meeting; and

(d) a specific statement is made in the information circular or in the form of proxy that the proxy is conferring such discretionary authority.

(9) A form of proxy sent to securityholders of a reporting issuer must not confer authority to vote

(a) for the election of any person as a director of a reporting issuer unless a bona fide proposed nominee for that election is named in the information circular or, in the case of a solicitation under subsection 9.2(4), the document required under paragraph 9.2(6)(a); or

(b) at any meeting other than the meeting specified in the notice of meeting or any adjournment of that meeting.

The requirements under NI 51-102 are aimed at ensuring that securityholders clearly understand the scope and limits of voting rights that they are assigning.

The proxy solicitation requirements under part 9 of NI 51-102 do not apply to a reporting issuer that complies with the requirements of the laws of the jurisdiction in which it is incorporated, organized, or continued, if the requirements are substantially similar (NI 51-102, s 9.5). For example, if an issuer complies with the proxy requirements under the *Canada Business Corporations Act*, RSC 1985, c C-44, as amended, where it is incorporated under that statute, the *Securities Act* requirements in respect of proxies do not apply.

There are also provisions for securityholders soliciting proxies: see Chapter 7 for a discussion of these requirements.

Disclosure in a circular may be sufficient to allow a director to vote where the director was affiliated. Where a circular discloses information regarding conflicts of interest, such as in disclosing that a party is affiliated with a company that gave a fairness opinion, the court has held that a director did not act improperly in voting because the circular disclosure was sufficient (*Renaissance Energy*, [2000] AJ No 1030 (QL) (QB)).

c. *Beneficial Owners of Securities*

Most securityholders today are beneficial, as opposed to registered, holders because securities are increasingly registered in the name of depositories or their nominees that hold securities on behalf of dealers, trust companies and other intermediaries, and not in the name of the beneficial owners. While the holding of securities in central depositories has increased the liquidity of capital markets, there has been concern that beneficial owners did not have any voice in the activities of the issuer similar to that held by registered securityholders. There are now special rules where proxies are being solicited from the non-registered beneficial owners of securities (NI 54-101, *Communication with Beneficial Owners of Securities of a Reporting Issuer* (2003), as amended 2013). NI 54-101 uses the terms NOBO and OBO to address different kinds of beneficial owners. If the beneficial owner chooses to have the name and securities disclosed, the owner is considered a "non-objecting beneficial owner" (NOBO) for purposes of the instrument. If not, the beneficial owner is an "objecting beneficial owner" (OBO) (NI 54-101, s 1.1).

NI 54-101 places obligations on reporting issuers to allow for the participation of non-registered beneficial owners in the proxy process. The instrument is a recognition of the growing number of beneficial securityholders. According to NI 54-101CP (2003, as amended 8 February 2013), the instrument's underlying fundamental principles are to give all securityholders of a reporting issuer, whether they are registered or beneficial owners, the opportunity to be treated alike as far as practicable, to encourage efficiency, and to ensure that the obligations of each party in the securityholder communication process are equitable and clearly defined (NI 54-101CP, s 1.2). The reporting issuer must send a notification of meeting and record date, requesting beneficial ownership information from proximate intermediaries within a specified period prior to an annual or special general shareholder meeting.

The intermediaries are to respond with the information within three business days of receipt of the request (NI 54-101, ss 4.1, 3.1). If it is able to do so, a proximate intermediary is required to respond to a request for a NOBO list by providing the NOBO list in electronic format. Section 2.5(4) provides that a request for beneficial ownership information must be made through a transfer agent. However, where only a NOBO list is being requested, the request may be made by the reporting issuer or another person or company retained by the reporting issuer, provided the requester has provided the necessary undertaking in Form 54-101F10. Section 3.5(1) specifies that voting instructions that the reporting issuer requests directly from NOBO will be returned directly to the reporting issuer; and management of the reporting issuer will then vote the securities beneficially owned by NOBO according to the instructions received from the NOBO to the extent that management has the corresponding proxy. The proximate intermediary that provides the NOBO list under s 4.1 of the Instrument gives management that proxy. The Instrument sets out the permitted uses of a NOBO list as follows:

Part 6 Use of NOBO Lists

6.1 Permitted Uses

A person or company that is not a reporting issuer may only use the NOBO list and the procedures in sections 2.9 or 2.12 of the Instrument in connection with an effort to influence voting or an offer to acquire securities of a reporting issuer. In our view, a person or company may obtain the NOBO list if the person or company, acting reasonably and in good faith, intends to use the NOBO list to determine whether to begin an effort to influence securityholder voting or an offer to acquire securities of the reporting issuer.

Using a NOBO list contrary to Part 7 of the Instrument will constitute a breach of the Instrument and securities legislation. Penalty provisions of securities legislation may be applied.

There are also provisions for notice of change of the meeting or the substantive content that will be decided at the meeting so that a beneficial owner that originally declined to participate is given another opportunity based on information about the change. NOBO are then entitled to receive whatever proxy-related materials that registered owners are entitled to receive, including seeking voting instructions from the beneficial owner. The materials must explain in plain language how the NOBO may exercise voting rights attached to the securities, including the right to attend and vote the securities directly at the meeting (NI 54-101, s 2.16). The instrument also allows for electronic communication in order to facilitate disclosure requirements.

C. Continuing Challenges for Financial Reporting

As Sections I and II of this chapter illustrate, there have been ongoing efforts by securities regulators to enhance the quality, consistency and timeliness of disclosures by issuers. These periodic disclosure requirements offer some certainty to investors that they are receiving information that will be sufficient for them to make their investment decisions. Even with codification, however, there will be issuers who use any malleability or lack of clarity in reporting requirements to shirk their obligations or engage in self-dealing. Hence, enforcement of securities law requirements is essential to the integrity of the system, both to protect investors and to act as a deterrent to misconduct.

The case of *Re Livent Inc* illustrates the ongoing problems with financial reporting. In this case, the Ontario Securities Commission alleged that the issuer made statements in its interim and annual financial statements that were misleading, untrue, or failed to state facts that required to be stated (OSC Notice of Hearing, *Re Livent Inc* (2001), 24 OSCB 3987). The OSC alleged that the issuer disclosed improper records of transactions, modified the accounting computer system, made changes to ledger entries for which there was no audit trail, improperly recognized certain revenues, and thus overstated net income, failed to disclose side deals that materially modified the substance of transactions, and committed a host of other alleged violations of financial reporting. The case involved periods in which the securities of the issuer were cease-traded and considerable litigation regarding the scope of disclosure required. The OSC's proceedings were suspended pending the outcome of criminal action; however, the case against the three former executives was subsequently reopened and on September 9, 2014, the OSC approved a settlement agreement reached between OSC staff and Gottlieb. The hearing regarding the other two executives is now scheduled to commence on September 19, 2016; *In the Matter of the Securities Act, RSO 1990, c S.5, as Amended and in the Matter of Garth H Drabinsky, Myron I Gottlieb and Gordon Eckstein*, order dated 24 February 2015, (<http://www.osc.gov.on.ca/en/SecuritiesLaw_ord_20160303_222_garth.htm>). The criminal cases are excerpted in Chapter 11, Enforcement.

III. MATERIAL CHANGE REPORTING

In addition to periodic reporting requirements discussed above, issuers have ongoing obligations to make timely disclosure of material changes that affect an issuer as these changes occur. A reporting issuer in Canada must comply with continuous disclosure requirements through electronic filings on the SEDAR system and its public website. In terms of specific disclosure requirements, there is some latitude in defining what is a "material" event, such that it should be disclosed. An underlying premise of material change reporting is that continuous disclosure is essential to promotion of active capital markets and enhanced investor protection.

The term "material change" was discussed at length in Chapter 4. It is defined under OSA, s 1(1) as follows:

> "material change,"
> (a) when used in relation to an issuer other than an investment fund, means,
> (i) a change in the business, operations or capital of the issuer that would reasonably be expected to have a significant effect on the market price or value of any of the securities of the issuer, or
> (ii) a decision to implement a change referred to in subclause (i) made by the board of directors or other persons acting in a similar capacity or by senior management of the issuer who believe that confirmation of the decision by the board of directors or such other persons acting in a similar capacity is probable, and
> (b) when used in relation to an issuer that is an investment fund, means,
> (i) a change in the business, operations or affairs of the issuer that would be considered important by a reasonable investor in determining whether to purchase or continue to hold securities of the issuer, or
> (ii) a decision to implement a change referred to in subclause (i) made,
> (A) by the board of directors of the issuer or the board of directors of the investment fund manager of the issuer or other persons acting in a similar capacity,
> (B) by senior management of the issuer who believe that confirmation of the decision by the board of directors or such other persons acting in a similar capacity is probable, or
> (C) by senior management of the investment fund manager of the issuer who believe that confirmation of the decision by the board of directors of the investment fund manager of the issuer or such other persons acting in a similar capacity is probable;

This definition is almost identical to the definition under NI 51-102, discussed below.

Once an issuer determines that a material change has occurred within the meaning of securities legislation, the statutes impose a reporting obligation. The provisions in Ontario are illustrative.

Ontario *Securities Act*
RSO 1990, c S.5, as amended by SO 2004, c 31,
Schedule 34; SO 2016, c 5, Schedule 26

Part XVIII Continuous Disclosure

Publication of Material Change

75(1) Subject to subsection (3), where a material change occurs in the affairs of a reporting issuer, it shall forthwith issue and file a news release authorized by a senior officer disclosing the nature and substance of the change.

Report of material change

(2) Subject to subsection (3), the reporting issuer shall file a report of such material change in accordance with the regulations as soon as practicable and in any event within ten days of the date on which the change occurs.

Exception

(3) A reporting issuer may, instead of complying with subsection (1), promptly file with the Commission the report required under subsection (2), marked as confidential, and its written reasons for doing so if,

(a) the reporting issuer reasonably believes that a disclosure required under subsections (1) and (2) would be unduly detrimental to its interests; or

(b) the material change consists of a decision made by the senior management of the reporting issuer to implement a change and the senior management,

(i) believes that confirmation by the board of directors of the decision to implement the change is probable, and

(ii) has no reason to believe that any person or company with knowledge of the material change has purchased or sold the reporting issuer's securities or traded a related derivative. [SO 2010, c 26, Schedule 18, s 29(1).]

Idem

(4) Where a report has been filed with the Commission under subsection (3), the reporting issuer shall advise the Commission in writing where it believes the report should continue to remain confidential within ten days of the date of filing of the initial report and every ten days thereafter until the material change is generally disclosed in the manner referred to in subsection (1) or, if the material change consists of a decision of the type referred to in clause (3)(b), until that decision has been rejected by the board of directors of the issuer.

Requirement to disclose subsequently

(5) A reporting issuer that has filed a report under subsection (3) shall promptly disclose the material change in the manner referred to in subsection (1) if the reporting issuer becomes aware or has reasonable grounds to believe that a person or company

having knowledge of the material change is purchasing or selling securities of the reporting issuer or trading a related derivative. [SO 2010, c 26, Schedule 18, s 29(2).]

Trading where undisclosed change

76(1) No person or company in a special relationship with a reporting issuer shall purchase or sell securities of the issuer with the knowledge of a material fact or material change with respect to the reporting issuer that has not been generally disclosed. [RSO 1990, c S.5, s 76(1); SO 2015, c 20, Schedule 39, ss 2(1)-(3).]

Tipping

(2) No issuer and no person or company in a special relationship with an issuer shall inform, other than in the necessary course of business, another person or company of a material fact or material change with respect to the issuer before the material fact or material change has been generally disclosed. [RSO 1990, c S.5, s 76(2); SO 2015, c 20, Schedule 39, ss 2(1)-(4).]

Same

(3) No person or company that is considering or evaluating whether, or that proposes,

(a) to make a take-over bid, as defined in Part XX, for the securities of an issuer;

(b) to become a party to a reorganization, amalgamation, merger, arrangement or similar business combination with an issuer; or

(c) to acquire a substantial portion of the property of a reporting issuer,

shall inform another person or company of a material fact or material change with respect to the issuer before the material fact or material change has been generally disclosed except where the information is given in the necessary course of business relating to the take-over bid, business combination or acquisition. [RSO 1990, c S.5, s 76(3); SO 2013, c 2, Schedule 13, ss 2(1), (2); SO 2015, c 20, Schedule 39, ss 2(1)-(3).]

Defence

(4) No person or company shall be found to have contravened subsection (1), (2) or (3) if the person or company proves that the person or company reasonably believed that the material fact or material change had been generally disclosed.

These provisions create an overall obligation to disclose a material change in the affairs of the reporting issuer. Most jurisdictions repealed their statutory language regarding material change reporting after adopting NI 51-102, which sets out material change disclosure requirements for reporting issuers. It focuses on public disclosure of material change through news releases and subsequent filing of material change reports as soon as practicable. It provides limited relief where such a disclosure would be unduly detrimental to the interests of the issuer and where that decision is arrived at in a reasonable manner. In such an instance, there is an obligation to report that decision to the securities regulator, with an ongoing obligation to report to the commission every ten days where the issuer believes that the report should continue to remain confidential. As you read, notice that it incorporates the same kind of relief from public disclosure as securities legislation, where the reporting issuer concludes that it would be unduly detrimental to the interests of the reporting issuer to disclose.

National Instrument 51-102, *Continuous Disclosure Obligations*
In force 30 March 2004, as amended effective 17 November 2015

1.1 "material change" means

(a) a change in the business, operations or capital of the reporting issuer that would reasonably be expected to have a significant effect on the market price or value of any of the securities of the reporting issuer; or

(b) a decision to implement a change referred to in paragraph (a) made by the board of directors or other persons acting in a similar capacity or by senior management of the reporting issuer who believe that confirmation of the decision by the board of directors or any other persons acting in a similar capacity is probable;

. . .

Part 7 Material Change Reports

7.1 Publication of Material Change

(1) Subject to subsection (2), if a material change occurs in the affairs of a reporting issuer, the reporting issuer must

(a) immediately issue and file a news release authorized by an executive officer disclosing the nature and substance of the change; and

(b) as soon as practicable, and in any event within 10 days of the date on which the change occurs, file a Form 51-102F3 Material Change Report with respect to the material change.

(2) Subsection (1) does not apply if,

(a) in the opinion of the reporting issuer, and if that opinion is arrived at in a reasonable manner, the disclosure required by subsection (1) would be unduly detrimental to the interests of the reporting issuer; or

(b) the material change consists of a decision to implement a change made by senior management of the reporting issuer who believe that confirmation of the decision by the board of directors is probable, and senior management of the reporting issuer has no reason to believe that persons with knowledge of the material change have made use of that knowledge in purchasing or selling securities of the reporting issuer, and the reporting issuer immediately files the report required under paragraph (1)(b) marked so as to indicate that it is confidential, together with written reasons for nondisclosure.

(3) [Repealed]

(4) [Repealed]

(5) If a report has been filed under subsection (2), the reporting issuer must advise the regulator or securities regulatory authority in writing if it believes the report should

continue to remain confidential, within 10 days of the date of filing of the initial report and every 10 days thereafter until the material change is generally disclosed in the manner referred to in paragraph (1)(a), or, if the material change consists of a decision of the type referred to in paragraph (2)(b), until that decision has been rejected by the board of directors of the reporting issuer.

(6) Despite subsection (5), in Ontario, the reporting issuer must advise the securities regulatory authority.

(7) If a report has been filed under subsection (2), the reporting issuer must promptly generally disclose the material change in the manner referred to in subsection (1) upon the reporting issuer becoming aware, or having reasonable grounds to believe, that persons or companies are purchasing or selling securities of the reporting issuer with knowledge of the material change that has not been generally disclosed.

These provisions of NI 51-102 are aimed at harmonization of material change reporting in jurisdictions across Canada. NI 51-102 has a specific form dealing with material change reporting that has encouraged more consistency in reporting (Form 51-102F3).

A number of important decisions have considered the definition of "material change." In *Pezim v British Columbia (Superintendent of Brokers)*, below, the Supreme Court of Canada dealt with both the definition of materiality and the issue of the standard of review of decisions of securities regulators. The respondents in *Pezim* were the president, chair of the board, and the vice-president responsible for internal administration of Prime, a company holding several wholly owned subsidiaries and controlling or managing about 50 public junior resource companies. The officers were also directors of Calpine, a company controlled and managed by Prime. Both companies were reporting issuers listed on the (then) Vancouver Stock Exchange and subject to the continuing and timely disclosure requirements of the British Columbia *Securities Act*. In the spring of 1990, BCSC's Superintendent of Brokers instituted proceedings against the respondents in connection with various transactions that occurred in 1989, alleging that the respondents had violated timely disclosure provisions and insider-trading prohibitions in three categories of impugned transactions: the drilling results and share options transactions, the private placement, and the ALC withdrawal.

Pezim v British Columbia (Superintendent of Brokers)
[1994] 2 SCR 557

IACOBUCCI J (Lamer CJ and La Forest, Sopinka, Gonthier, and Major JJ concurring): …

[79] Both "material change" and "material fact" are defined in s. 1 of the Act. They are defined in terms of the significance of their impact on the market price or value of the securities of an issuer. The definition of "material fact" is broader than that of "material change"; it encompasses any fact that can "reasonably be expected to significantly affect" the market price or value of the securities of an issuer, and not only changes in the "business, operations, assets or ownership of the issuer" that would reasonably be expected to have such an effect.

[80] The use of these two terms in the Act also reflects the differences in their scope. For example, a prospectus relating to a public distribution of securities must disclose all

material facts relating to the issuer: ss. 44(1), 45(2), 49(1) and 50(1). However, the prospectus need be amended only when a material change occurs: ss. 47(1), (2) and 48(1). [Note: Sections 43-47 have since been repealed.]

[81] [Then] sections 67 and 68 of the Act also reflect the differences between a material change and a material fact. As Victor p. Alboini points out in *Securities Law and Practice*, 2nd ed., vol. 2 (1984), at p. 18-13, "[t]he concept of 'material change' should be distinguished from that of 'material fact.' Undisclosed material facts concerning a reporting issuer may not require timely disclosure … although they do restrict trading." Under the timely disclosure provision of the Act, s. 67, only material changes require that a press release be issued and that a report be filed. In contrast, under the insider trading provision, s. 68, a person who is in a special relationship with a reporting issuer is prohibited from buying or selling securities of the issuer when the person knows of either a material change or a material fact which has not been publicly disclosed.

[82] As already mentioned, the present case turns partly on the definition of "material change." Three elements emerge from that definition: the change must be (a) "in relation to the affairs of an issuer," (b) "in the business, operations, assets or ownership of the issuer" and (c) material, i.e., would reasonably be expected to have a significant effect on the market price or value of the securities of the issuer. Thus, not all changes are material changes; the latter are set in the context of making sure that issuers keep investors up to date. Consequently, it would seem wholly uncontroversial that the determination of what information should be disclosed is an issue which goes to the heart of the regulatory expertise and mandate of the Commission, i.e., regulating the securities markets in the public's interest.

[83] This case also turns on the meaning of the words "as soon as practicable" in s. 67 of the Act which reveal when a material change should be disclosed to the public. In my view, the timeliness of disclosure also falls within the Commission's regulatory jurisdiction.

[84] In summary, having regard to the nature of the securities industry, the Commission's specialization of duties and policy development role as well as the nature of the problem before the court, considerable deference is warranted in the present case notwithstanding the fact that there is a statutory right of appeal and there is no privative clause.

2. *In the Case at Bar, Did the British Columbia Court of Appeal Exercise the Appropriate Standard of Review?*

A. *The Drilling Results and Share Options Transactions*

[85] The Commission's conclusion that s. 67 was violated in the context of the share options transactions can be subdivided into two parts. The first element of the conclusion is that undisclosed drilling results can constitute a material change in the affairs of a reporting issuer. …

[86] As already mentioned, the determination of what constitutes a material change for the purposes of general disclosure under s. 67 of the Act is a matter which falls squarely within the regulatory mandate and expertise of the Commission. Consequently, when the majority of the Court of Appeal rejected the Commission's findings on this matter, it fell into error. Furthermore, the majority's view on this point is, in my opinion, clearly

wrong and is inconsistent with the economic and regulatory realities the Act sets out to address. Counsel for the respondents conceded this point, during the hearing of this appeal, and stated that "information from a drilling program can be tantamount to a material change."

• • •

[88] Can the Court really suggest that there has not been a change in a company's assets when, following adequate sampling, a discovery is made on a portion of its property that had been previously categorized as having no known mineralization? Surely, given the basic aim of the Act—to protect the investing public through full, true and plain disclosure of all material facts relating to securities—one could conclude (as did Mr. Justice Locke, the dissenting judge) that the Commission did not make a "plain and vital mistake" in the application of the words in s. 67 of the Act to the facts before it. …

[89] Consequently, I am of the view, as found by the Commission and Locke JA, that the assay results constituted a change with respect to or in the companies' assets and is "material" for the purposes of the Act.

[90] The second element of the Commission's conclusion that s. 67 was violated in the context of the share options transactions is that the obligation to disclose "as soon as practicable" takes on a different meaning when an issuer is about to engage in a securities transaction. …

[94] It must be noted that a duty to inquire under s. 67 is not incompatible with the insider trading provision of the Act, s. 68. If an issuer wishes to engage in a securities transaction, its directors must inquire about all material changes in the issuer's affairs. Consequently, the directors will have, at one point in time, knowledge of undisclosed material facts and material changes which constitute inside information. However, as long as the material facts and material changes are adequately disclosed prior to the transaction, there will be no possibility of insider trading. It must also be noted that the erecting of a Chinese Wall, which prevents directors of a company from having inside information, does not erase the duty imposed on directors to inquire about material changes, as the disclosure requirements under s. 67 are on the issuer.

[95] Having concluded that information contained in drilling results can constitute a material change in the affairs of a reporting issuer and that s. 67 imposes on senior management a duty to inquire as to the existence of material changes before causing a reporting issuer to engage in a securities transaction, the Commission went on to review the circumstances surrounding the share options transactions of July 12 and 31, August 15 and 17, 1989. The Commission made the following findings: (1) The July 12 transaction was completed after a new zone of mineralization had been identified, as well as a possible doubling of the reserves, but before the news release of July 13 was issued. (2) The July 31 transaction was concluded after the discovery of visible gold and extensive other mineralization in hole 109, but before the news release of August 2. (3) The August 15 transaction was completed after Prime was in possession of the assay results for holes 93 and 101 but before the news release was issued that afternoon. (4) The August 17 transaction followed the arrival of the gold assays for hole 109; the news release relating to these assays was issued on August 22. Based on these findings, the Commission held that the respondents failed to disclose various material changes in the affairs of Prime and Calpine before causing these two companies to engage in securities transactions. Consequently, the respondents had contravened s. 67 of the Act.

[96] Like Locke JA, I find that there was overwhelming evidence to support each of the Commission's findings and I would not disturb any of them. Consequently, the majority of the Court of Appeal erred in interfering with the Commission's conclusion that, with respect to the share options transactions, the respondents breached their timely disclosure obligations under s. 67 of the Act. …

B. The Private Placement

[98] The majority of the Court of Appeal agreed with the Commission that s. 67 of the Act was breached when Calpine failed to disclose the identity of the placee or the fact that Prime was to increase its control over Calpine from 23 to 36 percent, assuming exercise of the warrants. In this respect, it is worth noting that by obtaining a 36 percent holding in Calpine, Prime thereby could prevent the passing of a special resolution as defined in s. 1 of the *Company Act*, which in turn empowered Prime to prevent a number of important transactions for which a special resolution of shareholders is required under the *Company Act* (see, for example, ss. 255, 267 and 272). [Note: Now the *Business Corporations Act.*]

[99] The majority also agreed that Calpine misled the VSE on July 17, 1989 by representing that the private placement was to be brokered by Prime Equities. However, the majority overturned the Commission's finding that Page falsely certified to the VSE on August 18, 1989 that there were no material changes in the affairs of Calpine that had not been publicly disclosed. It predicated its conclusion on the fact that undisclosed assays cannot constitute a material change.

[100] As already mentioned, the determination of what constitutes a material change goes to the heart of the expertise and mandate of the commission. Furthermore, having regard to the realities of the mining industry, information from assay results can properly be characterized as a material change in the business, operations, assets or ownership of a reporting issuer. To conclude, I agree with Locke JA that the findings of the Commission on the private placement issue reveal no error.

C. The ALC Withdrawal

[101] The majority of the Court of Appeal overturned the Commission's finding that s. 67 had been breached by not disclosing the ALC withdrawal. The majority viewed the ALC withdrawal in contractual terms and stated that it did not have to be disclosed until there was repudiation of the contract and such repudiation was accepted by Prime.

[102] In my view, this narrow approach is wrong and is inconsistent with the purpose of the Act, i.e., to protect the investing public. Again, like Locke JA, I find there is little basis for disagreeing with the Commission's conclusions. ALC's withdrawal represented a $4.25 million contractual dispute. It would seem wholly uncontroversial to consider such a dispute a change in the business, operations, ownership or affairs of a reporting issuer. As Stevens and Wortley point out, *supra*, at p. 338, "an account receivable that was to be transformed into cash on September 29 became instead nothing more than a disputed claim for breach of contract." Accordingly, non-disclosure of this dispute constituted a failure to disclose a material change. Thus, the majority of the Court of Appeal erred in rejecting the Commission's findings on this point.

[103] In stating the above, I do not wish to imply that it is always self-evident as to what constitutes a material change. In this respect, it is interesting to note that the Chair of the Ontario Securities Commission has encouraged in that province an early warning system which allows informal disclosure to the Commission of a proposed transaction on a confidential basis. According to Alboini, *supra*, at pp. 18-14 and 18-15, such a system "allows for appropriate steps to be taken by the Commission to permit stock watches, while also creating an opportunity to discuss with Commission members or staff possible orders or applications that may be required in order to facilitate the transaction from a regulatory point of view."

...

VI. Conclusion and Disposition

[111] The majority of the Court of Appeal erred in failing to appreciate the Commission's role in an area requiring special knowledge and sophistication. It also failed to recognize the Legislature's intent to confer a broad public interest mandate on the Commission to carry out its role. There was ample evidence to support each of the Commission's findings. There being no reviewable error of law, the majority of the Court of Appeal erred in interfering with the Commission's findings. Consequently, I would allow the appeal, set aside the judgment of the British Columbia Court of Appeal and substitute therefor the findings and orders of the Commission. The appellants shall have their costs here and in the court below.

In *Kerr v Danier Leather Inc*, the Supreme Court of Canada further clarified the difference between material fact and material change, holding that when a prospectus or amendment to a prospectus contains no misrepresentation on the date the document is filed, information amounting to material facts, but not material changes that arises subsequently cannot support an action under s 130(1). In this respect, the court is signalling that the wording of the statute is extremely important in determining the scope of disclosure obligations.

Kerr v Danier Leather Inc
2007 SCC 44, [2007] 3 SCR 331

BINNIE J (McLachlin CJ and Bastarache, LeBel, Deschamps, Fish, Abella, Charron, and Rothstein JJ concurring): ...

[35] Was the sales forecast, though found not to be a "material change," nevertheless a "misrepresentation" as of May 16, 1998? According to s. 1, a "misrepresentation" can occur by:

...

> ... an omission to state a material fact that is necessary ... to make a statement not misleading in the light of the circumstances in which it was made.

The argument, therefore, is that failure to disclose the intra-quarterly results prior to closing rendered the prospectus forecast "misleading" at the "time of purchase" to the knowledge of the respondents, and therefore actionable under s. 130(1). This is because a "material fact" is defined in the Act more broadly than a "material change" and includes "a fact that significantly affects, or would reasonably be expected to have a significant effect on, the market price or value of … securities" (s. 1). The trial judge concluded that the intra-quarterly results constituted a "material fact."

[36] The appellants further submit that nothing in s. 130(1) suggests any legislative intent to alter the basic common law principle that requires a representation that becomes untrue to the maker's knowledge to be corrected before it is acted upon (see S.M. Waddams, *The Law of Contracts* (4th ed. 1999), at p. 315). In this vein, the appellants, as did the trial judge, observe that s. 130(1) (as it stood in 1998) deems an investor to have relied on a misrepresentation "if it was a misrepresentation at the time of purchase." Reference to "the time of purchase," they say, further indicates that an issuer's duty to disclose material facts continues until the closing date.

[37] In my opinion, with respect, these submissions are not persuasive. Prospective purchasers were entitled to assume that no material *changes* (as defined in the Act) had occurred to the material facts disclosed in the prospectus between the filing date and the closing date, but that is the extent of the assurance given by the Act to prospective investors.

[38] The appellants submit that s. 57(1) should not be used as a guide to the interpretation of s. 130(1), relying in part on the argument that "s. 57(1) says nothing about whether a material fact if disclosed may remain uncorrected if it becomes untrue by the date of purchase, and thus the section does nothing to limit any such duty that may otherwise exist," as discussed by H. Underwood and R. Sorell in "Danier Leather Inc. and the Duty to Update a Prospectus" (2006), 43 *Can. Bus. LJ* 134, at pp. 144-45. However, such an interpretation would disregard the court's duty to interpret the statute "harmoniously" as a whole. Imposition of civil liability under s. 130(1) for an omission to do what the legislature as a matter of policy has declined to require in s. 57(1) would simply be to substitute the court's view of policy for that adopted by the legislature. The distinction between "material change" and "material fact" is deliberate and policy-based, as explained by a former chairman of the OSC:

> The term "material fact" is necessary when an issuer is publishing a disclosure document, such as a prospectus or a take-over bid circular, where all material information concerning the issuer *at a point in time* is published in one document which is convenient to the investor. The term "material change" is limited to a change in the business, operations or capital of the issuer. *This is an attempt to relieve reporting issuers of the obligation to continually interpret external political, economic and social developments as they affect the affairs of the issuer,* unless the external change will result in a change in the business, operations or capital of the issuer, in which case, timely disclosure of the change must be made. [Emphasis added.]
>
> (Remarks of Peter J. Dey concerning disclosure under the *Securities Act* made to securities lawyers in Calgary and Toronto on June 7 and 9, 1983.)

As to the current state of this policy, it is worth noting that both the Toronto Stock Exchange Committee on Corporate Disclosure, *Final Report: Responsible Corporate Disclosure: A Search for Balance* (1997) ("Allen Report") and the Ontario, *Five Year Review Committee Final Report: Reviewing the Securities Act (Ontario)* (2003) ("Crawford Report"), considered whether the *Securities Act* should be amended to require continuing disclosure by issuers of material facts or whether the policy of requiring the disclosure of only material changes should be continued. Both committees recommended against a modification of the statutory policy.

[39] Firstly, if an issuer has fully complied with its regulatory obligations under ss. 56 to 58 of the Act it would be contrary to the scheme of the Act, and to the intent of the Ontario legislature reflected therein, to find civil liability against an issuer under s. 130(1) for failing to disclose post-filing information that does not amount to a material change.

[40] Secondly, the statutory definition of "misrepresentation" uses the past tense in the phrase "in the light of the circumstances in which it was made." The appellants say the past tense "contemplates that a statement may need correction later" (A.F., at para. 51). In my view, however, this past tense simply signals that the relevant date for assessing the accuracy of a statement is the effective date when the statement *was* made, i.e., the date the prospectus (or an amendment) was filed.

[41] Thirdly, the appellants rely on the phrase "if it was a misrepresentation at the time of purchase" but this reliance too, in my view, is misplaced. These are words of limitation designed to ensure that s. 130(1) does not impose civil liability for a representation that had become cured or corrected at the date of purchase. Suppose, for example, that Danier owned an important patent on a process for working leather, and trumpeted this fact in its prospectus, inadvertently failing to disclose that a competitor had mounted a serious court challenge to the patent's validity. The Act gives the purchasers the benefit of "deemed" reliance. The existence of a serious court challenge would be a material fact. Yet if the challenge were settled or discontinued and the patent thus vindicated *before* the time of purchase, why should the omission attract damages or rescission? The answer, according to the language of s. 130(1), is that it does not.

[42] The appellants' reliance on the common law as a guide to the interpretation of s. 130(1) is also unconvincing. The common law does not require a person selling shares to issue a prospectus. It does not define or distinguish between material facts and material changes. It does not create a scheme of compelled disclosure with its own requirements and limits on those requirements. It is the Act and not the common law that settles the policy.

[43] In summary, when (as here) a prospectus (or an amendment) contains no misrepresentation *on the date the document is filed*, information amounting to material *facts* (but not material *changes*) that arises subsequently cannot support an action under s. 130(1). (Of course, if a material *change* arises during the period of distribution, failure to disclose this change as required by s. 57(1) could support an action under s. 130(1).) In the case at bar, however, the trial judge found that the intra-quarterly results were *not* a material change, and as will be explained, I agree with the trial judge in this regard. Such is the prospectus disclosure policy presently mandated by the Act and the courts are obliged to give effect to it. In contexts other than "prospectus misrepresentation," including regulatory or stock exchange oversight, a different policy may prevail, depending on the governing rules and enactments. This appeal is concerned only with s. 130(1).

...

[46] The appellants rely in this respect on *Pezim*, at p. 600, where the Court agreed with the BC Securities Commission that "a change in assay and drilling results can amount

to a material change depending on the circumstances." A change in assay or drilling results is itself a change in the issuer's "assets" (the term then used in the BC *Securities Act*), but a change in intra-quarterly results is not itself a change in the issuer's business, operations or capital and, for that matter, does not necessarily signal that a material change has occurred. Sales often fluctuate (as here) in response to factors that are external to the issuer.

[47] It almost goes without saying that poor intra-quarterly results may *reflect* a material change in business operations. A company that has, for example, restructured its operations may experience poor intra-quarterly results because of this restructuring, but it is the restructuring and not the results themselves that would amount to a material change and thus trigger the disclosure obligation. Additionally, poor intra-quarterly results may motivate a company to implement a change in its business, operations or capital in an effort to improve performance. Again, though, the disclosure obligation would be triggered by the change in the business, operations or capital, and not by the results themselves.

[48] In the present case, there is no evidence that Danier made a change in its business, operations or capital during the period of distribution. It is not disputed that the revenue shortfall as of May 16 was caused by the unusually hot weather, a factor external to the issuer. Consequently, Danier experienced no material change that required disclosure and did not breach s. 57(1).

In *Re AiT Advanced Information Technologies Corp*, 2008 LNONOSC 22, 31 OSCB 712, the Ontario Securities Commission considered whether directors authorized, permitted, or acquiesced in a breach of the Ontario *Securities Act* and acted contrary to the public interest by authorizing, permitting, or acquiescing in Advanced Information Technologies Corporation's failure to disclose forthwith a merger transaction between AiT and 3M Company as a material change. Its consideration of the concept of materiality and its determination that assessment of material change is not a bright-line decision is helpful to understanding the sometimes difficult decision that directors must make in determining the timing of their disclosure. In this respect, the decision is arguably more contextual than the reasoning in *Kerr v Danier Leather Inc*.

Re AiT Advanced Information Technologies Corp
2008 LNONOSC 22, 31 OSCB 712

C. *The Concept of Materiality*

[203] In any interpretation of material fact or material change, it is first necessary to review and understand the concept of "materiality" in our disclosure regime:

> The test for materiality in the Act is objective and is one of market impact. An investor wants to know facts that would reasonably be expected to significantly affect the market price or value of securities. (*Re YBM Magnex et al., supra* at para. 91)

[204] The British Columbia Securities Commission has addressed the issue of materiality in the context of negotiations leading up to a transaction (although in the context

of a broader "material information" regime). The following principles were articulated in *Re Siddiqi*, 2005 LNBCSC 375 at paragraph 87:

> Whether information is material depends on the facts of each case. The test is the expected impact the information would have on the market price or value of the issuer's securities. Where transactions are involved, it is not enough to consider only the materiality of the transaction itself, but also the materiality of the information that negotiations are underway that could lead to a possible transaction. In some cases, the existence of negotiations would or could reasonably be expected to affect the stock price, and is therefore material. (Of course, the existence of negotiations about a proposed transaction can be material only if the underlying transaction itself, if completed, would be material.)

[205] Staff also referred us to the applicable test used in the United States, the probability/magnitude test. Staff referred us to the cases: *SEC v. Texas Gulf Sulphur*, 401 F. 2d 833 (2nd Cir., 1968) aff'd F. 2d 1301 (USCA 2nd Cir., 1971); *TSC Industries, Inc. v. Northway, Inc.*, 426 US 438 (1976); and *Basic v. Levinson* (1988), 485 US 224 (USSC) (WL). In particular, Staff points out that the probability/magnitude test has been applied in the context of merger and acquisition transactions in the United States.

[206] However, we note that the law in the United States does not include the concept of a "material change" as defined in our Act. The probability/magnitude test was formulated as an appropriate test for determining the materiality of speculative or contingent information. Although the American probability/magnitude test may be useful with respect to materiality, it is not particularly useful in determining whether a change has occurred, which is crucial in this case. As a result, we are wary of quoting and adhering to the American case law, especially when the American law does not incorporate the concept of a "material change" as the Ontario statute does.

[207] In the present case, the negotiations between AiT and 3M were material in relation to AiT as a reporting issuer: negotiations of a potential acquisition transaction by 3M could reasonably be expected to affect the market price or value of AiT's shares and were therefore material. AiT was also a small company relative to 3M, and materiality often occurs at a much earlier stage for smaller issuers than larger issuers.

...

E. *The Assessment of a Material Change Is Not a Bright-Line Test*

[213] Staff in its submissions placed great emphasis on the addition of the words "a decision to implement such a change made by the board of directors of the issuer" to support the proposition that a material change can occur in advance of the execution of a definitive binding agreement and therefore the determination of whether a material change has occurred is not a "bright-line" test.

[214] We agree that there is no "bright-line test." Instead, the assessment of whether a material change has taken place will depend on the circumstances and series of events that took place. This is because the determination of a material change is a question of mixed fact and law (*Re YBM Magnex et al.*, *supra* at para. 94). This determination requires ascertaining whether the existing facts fulfill the legal test. Each case will be unique, and the specific facts and circumstances will vary case by case. Since the fact scenarios will

differ in all cases, it is impossible to articulate a bright-line test that will apply in all circumstances.

F. Interpretation of "Decision to Implement a Change" by a Board of Directors

[215] The definition of a "material change" in the 1978 legislation was the first time a reference to a material change included "a decision to *implement* such a change made by the board of directors of the issuer" [emphasis added]. The word "implement" is not defined in the Act, however, we note that the *Canadian Oxford Dictionary* defines the word "implement" as "to put into effect." (*The Canadian Oxford Dictionary*, 2001, s.v. "implement").

[216] Anisman noted in his expert report:

> As a "material change" must be reported when it occurs, the question of what may constitute a change is frequently characterized in terms of when a change occurs, particularly in the context of negotiated transactions involving mergers and acquisitions. Such negotiations may move from overtures, through tentative discussions, into exclusive or non-exclusive arrangements involving confidentiality agreements, to letters of intent and agreements in principle, preparation of a definitive agreement, submission to shareholders for approval, fulfillment of conditions, and ultimately to closing and implementation. Any or all of these steps may be material, as outlined above. *A change will occur when a decision has been made indicating a substantial likelihood that implementation will be forthcoming.* [emphasis added]
>
> (Philip Anisman, *Expert Report prepared for Re AiT Advanced Information Technologies Corporation, et al.*, dated August 31, 2007, p. 12)

[217] While the Act is silent regarding the definition of "implement" we note that the Commission has addressed this issue in *Re Burnett* (1983), 6 OSCB 2751. The Commission stated that:

> An intention by a person or company to do something, which once implemented would constitute a material change in the affairs of the reporting issuer, but which at the time the intention is formed, *for reasons beyond the control of the person or company is still not capable of achievement is not ordinarily a material change* in the affairs of the issuer. [emphasis added] (*Re Burnett, supra* at para. 7)

[218] A decision by a board of directors of an issuer to pursue a potential transaction that is not yet within its control to put into effect (and therefore is not then capable of achievement), would not ordinarily be a material change in the business, operations or capital of an issuer at that point in time unless the board has reason to believe that the other party is also committed to completing the transaction, as discussed below.

[219] Staff also referred us to *Re Bennett (Doman)*, 1996 LNBCSC 38 (QL), rev'd in part [1998] BCJ No. 2378 (BCCA), leave to SCC refused [1998] SCCA No. 601. Staff takes the position that this case stands for the proposition that a decision to sell a control block of shares is a material change even though there was no agreement and no purchaser had been identified. The British Columbia Securities Commission noted that since legal and financial advisors had been retained for a possible transaction and serious discussions had taken place, this constituted a material change.

[220] The present case can be distinguished from the British Columbia Securities Commission case *Re Bennett (Doman)*. First, *Re Bennett (Doman)* was an insider trading case. Second, Doman was a controlling majority shareholder of Doman Industries:

> Doman controlled Doman Industries. If he decided to sell Doman Industries, Doman Industries would be sold. It would be irrelevant what the directors had to say. The decision to sell Doman Industries was his alone to make. (*Re Bennett (Doman)*, *supra* at 99 and 100)

[221] In any event, we find that there is no bright-line test with respect to a material change, and the fact that legal and financial advisors are retained will not on its own be sufficient to demonstrate that a material change has occurred. Therefore, the fact that legal and financial advisors are retained is not determinative of the existence of a material change.

[222] However, in our view, in the context of a proposed merger and acquisition transaction, where the proposed transaction is speculative, contingent and surrounded by uncertainties, a commitment from one party to proceed will not be sufficient to constitute a material change. In the context of a merger and acquisition transaction, it is necessary to establish whether there is sufficient commitment from both parties of the transaction to determine whether a "decision to implement" the transaction has taken place. Therefore, in the case at bar, we need to establish whether a sufficient indication of commitment was made by AiT and 3M during the Relevant Period.

[223] We rely on Anisman's wording "when a decision has been made indicating a substantial likelihood that implementation will be forthcoming." In our view, for there to be a substantial likelihood that a proposed transaction will be completed, there needs to be sufficient signs of commitment on behalf of all the parties involved to proceed with the transaction.

See also the discussion in *YBM Magnex International Inc* (2003), 26 OSCB 5285 as to whether an audit suspension would constitute a material change required to be disclosed.

QUESTIONS

1. What, in the court's view in *Kerr v Danier Leather*, is the difference between a material fact and a material change, and why was it relevant in terms of the disclosure requirements?
2. The Supreme Court in *Pezim* accorded a high level of deference to the securities commission on the issue of what was a material change. In your view, does this deference create sufficient certainty, or should "material" be more codified in the statute?
3. What test does the Ontario Securities Commission find is the appropriate test in the context of a proposed merger and acquisition transaction? Consider this question again below, when you read the more recent *Coventree* decision.
4. The Supreme Court of Canada in *Kerr v Danier Leather* signals that regulators and judges should pay close attention to statutory language in determining material change allegations, while, arguably, the commission in *Re AiT Advanced Information Technologies Corp* offers a contextual approach to the determination of material change. Are these decisions compatible? Why or why not?

The Supreme Court of Canada discussed the secondary market liability provisions and their relationship to continuous disclosure in a recent case under the new class action provisions of Québec securities legislation (*Theratechnologies Inc v 121851 Canada Inc*, 2015 SCC 18, [2015] 2 SCR 106). In the spring of 2010, the issuer, Theratechnologies Inc (Thera) was awaiting the approval of the United States Food and Drug Administration (FDA) for a new drug to reduce excess abdominal fat among HIV patients. As its application proceeded, Thera regularly updated its shareholders and the Commission des valeurs mobilières du Québec about developments in the FDA process. It also regularly informed its shareholders about the results of its clinical trials measuring the safety and efficacy of the drug, including potential side effects. However, when questions posed by the FDA were publicized by stock quotation enterprises, the price of the company's shares dropped. 121851 Canada Inc, a holding company, sold its shares in Thera during this period and sought authorization under s 225.4 of the Québec *Securities Act* to bring a class action for damages against Thera, claiming that the information about the potential side effects of the drug and the FDA's questions about those side effects amounted to a material change in Thera's business, operations or capital, triggering the timely disclosure obligations under s 73 of the *Securities Act*. The Superior Court motions judge concluded that the authorization mechanism in s 225.4 of the *Securities Act* imposed a higher threshold than art 1003 of the *Code of Civil Procedure*, CQLR c C-25 (CCP), which deals with the authorization of class actions generally, but found sufficient evidence to support the conclusion that 121851's action had a reasonable possibility of success. An appeal by Thera to the Court of Appeal was dismissed. The Supreme Court of Canada allowed the appeal. The issues in the case are discussed at length in Chapter 10 on civil liability; the excerpt below is the court's reasoning on the substantive aspects of a material change.

Theratechnologies Inc v 121851 Canada Inc
2015 SCC 18, [2015] 2 SCR 106

ABELLA J (McLachlin CJ and Rothstein, Cromwell, Moldaver, Karakatsanis, and Wagner JJ concurring): …

[40] 121851 alleges that Thera breached its obligation under s. 73 of the *Securities Act* to provide timely disclosure of material changes to its investors. Section 5.3 of the *Securities Act* defines a "material change" as

> a *change in the business, operations or capital of the issuer* that would reasonably be expected to have a significant effect on the market price or value of any of the securities of the issuer, or a decision to implement such a change made by the directors or by senior management of the issuer who believe that confirmation of the decision by the directors is probable.

As this statutory definition makes clear, a material change has two components. There must be a change in the business, operations or capital of the issuer and the change must be material, which means it would reasonably be expected to have a significant effect on the market price or value of the securities of the issuer: *Securities Act*, s. 5.3. Both elements are required to trigger an obligation of timely disclosure.

[41] 121851 argues that a material change occurred on May 11, 2010, when Thera received the FDA briefing materials, which included a Background Introductory Memorandum asking the Advisory Committee to comment on "the findings of glucose intolerance and development of diabetes associated with Egrifta [tesamorelin] therapy and its impact on longterm cardiovascular risk." This information was made public on May 25, 2010, when the FDA posted the memorandum, alongside all the briefing materials it had generated on tesamorelin, on its website.

[42] In my view, however, 121851 has not pointed to any evidence that could qualify as a material change in Thera's operations, capital or business as described in s. 5.3 of the *Securities Act*. And without some evidence of a material change that corresponds to the statutory requirements, 121851's action cannot reasonably hope to succeed.

[43] Tesamorelin operates by activating a growth hormone, which, in other contexts, has been associated with an increased risk of diabetes. Thera's phase-three clinical trials measured the blood sugar levels of participating patients to evaluate the risk associated with this potential side effect. The trials compared five glycemic parameters recognized by the scientific community and the American Diabetes Association in patients taking tesamorelin and patients taking a placebo, and revealed that tesamorelin did not have a clinically significant effect on the glucose levels of patients.

[44] The results of the clinical trials were disclosed to shareholders as they became available. In its November 2008 Annual Notice, for example, Thera summarized its clinical results to date and noted that

> [t]he administration of [the hormone] is not indicated in glucose-intolerant patients, a condition often observed in these patients. Consequently, Theratechnologies decided to study the effect of tesamorelin in the treatment of this condition. Highlights of the study included a good safety profile, a clear effect on body composition and a clinically relevant reduction in visceral fat while subcutaneous fat was preserved.

[45] On November 11, 2009, Thera, in collaboration with two external experts, presented the combined results of its two phase-three clinical trials at the 12th European AIDS Conference. The fact of this presentation and its content were disclosed to investors via a press release, which stated that "[n]o clinically important changes in glucose parameters were observed after treatment with tesamorelin."

[46] On March 1, 2010, Thera issued a press release announcing the publication of a study detailing its combined clinical results in the publicly available *Journal of Acquired Immune Deficiency Syndromes*. The press release provided a link to the study, which included an abstract highlighting the clinical results and concluding that the potential side effects of tesamorelin were not significant:

> Tesamorelin reduces visceral fat by approximately 18% and improves body image distress in HIV-infected patients with central fat accumulation. These changes are achieved without significant side effects or perturbation of glucose [p. 311].

[47] Through these press releases, Thera disclosed to its shareholders that it was monitoring tesamorelin's side effects, including on patients' blood sugar levels. It provided both summaries and full studies detailing the results of its clinical trials. There is no allegation that any of these reports were either false or misleading. A reasonable investor who read Thera's news releases would have known that blood sugar issues and diabetes

were potential side effects of the drug, and that Thera's clinical trials had found they were not clinically significant.

[48] As a result, this case can be distinguished from *Pezim v. British Columbia (Superintendent of Brokers)*, [1994] 2 S.C.R. 557, in which the Court held that information contained in drilling results regarding a mining company's exploration site could constitute a material change in the "business, operations, assets or ownership of the issuer," since they could reasonably be expected to significantly affect the company's assets. Unlike the drilling results at issue in *Pezim*, the potential side effects of tesamorelin had already been disclosed to shareholders well before the FDA published its questions and the rest of its briefing materials. There was no new information about the side effects of tesamorelin that required timely disclosure as of May 11, 2010.

[49] 121851's argument is more analogous to the claim in *Kerr v. Danier Leather Inc.*, [2007] 3 S.C.R. 331. The company, which was making an initial public offering (IPO) of its shares, had issued preliminary prospectuses which included a sales forecast for the fourth quarter of the fiscal year to its potential investors. Unseasonably warm weather, however, knocked the company sales forecasts off track as the quarter progressed. After its IPO had closed, the company's disclosed its intra-quarterly results in a press release, triggering a sharp drop in its share value. Although the company ultimately realized its initial sales forecasts, the claimants launched a class action, alleging that the company had withheld the intra-quarterly results to ensure the success of its IPO.

[50] This Court held that the intra-quarterly results did not constitute a material change to the business, operations or capital of the company because the warm weather that triggered the drop in sales was external to the company and its business:

> ... a change in intra-quarterly results is not itself a change in the issuer's business, operations or capital and, for that matter, does not necessarily signal that a material change has occurred. Sales often fluctuate (as here) in response to factors that are external to the issuer.
>
> It almost goes without saying that poor intra-quarterly results may *reflect* a material change in business operations. A company that has, for example, restructured its operations may experience poor intra-quarterly results because of this restructuring, but it is the restructuring and not the results themselves that would amount to a material change and thus trigger the disclosure obligation. Additionally, poor intra-quarterly results may motivate a company to implement a change in its business, operations or capital in an effort to improve performance. Again, though, the disclosure obligation would be triggered by the change in the business, operations or capital, and not by the results themselves. [Emphasis in original; paras. 46-47.]

[51] The same is true in this case. 121851 argues that the FDA's preoccupation with the side effects represents a material change in Thera's operations, business or capital. But it has not pointed to any evidence to suggest that the questions the FDA posed to its Advisory Committee about these side effects, or the contents of its Briefing Package more generally, departed in any way from the regular and routine process through which the FDA assesses whether a drug should be approved. Nor is there any evidence that the questions reflected new and undisclosed information about tesamorelin. In fact, the evidence on the record suggests the opposite. It is FDA policy to prepare briefing materials for an Advisory Committee, including information compiled by both the FDA and the sponsoring company, and to post those materials two days before an Advisory Committee meeting.

Questions from the FDA to its expert Advisory Committee about the side effects of a drug do not constitute a departure from the normal FDA process, or, necessarily an indication of whether the drug will be approved. Rather, they are a routine step in the FDA's work to determine whether a drug's benefits outweigh its risks. As such, it is difficult to characterize these questions as any kind of change to Thera's business, operations, or capital requiring a reassuring public response from Thera.

[52] 121851 argues that the market's reaction demonstrates that the FDA's concerns about side effects constitute a material change. It points out that the Canadian Securities Administrators' "National Policy 51-201 Disclosure Standards" includes among its list of potentially "material" information "any development that affects the company's resources, technology, products or markets": Article 4.3. Because this example falls under the subheading of "changes in business and operations," 121851 submits that the FDA's questions are a development that could be considered a material change.

[53] This section of the policy, however, deals with the market impact of events, not whether they are best characterized as material facts or material changes. To adopt this list as dispositive of whether there was a change in the business, operations or capital of a reporting issuer would collapse the distinction between material facts and material changes, significantly expanding timely disclosure obligations beyond what is required by statute. This would, in effect, allow the Canadian Securities Administrators' policy to amend Québec's securities legislation, contrary to this Court's ruling in *Pezim*.

[54] It is true that Thera had sometimes disclosed routine aspects of the FDA process in press releases to its shareholders in the months leading up to the Advisory Committee meeting, but this does not bring the FDA's questions to its Advisory Committee within the statutory definition of a material change. Thera had a statutory duty to disclose material changes in its operations, capital or business in a timely manner, not to reassure its investors at every stage of the FDA approval process.

[55] Finally, even if Thera had issued a press release on May 11, 2010 after it received the FDA's briefing materials, it is not clear what reassurance Thera could have provided at this stage, given that the outcome of the FDA process, as every reasonable investor would have known and as Thera repeatedly made clear, is always uncertain. As the U.S. Supreme Court acknowledged in *TSC Industries, Inc. v. Northway, Inc.* 426 U.S. 438 (1976), there are risks of excessive disclosure, which could "simply … bury the shareholders in an avalanche of trivial information—a result that is hardly conducive to informed decision making": pp. 448-49, cited in *Cornish*, at para. 41.

[56] Because the evidence does not credibly point to a material change that could have triggered timely disclosure obligations, there is no reasonable possibility that 121851's action under s. 73 of the *Securities Act* could succeed. I would allow the appeal with costs.

QUESTIONS

1. What, in the court's view, is the test for "reasonable possibility" of success within the meaning of the relevant provision of the Québec *Securities Act*? How does this standard differ from the general threshold for the authorization of a class action under art 1003 of the *Code of Civil Procedure*?
2. What is the test used by the court to determine material change?

3. What is your view of the court's discussion regarding disclosure obligations regarding the market impact of events under National Policy 51-201, *Disclosure Standards*, and material changes and material facts? Is it time to consider one standard of "material information"?

Recall that Chapter 4 discussed the *Coventree* case in the context of prospectus disclosure in an offering of common shares for sale to the public. That judgment runs to 827 paragraphs. The Ontario Securities Commission in that judgment also advanced its thinking on the issue of material changes and obligations to disclose. As you read it, consider how its reasoning aligns or differs from the Supreme Court's analysis in *Kerr v Danier Leather.*

In the Matter of Coventree Inc, Geoffrey Cornish and Dean Tai

Ontario Securities Commission, Reasons for Decision (28 September 2011)

[148] The definition of "material fact" is broader than that of "material change." Not all material facts will arise from a "change in the business, operations or capital of the issuer." This distinction is fundamental to the application of section 75 of the Act, which applies only to material changes, and is a key consideration in this proceeding.

(c) Materiality

[149] The standard of materiality for both a material fact and material change is the same. A fact or change is considered to be material if it "would reasonably be expected to have a significant effect on the market price or value" of an issuer's securities. When we refer to "materiality" in these reasons, we are referring to the application of that test. Clearly, such a fact or change would be important to a reasonable investor in making an investment decision with respect to the relevant securities.

[150] The interpretation of the disclosure provisions of the Act are also informed by National Policy 51-201—*Disclosure Standards* (2002), 25 OSCB 4492 ("NP 51-201"), which provides guidance on best disclosure practices.

[151] In general, the concept of materiality in the Act is a broad one that varies with the characteristics of the reporting issuer and the particular circumstances involved. NP 51-201 states that:

> In making materiality judgements, it is necessary to take into account a number of factors that cannot be captured in a simple bright-line standard or test. These include the nature of the information itself, the volatility of the company's securities and prevailing market conditions. The materiality of a particular event or piece of information may vary between companies according to their size, the nature of their operations and many other factors.

[152] Section 4.4 of NP 51-201 also provides as follows:

> Companies are not generally required to interpret the impact of external political, economic and social developments on their affairs. However, *if an external development will have or has had a direct effect on the business and affairs of a company that is both material and uncharacteristic of the effect generally experienced by other companies engaged in the same*

> *business or industry, the company is urged to explain, where practical, the particular impact on them.* For example, a change in government policy that affects most companies in a particular industry does not require an announcement, but if it affects only one or a few companies in a material way, such companies should make an announcement. [emphasis added]
>
> . . .

[156] Accordingly, the assessment of the materiality of an event or development is a question of mixed fact and law that requires a contextual determination that takes into account all of the relevant circumstances, including the size and nature of the issuer and its business, the nature of the event or development and the consequences to the issuer's business, operations or capital. That assessment requires the application of judgement and common sense. In assessing whether a fact is a "material fact" or whether a "material change" has occurred, one must take into account both quantitative and qualitative considerations or factors.

(d) The Commission Is a Specialized Tribunal

[157] The materiality standard applicable in this case is an objective test based on reasonable expectation. Determining questions such as whether a fact is a material fact, whether a material change has occurred, the effect of events or developments on the market price or value of securities and the adequacy of disclosure made, are matters squarely within our expertise as a specialized tribunal. While the evidence of experts, shareholders or investors may be relevant or useful, we do not need such evidence in order to make these decisions (see *Re Donnini* (2002), 25 OSCB 6225 at para. 123, *Rex Diamond (Div. Ct.), supra*, at para. 3 and *Re Biovail, supra*, at para. 80). No evidence of experts or of Coventree public shareholders was introduced. We did hear evidence from a number of individuals involved in the purchase of ABCP by investors.

[158] In *Rex Diamond (Div. Ct.)* (*supra*, at para. 3), the Court recognized the Commission's expertise when it stated that "whether a material change occurred is a matter that is central to the expertise of the Commission." The same principle applies to the Commission's determination of whether a fact constitutes a "material fact."

(e) Hindsight

[159] The Commission has made clear that assessments of materiality are not to be made with the benefit of hindsight. The Commission stated in *Re AiT* that:

> Instead, we must objectively assess the facts that were available to the AiT Board during the Relevant Period, to determine in all the circumstances whether the three events constituted a material change in the business, operations or capital of AiT that triggered its disclosure obligation under section 75. It is important therefore, to recognize the dangers of hindsight in coming to this conclusion and to be careful not to look at the situation based on what subsequently happened. (*Re AiT, supra*, at para. 228)

[160] Further, in *Re YBM Magnex* (*supra*, at para. 90), the Commission stated that

> "[a]ssessments of materiality are not to be judged against the standard of perfection or with the benefit of hindsight. It is not a science and involves the exercise of judgement and common sense."

[161] Coventree should not be held to a standard of perfection and must not be judged with the benefit of hindsight. In particular, we must not judge the Respondents with the benefit of the hindsight that a market disruption in the ABCP market occurred on August 13, 2007. In our view, we have not so judged the Respondents.

...

[163] ... [T]he business judgement rule does not apply to the determination of whether the Prospectus failed to disclose a "material fact" or whether a "material change" occurred within the meaning of section 75 of the Act. Disclosure decisions under the Act are not sheltered by the business judgement rule.

...

[337] Accordingly, in our view, the DBRS January Release constituted a change in Coventree's business that would reasonably be expected to have had a significant effect on the market price or value of Coventree shares within the meaning of the term material change" in the Act. As a result, we conclude that Coventree was obligated to disclose that material change in accordance with section 75 of the Act on January 22, 2007, the day that Coventree confirmed with DBRS that the DBRS January Release required global style liquidity for CDO related SFA transactions.

[338] Further, by April 25, 2007, Coventree knew that DBRS was applying the DBRS January Release to all credit arbitrage transactions, not just CDO related SFA transactions. Credit arbitrage transactions represented approximately 60% of conduit assets (40% of assets attributed to CDO related SFA transactions and 20% to credit arbitrage transactions not involving CDOs (see paragraph 336 of these reasons)) and approximately 80% of Coventree's revenues for its first, second and third quarters of 2007. In our view, a reasonable shareholder or investor would consider Coventree's inability to carry out any future credit arbitrage transactions important information in making an investment decision with respect to Coventree shares. Even if the materiality of the DBRS January Release was not reasonably apparent to Coventree on January 22, 2007 (which we do not accept), the materiality of that release should have been clear to Coventree by April 25, 2007 (see paragraph 322 of these reasons).

...

[590] In our view, the following changes in Coventree's business or operations had occurred by the close of business on August 1, 2007:

(i) Inability to Issue New ABCP

By August 1, 2007, Coventree sponsored conduits were unable to issue any new ABCP because of the lack of liquidity in the market. As a result, Coventree could not, through those conduits, carry out any traditional securitization transactions and could not purchase assets from its traditional asset providers. That resulted in Coventree being unable to fund the purchase of mortgages from Xceed, one of its important asset providers, on July 30, 2007. Further, Coventree sponsored conduits could not enter into new credit arbitrage transactions because of the lack of liquidity in the market and because of the DBRS January Release. (We recognise, in this respect, that we have previously concluded that the DBRS January Release itself constituted a material change with respect to Coventree.) That meant that by August 1, 2007, Coventree was unable to carry out through Coventree or Nereus sponsored conduits either traditional securitizations or credit arbitrage transactions. Those transactions represented approximately 90% of Coventree's revenues for the period ending June 30, 2007. Further, because Coventree was unable to issue any new ABCP, it could not fund the purchase of maturing ABCP or potential collateral calls, or replace assets that were sold by the conduits to generate cash. In effect, Coventree could not carry on its securitization business because its sponsored conduits could not do any new fundings.

(ii) Difficulty Rolling Outstanding ABCP

By August 1, 2007, Coventree sponsored conduits were having difficulty rolling outstanding ABCP as it matured because of the lack of liquidity in the ABCP market. Coventree knew from conversations with its dealers that the dealers were finding it increasingly difficult to roll Coventree sponsored ABCP and were having to purchase Coventree sponsored ABCP into inventory pursuant to their market-making lines. By August 1, 2007, those dealers were expressing high levels of concern that their marketmaking lines were fully or close to fully extended. The lack of liquidity in the market also meant that a substantial amount of ABCP was being rolled on an overnight basis. That increased the amount of maturing ABCP on the following days. Coventree knew that if any maturing ABCP did not roll, there would be a default. Increased overnight rolls also required Coventree to monitor the liquidity agreements related to A notes, on a daily basis, to ensure compliance with those agreements (see paragraphs 466 and 467 of these reasons). Overnight rolls increased the risk that holders of A notes might lose the benefit of the liquidity agreements. Coventree also knew that the Caisse wished to reduce its holdings of Coventree sponsored ABCP as well as its overall exposure to the ABCP market. While the Caisse supported the ABCP market for the short-term after the August 4, 2007 long weekend, the decision by the Caisse to reduce its holdings had the potential to significantly and adversely affect the ABCP market as a whole, and Coventree's business in particular. By saying that, we are not suggesting that the Caisse's decision to reduce its overall holdings of ABCP constituted a change in Coventree's business. Rather, that was an important factor, known by Coventree, affecting market liquidity for Coventree sponsored ABCP.

The ability of Coventree sponsored conduits to roll maturing ABCP was a critical element of Coventree's business. If there were no purchasers of Coventree sponsored ABCP, there would be a default by its conduits in repaying maturing ABCP regardless of the credit quality of the assets backing that ABCP. Adequate market liquidity and the ability to roll ABCP were essential to a business model that used short-term borrowings (in the form of ABCP) to finance longer-term assets (held by Coventree sponsored conduits or to which those conduits had exposure).

(iii) ABCP Spread Widening

There was a very substantial widening of interest rate spreads for Coventree sponsored ABCP on August 1, 2007 (see paragraph 499 of these reasons). That spread widening was, at least in part, the reason for Coventree calling the August Board Meeting and led Cornish to prepare the Draft Press Release describing the impact of spread widening on Coventree's revenues. While we recognise that by August 1, 2007, spread widening had occurred over only a relatively few days, nonetheless we believe, based on the evidence, that Coventree viewed that spread widening as unprecedented with respect to Coventree sponsored ABCP. Child's e-mail to the Board calling the August Board Meeting indicated that "the markets are going crazy." In addition, spreads on Coventree sponsored ABCP relative to the spreads on bank sponsored ABCP had widened dramatically. Spread widening affected Coventree's revenues and net income as ABCP matured and was rolled at higher interest rates. It also affected the viability of Coventree's securitization business. If spread widening made the cost of funds from issuing ABCP too high, then the return on the underlying assets of a conduit would not be able to support the payment of interest on the ABCP. That meant that Coventree had to also consider whether spread widening had reached a level at which Coventree would not be able to compete for the business of its traditional asset originators (see paragraphs 526 and 527 of these reasons).

While significant spread widening had occurred in the past based on extraordinary events such as the Russian debt crisis (see paragraph 573 of these reasons), there is no question that the spread widening that occurred in the ABCP market by the close of business on August 1, 2007 was unprecedented with respect to Coventree sponsored ABCP and reflected very significant changes in the level of liquidity available in the market.

We reach that conclusion notwithstanding the fact that Coventree concluded that the immediate financial impact of increased interest rate spreads was negligible and had not reached a level of materiality by August 1, 2007. We recognise that increased spreads only affect ABCP as it matures. However, the immediate financial impact of spread widening was only one quantitative consideration in assessing the materiality of spread widening. The qualitative impact of spread widening on Coventree's business also had to be considered.

ABCP was sold as a very safe short-term investment and historically was issued at very small interest rate spreads above CDOR (A notes were typically issued, for example, at one to three basis points over CDOR). Any substantial increase in interest rate spreads could affect the viability of Coventree's business.

(iv) Credit Default Swap Spread Widening

Spread widening with respect to credit default swaps meant that Coventree sponsored conduits were close to triggers for collateral calls on LSS transactions. If collateral calls occurred, the financial impact could be extreme given the high leverage inherent in LSS transactions. Coventree did not have the ability to issue new ABCP to fund collateral calls. The conduits' only source of cash for this purpose came from normal course amortization of transactions and asset sales.

Childs' notes of the August Board Meeting indicate that "we've had unprecedented movement with both spreads + correlation" (see paragraph 559 of these reasons).

It is clear from the evidence that, by August 1, 2007, Coventree, Cornish, Tai and Allan were extremely concerned about the possibility of collateral calls.

(v) Sales of Assets

By July 20, 2007, Coventree was selling conduit assets to generate cash in the conduits. That was a change made by Coventree in its business in response to external events and developments in credit markets. By August 1, 2007, Coventree sponsored conduits had accumulated cash of approximately $188 million that was expected to increase to $610 million by Tuesday, August 7, 2007 (see paragraphs 513 and 667 of these reasons). The sale of assets to generate that cash reduced Coventree's revenue backlog, although we note that Coventree had concluded that the reduction in revenue backlog was not material at that time because of the particular assets that had been sold. In addition, where assets were sold by the conduits to generate cash, there were potential losses on those sales and "negative carry" in terms of the return on the liquid assets held relative to the interest being paid on the affected ABCP (see paragraphs 517 to 520 of these reasons).

[591] In our view, each of the events and developments referred to in paragraph 590 of these reasons, were changes in Coventree's business or operations. Among other changes in its business, Coventree was unable to carry out through its sponsored conduits any traditional securitization transactions or any credit arbitrage transactions and there was increasing difficulty rolling Coventree sponsored ABCP as it matured. Spread widening was beginning to affect Coventree's financial returns but, more important, had implications for the ongoing viability of its business. In response to these developments, Coventree sponsored conduits were selling assets worth millions of dollars to generate cash for possible collateral calls. Coventree sponsored conduits were "perched on" collateral call triggers. In our view, these events and developments were changes in Coventree's business or operations. While external events and developments gave rise to those changes, it is the changes in Coventree's business or operations as a result that form the basis for a potential material change.

[592] *We would add that public shareholders and investors would have been unaware of the changes in Coventree's business or operations referred to in paragraph 590 of these reasons.*

(c) Material Changes Occurred

[593] In our view, the events and developments referred to in clause (i) of paragraph 590 of these reasons constituted changes in Coventree's business or operations that would reasonably be expected to have had a significant effect on the market price or value of Coventree shares. Those events and developments therefore constituted a "material change" with respect to Coventree, within the meaning of section 75 of the Act, that occurred by the close of business on August 1, 2007.

[594] Further and in any event, the events and developments referred to in clauses (i) to (v) inclusive of paragraph 590 of these reasons, taken together, constituted changes in Coventree's business or operations that would reasonably be expected to have had a significant effect on the market price or value of Coventree shares. Those events and developments therefore constituted a "material change" with respect to Coventree within the meaning of section 75 of the Act, that occurred by the close of business on August 1, 2007.

[595] As a result of our conclusions in paragraphs 593 and 594 of these reasons, Coventree was required to forthwith issue a news release on August 2, 2007, and to file a material change report as soon as practicable and in any event within 10 days following that date. Coventree failed to do so. Coventree thereby breached subsections 75(1) and (2) of the Act.

. . .

[610] In our view, there is a real legal question whether a change in a risk to which a business is subject constitutes a change in the business itself that can form the basis of a "material change" within the meaning of the Act. In this respect, it may be that some risks form part of an issuer's business while other risks are properly viewed as outside or external risks not forming part of the business.

[611] The Commission concluded in *Re YBM Magnex* that "facts that give rise to a material risk are material facts" within the meaning of the Act (*Re YBM Magnex, supra*, at para. 87). As a result, material risks were required to be disclosed by YBM in its prospectus and certain of those material risks were not disclosed. The Commission also considered whether the audit suspension by YBM's auditors was a change in the business, operations or capital of YBM within the meaning of the definition of "material change" in the Act. The Commission stated that, in the particular circumstances, "the risk regarding the filing deadline and likely cease trade order constituted a material change." That conclusion was reached, however, based on the auditors' communication to YBM that they would not carry out the YBM audit unless a forensic audit was done. As a practical matter, YBM knew that it would not be able to file audited financial statements by the filing deadline and that, as a result, a cease trade order would be issued by the Commission in respect of YBM securities.

. . .

[616] In the circumstances before us, we are not prepared to conclude that the change in the risk of occurrence of a market disruption in the ABCP market in the days leading up to August 13, 2007, constituted a change in Coventree's business or operations for purposes of the definition of "material change" in the Act. That was an external risk dependent on a complex interaction of market forces and the individual actions of market participants, that were beyond the control and knowledge of Coventree. We do not believe that the obligation to disclose material changes under the Act required Coventree to issue a news release speculating on or attempting to predict whether a market disruption would occur.

[617] At some point, a material risk may, for practical purposes, become a reality. That was the case in *Re YBM Magnex* and *Re Rex Diamond*. In our view, it was not the case in this matter.

[618] We have concluded that there were changes in Coventree's business or operations as a result of the events and developments referred to in paragraph 590 of these reasons that constituted a "material change" within the meaning of the Act. Further, in our view, the imminent risk of a market disruption in the days leading up to August 13, 2007 constituted a "material fact" with respect to Coventree within the meaning of the Act. In our view, however, the change in the risk of occurrence of a market disruption did not constitute a "material change" within the meaning of the Act.

[619] Determining whether a change has occurred in an issuer's business, operations or capital is a different question than determining the materiality of a contingent or speculative event. The Commission has in certain decisions applied the "probability/magnitude test" under U.S. securities law in making determinations as to the materiality of contingent or speculative events (see, for instance, *Re Donnini, supra*, at para. 131, and *Re YBM Magnex, supra*, at para. 92). The Commission stated in *Re AiT*, however, that the probability/magnitude test "is not particularly useful in determining whether a change has occurred, which is crucial in this case" (*Re AiT, supra*, at para. 207, *Re Rex Diamond*,

supra, at para. 202). The question whether a change had occurred in Coventree's business or operations is the crucial question in this case. Further, in determining materiality in this matter, we are applying a statutory definition that requires a determination whether an event or development would reasonably be expected to have had a significant effect on the market price or value of Coventree shares. *In our view, there is no question as to the materiality to public shareholders and investors of the events and developments affecting Coventree and its business by the close of business on August 1, 2007.*

[620] Finally, we note that an issuer is required to disclose material risks in a prospectus and in its MD&A. Section 21.1(3) of the Prospectus Form requires an issuer to "describe any risk factors material to the issuer that a reasonable investor would consider relevant to an investment in the securities being distributed ..." Further, Part 1(a) of Form 51-102F1—*Management's Discussion and Analysis*—requires an issuer to "discuss important trends and risks that have affected the financial statements, and trends and risks that are reasonably likely to affect them in the future ... ." Accordingly an issuer is required to disclose material risks and significant changes in those risks in its MD&A.

. . .

[636] We recognise that Coventree did not have clear or complete information as to what was happening in credit markets in late July and early August 2007 or why. Coventree was striving to obtain as much guidance as possible from the dealers as to market developments and the reasons for them. Further, Coventree was not able to predict, and cannot be expected to speculate on, what dealers, investors or the Caisse might do in terms of purchasing or rolling maturing ABCP. Nor should Coventree be expected to have predicted the market disruption that occurred on August 13, 2007.

[637] Having said that, we have concluded that there were direct changes in Coventree's business as a result of the events and developments that had occurred by the close of business on August 1, 2007 and those changes were material. It is not premature disclosure to disclose those actual events and developments, and their consequences to Coventree's business, even if there is uncertainty as to their causes, future effects, financial impact or duration. An issuer can make appropriate disclosure of relevant events and developments as they exist and have occurred, even if the future is uncertain. An issuer does not subject itself to any liability (as suggested by Coventree) for premature disclosure where the disclosure made relates to events and their consequences that have occurred and is accurate, balanced and appropriately qualified.

[638] Further, in assessing whether changes that had occurred in Coventree's business were material, Coventree had to consider the likely future effects and consequences of those changes on its business, both as a quantitative and qualitative matter. That is not the same as requiring premature disclosure of uncertain future events or predicting future financial performance. It is requiring an assessment of the significant effects and consequences that changes in its business or operations may have going forward. That assessment is inherent in determining whether any change in business is material.

[639] Disclosure in this matter was for the benefit of public shareholders and potential investors in Coventree shares. It was not for the benefit of credit markets and purchasers of ABCP (although they would also have benefited from the disclosure). The potential negative impact of disclosure by Coventree on credit markets or its share price did not justify Coventree's failure to comply with its disclosure obligations under section 75 of the Act.

In dismissing an appeal of *Coventree*, the Ontario Divisional Court in *Cornish v Ontario (Securities Commission)*, below, held that materiality is a highly contextual issue that requires the commission to apply statutory obligations to a particular company in the context of its industry and the market. It further held that the disclosure requirements under the *Securities Act* are not to be subordinated to the exercise of business judgment, and that mandatory disclosure cannot be avoided in circumstances where senior management or directors of a company believed or hoped that things would change. The court held that the test for the determination of material change is objective, and does not depend on the subjective assessment or optimistic personal views of company executives.

Cornish v Ontario Securities Commission

2013 ONSC 1310 (Sup Ct J (Div Ct)) (footnotes omitted)

DUCHARME J:

[1] Coventree Inc. ("Coventree") is an Ontario company that was incorporated in 1998. It became a reporting issuer following an initial public offering on November 15, 2006. At the relevant time, Coventree described itself as a niche investment bank specializing in structured finance. The appellant, Geoffrey Cornish, is a founder, President and a former CEO of Coventree Inc. The appellant, Dean Tai, was also a founder, director and officer of Coventree.

[2] On September 28, 2011, following a 45-day hearing that ran from May 12, 2010 to December 9, 2010, the Ontario Securities Commission ("OSC" or the "Commission") found that the appellants authorized, permitted or acquiesced in Coventree's non-compliance with Ontario securities law, and thereby failed to comply with Ontario securities law pursuant to s. 129.2 of the *Securities Act*, R.S.O. 1990, c. S.5, as amended (the "Act"). The conduct of each of the appellants in contravening Ontario securities law was also found to be contrary to the public interest.

[3] Following a separate hearing on October 26 and 27, 2011 to consider the appropriate sanctions, the Commission issued its sanctions order on November 8, 2011. It publicly reprimanded Mr. Cornish and Mr. Tai and:

(a) required them to resign as a director or officer of any reporting issuer, other than Coventree;
(b) prohibited them from becoming or acting as a director or officer of a reporting issuer for one year; and
(c) levied a $500,000 administrative monetary penalty against each.

[4] The appellants seek to have the September 28, 2011 order and the November 28, 2011 sanctions order set aside, and, in their place, request an order be made dismissing the Statement of Allegations of the Commission dated December 7, 2009 against the appellants.

[5] The appellants challenge the Commission's interpretation and application of its enabling statute. In particular, they challenge the Commission's interpretation and application of the definition of "material change" under the Act, and the Commission's discretionary application of its public interest jurisdiction under s. 127 of the Act. The appellants also

argue that the Commission in its reasons for decision made inappropriate credibility findings as well as other irrelevant and prejudicial findings against them. The appellants characterize these issues as a denial of procedural fairness and a breach of natural justice.

[6] For the reasons that follow, I would dismiss the appeals. The Commission made no error in law and reached a reasonable decision based on the evidence before it.

. . .

V. Were the Commission's Findings That There Were Material Changes Within the Meaning of the Securities Act Reasonable?

(A) Overview

[37] Section 75 requires forthwith disclosure of material changes to a reporting issuer's business, operations or capital. The appellants both emphasize that s. 75 of the *Securities Act* must be read in light of the entire mandatory disclosure regime. Therefore, before considering their specific grounds of appeal, it will be helpful to review: (1) the importance of public disclosure in the regulation of securities markets; (2) the public disclosure requirements under the *Securities Act*; and (3) the proper approach to the determination of when a material change has occurred.

(1) The Importance of Public Disclosure in the Regulation of Securities Markets

[38] One of the central policies underlying the *Securities Act* and its predecessors is the "protection of the investing public through full, true and plain disclosure of all material facts relating to securities being issued." The importance of public disclosure in securities markets cannot be underestimated. Disclosure is fundamental to the fairness of Ontario's capital markets, and to the protective mandate of the Act. The Commission has repeatedly identified disclosure as the cornerstone of securities regulation:

> *Disclosure is the cornerstone principle of securities regulation.* All persons investing in securities should have equal access to information that may affect their investment decisions. *The Act's focus on public disclosure of material facts in order to achieve market integrity would be meaningless without a requirement that such disclosure be accurate and complete and accessible to investors.* [Emphasis added]

[39] In *British Columbia Securities Commission v. Branch*, the Supreme Court of Canada acknowledged the centrality of disclosure to the regulation of the securities industry:

> [A]lthough activity in the securities sphere is of immense economic value to society generally, it must be remembered that participants engage in this licensed activity of their own volition and ultimately for their own profit. In return for permitting persons to obtain the fruits of participation in this industry, society requires that market participants also undertake certain corresponding obligations in order to safeguard the public welfare and trust. *Participants must conform with the extensive regulations and requirements set out by the provincial securities commissions. Many of these requirements are fundamental to maintaining an efficient, competitive market environment in a context where imperfect information is endemic. They are also essential to prevent and deter abuses of such asymmetries of information, and therefore to maintain the integrity of the securities system and protect the public interest.* [Emphasis added.]

[40] Disclosure also acts to enhance the accountability of corporate management, serves to level the playing field such that all investors have access to the same information upon which to make pricing and investment decisions, and contributes to the efficiency of capital markets by permitting investors to target particular securities. The policy of equal access to information that is reflected in the disclosure requirements under the Act has been characterized as the "most fundamental principle of securities regulation."

[41] However, while disclosure is important "[t]oo much disclosure or information overload can be counter-productive" in terms of enabling investors to make informed choices. As the U.S. Supreme Court noted in *TSC Industries, Inc. v. Northway, Inc.*:

> We are aware, however, that the disclosure policy embodied in the proxy regulations is not without limit. … *Some information is of such dubious significance that insistence on its disclosure may accomplish more harm than good.* The potential liability for a Rule 14a-9 violation can be great indeed, and if the standard of materiality is unnecessarily low, not only may the corporation and its management be subjected to liability for insignificant omissions or misstatements, but also management's fear of exposing itself to substantial liability may cause it simply to bury the shareholders in an avalanche of trivial information—a result that is hardly conducive to informed decision making. [Emphasis added.]

Thus, a central tenet of securities law is that disclosure obligations are limited to material matters.

• • •

(3) The Determination of When a Material Change Has Occurred

[45] This is the central question in cases under s. 75 of the Act. A "material change" is defined in s. 1.1 of the Act as including:

> [A] change in the business, operations or capital of the issuer that would reasonably be expected to have a significant effect on the market price or value of any of the securities of the issuer.

[46] The first part of the analysis under s. 75 of the Act requires a determination as to whether a change in the "business, operations or capital" of the issuer has occurred and, if so, when. The second part of the analysis requires an assessment of whether the change was material in the sense that it "would reasonably be expected to have a significant effect on market price or value of the securities."

[47] *In Re YBM Magnex International* (OSC), the Commission found that materiality should be assessed objectively from the perspective of an investor and prospectively through the lens of expected market impact:

> The test for materiality in the Act is objective and is one of market impact. *An investor wants to know facts that would reasonably be expected to significantly affect the market price or value of the securities.* The investor is an economic being and materiality must be viewed from the perspective of the trading markets, that is, the buying, selling or holding of securities. [Emphasis added]

Or as the Commission put it "[t]he materiality standard applicable in this case is an objective test based on reasonable expectation."

[48] The Commission has recognized that the concept of material change involves an exercise of judgment and that "a supercritical interpretation of the meaning of material change does not support the goal of promoting disclosure or protecting the investing public." Thus, a technical interpretation of the language of the Act should not be relied upon to justify non-disclosure of material changes. Importantly, the Commission has recognized that "[i]f the decision is borderline, then the information should be considered material and disclosed."

[49] Assessments of materiality are not to be made against a standard of perfection or with the benefit of hindsight. In *Re AiT Advanced Information Technologies Corp.*, the OSC found that it was unfair to judge the respondents' disclosure decisions on the basis of what subsequently happened:

> Instead, we must objectively assess the facts that were available to the AiT board during the [r]elevant [p]eriod, to determine in all the circumstances whether the three events constituted a material change in the business, operations or capital of AiT that triggered its disclosure obligation under section 75. *It is important therefore, to recognize the dangers of hindsight in coming to this conclusion and to be careful not to look at the situation based on what subsequently happened.* [Emphasis added.]

[50] When a reporting issuer is considering material change disclosure, it must apply an objective test as to the expected market impact as it will not have the benefit of actual market impact information.

[51] Materiality is a highly contextual issue that requires the Commission to apply statutory obligations to a particular company in the context of its industry and the market. No single factor will be determinative of whether a material change occurred:

> Materiality is a question of mixed law and fact, i.e. do the facts satisfy the legal test? Some facts are material on their own. When one or more facts do not appear to be material on their own, materiality must also be considered in light of all the facts available to the persons responsible for the assessment.

[52] In making determinations about materiality, common sense must prevail in assessing the broader factual context, or the "total mix":

> [T]he application of the probability/magnitude test to the investigation by U.S. law enforcement agencies as a discrete event is problematic. In essence, the fact of the investigation was incapable of the application of the probability/magnitude test. Probability could not be determined with perfect certainty. However, this does not mean that a fact cannot meet the test for materiality set out in the Act. *One should not lose sight of the forest for the trees by assessing the materiality of individual facts piecemeal when the broader factual context suggests a risk faced by an issuer. Some facts may be material on their own, while others may only be material in the context of other facts. The probability/magnitude test is useful in assessing the occurrence of a future event, but common sense must prevail. The broader factual context, or total mix, must not be overlooked when the risk facing the company is a current one.* [Emphasis added.]

[53] Since materiality is highly contextual, there is no "bright line" test to determine whether a material change has occurred. That assessment depends on particular circumstances and events. National Policy 51-201, the relevant Commission policy statement, which gives non-binding guidance to reporting issuers such as Coventree, states under

the heading "Materiality Determinations" that many different factors should be taken into account, including the size of the company, the nature of its operations, the volatility of the company's securities, and prevailing market conditions. Accordingly, a single factor such as share price movement will not conclusively determine whether a material change has occurred.

[54] A disclosure obligation arises when the material change actually occurs and, if the financial impact is experienced at a later date, the disclosure obligation is not delayed to that later date. This concept was made clear in the decision of the Supreme Court of Canada in *Kerr v. Danier Leather*:

> It almost goes without saying that poor intra-quarterly results may reflect a material change in business operations. A company that has, for example, restructured its operations may experience poor intra-quarterly results because of this restructuring, *but it is the restructuring and not the results themselves that would amount to a material change and thus trigger the disclosure obligation.* Additionally, poor intra-quarterly results may motivate a company to implement a change in its business, operations or capital in an effort to improve performance. *Again, though, the disclosure obligation would be triggered by the change in the business, operations or capital, and not by the results themselves.* [Emphasis added.]

[55] In addition, the determination of whether a material change has occurred does not require deference to the business judgment of management. On the contrary, the "disclosure requirements under the *Securities Act* are not to be subordinated to the exercise of business judgment." Mandatory disclosure cannot be avoided in circumstances where senior management or directors of a company believed or hoped that things would change. In *Rex Diamond Mining Corp. v. Ontario (Securities Commission)*, this Court confirmed that the test for the determination of material change is objective, and does not depend on the subjective assessment or optimistic personal views of company executives.

[56] The determination of whether a material change has occurred may be assisted by evidence of price and volume fluctuations for a reporting issuer's shares. Thus, in *Rex Diamond*, where the issuer disclosed the material change at a later date by way of news release rather than disclosing it forthwith as required by the Act, there was evidence of share price and volume fluctuations following the disclosure. Additionally, there were accurate rumours in the market before Rex Diamond ultimately disclosed the information, and the share price and volume experienced abnormal fluctuations during that period. The Commission found that both of these market reactions demonstrated that the information was important to the investing public and therefore material.

[57] However, the Commission does not always need evidence of effect on market price to find a material change. As Iacobucci J. stated for a unanimous court in *Pezim:*

> As already mentioned, the present case turns partly on the definition of "material change." … Thus, not all changes are material changes; the latter are set in the context of making sure that issuers keep investors up to date. Consequently, *it would seem wholly uncontroversial that the determination of what information should be disclosed is an issue which goes to the heart of the regulatory expertise and mandate of the Commission*, i.e., regulating the securities markets in the public's interest. [Emphasis added.]

[58] Thus, no issue can be taken with the Commission's statement in this case that "[d]etermining questions such as whether a fact is a material fact, whether a material

change has occurred, the effect of events or developments on the market price or value of securities and the adequacy of disclosure made, are matters squarely within our expertise as a specialized tribunal." The Commission has repeatedly held that, as an expert tribunal, it does not require evidence from experts or investors in order to determine questions of disclosure and materiality. Thus, "such opinion or evidence may be relevant or useful but is not necessary."

[59] Not only is such evidence not necessary, but it may not always be of assistance in a materiality analysis. There are at least three reasons why evidence of historical price and volume fluctuations for a reporting issuer's shares may not always be of assistance in this regard. First, if the reporting issuer is a new issuer, or if the issuer has never disclosed the same type of material change in the past, there may not be any relevant trading data to refer to for the purpose of determining how the market might react to a particular type of information. Second, where disclosure of the material change is limited or not made at all, a review of the market price and trading volume may not assist in the analysis of materiality. Third, if the material change is disclosed by the issuer along with other information, the market reaction to the combined disclosure may not be a reliable indicator of the market impact of the disclosure of one particular piece of information in isolation.

(B) Were the Commission's Findings That There Were Material Changes Within the Meaning of S. 1 of the Securities Act Reasonable?

(1) Did the Commission Err in Applying the "Reasonable Investor Test" to Determine Materiality Instead of the Statutorily Mandated "Market Impact Test"?

...

[65] The short answer to the appellants' complaint is that the Commission clearly recognized and applied the statutory market impact test for materiality. The Commission made repeated references to the proper test, including the following:

> In considering Staff's allegations and in determining materiality for purposes of this proceeding, the principal question we must address is what effect certain facts, events or developments *would reasonably be expected to have had on the market price or value of Coventree shares.* ...
>
> Accordingly, in order for a "material change" to have occurred, there must be "a change in the business, operations or capital" of the issuer and that change *must reasonably be expected to have a significant effect on the market price or value of the relevant securities.* The latter element of that definition is the same objective test for materiality contained in the definition of "material fact." ...
>
> The standard of materiality for both a material fact and material change is the same. A fact or change is considered to be material if it *"would reasonably be expected to have a significant effect on the market price or value" of an issuer's securities. When we refer to "materiality" in these reasons, we are referring to the application of that test.* Clearly, such a fact or change would be important to a reasonable investor in making an investment decision with respect to the relevant securities. [Emphasis added]

[66] The Commission did not only refer to the market impact test in its general discussion of the relevant law; it also specifically applied the test to its analysis of all four particulars, both those found to be substantiated and those that were not.

...

[71] …

We would add that *the test to determine materiality is whether any of the events and developments referred to in paragraph 590 of these reasons, considered separately or together, would reasonably be expected to have had a significant effect on the market price or value of Coventree shares.* Clearly, an event or development that would have that effect would be important to a reasonable shareholder or investor in making an investment decision with respect to Coventree shares. It is clear to us that if Coventree had informed a reasonable shareholder or investor of the facts that:

(a) its conduits were unable to carry out any new securitization transactions, whether traditional securitizations or credit arbitrage transactions;
(b) its conduits were unable to purchase assets from Coventree's traditional asset originators;
(c) its credit arbitrage business, which until very recently had represented approximately 80% of its revenues, was viewed by Coventree as dead or dying;
(d) the business of its wholly-owned subsidiary, Nereus, was no longer viable;
(e) its conduits were unable to issue any new ABCP for any purpose including for buying back maturing ABCP or funding possible collateral calls;
(f) its conduits were having increasing difficulty rolling their maturing ABCP and were doing so only with the reluctant market support of the Caisse de Dépôt et Placement du Quebec (the "Caisse") in rolling its holdings of Coventree sponsored ABCP;
(g) interest rate spreads on Coventree sponsored ABCP had widened to an unprecedented level;
(h) its conduits were "perched on" collateral call triggers;
(i) its conduits were selling assets worth millions of dollars to accumulate cash to fund possible collateral calls;
(j) there was a very substantial supply/demand imbalance in the ABCP market (see paragraph 598 below); and
(k) Coventree had no way of knowing if or when market conditions would return to normal;

that shareholder or investor would have considered that information critically important in making an investment decision with respect to Coventree shares. That means, in our view, that *those events and developments would reasonably be expected to have had a significant effect on the market price or value of Coventree shares.* That is the common sense conclusion in all of the circumstances. [Emphasis added.]

[72] … Rather than parsing a few sentences, taken alone, the Commission's reasons must be read as a whole and in context. When this is done, it is abundantly clear that, throughout its reasons, the Commission analyzed materiality in terms of the market impact test as required by the definition of a material change in s. 1.1. of the Act.

…

[91] The Commission arrived at its conclusions after carefully reviewing extensive evidence, most of which was not in dispute. Also, unlike *Cartaway*, this case turned primarily on direct, rather than circumstantial, evidence. As the foregoing analysis demonstrates, the Commission based its conclusion not on speculation, but on a thorough review of all of the evidence. The evidence that was before the Commission supports its conclusions.

A. Timing of Disclosure

As we saw in *Pezim v British Columbia (Superintendent of Brokers)*, the issuer has an obligation to disclose material changes as soon as practicable, and the notion of "as soon as practicable" takes on a different meaning when an issuer is about to engage in a securities transaction. The directors of the issuer have a positive duty to inquire about material changes and to ensure that any such changes are disclosed prior to the transaction. The Supreme Court of Canada in *Pezim* held that although a duty to inquire was not expressly stated in the statute, an interpretation that there is a duty to inquire as part of the general obligation to disclose material changes helps guarantee the fairness of the market, a key underlying objective of the legislation (*Pezim*, at para 93). Hence, timely disclosure is a fundamental requirement of the continuous disclosure system, aimed at the protection of investors.

B. Probability/Magnitude Test

In some instances, material changes are contingent or uncertain, although directors and officers of the reporting issuer may have some information regarding the possibility of such a change. The probability/magnitude test, imported from the United States, is a method sometimes used by securities regulators to analyze when contingent events like mergers or lawsuits become sufficiently crystallized that they are required to be disclosed as material changes. It requires an assessment of the probability that an event will occur, having regard to all the known or ascertainable facts. It also requires some assessment of the magnitude or significance of the change, in terms of whether the information would be viewed by reasonable investors as important information for making a decision to buy, sell, or continue to hold their securities. A key decision outlining this test is *YBM Magnex*, which held that the test encompasses an assessment of the current value of the information as it affects the price of securities, discounted by the chances of it occurring. *YBM Magnex* was first discussed in Chapter 4 in regard to failure to disclose in the prospectus. The excerpt below discusses material change and the use by securities regulators of the probability/magnitude test in determining whether a change is material such that it should have been reported.

YBM Magnex International Inc
(2003), 26 OSCB 5285

[91] The test for materiality in the Act is objective and is one of market impact. An investor wants to know facts that would reasonably be expected to significantly affect the market price or value of the securities. The investor is an economic being and materiality must be viewed from the perspective of the trading markets, that is, the buying, selling or holding of securities. Price in an open market normally reflects all available information. YBM was not a thinly traded stock. As such, its price more likely reflected the information disclosed to the public market. Full disclosure of adverse information may lower the price but it does not shut out a security from the market.

[92] There was extensive reference to the US law on materiality. The reasonable investor test or substantial likelihood test is found in *TSC Industries, Inc. v. Northway, Inc.*, 426 US 438 (1976) (*TSC Industries*). Generally, for historic information like past financial results or completed business transactions this test frames the materiality

assessment. When facts point to a future event, the US courts have applied the probability/magnitude test; *Basic Inc. v. Levinson*, 485 US 224 (1988). This test analyses the current value of information as it affects the price of securities discounted by the chances of it occurring. This test has been applied by the Commission in *Re Sheridan* (1993), 16 OSCB 6345, and in *Re Donnini* (2002), 25 OSCB 6225.

. . .

[495] On April 19, D&T by phone advised Mitchell, Antes and Abbe Fletman of Wolf, Block (who had been retained as counsel to the Audit Committee) that D&T would not perform any further audit procedures in connection with the 1997 audit. D&T had reached a high level of anxiety. It was concerned that: (1) entities involved in the aforementioned transactions may not exist as legal entities; (2) certain individuals associated with these entities may have ties to organized crime; and (3) the transactions may be bogus and were being used to cover the flow of money between these companies for other purposes. It rejected the Audit Committee's extensive investigation plan as insufficient, requested that an in-depth forensic investigation be performed by outside counsel and an experienced forensic investigation firm, and that YBM management not be involved in the investigation.

[496] D&T further advised the Audit Committee that it would not perform any further audit procedures or services for YBM until the Audit Committee completed its investigation and all matters were resolved to D&T's satisfaction. Upon completion of the investigation, D&T would determine whether it would continue to be associated with YBM, whether it would be able to issue an opinion on YBM's 1997 financial statements, and whether it would continue to be associated with YBM's 1996 financial statements. D&T believed it unlikely that these issues could be resolved by YBM's filing deadline with the securities commissions, which D&T understood to be April 30. In fact, the deadline was May 20.

[497] On April 20, Coulter faxed Mitchell a letter confirming the telephone discussion. It is at this time that staff submit a press release should have been issued disclosing the audit suspension. Mitchell discussed with counsel that if YBM did not get its audit opinion, YBM's shares could be cease-traded. Mitchell relied on counsel's advice that no disclosure was required at this time.

. . .

[518] An issuer is obliged to disclose material changes. That enhances the fairness of the market. The definition of material change acts as a brake on premature and undesirable disclosure. The concept of material change, like that of material fact, requires an exercise of judgement. If the decision is borderline, then the information should be considered material and disclosed. In our opinion, a supercritical interpretation of the meaning of material change does not support the goal of promoting disclosure or protecting the investing public; sections 1.1 and 2.1 of the Act.

[519] The requirement for an annual audit by an independent auditor is intended to provide the public with an independent and objective check on the fairness of the presentation of the company's financial position at fiscal year end. That information is not only crucial to investors in the secondary market but also to an issuer's ability to raise capital. An auditor, while not a guarantor of financial statement accuracy, assumes a special role vis-à-vis the public. There was no disagreement with respect to the crucial role of auditors in public companies.

[520] There was also no disagreement that YBM faced a serious risk if it did not file its audited financial statements by May 20, or obtain an exemption from the filing deadline. Failure to file on time or obtain an exemption would result in the issuance of a cease trade order against YBM's securities.

[521] Was the audit suspension a change in the business, operations or capital of YBM that would reasonably be expected to have a significant effect on the market price or value of its securities? "Business, operations or capital" is not defined in the Act. In *Pezim v. British Columbia (Superintendent of Brokers)*, [1994] 2 SCR 557 at 561-562 (*Pezim*), Iacobucci J noted that: [t]hree elements emerge from [the definition of a material change in the BC legislation]: a) the change must be in relation to the affairs of an issuer, b) in the business, operations, assets or ownership of the issuer and c) material, i.e., would reasonably be expected to have a significant effect on the market price or value of the securities of the issuer … . This case also turns on the meaning of the words "as soon as practicable" … as to when a material change should be disclosed to the public. The timeliness of disclosure also falls within the [BC] Commission's regulatory jurisdiction.

…

[525] We agree with the respondents that the probability/magnitude test is a useful tool in this context, as the issue is the materiality of a discrete event, namely YBM missing its filing deadline and having its securities cease-traded. We believe the potential magnitude of a publicly traded company missing its filing deadline and having its securities cease-traded is self-evident. We are left with the question of what the probability was of not obtaining an audit opinion by May 20 based upon the audit suspension on April 20. Alternatively, even if probability was difficult to determine herein, was the emergence of the present risk regarding the filing deadline and ensuing cease trade order material based on the events of April 19 and 20 as informed by earlier events?

…

[530] The concerns presented to Mitchell and Antes on April 19 which led to the audit suspension and the request for a forensic investigation were extraordinary in nature. This was much more than a disagreement between D&T and management over the application of accounting principles, for example. D&T was concerned about (a) the validity of transactions, (b) whether counterparties to YBM's agreements were legal entities, and (c) organized crime and the possible cover-up of the flow of money.

…

[538] In our opinion, given: (1) the extraordinary nature of the concerns expressed by D&T on April 20; (2) D&T's request for a forensic investigation on April 20; and (3) the fact that D&T advised that it would need to consider whether it was willing to continue being associated with YBM and able to issue an opinion on YBM's 1997 financial statements upon completion of the Audit Committee's investigation, it was probable as of April 20 that YBM would be unable to obtain an audit opinion and make its May 20 filing deadline. Given the events of April 19 and 20, as informed by earlier events, the emergence by April 20 of the risk regarding the filing deadline and likely cease trade order constituted a material change.

[539] The press release was issued approximately 18 days after notice of the audit suspension was provided. Staff contend this was not "forthwith," particularly in light of the ten-day period set out in subsection 75(2) of the Act. We agree with this submission.

[540] For the foregoing reasons, we find that YBM breached subsection 75(1) of the Act by failing to disclose the audit suspension forthwith.

[541] We have found that YBM failed to disclose the audit suspension forthwith and therefore failed to comply with its continuous disclosure obligations under the Act. The press release was issued approximately 18 days after notice of the audit suspension was provided.

The probability/magnitude test is also discussed in *Donnini* in Chapter 8.

C. Disclosure of Significant Acquisition

All reporting issuers are required to file a business acquisition report (BAR) within 75 days after the date of acquisition of a business or related businesses, as determined under NI 51-102, s 8.3.

While all reporting issuers are required to file a BAR within the 75 days, NI 51-102 sets different filing deadlines if the most recently completed financial year of the acquired business ended 45 days or less before the date of acquisition, in which case a reporting issuer must file a BAR within 90 days after the date of acquisition, but a venture issuer has 120 days after the date of acquisition (NI 51-102, s 8.2).

There are several specified "significance tests" in respect of what is defined as a significant acquisition under s 8.3(2), any one of which applies to non-venture issuers:

(2) Required Significance Tests

For the purposes of subsection (1) and subject to subsections (4.1) and (4.2), the significance tests are:

(a) The Asset Test. The reporting issuer's proportionate share of the consolidated assets of the business or related businesses exceeds 20 percent of the consolidated assets of the reporting issuer calculated using the audited annual financial statements of each of the reporting issuer and the business or the related businesses for the most recently completed financial year of each that ended before the acquisition date.

(b) The Investment Test. The reporting issuer's consolidated investments in and advances to the business or related businesses as at the acquisition date exceeds 20 percent of the consolidated assets of the reporting issuer as at the last day of the most recently completed financial year of the reporting issuer ended before acquisition date, excluding any investments in or advances to the business or related businesses as at that date.

(c) The Profit or Loss Test. The reporting issuer's proportionate share of the consolidated specified profit or loss of the business or related businesses exceeds 20 percent of the consolidated specified profit or loss of the reporting issuer calculated using the audited annual financial statements of each of the reporting issuer and the business or related businesses for the most recently completed financial year of each ended before the acquisition date.

There are variations on the tests for venture issuers; specifically, for a venture issuer, the acquisition satisfies either of the significance tests set out if "20 percent" is read as "100 percent" (NI 51-102, s 8.3(1)). There are always variations for venture issuers on the profit or loss test where a loss occurred or is lower than average for the most recent year (NI 51-102, ss 8.3(7), (8)), for situations in which there is a step-by-step acquisition (NI 51-102, s 8.3(11)), and related businesses (NI 51-102, s 8.3(12)).

The business acquisition report must include a statement of comprehensive income, a statement of changes in equity, and a statement of cash flows; a statement of financial position; and notes to the financial statements and the annual financial statements must be audited (NI 51-102, s 8.4).

NI 51-102 specifies when interim financial reports must be filed with a BAR (NI 51-102, ss 8.4(3), (3.1), (4)). The BAR must also include a *pro forma* balance sheet of the reporting issuer as at the date of the reporting issuer's most recent statement of financial position filed, which gives effect, as if it had taken place as of the date, to significant acquisitions that have taken place but are not reflected in the reporting issuer's most recent statement of financial position (NI 51-102, s 8.4(5)). This disclosure must include the underlying assumptions on which the *pro forma* financial statements are prepared and provide a "constructed income statement" where financial year-ends of the reporting issuer and the acquisition are more than 93 days apart from each other, with notes on how it was calculated (NI 51-102, s 8.4(7)).

The objective of the BAR requirements is to allow transparency and comparability in the financial data underpinning the significant acquisition. There are some exemptions for acquisitions reporting, particularly where the financial information is very recent. For example, an exemption to this disclosure requirement is available where the reporting issuer's acquisition is accounted for using the equity method (NI 51-102, s 8.6).

NI 62-103, *The Early Warning System and Related Takeover Bid and Insider Reporting Issuers* (2000, as amended effective 9 May 2016), sets out which particular disclosures are required, as discussed in Chapter 8, Insider Trading.

D. Rumours

Although there is an obligation to disclose material changes, securities regulators have recognized that certain disclosures can be delayed for strategic reasons, if they are filed with the regulator and updates are regularly filed, as discussed above. Even where information is confidential, there are, however, sometimes rumours that a particular change has occurred or is about to occur. The challenge is to ensure that some investors do not receive an unfair advantage from information that has not yet been made public. Regulators have tried to find the appropriate balance between confidentiality and requiring issuers to disclose as a result of rumours circulating in the market.

Confidentiality is also permitted in situations where the material change consists of a decision to implement a change made by the company's senior management, who believe that confirmation of the decision by the company's board of directors is probable. While the Québec *Securities Act* does not require a confidential filing, it does relieve a company from the obligation to disclose a material change if senior management reasonably believes that disclosure would be seriously prejudicial to it and no one has purchased or sold, or will purchase and sell its securities based on the undisclosed information (NP 51-201, *Disclosure Standards*, s 2.2). A company must issue and file a press release once the reasons for not disclosing no longer exist (NP 51-201).

National Policy 51-201, *Disclosure Standards*
In force 2002, as amended effective 31 May 2013

2.2 Confidentiality

(1) Securities legislation permits a company to delay disclosure of a material change and to keep it confidential temporarily where immediate release of the information would be unduly detrimental to the company's interests. For example, immediate disclosure

might interfere with a company's pursuit of a specific objective or strategy, with ongoing negotiations, or with its ability to complete a transaction. If the harm to a company's business from disclosing outweighs the general benefit to the market of immediate disclosure, withholding disclosure is justified. In such cases a company may withhold public disclosure, but it must make a confidential filing with the securities commission. Certain jurisdictions also require companies to renew the confidential filing every 10 days should they want to continue to keep the information confidential.

(2) We discourage companies from delaying disclosure for a lengthy period of time as it becomes less likely that confidentiality can be maintained beyond the short term.

2.3 Maintaining Confidentiality

(1) Where disclosure of a material change is delayed, a company must maintain complete confidentiality. During the period before a material change is disclosed, market activity in the company's securities should be carefully monitored. Any unusual market activity may mean that news of the matter has been leaked and that certain persons are taking advantage of it. If the confidential material change, or rumours about it, have leaked or appear to be impacting the share price, a company should take immediate steps to ensure that a full public announcement is made. This would include contacting the relevant exchange and asking that trading be halted pending the issuance of a news release.

(2) Where a material change is being kept confidential, the company is under a duty to make sure that persons with knowledge of the material change have not made use of such information in purchasing or selling its securities. Such information should not be disclosed to any person or company, except in the necessary course of business.

E. Policy Developments in Respect of Continuous Disclosure

Notwithstanding the convergence of regulatory authority in respect of continuous disclosure and thus a reduction in fragmentation of regulatory requirements, there are still issues in terms of how best to communicate information to the market in a way that is timely and meaningful for a broad range of investors. The IDA Task Force to Modernize Securities Legislation identified this challenge as one of the most important for modern capital markets. One of its background research studies made the following observations.

Janis Sarra, "Modernizing Disclosure in Canadian Securities Law: An Assessment of Recent Developments in Canada and Selected Jurisdictions"

Research Study for the Task Force to Modernize Securities Legislation (29 May 2006) at 35-36, 37, 39, 119 (footnotes omitted), online: <http://www.tfmsl.ca/docs/V2(1A)%20Sarra.pdf>

iii. Fragmentation of Information

Under most jurisdictions in Canada, primary market disclosure is contained in several documents, notably the prospectus and the AIF. For specialized offerings, such as the prompt offering prospectus, the information is disclosed in the prospectus, the AIF, the financial statements and any material change reports, which can lead to fragmentation of information, particularly with the increase in web-based disclosure. In secondary market disclosure, information is disclosed in financial statements, AIFs, MD&As, proxy circulars and material change reports, often located in different places. The titles of documents do not provide a clear indication of the material contained in the documents. There is overlap, duplication and fragmentation. One example is governance disclosures; board information can be located in proxy circulars whereas audit committee disclosures are in the AIF. While there should be cross-referencing of such disclosures, this is not always clear to investors. This fragmentation is costly to market participants and creates inefficiencies in the system.

The different statutory standards of disclosure between primary and secondary market disclosure means that information is located in different places during different periods of the issuers' distribution and continuous disclosure life cycles, often inaccessible to retail investors.

One possible option for a modernized securities system is to locate disclosure in one "living" document that investors can access at any point in the life cycle of the issuer, whether it is making an offer of securities to the market or meeting its continuous disclosure obligations. The current system means that investors do not necessarily get all the information that is referenced in required disclosure, and that they must spend additional time and resources to receive those disclosures, and then have the time, resources and capacity to analyze and apply that information to their investment decisions. Another possibility … is to have "one-click full access" electronic disclosure.

• • •

For the investor, the accessibility of information is critically important. Scholars, practitioners and regulators have identified the problems faced by two types of investors—retail and institutional—and have considered how to reconcile the different information needs of these investor types. Yet with the increased involvement of retail investors in the market, both directly through on-line facilities and through managed investment funds, the nature of investor interests lies more along a continuum of interest, information and sophistication, rather than a two-tier dichotomy between retail and institutional investors. Institutional investors also run along that continuum in that while they are sophisticated investors, they have different interests, time horizons and priorities in their market activity, and hence may have different disclosure needs. For example, institutional investors interested in longer term investments view governance disclosure as an important aspect of the disclosure regime, as these investors are looking at long timelines of investment and are interested in the long term strategic plans of the issuer. These investors use governance and other disclosures as the basis on which to exercise "voice" in activities of the issuer. Full, true and plain disclosure must be tailored to meet a broad range of investor needs.

• • •

In thinking about how disclosure could be recast to meet the objectives of full, plain and true disclosure, one needs to conceptualize documents that contain different parts. While the plain language may be necessary for unsophisticated retail investors or those investors without the time or resources to analyze all disclosure documents, disclosure requirements must nevertheless continue to provide analysts, institutional investors, regulators and other market participants with the level of detail that they require to make informed judgments about their investment advice. Detail, however, does not mean that disclosure must necessarily be overly complex. Full, true and plain can mean complete, correct and readily understood information for all market participants. The 1998 Review of the *OSA* found that effective disclosure is the timely, meaningful and relevant dissemination of information to the market in a form that is capable of being understood by investors who are reasonable persons acting reasonably.

. . .

The SEC is promoting a new electronic platform or business reporting language for delivering disclosure of the numbers in financial statements; a reporting language that can perform fast and flexibly, reducing cost and inefficiency. The platform is called eXtensible Business Reporting Language (XBRL) and it is being developed by an international consortium of 400 major companies, organizations and government agencies. The SEC has introduced a voluntary XBRL filing program. XBRL is also being tested in Europe and other jurisdictions, and there is now "XBRL Canada" as a member of the international nonprofit consortium promoting the use of this electronic business reporting language.

XBRL attaches electronic tags to elements of information; the tags indicating particular items on financial statements. The electronic tags are standardized, regardless of the XBRL-enabled software application that is used to read the XBRL data file. The tagged data can then be pulled out of the comprehensive electronic disclosures, allowing easy and improved access to information. The tagging allows investors to draw out the information they are interested in examining on a selective basis. The tagging also allows software programs to calculate ratios and perform other analyses without having to re-input financial data, providing enhanced access to information for analysts and other financial intermediaries.

... Rather, with interactive data on XBRL, each investor is able to order up his or her own custom model with "just a few clicks of the mouse." The information is called up instantly to one page, removing the necessity of culling through data where originally entered. If the platform is as easy and accessible as the SEC believes, this could revolutionize electronic disclosure.

The IDA Task Force to Modernize Securities Legislation in its final report, *Canada Steps Up* (2006), made a series of recommendations regarding how disclosure requirements could better meet investors' needs.

IDA Task Force on the Modernization of Securities Law, *Canada Steps Up*
Final Report (2006)

Recommendations

12. The Task Force encourages securities regulators to work to make disclosure documents more effective by improving the method by which information is made available to investors to enhance the penetrability and comprehensibility of that information.

13. The Task Force recommends that the search features of SEDAR be expanded to allow for more detailed searches of disclosure documents, and the taxonomy for disclosure documents filed on SEDAR be further refined to reduce the dependence on the use of "catch-all" categories.

14. The Task Force recommends the adoption of a full "access equals delivery" system. Specifically, we recommend that all requirements for the delivery of disclosure documents

be abolished and, instead, that all disclosure documents be required to be filed on SEDAR and on the issuer's website, and that the elimination of any requirement to "deliver" a document would render investor consent to "access equals delivery" unnecessary.

15. The Task Force recommends that MERIT (Model for Effective Regulatory Information Transfer) be thoroughly considered and that securities regulators encourage and facilitate the use of XBRL, information layering and interactivity within electronic disclosure documents, all as detailed in the technical white paper included at Schedule 4-A.

16. The Task Force recommends that, until MERIT and the use of XBRL can be implemented, paper-based disclosure be presented in layered format with each layer being of increasing depth and complexity thereby allowing investors to determine the depth of disclosure which is informative for them.

17. The Task Force recommends that financial literacy be treated as a matter of national priority.

18. The Task Force recommends the creation of a national coordinator of public and private sector investor education initiatives.

19. The Task Force recommends that further study be undertaken by capital markets stakeholders to design programmes that ensure that the objective of financial literacy as a national priority is achieved.

20. The Task Force recommends that insiders of an issuer be obliged to give at least two business days' advance notice of their intention to sell some or all of their securities in the issuer.

The Expert Panel on Securities Regulation, in its final report in January 2009, proposed draft national securities legislation (*Draft Securities Act*), which took a more principles-based approach to securities regulation, including a core set of objectives and proposed creation of a national securities regulator and more streamlined continuous disclosure requirements (Expert Panel on Securities Regulation, *Creating an Advantage in Global Capital Markets, Final Report and Recommendations*, January 2009). As discussed earlier in this text, the draft legislation was not upheld in a constitutional challenge, the Supreme Court of Canada finding that "[t]he *Securities Act* as presently drafted is not valid under the general branch of the power to regulate trade and commerce under s. 91(2) of the *Constitution Act, 1867*": *Reference re Securities Act*, 2011 SCC 66, [2011] 3 SCR 837 at para 134. Participating provincial regulators and governments are now considering a proposed provincial Capital Markets Act (PCMA). However, the expert panel's earlier observations in respect of risk-based regulation and disclosure continue to be helpful in considering further refinement to the continuous disclosure system.

Expert Panel on Securities Regulation, *Creating an Advantage in Global Capital Markets*

Final Report and Recommendations (January 2009) at 26

D) Risk-Based Securities Regulation

We believe that the resources of a securities regulator should be allocated to market participants, such as issuers and securities firms, and investment products that pose the greatest risk to the economy generally and the investor in particular. We understand that this risk-based approach to securities regulation is used by many securities regulators in Canada. For example, the Ontario Securities Commission and those of several other provinces use a risk-based approach to select prospectuses for more detailed review and to select reporting issuers for a continuous disclosure review. They also use this approach to determine the frequency of compliance reviews of advisors and fund managers as well as to determine which enforcement matters will be pursued through full investigations.

The Expert Panel's *Draft Securities Act* (DSA) would impose continuous disclosure requirements on reporting issuers and give the regulator the ability to review such disclosure. The timely disclosure obligations are aimed at fostering fairness and confidence in markets by ensuring that disclosure of material change is provided in a timely manner. The approach taken to the regulation of continuous disclosure in the DSA aligns with NI 51-102 continuous disclosure obligations for reporting issuers and NI 81-106 continuous disclosure requirements for investment funds. As a result of the introduction of NI 51-102 and NI 81-106 addressing proxy solicitation, the approach taken in the DSA is to move substantive proxy related requirements from the DSA to the rules and to give the proposed national securities commission the rule-making authority to implement these requirements. Below is the proposed DSA provision in respect of continuous disclosure requirements (Expert Panel, Commentary on *Draft Securities Act*).

IV. CHAPTER SUMMARY AND FURTHER PUBLIC POLICY CONSIDERATIONS IN THE CONTINUOUS DISCLOSURE REGIME

The continuous disclosure system is a critically important aspect of Canadian capital markets, aimed at providing transparent and efficient access to information about issuers. NI 51-102 is aimed at bringing greater clarity and harmonization to continuous disclosure reporting. The two elements of the system are timely reporting on a periodic basis, as required for financial statements, MD&As, and AIFs, and timely reporting of material changes that affect the issuer.

Although recent regulatory changes have been aimed at enhancing the transparency of financial reporting as part of an effort to increase confidence in capital markets, there are still considerable barriers to meaningful participation. As the number of national and multilateral instruments increase, it is harder for investors to discern whether the issuer is meeting its disclosure obligations. The complexity of reporting instruments also means that the information is increasingly inaccessible to smaller investors who do not have the time or resources to scrutinize disclosures and who must rely on industry professionals to give advice. Yet those professionals are faced with multiple conflicts of interest in their analysis and promotion of financial instruments, easily the subject of another full chapter.

Another issue is the continuing debate regarding increased codification of disclosure requirements. British Columbia has long advocated moving toward less codification and more simplified outcomes-based disclosure, based on a combination of rules and principles. The rest of Canada is considering the potential for a more principles-based system, but equally has moved closer to the US model of highly codified requirements. It is unclear as to whether there will be common ground such that all of the objectives of securities legislation are met with some uniformity across Canada, although the agreement by securities regulators on national instruments on continuous disclosure offer positive signs for the future convergence of disclosure standards. This issue of disclosure is complicated by global moves toward convergence with the United States, shifts that may ultimately dictate the outcome of public policy debates in Canada if it is to remain competitive in international capital markets. Part of this debate also involves consideration of a shift to an integrated disclosure system that is issuer-based as opposed to the current largely transaction-based regime and consideration of whether proportionate regulation, whereby junior issuers may have differently focused disclosure requirements, should be adopted. Regulators nationally through their collaboration in the CSA are seriously considering these issues as the next evolution in securities law development.

A final public policy consideration is the focus of the securities regime on the protection of property of equity investors. In this respect, it is a regulatory function that assists in promoting economic growth and productive activity, but its narrow construction as consumer protection legislation for securities investors must be borne in mind in considering its scope. One way that shareholders may be protected is through a regime that provides sufficient warning of corporate transactions that may adversely affect their holdings, such that they can decide whether to exercise their voice or exit in response. Materiality disclosure is one of the tools that offers this protection. Corporate officers, accountants, or other agents of the issuer may meet the letter of the continuous disclosure regime without meeting its spirit and intent by providing investors with disclosure such that they can make informed choices. Short-term advantage gained from a liberal interpretation of "non-material" can cause a loss of investor and market confidence, and have negative financial consequences for the issuer. In addition to the investor empowerment argument for disclosure, it is equally important to recognize that not requiring disclosure of these harms as part of the securities regime creates *ex ante* incentives on the part of corporate officers to externalize the costs of some activities. Externalization results in the activity either not being reported or reported as benefits to the issuer.

"Material" in most securities and corporate law statutes refers to events or transactions that may affect share or property value. Thus harms that are externalized need not be costed on the issuer's balance sheet and are not required to be reported as material because they allegedly do not have a material impact on shareholder value. Harms considered to be part of the public law regime such as the infractions of labour standards or environmental law are thus not part of the securities law regime except where particular events have impacted on shareholder value. Given this definition of "material," investors are frequently not exposed to the social and economic costs of other harms being perpetrated by the issuer unless they are likely to influence the bottom line. The bottom line in this sense is short-term financial results, as opposed to long-term sustainability of the issuer. However, there is some recent indication that the definition of materiality is expanding. As discussed earlier in this chapter, there are the relatively new disclosure requirements on the AIF form under NI 51-102. The issuer must disclose social and environmental policies that are fundamental to the issuer's operations, such as policies regarding the issuer's relationship with the environment or with the communities in which it does business or human rights policies, including an obligation to describe steps that the issuer has taken to implement the policies. The form also requires the issuer to disclose risks to the issuer, including environmental and health risks and economic or political conditions that would be most likely to influence an investor's decision to purchase securities (Form 51-102F2). This requirement may begin to open up disclosure and enhance accountability of issuers for decisions that affect more than narrow financial reporting. It will be interesting to see how these requirements are interpreted by both issuers and securities regulators.

As in Canada, there has been considerable debate internationally regarding what constitutes a material transaction. Regulations that define material in relation to market price or value may exclude other material information that will influence investors' decision-making. Absent a universal shared understanding of this notion, many transactions that are considered material by some investors or jurisdictions, but not others, are not clearly disclosed. It means that securityholders are unlikely to have confidence in the quality of disclosure; in turn, this lack of confidence acts as a deterrent to the effective operation of capital markets. The Global Reporting Initiative, the International Corporate Governance Network, and other cross-border organizations advocate more fulsome disclosure of material risks to particular transactions. At the heart of these debates is how to create meaningful ongoing disclosure while ensuring that the costs of disclosure are not prohibitive.

An issuer should be obligated to disclose all costs associated with its activities so that investors, creditors, and other stakeholders can assess their continued investments. Such costs are quantifiable using IFRS and economic indicators. Securities law is highly integrated with other public law protections such as consumer protection, occupational health and safety law, employment standards and environmental protection. To treat these laws separately, or cast some activity as private and the rest as public law issues, ignores the highly integrated public/private regulatory regime in which issuers operate internationally.

V. FURTHER READING

Lin, Tom CW. "Reasonable Investor(s)" (2015) 95 BUL Rev 461.

Lin, Tom CW. "A Behavioral Framework for Securities Risk" (16 April 2012) 34 Seattle UL Rev 325, online: <http://ssrn.com/abstract=2040946>.

Dhir, Aaron A. "Shadows and Light: Addressing Information Asymmetries Through Enhanced Social Disclosure in Canadian Securities Law" (2008) 47 Can Bus LJ 435.

Black, Julia. "Involving Consumers in Securities Regulation," Research study for the IDA Task Force on the Modernization of Securities Regulation (2006).

Smith, Dimity Kingsford. "Importing the E-World into Canadian Securities Regulation," Research study for the IDA Task Force on the Modernization of Securities Regulation (2006).

Condon, Mary & Anita Anand. "Weather, Leather, and the Obligation to Disclose: Kerr v. Danier Leather Inc" (2005) 44:4 Osgoode Hall LJ 727.

CHAPTER SEVEN

Securities Regulators and Corporate Governance

I. INTRODUCTION

In addition to the regulation of market activity, Canadian securities regulators are increasingly involved in the internal governance of reporting issuers. These recent initiatives with respect to corporate governance can be categorized as both investor confidence and investor participation measures. This chapter examines the relationship between securities law and corporate law in four critically important areas: the proxy solicitation process, corporate governance disclosure, officer certification requirements, and audit committee independence. All of these aspects of corporate and securities law are related to the disclosure system and the statutory objectives of investor protection and efficiency of the capital markets. Hence, the governance aspects of securities law must be read and understood in conjunction with the requirements of the continuous disclosure system, discussed in Chapter 6, as well as general corporate law requirements. The chapter ends with a brief discussion of how securities law has developed to regulate some governance aspects of income trusts.

In the past decade, Canadian securities regulators have been engaged in a series of reforms to securities law that are aimed at increasing the transparency of issuer decisions regarding effective governance and enhancing the participation rights of securityholders. Increased codification of governance was driven in part by the corporate and securities scandals in the United States, the subsequent enactment of the *Sarbanes-Oxley Act* (discussed in Chapter 3), and the Securities and Exchange Commission's (SEC's) aggressive move into the area of corporate governance and increased enforcement. Given the number of large Canadian-based issuers that are cross-listed on US exchanges and the existence of the multijurisdictional disclosure system (MJDS) discussed in Chapters 4 and 6, there has been considerable pressure on regulators to ensure that securities law requirements in Canada continue to align with the US requirements in order that Canadian-based issuers have continued cost-effective and timely access to US capital markets. Many Canadian-based issuers are dependent on access to the larger US market and, hence, are anxious to meet US requirements in order to provide investors with confidence in their governance and oversight activities. Given the wholesale move to regulate corporate governance by US securities regulators, Canadian regulators have followed suit.

Although Canada has not had the colossal corporate failures that the United States experienced with Enron, WorldCom, Lehman Brothers, and other scandals, there have been several cases that have raised questions about the sufficiency of regulation and enforcement of Canadian securities law, such as Livent, YBM Magnex, Bre-X, Nortel Networks, and Sino Forest. Hence, securities regulators have moved toward both enhanced enforcement of existing law and increased codification of the governance and oversight aspects of issuer conduct. At the same time, however, Canadian securities regulators have considered a move toward more principles-based regulation of corporate governance, away from the degree of codification seen in the United States.

In some instances regulators have also funded initiatives designed to educate investors on governance issues and their relationship to investor protection. For example, in 2001 the OSC established the Investor Education Fund (IEF) to develop and promote independent financial information, programs, and tools to help consumers make better financial and investing decisions. The IEF is funded by settlements and fines from OSC enforcement proceedings, and began as a non-profit organization before being merged with the OSC Investor Office in 2014 (<http://www.osc.gov.on.ca/en/NewsEvents_nr_20141126_investor-protection.htm>). In May 2004, Québec's minister of finance and the Autorité des marchés financiers (AMF) announced the launch of a new fund, later named as the *Fonds pour l'éducation et la saine gouvernance*, translated as the Education and Good Governance Fund (EGGF). The EGGF supports projects focusing on investor protection and education, the promotion of good governance, and the advancement of knowledge in all areas associated with the AMF's mission. The fund consists of a reserve from the AMF, made up of various fees collected and administrative penalties imposed on those individuals and issuers who fail to comply with regulatory requirements. Since its inception in 2004, the EGGF has allocated over $29 million to 191 projects. Projects in 2014 included: corporate governance and management control systems, organizational governance, and the ethical alert process within regulated organizations (<http://www.lautorite.qc.ca>).

This move into the corporate governance market by Canadian securities regulators is somewhat contested. The issue of what appropriately belongs to corporate law and what is properly within the purview of securities regulation is not always clear. Although the relatively new governance requirements will likely ensure that there is greater transparency and protection for securityholders, it raises a fundamental question of whether regulators are improperly regulating what ought to be the domain of corporate law statutes and the courts that supervise their compliance. As you read through this chapter, consider the issues that arise from the recent regulatory requirements by Canadian securities regulators that touch on key aspects of corporate governance.

We first address the proxy solicitation process. Recall that we discussed an issuer's disclosure obligations with respect to information circulars in Chapter 6. Here, we discuss the governance aspects of the proxy process and the rules set under both corporate and securities law, in part aimed at enhancing participation rights for beneficial securityholders. Next, we examine the certification obligations under securities law as a governance measure aimed at providing investors with enhanced confidence in the accuracy and timeliness of the issuer's financial disclosures. Third, we examine provisions for audit committee independence, in particular, a national instrument that codifies the roles and responsibilities of audit committees of reporting issuers as a key gatekeeping function. Fourth, we look at the national policy and instrument on corporate governance and assess whether the move by securities regulators into monitoring of various aspects of corporate governance practice is a positive or negative development in the securities law regime. Corporate law, like securities law, is an intensely rich and deep area of the law and it is important to remember that the four issues discussed in this chapter are only a small part of a much broader system of corporate law in Canada. The chapter ends with a discussion of income trusts as a form of business entity that does not fall within the ambit of corporate law, but for which some aspects of governance are regulated by securities law where the income trust is a distributing entity.

II. PROXY SOLICITATION AND CORPORATE GOVERNANCE

In Chapter 6 we learned of the issuer's obligation to communicate with investors and to provide them with information on a periodic and timely basis. The information circular and proxy process allows securityholders to make informed decisions as to whether to purchase, sell, or continue to hold their securities. It can also allow investors to exercise their rights to participate through voting and shareholder proposal mechanisms, granted to them by both corporate and securities law statutes. The sale of shares by investors if they are dissatisfied with the overall governance and direction of the issuer is called "exit," whereas the exercise of securityholder rights through the proxy process is often referred to as "voice." Both have a governance role in that they may signal to directors and officers that there is a lack of confidence in the oversight or management of the issuer's business or operations. However, exit as a governance tool is imprecise and can send mixed messages to managers regarding their governance activities. In contrast, the exercise of participation rights by securityholders can serve as a direct communication device to directors regarding investors' confidence in the current management or strategic planning of the issuer. Where institutional investors are actively exercising their participation rights, it can also serve as a signalling device for retail investors who may not have the time or resources to fully review the activities of the issuer.

In the mid-1990s, the Senate Standing Committee on Banking Trade and Commerce commented on the importance of the governance aspects of the proxy solicitation process, setting the stage for regulatory reform of both corporate and securities law.

Canada, Senate, *Report of the Senate Standing Committee on Banking, Trade, and Commerce on Corporate Governance*
(Ottawa: Public Works and Government Services, August 1996)

Effective corporate governance is an ongoing process built on the foundation of continuing involvement by shareholders in the affairs of the corporation and with one another. Shareholders must be informed. They must conduct continual research on the company.

They must review policies, prospects and decisions. When questionable decisions are made, they must indicate their concern. When good ideas surface that the company should review, shareholders must prod the company to consider them. The company, for its part, must assess the preference of shareholders and the views of the market, which is its best critic, on whether value is being realized. This process is founded on continual communication. Shareholders must speak with many people in the market. They must speak with each other to learn whether their views are widely shared or are a minority opinion. They must be able to speak with the company, as individuals or as a group. When a problem surfaces, they must be able to discuss their concerns; when a corporate proposal is made that demands opposition, they must be able to act. The Canadian proxy rules … create substantial barriers to this kind of continued, informal communication among shareholders. As a result, they reduce the effectiveness of the oversight process. The result is detrimental to shareholders, corporations and the integrity of the process itself. The reforms proposed in the directorate's discussion paper would rectify the most significant problems with the rules and thereby spur a healthier, more-effective and, importantly, less contentious governance process. The current proxy rules were designed to protect investors from being misinformed, misled or manipulated by proxy solicitation undertaken either by management or by outside investors. They accomplish this task by requiring soliciting parties to prepare, distribute and file a dissident proxy circular and to make detailed disclosure about his or her organization, investment intent and trading history. In addition, each specific communication, whether it be a letter, advertisement or speech, triggers a dissident proxy circular obligation. In contentious, heated proxy contests for control waged between a determined raider and an entrenched management team, there is conceivably an argument that such dissident proxy circular requirements make sense. Even in these situations, though, one can make a strong argument that the rules interfere in a fundamental way with freedom of speech and with investors' rights to communicate freely about property that they own. However, the impact of the rules on contentious control situations is not my concern here. The reason that the present laws have a deep impact on corporate governance lies in the fact that they do not solely apply to such extreme situations. Instead, they apply to virtually any communication among investors about a significant issue of corporate policy. The key factor in the rules that leads to this result is the definition of the term "solicitation." Solicitation is defined to involve any communication that can reasonably be calculated to result in the giving, withholding or revoking of a proxy. This means, as a practical matter, that virtually any expression of opinion by one shareholder to another can be construed to be solicitation. The rules were written with one reason; the intent was sound. The idea was to prevent unscrupulous shareholders and management from front-running the solicitation process. …

In our view, the changes to the rules that have been proposed by the directorate are an entirely appropriate redress to the present situation. Disinterested investors under the proposed rules would be allowed to communicate freely with fellow shareholders without the problems associated with preparing a dissident proxy circular. We believe that this proposed change would have a profound effect on efficiency of the corporate governance process and would free us and other institutions to communicate informally with one another about the companies in which we invest. It is our belief that changing the proxy rules in the manner contemplated by the directorate would eventually lead to a higher level of corporate governance.

Information circulars and proxy solicitation requirements engage both securities law and corporate law. Canadian corporate law requires that an annual general meeting (AGM) of shareholders be convened, at which shareholders elect directors, receive annual financial statements, and appoint the company's auditor. The AGM is held annually, although different statutes have provisions such that the period between annual meetings can be up to a maximum of 15 months (see e.g. *Canada Business Corporations Act*, RSC 1985, c C-44 (CBCA), s 133).

While corporate officers manage the operations, and directors engage in oversight of the issuer, shareholders' fundamental power is to express their displeasure with the governance or accountability of the issuer by appointing new directors or auditors at the AGM. Shareholders also have the right to participate in special general meetings, and to vote on issues such as changing the capital structure of the issuer or other "fundamental" changes.

In addition to corporate law requirements in respect of shareholder rights and the company's obligation to hold annual and special general meetings, a reporting issuer has additional obligations under securities legislation. While corporate law is aimed at enabling the corporation to operate, setting out the respective rights and obligations of directors, officers, and shareholders, securities law is fundamentally concerned with the need to protect the integrity of capital markets by ensuring that investors' rights to information and exercise of voting are not compromised. Specifically, shareholders who are not able to attend general meetings are granted a voice in decisions at the meeting through the proxy process. Management's obligation is to ensure that shareholders are notified of their right to participate in the meeting by proxy and given the opportunity to exercise this right. As discussed in Chapter 6, the securityholder, by signing a proxy form, authorizes someone to vote on the shareholder's behalf at the meeting, thus allowing the shareholder a "voice" at the meeting. The proxy solicitation provisions are also designed to provide an alternative to exit—that is, selling shares if securityholders are dissatisfied with the governance of the company.

Professor Hillary Sale has commented on the relationship of proxy provisions to securities regulators in the context of US securities law. Note that Canadian regulators, like the SEC, are engaged in much more than regulating issuers' disclosure.

Hillary A Sale, "Of Corporate Suffrage, Social Responsibility and Layered Law: Teaching Basic Business Law Through Federal Securities Law"

(2000) 34 Ga L Rev 809 at 817-18

Thus, the SEC is not just a "disclosure regulator." Through its regulations and the no-action process, the SEC actually arbitrates the balance of power between shareholders and management, and even between some shareholders and others. Unlike much of the default state corporate law, these rules are mandatory in nature. Thus, shareholders in publicly held companies who want to engage in a debate with management and other shareholders about the company's policies must comply with section 14 of the Securities Exchange Act and the accompanying regulations. Finally, the proxy material allows for consideration of whether, by occupying much of the field, the federal government has impeded the development of state law, such as that on shareholder voting and company bylaws and charters.

Proxies also serve an important role as an ex ante governance mechanism or a "consultative" approach to shareholder/manager interactions. The possible issues cover a broad spectrum, from shareholder attempts to access the ballot to change the board of directors from classified to non-classified, to a shareholder who wants the company to stop importing pâté de foie gras because of the force-feeding techniques used on the geese whose livers become the pâté.

Thus under both corporate and securities legislation, proxy and proposal provisions provide a means for shareholders to express their preferences and to exercise some limited control rights over the strategic direction of the corporation. They are the principal mechanisms through which shareholders review the stewardship of the issuer. Proxy voting is the exercise of control rights, either on a proactive or default control basis. Regulation of management proxy solicitation is the recognition of the strong normative influence of corporate managers. It tempers their conduct by setting basic standards of what they are required to communicate, including disclosure of conflicts of interest, and at least some transparency aimed at encouraging investors to exercise their proxy voting power in an informed manner. Management must solicit proxies for each meeting called and provide a proxy form to all shareholders. It must issue an information circular that provides detailed information as to the purpose for which the proxy is being solicited. The reporting issuer must also file a copy of any information circular in accordance with securities regulations.

The genesis of the current proxy system was a 1965 report on securities legislation in Ontario, dubbed the Kimber Report after its chair (*Report of the Attorney General's Committee on Securities Legislation in Ontario* (Toronto: Queen's Printer, 1965)). The Kimber Report made a strong case for greater accountability and participation rights for securityholders. In particular, it sought to ensure that securityholders could vote against management proposals, not solely support them or not have their voice counted, as was the practice at the time (Kimber Report, para 6.12). The findings of the Kimber Report formed the underpinning for the expansion of proxy rights and obligations under modern securities law. Currently, all Canadian securities legislation includes mandatory proxy solicitation provisions. These provisions specify how securityholders communicate a wish to vote for or against proposals that are included in a notice of annual general meeting or a special general meeting. In respect of elections of directors and the appointment of auditors, proxy-holders can either vote in favour of the appointment of directors proposed by management or auditors or withhold their votes.

Canadian securities law requires management to solicit proxies in order to ensure that investors are advised of their ability to participate and are given the opportunity to exercise their proxy rights. Management solicitation must occur for every annual general meeting and special meeting that the issuer calls, and the proxy must be very explicit regarding the scope of authority sought.

Given the nature of proxy rights, the provisions in securities and corporate law statutes overlap in their requirements. In some instances, securities legislation recognizes and addresses this overlap by relieving a reporting issuer from complying with the proxy requirements if the issuer is complying with the proxy requirements contained in the law of the jurisdiction in which the issuer carries on business or is incorporated, so long as those requirements are substantially similar to the securities law requirements that would otherwise apply; hence compliance with the proxy requirements of corporate law is deemed compliance with the requirements of securities law (e.g., Ontario *Securities Act*, RSO 1990, c S.5 (OSA), ss 88, 121; British Columbia *Securities Act*, RSBC 1996, c 418 (BCSA), s 119). It is important to consider securities legislation, corporate law, and national instruments in determining whether or not the issuer has complied with proxy circular and solicitation requirements. In Chapter 6 we discussed the proxy and information circular requirements under NI 51-102, *Continuous Disclosure Obligations* (2004, as amended 2015). The information circular is required to provide background information such that investors can exercise their proxy rights on an informed basis. NI 51-102 is aimed at bringing transparency and continuity to the proxy provisions of securities laws.

In addition to management's obligations under corporate and securities statutes to issue and disseminate proxy circulars, securityholders may wish to communicate with one another in order to influence the governance of the issuer or to influence the outcome of a particular issue or proposed vote. Hence, securityholders can also solicit proxies, and the rules governing such solicitations are highly codified. Unlike management, which issues the circular at the expense of the company, proxy solicitation undertaken by securityholders is paid for directly and can be very costly.

The definition of what constitutes a proxy solicitation has been contested over the years because of the significant implications of such a determination. If shareholder communication is found to be a proxy solicitation within the meaning of corporate or securities legislation, costly dissident proxy solicitation requirements are triggered. Legislative amendments have relaxed these definitions somewhat to allow increased communication among securityholders without activating the proxy solicitation requirements, such as CBCA amendments in 2001, which were aimed at increasing the voice aspect of the shareholder relationship (*Canada Business Corporations Regulations*, SOR/2001-512, *Canada Gazette*, online <http://canadagazette.gc.ca>). The principal amendments were aimed, in part, at enhanced shareholder participation, including permitting corporations to have electronic shareholder meetings and voting through the use of new technologies, new provisions for shareholder proposals, and revised proxy rules aimed at facilitating shareholder communication (CBCA, s 132). The following excerpt explains the significance of these amendments for proxy provision.

Janis Sarra, "The Corporation as Symphony: Are Shareholders First Violin or Second Fiddle?"
(2003) 36 UBC L Rev 403

The most recent amendments to the CBCA were aimed at removing impediments to shareholder communication and thus promoting shareholder activism and accountability. Prior to 2001, most forms of communication to a shareholder could be deemed to be a solicitation (CBCA, s. 147(c) [RSC 1985, c C-44], prior to the 2001 amendments). Solicitation was defined to include: "the sending of a form of proxy or other communication to a shareholder under circumstances reasonably calculated to result in the procurement, withholding or revocation of a proxy," a provision now repealed. Any solicitation required a dissident proxy circular to be issued and circulated to all shareholders, an extremely expensive and time consuming process.

Solicitation has now been redefined to allow broader communication without triggering dissident proxy requirements under the CBCA, including a public announcement by a shareholder of how the shareholder intends to vote and the reasons for that decision, or a communication for the purposes of obtaining the number of shares required for a shareholder proposal. CBCA, ibid., s. 147. The Regulations further codify solicitation, specifying that solicitation does not include a public announcement that is made by a speech in a public forum; or a press release, an opinion, a statement or an advertisement provided through a broadcast medium or by a telephonic, electronic or other communication facility, or appearing in a newspaper, a magazine or other publication generally available to the public (s. 67, Regulations). A person may now solicit proxies without sending a dissident's proxy circular, if the total number of shareholders whose proxies are solicited is fifteen or fewer. There is a further exception for solicitation by "public broadcast," where a person may solicit proxies without sending a dissident's proxy circular if the solicitation is conveyed by public broadcast, speech or publication (s. 150(1.1), (1.2)). The new communication provisions will allow shareholders that were previously distanced by proxy solicitation prohibitions, to communicate and build support for particular governance strategies. The proxy requirements of corporate and securities statutes frequently overlap, often with express statutory language specifying that compliance with the proxy requirements of one is deemed compliance with the other (See, for example, Ontario *Securities Act*, RSO 1990, c. S.5, as amended, ss. 116-119.) [Note: Section 118 was repealed since this article was written: SO 2009, c 18, Schedule 26, s 15].

In *Re Pacifica Papers Inc*, [2001] BCJ No 1714 (QL) (CA), the British Columbia Court of Appeal dealt with the issue of proxy requirements in the context of lockup or support agreements in a negotiated merger transaction. A lockup agreement in this context is a promise by a securityholder to support a proposal of the issuer and is a means whereby the issuer can secure support for an initiative from a key securityholder. Cerberus, the largest shareholder in Pacifica, holding 18 percent of its shares, appealed a lower court approval of a plan of arrangement under which each Pacifica shareholder would receive 2.1 Norske shares or 1 Norske share and $7.50 for each Pacifica share. Cerberus opposed the plan, arguing that the process to obtain shareholder approval was illegal and that Pacifica shareholders would not receive maximum value for their shares. The lower court had held that the arrangement was fair and reasonable. The court found that the proxies were solicited in a manner that contravened the *Canada Business Corporations Act*, but concluded that this solicitation was a technical non-compliance and insufficient for the judge to refuse his discretion to approve the arrangement. As you read the excerpts below from both the BC Supreme Court and the BC Court of Appeal, consider what they are saying about support agreements committing proxies to vote in favour of the arrangement and about the timing of when information circulars need to be sent.

Re Pacifica Papers Inc
[2001] BCJ No 1484 (QL) (SC)

[86] Mr. Nystrom and Cerberus contend that the support agreements made between Norske and ten of Pacifica's larger shareholders were obtained by Pacifica in contravention of the CBCA. As indicated, the support agreements are commitments to give proxies to

vote in favour of the Arrangement that were made prior to the completion of the Agreement on March 25th. In seeking the support agreements, Pacifica was soliciting proxies. This is said to have contravened s. 150(1) of the CBCA which is said to have prohibited the solicitation of any proxies before the information or proxy circular, and a notice of the shareholders meeting, were distributed to the shareholders on May 8th. The contention is that the contravention of the CBCA rendered the shareholders' vote invalid and that is fatal to the approval of the Arrangement.

[87] Pacifica maintains that there was no contravention of the CBCA in obtaining the support agreements or the proxies for Norske and that the Arrangement ought to be approved in any event.

[88] It is important to understand that there is no basis on which it can be said that those who signed the support agreements were not sufficiently informed. What Mr. Nystrom and Cerberus contend is that the agreements obtained by Pacifica undermined the shareholders meeting and rendered the vote a foregone conclusion. But they would have to accept that the result would have been no different in that regard if there had been no support agreements but the same proxies had been given after the proxy circular had been distributed. Indeed, it seems to me, that if their position on the point is sound, it may result in nothing more than the convening of a second meeting of the shareholders following a second round of proxy solicitation with respect to which the current complaint could not be raised.

[89] Section 150 of the CBCA provides:

> 1) A person shall not solicit proxies unless
>
> a) in the case of solicitation by or on behalf of the management of a corporation, a management proxy circular in prescribed form, either as an appendix to or as a separate document accompanying the notice of the meeting, or
>
> b) in the case of any other solicitation, a dissident's proxy circular in prescribed form stating the purposes of the solicitation is sent to the auditor of the corporation, to each shareholder whose proxy is solicited, to each director and, if paragraph (b) applies, to the corporation.
>
> • • •
>
> 3) A person who fails to comply with subsections (1) and (2) is guilty of an offence and liable on summary conviction to a fine not exceeding five thousand dollars or to imprisonment for a term not exceeding six months or to both, whether or not the body corporate has been prosecuted or convicted.

A "proxy" and a "form of proxy" are defined in s. 147 as follows:

> "form of proxy" means a written or printed form that, on completion and execution by or on behalf of a shareholder, becomes a proxy; [Note: The language has changed since this judgment to read: "'form of proxy' means a written or printed form that, on completion and execution or, in Québec, on signing by or on behalf of a shareholder, becomes a proxy."]
>
> "proxy" means a completed and executed form of proxy by means of which a shareholder appoints a proxyholder to attend and act on his behalf at a meeting of shareholders .... [Note: The language has changed since this judgment to read: "'proxy' means a completed and executed or, in Québec, signed form of proxy by means of which a shareholder appoints a proxyholder to attend and act on the shareholder's behalf at a meeting of shareholders."]

[90] Pacifica says that s. 150(1) cannot be interpreted as prohibiting Pacifica's solicitation of the support agreements for Norske prior to the mailing of a proxy circular. It says that would require the addition of the words "prior to or concurrently with the solicitation" at the end of the subsection which Parliament did not see fit to add. Pacifica maintains that proxy solicitation is permitted before a proxy circular is sent to a shareholder whose proxy is solicited providing a circular is at some time sent with a notice of a meeting.

[91] This court considered a section of the Companies Act, 1973 (BC) c. 18 that was worded materially the same in *Re Ardiem Holdings Ltd.* (1975), 61 DLR (3d) 725, reversed on other grounds (1976), 67 DLR (3d) 253. The issue was not whether solicitation prior to the delivery of a proxy circular was prohibited but rather whether, where a circular had been distributed, it was necessary to distribute a copy whenever proxies were subsequently solicited. It was held that it was not necessary, but in considering s. 177(1) of the Act the learned chambers judge said at pp. 730-31:

> The argument turns on the use of the word "is" in conjunction with the word "sent" … . In my view, the plain meaning of s. 177(1), although it is a little clumsily phrased, is this: that as a condition precedent to management being lawfully able to solicit proxies an information circular must be sent, either as an appendix to or as a separate document accompanying the notice of the meeting, by prepaid mail to every member of the company, etc. I think the meaning to be plain enough and management in the present case sent out an information circular as required.

[92] The issue may have been somewhat different, but this is a considered view of essentially the same wording by a judge of this court who concluded that the distribution of an information circular was a condition precedent to soliciting proxies. I take a condition precedent to mean something that must be done before, or at least at the same time as, the solicitation occurs to render it permissible, and I would be hard pressed not to follow this court's interpretation.

[93] In view of what was said in *Ardiem Holdings*, I could not give s. 150(1) the interpretation for which Pacifica contends, although the section could be better worded. The meaning may have been clearer if the words "has been" were employed instead of the word "is," but it seems to me that the interpretation for which Pacifica contends is at odds with what must be the obvious purpose of the section—shareholder protection. Shareholders must be given the statutory prescribed information about a transaction upon which they are to vote, and the notice of a meeting to be convened for that purpose, before their proxies, are solicited.

…

[95] Nonetheless, I find that there was a contravention of s. 150(1).

[96] The question then is whether, as Mr. Nystrom and Cerberus maintain, the contravention of s. 150(1) is fatal to the approval of the Arrangement. Pacifica says that the remedy for the contravention is limited to a prosecution under s. 150(3), but I do not consider the provision for a summary conviction proceeding precludes a civil remedy. Pacifica then says that the contravention should not in the circumstances be permitted to defeat the Arrangement.

[97] In my view, it is necessary to consider first whether the contravention of s. 150(1) rendered the shareholders' vote invalid and then whether it renders the Arrangement unfair in any event.

[98] With respect to the first, it seems to me that it was clearly open to all of the shareholders to give or withhold their proxies regardless of whether they signed a support agreement. That is because the agreements were clearly unenforceable. Quite apart from whether there was any consideration given by Norske, which appears to be open to question, all of the agreements were illegal. They were the product of an unlawful solicitation prohibited by the CBCA. Norske had no recourse that I can see against any shareholder who, upon receiving Pacifica's information circular, chose not to give its proxy.

[99] At least in a legal sense, the proxies can only then have been given by the shareholders in the exercise of their right to vote their shares. The votes cast were accordingly valid. It is said that some or all of the shareholders who signed a support agreement may have felt compelled to give their proxies, but there is no evidence to that effect, and they were in fact under no legal compulsion to do so. Given that the support agreements, as the subject of an unlawful solicitation, were of no force or effect, I consider that the inference, in the absence of any evidence to the contrary, must be that the proxies were given because the shareholders were content to vote for the Arrangement after the information circular was distributed and they had the opportunity to consider it. The solicitation did not render the shareholders' vote invalid.

An appeal from this judgment was dismissed, with the BC Court of Appeal finding that the judge did not err regarding the finding of the violation of the CBCA or when he concluded that the arrangement was fair and reasonable. With respect to the lower court's findings on the interpretation of s 150(1) support agreements, the Court of Appeal made the following observations.

Re Pacifica Papers Inc
[2001] BCJ No 1714 (QL) (CA)

[11] Although I am in general agreement with the Reasons of the learned Chambers judge, I would express two reservations. The first reservation is with respect to his conclusion that Pacifica was in breach of s. 150(1) of the Act which provides:

> 150(1) Soliciting proxies—A person shall not solicit proxies unless
> (a) in the case of solicitation by or on behalf of the management of a corporation, a management proxy circular in prescribed form, either as an appendix to or as a separate document accompanying the notice of the meeting, or
> (b) in the case of any other solicitation, a dissident's proxy circular in prescribed form stating the purposes of the solicitation is sent to the auditor of the corporation, to each shareholder whose proxy is solicited, to each director and, if paragraph (b) applies, to the corporation.

[12] The learned Chambers judge held that the words "is sent" following s-s. (b) in s. 150(1) are to be interpreted as meaning "has been sent," so as to require compliance with either s-s. (a) or (b) of s. 150(1) before proxies may be solicited. Counsel for the appellants contend that the section, properly construed, requires that any management proxy solicitation must be sent concurrently with the management circular and the notice

of meeting. In other words, proxies may not be solicited unless and until the other documents specified in the section are sent to shareholders.

[13] It is unnecessary for the disposition of this appeal to express any firm view on the correctness of the judge's interpretation. However, as presently advised, the learned Chambers judge's interpretation, and the position contended for by the appellants, appear to import into s. 150 a restriction on proxy solicitation that the language, on a plain reading, does not bear.

[14] In any event, whether his interpretation of that section is correct or not, the learned Chambers judge did not err in concluding that the alleged contravention of s. 150(1) was not fatal to the exercise of his discretion to grant approval of this arrangement.

[15] The second reservation I would express is with respect to the learned Chamber judge's finding that those shareholders who signed support (or lockup) agreements could not be required to vote for the arrangement because the support was obtained illegally. It was correct to say that those shareholders who signed support agreements could not be required to vote for the arrangement, but it seems to me that the reason for that would be that proxies are always revocable, rather than any alleged illegality. The judge's inference that the proxies were given because shareholders were content to vote for the arrangement after receipt of the information circular that was distributed, and they had an opportunity to consider it, is therefore one that I would not be prepared to interfere with.

[16] Apart from those two caveats, I am, as I have said, in general agreement with the Reasons of the trial judge, and I expressly agree with the conclusion he reached.

QUESTIONS

1. On what basis does the Court of Appeal disagree with the lower court in its interpretation of s 150?
2. Are you persuaded that the courts arrived at the appropriate outcome in finding that a violation of proxy solicitation rules occurred but proceeding to approve the plan of arrangement? Why or why not?
3. If the Court of Appeal was not deciding the question on the basis of this reasoning, why include such *obiter* statements in the judgment?
4. The Court of Appeal held that proxies under lockup agreements are always revocable and those who signed could not be required to vote for the arrangement, and thus found that this approach was better than finding they were not binding due to illegality. Do you agree?
5. What would be the effect of the recent amendment to the CBCA making lockup agreements enforceable on the reasoning in the BCSC decision in *Pacifica*?

In 2001, amendments to the CBCA relaxed the rules relating to proxy solicitation. Similar amendments to the Ontario *Business Corporations Act*, RSO 1990, c B.16 (OBCA) came into force in 2007. These amendments permit a dissident shareholder to solicit proxies without preparing and sending an information circular to shareholders if the solicitation is, in the prescribed circumstances, conveyed by public broadcast, speech, or publication. Although corporate law exempts these types of solicitations, dissident shareholders of reporting issuers governed by that legislation were unable to take advantage of the exemptions because there was no corresponding exemption from the proxy solicitation and information circular provisions of NI 51-102.

In 2008, NI 51-102 and its companion policy and forms were amended to align securities regulation with the CBCA. The amendments to NI 51-102 added a new exemption from the information circular requirements for certain proxy solicitations made to the public by broadcast, speech, or publication, and provide guidance in NI 51-102CP on what constitutes a solicitation to the public. The exemption from the information circular requirements for certain proxy solicitations made to the public by broadcast, speech, or publication generally corresponds to the exemption in s 150(1.2) of the CBCA. The amendments to s 9.5 of NI 51-102 extend the existing exemption to a person or company that solicits proxies and complies with substantially similar requirements of the laws under which the relevant reporting issuer is incorporated, organized, or continued, expanding the exemption from just issuers.

In Chapter 6, we discussed how most securityholders today are beneficial, as opposed to registered, securityholders and how continuous disclosure obligations under NI 54-101, *Communication with Beneficial Owners of Securities of a Reporting Issuer* (2003), 26 OSCB 2641 (as amended February 2013), are aimed at enhancing access to information for beneficial securityholders. NI 54-101 also encourages participation of non-registered beneficial owners in the proxy process, and is aimed at remedying previous problems associated with beneficial owners trying to use the proxy process. The following excerpts by Janis Sarra and Stuart Morrow, respectively, discuss some of the barriers to participation that shareholders have faced in their efforts to exercise proxy voting rights.

Janis Sarra, "The Corporation as Symphony: Are Shareholders First Violin or Second Fiddle?"
(2003) 36 UBC L Rev 403

iii. Missing Refrains: De Facto Exclusion of Smaller Investors

One disturbing factor in the new "score" is the risk of diminution of smaller investors' ability to exercise "voice." The advent of book-entry or book-based securities record systems means that the Canadian Depository for Securities and other depositories are frequently the registered holder of share certificates. The introduction of computerized purchase and sale records and use of centralized depositories has assisted capital markets and reduced the transaction costs of trading. Yet there have been problems with the ability of beneficial shareholders whose shares are registered under the depository to exercise voting rights and survive challenges to the validity of proxies when they attempt to vote on their own behalf (see for example, *Re Coral Gold Corporation* [1999] BCJ 22 (BCSC) where the court held that the corporation was not required to provide a list of beneficial shareholders. See also *Fama Holdings Ltd. v. Powertech Industries Inc.* [1997] BCJ No. 994 (BCCA) and *Vella-Zarb v. Canhorn Chemical Corp.* [1996] OJ No. 2495 (Ont. CJ)). Often small retail investors do not appreciate that their status is that of beneficial as opposed to registered shareholder.

There is a tension between the need to have a form of proxy that protects the integrity of the shareholder voting process and the litigation over alleged defects in form of proxy that consume considerable resources and act as a serious deterrent to exercise of shareholder voice (*Langset v. Langtec Capital Corp.* [1997] BCJ No. 137 (BCSC); *Re Sepp's Gourmet Foods Ltd.* [2002] BCJ No. 33 (BCSC), reversed [2002] BCJ No. 289 (BCCA), application for leave to appeal dismissed [2002] SCCA No. 144; *Ambassador Industries v. Camfrey Resources Ltd.* [1991] BCJ No. 1073 (BCSC); *Value Investment Corp. v. Caldwell Gundy Inc.* [1989] BCJ No. 1680 (BCSC); *Pressello v. Venture Pacific Development* [2001] BCJ No. 2617). This has serious and as yet unresolved challenges for any increased shareholder democracy. The recent CSA National Instrument on Communication with Beneficial Owners of Securities of a Reporting Issuer and delivery of documents by electronic means is aimed at increasing shareholder communication, allowing for enhanced delivery of documents via the internet and facilitating the use of electronic communication in the proxy solicitation process (NI 54-101). It is likely to counter balance some of the deterrent effects of the registry system in regard to shareholder participation, but in itself is not sufficient to address these problems.

Stuart Morrow, "Proxy Contests and Shareholder Meetings"
(2003) 36 UBC L Rev 483

On July 1, 2002, the Canadian Securities Administrators ("CSA") implemented National Instrument 54-101 *Communication with Beneficial Owners of Securities of a Reporting Issuer* ("NI 54-101") and simultaneously rescinded National Policy 41 *Shareholder Communication* ("NP 41"). NP 41 had been adopted in 1987 to address the concern that a growing proportion of public company shareholders who no longer held their stock in registered form were literally "unknown" to the issuer and hence, unable to be contacted by the issuer. The procedures under NP 41 were meant to assure both issuers and their shareholders of a reliable mechanism through which shareholders who did not object to being identified as beneficial holders of the issuer's stock ("NOBOs") would receive proxy materials and other shareholder information distributed by the issuer. Beneficial owners who wished to remain anonymous ("OBOs") could still elect to do so.

The industry's experience with NP 41 was varied. Industry professionals such as market intermediaries, financial institutions, brokerage houses and institutional investors were able to adapt to changing rules and put internal procedures in place to ensure that their clients' interests were safeguarded. However, the experience among smaller, retail investors was quite different. The fundamental distinction between "registered" and "beneficial" shareholders is lost on most retail (typically individual) investors. The relative complexity of completing proxy forms and returning those to brokerage houses or other intermediaries, within tight time periods, to have their votes recorded or to give them the opportunity to appear and be heard at shareholder meetings was widely misunderstood. Beneficial shareholders' confusion with the NP 41 rules and related corporate and securities proxy regulations was widespread and constant, much to the exasperation of corporate secretaries and transfer agents, to say nothing of the beneficial shareholders who often found themselves being denied access to meetings or, if admitted, being denied the right to vote at the meeting. …

The recent MRRS Order *In the Matter of Bradstone Equity Partners, Inc. et al.*, [2002] BCSCD No. 472. is an example of the practical application of the principles enunciated in both NI 54-101 and NP 11-201. In the decision, four parties to a plan of arrangement were permitted to save on relatively significant printing and mailing costs by making the joint information circular available electronically to shareholders, subject to a detailed summary being mailed to all shareholders and printed copies of the full circular being provided on request. The Order reflected regulators' creative application of the principles of NP 11-201 in circumstances where the prior solicitation of shareholder consents to receipt of materials electronically would have been impractical.

Fundamental to the exercise of shareholder rights under both corporate and securities legislation is that those rights are only exercisable by or on behalf of *registered* shareholders. Issuers are only bound to recognize as its shareholders those persons recorded on its share register or who either derive their rights from the registered shareholder (i.e. those who can establish the chain of title, or "connect the dots" so to speak, from the registered shareholder to the beneficial shareholder) or who can demonstrate an entitlement to have their names entered on the share register. NI 54-101 not only facilitates the delivery of proxy-related materials to beneficial shareholders, but it also allows for issuers to send materials directly to NOBOs, thereby according beneficial shareholders similar recognition as their registered counterparts.

The distinction between registered and beneficial shareholders has subtle implications. The case of *Fama Holdings Ltd. v. Powertech Industries Inc.*, [1997] BCJ No. 994 (BCCA) provides a good illustration of the confusion that can arise in the administration of proxies voted through the book-based system. A brokerage firm held about 2.2 million shares of the subject company's stock, some 300,000 of which it held directly as a registered shareholder and the balance being held by it by two depository companies in which it participated. The brokerage purported to vote substantially all the shares held by it for client accounts on the basis of the two omnibus proxies provided by the depository corporations, having neglected that part of the shares to be voted were in registered form. The proxies submitted by it were held to be valid as it was able to establish that it had not voted more shares than it was entitled to vote directly (the registered shares) or by proxy at the meeting.

A common misconception is that a beneficial shareholder who has himself appointed as his own proxyholder, by filling in his own name in lieu of management's nominee on the form of proxy, will be put in the same position as a registered holder at the meeting. In most circumstances, that may work out to be the case, *provided* the form of proxy contains a grant of discretionary authority to deal with other business at the meeting (a right that is *not* statutorily required to be granted in a solicited proxy), and has not otherwise been completed such that the proxyholder will be bound on how to vote at the meeting. The proxyholder has no choice but to execute the instructions completed on the proxy and to be bound by any other restrictions contained in the form of proxy. A registered holder has discretion to decide how to vote right up to the time the question is put to the meeting—the beneficial shareholder, acting as his own proxyholder may not have the same freedom if there are voting restrictions on his proxy.

Although the scope of NI 54-101 does not address the preservation of a beneficial shareholder's rights at a meeting, the new instrument dramatically improves the procedures for delivery of proxy-related information to non-objecting beneficial owners (NOBOs) and objecting beneficial owners (OBOs). The obligation of intermediaries under NI 54-101 to provide reporting issuers with NOBO lists on request creates transparency in the beneficial ownership of the issuer, and also permits a reporting issuer to communicate directly with its non-objecting beneficial shareholders. The direct communication afforded by the instrument is a fundamental change from National Policy 41, *Shareholder Communication* (expired 30 June 2002 (2002), 25 OSCB 3361) and represents a marked improvement of the shareholder communication process. NI 54-101 has been amended several times, most recently February 11, 2013, to clarify notification obligations to beneficial shareholders. Form 54-101F1 sets out the explanation that is to be given to beneficial shareholders regarding their rights to information and voting.

National Instrument 54-101, *Communication with Beneficial Owners of Securities of a Reporting Issuer*, Form 54-101F1, *Explanation to Clients and Client Response Form*
As amended effective 1 January 2011

Note: Terms used in this Form have the meanings given to them in National Instrument 54-101. The use of this Form is referenced in sections 1.1, 3.2, 3.3, 3.4 and 3.5 of National Instrument 54-101.

Explanation to Clients

[Letterhead of Intermediary]

Based on your instructions, the securities in your account with us are not registered in your name but in our name or the name of another person or company holding your securities on our behalf. The issuers of the securities in your account may not know the identity of the beneficial owner of these securities.

We are required under securities law to obtain your instructions concerning various matters relating to your holding of securities in your account.

Disclosure of Beneficial Ownership Information

Securities law permits reporting issuers and other persons and companies to send materials related to the affairs of the reporting issuer directly to beneficial owners of the reporting issuer's securities if the beneficial owner does not object to having information about it disclosed to the reporting issuer or other persons and companies. Part 1 of the client response form allows you to tell us if you OBJECT to the disclosure by us to the reporting issuer or other persons or companies of your beneficial ownership information, consisting of your name, address, electronic mail address, securities holdings and preferred language of communication. Securities legislation restricts the use of your beneficial ownership information to matters relating to the affairs of the reporting issuer.

If you DO NOT OBJECT to the disclosure of your beneficial ownership information, please mark the first box in Part 1 of the form. In those circumstances, you will not be charged with any costs associated with sending securityholder materials to you.

If you OBJECT to the disclosure of your beneficial ownership information by us, please mark the second box in Part 1 of the form. If you do this, all materials to be delivered to you as a beneficial owner of securities will be delivered by us. [*Instruction: Disclose particulars of any fees or charges that the intermediary may require an objecting beneficial owner to pay in connection with the sending of securityholder materials.*]

Receiving Securityholder Materials

For securities that you hold through your account, you have the right to receive proxy-related materials sent by reporting issuers to registered holders of their securities in connection with meetings of such securityholders. Among other things, this permits you to receive the necessary information to allow you to have your securities voted in accordance with your instructions at a securityholder meeting. [*Optional: Revise this paragraph, if appropriate, to state that objecting beneficial owners will not receive materials unless they or the relevant issuers bear the costs.*]

In addition, reporting issuers may choose to send other securityholder materials to beneficial owners, although they are not obliged to do so.

Securities law permits you to decline to receive securityholder materials. The three types of materials that you may decline to receive are:

(a) proxy-related materials, including annual reports and financial statements, that are sent in connection with a securityholder meeting;

(b) annual reports and financial statements that are not part of proxy-related materials; and

(c) materials that a reporting issuer or other person or company sends to securityholders that are not required by corporate or securities law to be sent to registered holders.

Part 2 of the client response form allows you to receive all materials sent to beneficial owners of securities or to decline to receive the three types of materials referred to above.

In *Hastman v St Elias Mines Ltd*, 2013 BCSC 1069, in the context of an oppression application under s 227 of the *Business Corporations Act*, SBC 2002, c 57 (BCA), the BCSC discussed misrepresentations in a dissident shareholders' circular, proposing the election of five nominees as directors at the AGM. At a meeting with the chair, prior to the AGM, counsel for the petitioners urged the chair to accept the proxies. The chair decided not to accept the proxies. The dissident shareholders did not change the circular and ultimately obtained in excess of 90 percent of the proxy votes in favour of their candidates. At the AGM, the chair was asked to accept the proxies obtained on the basis of the dissident circular, and she confirmed her previous decision not to accept them. The dissident shareholders alleged oppression and sought a declaration setting aside the AGM and an order requiring a new meeting and elections. The dissident shareholders also alleged a violation of NI 54-101. As you read through the excerpt, consider the interrelationship between corporations legislation, securities legislation, and the national instrument addressing the communication with beneficial shareholders.

Hastman v St Elias Mines Ltd
2013 BCSC 1069

[13] St. Elias Mining Ltd. is a publicly traded company incorporated under the *BCA*. It has 110 registered shareholders and about 7,500 beneficial shareholders. The majority of the shareholders are retail investors and many are resident in Alberta, Saskatchewan, and Manitoba.

[14] St. Elias Mining Ltd. is subject to the policy of the TSXV. Policy 3.1: "Directors, Officers, Other Insiders & Personnel and Corporate Governance," is applicable to the issues in this application. … [Excerpts omitted.]

[15] The petitioners, Gilby Hastman and Darcy Hastman, are registered and beneficial shareholders of St. Elias Mining Ltd. They live in Alberta where they operate other businesses. The former has been very active in the facts underlying this application, and I will refer to him below as Mr. Hastman.

[16] Some time in or about 2012 there was considerable dissatisfaction among shareholders with the performance of St. Elias Mining Ltd. and its management. The stock price has fallen recently. There is an allegation that management has been hiding a gold discovery, and, unfortunately, there are allegations about threats of personal violence between shareholders.

. . .

[22] On December 10, 2012, a group of dissident shareholders sent out a circular to shareholders; published on SEDAR on December 12, 2012. I reproduce the relevant parts of that document as follows:

> The Concerned Shareholders believe that the Company's future is in jeopardy if the Management Nominees are elected at the AGM. The Concerned Shareholders strongly believe that management of the Company needs to be changed and have lost confidence in the ability of the Current Directors to maximize shareholder value while preserving the Company's resources, for the following reasons:
>
> . . .
>
> The Concerned Shareholders have nominated the following Dissident Nominees for election as directors of the Company at the AGM:
>
> Gllby Len Hastman;
> Darcy Kim Hastman;
> Ted E.R. Rutherglen;
> James E. Rainbird; and
> Richard Alexander Defreitas

. . .

[46] I will consider, first, whether the dissident circular contains material misrepresentations. I will then consider the petitioners' claims of oppression.

Material Misrepresentation

[47] The dissident circular provided the information upon which proxy voters exercised their votes. What is in dispute is whether this information contains material misrepresentations.

[53] …

. . .

> [61] In sum, the important aspects of the test for materiality are:
>
> i. Materiality is a question of mixed law and fact, determined objectively, from the perspective of a reasonable investor;
>
> ii. An omitted fact is material if there is a substantial likelihood that it *would* have been considered important by a reasonable investor in making his or her decision, rather

> than if the fact merely *might* have been considered important. In other words, an omitted fact is material if there is a substantial likelihood that its disclosure would have been viewed by the reasonable investor as having significantly altered the total mix of information made available;
>
> iii. The proof required is not that the material fact would have changed the decision, but that there was a substantial likelihood it would have assumed actual significance in a reasonable investor's deliberations;
>
> iv. Materiality involves the application of a legal standard to particular facts. It is a fact-specific inquiry, to be determined on a case-by-case basis in light of all of the relevant considerations and from the surrounding circumstances forming the total mix of information made available to investors; and
>
> v. The materiality of a fact, statement or omission must be proven through evidence by the party alleging materiality, except in those cases where common sense inferences are sufficient. A court must first look at the disclosed information and the omitted information. A court may also consider contextual evidence which helps to explain, interpret, or place the omitted information in a broader factual setting, provided it is viewed in the context of the disclosed information. As well, evidence of concurrent or subsequent conduct or events that would shed light on potential or actual behaviour of persons in the same or similar situations is relevant to the materiality assessment. However, the predominant focus must be on a contextual consideration of what information was disclosed, and what facts or information were omitted from the disclosure documents provided by the issuer.

[emphasis in original]

[54] As can be seen in the above (also para. 69 in *Sharbern*), the onus to prove materiality lies with the party that is alleging materiality, in this case the respondents.

[55] I turn next to the evidence on the allegations. Does it support the respondents' allegations that the dissident circular contains material misrepresentations?

...

[62] I conclude that a reasonable shareholder would have considered it important to know whether two out of five candidates nominated by the dissidents could not hold office if they were elected. In this case, they could not stand for nomination, for reasons of their own doing; they had not complied with the time limits for filing consents. In my view, there was a substantial likelihood that the disclosure of this fact would have been viewed by the reasonable investor as having significantly altered the "total mix" of information made available to him or her. It may not have changed the decision of shareholders, but there is, in my view, a substantial likelihood it would be significant to the deliberations of shareholders.

...

[69] I conclude that a reasonable shareholder would consider it important in deciding how to vote to know whether the nominees being presented met the requirements of TSXV policy. At a minimum a shareholder would consider it important to know the existence of the TSXV policy and its potential application to the group of nominees, if elected. Further, the application of that policy would be something a reasonable shareholder would want to know because of the uncertainty and disruption of having a board that did not meet TSXV policy. The prospect of another shareholder meeting to elect a

group of electors or even one director was a real one and a vote for the dissident nominees shareholders was essentially a vote for the uncertainty, conflict and cost of subsequent elections. I conclude that reasonable shareholders would want to know that before casting their votes.

. . .

[80] In the dissident circular his [Mr. Rainbird's] work history is stated as including being a president and chief executive officer of a mining company from August 2007 to December 2011, a period of about four years. In fact he held those positions from October 26, 2010, to December 21, 2011, a period of fourteen months. The circular also states that Mr. Rainbird was a director and chief financial officer for another company from April 2007 to January 2010, about three years. In fact, he held those positions from late October 2010 to December 3, 2010; a period of five weeks.

[81] This information was communicated to the dissident shareholders on December 13, 2012, the day after the circular was published. The reply made on behalf of the petitioners was a generic one, that the information in the circular was correct and it would not be changed.

[82] I find that the information in the dissident circular about Mr. Rainbird's previous work history was not correct. Further it misstated that history by embellishing it and it was, therefore, a misrepresentation. I find that it was also a material misrepresentation. It was not corrected when given the opportunity to do so and it can be properly viewed as done for the purpose of influencing the choices of voting shareholders.

. . .

[86] I have found above that the respondents have proven there are material misrepresentations in the December 2012 dissident circular. One of these was the failure of Mr. Rainbird and Mr. Defreitas to file timely consents to be nominated as directors. A second follows from the first: Mr. Rainbird was the only dissident nominee with public issuer experience and, if he could not serve as a director because of the timeliness problem with his consent, then the dissident shareholders as a group would not constitute a valid board of directors under the policy of TSXV. Third, Mr. Rainbird could not serve as a director without the written consent of the TSXV because of the settlement agreement he was a party to as a result of problems with another company. There are others, above.

[87] There are other issues that apply to the dissident circular as a whole and to how it was produced.

[88] There is something of an issue about whether the material misrepresentations existed at the time of the release of the circular. In this regard, apart from the problems identified above, it stated, "It is not contemplated that any of the Dissident Nominees will be unable to serve if elected." One could perhaps parse this statement by asking who was doing the contemplating. However, the evidence is that the petitioners knew the untimely consents from Mr. Rainbird and Mr. Defreitas were a concern for management before the circular was released. They also knew about the disciplinary history of Mr. Rainbird, that written consent from the TSXV was required before he could serve as a director and that consent had not been given at the time the circular was released.

[89] To say that it was not contemplated that any of the dissident nominees would be unable to serve is a material misrepresentation on its own. It misleads shareholders and affects their ability to properly deliberate the choices they had to make for election of directors. Further, the circular stated that, if there was a vacancy in the dissident nominees,

the dissident shareholders "may appoint a substitute nominee selected by them." This is also a material misrepresentation since it held out an alternative that does not exist in the articles of the respondent St. Elias Mining Ltd. or anywhere else. I conclude that there were material misrepresentations in the dissident circular at the time it was issued and the petitioners knew there were material misrepresentations at that time.

[90] Another issue is that Mr. Hastman, in cross-examination, defended the dissident circular by saying there was no need to change it. This was cast in terms of, according to Mr. Hastman, the circular being correct. However, the circular was not correct and it omitted information that was significant for the deliberations of shareholders. If it is an issue, I also conclude that the dissident shareholders had a responsibility to ensure that their circular was complete and correct before it was released. They did not meet that responsibility. Instead they fashioned a document that left out significant information and misstated other information. I accept that a proxy battle does not always operate by Marquess of Queensberry Rules. It is nonetheless important that documents with significant legal consequences, such as information circulars that inform shareholders about their voting choices, be complete and accurate.

[91] The dissident shareholders had a second option. They could have amended their circular when it was made clear that management was opposed to it. As above, this opportunity arose the day after the dissident circular was published when counsel for the respondents wrote a detailed letter setting out the problems. At a minimum, the dissidents could have issued a press release to amend the circular. Press releases were issued after the circular and they were, according to Mr. Hastman, simple to do. A press release does not have the same legal significance as a circular but it would have been an opportunity to get complete and accurate information to shareholders.

Oppression

. . .

[93] Under s. 227(3) of the *BCA* there are a number of interim and final remedies to remedy or to bring an end to acts of oppression.

[94] The Supreme Court of Canada has discussed oppression using the following general principles, as applied to the *Canada Business Corporations Act*, R.S.C. 1985, C-44 (*BCE Inc. v. 1976 Debentureholders,* 2008 SCC 69 [*BCE*]):

> [57] We preface our discussion of the twin prongs of the oppression inquiry by two preliminary observations that run throughout all the jurisprudence.
>
> [58] First, oppression is an equitable remedy. It seeks to ensure fairness—what is "just and equitable." It gives a court broad, equitable jurisdiction to enforce not just what is legal but what is fair: *Wright v. Donald s. Montgomery Holdings Ltd.* (1998), 1998 CanLII 14805 (ON SC), 39 B.L.R. (2d) 266 (Ont. Ct. (Gen. Div.)), at p. 273; *Re Keho Holdings Ltd. and Noble* (1987), 1987 ABCA 84, 38 D.L.R. (4th) 368 (Alta. C.A.), at p. 374; see, more generally, Koehnen, at pp. 78-79. It follows that courts considering claims for oppression should look at business realities, not merely narrow legalities: *Scottish Co-operative Wholesale Society*, at p. 343.
>
> [59] Second, like many equitable remedies, oppression is fact-specific. What is just and equitable is judged by the reasonable expectations of the stakeholders in the context and in regard to the relationships at play. Conduct that may be oppressive in one situation may not be in another.

[95] More specifically, the court described the "best approach" to the interpretation of the oppression provisions of the *CBCA* as one that combines two approaches developed in the cases (para. 56):

> One should look first to the principles underlying the oppression remedy, and in particular the concept of reasonable expectations. If a breach of reasonable expectation is established, one must go on to consider whether the conduct complained of amounts to "oppression," "unfair prejudice," or "unfair disregard" [in the oppression provisions of the CBCA].

[96] I also take the following from the *BCE* decision:

a) A claimant pursuing an oppression claim must identify the alleged expectations that form the basis of the claim and must establish that such expectations were reasonable (para. 70).

b) Oppression is an equitable remedy and it seeks to ensure fairness (para. 58).

c) Like many equitable remedies, depression is fact specific. Conduct that may be oppressive in one situation may not be in another. What is just and equitable is judged by the reasonable expectations of the stakeholders in the context and in regard to the relationships at play (para. 59).

d) The concept of reasonable expectations is objective and contextual. The actual expectation of a particular stakeholder is not conclusive (para. 62).

e) An expectation is not reasonable if it would require directors to act in a manner that is not in the best interests of the company (para. 66).

f) Where the interests of a particular shareholder are not co-extensive with that of the company, the duty of the directors is to the company, not the shareholder. In such cases, "the reasonable expectation of stakeholders is simply that the directors acted in the best interests of the corporation" (para. 66).

g) Not every unmet expectation gives rise to a claim (para. 67).

h) Courts should defer to the business decisions of directors, so long as they lie within the range of reasonable alternatives (para. 40). The oppression remedy does not replace or override the business judgment rule (para. 81-84).

. . .

[104] … I have found that there were material misrepresentations in the dissident circular published on December 13, 2012. Those findings inform the discussion to follow.

[105] I next turn to the specific issues in dispute with regards to the claim of oppression by the petitioners.

Reasonable Expectation

[106] The petitioners submit that they had a reasonable expectation that the chair of the respondent St. Elias Mining Ltd. would act fairly in her dealings with them and her conduct of the AGM.

[107] Stated that broadly, I can agree that was a reasonable expectation. The respondents also agree. As might be expected, the parties disagree over whether the chair, in fact, acted fairly.

[108] There is an element of fairness to the principles of oppression. As above, this is evident from s. 227 of the BCA which states that one ground for an application of oppression is that some act or resolution of a company is "unfairly prejudicial." As well, as discussed

in *BCE*, looking at business realities, not just narrow legal realities, oppression gives the courts a broad equitable jurisdiction to consider what is fair, not just what is legal. Further, in a claim for oppression, the claimant must show the failure to meet the reasonable expectation of being treated in a certain way. However, to complete a claim for oppression, the party making the claim must show that the expectation involved unfair conduct (and prejudicial consequences) (*BCE* at paras. 57, 71, 89; see also: *Blair v. Consolidated Enfield Corp*, 1995 CanLII 76 (SCC), [1995] 4 S.C.R. 5 at para. 46, 128 D.L.R. (4th) 73; *International Energy and Mineral Resources Investment (Hong Kong) Company Limited v. Mosquito Consolidated Gold Mines Limited*, 2012 BCSC 1191 at para. 48 [*Mosquito Consolidated Gold Mines*]).

[109] This requirement of fairness on the part of a chair does not extend to the point of a chair having quasi-judicial status. That status is inappropriate because, in many cases, the chair will also be a shareholder and therefore interested in the issues being deliberated. The term "quasi-judicial" imports the idea of a wholly disinterested person and a chair will often not be wholly disinterested (*Blair* at para. 45).

[110] Under *BCE* the next step is to consider whether there was a breach of this expectation by means of oppression, unfair prejudice or unfair disregard.

...

[121] From these authorities I conclude that the chair at the AGM on December 27, 2012, had broad discretion to make a number of decisions. These can be procedural and substantive, including questions of law and fact. This is generally consistent with the chair's authority to "preside" over meetings as set out in Article 11.9. Further, a chair's decisions are entitled to deference from the courts and the latter will not readily intervene in those decisions. A chair can be wrong on an issue that does not involve an error of law without interference from the court. An example of a decision where this deference may arise is a decision by the chair to rule certain motions out of order, including situations where proxies are invalid. However, errors of law are reviewable by the courts, as are decisions by the chair that are unreasonable.

[122] With this legal framework in mind, there remains the issue of whether, in the circumstances of this case, the chair was acting within her authority when she rejected the green proxies at the December 2012 AGM. I put the issue that way because the petitioners submit that a chair cannot disallow proxies at a meeting. As Mr. Hastman put it in his evidence, only a court or the securities commission can make that decision. The petitioners say that it was an act of oppression for the chair to do otherwise.

[123] As a starting point for the petitioners' submission I note that the general thrust of the above discussion does not favour the petitioners' position. In addition, there are the above conclusions that the dissident circular contained material misrepresentations. Further, these misrepresentations were significant to how shareholders would exercise their franchise to elect directors at the AGM. For example, it would be significant for shareholders to know before casting their vote that Mr. Rainbird and Mr. Defreitas could not serve as directors because they did not file their consents to serve in compliance with the articles of the respondent company. It would also have been significant for shareholders to know that Mr. Rainbird could not serve as a director because unless he had written consent to do so from the TSXV.

[124] Therefore, the critical question is what should have been done about the dissident circular? It could not stand as it was originally drafted because it did not permit

an informed decision by shareholders on the important issue of who the directors should be. In this regard I note that *Nathan's Company Meetings* states that proxies obtained on the basis of information that is contrary to law, false or misleading are nullified (para. 212).

. . .

[135] The overall result is that I have some difficulty understanding what else the respondents could have done with regards to the situation facing them from the time they received the dissident circular. I am urged by the petitioners to find that the respondents could have fashioned an application to come to court. But that would have prevented the completion of the AGM in 2012. As well, again, there is no equivalent provision in the *BCA* to that in the Ontario legislation relied on in *Kluwak*. The petitioners had the opportunity to, first of all, prepare a circular that was complete and accurate and then they had the opportunity to amend their circular or provide new information through the simple expedient of a press release. They did not take those opportunities.

[136] I also consider the meeting just prior to the AGM to be significant. The chair met with the petitioners and their counsel, the latter made their points about the green proxies and the chair then excused herself to consider those points. She returned to the meeting and advised the petitioners that she was going to reject the green proxies. The petitioners question this process. First they suggest that it was legal counsel's decision and not the chair's decision. There is no evidence to support that proposition. Previously, counsel for the respondents had been clear that any decision would be that of the chair. In any event, the chair was entitled to take legal advice on the decision she was to make although, properly so, there is no evidence that she did or did not take advice. There is also a suggestion that the chair had a closed mind before the meeting but it is no more than a suggestion.

. . .

[141] I conclude that the chair had the authority and she had the reasons to reject the green proxies prior to the AGM and then, when she was asked to admit the green proxies in any event at the AGM, to confirm her previous decision. There was no unfair prejudice in her actions and, indeed, the meeting before the AGM with the petitioners was a significant indication of the fairness of the process. The petitioners claim that the denials of their objections at the AGM were acts of oppression but there are no claims that the meeting itself was run unfairly. I also conclude that to allow the green proxies to be admitted to the AGM would have put the directors in the position of making voting choices based on incomplete or accurate information. That would not have been in the best interests of the company.

[142] Accordingly, I conclude that the respondents' denial of the petitioners' "Green Proxy Objection" and their "Elected Directors Objection" were not acts of oppression.

The NI 54-101 Objection

[143] The petitioners allege that the respondents failed to comply with NI 54-101 because materials for the December 27, 2012, were not sent out in accordance with the time requirements in that document.

[144] The allegation arises from para. 34 of the Petition:

> 34. On December 5, 2012 Olympia filed on SEDAR a certificate that the proxy materials to be indirectly sent to beneficial shareholders of the Company were sent to the respective

intermediaries on December 5, 2012. Pursuant to minimum period prescribed in s. 2.12(b) of NI 54-101, the AGM could not have been lawfully scheduled until on or after January 1, 2013. [*sic* throughout].

[145] Apart from the language, this is not a clear pleading. For example, there are three ss. (b)'s in s. 2.12: ss. 2.12(1)(b), 2(b) and 3(b). Paragraph refers to "s. 2.12(b)." Complicating things further, the sub-section that appears to be relied on by the petitioners is ss. 2.12(2)(a) which states that materials are to be sent to beneficial shareholders through their intermediaries "at least 3 business days before the 21st day before the date of the meeting."

[146] A further problem with this issue is that there is no evidence on it other than the affidavit of Mr. Hastman, who simply deposes that documents from management on the delivery of documents are true copies. A further difficulty is that, in cross-examination on his affidavit, Mr. Hastman agreed that he was not familiar with NI 54-101 or its timing requirements for sending out materials. And there is no evidence from any shareholder, including Mr. Hastman, that the documents were delivered late.

[147] Turning to another aspect of this issue, assuming for the moment that the delivery of documents was late, there is no evidence that it had any impact on the dissident circular or that an issue of fairness arises from it. And I note a previous decision of this court where there was no dispute that certain documents in question were not delivered at all (*Financial Network Guaranty Ltd. v. Terra Nova Energy Inc.*, [1987] B.C.J. No. 2646). However, there was no evidence that the petitioner in that case was prejudiced in any way and there was no unfairness. I adopt the conclusion of that decision: the petitioners in the subject case have not demonstrated that their equitable or legal rights have been affected by the assumed late delivery of documents.

[148] The chair's ruling on the petitioners' "NI 54-101 objection" was not an act of oppression.

Canadian legislation specifically provides for the revocability of proxies through the deposit of the appropriate instrument in writing at the issuer's offices or as otherwise permitted by law. The courts have the power to rectify errors in proxy-related decisions.

US Gold Corp v Atlanta Gold Corp

(1989), 43 BCLR (2d) 71 (CA)

There are hundreds and perhaps thousands of corporations in this province, large and small, public and private, active and passive, with an infinite variety of assets and liabilities and objectives. Not all are efficiently administered by persons cognisant of all the nuances of the Articles or of the provisions of the statute. Mistakes in compliance are inevitable. It seems to me that by empowering the court to remedy omissions, defects, errors, or irregularities, Section 230 [now s 206 of the BCCA] represents tacit recognition that there will be mistakes and that a simple method of correcting the mistakes or alleviating adverse consequences flowing therefrom is a necessary and integral part of a sensible and workable system of corporate law.

It seems to me, further, that when the omission, defect, error or irregularity is what is commonly called "technical," as is the case here, the court ought not to be reluctant to rectify it. And there ought to be an even lesser degree of reluctance when, as is also the case here, the consequence of declining to rectify it is to deny to shareholders the right to have their proxy votes tabulated at the annual general meeting.

By codifying the rules where proxies are solicited from non-registered beneficial owners of securities, NI 54-101 should remedy some of the problems highlighted above. Beneficial owners can consent to receive documents by electronic means. An objective of NI 54-101 is to give all securityholders of a reporting issuer the opportunity to be treated alike, as far as practicable, and to clearly define the obligations to both registered and beneficial securityholders. It is also intended to provide greater transparency for beneficial owners, in terms of advising them how they can exercise the voting rights attached to their securities. While the provisions are aimed at enhancing participation, it is not yet clear whether the provisions have been effective in increasing the voice of beneficial owners of securities.

Kahan and Rock make a number of observations regarding the challenges for meaningful shareholder voice, even with changes to US proxy voting rules, and the negative consequences of a number of current voting practices.

Marcel Kahan & Edward Rock, "The Hanging Chads of Corporate Voting"
(2008), online: <http://ssrn.com/abstract=1007065>

There are around 12,000 reporting companies. All of these companies hold annual meetings and are subject to the SEC proxy rules when they solicit proxies. Finally, annual meetings are seasonal, with most taking place during the second quarter of the calendar year. Broadridge delivers more than one billion communications to investors per year. It is an accident waiting to happen. An aggravating factor is that, for both issuers and custodians, the voting process is a necessary chore, not a profit center. The issuers must solicit proxies because they need a quorum to act. Federal law requires custodians to assist in the identification of beneficial owners, distribution of materials, and collection of proxies. Custodians typically delegate that task to Broadridge, which is in the happy position of being hired by the custodians but presenting its bill to the issuers. This system produces three types of pathologies. First, there are pathologies caused by the sheer complexity of the system. Second, there are pathologies caused by a misalignment of the property concepts implicit in the beneficial-owner-as-shareholder paradigm and the property rules that, in fact, govern the voting of shares held by nominees. Third, there are pathologies caused by a misalignment between voting rights and economic interests.

a. Pathologies of Complexity

i. Pathology 1: Materials Don't Arrive

The corporate voting system operates on a tight schedule. As noted earlier, the record date, under Delaware law, cannot be more than 60 days before the meeting. For shares held in nominee name, the following steps must occur before the materials are mailed out: the issuer sends an inquiry to DTC; DTC must respond; the issuer must send out search cards to the custodians; the custodians must respond; often this process has to be repeated for multiple tiers of custodians; then, and only then, can the issuer mail the materials to Broadridge, which then distributes them to the shareholders. Given this complexity, there will be numerous cases in which the proxy materials and the request for voting instructions simply do not make it to the beneficial owner in time for the beneficial owner to vote. Why does it matter if materials do not arrive? Most obviously, it deprives the beneficial owners of their right to vote. Moreover, it is likely that the beneficial owners most affected by materials not arriving are individual investors. The failure of materials to arrive will correspondingly increase the relative influence of the institutional shareholders.

But the effects are more complex. "Non-votes" resulting from the non-delivery of proxy materials are, for legal purposes, treated identically with non-votes because of apathy or carelessness. Under NYSE Rule 452, brokers may use their discretion to vote shares on routine and uncontested matters as to which the broker does not receive instructions ten days in advance of the meeting. At least until recently, brokers have tended to vote uninstructed shares in accordance with recommendations of the board of directors. Thus, with respect to such shares, any non-arrival of materials translates into more pro-management votes.

. . .

ii. Pathology 2: Votes That Are Not Counted

. . .

What is the effect of the non-counting of votes? If votes are not counted by mistake, the effect is similar to the one resulting from the non-arrival of materials. And even if the tabulator stops counting early because there are already enough votes in to determine the outcome, there may be an important, albeit symbolic, effect: the margin of victory (in particular the percentage of withheld votes in director elections or the percentage supporting a shareholder resolution) can be an important indicator of the support that management enjoys.

iii. Pathology 3: The Nightmare of Verification

The most troubling pathology of complexity is the system's inability to provide vote verification and an end-to-end audit trail. Any voting system is only as good as its post-voting system of verification. The complex system of holdings, combined with the circuitous system of distributing materials, soliciting proxies and collecting voting instructions, creates a nightmare of verification …. These partial are cumulative, which means that substantial care is required to prevent the custodian from voting more shares than it is entitled to. With respect to nominee shares, the custodians are voting on behalf of their customers who may have differing views. The proxies will thus be split between "for" and "against" and "abstain." With this complexity, problems are common.

. . .

The verification nightmare suggests that there may well be discrepancies—sometimes significant ones—between the ballots cast and the voting instructions given by the beneficial holders. This generates random "noise" in the tabulation of votes, which may sometimes favor and sometimes disfavour management, but which always makes the reported results less reliable. If one believes not only that a decision by shareholders (when they are entitled to vote) is important for legitimacy purposes, but also that shareholder support is related to whether this decision is a good one, then even random noise means that worse decisions will be certified as having received the requisite shareholder support.

b. Pathologies of Ownership: Confusions as to Who "Really" Owns the Shares

The second set of pathologies arises because of a misalignment of the property concepts implicit in the beneficial-owner-as-shareholder paradigm and the property rules that, in fact, govern the voting of shares held by nominees, combined with wide-spread securities lending and short selling.

. . .

There is an active market for the borrowing and lending of securities. Securities lending serves a variety of purposes, including importantly that it enables short selling. When an investor believes that shares are over-valued and will soon decline in price, it can profit by selling the shares now (at the high price) and then covering the position later once the price has declined. Because "naked" short selling is illegal, the investor must "borrow" shares in order to sell them now at the high price. Later, it will buy the same shares, hopefully at a lower price, and restore them to the lender. As this example demonstrates, the terms "lending" and "borrowing" are not accurate. The standard form contract governing equity lending prepared by the Securities Industry and Financial Markets Association (SIFMA) is a "Master Repurchase Agreement." The securities "loan" is really a transfer by a seller (e.g., an institutional investor) of full legal title in securities to a buyer (e.g., a hedge fund). In exchange, the buyer promises to sell back equivalent (but different) shares in the future and to make the lender whole for any dividends paid during the loan period, pays a fee and provides collateral. If a shareholder "lends" its shares out before the record date, the shareholder is no longer a shareholder as of the record date and is not entitled to vote, whether or not the "returned" shares are received prior to the meeting. As noted earlier, securities lending is a huge market and a highly profitable business. Firms are estimated to make around $5 billion per year from securities lending, with CalPERS alone making about $130 million per year from its operations. Typically, large institutional investors will either have the custodian bank handle the securities lending or will put the business out to bid to a third party specialist. As a result, the personnel in the institutional investor with responsibility for voting the shares may not even be aware that the shares are out "on loan."

Institutional investors have access to records of their securities lending operations and can, if they choose, decline to lend out their shares or recall them in advance of record dates for meetings at which they intend to raise issues or want to vote. But doing so would sacrifice substantial revenue. Here's why. Most securities lending programs combine the shares of a large number of customers. Recalls of lent shares or freezes on lending increase the transaction costs of the entity that handles the lending program. If a participant in a securities lending program regularly recalls or freezes shares in advance of a record date, that entity will simply give preference to the many participants who do not impose such limitations, and will not lend the participant's shares out unless no other shares are available. The effect of such a policy is thus effectively to opt out of securities lending, a very expensive decision.

. . .

c. *Pathologies of Misalignment Between Voting Rights and Economic Interest*

The concepts of record dates and record holders—albeit necessary (to some extent) to the make a voting system for public corporations workable—result in a discrepancy between beneficial economic stakes in the company on one hand and voting rights on the other hand. Voting rights rest with the record holder on the record date. But that record holder may not have beneficial economic ownership in the company for three reasons:

- The record holder is a street name holder (a bank or broker) who never had a beneficial economic interest.
- The shares have been sold after the record date and before the vote.
- The holder has hedged her economic exposure to the company.

By the same token, a holder may have a beneficial economic interest, but no voting rights (because she is not a record holder, because she has bought the shares after the record date, or because she is a counterparty to a hedging transaction). The various regulations discussed above are designed (largely, but not wholly, successfully) to deal with the first of these reasons. But they do not address at all the other two reasons for the discrepancy. Thus, in the present regime, there will be some persons with voting rights and no beneficial interest, and others with a beneficial interest and no voting rights. And the number of such persons is larger the more liquid the market for the shares, and the larger the market for derivatives. Discrepancies between voting rights and beneficial interests can arise in two contexts: first, as an unintended consequence of a transaction undertaken for other reasons (e.g. when a person buys shares after the record date because she believes the stock price will increase); second, for the purpose of obtaining votes without an equivalent economic exposure (e.g. when a person buys shares before and sells them after the record date so that she can vote the shares without having any economic exposure).

The challenges identified by Kahan & Rock have also long been recognized in the Canadian context, and the CSA has recently sought to address these challenges by initiating a review of the Canadian proxy voting infrastructure. In August 2013, the CSA published Consultation Paper 54-401, *Review of the Proxy Voting Infrastructure,* followed by an in-depth, technical examination of the issues raised. The review and analysis concluded with the publication of CSA Multilateral Staff Notice 54-304, *Final Report on Review of the Proxy Voting Infrastructure and Request for Comments on Proposed Meeting Vote Reconciliation Protocols* on March 31, 2016.

CSA Multilateral Staff Notice 54-304, *Final Report on Review of the Proxy Voting Infrastructure and Request for Comments on Proposed Meeting Vote Reconciliation Protocols*

(31 March 2016)

Background

Shareholder voting is one of the most important methods by which shareholders can affect governance, communicate preferences and signal confidence or lack of confidence in an issuer's management and oversight. Issuers also rely on shareholder voting to approve corporate governance matters and certain fundamental changes and transactions.

Shareholder voting is fundamental to, and enhances the quality and integrity of, our public capital markets.

Shareholder voting in Canada generally occurs through *proxy voting*, whereby management or another individual is given the authority to attend and vote at the meeting on behalf of a shareholder through an instrument known as a *proxy*.

Furthermore, proxy votes typically are submitted by intermediaries and not the actual shareholders. This is because most shareholders are not registered shareholders and hold their shares through intermediaries, which in turn hold their shares with the central depository, the Canadian Depository for Securities Limited (*CDS*). This system of holding shares is known as the *intermediated holding system*.

In order to facilitate proxy voting in the intermediated holding system, a complex, opaque and fragmented *proxy voting infrastructure* has developed. The key entities that operate this infrastructure are CDS, intermediaries, Broadridge Investor Communication Solutions Canada (*Broadridge*) (the main proxy voting agent for intermediaries) and the transfer agents who act as meeting tabulators. These entities implement the processes used to tabulate proxy votes for shares held through intermediaries. We refer to these processes as *meeting vote reconciliation*.

For some time, issuers and investors have expressed concerns that the proxy voting infrastructure and meeting vote reconciliation are inaccurate, unreliable and non-transparent. They pointed to two specific problems as evidence:

- *Over-voting*: Over-voting occurs when an intermediary submits proxy votes and the meeting tabulator cannot establish that the intermediary has any vote entitlements, or the number of proxy votes submitted exceeds the number of vote entitlements for that intermediary as calculated by the tabulator.
- *Missing votes*: Beneficial owners generally have no way of knowing whether a tabulator or meeting chair accepted their intermediary's proxy votes. Investors have identified instances where the voting results suggested their proxy votes were not included in the tabulation and therefore went "missing."

We decided to take a leadership role in addressing these concerns because we were best positioned to investigate, analyze and develop solutions to these issues in a sustained and systematic way. We therefore initiated a review of the proxy voting infrastructure by publishing CSA Consultation Paper 54-401 Review of the Proxy Voting Infrastructure in August 2013.

A central objective of our review was to understand how meeting vote reconciliation occurred in practice. We therefore conducted a detailed review of six shareholder meetings (the Shareholder Meeting Reviews) with the assistance of a proxy solicitor. Based on our review, we identified a number of problems that could undermine the accuracy, reliability and accountability of meeting vote reconciliation. We reported our findings in the Progress Report published in January 2015.

Through the Shareholder Meeting Reviews, we determined that there were two significant underlying gaps in meeting vote reconciliation.

- *Information gaps*

  Meeting tabulators do not always have the accurate and complete vote entitlement information they require to properly establish which intermediaries have vote entitlements for a meeting and how many vote entitlements these intermediaries have. Missing, incomplete or inaccurate vote entitlement information can cause an intermediary that submits proxy votes to be in an over-vote position from the meeting tabulator's perspective. Meeting tabulators use different methods to address over-vote situations. Depending on the tabulator, the same proxy votes could be accepted, rejected or pro-rated. Rejected or pro-rated votes could result in the appearance of missing votes.

- *Communication gaps*

  There are no standard communication channels between intermediaries and tabulators. The lack of such communication channels means there is no way to efficiently and accurately

  - confirm that all necessary information has been sent and received, or
  - detect and resolve information problems that could lead to proxy votes being rejected or pro-rated at a meeting.

  Furthermore, intermediaries are not routinely notified if a meeting tabulator rejects or pro-rates their proxy votes due to missing or incomplete vote entitlement information.

  We therefore determined that there was a need to develop protocols for meeting vote reconciliation that would enhance accuracy, reliability and accountability of meeting vote reconciliation by

  - delineating clear roles and responsibilities for CDS, intermediaries, Broadridge and the meeting tabulator at each stage of meeting vote reconciliation, and
  - outlining the operational processes that each of these key entities should implement to fulfil their roles and responsibilities.

...

Overview of the Protocols

The Protocols contain CSA staff expectations on the roles and responsibilities of the key entities and guidance on the kinds of operational processes that they should implement to support accurate, reliable and accountable meeting vote reconciliation. The Protocols have been developed taking into account existing operational processes, and in our view should not require a major technological overhaul of existing systems.

The protocols themselves were published as annexes to the final report and subject to industry consultation and refinement. Intermediaries engaged in the proxy-voting infrastructure in Canada are expected to voluntarily implement the improvements contemplated by the protocols for the 2017 proxy season, and the CSA technical committee will monitor this implementation; measure the resulting impact on improving the accuracy, reliability, and accountability of meeting vote reconciliation; and consider whether any additional rules and policy guidance may be required.

III. CORPORATE GOVERNANCE DISCLOSURE

Securities regulators have moved in recent years to require disclosure in respect of numerous aspects of corporate governance practice. Historically, corporate governance was considered primarily the domain of corporate law, and disclosures respecting corporate governance were chiefly dealt with by the listing requirements of the stock exchanges. Corporate governance had been thought of as an essential element of corporate law, not securities law. Securities law was traditionally aimed at protection of investors and the efficiency of, and confidence in, capital markets through regulation of the activities of issuers.

There had been considerable debate as to whether corporate governance rules or guidelines properly fit under corporate law rather than securities regulation, and, until recently, corporate governance was not an area that securities regulators sought to regulate. That situation changed with the introduction of US corporate governance rules as a requirement for listing on the New York Stock Exchange (NYSE) and other exchanges. In an effort to harmonize regulatory approaches in Canada and the United States, the CSA proposed best corporate governance practices that were based on the NYSE corporate governance rules implemented after the US *Sarbanes-Oxley Act* came into force. Unlike the NYSE rules that are mandatory listing standards, however, Canadian regulators implemented voluntary compliance with a mandatory disclosure requirement in terms of requiring reporting issuers to describe how they meet the objectives of a guideline if they have not implemented the specific governance standards suggested by the guideline. This is known as a "comply or explain" system.

Hence corporate governance standards are voluntary in Canada, but securities regulation requires disclosure of governance practices. This policy choice reflects the distinct policy development of securities law in Canada. One of the earliest studies on corporate governance, commissioned by the TSX and chaired by Peter Dey, *Where Are the Directors?*, proposed a comply-or-explain approach to corporate governance rather than prescriptive rules. That report set the stage for policy debates that followed, and Canada adopted voluntary standards rather than prescribed governance rules. NI 58-101, *Disclosure of Corporate Governance Practices* (effective 17 March 2008, as amended 17 November 2015), sets out a series of disclosure requirements.

In December 2008, the CSA announced that it was considering revisions to corporate governance requirements and proposed the repeal and replacement of NI 58-101. The CSA proposed replacing the current governance policy with a more principles-based policy that would be broader in scope, with nine corporate governance principles and commentary explaining those principles. The CSA considered replacing existing disclosure requirements with a new set of disclosure requirements that would be more general in nature, rather than based on a comply-or-explain model, and they would have applied to both venture and non-venture issuers (CSA, *Request for Comment, Proposed Repeal and Replacement of NP 58-201 Corporate Governance Guidelines* (19 December 2008)). However, in late 2009, the CSA announced that, after consulting with the issuer community, it had concluded that it was not the time to introduce significant changes because issuers were focused on business sustainability in the wake of the 2009 financial crisis (CSA Staff Notice 58-305, *Status Report on the Proposed Changes to the Corporate Governance Regime* (3 November 2009)).

NI 58-101, *Disclosure of Corporate Governance Practices* (effective 17 March 2008, as amended 2014), sets out differing disclosure requirements for venture and non-venture issuers. All reporting issuers are required to disclose the identity of independent and non-independent directors and describe the basis for that determination; however, the requirements for non-venture issuers are considerably more detailed. They must also disclose board attendance records; the identity, role, and responsibilities of an independent chair or lead director; or, if the board does not have one, a description of what the board does to provide leadership for its independent directors (Form 58-101F1, s 1). The non-venture issuer must also describe what the board of directors does to facilitate its exercise of independent judgment in carrying out its responsibilities if a majority of directors are not independent, and disclose whether or not the independent directors hold regularly scheduled in-camera meetings, including particulars on the number of meetings and what the board does to facilitate open and candid discussion among its independent directors. Venture issuers do not face such requirements.

Venture issuers are also not required to disclose the board's written mandate or delineation of board roles and responsibilities; nor are they required to disclose written position descriptions or delineated roles for the board chair and chair of each board committee (Form 58-101F1, s 2). All issuers must disclose orientation and continuing education initiatives for directors; but only non-venture issuers must describe how the board ensures that its directors maintain the skill and knowledge necessary to meet their obligations as directors. All issuers must disclose if any of their directors are also a director of any other issuer that is a reporting issuer in Canada or a foreign jurisdiction, identifying both the director and the other issuer (Forms 58-101F1, 58-101F2).

While venture issuers must disclose what steps, if any, the board takes to encourage and promote a culture of ethical business conduct, non-venture issuers must provide more detailed disclosure, including whether or not the board has adopted a written code for the directors, officers, and employees; describe how the board monitors compliance with its code or, if the board does not monitor compliance, explain how the board satisfies itself regarding compliance with its code; provide a cross-reference to any material change report filed since the beginning of the issuer's most recently completed financial year that pertains to any conduct of a director or executive officer that constitutes a departure from the code; and describe any steps the board takes to ensure directors exercise independent judgment in considering transactions where a director or executive officer has a material interest (Form 58-101F2, s 4; Form 58-101F1, s 5).

While both types of issuers must describe how the board satisfies itself that the board, its committees, and its individual directors are performing effectively, non-venture issuers must disclose whether or not the board, its committees, and individual directors are regularly assessed with respect to their effectiveness and contribution, and describe the process used for the assessments (Form 58-101F1, s 9; Form 58-101F2, s 8).

Hence, the scope, breadth, and detail of required corporate governance disclosure are proportionate to the issuer's status as a venture or non-venture issuer. Another principal difference is that where the non-venture issuer board does not have formal policies and practices in place, it must disclose initiatives that it has undertaken to ensure independence and objectivity in the process—a requirement not imposed on venture issuers.

The TSX, which previously had a "comply or explain" approach that required disclosure with reference to 14 TSX corporate governance best practice guidelines, modified its company manual to align with the requirements of NI 58-101. NI 58-101 was amended in 2008 to cover disclosure for proxy solicitation.

In 2014, further amendments to NI 58-101 were made requiring non-venture issuers to disclose additional corporate governance information, including whether the issuer imposed director term limits and the representation of women on boards and at executive levels (Amendment Instrument for National Instrument 58-101, *Disclosure of Corporate Governance Practices 1*, effective 31 December 2014). At the same time, s 1.1 of NI 58-101 was amended to specify that the definition of "major subsidiary" has the same meaning as in National Instrument 55-104, *Insider Reporting Requirements and Exemptions*; applying to management information circulars and AIFs that are filed following an issuer's financial year ending on or after December 31, 2014 (Amendment Instrument for National Instrument 58-101).

The December 2014 amendments require issuers to disclose whether or not they have adopted term limits for the directors or other mechanisms of board renewal and, if so, to include a description of those term limits or other mechanisms of board renewal. If an issuer has not adopted director term limits or other mechanisms of board renewal, it is required to disclose why it has not done so.

The amendments also require disclosure of whether the issuer has adopted a written policy relating to the identification and nomination of women directors and, if not, why not; whether and how the board or nominating committee considers the level of representation of women on the board in identifying and nominating director candidates and, if not, why not; disclosure of whether the issuer has adopted a target regarding women in executive officer positions of the issuer and what those targets are; and if the issuer has not adopted a target, disclose why it has not done so. The amendments are intended to increase transparency for investors and other stakeholders regarding issuers' commitment to board renewal and the representation of women on boards and in senior management in order to assist investors in making investment and voting decisions.

Prior to these amendments, in November 2013, Ontario Securities Commission staff issued a survey to approximately 1,000 TSX-listed issuers regarding gender diversity. It received 448 responses to the survey, about a 45 percent response rate. The issuers that responded to the survey had a range of market capitalizations, with 29 percent having a market capitalization of less than $75 million and 26 percent having a market capitalization of $1 billion or more. The issuers also were from a range of industries, with 26 percent being from the diversified metals and mining industry, 17 percent from the energy industry, and 9 percent from the financial industry. The survey found that the level of representation of women on boards and in executive officer positions with responding firms was low. Out of all respondents, 57 percent had no women directors, 28 percent had one woman director, and 3 percent had three women directors. Only three issuers who responded had women representing 50 percent or more of their board membership. In addition, only 3 percent of respondents had a woman chair of the board, and 3 percent of respondents had a female lead director. Out of all respondents, 53 percent indicated that women hold less than 10 percent of their executive officer positions. The level of transparency regarding the representation of women by the respondents was also low. Out of all respondents, 88 percent did not publicly disclose the proportion of women employees in the whole organization; 80 percent did not publicly disclose the proportion of women in executive officer positions; 61 percent did not publicly disclose the proportion of women on the board; 91 percent did not have a policy for the identification and nomination of women directors; 94 percent had not adopted a target regarding the representation of women on its board by a specific date; and 94 percent had not adopted a target regarding the representation of women in executive officer positions by a specific date (Proposal for Public Comment, Proposed OSC Amendments to Form 58-101F1, Corporate Governance Disclosure of NI 58-101, Disclosure of Corporate Governance Practices—Proposed Disclosure Requirements Regarding the Representation of Women on Boards and in Senior Management).

The new requirements for disclosure of director term policies and gender representation at the executive and board level apply to all non-venture issuers reporting in the participating jurisdictions. The underlying rationale is that the ability to recruit qualified directors is critical to an effective board and that it is important to consider a broad pool of qualified directors when considering possible new board candidates. Corporate decision-making benefits from a diversity of opinions and viewpoints, and diversity is enhanced when leadership roles are filled with individuals who have different professional experience, education, skill, and genders, as well as other individual qualities and attributes. The amendments to Form 58-101F1 relating to the disclosure of director term limits and representation of women was adopted by all Canadian securities regulators except those in British Columbia and Alberta. Form 58-101F1 for the filing of corporate governance disclosures is set out below.

Form 58-101F1, *Corporate Governance Disclosure*
As amended effective 31 December 2014

1. Board of Directors

(a) Disclose the identity of directors who are independent.

(b) Disclose the identity of directors who are not independent, and describe the basis for that determination.

(c) Disclose whether or not a majority of directors are independent. If a majority of directors are not independent, describe what the board of directors (the board) does to facilitate its exercise of independent judgement in carrying out its responsibilities.

(d) If a director is presently a director of any other issuer that is a reporting issuer (or the equivalent) in a jurisdiction or a foreign jurisdiction, identify both the director and the other issuer.

(e) Disclose whether or not the independent directors hold regularly scheduled meetings at which non-independent directors and members of management are not in attendance. If the independent directors hold such meetings, disclose the number of meetings held since the beginning of the issuer's most recently completed financial year. If the independent directors do not hold such meetings, describe what the board does to facilitate open and candid discussion among its independent directors.

(f) Disclose whether or not the chair of the board is an independent director. If the board has a chair or lead director who is an independent director, disclose the identity of the independent chair or lead director, and describe his or her role and responsibilities. If the board has neither a chair that is independent nor a lead director that is independent, describe what the board does to provide leadership for its independent directors.

(g) Disclose the attendance record of each director for all board meetings held since the beginning of the issuer's most recently completed financial year.

2. *Board Mandate*

Disclose the text of the board's written mandate. If the board does not have a written mandate, describe how the board delineates its role and responsibilities.

3. *Position Descriptions*

(a) Disclose whether or not the board has developed written position descriptions for the chair and the chair of each board committee. If the board has not developed written position descriptions for the chair and/or the chair of each board committee, briefly describe how the board delineates the role and responsibilities of each such position.

(b) Disclose whether or not the board and CEO have developed a written position description for the CEO. If the board and CEO have not developed such a position description, briefly describe how the board delineates the role and responsibilities of the CEO.

4. *Orientation and Continuing Education*

(a) Briefly describe what measures the board takes to orient new directors regarding

(i) the role of the board, its committees and its directors, and

(ii) the nature and operation of the issuer's business.

(b) Briefly describe what measures, if any, the board takes to provide continuing education for its directors. If the board does not provide continuing education, describe how the board ensures that its directors maintain the skill and knowledge necessary to meet their obligations as directors.

5. *Ethical Business Conduct*

(a) Disclose whether or not the board has adopted a written code for the directors, officers and employees. If the board has adopted a written code:

(i) disclose how a person or company may obtain a copy of the code;

(ii) describe how the board monitors compliance with its code, or if the board does not monitor compliance, explain whether and how the board satisfies itself regarding compliance with its code; and

(iii) provide a cross-reference to any material change report filed since the beginning of the issuer's most recently completed financial year that pertains to any conduct of a director or executive officer that constitutes a departure from the code.

(b) Describe any steps the board takes to ensure directors exercise independent judgement in considering transactions and agreements in respect of which a director or executive officer has a material interest.

(c) Describe any other steps the board takes to encourage and promote a culture of ethical business conduct.

6. *Nomination of Directors*

(a) Describe the process by which the board identifies new candidates for board nomination.

(b) Disclose whether or not the board has a nominating committee composed entirely of independent directors. If the board does not have a nominating committee composed entirely of independent directors, describe what steps the board takes to encourage an objective nomination process.

(c) If the board has a nominating committee, describe the responsibilities, powers and operation of the nominating committee.

7. *Compensation*

(a) Describe the process by which the board determines the compensation for the issuer's directors and officers.

(b) Disclose whether or not the board has a compensation committee composed entirely of independent directors. If the board does not have a compensation committee composed entirely of independent directors, describe what steps the board takes to ensure an objective process for determining such compensation.

(c) If the board has a compensation committee, describe the responsibilities, powers and operation of the compensation committee.

8. *Other Board Committees*

If the board has standing committees other than the audit, compensation and nominating committees, identify the committees and describe their function.

9. *Assessments*

Disclose whether or not the board, its committees and individual directors are regularly assessed with respect to their effectiveness and contribution. If assessments are regularly conducted, describe the process used for the assessments. If assessments are not regularly conducted, describe how the board satisfies itself that the board, its committees, and its individual directors are performing effectively.

10. Director Term Limits and Other Mechanisms of Board Renewal (Manitoba, New Brunswick, Newfoundland and Labrador, Northwest Territories, Nova Scotia, Nunavut, Ontario, Québec and Saskatchewan only)

Disclose whether or not the issuer has adopted term limits for the directors on its board or other mechanisms of board renewal and, if so, include a description of those director term limits or other mechanisms of board renewal. If the issuer has not adopted director term limits or other mechanisms of board renewal, disclose why it has not done so.

11. Policies Regarding the Representation of Women on the Board (Manitoba, New Brunswick, Newfoundland and Labrador, Northwest Territories, Nova Scotia, Nunavut, Ontario, Québec and Saskatchewan only)

(a) Disclose whether the issuer has adopted a written policy relating to the identification and nomination of women directors. If the issuer has not adopted such a policy, disclose why it has not done so.

(b) If an issuer has adopted a policy referred to in (a), disclose the following in respect of the policy:

(i) a short summary of its objectives and key provisions,

(ii) the measures taken to ensure that the policy has been effectively implemented,

(iii) annual and cumulative progress by the issuer in achieving the objectives of the policy, and

(iv) whether and, if so, how the board or its nominating committee measures the effectiveness of the policy.

12. Consideration of the Representation of Women in the Director Identification and Selection Process (Manitoba, New Brunswick, Newfoundland and Labrador, Northwest Territories, Nova Scotia, Nunavut, Ontario, Québec and Saskatchewan only)

Disclose whether and, if so, how the board or nominating committee considers the level of representation of women on the board in identifying and nominating candidates for election or re-election to the board. If the issuer does not consider the level of representation of women on the board in identifying and nominating candidates for election or re-election to the board, disclose the issuer's reasons for not doing so.

13. Consideration Given to the Representation of Women in Executive Officer Appointments (Manitoba, New Brunswick, Newfoundland and Labrador, Northwest Territories, Nova Scotia, Nunavut, Ontario, Québec and Saskatchewan only)

Disclose whether and, if so, how the issuer considers the level of representation of women in executive officer positions when making executive officer appointments. If the issuer does not consider the level of representation of women in executive officer positions when making executive officer appointments, disclose the issuer's reasons for not doing so.

14. Issuer's Targets Regarding the Representation of Women on the Board and in Executive Officer Positions (Manitoba, New Brunswick, Newfoundland and Labrador, Northwest Territories, Nova Scotia, Nunavut, Ontario, Québec and Saskatchewan only)

(a) For purposes of this Item, a "target" means a number or percentage, or a range of numbers or percentages, adopted by the issuer of women on the issuer's board or in executive officer positions of the issuer by a specific date.

(b) Disclose whether the issuer has adopted a target regarding women on the issuer's board. If the issuer has not adopted a target, disclose why it has not done so.

(c) Disclose whether the issuer has adopted a target regarding women in executive officer positions of the issuer. If the issuer has not adopted a target, disclose why it has not done so.

(d) If the issuer has adopted a target referred to in either (b) or (c), disclose:

(i) the target, and

(ii) the annual and cumulative progress of the issuer in achieving the target.

15. Number of Women on the Board and in Executive Officer Positions (Manitoba, New Brunswick, Newfoundland and Labrador, Northwest Territories, Nova Scotia, Nunavut, Ontario, Québec and Saskatchewan only)

(a) Disclose the number and proportion (in percentage terms) of directors on the issuer's board who are women.

(b) Disclose the number and proportion (in percentage terms) of executive officers of the issuer, including all major subsidiaries of the issuer, who are women.

Also effective 31 December 2014, the Instructions of Form 58-101F1 are amended by adding the following sections:

(4) An issuer may disclose any additional information that is relevant in order to understand the context of the information disclosed by the issuer under Item 15(a) or (b) of this Form.

(5) An issuer may incorporate information required to be disclosed under Items 10 to 15 by reference to another document. The issuer must clearly identify the reference document

or any excerpt of it that the issuer incorporates into the disclosure provided under Items 10 to 15. Unless the issuer has already filed the reference document or excerpt under its SEDAR profile, the issuer must file it at the same time as it files the document containing the disclosure required under this Form.

For a comparative perspective on issues of gender diversity on corporate boards, see Aaron Dhir, *Challenging Boardroom Homogeneity* (New York: Cambridge University Press, 2015). Anita Anand and Vijay Jog have suggested that efforts to increase the number of women on boards and in executive roles may not be sufficient to truly enhance corporate governance and that diversity on boards should also include visible minority directors.

Anita Anand & Vijay Jog, "Diversity on Boards"
(2014) Canadian Law and Economics Association, Working Paper at 1-2, 30

Examinations of board composition in public companies focus on the absence of women but rarely on the absence of visible minority directors (VMDs). In countries such as Canada, the United States and Australia, where visible minorities contribute significantly to GDP and represent a high growth segment of the population, a question arises as to whether boards should bear some demographic similarity to the society in which the firm operates. In order to understand board composition and its potential impact on a firm's performance, more information is required about the complement of VMDs on boards of directors. This study fills this gap in the literature.

"Diversity" in the corporate context refers to the composition of the board, taking into account individual characteristics of board members, such as gender, race, disability, age and ethnicity. The relative paucity of women on boards has dominated the academic debate (Francoeur et al, 2007; Terhesen et al, 2009; Peterson and Philpot, 2006) with visible minority representation falling a distant second (Brammer et al, 2007). We begin by questioning this divide in the literature and argue that characteristics other than gender are relevant to the discussion about board diversity. Indeed, the aim of this study is to provide a deeper look at board composition by examining VMDs and subgroups of VMDs.

To this end, we analyze board composition and performance of sample firms listed on the Toronto Stock Exchange as well as visible minorities in the graduating classes of director programs (DPs) in Canada. Our preliminary analysis indicates that the representation of VMDs on boards and in DPs is less than 5.5 percent in both cohorts (and less in the TSX group of companies if six foreign-owned firms are excluded). Certain visible minority groups, including those from South Asia, are more prevalent on public company boards than other visible minority groups, such as Aboriginal peoples. Finally, firms in consumer-based industries (such as financial services) demonstrate a higher propensity than other industries (such as mining) to place VMDs on their boards.

We believe that additional attention should be paid to potential contributions that VMDs can make to corporate boards. Building on Becker (1957), we hypothesize that VMDs may bring specific advantages to the firm and as a result firms will be at a competitive disadvantage if firms fail to hire these directors. Specifically, VMDs may have a unique ability to understand diverse labour and consumer markets, to provide access to untapped and new networks, and to exercise useful approaches in negotiations around the boardroom table.

. . .

In this study, we examine the complement of VMDs on boards of companies listed on the TSX. We find that the proportion of VMD is less than 5 percent of the sample with some visible minority groups completely unrepresented (Filipinos, West Asians and Aboriginals). Our results related to the financial performance of companies in four subgroups indicate that companies with only white males actually have inferior stock market performance than companies with more diverse boards based both on absolute and "relative to the sector" basis. We also find that firms with boards with only white males do not show significantly better performance than firms with boards comprised of females and VMDs. We do not claim that these results show causality since it is possible that firms that demonstrate superior stock performance are forward-thinking or better able to conduct searches that lead to a diverse board. However, if nothing else, our results do show that there is no performance deterioration by having a diverse board.

In 2015, the CSA conducted a review to assess the new disclosure requirements of NI58-101. The findings of this study were published in CSA Multilateral Staff Notice 58-307, *Staff Review of Women on Boards and in Executive Officer Positions—Compliance with NI 58-101 Disclosure of Corporate Governance Practices* (28 September 2015). The review reported that as of June 2, 2015 there were 886 reporting issuers listed on the TSX that were required to report under the new disclosure rules. Of these, 722 had a year-end between December 31, 2014 and March 31, 2015 and released their disclosure on corporate governance by July 31, 2015. Among this issuer sample, the CSA reviewers found that:

- 49 percent of these issuers had at least one woman on their board.
- 60 percent had at least one woman in an executive officer position.
- 15 percent had added one or more women to their board in the prior year.
- Over 30 percent of the issuers with a market capitalization above $2 billion had adopted a written policy for identifying and nominating women directors.
- Of those with written policies, 48 percent disclosed that they were adopted or updated in the prior year.
- 60 percent of the issuers with a market capitalization above $2 billion had two or more female directors.
- 19 percent of issuers had adopted director term limits, while 56 percent have adopted other mechanisms of board renewal.

QUESTIONS

1. The principles proposed by the CSA in 2008, but not proceeded with, would have amended Form 58-101F1 to incorporate nine broad principles—specifically:

1) Create a Framework for Oversight and Accountability,
2) Structure the Board to Add Value,
3) Attract and Retain Effective Directors,

4) Continuously Strive to Improve the Board's Performance,
5) Promote Integrity,
6) Recognize and Manage Conflicts of Interest,
7) Recognize and Manage Risk,
8) Compensate Appropriately, and
9) Engage Effectively with Shareholders.

The requirements under these broad categories were less detailed but required an equal amount of disclosure, aimed at meeting these principles. What was the purpose of the proposed move toward principles-based reporting of corporate governance?

2. In your view, should the CSA have suspended its efforts to move toward more principles-based corporate governance disclosure?

3. Why do you think British Columbia and Alberta securities regulators did not adopt the changes to Form 58-101F1 that require disclosure of director term limits, board renewal efforts, and the representation of women on boards and at executive officer levels of the issuer?

4. Should Canadian securities regulators adopt a comply-or-explain approach to the issue of representation of visible minority directors on boards?

The CSA also published a national policy on corporate governance guidelines in 2005. The purpose of the policy is to provide guidance on corporate governance practices, taking account of the best practices at the time (National Policy 58-201NP, *Corporate Governance Guidelines*, effective 30 June 2005). Its express purpose was to provide guidance on corporate governance practices that had been formulated to achieve a balance between providing protection to investors and fostering fair and efficient capital markets and confidence in capital markets. It also sought to be sensitive to the realities of the greater numbers of small companies and controlled companies in the Canadian corporate landscape; and take account of the impact of corporate governance developments in the United States and globally, recognizing that corporate governance was evolving (58-201NP, s 1.1).

One can contrast the situation in the United States and Canada with respect to corporate governance guidelines as one in which self-regulating organizations such as the NYSE and TSX are given the power to delist an issuer for failure to comply. However, non-compliance means something different in each jurisdiction. In the United States, it means failure to adhere to the guidelines. In Canada, it means the issuer's failure to disclose its non-adherence to the guidelines. Thus, in Canada, the non-adhering issuer remains listed as long as it is disclosing, and the only sanction is the potential for shareholder exit. While the regime adopted in Canadian jurisdictions is consistent with the use of disclosure as a major regulatory tool, one may question whether securities regulation of corporate governance using this tool will result in any measurable change in an issuer's governance. One can also question whether a major departure from the guidelines may form the basis of a legal action against directors under the applicable corporate law statutes, such as a claim that the departure constitutes a breach of the directors' duties of loyalty and care, or oppressive conduct toward investors.

IV. CERTIFICATION OF DISCLOSURE

Another aspect of corporate governance of issuers is the certification requirements that are aimed at holding corporate officers accountable for the quality and accuracy of the issuer's disclosures. In 2008, Canadian securities regulators undertook initiatives to assist with the integrity of disclosures through new certification requirements. These initiatives were based in part on similar changes in the United States, where legislative initiatives such as the *Sarbanes-Oxley Act of 2002* (Pub L 107-204, 116 Stat 745 (2002)) were aimed at protecting investors by improving the accuracy and reliability of corporate disclosure pursuant to US securities laws. However, Canadian regulators have made distinct choices about the scope of required disclosure and certification—for example, expressly declining to adopt the external auditor attestation requirements in the US *Sarbanes-Oxley Act* (*S-Ox 404*).

NI 52-109, *Certification Disclosure in Issuer's Annual and Interim Filings* (effective 15 December 2008, as amended effective 5 November 2015), created a new national instrument on officer certification. The Instrument replaced Multilateral Instrument (MI) 52-109, which had been effective for all jurisdictions except British Columbia, on 30 March 2004 (NI 52-109, *Certification of Disclosure in Issuers' Annual and Interim Filings* (2002), 27 OSCB 3230, s 5.1). NI 52-109 sets out disclosure and filing requirements for all reporting issuers other than investment funds. The objective of the requirements is to improve the quality, reliability, and transparency of annual filings, interim filings, and other materials that issuers file or submit under securities legislation. The Instrument applies to both corporate and non-corporate entities.

NI 52-109 requires an issuer's chief executive officer (CEO) and chief financial officer (CFO), or persons performing similar functions to a CEO or CFO (certifying officers), to personally certify that the issuer's annual filings and interim filings do not contain any misrepresentations; that the financial statements and other financial information in the annual and interim filings fairly present in all material respects the financial condition, results of operations, and cash flows of the issuer; that they have designed or supervised design of disclosure controls and procedures (DC&P) and internal control over financial reporting (ICFR); that they have caused the issuer to disclose in its MD&A any change in the issuer's ICFR that has materially affected the issuer's ICFR; and, on an annual basis, that they have evaluated the effectiveness of the issuer's DC&P and caused the issuer to disclose their conclusions about the effectiveness of DC&P in the issuer's MD&A.

NI 52-109 does not define "financial condition," but its companion policy notes that the term "financial condition" in the annual certificates and interim certificates is to reflect the overall financial health of the issuer and includes the issuer's financial position, as shown on the balance sheet, and other factors that may affect the issuer's liquidity, capital resources, and solvency (NI 52-109CP, s 4.2).

NI 52-109 defines "DC&P" and "IFCR" as follows:

> "disclosure controls and procedures" means controls and other procedures of an issuer that are designed to provide reasonable assurance that information required to be disclosed by the issuer in its annual filings, interim filings or other reports filed or submitted by it under securities legislation is recorded, processed, summarized and reported within the time periods specified in the securities legislation and include controls and procedures designed to ensure that information required to be disclosed by an issuer in its annual filings, interim filings or other reports filed or submitted under securities legislation is accumulated and communicated to the issuer's

> management, including its certifying officers, as appropriate to allow timely decisions regarding required disclosure;
>
> "internal control over financial reporting" means a process designed by, or under the supervision of, an issuer's certifying officers, and effected by the issuer's board of directors, management and other personnel, to provide reasonable assurance regarding the reliability of financial reporting and the preparation of financial statements for external purposes in accordance with the issuer's GAAP and includes those policies and procedures that: (a) pertain to the maintenance of records that in reasonable detail accurately and fairly reflect the transactions and dispositions of the assets of the issuer; (b) are designed to provide reasonable assurance that transactions are recorded as necessary to permit preparation of financial statements in accordance with the issuer's GAAP, and that receipts and expenditures of the issuer are being made only in accordance with authorizations of management and directors of the issuer; and (c) are designed to provide reasonable assurance regarding prevention or timely detection of unauthorized acquisition, use or disposition of the issuer's assets that could have a material effect on the annual financial statements or interim financial reports;

Thus, the certifying officers are required to certify that the financial statements fairly present the financial condition of the issuer, that there are internal controls to ensure that material information is conveyed to decision-makers, and that they have disclosed to the auditor and audit committee any significant deficiencies in internal control and any fraud, material or not, that involved managers or other employees who have a significant role in the company's internal controls. Canadian issuers listed in the United States must comply with the *Sarbanes-Oxley Act of 2002*.

The CSA has observed that the certification of fair presentation is not qualified by the phrase "in accordance with generally accepted accounting principles," which is typically included in audit reports accompanying annual financial statements. The forms specifically exclude this qualification to prevent certifying officers from relying entirely on compliance with the issuer's generally accepted accounting principles (GAAP) in this representation, particularly as the issuer's GAAP financial statements might not fully reflect the financial condition of the issuer. Certification is intended to provide assurance that the financial information disclosed in the annual filings or interim filings, viewed in its entirety, provides a materially accurate and complete picture that may be broader than financial reporting under the issuer's GAAP (Companion Policy 52-109CP to NI 52-109, *Certification of Disclosure in Issuers' Annual and Interim Filings*).

The concept of fair presentation encompasses a number of quantitative and qualitative factors, including selection of appropriate accounting policies; proper application of appropriate accounting policies; disclosure of financial information that is informative and reasonably reflects the underlying transactions; and additional disclosure necessary to provide investors with a materially accurate and complete picture of financial condition, financial performance, and cash flows (NI 52-109CP, s 4.1).

NI 52-109 does not prescribe the approach that certifying officers should use to design the issuer's DC&P or ICFR. However, the CSA suggests that a top-down, risk-based approach is an efficient and cost-effective approach. Under a top-down, risk-based approach to designing DC&P and ICFR, certifying officers first identify and assess risks faced by the issuer in order to determine the scope and necessary complexity of the issuer's DC&P or ICFR, focusing their resources on the areas of greatest risk and avoid expending unnecessary resources on areas with little or no risk. Identifying risks involves officers considering the size and nature of the issuer's business and the structure and complexity of business operations. If an issuer has multiple locations or business units, certifying officers are to identify the risks that could reasonably result in a material misstatement and then consider the significance of these risks at individual locations or business units (NI 52-109CP, s 6.6).

The CSA has observed that a key element of an issuer's control environment is the attitude toward controls demonstrated by the board of directors, audit committee, and senior management through their direction and actions in the organization. Certifying officers should also consider the organizational structure of the issuer; management's philosophy and operating style, integrity, ethics, and competence of personnel; external influences that affect operations and risk management practices; and human resources policies and procedure (NI 52-109CP, s 6.7).

The certifying officers are to certify that they have evaluated, or supervised, the evaluation of, the issuer's DC&P and ICFR. They must maintain documentary evidence sufficient to provide reasonable support for their certification of design of DC&P and ICFR. The extent of documentation will vary depending on the size and complexity of the issuer's DC&P and ICFR. Certifying officers should exercise their judgment, acting reasonably, and should apply their knowledge and experience in determining the nature and extent of documentation and evaluation (NI 51-109CP, ss 6.15(1), 7.3). Employees or third parties, supervised by the certifying officers, may conduct the evaluation of the issuer's DC&P and ICFR; however, such employees should have the necessary knowledge, skills, information, and authority to evaluate the DC&P and ICFR for which they have been assigned responsibilities (NI 51-109CP, s 7.4). The certifying officers can engage external auditors or other professionals to assist with their DC&P or ICFR evaluations. The companion policy describes a number of tools that certifying officers can use to perform their DC&P and ICFR evaluations (NI 51-109CP, s 7.6). It also introduces the notion of "reperformance," which is the independent execution of certain components of the issuer's DC&P or ICFR that were performed previously to test their reliability (NI 51-109CP, s 7.9).

NI 51-109 introduces the concept of material weakness in design of controls, based in part on the US definition of material weakness. The companion policy to NI 52-109 sets out how to identify a deficiency in the design or operation of ICFR, how to assess its significance, and the obligation to disclose a material weakness relating to design or operation of IFCR, including how to assess certain long-term investments (NI 52-109CP, ss 9.2, 9.6, 13). It also introduces the concept of "compensating control," which is where a deficiency has been identified, but some other part of the financial reports compensates in terms of reducing risk (NI 52-109CP, s 9.1(3)).

If the certifying officers become aware of a material weakness relating to the design of ICFR that existed at the end of the annual or interim period, the issuer's annual or interim MD&A must describe each material weakness relating to design, the impact of each material weakness on the issuer's financial reporting and its ICFR, and the issuer's current plans or actions to remediate each material weakness. If officers become aware of a material weakness relating to the operation of ICFR, the issuer's annual MD&A must describe each material weakness relating to operation, the impact of each material weakness on the issuer's financial reporting and its ICFR, and the issuer's current plans to remediate each material weakness (Form 52-109F1, s 6(b)). The certifying officer is required to give investors an accurate and complete picture of the material weakness and actions taken to remedy the weakness. If the certifying officers identify a weakness in the design or operation of DC&P that is significant and exists as at the period end date, they are not allowed to conclude that the issuer's DC&P is effective.

Form 52-109F1 requires the certifying officers to represent that the issuer has disclosed in its annual MD&A certain information about the certifying officers' evaluation of the effectiveness of the DC&P. Form 52-109F1 also requires the certifying officers to represent that the issuer has disclosed in its annual MD&A certain information about the certifying officers' evaluation of the effectiveness of the ICFR. Under NI 51-102, the board of directors must approve the issuer's annual MD&A, including the required disclosure concerning DC&P and ICFR, before it is filed. To provide reasonable support for the board of directors' approval of an issuer's MD&A disclosure concerning ICFR, including any material weaknesses, the board of directors should understand the basis on which the certifying officers concluded that any particular deficiency or combination of deficiencies did or did not constitute a material weakness (NI 52-109CP, s 12).

NI 52-109 creates a "Venture Issuer Basic Certificate" for venture issuers, in which certifying officers of venture issuers are no longer required to include representations in their certificates relating to the establishment and maintenance of DC&P and ICFR, whereas non-venture issuers are required to use a control framework in the design of ICFR (NI 52-109, s 3.1). The venture issuer basic certificate includes a note to investors and others reading the materials explaining how it differs from the full certificate required to be filed by reporting non-venture issuers.

NI 52-109 also requires that issuers use a control framework to design their ICFR, whereas venture issuers are not so required (NI 52-109, s 3.4). The CSA has also suggested that smaller issuers can also refer to *Internal Control Over Financial Reporting—Guidance for Smaller Public Companies* published by the Committee of Sponsoring Organizations of the Treadway Commission (COSO), for guidance to smaller public companies on the implementation of the COSO framework. However, if a venture issuer files a Form 52-109F1 or Form 52-109F2 for a financial period, the venture issuer must use a control framework to design the issuer's ICFR (NI 52-109, s 3.4).

NI 52-109 also makes a distinction between non-venture issuers and venture issuers in terms of new requirements to report material weakness in internal controls. "Material weakness" means a deficiency, or a combination of deficiencies, in the ICFR such that there is a reasonable possibility that a material misstatement of the reporting issuer's annual or interim financial statements will not be prevented or detected on a timely basis. If a non-venture issuer determines it has a material weakness that exists as at the end of the period covered by its annual or interim filings, it must disclose in its annual or interim MD&A a description of the material weakness; its impact on the issuer's financial reporting and its ICFR; and the issuer's current plans, if any, or any actions already undertaken, for remediating the material weakness (NI 52-109, s 3.2).

A venture issuer is not required to file an AIF; however, if it voluntarily files an AIF for a financial year after it has filed its annual financial statements, annual MD&A, and annual certificates for the financial year, the venture issuer must file on the same date that it files its AIF a separate annual certificate signed by a certifying officer (NI 52-109, s 4.1). Under the Venture Issuer Basic Certificate, the certifying officer must certify that he or she has reviewed the annual financial statements and annual MD&A of the venture issuer for the financial year ended, and, based on the officer's knowledge, having exercised reasonable diligence, the annual filings do not contain any untrue statement of a material fact or omit to state a material fact required to be stated or that is necessary to make a statement not misleading in light of the circumstances under which it was made, for the period covered by the annual filings (Form 52-109FV1, *Certification of Annual Filings*). The officer must also certify that based on his or her knowledge, having exercised reasonable diligence, the annual financial statements together with the other financial information included in the annual filings fairly present in all material respects the financial condition, results of operations and cash flows of the issuer, as of the date of and for the periods presented in the annual filings.

The Instrument requires a cautionary note to investors that there is not the same level of assurances given by officers of venture issuers. The explanatory note is to alert investors that inherent limitations on the ability of certifying officers of a venture issuer to design and implement on a cost effective basis DC&P and ICFR may result in additional risks to the quality, reliability, transparency, and timeliness of interim and annual filings and other reports provided under securities legislation (Companion Policy 52-109CP to NI 52-109, *Certification of Disclosure in Issuers' Annual and Interim Filings*).

Certification of annual and interim filings following an initial public offering, reverse takeover, or becoming a non-venture issuer contains similar scaled requirements and an abbreviated similar note to readers (NI 52-109, s 4.5; Form 52-109F1; Form 52-109FV2; Form 52-109F2).

The underlying policy rationale for this proportionate regulation is that many venture issuers have few employees and limited financial resources, which make it difficult for them to design DC&P and ICFR without incurring significant additional costs, hiring additional employees, or restructuring the board of directors and audit committee. Hence, they are not required to make representations relating to the establishment and maintenance of DC&P and ICFR. However, a venture issuer may elect to file Form 52-109F1 or 52-109F2, which include representations regarding the establishment and maintenance of DC&P and ICFR.

Where an issuer does not have a chief executive officer or chief financial officer, each person who performs similar functions to a CEO or CFO must certify the annual filings and interim filings. It is left to the issuer's discretion to determine who those persons are. In the case of an income trust reporting issuer (as described in NP 41-201, *Income Trusts and Other Indirect Offerings*, effective 31 December 2007, as amended effective 13 August 2013), where executive management resides at the underlying business entity level or in an external management company, the CEO or CFO of the underlying business entity or the external management company is considered to be the person performing functions in respect of the income trust similar to a CEO or CFO. In the case of a limited partnership reporting issuer, the CEO or CFO of its general partner would generally be considered to be the person performing functions in respect of the limited partnership reporting issuer similar to a CEO or CFO. There are also provisions for deeming CEOs and CFOs to have designed the disclosure controls and procedures if they assumed the role after they were designed and the new CEO or CFO has reviewed them and made any appropriate modifications or enhancements to existing controls and procedures.

The officer certification requirements are considered to be an important initiative in maintaining integrity in the capital markets and thereby enhancing investor confidence. NI 52-109 defines "disclosure controls and procedures" and "internal control over financial reporting," but does not prescribe any specific policies or procedures that must make up those controls and procedures. Regulators decided that this decision was best left to management's judgment based on various factors that may be particular to an issuer, including its size, the nature of its business, and the complexity of its operations.

Form 52-109F1 illustrates the kind of assurances that officers are required to make under the National Instrument. Originally effective in 2008, Form 52-109F1 was amended in 2011 to reflect the changeover in Canada's accounting practices to International Financial Reporting Standards (IFRS).

Form 52-109F1, *Certification of Annual Filings: Full Certificate*
As amended effective 1 January 2011

I, [identify (i) the certifying officer, (ii) his or her position at the issuer, (iii) the name of the issuer and (iv) if the certifying officer's title is not "chief executive officer" or "chief financial officer," indicate in which of these capacities the certifying officer is providing the certificate], certify the following:

1. *Review:* I have reviewed the AIF, if any, annual financial statements and annual MD&A, including, for greater certainty, all documents and information that are incorporated by reference in the AIF (together, the "annual filings") of [*identify issuer*] (the "issuer") for the financial year ended [*state the relevant date*].
2. *No misrepresentations:* Based on my knowledge, having exercised reasonable diligence, the annual filings do not contain any untrue statement of a material fact or omit to state a material fact required to be stated or that is necessary to make a statement not misleading in light of the circumstances under which it was made, for the period covered by the annual filings.
3. *Fair presentation:* Based on my knowledge, having exercised reasonable diligence, the annual financial statements together with the other financial information included in the annual filings fairly present in all material respects the financial condition, financial performance and cash flows of the issuer, as of the date of and for the periods presented in the annual filings.
4. *Responsibility:* The issuer's other certifying officer(s) and I are responsible for establishing and maintaining disclosure controls and procedures (DC&P) and internal control over financial reporting (ICFR), as those terms are defined in National Instrument 52-109 *Certification of Disclosure in Issuers' Annual and Interim Filings*, for the issuer.
5. *Design:* Subject to the limitations, if any, described in paragraphs 5.2 and 5.3, the issuer's other certifying officer(s) and I have, as at the financial year end
   (a) designed DC&P, or caused it to be designed under our supervision, to provide reasonable assurance that
      (i) material information relating to the issuer is made known to us by others, particularly during the period in which the annual filings are being prepared; and
      (ii) information required to be disclosed by the issuer in its annual filings, interim filings or other reports filed or submitted by it under securities legislation is recorded, processed, summarized and reported within the time periods specified in securities legislation; and

(b) designed ICFR, or caused it to be designed under our supervision, to provide reasonable assurance regarding the reliability of financial reporting and the preparation of financial statements for external purposes in accordance with the issuer's GAAP.

5.1 *Control framework:* The control framework the issuer's other certifying officer(s) and I used to design the issuer's ICFR is <*insert the name of the control framework used*>.

<insert paragraph 5.2 or 5.3 if applicable. If paragraph 5.2 or 5.3 is not applicable, insert "5.2 N/A" or "5.3 N/A" as applicable. For paragraph 5.3, include (a)(i), (a)(ii) or (a)(iii) as applicable, and subparagraph (b).>

5.2 *ICFR—material weakness relating to design:* The issuer has disclosed in its annual MD&A for each material weakness relating to design existing at the financial year end

(a) a description of the material weakness;

(b) the impact of the material weakness on the issuer's financial reporting and its ICFR; and

(c) the issuer's current plans, if any, or any actions already undertaken, for remediating the material weakness.

5.3 *Limitation on scope of design:* The issuer has disclosed in its annual MD&A

(a) the fact that the issuer's other certifying officer(s) and I have limited the scope of our design of DC&P and ICFR to exclude controls, policies and procedures of

(i) a proportionately consolidated entity in which the issuer has an interest;

(ii) a special purpose entity in which the issuer has an interest; or

(iii) a business that the issuer acquired not more than 365 days before the issuer's financial year end; and

(b) summary financial information about the proportionately consolidated entity, special purpose entity or business that the issuer acquired that has been proportionately consolidated or consolidated in the issuer's financial statements.

<insert subparagraph 6(b)(ii) if applicable. If subparagraph 6(b)(ii) is not applicable, insert "(ii) N/A.">

6. *Evaluation:* The issuer's other certifying officer(s) and I have

(a) evaluated, or caused to be evaluated under our supervision, the effectiveness of the issuer's DC&P at the financial year end and the issuer has disclosed in its annual MD&A our conclusions about the effectiveness of DC&P at the financial year end based on that evaluation; and

(b) evaluated, or caused to be evaluated under our supervision, the effectiveness of the issuer's ICFR at the financial year end and the issuer has disclosed in its annual MD&A

(i) our conclusions about the effectiveness of ICFR at the financial year end based on that evaluation; and

(ii) for each material weakness relating to operation existing at the financial year end

(A) a description of the material weakness;

(B) the impact of the material weakness on the issuer's financial reporting and its ICFR; and

(C) the issuer's current plans, if any, or any actions already undertaken, for remediating the material weakness.

7. *Reporting changes in ICFR:* The issuer has disclosed in its annual MD&A any change in the issuer's ICFR that occurred during the period beginning on [insert the date immediately following the end of the period in respect of which the issuer made its most recent interim or annual filing, as applicable] and ended on <insert the last day of the financial year> that has materially affected, or is reasonably likely to materially affect, the issuer's ICFR.

8. *Reporting to the issuer's auditors and board of directors or audit committee:* The issuer's other certifying officer(s) and I have disclosed, based on our most recent evaluation of ICFR, to the issuer's auditors, and the board of directors or the audit committee of the board of directors any fraud that involves management or other employees who have a significant role in the issuer's ICFR.

Date: <insert date of filing>

[Signature]

[Title]
<If the certifying officer's title is not "chief executive officer" or "chief financial officer," indicate in which of these capacities the certifying officer is providing the certificate.>

The companion policy to NI 52-109 sets out sanctions for false certification, as follows.

Companion Policy 52-109CP to NI 52-109, *Certification of Disclosure in Issuers' Annual and Interim Filings*
As amended effective 1 January 2011

Part 18 Liability for Certificates Containing Misrepresentations

18.1 Liability for certificates containing misrepresentations

A certifying officer providing a certificate containing a misrepresentation potentially could be subject to quasi-criminal, administrative or civil proceedings under securities law.

A certifying officer providing a certificate containing a misrepresentation could also potentially be subject to private actions for damages either at common law or, in Quebec, under civil law, or under the statutory civil liability regimes in certain jurisdictions.

Fair Presentation

The certification that the financial information fairly presents the issuer's financial condition is an important aspect of the assurances given by the issuer's officers, because it is broader than affirming that documents comply with GAAP (soon to be IFRS). "Fairly present" means a materially accurate and complete picture of the issuer's financial condition. Fair presentation includes but is not necessarily limited to selection of appropriate accounting policies; proper application of appropriate accounting policies; disclosure of financial information that is informative and reasonably reflects the underlying transactions; and inclusion of additional disclosure necessary to provide investors with a materially accurate and complete picture of financial condition, results of operations, and cash flows (NI 52-109CP). Where an issuer is of the view that there are limitations to the issuer's GAAP-based financial statements as an indicator of its financial condition, the issuer should provide additional disclosure in its MD&A necessary to provide a fair and complete picture of the issuer's financial condition, financial performance, and cash flows (NI 52-109CP, s 4.1).

The British Columbia Court of Appeal has commented on what constitutes fair presentation in *Kripps v Touche Ross*, an excerpt of which is set out below.

Kripps v Touche Ross and Co
(1997), 33 BCLR (3d) 254 (CA)

[62] In my respectful view, the statement that "financial statements present fairly the financial position of the company in accordance with generally accepted accounting principles" is ambiguous. It is neither a clear statement of opinion by the professional auditor that the financial statements present fairly the financial position of the company, nor that the financial statements are in accordance with generally accepted accounting principles. In the case at bar, the defendant argued that while the financial statements may present unfairly the financial position of the company (i.e., misrepresent that position), they are nevertheless in accordance with GAAP. Therefore, the defendant says, it is true to say that the financial statements present fairly the financial position according to GAAP. Therefore, it has made no misrepresentation in its auditor's report and is not liable.

[63] In my view, the critical issue is the effect of the auditor's report. The learned trial judge concluded that the failure to disclose the amount of arrears was an omission of a piece of material information, but that the capitalization of unpaid interest was the universal practice at the time and was in accordance with GAAP. He therefore concluded that since the capitalization of arrears was in accordance with GAAP, the defendant could not refuse to sign the standard form of auditor's report, regardless of whether the practice was misleading (at para. 93):

> If it was only a question of whether there was a fair presentation of the financial position, the qualifying words "in accordance with GAAP" would serve no purpose. But, as the *Handbook* provides, GAAP is the standard against which fair presentation is to be judged. The opinion auditors give is that the financial position is, in accordance with accepted principles, fairly presented. It is, in that sense, a qualified opinion of fair presentation, and the qualification cannot be ignored.

[64] It is my view that the aim of an auditor's report is to allow auditors to provide their professional opinion which may be relied upon as a guide to business planning and investment. GAAP may be their guide to forming this opinion, but auditors are retained to form an opinion on the fairness of the financial statements, not merely on their conformity to GAAP. A person to whom the auditor owes a duty of care who reads a standard auditor's report and concludes in reliance on it that the financial statements are fair is acting reasonably.

[65] I find support for this view in Section 5400 of the Handbook. 5400.14 sets out the standard form of auditor's report. 5400.16 states, in part:

> To permit all auditors to judge in a consistent manner whether financial statements "present fairly," there must be a standard against which those judgments can be made; generally accepted accounting principles provide such a standard.

It is clear from the *Handbook* that the paramount aim in auditing and in providing an unqualified audit is to ensure that the financial statements "present fairly" the financial position of the company being audited. GAAP is a tool to achieve that fair presentation. But in my view auditors intend unqualified auditor's reports to mean that the financial statements present fairly the financial position. The tool used, GAAP, is intended to result in such fair presentation and when it does not the tool is revised, as it was in 1985 when it became clear that the practice of capitalizing unpaid interest could be misleading. Further, auditors, as professionals rendering their considered opinion, expect to induce reliance on that opinion whether the reliance that they expect to induce is merely by company management or by a broad class of investors. Reliance is only reasonable if the unqualified auditor's report is taken to mean that the financial statements do present fairly the financial position of the company.

[66] Given the aim in auditing, the understanding of audits that those who might rely on them have, and that auditors know of this understanding, auditors cannot hide behind the qualification to their reports ("according to GAAP") where the financial statements nevertheless misrepresent the financial position of the company. This does not open the floodgates to liability for auditors. The CICA has carefully drafted, and continues to improve and adapt with changing conditions, the Handbook and GAAP.

[67] The defendant relies upon *Lapointe v. Hôpital le Gardeur*, [1992] 1 SCR 351 and *Sceptre Resources Ltd. v. Deloitte Haskins & Sells* (1991), 83 Alta. LR (2d) 157 (CA) as exemplifying the line of cases which hold that a professional defendant may avoid liability where the impugned conduct is in accordance with standard and approved professional practice.

[68] The plaintiffs, on the other hand, referred us to what was said by McEachern CJSC (as he then was) in *Revelstoke Credit Union v. Miller*, [1984] 2 WWR 297 at 303 (BCSC) and say that the standard of care should not be limited to GAAP. They submit that the standard of care as defined by law is to exercise such reasonable care as the circumstances require to ensure that representations made are accurate and not misleading. And, more specifically, that the defendant was required to exercise the care and skill which other competent auditors would have used in identical circumstances to ascertain whether the balance sheet truly exhibited the company's financial position according to the books and information obtained.

[69] The present judicial attitude towards standards set by professions is set out by Sopinka J for a majority of the Supreme Court of Canada in *ter Neuzen v. Korn* (1995), 11 BCLR (3d) 201 at para. 51:

> I conclude from the foregoing that, as a general rule, where a procedure involves difficult or uncertain questions of medical treatment or complex, scientific or highly technical matters that are beyond the ordinary experience and understanding of a judge or jury, it will not be open to find a standard medical practice negligent. On the other hand, as an exception to

> the general rule, if a standard practice fails to adopt obvious and reasonable precautions which are readily apparent to the ordinary finder of fact, then it is no excuse for a practitioner to claim that he or she was merely conforming to such a negligent common practice.

While this test does not allow a professional to be completely insulated from liability where a standard practice is followed, it is very deferential to standard practices: only "if a standard practice fails to adopt obvious and reasonable precautions which are readily apparent to the ordinary finder of fact" may the standard practice be held to fall below the standard of care. Auditors should state plainly their professional opinion that a set of financial statements present fairly the financial position of the company and have no fear that there will be an explosion of liability.

[70] However, while deference will be shown to the professional standard, the court will not blindly accept it: a study of the authorities shows that selection of the appropriate standard of care is a question of law. In *CNR v. Vincent*, [1979] 1 SCR 364, Pratte J said at 375:

> [I]t is up to the judge to lay down the criterion that will be used to determine whether there has been fault; this is undoubtedly a question of law.
>
> [T]he role of the jury is much broader, in my view, where the criterion that is to be used to determine whether there has been a quasi-delict is, as in the case at bar, the conduct of a prudent and reasonable man. In this case, while it is up to the judge to explain to the jury what is meant by this prudent and reasonable man whose behaviour is to be used as a criterion, it is up to the jury, on the other hand, to decide whether the conduct of the party being sued meets the requirements of this criterion. See also *Wade v. CNR*, [1978] 1 SCR 1064.

[71] This view is also evidenced by the text writers. In J. Fleming, *The Law of Torts*, 8th ed. (Sydney: The Law Book Company Limited, 1992) the learned author says at 106:

> It is for the court to determine the existence of a duty relationship and to lay down in general terms the standard of care by which to measure the defendant's conduct; it is for the jury to translate the general into a particular standard suitable for the case in hand and to decide whether that standard has been attained. …

[72] This conclusion is also reached in *ter Neuzen* at para. 52:

> The question as to whether the trier of fact can find that a standard practice is itself negligent is a question of law to be determined by the trial judge irrespective of the mode of trial.

[73] In my view, therefore, while professional standards would normally be a persuasive guide as to what constitutes reasonable care, those standards cannot be taken to supplant or to replace the degree of care called for by law. A professional body cannot bind the rest of the community by the standard it sets for its members. Otherwise, all professions could immunize their members from claims of negligence. A partial immunization would be the result of giving effect to the "qualification" in unqualified auditor's reports that the financial statements present fairly the financial position "in accordance with GAAP." It is for this reason that I respectfully disagree with the learned trial judge that it is appropriate for auditors to sign unqualified auditor's reports if the financial statements are prepared in accordance with GAAP, if the auditors know or ought to know that the financial statements are misleading.

QUESTIONS

1. What does "fairly present" mean in terms of securities statutory requirements?
2. On the basis of the reasoning in this case, would auditors be able to determine with sufficient certainty the standard they are required to meet in reporting that the financial statements fairly present the financial position of the issuer?

The audit committee is required to review an issuer's financial disclosure and to establish procedures for dealing with complaints and concerns about accounting or auditing matters (NI 52-110). Certifying officers must disclose to the issuer's auditors, the board of directors, or the audit committee of the board of directors any fraud that involves management or other employees who have a significant role in the issuer's ICFR (Form 52-109F1, s 8).

V. THE ROLE OF AUDIT COMMITTEES IN THE CONTINUOUS DISCLOSURE SYSTEM

Under corporate law, an issuer's external auditors are responsible to the shareholders. In reality, shareholders face collective action problems in that they are dispersed and frequently hold too small a stake in the issuer to invest time and energy in effectively exercising meaningful oversight. Hence, corporate officers have undertaken this role, which can create problems of accountability, given that the auditor is assessing the officers' work.

In Chapter 6, we discussed the problem of financial statement manipulation and the adverse effect on securities markets when detected or recognized in restatements of previous financial statements. One concern that has arisen following the Enron collapse is the problem of auditor "capture" when the lucrative fees for consulting services to corporate clients and other non-audit work far exceed audit fees. Hence, auditors may not be independent or effective in their gatekeeping role. Another concern is that audit committees of issuers' boards of directors are insufficiently independent of management and/or financially literate to serve as a check on auditor capture. One reform requires issuers to disclose information about their audit committees, the independence of its members, and their degree of financial literacy or expertise. Another step imposes substantive standards for audit committees in securities regulation. Clearly the intent is to lessen the concerns of market participants regarding the audit process and the financial statements generated.

Canadian regulators adopted MI 52-110, *Audit Committees* (2003), 26 OSCB 4884 to ensure that external audits are conducted independently of the issuer's management by assigning oversight duties to an independent audit committee. MI 52-110 became effective in March 2004 for all provinces and territories except British Columbia (Rules and Policies, 26 March 2004 (2004), 27 OSCB 3252). It has subsequently been amended to become NI 52-110, to reflect that it now covers all Canadian regulators, effective 17 March 2008 (as amended effective 17 November 2015).

The objective of NI 52-110 is to encourage reporting issuers to establish and maintain strong, effective, and independent audit committees that will enhance the quality of financial disclosure made by reporting issuers. NI 52-110 applies to both corporate and non-corporate entities such as income trusts and limited partnerships (NI 52-110, s 2.1). It establishes requirements for the responsibilities, composition, and authority of audit committees.

Section 1.2 sets out to whom the instrument applies.

National Instrument 52-110, *Audit Committees*
As amended effective 17 November 2015

1.2 Application

This Instrument applies to all reporting issuers other than:

(a) investment funds;

(b) issuers of asset-backed securities;

(c) designated foreign issuers;

(d) SEC foreign issuers;

(e) issuers that are subsidiary entities, if

(i) the subsidiary entity does not have equity securities (other than non-convertible, non-participating preferred securities) trading on a marketplace, and

(ii) the parent of the subsidiary entity is

(A) subject to the requirements of this Instrument, or

(B) an issuer that (1) has securities listed or quoted on a U.S. marketplace, and (2) is in compliance with the requirements of that U.S. marketplace applicable to issuers, other than foreign private issuers, regarding the role and composition of audit committees;

(f) exchangeable security issuers, if the exchangeable security issuer qualifies for the relief contemplated by, and is in compliance with the requirements and conditions set out in, section 13.3 of NI 51-102; and

(g) credit support issuers, if the credit support issuer qualifies for the relief contemplated by, and is in compliance with the requirements and conditions set out in, section 13.4 of NI 51-102.

An audit committee is a committee of the board of directors that has responsibility for oversight of the financial reporting process, which includes helping directors meet their responsibilities, providing better communication between the directors and the external auditors, enhancing the independence of the external auditor, increasing the credibility and objectivity of financial reports, and strengthening the role of the directors by facilitating in-depth discussions among directors, management, and the external auditor. An audit committee of a reporting issuer must be made up of a minimum of three directors of the issuer (NI 52-110, ss 3.1(1)-(2)). NI 52-110 requires that the audit committee must also be responsible for managing the relationship between the issuer and the external auditor by requiring the external auditor to report directly to the audit committee (NI 52-110, s 2.2). In particular, it provides that an audit committee recommend to the board of directors the nomination and compensation of the external auditors (NI 52-110, s 2.3).

Section 2.3(3) of NI 52-110 specifies that an audit committee must be directly responsible for overseeing the work of the external auditor engaged for the purpose of preparing or issuing an auditor's report or performing other audit, review, or attestation services for the issuer, including the resolution of disagreements between management and the external auditor regarding financial reporting. The audit committee's responsibilities are set out in NI 52-110, part 2.

National Instrument 52-110, *Audit Committees*
As amended effective 17 November 2015

Part 2 Audit Committee Responsibilities

2.1 Audit Committee

Every issuer must have an audit committee that complies with the requirements of the Instrument.

2.2 Relationship with External Auditors

Every issuer must require its external auditor to report directly to the audit committee.

2.3 Audit Committee Responsibilities

(1) An audit committee must have a written charter that sets out its mandate and responsibilities.

(2) An audit committee must recommend to the board of directors:

(a) the external auditor to be nominated for the purpose of preparing or issuing an auditor's report or performing other audit, review or attest services for the issuer; and

(b) the compensation of the external auditor.

(3) An audit committee must be directly responsible for overseeing the work of the external auditor engaged for the purpose of preparing or issuing an auditor's report or performing other audit, review or attest services for the issuer, including the resolution of disagreements between management and the external auditor regarding financial reporting.

(4) An audit committee must pre-approve all non-audit services to be provided to the issuer or its subsidiary entities by the issuer's external auditor.

(5) An audit committee must review the issuer's financial statements, MD&A and annual and interim profit or loss press releases before the issuer publicly discloses this information.

(6) An audit committee must be satisfied that adequate procedures are in place for the review of the issuer's public disclosure of financial information extracted or derived from the issuer's financial statements, other than the public disclosure referred to in subsection (5), and must periodically assess the adequacy of those procedures.

(7) An audit committee must establish procedures for:

(a) the receipt, retention and treatment of complaints received by the issuer regarding accounting, internal accounting controls, or auditing matters; and

(b) the confidential, anonymous submission by employees of the issuer of concerns regarding questionable accounting or auditing matters.

(8) An audit committee must review and approve the issuer's hiring policies regarding partners, employees and former partners and employees of the present and former external auditor of the issuer.

It is important to note that external auditors continue to be retained by, and are ultimately accountable to, the shareholders. Hence auditors have a right and duty to provide their views directly to the shareholders if they disagree with an approach being taken by the audit committee.

A. Independence of the Audit Committee

NI 52-110 sets independence requirements, specifically, that every member of an audit committee is to be independent. The definition of "independence" under NI 52-110 is drawn from both the rules promulgated by the SEC in response to the *Sarbanes-Oxley Act* and the corporate governance rules issued by the New York Stock Exchange. Independence means the absence of any direct or indirect material relationship between the director and the issuer that, in the view of the issuer's board of directors, could be reasonably expected to interfere with the exercise of a member's independent judgment (NI 52-110, s 1.4).

Section 1.4(3) sets out a list of relationships with an issuer that would reasonably interfere with the exercise of the person's independent judgment and a list of related persons that are not eligible to serve on the issuer's audit committee. A person or company is considered to be an affiliated entity of another person or company if one of them controls or is controlled by the other or if both persons or companies are controlled by the same person or company, or the person is both a director and an employee of an affiliated entity, or an executive officer, general partner, or managing member of an affiliated entity (NI 52-110, s 1.3(1)). "Control" in the context of this instrument means the direct or indirect power to direct or cause the direction of the management and policies of a person or company, whether through ownership of voting securities or otherwise. A person is not considered to control an issuer if the person owns 10 percent or less of any class of voting securities of the issuer and is not an executive officer of the issuer (NI 52-110, s 1.3(4)).

Below is the current definition of independence. Immediately following is the definition that the CSA proposed in 2008, but with which it is not proceeding. Note how the current definition would have been replaced with a more principles-based statement under proposed amendments to NI 52-110.

National Instrument 52-110, *Audit Committees*
As amended effective 17 November 2015

1.4 Meaning of Independence

(1) An audit committee member is independent if he or she has no direct or indirect material relationship with the issuer.

(2) For the purposes of subsection (1), a "material relationship" is a relationship which could, in the view of the issuer's board of directors, be reasonably expected to interfere with the exercise of a member's independent judgment.

(3) Despite subsection (2), the following individuals are considered to have a material relationship with an issuer:

(a) an individual who is, or has been within the last three years, an employee or executive officer of the issuer;

(b) an individual whose immediate family member is, or has been within the last three years, an executive officer of the issuer;

(c) an individual who:

(i) is a partner of a firm that is the issuer's internal or external auditor,

(ii) is an employee of that firm, or

(iii) was within the last three years a partner or employee of that firm and personally worked on the issuer's audit within that time;

(d) an individual whose spouse, minor child or stepchild, or child or stepchild who shares a home with the individual:

(i) is a partner of a firm that is the issuer's internal or external auditor,

(ii) is an employee of that firm and participates in its audit, assurance or tax compliance (but not tax planning) practice, or

(iii) was within the last three years a partner or employee of that firm and personally worked on the issuer's audit within that time;

(e) an individual who, or whose immediate family member, is or has been within the last three years, an executive officer of an entity if any of the issuer's current executive officers serves or served at that same time on the entity's compensation committee; and

(f) an individual who received, or whose immediate family member who is employed as an executive officer of the issuer received, more than $75,000 in direct compensation from the issuer during any 12 month period within the last three years.

(4) Despite subsection (3), an individual will not be considered to have a material relationship with the issuer solely because

(a) he or she had a relationship identified in subsection (3) if that relationship ended before March 30, 2004; or

(b) he or she had a relationship identified in subsection (3) by virtue of subsection (8) if that relationship ended before June 30, 2005.

(5) For the purposes of clauses (3)(c) and (3)(d), a partner does not include a fixed income partner whose interest in the firm that is the internal or external auditor is limited to the receipt of fixed amounts of compensation (including deferred compensation) for prior service with that firm if the compensation is not contingent in any way on continued service.

(6) For the purposes of clause (3)(f), direct compensation does not include:

(a) remuneration for acting as a member of the board of directors or of any board committee of the issuer, and

(b) the receipt of fixed amounts of compensation under a retirement plan (including deferred compensation) for prior service with the issuer if the compensation is not contingent in any way on continued service.

(7) Despite subsection (3), an individual will not be considered to have a material relationship with the issuer solely because the individual or his or her immediate family member

(a) has previously acted as an interim chief executive officer of the issuer, or

(b) acts, or has previously acted, as a chair or vice-chair of the board of directors or of any board committee of the issuer on a part-time basis.

(8) For the purpose of section 1.4, an issuer includes a subsidiary entity of the issuer and a parent of the issuer.

1.5 Additional Independence Requirements

(1) Despite any determination made under section 1.4, an individual who

(a) accepts, directly or indirectly, any consulting, advisory or other compensatory fee from the issuer or any subsidiary entity of the issuer, other than as remuneration for acting in his or her capacity as a member of the board of directors or any board committee, or as a part-time chair or vice-chair of the board or any board committee; or

(b) is an affiliated entity of the issuer or any of its subsidiary entities,

is considered to have a material relationship with the issuer.

(2) For the purposes of subsection (1), the indirect acceptance by an individual of any consulting, advisory or other compensatory fee includes acceptance of a fee by

(a) an individual's spouse, minor child or stepchild, or a child or stepchild who shares the individual's home; or

(b) an entity in which such individual is a partner, member, an officer such as a managing director occupying a comparable position or executive officer, or occupies a similar position (except limited partners, non-managing members and those occupying similar positions who, in each case, have no active role in providing services to the entity) and which provides accounting, consulting, legal, investment banking or financial advisory services to the issuer or any subsidiary entity of the issuer.

(3) For the purposes of subsection (1), compensatory fees do not include the receipt of fixed amounts of compensation under a retirement plan (including deferred compensation) for prior service with the issuer if the compensation is not contingent in any way on continued service.

Proposed National Instrument 52-110, *Audit Committees*
Proposed December 2008; CSA not proceeding to implement,
CSA Staff Notice 58-305, 13 November 2009

1.4 Independence

For the purpose of this Instrument, a director is independent if he or she

(a) is not an employee or executive officer of the issuer, and (b) does not have, or has not had, any relationship with the issuer, or an executive officer of the issuer, which could, in the view of the issuer's board of directors having regard to all relevant circumstances, be reasonably perceived to interfere with the exercise of his or her independent judgment.

The current Instrument also contains provisions dealing with replacement of audit committee members where they cease to be independent, resign, or die (NI 52-110, ss 3.4, 3.5). Temporary exceptions to the independence requirements are available if the member is able to exercise the impartial judgment necessary for the member to fulfill his or her responsibilities as an audit committee member (NI 52-110, s 3.6). The individual granted the exemption cannot be the chair of the committee and the exemption is not available unless the majority of the audit committee members are still independent (NI 52-110, ss 3.6, 3.7). The board of directors must first determine that reliance on the exemption will not materially adversely affect the ability of the audit committee to act independently (NI 52-110, s 3.9). An audit committee must have the authority to engage independent counsel and other advisers as it determines necessary to carry out its duties, to set and pay the compensation for any advisers employed by the audit committee, and to communicate directly with the internal and external auditors (NI 52-110, s 4.1).

There are provisions that give some time relief with respect to membership requirements for initial public offerings (NI 52-110, s 3.2). There are also some exemptions from the requirements for controlled companies—for example, the audit committee member cannot act as the chair of the audit committee; the board determines in its reasonable judgment that the member is able to exercise the impartial judgment necessary to fulfill his or her responsibilities as an audit committee member; and the appointment of the member is required in the best interests of the issuer and its shareholders (NI 52-110, s 3.3).

The proposed definition of independence that did not go ahead would have captured relationships that are reasonably *perceived* to interfere with the exercise of independent judgment, whereas the current definition captures relationships that are reasonably *expected* to interfere with the exercise of independent judgment. The CSA has observed that the concept of perception is broader than that of expectation and suggested that it might be appropriate to include in the definition of independence as it is removing the "bright-line" tests in s 1.4 (*Request for Comment Proposed Repeal and Replacement of NP 58-201*, CSA not proceeding to implement, CSA Staff Notice 58-305, 13 November 2009).

B. Financial Literacy

NI 52-110 also sets financial literacy requirements for audit committee members. An individual is financially literate if he or she has the ability to read and understand a set of financial statements that present a breadth and level of complexity of accounting issues that are generally comparable to the breadth and complexity of the issues that can reasonably be expected to be raised by the issuer's financial statements (NI 52-110, s 1.6). A comprehensive knowledge of GAAP and generally accepted auditing standards (GAAS) and IFRS is not part of the definition of financially literate. An issuer is required to disclose in its AIF the education and experience of each audit committee member that is relevant to the performance of his or her responsibilities as an audit committee member and, in particular, any education or experience that would provide the member with an understanding of the accounting principles used by the issuer to prepare its financial statements as well as the ability to assess the general application of such accounting principles in connection with the accounting for estimates, accruals, and reserves (Form 52-110F1, s 3). The issuer must also disclose any experience that the member has in actively supervising persons engaged in preparing, auditing, analyzing, and evaluating financial statements. A director that is not financially literate can be appointed to the audit committee provided that the member becomes financially literate within a reasonable period of time following the appointment and the board of directors has determined that the appointment will not materially adversely affect the ability of the audit committee to act independently (NI 52-110, ss 3.8, 3.9).

While there are financial literacy requirements in NI 52-110 and extensive disclosure is required in terms of experience and expertise on the audit committee, NI 52-110 does not go as far as the *Sarbanes-Oxley Act*, which requires that there be at least one "financial expert" on the committee, as defined by the statute and US regulations (116 Stat 745 at 790). A number of Canadian issuers must, however, meet these requirements because they are cross-listed in the United States and subject to the requirements of the *Sarbanes-Oxley Act*.

The issuer must also disclose whether the issuer has relied on any of the audit committee exemptions, such as in connection with an IPO or *de minimis* non-audit services exemptions, including disclosing the name of the member appointed under an exemption, the nature of the exemption, and the rationale for the appointment (Form 52-110F1, ss 4-5).

C. Pre-Approval of Non-Audit Services

Prior to recent corporate scandals in the United States, audit firms provided many non-audit services to issuers, which were often more lucrative than the audit fees they received from the issuer. This practice led in some instances to auditor capture and the failure of auditors to alert investors to the self-dealing practices of corporate officers. NI 52-110 now requires the pre-approval of non-audit services by the audit committee (NI 52-110, ss 2.3(4), 2.6). Audit committees must adopt policies and procedures for the engagement of non-audit services, including that the audit committee is informed of non-audit services (NI 52-110, s 2.6). The information required under the procedure should be detailed such that the audit committee can make an informed assessment of the impact of the particular service on the auditor's independence. The audit committee cannot delegate its responsibilities to make the pre-approval determination to management, but it can delegate the authority to approve non-audit services to one or more independent members if any pre-approval is brought to the audit committee at its first scheduled meeting following such pre-approval (NI 52-110, s 2.5). There are also provisions for *de minimis* non-audit services in which an audit committee satisfies the pre-approval requirement if the aggregate amount of all the non-audit services is reasonably expected to constitute no more than 5 percent of total fees paid by the issuer and its subsidiary entities to the issuer's external auditor during the fiscal year in which the services are provided (NI 52-110, s 2.4). Where the issuer or its subsidiary did not recognize the services as non-audit services at the time of the engagement and the services are promptly brought to the attention of, and approved by, the audit committee or its designated member prior to the completion of the audit, the pre-approval conditions are satisfied (NI 52-110, s 2.4). Disclosure provisions under NI 52-110 are aimed at alignment with the provisions of NI 51-102. Any disclosure required by NI 52-110 to be included in an issuer's AIF or management information circular may also be incorporated by reference, provided that the procedures set out in NI 51-102 are followed.

Venture issuers were previously exempted from some of the audit committee composition and reporting obligations, but must complete a separate form for disclosure (NI 52-110, ss 6.1-6.2; Form 52-110F2). However, effective 30 June 2015, part 6 of NI 52-110 was amended to specifically address composition of audit committees of venture issuers:

> **6.1.1 Composition of Audit Committee**
>
> (1) An audit committee of a venture issuer must be composed of a minimum of three members.
>
> (2) Every member of an audit committee of a venture issuer must be a director of the issuer.
>
> (3) Subject to subsections (4), (5) and (6), a majority of the members of an audit committee of a venture issuer must not be executive officers, employees or control persons of the venture issuer or of an affiliate of the venture issuer.

(4) If a circumstance arises that affects the business or operations of the venture issuer, and a reasonable person would conclude that the circumstance can be best addressed by a member of the audit committee becoming an executive officer or employee of the venture issuer, subsection (3) does not apply to the audit committee in respect of the member until the later of:

(a) the next annual meeting of the venture issuer;

(b) the date that is six months after the date on which the circumstance arose.

A US-listed issuer is also exempted from the audit committee composition, responsibilities, and reporting obligations if it is in compliance with requirements of the US marketplace. If it is incorporated or continued in a jurisdiction in Canada, it must include the required disclosures in its AIF (NI 52-110, s 7.1; Form 52-110F1).

VI. GOVERNANCE OF INCOME TRUSTS

A major theme of this chapter has been the possibility for tension or overlap between securities law and corporate law, because both bodies of law are concerned about good governance practices. One possible justification for the entry of securities regulators into the field of promoting good governance practices is that many significant business entities in Canada are not in fact organized as corporations and, therefore, are not regulated by corporate law. An important example in the Canadian context is the business entity known as an income trust. Income trusts, which can have many features of the corporate form, have been used in Canada as an organizational form in a business or investment context for a number of years. Income trusts include real estate investment trusts, oil and gas trusts, energy trusts, and business income trusts, the latter of which can have any kind of underlying business. The use of a business income trust structure allows the income of the operating entity through which the business is carried on to flow through to investors without being taxed at the level of the operating business entity.

The excerpt below discusses how securities law has developed to regulate some of the governance aspects of the income trust.

Robert Yalden et al, *Business Organizations: Principles, Policies, and Practice*
(Toronto: Emond Montgomery, 2007) at 1122, 1154,
1163-65, 1166 (footnotes omitted)

If a business is operated through a trust instead of a corporation, there will be no incorporation under a corporate statute such the *Canada Business Corporations Act* (CBCA). Consequently, provisions in the CBCA that set out basic corporate governance features such as powers of directors, the delegation of powers of directors, shareholders' meetings, shareholder proposals, shareholder requisitioned meetings, removal of directors, supermajority voting for fundamental changes, and remedies such as the appraisal remedy, the oppression remedy, derivative actions, and investigations will not apply to the trust.

...

The absence of statutes addressing business trust governance concerns has not meant that business trust governance concerns go unaddressed in Canada. Securities regulation will apply when units of a business trust are publicly distributed to investors. In the types of business trusts that are used in Canada, one usually finds that the declaration of trust contains extensive provisions on the governance of the business trust and these usually replicate many of the provisions one normally finds in corporate statutes such as the CBCA. There are notable absences, such as shareholder proposals, derivative action provisions, the appraisal remedy, and the oppression remedy.

. . .

... The "public interest" discretion of securities regulators on the distribution of securities may give securities regulators a basis for requiring investor protection provisions for publicly traded business trust units. Stock exchange listings also provide an opportunity for stock exchange regulation of business trusts. The stock exchange could require investor protection provisions before accepting a listing application for units of a business trust. Market forces might also play a role in encouraging issuers to adopt investor protection provisions.

. . .

The Canadian Securities Administrators issued National Policy 41-201 *Income Trusts and Other Indirect Offerings* in December of 2004. It addresses concerns with respect to income trusts, particularly disclosure concerns.

In terms of prospectus disclosure, National Policy 41-201 focuses on distributable cash, material debt, stability ratings, external management contracts, risk factors, and corporate governance. While other structures have material debt, disclosure of which is important to investors, the disclosure of material debt may be more significant for income trusts because income trusts tend to emphasize cash distributions, and material debt obligations may have a significant impact on the cash flows available for distribution.

. . .

There may have been a tendency to read the securities law requirements on the disclosure of executive compensation to apply only to the reporting issuer itself. Since it is the trust and not the operating entity that is the reporting issuer, this interpretation would lead to only disclosing the executive compensation of the trustees or senior trust management and not executive compensation of the senior managers of the operating entity. For investors, probably the most relevant executive compensation is that of the persons managing the operating entity. Thus, the CSA indicates in National Policy 41-201 that it expects the income trust to provide executive compensation information in the prospectus concerning the operating entity as if it were a subsidiary of the income trust (para. 3.8). The Policy also indicates the expectation that the external management contracts entered into with respect to the operating entity will be disclosed, that the contracts will be filed on SEDAR, and that the prospectus will also provide information about why external management was obtained rather than using internal management (paras. 3.9 and 3.10).

The CSA also indicates in National Policy 41-201 that it is concerned that a unitholder in an income trust may not have the same protections, rights, or remedies as shareholders in corporations. They thus recommend that the prospectus provide disclosure indicating either that the declaration of trust provides unitholders with substantially the same protections, rights, and remedies as a shareholder would have under the *Canada Business Corporations Act*, or that the prospectus list the protections, rights, or remedies under the *Canada Business Corporations Act* that would not be available to the unitholder (para. 7.2).

As noted above, in an income trust structure, it is the trust that is a reporting issuer, not the operating entity. This may create ambiguity under securities laws in some Canadian jurisdictions as to whether continuous disclosure concerning the operating entity is required. In National Policy 41-201, the CSA indicates that, to the extent there is ambiguity, the issuer must provide an undertaking that it will treat the operating entity as a subsidiary of the income trust and comply with continuous disclosure obligations accordingly (para. 6.1). With respect to reporting of insider trades, the Policy also makes it clear that the CSA considers insiders of the operating entity to be insiders of the income trust (para. 6.4).

...

The CSA issued Staff Notice 51-319 reporting on its findings from a review of continuous disclosure by income trust issuers. They found deficiencies in management discussion and analysis disclosure concerning liquidity, risks and uncertainties, and overall performance and results of operations. In terms of liquidity, it was found that in many cases income trusts did not provide sufficient disclosure about sources of funding relating to current and future cash distributions. According to the CSA, this sort of disclosure helps investors assess a trust's ability to sustain distributions over the long term. Discussions of risks and uncertainties were found deficient in some cases because boilerplate language was used that provided little information to investors. Investors, the CSA says, need to know about the risk associated with the maintenance and replacement of the operating entity's capital assets in order to assess the trust's ability to sustain distributions over the long term. The CSA suggests that issuers should, if possible, quantify the past and expected future impact of each risk to facilitate the analysis of the impact of each risk. A sensitivity analysis, it is suggested, could serve this purpose. The CSA also found a tendency of income trusts to provide superficial discussions of overall performance and results of operations and suggested that there should be an attempt to quantify specific factors that caused variances in performance from previous periods.

...

The CSA has published staff notices on non-GAAP measures and has commented on the use of distributable cash measures. In Staff Notice 52-306 (2006) 29 OSCB 6269, the CSA indicated that it expects that disclosure of distributable cash will include a reconciliation to the most comparable GAAP measure and expressed the view that the most directly comparable GAAP measure would be cash flows from operating activities. The CSA also suggested in Staff Notice 52-306 that if cash distributions are not equal to distributable cash, the issuer should discuss the reasons for the difference. The CSA has also been giving further consideration to the disclosure of distributable cash.

In their 2008 study of the governance choices of 187 income trusts listed on the TSX between 1996 and 2005, Anita Anand and Edward Iacobucci found that declarations of trust sometimes mimic the CBCA, as in the case of proxy voting and annual meeting requirements. In other areas, however, income trust governance diverges significantly from the CBCA, as in the case of remedies, where none of the 187 trusts adopted a derivative action or oppression remedy procedure. (See Anita Anand & Edward Iacobucci, "An Empirical Examination of the Governance Choices of Income Trusts" [unpublished paper on file with the authors].) In regulating some of the governance and other disclosures of income trusts, securities regulators are ensuring that the practices of these business entities are more transparent to the investing public.

VII. CHAPTER SUMMARY

This chapter has explored the relationship between securities law and corporate law in the proxy solicitation process and examined recent developments in terms of investor participation rights, including provisions that create access for beneficial securityholders. It has examined a number of corporate governance disclosures that have come into effect since 2005, and examined certification requirements as a governance measure. The chapter also examined the relatively new requirements for audit committees that are designed to increase accountability for financial disclosures by issuers.

The question of whether corporate governance regulation is more appropriately the domain of corporate law or securities law has been debated in the past, and is likely to resurface, including the question of the degree to which corporate governance standards can or should be codified. The issue of corporate governance and director oversight is also significant in takeover situations, and these issues are canvassed in Chapter 9. The scope of director and officer fiduciary obligation and responsibility for effective oversight has been the subject of judicial consideration under corporate law statutes (see e.g. *Peoples Department Stores Inc (Trustee of) v Wise*, 2004 SCC 68, [2004] 3 SCR 461; *BCE Inc v 1976 Debentureholders*, 2008 SCC 69, [2008] 3 SCR 560). It is not yet clear how, if at all, new securities law initiatives will interact with potential liability of directors and officers for their governance activities and, if they do, what remedies may be available to investors and other stakeholders for any failure to engage in effective oversight.

CHAPTER EIGHT

Insider Trading

I. INTRODUCTION

Insider trading is one of the more recognizable areas of securities regulation. Many students will be familiar with high-profile insider trading cases in the United States involving well-known names like Martha Stewart and Jeff Skilling. Yet the term "insider trading" is, generally speaking, poorly understood. In this chapter, we set forth an explanation of insider trading in the context of provincial securities legislation, the circumstances in which it arises and the relevant law. At the outset, it is important to know that insider trading is not illegal in all circumstances. As long as those individuals who fall under the definition of "insider" disclose their trades, and the trades do not result from material undisclosed information, trading by insiders is permissible. Furthermore, the Internet has greatly facilitated the ability of investors to view insider reports. This technological development has fuelled changes in the law as will be seen below. After reviewing the background of insider trading law, we will examine legal insider trading and illegal insider trading.

We should note that there are various policy issues at play in the regulation of insider trading. The regulation is built on concerns relating to fairness and, in particular, the idea that the law and its enforcers must seek to build confidence in the capital markets. On this analysis, investors should feel confident that there is a level playing field and that individuals with access to confidential information will not benefit from their special connections with an issuer.

Some argue that insider trading should not be policed at all and that insiders should be permitted to trade whether or not the information that forms the basis of their trades has been disclosed. First, insiders and other individuals will surely have access to information regarding the issuer earlier than the general public. If these individuals are able to trade on the basis of that information, they are rewarded for the work they do as issuer insiders. This reward will operate as an incentive for their continued performance for the company and its shareholders (see Jeffrey G MacIntosh & Christopher C Nicholls, *Securities Law* (Toronto: Irwin Law, 2002) 227). Second, directors and officers benefit from their positions in many ways, such as receiving salaries and stock options. Why shouldn't they be able to benefit from the information they learn as a result of being in their positions? To prevent them from doing so is inconsistent with other advantages that directors and officers receive as a result of their positions (see Ian B Lee, "Fairness and Insider Trading" (2002) 1 Colum Bus L Rev 119 at 133). Finally, McNally and Smith have observed that insider trading regulation is expensive to enforce and, as will be noted, detections are both difficult and rare. How can the law deter would-be violators if they believe that they will not be caught? (See William J McNally & Brian F Smith, "Do Insiders Play by the Rules?" (2003) 29:2 Can Pub Pol'y 125 at 127, excerpted below.)

The regulation of insider trading in Canada is not based on arguments such as these. As mentioned above, the legislation is built on concerns relating to fairness among those who trade in securities of the issuer. We will now examine this principle in more detail.

II. BACKGROUND

The 1965 Kimber Report (*Report of the Attorney General's Committee on Securities Legislation in Ontario* (Toronto: Queen's Printer, 1965)) established a scheme for regulating insider trading. The excerpt below sets forth some of the basic elements of the proposal. The report makes clear that, in certain instances, allowing insiders to purchase and sell securities of the company with which they have a close relationship should be permissible. However, such persons should not be allowed to profit from information that they have exclusively.

Report of the Attorney General's Committee on Securities Legislation in Ontario

(Toronto: Queen's Printer, 1965) (Kimber Report)

2.01 In the securities industry, the phrase "insider trading" is generally used to denote purchases or sales of securities of a company effected by or on behalf of a person whose relationship to the company is such that he is likely to have access to relevant material information concerning the company not known to the public. …

2.02 In our opinion, it is not improper for an insider to buy or sell securities in his own company. Indeed, it is generally accepted that it is beneficial to a company to have officers and directors purchase securities in the company as they thereby acquire a direct financial interest in the welfare of the company … . However, … it is improper for an insider to use confidential information acquired by him by virtue of his position to make profits by trading in the securities of his company. The ideal securities market should be a free and open market with the prices thereon based upon the fullest possible knowledge of all relevant facts among traders. Any factor which tends to destroy or put into question this concept lessens the confidence of the investing public in the market place and is, therefore, a matter of public concern.

2.03 … We believe that the law should clearly provide that the use by insiders, for their own profit or advantage, of particular information known to them but not available to the general public is wrong and that the law should give appropriate remedies to those aggravated by such misuse.

2.04 The Committee has concluded that the legislation required to meet the problems should provide for full and public disclosure of all transactions effected by insiders in the securities of their companies. This is the primary requirement. The insider who knows that his trading will become public knowledge will be less likely to engage in improper trading. Such disclosure will also lead to greater investor confidence in the securities market. However, disclosure, while a deterrent, is not, in our view, sufficient by itself. The possibility that improper trading may occur requires that there be a sanction against those who engage in it. Consequently, the law should provide an effective procedure to recover any benefits derived by those who engage in improper insider trading.

III. LEGISLATIVE SCHEME

The legislative scheme to regulate trades by insiders is two-pronged. First, the legislation stipulates that under prescribed circumstances, trading by insiders is legal. Specifically, if insiders report trades within a certain time period, such trades are permissible providing they are not based on undisclosed material information. Second, the legislation identifies certain illegal insider trading. No insider, or any other person in a "special relationship" with the issuer, can trade on material undisclosed information. Thus, as we will see, the prohibition on insider trading actually covers a much broader class of individuals than simply insiders as that category is defined under statute.

Before we address these two prongs of the legislation, it is important to understand who, under the law, is deemed to be an "insider." Section 1(1) of the Ontario *Securities Act*, RSO 1990, c S.5 (OSA), which mirrors legislation in other provinces, states:

"insider" means,

(a) a director or officer of a reporting issuer,

(b) a director or officer of a person or company that is itself an insider or subsidiary of a reporting issuer,

(c) a person or company that has,

(i) beneficial ownership of, or control or direction over, directly or indirectly, securities or a reporting issuer carrying more than 10 per cent of the voting rights attached to all the reporting issuer's outstanding voting securities, excluding, for the purpose of the calculation of the percentage held, any securities held by the person or company as underwriter in the course of a distribution, or

(ii) a combination of beneficial ownership of, and control or direction over, directly or indirectly, securities of a reporting issuer carrying more than 10 per cent of the voting rights attached to all the reporting issuer's outstanding voting securities, excluding, for the purpose of the calculation of the percentage held, any securities held by the person or company as underwriter in the course of a distribution,

(d) a reporting issuer that has purchased, redeemed or otherwise acquired a security of its own issue, for so long as it continues to hold that security,

(e) a person or company designated as an insider in an order made under subsection (11),

(f) a person or company that is in a class of persons or companies designated under subparagraph 40 v of subsection 143(1).

(Alberta, *Securities Act*, RSA 2000, c S-4 (ASA), s 1(aa); British Columbia, *Securities Act*, RSBC 1996, c 418 (BCSA), s 1(1); Québec, *Securities Act*, CQLR c V-1.1 (QSA), s 89; Newfoundland and Labrador, *Securities Act*, RSNL 1990, c S-13 (Nfld SA), s 2(1)(s).)

This definition identifies the class of individuals subject to reporting obligations (permissible insider trading). They also establish one group of individuals who will be subject to legislative prohibitions relating to trading on material undisclosed information (impermissible insider trading). We will use this division in our analysis of the legislation.

A. Legal Insider Trading

1. *Legislative Provisions and Exemptions*

In the excerpt below, Johnston, Rockwell, and Ford discuss the legal obligation on insiders to file reports of their trades. The authors also discuss developments brought about by the emergence of the Internet, including the System for Electronic Disclosure by Insiders (SEDI). Note that, at the end of the excerpt, the authors describe exemptions from the obligation to file insider trading reports.

David Johnston, Kathleen Doyle Rockwell & Cristie Ford,
Canadian Securities Regulation
5th ed (Markham, Ont: LexisNexis Canada, 2014)
at 351-55 (footnotes omitted)

C. *Insider Profiles and Issuer Profile Supplements*

NI 55-102 *System for Electronic Disclosure by Insiders* (SEDI) requires reporting insiders and reporting issuers to file "insider profiles" and "issuer profile supplements," respectively [NI 55-102, ss 2.1(2), 2.3(1)]. An insider profile must conform to Form 55-102F1 and contain information about the insider's relationship to the reporting issuer, including the date on which the insider became an insider (and ceased to be an insider, if applicable). The profile must also list information such as the insider's address, telephone number and e-mail address.

Reporting issuers ("SEDI issuers") must file "supplements" because their continuous disclosure obligations already require them to file "issuer profiles" on the System for Electronic Document Analysis and Retrieval (SEDAR) [Form 55-102F3, s 1]. An issuer profile supplement must conform to Form 55-102F3 and contain information about the reporting issuer's classes of securities, as well as coordinates for an "insider affairs contact."

D. *Insider Trading Reports*

A person must file an ITR within 10 days of first becoming a reporting insider, disclosing (i) the reporting insider's "beneficial ownership of, or control or direction over," the reporting issuer's securities; and (ii) the reporting insider's "interest in, or right or obligation associated with, a related financial instrument involving" the reporting issuer's securities (*i.e.*, a derivative) [NI 55-104, ss 3.2, 1.1(1)]. Subsequently, the reporting insider must file an ITR within five days of any change to either of those positions [NI 55-104, s 3.3]. This requirement for a "related financial instrument" is necessary because, without it, an insider could use equity derivatives to achieve the same result as selling or buying the issuer's securities without triggering the filing requirement [55-104CP, part 4; CSA Staff Notice 55-312].

ITRs must include the information required by Form 55-102F2 [NI 55-102, part 3]. The insider must disclose the nature of its ownership—whether it owns, controls or directs the securities that are the subject of the transaction being reported. The insider must disclose other information, including the number and value of the securities acquired or disposed of, the date of the transaction and the closing balance of the securities held by the insider.

E. Exemptions from the ITR Filing Requirement

NI 55-104 provides for numerous exemptions from the ITR filing requirement [NI 55-104, parts 5-9]. The Commissions are also empowered to grant discretionary exemptions [NI 55-104, s 10.1]. Some exemptions relieve the insider of the obligation to file an ITR, and others merely permit the insider to delay its report. These exemptions prevent the ITR requirement from unduly undermining capital market efficiency. Sometimes the costs of ITRs outweigh their benefits.

Here we discuss six significant categories of ITR exemptions, as well as discretionary exemptions (along with the underlying policy rationale).

1. Automatic Securities Purchase Plans

There is a reporting exemption for a director or officer who acquires securities through an "automatic securities purchase plan" (or disposes of such securities in a specified way) [NI 55-104, part 5 and s 1.1]. This is allowed because the number, value and date of acquisition of securities under an automatic securities purchase plan are determined in advance, and the specified dispositions are ones that also do not involve discretion or discrete investment decisions by the directors or officers. In such cases, the ITR may be delayed until five days after the disposition; if not yet disposed of or if through specified dispositions, the delay may be until March 31 of the next calendar year.

Importantly, this exemption does not apply to directors or officers who receive stock options or similar securities as part of their compensation [NI 55-104, s 5.3]: there is a separate exemption for these arrangement [NI 55-104, s 6.2].

2. Issuer Events

An "issuer event"—defined as "a stock dividend, stock split, consolidation, amalgamation, reorganization, merger or other similar event" [NI 55-102, s 1.1]—typically changes a securityholder's holding automatically, without the securityholder exercising any discretion. In these circumstances, reporting insiders may defer their reports of the changes to their holdings. Reporting insiders are not required to file ITRs, but they must report the change on the next ITR they are required to file [NI 55-104, part 8].

There is still a filing requirement, however, as reporting issuers must file an "issuer event report" (IER) within one business day of an issuer event. An IER must contain the information in Form 55-102F4, including a plain language description of the event and disclosure about the ways in which the issuer event will affect securityholders [NI 55-102, s 2.4(1)].

3. *Issuer Grants as Compensation*

It is quite common for directors and officers to be compensated partly in stock or stock options. Where a director or officer acquires securities pursuant to a compensation plan (or disposes of such securities in a specified way)—the existence and material terms of which have been previously disclosed on SEDAR, and relating to which the reporting issuer has filed the required issuer grant report on SEDI—the director or officer need not file an ITR within five days [NI 55-104, s 6.2]. In such cases, the ITR may be delayed until five days after the disposition; if not yet disposed of or if through specified dispositions, the delay may be until March 31 of the next calendar year or, if the director or officer disposes of the securities received under the grant, within five days of the disposition [NI 55-104, s 6.4(2)].

4. *Normal Course Issuer Bids and Publicly Disclosed Transactions*

A reporting issuer that has purchased, redeemed or otherwise acquired any of its own securities is a reporting insider of itself [NI 55-104, s 1.1(1)(h)]. This would normally trigger an ITR obligation to be discharged within five days. However, if an issuer acquires its own securities under a "normal course issuer bid," it need not file an ITR until 10 days after the end of the month in which the acquisition occurred [NI 55-104, ss 7.1-7.2]. An issuer bid is an offer, by the issuer, to purchase some or all of its own securities in the secondary market. A normal course issuer bid is one that involves fewer than 5 per cent of the class or classes of the issuer's outstanding securities within a 12-month period, or one that is conducted in accordance with the rules of a recognized exchange [NI 55-104, s 1.1(1); MI 62-104, s 4.8].

Similarly, if an issuer is involved in a transaction in connection with any of its own securities, the existence and material terms of which have been previously disclosed on SEDAR, the issuer need not file an ITR [NI 55-104, s 7.3].

5. *Insiders of U.S. Issuers*

NI 71-102 *Continuous Disclosure and Other Exemptions Relating to Foreign Issuers* exempts insiders of an "SEC foreign issuer" from the ITR requirement, provided they comply with U.S. insider trading reporting requirements [NI 71-102, s 4.12].

6. *General Exemptions*

There are certain additional exemptions in various circumstances. For example, if a reporting insider has no beneficial ownership, or control or direction over, any security of the issuer, or any interest in a related financial instrument, that reporting insider has no filing obligation [NI 55-104, s 9.4]. Insiders of issuers that are mutual funds are not required to file ITRs [NI 55-104, s 9.1]. Mutual funds are regulated as a separate category under separate National Instruments.

7. *Discretionary Exemptions*

Reporting insiders may apply to the Commission for a discretionary exemption from the insider reporting requirements [NI 55-104, part 10; OSA, s 121(2); ASA, s 213; BCSA, s 91(b); QSA, s 263]. The provincial securities legislation is somewhat inconsistent with respect to when the Commission may grant an exemption. The *OSA provides than an exemption may be granted if there is a conflict between the reporting requirements and a requirement of the laws where the reporting issuer is incorporated, organized or continued, or if the OSC believes there is "adequate justification" for the exemption [OSA, s 121(2)(a)(ii)]. The BCSA's first branch is similar to that of the OSA, but the BCSA's second branch provides that an exemption may be granted when the BCSC believes it would not be "prejudicial to the public interest" [BCSA, s 91(b)]. The QSA provides that an exemption may be granted when the AMF believes the exemption is not "detrimental to the protection of investors" [QSA, s 263]. The ASA's provision is general, so does not address such specifics, although all decisions would be animated by the ASC's public interest jurisdiction [ASA, s 213].*

In any event, in assessing whether to grant an exemption, the Commission's overriding test is access to specific undisclosed material information. For example, some of those who fit the definition of "reporting insider" may not ever have the chance to know material information before it is publicly disclosed, in which case the ITR requirement serves no useful purpose. One of the first decisions based on the modern legislation was Re British American Oil Co., which involved dozens of subsidiaries. The OSC ruled that "in the complex of companies there are only certain groups of individuals who are privy to what might be viewed as executive or policy knowledge which would affect their market decisions." Everyone who fit within the definition of "insider" but was not privy to material non-public information was granted an exemption from the ITR requirements.

In addition to the exemptions noted by Johnston, Rockwell & Ford, there are a number of exemptions from the requirements to file insider trading reports. For example, under National Instrument (NI) 62-103 (2000), 23 OSCB 1315, "eligible institutional investors" as defined in the Instrument are exempt from insider reporting requirements if they have filed an early warning report and do not have knowledge of any material fact or change, among other things. As we will see in our discussion of takeover bids in Chapter 9, an early warning report is a means of providing disclosure to the market of a purchase of an issuer's shares if the amount purchased together with the amount held at the time of purchase is 10 percent or more of the outstanding securities of that class. Every subsequent purchase of an additional 2 percent of the issuer's securities must thereafter be disclosed (Multilateral Instrument (MI) 62-104, *Take-Over Bids and Issuer Bids* (16 November 2007) s 5.2; OSA, s 101).

As noted in the Johnston, Rockwell & Ford excerpt, NI 55-104, *Insider Reporting Requirements and Exemptions* (2007), 33 OSCB 3673, provides certain blanket exemptions, one being an exemption for directors and senior officers of some subsidiaries of a reporting issuer. These individuals are exempt if they do not ordinarily have inside information. There is also an exemption for some directors and senior officers of the reporter issuer itself, so long as those individuals do not normally receive undisclosed material information. The rationale for this exemption is that it has become industry practice for some employees to be granted "vice-president" titles for marketing purposes. Thus, the so-called non-executive officer exemption recognizes that these individuals do not ordinarily have access to material information prior to its general disclosure and that they would not reasonably be considered to be senior officers from a functional point of view.

Insiders are also subject to rules relating to so-called equity monetizations. These are transactions in derivatives that allow an investor to "cash out" an equity position without completing a formal sale of the securities that make up the positions. If these transactions are not disclosed, an insider's public disclosure regarding its holdings would not accurately reflect its true economic position in the issuer. Thus, MI 55-103, *Insider Reporting for Certain Derivative Transactions (Equity Monetization)* (2004), 27 OSCB 2361, requires insiders who cash out an equity position through an equity monetization to disclose that transaction. Under the MI, equity monetizations are not prohibited, but they must be disclosed.

In summary, the legislative scheme regarding permissible insider trading is straightforward. If an individual or entity falls under the definition of "insider," then reporting obligations attach on the ascension into office as well as on every trade in the issuer thereafter. Exemptions from the reporting obligations are available for certain individuals and entities, such as institutional investors and directors and senior officers of subsidiaries. These exemptions are only available in limited instances and students should be sure to note the particulars of the applicable statute and other legislation. A key question, to which we now turn, is whether the legislative regime is effective.

2. *Assessment of the Legislative Scheme*

One of the vexing questions about legal insider trading is whether filing insider trading reports is an effective means to disseminate information to the market. Students should remember that the very purpose of disseminating this information is to ensure that all securityholders are trading on a "level playing field" in that they have access to the same information. The introduction of SEDI, the electronic-based disclosure system, is certainly a welcome development in this regard because it speeds up the time between the insider's filing and the receipt of the information by the investor. But questions arise as to whether SEDI will enhance the quality and accuracy of insider trading reports. A subsequent question is whether there is adequate enforcement for failure to file insider trading reports.

In their study of insider trading in Canada, William J McNally & Brian F Smith, "Do Insiders Play by the Rules?" (2003) 29:2 Can Pub Pol'y 125, found that there have been only two cases in which insiders were found to have failed to report their trading activity. The study, excerpted at the end of this chapter, suggests that either there is nearly 100 percent compliance with the disclosure requirements relating to filing insider trading reports or the surveillance and enforcement of this aspect of disclosure are weak. Of course, the McNally & Smith study does not reveal how many investigations have been carried out with respect to failure to file insider trading reports. Although this information is difficult to obtain, it would be useful in terms of assessing the efficacy of the securities regulators in policing this aspect of capital markets activity.

It is also worth noting the role of internal corporate insider trading policies that restrict the ability of insiders to trade securities of the issuer beyond what the law requires. Law and economics theory predicts that shareholders would seldom, if ever, negotiate private contracts with the corporation banning insider trading if it were not illegal. However, empirical work by Laura Nyantung Beny & Anita Anand, "Private Regulation of Insider Trading in the Shadow of

Lax Public Enforcement: Evidence from Canadian Firms" (2008) 3:2 Harv Bus L Rev 215, indicates that issuers will impose private insider trading policies to enhance corporate performance. In particular, issuers with controlling shareholders are more likely to voluntarily adopt internal insider trading policies that impose trading restrictions on their insiders that are more stringent than insider trading laws themselves. This evidence suggests that, even in the absence of insider trading laws, private restrictions on insider trading may nonetheless arise as a matter of internal corporate policy. We will now move on to discuss illegal insider trading.

B. Illegal Insider Trading and Tipping

The more complex (and perhaps more controversial) of the two prongs of legislation dealing with insider trading relates to the prohibitions against illegal insider trading and tipping. Generally, it is illegal for persons or companies in a "special relationship" with a reporting issuer to trade in securities of the reporting issuer if they have knowledge of a material fact or material change with respect to the reporting issuer that has not been generally disclosed. This is sometimes referred to as "illegal insider trading." The legislation also prohibits someone in a special relationship with the issuer from sharing information with respect to a material fact or material change that has not been generally disclosed. This is referred to as "tipping." We will discuss both of these prohibitions below.

The basic prohibition against illegal insider trading is as follows:

> No person or company in a special relationship with an issuer shall purchase or sell securities of the issuer with the knowledge of a material fact or material change with respect to the issuer that has not been generally disclosed (OSA s. 76(1); ASA s. 147(3); and NBSA s. 147(2)).

According to s 76(5) of the OSA, an "issuer" is defined as

> (a) a reporting issuer; or
> (b) any other issuer whose securities are publicly traded.

Students should note that s 76(1) of the OSA was recently amended, with all references to "a reporting issuer" being changed to "an issuer." Similar language is used in the ASA and the NBSA; however, the Nfld SA and the QSA still employ the "reporting issuer" language. This amendment now ensures that public and private corporations (and not only reporting issuers per se) can fall within the insider trading provisions.

Note that the provision applies to anyone in a special relationship with the issuer (as noted previously, not simply insiders as defined in the statute) who has bought or sold the issuer's securities. Furthermore, the knowledge must consist of a material fact or a material change, and the information cannot have been generally disclosed already. If these elements are present, then the legislation has been breached. To clarify, the elements are as follows: (1) special relationship; (2) purchase or sale with knowledge of a material fact or change; and (3) not generally disclosed.

1. Special Relationship

The definition of "special relationship" is of crucial importance. In particular, if there is a claim against *x* for illegal insider trading, then *x* must have been in a special relationship with the issuer. This means that *x* must be, according to OSA, s 76(5) (see also ASA, s 9; BCSA, s 3; Nfld SA, s 77(5); and QSA, s 189):

"person or company in a special relationship with an issuer" means,

(a) a person or company that is an insider, affiliate or associate of,

(i) the issuer,

(ii) a person or company that is considering or evaluating whether to make a take-over bid, as defined in Part XX, or that proposes to make a take-over bid, as defined in Part XX, for the securities of the issuer, or

(iii) a person or company that is considering or evaluating whether to become a party, or that proposes to become a party to a reorganization, amalgamation, merger or arrangement or similar business combination with the issuer or to acquire a substantial portion of its property,

(b) a person or company that is engaging in any business or professional activity, that is considering or evaluating whether to engage in any business or professional activity, or that proposes to engage in any business or professional activity if the business or professional activity is

(i) with or on behalf of the issuer, or

(ii) with or on behalf of a person or company described in subclause (a)(ii) or (iii),

(c) a person who is a director, officer or employee of

(i) the issuer [or]

. . .

(iv) a person or company described in subclause (a)(ii) or (iii) or clause (b),

(d) a person or company that learned of the material fact or material change with respect to the issuer while the person or company was a person or company described in clause (a), (b) or (c),

(e) a person or company that learns of a material fact or material change with respect to the issuer from any other person or company described in this subsection, including a person or company described in this clause, and knows or ought reasonably to have known that the other person or company is a person or company in such a relationship.

This definition is undoubtedly broad. Directors, officers, and employees generally fall under this definition, as do directors, officers, or employees of bidders and parties contemplating or engaging in business or business combinations with the issuer (see (c)). Perhaps the broadest part of the definition is (e), in which anyone who learns of a material fact or change from anyone described in the definition as a whole and who should have known that the person was in a special relationship with the issuer can come within the definition. For instance, in *Re Waheed* (2014), 37 OSCB 8007, a strategic consultant was found to have been in a special relationship with the issuer under both ss 76(5)(d) and (e), as he gained knowledge about the issuer while acting in a professional relationship with the issuer as a strategic adviser and, further, he gained such knowledge from the directors and officers of the issuers. Notwithstanding the tribunal's findings in respect of this component of the offence, the insider trading and tipping allegations by OSC staff failed on separate grounds relating to the defendants' knowledge of certain material facts. Even so, it is important to note that this provision is based on a reasonableness standard but nevertheless potentially implicates those who *learn* of the information, not simply those who convey it.

It is also important to note that people in a special relationship are not only insiders but also parties contemplating, or associated with making, a takeover bid or contemplating or engaged in some other proposed transaction with the issuer (see (a)(ii) and (iii) above). Under the former s 76(5), only parties proposing a take-over bid or other transaction were caught by the definition of special relationship. The new s 76(5), passed in 2013, broadened this definition to include parties considering or evaluating whether to make a take-over bid or other transaction. *Re Donald*, excerpted below, highlights the difficulties associated with the former definition.

Re Donald
(2012), 35 OSCB 7383

[2] Staff alleges that Donald purchased securities of Certicom Corp. in August and September 2008 while he was a person in a special relationship with Certicom and while he had knowledge of material facts with respect to Certicom that had not been generally disclosed, contrary to subsection 76(1) of the Act.

[3] In 2008, Certicom was a provider of cryptography used by software vendors and wireless device manufacturers, including Research in Motion, to provide security in their products.

[4] RIM is a designer, manufacturer and marketer of wireless devices for the mobile communications market.

[5] During the relevant period of time, Donald was RIM's Vice President for Code Division Multiple Access.

[6] On August 20, 2008, RIM hosted a golf tournament and dinner for its executives (at the Redtail Golf Course, a private golf course in Port Stanley, Ontario). Following a day of golf, a private dinner was served in Redtail's dining room. During the dinner, Donald had a conversation regarding Certicom with Chris Wormald, RIM's Vice President of Strategic Alliances, one of the other RIM officers who were seated at the same table. Staff alleges that during this conversation, Donald became aware of material facts relating to Certicom that had not been generally disclosed.

[7] On the following day, August 21, 2008, Donald instructed his broker to purchase $300,000 worth of Certicom shares at a price not to exceed $1.55 per share. Between August 21, 2008 and September 15, 2008, Donald acquired 200,000 shares of Certicom through his broker at a total cost of $305,000.

[8] On December 3, 2008, RIM announced its intention to make an offer to acquire all of Certicom's shares at a price of $1.50 per share. Following a number of intervening events, on February 10, 2009, Certicom announced that it had entered into an arrangement agreement with RIM pursuant to which RIM would acquire all of Certicom's common shares at a price of $3.00 per share. On March 26, 2009, following the implementation of RIM's plan of arrangement, Donald received the proceeds of the sale of his Certicom shares in the amount of $600,000.

...

Allegations

[10] Staff alleges that, at the time of his purchases of Certicom shares, Donald was in a special relationship with Certicom because:

(a) He learned of material facts with respect to Certicom that had not been generally disclosed while he was an insider, officer and employee of RIM, at a time when RIM was a company:
   (i) proposing to make a take-over bid for Certicom;
   (ii) proposing to become a party to a reorganization, amalgamation, merger or arrangement or similar business combination with Certicom; and/ or
   (iii) engaging in business with Certicom; and

(b) He learned of material facts with respect to Certicom from Wormald, who was in a special relationship with Certicom, in circumstances where Donald knew or ought reasonably to have known that Wormald was a person in such a relationship.

[11] Staff alleges that, at the time of his purchases of Certicom shares, Donald had knowledge of material facts relating to Certicom that had not been generally disclosed. More specifically, the material facts of which Staff alleges Donald had knowledge were that:

(a) RIM had been in confidential discussions with Certicom relating to a potential acquisition of Certicom by RIM;
(b) RIM was in talks with Scott Vanstone ("Vanstone"), Certicom's founder and a former Chief Executive Officer ("CEO") and a member of Certicom's board of directors;
(c) RIM had a continuing interest in the acquisition of Certicom; and
(d) Donald understood from Wormald that Certicom's then current share price was dramatically undervalued based on Certicom's licensing agreements.

. . .

Finding

[53] It is clear from the evidence that Wormald communicated to Donald that (i) RIM was interested in acquiring Certicom; (ii) Certicom was not at the time demonstrating any interest in dealing with RIM; (iii) Wormald had been speaking to Vanstone; and (iv) Wormald thought that Certicom's share price was undervalued based on its licence agreements. It is also clear from Donald's evidence that Wormald told him that Certicom's shares were worth approximately $5.00 per share, which we note was more than three times the price at which the shares were trading at the time.

. . .

Special Relationship with Certicom

[146] Staff submits that Donald falls under the definition of a person in a special relationship with Certicom in three possible ways.

[147] First, and Staff submits, most compellingly, Donald was in a special relationship pursuant to subsection 76(5)(e) of the Act because he learned of material facts with respect to Certicom from Wormald who was himself in a special relationship with Certicom in circumstances where Donald knew or ought reasonably to have known that Wormald was a person in such a relationship. Staff submits that RIM possessed confidential information about Certicom that was provided to it for the very purpose of assessing the desirability of an acquisition, and that Wormald was the officer in charge of RIM's assessment of Certicom as an acquisition opportunity.

[148] Second, Staff submits that it is also arguable that Donald was in a special relationship under subsection 76(5)(c) of the Act because he learned of material facts with respect to Certicom while he was an insider, officer and employee of RIM when RIM was proposing to make a take-over bid for Certicom (i.e. while RIM was a company described in subsection 76(5)(a)(ii) of the Act). Staff submits that contemplating a hostile bid would

be sufficient to constitute "proposing" since to find otherwise would exempt such transactions from the application of subsection 76(5) of the Act which Staff contends is clearly not its intention.

. . .

[154] Finally, Staff submits that Donald may also have been in a special relationship under subsection 76(5)(c) of the Act because he learned of material facts with respect to Certicom while he was an insider, officer and employee of RIM at a time when RIM was a company that was engaging in or proposing to engage in a business or professional activity with or on behalf of the reporting issuer (i.e. while RIM was a company described in subsection 76(5)(b) of the Act). Staff submits that there is no requirement that the business activity referred to in subsection 76(5)(b) relates directly to a potential transaction. Staff also submits that it was sufficient that RIM was engaging in business with Certicom and licensing Certicom's ECC technology for use in the BlackBerry since 2000, which Donald knew. Staff characterizes the relationship between RIM and Certicom as very important, and given the fact that RIM thought it would be of great benefit to acquire Certicom's technology which represents the core marketing niche of the BlackBerry device, the business relationship was sufficient for subsection 76(5)(b) of the Act to apply.

. . .

No Special Relationship with Certicom

[169] Donald submits that Wormald and Donald were never insiders of Certicom, nor were they in a special relationship with Certicom.

[170] Donald contends that his conversation with Wormald on August 20, 2008 had none of the hallmarks of a "tip"; it did not happen in secret, it was not in a business setting and it was not hushed or hurried. He submits that the information provided was non-specific, conjectural, full of opinion and publicly available.

. . .

[173] Donald submits that, whatever RIM may have been *thinking*, it was not *proposing* to make a take-over bid or *proposing* to become party to an arrangement in August or September 2008. Accordingly, Donald was not, therefore, a person in a special relationship with Certicom on August 20, 2008 pursuant to subsections 76(5)(a)(ii) or (iii) of the Act. Donald relies on the finding in *Donnini* that the special relationship in that case began when Yorkton proposed a special warrants financing to the Chief Financial Officer of KCA. In this case, Donald argues that the special relationship began when Balsillie proposed the acquisition of Certicom by RIM to Gupta on October 28, 2008. Donald submits that the evidence falls far short of establishing that RIM had made or even decided on any proposal to make a take-over bid or become a party to a reorganization, amalgamation, merger or arrangement with Certicom as of August 2008.

. . .

Findings with Respect to Proposing to Make a Take-Over Bid

[229] In our view, the evidence is clear that, as of the date of the 2008 RIM Golf Event and the day thereafter when Donald placed his order to purchase shares of Certicom, and notwithstanding the considerable amount of due diligence that had been undertaken by the Strategic Alliances Group, RIM's interest in acquiring Certicom had not evolved into

a proposal to do so. The evidence does not establish that RIM had made a decision that it should be or would be proposing to make a take-over bid to acquire Certicom within the meaning of subsection 76(5)(a)(ii) of the Act.

[230] In coming to the foregoing conclusion, we take into account the following factors:

(a) Balsillie, the Co-CEO of RIM with the greatest knowledge of and involvement with the matter, had not made a decision to proceed with the acquisition of Certicom or any portion of its business and had made it clear to Wormald that he wished to be consulted and to approve any "concrete steps we took before passing any milestones or crossing any lines" (Hearing Transcript, March 22, 2011 at page 117, lines 13 to 17).

(b) Although the members of the Strategic Alliances Group appear to have been close to completing an analysis of Certicom's patents and licence agreements and a valuation of Certicom based on Certicom's intellectual property and the cash flow savings to RIM in the event of a successful acquisition of Certicom, as of August 21, 2008, neither this information nor the report on the due diligence process, including a recommended bid range, had been seen or reviewed by either Balsillie or RIM's board of directors. In short, as of August 21, 2008, neither RIM's senior management nor its board of directors had expressed an interest in acquiring Certicom or made a decision to do so.

(c) There was no direct communication between Balsillie and Gupta between March 9, 2008 when Balsillie telephoned Gupta to suggest the reinstatement of discussions relating to a potential acquisition of Certicom by RIM and Balsillie's telephone call to Gupta on October 28, 2008 to inform him that RIM's board of directors had approved the acquisition of Certicom and that RIM wanted to proceed in a friendly manner.

(d) As the evidence disclosed that RIM had never previously made a take-over bid for an issuer, it would be reasonable to expect that RIM would seek advice about the process, the legal requirements and the associated risks before agreeing or committing to initiate such a bid. The need to undertake these steps was clearly reflected in the Pitch Book as noted in paragraph [129] above. Speaking about the likelihood of a hostile bid at the time the Pitch Book was created, Wormald testified: "We just were unaware of all the mechanics behind a hostile offer and, you know, what the requirements were. So, you know, to say—today we were firm in our desire to do it is a little premature because we hadn't really spun up the discussion with investment bankers or lawyers to be sure that it was a path we could take" (Hearing Transcript, March 22, 2011 at page 116, lines 1 to 7).

(e) RIM had not retained external financial or legal advisors, which is typically one of the first steps taken when the acquisition of a publicly-traded company is contemplated, and had not addressed the manner in which any proposed acquisition would be financed.

(f) No trading ban relating to Certicom shares was implemented and no formal In-the-Know List was created until the Strategic Alliances Group was provided with an initial draft by Gardiner, RIM's internal legal counsel, on November 20, 2008. While it might be argued that RIM was unfamiliar with the need for such a List given the lack of prior experience with a take-over bid, the absence of an

> In-the-Know List suggests that RIM had not received legal advice about the steps that it needed to undertake if a decision was made to proceed with a bid.
>
> . . .
>
> *Was Donald in a Special Relationship with Certicom?*
>
> [240] Donald was a Vice President of RIM when he discussed Certicom with Wormald at the 2008 RIM Golf Event. As such, he was an officer or employee of RIM within the meaning of subsection 76(5)(c) of the Act. Had we found that RIM was proposing to make a take-over bid for Certicom or proposing to enter into some other business relationship with Certicom, we would have concluded that Donald, as an officer and employee of RIM, was in a special relationship with Certicom. As we have concluded that RIM was not in a special relationship with Certicom, we cannot conclude that Donald was in a special relationship with Certicom in his capacity as an officer or employee of RIM.
>
> *Did Donald Learn of a Material Fact from a Person in a Special Relationship with Certicom (Subsection 76(5)(e) of the Act)?*
>
> [241] Our analysis of the materiality of what Wormald communicated to Donald at the 2008 RIM Golf Event is addressed below.
>
> [242] For the same reasons that we could not find that Donald was in a special relationship with Certicom, we cannot find that Wormald was in a special relationship with Certicom.

2. Material Information

In addition to the complex definition of "special relationship," students need to be aware of the definitions of the terms "material fact" and "material change" because the knowledge on which an individual purchases or sells securities must meet the materiality standard contained in the definitions of these terms in the relevant legislation. If the information passed between or among individuals does not meet the materiality threshold, no claim of illegal insider trading can be founded.

As we saw in Chapters 4 and 6, the Ontario and New Brunswick definitions of "material fact" require disclosure of facts that would reasonably be expected to have a significant effect on the market price or value of securities. The Alberta, Nova Scotia, Saskatchewan, Newfoundland and Labrador, and Prince Edward Island definitions are similar except that they both have a requirement to disclose any "fact that significantly affects, or would reasonably be expected to have a significant effect on, the market price or value of the securities" (ASA, s 1(gg); Nova Scotia, *Securities Act*, RSNS 1989, c 418 (NSSA), s 2(1); Saskatchewan, *The Securities Act, 1988*, SS 1988-89, c S-42.2 (SSA), s 2(1)(z); Nfld SA, s 2(1)(x); Prince Edward Island, *Securities Act*, RSPEI 1988, c S-3 (PEISA), s 1(ff)).

In most Canadian provinces (the exceptions being Manitoba, Québec, and Nova Scotia), the definition of material change is the same. It is "a change in the business, operations or capital of the issuer that would reasonably be expected to have a significant effect on the market price or value of any of the securities of the issuer." See Chapter 6 for a more extensive discussion of materiality.

A recent and useful case on the issue of materiality in the context of insider trading relates to the actions of Piergiorgio Donnini, who was at the time of the imputed trades head trader for Yorkton Securities, a Toronto investment firm. Donnini had a discussion with Yorkton's chair, Scott Paterson, concerning the initiation of a second financing for a company called Kasten Chase. That day and the day after, Donnini traded an unusually high volume of Kasten stock, while also acting to conceal the identity of his firm. The Ontario Securities Commission (OSC) concluded that Donnini engaged in insider trading and that his actions could not be excused on the basis of reasonable mistake.

Students should continue to bear in mind the decision in *Pezim v British Columbia (Superintendent of Brokers)*, [1994] 2 SCR 557 (discussed in Chapter 6 and below in this chapter), which held that a fact need not be a material change in order to be a material fact. Students should also note that the crucial issue raised in the following excerpt is that the material fact at issue in *Donnini* related to a transaction (the second special warrant deal) that was not certain to occur at the time the trading took place.

As a final note of introduction, the case refers to Donnini's "short trading" activities. Short trading (sometimes referred to as "short selling") is a technique whereby a person sells securities that he or she does not own in an attempt to take advantage of an expectation that the price for the security will decrease. A short seller borrows shares from a person/broker who owns them (the lender). He or she then sells the borrowed shares. Once the share price has decreased, he or she buys back the shares to return them to the lender. The profit is the difference between the price at which the shares were originally sold and the buy-back price. Short trading is considered risky because it requires precise timing and there is no limit to the losses that could theoretically be incurred. Short selling is a common practice among hedge funds and is sometimes used to mitigate or manage risk because a portfolio that includes both long and short positions in shares that tend to move together is generally believed to have lower volatility than a portfolio with only long positions.

Re Donnini

(2002), 25 OSCB 6225

[5] The principal question in this case was whether Donnini had knowledge of a material fact that had not been generally disclosed when he purchased and sold shares of KCA after 2:45 p.m. on February 29, 2000 and on March 1, 2000.

[6] The issues were (i) whether information concerning a proposed second special warrants financing for KCA was material, (ii) whether the information constituted a fact, and (iii) whether Donnini's knowledge of the information was knowledge of a material fact.

...

[114] We were satisfied that the evidence, without taking into account use or benefit, was sufficient for us to find the necessary knowledge. Nevertheless, we also determined that Donnini did, indeed, use undisclosed material facts. His use of undisclosed material facts further confirmed our conclusion that Donnini had the necessary knowledge.

[115] Donnini used the undisclosed material facts as follows. After the 2:45 p.m. meeting in Paterson's office, Donnini continued his trading activities. Donnini testified that he used jitney traders to short KCA shares because he believed, based on his second

telephone conversation with Milligan [from KCA], that Milligan would be upset that Yorkton was shorting the stock. Donnini testified that Yorkton clients did not always understand that Yorkton had the right to mitigate risk, which is how Donnini consistently characterized his trading activities in KCA. The trade orders were large and the evidence showed that in one case a price limit of $6.90 was given for the short sale orders. It does appear that initially Donnini was mitigating the risk of Yorkton's long position in KCA stock held after the completion of the first special warrants financing on February 24, 2000. However, once that initial risk was completely hedged, Donnini continued to short KCA stock subsequent to learning about the second special warrants financing and prior to its public announcement.

...

[118] We did not accept the assertion of respondent's counsel that Donnini and Yorkton did not benefit from such trading to the detriment of others. He had material information other traders did not have. Furthermore, hedge funds and other investors who might have wished to short the shares of KCA and to buy under the second special warrants transaction were not provided with the same opportunities that Yorkton had when Donnini, with the material information he had, sold short shares of KCA February 29 and March 1, 2000.

5. *Can a Contingent Event Be a Fact?*

[119] Counsel for the respondent argued that before a fact can become material, it has to be established. ...

[120] A similar stance was taken by the majority of the British Columbia Court of Appeal in *Pezim v. British Columbia (Superintendent of Brokers)* ... (*Pezim* BCCA). The central issue involved whether assay results constituted a change with respect to or in the companies' assets, and were material for the purposes of the British Columbia Securities Act. The majority of the Court of Appeal disagreed with the British Columbia Securities Commission with respect to the meaning of a material change. Writing for the majority, Justice Lambert stated, at 148, that undisclosed assay results could not constitute a material change:

> In my opinion, geological information of the nature obtained on a continuing basis as a result of a planned drilling program does not constitute a change in the business, the operations, the assets or the ownership of the issuer, no matter what information is obtained from the drilling results. Such information may constitute a basis for a perception that there has been a change in the value of an asset. But that is a far different thing than a change in an asset.

Justice Lambert distinguished between a reporting provision of the *British Columbia Securities Act* dealing with a material change and another provision, a prohibitory provision, dealing with material facts. Having made the distinction between material facts and material changes, the majority of the Court of Appeal further held that the reporting requirement section of the *British Columbia Securities Act* does not impose a duty to inquire into material facts prior to engaging in securities transactions.

[121] Speaking for a unanimous Supreme Court of Canada in *Pezim*, at 597-98, Justice Iacobucci reversed the decision of the majority of the Court of Appeal. ...

[122] US materiality rules, at least prior to the *Sarbanes-Oxley Act* of 2002, Pub. L No. 107-204, 116 Stat. 745, did not require immediate disclosure of material changes. They

did, however, deal with selective disclosure and disclosure of material facts in documentation that needs to be filed from time to time, e.g. prospectuses, 10Ks, etc. Under our securities law, in contrast, we have a positive disclosure obligation when a material change occurs. In addition, under our securities law, when certain documents are filed, such as prospectuses and continuous disclosure documentation, there is an obligation to disclose material facts. In addition, our law imposes restrictions on certain persons trading with knowledge of either a material fact or material change with respect to reporting issuers before the material fact or material change has been generally disclosed. As indicated in *Pezim*, facts may be a material fact without being a material change. A material change, on the other hand, will always also be a material fact. In the case before us, we were concerned with whether a material fact existed, not with whether the material fact had matured into a material change requiring immediate timely disclosure pursuant to section 75 of the Act.

. . .

[128] *Re Sheridan* (1993), 16 OSCB 6345 (*Sheridan*) dealt with whether a fact was a material change and whether Sheridan failed to cause a timely disclosure of the change. In the present case, we were not dealing with an alleged material change. Indeed, if we were to determine when a material change occurred, we believe it more likely to have been when the parties reached agreement in principle sometime on March 1, 2000, or, perhaps, on March 2, 2000, after the board of directors of KCA and the bought deal committee of Yorkton had approved the transaction. However, we did not need to decide this question because the matter at issue was not whether and when a material change occurred in the affairs of KCA with respect to the special second warrants financing, but rather whether the information which Donnini had after his meeting with Paterson and McQueen on the afternoon of February 29, 2000 constituted a material fact.

[129] We determined that the negotiations for the second special warrants financing were sufficiently advanced at 2:45 p.m. on February 29, 2000 that the information about the proposed transaction at that time was a fact for purposes of the definition of "material fact" in the Act.

6. *Probability/Magnitude Test*

[130] In *Sheridan*, in the course of its materiality analysis, the Commission specifically referred to the leading US cases of *Basic Inc. v. Levinson*, 485 US 224 (1988) (*Basic*), and *Securities and Exchange Commission v. Texas Gulf Sulphur Co.*, 401 F.2d 833 (2d Cir. 1968) (*Texas Gulf Sulphur*). Quoting *Texas Gulf Sulphur* at 849, the Commission observed at 6350 that materiality in cases of contingent or speculative developments depends:

> at any given time upon a balancing of both the indicated probability that the event will occur and the anticipated magnitude of the event in light of the totality of the company activity.

Immediately thereafter, the Commission also quoted J.W. Bagby & J.C. Ruhnka, "The Predictability of Materiality in Merger Negotiations Following *Basic*" (1988) 16 Sec. Reg. LJ 245 as follows:

> Materiality is reached when some unspecified minimum threshold of both probability and magnitude is reached. Only when there is some probability of the event's occurrence and some magnitude to the event can it be expected that a reasonable investor would consider

> the disclosure a factor in making an investment decision. Materiality is indicated when there are high probabilities the event will occur and high magnitudes of the event's impact on the registrant … . Instead of balancing the two against each other, the materiality analyst will weigh both of them separately and then discount the potential magnitude by the probability of non-occurrence. …

[131] In *Texas Gulf Sulphur*, in addressing whether a reasonable person would attach importance to the facts in question in determining his or her course of action in the transaction in question, the United States Court of Appeals for the Second Circuit stated at 849 that, "The speculators and chartists of Wall and Bay Streets are also 'reasonable' investors entitled to the same legal protection afforded conservative traders." Therefore, the Court concluded in their next sentence, material facts include not only information in respect of earnings and distributions, but also "facts which affect the probable future of the company and those which may affect the desire of investors to buy, sell or hold the company's securities." After that, at 849-850, the Court articulated the probability/magnitude test:

> In each case, then, whether facts are material within Rule 10b-5 when the facts relate to a particular event and are undisclosed by those persons who are knowledgeable thereof will depend at any given time upon a balancing of both the indicated probability that the event will occur and the anticipated magnitude of the event in light of the totality of the company activity. Here, notwithstanding the trial court's conclusion that the results of the first drill core, K-55-1, were "too 'remote' to have had any significant impact on the market, i.e. to be deemed material," … knowledge of the possibility, which surely was more than marginal, of the existence of a mine of the vast magnitude indicated by the remarkably rich drill core located rather close to the surface (suggesting mineability by the less expensive open-pit method) within the confines of a larger anomaly (suggesting an extensive region of mineralization) might well have affected the price of TGS stock and would certainly have been an important fact to a reasonable, if speculative, investor in deciding whether he should buy, sell or hold.

[132] Since the potential magnitude of the second special warrants financing was highly significant for the value of KCA shares, a lower probability of occurrence than we determined was actually present would still have led us to conclude that each of the financing, the negotiations and the potential price and size of the financing was a material fact.

[133] In *Basic*, in the context of preliminary corporate merger discussions, the United States Supreme Court at 239 explicitly adopted the probability/magnitude test from *Texas Gulf Sulphur*, and endorsed the following approach to the application of that standard:

> Whether merger discussions in any particular case are material therefore depends on the facts. Generally, in order to assess the probability that the event will occur, a fact finder will need to look to indicia of interest in the transaction at the highest corporate levels. Without attempting to catalog all such possible factors, we note by way of example that board resolutions, instructions to investment bankers, and actual negotiations between principals or their intermediaries may serve as indicia of interest … . No particular event or factor short of closing the transaction need be either necessary or sufficient by itself to render merger discussions material.

[134] Paterson wanted to do the deal and had already instructed McQueen to begin to prepare an engagement letter. Accordingly, the second special warrants financing met the test of interest at the highest levels of both KCA and Yorkton by 2:45 p.m. on February 29, 2000.

...

[137] ... Our Act includes the test of whether a fact "would reasonably be expected to have a significant effect on the market price or value" of securities. In determining what would reasonably be expected to have a significant effect on the market price or value of KCA shares on February 29, 2000, we believe the American test of market interest, i.e. investor and potential investor interest, to be very useful. Although the US and Ontario tests for determining materiality are worded differently, the American test is helpful, if not analogous, in coming to a determination under the Ontario test.

[138] We concluded that there would have been a substantial likelihood on February 29, 2000 that the disclosure of the information that Donnini had about the proposed second special warrants financing would have been viewed by reasonable investors as important information for making a decision to buy, sell or hold shares of KCA after 2:45 p.m. on February 29 and on March 1, 2000.

...

[143] ... [W]e have no doubt that it would have been reasonable at the time to conclude that the second special warrants financing would add significantly to the intrinsic value of KCA shares. Furthermore, we determined that under all the circumstances that existed at 2:45 p.m. on February 29, 2000, the fact that KCA and Yorkton were in negotiations for a second special warrants financing with a likely size of $10 million and a likely price of $6.75 per share would have reasonably been expected to have a significant effect on the market price or value of the shares of KCA. As a result, we concluded that each of (i) the proposed second special warrants financing, (ii) the negotiation concerning it and (iii) the proposed price and size of it, were material facts.

8. *Donnini's Knowledge*

[144] Counsel for the respondent kept stressing that what was at issue here was a three-minute "hallway-type" conversation. We disagreed. In determining the state of Donnini's knowledge, we took into consideration all facts and circumstances.

[145] Donnini, although not an officer or director of Yorkton Securities Inc., was a director and the fourth largest shareholder of Yorkton's parent company. He was more than a common employee or foot soldier of the organization. He was the head liability and head institutional trader at Yorkton. He was a colleague of Paterson. He described their relationship as akin to a partnership. He was a chief lieutenant of Paterson. He was intimately involved in managing Yorkton's exposure to KCA, at least from February 15 on through the material time of February 29 and March 1, 2000. He kept Paterson informed on a daily basis of Yorkton's exposure to KCA and of his risk management activities. He knew that Paterson was a superior dealmaker who made things happen. Paterson was "king" of the corporate finance department at Yorkton. Paterson's instincts were extremely important in ascertaining the probability of what eventually might happen with respect to projects on which Paterson was working. Donnini knew this.

[146] It was not appropriate to exclude from our minds the context of all the other information Donnini had about KCA, Milligan, Paterson and McQueen in addition to what he learned in the three-minute meeting. The two telephone conversations between Milligan and Donnini were relevant to the question of Donnini's knowledge. They confirmed that Donnini knew that Paterson had been speaking to Milligan that day. Furthermore, McQueen, a member of the corporate finance team of Yorkton, went and got Donnini for the 2:45 p.m. meeting and stayed in the room for the meeting. Therefore, in Donnini's mind, Yorkton's corporate finance group was obviously involved with Paterson in moving the second special warrants financing forward.

[147] On June 11, 2002, we announced our findings that Donnini had the following knowledge after the conversation with Paterson in the presence of McQueen on February 29, 2000. Paterson had proposed a second transaction. Milligan was negotiating with Paterson. KCA was cash starved and, by any reasonable standard, could be expected to be enthusiastic about proceeding with the transaction. The market for shares of high technology companies, including shares of KCA, was "unbelievable," "unprecedented" at that time. Paterson was comfortable with proceeding with the transaction. Hedge funds would be the principal purchasers.

[148] As we stated earlier in these reasons, we were satisfied that the evidence, without taking into account Donnini's trading activities, was sufficient for us to find that Donnini had knowledge of the material facts in question. Donnini's trading on February 29 and March 1, 2000 further confirmed our conclusion that Donnini indeed had knowledge of the material facts.

[149] Donnini consistently characterized his trading activities in KCA shares as mitigating risk, and not speculating. However, once Yorkton's initial risk relating to the positions it acquired from the first special warrants financing had been fully mitigated, Donnini continued to short KCA stock subsequent to learning about the second special warrants financing and prior to its public announcement, and went "naked short," i.e., he took a speculative position. Of course, he would not really have been "naked short" if his true intention (as we believed it was) had been to mitigate risk from an anticipated position of Yorkton in the second special warrants financing. In continuing to short the stock of KCA after the three-minute meeting on February 29 and on March 1, 2000, Donnini acted in the same manner that a hedge fund intending to participate in the second special warrants financing might have behaved. Donnini's pattern of trading gave us no reason to believe that he did not have the necessary knowledge of the material facts. To the contrary, as we stated above, it further confirmed that Donnini did, indeed, have the necessary knowledge.

[150] During the three-minute meeting, when Paterson advised Donnini of the probable size of $10 million and probable price of $6.75, Paterson also asked Donnini about Yorkton's short position in KCA. Thereby, he connected, or juxtaposed the second special warrants offering and Yorkton's short position. Donnini replied that Yorkton was half a million to a million shares short. Paterson then asked the average price of the short position, and when Donnini replied with a number greater than $7.00 a share, Paterson mused aloud about the difference between $6.75 and $7.00 and how anything greater than 25 cents could be shared with KCA. The content of this conversation had a level of specificity that indicated a potential deal was well advanced. It also suggested that the financing

had the potential to provide a locked-in profit on a hedge transaction if Yorkton retained a portion of the offering to cover the short position Donnini was putting in place. (This ultimately occurred.)

[151] In summary, we believed that much of the evidence we heard, in addition to the evidence relating to the three-minute meeting between Paterson and Donnini in the presence of McQueen, was relevant in determining the state of Donnini's knowledge.

...

[153] In conclusion, taking into account the foregoing and based on clear and convincing facts, including the agreed facts, the undisputed facts and the facts found by us based on cogent evidence, we determined that Donnini, after 2:45 p.m. on February 29 and on March 1, 2000, had knowledge of material facts with respect to KCA that had not generally been disclosed.

[154] Finally, in view of the high volume of short sale orders placed on February 29 and March 1, 2000, we concluded that Donnini's actions were deliberate and intentional, and that his trades could not be excused on the basis of reasonable mistake. Accordingly, when Donnini purchased and sold shares of KCA after 2:45 p.m. on February 29 and on March 1, 2000 he breached section 76(1) of the Act.

3. *Generally Disclosed*

One of the vexing questions in determining whether illegal insider trading has occurred is: what counts as "general disclosure"? The legislation does not define this phrase, but a 1976 OSC decision suggests that two factors must be examined when determining whether information has been generally disclosed. In *Re Harold P Connor* (1976), OSCB 149, the OSC stipulated that the information must be "disseminated to the trading public," and the public must then be given a sufficient amount of time to "digest such information given its nature and complexity." In this case, which is excerpted below, the OSC suggested that one full trading day following the release of the information should pass before insiders trade. These two factors are embodied in National Policy (NP) 51-201, *Disclosure Standards* (2002), 25 OSCB 4492, s 3.5(2), which states:

(2) Securities legislation does not define the term "generally disclosed." Insider trading court decisions state that information has been generally disclosed if:

(a) the information has been disseminated in a manner calculated to effectively reach the marketplace; and

(b) public investors have been given a reasonable amount of time to analyze the information.

In short, the term "generally disclosed" requires one to assess whether information has been released to the public and whether enough time has passed so that investors can analyze it.

This two-pronged approach was also adopted in *Pezim v British Columbia*. This case is also important because it addresses the question whether there is a duty to inquire about material changes in an issuer's affairs. The excerpt below relates to the now-repealed s 67 of the BCSA, which read as follows:

67(1) If, after a receipt is issued for a prospectus but before the completion of the distribution under it, a material change occurs in the affairs of an issuer, the person who is making the distribution must file an amendment to the prospectus disclosing the change, as soon as practicable, and in any event no later than 10 days after the change occurs.

(2) If, after a receipt is issued for a prospectus but before the completion of the distribution under it, additional securities of the same class of securities previously disclosed in the prospectus are to be distributed, the person making the distribution must file an amendment to the prospectus disclosing the additional securities, as soon as practicable, and in any event no later than 10 days after the decision to increase the number of securities offered is made.

(3) If, after a receipt is issued for the prospectus but before the completion of the distribution under it, the terms or conditions of the offering disclosed in the prospectus are to be altered, the person making the distribution must file an amendment to the prospectus disclosing the change, as soon as practicable, and in any event no later than 10 days after the decision to alter the terms or conditions is made.

(4) The executive director must issue a receipt for an amendment to a prospectus filed under this section and section 65(2) and (3) applies.

(5) Except with the written permission of the executive director, a distribution or an additional distribution must not proceed until a receipt for an amendment to a prospectus that is required to be filed under this section is issued by the executive director.

Pezim v British Columbia (Superintendent of Brokers)

[1994] 2 SCR 557

[93] … [I]t appears that the majority of the Court of Appeal is itself unclear as to whether or not there is a duty under s. 67 to inquire as to the existence of material changes before causing a reporting issuer to engage in securities transactions. In any event, I find that it was well within the Commission's jurisdiction to interpret s. 67 in the manner it did, and I fully agree with its position on this point. Although a duty to inquire is not expressly stated in s. 67, such an interpretation contextualizes the general obligation to disclose material changes and guarantees the fairness of the market, which is the underlying goal of the Act. Stevens and Wortley [George C Stevens & Stephen D Wortley, "Murray Pezim in the Court of Appeal: Draining the Lifeblood from Securities Regulation" (1992) 26 UBC L Rev 331] … also support this position, at pp. 338-39:

> Now the duty to disclose all material facts arises when a company enters the public market. Its prospectus must contain full, true and plain disclosure of all material facts. Compliance with that fundamental rule does indeed put a duty of inquiry on those who sign the prospectus, Lambert JA's statement notwithstanding. Thereafter, the duty to disclose material facts is really a duty to disclose *changes* from the basket of facts disclosed originally and from time to time afterwards. That is why the *Act* uses "material facts" and "material changes" in different contexts.
>
> Nowhere, however, in this underlying statutory scheme of continuous disclosure is there a principle that states the duty of inquiry imposed upon management when a company first enters the securities markets is in some way lessened thereafter. On this point the Court has made unhappy new law. [Emphasis in original.]

[94] It must be noted that a duty to inquire under s. 67 is not incompatible with the insider trading provision of the Act, s. 68. If an issuer wishes to engage in a securities transaction, its directors must inquire about all material changes in the issuer's affairs.

Consequently, the directors will have, at one point in time, knowledge of undisclosed material facts and material changes which constitute inside information. However, as long as the material facts and material changes are adequately disclosed prior to the transaction, there will be no possibility of insider trading. It must also be noted that the erecting of a Chinese wall, which prevents directors of a company from having inside information, does not erase the duty imposed on directors to inquire about material changes, as the disclosure requirements under s. 67 are on the issuer.

It will come as little surprise that there are no rigid rules for determining whether dissemination has been adequate. Tribunals and courts regard a variety of factors, including the information, the type of security, the issuer, the medium adopted for communicating the information, and any alternative disclosure methods. As NP 51-201, *Disclosure Standards* (2002), 25 OSCB 4493 suggests, an issuer's disclosure practices should be consistent.

C. Tipping

The second aspect of illegal insider trading is referred to as "tipping." The relevant statutory provision, OSA, s 76(2) (ASA, ss 147(3), (4); Nfld SA, s 77(2); QSA, s 188), reads as follows:

> 76(2) No issuer and no person or company in a special relationship with an issuer shall inform, other than in the necessary course of business, another person or company of a material fact or material change with respect to the issuer before the material fact or material change has been generally disclosed.

Thus, tipping occurs if *x* is in a special relationship with an issuer and reveals a material fact or a material change to *y*, other than in the necessary course of business, before such information has been disclosed to the public. In this example, *x* is commonly referred to as the "tipper" and *y* is the "tippee." There are three basic elements of the offence of tipping:

1. the tipper must be in a special relationship with the issuer;
2. the tipper informs the tippee of a material fact or material change other than in the necessary course of business; and
3. the information has not been generally disclosed.

As the definition of special relationship suggests (OSA, s 76(5)(e); ASA, s 9; BCSA, s 3; QSA, s 189; New Brunswick *Securities Act*, SNB 2004, c S-5.5 (NBSA), s 147(1)(c); Nfld SA, s 77(5)), a tippee can also be a tipper if he or she, like the original tipper, is also in a special relationship with the issuer and passes material undisclosed information along to another person. If this other person also classifies as a tipper and passes information on to yet another person, it is easy to see how a chain of tippers can be formed. As the chain becomes longer, it becomes more and more difficult to isolate and detect insider trading.

Thus, the tipper will be guilty of tipping even if the recipient of the information does not know that the tipper is in a special relationship with the issuer. For example, if I am a lawyer working on a deal and I tell my grandmother about it, my grandmother does not have to know that I am in a special relationship for me to be guilty of tipping. However, for my grandmother herself to be guilty of either trading or tipping, she would have to be in a special relationship or know that I am in such a relationship.

One of the most high-profile cases in the recent past relating to tipping was the case of *R v Rankin*, 2005 CarswellOnt 4068 (Ont Sup Ct J); (2006), 42 CR (6th) 297 (Ont Sup Ct J); 2007 ONCA 127, 216 CCC (3d) 481, 221 OAC 184. In this case, Andrew Rankin, a managing director in the mergers and acquisitions department of RBC Dominion Securities (DS), was charged with 20 counts of insider trading and tipping under ss 76(1) and (2) of the OSA. The Ontario Securities Commission began the investigation after an unknown person (later found to be Rankin's childhood friend, Daniel Duic) made a number of suspicious stock trades involving DS clients. Over a period of 14 months, Duic bought stock in DS's clients immediately before or after deals that affected the price of the stock. Duic agreed to testify against Rankin. Aside from Duic's testimony, the main source of evidence against Rankin was circumstantial evidence that documented the timing of Duic's trades and his connection with Rankin, the alleged source of the confidential information. Khawly J of the Ontario Court of Justice did not find Rankin's denial of the allegations and accompanying testimony credible nor did he find that the testimony raised a reasonable doubt that Rankin had tipped Duic. Khawly J acquitted Rankin on the ten counts of insider trading, but convicted him on the tipping charges and sentenced him to six months in prison concurrent on each count.

Rankin appealed his conviction on the tipping charges and the Crown appealed the sentence. Nordheimer J allowed Rankin's appeal, set aside the conviction, and ordered a new trial. Nordheimer J found that the trial judge had erred in making global findings of credibility and liability instead of considering each count individually. Moreover, the judge's reasons were unintelligible for the parties and did not provide for meaningful appellate review. In addition, Duic was a problematic witness whose motives and conflicting evidence should have warranted a greater degree of caution than was exhibited by the trial judge.

The Crown then sought leave to appeal from Nordheimer J's decision under s 131 of the *Provincial Offences Act*, RSO 1990, c P.33. Gillese JA, writing for the Ontario Court of Appeal, denied the motion because the case did not meet the high threshold set by s 131. The three grounds that the OSC would have advanced if leave had been granted—first, that the appeal court judge substituted his view of Mr. Duic's credibility for that of the trial judge; second, that the appeal court judge misapplied the law on similar fact evidence; and third, that the appeal court judge misapplied the standard of review—were based either on settled law or did not raise issues of statutory interpretation requiring additional clarification.

Gillese JA found that whether a proposed appeal is of sufficient public importance is not determined by the subject matter of the appeal, but rather on the questions of law that would be resolved on appeal. This is so notwithstanding the negative publicity faced by the OSC as a result of having its first tipping conviction overturned, and the importance of market integrity and investor confidence.

The case was initially significant because it was the first Canadian case to yield a conviction of tipping. However, when the case was overturned and leave to appeal denied, the case came to stand as another example of how difficult enforcing insider trading and tipping is. On this issue, see The Hon Peter de C Cory & Marilyn L Pilkington, "Critical Issues in Enforcement" (Task Force to Modernize Securities Legislation in Canada, 28 June 2006), online: <http://www.tfmsl.ca/docs/V6(4)%20CoryPilkington.pdf>.

Ultimately, the OSC settled with Rankin on February 19, 2008. He was permanently prohibited from registering under Ontario securities law or serving as a director or officer in any reporting issuer. Rankin also agreed to cease trading securities for ten years, and to pay $250,000 in costs for the investigation.

Another recent high-profile case relating to tipping was that of *Re Azeff et al* (2015), 38 OSCB 2983. In this case, OSC Staff alleged that Mitchell Finklestein, a partner at a downtown Toronto law firm, tipped his former undergraduate fraternity brother, now working as an investment adviser at CIBC in Montreal, about material non-public information relating to six impending transactions on which his law firm advised. In turn, the investment adviser, Paul Azeff, passed this material non-public information along to his business partner, Kevin Bobrow. The pair used this information to purchase securities for friends, family members, and themselves. Some of the friends they tipped extended the tipping chain by conveying the information to two investment advisers, Howard Miller and Man Kin Cheng.

The OSC found that Finklestein breached s 76(2) of the OSA in three of the six impugned transactions for conveying material facts that had not been generally disclosed to Azeff while in a special relationship with the relevant issuers by virtue of his position as a partner at a law firm advising on these transactions. For his part, Azeff was found to have contravened s 76(1) of the OSA for trading on the information he had received from Finklestein.

Relying primarily on circumstantial evidence and evidentiary inferences, the OSC also found Bobrow, Miller, and Cheng in contravention of s 76(1) of the OSA. Recall that s 76(5) defines "special relationship" to include individuals who learn of material non-public information from an individual they know or reasonably ought to have known was in a special relationship with the issuer. Although Bobrow, Miller, and Cheng were each two or three links down the tipping chain, the OSC found that they ought to have reasonably known that the material non-public information they received originated from a "knowledgeable person." To reach this conclusion, the OSC examined the nature of the relationships between the respective members of the tipping chain, the specific nature of the information they received, and the anomalous trading behaviour engaged in by the defendants upon learning of the material non-public information. Unless the case is successfully appealed by the defendants, this decision appears to signal a willingness on the part of securities tribunals to apply the constructive knowledge portion of the definition of "special relationship" to "downstream" members of the tipping chain. In this way, *Re Azeff* appears to mark an extension of the tipping chain.

D. Insider Trading, Tipping, and the Criminal Code

In addition to illegal insider trading and tipping under provincial securities legislation, Canada also creates an offence for prohibited insider trading and tipping under the *Criminal Code*, RSC 1985, c C-46. Under s 382.1(1) of the *Criminal Code*, a person is guilty of an indictable offence of up to ten years for, directly or indirectly, buying or selling a security while knowingly using inside information that they

> (a) possess by virtue of being a shareholder of the issuer of that security;
>
> (b) possess by virtue of, or obtained in the course of, their business or professional relationship with that issuer;
>
> (c) possess by virtue of, or obtained in the course of, a proposed takeover or reorganization of, or amalgamation, merger or similar business combination with, that issuer;
>
> (d) possess by virtue of, or obtained in the course of, their employment, office, duties or occupation with that issuer or with a person referred to in paragraphs (a) to (c); or
>
> (e) obtained from a person who possesses or obtained the information in a manner referred to in paragraphs (a) to (d).

The primary difference between the offences under the OSA and the *Criminal Code* is that the criminal offences of insider trading and tipping impose a *mens rea* requirement: the individual must have "knowingly" bought or sold securities with the use of inside information. In addition to the higher burden of proof in criminal, as opposed to civil, cases, this *mens rea* requirement makes it more difficult to prosecute illegal insider trading and tipping under the *Criminal Code* than under the OSA. Although securities regulators have recently undertaken efforts to bolster their enforcement of illegal insider trading and tipping, including the use of wiretaps and increased coordination with the RCMP, it remains difficult to prosecute these offences under the *Criminal Code*. Indeed, only one individual has been jailed for illegal insider trading under the *Criminal Code*.

A secondary difference between the offences under the OSA and the *Criminal Code* relates to the *Criminal Code* provisions' use of the term "shareholders." This language is arguably underinclusive, because it will not catch businesses that are not organized as corporations.

IV. DEFENCES TO LIABILITY FOR ILLEGAL INSIDER TRADING

A. Reasonable Belief That Information Has Been Generally Disclosed

Like other offences found in securities legislation, there are defences for those who have engaged in illegal insider trading and tipping. One statutory defence available depends on whether the accused reasonably believed that the information had been generally disclosed prior to the trade that gives rise to the allegation of illegal insider trading. For example, OSA, s 76(4) (ASA, s 147(6)(a); QSA, ss 187(1), 188(1)) reads as follows:

> No person or company shall be found to have contravened subsection (1), (2) or (3) if the person or company proves that the person or company reasonably believed that the material fact or material change had been generally disclosed.

The onus is on the accused to prove that he or she had a reasonable belief that the information had been "generally disclosed." We discussed the meaning of this term above. In addition to that discussion, students should note that the case law is very important in determining whether adequate disclosure has been made. The Ontario Court of Appeal considered the issue in *Green v Charterhouse Group Can Ltd*. The court held that a limited discussion of the relevant information in a letter was inadequate disclosure. The following excerpt sets forth the court's finding on this issue.

Green v Charterhouse Group Can Ltd
(1976), 12 OR (2d) 280 (CA)

[Arthur Green, the plaintiff, had an agreement with the defendants that he would offer to sell his shares in Imbrex Ltd to them before attempting to sell them to others. Thinking the market price of the shares was going to decline, Green was anxious to sell his shares. He offered his shares to the defendant shareholders under the agreement, which was accepted. Prior to the sale the defendants gained the knowledge of a possible takeover of the company under which an offer might be made for the shares at a much higher price than the price agreed upon with the plaintiff. This takeover possibility was not certain to occur. The plaintiff was notified in general terms of the possibility of an offer. On the materialization of the takeover the shares rose in value. Green brought an action under former s 113 of the *Securities Act* (Ontario) to impose liability on the defendants for making use of specific confidential information for their own benefit. The trial judge dismissed this action. Green then appealed this decision to the Ontario Court of Appeal.]

ARNUP JA (delivering the judgment of the court): …

I should comment upon Sinclair's so-called "warning letter" of April 30, 1968. Whatever may be said of this letter as being a discharge of the "moral obligations" which Godbout thought Green's former associates owed to Green, the letter was not the disclosure which may provide a defence to an action under s. 113(1) of the *Securities Act*. While the letter does not say so, the writer is really saying that "confidential information exists which might be of substantial significance to you but which I am not at liberty to disclose." Once the necessary ingredients of a cause of action against an insider under s. 113(1) are shown to exist, then the resulting obligation is discharged by disclosure of "such information." It is not discharged by disclosing it exists, without saying what it is.

. . .

I would dismiss the appeal with costs.

Another case relating to this defence is *Harold P Connor*. One of the defendants in the case, CJ Morrow, believed that certain information had been disclosed before he traded because a press release had been issued. The OSC nevertheless found Morrow guilty of insider trading because not enough time had passed after the issuance of the press release. The case dealt with s 19(5) of the OSA, which, at the time, permitted the commission to deny a trading exemption if it was in the public interest to do so, but required a hearing before an order in this regard could be granted.

Re Harold P Connor

(1976), OSCB 149

This was a hearing pursuant to s. 19(5) of *The Securities Act*, RSO 1970, ch. 426 as amended (the Act), to determine whether it was in the public interest to deny trading exemptions under s. 19 of the Act to Harold P. Connor (Connor), William Owen Morrow (W.O. Morrow), James Benjamin Morrow (J.B. Morrow), Charles Ross MacFadden (MacFadden), and Jack Burton Estey (Estey), because as members of the Executive Committee of National Sea Products Limited (National Sea) they did not cause it to comply with Uniform Act Policy #2-12 (Policy #2-12) in respect to a material change in its affairs alleged to have occurred from the period September 1st, 1973, to June 1st, 1974, inclusive.

In addition to the allegation of failing to cause National Sea to comply with Policy #2-12, there were eight separate allegations against the five above-noted individuals and Clarence J. Morrow (C.J. Morrow) with respect to trading by them as insiders of National Sea for their own account or through companies which they control at a time when they had knowledge of a material change in the affairs of National Sea that had not been publicly disclosed. The hearing against the respondents in their individual capacities was also pursuant to s. 19(5) of the Act to determine whether certain trading exemptions under s. 19 should be withdrawn in the public interest.

• • •

… [T]he first six months of fiscal 1974 were ahead of the comparative quarters for fiscal 1973 and gave every indication that the record earnings of 1973 would be exceeded. … [T]he third quarter did not produce satisfactory results and showed a loss … . This third quarter swing of almost $2 million resulted in a net profit of $1,164,571 (73 cents a common share) for the nine month period ended June 1st, 1974, compared with $2,430,525 ($1.56 a common share) for the previous year. In the normal course of events the third quarter statement would not have been released to shareholders until July 15th, 1974, but at the regular meeting of the Board of Directors on June 25th it was decided to release the statement immediately because of the evidence of a turnaround in the company's affairs and because of the changed outlook for the remainder of the year.

It was the allegation of Commission counsel that a material change had occurred in National Sea's affairs as of June 1st, 1974, and that the existence of this material change had become known to the five respondents … . All were directors and members of the Executive Committee and Management Committee of National Sea. As such it is alleged that they had knowledge of the existence of a material change in the company's affairs … . It was also alleged that these five respondents along with C.J. Morrow, who had retired from active participation in the company but remained a director, engaged in insider trading between June 4th and June 26th, 1974, in that they had confidential information of a material nature that they had not been disclosed to the public at the time that they traded their shares. Between June 4th and June 26th the six respondents and other insiders who are not party to this action sold, either individually or through companies they controlled, 117,500 shares of National Sea for a total consideration of $1,827,745. It should be noted that prior to the press release of June 26th, the market for National Sea stock during June traded in the $15-$16 range and that subsequent to the release it dropped to $9.25 bid on July 2nd and continued to decline for the balance of the year.

• • •

[The commission found that a claim of insider trading under s 113(1) of the *Securities Act* was not made out as the respondents satisfied on a balance of probabilities that they did not make use of the specific confidential information for their own benefit or advantage. This was for all except one transaction by CJ Morrow.]

This concludes all of the trading transaction of National Sea under review with the exception of the sale of 1,000 shares by C.J. Morrow on June 26th, 1974. On the afternoon of June 25th, C.J. Morrow attended a directors meeting of National Sea which was held in Lunenberg, Nova Scotia. At that meeting it was decided to issue a press release with respect to the third quarter loss rather than wait for the release of the third quarter earnings on the normal July 15th date. This was pursuant to a recommendation of the Executive Committee which considered it advisable to explain the situation immediately to the company's shareholders. The evidence of all the parties concerned was that the meeting lasted quite late and broke up somewhere between 5 and 5:30 pm. The evidence was that it is the usual practice when a press release with respect to earnings or any other matter is sent out as a result of a directors meeting for the company's secretary, Mrs. Campbell (Campbell), to leave the meeting and send a telex to the Dow Jones wire service immediately. Because of the late hour at which the directors meeting ended on June 25th, 1974, Campbell did not telephone the message to National Sea's Halifax office from where a telex would have been sent, but instead sent the telex herself from Halifax on the morning of June 26th. On June 26th at 10:33 am Halifax time, 9:33 am Toronto time, C.J. Morrow entered an order with the brokerage firm of Pitfield, MacKay, Ross & Company Limited to sell 1,000 shares of National Sea stock. The evidence was that the order was sent to Pitfield's order desk which covers both the Montreal and Toronto Stock Exchanges at 9:37 am Toronto time which means that it was placed on the floor of both exchanges at that time.

There is no doubt that the trade of C.J. Morrow on June 26th, in the absence of any public disclosure, would meet all the tests of s. 113(1). C.J. Morrow testified that he assumed that the third quarter loss was public knowledge at the time he put his sell order in on the morning of June 26th. He believed that that Campbell, as was her usual practice, had telexed the press release to Dow Jones either during or at the conclusion of the meeting. It was the testimony of Connor, however, that Campbell did not leave the room during the directors meeting of June 25th, and so it is reasonable to assume that C.J. Morrow believed that the telex was sent some time after 5:30 pm Halifax time, June 25th. The trade by C.J. Morrow must be considered from the point of view of two separate situations. The first is that a telex of the press release had, in fact, been sent out on the evening of June 25th; the second is that the telex was sent to Dow Jones early in the morning of June 26th. In either case we hold that C.J. Morrow was in breach of his obligations as an insider of National Sea in entering an order to sell 1,000 shares at 9:33 am. Toronto time, June 26th. We would say immediately that there was no conscious wrongdoing on C.J. Morrow's part.

This is the first opportunity the Commission has had to express its views with respect to the time interval during which those possessing inside information must refrain from trading after the information is first released. C.J. Morrow believed that he was acting reasonably on the basis of past practice, and honourably in the sense that the third quarter loss had been made public. In saying that he breached his obligation as an insider, we are in no way implying that C.J. Morrow consciously wished to beat the release of the news to the public by trading on the morning of June 26th. We do wish to stress, however, that an insider is not in all cases free to trade as soon as a press release with respect to the specific confidential information is put over the Dow Jones wire. The appropriate standard is a two part one: the information must be disseminated to the trading public and the trading public must have it in its possession for a period of time that will allow it to digest such information given its nature and complexity. There can be no firm rule as to what depends upon the nature and complexity of the information, the nature of the market for the stock, the place of the market for the stock, the place of dissemination of the news release. We do feel confident in saying, however, that an insider may not trade with the release of the news as was literally the case here. A safe working rule would be that an insider should wait a minimum of one full trading day after the release of the information before trading.

That information is not considered to be disclosed to the public coincidentally with it being put over the Dow Jones wire was confirmed by the Ontario Court of Appeal in *Green v. Charterhouse.*

Harold P Connor and *Green v Charterhouse* give a good introduction to the defence of reasonable belief in general disclosure. They show that the disclosure must be completely honest and forthright (that is, not a letter containing limited information), and that the information is not disclosed to the public the minute it is sent over the news wire. In short, there must be a reasonable belief that plain disclosure had been released and the public has had adequate time to digest it.

QUESTIONS

1. Do you feel the safe working rule (set down by the OSC in *Harold P Connor*) of waiting one full trading day after the release of information before trading is still relevant today? Keep in mind the speed at which information disseminates globally.
2. Do you think that the legislation should be more specific about available defences, as well as the points raised in *Harold P Connor* relating to the safe working rule?
3. In this chapter, as well as in Chapter 10, Civil Liability, we will see that there are a host of defences available to persons who are found to have breached the relevant securities act. Is there a justification for such defences?

The legislation contains specific defences for professionals. In particular, s 175 of the OSA regulations (RRO 1990, Reg 1015; Nfld SA Reg CNLR 805/96, s 149D; SSA Reg RRS c S-42.2, Reg 1, s 173.1) provides limited exemptions from insider trading rules. The legislation seeks to address the problem that arises in integrated securities firms where employees of the firm may obtain inside information through an activity that may provide them with an opportunity for profit in the process of trading or advising. The prohibitions against trading or informing would place the firm at risk in terms of possible enforcement proceedings if it continued its normal trading or advising activities. Thus, s 175(1) of the regulation provides, in effect, that a person or company (that is, both the firm and the responsible employees) may avoid quasi-criminal and civil liability under the OSA if the firm or employee can prove that no individual with actual knowledge of an undisclosed material fact or material change made, or participated in the making of, the decision to buy or sell a security to which the material fact or material change relates. Note that these provisions were discussed in paras 161-170 of *Donnini*, above.

Policy 33-601, *Guidelines for Policies and Procedures Concerning Inside Information* (1998), 21 OSCB 619, enhances the legislation in this area by setting out general guidelines for securities firms' policies and procedures that concern inside information. These guidelines cover such areas as employee education, containment of inside information, procedures to restrict transactions, use of grey and restricted lists, and compliance. In particular, when a registrant is, or may be, in receipt of inside information about an issuer, Policy 33-601 recommends that the registrant consider whether to monitor, restrict, or discontinue certain activities of the registrant and its employees with regard to the securities of that issuer. This would include trading, advising, and dissemination of research material. Policy 33-601 further recommends that the registrant place an issuer on a grey list when it has received inside information about the issuer—for example, when the registrant has been invited to manage or participate in a possible offering or to act concerning a possible merger or acquisition or other corporate assignment. For further discussion of grey lists, see *Donnini*, above at paras 161-170.

B. Reasonable Mistake of Fact

The next case is one of the leading cases on insider trading in Canada and is useful in assessing the reasonableness standard in relation to defences. This case was brought by the Ontario Securities Commission against Harper for insider trading in a mineral exploration company called Golden Rule Resources. In particular, the OSC alleged that Harper was in a special relationship with the company and that he sold shares contrary to s 76(1) of the OSA, which forbids trading that is based on material undisclosed information. The OSC alleged that Harper knew about reports on soil results that indicated much less gold in the land that Golden Rule was mining than the public was aware of ("the 800 soil sample results and 37 Teck samples"). Despite Harper's knowledge of these material facts, he continued to send out positive press releases and indicated that there were no other reports. The stock price of Golden Rule increased but fell dramatically when the information was subsequently released to the public. By this time, Harper had sold most of his shares in Golden Rule. While Harper agreed that he was in a special relationship with Golden Rule and that he had sold the shares in question, he argued that the information was not material and, even if it was, he had a genuine and reasonable belief that it was not.

R v Harper
[2000] OJ No 2791 (QL) (Sup Ct J)

SHEPPARD J:

...

[1] This prosecution concerns two counts of insider trading in shares of a junior mineral exploration company during a five month period in 1997 while the company was exploring for gold in Ghana, West Africa. The exploration activities consisted of hiring site geological and labouring staff and conducting a geochemical soil survey plus additional trench digging as a lead-up to potential diamond drilling on the site. Progress on the property was reported by means of site grid maps and assay results/certificates.

[2] It is common ground and not disputed that Glen Harvey Harper ("Harper") was a person in a special relationship to this company ("Golden Rule"). The prosecution ("OSC") alleges that Harper, having knowledge of undisclosed material facts in the form of assay results, sold 227,600 shares of Golden Rule for $2,058,580 and 197,102 shares of Golden Rule for $1,983,889 during two time periods.

...

[38] If good results are material fact which this court finds were required to be released and were released, then bad results or "duds," as the defence describes the 800 sample results, are for same reasons required to be released but were not released.

[39] Defence argues that through cross examinations of the OSC witnesses, particularly Messieurs Embry, Farquharson and Burk, this position has been undermined. This court does not agree: the witnesses' opinions and their bases remained unshaken. Their evidence satisfies this court beyond a reasonable doubt that disclosure of the 800 sample results and the Teck trench results might reasonably be expected to affect the Golden Rule share price. It is noteworthy that in a one-week period after becoming aware of at least 33 of the 37 Teck assay results, Harper sold $1,345,630 of Golden Rule shares and bought

none. These sales all occurred in the $10.00 to $11.00 per share range. This occurred, notwithstanding the confidentiality agreement with Teck.

[40] The OSC proved, from the evidence of exploration developments before, at the beginning of and after the time period of these two counts, that good news and bad news press releases … did affect the price of the Golden Rule shares. … [T]his was the only significant factor driving the price of Golden Rule shares at that time.

[41] The first question now being answered beyond a reasonable doubt in the affirmative, the Court must turn its consideration to the second contested question.

2. Did Harper have a genuine and reasonable belief at the relevant time that the results of the 800 soil samples and the results of the Teck trench samples did not constitute material facts?

[42] In addressing the question, the evidentiary test becomes has Harper demonstrated on a balance of probabilities an honest and reasonable mistaken belief to refute his knowledge of facts which the Court finds to be material and which Harper admits to being in possession.

2(a) The 800 Soil Sample Results of January 2 and/or 3, 1997

[43] This Court finds that Harper knew his previously reported gold-in-soil assay results (the 1,394 samples) were high, in fact "amazing." They were reported to the public. This Court finds that Harper knew the January 2 and/or 3, 1997, 800 sample results were duds, and inconsistent with the previous results.

[44] Harper states he released the 1,394 results on November 29, 1996, (supra) because in his view, the results were material information. He released further favourable soil sample results February 5, 1997. At no time did he release the negative 800 soil sample results. It is not reasonable that good news results are material and bad news results are not material. When Harper said [to] everyone on December 31, 1996 that he was anxious for the results of the 800 samples, he was anxious to release more good news to an ever hotter equity market for Golden Rule shares and to encourage analyst's coverage.

[45] For these reasons, a determination of when Harper knew the 800 samples all showed results below 1 g/t is important. He admits to knowing this on January 22 or 23, 1997. However, Harper released good trench results received at the same time as the 800 soil samples on January 7 and 10, 1997. No press release of the 800 soil sample results came either at that time or after January 22 or 23, 1997. The Court rejects that Harper relied on his project geologist's advice that he needed more time to analyze the 800 sample results vis-à-vis the 1,394 sample as there never was a release. It was not shown by the defence that any analysis entailed a complexity that was time consuming.

[46] From this time onward, Harper buried the results of the 800 sample, contrary to his press release promise of December 19, 1996, (supra). They were counter to Golden Rule and his personal financial interests.

…

[48] The defence has argued that the reason for the mistake of fact by Harper which gave rise to his genuine and reasonable belief that neither the 800 samples nor the 37 Teck samples were material facts was his reliance on express advice from the project geologist, Dr. Mark Nebel. Harper claims Nebel advised that the information was not significant

and in no way undermined the previous Golden Rule gold-in-soil and trench results assay results.

[49] Given Harper's decades of experience with Golden Rule, its related mining companies, prior employment and his industrial/financial involvement in general, such reliance would be unreasonable.

. . .

[59] The Court finds the 800 soil sample results were a material fact which Harper ought to have disclosed in a timely fashion. Harper has not demonstrated an honest and reasonable belief on the accepted evidence to refute his knowledge of the found material fact.

2(b) Teck Trench Sample Results March 12, 1997

[60] Harper made it clear in his evidence that he rejected the Teck trench sample results as unreliable. Therefore, the results were not significant and should not be reported. The procedural factors raised by Harper to support or justify a conclusion of unreliability were speculative and not supported by any evidence that might give rise to an actual problem. If he felt the Teck process for taking trench samples and delivering them to the assay lab was flawed (a process which paralleled Golden Rule's existing methods), he never advised Teck to use a different method and/or not to use Golden Rule field staff to gather the samples. It was unreasonable for Harper (a) to question Teck's use of Golden Rule field staff including a field geologist, and (b) to come to a conclusion that the results from samples they gathered were unreliable. If this was so, all of Golden Rule's similar sample results would be unreliable because they were produced in the same manner by the same staff.

[61] There was no evidence of other persons outside Golden Rule's employees being involved with field transport of Teck's samples for geologist Burk. To suggest such, as Harper did, was speculation and unreasonable unless supported by evidence which it was not.

[62] Trusted Golden Rule staff had assumed responsibility for storing these samples as it appears they had done with hundreds of other Stenpad trench and soil samples over the previous seven months. It was unreasonable to find these Teck results unreliable, while accepting and publicizing the spectacular results from samples gathered in the same way in fall of 1996. Further, Burk examined the samples bags in the presence of Harper and saw no indications of tampering with the bags as they were being loaded for transport to the lab.

[63] Harper's concerns leading him to a belief in the unreliability of the assay results on these samples is a retrospective rationalization. As such, it is neither genuine nor reasonable. It is an irrational attempt to look for someone else to blame for the bad news results, whether it be the Teck geologist, Golden Rule's geologist, Golden Rule's local manager, or Golden Rule local field staff. There is no evidence to raise, on a balance of probabilities, an honest and reasonable mistaken belief. Therefore, Harper's evidence is rejected on this issue.

[64] Further, within hours of Harper reviewing the Teck results, he was informed by Burk that Burk's instructions were to leave Ghana and return to Canada. Teck was walking away from its interest in the project having received the trench sample results. A reasonably competent geologist/financier would realize that there had been a material change

in Teck interest in the Stenpad property as a result of this assay report. The assay report was a material fact for Teck. As noted above, Harper proceeded to make between six (6) and eleven (11) share sales day for the next week. Total value of the sales was $1,345,630.

[65] The Court finds the Teck trench results were a material fact which Harper ought to have disclosed in a timely fashion. Harper has not demonstrated an honest and reasonable belief on accepted evidence to refute his knowledge of the material fact as previously found.

Conclusion

[66] This court has found above that the evidence establishes beyond a reasonable doubt that Harper is guilty as charged. The evidence before the Court supports a finding that, by any geological or investor standard, the 800 soil samples and the 37 Teck samples were material facts, and that Harper had knowledge of those facts at a time that he admits he was trading in shares of Golden Rule. The Court rejects Harper's claim that he did not believe that the 800 soil samples and the 37 Teck samples were material facts, and has found on the evidence his alleged belief to be neither genuine, nor reasonable. The Court has found that the evidence establishes that rather than disclosing this material information to the public, Harper held it back from public view. Many appropriate moments to share the material information with the public were shown in the evidence … . Harper sold into the public market millions of dollars of Golden Rule shares for his own or his immediate family's personal gain.

[Harper appealed this decision, and the conviction was upheld, although the sentence was slightly reduced: *R v Harper*, [2003] OJ No 4196 (QL) (CA). See Chapter 11, Enforcement.]

Harper indicates that when there is a definite finding of insider trading, the accused can nevertheless attempt to argue that he or she reasonably believed that the information was not material. This is a difficult argument to make (and one that will often be unsuccessful), especially given the need for the accused to demonstrate that his or her belief was reasonable. As the case indicates, much will turn on the evidence adduced.

C. Necessary Course of Business

Although not a true defence in that information disclosed in the "necessary course of business" is an explicit exception in the statutory language, the accused in many tipping cases will nonetheless rely on this exception and offer it as a defence to the allegation. In this event, there is no liability. NP 51-201 sets forth situations in which information will be conveyed in the necessary course of business. The policy was originally introduced to address the issue of selective disclosure (that is, the practice whereby companies release information to select individuals, such as analysts, prior to the public at large). As you will note from the introduction, the policy is based on the notion that everyone should have equal access to information, and an equal opportunity to trade on that information. The policy provides a good summary of the law relating to insider trading, especially tipping, and the relevant defences. Following the excerpt of the policy, we provide an example of a case in which the necessary course of business exception was discussed.

National Policy 51-201, *Disclosure Standards*
(2002), 25 OSCB 4493

Part I Introduction

1.1 Purpose

(1) It is fundamental that everyone investing in securities have equal access to information that may affect their investment decisions. The Canadian Securities Administrators ("the CSA" or "We") are concerned about the selective disclosure of material corporate information by companies to analysts, institutional investors, investment dealers and other market professionals. Selective disclosure occurs when a company discloses material nonpublic information to one or more individuals or companies and not broadly to the investing public. Selective disclosure can create opportunities for insider trading and also undermines retail investors' confidence in the marketplace as a level playing field.

(2) This policy provides guidance on "best disclosure" practices in a difficult area involving competing business pressures and legislative requirements. Our recommendations are not intended to be prescriptive. We encourage companies to adopt the suggested measures, but they should be implemented flexibly and sensibly to fit the situation of individual companies.

. . .

Part III Overview of the Statutory Prohibitions Against Selective Disclosure

. . .

3.3 Necessary Course of Business

(1) The "tipping" provision allows a company to make a selective disclosure if doing so is in the "necessary course of business." The question of whether a particular disclosure is being made in the necessary course of business is a mixed question of law and fact that must be determined in each case and in light of the policy reasons for the tipping provisions. Tipping is prohibited so that everyone in the market has equal access to, and opportunity to act upon, material information. Insider trading and tipping prohibitions are designed to ensure that anyone who has access to material undisclosed information does not trade or assist others in trading to the disadvantage of investors generally.

(2) Different interpretations are being applied, in practice, to the phrase "necessary course of business." As a result, we believe interpretive guidance in this regard is necessary. The "necessary course of business" exception exists so as not to unduly interfere with a company's ordinary business activities. For example, the "necessary course of business" exception would generally cover communications with:

(a) vendors, suppliers, or strategic partners on issues such as research and development, sales and marketing, and supply contracts;

(b) employees, officers, and board members;

(c) lenders, legal counsel, auditors, underwriters, and financial and other professional advisors to the company;

(d) parties to negotiations;

(e) labour unions and industry associations;

(f) government agencies and non-governmental regulators; and

(g) credit rating agencies (provided that the information is disclosed for the purpose of assisting the agency to formulate a credit rating and the agency's ratings generally are or will be publicly available).

(3) Securities legislation prohibits any person or company that is proposing to make a take-over bid, become a party to a reorganization, amalgamation, merger, arrangement or similar business combination or acquire a substantial portion of a company's property from informing anyone of material information that has not been generally disclosed. An exception to this prohibition is provided where the material information is given in the "necessary course of business" to effect the take-over bid, business combination or acquisition.

(4) Disclosures by a company in connection with a private placement may be in the "necessary course of business" for companies to raise financing. The ability to raise financing is important. We recognize that select communications between the parties to a private placement of material information may be necessary to effect the private placement. Communications to controlling shareholders may also, in certain circumstances, be considered in the "necessary course of business." Nevertheless, we believe that in these situations, material information that is provided to private placees and controlling shareholders should be generally disclosed at the earliest opportunity.

(5) The "necessary course of business" exception would not generally permit a company to make a selective disclosure of material corporate information to an analyst, institutional investor or other market professional.

(6) There may be situations where an analyst will be "brought over the wall" to act as an advisor in a specific transaction involving a reporting issuer they would normally issue research about. In these situations, the analyst becomes a "person in a special relationship" with the reporting issuer and is subject to the prohibitions against tipping and insider trading. This means that the analyst is prohibited from further informing anyone of material undisclosed information they learn in this advisory capacity, including issuing any research recommendations or reports.

A good example of the "necessary course of business" defence is shown in *Re Royal Trustco Ltd et al v Ontario Securities Commission*. In this case, it was found that disclosing information to a shareholder as part of an attempt to defend against a takeover bid was not in the "necessary course of business."

Re Royal Trustco Ltd et al and Ontario Securities Commission
(1983), 42 OR (2d) 147 (H Ct J (Div Ct))

REID J (delivering the judgment of the court):

[1] Kenneth Alan White (White) and John Merton Scholes (Scholes) appeal from an order of the respondent (the Commission) depriving them of the exemptions to which they were otherwise entitled under s. 34(1) of the *Securities Act*, RSO 1980, c. 466 (the Act), for periods respectively of 60 and 30 consecutive days. …

[2] The order stemmed from an abortive take-over bid which Campeau Corporation (Campeau) made on August 29, 1980, for all of the common and convertible preferred

shares of Royal Trustco Limited (Trustco), the publicly traded parent holding company of the Royal Trust group of companies.

. . .

The allegations read: …

> 6. On or about September 17, 1980, White and Scholes, both being in a special relationship with Royal Trustco, met with certain personnel of The Toronto- Dominion Bank and revealed to them, other than in the necessary course of business, certain material facts in relation to the affairs of Royal Trustco which had not been generally disclosed, including the following:
>
> (a) that approximately 60% of the shares of Royal Trustco were owned by persons or companies who White and Scholes knew or had reason to believe would not tender pursuant to the Bid, some or all of whom were named or otherwise identified, and
>
> (b) that Royal Trustco management was considering recommending to the Board that the dividends payable on Royal Trustco shares be increased.

… In my opinion, the tipping allegation was established, if not in the exact terms of 6(a) in terms that were reasonably like them, like enough to dispose of any suggestion that the notice was not sufficiently clear or that respondents suffered any denial of natural justice because of any discrepancy between the notice and the evidence, or the notice, the evidence and the finding.

[20] Section 75(1)(b) [now s 76(2)] of the Act reads:

> 75(1) No person or company in a special relationship with a reporting issuer shall, …
>
> (b) inform, other than in the necessary course of business, another person or company about a fact or change which he knows is a material fact or material change before the material fact or material change had been generally disclosed.

[21] There is no question that s. 75(1) of the Act is intended to prevent disclosure by persons in the position of White and Scholes of material facts before they have been generally disclosed. In my opinion, the information disclosed fell easily within the category of material facts within the context of the legislation and in the prevailing circumstances. That the respondents could not guarantee that the known holders of Trustco's shares would not sell or deposit their shares does not reduce the disclosure to a level less than fact. It was made clearly to encourage the officers of the bank not to sell or deposit the 10 per cent of the outstanding shares of Trustco that it had acquired after earlier representations to it by White and Scholes and it achieved that purpose. Having in mind the general object of s. 75, which is to prevent improper or unfair disclosure, I do not think the term "fact" should be read supercritically. In my opinion, the information was sufficiently factual or a sufficient alteration of circumstances to be a material "change" to fall within the section. In my opinion the Commission was justified in holding that the section had been breached.

[22] Once it is accepted that a disclosure was made to some shareholders but not to others contrary to the Act it is better, in my opinion, to leave its significance to the Commission than to this Court. In saying that, I do not deny the scope of our powers. I seek merely to call attention to the fact that the regulation of the securities industry is the function of the Commission, not of the Court, and unless the Commission can be shown to have been seriously in error in law or fact this Court should be slow to intervene. There

is no question in my mind that the evidence amply supported a finding that allegation 6(a) had been established. In my opinion, the Commission would have been justified in imposing the penalties it chose had that allegation alone been established.

[23] I am far from believing that "the gentlemen in Whitehall are always right" but in this case I can find no error, after an exhausting analysis that was a tribute to the resourcefulness and assiduity of counsel, that would justify any intervention by this Court.

[24] The appeal should be dismissed with costs.

Appeal dismissed.

QUESTIONS

1. What is "tipping"?
2. What are some of the defences to illegal insider trading? Are the same defences available for both illegal insider trading and tipping?
3. Do you think that those who have been found to have engaged in illegal insider trading should have a defence to liability?

V. ASSESSMENT OF ILLEGAL INSIDER TRADING

When we discussed legal insider trading, we questioned whether the legislative regime, and the enforcement of that regime, was effective. Similar questions arise with respect to illegal insider trading. In 2002, the CSA established an independent task force to examine illegal insider trading in Canadian capital markets. The task force included representatives from the Ontario, Québec, British Columbia, and Alberta securities commissions, the IDA, the Bourse de Montréal, and Market Regulation Services Inc. The following excerpt from the task force discusses the difficulties in detecting insider trading.

Insider Trading Task Force, *Illegal Insider Trading in Canada: Recommendations on Prevention, Detection, and Deterrence*
(November 2003) at 7-8, online: <investorvoice.ca/Research/CSA_InsiderTradingTaskForce_12Nov03.pdf>

Incidence of Illegal Insider Trading

Economists have been presenting consistent empirical evidence of widespread insider trading on various markets around the world for over a decade. Economists define insider trading broadly as trading on inside information, being material facts or changes that have not been publicly disclosed through a media report or other official means of general dissemination. It is difficult, however, to determine how much of that trading would represent illegal insider trading as defined in Canada under provincial securities statutes.

The methodology used to date to quantify insider trading relies on identifying statistically abnormal changes in market price and volume before announcements of material events. These methods, however, are not sufficiently refined to do more than identify an apparent order of magnitude of trading on inside information, including for example speculative trading that derives from the leakage of inside information but does not meet the definition of illegal insider trading. Better analytical tools are becoming available and will over time yield more information about the nature and extent of illegal insider trading than traditional models are currently capable of doing.

Canadian markets are founded on the basis of fairness, which suggests that investors, whether insiders or not, should not be allowed to trade on inside information, however it was obtained. Market efficiency, the other central principle of market regulation, is directly tied to how quickly material information flows through the market and is incorporated into securities prices. Any trading on inside information that occurs on Canadian markets has a direct adverse impact on the fairness and efficiency of those markets and, as various academic research papers have concluded, consequently on market liquidity and the cost of capital.

Examples of proven illegal insider trading that has occurred over the past 15 years in Canada include: Russell J. Bennett, William R. Bennett and Harbanse S. Doman (approximately $2.3 million in losses avoided from sales of Doman Industries Ltd. shares in 1988); Seakist Overseas Ltd., Michael G. de Groote et al. (approximately $16.5 million in net profits from the short sale of Laidlaw Inc. shares in 1991); Glen Harper (approximately $3.6 million in losses avoided from selling shares of Golden Rule Resources Ltd. in 1997); and MCJC Holdings Inc. (unreported net profits from the sale of $20.4 million in Corel Corporation shares in 1997).

Due to data limitations, it is currently very difficult to establish accurately the extent of insider trading, much less illegal insider trading, that occurs on Canadian markets. Nevertheless, academic research consistently evidences trading on inside information on markets around the world. There is no reason to believe that Canadian markets would not also be victimized by these activities. With increased ease of access to offshore trading and the continued development of the options and single stock futures markets, illegal insider trading threatens to become more prevalent and profitable over time without strategies to mitigate the risk.

Earlier in the chapter, we referred to a study on insider trading by McNally and Smith. In this important study, the authors show that insiders do not avoid trading prior to announcements of material information. They also suggest that insider trading violations are infrequently enforced.

William J McNally & Brian F Smith, "Do Insiders Play by the Rules?"
(2003) 29:2 Can Pub Pol'y 125

In this article, we make three contributions to the study of insider trading in Canada. First, we provide a history of illegal insider trading prosecutions in Canada. Second, we document how well insiders comply with the *Ontario Securities Act* (OSA) and Toronto Stock Exchange (TSX) bylaws and third, we present circumstantial evidence of the amount of illegal insider trading. The last contribution addresses a primary objective of the CSA/SRO task force. As noted in an article describing the mandate of the task force, "regulators are unable to estimate how many individuals are slipping through the cracks each year and profiting on the basis of undisclosed material information." ...

Estimation of the extent of illegal insider trading faces two obstacles. First, if illegal trades are not disclosed, then their detection is difficult. Second, even if the trades are disclosed, proving that they were made on the basis of undisclosed material information is difficult. We address both issues in this article. ...

We assess firms' compliance with four securities (OSA/TSX) regulations. First, TSX-listed companies that buy back their own shares are deemed to be insiders and must report their repurchases to both the OSC and the Exchange. We compare the quantity of shares reported to the two organizations. Second, we test whether firms comply with the limits on the percentage of shares that can be acquired in 30-day periods. Third, we compare OSC trade records with trade-to-trade data from the TSX to ensure compliance with price regulations on repurchases. Fourth, we explore whether the prohibition against prearranged repurchases from insiders is being followed.

• • •

The Cost and Benefits of Insider Trading Restrictions

• • •

... [L Harris, *Trading and Exchanges* (New York: Oxford University Press, 2003)] argues that unrestricted insider trading makes prices more informative because trading by insiders moves stock prices toward their fundamental value. But this is only a benefit to the extent that firms are slow in releasing information to the investing public.

Another argument against insider trading restrictions is that they are expensive to enforce, particularly because it is difficult to prove that insiders have knowledge of material information when they trade. If illegal insider trading is difficult to prosecute, then there will be a negligible risk of being caught. The popular press notes that this problem is especially troublesome in Canada .... If convictions are rare, then unethical individuals will not be deterred from engaging in illegal insider trading.

Convictions are rare because prosecutions often rely on circumstantial evidence which gives defendants the opportunity to claim arbitrary and discriminatory treatment (*BC Business* 1996). Furthermore, it is claimed, the OSC's past enforcement efforts have been restricted by its limited resources. If scarce resources explain the poor conviction record, then the conviction rate should rise soon, because, since 1998, the OSC's budget has tripled to more than $50 million, the number of employees has doubled to 350 and the enforcement staff has doubled to 80 (*The Record* 2003).

A recent international study of 103 countries shows that there is a net benefit to restricting insider trading only when the restrictions are enforced and they result in convictions [Uptal Bhattacharya & Hazem Daouk, "The World Price of Insider Trading" (2002) 57:1 *Journal of Finance* 75-108].

• • •

Recent History of Insider Trading Convictions in Canada

The efficacy of insider trading laws is affected by the extent to which they are enforced. If they are not enforced, then insider trading is limited only by the compunction of capital market participants not to violate the law. Worse, a lack of enforcement may send a signal to market participants that insider trading is not a serious crime.

We investigated the frequency of insider trading prosecutions by provincial securities commissions from January 1980 to October 2002. … [T]here are 15 convictions for insider trading with penalties ranging from $1,200 to $23 million. Five cases were dismissed and three decisions are pending. The commissions took an average of four years to reach a decision (from the time of the insider trading). The time varied from one-half year to 11 years. In summary, insider trading convictions are infrequent (fewer than one a year), the fines vary considerably and the securities commissions take a long time to prosecute cases.

We also note that there are two cases where the penalties imposed for illegal insider trading are less than the profit generated from the crime. First, Bennetts made a profit of $2 million based on a tip from a friend who was a CEO of a company that was the target of a takeover offer, but they only faced a $667,000 monetary fine. Second, Michael Cowpland, through his holding company M.C.J.C. Holdings, avoided a loss of $10 million by selling before Corel issued a profit warning. Although the OSC is seeking further penalties, the fine imposed to date is just $1 million. When the monetary penalty is less than the profits of the crime, as in these two cases, a perverse incentive for illegal insider trading is created.

… [W]e identify only two convictions for failure to report insider trading. In one of these cases the insiders were reprimanded and in the other there was a fine of $25,000.

Given the scarcity of convictions for both reporting and trading, one can conclude either that nearly all corporate insiders in Canada are law-abiding or that illegal insider is occurring but remains largely undetected. To assess which of these conclusions to draw, we next study compliance with five rules governing insider trading.

Tests of Compliance with the OSA and TSX Insider Trading Rules

Insider Trading Reporting

… We assess whether firms are complying with the OSC and TSX reporting requirements by comparing data collected by both organizations. We examine the data from 1,812 repurchase programs in which repurchases were reported over the period 1987 to 2000 to either the OSC or TSX. …

… [W]e note that identical numbers of shares (+/−5 percent) are reported to both the OSC and TSX in only 25 percent of repurchase programs. In two-thirds of all programs, the TSX reports more shares repurchased than the OSC. For most of those programs, (869 of 1,211) the OSC has no record of the repurchase at all. …

… We speculate that the reason that the TSX is more effective at gathering repurchase data is that a firm can be delisted from the TSX for not complying with the bylaws of the Exchange. On the other hand, the OSC has never prosecuted a company for non-compliance with repurchase disclosure regulations. …

… [There is] a significant and persistent gap between the levels of repurchase activity reported by the two agencies, although the gap is slowly diminishing. Given the common goal of providing shareholders with satisfactory disclosure, there is a clear need for the OSC and TSX to work together to improve reporting compliance of listed firms.

The gap in reporting by the OSC is of serious concern for three reasons. First, there is a very big compliance problem regarding reporting of repurchases to the OSC. Second, this finding leads one to question whether a large proportion of other insiders are also not reporting their trades to the OSC. Finally, since the TSX provides no information on the exact date and prices paid in individual repurchases trades as the OSC does, the public cannot rely on the TSX as a complete secondary source of information about repurchases. The public's ignorance of the detailed trade information leads the stock market to be less efficient.

Monthly Purchase Restrictions

The TSX limits the number of shares that a firm may repurchase over any given 30-day period to a maximum of 2 percent of the shares outstanding .... In this section we evaluate whether firms abide by this maximum. ...

In only 61 (0.65 percent) of the months [analyzed] did firms buy back more than 2 per cent of their shares outstanding. In such cases, the median repurchased was only 2.16 percent. Thus, nearly all firms are complying with the monthly limit and the exceptions are relatively small.

Price Restrictions

TSX rules stipulate that repurchases should not be made at a price that is higher than the last independent trade of a board lot of shares .... We examine the price of the last board lot of shares traded prior to the repurchase trade. ...

... Of the 62, 658 repurchase trades, 51, 334 of them have a trade in the prior period. Of these 51,334, we find that there are 6,490 (12.6 percent) repurchase trades with a price higher than that of the last independent trade of a board lot of shares. In such trades, the mean (median) excess price of the repurchase trade over that of the last independent trade of a board lot of shares is 1.06 percent (0.52 percent). The finding that one in eight repurchase trades violates the TSX price rules suggest that the TSX is not aggressively reviewing and enforcing compliance by issuer firms.

Repurchases from Insiders

We next examine evidence as to whether firms follow the TSX trading rule which prohibits trades in repurchases that are pre-arranged (crosses) between a seller who is an insider and the firm as a buyer .... Using the Insider Reporting Database, we find that there are 23,371 days on which companies buy back shares and 7,734 days when insiders sell [see WJ NcNally, BF Smith & T Barnes, "Underreaction, Abnormal Returns and Supply Curve Elasticity: Evidence from Open Market Share Repurchases" (Waterloo, Ont: Wilfrid Laurier University, 2002)]. However, there are only 772 days on which both insiders sell and companies repurchase. Thus, in 90 percent of the days when insiders are selling, companies are not buying back their shares. Since there are relatively few days when insiders are selling and companies are repurchasing, it is not common that firms pre-arrange to buy from insider sellers.

Trading with Material Information

Insiders are prohibited from trading when they have access to material information that is not available to the rest of the market (OSA, section 134). While there is no explicit restriction from trading a particular number of days before material announcements in Canada, we assume that insiders are aware of the news contained in public releases in the days and even the weeks prior to their release. …

To evaluate whether insiders are trading with material information, we compare the volume of trades that occur in the 22 trading days preceding significant public announcements to the volume traded after the announcements. …

We classified all news releases issued by repurchasing firms over the year of their repurchase (23,121 press releases) [as good news or bad news]. …

… [T]here is no difference between the daily volume of shares repurchased over the 22 trading days before and after positive announcements … . Thus, firms do not appear to be holding back from repurchasing prior to good news events.

… The "other" insiders include directors, senior officers and large shareholders. The spikes in Figure 4 just preceding the announcement day suggest a concentration of trading prior to good news announcements. A further examination of the five days preceding the announcement reveals that insiders do 16.7 percent of their total buying in that period. This concentration is substantial, since five days constitutes only 2 percent of the trading year. The Wilcoxon test indicates that the average volume of trading over the 22 days prior to the announcement of good news is not significantly different from the volume after (p-value of 0.35). Thus, there is no evidence that insiders postpone their purchases until after significant news is released.

Since postponing purchases is what we would expect if insider trading rules were being followed, our finding suggests that insiders are illegally buying on the basis of undisclosed information.

The level of insider sales before bad news also provides evidence of illegal insider trading. … [T]here is a larger volume of shares sold before bad news than after. The Wilcoxon test … indicates a higher volume of sales in the period before the bad news is announced at the 10 percent significant level (p-value of 0.02). Some insiders appear to be actively selling in the weeks before significantly negative news. However, the scale of this informed selling is small, as the volume of shares sold in the five days preceding the bad news constitutes only 2.1 percent of the total number of shares sold by all insiders during the repurchase program.

Our results show that insiders do not avoid trading prior to announcements of material information. If we assume that insiders know this information in the weeks prior to the announcement, then our findings provide circumstantial evidence of the scope of illegal insider trading on the TSX.

Conclusions

In Canada, there is a small likelihood of being prosecuted for insider trading violations. On average, there has been less than one insider trading conviction a year since 1980. There have been only two cases where insiders were charged with failure to report their trading activity.

In contrast to the scarcity of prosecutions for reporting violations, we find that almost half of the repurchasing firms fail to report their trades to the OSC. There is clearly a sizable reporting deficiency for the OSC. Yet no firm has been prosecuted by a provincial securities commission for failure to report a buyback program. This failure is surprising in light of how easy it is to verify compliance.

To the extent that so many firms are not providing information on their buyback activity to the OSC, we suspect that the directors, senior officers and large shareholders of many of these same firms are not reporting their trades. This suspicion should be a basis for further investigation by the OSC.

Another serious rule violation is that one-eighth of all repurchase trades occur at prices above the last traded board lot. This is surprising because compliance with this rule can easily be checked with readily available TSX trading records. However, firms have a very high level of compliance with the 2 percent limit on 30-day share repurchases and the prohibition against pre-arranged purchases from insiders.

Insiders do not desist from trading in the period immediately prior to material company news releases. Insider sales are significantly higher before than after bad news; 16.7 percent (2.1 percent) of all insider purchases (sales) occur in the five-day period preceding good (bad) news. This pattern of trading provides circumstantial evidence that many insiders are taking advantage of their privileged position. This result is contrary to the view of an OSC official who stated that "it's hard to imagine that these tools [used for market surveillance] are missing tons of it." It appears that insiders do not fear prosecutions by the OSC, which is probably due to the fact that the OSC has seldom enforced its own rules and has secured relatively few convictions.

There are a number of policy prescriptions that follow from this research. First, the relative paucity of prosecutions in Canada relative to the United States suggest that the OSC should consider approaches used by the American regulators for dealing with illegal insider trading. For example, in the United States, individuals who provide regulators with information on the illegal insider trading of others are entitled to a portion of the fines levied on convicted individuals.

Second, compliance with insider trading reporting rules should be improved. Repurchase data sent to the OSC can be checked easily with that sent to the TSX. Third, reporting of other insider trades should be checked for consistency with changes in the ownership figures which are published in year-end proxy circulars. Fourth, to reduce compliance costs for firms, the TSX and OSC should explore a common repurchase reporting system. A common company report detailing repurchase trades' quantities, times and prices would allow the TSX to measure compliance of repurchase trades with the price rule.

Fifth, given the paper's finding that insiders appear to be trading with asymmetric information, we recommend that announcements of insider trading should be made much faster than current rules prescribe. In fact, we recommend that the OSC require insider trades to be flagged at the time of each trade. This will prevent insiders from quietly disposing of or acquiring a position in their firm's stock on the basis of material information. Finally, we recommend that insiders be restricted from trading in a period just prior to pre-planned announcements such as earnings releases. This will limit the potential gains from illegal trading activity while placing only a relatively small time restriction on insiders. Indeed, many scrupulous companies already impose such a ban on their insiders.

One of the thrusts of the McNally & Smith article is that insider trading exists and that it is difficult to detect and regulate. The *Rankin* case, discussed above, is a prime example of the difficulty involved in securing a conviction in the insider trading and tipping context. Another recent case in which a conviction was not obtained is *R v Felderhof*, 2007 ONCJ 345.

In the light of *Rankin* and *Felderhof*, we must ask whether there is a particular reason that insider trading convictions, and indeed convictions relating to financial crimes, are not common. One reason is that the burden of proof (that is beyond a reasonable doubt) in provincial court is high, certainly higher than it would be if the hearing occurred within the administrative tribunal. Furthermore, as the *Felderhof* case suggests, the concepts at the heart of securities regulation generally, and insider trading specifically, are very difficult to apply in practice. For example, in the *Felderhof* case, the trial court engaged in a detailed analysis of materiality.

Applying the approach of the Ontario Securities Commission in *Re Donnini* (2002), 25 OSCB 6225 at para 110, Hryn J approached the question in three stages over 103 pages: first, whether the OSC had proven the alleged particulars; second, whether they constituted "facts"; and third, whether they were material. The court also relied on the OSC ruling in *YBM Magnex International Inc* (2003), 26 OSCB 5285, arguing that the test for materiality is an objective one and, further, that "[w]hen one or more facts do not appear to be material on their own, materiality must also be considered in light of all the facts available to the persons responsible for the assessment" (*YBM*, at para 94). However, Hryn J found that the OSC had not met the burden of proof for any of the five counts against Felderhof since its expert witness on materiality, Dr Juneja, had only assessed whether all of the alleged information and the resulting consequences, taken together, were material. The court held that the consequences were not a component of the actus reus: "S. 76(1) requires the OSC to prove the material fact beyond a reasonable doubt. Dr. Juneja did not testify that the particulars were material facts. The particulars are the alleged material facts and are part of the information charging Felderhof with insider trading. The potential consequences are not part of the charges Felderhof is facing" (para 2340).

Similarly, in *R v Landen*, the Crown was able to prove—beyond a reasonable doubt—that one of the accused (Landen) had engaged in insider trading contrary to OSA, s 76(1)(a). However, there remained reasonable doubt as to the tipping charges facing Landen, as well as to the assertion that the co-accused (Diamond) possessed insider information. Only an insider trading conviction against Landen was secured, with all remaining charges being dismissed. The *Landen* case is discussed in greater detail in Chapter 11.

A main challenge in bringing cases before the provincial court is meeting the very high burden of proof. This may be one reason that convictions under s 122 are difficult to secure. The *Felderhof* and *Landen* cases are prime examples of this point.

QUESTIONS

1. Why is detecting insider trading difficult?

2. Is the problem purely an enforcement issue or is the structure of the legislation itself problematic? If so, why?

3. Do you agree that investors are harmed if insider trading goes undetected and unpunished?

4. Clearly there are public policy considerations in the regulation of insider trading that relate to fairness and investor protection. Are there any valid arguments in favour of allowing insiders to trade based on material undisclosed information? In other words, what are some alternatives to the current legislative regime? Consider voluntary conduct by firms to regulate insider trading via the establishment of insider trading policies. See Beny & Anand, above.

Additional policy considerations arise in the context of options backdating. Compton, Nicholls, Sandler, and Tedds examined whether or not insider reporting rules and regulations were effective in deterring options backdating. The CSA, in adopting amendments to NI 55-104, noted that changes to the insider reporting deadlines were connected in part to a desire to deter "improper options backdating" (Compton et al at 474). See Ryan A Compton, Christopher C Nicholls, Daniel Sandler & Lindsay M Tedds, "Insider Reporting Obligations and Options Backdating" (2011) 26:3 BFLR 473, in which the authors discuss whether the new insider trading rules have been effective in this regard.

VI. CHAPTER SUMMARY

Insider trading is permissible when those individuals or entities defined as insiders under the legislation file insider trading reports to disclose their trades. Insider trading is not permissible, however, when the individual or entity is in a special relationship with the issuer and trades based on material information that has not been generally disclosed. Questions have been raised about the efficacy of the legal regime: Is the definition of "special relationship" too broad? Is it impossible to determine where in the "chain" of passing on information illegal insider trading stops? How effective is the enforcement of insider trading? These are questions to which there are no definitive responses, but which force us to consider the current legal regime and the relevance of its underlying policy.

CHAPTER NINE

Takeover Bids

I. INTRODUCTION

In this chapter, we outline the law relating to takeover bids. We begin with a definition of "takeover bid." We then discuss the history of the law, the legislative scheme, disclosure issues, exemptions from the takeover bid requirements, defensive tactics, and the duties of the target board in a takeover bid.

A takeover bid occurs when a corporation ("the bidder") makes an offer to purchase outstanding shares of another corporation ("the target"). Under securities legislation, such an offer is a takeover if it would, on its own or in combination with shares already held by the bidder, result in the bidder acquiring 20 percent or more of the target's shares. Takeovers are usually described as "hostile" or "friendly." Hostile bids occur when target management and/or the board of directors do not invite the bid and are not generally in favour of the bid. In contrast, friendly takeovers occur when target management and the board approve of the bid and cooperate with the bidder in selling the bid to target shareholders (that is, shareholders of the firm that is the subject of the takeover bid). Students should note that formal takeover bids that follow the procedure set forth in the legislation constitute one of many different types of change of control transactions. Others, which will not be covered in this chapter, include going-private transactions, arrangements, and asset purchase deals.

Takeover bids occur for various reasons, some of which may overlap. The bidder may seek to acquire the target for strategic reasons relating to the development and expansion of its business. The bidder may seek to expand its business into a new geographic area or into a new sector of the consumer market. An acquisition may also be consistent with a diversification strategy that the bidder envisions for itself. In addition, the target may be a competitor that impedes the growth of the bidder. (Note, however, that the *Competition Act*, RSC 1985, c C-34, applies to certain takeover bids.) The bidder may believe that target management is inefficient and that it could run the firm in a more efficient and more profitable manner. Alternatively, the bidder may believe that the target is undervalued and therefore attempt to buy the target at a low price, thereby getting "value for its money." Other motives, such as those relating to tax law, may also drive a decision to complete a takeover bid.

Apart from being friendly or hostile, takeover bids can take a variety of forms in terms of the consideration that is paid to target shareholders. In particular, the bidder may offer target shareholders cash, shares, or a combination of cash and shares. Where shares are offered, target shareholders are offered a per share ratio of the bidder's shares in exchange for their shares in the target. In the bidder's decisions relating to consideration to be paid, the value of the target's shares is of primary importance. The bidder analyzes the target's current and historical stock price as well as other relevant financial information that the target has disclosed. Note, however, that in a hostile bid, the bidder does not have access to some financial information that it would find useful. The target may open a "data room" of otherwise confidential information for a takeover auction or for an alternative friendly bidder, sometimes referred to as a "white knight."

In takeover bids generally, and in hostile bid situations especially, the target board has a number of legal obligations to observe in responding to the bid. It must comply with securities legislation. In Ontario, these obligations include part XX of the *Securities Act*, RSO 1990, c S.5 (OSA). and NI 62-104, *Take-Over Bids and Issuer Bids* (9 May 2016).[1] A target board must also adhere to its fiduciary duties under corporate law. In addition, NP 62-202, *Take-Over Bids—Defensive Tactics* (1997), 20 OSCB 3526, discussed below, applies throughout the country and sets forth guidelines that govern defensive tactics that a target company may

1 Recent amendments to Canada's takeover bid regime involved the adoption of NI 62-104 by the Ontario Securities Commission on May 5, 2016. This coincided with the repeal of OSC Rule 62-504 and legislative amendments to part XX of the Ontario *Securities Act*. As such, there is now a harmonized takeover bid national instrument in force in all Canadian jurisdictions.

employ in response to a takeover bid. Ultimately, the law seeks to protect the interests of target shareholders. Specifically, target shareholders must be given ample opportunity to consider various bids for their shares and the opportunity to change their mind if they decide to withdraw their shares after tendering. All target shareholders must be treated equally in terms of the consideration that the bidder offers to them. They must be able to make fully informed decisions, including the ultimate decision on whether or not to tender to the bid. Thus, as we will see, the legislation and case law have developed so as to protect the interests of target shareholders by ensuring that the bidder (and even the directors of the target in some cases) provide full disclosure, equal treatment, and adherence to time periods.

As we will discuss later in this chapter, significant changes to Canada's harmonized takeover bid regime came into force on May 9, 2016. After receiving comments and feedback from various stakeholders and interested parties, the Canadian Securities Administrators (CSA) extended the minimum bid period to 105 days, established a minimum deposit requirement of 50 percent, and introduced a 10-day bid period extension requirement. In its notice of amendment, the CSA explained that these changes:

> will enhance the quality and integrity of the take-over bid regime and rebalance the current dynamics among offerors, offeree [that is, target] issuer boards of directors (offeree boards), and offeree issuer securityholders by (i) facilitating the ability of offeree issuer securityholders to make voluntary, informed and co-ordinated tender decisions, and (ii) providing the offeree board with additional time and discretion when responding to a take-over bid (CSA Notice of Amendments to Takeover Bid Régime, Feb. 26, 2016).

As these amendments demonstrate, protecting the interests of target shareholders and the target's board of directors remains a primary policy consideration for Canadian securities regulators.

Takeover bid legislation generally does not address the interests or needs of the shareholders of the bidder. This regulatory gap seems odd in light of the fact that it is the bidder's shareholders who bear the brunt, or reap the gain, of the bidder's decision to make a takeover bid. A clear objective of takeover bid legislation in Canada is to encourage takeover bids. The assumption is that takeover bids are good for the economy. Firms being run by inefficient managers lead to depressed stock prices that do not exhibit the true value of the firm. Thus, a takeover bid that results in the replacement of inefficient managers will enable the firm to operate more efficiently overall. Limiting the class of persons who are protected is thus one means that legislators have sanctioned to encourage takeover bids.

To some extent, academic research supports this view. This research has shown that takeover bids lead to increased share prices for target shareholders.[2] While this evidence may demonstrate certain benefits of the takeover bid process, it is not entirely clear that the

2 M Jensen & R Ruback, "The Market for Corporate Control: The Scientific Evidence" (1983) 11 J Fin Econ 5 at 8: "[T]arget firms in successful takeovers experience statistically significant abnormal stock price changes of 20% in mergers and 30% in tender offers." G Jarrell & A Poulsen, "Shark Repellents and Stock Prices: The Effects of Anti-Takeover Amendments Since 1980" (1987) 19:1 J Fin Econ 127 at 154-55. Jarrell & Poulsen studied the effects of anti-takeover amendments and whether they harm target shareholders by deterring valuable takeover bids. Gregg A Jarrell, James A Brickley & Jeffry M Netter, "The Market for Corporate Control: The Empirical Evidence Since 1980" (1988) 2:1 J Econ Perspectives 49 at 51.

resulting entity itself benefits.[3] Indeed, there is little evidence about the profitability of the merged entity following a takeover bid. Furthermore, one should also examine the issue by stakeholder group: while the target shareholders may benefit on the whole, other stakeholders, such as the bidder's shareholders and perhaps society at large, may not. In short, students should be aware that the issue of whether takeover bids are "all they are cracked up to be" is a live one that is open to debate based on both theoretical argument and empirical evidence.

QUESTIONS

1. List the various stakeholders in a takeover bid and their respective interests in the bid. What does each stakeholder group seek in the transaction?
2. The introduction to this chapter lists some of the reasons for takeover bids. Are you convinced that these reasons are accurate? Can you think of any others?
3. Should the law seek to facilitate takeover bids? Whose interests must be protected if it does?

II. HISTORY AND PROCESS ISSUES

During the past 30 years, takeover bid law in Canada has proliferated to include not only provincial and territorial statutes but also national policies, case law, and legislative instruments issued by provincial regulatory bodies. Though this proliferation has been gradual, a great moment of change occurred with the publication of the Kimber Report, *Report of the Attorney General's Committee on Securities Legislation in Ontario* (Toronto: Queen's Printer, 1965). The Kimber Report set forth a number of recommendations relating to change of control transactions, which were codified in Ontario's *Securities Act*, SO 1966, c 142 and adopted in all of the western provinces and eventually throughout Canada (Alberta, *Securities Act*, SA 1967, c 76; British Columbia, *Securities Act*, SBC 1967, c 45; Manitoba, *Securities Act*, SM 1968, c 57).

The Kimber Report contained a number of recommendations, including stipulations relating to insider trading in anticipation of a takeover bid; the definition of takeover and the establishment of the 20 percent threshold; an allowance for changes of control by private agreement; the establishment of a 21-day period during which a takeover bid must remain open; the implementation of pro rata take-up rules; a requirement to provide shareholder lists and information regarding financing arrangements; and variation in the offer price and takeover bid circulars. Because of the pervasiveness of the recommendations, and the

---

3 Simon Deakin & Giles Slinger, "Hostile Takeovers, Corporate Law, and the Theory of the Firm" (1997) 24:1 JL & Soc'y 124 at 144 state: "Several studies have identified long-term share-price declines following mergers, whether resulting from a hostile or an agreed bid, and the most comprehensive study has found that this negative effect intensifies over time. Companies which made hostile takeovers did better than those which made agreed mergers, but nevertheless on average showed neither gains nor losses to a significant degree over the post-merger period. This finding broadly confirms earlier research which, rather than taking share price movement as the benchmark of company performance, was based on accounting data concerning companies' sales, assets and profits. This found that companies which have acquired by tender offers had slightly below industry-average cash flow and sales performance both before and after takeover, so that 'the hypothesis that takeovers improve performance is not supported.'"

almost universal adoption of the recommendations across Canada, the Kimber Report is certainly the watershed of the modern era in securities regulation (see David Johnston & Kathleen Doyle Rockwell, *Canadian Securities Regulation*, 4th ed (Markham, Ont: Butterworths, 2006) at 3).

Following the implementation of the 1966 OSA, corporate business combinations including takeover bids, private acquisitions, and mergers increased (see *Report of the Committee of the Ontario Securities Commission on the Problems of Disclosure Raised for Investors by Business Combinations and Private Placements* (Toronto: Department of Financial and Commercial Affairs, 1970) ("merger study")). The increase in change-of-control transactions heightened the need for an examination into the adequacy of the regime governing disclosure of information. Hence, the Ontario Securities Commission (OSC), at the request of the province of Ontario, struck a committee to "review and report upon existing legislation, regulation and policy relating to consolidations, amalgamations, mergers, re-organizations, take-overs … and … to recommend what, if any, changes in the law appear desirable" (merger study at 2).

In accordance with its mandate, the merger study discussed disclosure issues in a number of contexts. With respect to takeover bids, the merger study concluded that the disclosure required by present legislation—specifically, the takeover bid circular—had worked effectively, but that certification should be required, as it is with the prospectus. The study suggested that the identity of the offeror should be disclosed in the case of a partial bid and that withdrawal rights should be extended where the offeror amends the terms of the original offer.

Another important review of takeover bid legislation occurred in 1983 when the chair of the OSC asked Gordon Coleman, Garfield Emerson, and David Jackson to review and make recommendations concerning the full scope of the application of Ontario's takeover bid legislation. They wrote the *Report of the Committee to Review the Provisions of the Securities Act (Ontario) Relating to Take-Over Bids and Issuer Bids* (Toronto: Ontario Securities Commission, 1983), better known as "the report of the Three Wise Men," which is excerpted later in this chapter. Some of their significant recommendations included lowering the threshold for takeover bids from 20 to 10 percent, extending the period during which securities deposited under a bid may be withdrawn to 21 days from the date of the bid, and suggesting the removal of limitations on the conditions that an offeror may attach to a bid or on the length of time a bid may remain open. The "Three Wise Men" also provided a clear jurisdiction for the courts to play an enlarged role in hearing and deciding questions of law arising from takeover bids (at 27). The takeover bid provisions of the 1966 OSA were revised as a result of the recommendations of this report.

The next major review of takeover bid law in Canada did not occur until 1996. The Committee to Review Take-Over Bid Time Limits, chaired by Adam Zimmerman (Investment Dealers Association, *Report of the Committee to Review Take-Over Bid Time Limits* (May 1996) ("Zimmerman Report"), reproduced at (1996), 19 OSCB 4469), had as its mandate a consideration of whether takeover bid time limits appropriately balance the interests of target companies and their shareholders with those of acquiring companies. The Zimmerman committee made two main recommendations: (1) the minimum deposit period for formal takeover bids should be extended from 21 to 35 days and (2) a bidder can begin a takeover bid by placing an advertisement containing its offer to purchase and an appropriate summary of its offering in the financial newspapers. The circular must be mailed to shareholders within two business days. The committee made a number of other recommendations, including broader withdrawal rights and time periods for delivery of directors' circulars. Ontario was the first province to adopt the recommendations of the Zimmerman committee, with all the other provinces following suit by mid-2003.

The Canadian Securities Administrators later issued MI 62-104, mentioned above. Since then, MI 62-104 has been replaced by NI 62-104, also mentioned above. This chapter will focus on the substantive provisions of this new national instrument, as it forms the basis of takeover bid law in Canada.

While takeover bid legislation is, generally speaking, harmonized in all Canadian jurisdictions (especially since the introduction of NI 62-104), certain provinces (for example, Ontario and Québec) have *Protection of Minority Securityholders in Special Transactions*, MI 61-101 (14 December 2007), a set of separate rules specifically relating to conflict-of-interest transactions. Though we will not discuss this legal instrument here, it is an important facet of the legal regime concerning related-party transactions, business combinations, issuer bids, and insider bids.

As a final introductory comment, students will note that a strong theme throughout this chapter, and perhaps the book as a whole, is the close relationship between corporate and securities law. One of the objectives of securities law is investor protection. In seeking to achieve this goal, securities regulators monitor the actions of the target board to ensure that it does not sacrifice the interests of its shareholders, and particularly the maximization of shareholder value, in responding to a takeover bid. However, the analysis of target conduct often includes an examination of the conduct of its board of directors. As you are aware, the legal requirements that govern the board are set forth in corporate statutes—in particular, the best interests of the corporation test. Thus, securities regulation in the takeover bid sphere steps into the corporate law domain. In light of this intrusion, some argue that corporate and securities law are duplicative. They urge legislators and regulators to consider whether this regulatory regime is optimal or whether another alternative is preferable. In particular, they ask whether securities regulators should be in the business of determining the appropriate actions of a company's board of directors.

The debate over the appropriate role of securities regulators often plays out in a discussion of whether regulatory bodies or courts are the appropriate forum for hearing disputes that arise in the context of the takeover bid. This issue was addressed in *Re CW Shareholdings Inc v WIC Western International Communications Ltd* (1998), 21 OSCB 2910. The facts of the case will be discussed later in this chapter. For now, it is important to note that the Alberta, British Columbia, and Ontario securities commissions agreed that there are certain issues that courts, not commissions, are more suited to rule on. In the case, CW argued that the commissions, not the courts, were the appropriate venue for consideration of CW's cease-trade application. At para 36, CW argued that:

> (a) Procedural and evidentiary flexibility enabled the Commissions to cope with compressed timeframes of bids.
> (b) Only the Commissions have the necessary understanding of the capital markets backdrop.
> (c) Courts have erected jurisprudential impediments to their dealing with take-over bid issues. The bidder is the natural applicant, but courts have said that bidders have no standing to make oppression or fiduciary duty claims arising from defensive tactics. Courts have said target shareholders must be represented on a hearing challenging defensive tactics, but there was no practical mechanism for accomplishing this.

(d) On the facts of the case, the Court did not offer an advantage as a venue to compensate for the disadvantages.

(e) Although the Court was not CW's first choice as a venue, CW initiated the Court proceedings at a time when it was unclear whether the Commissions would hear the application, and there were concerns as to whether an internal re-organization of WIC was being proceeded with at the instance of Shaw.

The first argument relating to procedural and evidentiary flexibility is one that is often cited. Indeed, as will be discussed in the chapter relating to enforcement, some criticize hearings before commissions because they need not follow the rules of process and evidence employed in the courts. The following excerpt from the OSC decision indicates how the CW claim was adjudicated. Ultimately, it was found that the securities commissions are not the appropriate venue to decide some of the issues raised.

Re CW Shareholdings Inc v WIC Western International Communications Ltd
(1998), 21 OSCB 2910

It is CW's position that the Pre-Acquisition Agreement, and specifically the break-up fee and option on WIC's radio assets, constitute improper defensive tactics which were intended to, and have the effect of, stopping the auction process.

Shaw and WIC argue that, to the contrary, the Pre-Acquisition Agreement was necessary to obtain from Shaw a higher bid than that of CW under the CW Bid, and that without the Pre-Acquisition Agreement there would not have been an auction process at all.

Staff of the Commissions submitted that, unless the Commissions were prepared to say that break-up fees or asset options would always constitute improper defensive tactics, the Commissions would not be in a position to deal with the question without first dealing with the question of breach of fiduciary duty.

Commission Jurisprudence on Choice of Forum

It was acknowledged by all of the parties that the Commissions clearly have the jurisdiction to cease trade a take-over bid where it would be in the public interest to do so, and that the existence of improper defensive tactics on the part of the target company could constitute an appropriate basis on which the Commissions could exercise their cease trade powers.

It is clear that something which, for corporate law purposes, may constitute a breach of fiduciary duties may also, for securities law purposes, properly result in a decision by a securities commission to exercise its discretionary powers, including its cease trade power. The question is not whether a securities commission can look into the question of whether there has been a breach of fiduciary duties, but rather whether it is in the public interest for it to do so in the particular case.

However, there appears to be little in the way of Commission decisions dealing directly with the question of when the Commission should investigate alleged breaches of fiduciary duties.

In *In the Matter of Cablecasting Limited* … , the Commission had the following to say:

> After hearing counsel, the Commission concluded that section 144 would enable the Commission, if it felt that the action was in the public interest, to issue a cease trading order on either of the bases argued by Mr. Cameron. Specifically, the section 144 authority could be used where the Commission concludes that a proposed transaction
>
> - would contravene the OBCA (or some other statute reflecting public policy considerations); or
> - while consistent with the language of prior policy rulings and statements of the Commission, would contravene the intent of these rulings and statements and detract from the credibility of the capital markets or be otherwise inconsistent with the best interests of investors.

Each of these points is potentially controversial. They require separate analysis.

As to the first, it seems clear to the Commission that availability of some other remedy does not preclude it from granting an application such as this. Mr. Cameron readily acknowledged that, if his allegations are correct, the Davisons could have elected to initiate litigation to delay the shareholders' meeting. He also pointed out, rightly in our view, that an application before the Commission can be processed more quickly and cheaply than could a formal court proceeding on the same facts. To conclude that availability to the applicant of a remedy in the courts ousts the jurisdiction of the Commission would, in our view, be inconsistent with the principles of *The Securities Act*. If a clear abuse of investors is demonstrated, the Commission should not be forced to rely on a single minority shareholder to initiate legal proceedings on behalf of all.

But there is another side to the case. The very expedition with which applications to the Commission of this type are processed precludes the level of refinement of fact-finding that is attained by the exchange of pleadings, the examinations for discovery, the formal trials and the adversary relationship that characterize judicial proceedings. The Commission's staff includes a number of highly qualified investigators, but it is not appropriate to call upon them to become involved in a situation of this type unless there is reason to believe that fraud has occurred or that the transaction constitutes a flagrant abuse in some other respect. Also, when a dispute of this type is litigated, the usual procedure is for the complaining shareholder to apply for and obtain an injunction preventing consummation of the transaction pending judicial resolution of the matters in issue. Presumably, the Commission could exercise its authority under section 144 to have the same effect as an injunction, but this novel use of that authority should be essayed only in rare circumstances. For these reasons, and because it would be presumptuous for the Commission to make a practice of enforcing statutes not assigned to it, this basis for a cease trading order ought to be applied only where a significant contravention of another statute can be expeditiously demonstrated.

In *In the Matter of Canadian Tire Corporation et al.* (1987) … , the Commission said the following:

> Counsel for the Billeses and the Dealers also argued that the Commission is not the proper forum for this case. The contention was that this is a private matter between the Class A shareholders and the controlling shareholders. Accordingly, the Class A shareholders should

pursue their remedies in the Courts where the issues can more properly be sorted out through the trial process. This contention is supported by the fact that the notice of hearing in para. 14 alleges breaches of fiduciary duty, and such breaches are properly matters to be tried in the Courts, either under the oppression remedy or in a derivative action.

The contention that the issue here is a private one between two classes of shareholders is far wide of the mark. A purported sale of control in the circumstances set out above, where the rights of the holders of some 83 million Class A shares are concerned, is not a private matter, although individual rights in terms of a particular shareholding are involved. This is demonstrably a public matter involving a major public company and one that concerns and impacts on the public marketplace. In the sense in which counsel were using the idea of a private list, any takeover bid would, according to their analysis, be a private matter between shareholders. Yet it is well known that take-over bids, the rules applying to them and how they are conducted, are very much a public matter in the sense of their concern to, and impact on the marketplace and its perceived integrity. The Commission, accordingly, has always played a major role in overseeing such transactions.

Moreover, the argument that this matter more properly belongs before the Courts, mistakes the respective roles of the Courts and the Commission in overseeing the management and actions of public companies and protecting shareholders' interests. The Commission is vested with the power to regulate the capital markets in the public interest and is given broad powers to do so. The power to intervene includes the power to cease trade and to do so, at least initially, without a public hearing if satisfied of the necessity. In carrying out its regulatory function, the Commission necessarily impacts on the rights and obligations of companies, directors and shareholders. But it does so from the perspective of the regulation of the public markets and their fair and efficient operation. The subjecting of take over bids to an elaborate code of rules and regulations, backed by the power to issue a cease-trade order, if conduct during the course of a bid calls for it, is perhaps the best known example of this regulatory function.

The Courts, on the other hand, adjudicate rights between shareholders and their companies. In so doing, the judicial process has the advantage of the refinement of issues provided by pleadings, examinations for discovery and the trial process. Moreover, the Courts are able to provide remedies appropriate to the individual case. What the Courts are not structured to do, is to move quickly to regulate public markets through regulating shareholder and/or corporate conduct. To be sure, the injunction remedy is available in the proper case, but it is not a remedy designed to be used as a regulatory tool.

The line between when Commission action or judicial process is appropriate in shareholder and corporate matters is, of course, not so clearly marked as the foregoing comments would indicate. There is bound to be overlap as there is no clear line between securities and corporate matters and many issues before the Commission involve the conduct of fiduciaries. But the role of the Commission is not to determine breaches of fiduciary duty, or to deal with a breach of a corporate statute, in order to provide a private remedy. Rather, it is to regulate shareholder and corporate conduct in the context of, and for the purpose of, regulating the public securities markets. Again, the line will not always be clear as intervention in matters that from one aspect are of a private nature will, from another aspect, be seen to have public market implications. If the Commission should mistake its role in a particular case, or act beyond the jurisdiction granted, the Courts can rectify the matter and set out a new balance through the appeal procedure granted under s. 9 of the Act.

Conclusions on Forum Motion

We agree with the submissions made by Shaw, WIC and the staffs of the Commissions that essentially the relief requested by CW in its application for cease trade-orders and that requested in its application to the Court are the same thing, and are bottomed on an attack against the Pre Acquisition Agreement and the question of whether the Board properly performed its fiduciary duties in entering into that agreement. We also agree that the Court can more appropriately deal with questions of this sort, at least in the circumstances of this case, than the Commissions, especially since there is no jurisdiction in the Commissions to set aside the Pre-Acquisition Agreement, while the Court can do so.

We do not accept Mr. Tory's argument to the effect that the Court will not be able to deal appropriately with these issues, or to do so on a timely basis.

QUESTIONS

1. Consider the August 8, 2006 case of *Sears Canada* in which the OSC held that Sears Canada acted coercively and against the public interest by granting improper benefits to certain of their shareholders. Does the case suggest circumstances in which the OSC will intervene in a case?
2. Do you agree with allowing a bid to commence via advertisement in a financial newspaper? What is the purpose underlying this reform?
3. What is the proper forum to hear disputes concerning takeover bids: courts or securities commissions? Are you concerned with the overlap between corporate and securities law?

III. LEGISLATION

A. Definition of Takeover Bid

As stated in s 1.1 of NI 62-104, a "takeover bid"[4] is:

> an offer to acquire outstanding voting securities or equity securities of a class made to one or more persons, any of whom is in the local jurisdiction or whose last address as shown on the books of the offeree issuer is in the local jurisdiction, where the securities subject to the offer to acquire, together with the offeror's securities, constitute in the aggregate 20% or more of the outstanding securities of that class of securities at the date of the offer to acquire but does not include an offer to acquire if the offer to acquire is a step in an amalgamation, merger, reorganization or arrangement that requires approval in a vote of securityholders.

This definition differs slightly from part XX of the OSA, which applies in Ontario. In this definition, note that "offeror" is the bidder and "offeree issuer" is the target in the takeover bid. Also note that the takeover bid occurs with the making of an offer, not with the completion of a transaction itself. Of crucial importance is the 20 percent threshold identified in the definition. The figure is arbitrary but appears to refer to some level in which a person holds

4 OSA, s 89(1) defines a "take-over bid" as "a direct or indirect offer to acquire a security that is, (a) made by a person or company other than the issuer of the security; and (b) within a prescribed class of offers to acquire."

substantial control of the target. The definition itself derives from the Kimber Report. The following excerpt from this report discusses the 20 percent threshold and its rationale.

Report of the Attorney General's Committee on Securities Legislation in Ontario
(Toronto: Queen's Printer, 1965)

3.11 In view of the conclusion reached by the Committee as to the proper objectives of legislation concerning take-over bids, the Committee does not think it desirable to define a take-over bid in terms of attempted control of a corporation. To define a take-over bid in terms of the intended acquisition of legal control would leave free from regulation a substantial number of offers where the objective is to acquire effective, not legal, control. The point at which effective control is achieved may vary widely from one case to another. As a result, we have concluded that for the purposes of the recommendations which follow, a take-over bid should be defined as an offer (other than by way of private agreement or by way of purchase on a stock exchange or in the over-the-counter market) made to any number of the holders of any class of outstanding voting shares of a company, other than a private company, to purchase a number of such shares which, together with the number of such shares beneficially owned, directly or indirectly, by the offeror and any person or company associated with the offeror at the time of making such offer, will amount in the aggregate to more than 20 per cent of the outstanding voting shares of such class.

While the basic threshold set down in the legislation is 20 percent, there are provisions relevant to discerning whether this threshold has been reached. To begin, in some circumstances, a bidder may be acting "jointly and in concert" with another person or company. In these circumstances, the legislation requires both the bidder and the person with whom it is acting jointly and in concert to count their shares together for the purposes of analyzing whether the 20 percent threshold has been reached. Thus, two or more parties cannot divide up the number of securities that they are bidding for in order to avoid the takeover bid rules (NI 62-104, s 1.8(3); OSA s 90).

In addition, if the bidder or any person acting jointly and in concert with the bidder has a right to acquire the securities of the target through conversion privileges attaching to securities of another class, those securities must be included in the calculation of the number of shares the bidder owns (NI 62-104, s 1.7). The legislation provides some indication of which acts will be considered "jointly and in concert." For example, any agreement, commitment, or understanding, whether informal or formal, with a bidder under which a person or company offers to acquire the same securities as those the bidder is seeking to acquire will constitute joint and in-concert acts (NI 62-104, ss 1.9(1) to (3)).

B. Launching a Takeover Bid

Following the Zimmerman amendments (discussed above), there are now two means of commencing a takeover bid. First, the traditional means of delivering a takeover bid circular to all of the shareholders of the target (NI 62-104, s 2.9(1)). Second, the innovative means of publishing an announcement of the takeover bid in a major daily newspaper. If the bidder chooses the second option, it must also file and deliver a copy of the bid to the target company's office (NI 62-104, s 2.10(2)). This copy of the bid must be accompanied by a takeover bid circular (NI 62-104, s 2.10(1)). In addition, within two days of receiving a list of the target's shareholders, the bidder must deliver the circular to all the shareholders of the target.

While bidders prefer the bid process to conclude as quickly as possible, the target company prefers a longer bid period so that it can survey alternatives. The provision permitting commencement by advertisement provides a definite advantage to the bidder. One of the first takeover bids in which the bid was commenced by advertisement was the Sherritt/Ontario Teachers' Pension Plan bid for Fording in October 2002. On October 21, 2002, the following news release was placed over Canada NewsWire:

> TORONTO, Oct. 21 /CNW/—Sherritt Coal Partnership II, a partnership of Sherritt International Corporation (Sherritt) (TSX: S) and Ontario Teachers' Pension Plan (Teachers'), today announced its intention to make a cash takeover bid to purchase all of the outstanding shares of Fording Inc. (TSX and NYSE: FDG) (approximately 51.3 million shares outstanding) for C$29.00 per share (approximately equal to US$18.45). The total value of the transaction is C$1.6 billion (approximately equal to US$1.0 billion), comprised of C$1.5 billion in equity, including the value of the 6.2% of Fording shares already owned by Teachers', and C$128 million net debt. This offer price will provide Fording shareholders with a 25% premium to the 20-day average closing stock price of Fording.
>
> The offer will be subject to Fording shareholders tendering a minimum of 66⅔% of the outstanding shares of Fording and will also be subject to normal conditions and regulatory approvals. The offer will be open for acceptance by Fording shareholders for a period of 60 days and will be made by means of a takeover bid circular to be mailed shortly to shareholders.

This news release is an example of the type of information that a bidder would publish if it were commencing its bid by advertisement. In addition, an advertisement, which looked similar to the cover page of the takeover bid circular itself, also appeared in Canada's main business newspapers.

C. Equality, Disclosure, and Timing

As noted above, the legislative provisions relating to takeover bids essentially seek to protect the interests of the target shareholders. Thus, the scheme set forth in the legislation consists of a series of obligations that govern the bidder's behaviour in the making of a takeover bid. These obligations can be broken down into three distinct categories: obligations that relate to equal treatment, those that relate to disclosure, and those that concern timing. In other words, the legislation seeks to ensure that shareholders are treated equally, that they have full information in making their decisions regarding the bid, and they have ample opportunity to consider the bid. Before reading the following summary of the formalities in the legislation, students should read the takeover bid sections of the securities legislation.

1. Equal Treatment

There are two main provisions in securities legislation that seek to ensure equal treatment. The first is pro rata take-up and the second is identical consideration. Before we discuss these provisions, students should note the contents of a 1983 report prepared for the

Ontario Securities Commission. The OSC Report discusses the importance of equal treatment in the context of a takeover bid.

Gordon Coleman, Garfield Emerson & David Jackson, *Report of the Committee to Review the Provisions of the Securities Act (Ontario) Relating to Take-Over Bids and Issuer Bids*
(Toronto: Ontario Securities Commission, 1983)

Fundamental Principles

1.01 In reviewing Part XIX, we have regarded as fundamental the principles that all holders of the same class of securities be treated equally and that adequate relevant information be made available on a timely basis to all offeree security holders. We emphasize the conclusion of the Kimber Committee that:

> the primary objective of any recommendations for legislation with respect to the take-over bid transaction should be the protection of the bona fide interests of the shareholders of the offeree company. Shareholders should have made available to them, as a matter of law, sufficient up-to-date relevant information to permit them to come to a reasoned decision as to the desirability of accepting a bid for their shares. In arriving at its conclusions, however, the Committee attempted to ensure that its recommendations would not unduly impede potential bidders or put them in a commercially disadvantageous position vis-à-vis an entrenched and possibly hostile board of directors of an offeree company. (Kimber report, para. 3.10)

1.02 It was the basic view of the Kimber Committee that a statutory code should, without working a hardship on offerors, ensure (i) that management of an offeree issuer have ample opportunity to inform offeree shareholders of its analysis of the bid; and (ii) that offeree shareholders are given adequate information and sufficient time to form a reasoned judgment whether or not to sell their shares to the offeror. In addition, we believe that shareholders of an offeree issuer and public investors generally should be confident that transactions which may affect the *de facto* control of public security issuers will be made, as a matter of principle, on a basis which requires identical treatment of holders of the same class of securities and that all such shareholders will have an equal opportunity to participate in the benefits which may accompany a change of effective control of public issuers. Beyond these goals of fairness to and even-handed treatment of shareholders of any particular target company, there are also legitimate national and provincial concerns that the capital markets in Canada, as well as in any local market, function and are perceived to function not only efficiently but in the best interests of all public investors who commit their funds to management by others. The rights of minority shareholders should be protected so that the essential elements of shareholder democracy in the context of public issuers are honoured in the arena of take-over transactions.

1.03 These goals are not achieved, however, without costs. Increasing the information available to the management and shareholders of an offeree issuer and ensuring that all offerees are treated equally in a take-over bid not only increases the burden on bidders but also adds complexity to the statutory rules governing take-over bids. Burdensome and complex regulatory provisions impede the economic efficiencies of the markets and impose direct costs on participants in the take-over bid process. There are also real but unmeasured indirect costs that result from excessive regulation, including imbalances in capital flows, imperfect competition, reduced innovation in take-over techniques and inadvertent and unnecessary non-compliance. Ultimately these economic inefficiencies and costs are borne by the economy as a whole.

1.04 Another factor affecting the regulation of bids is that, in order to protect the interests of the shareholders of the target company, the focus of securities legislation is principally on the conduct of the offeror and those acting jointly with the offeror. This focus may lead to an unintended tipping of the balance of the regulatory scheme in favour of the directors and management of an offeree issuer seeking to defend against what they perceive to be a hostile bid. The weighing of the statutory rules against the bidder may arise because the conduct of the directors and management of the target remain essentially unregulated by provincial securities legislation. Protection of the interests of the shareholders of the target company, as well as other public goals, including the neutrality of the rules to permit competitive free market forces to operate, may require the adoption of restraints on certain types of conduct by the target once a take-over is made.

These words stand as an important comment on the goals of takeover bid legislation. Note how the authors of the OSC Report express the number of competing interests at stake in a takeover bid. We will now discuss two legislative provisions that manifest the presence of an equal treatment principle in the legislation.

a. Pro Rata Take-up

It may happen that a bidder seeks to acquire less than 100 percent of the outstanding shares of the target. This strategy is often referred to as a "partial bid." In this case, a question arises as to how the bidder takes up or agrees to purchase the shares if more than the desired number of shares are tendered to the bid. Under NI 62-104, s 2.26.1(1), shareholders of the target are assured that the bidder will take up the shares on a pro rata basis so that the bidder purchases the same proportion of the shares from all tendering shareholders according to the number of shares each shareholder tendered. For this reason, the pro rata take-up requirement is sometimes also referred to as "proportionate take-up." It replaces the "first-come, first-served" system under which shareholders who tendered early got 100 percent of their shares taken up, whereas shareholders who tendered later were not so fortunate.

b. Identical Consideration

The rules relating to identical consideration stipulate that all holders of the target's securities shall receive identical consideration (NI 62-104, s 2.23). This rule may seem like a basic requirement, but the bidder could increase its offer price once the initial bid is made. Some shareholders may have already tendered to the original bid prior to the increase in price. The identical consideration provision states that the shareholders who tendered initially will not be deprived of the higher offer price. Rather, all shareholders must receive the same offer price. Thus, no shareholder will be disadvantaged by a decision to tender early.

The legislation also prevents the bidder from making side deals with certain securities holders, such as controlling shareholders who may be seeking a premium for their holdings over and above what the "masses" receive. The legislation stipulates that these shareholders are not entitled to any collateral benefits for their shares. Collateral benefits include any "consideration of greater value than that offered to the other holders." In other words, the collateral benefits contemplated in the legislation need not be purely monetary, but could also include, for example, tangible gifts.

2. Disclosure

As noted above, the takeover bid provisions in Canadian securities legislation aim to protect the interests of target shareholders. Disclosure of information to the target shareholders is a cornerstone of this objective. The underlying reasoning is that before shareholders can make a decision to tender, they must have the information at their disposal to make an informed decision. Disclosure ensures that shareholders have full information about the bid and the bidder. For example, shareholders will know what percentage of outstanding securities of the target the bidder owns; the terms and conditions of the bid; and the bidder's business plans for the target. The bidder is required to disclose information in response to a number of similar relevant issues under Form 62-104F1, *Take-Over Bid Circular* (NI 62-104, s 2.10).

The requirements relating to ensuring disclosure also contribute to equal treatment of shareholders. Under the legislation, all shareholders in a particular jurisdiction are entitled to receive the bid documents (NI 62-104, s 2.8). Even when the bid is commenced by advertisement, the bidder must still deliver a bid circular to all shareholders of the target, yet need do so only after receiving a list of the target's shareholders. Thus, in theory under the rules, no one shareholder is disadvantaged by having less information than any other.

a. Circulars

Once the bid has been commenced by either of the two means (by mailout of the circular or by advertisement), the target's board of directors has an obligation under the legislation to prepare a directors' circular and deliver it to target shareholders (NI 62-104, s 2.17(1)). The most important feature of the directors' circular is that it contains a recommendation to the target shareholders to either accept or reject the bid. If the directors believe that they are unable to make a recommendation or if they choose to make no recommendation, the legislation permits them to indicate this decision to target shareholders in the circular. The particular information required in the directors' circular is mandated in Form 62-104F3, *Directors' Circular*. This form requests information such as the relationship between target management/board and the bidder, trading by managers and directors, material changes in the target, etc.

What are the consequences for failing to follow the disclosure obligations in the legislation? Failure to deliver a takeover bid circular contravenes provincial securities law and is therefore punishable as a quasi-criminal offence (Alberta *Securities Act*, RSA 2000, c S-4 (ASA), s 194; British Columbia *Securities Act*, RSBC 1996, c 418 (BCSA), s 155; Newfoundland and Labrador *Securities Act*, RSNL 1990, c S-13 (Nfld SA), s 122; OSA, s 122(1); Québec *Securities Act*, CQLR c V-1.1 (QSA), s 195). Liability can also occur in some provinces if the takeover bid circular contains a statement that is misleading or untrue or contains a material omission (ASA, s 205(1); New Brunswick *Securities Act*, SNB 2004, c S-5.5 (NBSA), s 153(1); BCSA, s 132(1); OSA, s 131(1); Nfld SA, s 131(1)). The legislation imposes liability for a directors' circular as well (ASA, s 205(2); BCSA, s 132(3); NBSA, s 153(2); OSA, s 131(2); Nfld SA, s 131(2)). Furthermore, there is the possibility of administrative action by the regulatory body if the contravention of securities law violates the public interest (OSA, s 127; ASA, s 198; BCSA, s 161; NBSA, s 184; Nfld SA, s 127), or court proceedings under OSA, s 128 (ASA, s 219; BCSA, s 157; NBSA, s 187; Nfld SA, s 128.1). These provisions are discussed in greater detail in the enforcement chapter (Chapter 11) of this book. In addition to these possibilities of enforcement action, securities legislation in some jurisdictions provides for a civil right of action against the bidders in favour of all those entitled to receive a takeover bid circular but who did not in fact receive one (ASA, s 206(b); BCSA, s 135(b); Nfld SA, s 133; OSA, s 133; QSA, s 215).

It is possible for the bidder to amend the terms of the deal once the offer has been made. For example, the bidder may choose to increase the price of its offer. If there is any variation to the terms of a bid, the bidder must deliver a notice of the variation to every person or company to whom the takeover bid circular or issuer bid circular was required to be delivered and whose securities were not taken up at the date of the variation (NI 62-104, s 2.12(1)).

b. The "Early Warning" System

In addition to the disclosure that the bidder must make when launching a takeover bid, there are additional requirements that bind the bidder in its acquisition of shares of a company once a threshold number of securities have been purchased. The "early warning rule" is a link between the rules that relate to timely disclosure of material information and the rules that relate to takeover bids. The legislation requires any person who acquires control over 10 percent of voting or equity securities of an issuer to issue and file a press release. The press release must identify the person who has made the acquisition as well as the extent of his or her control in aggregate. Once the 10 percent threshold has been reached, every subsequent increase of 2 percent requires the person to issue a press release and file a report with the provincial regulator. As of May 9, 2016, decreases in ownership, control, or direction of 2 percent or more must also be disclosed by way of press release, and a press release will need to be issued if a securityholder's ownership, control, or direction falls below the 10 percent threshold. The effect of these provisions is to provide targets with a "heads up" or "warning" of potential takeovers, sometimes called "creeping takeover bids," where the potential bidder slowly approaches the 20 percent threshold. The early warning system also provides shareholders with an opportunity to find out other significant shareholders in the company.

There are certain exemptions from the early warning requirements. NI 62-103, *The Early Warning System and Related Take-Over Bid and Insider Reporting Issues* (2016), 22 OSCB 50; (2000), 23 OSCB 1315 provides exemptions for:

- mutual funds or "eligible institutional investors" as defined under the instrument;
- entities that have an increase in a class of securities of a reporting issuer that arose solely due to certain actions of the issuer;
- underwriters, if they own securities only as underwriters and have made certain disclosure by news release;
- lenders lending or transferring securities for the purposes of determining the early warning reporting threshold trigger if they lend securities pursuant to a specified securities lending arrangement; and
- borrowers under securities lending agreements borrowing securities for the purposes of determining the early warning reporting thresholder trigger in certain circumstances.

Part 11 of NI 62-103 provides a discretionary exemption to be made by the regulator that can be in whole or in part an exemption to the NI. Students should refer to the instrument itself for a complete description of requirements pertaining to each of the groups. Note also that if an exemption is available, it is usually accompanied by a requirement to file some type of report and/or news release. For example, under the underwriter's exemption, a news release must be issued that announces the proposed underwriting and identifies the reporting issuer and the designation and number or principal amount of the securities underwritten.

Students should note that the CSA recently introduced changes to the Early Warning System, which came into effect on May 9, 2016. Substantive amendments include a new requirement to disclose decreases in ownership of 2 percent or more, a new requirement to disclose when ownership levels drop below the 10 percent threshold and enhanced disclosure in the early warning report.

These changes are intended to increase the transparency of and information available under the system. The CSA had originally considered reducing the early warning threshold from 10 percent to 5 percent; however, those considerations were abandoned after a majority of commenters raised concerns and objections. For more information, students should consult CSA, *Notice of Amendments to Early Warning System* (25 February 2016).

3. *Timing*

Recent Changes to the Takeover Bid Regime

On May 9, 2016, significant changes to securities legislation came into force across all Canadian jurisdictions. As noted in this chapter's introduction, MI 62-104 was formally replaced by NI 62-104, which now represents the regulatory framework governing takeover bids in all provinces, including Ontario. The most substantive changes came in the form of amendments to the minimum deposit period, which was extended from 35 to 105 days. The CSA also introduced a mandatory 10-day extension rule and a 50 percent minimum tender requirement, both of which are discussed in more detail below.

The CSA has argued that these changes will provide the target's shareholders with more time to gather information related to the takeover bid in question. Moreover, the changes are designed to give targets' boards of directors greater flexibility and discretion in responding to takeover bids. It bears mentioning that originally, the Québec Autorité des marchés financiers (AMF) took a different approach from Ontario in the context of the CSA discussions. Québec's approach was even more board friendly than the approach that ultimately prevailed in NI 62-104, particularly with respect to the time proposed that a bid should remain open. The Québec approach is a good example of the competing considerations at play in regulating takeovers. See <https://www.lautorite.qc.ca/files/pdf/consultations/juin-2013/2013mars14-avis-amf-62-105-cons-publ-en.pdf> and <http://www.groupes.finances.gouv.qc.ca/GTPEQ/Documents/Rapport_ENG_GTPEQ.pdf>.

These arguments continue to be the subject of vigorous debate. In a 2015 *McGill Law Journal* article (excerpted below), University of Toronto Professor Anita Anand presents a skeptical view of the then-proposed amendments. Professor Anand makes the case that a longer minimum deposit (or "bid") period will have the effect of reducing the number of takeover bids that occur generally. She contends that the new rules will have a chilling effect on hostile takeover bids especially as bidders will not wish to remain "in limbo" while the bid period clock keeps ticking. For more information, see Anita Anand, "The Future of Poison Pills in Canada: Are Takeover Bid Reforms Needed?" (2015) 61:1 McGill LJ 1.[5]

a. The 105-Day Rule

Under securities legislation, takeover bids must be made to all securityholders. Bidders must send the takeover bid documents to these securityholders and to securityholders who hold convertible securities (that is, securities that can be converted into the class subject to the takeover bid) (NI 62-104, s 2.8). A crucial point to note is that the takeover bid must remain open for at least 105 days (NI 62-104, s 2.28.1) in order to provide target holders with ample time to consider the offer. Furthermore, in a hostile bid situation, target directors will seek time to examine other merger possibilities. We will discuss this issue again under defensive tactics below.

The bidder is not permitted to take up, or accept for purchase, any shares deposited by tendering shareholders (NI 62-104, s 2.29.1) during the 105-day period. Thus, shareholders who have deposited shares are permitted to withdraw them. NI 62-104, s 2.30(1) states:

> 2.30(1) A securityholder may withdraw securities deposited under a take-over or issuer bid
> (a) at any time before the securities have been taken up by the offeror,
> (b) at any time before the expiration of 10 days from the date of a notice of change under section 2.11 or a notice of variation under section 2.12 or
> (c) if the securities have not been paid for by the offeror within 3 business days after the securities have been taken up.

Withdrawal rights are fundamental to shareholders' rights under the statute. First, shareholders are permitted to change their minds rather than have to make a "once and for all" decision. Second, shareholders are encouraged to tender to the bid and thereby contribute to facilitating takeover bids on a broader level.

There are competing tensions at this stage of the takeover bid process. On the one hand, shareholders no doubt take comfort in knowing that they can withdraw their decision to deposit at any point during the 105-day period. On the other hand, bidders look forward to the end of the 105-day period when shareholders can no longer change their minds about the decision to tender. Securities legislation provides that once shares are taken up, they must be paid for within three business days. NI 62-104, s 2.32.1(2) states:

> 2.32.1(2) An offeror must pay for any securities taken up under a take-over bid as soon as possible, and in any event not later than 3 business days after the securities deposited under the bid are taken up.

Securities legislation stipulates a ten-day period within which all shares tendered to the takeover bid *must* be taken up (NI 62-104, s 2.32.1(1)). Thus, a bidder cannot wait indefinitely before taking up tendered shares.

---

5 Note that, at the time of the article's writing, the CSA was proposing a 120-day minimum deposit period. The CSA reduced the final legislation to 105 days after a lengthy comment- and feedback-gathering process.

b. The Mandatory 10-Day Extension Period

Under NI 62-104, offerors are required to extend the deposit period by ten days, following the expiry of the initial deposit period. NI 62-104, s 2.31.1 states:

> 2.31.1 If, at the expiry of the initial deposit period, an offeror is obligated to take up securities deposited under a take-over bid pursuant to subsection 2.32.1(1), the offeror must
>
> (a) extend the period during which securities may be deposited under the bid for a period of at least ten days.

NI 62-104, s 2.31.1(b) stipulates that a corresponding press release must be issued in conjunction with the ten-day extension. This press release must disclose whether the minimum tender requirement (discussed below) has been satisfied, the number of securities deposited and withdrawn as at the expiry of the initial deposit period, and that the bid's deposit period has been extended by the mandatory ten days.

c. The 50 Percent Minimum Tender Requirement

NI 62-104 also contains a minimum tender requirement, whereby offerors cannot take up securities deposited under a takeover bid unless

> 2.29.1(c) more than 50% of the outstanding securities of the class that are subject to the bid, excluding securities beneficially owned, or over which control or direction is exercised, by the offeror or by any person acting jointly or in concert with the offeror, have been deposited under the bid and not withdrawn.

In effect, s 2.29.1(c) means that a takeover bid must be approved by a majority of the target's independent shareholders.

d. Flexibility in the 105-Day Rule

What happens if the bidder is not satisfied with the number of tenders that it has received during the initial 105-day period? Bidders are permitted to extend the date on which the offer will expire in order to provide shareholders with more time to tender their shares. However, bidders are permitted to extend the bid only if the securities previously deposited are first taken up. NI 62-104, s 2.32.1(4) states:

> 2.32.1(4) In the case of a take-over bid that is not a partial take-over bid, an offeror must not extend its bid beyond the expiry of the mandatory 10-day extension period unless the offeror first takes up all securities deposited under the bid and not withdrawn.

However, there is an exception to this rule that arises if the takeover bid is extended during a period in which withdrawal rights still exist. NI 62-104, s 2.32.1(5) states:

> 2.32.1(5) Despite subsection (4), if the offeror extends the bid in circumstances where the rights of withdrawal conferred by paragraph 2.30(1)(b) are applicable, the offeror must extend the bid without the offeror first taking up the securities which are subject to the rights of withdrawal.

It is also important to note that the target board of directors has the ability to decrease the 105-day minimum deposit period to 35 days in the context of a friendly takeover transaction. It can do so if the takeover bid in question qualifies as an "alternative transaction" (NI 62-104, s 2.28.3). An "alternative transaction" is defined by NI 62-104, s 1.1 as:

> "alternative transaction" means, for an issuer:
>
> (a) an amalgamation, merger, arrangement, consolidation, or any other transaction of the issuer, or an amendment to the terms of a class of equity securities of the issuer, as a consequence of which the interest of a holder of an equity security of the issuer may be terminated without the holder's consent, regardless of whether the equity security is replaced with another security, but does not include
>
> (i) a consolidation of securities that does not have the effect of terminating the interests of holders of equity securities of the issuer in those securities without their consent, except to an extent that is nominal in the circumstances,
>
> (ii) a circumstance in which the issuer may terminate a holder's interest in a security, under the terms attached to the security, for the purpose of enforcing an ownership or voting constraint that is necessary to enable the issuer to comply with legislation, lawfully engage in a particular activity or have a specified level of Canadian ownership, or
>
> (iii) a transaction solely between or among the issuer and one or more subsidiaries of the issuer,
>
> (b) a sale, lease or exchange of all or substantially all the property of the issuer if the sale, lease or exchange is not in the ordinary course of business of the issuer, but does not include a sale, lease or exchange solely between or among the issuer and one or more subsidiaries of the issuer;

Under NI 62-104, s 2.28.2, the target can also issue a deposit period news release in respect of the offeror's takeover bid. In this context, NI 62-104, s 2.28.2(3) states:

> 2.28.2(3) For the purposes of subsections (1) and (2), an offeror must not allow securities to be deposited under its take-over bid for an initial deposit period of less than 35 days from the date of the bid.

At this point, students may question how these provisions operate in practice. Below is an excerpt from *Re Canfor Corp* that illustrates the application of takeover bid provisions, including take-up and withdrawal rights. *Canfor* presented a unique situation where the bidder (Canfor) was offering neither shares nor cash as consideration for the shares of the target's (Slocan's) shareholders. Rather, Canfor would exchange one "deposit receipt" for each common share of Slocan tendered, and these deposit receipts would later be converted into Canfor stock upon the fulfilment of certain conditions precedent. At issue was whether some aspects of the bid violated the Ontario *Securities Act*.

Re Canfor Corp

(1995), 18 OSCB 475

1. *Did the Structure of the Canfor Bid Breach the Act?*

Paragraph 95.9 [now 98.3(1)] of the Act provides that, subject to paragraphs 95.10 and 11 [now 98.3(2) and (3)], the offeror under a take-over bid must take up and pay for securities deposited under the bid, where all the terms and conditions of the bid have been complied with or waived, not later than 10 days after the expiry of the bid. Paragraph 95.10 [now 98.3(2)] requires that any securities that are taken up by the offeror under the bid shall be paid for by the offeror as soon as possible, and in any event not more than three days, after the taking up of the securities. Paragraph 95.11 [now 98.3(3)] is not relevant to these proceedings. It is the position of Slocan and of the Staff of the Commission that the provisions of the Canfor bid breach paragraphs 95.9 [now 98.3(1)] and 95.10 [now 98.3(2)].

Counsel for Slocan acknowledged that the Deposit Receipts would be securities within the meaning of the Act, and that securities can constitute the consideration payable under a bid. However, they argued that the delivery of Deposit Receipts would not constitute taking up and payment for the Slocan shares tendered to the Canfor bid, under either the Canfor Offer or the Act. In this connection, they made the following principal arguments.

(a) They submitted that on a proper reading of the Canfor Offer, the consideration being offered was Canfor shares, and not Deposit Receipts, so that the issuance of the latter could not constitute payment of the consideration offered.

While we agree that the expression of just what the consideration offered was, as it appeared in various places in the Canfor Offer, the Canfor Circular and the covering letter which went to Slocan shareholders with these documents, was somewhat confusing, in our opinion a reading of each of those documents as a whole makes it apparent that the consideration offered is in fact Deposit Receipts.

(b) They submitted that Part XX of the Act speaks of both taking up and payment, each of which terms must be given a meaning different from the other, and, accordingly, even if there was payment for the deposited Slocan shares they might not be taken up within the meaning of Part XX. They further argued that, if the consideration offered for the Slocan shares is Deposit Receipts and not Canfor shares, the issuance of the Deposit Receipts will not constitute an unconditional and irrevocable taking up of the Slocan shares since the offer made by the Canfor Offer is to buy the Slocan shares and, under the Indenture, the beneficial ownership of the Slocan shares will remain in the holders of the Deposit Receipts, who at least initially will be the tendering Slocan shareholders, so that the Slocan shares will not be taken up since the entire interest in the Slocan shares will not pass to Canfor on the delivery of the Deposit Receipts. They pointed out that, in certain circumstances within the control of Canfor, the Deposit Receiptholders might eventually receive, in exchange for Deposit Receipts, deposited Slocan shares rather than Canfor shares.

While, as asserted by counsel for Slocan, it might initially appear inconsistent that there could be a taking up of the deposited Slocan shares in such circumstances, we are of the view that, on the proper legal analysis, the Canfor bid does provide for the taking up of the deposited Slocan shares by the issuance of transferable Deposit Receipts. In our view, what is being offered for is apparent from the Canfor bid, read as a whole, and the fact that the Deposit Receipts represent beneficial ownership of the Slocan shares from the time of the issuance of the Deposit Receipts to the time, if any, that the Deposit Receipts are exchanged for Canfor shares, does not mean that there is no taking up under the terms of the Canfor bid. Nor does the fact that, under certain circumstances, the holders of the Deposit Receipts might receive therefor Slocan shares rather than Canfor shares. Legal title to the Slocan shares is to pass to the Trustee and Canfor will then have control over what happens with those shares. Taking up is not defined by the Act and, as was conceded by counsel for Slocan, is not a term of art which has the same meaning in all circumstances. In our view, taking up, when used in Part XX, means the communication by the offeror of its irrevocable decision to complete the purchase of the shares tendered under its offer, and must take place before or at the time of payment. In this transaction, taking up will occur, if at all, before or at the time of the issuance by Canfor of Deposit Receipts in payment for the tendered Slocan shares.

(c) They submitted that there was, as a matter of law, really only one transaction, the exchange of Canfor shares for Slocan shares, and not two transactions, the first involving the exchange of Deposit Receipts for Slocan shares, and the second involving the exchange of either Canfor shares or Slocan shares for Deposit Receipts. Accordingly, they argued, until such time as the later exchange takes place there will be no taking up and payment, and then only if it involves Canfor shares.

In our view, there are, as a matter of law, two transactions. The issuance of Deposit Receipts is not, in the unusual circumstances of the transaction resulting from the stringent provisions of the *Forest Act*, merely a sham or an artificial transaction. In our view, the issuance of Deposit Receipts in exchange for tendered Slocan shares will, as a matter of law, constitute payment for the Slocan shares being taken up. The fact that the two legal transactions are connected, arising out of the same offer, might well be relevant when we turn to consideration of the request that we exercise our cease trade power, but is not, in our view, relevant in determining what would constitute taking up and payment.

...

Counsel for Slocan and Counsel for the Staff of the Commission argued further that, if there is no taking up, then the Canfor bid will not satisfy the requirements of subparagraph 95.4 iii [now 98.1(c)] of the Act, which provides that, where the securities have not been taken up and paid for by the offeror, securities deposited pursuant to the bid may be withdrawn by or on behalf of a depositing security holder after 45 days from the date of the bid. Since we have decided that the taking up of the Slocan shares would occur before or at the time of issuance of the Deposit Receipts and that the Deposit Receipts would constitute payment therefor, this does not arise.

2. *Did the Canfor Circular Comply with the Disclosure Obligations Under the Act and the Regulation?*

Slocan, supported by the Staff of the Commission, also asserted that Canfor did not comply adequately with its disclosure obligations under the Act and the Regulation in respect of the Canfor bid. Form 32 [now 62-504F1] to the Regulation describes certain of the information required to be included in a take-over bid circular. Item 19 [now 23] of the Form requires the disclosure of any matters not otherwise required by the Form to be disclosed that have not previously been generally disclosed and are known to the offeror but which would reasonably be expected to affect the decision of the securityholders of the offeree issuer to accept or reject the offer. The Commission considered the approach to be taken, in a take-over bid situation, to allegations of this sort in *In the Matter of Standard Broadcasting Corporation Limited et al.* (1985), 8 OSCB 3672, where it stated, commencing at page 3676, as follows:

> As to the allegations of inadequate disclosure that were made and did surface at several points during the course of the hearing, none were, in our respectful opinion, material in the sense that the disclosure asked for would have been necessary to allow an investor to make an informed investment decision. We stress this last point, as it is often the case that allegations

> of non-disclosure or inadequate disclosure, are made during the course of a take-over bid. There is a difference between perfect disclosure (which no two opposing counsel likely would ever agree upon), acceptable disclosure and material non-disclosure or material misleading disclosure.

. . .

Slocan and Commission Staff argued that the Canfor offering documents did not contain adequate disclosure in a number of respects. (Some of the allegations by Slocan of inadequate disclosure had limited merit, in our view, and we will not deal with those.)

(a) They argued that Canfor did not clearly describe the consideration it was offering for the Slocan shares.

As we have indicated, we do agree that the fact that the consideration is to be Deposit Receipts and not Canfor shares is sometimes expressed less clearly than we might have liked. However, a complete reading of even the face page of the Canfor bid document, in our view, makes the position apparent.

(b) They argued that Canfor should have made it clear that its method of avoiding a change of control for purposes of the *Forest Act* was untested, and that it might violate the provisions of the *Forest Act*. We were advised by counsel for Canfor that Canfor had a clear legal opinion in this respect. Counsel for Slocan responded that Canfor should have known that the opinion was aggressive, and should have approached the Minister to make sure that he agreed.

While we do not agree that it was incumbent on Canfor to approach the Minister, we have concluded, on balance, that Canfor should have disclosed the fact that the method was untested. We are unable to conclude that the fact that Canfor had a legal opinion made such disclosure unnecessary. Given that the entire regulatory risk was on the Slocan shareholders (due to the fact that the Preservation Covenants effectively gave Canfor a complete "out" if it did not wish to complete the exchange of Deposit Receipts for Canfor shares and the fact that Canfor had a similar "out" if conditions of the Minister's consent were not satisfactory to Canfor), the fact that the issuance of Deposit Receipts might trigger the potentially severe change of control penalties of the *Forest Act* was, in our view, material to the decision by the Slocan shareholders of whether or not to tender to the Canfor bid. In our view this disclosure deficiency constituted a breach of the Act and the Regulation. In this connection, we understand that, subsequent to the Hearing and in connection with court proceedings in the province of British Columbia, Canfor agreed to amendments to the Indenture to restrict certain rights on its part as a result of concerns raised by the Minister that there would otherwise be a change of control of Slocan for the purposes of the *Forest Act* on the deposit under the Indenture of Slocan shares taken up by Canfor under the Canfor bid.

(c) They argued that further disclosure should have been made with respect to the length, complexity and difficulty of the approval process, and the risks concerning the conditions which the Minister might impose as a term of his granting approval, especially in view of the facts that the process was, as between the Slocan shareholders and Canfor, entirely in the hands of Canfor, and that the entire regulatory risk was on the Slocan shareholders.

As regards the conditions which might be imposed, we understand that these are not fixed, and that to a considerable extent all that Canfor would have been able to do in this regard was to speculate. Since it would be up to Canfor to decide whether the conditions to be imposed were satisfactory to it, telling the Slocan shareholders what conditions might be imposed would not provide them with useful information unless Canfor was also prepared to state whether it would accept those conditions. We think that it would be too much to ask Canfor to, in effect, advise the Minister as to which of the stringent conditions he might think of imposing would be acceptable to Canfor. As to the length of the process, it seems clear from the Canfor bid that the process could take in excess of 100 days, and, on balance, we cannot conclude that the failure to say this more clearly constituted a breach of the Act and the Regulation. However, as regards the complexity and difficulty of the approval process, we have, again on balance, decided that further and better information should have been provided by Canfor to the Slocan shareholders. In our view, this information would be material to the decision which the Slocan shareholders have to make and the failure to disclose it constituted a breach of the Act and the Regulation.

(d) They argued that Canfor should have disclosed more candidly the fact that, under the Indenture, Canfor would be able to extend the Termination Date in its sole discretion. The Canfor offering documents define Termination Date to mean the day that is 100 days after the Expiry Time or such later date "as may be permitted by the Deposit Receipt Indenture." The Indenture defines the term as the day which is 100 days after the Expiry Time or such later date "as the Company [i.e., Canfor] may determine as being reasonably necessary for the purpose of obtaining the *Forest Act* Consent."

Certainly, the use of the latter definition in the Canfor offering documents would have been more in the nature of full disclosure, and hardly longer. Slocan shareholders could not have been expected to ask for a copy of the Indenture so as to find out what it permitted in this respect. The use of the abridged definition was somewhat "cute." However, Canfor's power to extend is restricted to what it determines to be reasonably necessary for the purpose of obtaining the Minister's consent, and we do not think that the disclosure was so clearly inadequate as to constitute a breach of the Act and the Regulation.

• • •

We have some doubt as to whether the correction of serious disclosure deficiencies in a take-over bid circular by appropriate disclosure in the directors' circular would in all circumstances suffice to remedy the situation. However, in this case the Slocan directors did make appropriate disclosure in their circulars of the matters which we have found should have been, but were not, disclosed in the Canfor offering documents, and the deficiencies in the latter were, in our view, while material, not so significant as to demand an order correcting them in the circumstances. In addition, the directors of Slocan disclosed the omitted information in sufficient time to allow the Slocan shareholders to make a reasoned decision as to the desirability of accepting the Canfor bid. Accordingly, we have concluded that in the circumstances of this transaction it is not necessary for us to exercise our subsection 104(1) and clause 104(2)(b) jurisdiction or our clause 127(1)2 jurisdiction in order to remedy the deficiencies.

... We considered the fact that Canfor will be issuing Deposit Receipts to Slocan shareholders which will trade on the TSE. This will provide Slocan shareholders with some liquidity for their securities and allow them to conclude their exposure to the risks associated with the Deposit Receipts, for example in the event of an adverse material change in the affairs of Canfor (although the liquidity may be somewhat limited by the 20 percent cap). Slocan shareholders will have much of the protection they would have if they were to have withdrawal rights, although they will not have the ability to tender to another bid during the subject period. However, we recognized the reasons why Canfor may have considered that the granting of a withdrawal right in the event of another bid would expose it to commercial risks which it was not prepared to take in view of the time and effort which would inevitably be involved in pursuing the Minister's approval under section 50 of the *Forest Act*. We also noted that, in light of the terms of the Canfor bid and the Commission's order in this case, other interested bidders would have five weeks to come forward, although we appreciate that the circumstances may be such that another company that is not currently interested in making a bid might develop an interest subsequent to the closing of the Canfor bid. Finally, we were reluctant to impose a cease trade order which might result in the shareholders of Slocan not having the opportunity to consider a bid for their shares, absent compelling reasons for doing so.

We recognize that there may well be cases where structuring a bid in a manner similar to the Canfor bid and using deposit receipts as consideration may be contrary to the public interest. However, on balance, in the unusual circumstances of this case in which the stringent provisions of the *Forest Act* had to be accommodated, we were not satisfied that the Canfor bid was so abusive of investors or the capital markets as to warrant our intervention under clause 127(1)2 of the Act to, in effect, require the granting of a withdrawal right. In our view it was appropriate that the Canfor bid go to the Slocan shareholders for their decision.

Slocan argued that the Canfor bid failed to comply with the spirit of the Act in a number of other respects. We do not find it necessary to deal with each of these. Suffice it to say that, in our view, none of these alleged failures to comply came close to the "abusive" threshold. We should mention one, however, since Slocan made a good deal of it.

As we have said, the "Preservation Covenants" would likely have the effect of giving Canfor a complete "out," at its option. This is no doubt something which the Slocan shareholders should consider carefully in deciding whether or not to tender to the Canfor bid. In drafting these "covenants" it seems to us that Canfor did not lean over backwards to be fair to the Slocan shareholders. However, we do not consider this to be so abusive as to require our intervention. If Canfor had made a bid open for acceptance for 100 days or more, as Slocan said it should have, Canfor could have included precisely the same restraints as conditions of its offer without violating the letter or spirit of the Act. In such a case, the depositing shareholders would have had withdrawal rights after 45 days from the date of the bid, but, in our view, this goes to the question of whether we should have required such a withdrawal right, not to the question of the propriety of the Preservation Covenants. We cannot, therefore, conclude that it was abusive for Canfor to have provided for such restraints by way of the Preservation Covenants.

Accordingly, we are not prepared to cease trade the issuance of the Deposit Receipts.

We did, however, conclude that it would be in the public interest that the Slocan shareholders be given additional time to assess the Canfor bid and recent developments concerning it, including our decision. Accordingly, we ordered, pursuant to clause 104(2)(b) of the Act, that the time period during which Slocan shares may be tendered under the Canfor bid be varied by extending it for 10 days.

The *Canfor* decision highlights the importance of the bidder's circular as well as the take-up and payment provisions of securities legislation. The commission accepted that the issuance of the deposit receipts in exchange for the tendered Slocan shares constituted payment by the bidder.

D. Exemptions from the Takeover Bid Requirements

Takeover bid legislation offers a number of exemptions to the strict requirements of the statute or national instrument. If bidders qualify under any one of these exemptions, they are not compelled to follow the rules relating to disclosure and other provisions of the legislation. Some of these exemptions are discussed below. We will then discuss certain policy considerations underlying the legislation.

1. *NI 62-104, Section 4.1, Normal Course Purchase Exemption*

This exemption applies to takeover bids for 5 percent or less of the outstanding securities of a class of securities of the offeree issuer during a 12-month period. NI 62-104, s 4.1 states:

> 4.1 A take-over bid is exempt from Part 2 if all of the following conditions are satisfied:
> (a) the bid is for not more than 5% of the outstanding securities of a class of securities of the offeree issuer;
> (b) the aggregate number of securities acquired in reliance on this exemption by the offeror and any person acting jointly or in concert with the offeror within any period of 12 months, when aggregated with acquisitions otherwise made by the offeror and any person acting jointly or in concert with the offeror within the same 12-month period, other than under a bid that is subject to Part 2, does not exceed 5% of the securities of that class outstanding at the beginning of the 12-month period;
> (c) there is a published market for the class of securities that are the subject of the bid;
> (d) the value of the consideration paid for any of the securities acquired is not in excess of the market price at the date of acquisition, as determined in accordance with section 1.11, plus reasonable brokerage fees or commissions actually paid.

2. *NI 62-104, Section 4.2, Private Agreement Exemption*

This exemption allows an offeror to purchase securities from not more than five securityholders in the aggregate, so long as the bid is not made generally to securityholders of the issuer and the consideration paid for the securities does not exceed 115 percent of market value. NI 62-104, s 4.2 states:

> 4.2(1) A take-over bid is exempt from Part 2 if all of the following conditions are satisfied:
> (a) purchases are made from not more than 5 persons in the aggregate, including persons located outside the local jurisdiction;
> (b) the bid is not made generally to securityholders of the class of securities that is the subject of the bid, so long as there are more than 5 securityholders of the class;
> (c) if there is a published market for the securities acquired, the value of the consideration paid for any of the securities, including brokerage fees or commissions, is not greater than 115% of the market price of the securities at the date of the bid as determined in accordance with section 1.11;
> (d) if there is no published market for the securities acquired, there is a reasonable basis for determining that the value of the consideration paid for any of the securities is not greater than 115% of the value of the securities.

(2) In subsection (1), if an offeror makes an offer to acquire securities from a person and the offeror knows or ought to know after reasonable enquiry that

(a) the person acquired the securities in order that the offeror might make use of the exemption under subsection (1), then each person from whom those securities were acquired must be included in the determination of the number of persons to whom an offer to acquire has been made, or

(b) the person from whom the acquisition is being made is acting as a nominee, agent, trustee, executor, administrator or other legal representative for one or more other persons having a direct beneficial interest in those securities, then each of those other persons must be included in the determination of the number of persons to whom an offer to acquire has been made.

(3) Despite paragraph (2)(b), a trust or estate is to be considered a single securityholder in the determination of the number of persons to whom an offer to acquire has been made if

(a) an inter vivos trust has been established by a single settlor, or

(b) an estate has not vested in all persons who are beneficially entitled to it.

3. NI 62-104, Section 4.3, Non-Reporting Issuer Exemption

This exemption applies to targets that are not reporting issuers. For an offeree issuer to qualify for this exemption, NI 62-104, s 4.3 requires that:

4.3(a) the offeree issuer is not a reporting issuer;

(b) there is no published market for the securities that are the subject of the bid;

(c) the number of securityholders of that class of securities at the commencement of the bid is not more than 50, exclusive of holders who

(i) are in the employment of the offeree issuer or an affiliate of the offeree issuer, or

(ii) were formerly in the employment of the offeree issuer or in the employment of an entity that was an affiliate of the offeree issuer at the time of that employment, and who while in that employment were, and have continued after that employment to be, securityholders of the offeree issuer.

4. NI 62-104, Section 4.4, Foreign Takeover Bid Exemption

This exemption applies to transactions where the target issuer's securities are primarily traded on a foreign stock exchange. Moreover, securityholders of the target issuer residing in Canada must own less than 10 percent of the outstanding securities of the class of securities subject to the bid. For more information, students should consult NI 62-104, s 4.4.

5. NI 62 104, Section 4.5, De Minimis Exemption

This exemption applies to takeover bids made to a particularly small number of shareholders in the local jurisdiction. NI 62 104, s 4.5 states:

4.5 A take-over bid is exempt from Part 2 if all of the following conditions are satisfied:

(a) the number of beneficial owners of securities of the class subject to the bid in the local jurisdiction is fewer than 50;

(b) the securities held by the beneficial owners referred to in paragraph (a) constitute, in aggregate, less than 2% of the outstanding securities of that class;

(c) securityholders in the local jurisdiction are entitled to participate in the bid on terms at least as favourable as the terms that apply to the general body of securityholders of the same class;

(d) at the same time as material relating to the bid is sent by or on behalf of the offeror to securityholders of the class that is subject to the bid, the material is filed and sent to securityholders whose last address as shown on the books of the offeree issuer is in the local jurisdiction.

It is important to note that there are various policy considerations underlying the exemptions. For example, the control block exemption, also called the five-person exemption or the private agreement exemption, permits bidders to derogate from the principles of equal treatment. As we have seen, the legislation generally ensures that shareholders receive identical consideration and that no one shareholder, even a controlling shareholder, receives a collateral benefit for tendering its shares. Derogation from this basic principle is, however, viewed to be acceptable in the interests of facilitating changes of control in limited situations. As noted above, if the premium to be received on the sale of the control block is not substantial (that is, the sale price is not more than 15 percent above the current market price), the sale is permissible. In addition, the offer must be made to five or fewer persons, among other requirements.

E. Arrangements

Before turning to the defensive tactics available to a firm that is the target of a takeover bid, it is interesting to consider whether the rules governing takeover bids should be extended to apply to arrangements aimed at gaining control of a company as well, since both are a form of acquisition transaction. This question was addressed by the *Five Year Review Committee Final Report: Reviewing the Securities Act (Ontario)* (Toronto: Five Year Review Committee, 21 March 2003), online: <http://www.osc.gov.on.ca/documents/en/Securities/fyr_20030529_5yr-final-report.pdf>. The committee ultimately decided that maintaining separate regulations for each transaction was appropriate. One major reason that the transactions are governed separately is that the law pertaining to arrangements is intended to be inherently flexible and principles-based. This is in contrast to the statutory provisions on takeover bids, which tend to be more rules-based, stipulating, for example, how long a bid must remain open once it has been made and target shareholders' specific rights relating to withdrawal and take-up.

With the case of *BCE Inc v 1976 Debentureholders*, 2008 SCC 69, [2008] 3 SCR 560, the Supreme Court has both clarified and modified the law on arrangements such that some might question whether or not its characteristic flexibility remains intact. In *BCE*, the Ontario Teachers' Pension Plan Board announced that it intended to acquire BCE through a plan of arrangement in the form of a leveraged buyout. A group of debentureholders opposed this plan; however, they were not accorded a vote in the transaction. BCE eventually accepted the Teachers' bid of $51.7 billion, the largest leveraged buyout in Canadian history. The arrangement meant that the debentureholders' securities would be devalued to below investment grade as a result of the corporation taking on significantly more debt. The debentureholders brought an action in the Québec Superior Court claiming that the proposed arrangement was oppressive within the meaning of s 241 of the *Canada Business*

Corporations Act, RSC 1985, c C-44 (CBCA). The trial judge dismissed the debentureholders' claim, but the Québec Court of Appeal allowed the appeal.

The Supreme Court heard the case on the following issues: whether the Court of Appeal erred in dismissing the debentureholders' oppression claim, and whether the Court of Appeal erred in overturning the plan of arrangement. Part of the analysis was whether the "fair and reasonable" test in the arrangement context was distinct from the notion of reasonable expectations, a concept central to the analysis of oppression. An excerpt from their decision follows.

BCE Inc v 1976 Debentureholders
2008 SCC 69, [2008] 3 SCR 560

THE COURT: …

(d) Criteria for Court Approval

[136] Section 192(3) specifies that the corporation must obtain court approval of the plan. In determining whether a plan of arrangement should be approved, the court must focus on the terms and impact of the arrangement itself, rather than on the process by which it was reached. What is required is that the arrangement itself, viewed substantively and objectively, be suitable for approval.

[137] In seeking approval of an arrangement, the corporation bears the onus of satisfying the court that: (1) the statutory procedures have been met; (2) the application has been put forward in good faith; and (3) the arrangement is fair and reasonable: see *Trizec Corp., Re* (1994), 21 Alta. LR (3d) 435 (QB), at p. 444. This may be contrasted with the s. 241 oppression action, where the onus is on the claimant to establish its case. On these appeals, it is conceded that the corporation satisfied the first two requirements. The only question is whether the arrangement is fair and reasonable.

[138] In reviewing the directors' decision on the proposed arrangement to determine if it is fair and reasonable under s. 192, courts must be satisfied that (a) the arrangement has a valid business purpose, and (b) the objections of those whose legal rights are being arranged are being resolved in a fair and balanced way. It is through this two-pronged framework that courts can determine whether a plan is fair and reasonable.

[139] In the past, some courts have answered the question of whether an arrangement is fair and reasonable by applying what is referred to as the business judgment test, that is whether an intelligent and honest business person, as a member of the voting class concerned and acting in his or her own interest would reasonably approve the arrangement: see *Trizec*, at p. 444; *Pacifica Papers Inc. v. Johnstone* (2001), 15 BLR (3d) 249, 2001 BCSC 1069. However, while this consideration may be important, it does not constitute a useful or complete statement of what must be considered on a s. 192 application.

[140] First, the fact that the business judgment test referred to here and the business judgment rule discussed above (at para. 40) are so similarly named leads to confusion. The business judgment *rule* expresses the need for deference to the business judgment of directors as to the best interests of the corporation. The business judgment *test* under s. 192, by contrast, is aimed at determining whether the proposed arrangement is fair and

reasonable, having regard to the corporation and relevant stakeholders. The two inquiries are quite different. Yet the use of the same terminology has given rise to confusion. Thus, courts have on occasion cited the business judgment test while saying that it stands for the principle that arrangements do not have to be perfect, i.e. as a deference principle: see *Abitibi-Consolidated Inc. (Arrangement relatif à)*, [2007] QJ No. 16158 (QL), 2007 QCCS 6830. To conflate the business judgment test and the business judgment rule leads to difficulties in understanding what "fair and reasonable" means and how an arrangement may satisfy this threshold.

[141] Second, in instances where affected security holders have voted on a plan of arrangement, it seems redundant to ask what an intelligent and honest business person, as a member of the voting class concerned and acting in his or her own interest, would do. As will be discussed below (at para. 150), votes on arrangements are an important indicator of whether a plan is fair and reasonable. However, the business judgment test does not provide any more information than does the outcome of a vote. Section 192 makes it clear that the reviewing judge must delve beyond whether a reasonable business person would approve of a plan to determine whether an arrangement is fair and reasonable. Insofar as the business judgment test suggests that the judge need only consider the perspective of the majority group, it is incomplete.

[142] In summary, we conclude that the business judgment test is not useful in the context of a s. 192 application, and indeed may lead to confusion.

[143] The framework proposed in these reasons reformulates the s. 192 test for what is fair and reasonable in a way that reflects the logic of s. 192 and the authorities. Determining what is fair and reasonable involves two inquiries: first, whether the arrangement has a valid business purpose; and second, whether it resolves the objections of those whose rights are being arranged in a fair and balanced way. In approving plans of arrangement, courts have frequently pointed to factors that answer these two questions as discussed more fully below: *Canadian Pacific Ltd. (Re)* (1990), 73 OR (2d) 212 (HC); *Cinar Corp. v. Shareholders of Cinar Corp.* (2004), 4 CBR (5th) 163 (Que. Sup. Ct.); *PetroKazakhstan Inc. v. Lukoil Overseas Kumkol B.V.* (2005), 12 BLR (4th) 128, 2005 ABQB 789.

[144] We now turn to a more detailed discussion of the two prongs.

[145] The valid business purpose prong of the fair and reasonable analysis recognizes the fact that there must be a positive value to the corporation to offset the fact that rights are being altered. In other words, courts must be satisfied that the burden imposed by the arrangement on security holders is justified by the interests of the corporation. The proposed plan of arrangement must further the interests of the corporation as an ongoing concern. In this sense, it may be narrower than the "best interests of the corporation" test that defines the fiduciary duty of directors under s. 122 of the *CBCA* (see paras. 38-40).

[146] The valid purpose inquiry is invariably fact-specific. Thus, the nature and extent of evidence needed to satisfy this requirement will depend on the circumstances. An important factor for courts to consider when determining if the plan of arrangement serves a valid business purpose is the necessity of the arrangement to the continued operations of the corporation. Necessity is driven by the market conditions that a corporation faces, including technological, regulatory and competitive conditions. Indicia of necessity include the existence of alternatives and market reaction to the plan. The degree of necessity of the arrangement has a direct impact on the court's level of scrutiny. Austin J in *Canadian Pacific* concluded that

> while courts are prepared to assume jurisdiction notwithstanding a lack of necessity on the part of the company, *the lower the degree of necessity, the higher the degree of scrutiny that should be applied*. [Emphasis added; p. 223.]

If the plan of arrangement is necessary for the corporation's continued existence, courts will more willingly approve it despite its prejudicial effect on some security holders. Conversely, if the arrangement is not mandated by the corporation's financial or commercial situation, courts are more cautious and will undertake a careful analysis to ensure that it was not in the sole interest of a particular stakeholder. Thus, the relative necessity of the arrangement may justify negative impact on the interests of affected security holders.

[147] The second prong of the fair and reasonable analysis focuses on whether the objections of those whose rights are being arranged are being resolved in a fair and balanced way.

[148] An objection to a plan of arrangement may arise where there is tension between the interests of the corporation and those of a security holder, or there are conflicting interests between different groups of affected rights holders. The judge must be satisfied that the arrangement strikes a fair balance, having regard to the ongoing interests of the corporation and the circumstances of the case. Often this will involve complex balancing, whereby courts determine whether appropriate accommodations and protections have been afforded to the concerned parties. However, as noted by Forsyth J in *Trizec*, at para. 36:

> [T]he court must be careful not to cater to the special needs of one particular group but must strive to be fair to all involved in the transaction depending on the circumstances that exist. The overall fairness of any arrangement must be considered as well as fairness to various individual stakeholders.

[149] The question is whether the plan, viewed in this light, is fair and reasonable. In answering this question, courts have considered a variety of factors, depending on the nature of the case at hand. None of these alone is conclusive, and the relevance of particular factors varies from case to case. Nevertheless, they offer guidance.

[150] An important factor is whether a majority of security holders has voted to approve the arrangement. Where the majority is absent or slim, doubts may arise as to whether the arrangement is fair and reasonable; however, a large majority suggests the converse. Although the outcome of a vote by security holders is not determinative of whether the plan should receive the approval of the court, courts have placed considerable weight on this factor. Voting results offer a key indication of whether those affected by the plan consider it to be fair and reasonable: *St. Lawrence & Hudson Railway Co. (Re)*, [1998] OJ No. 3934 (QL) (Ont. Ct. (Gen. Div.)).

[151] Where there has been no vote, courts may consider whether an intelligent and honest business person, as a member of the class concerned and acting in his or her own interest, might reasonably approve of the plan: *Re Alabama, New Orleans, Texas and Pacific Junction Railway Co.*, [1891] 1 Ch. 213 (CA); *Trizec*.

[152] Other indicia of fairness are the proportionality of the compromise between various security holders, the security holders' position before and after the arrangement and the impact on various security holders' rights: see *Canadian Pacific*; *Trizec*. The court may also consider the repute of the directors and advisors who endorse the arrangement and the arrangement's terms. Thus, courts have considered whether the plan has been

approved by a special committee of independent directors; the presence of a fairness opinion from a reputable expert; and the access of shareholders to dissent and appraisal remedies: see *Stelco Inc. (Re)* (2006), 18 CBR (5th) 173 (Ont. SCJ); *Cinar*; *St. Lawrence & Hudson Railway*; *Trizec*; *Pacifica Papers*; *Canadian Pacific*.

[153] This review of factors represents considerations that have figured in s. 192 cases to date. It is not meant to be exhaustive, but simply to provide an overview of some factors considered by courts in determining if a plan has reasonably addressed the objections and conflicts between different constituencies. Many of these factors will also indicate whether the plan serves a valid business purpose. The overall determination of whether an arrangement is fair and reasonable is fact-specific and may require the assessment of different factors in different situations.

[154] We arrive then at this conclusion: in determining whether a plan of arrangement is fair and reasonable, the judge must be satisfied that the plan serves a valid business purpose and that it adequately responds to the objections and conflicts between different affected parties. Whether these requirements are met is determined by taking into account a variety of relevant factors, including the necessity of the arrangement to the corporation's continued existence, the approval, if any, of a majority of shareholders and other security holders entitled to vote, and the proportionality of the impact on affected groups.

While the Supreme Court in *BCE* has expanded the list of principles to be considered in the arrangement context, it has retained the principles-based flexibility that has traditionally characterized this area of the law. It therefore seems sound to maintain separate regimes for arrangements and takeover bids, because the rationale for their separate treatment is still applicable. (See Anita Anand, "Flexibility vs. Certainty: The Law Relating to Arrangements After BCE" (2009) 48:2 Can Bus LJ 173.)

QUESTIONS

1. Should takeover bid law protect the interests of the bidder's shareholders in addition to the target's shareholders? Why or why not?

2. Do you feel the takeover bid obligations of equality, disclosure, and timing are effective in protecting the target's shareholders?

3. The exemptions from the takeover bid requirements most certainly add to market efficiency, but do they serve investor protection well? Consider the control block purchase exemption and the fact that most Canadian corporations are controlled by one individual or group.

IV. DEFENSIVE TACTICS

When a hostile bid is made, the target board finds itself in a conflict of interest situation. On the one hand, directors are obliged to act in the best interests of the company under corporate law. On the other hand, in a takeover bid situation, target directors and management stand to lose their positions if the bid is successful. Thus, directors and senior management are in a conflict of interest position in a takeover bid and especially in adopting defensive tactics in response to the bid. Is the defensive tactic meant to thwart the takeover bid altogether or is it meant for another purpose, such as to "buy time" while the board seeks a higher offer?

In the light of this conflict of interest, the law relating to the actions that the target board can legitimately adopt in the face of a hostile bid is complicated. NP 62-202 and case law (both discussed later in the chapter) govern the issue. In Canada, unlike the United States, the rule appears to be that the board cannot "just say no" to a takeover bid. The board can, however, adopt "defensive tactics." A defensive tactic is a strategy or mechanism adopted by the target board in the face of a hostile bid in order to thwart or delay a takeover bid. In Canada, defensive tactics are permitted to delay the bid in order to give the board more time to consider it and to seek alternative offers. Some examples of defensive tactics include finding a "white knight" or alternative bidder; shareholder rights plans (SRPs) or "poison pills," sale of a "crown jewel" or key asset of the target; litigation; implementing an issuer bid; and negotiating a "break fee" with an alternative bidder. (These terms are explained later in this chapter. See "A. Different Types of Defensive Tactics," below.)

Before explaining these different terms, let us note that the defensive tactic that a company adopts is influenced to some degree by certain characteristics of the market. In the United States, capital markets tend to be populated by widely held public corporations. Thus, in the United States, target boards are more likely to adopt defensive tactics (for example, an issuer bid or a poison pill) that affect or potentially affect a broad range of target shareholders. On the contrary, Canadian markets exhibit a high degree of concentration in share ownership (Jeffrey G MacIntosh & Lawrence P Schwartz, "Do Institutional and Controlling Shareholders Increase Corporate Value?" in Ronald J Daniels & Randall Morck, eds, *Corporate Decision-Making in Canada* (Calgary: University of Calgary Press, 1995) 303). In a takeover bid, the target board and management are in many instances responding to the interests and concerns of the controlling shareholder, especially in the hostile bid situation. Some defensive tactics, such as break fees and sale of the crown jewel, are thus more important in the Canadian context where a number of listed companies have controlling shareholders and are not otherwise widely held. The implementation of a break fee or a sale of a crown jewel is often easier to effect for companies with a controlling shareholder. If a target is signing an agreement with a white knight, it will likely seek the approval of any controlling shareholder and this shareholder will likely have representation on the board. Once the approval of the controlling shareholder has been achieved, the company will be more confident about pursuing this strategy. On the other hand, in order for a poison pill to be effective, shareholder approval is required, but it may be difficult to achieve in the midst of a bid.

When faced with a hostile bid, target boards often set up a special committee of directors to review the terms of the bid and alternatives to the bid in order to make a recommendation to the board. The special committee typically comprises independent directors, although this is not a legal requirement. The apparent rationale for this practice is that non-independent directors suffer from the conflict of interest described above—that is, the conflict between acting in the best interests of the corporation and acting in their own self-interest when evaluating a bid. (See the discussion in *Maple Leaf Foods Inc v Schneider Corp* (1998), 42 OR (3d) 177 (CA) and *CW Shareholdings Inc v WIC Western International Communications Ltd* (1998), 39 OR (3d) 755 (Gen Div) below). A special committee comprising independent directors is not subject to this conflict. Their only incentive is to act in the company's best interests when reviewing alternatives.

The following excerpt from Drew Hasselback explains how securities regulators have approached the issue of defensive tactics. In particular, Hasselback focuses on the "poison pill," a popular defensive tactic that will be examined at length later in this chapter.

Drew Hasselback, "Poison Pills Are Proving Tough for Securities Commissions to Swallow"
Financial Post (27 January 2011)

M&A lawyers began 2010 wondering whether Canadian takeover rules were on the cusp of embracing the principle that directors could "Just Say No" to hostile bids. A year later, however, it seems that it is the securities commissions are just saying no to that "Just Say No" defence.

Two securities commission cases, *Baffinland* in Ontario and *Lions Gate* in British Columbia, were convened to decide the fate of so-called poison pills, and both pointed in a common direction: it should be up to shareholders, not corporate directors, to decide the fate of takeover bids.

Poison pills equip companies with the right to respond to a hostile bid by issuing a whack of new shares so the unwanted bidder can't follow through with its offer to buy them all. The reality is that they're never used for that purpose. Rather, company boards use them only to buy time while they look for white-knight bidders to trump the hostile offer.

"They are important in situations where a lot of hostiles show up and there's a lot of alternatives," says Jeff Barnes, a partner with Borden Ladner Gervais in Toronto.

At least that was the understanding until 2007, when the Alberta Securities Commission issued the *Pulse Data* decision. The ASC allowed Pulse Data's poison pill to stand because directors had shopped the company enough to demonstrate that a hostile bid launched by a company Seitel was way too cheap. What's more, Pulse Data's poison pill was approved by a healthy majority of shareholders after the Seitel bid was launched.

Then came the Supreme Court of Canada's 2008 *BCE* decision, which found that corporate directors owe a duty to the company itself. Lawyers debate the implications of this ruling, but it seems to mean that a board has the right to put the long-term interests of a company ahead of the short-term interests of shareholders.

Ontario's securities commission then took a crack at applying the lessons from Pulse Data and BCE in a case called *Neo Material Technologies.* As with Pulse Data, the poison pill at issue was introduced after Neo had received a hostile bid, and shareholders approved it by a wide majority. After discussing the implications of the BCE decision, the OSC found no reason to believe Neo Material's board was motivated by anything other than its duty to the corporation, so it let the pill stand.

"The *Neo* and *Pulse Data* cases, I think, raised the question of whether, 'Gosh, Can a Canadian board now use a pill to Just Say No?' " recalls David Woollcombe, a partner in the Toronto office of McCarthy Tétrault LLP. "There was lots of interest and excitement about that in the light of the *BCE* decision."

Indeed, the B.C. Securities Commission was the first to strike. In the summer of 2010, it came out with the decision in *Icahn Partners and Lions Gate Entertainment.* A majority of the commission panel found that a company's board has to pursue other bids, or the

> poison pill has to go—no matter how much support the "shareholder rights plan" or SRP has received from shareholders.
>
> The question was whether this decision was just a bump on the road to Just Say Now, or whether it represented a shift back to the pre-2007 understanding of the rules. The answer for Ontario came in November, when the OSC tossed out a poison pill that Baffinland Iron Mines was then using to fend off an unsolicited bid from Nunavut Iron Mines.
>
> "To the extent that a window opened giving boards greater discretion to defend unsolicited transactions for a period of time longer than traditionally permitted in Canada, that window has been largely, if not entirely, shut," says Mike Gans of Blakes.
>
> Ralph Shay of Fraser Milner Casgrain LLP in Toronto suggests the market could use some fresh guidance on takeover defences. As the year as shown, different provincial securities commissions can take different views on how to apply National Policy 62-202, the document that sets Canadian policy on takeover defences. "We need harmonization and clarification."
>
> Ed Waitzer, a partner with Stikeman Elliott LLP and a former chairman of the Ontario Securities Commission, takes a different tack. He suggests securities commissions get out of the takeover defence business entirely.

We now move to discuss various types of defensive tactics that the target board can adopt in the face of a hostile bid.

A. Different Types of Defensive Tactics

Let us turn now to examine some of the more prominent takeover bid defensive tactics in Canada.

1. White Knight

When a target board is faced with a hostile bid, it may strike a special committee to review the proposed transaction and alternatives to the bid. The law requires the special committee to "canvass the market" (see *Maple Leaf Foods Inc v Schneider Corp*, below). As part of this process, the special committee will consider other possible bidders. If a bid emerges that is "friendly," in the sense that it is invited, accepted, and favoured by management in the face of a hostile bid, the bidder is known as a "white knight." Of course, the target board may not strike a special committee. If the board in this situation seeks out and obtains an alternative friendly offer, the entity making the offer is also known as a "white knight." The target and the white knight typically negotiate a merger agreement that may contain terms that constitute other defensive tactics, such as the break fee discussed below.

2. Poison Pills or Shareholder Rights Plans

A shareholder rights plan (SRP), or the more derogatory term, poison pill, can be adopted by a corporation prior to or during a takeover bid. If the SRP is adopted during a bid without shareholder approval, the pill is referred to as "tactical." A typical SRP is a document that sets forth instances in which a takeover bid will be permitted by the company. Often, one of the terms is that the board of directors must approve the bid. The effect of this sort of provision is that it forces bidders to gain the approval of the board if they want to make a takeover bid for the target. If board approval is not obtained or if the bid otherwise falls outside the terms of the SRP then, technically speaking, the SRP is activated.

Once activated, the typical pill provides shareholders of the target company with the right to purchase additional shares of the class that is subject to the bid at a very low price. The shares are issued to all shareholders except the bidder. The effect of the SRP is therefore to dilute the bidder's holdings and to make it much more difficult to complete the takeover bid. Canadian law has not, to date, disallowed SRPs despite the fact that they discriminate among shareholders in this way. (See e.g. *347883 Alberta Ltd v Producers Pipelines Inc*, [1991] 4 WWR 577 (Sask CA).)

Students should note that the May 9, 2016 introduction of NI 62-104 is expected to have an influence on the viability of poison pills moving forward. In her 2015 *McGill Law Journal* article (see above, and excerpted below), Professor Anita Anand discusses the future of the SRP in light of the new regulatory regime.

Anita Anand, "The Future of Poison Pills in Canada: Are Takeover Bid Reforms Needed?"
(2015) 61:1 McGill LJ 1 (footnotes omitted)

II. Poison Pills

. . .

A. Underlying Rationale

Poison pills are a type of defensive tactic that enable the corporation to shield itself against hostile or unwelcome bidders. By adopting a poison pill, the target board deters potential acquirers from purchasing twenty per cent (i.e., the threshold that triggers the takeover bid rules) or more of the target's shares. The pill makes the acquisition expensive and is attractive for the board and management who may believe that a bid is not in the best interests of the corporation. They may wish to steer the corporation away from the bid and toward another transaction or approach for the corporation. In Canada, defensive tactics provide the board with flexibility to respond to the takeover bid rather than to eschew it altogether.

The target corporation's shareholders may adopt a poison pill prior to any hostile bid being launched or they may be asked to do so in the face of a bid (a so-called "tactical" pill). Once shareholders ratify the pill, technically the decision to trigger it rests with the board. In reality, this outcome rarely persists as the hostile bidder typically attempts to negotiate with the target or launches a proxy contest to replace the target board altogether. To be sure, if triggered, the poison pill would allow existing shareholders, except the bidder, to purchase shares at a discount so as to dilute the bidder's holdings in the target. In this way, the pill (and by implication, the legal rules that permit the use of this defensive tactic) discriminates (or allows discrimination) as between the bidder qua shareholder and all other shareholders of the target. This discrimination runs contrary to the principle of equal treatment in securities regulation that is embodied in provisions such as the identical consideration provision (which ensures that all shareholders receive the same price for their shares) and the pro rata take-up rules (which require bidders making partial bids to prorate their take-up of tendered shares in the event that the number of tendered shares exceeds the number of shares contained in a partial bid).

What then is the original rationale for poison pills? These defensive tactics were meant to prevent hostile bidders from encouraging target shareholders to tender to an unreasonably low bid. In theory, the pill makes it prohibitively costly for the hostile bidder to obtain control of the target without the target board's cooperation. But the pill also places a wedge between the bidder and the target shareholders to whom it has made the offer. It puts management and the board in the driver's seat by increasing the cost of the bid and by forcing the bidder to negotiate with the board as opposed to the shareholders. The pill allows management and the board to bargain on behalf of shareholders to seek out a higher or more attractive offer so that shareholders do not fall prey to the tactics of the hostile bidder. Without a pill, a bidder could exploit coordination problems among widely disseminated shareholders and pay less for control than if the target were to face an auction.

But placing the bargaining power with the board and management gives rise to a concern that these groups may be conflicted in terms of their loyalties. As Weisbach explains: "Managerial entrenchment occurs when managers gain so much power that they are able to use the firm to further their own interests rather than the interests of shareholders." As a rational, self-interested actor, the agent may well act in his or her own best interests rather than in the corporation's, regardless of his or her ongoing fiduciary duty. In the face of a hostile takeover bid where they may lose their positions following a change of control, management and the board may make efforts to perpetuate themselves in their respective offices. They may simply seek to retain their current position or even to "extract higher wages and larger perquisites from shareholders, and obtain more latitude in determining corporate strategy."

The concern with management entrenchment provides the historic rationale of takeover bid law in Canada. Yet some may question the validity of the management entrenchment hypothesis. First, the theory is based in agency cost analysis, but it cannot be proven definitively: one cannot determine with certainty that directors and management seek to entrench themselves in any given situation. Second, the theory ignores senior managers' and directors' attempts to fulfill their fiduciary duties. The Ontario Securities Commission has recognized that target boards of directors genuinely attempt to fulfill their fiduciary duties to the corporation, holding that a measure of deference should be accorded to board decisions. However, it is not necessarily the case that directors will be unconflicted in the takeover context; when faced with a hostile bid, directors may indeed seek to entrench themselves. The question is not whether managers and the board will in fact put their own interests ahead of the corporation and its stakeholders but rather whether this possibility may arise. As long as management and the board have the opportunity to prioritize their own interests above the corporation's, the concept of management entrenchment remains relevant.

In response, one could ask: why not strip senior management and the board of their powers and let shareholders make all major decisions? As argued below, takeover contests are not the ordinary course of business. On the contrary, they disrupt the ordinary course, possibly permanently. Given that there is a change of control on the immediate horizon, takeovers intensify the threat of management entrenchment as directors and senior managers contemplate a potential loss of board seats or employment. Thus the applicable legal regime must minimize the impact of potential conflicts of interest at the board and senior management levels.

B. Applicable Law

. . .

The poison pill case law has resulted in complex, inconsistent, and ambiguous law: neither bidder nor target can know definitively ex ante whether a bidder's request to the commission for it to cease trade a pill will be decided in the affirmative or the negative. One could argue that uncertainty is not necessarily wholly disadvantageous to the target shareholders if it results from a period during which the board is exploring alternatives. While this argument has merit, it does not take into account the potential for management and the board to search for alternatives that are more self-serving than the original offer. The lengthier the bid period, the more leeway for the board to delay or forgo decisions that may be in the shareholders' best interests. Indeed, as argued below in reference to the 120-bid period proposed by the CSA, these are decisions that should rest with shareholders given the extraordinary implications for shareholders themselves. This argument does not imply that *every* takeover bid should be treated identically, but that the decision about an individual takeover bid should be made on the basis of how many shareholders have tendered to the bid itself.

3. Sale of Crown Jewel

A target may attempt to discourage an initial bidder by entering into an agreement with a third party to sell a significant asset if the initial bidder is successful in its quest to take over the target. The significant asset is known as the "crown jewel" and may constitute the initial bidder's reason for making the takeover bid in the first place. Thus, if it appears that the crown jewel will be sold to a third party, the bidder's incentive for making the acquisition largely falls away.

A prime example of the crown jewel defensive tactic arose in the 1998 case of *Re CW Shareholdings Inc*, discussed earlier. The case was heard before three securities commissions and subsequently by the Ontario Court General Division. The case arose out of the hostile takeover bid for WIC made by CanWest (CW). WIC sought out alternative bidders and signed a "pre-acquisition agreement" with Shaw Communications, its white knight. The agreement contained an option in favour of Shaw on the WIC radio broadcasting business, a jewel in WIC's crown. The option was exercisable at a price of $160 million. CW argued that the agreement was unprecedented in the inducements it offered to Shaw partly in respect of the generosity of the option granted on the WIC radio broadcasting business. As noted in the excerpt from the case below, both the commissions and the court disagreed with CW's argument.

4. Litigation

Another defensive tactic often used is litigation. This may sound strange, but the target initiating litigation will delay and possibly thwart the bid process. Examples are difficult to come by because litigation is obviously not initiated with the express purpose of slowing down the clock during a bid. One example may be found in *Re Chapters Inc* (2001), 24 OSCB

1064. In this case, the target, Chapters Inc, applied to the Ontario Securities Commission for relief under s 104 of the Ontario *Securities Act*, requesting that the commission issue an order requiring Trilogy Enterprises LP (the bidder) to amend its takeover bid circular to include the historical and current year pro forma financial statements of Indigo Books & Music Inc. The OSC dismissed the application. An ulterior motive of the application may have been to buy more time for the target shareholders to consider the bid or for the board to search out alternative competing offers.

Another example can be found in *Re Canfor Corp*, above. As noted earlier in this chapter, the target, Slocan, applied to the Ontario Securities Commission and to the BC Securities Commission for a hearing alleging that

> (d) the Canfor bid offended the "take-up and payment" provisions of Part XX (the take-over bid provisions) of the Act, and, in particular, the provisions of paragraphs 95.9 [now 98.3(1)] and 95.10 [now 98.3(2)] of the Act;
>
> (e) the Canfor bid was not consistent with the withdrawal rights afforded by Part XX of the Act, and, in particular, the provisions of subparagraph 95.4 iii [now 98.1(c)] of the Act; and
>
> (f) the Canfor Offer and Canfor Circular failed to disclose all material facts which would reasonably be expected to affect the decision of a holder of Slocan shares to accept or reject the Canfor bid, as required by the Act and the regulation made pursuant thereto (the "Regulation").

Slocan's application was supported by the staff of the Ontario Securities Commission and opposed by Canfor and staff of the BC Securities Commission. Although the commissions decided in favour of Canfor, they did extend the time during which Slocan shares might be deposited under the bid to ten days in order to provide Slocan shareholders additional time to assess the offer and recent developments, including the decision itself. A combined hearing involving two or more securities commissions has become common and lessens issuers' ability to engage in "regulatory arbitrage" whereby they bring similar actions in different jurisdictions. The applicant's intention may be to delay a transaction or obtain conflicting results in different hearings.

As an aside, students should note that bidders may also use litigation before the courts as a strategic measure, albeit not a "defensive" measure. For example, bidders in the hostile bid situation have claimed that the target's decision to conclude a deal with a white knight constitutes oppressive conduct to them *qua* shareholder (*Rogers Communications Inc v MacLean Hunter Ltd* (1994), 2 CCLS 233 (Ont Gen Div)). In general, courts have been reluctant to accept this argument, noting that would-be acquirors are, in these instances, just "bitter bidders" and that the purpose of the oppression remedy is not to grant shareholders standing in court *qua* bidders but *qua* shareholders. (See also *CW Shareholdings Inc v WIC Western International Communications* (1998), 39 OR (3d) 755 (Gen Div).)

5. Break Fee

This type of defensive tactic is also known as a "bust-up fee" or a "break fee." The merger or acquisition agreement that is negotiated between the target and a white knight may contain a clause indicating that if the merger between the target and the white knight does not occur, the target will pay a certain fee to the white knight. Break fees thus deter the target from breaking its agreement with the white knight, and they can also induce the white knight to enter an agreement with the target to begin with. Break fees range from 3 to 5 percent of the value of the target company. This amount thus adds to the cost of the acquisition by a bidder other than the white knight. In the following article, Professor Anand distinguishes between corporate law and securities law relating to break fees.

Anita Anand, "Break Fees: Loathed but Legal"
National Post (5 March 2002) FP11

The hearing process at the commission begins when a party brings an application. In the poison pill context, the application is usually to cease to trade the pill which the commission has the authority to do under its public interest power in the *Securities Act*. But break fees are very different beasts. They do not involve the issuance or potential issuance of a corporation's securities. Rather, they involve the allocation of corporate assets. They are terms of an elaborate corporate contract. Securities regulators do not have jurisdiction to strike down a contract that shareholders may not like.

The corporate law regime, on the other hand, offers shareholders avenues of recourse such as the shareholders' meeting (with the accompanying proxy solicitation process). In this case, the shareholders' meeting is the right avenue for disgruntled shareholders to air their differences with corporate management. In fact, the corporate statute seeks to balance the very different interests represented here by according shareholders certain rights as against management.

Apart from the shareholders' meeting, shareholders also can exercise their rights under the oppression remedy or the derivative action. Admittedly, these remedies could only kick in after the deal is approved. They can be cumbersome and involve substantial legal fees with no guaranteed reward. But if shareholders find the corporate law regime wanting because of its lack of immediacy, then this is an issue for corporate reform lobbyists—not securities regulators.

The aggrieved investor may reply that this particular contract involves a change of control which affects the target's shareholders. Therefore, from an investor protection standpoint, securities regulators must assert jurisdiction. However, in the takeover bid context, the commission would likely only assert jurisdiction if a break fee would prevent shareholders from receiving a higher offer. Where a break fee is within a generally accepted range (i.e. the amount of the fee does not preclude a competing bid), the commission need not and should not take a position. In those circumstances, payment of the break fee is a matter of corporate governance.

The issue, then, is whether 4.5% is within the generally accepted range. In a takeover bid case, an Ontario court has held that break fees must represent a reasonable balance between their effect as an "auction inhibitor" and an "auction stimulator." …

Investors and their counsel must step back and realize that break fees are not so much a capital markets concern as they are a corporate governance issue. The commission need not take jurisdiction here. This is a corporate law issue to be dealt with within the parameters of the corporate law statute.

This argument has been disputed by those who argue that securities commissions have jurisdiction to disallow break fees if they pose a threat to the "public interest." See Philip Anisman, "It's Break Point for Break Fees," *National Post* (18 March 2002) FP15. Note, however, that although this argument is valid in theory, securities regulators have not, as of yet, disallowed break fees in practice.

B. Additional Defensive Tactics

Students should consider whether or not the adoption of NI 62-104 and the corresponding changes to Canada's takeover bid regime will give rise to new defensive tactics. The attempted hostile takeover of Dolly Varden Silver Corp (a junior issuer based in British Columbia) by Idaho's Hecla Mining Co is perhaps instructive in this regard. Varden planned to undertake a $6 million private placement involving its issued securities. In an article published in the *Globe and Mail*, Professor Anita Anand weighed in on whether or not this might be considered a dilutive defensive tactic by Varden.

Anita Anand, "One Case, Two Commissions, Several Novel Securities Issues"
The Globe and Mail (22 July 2016)

This week, the Ontario Securities Commission and British Columbia Securities Commission simultaneously heard a case relating to the hostile takeover bid that Idaho's Hecla Mining Co. has launched for Dolly Varden Silver Corp., a junior issuer based in British Columbia. Hecla seeks to acquire all of the Varden shares it does not already own (it owns just less than 20 per cent).

To begin, it is important that two provincial securities commissions are co-ordinating to hear this case, undeterred by the fragmented system of regulating capital markets in this country.

A key point of law at issue is whether Varden's planned private placement totalling $6-million in issued securities is a dilutive defensive tactic designed to thwart Hecla's bid. In this case, securities regulators must go where they have historically feared to tread: Should exempt market distributions in the face of a takeover bid be regulated and possibly prevented?

Securities regulators have been usefully studying and making necessary amendments to the regime governing takeover bids, most recently in Multilateral Instrument 62-104, which sought to standardize rules that had historically been applied in an inconsistent fashion by securities tribunals. Takeover bids now have an irrevocable 50-per-cent minimum tender condition and must remain open for a minimum of 105 days. But, importantly, the instrument says nothing about the use of defensive tactics other than a shareholder rights plan or "poison pill."

Securities regulators certainly have jurisdiction to hear the Hecla-Varden case under their public-interest power, a broad, undefined power that allows them to intervene in transactions in which they foresee the public interest being violated. They also have the ability to make rules relating to defensive tactics should they determine that longstanding National Policy 62-202 is insufficient to guide issuers in these matters.

On the point of target private placements in the face of a hostile bid, securities regulators should be reticent to exercise their public-interest power to prevent them. The Varden board is bound by its (corporate law) fiduciary duty to act in the best interests of the corporation, including a corporation that is in dire financial straits. It also has the clear legal right under current securities law—at least at present—to issue securities via a private placement. Securities regulators should therefore not prevent the distribution from occurring, especially in the absence of clear evidence that the private placement was initiated in response to the bid rather than as part of a long-term strategy for Varden.

The familiar argument regarding whether boards can "just say no" to a hostile offer will be raised, since a private placement may actually thwart a bid as opposed to simply buying more time for the target board (as in the case of poison pills). This is a legitimate issue, but it is not one to be sorted out by use of the public-interest power in a single case.

Rather, securities regulators need to turn to the broader issue of defensive tactics and address this point through the rule-making process with input from all stakeholders. Corporate law and securities regulation intersect here, and the overlap in the law must also be explicitly addressed.

Finally, note that regardless of the outcome, this case is not precedent-setting. Although this transaction raises novel regulatory issues, decisions by securities tribunals—as administrative bodies—do not create legal precedents or form common law. Even after the case, market participants will still need to hear from securities regulators in the form of a policy statement or rule regarding the state of the law on defensive tactics. The time to update the rules relating to defensive tactics has arrived.

C. Guidelines for Target's Use of Defensive Tactics

NP 62-202, mentioned above, sets forth guidelines that govern the board's conduct with regard to defensive tactics. The policy sets forth the primary objective of takeover bid law in Canada, which is to protect the bona fide interests of target shareholders. It states that companies are permitted to adopt defensive tactics, but they must not deny shareholders the ability to make their own decisions and they must not frustrate an open bidding process. NP 62-202, s 1.1(4) further outlines defensive tactics that may come under scrutiny, including

> (a) the issuance, or the granting of an option on, or the purchase of, securities representing a significant percentage of the outstanding securities of the target company,
>
> (b) the sale or acquisition, or granting of an option on, or agreeing to sell or acquire, assets of a material amount, and
>
> (c) entering into a contract other than in the normal course of business or taking corporate action other than in the normal course of business.

Thus, NP 62-202 provides guidance to issuers relating to defensive tactics. Students should note that the policy is not mandatory and therefore contains only recommendations, not prescriptive law.

The *WIC* case, heard before the Alberta, BC, and Ontario securities commissions, raised issues of whether certain defensive mechanisms are permissible. The following excerpt from the case highlights the commissions' findings on these issues. (The case picks up at the point where the excerpt at the beginning of the chapter left off. See Section II, "History and Process Issues," above.)

Re CW Shareholdings Inc v WIC Western International Communications Ltd
(1998), 21 OSCB 2910

We do not accept Mr. Tory's [counsel for CW] argument to the effect that the Court will not be able to deal appropriately with these issues, or to do so on a timely basis.

This is not to say, however, that, if the Commissions were able to conclude, for instance, that a break-up fee or an asset option was always an improper defensive tactic, it would not be appropriate for them, if they considered that the public interest so required, to cease trade the Shaw Bid without forming a conclusion on the fiduciary arguments.

Although break-up fees have become a more or less usual feature of the take-over bid landscape, the quantum of a specific fee could, in our view, result in the agreement to pay such a fee being an improper defensive tactic. However a break-up fee in an appropriate amount could, in our view, be properly agreed to by a target company if it were necessary to agree to it in order to induce a competing bid to come forward. As a result, we are unable to conclude, without entering into an examination of the factual background, that the mere existence of the break-up fee constitutes an improper defensive tactic. This examination would have to include consideration of the unusual pre-existing relationship between WIC and Shaw.

As regards the option on WIC's radio assets, we have a greater concern. It has certain aspects which seem to us to be unusual, in particular the fact that the option will be exercisable even if the CW Bid, made before the entering into of the Pre-Acquisition Agreement, is successful, thus having what amounts to a retroactive effect. However, we are unable to conclude, without entering into an examination of the factual background, that the mere existence of these features results in the option constituting an improper defensive tactic. A particular asset option may or may not be offensive, depending on whether it is necessary to obtain a competing bid and whether it has the effect of depriving shareholders of the ability to respond to a take-over bid or to a competing bid or is likely to deny or limit severely the ability of the shareholders of the target company to respond to a take-over bid or a competing bid. (See NP 62-202.)

Mr. Tory argued that the effect of the Pre-Acquisition Agreement was to kill competitive bidding because a successful counter-bid would trigger an immediate and substantial per share loss of value, and that the agreement denied shareholders access to the CW Bid. In our Decision with respect to the Rights Plan we concluded that the only realistic potential counter-bidders against the CW Bid were Shaw and, less likely, Cathton. We think it unlikely that Cathton will come forward with a bid at this stage in the bidding process. Accordingly, at the moment, the auction appears to us to be between CW and the Shaw Companies.

Mr. Tory assured us that CW will neither make a higher bid nor take-up and pay under the CW Bid unless the option disappears.

Given the prior history in connection with CanWest's interest in WIC, we think it quite possible that this position will change if the Court does not strike down the Pre-Acquisition Agreement. In our view, the effect of the Pre-Acquisition Agreement will not be to "kill competitive bidding."

As we know from the discussion above, the securities commissions' decision in *WIC* was not the final word because the commissions decided that they were not the forum to hear the case. Thus, CW brought the case before the Ontario court where Justice Blair discussed the legality of the defensive tactics approved in the case.

CW Shareholdings Inc v WIC Western International Communications Ltd
(1998), 39 OR (3d) 755 (Gen Div)

BLAIR J:

Break Fees

[50] A break fee—or "bust-up fee," as it is sometimes called—is a payment employed by the target corporation for the purpose of enticing another competitive bidder to enter the fray. It is paid to the competitive bidder when its bid fails or is superseded by a better offer. Partly, the inducement is paid to compensate the bidder being-wooed for its time, effort, costs and lost opportunity in putting forward the opposing bid; partly the break fee is purely and simply bait to lure another party into the arena in order to generate a free-for-all for the prize. Such fees are effective inducements, and they are common in take-over bid situations and accepted as proper techniques in appropriate circumstances. The Ontario, Alberta and British Columbia Securities Commissions have acknowledged this concept only a few days ago, in this particular takeover battle—on an application by CanWest to cease trade the Shaw bid as being contrary to the public interest. On May 5, 1998, the Commissions stated:

> Although break-up fees have become a more or less usual feature of the take-over bid landscape, the quantum of a specific fee could, in our view, result in the agreement to pay such a fee being an improper defensive tactic. However a break-up fee in an appropriate amount could, in our view, be properly agreed to by a target company if it were necessary to agree to it in order to induce a competing bid to come forward.

[51] In both *Corona Minerals Corp. v. GSA Management Ltd.*, supra, and in *Re Everfresh Beverages Inc.* … this Court has accepted as valid transactions which involved break fees and which resulted in "excess value realized." I accept that break fees are appropriate in such circumstances where,

(a) as the Commissions have noted, they are "necessary … in order to induce a competing bid to come forward";
(b) that bid represents a better value for the shareholders, and where
(c) the break fee represents a reasonable commercial balance between its potential negative effect as an auction inhibitor and its potential positive effect as an auction stimulator.

Asset Options

[52] The WIC directors have granted Shaw an option to purchase WIC's radio assets as a further inducement to enter the bidding.

[53] Asset options are a rarer species of inducement technique in takeover bid situations that are break fees, but they are not unknown. They have been used in Canadian and American takeover bid contexts in the past. Mr. Spafford of Wood Gundy and Mr. Buzzi of RBC DS both testified to this effect. Mr. Spafford identified the 1995 Labatt/Interbrew takeover and the 1997 Ault Foods/Parmalat Food takeover as two examples in which he had been involved where asset options had been granted, as well as a break fee, in order to induce a competing bid. In the *Hiram Walker Resources* case, supra, the Court refused in the circumstances to set aside a transaction which involved the sale of the Hiram Walker distillery assets, representing approximately 47% of the company's total assets.

[54] The use of asset options to obtain a better offer in takeover bid situations has been recognized by securities administrators in Canada in National Policy 62-202, and its predecessor National Policy 38. It is also recognized as a defensive tactic which may come under scrutiny in the circumstances described below. See NP 62-202, Part I (Take-over Bids—Defensive Tactics), article 1.1(1)-(6). Again, in their decision respecting this particular takeover situation on May 5, 1998, the Securities Commissions recognized the dichotomy allying to asset options, expressing the philosophy reflected in NP 62-202 in this way (at p. 31):

> A particular asset option may or may not be offensive, depending on whether it is necessary to obtain a competing bid and whether it has the effect of depriving shareholders of the ability to respond to a take-over bid or to a competing bid or is likely to deny or limit severely the ability of the shareholders of the target company to respond to a take-over bid or a competing bid.

[55] In my view the granting of an asset purchase option (or "asset lock-up," as it is sometimes called, in the jargon of the trade) to a potential bidder may be a proper and acceptable measure for a target corporation to adopt as a competitive-bid-stimulating inducement where—viewed in the context of the entire negotiated transaction, as in the case of break fees—it strikes a reasonable commercial balance between its potential negative effect as an auction inhibitor depressing shareholder value and its potential positive effect as an auction stimulator enhancing shareholder value. On which side of this dichotomy a particular asset lock-up agreement falls will depend upon the circumstances of each particular case. Without attempting to create an exhaustive list, the factors to be considered will include, for example:

A. Whether the process by which the directors of the target company exercised their obligation to maximize shareholder value complied with their duties as target-corporation directors;
B. Whether the overall commercial balance and proportion between the auction inhibiting and auction stimulating effect of such an agreement in the circumstances has been struck, i.e., whether the agreement is likely to preclude further bidding, in the sense of harming or significantly dampening the auction process, and thus deprive the shareholders of potential additional value;
C. Whether the price for the optioned asset is within the range of reasonable value attributed to that asset, or whether it represents such a discount that it would result in a disproportionate erosion in the value of the corporation making it uneconomical for others to bid;

D. Whether the competing bid induced by the asset lock-up agreement provides enough additional value to the shareholders to justify the granting of the option.

. . .

[57] If an asset lock-up agreement is not per se illegal—as I agree it is not—it seems to me that a break fee is similarly not per se illegal, as I have already concluded. Furthermore, if neither inducement is per se illegal in and of itself, I do not think it can be said that they fall into that category when utilized together. Again, whether the tactic is appropriate or inappropriate will depend on the circumstances of the case. It is of considerable importance in these kinds of situations, however, that directors of target corporations be left with as much flexibility as possible to deal with the circumstances which face them, in order to carry out their duties to maximize shareholder value.

Thus, Justice Blair held that the defensive tactics used by the target in the case were not per se, illegal, but they could become illegal depending on the circumstances of the case. Blair J's list of factors will, without doubt, be referred to in subsequent decisions when evaluating the legality of defensive tactics. Blair J appears to have two overarching considerations: first, he is reluctant to intervene in decisions of the target board; second, he seeks to ensure that target boards have flexibility in responding to a bid.

Over time, the way in which SRPs operate has evolved as has the law relating to SRPs. One of the leading cases on SRPs is *Re Royal Host Real Estate Investment Trust* (1999), 22 OSCB 7819. The *Royal Host* case was heard by the securities commissions of Alberta, British Columbia, and Ontario. The commissions discussed the issue of when a "pill must go" and decided that there is no "holy grail" that determines when the time has come. Rather, the facts and the circumstances of every case will be extremely important in the determination. The commissions considered past case law and set forth a number of factors that they will review in deciding when and whether a pill must go. These factors were discussed further in *Re Chapters Inc* and *Trilogy Retail Enterprises LP* (2001), 24 OSCB 1663. The excerpt from *Royal Host*, below, focuses on the parts of the judgment that address the state of the law regarding poison pills.

Re Royal Host Real Estate Investment Trust
(1999), 22 OSCB 7819

[1] On June 22, 1999, the British Columbia Securities Commission, the Alberta Securities Commission and the Ontario Securities Commission jointly heard an application by Royal Host Real Estate Investment Trust ("Royal Host") in respect of a take over bid it had made for the units of Canadian Hotel Income Properties Real Estate Investment Trust ("CHIP").

[2] Royal Host publicly announced on May 19, 1999, that it would make the bid for CHIP. On May 21, the trustees of CHIP adopted a unitholder rights plan, without the approval of the holders. Royal Host made the bid on May 31 and, on June 15, amended the bid so that it would remain open until June 25.

[3] In its application to the commissions, Royal Host sought orders terminating the operation of the CHIP rights plan against its bid, specifically:

- orders cease trading the CHIP unit rights issued pursuant to the rights plan and any CHIP units issued on exercise of the unit rights, and
- orders that certain exemptions not apply to any trades in securities issued by CHIP in connection with the distribution of the unit rights.

. . .

Analysis

[36] The starting point for our analysis of whether we should terminate the operation of the CHIP rights plan against the Royal Host bid is National Policy 62-202, Take-Over Bids—Defensive Tactics, which came into force on August 4, 1997. It replaced the substantially identical national policy statement, National Policy 38, adopted in 1986. National Policy 62-202 sets out our goal in regulating take over bids. …

. . .

[38] Over the past decade, the four major Canadian securities commissions have issued a series of decisions respecting applications to terminate the operation of rights plans, or "poison pills," adopted as defensive tactics.

[39] The first of these was *Canadian Jorex Ltd., Re* … . Jorex adopted a rights plan, without shareholder approval, nine days after Mannville made an offer to acquire all of Jorex's shares. A rival bid was made shortly thereafter by Canadian Trans-Arctic & Southern International Corp. Jorex subsequently waived its plan in respect of Trans-Arctic's bid, but not Mannville's. Mannville complained to staff of the Ontario Commission that the plan was contrary to the public interest and should be stopped. The hearing was the result of that complaint.

. . .

[41] After considering the facts of the case, the Commission concluded that the time had come for the pill to go. They observed at page 266:

> Underlying our conclusion was our view of the public interest in matters such as this. As is amply reflected in National Policy 38, the primary concern of the Commission in contested take-over bids is not whether it is appropriate for a target board to adopt defensive tactics, but whether those tactics "are likely to deny or severely limit the ability of the shareholders to respond to a take-over bid or a competing bid" (paragraph 6) or "may have the effect of denying to shareholders the ability to make a [fully informed] decision and of frustrating an open take-over bid process" (paragraph 2). If so, then as National Policy 38 clearly indicates, the Commission will be quite prepared to intervene to protect the public interest as we see it. For us, the public interest lies in allowing shareholders of a target company to exercise one of the fundamental rights of share ownership—the ability to dispose of shares as one wishes—without undue hindrance from, among other things, defensive tactics that may have been adopted by the target board with the best of intentions, but that are either misguided from the outset or, as here, have outlived their usefulness.

[42] The Ontario Commission applied National Policy 38 and the principles set out in *Jorex* in the reasons for its decision in *Lac Minerals Ltd., Re* … , where it observed at page 4963 that: "All parties agreed that the critical issue that the Commission had to decide was 'is it time for the poison pill to go?' "

. . .

[44] This issue involved interesting questions about the relationship between securities law and corporate law. It raised the tension between (i) the board's duty to manage the corporation honestly and in good faith with a view to the best interests of the corporation; and (ii) the shareholders' "right" to decide whether to sell their shares in response to a take-over bid.

[45] The Commission then referred to *Jorex* and continued at page 4969:

> In a case such as this, the Commission's main concern is the interests of the shareholders of the target company. Would the interests of the Lac shareholders be prejudiced by the continued operation of the Lac Rights Plan in the face of the outstanding bids by Royal Oak and American Barrick?

… Accordingly, we decided that it was in the public interest to indicate that in those circumstances, should the Lac Board not do so, we would make an order cease trading any securities issued or to be issued in connection with the Lac Rights Plan in respect of that bid.

[47] On the same day the Ontario Commission released the reasons for its decision in *Lac Minerals Ltd.*, it also released the reasons for its decision in *MDC Corp., Re.* …

[48] As in *Lac Minerals Ltd.*, Regal had adopted and obtained shareholder approval of its rights plan before MDC publicly announced its intention to make a bid. However, in this case, shareholder approval was obtained only shortly before MDC's announcement.

[49] Again as in *Lac Minerals Ltd.*, the Commission applied National Policy 38 and the principles in *Jorex* and identified the only real issue before it as "when does the pill go."

[50] In our view, our determination of where the public interest lies required us, in this case, to consider two principal questions.

1. If the Plan is permitted to remain in effect for a reasonable further period, is there, on the evidence, a reasonable possibility that a better offer will come along during the period so that, whether or not this results in MDC raising its bid, the shareholders of Regal will be advantaged?
2. If the Plan is not terminated prior to the end of the current period for the acceptance of the bid, is it likely that [MDC] will not extend the period for acceptance for such "reasonable further period," and thus deprive the Regal shareholders of the opportunity to decide whether they wish to accept the [MDC] bid?

[51] After reviewing the evidence, the Commission concluded that there was a reasonable possibility that a better offer would come along if the rights plan was permitted to remain in effect for a further three weeks and that MDC was likely to extend its bid for some reasonable period if it was likely that the operation of the plan would be terminated by the end of that period.

[52] After reaching these conclusions, the Commission continued at page 4980:

> … It is all very well for us to conclude that there is a real possibility that shareholder value will be increased as a result of our deciding that the "time has not yet come," but we would not have been prepared to do so if it was clear to us that the shareholders of Regal felt otherwise.

• • •

[56] Approximately three years after *Regal*, National Policy 38 was replaced by National Policy 62-202. Subsequently, each of the four commissions participated in one or both of two hearings respecting the validity of "tactical" rights plans, namely plans

implemented by a target company without shareholder approval in the face of a hostile take over bid. Those two decisions have been interpreted as imposing a different test from that established in *Regal.*

[57] In *CW Shareholdings Inc., Re* … , the Ontario, Alberta and British Columbia Commissions considered a rights plan that had been adopted by WIC in the face of a take over bid by CW Shareholdings without shareholder approval. …

[58] The Rights Plan was put into place in the face of the Bid and without a vote of shareholders. In such circumstances, it is, at the very least, necessary for the target company to demonstrate that it was necessary to do so because of the coercive nature of the Bid or some other very substantial unfairness or impropriety. This was not done by WIC in this case.

[59] In *Ivanhoe III Inc., Re* … , the Ontario and Québec Commissions let stand a rights plan adopted by Cambridge without shareholder approval in the face of a partial bid by Ivanhoe. The reasons issued by the two commissions were, in substance, identical. In its reasons, the Ontario Commission referred to the above quoted paragraph from *WIC* and applied a two step procedure, as described at page 1329:

> The two principal issues which had to be considered by the Commission were:
>
> 1. in view of the facts that the Plan had been adopted in the face of the Bid and had not received shareholder approval, should it be permitted to stand; and
> 2. if the Plan was permitted to stand, had the time come for it to be terminated by the Commission.
>
> …

[61] Had we not concluded that the Bid was coercive, we would have immediately cease traded the Plan, since we agree with the Commission's determination in WIC that, if a rights plan is put into place in the face of a bid and without a vote of shareholders, it is, at the very least, necessary for the target company to demonstrate that it was necessary to do so because of the coercive nature of the bid or some other very substantial unfairness or impropriety.

[62] The Commission then turned to the second issue and applied the *Regal* test in determining whether the time had come to terminate the rights plan. It found that there was a reasonable possibility that a better offer would come along and that there was every reason to believe that Ivanhoe would extend its bid, if the plan was to remain in place until its expiry. Accordingly, the Commission denied the application but stated that it would terminate the operation of the plan if the trustees amended it to remain in effect after its original expiry date.

[63] Shortly after *Cambridge,* the Alberta Commission issued the reasons for its decision in *Samson Canada Ltd., Re* … . The shareholders of Highridge had approved a rights plan almost two years before Samson publicly announced its intention to make a bid for all of the Highridge shares.

[64] In its decision, the Commission noted that both parties had agreed that the relevant test was that set out in *Regal.* In applying the *Regal* test, the Commission observed at page 1794:

> … Shareholder approval of the Plan is powerful, but not necessarily conclusive, evidence of how the shareholders want their collective interests to be protected in a take-over bid situation.

The Commission agreed that the offer was opportunistic but that that, in and of itself, did not make it coercive. The Commission continued at page 1795:

> Whether an offer is coercive is only one factor to be considered in assessing a shareholder rights plan. Like prior shareholder approval, coerciveness is a powerful but not necessarily conclusive factor to be considered in applying the *Regal* test.
>
> Striking a balance between these objectives in any particular case is highly dependent on the specific facts. Relevant factors include: whether shareholder approval was obtained; whether broad shareholder support is evident; when the poison pill was adopted; the nature of the bid, including whether it is coercive or unfair to the target company shareholders; the size and complexity of the target company and the number of potential, viable offerors; the likelihood of the existing bid or bids falling away if the pill is not removed; and the likelihood that, if given further time, the target company can find a better offer.

. . .

[74] In applying these principles to the determination of the public interest in a particular case, the challenge we face is finding the appropriate balance between permitting the directors to fulfill their duty to maximize shareholder value in the manner they see fit and protecting the right of the shareholders to decide whether to tender their shares to the bid. We can make this determination only after considering all of the relevant factors in that particular case. While it would be impossible to set out a list of all of the factors that might be relevant in cases of this kind, they frequently include:

- whether shareholder approval of the rights plan was obtained;
- when the plan was adopted;
- whether there is broad shareholder support for the continued operation of the plan;
- the size and complexity of the target company;
- the other defensive tactics, if any, implemented by the target company;
- the number of potential, viable offerors;
- the steps taken by the target company to find an alternative bid or transaction that would be better for the shareholders;
- the likelihood that, if given further time, the target company will be able to find a better bid or transaction;
- the nature of the bid, including whether it is coercive or unfair to the shareholders of the target company;
- the length of time since the bid was announced and made;
- the likelihood that the bid will not be extended if the rights plan is not terminated.

. . .

[76] After reviewing these decisions and the fact patterns on which they were based, we have come to the conclusion that it is fruitless to search for the "holy grail" of a specific test, or series of tests, that can be applied in all circumstances. Take over bids are fact specific; the relevant factors, and the relative importance to be attached to each, will vary from case to case. As a result, a test that focuses on certain factors to the exclusion of others will almost certainly be inappropriate in some of the cases to which we attempt to apply it.

QUESTIONS

1. In Canada it has not been legally permissible to thwart a bid altogether, yet this has been permissible in the United States. Do you think this difference possibly stems from the differences between Canadian and US capital markets?

2. *Producers Pipelines* discusses two hypotheses for the purpose of poison pills: shareholder interest and management entrenchment. Which hypothesis do you favour and why? To what extent are they both relevant in determining the legality of poison pills?

3. Shareholder approval is usually important for a poison pill to stand. In the case of a tactical pill where no shareholder approval has been obtained, however, can it be said that management knows better than the shareholders themselves what is best for them?

V. DUTIES OF THE TARGET BOARD

A main contribution of the *Producers Pipelines* case, above, was that it set forth a proportionality test that governs board conduct in the takeover bid context. *Producers Pipelines* also exemplifies that courts have struggled to delineate the precise duties owed by directors in the context of a takeover bid. The courts first applied a "proper purpose" test, which is founded on the notion that a board could not exercise its powers for an improper motive or purpose. In recent decades, Canadian courts have reformulated this test. In *Teck v Millar* (1972), 33 DLR (3d) 288 (BCSC), directors who acted in what they considered to be the best interests of the company were held to have satisfied their fiduciary obligations. It is not clear whether the proper purpose test and the best interest of the corporation test are two different tests. In some respects, they do not seem to be distinct because, in both cases, directors need to have acted "properly."

Though not a takeover bid case, the decision in *Peoples Department Stores Inc (Trustee of) v Wise*, 2004 SCC 68, [2004] 3 SCR 461 (excerpted below) should also be mentioned here. In this case, the Supreme Court of Canada cited *Teck* and held that the directorial duty is not owed to any one particular shareholder but to the corporation as a whole. The case thus firmly supports the *Teck* best interests of the corporation rule. (See A Anand, "Supreme Ambiguity," *National Post* (18 November 2004) FP15.) Of course, the analysis of the target board's legal duties cannot occur without reference to corporate statutes in Canada that state that directors must "act honestly and in good faith with a view to the best interests of the corporation." (See CBCA, s 122.) Reference should also be made to the *BCE* case (excerpted below) in which the Supreme Court of Canada provides further explanation of this wording in the corporate statute. However, both *Peoples* and *BCE* are somewhat ambiguous. *BCE* does not overturn *Peoples*—both uphold the corporate statute but both cast the net widely (too widely) in terms of the scope of directors' duties. (For further analysis, see (2009) 48:2 Can Bus LJ, a special edition on the *BCE* case.)

A related issue that arises in the takeover bid context is whether directors have a positive duty to maximize shareholder value. In the 1998 decision of *CW Shareholdings Inc v WIC Western International Communication Ltd*, already discussed and excerpted in this chapter, the Ontario Court General Division held that boards must seek to maximize shareholder value by conducting an auction. The court considered a bidding war by two shareholders, CanWest and Shaw Communications, for Western International Communications (WIC). WIC ultimately signed a lockup agreement with Shaw, its white knight. CanWest sought relief under the oppression remedy of the CBCA.

In considering the duties of the WIC board, the court held that although boards are subject to the business judgment rule, they are not bound by an "enhanced scrutiny" standard, which circumscribes activities of target boards in the United States. In addition, the court held (at 40) that in the context of a hostile bid situation where the target corporation is in play, "the duty of the directors is to act in the best interests of the shareholders as a whole and to take active and reasonable steps to maximize shareholder value by conducting an auction." Following the *WIC* decision, the Ontario Court of Appeal had an opportunity to consider again the duties of the target board in a takeover bid. In *Maple Leaf Foods Inc v Schneider Corporation*, the target board (Schneider) rejected numerous increasing bids from the original bidder (Maple Leaf) in favour of a bid from another bidder (Smithfield Foods), preferred by the target's controlling shareholder. The court held that the Schneider board had not acted improperly in rejecting the Maple Leaf bid. With respect to determining whether the directors complied with their duty to act in the best interests of the corporation, the Court of Appeal upheld the application of the business judgment rule, adopting a "reasonable analysis of the situation" test. The court drew a distinction between a duty to auction and a duty to "canvass the market." The court held that an auction need not be held in each change of control situation and that a "market canvass" may be acceptable if a board is unable to judge the adequacy of a bid. It appears that a market canvass is a lesser obligation than a full-fledged auction, though the precise parameters of the market canvass are not discussed in the case.

As discussed above, the *Peoples* decision reaffirmed *Teck* and the best interests of the corporation rule. In the following excerpt, the court considers to whom the directorial duty is owed.

Peoples Department Stores Inc (Trustee of) v Wise
2004 SCC 68, [2004] 3 SCR 461

MAJOR and DESCHAMPS JJ:

I. Introduction

[1] The principal question raised by this appeal is whether directors of a corporation owe a fiduciary duty to the corporation's creditors comparable to the statutory duty owed to the corporation. For the reasons that follow, we conclude that directors owe a duty of care to creditors, but that duty does not rise to a fiduciary duty. We agree with the disposition of the Quebec Court of Appeal. The appeal is therefore dismissed.

[2] As a result of the demise in the mid-1990s of two major retail chains in eastern Canada, Wise Stores Inc. ("Wise") and its wholly-owned subsidiary, Peoples Department Stores Inc. ("Peoples"), the indebtedness of a number of Peoples' creditors went unsatisfied. In the wake of the failure of the two chains, Caron Bélanger Ernst & Young Inc., Peoples' trustee in bankruptcy ("trustee"), brought an action against the directors of Peoples. To address the trustee's claims, the extent of the duties imposed by s. 122(1) of the *Canada Business Corporations Act*, R.S.C. 1985, c. C-44 ("CBCA"), upon directors

with respect to creditors must be determined; we must also identify the purpose and reach of s. 100 of the *Bankruptcy and Insolvency Act*, R.S.C. 1985, c. B-3 ("BIA").

[3] In our view, it has not been established that the directors of Peoples violated either the fiduciary duty or the duty of care imposed by s. 122(1) of the CBCA. As for the trustee's submission regarding s. 100 of the BIA, we agree with the Court of Appeal that the consideration received in the impugned transactions was not "conspicuously" less than fair market value. The BIA claim fails on that basis.

. . .

III. Analysis

. . .

A. *The Statutory Fiduciary Duty: Section 122(1)(a) of the CBCA*

. . .

[42] This appeal does not relate to the non-statutory duty directors owe to shareholders. It is concerned only with the statutory duties owed under the CBCA. Insofar as the statutory fiduciary duty is concerned, it is clear that the phrase the "best interests of the corporation" should be read not simply as the "best interests of the shareholders." From an economic perspective, the "best interests of the corporation" means the maximization of the value of the corporation: see E.M. Iacobucci, "Directors' Duties in Insolvency: Clarifying What Is at Stake" (2003), 39 *Can. Bus. L.J.* 398, at pp. 400-1. However, the courts have long recognized that various other factors may be relevant in determining what directors should consider in soundly managing with a view to the best interests of the corporation. For example, in *Teck Corp. v. Millar* (1972), 33 D.L.R. (3d) 288 (B.C.S.C.), Berger J. stated, at p. 314:

> A classical theory that once was unchallengeable must yield to the facts of modern life. In fact, of course, it has. If today the directors of a company were to consider the interests of its employees no one would argue that in doing so they were not acting *bona fide* in the interests of the company itself. Similarly, if the directors were to consider the consequences to the community of any policy that the company intended to pursue, and were deflected in their commitment to that policy as a result, it could not be said that they had not considered *bona fide* the interests of the shareholders.
>
> I appreciate that it would be a breach of their duty for directors to disregard entirely the interests of a company's shareholders in order to confer a benefit on its employees: *Parke v. Daily News Ltd.*, [1962] Ch. 927. But if they observe a decent respect for other interests lying beyond those of the company's shareholders in the strict sense, that will not, in my view, leave directors open to the charge that they have failed in their fiduciary duty to the company.

The case of *Re Olympia & York Enterprises Ltd. and Hiram Walker Resources Ltd.* (1986), 59 O.R. (2d) 254 (Div. Ct.), approved, at p. 271, the decision in *Teck, supra*. We accept as an accurate statement of law that in determining whether they are acting with a view to the best interests of the corporation it may be legitimate, given all the circumstances of a given case, for the board of directors to consider, *inter alia*, the interests of shareholders, employees, suppliers, creditors, consumers, governments and the environment

[43] The various shifts in interests that naturally occur as a corporation's fortunes rise and fall do not, however, affect the content of the fiduciary duty under s. 122(1)(a) of the CBCA. At all times, directors and officers owe their fiduciary obligation to the corporation. The interests of the corporation are not to be confused with the interests of the creditors or those of any other stakeholders.

[44] The interests of shareholders, those of the creditors and those of the corporation may and will be consistent with each other if the corporation is profitable and well capitalized and has strong prospects. However, this can change if the corporation starts to struggle financially. The residual rights of the shareholders will generally become worthless if a corporation is declared bankrupt. Upon bankruptcy, the directors of the corporation transfer control to a trustee, who administers the corporation's assets for the benefit of creditors.

[45] Short of bankruptcy, as the corporation approaches what has been described as the "vicinity of insolvency," the residual claims of shareholders will be nearly exhausted. While shareholders might well prefer that the directors pursue high-risk alternatives with a high potential payoff to maximize the shareholders' expected residual claim, creditors in the same circumstances might prefer that the directors steer a safer course so as to maximize the value of their claims against the assets of the corporation.

[46] The directors' fiduciary duty does not change when a corporation is in the nebulous "vicinity of insolvency." That phrase has not been defined; moreover, it is incapable of definition and has no legal meaning. What it is obviously intended to convey is a deterioration in the corporation's financial stability. In assessing the actions of directors it is evident that any honest and good faith attempt to redress the corporation's financial problems will, if successful, both retain value for shareholders and improve the position of creditors. If unsuccessful, it will not qualify as a breach of the statutory fiduciary duty.

[47] For a discussion of the shifting interests and incentives of shareholders and creditors, see W.D. Gray, "*Peoples v. Wise* and *Dylex*: Identifying Stakeholder Interests upon or near Corporate Insolvency—Stasis or Pragmatism?" (2003), 39 *Can. Bus. L.J.* 242, at p. 257; E.M. Iacobucci and K.E. Davis, "Reconciling Derivative Claims and the Oppression Remedy" (2000), 12 *S.C.L.R.* (2d) 87, at p. 114. In resolving these competing interests, it is incumbent upon the directors to act honestly and in good faith with a view to the best interests of the corporation. In using their skills for the benefit of the corporation when it is in troubled waters financially, the directors must be careful to attempt to act in its best interests by creating a "better" corporation, and not to favour the interests of any one group of stakeholders. If the stakeholders cannot avail themselves of the statutory fiduciary duty (the duty of loyalty, *supra*) to sue the directors for failing to take care of their interests, they have other means at their disposal.

In *BCE*, the court considered the central question to whom directors owe a duty. In the context of this discussion, the court considered whether directors have a duty to maximize shareholder value.

BCE Inc v 1976 Debentureholders
2008 SCC 69, [2008] 3 SCR 560

THE COURT:

I. Introduction

[1] These appeals arise out of an offer to purchase all shares of BCE Inc. ("BCE"), a large telecommunications corporation, by a group headed by the Ontario Teachers Pension Plan Board ("Teachers"), financed in part by the assumption by Bell Canada, a wholly owned subsidiary of BCE, of a $30 billion debt. The leveraged buyout was opposed by debentureholders of Bell Canada on the ground that the increased debt contemplated by the purchase agreement would reduce the value of their bonds. Upon request for court approval of an arrangement under s. 192 of the *Canada Business Corporations Act*, RSC 1985, c. C-44 ("*CBCA*"), the debentureholders argued that it should not be found to be fair. They also opposed the arrangement under s. 241 of the *CBCA* on the ground that it was oppressive to them.

[2] The Quebec Superior Court, *per* Silcoff J, approved the arrangement as fair under the *CBCA* and dismissed the claims for oppression. The Quebec Court of Appeal found that the arrangement had not been shown to be fair and held that it should not have been approved. Thus, it found it unnecessary to consider the oppression claim.

[3] On June 20, 2008, this Court allowed the appeals from the Court of Appeal's disapproval of the arrangement and dismissed two cross-appeals from the dismissal of the claims for oppression, with reasons to follow. These are those reasons. …

. . .

[35] A share "is not an isolated piece of property … [but] a 'bundle' of interrelated rights and liabilities": *Sparling v. Quebec (Caisse de dépôt et placement du Québec)*, [1988] 2 SCR 1015, at p. 1025, *per* La Forest J. These rights include the right to a proportionate part of the assets of the corporation upon winding-up and the right to oversee the management of the corporation by its board of directors by way of votes at shareholder meetings.

[36] The directors are responsible for the governance of the corporation. In the performance of this role, the directors are subject to two duties: a fiduciary duty to the corporation under s. 122(1)(a) (the fiduciary duty); and a duty to exercise the care, diligence and skill of a reasonably prudent person in comparable circumstances under s. 122(1)(b) (the duty of care). The second duty is not at issue in these proceedings as this is not a claim against the directors of the corporation for failing to meet their duty of care. However, this case does involve the fiduciary duty of the directors to the corporation, and particularly the "fair treatment" component of this duty, which, as will be seen, is fundamental to the reasonable expectations of stakeholders claiming an oppression remedy.

[37] The fiduciary duty of the directors to the corporation originated in the common law. It is a duty to act in the best interests of the corporation. Often the interests of shareholders and stakeholders are co-extensive with the interests of the corporation. But if they conflict, the directors' duty is clear—it is to the corporation: *Peoples Department Stores*.

[38] The fiduciary duty of the directors to the corporation is a broad, contextual concept. It is not confined to short-term profit or share value. Where the corporation is

an ongoing concern, it looks to the long-term interests of the corporation. The content of this duty varies with the situation at hand. At a minimum, it requires the directors to ensure that the corporation meets its statutory obligations. But, depending on the context, there may also be other requirements. In any event, the fiduciary duty owed by directors is mandatory; directors must look to what is in the best interests of the corporation.

[39] In *Peoples Department Stores*, this Court found that although directors *must* consider the best interests of the corporation, it may also be appropriate, although *not mandatory*, to consider the impact of corporate decisions on shareholders or particular groups of stakeholders. As stated by Major and Deschamps JJ, at para. 42:

> We accept as an accurate statement of law that in determining whether they are acting with a view to the best interests of the corporation it may be legitimate, given all the circumstances of a given case, for the board of directors to consider, *inter alia*, the interests of shareholders, employees, suppliers, creditors, consumers, governments and the environment.

As will be discussed, cases dealing with claims of oppression have further clarified the content of the fiduciary duty of directors with respect to the range of interests that should be considered in determining what is in the best interests of the corporation, acting fairly and responsibly.

[40] In considering what is in the best interests of the corporation, directors may look to the interests of, *inter alia*, shareholders, employees, creditors, consumers, governments and the environment to inform their decisions. Courts should give appropriate deference to the business judgment of directors who take into account these ancillary interests, as reflected by the business judgment rule. The "business judgment rule" accords deference to a business decision, so long as it lies within a range of reasonable alternatives: see *Maple Leaf Foods Inc. v. Schneider Corp.* (1998), 42 OR (3d) 177 (CA); *Kerr v. Danier Leather Inc.*, [2007] 3 SCR 331, 2007 SCC 44. It reflects the reality that directors, who are mandated under s. 102(1) of the *CBCA* to manage the corporation's business and affairs, are often better suited to determine what is in the best interests of the corporation. This applies to decisions on stakeholders' interests, as much as other directorial decisions.

[41] Normally only the beneficiary of a fiduciary duty can enforce the duty. In the corporate context, however, this may offer little comfort. The directors who control the corporation are unlikely to bring an action against themselves for breach of their own fiduciary duty. The shareholders cannot act in the stead of the corporation; their only power is the right to oversee the conduct of the directors by way of votes at shareholder assemblies. Other stakeholders may not even have that.

[42] To meet these difficulties, the common law developed a number of special remedies to protect the interests of shareholders and stakeholders of the corporation. These remedies have been affirmed, modified and supplemented by the *CBCA*.

[43] The first remedy provided by the *CBCA* is the s. 239 derivative action, which allows stakeholders to enforce the directors' duty to the corporation when the directors are themselves unwilling to do so. With leave of the court, a complainant may bring (or intervene in) a derivative action in the name and on behalf of the corporation or one of its subsidiaries to enforce a right of the corporation, including the rights correlative with the directors' duties to the corporation. (The requirement of leave serves to prevent frivolous and vexatious actions, and other actions which, while possibly brought in good faith, are not in the interest of the corporation to litigate.)

[44] A second remedy lies against the directors in a civil action for breach of duty of care. As noted, s. 122(1)(b) of the *CBCA* requires directors and officers of a corporation to "exercise the care, diligence and skill that a reasonably prudent person would exercise in comparable circumstances." This duty, unlike the s. 122(1)(a) fiduciary duty, is not owed solely to the corporation, and thus may be the basis for liability to other stakeholders in accordance with principles governing the law of tort and extracontractual liability: *Peoples Department Stores*. Section 122(1)(b) does not provide an independent foundation for claims. However, applying the principles of *The Queen in right of Canada v. Saskatchewan Wheat Pool*, [1983] 1 SCR 205, courts may take this statutory provision into account as to the standard of behaviour that should reasonably be expected.

[45] A third remedy, grounded in the common law and endorsed by the *CBCA*, is a s. 241 action for oppression. Unlike the derivative action, which is aimed at enforcing a right of the corporation itself, the oppression remedy focuses on harm to the legal and equitable interests of stakeholders affected by oppressive acts of a corporation or its directors. This remedy is available to a wide range of stakeholders—security holders, creditors, directors and officers.

[46] Additional "remedial" provisions are found in provisions of the *CBCA* providing for court approval in certain cases. An arrangement under s. 192 of the *CBCA* is one of these. While s. 192 cannot be described as a remedy *per se*, it has remedial-like aspects. It is directed at the situation of corporations seeking to effect fundamental changes to the corporation that affects stakeholder rights. The Act provides that such arrangements require the approval of the court. Unlike the civil action and oppression, which focus on the conduct of the directors, a s. 192 review requires a court approving a plan of arrangement to be satisfied that: (1) the statutory procedures have been met; (2) the application has been put forth in good faith; and (3) the arrangement is fair and reasonable. If the corporation fails to discharge its burden of establishing these elements, approval will be withheld and the proposed change will not take place. In assessing whether the arrangement should be approved, the court will hear arguments from opposing security holders whose rights are being arranged. This provides an opportunity for security holders to argue against the proposed change.

. . .

(VII) FAIR RESOLUTION OF CONFLICTING INTERESTS

[81] As discussed, conflicts may arise between the interests of corporate stakeholders *inter se* and between stakeholders and the corporation. Where the conflict involves the interests of the corporation, it falls to the directors of the corporation to resolve them in accordance with their fiduciary duty to act in the best interests of the corporation, viewed as a good corporate citizen.

[82] The cases on oppression, taken as a whole, confirm that the duty of the directors to act in the best interests of the corporation comprehends a duty to treat individual stakeholders affected by corporate actions equitably and fairly. There are no absolute rules. In each case, the question is whether, in all the circumstances, the directors acted in the best interests of the corporation, having regard to all relevant considerations, including, but not confined to, the need to treat affected stakeholders in a fair manner, commensurate with the corporation's duties as a responsible corporate citizen.

[83] Directors may find themselves in a situation where it is impossible to please all stakeholders. The "fact that alternative transactions were rejected by the directors is irrelevant unless it can be shown that a particular alternative was definitely available and clearly more beneficial to the company than the chosen transaction": *Maple Leaf Foods*, *per* Weiler JA, at p. 192.

[84] There is no principle that one set of interests—for example the interests of shareholders—should prevail over another set of interests. Everything depends on the particular situation faced by the directors and whether, having regard to that situation, they exercised business judgment in a responsible way.

[85] On these appeals, it was suggested on behalf of the corporations that the "*Revlon* line" of cases from Delaware support the principle that where the interests of shareholders conflict with the interests of creditors, the interests of shareholders should prevail.

[86] The "*Revlon* line" refers to a series of Delaware corporate takeover cases, the two most important of which are *Revlon, Inc. v. MacAndrews & Forbes Holdings, Inc.*, 506 A 2d 173 (Del. 1986), and *Unocal Corp. v. Mesa Petroleum Co.*, 493 A 2d 946 (Del. 1985). In both cases, the issue was how directors should react to a hostile takeover bid. *Revlon* suggests that in such circumstances, shareholder interests should prevail over those of other stakeholders, such as creditors. *Unocal* tied this approach to situations where the corporation will not continue as a going concern, holding that although a board facing a hostile takeover "may have regard for various constituencies in discharging its responsibilities, … such concern for non-stockholder interests is inappropriate when … the object no longer is to protect or maintain the corporate enterprise but to sell it to the highest bidder" (p. 182).

[87] What is clear is that the *Revlon* line of cases has not displaced the fundamental rule that the duty of the directors cannot be confined to particular priority rules, but is rather a function of business judgment of what is in the best interests of the corporation, in the particular situation it faces. In a review of trends in Delaware corporate jurisprudence, former Delaware Supreme Court Chief Justice E. Norman Veasey put it this way:

> [I]t is important to keep in mind the precise content of this "best interests" concept—that is, to whom this duty is owed and when. Naturally, one often thinks that directors owe this duty to both the corporation and the stockholders. That formulation is harmless in most instances because of the confluence of interests, in that what is good for the corporate entity is usually derivatively good for the stockholders. There are times, of course, when the focus is directly on the interests of stockholders [i.e., as in *Revlon*]. But, in general, the directors owe fiduciary duties to the *corporation*, not to the stockholders. [Emphasis in original.]
>
> (E. Norman Veasey with Christine T. Di Guglielmo, "What Happened in Delaware Corporate Law and Governance from 1992-2004? A Retrospective on Some Key Developments" (2005), 153 *U. Pa. L. Rev.* 1399, at p. 1431)

[88] Nor does this Court's decision in *Peoples Department Stores* suggest a fixed rule that the interests of creditors must prevail. In *Peoples Department Stores*, the Court had to consider whether, in the case of a corporation under threat of bankruptcy, creditors deserved special consideration (para. 46). The Court held that the fiduciary duty to the corporation did not change in the period preceding the bankruptcy, but that if the directors breach their duty of care to a stakeholder under s. 122(1)(b) of the *CBCA*, such a stakeholder may act upon it (para. 66).

…

[102] The evidence, objectively viewed, supports a reasonable expectation that the directors would consider the position of the debentureholders in making their decisions on the various offers under consideration. As discussed above, reasonable expectations for the purpose of a claim of oppression are not confined to legal interests. Given the potential impact on the debentureholders of the transactions under consideration, one would expect the directors, acting in the best interests of the corporation, to consider their short and long-term interests in the course of making their ultimate decision. …

[103] Indeed, the evidence shows that the directors did consider the interests of the debentureholders. A number of debentureholders sent letters to the Board, expressing concern about the proposed leveraged buyout and seeking assurances that their interests would be considered. One of the directors, Mr. Pattison, met with Phillips, Hager & North, representatives of the debentureholders. The directors' response to these overtures was that the contractual terms of the debentures would be met, but no additional assurances were given.

[104] It is apparent that the directors considered the interests of the debentureholders and, having done so, concluded that while the contractual terms of the debentures would be honoured, no further commitments could be made. This fulfilled the duty of the directors to consider the debentureholders' interests. It did not amount to "unfair disregard" of the interests of the debentureholders. As discussed above, it may be impossible to satisfy all stakeholders in a given situation. In this case, the Board considered the interests of the claimant stakeholders. Having done so, and having considered its options in the difficult circumstances it faced, it made its decision, acting in what it perceived to be the best interests of the corporation.

[105] What the claimants contend for on this appeal, in reality, is not merely an expectation that their interests be considered, but an expectation that the Board would take further positive steps to restructure the purchase in a way that would provide a satisfactory purchase price to the shareholders and preserve the high market value of the debentures. At this point, the second, softer expectation asserted approaches the first alleged expectation of maintaining the investment grade rating of the debentures.

[106] The difficulty with this proposition is that there is no evidence that it was reasonable to suppose it could have been achieved. BCE, facing certain takeover, acted reasonably to create a competitive bidding process. The process attracted three bids. All of the bids were leveraged, involving a substantial increase in Bell Canada's debt. It was this factor that posed the risk to the trading value of the debentures. There is no evidence that BCE could have done anything to avoid that risk. Indeed, the evidence is to the contrary.

[107] We earlier discussed the factors to consider in determining whether an expectation is reasonable on a s. 241 oppression claim. These include commercial practice; the size, nature and structure of the corporation; the relationship between the parties; past practice; the failure to negotiate protections; agreements and representations; and the fair resolution of conflicting interests. In our view, all these factors weigh against finding an expectation beyond honouring the contractual obligations of the debentures in this particular case.

[108] Commercial practice—indeed commercial reality—undermines the claim that a way could have been found to preserve the trading position of the debentures in the context of the leveraged buyout. This reality must have been appreciated by reasonable debentureholders. More broadly, two considerations are germane to the influence of

general commercial practice on the reasonableness of the debentureholders' expectations. First, leveraged buyouts of this kind are not unusual or unforeseeable, although the transaction at issue in this case is noteworthy for its magnitude. Second, trust indentures can include change of control and credit rating covenants where those protections have been negotiated. Protections of that type would have assured debentureholders a right to vote, potentially through their trustee, on the leveraged buyout, as the trial judge pointed out. This failure to negotiate protections was significant where the debentureholders, it may be noted, generally represent some of Canada's largest and most reputable financial institutions, pension funds and insurance companies.

[109] The nature and size of the corporation also undermine the reasonableness of any expectation that the directors would reject the offers that had been presented and seek an arrangement that preserved the investment grade rating of the debentures. As discussed above (at para. 74), courts may accord greater latitude to the reasonableness of expectations formed in the context of a small, closely held corporation, rather than those relating to interests in a large, public corporation. Bell Canada had become a wholly owned subsidiary of BCE in 1983, pursuant to a plan of arrangement which saw the shareholders of Bell Canada surrender their shares in exchange for shares of BCE. Based upon the history of the relationship, it should not have been outside the contemplation of debentureholders acquiring debentures of Bell Canada under the 1996 and 1997 trust indentures, that arrangements of this type had occurred and could occur in the future.

[110] The debentureholders rely on past practice, suggesting that investment grade ratings had always been maintained. However, as noted, reasonable practices may reflect changing economic and market realities. The events that precipitated the leveraged buyout transaction were such realities. Nor did the trial judge find in this case that representations had been made to debentureholders upon which they could have reasonably relied.

[111] Finally, the claim must be considered from the perspective of the duty on the directors to resolve conflicts between the interests of corporate stakeholders in a fair manner that reflected the best interests of the corporation.

[112] The best interests of the corporation arguably favoured acceptance of the offer at the time. BCE had been put in play, and the momentum of the market made a buyout inevitable. The evidence, accepted by the trial judge, was that Bell Canada needed to undertake significant changes to continue to be successful, and that privatization would provide greater freedom to achieve its long-term goals by removing the pressure on short-term public financial reporting, and bringing in equity from sophisticated investors motivated to improve the corporation's performance. Provided that, as here, the directors' decision is found to have been within the range of reasonable choices that they could have made in weighing conflicting interests, the court will not go on to determine whether their decision was the perfect one.

[113] Considering all the relevant factors, we conclude that the debentureholders have failed to establish a reasonable expectation that could give rise to a claim for oppression. As found by the trial judge, the alleged expectation that the investment grade of the debentures would be maintained is not supported by the evidence. A reasonable expectation that the debentureholders' interests would be considered is established, but was fulfilled. The evidence does not support a further expectation that a better arrangement could be negotiated that would meet the exigencies that the corporation was facing, while better preserving the trading value of the debentures.

[114] Given that the debentureholders have failed to establish that the expectations they assert were reasonable, or that they were not fulfilled, it is unnecessary to consider in detail whether conduct complained of was oppressive, unfairly prejudicial, or unfairly disregarded the debentureholders' interests within the terms of s. 241 of the *CBCA*. Suffice it to say that "oppression" in the sense of bad faith and abuse was not alleged, much less proved. At best, the claim was for "unfair disregard" of the interests of the debentureholders. As discussed, the evidence does not support this claim.

The *BCE* decision is ambiguous—the case seems to stand for the principle that directors may seek to maximize shareholder value in the context of a takeover bid, but they are under no legal obligation to do so. The court has left the fiduciary obligation wide open by holding that the duty of the board is to act in the best interests of the corporation without explaining what this means in practice. As Edward Iacobucci has stated, "by holding that in substance directors have only a duty to act in the interests of the corporation and not any particular stakeholder, *BCE* precludes directors from being required to make a decision that substantively advances the interests of creditors (or any other stakeholder for that matter)." (See Edward Iacobucci, "Indeterminacy and the Canadian Supreme Court's Approach to Corporate Fiduciary Duties" (2009) 48:2 Can Bus LJ 232.)

QUESTIONS

1. After *BCE*, does the target board have a duty to maximize shareholder value?
2. What considerations are relevant in determining the best interests of the shareholders? Should the board automatically concede to the highest bidder in order to maximize share value?
3. Should securities commissions adjudicate takeover bid issuers, or is it better to leave these cases to be heard by the courts?

VI. CHAPTER SUMMARY

One of the themes of this chapter has been the evolution of takeover bid legislation over the past 40 years. Beginning with the Kimber Report in 1965, takeover bid law has grown to be a complex, yet harmonized, body of law that compels the bidder to adhere to certain practices when making a bid or when seeking to be exempted from a bid. Another theme of the chapter has been the various ways in which the takeover bid legislation attempts to protect the interests of target shareholders. Such protection is afforded through provisions that ensure that target shareholders have ample opportunity to consider the original and any competing bids, receive equal treatment, and receive proper disclosure regarding the bid and the bidder. A final theme of this chapter has been the interrelationship between corporate and securities law. We saw this interrelationship particularly in the duties of the target board in the face of a takeover bid. The board is bound by its corporate law duties. Yet the defensive tactics it employs raise securities law issues because the tactics have the potential to negatively affect the target shareholders and thereby raise investor protection concerns.

CHAPTER TEN

Civil Liability

I. INTRODUCTION

In previous chapters, we discussed the issuer's obligation to provide full, true, and plain disclosure of all material facts in its prospectus. In this chapter, we discuss the consequences of failing to meet this obligation. The starting point for the chapter is, therefore, to appreciate the vast importance of the adjectives "full, true, and plain" in describing the type of disclosure contained in the prospectus. Failure to meet this standard supports the claim that the prospectus contains a misrepresentation in its disclosure. Until recently, the civil liability provisions in provincial securities laws applied only to the disclosure made in three types of documents: prospectuses, offering memoranda, and takeover bid circulars (including directors' circulars and issuer bid circulars). Legislation has been enacted in all provincial jurisdictions invoking liability for misrepresentations in continuous disclosure documents.

The remedies available to investors under securities legislation for misrepresentations are in addition to the remedies available to them at common law. You will recall from the law of torts that the common law requires an investor claiming a misrepresentation to prove the existence of a misstatement, reliance on that misstatement, and causation between the reliance and the damages suffered. However, the civil liability provisions contained in securities legislation differ from the common law in a number of respects. To begin with, "misrepresentations" are defined in the legislation to include omissions as well as misstatements. Furthermore, there is no need for an investor to prove each of the elements of a negligence claim, such as reliance, as he or she must do at common law. Finally, securities legislation contains a number of defences to the statutory civil liability provisions. Note the discussion of the common law position in *Kerr v Danier Leather Inc* (2004), 46 BLR (3d) 167 (Ont Sup Ct J), below.

Statutory remedies are extremely important for the development of financial markets. Their existence arguably contributes to investor confidence and the integrity of the market. There may, however, be another more persuasive reason that strong securities regimes are beneficial for financial markets. Rafael La Porta, Florencio Lopez-de-Silanes & Andrei Shleifer, "What Works in Securities Laws?" (2006) 61:1 J Fin 1, have found that countries with better legal protections for investors have more developed financial markets. They analyzed the securities laws of 49 countries and found that financial markets do not prosper when left to market forces alone. Both disclosure rights and liability standards were positively correlated with larger stock markets, while public enforcement, such as having an independent regulator or access to criminal sanctions, played a modest role in the development of stock markets. Highlighting a law and economics approach to capital market regulation, their findings suggest that securities laws matter because they facilitate private contracting rather than providing for public regulatory enforcement. As La Porta et al state:

> A different view of why securities law matters holds that its principal benefit is not the creation of a public enforcer, but rather the direct reduction in the costs of private contracting and enforcement. Regulation can standardize securities contracts by mandating disclosure requirements or limiting certain kinds of transactions as well as simplify private litigation. Without standardized contracts, litigation would be governed by contract and tort law, with grave uncertainty about outcomes because such matters as intent and negligence need to be sorted out in court. Securities law can structure contracting and litigation by explicitly describing the obligations of various parties and burdens of proof, thereby reducing the costs to them and to the court of establishing liability. With standardized contracts and litigation, the costs of writing and enforcing contracts decline, benefiting markets.

Of course, there are limitations to statutory remedies, including a host of defences available to would-be defendants. These defences weaken the ability of investors to succeed via the statutory remedy, as highlighted in *YBM Magnex International Inc* (2003), 26 OSCB 5285, excerpted below.

Before beginning, a word on the onus of proof. Usually, in civil cases, the person who is asserting the violation of the law has the onus of proof. For example, in a case concerning negligence, the plaintiff must prove negligence while the defendant has the onus of proving the defence of contributory negligence, if applicable. It is the same in securities regulation: the plaintiff must prove a breach of the relevant securities act provisions. The defendant can certainly rely on available defences and usually must prove the defence. However, in the securities realm, the onus of proof when a defence is invoked is not always clear. In some cases, the statute suggests that the defendant must prove that he, she, or it meets the requirements of the defence, but in other cases, who bears the onus of proof is ambiguous. Students, like legal counsel, must read the statutory provisions and the relevant defences closely when analyzing civil liability and applicable defences.

II. PRIMARY MARKET LIABILITY

The typical provision setting forth the cause of action stipulates that a number of parties, not simply the issuer, are potentially liable for a misrepresentation in one of the relevant documents. For example, s 130(1) of the Ontario *Securities Act*, RSO 1990, c S.5 (OSA) states as follows:

> 130(1) Where a prospectus, together with any amendment to the prospectus, contains a misrepresentation, a purchaser who purchases a security offered by the prospectus during the period of distribution or during distribution to the public has, without regard to whether the purchaser relied on the misrepresentation, a right of action for damages against,
>
> (a) the issuer or a selling securityholder on whose behalf the distribution is made;
>
> (b) each underwriter of the securities who is required to sign the certificate required by section 59;
>
> (c) every director of the issuer at the time the prospectus or the amendment to the prospectus was filed;
>
> (d) every person or company whose consent to disclosure of information in the prospectus has been filed pursuant to a requirement of the regulations but only with respect to reports, opinions or statements that have been made by them; and
>
> (e) every person or company who signed the prospectus or the amendment to the prospectus other than the persons or companies included in clauses (a) to (d),
>
> or, where the purchaser purchased the security from a person or company referred to in clause (a) or (b) or from another underwriter of the securities, the purchaser may elect to exercise a right of rescission against such person, company or underwriter, in which case the purchaser shall have no right of action for damages against such person, company or underwriter.

See also Alberta *Securities Act*, RSA 2000, c S-4 (ASA), ss 203(1)-(3); British Columbia, *Securities Act*, RSBC 1996, c 418 (BCSA), ss 131(1)-(3); Newfoundland and Labrador, *Securities Act*, RSNL 1990, s S-13 (Nfld SA), s 130(1).

Securities legislation contains comparable provisions relating to misrepresentations in offering memoranda and circulars in the case where a material fact or change has not been disclosed. Students will note that the cause of action is against the issuer or selling securityholder (that is, sales from a control block); the underwriter required to sign the certificate in the prospectus; directors of the issuer; any person who prepared and filed reports, opinions, or statements, usually professionals like accountants or lawyers; and anybody else who signed the prospectus or amending document.

When an investor purchases a security under a prospectus during the period of distribution, liability can arise if the prospectus contained a misrepresentation at the time of purchase (students should note that, according to *Kerr v Danier*, misrepresentations can include future-oriented financial information in some circumstances, as discussed in Chapter 4). Liability can arise under similar circumstances for offering memoranda (OSA, s 130.1; ASA, s 204(1); BCSA, s 132.1 ("prescribed disclosure documents")). In a takeover bid situation, the party that issues the circular (that is, the offeror, bidder, or directors of the target), any person who signed the document as an officer or director and any person who provided a consent in the use of a report, opinion, or statement can be liable when the document is sent to the shareholders. The legislation contains a "deemed reliance" provision whereby shareholders need not prove that they received, understood, or relied on the document (OSA, s 131(1); ASA, s 205(1); BCSA, s 132(1); Nfld SA, s 131(1)).

If a party is found to have breached the statutory civil liability provisions, the investor who purchased, based on the misrepresentation or omission, has one of two possible remedies: rescission or damages. Both these remedies are available against the issuer or underwriter in the case of a firm commitment underwriting. However, only damages are available against directors, persons who consented to any part of the prospectus (but only with regard to the part they consented to), or any other person who signed the prospectus or amendment. The effect of rescission is that it voids the contract and attempts to place the parties in the position they were in before the contract had been performed. This remedy may mean returning the purchase price of the securities to the investor (OSA, ss 130(1) and 131(1); ASA, ss 203(2), 204(1)(b), 205(1); BCSA, ss 131(3), 132.1(2), 132(1)(a)).

Where damages are claimed, they are limited by statute to the price at which they were offered to the public (OSA, s 130(9); ASA, s 203(13); BCSA, s 131(13); Nfld SA, s 130.1(4)). In particular, damages are calculated based on the difference between the price paid for the shares and their value once the misrepresentation is disclosed as such or the omission is rectified. As stated in *Kerr v Danier*, at para 353, below,

> [t]he *prima facie* measure of such damages is the depreciation in the price of the security, which is equal to the price paid less the post-misrepresentation price. This amount may then be reduced under s. 130(7) if the defendant proves that: (1) the depreciation in price was caused in all or in part by factors other than its misrepresentation; and (2) that the depreciation in price is not reflective of the depreciation in value experienced by the plaintiff.

OSA, s 130(7) states that the defendant will not be liable for damages that "do not represent the depreciation in value of the security as a result of the misrepresentation relied upon." See also ASA, s 203(9); BCSA, s 131(10); Nfld SA, s 130.1(6).

The underwriter can be liable for no more than the total public offering price represented by the portion of the distribution underwritten by the underwriter (OSA, s 130(6); ASA, s 203(8); BCSA, s 131(9); Nfld SA, s 130(6)). The liability of persons under the statutory civil action is joint and several (OSA, s 130(8); ASA, s 203(10); BCSA, s 131(11); Nfld SA, s 130(8)).

The line between primary and secondary market liability can be a blurry one, however, because of multiple disclosure documents involved as evidenced by *Lawrence v Atlas Cold Storage Holdings Inc* (2006), 34 CPC (6th) 41 (Ont Sup Ct J) (excerpted below) and *Lawrence v Atlas Cold Storage Holdings Inc* (2009), 78 CPC (6th) 142 (Ont Sup Ct J). In approving the settlement of a class action proceeding against Atlas Cold Storage, Ernst & Young LLP, and BMO Nesbitt Burns Inc (among others), Lax J discussed when a supposedly secondary market transaction might still fall within the ambit of OSA, s 130.

The case is pertinent to the interrelationship between class actions and securities law. Prior to the introduction of the *Class Proceedings Act, 1992* (SO 1992, c 6) (CPA), individual plaintiffs could be effectively prevented from bringing an action for misrepresentation because they lacked the financial resources to do so. With the ability to gather a class together under the CPA, the securities act provisions relating to misrepresentation may be invoked more often, as the two excerpts from the Atlas case seem to suggest.

Lawrence v Atlas Cold Storage Holdings Inc
(2006), 34 CPC (6th) 41 (Ont Sup Ct J)

[28] The following is the admission at issue:

Q: Now, in the confirmation of purchase, Mr. Simon, it says that the shares were bought on the Toronto Stock Exchange. Is that so?

A: Yes.

Q: It would appear that they were bought at a price a cent above the issue price. Is that your understanding?

A: I don't know. I can just see what the price is here. I don't know what the issue price was.

Q: The issue price was $11.55.

A: Then that is fine, yes.

Q: Do you know how you came to pay a cent above the issue price?

A: No.

Q: In any event, there is no question they were bought on the Exchange?

A: Right.

Q: In other words, in the secondary market?

A: Right, that is right.

[29] A "Member of Royal Bank Financial Group" issued the confirmation of purchase at $11.56 per unit to the Charles Trust. It indicates, "As agents, we today confirm the following buy for your account on the Toronto Stock Exchange ..." It is not clear from the evidence which member of the Royal Bank Financial Group issued the confirmation of purchase. Nor does the confirmation of purchase indicate who the seller was.

[30] RBC Capital Markets was one of the underwriters of the offering of units pursuant to the October 15, 2002 prospectus.

(ii) Is it clearly inconsistent with a pleading that he purchased units offered under the Atlas prospectus, such that the amendment would constitute an abuse of process and should be denied? (Can a person who purchases units on the Toronto Stock Exchange on the closing date of an offering of units under a prospectus constitute "a purchaser who purchases a security offered by the prospectus" for the purpose of section 130 of the Securities Act?)

[31] Section 130 of the *Securities Act* creates civil liability for a misrepresentation in a prospectus to, "... a purchaser who purchases a security offered by the prospectus during the period of distribution or during distribution to the public ... without regard to whether the purchaser relied on the misrepresentation ... ."

[32] Counsel for the plaintiffs argue that, for the purpose of s. 130, a purchaser purchases a security offered by a prospectus as long as during the period of distribution for that prospectus he purchases the same kind of security as the kind of security offered by the prospectus, whether from an underwriter or through the facilities of a stock exchange.

[33] The proposed amended pleading is that the Charles Trust purchased units offered under the Atlas prospectus dated October 15, 2002. The Claim indicates that Atlas offered 7,620,000 units pursuant to the October 15, 2002, prospectus. On the plaintiffs' argument, a person who, through the facilities of a stock exchange, acquired some of the 4,250,000 units initially offered by, for example, the Atlas prospectus dated February 27, 2001, which is not alleged to have contained a misrepresentation, during the period of distribution for the October 15, 2002, prospectus, "purchases a security offered by the [October 15, 2002] prospectus," for the purpose of s. 130.

[34] In the alternative, counsel for the plaintiffs argue that, for the purpose of s. 130, a purchaser purchases a security offered by a prospectus as long as during the period of distribution for that prospectus he purchases one of the securities qualified by that

prospectus, whether from an underwriter or over the facilities of a stock exchange. This alternative requires a purchaser to trace the chain of title of the security that he acquires. Hence, on this argument, the Charles Trust purchases units offered under the Atlas prospectus dated October 15, 2002, even if purchased on the exchange, at a price greater than the offering price, as long as the units purchased can be traced to the 4,250,000 units qualified by the October 15, 2002, prospectus.

[35] Counsel for the plaintiffs concede that the B.C. Court of Appeal, in *Pearson v. Boliden Inc.* (2002), 222 D.L.R. (4th) 453 (B.C. C.A.), paras. 76 and 86, held that the cause of action in s. 130 of the *Securities Act* is not available to persons buying securities on the "secondary market," which it defined for the purposes of its decision as purchases from persons other than the underwriters. Plaintiffs' counsel says the B.C. Court of Appeal's decision is wrong, and that as an Ontario Superior Court judge I am not bound by it.

[36] Counsel for the plaintiffs argue that the boundary between primary and secondary market transactions is the termination of the period of distribution, and cites *Kerr v. Danier Leather Inc.*, [2004] O.J. No. 1916 (S.C.J.) para. 120; reversed on a separate point on appeal (2005), 77 O.R. (3d) 321 (C.A.); leave to appeal to the Supreme Court of Canada granted, [2006] S.C.C.A. No. 56. *Kerr v. Danier* dealt with an initial public offering.

[37] Counsel for the plaintiffs submits that in any event the defendants have not proven that the Charles Trust did not buy its units from an underwriter.

[38] It is clear that the Charles Trust purchased its units during the period of distribution in respect of the October 15, 2002, prospectus.

[39] There is no evidence that a sale from an underwriter to a member of the public would not or could not be effected through the facilities of the exchange, or that in any event the Charles Trust did not purchase its units from an underwriter.

[40] Counsel for the plaintiffs submitted that the seller of the units acquired by the Charles Trust could be identified, but that in this motion the onus was not on the plaintiffs to do so.

[41] In his examination, Mr. Simon equates buying units on the stock exchange with buying units on the secondary market. I do not take that as a statement that he knew the identity of the seller, and the seller was not an underwriter.

[42] Without the need to be convinced that either of the interpretations of s. 130 that plaintiffs' counsel advances has any merit, on the evidence before me, I am not prepared to conclude that it is an abuse of the courts process to permit an amendment to the Claim to plead that Mr. Simon in his capacity as trustee of the Charles Trust purchased units offered under the Atlas prospectus dated October 15, 2002.

In *Lawrence v Atlas Cold Storage Holdings Inc* (2009), 78 CPC (6th) 142 (Ont Sup Ct J), Lax J approved a settlement of the action. The parties agreed to settle the matter for the following reasons:

> [15] Shortly after the release of reasons on the preliminary motions, class counsel discovered that a third party had acquired Atlas Holdings and its subsidiaries by way of a leveraged buyout and later learned that $500 million of fresh encumbrances had been registered against its assets. The assets had been encumbered to their approximate book value. This meant that in order for class members to execute on any judgment against Atlas Holdings, they would have to first commence a second action to set aside the $500 million in encumbrances. Class counsel

took steps to put the leveraged buyout parties on notice of their intended action. They appreciated that if settlement discussions were to take place, the $500 million in encumbrances would provide the defendants with significant leverage. They hoped that the prospect of defending a second action might, at least in part, neutralize that leverage.

[16] Then, evidence was discovered which established that the trust units purchased by the Charles Trust had no connection with the distributions underwritten by Nesbitt, but were purchased in the secondary market before the Nesbitt distributions. The cause of action provided by s. 130 of the *OSA* was therefore vulnerable to attack on the basis of the plaintiffs' theory that the purchase had taken place in the primary market. The certification motion was to be heard over five days commencing on January 14, 2008. E&Y and Nesbitt brought motions for summary judgment returnable on the date scheduled for the certification motion.

Without recourse to s 130 of the OSA, the class would have needed to pursue the common law torts of conspiracy, fraudulent misrepresentation, and negligent misrepresentation. In other words, the class would have needed to prove reliance—something which the OSA's primary market liability provisions do not require.

QUESTIONS

1. List all of the parties who are required to sign the prospectus. Is each of these parties potentially liable for misrepresentation or omissions in the prospectus?
2. Are any other parties potentially liable (that is, parties who have not signed the prospectus)? If so, which parties are potentially liable in the case of a misrepresentation or omission?
3. Why is the remedy of rescission available against only certain parties but not others?
4. Do the statutory civil liability provisions extend to documents other than the prospectus? If so, which documents?
5. Why do you think the onus is on the defendant to limit its damages by proving that factors other than its misrepresentation resulted in a decrease in share price? Why not have the plaintiff prove that the misrepresentation resulted in the loss in share value?

III. DEFENCES

One of the primary distinctions between the common law right of action for misrepresentation and the statutory civil liability provisions is the existence in the statute of a host of defences against claims of misrepresentation. The legislation seeks to balance investor remedies with allowing good faith transactions that violate statutory provisions. One could argue that the statutory defences tip the balance toward exonerating transactions that violate the statute. The defences are broad and must be read in the light of recent decisions (see *YBM* and *Danier*, discussed below). As mentioned, in order to succeed under some of the defences, the party claiming protection under the defence must prove its applicability to him or her.

A. Purchaser Had Knowledge of the Misrepresentation

There is a complete defence available for a misrepresentation in a prospectus if the defendant proves that the purchaser had knowledge of the misrepresentation when he or she purchased the securities. This is the only defence available to the issuer other than the defence discussed above, that the depreciation in the price of the securities was not caused by the misrepresentation. OSA, s 130(2) provides for this defence:

> 130(2) No person or company is liable under subsection (1) if he, she or it proves that the purchaser purchased the securities with knowledge of the misrepresentation.

See also ASA, s 203(4); BCSA, s 131(4); Nfld SA, s 130(2).

This defence is also available for misrepresentations in an offering memorandum or takeover bid document. These two provisions form the only defence available for a control block issuer or an offeror. OSA, ss 130.1(2) and 131(4) provide:

> 130.1(2) No person or company is liable under subsection (1) if he, she or it proves that the purchaser purchased the securities with knowledge of the misrepresentation.
>
> 131(4) No person or company is liable under subsection (1), (2) or (3) if the person or company proves that the securityholder had knowledge of the misrepresentation.

See also ASA, ss 204(3), 205(4); BCSA, ss 132.1(3), 132(4).

B. Defendant Had No Knowledge

Securities legislation also allows a "no knowledge" defence if the defendant can prove that the document containing the misrepresentation was filed without his, her, or its knowledge or consent. In particular, OSA, s 130(3)(a) reads as follows:

> 130(3) No person or company, other than the issuer or selling securityholder, is liable under subsection (1) if he, she or it proves,
>
> (a) that the prospectus or the amendment to the prospectus was filed without his, her or its knowledge or consent, and that, on becoming aware of its filing, he, she or it forthwith gave reasonable general notice that it was so filed.

See also ASA, s 203(5)(a); BCSA, s 131(5)(a).

The defence is also available in connection with suits for misrepresentations (which, by definition, include omissions) in a takeover bid circular. OSA, s 131(5)(a) specifies:

> 131(5) No person or company, other than the offeror, is liable under subsection (1), (2) or (3) if he, she or it proves,
>
> (a) that the take-over bid circular, issuer bid circular, directors' circular or director's or officer's circular, as the case may be, was sent without his, her or its knowledge or consent and that, on becoming aware of it, he, she or it forthwith gave reasonable general notice that it was so sent.

See also ASA, s 205(5)(a); BCSA, s 132(5)(a); Nfld SA, s 131(5). BCSA, s 132.1(4)(a), prior to the most recent legislative proposals, also provides this defence for "disclosure documents" (which essentially refers to offering memoranda) in addition to the defence for takeover bid circulars and prospectuses. The rationale for the "no knowledge" defence is likely that defendants who are unaware of the filing of a document containing a misrepresentation should not be penalized for it. This policy rationale does, however, raise the question of the extent of investigation that one must undertake to become aware of filing activity or intentions. The "no knowledge" defence might seem to reward a lack of attention to the business of the issuer. Presumably, its use would be circumscribed by the courts to avoid that outcome.

C. Defendant's Withdrawal of Consent

A defendant can also avoid liability if he or she withdraws consent previously given to a prospectus or a takeover bid circular. The withdrawal of consent must occur "after the issue of a receipt for the prospectus and before the purchase of securities by the purchaser" (OSA, s 130(3)(b); BCSA, s 131(5)(b); ASA, s 203(5)(b); Nfld SA, s 130(3)(b)). The withdrawal of consent must occur as soon as the defendant becomes aware of the misrepresentation, in accordance with the wording of the statute. Furthermore, the defendant must provide "reasonable general notice" of the withdrawal. It is unclear how and to whom this notice must be provided. However, it is likely that it must be provided to investors or those individuals who purchased on the basis of the misrepresentation. Because an individual defendant is unlikely to know who such purchasers are, the term "general" seems to mean by dissemination in a public manner.

The defence is also available in the takeover bid context. OSA, s 131(5)(b) specifies:

> 131(5) No person or company, other than the offeror, is liable under subsection (1), (2) or (3) if he, she or it proves, ...
>
> (b) that, after the sending of the take-over bid circular, issuer bid circular, directors' circular or director's or officer's circular, as the case may be, on becoming aware of any misrepresentation in the take-over bid circular, issuer bid circular, directors' circular or director's or officer's circular, he, she or it withdrew the consent thereto and gave reasonable general notice of the withdrawal and the reason therefor.

See also ASA, s 205(5)(b); BCSA, s 132(5)(b). BCSA also provides this defence for disclosure documents, under s 132.1(4)(b).

D. Defendant's Reliance on an Expert

If the misrepresentation is contained in a portion of the prospectus made on the authority of an expert, or in a portion of the prospectus that is purported to be an extract or copy of an expert's report or opinion, a statutory defence is available. In order for the defendant to be relieved of liability, the defendant must prove that he or she had no reasonable grounds to believe and did not believe that there had been a misrepresentation or an inaccurate representation of the expert's report (OSA, s 130(3)(c); ASA, s 203(5)(c); BCSA, ss 131(5)(c), 131(5)(d)(i)-(ii)). For example, imagine a prospectus that contains a report from an engineering firm and that report contains a misrepresentation. If a director of the issuer did not believe, and had no reasonable grounds to believe, that the report contained a misrepresentation, then the director can be relieved of liability. It is not completely clear from the wording of the statute who must prove "reasonable grounds for belief," but it would seem that the defendant would be in the best position to indicate what he or she believed and whether there were reasonable grounds for that belief. This defence is also available for misrepresentations in takeover bid circulars (OSA, s 131(5)(c); ASA, s 205(5)(c); BCSA, s 132(5)(c)).

E. Defences Available to Experts Themselves

Securities legislation also provides a defence for experts, such as the engineering firm in the example above, that provide the opinions and reports contained in a prospectus. The legislation states clearly that the onus of proof rests with the expert to prove that he or she had reasonable grounds to believe and did believe that the impugned part of the prospectus was a fair representation of the opinion or report (OSA, s 130(3)(d)(i); ASA, s 203(5)(d)(i); BCSA, s 131(5)(d)(iii)). A further defence is available if the expert became aware of the misrepresentation and then advised the securities commission and gave "reasonable general notice that such use had been made and that he, she, or it would not be responsible for that part of the prospectus or the amendment to the prospectus" (OSA, s 130(3)(d)(ii); ASA, s 203(5)(d)(ii); BCSA, s 131(5)(d)(iv)). As mentioned above, these defences are also available for takeover bid circulars (OSA, s 131(5)(d); ASA, s 205(5)(d); BCSA, s 132(5)(d)).

F. Defendant's Due Diligence Defence

A due diligence defence is available for misrepresentations made in a prospectus or takeover bid document. The defence is available for experts in respect of their opinions and reports as well as for other individuals, such as directors, in respect of other portions of the prospectus. These "other" portions are sometimes referred to as the "non-expertised" parts of the prospectus.

Under the legislation, a defendant is not liable unless he, she, or it failed to conduct "such reasonable investigation as to provide reasonable grounds for a belief that there had been no misrepresentation." The legislation is ambiguously worded and also contains a stipulation that the defendant must not have believed that there had been a misrepresentation (OSA, ss 130(4), (5); ASA, ss 203(6), (7); BCSA, ss 131(6), (7)). Note that the requirements seem to operate conjunctively. As MacIntosh and Nicholls state, a defence is available if "the defendant did not, in fact, believe there had been a misrepresentation and conducted a 'reasonable investigation as to provide reasonable grounds for a belief that there had been no misrepresentation'" (Jeffrey G MacIntosh & Christopher C Nicholls, *Securities Law* (Toronto: Irwin, 2002) at 163).

The onus of proof with respect to the due diligence defence is not clear from the legislation because it does not specifically provide that the onus rests with the defendant. The *Danier* case (discussed in Chapter 4) (*Kerr v Danier Leather Inc* (2004), 46 BLR (3d) 167 (Ont Sup Ct J)) suggests that the onus is on the plaintiff to prove that the defendant did not act diligently:

> [196] …
>
> Section 130(4) does not contain the words "if he, she or it proves" as does s. 130(3). In the defences under s. 130(3), it is clear that the defendant must prove his or her defence once the plaintiff has established the existence of a misrepresentation. The absence of the words "if he, she or it proves" appears to confirm that the plaintiff retains the burden of proof to establish that the auditor [or other expert] failed to meet his or her due diligence standard. In addition, the standard is cast in the negative, i.e., a failure to meet a due diligence standard, and this is suggestive of the plaintiff bearing the burden of proof. This analysis also applies with respect to the defence in s. 130(5). …
>
> [197] Thus, for Wortsman and Tatoff to be liable, in addition to proving that the prospectus contained a misrepresentation, the plaintiffs must also prove that these defendants: "(a) failed to conduct such reasonable investigation as to provide reasonable grounds for a belief that there had been no misrepresentation; or (b) believed there had been a misrepresentation."

Thus, it appears that the plaintiff bears the onus of proof in the due diligence defence because the statute does not specify otherwise. After *Danier*, a question still remains as to whether the onus of proof rests with the plaintiff in the other defences, which do not stipulate that the defendant bears the onus of proof. One would presume so, but this issue must still be litigated. Indeed, there seem to be strong policy arguments in favour of reversing the onus of proof in the due diligence defence from the plaintiff to the defendant given that the defendant likely has more evidence regarding whether a reasonable investigation was undertaken. See also the provisions of OSA, s 138, below.

QUESTIONS

1. List the parties that can, under the wording of the legislation, gain protection under the defence provisions.
2. Imagine a circumstance in which each defence to liability might arise.
3. What are the implications for investors of having a range of defences to liability? In your view, how broad is this range?
4. What is the threshold test in the legislation for most of the defences?

IV. CASE LAW

Escott v BarChris Construction Corp et al, 2 ALR Fed 86 (SDNY 1968) considered statutory provisions for civil liability under the US *Securities Act of 1933*, 15 USC (§§ 77a–77bbbb), which are similar to that provided for under most Canadian securities acts. Historically, because of the lack of Canadian jurisprudence on due diligence defences, *Escott v BarChris* has been considered by some to be a leading authority on reasonableness in the case of these defences.

The case involved incorporators of a construction company whose founders did not speak English. The company was expanding and went public. The founders signed the prospectus, referred to using the US term "registration statement," and were held to be liable because of omissions and misrepresentations contained in the prospectus. They were held to be liable regardless of the fact that they could not even read the document containing the misrepresentations and omissions. Note that the standard used in the case to assess the actions of the defendants, at least those who were insiders of the company, seems to be an objective standard. You will also note a shift from this position in the *YBM* case discussed below. The excerpt from the following case deals with only those individuals who signed the registration statement. However, the case itself deals with a number of other parties.

Escott et al v BarChris Construction Corp et al
2 ALR Fed 86 (SDNY 1968)

McLEAN DIST J: This is an action by purchasers of 5½ per cent convertible subordinated fifteen year debentures of BarChris Construction Corporation (BarChris).

The action is brought under Section 11 of the *Securities Act of 1933* … . Plaintiffs allege that the registration statement with respect to these debentures filed with the Securities and Exchange Commission, which became effective on May 16, 1961, contained material false statements and material omissions.

…

The signers, in addition to BarChris itself, were the nine directors of BarChris, plus its controller, defendant Trilling, who was not a director. Of the nine directors, five were officers of BarChris, i.e., defendants Vitolo, president; Russo, executive vice president; Pugliese, vice president; Kircher, treasurer; and Birnbaum, secretary. Of the remaining four, defendant Grant was a member of the firm of Perkins, Daniels, McCormack & Collins, BarChris's attorneys. Defendant Coleman, a partner in Drexel … Auslander and Rose, who were not otherwise connected with BarChris.

• • •

At the time relevant here, BarChris was engaged primarily in the construction of bowling alleys, somewhat euphemistically referred to as "bowling centers." … BarChris was an outgrowth of a business started as a partnership by Vitolo and Pugliese in 1946 … . The introduction of automatic pin setting machines in 1952 gave a marked stimulus to bowling. It rapidly became a popular sport, with the result that "bowling centers" began to appear throughout the country in rapidly increasing numbers. BarChris benefited from this increased interest in bowling. Its construction operations expanded rapidly … . BarChris's sales increased dramatically from 1956 to 1960 … . For some years the business had exceeded the managerial capacity of its founders. Vitolo and Pugliese are each men of limited education … . Pugliese devoted his time to supervising the actual construction work. Vitolo was concerned primarily with obtaining new business. Neither was equipped to handle financial matters … . Rather early in their career they enlisted the aid of Russo, who was trained as an accountant … . He eventually became executive vice president of BarChris. In that capacity he handled many of the transactions which figure in this case.

In 1959 BarChris hired Kircher, a certified public accountant who had been employed by Peat, Marwick. He started as controller and became treasurer in 1960. In October of that year, another ex-Peat, Marwick employee, Trilling, succeeded Kircher as controller. At approximately the same time Birnbaum, a young attorney, was hired as house counsel. He became secretary on April 17, 1961.

• • •

In general, BarChris's method of operation was to enter into a contract with a customer, receive from him at that time a comparatively small down payment on the purchase price, and proceed to construct and equip the bowling alley. When the work was finished and the building delivered, the customer paid the balance of the contract price in notes, payable in installments over a period of years … . In 1960 BarChris began a practice which has been referred to throughout this case as the "alternative method of financing." In substance this was a sale and leaseback arrangement. … Under either financing method, BarChris was compelled to expend considerable sums in defraying the cost of construction before it received reimbursement. As a consequence, BarChris was in constant need of cash to finance its operations, a need which grew more pressing as operations expanded.

In December 1959, BarChris sold 560,000 shares of common stock to the public at $3.00 per share. This issue was underwritten by Peter Morgan & Company, one of the present defendants.

By early 1961, BarChris needed additional working capital. The proceeds of the sale of the debentures involved in this action were to be devoted, in part at least, to fill that need.

The registration statement of the debentures, in preliminary form, was filed with the Securities and Exchange Commission on March 30, 1961 … . The closing of the financing took place on May 24. On that day BarChris received the net proceeds of the financing.

By that time BarChris was experiencing difficulties in collecting amounts due from some of its customers. … As time went on those difficulties increased … . In October

1962 BarChris came to the end of the road. On October 29, 1962, it filed in this court a petition for an arrangement under Chapter XI of the Bankruptcy Act. BarChris defaulted in the payment of the interest due on November 1, 1962 on the debentures. …

The Debenture Registration Statement

… The registration statement in its final form contained a prospectus as well as other information. Plaintiffs' claims of falsities and omissions pertain solely to the prospectus, not to the additional data. … I turn now to the question of whether defendants have proved their due diligence defenses. The position of each defendant will be separately considered.

Russo

Russo was, to all intents and purposes, the chief executive officer of BarChris. He was a member of the executive committee. … He was thoroughly aware of BarChris's stringent financial condition in May 1961. … In short, Russo knew all the relevant facts. He could not have believed that there were no untrue statements or material omissions in the prospectus. Russo has no due diligence defenses.

Vitolo and Pugliese

They were the founders of the business who stuck with it to the end. Vitolo was president and Pugliese was vice president. Despite their titles, their field of responsibility in the administration of BarChris's affairs during the period in question seems to have been less all-embracing than Russo's. … Vitolo and Pugliese are each men of limited education. It is not hard to believe that for them the prospectus was difficult reading, if indeed they read it at all.

But whether it was or not is irrelevant. The liability of a director who signs a registration statement does not depend upon whether or not he read it or, if he did, whether or not he understood what he was reading.

And in any case, Vitolo and Pugliese were not as naive as they claim to be. They were members of BarChris's executive committee … . They must have known what was going on. Certainly they knew of the inadequacy of cash in 1961 … . All in all, the position of Vitolo and Pugliese is not significantly different, for present purposes, from Russo's.

And in any case, there is nothing to show that they made any investigation of anything which they may not have known about or understood. They have not proved their due diligence defenses.

Kircher

Kircher was treasurer of BarChris and its chief financial officer. He is a certified public accountant and an intelligent man. He was thoroughly familiar with BarChris's financial affairs … . Kircher worked on the preparation of the registration statement. … He read the prospectus and understood it. He knew what it said and what it did not say.

Kircher's contention is that he had never before dealt with a registration statement, that he did not know what it should contain, and that he relied wholly on Grant, Ballard and Peat, Marwick to guide him. He claims that it was their fault, not his, if there was anything wrong with it. He says that all the facts were recorded in BarChris's books where these "experts" could have seen them if they had looked. He says that he truthfully answered all their questions. In effect, he says that if they did not know enough to ask the right questions and to give him the proper instructions, that is not his responsibility. … Knowing the facts, Kircher had reason to believe that the expertised portion of the prospectus, i.e., the 1960 figures, was in part incorrect. He could not shut his eyes to the facts and rely on Peat, Marwick for that portion.

As to the rest of the prospectus, knowing the facts, he did not have a reasonable ground to believe it to be true. On the contrary, he must have known that in part it was untrue. Under these circumstances, he was not entitled to sit back and place the blame on the lawyers for not advising him about it.

Kircher has not proved his due diligence defenses.

Trilling

Trilling's position is somewhat different from Kircher's. He was BarChris's controller. He signed the registration statement in that capacity, although he was not a director.

… He was a comparatively minor figure in BarChris … . Trilling may well have been unaware of several of the inaccuracies in the prospectus. But he must have known of some of them. As a financial officer, he was familiar with BarChris's finances and with its books of account. … In the light of these facts, I cannot find that Trilling believed the entire prospectus to be true.

But even if he did, he still did not establish his due diligence defenses. He did not prove that as to the parts of the prospectus expertised by Peat, Marwick he had no reasonable ground to believe that it was untrue. He also failed to prove, as to the parts of the prospectus not expertised by Peat, Marwick, that he made a reasonable investigation which afforded him a reasonable ground to believe that it was true. As far as appears, he made no investigation. He did what was asked of him and assumed that others would properly take care of supplying accurate data as to the other aspects of the company's business. This would have been well enough but for the fact that he signed the registration statement. As a signer, he could not avoid responsibility by leaving it up to others to make it accurate. Trilling did not sustain the burden of proving his due diligence defenses.

Ultimately, the relevance of the *BarChris* case may be questioned because it is a US decision, and American law is in some respects different from Canadian law on the issue of civil liability. However, as noted above, historically, there has been a lack of Canadian decisions on due diligence defences, and so *BarChris* has been influential. The differences between US and Canadian law on burden of proof were raised in the *Kerr v Danier* decision discussed later in the chapter (see para 196 of the excerpt).

When the *YBM* case was decided by the Ontario Securities Commission, it provided a regulatory interpretation of Canadian law on due diligence. Recall that *YBM* was discussed in Chapter 4 with respect to prospectus requirements. As mentioned earlier, there is a shift from *BarChris* to *YBM* in terms of the standards to be applied to the defendants' actions. After the excerpt of the case below, we will discuss this shift.

YBM Magnex International Inc
(2003), 26 OSCB 5285

[Summary of facts: YBM Magnex made a public offering in 1997. The company had investigated and learned that the US Attorney's office was investigating them for illegal activity as well as the existence of allegations in Europe linking the company to organized crime. In August 1996, YBM's board of directors set up a special committee of outside directors to investigate the allegations. They concluded that no disclosure was required due to a lack of clarity in the allegations.

In May 1997, YBM filed its AIF on SEDAR, which contained some general disclosure regarding the special committee and mentioned that the company was subject only to risks generally associated with companies doing business in Eastern Europe.

The preliminary prospectus was filed June 1997 and incorporated the AIF by reference. It contained no further disclosure regarding the special committee and the allegations.

In May 1998, the US government executed search warrants against the company's US offices and staff, and issued a temporary cease-trade order with respect to the company's shares. OSC staff sought orders in the public interest alleging that the preliminary and final prospectus failed to contain full, true, and plain disclosure and that the issuer had failed to make timely disclosure of material changes.]

PER CURIAM:

[179] We think it best to consider the reasonableness of the respondents' diligence and their belief from the perspective of a prudent person in the circumstances. This necessarily entails both objective and subjective considerations including their degree of participation, access to the information and skill.

. . .

[197] The [Special] Committee was independent of management, but was not without a manifest conflict of interest. Mitchell chaired the Special Committee and was very active as YBM's co-lead underwriter.

. . .

[253] Generally speaking, a board is entitled to rely on special committees. However, as indicated above, Mitchell's independence and the non-participation of the other two members were questionable. The absence of Schmidt and Davies [other members of the special committee] from meetings with Fairfax or Mitchell rendered them ill-suited to discharge their role. The failure to participate, particularly given Davies' information, seriously limited the exchange of ideas and prevented the Special Committee from being a committee upon which the Board could fully rely. In addition, we note the serious nature of information conveyed to the Board by the Special Committee. This should have resulted in a call to action in light of the pending acquisition of Crucible and the public financing. Instead, we note some additional weaknesses in the process followed by the board:

1. Relying on US legal advice provided months before regarding potential defamation concerns, the Directors did not even get a copy of the Report. This could have aided the questioning and decision around disclosure. More than a one shot briefing from Mitchell was required.
2. The entire Board should have requested a meeting with Fairfax to discuss Fairfax's unfiltered continuing concerns regarding YBM's end users or money laundering.

> Fairfax wanted to do more work including interviewing the auditors, reviewing their work papers, conducting a complete investigation of customers and vendors including knocking on doors and checking all invoices, and explaining the actions taken by the Board to the US Government. Fairfax's services were not inexpensive, but, in relative terms, the financing raised $106 million. Fairfax's additional services were not called upon.

. . .

[264] Overall, we are satisfied that significant efforts were made by the Directors to ascertain the facts and assess their materiality. However, we find that the process adopted by the Directors to support their judgement and belief that the mandate, information obtained by and findings of the Special Committee were not material, and that the disclosure provided was full, true and plain, was deficient. YBM's Directors are not a homogenous group and therefore we must consider each director according to his degree of participation, access to information and skill.

. . .

[273] Mitchell, as an underwriter, was largely compensated based upon a direct drive compensation scheme. Clearly, First Marathon and Mitchell would benefit if YBM completed the Crucible acquisition and the offering. Simply put, Mitchell was in a conflict of interest. We do not view the conflict of interest as a matter of intention or lack of good faith on his part. Rather, it compromised both his time and judgement. …

[274] As an experienced director and underwriter, Mitchell ought to have known better. If Mitchell was not alert to this issue on August 29, 1996 when the Special Committee was created, he should have been on November 1, 1996 when the financing for the Crucible acquisition was first discussed by the Board. Mitchell submitted that he addressed the conflict by not advising First Marathon about the Special Committee without first obtaining Board approval. Unfortunately, the Board's approval came late in the Special Committee process. In any event, it did not address the essential problem. The Board's approval did little to protect investors because the basis for Mitchell's conflict remained and the Board proceeded with its decision regarding disclosure based upon the Report. The potential for divided loyalties makes it more difficult for Mitchell to justify the reasonableness of his belief that YBM made full, true, and plain disclosure.

. . .

[282] Mitchell took a number of positive steps [through his work as Chair of the Special Committee] towards uncovering facts that could have had an adverse economic impact on the business. However, the risks at issue left little margin for error. Mitchell had considerable skill, access to the most information and extensive participation in the offering, the investigation of the facts, their materiality and their disclosure. He developed a belief in the legitimacy of the business. However, that did not in our view justify a reasonable basis for his belief that YBM made full, true and plain disclosure of all material facts. Consequently, a defence of due diligence is unavailable to him.

. . .

[289] Davies was the only outside director who had a personal visit from the FBI in April 1996. While the FBI only disclosed that there was an investigation and asked no specific questions about YBM's business, it is clear that their visit related to YBM. The FBI wanted Davies to work in a somewhat clandestine manner on its behalf but he declined. Davies did not discuss this visit or the likely subject matter with the Board or

its counsel, only with his daughter. He explained that the FBI advised him to keep the interview in confidence. He compared his decision to do so with staff's responsibility with respect to their public law duties. We have some difficulty understanding Davies' motivation in this situation. Having heard his testimony, we are of the opinion that having regard to his skill and business experience, he failed to act prudently. A director has a positive duty to act when he or she obtains information, or becomes aware of facts, which might lead one to conclude that there may be an issue that may adversely affect the company; *Soper* at para. 53. We must consider his belief that there were no material facts omitted. A director's belief cannot be considered reasonable when he is aware of circumstances of such a character, so plain, so manifest, that a person with any degree of prudence would not have acted in this manner.

. . .

[292] There are no stringent prerequisites for becoming a director of a public company and the nature of that office involves the exercise of business judgement; *Soper* at para. 28. What Davies did not get by way of information, he could have asked for. The standard of care is intended to encourage responsibility not passivity. It is said that an obvious characteristic of a reasonable director is one who is prepared to ask tough questions not only of management but also of other directors. Davies' unique knowledge and role on the Special Committee presented him with an opportunity to do so. It is apparent that he declined.

. . .

[306] At the time, despite his passive role on the Special Committee, and given his relative age and inexperience, we would not put him [Schmidt] in the same position as Davies. It was more reasonable for him to rely on experienced counsel and financial advisors since his level of experience would make it more difficult for him to judge the advice as being right or wrong. Schmidt considered the information, relied on other professionals with more experience in disclosure and materiality and applied his own judgment. That belief was reasonable in the circumstances for the reasons discussed earlier.

[307] Schmidt, unlike Mitchell and Davies, did not have any information that other directors did not have or did not share with the board. His belief in the legitimacy of the business and no managerial improprieties was not unreasonable. He admittedly gave more weight to these factors than to other risks that YBM might face. He clearly could have done more on the Special Committee and he should have. Nevertheless, he had no knowledge of any facts not known to the directors generally and to Mitchell and Davies more specifically.

. . .

[309] Peterson is the Chair of the partnership at Cassels Brock and was the Premier of Ontario from 1985 to 1990. He was called to the Bar of Ontario in 1969. He is Wilder's partner. Peterson gives strategic advice but does not have a traditional law practice. He is an experienced corporate director who serves on many public boards. He has served on special committees and signed a number of prospectus certificates on behalf of other issuers.

[310] Peterson was an outside director who had been on the Board for four months at the time of the August 15, 1996 meeting. While he was a Director of YBM he invested $50,000 in shares of the company at $6.00 per share in the beginning and later at $15.00 per share. He never traded the stock. As such, he lost his investment along with other investors. He was not on the Special Committee. He signed the prospectus certificate on

behalf of the Board, but was not substantially involved in the offering process. He attended only one meeting with staff on November 4, 1997. He did attend all of the relevant board meetings and was fully aware of the mandate of the Special Committee. He also met with First Marathon on one occasion on May 12, 1997 to discuss the report of the Special Committee. At that time, he expressed his confidence in the management of YBM.

. . .

[321] While we believe Peterson could have done more, we have concluded that Peterson acted reasonably based on his involvement in the matter, his skill and his access to information in the circumstances. Accordingly, his due diligence defence is available to him, but just barely. We are of the view that Peterson brought a unique perspective to the board. His professional reputation as testified to by Mr. Michael Wilson, Mr. David Beatty and Mr. John Tory, and his experience in many other public company boards, was not in any way equalled by any other director. He had unique access to counsel to the Special Committee, whom he supported as counsel both to YBM and the Special Committee. He was appointed to add to the prestige and status of YBM. While Peterson meets the legal test of due diligence, the panel remains disappointed that he did not offer more insight and leadership to the board in these circumstances.

. . .

[332] Antes and Greenwald brought different skills to the Board than the other YBM directors. Skill is that proficiency that comes from training and experience. They did not have the public company or business experience of other YBM directors. They relied on the members of the Special Committee to fulfill the duties assigned to them. For all their involvement in identifying and recommending the acquisition of Crucible, Antes and Greenwald had no material role in the financing. They relied on counsel for the drafting of disclosure that was to comply with Ontario securities law. Legal advice must be considered in the context in which it was given, and in this context, given their level of experience and skill, it was reasonable for Antes and Greenwald to rely on counsel. They did not participate in the drafting of the AIF, the Preliminary Prospectus or the Final Prospectus, and did not participate in any of the meetings with staff. Despite the reasonableness of their reliance on counsel and even with their limited knowledge, they should have been alive to the muddled nature of the disclosure in the prospectuses when those two documents were presented for Board approval. Even without public board expertise, their knowledge of the mandate, information obtained by and findings of the Special Committee should have put them on notice.

[333] Antes and Greenwald, although members of the Audit Committee, were not involved in selecting or instructing D&T [Deloitte & Touche]. Their knowledge of staff's concerns and the D&T engagement came from board meetings in the summer of 1997. Antes believed that the high-risk audit being performed by D&T was akin to a forensic investigation and would unearth wrongdoing. Greenwald had no specific understanding of the investigation. When D&T's clean audit opinion emerged, they both viewed it as confirmation of their long-standing belief that YBM was a legitimate business. Their reliance on the D&T clean audit opinion was reasonable.

[334] Accordingly, their belief as to full, true and plain disclosure is justified in the circumstances of the case. Therefore, a due diligence defence is available to both Antes and Greenwald.

. . .

[357] Gatti had no experience in such matters. He relied on the Special Committee. He relied on the experience of underwriters and securities lawyers for the issuer and underwriters. While Gatti knew a great deal, the Special Committee knew more. The disclosure at issue was not financial disclosure. The Special Committee was independent of management. As such, his reliance was in good faith and honest in the circumstances. As indicated previously, a material fact is a question of fact and law. The assessment of and reliance on legal advice is most pertinent to the reasonableness of the investigation. Gatti was influenced by the fact that while the investigation may have existed, counsel advised that it was not disclosable. Indeed Gatti received correspondence with regard to a Parente audit inquiry letter with a marginal note that reads: "no required disclosure—per CBB." Finally on May 28, 1997, Gatti, Bogatin and James Held of YBM participated in a due diligence conference call with the underwriters, auditors and lawyers in which it was concluded that no material fact, including the fact of any pending investigation, was omitted from the preliminary prospectus. The prospectus was signed two days later. The question is, did he reasonably believe that the disclosure was adequate and that it was true?

• • •

[359] It was clear that Gatti was subordinate to Bogatin [CEO and President] and to the decisions of Mitchell and Wilder. What should he have done? In our opinion, in such circumstances an engaged CFO should communicate directly with the board of directors of the company. …

[360] In conclusion, we find that, at the relevant time, Gatti had a reasonable belief that the prospectus disclosure was true and that no material facts were omitted. In the circumstances of this case, we find that Gatti has proved his due diligence, but just barely.

• • •

[429] … The reasonableness of First Marathon's belief can only be assessed in the context of the collective knowledge of First Marathon. …

[430] … National Bank acknowledges that Mitchell "should not have been permitted to have been involved in investment banking functions in this financing."

• • •

[434] … [T]he investigation undertaken by the underwriters in this case was extensive. A significant shortcoming of Jones' investigation [on behalf of First Marathon], however, was that he was unaware of all the facts [that Mitchell was].

• • •

[437] In addition to these failures to communicate, the evidence suggests other shortcomings in First Marathon's due diligence process. Most notably, the process was not complete at the time First Marathon agreed that the preliminary prospectus could be filed … . It is unclear how First Marathon could certify to the best of its knowledge, information and belief given the circumstances. We recognize the commercial reason for proceeding in this manner, but the desire to get on with the Crucible acquisition was simply too high-risk at this stage.

• • •

[441] … First Marathon was a sophisticated and experienced underwriting firm. Unlike the officers and directors of YBM, conducting public offerings was First Marathon's lifeblood. Moreover, First Marathon, through Mitchell's involvement with YBM, was more knowledgeable than the typical underwriter … . While clearly not the guarantor of full, true and plain disclosure, the underwriter is a gatekeeper. …

> [442] … There can be little doubt that First Marathon exerted significant efforts to investigate YBM. We do not believe it sought to deliberately mislead investors. However, given its knowledge, access to information, involvement and skill, we do not find that National Bank has established that the belief that the prospectus contained full, true and plain disclosure was justified. Accordingly a defence of due diligence is unavailable.
>
> …
>
> [444] … While GMP was less knowledgeable regarding the mandate, information obtained by and findings of the Special Committee, it was not completely uninformed.
>
> …
>
> [448] … While not a guarantor of YBM's disclosure, McBurney understood that a diligent investment banker would be expected to "drill down" on sensitive issues and agreed that his experience as both a securities lawyer and investment banker would help him in identifying sensitive areas of a company's business. Why did GMP possess the limited knowledge that it did? It is clear that GMP relied upon Mitchell and First Marathon. McBurney knew that Mitchell's dual role had the potential for conflict.
>
> …
>
> [450] … In principle, we see no reason why one member of an underwriting syndicate cannot or should not rely on another, but where a co-lead underwriter falls down in the conduct of its due diligence, the other co-lead may have to bear the risk of its reliance … . We believe that GMP understood that its reliance on First Marathon was subject to certain risks given Mitchell's roles.
>
> …
>
> [460] There is no doubt that GMP, along with the other respondents, drew great comfort from the D&T audit which, by all accounts, was an exceptional measure to institute in the midst of a prospectus offering. However, GMP also relied on First Marathon's flawed investigation. GMP was fully aware of those risks. If it was not it should have been. GMP should have taken certain steps that would have been consistent with its role as a co-lead underwriter. Accordingly, we find that a defence of due diligence is unavailable to GMP.

In *YBM*, the actions of the directors and the information that they possessed were clearly relevant in leading to successful reliance on the due diligence defence in certain cases so as to avoid being sanctioned by the OSC. The decision seems to suggest that individuals in positions of responsibility, such as a member of a special committee or the board, may not always need to make inquiries about potential omissions or misrepresentations. Rather, in certain cases, members may be permitted to rest on information that was "given to them."

Specifically, whereas the *BarChris* case appears to lay down an objective test for analyzing the actions of defendants, *YBM* illustrates a mix of objective and subjective tests. The conclusion regarding certain defendants, such as Mitchell and Davies, contained an objective element in that the Commission held that they "ought to have known better" (*YBM* at paras 274 and 292). These conclusions are consistent with *BarChris* in which the court examined the position and the level of responsibility of the various parties and drew conclusions about what each should have known. However, for the other members of the board in *YBM*, such as Antes, Greenwald, and Gatti, the standard seems to have been subjective in that the commission analyzed the knowledge and actions of each individual so as to determine whether he qualified under the defence at issue (see paras 307, 332-334, 357, and 360). The variation in treatment of the various individuals in the case is conspicuous with little apparent consistency in the tests applied (see paras 253, 264, 274, 289, 292, and 306).

Students should also note that the Ontario Securities Commission (OSC) is pronouncing on the due diligence issue in the context of a s 127 hearing. Typically, the due diligence defence is available either in the context of a civil action under s 130 or as a defence to charges under s 122, the quasi-criminal provision. Section 127, on the one hand, contains the "public-interest" power of the OSC, as will be discussed in the next chapter (ASA, s 198; BCSA, s 161; Nfld SA, s 127). The discussion of the due diligence defence in the context of a s 127 hearing raises jurisdictional issues concerning the respective roles of courts and regulators. It is also curious that the OSC concludes that it might still hold that an order under s 127 is warranted even where the parties have met their due diligence standards. This raises the question of why the OSC spent so much time on the issue of due diligence in the first place.

A number of YBM shareholders brought a class action suit in relation to the prospectus disclosure issues as well as the failure to make timely disclosure. The plaintiff shareholders alleged that there was a massive conspiracy and fraud perpetrated upon the investors in YBM by organized crime. In particular, the plaintiffs claimed that members of Russian organized crime caused YBM to enter into contracts and that these contracts depleted the financial resources of YBM, including the proceeds of the securities offering. It was alleged that there were misrepresentations in the prospectus and the shareholders suffered losses arising out of their purchase of shares pursuant to the prospectus. Lengthy settlement discussions were held and, under the supervision of Winkler J, the parties reached a settlement. The settlement was approved by the Ontario Superior Court of Justice on May 2, 2002 in *Mondor v Fisherman*, [2002] OJ No 1855 (QL) (Sup Ct J). In that case, the court held that the proposed settlement was fair, reasonable, and in the best interests of all class members and that there was significant risk and cost to both sides in proceeding to trial. Under the settlement, the net amount that could be distributed to members of the class was approximately $110 million. On the issue of other litigation following the OSC decision in *YBM*, see also the decision in *Wilder v Ontario Securities Commission*, discussed in Chapter 11.

QUESTIONS

1. What does the OSC mean when it states that Peterson and Gatti "just barely" proved their individual due diligence? (See *YBM* at paras 321 and 360, above.)
2. Would the OSC have reached a different decision regarding the actions of the individuals discussed above if it had applied the more objective standard contained in *BarChris*?
3. Should the individual's particular skills, access to information, and participation be relevant to a decision regarding reasonable reliance? (See *YBM* at para 332, for example.)
4. After *YBM*, does an issuer have a legal obligation to report rumours? When do rumours become material?

Kerr v Danier Leather Inc, a class action suit, is a case that deals with statutory civil liability. The case was discussed at some length in Chapters 4 and 6 dealing with prospectus and continuous disclosure requirements and students should refer to those discussions, as well as the excerpt below, when studying this case. The plaintiffs were investors who purchased Danier

Leather Inc shares pursuant to the company's 1998 initial public offering (IPO). The plaintiffs sued Danier, its president/chief executive officer (CEO) (Wortsman) and its chief financial officer (CFO) (Tatoff) under s 130 of the OSA, claiming damages for alleged misrepresentations in the IPO final prospectus receipted on May 6, 1998. In its judgment, the court addresses the issues of the governing law, applicability of the law to the facts, liability, and damages. Students should follow this breakdown in their analysis of the case.

Kerr v Danier Leather Inc

(2004), 46 BLR (3d) 167 (Ont Sup Ct J)

[Summary of facts: Danier Leather issued a prospectus pursuant to an initial public offering, setting out a forecast of its revenues for the fourth quarter of 1998 and the fiscal year ending with that quarter. The prospectus contained some cautionary language stating that assumptions were used to create the forecast which could turn out to be inaccurate and that there was no guarantee that the projections would be met. A receipt for this prospectus was obtained on May 6, 1998. The shares were issued at $11.25 per share. On May 16, the CEO and CFO of Danier became aware that the fourth quarter revenues were falling short. However, they claimed that they still believed the forecast would be achieved by the end of the year and so did not investigate further. The IPO closed on May 20. On June 4, Danier issued a press release revealing the lower revenues. The shares dropped to $10.25, and on June 10, the share price was $8.90. The forecast was substantially achieved by the year-end.]

The trial judge agreed with Danier that the poor results were caused by warm weather and not a "material change" requiring an amendment prospectus under s 57(1). However, he also found an obligation under s 130(1) to disclose material facts. He awarded shareholders who sold their shares after June 10 the difference between the IPO price and the price of the securities on June 10. The Court of Appeal reversed the lower court and allowed the appeal of the liability. It found that there were no material changes during the period of distribution which required disclosure. The court also found that the trial judge had erred in not giving sufficient deference to the business judgment of Danier's senior management. The plaintiffs appealed to the Supreme Court of Canada, which dismissed the appeal. The Supreme Court held that prospectuses need not be updated where new material facts come to light after the prospectus has been filed. These subsequent material facts cannot support an action pursuant to s 130(1). The Supreme Court's decision is excerpted below.

Kerr v Danier Leather Inc

2007 SCC 44, [2007] 3 SCR 331

BINNIE J (McLachlin CJ and Bastarache, LeBel, Deschamps, Fish, Abella, Charron, and Rothstein JJ concurring):

[32] The *Securities Act* is remedial legislation and is to be given a broad interpretation: *Pezim v. British Columbia (Superintendent of Brokers)*, [1994] 2 SCR 557. It protects investors from the risks of an unregulated market, and by its assurance of fair dealing and

by the promotion of the integrity and efficiency of capital markets it enhances the pool of capital available to entrepreneurs. The Act supplants the "buyer beware" mind set of the common law with compelled disclosure of relevant information. At the same time, in compelling disclosure, the Act recognizes the burden it places on issuers and in Part XV sets the limits on what is required to be disclosed. The problem for the appellants is that when a prospectus is accurate at the time of filing, s. 57(1) of the Act limits the obligation of post-filing disclosure to notice of a "material change," which the Act defines in s. 1 in relevant part as a change in the business, operations or capital of the issuer that would reasonably be expected to have a significant effect on the market price or value of any of the securities of the issuer … . An issuer has no similar express obligation to amend a prospectus or to publicize and file a report for the modification of material *facts* occurring after a receipt for a prospectus is obtained. That is where the legislature has drawn the line.

[33] The appellants no longer dispute the trial judge's finding that Danier's prospectus provided "full, true and plain disclosure of all material facts" when it was receipted on May 6, 1998. However, they cite *Shaw v. Digital Equipment Corp.*, 82 F3d 1194 (USCA 1st Cir. 1996), for the proposition that an issuer should not be allowed to "exploit its informational trading advantage, at the expense of investors, by delaying disclosure of material non public negative news until after completion of the offering" (p. 1204). As to intra-quarterly results, *Shaw* states:

> [G]iven that at any point in a quarter, the remainder of the period may not mirror the quarter-to-date, is there a sufficient probability that unexpectedly disastrous quarter-to-date performance will carry forward to the end of the quarter, such that a reasonable investor would likely consider the interim performance important to the overall mix of information available? … [T]he question is whether the nondisclosure of interim facts rendered the prospectus materially incomplete. [p. 1210]

The appellants argue that *Shaw*'s "materially incomplete" test applies at least to the extent of obliging issuers to correct misinformation, and this duty (grounded in s. 130(1) itself) exists independently of the prospectus disclosure requirements of ss. 56 to 58. The separate and continuing obligation on issuers is to disclose any material facts arising after the date of the prospectus and before closing that make any of the factual assertions implied in the forecast untrue. The gist of the appellants' complaint is succinctly summarized in their factum as follows:

> … Danier management decided not to disclose this [the intra-quarterly] information to Danier's board, counsel, auditors, underwriters, or to the market. Rather, they closed the offering and collected $67,950,000 in proceeds. Two weeks after closing, [Danier] finally disclosed the information and a revised, substantially lower, forecast for Q4 and FY 1998. The market price of Danier's shares immediately fell. In contrast to the Wortsman Family Trust, which reaped $27,500,000, Danier's investors lost 22% of their investment. [para. 1]

A. *Did Section 130(1) Oblige Danier to Disclose Material Facts Arising After Its Prospectus Was Filed?*

[34] The appellants argue that post-filing information falling short of "material change" can nevertheless base an action for prospectus misrepresentation because of the wording, as they interpret it, of s. 130(1) which reads:

> 130(1) Where a prospectus together with any amendment to the prospectus *contains a misrepresentation*, a purchaser who purchases a security offered thereby during the period of distribution or distribution to the public shall be deemed to have relied on such misrepresentation *if it was a misrepresentation at the time of purchase* and has a right of action for damages against,
>
> (a) the issuer or a selling security holder on whose behalf the distribution is made; …
>
> (e) every person or company who signed the prospectus or the amendment to the prospectus other than the persons or companies included in clauses (a) to (d) … .

[35] Was the sales forecast, though found not to be a "material change," nevertheless a "misrepresentation" as of May 16, 1998? According to s. 1, a "misrepresentation" can occur by:

> … an omission to state a *material fact* that is necessary … to make a statement not misleading in the light of the circumstances in which it was made.

The argument, therefore, is that failure to disclose the intra-quarterly results prior to closing rendered the prospectus forecast "misleading" at the "time of purchase" to the knowledge of the respondents, and therefore actionable under s. 130(1). This is because a "material fact" is defined in the Act more broadly than a "material change" and includes "a fact that significantly affects, or would reasonably be expected to have a significant effect on, the market price or value of … securities" (s. 1). The trial judge concluded that the intra-quarterly results constituted a "material fact."

[36] The appellants further submit that nothing in s. 130(1) suggests any legislative intent to alter the basic common law principle that requires a representation that becomes untrue to the maker's knowledge to be corrected before it is acted upon (see S.M. Waddams, *The Law of Contracts* (4th ed. 1999), at p. 315). In this vein, the appellants, as did the trial judge, observe that s. 130(1) (as it stood in 1998) deems an investor to have relied on a misrepresentation "if it was a misrepresentation at the time of purchase." Reference to "the time of purchase," they say, further indicates that an issuer's duty to disclose material facts continues until the closing date.

[37] In my opinion, with respect, these submissions are not persuasive. Prospective purchasers were entitled to assume that no material *changes* (as defined in the Act) had occurred to the material facts disclosed in the prospectus between the filing date and the closing date, but that is the extent of the assurance given by the Act to prospective investors.

[38] The appellants submit that s. 57(1) should not be used as a guide to the interpretation of s. 130(1), relying in part on the argument that "s. 57(1) says nothing about whether a material fact if disclosed may remain uncorrected if it becomes untrue by the date of purchase, and thus the section does nothing to limit any such duty that may otherwise exist," as discussed by H. Underwood and R. Sorell in "Danier Leather Inc. and the Duty to Update a Prospectus" (2006), 43 *Can. Bus. L.J.* 134, at pp. 144-45. However, such an interpretation would disregard the court's duty to interpret the statute "harmoniously" as a whole. Imposition of civil liability under s. 130(1) for an omission to do what the legislature as a matter of policy has declined to require in s. 57(1) would simply be to substitute the court's view of policy for that adopted by the legislature. The distinction between "material change" and "material fact" is deliberate and policy-based … .

• • •

As to the current state of this policy, it is worth noting that both the Toronto Stock Exchange Committee on Corporate Disclosure, *Final Report: Responsible Corporate Disclosure: A Search for Balance* (1997) ("Allen Report") and the Ontario, *Five Year Review Committee Final Report: Reviewing the Securities Act (Ontario)* (2003) ("Crawford Report"), considered whether the *Securities Act* should be amended to require continuing disclosure by issuers of material facts or whether the policy of requiring the disclosure of only material changes should be continued. Both committees recommended against a modification of the statutory policy.

[39] Firstly, if an issuer has fully complied with its regulatory obligations under ss. 56 to 58 of the Act it would be contrary to the scheme of the Act, and to the intent of the Ontario legislature reflected therein, to find civil liability against an issuer under s. 130(1) for failing to disclose post-filing information that does not amount to a material change.

[40] Secondly, the statutory definition of "misrepresentation" uses the past tense in the phrase "in the light of the circumstances in which it *was* made." The appellants say the past tense "contemplates that a statement may need correction later" (A.F., at para. 51). In my view, however, this past tense simply signals that the relevant date for assessing the accuracy of a statement is the effective date when the statement *was* made, i.e., the date the prospectus (or an amendment) was filed.

[41] Thirdly, the appellants rely on the phrase "if it was a misrepresentation at the time of purchase" but this reliance too, in my view, is misplaced. These are words of limitation designed to ensure that s. 130(1) does not impose civil liability for a representation that had become cured or corrected at the date of purchase. Suppose, for example, that Danier owned an important patent on a process for working leather, and trumpeted this fact in its prospectus, inadvertently failing to disclose that a competitor had mounted a serious court challenge to the patent's validity. The Act gives the purchasers the benefit of "deemed" reliance. The existence of a serious court challenge would be a material fact. Yet if the challenge were settled or discontinued and the patent thus vindicated *before* the time of purchase, why should the omission attract damages or rescission? The answer, according to the language of s. 130(1), is that it does not.

[42] The appellants' reliance on the common law as a guide to the interpretation of s. 130(1) is also unconvincing. The common law does not require a person selling shares to issue a prospectus. It does not define or distinguish between material facts and material changes. It does not create a scheme of compelled disclosure with its own requirements and limits on those requirements. It is the Act and not the common law that settles the policy.

[43] In summary, when (as here) a prospectus (or an amendment) contains no misrepresentation *on the date the document is filed*, information amounting to material *facts* (but not material *changes*) that arises subsequently cannot support an action under s. 130(1). (Of course, if a material *change* arises during the period of distribution, failure to disclose this change as required by s. 57(1) could support an action under s. 130(1).) In the case at bar, however, the trial judge found that the intra-quarterly results were *not* a material change, and as will be explained, I agree with the trial judge in this regard. Such is the prospectus disclosure policy presently mandated by the Act and the courts are obliged to give effect to it. In contexts other than "prospectus misrepresentation," including regulatory or stock exchange oversight, a different policy may prevail, depending on the governing rules and enactments. This appeal is concerned only with s. 130(1).

...

B. Did the Courts Below Err in Failing to Find that the Intra-Quarterly Results Amounted to a Material Change?

[45] In an alternative argument, the appellants insist that the trial judge erred in failing to find that the intra-quarterly results constituted a "material change" that should have been disclosed pursuant to s. 57(1). For ease of reference, I repeat the definition of a "material change" in s. 1(1) of the Act:

> … a change in the *business, operations or capital* of the issuer that would reasonably be expected to have a significant effect on the market price or value of any of the securities of the issuer … .

The appellants submit that "the change in the *results* of Danier's operations amounted to a material change" (emphasis added; A.F., at para. 56), but this submission conflates "operations" with "results of operations." The shortfall in sales noted on May 16, 1998 is properly characterized as "results of operations," a term which is now found in ss. 1(1), 3.9 and 138.1 of the Act. Again, the legislature could have included "results of operations" in the definition of "material change" if it had intended to cast the disclosure obligation so widely, but they did not.

• • •

[48] In the present case, there is no evidence that Danier made a change in its business, operations or capital during the period of distribution. It is not disputed that the revenue shortfall as of May 16 was caused by the unusually hot weather, a factor external to the issuer. Consequently, Danier experienced no material change that required disclosure and did not breach s. 57(1).

The *Danier* case is significant. It is the first action under s 130 to go to trial (that is, before a court as opposed to a hearing before a securities commission) in Ontario. It is also the first Canadian securities class action to go to trial. It also addresses the issue of forward-looking financial information directly, including the obligation to disclose changes in such information. It sets out the parameters of the obligation to update a prospectus and in that vein highlights the importance of whether something is classified as a "material fact" or a "material change." The former is not caught by OSA s 57(1). Although the test in the case is applied to prospectus disclosure, it is conceivable that the principles could extend to other disclosure documents, certainly now that there is liability for secondary market disclosures as will be discussed below.

The court's approach to defining "material changes" and deciding that they do not include the changes at issue in *Danier* may be problematic. Commenting on the trial and appellate decisions in *Danier* before the Supreme Court ruling on the case, Professors Anita Anand and Mary Condon question the ease with which the corporation's lower fourth-quarter results were found not to be a "material change."

Anita Anand & Mary Condon, "Weather, Leather, and the Obligation to Disclose: *Kerr v Danier Leather Inc*"
(2006) 44 Osgoode Hall LJ 727 at 730-31 (footnotes omitted)

Neither the trial judge nor the Court of Appeal spent much time explaining the conclusion that the poor intra-quarterly results could not be characterized as a "material change" because the agreed *cause* of the depressed results was unseasonably warm weather, which was an event external to the issuer. It is unclear why both levels of court focused on the "cause" of the results rather than the results themselves. The definitions of "material fact" and "material change" do not advert to the idea of the "cause" of the material fact or change, but to the existence of the fact or change itself. Extrapolating from the reasoning of both levels of the court, had the "cause" of the poor results been instead a workers' strike that adversely affected sales, the results might have been disclosable. It is difficult to see how this distinction makes sense, despite the Court of Appeal's admission that "poor intra-quarterly results, could, under certain circumstances, in themselves amount to a material change."

The fact that some intra-quarterly results are disclosable and some are not *on the basis of an interpretation of their root causes* builds unnecessary inconsistency and a lack of predictability into the obligations of issuers. Rather, in a modern securities marketplace, it is the results themselves that investors will consider material to their investment decisions, at least as much, if not more than, how they were caused. However, it is indeed possible that investors may weigh poor results caused by a one-time-only problem over which the issuer has no control differently from an ongoing deficit within the company's operations. If the logic underlying the *Securities Act*, particularly as expressed in sections 1(1) and 56(1), is to give investors relevant information to make good investment decisions, then significant results themselves matter more than their cause. In other words, if the intra-quarterly results themselves are good or bad enough to have a material impact on the price or value of the issuer's securities, then how they were caused is somewhat beside the point.

For further discussion of the *Danier* case, see Edward M Iacobucci, "On Lemons and Leather: Liability for Misrepresentations of Forward-Looking Information Following *Danier Leather*" (2009) 48:1 Can Bus LJ 3.

V. SECONDARY MARKET LIABILITY

Until recently, issuers bore no statutory civil liability for misrepresentations made in continuous disclosure documents. For example, if an issuer misrepresented its financial position in its quarterly financials, securities legislation offered no protection to investors if they happened to rely on this misinformation in making their investment decisions. The absence of statutory civil liability for misrepresentations in continuous disclosure documents was a source of much controversy over the past decade. One of the reasons for this controversy, and especially the view that liability for misrepresentations in continuous disclosure documents is necessary, was that a vast majority of all securities trades occur in the secondary market. Indeed, the controversy regarding continuous disclosure liability is so pronounced that it prompted numerous studies of the issue, including a report from a committee of the Toronto Stock Exchange (*TSE Committee on Corporate Disclosure Final Report: Responsible Corporate Disclosure—A Search for Balance* (Toronto: Toronto Stock Exchange, 1997) (the Allen report), recommendations from a provincial committee reviewing the securities legislation in Ontario (Ministry of Finance, *Five Year Review Committee Final Report—Reviewing the Securities Act (Ontario)*, Ontario's Five Year Review Committee Final Report (Toronto: Queen's Printer for Ontario, 2003), as well as legislative initiatives in Ontario (Bill 198, *Keeping the Promise for a Strong Economy Act (Budget Measures)*, SO 2002, c 22 and Bill 41, *The Right Choices Act (Budget Measures), 2003, Schedule K Amendments to the Securities Act* (2003), 26 OSCB 4776). See also Bill 149, *Budget Measures Act (Fall), 2004 (Government Bill)*, 1st Sess, 38th Leg.

All provinces eventually adopted statutory amendments that were largely in response to the collapse of Enron and the waning investor confidence in capital markets perceived by the provinces. The statutory amendments give investors in the secondary market the right to sue issuers, officers, directors, and experts such as accountants, lawyers, geologists, and engineers for making public material misrepresentations, written or oral, about the company or for failing to comply with continuous disclosure requirements. Under the new rules, reliance need not be proven (OSA, s 138.3(1); ASA, s 211.03(1); BCSA, s 140(3)). The rules distinguish between "core" and "non-core" documents and statements. What type of document is a "core" document? The legislation states that for officers of the issuer, core documents include a prospectus, a takeover bid or issuer bid circular, a directors' circular, a rights offering circular, the AIF, MD&A, and annual financial statements. For directors who are not officers, a core document includes these documents as well as material change reports and interim financial statements. The following is an excerpt from the Ontario legislation:

> 138.3(1) Where a responsible issuer or a person or company with actual, implied or apparent authority to act on behalf of a responsible issuer releases a document that contains a misrepresentation, a person or company who acquires or disposes of the issuer's security during the period between the time when the document was released and the time when the misrepresentation contained in the document was publicly corrected has, without regard to whether the person or company relied on the misrepresentation, a right of action for damages against,
>
> (a) the responsible issuer;
>
> (b) each director of the responsible issuer at the time the document was released;
>
> (c) each officer of the responsible issuer who authorized, permitted or acquiesced in the release of the document;
>
> (d) each influential person, and each director and officer of an influential person, who knowingly influenced,
>
> (i) the responsible issuer or any person or company acting on behalf of the responsible issuer to release the document, or
>
> (ii) a director or officer of the responsible issuer to authorize, permit or acquiesce in the release of the document; and
>
> (e) each expert where,
>
> (i) the misrepresentation is also contained in a report, statement or opinion made by the expert,
>
> (ii) the document includes, summarizes or quotes from the report, statement or opinion of the expert, and
>
> (iii) if the document was released by a person or company other than the expert, the expert consented in writing to the use of the report, statement or opinion in the document.

Public oral statements by responsible issuer

(2) Where a person with actual, implied or apparent authority to speak on behalf of a responsible issuer makes a public oral statement that relates to the business or affairs of the responsible issuer and that contains a misrepresentation, a person or company who acquires or disposes of the issuer's security during the period between the time when the public oral statement was made and the time when the misrepresentation contained in the public oral statement was publicly corrected has, without regard to whether the person or company relied on the misrepresentation, a right of action for damages against,

(a) the responsible issuer;

(b) the person who made the public oral statement;

(c) each director and officer of the responsible issuer who authorized, permitted or acquiesced in the making of the public oral statement;

(d) each influential person, and each director and officer of the influential person, who knowingly influenced,

(i) the person who made the public oral statement to make the public oral statement, or

(ii) a director or officer of the responsible issuer to authorize, permit or acquiesce in the making of the public oral statement; and

(e) each expert where,

(i) the misrepresentation is also contained in a report, statement or opinion made by the expert,

(ii) the person making the public oral statement includes, summarizes or quotes from the report, statement or opinion of the expert, and

(iii) if the public oral statement was made by a person other than the expert, the expert consented in writing to the use of the report, statement or opinion in the public oral statement.

. . .

Burden of proof and defences

Non-core documents and public oral statements

138.4 (1) In an action under section 138.3 in relation to a misrepresentation in a document that is not a core document, or a misrepresentation in a public oral statement, a person or company is not liable, subject to subsection (2), unless the plaintiff proves that the person or company,

(a) knew, at the time that the document was released or public oral statement was made, that the document or public oral statement contained the misrepresentation;

(b) at or before the time that the document was released or public oral statement was made, deliberately avoided acquiring knowledge that the document or public oral statement contained the misrepresentation; or

(c) was, through action or failure to act, guilty of gross misconduct in connection with the release of the document or the making of the public oral statement that contained the misrepresentation.

Same

(2) A plaintiff is not required to prove any of the matters set out in subsection (1) in an action under section 138.3 in relation to an expert.

Failure to make timely disclosure

(3) In an action under section 138.3 in relation to a failure to make timely disclosure, a person or company is not liable, subject to subsection (4), unless the plaintiff proves that the person or company,

(a) knew, at the time that the failure to make timely disclosure first occurred, of the change and that the change was a material change;

(b) at the time or before the failure to make timely disclosure first occurred, deliberately avoided acquiring knowledge of the change or that the change was a material change; or

(c) was, through action or failure to act, guilty of gross misconduct in connection with the failure to make timely disclosure.

Same

(4) A plaintiff is not required to prove any of the matters set out in subsection (3) in an action under section 138.3 in relation to,

(a) a responsible issuer;

(b) an officer of a responsible issuer;

(c) an investment fund manager; or

(d) an officer of an investment fund manager.

Knowledge of the misrepresentation or material change

(5) A person or company is not liable in an action under section 138.3 in relation to a misrepresentation or a failure to make timely disclosure if that person or company proves that the plaintiff acquired or disposed of the issuer's security,

(a) with knowledge that the document or public oral statement contained a misrepresentation; or

(b) with knowledge of the material change.

Reasonable investigation

(6) A person or company is not liable in an action under section 138.3 in relation to,

(a) a misrepresentation if that person or company proves that,

(i) before the release of the document or the making of the public oral statement containing the misrepresentation, the person or company conducted or caused to be conducted a reasonable investigation, and

(ii) at the time of the release of the document or the making of the public oral statement, the person or company had no reasonable grounds to believe that the document or public oral statement contained the misrepresentation; or

(b) a failure to make timely disclosure if that person or company proves that,

(i) before the failure to make timely disclosure first occurred, the person or company conducted or caused to be conducted a reasonable investigation, and

(ii) the person or company had no reasonable grounds to believe that the failure to make timely disclosure would occur.

See Mary Condon, "Rethinking Enforcement and Litigation in Ontario Securities Regulation" (2006) 32 Queen's LJ 1 for a discussion of these provisions.

The new rules help to ensure accountability by removing the common law requirement for plaintiffs to show reliance. The touchstone of liability is whether the misrepresentations are made knowingly or not, rather than whether or not investors "relied" on the misrepresentation. For misrepresentations made unknowingly, liability is capped and is proportionate. For misrepresentations made knowingly, liability is not capped and is joint and several. For an excellent discussion of secondary market liability, see Adam C Pritchard & Janis P Sarra, "Securities Class Actions Move North: A Doctrinal and Empirical Analysis of Securities Class Actions in Canada" (2009) 47:4 Alta L Rev 881. The authors conducted an empirical study of class actions for Canadian issuers in Canada and the United States, current to mid-2009. They observed:

Two salient features emerge from this tally of lawsuits. First, the overall number of lawsuits remains relatively low, with no more than a handful in any given year. With a total of 90 lawsuits, the average is a mere five suits per year. Given the need for adequate damages to support a contingent fee recovery, the main litigation targets are likely to be issuers listed on the TSX. The total translates to approximately 0.3% chance of being sued in a securities class action in a given year for the approximately 1500 TSX issuers. By way of comparison, NERA reports that the overall probability of lawsuit for all US-listed companies has ranged from 1.8% to 1.3% over that same period.

The second salient feature is that, until quite recently, the litigation exposure faced by Canadian companies was overwhelmingly in US courts. The action is exclusively in the US until mid-1990s, with a very small number of Both and Canada only suits until the last few years, when we begin to see an uptick in Canada suits. We speculate that the class action bar in Canada is still finding its feet with respect to securities class actions; the recent adoption of the secondary market legislation greatly expands the number of available targets.

… one prominent feature of the lawsuits with proceedings in Both jurisdictions is that the fraud allegations are relatively serious. Nearly two thirds of the companies sued were the subject of some sort of regulatory investigation. "Govt. Enforcement" is defined to include a government investigation, such as RCMP, provincial securities commission, SEC, or FBI, whether formal or informal, against the sued company or officers, as well as an investigation by a stock exchange. A government investigation is regarded as a proxy for cases of intentional fraud, and disclosure of such an investigation is a prominent signal for the plaintiffs' bar.

Another prominent signal is the announcement of a restatement of earnings or revenues by a company, which is essentially an admission that its prior financial statements included a material misrepresentation. Half of the Both suits involve a restatement, and 43% of all actions involve accounting allegations, which are often revealed in either restatements or public disclosure to investors.

Half of all actions involved forward-looking information. This figure suggests that not withstanding the existence of defences through the use of cautionary language when issuing forward looking information, there is a risk, at least at the stage of commencement of actions, of being sued for the content of the forward information, particularly for cross-listed issuers. This suggests that Canadian issuers are not any more likely to face a suit for forward-looking information than are US issuers sued in the US. The incidence of forward-looking allegations remains relatively high in the US, despite the more stringent version of safe harbor in effect there, although there are very few complaints that allege forward-looking misstatements standing alone.

Overall, 83% of the cases involve secondary market civil liability actions and they comprise 100% of the cases in which issuers are sued in Both jurisdictions. Given how recent the Canadian secondary market provisions are, this figure is likely to increase in the future because of the greater scope of available damages. The initial cases under the Canadian secondary market provisions appear to support the supposition that restatements or admission of misrepresented information are the most likely to result in initial applications for class actions to be certified.

Cases

On December 14, 2009, van Rensburg J of the Ontario Superior Court of Justice certified the first class action under the OSA, s 138.3 secondary market liability provisions (*Silver v IMAX* (2009), 66 BLR (4th) 222 (Ont Sup Ct J)). In the following excerpt, Heintzmann, Schafler & Lam of Fraser Milner Casgrain LLP discuss the test for leave established in *IMAX*.

Robb C Heintzmann, Michael D Schafler & Solomon Lam, "Secondary Market Liability in Canada: Securities Class Actions"
Fraser Milner Casgrain LLP, March 2012

Interpreting the Test for Leave: Silver v IMAX

Silver v IMAX (2009), 66 B.L.R. (4th) 222 (Ont. S.C.) was the first case in Canada where leave to prosecute a secondary market claim was granted. In early 2006, IMAX had announced higher than expected revenues for the 2005 fiscal year. It turned out that these revenue figures had been inflated because IMAX had adopted an approach to income recognition that was not in accordance with generally accepted accounting principles (GAAP). When this information was publicly disclosed, IMAX's share price fell by 40%. IMAX later issued amended 2005 financial statements, acknowledging that its initial statements had not conformed to GAAP. Investors who traded shares of IMAX on NASDAQ or the Toronto Stock Exchange commenced a proposed global class action in Ontario and sought the leave of the court to assert a statutory claim for secondary market misrepresentation.

Justice van Rensburg of Ontario's Superior Court of Justice certified the class action and granted leave under section 138.8 to proceed with the secondary market representation claim. The main point of contention was how the elements of the test for leave under section 138.8 of the Securities Act should be construed:

- Good faith requirement. Justice van Rensburg held that this required the claimants to establish that they are bringing their action in "the honest belief that they have an arguable claim, and for reasons that are consistent with the purpose of the statutory cause of action and not for an oblique or collateral purpose."
- Reasonable possibility of success at trial. Justice van Rensburg held that this was a "relatively low threshold" for the claimant to satisfy. It only required the claimant to provide credible evidence that would permit the court to conclude that the claimant had more than a *de minimis* possibility of success at trial. While a claimant must satisfy only a very low threshold, a defendant relying on a statutory defence has a correspondingly high evidentiary burden to dissuade the court to grant leave.

IMAX sought leave to appeal Justice van Rensburg's decision to the Divisional Court. However, on 14 February 2011, Justice Corbett denied the motion, holding that there was no reason to doubt the correctness of Justice van Rensburg's decision or her interpretation of the test for leave. Justice Corbett cautioned that while Justice van Rensburg's decision was the first word on the test for leave for secondary market liability, "doubtless it is not the last."

In *Dobbie v Arctic Glacier Income Fund*, 2011 ONSC 25, Justice Tausendfreund of the Superior Court of Justice affirmed and adopted the principles of the test for leave enunciated in *IMAX*.

The case of *Silver v IMAX Corp.* represented the first Canadian case where leave to prosecute a secondary market claim was granted. Leave was granted under s 138.8 of the *Securities Act*:

138.8(1) No action may be commenced under section 138.3 without leave of the court granted upon motion with notice to each defendant. The court shall grant leave only where it is satisfied that,

(a) The action is being brought in good faith; and

(b) There is reasonable possibility that the action will be resolved at trail in favour of the plaintiff.

Justice van Rensburg of Ontario Superior Court of Justice was called to interpret both the "good faith" requirement and the "reasonable possibility of success at trial" requirement.

The following are excerpts of both the Ontario Superior Court of Justice decision to grant leave and the subsequent appeal of that decision. Students should pay close attention to van Rensburg J's interpretation of the leave requirements under OSA s 138.8.

Silver v IMAX Corporation

(2009), 66 BLR (4th) 222 (Ont Sup Ct J) (footnotes omitted)

VAN RENSBURG J:

[1] IMAX Corporation ("IMAX" or the "Company") is a public company that sells and leases its 3D theatre systems, which are installed in customers' theatres throughout the world. Its shares are listed on the TSX and NASDAQ.

[2] On February 17, 2006 IMAX issued a press release announcing: (a) that it had completed a record 14 theatre installations in the fourth quarter of 2005, ("Q4 2005"); (b) that it expected to meet or exceed its full year earnings guidance for 2005 of US $0.35 to $0.38 in net earnings per share ("EPS"); and (c) that it would release its fourth quarter and full year financial results on March 9th.

[3] On March 9, 2006, IMAX filed its Form 10-K containing its 2005 annual financial statements, with the U.S. Securities and Exchange Commission (the "SEC") and on SEDAR, and issued a press release reporting on its earnings and revenues. IMAX reported revenues of $144,930,000, including theatre system revenues of $97,753,000, with net earnings of $0.40 per share for the year ended December 31, 2005, an increase of 62% over the previous year. IMAX issued a second press release announcing the decision of its board of directors (the "Board") to explore strategic alternatives, including a sale or merger.

[4] Five months later, on August 9, 2006, IMAX issued another press release reporting on its second quarter results, noting that, although the process was ongoing, there was presently no buyer interested in acquiring the Company at a valuation sought by the Board.

[5] The press release also indicated that that the Company was in the process of responding to an informal inquiry from the SEC regarding the timing of its revenue recognition, and in particular its use of multiple element arrangement accounting to recognize revenue on theatre systems that were not yet open, including theatres where the 3D screen had not yet been installed.

[6] The following day IMAX's share price dropped 40%.

[7] In 2007, IMAX restated its financial statements for a number of years, including 2005 (the "Restatement"). The Restatement acknowledged that the Company had erred in recognizing revenue for theatre systems that were not completely installed, and that the Company had not complied with GAAP (generally accepted accounting principles). Theatre system revenues of US $17.5 million (and net earnings of US $9.7 million) had been prematurely recorded in fiscal 2005.

[8] In this proposed class action, it is alleged that IMAX misrepresented that: (a) its revenue for fiscal 2005 met or exceeded the Company's previously issued earnings guidance; (b) it had complied with GAAP; and (c) it had completed 14 theatre system installations in Q4 2005. The misrepresentations are alleged to have been made in IMAX's Form 10-K (including its Annual Report) and the February and March 2006 press releases.

• • •

[17] In the first motion, the plaintiffs seek leave under s. 138.8 of the OSA to proceed with the statutory cause of action contained in s. 138.3. Leave is mandatory if the plaintiffs establish that the action is brought in good faith and there is a reasonable possibility of success at trial.

[18] This is the first case in Ontario in which the court has been asked to grant leave in such an action. My main task on this motion will be to interpret and apply the leave requirement of s. 138.8 of the OSA.

[19] The statutory leave test involves a preliminary consideration of the merits of the action. In this regard, the parties filed more than 30 volumes of materials, consisting of affidavits, expert reports and public and non-public documents. A substantial part of these lengthy reasons is devoted to a review of the evidence, in order to determine whether the plaintiffs have a reasonable possibility of success in pursuing the statutory claims at trial.

• • •

[274] Subsection 138.8(1) of the OSA requires that any action claiming secondary market misrepresentation requires leave of the court, and provides as follows:

> No action may be commenced under section 138.3 without leave of the court granted upon motion with notice to each defendant. The court shall grant leave only where it is satisfied that,
>
> (a) the action is being brought in good faith; and
>
> (b) there is a reasonable possibility that the action will be resolved at trial in favour of the plaintiff.

[283] This section of the OSA has never been interpreted previously, and there are no other statutory provisions in force in a Canadian jurisdiction, that adopt the same type of test.

[284] How high the court should set the bar for a prospective plaintiff seeking to bring a claim for secondary market misrepresentation was the subject of extensive argument at the hearing of the motion, particularly in respect of how the court should interpret whether the plaintiffs have "a reasonable possibility of success at trial."

[285] The plaintiffs argue for a low threshold. The low bar would permit actions to proceed unless they are clearly an abuse of process or a "strike suit." The respondents, acknowledging in their factum that this action is not in fact a "strike suit," contend that the object of the leave test is to screen out unmeritorious actions. They argue for a more

stringent test, with onerous obligations on a plaintiff to establish their good faith and that the case has obvious merit.

. . .

[308] Accordingly, I interpret "good faith" in the context of s. 138.8, to require the plaintiffs to establish that they are bringing their action in the honest belief that they have an arguable claim, and for reasons that are consistent with the purpose of the statutory cause of action and not for an oblique or collateral purpose. "Good faith" involves a consideration of the subjective intentions of the plaintiffs in bringing their action, which is to be determined by considering the objective evidence.

[309] I am satisfied that the plaintiffs are acting in good faith in pursuing these proceedings. They have a personal financial interest in the action, as persons who acquired IMAX shares during the Class Period and continued to hold such shares on August 9, 2006. They have also asserted altruistic reasons for commencing the action, to hold the defendants accountable for misrepresentations to the public, and to send a message to directors and officers of other public companies that they too will be held accountable for misrepresentations to the public. These reasons for pursuing the action are consistent with the legislative purpose of the statutory remedy, which is deterrence. The plaintiffs have pleaded a misrepresentation that is supported by the evidence of the Company's Restatement. There is no evidence of any ulterior motive or conflict of interest. Accordingly, they meet the first branch of the test for leave to assert a claim for secondary market misrepresentation.

. . .

[334] Considering all of the factors noted above, I have approached part two of the leave test by asking myself whether, on the evidence that is before the court on this motion—that is the affidavits and transcripts of examinations, as well as the various documents that have been tendered as exhibits, and produced in response to undertakings and ordered to be produced during the cross-examination process—as well as reasonable inferences to be drawn from such evidence, and considering the onus of proof for each of the cause of action and the defences, as well as the limitations of evaluating credibility in a motion, is there a reasonable possibility that the plaintiffs will succeed at trial in proving:

> (i) that IMAX's Form 10-K/Annual Report and/or its February and March press releases contained a misrepresentation as alleged by the plaintiffs;
>
> (ii) with respect to Joyce and Gamble, that they authorized, permitted or acquiesced in the release of a document containing the misrepresentation;
>
> (iii) if the alleged misrepresentations were contained only in the press releases (as non-core documents), that the Individual Defendants and Gamble knew of the misrepresentation, deliberately avoided acquiring knowledge or were guilty of gross misconduct in connection with their release;

and, with respect to the defences relied upon by each respondent, is there a reasonable possibility that such respondent will not be able to establish at trial both elements of the defence of "reasonable investigation"; namely:

> (i) that the respondent conducted or caused to be conducted a "reasonable investigation"; and

(ii) at the time of the release of the document the respondent had no reasonable grounds to believe that the document contained the misrepresentation;

or, to the extent the expert reliance defence is applicable:

(i) that the respondent did not know that there had been a misrepresentation in the part of the document made on the authority of the expert; and

(ii) the respondent had no reasonable grounds to believe that there had been a misrepresentation in the part of the document made on the authority of the expert.

[335] With respect to the loss causation defence in s. 138.5(3), is there a reasonable possibility that the respondents will not be able to establish that the plaintiffs' entire loss is attributable to a change in the market price of securities that is unrelated to the misrepresentation?

[336] While the statute speaks of leave in the general sense, that is leave to proceed with the action, I have approached this task individually with respect to each respondent. If on the evidence at this stage, the plaintiffs do not have a reasonable possibility of success at trial against a specific Individual Defendant or proposed defendant, the statutory action will not be permitted to proceed against that person.

[337] I reach this conclusion because of the requirement under s. 138.8(2) for each defendant to deliver an affidavit setting forth the material facts upon which he or she intends to rely, and s. 138.8(3) providing for the examination of each affiant. Indeed in this case, each respondent filed an affidavit and has been cross-examined with respect to the statutory defences, and an examination of the defences as they would apply to each individually is possible and appropriate.

[338] With respect to the application of the damages cap, the respondents assert that the court must consider whether to grant leave to assert a claim exceeding the damages cap for the individual respondents based on whether they authorized, permitted, acquiesced in or influenced the making of the misrepresentation while knowing that it was a misrepresentation (s. 138.7(2)).

[339] As noted, the plaintiffs have pleaded facts that would exceed the damages cap only in respect of the Individual Defendants and Gamble. It is unnecessary at the leave stage to determine whether there is a reasonable possibility that the damages cap will be exceeded. The statutory threshold speaks of a reasonable possibility of success at trial, and does not invite the court to make specific findings with respect to the measure of success the plaintiffs might hope to achieve against a particular respondent. Provided that there is a reasonable possibility that the action will succeed against a particular respondent, the claim against that person should be permitted to proceed.

Silver v IMAX Corp

Appeal Book Endorsement, [2010] OJ No 6242 (QL) (CA)

THE COURT:

Disposition of Motion

[1] This is an action that has been certified as a class proceeding. At the same time as she made an order certifying the proceeding, Justice van Rensburg of the Superior Court of Justice made an order granting leave to the plaintiffs to plead secondary market misrepresentation pursuant to s. 138.3 of the Securities Act, R.S.O. 1990, c. 5.5. The defendants seek to appeal the order granting leave.

[2] The plaintiffs move to quash the appeal on the basis that the leave order is an interlocutory order rather than a final order and that the appeal therefore lies to the Divisional Court with leave of that Court. We agree.

[3] The leave order is a procedural interlocutory order. It does not finally dispose of the matter at issue between the parties or decide the issue in the action or proceeding: *Hendrickson v. Kallio*, [1932] O.R. 675; *Buck Brothers Ltd v. Frontenac Builders Ltd.* (1994), 19 O.R. (3d) 97 (C.A.); *Bell Canada v. The Plan Group* (2009), 96 O.R. (3d) 81 (C.A.). It does not eliminate a defence open to the defendants and "thereby deprive the defendant of a substantive right which could be determinative of the entire action": *Ball v. Donis* (1993), 13 O.R. (3d) 322 (C.A.). Imax's argument that the leave order finally determines the issue of whether an action can be commenced at all, is simply another way of saying that the order determines the question raised on the motion; but that basis for saying that an order is "final" has been consistently rejected since *Hendrickson v. Kallio*. Imax remains able to raise any and all defences available to it in response to the secondary market misrepresentation proceeding. If successful, it will defeat the claim. Until that issue is finally disposed of, however, the leave order is simply a procedural step in the action permitting the claim to proceed.

[4] The motion to quash is therefore granted.

[5] Cost to the moving party fixed of $5,000 all inclusive.

Originally, the certified class was to include all persons who purchased or acquired IMAX securities on or after February 17, 2006 and continued to hold some or all of the securities at the close of trading on the TSX and NASDAQ on August 9, 2006. In other words, the class was a global one. But on March 19, 2013, the defendants brought a motion to amend the class definition. Settlement proceedings had since been concluded in the United States, and the defendants argued that "overlapping" class members—those investors who could have their claims settled in both Ontario and US proceedings—should be excluded from the Ontario class. In the following excerpt, the court considers the defendants' arguments in the context of global securities class actions.

Silver v IMAX
2013 ONSC 1667 (footnotes omitted)

VAN RENSBURG J:

I. Nature of the Motion

[1] This is another chapter in the proceedings involving alleged misrepresentation to the secondary market in respect of the financial reporting and recognition of revenue for theatre systems of IMAX Corporation ("IMAX"), a Canadian public company whose shares are dual-listed on the TSX and the NASDAQ.

[2] This motion arises out of the fact that there are overlapping class proceedings in Ontario and in the U.S. with respect to the subject matter of this action. The U.S. Proceedings were described in my decision certifying a global class in this action (the "Certification Decision"). My decision respecting the timing, content and distribution of the notice of certification (the "Notice Decision") referred to the developments that had occurred by that stage, when a proposed settlement was pending in the U.S. Proceedings. The settlement has now received approval from the U.S. Court, subject to an order amending the class definition in these proceedings.

[3] In this motion, the defendants seek an order amending the class definition in this action to exclude from the certified class all persons who will be bound by a final judgment approving the pending settlement of the U.S. Proceedings.

[4] The settlement in the U.S. Proceedings is conditional on an order from this court amending the class in this way. If the order is granted, there will be no further review by the U.S. Court, and the settlement in the U.S. Proceedings will be concluded. If the order is not granted, the settlement will not proceed, and the U.S. Action will revert to the stage it was at when the settlement was reached, that is, as a proposed class action that had not yet been certified.

[5] The defendants assert that this court has authority under the *Class Proceedings Act*, 1992, S.O. 1992, c. 6 (the "CPA") to amend the class definition, and that, consistent with the principles of comity, the court should respect the jurisdiction and authority of the U.S. court that has already considered, among other things, the fairness of the proposed settlement.

[6] *In Currie v. McDonald's Restaurants of Canada Ltd.*, (2005), 74 O.R. (3d) 321 (C.A.), the Court of Appeal established the test for recognition by an Ontario court of a foreign judgment approving a class action settlement, so as to preclude an action for the same relief in our jurisdiction. The case involved the enforcement of a U.S. judgment approving a class action settlement that purported to bind Ontario residents. The defendants in the present case assert that the order requested should be granted because the U.S. Court, which had jurisdiction, has already approved the settlement. In the alternative, they argue that this court should apply the factors in *Currie*, to grant the order requested, and to thereby facilitate the conclusion of the settlement reached in the U.S. Proceedings.

[7] The plaintiffs' counsel contend that this motion is in substance a request for the court to approve a settlement, and that the court should decline to do so because the settlement is insufficient and unfair. They point out that this is a case of first impression, that there is no precedent for the relief that the defendants are seeking, and that, if the order is granted, as they put it, the effect will be to "rip the guts out" of the pending Ontario class

action. Since almost no one opted out of the U.S. settlement class, what will be left in the Ontario action will be a much smaller class, comprised almost entirely of only TSX purchasers (approximately 15% of the global class certified by this court).

[8] I have set out the arguments of the parties only briefly at this stage. Later in this decision I will consider their submissions in greater detail.

II. The Cross-Border Context

[9] In his decision refusing leave to appeal from both the Certification Decision and my decision granting leave for the plaintiffs to pursue a statutory claim for secondary market misrepresentation (the "Leave Decision"), Corbett J. had this to say about the parallel proceedings:

> van Rensburg J. accurately stated and applied the test for defining classes in class proceedings. The implementation of Her Honour's decision, in a manner harmonious with proper respect for the exercise of jurisdiction by the American courts, will, no doubt, unfold over time as the two cases proceed. …
>
> … [The U.S. Action and the Ontario Action] are and should be complementary, to achieve a proper vindication of the rights of plaintiffs, fair process for the defendants and plaintiffs, respect for the autonomous jurisdictions involved, and an integrated and efficient resolution of claims. This requires common sense, judicial comity, and fair process. It does not require balkanization of class proceedings, but rather sensitive integration of them.

[10] Corbett J.'s hope for a "sensitive integration" of the parallel proceedings does not appear to have been realised. Nevertheless, he identified certain objectives that in my view are relevant here: the vindication of the rights of plaintiffs, fair process for the defendants and plaintiffs, and respect for the autonomous jurisdictions involved.

[11] There have been numerous settlements of parallel class actions approved by Canadian courts that have involved a resolution of all pending proceedings. While this may be the typical practice, and while there have been calls for reform, especially in respect of parallel class actions in Canadian provinces, there is currently no legal requirement for the integration of parallel class proceedings, or for the co-operation of cross-border counsel and courts in the litigation or resolution of such proceedings.

[12] The legal position is therefore that the court in each jurisdiction where an overlapping class proceeding is pending, is autonomous. Parallel proceedings are permissible and not uncommon. The actions may or may not proceed in tandem; counsel may or may not consult with or work with one another. Ultimately, one case may reach judgment before the other. This is, as U.S. conflicts of laws expert, Professor Patrick Borchers, puts it, "the day of reckoning," after which the second court would be asked to recognize the judgment of the other court, so as to preclude the continuation of the parallel proceedings in favour of persons bound by the settlement.

[13] The defendants could have settled the U.S. Proceedings, and obtained the approval of the U.S. Court, and then sought to enforce the settlement here by precluding the claims of the overlapping class members. They did not proceed in this manner, instead seeking in advance an order that would have the effect of preclusion of the claims of overlapping class members who did not opt out of the U.S. Settlement, by removing such persons from the certified Ontario class.

[14] The defendants contend that it was necessary and reasonable to proceed in this manner rather than to face the uncertainty of not knowing whether a judgment approving a U.S. settlement would be given preclusive effect in Ontario. In *Currie*, after all, the Ontario court refused to enforce a U.S. judgment approving a settlement to preclude a pending Ontario proceeding. In *Canada Post Corporation v. Lépine*, 2009 SCC 16, [2009] 1 S.C.R. 549, the decision of a Québec court refusing to give preclusive effect to an Ontario judgment approving the settlement of a national class action, was upheld on appeal. In *Hocking v. Haziza*, 2008 QCCA 800, [2008] Q.J. No. 3423 (C.A.), the Québec Court of Appeal upheld a decision refusing to recognize and enforce an Ontario judgment approving a national class action settlement. In *Meeking v. The Cash Store Inc.*, 2012 MBQB 58, [2012] M.J. No. 60 (Q.B.), the Manitoba Court of Queen's Bench recognized the preclusive effect of an Ontario judgment approving a multi-provincial class action settlement (except with respect to certain claims where inadequate notice had been given).

[15] In an expert report filed by the defendants in support of this motion, Professor John Coffee, a U.S. class actions expert, observed:

> … [N]o rational defendant will be willing to settle under a procedure that gives those class members who are currently covered by both classes the right to claim compensation under the U.S. Action, while also reserving the right to share under a potentially higher judgment (or settlement) later obtained in the Ontario Action. If the class members in the Ontario Action who purchased on Nasdaq were allowed to remain in both classes, the defendants could be required to fund two overlapping resolutions on both sides of the border (either two settlements, or the present settlement in the U.S. Action and a later judgment in the Ontario Action). …
>
> This prospect makes it foolish for defendants to settle in the U.S. Action because that earlier settlement would be an illusory settlement that did not cap their liability to the overlapping members of these two classes. Faced with this two-front war, defendants cannot settle—unless the class definition in the second action is adjusted to eliminate the overlap, or a global settlement is reached.

[16] Accordingly, the central issue in this motion is whether this court should recognize the settlement that has been approved by the U.S. Court and give effect to the settlement by carving out of the certified global class those persons who would be covered by the U.S. Settlement, or whether such persons should remain in the Ontario class until their claims are determined in these proceedings, whether on the merits, or in the context of a court-approved settlement of these proceedings.

III. Decision

[17] For the reasons that follow, the relief sought by the defendants is granted. The class in these proceedings is amended as per the proposed wording in paragraph 25 of the Defendants' Reply Factum.

[18] In arriving at this decision, I have applied the factors from the Court of Appeal's decision in *Currie* with respect to when a decision of a foreign court purporting to settle claims of class members that are the subject of parallel proceedings in Ontario, will be given preclusive effect. Having determined that the U.S. Court has a "real and substantial

connection" with the claims of the overlapping class members, I have considered whether there was procedural fairness in the treatment of such claims (including the adequacy of notice and representation in the proceedings). Having found that the U.S. Settlement should be recognized, I have considered all of the circumstances, including the current status of these proceedings, before concluding that the Ontario Action is no longer the "preferable procedure" for the determination of the claims of class members whose claims are covered by, and who have not opted out of, the U.S. Settlement. The class definition in these proceedings is amended accordingly.

Canadian Imperial Bank of Commerce v Green, 2015 SCC 60, [2015] 3 SCR 801 is related to the *IMAX* case. The SCC was forced to consider the relationship between CPA s 28 and the statutory limitation period specified by OSA s 138.14, which reads:

> 138.14(1) No action shall be commenced under section 138.3,
> (a) in the case of misrepresentation in a document, later than the earlier of,
> (i) three years after the date on which the document containing the misrepresentation was first released, and
> (ii) six months after the issuance of a news release disclosing that leave has been granted to commence an action under section 138.3 or under comparable legislation in the other provinces or territories in Canada in respect of the same misrepresentation;
> (b) in the case of a misrepresentation in a public oral statement, later than the earlier of,
> (i) three years after the date on which the public oral statement containing the misrepresentation was made, and
> (ii) six months after the issuance of a news release disclosing that leave has been granted to commence an action under section 138.3 or under comparable legislation in another province or territory of Canada in respect of the same misrepresentation; and
> (c) in the case of a failure to make timely disclosure, later than the earlier of,
> (i) three years after the date on which the requisite disclosure was required to be made, and
> (ii) six months after the issuance of a news release disclosing that leave has been granted to commence an action under section 138.3 or under comparable legislation in another province or territory of Canada in respect of the same failure to make timely disclosure.

This limitation period was set to run out before leave for the statutory cause of action under OSA s 138.3 could be obtained. However, s 28 of the CPA states:

> 28(1) Subject to subsection (2), any limitation period applicable to a cause of action asserted in a class proceeding is suspended in favour of a class member on the commencement of the class proceeding and resumes running against the class member when,
> (a) the member opts out of the class proceeding;
> (b) an amendment that has the effect of excluding the member from the class is made to the certification order;
> (c) a decertification order is made under section 10;
> (d) the class proceeding is dismissed without an adjudication on the merits;
> (e) the class proceeding is abandoned or discontinued with the approval of the court; or
> (f) the class proceeding is settled with the approval of the court, unless the settlement provides otherwise.

The question, then, was whether s 28 of the CPA had worked to suspend the three-year limitation period set out in OSA s 138.14(1). That is, could the limitation period be suspended, even if the class members had not yet received leave to commence a statutory action? The SCC in *Green* answered in the negative, holding:

> Pleading an intention to seek leave in respect of a s. 138.3 *OSA* claim in a class proceeding together with a common law cause of action amounts to neither the assertion of the statutory cause of action nor the commencement of a class proceeding for that statutory cause of action under s. 28 *CPA*. Accordingly, the limitation period at s. 138.14 *OSA* cannot be suspended in favour of the class members under s. 28 *CPA* before leave is granted under s. 138.8 *OSA* to commence the statutory action.

Students should note that Ontario had actually already answered this question by the time the SCC delivered its decision in *Green*. The legislature introduced OSA, s 138.14(2) in 2014:

> 138.14(2) A limitation period established by subsection (1) in respect of an action is suspended on the date a notice of motion for leave under section 138.8 is filed with the court and resumes running on the date,
> (a) the court grants leave or dismisses the motion and,
> (i) all appeals have been exhausted, or
> (ii) the time for an appeal has expired without an appeal being filed; or
> (b) the motion is abandoned or discontinued.

In December 2015, the SCC rendered its decision in *Theratechnologies Inc v 121851 Canada Inc*, excerpted below. This judgment is now the leading case on the test for leave to pursue a secondary market liability claim. Although decided in reference to the Québec *Securities Act*, *Theratechnologies* provides an in-depth discussion of what a plaintiff must show in order to move forward with a secondary market liability claim. Students should pay close attention to the SCC's reasons for finding that the relevant threshold requirements had not been met by 121851.

Theratechnologies Inc v 121851 Canada Inc

2015 SCC 18, [2015] 2 SCR 106

ABELLA J (McLachlin CJ and Rothstein, Cromwell, Moldaver, Karakatsanis, and Wagner JJ concurring):

[1] The genesis of this case was a new drug application to the U.S. Food and Drug Administration (FDA) by a pharmaceutical research and development company based in Montréal. As is common during the new drug approval process, the FDA referred a number of questions about this drug to an expert Advisory Committee, including questions about the drug's potential side effects. The FDA also made these questions public as part of a package of briefing materials on its website. When the questions were publicized by stock quotation enterprises, the price of the company's shares dropped sharply.

[2] A holding company that sold its shares during this period sought authorization to bring a class action for damages under s. 225.4 of the *Securities Act*, CQLR, c. V-1.1, alleging a breach of statutory disclosure obligations.

[3] In 2007, changes to the *Securities Act* created a new statutory cause of action that enabled investors to bring claims against reporting issuers who breach their obligation

to disclose material facts and changes to their shareholders. Actions for damages may not be brought without the prior authorization of the court pursuant to s. 225.4. A court will grant authorization "if it deems that the action is in good faith and there is a reasonable possibility that it will be resolved in favour of the plaintiff." The issue in this appeal is whether there was a "reasonable possibility" of success within the meaning of this provision.

[4] I agree with the Court of Appeal that the threshold set out in s 225.4 for authorization requires more than a mere possibility of success, but, with great respect, do not share its conclusion that the threshold was met in this case.

Background

. . .

[17] … Section 225.4 states:

> 225.4 No action for damages may be brought under this division without the prior authorization of the court.
>
> The request for authorization must state the facts giving rise to the action. It must be filed together with the projected statement of claim and be notified by bailiff to the parties concerned, with a notice of at least 10 days of the date of presentation.
>
> The court grants authorization if it deems that the action is *in good faith* and there is *a reasonable possibility that it will be resolved in favour of the plaintiff*.

[18] The Motions Judge concluded that the authorization mechanism in s. 225.4 of the *Securities Act* imposed a higher threshold than art. 1003 of the *Code of Civil Procedure*, CQLR, c. C-25 (C.C.P.), which deals with the authorization of class actions generally, but found sufficient evidence to support the conclusion that 121851's action had a reasonable possibility of success.

[19] An appeal by Thera to the Court of Appeal was dismissed. The Court of Appeal agreed with the Motions Judge that the screening mechanism under s. 225.4 was more stringent than for the authorization of a class action under art. 1003 of the *Code of Civil Procedure* and required more than a mere possibility of success. It noted that the legislative intention behind s. 225.4 was to make the provision a more robust screening mechanism.

[20] Based on documentary evidence and Mr. St-Germain's testimony, the Court of Appeal was of the view that there was a reasonable possibility that the action would be resolved in his company's favour. As a result, it upheld the order authorizing an action for damages.

Analysis

[21] Section 225.4 of the *Securities Act* is part of a new regime of statutory civil liability to address breaches of disclosure obligations in the secondary market, the market in which a company's shares are traded publicly after they have been issued or distributed by the company. This provision sets out two substantive criteria for the authorization of an action for damages: the action must be brought in good faith and there must be a reasonable possibility that it will be resolved in favour of the claimant. There is no dispute that 121851's action is brought in good faith. This case turns then on the interpretation of "a reasonable possibility" that 121851's action will be resolved in its favour. The history and

objectives of the authorization mechanism set by s. 225.4 in the context of the *Securities Act* as a whole assist in this exercise.

[22] Like its counterparts elsewhere in Canada, Quebec's *Securities Act* requires companies whose shares are traded in the secondary market to regularly disclose certain information to their security holders and the provincial securities regulator: s. 73; *Securities Act*, R.S.B.C. 1996, c. 418, s. 85; *Securities Act*, R.S.A. 2000, c. S-4, s. 147; *Securities Act*, R.S.O. 1990, c. S.5, s. 75; *Securities Act*, R.S.N.S. 1989, c. 418, s. 81; *Securities Act*, S.N.B. 2004, c. S-5.5, s. 89(1).

[23] Continuous disclosure obligations fall into two categories: periodic disclosure and timely disclosure. Periodic disclosure must be made at regular intervals, typically through the regular provision of documents such as proxy circulars, financial statements and insider trading reports. In these regularly issued documents, companies must disclose all material *facts*—that is, anything "that may reasonably be expected to have a significant effect on the market price or value of securities issued": *Securities Act* (Quebec), s. 5 "material fact."

[24] Timely disclosure obligations, on the other hand, are imposed only when there has been a material *change* in the issuer's affairs. Material changes, which arise from changes in the issuers' business, operations or capital, must be disclosed at the time they occur: *Securities Act* (Quebec), s. 5.3; Mark R. Gillen, *Securities Regulation in Canada* (3rd ed. 2007), at p. 211; David Johnston, Kathleen Doyle Rockwell and Cristie Ford: *Canadian Securities Regulation* (5th ed. 2014), at p. 249.

[25] Both periodic and timely disclosure obligations are designed to increase fairness in the secondary market:

> [Continuous disclosure] ... is designed to create a "level playing field" where all investors have access to the same information and all pricing and investment decisions are made from the same starting point. Of course, investors may still value securities differently, depending on how they interpret that information. Different investors have different goals, typically balanced between risk and return. Riskier investments generally yield higher returns, and vice versa. Securities regulation does not tell investors what to do, nor steer them toward or away from particular investments. It should, however, ensure that they have enough information to assess properly the risks involved and make fully informed decisions. [Footnote omitted; Johnston, Rockwell and Ford, at p. 249.]

As a result, the policy of ensuring this "level playing field" reified in statutory continuous disclosure obligations has been called "the most fundamental principle of securities regulation": *Cartaway Resources Corp. (Re)*, [2000] B.C.S.C.D. No. 92 (QL), at para. 216; *Cornish v. Ontario Securities Commission* (2013), 2013 ONSC 1310, 306 O.A.C. 107 (S.C.J.), at para. 40.

[26] Disclosure also supports capital market efficiency by helping investors target the most deserving securities and enhancing the accountability of corporate management: *Cornish*, at para. 40. As investors realize that they have the necessary information, they become more confident in the securities market, and their consequent increased participation leads to more efficient markets: Johnston, Rockwell and Ford, at p. 249.

[27] Section 225.4 emerged directly out of Canada-wide efforts to develop a more meaningful and accessible form of recourse for investors. Historically, Canadian investors in the secondary trading market did not have access to a statutory cause of action when

they suffered losses as a result of breaches of legislated continuous disclosure obligations. In common law jurisdictions, investors had to rely on the tort of negligent misrepresentation, which required, among other things, that investors prove that they had relied on the misinformation or omission of information to their detriment: A. C. Pritchard and Janis p. Sarra, "Securities Class Actions Move North: A Doctrinal and Empirical Analysis of Securities Class Actions in Canada" (2010), 47 *Alta. L. Rev.* 881, at p. 885. Because it was extremely difficult to prove such reliance when securities were purchased in the secondary market, this requirement put meaningful redress out of reach for many who were harmed by dubious disclosure practices: Joseph Groia and Pamela Hardie, *Securities Litigation and Enforcement* (2nd ed. 2012), at p. 352.

[28] In Quebec, investors faced a similarly heavy burden under the *Civil Code*. To establish civil liability, claimants were required to prove a fault, such as the publication of misinformation or the failure to meet a statutory disclosure obligation; that they suffered prejudice; and that there was a causal link between the fault and the prejudice—that is, that they had relied on the misinformation in making the trade: arts. 1457 and 1607 of the *Civil Code of Québec*. Demonstrating the requisite causal link proved to be particularly onerous in the securities context: Quebec, National Assembly, Committee on Public Finance, "Étude détaillée du projet de loi n° 19—Loi modifiant la Loi sur les valeurs mobilières et d'autres dispositions législatives," *Journal des débats de la Commission permanente des finances publiques*, vol. 40, No. 10, 1st Sess., 38th Leg., October 25, 2007 ("Étude detaillée"), at p. 2.

[29] During the 1990s, following a series of high profile misrepresentations and incidents of questionable disclosure practices among publicly traded companies in Canada, the Toronto Stock Exchange created the Allen Committee to re-examine the regime governing disclosure in the secondary market. The Allen Committee concluded that the "current sanctions and funding available to regulators … are inadequate" and "the remedies available to investors in secondary trading markets who are injured by misleading disclosure are so difficult to pursue that they are, as a practical matter, largely hypothetical": Committee on Corporate Disclosure, *Final Report—Responsible Corporate Disclosure: A Search for Balance* (Toronto Stock Exchange, 1997), at p. 5. It recommended the creation of a statutory civil liability regime that would help investors sue issuers, directors, and officers who violated their statutory disclosure obligations.

[30] The Canadian Securities Administrators, an umbrella organization of Canada's provincial and territorial securities regulators, adopted most of the Committee's recommendations and began developing proposals to implement them across Canada: "Proposal for a Statutory Civil Remedy for Investors in the Secondary Market and Response to the Proposed Change to the Definitions of 'Material Fact' and 'Material Change,'" CSA Notice 53-302, reproduced in (2000), 23 OSCB 7383. Despite the fact that the Allen Committee had not recommended it, and in order to discourage the kind of strike suits that had become common in the United States under more investor-friendly regimes, the Canadian Securities Administrators recommended that in addition to reducing the burden of proof on investors, the new liability regime should include a "screening mechanism" to ensure that only claims with a reasonable chance of success would be brought:

> This screening mechanism is designed not only to minimize the prospects of an adverse court award in the absence of a meritorious claim but, more importantly, *to try to ensure that unmeritorious litigation, and the time and expense it imposes on defendants, is avoided or*

> *brought to an end early in the litigation process.* By offering defendants the reasonable expectation that an unmeritorious action will be denied the requisite leave to be commenced, the 2000 Draft Legislation should better enable defendants to fend off coercive efforts by plaintiffs to negotiate the cash settlement that is often the real objective behind a strike suit. [Emphasis added; *ibid.*, at p. 7390.]

[31] In 2002, Ontario became the first province to implement the Canadian Securities Administrators' recommendations by inserting a new liability regime into its *Securities Act*. The legislation included a screening mechanism that limited actions against public companies for breaches of continuous disclosure obligations to those actions instituted in good faith with "a reasonable possibility" of being resolved at trial in favour of the plaintiff: s. 138.8(1).

[32] Quebec implemented the recommendations of the Canadian Securities Administrators through Bill 19, *An Act to amend the Securities Act and other legislative provisions*, S.Q. 2007, c. 15, which received assent on November 9, 2007. When Bill 19 was before the legislature, Monique Jérôme-Forget, the Minister of Finance at the time, said:

> [TRANSLATION] The recourse proposed in Bill 19 is highly harmonized with that in place in Ontario, which is recourse that strongly inspired the other provinces and territories. Only the necessary adjustments were made to reflect civil law notions and vocabulary, and to ensure its harmonious integration into the Québec legislative corpus, including the Securities Act, into which it will be incorporated. ("Étude détaillee," at p. 1).

[33] Under this regime, when a security is acquired or transferred at the time of a false declaration or omission of information that should have been disclosed, the fluctuation in the value of the security is presumed to be attributable to that fault. Investors were thereby released from the heavy burden of demonstrating that the variation in the market price of the security was linked to the misinformation or omission, and from demonstrating that they personally relied on that information or omission in buying or transferring the security.

[34] The scheme also establishes an authorization mechanism to permit only actions in good faith with a "reasonable possibility of success." As the Court of Appeal noted, Quebec's new regime therefore reflected an attempt to strike a balance between preventing unmeritorious litigation and strike suits and, at the same time, ensuring that investors have a meaningful remedy when issuers breach disclosure obligations.

[35] Given this history, I agree with the Court of Appeal and Motions Judge that the "reasonable possibility" of success required under s. 225.4 sets out a different and higher standard than the general threshold for the authorization of a class action under art. 1003 of the *C.C.P.* Under art. 1003, the court seeks only to identify whether "the facts alleged seem to justify the conclusions sought"—that is, whether the applicant has established "a good colour of right": *Infineon Technologies AG v. Option consommateurs*, 2013 SCC 59, [2013] 3 S.C.R. 600, at para. 62; *Guimond v. Quebec (Attorney General)*, [1996] 3 S.C.R. 347, at paras. 5 and 9-10; *Marcotte v. Longueuil (City)*, 2009 SCC 43, [2009] 3 S.C.R. 65, at para. 94. As this Court pointed out in *Infineon Technologies*, the low threshold for authorizing a class action under art. 1003 of the *C.C.P.* reflects the "twin objectives of deterrence and compensation that animate the class action system": para. 125.

[36] The Quebec legislature used different language in s. 225.4 to create a more meaningful screening mechanism in the securities context so that costly strike suits and unmeritorious claims would be prevented. Courts are given an important gatekeeping role, which requires them to conduct a preliminary examination of the impugned action or inaction to assess whether it could be said to have a reasonable possibility of success: Pritchard and Sarra, at p. 893. The question before us is as Belobaba J. asked in *Ironworkers Ontario Pension Fund (Trustee of) v. Manulife Financial Corp.* (2013), 2013 ONSC 4083, 44 C.P.C. (7th) 80 (Ont. S.C.J.):

> Is this simply a screening mechanism to keep out "strike suits" that are plainly unmeritorious and have no chance of success? Or, is this a preliminary merits test that should have more bite? [para. 36]

[37] I am aware that there has been some discussion in the Ontario and British Columbia courts about what the threshold is, all seeking to find a balance between preventing cases without a realistic prospect of success but encouraging those with a likelihood of success: *Silver v. Imax Corp.* (2009), 66 B.L.R. (4th) 222 (Ont. S.C.J.), at para. 324, leave to appeal refused (2011), 105 O.R. (3d) 212 (Div. Ct.); *Dobbie v. Arctic Glacier Income Fund* (2011), 2011 ONSC 25, 3 C.P.C. (7th) 261 (Ont. S.C.J.), at paras. 129-30; *Round v. MacDonald, Dettwiler and Associates Ltd.*, 2011 BCSC 1416, at para. 76, aff'd (2012), 39 B.C.L.R. (5th) 44 (C.A.); *Millwright Regional Council of Ontario Pension Trust Fund (Trustees of) v. Celestica Inc.* (2014), 2014 ONSC 1057, 49 C.P.C. (7th) 12 (Ont. S.C.J.), at para. 112; *Millwright Regional Council of Ontario Pension Trust Fund (Trustees of) v. Celestica Inc.* (2014), 2014 ONCA 90, 118 O.R. (3d) 641 (C.A.), at paras. 81-89.

[38] In my view, as Belobaba J. suggested in *Ironworkers*, the threshold should be more than a "speed bump" (para. 39), and the courts must undertake a reasoned consideration of the evidence to ensure that the action has some merit. In other words, to promote the legislative objective of a robust deterrent screening mechanism so that cases without merit are prevented from proceeding, the threshold requires that there be a reasonable or realistic chance that the action will succeed.

[39] A case with a reasonable possibility of success requires the claimant to offer both a plausible analysis of the applicable legislative provisions, and some credible evidence in support of the claim. This approach, in my view, best realizes the legislative intent of the screening mechanism: to ensure that cases with little chance of success—and the time and expense they impose—are avoided. I agree with the Court of Appeal, however, that the authorization stage under s. 225.4 should not be treated as a mini-trial. A full analysis of the evidence is unnecessary. If the goal of the screening mechanism is to prevent costly strike suits and litigation with little chance of success, it follows that the evidentiary requirements should not be so onerous as to essentially replicate the demands of a trial. To impose such a requirement would undermine the objective of the screening mechanism, which is to protect reporting issuers from unsubstantiated strike suits and costly unmeritorious litigation. What *is* required is sufficient evidence to persuade the court that there is a reasonable possibility that the action will be resolved in the claimant's favour.

[40] 121851 alleges that Thera breached its obligation under s. 73 of the *Securities Act* to provide timely disclosure of material changes to its investors. Section 5.3 of the *Securities Act* defines a "material change" as

> a *change in the business, operations or capital of the issuer* that would reasonably be expected to have a significant effect on the market price or value of any of the securities of the issuer, or a decision to implement such a change made by the directors or by senior management of the issuer who believe that confirmation of the decision by the directors is probable.

As this statutory definition makes clear, a material change has two components. There must be a change in the business, operations or capital of the issuer and the change must be material, which means it would reasonably be expected to have a significant effect on the market price or value of the securities of the issuer: *Securities Act*, s. 5.3. Both elements are required to trigger an obligation of timely disclosure.

[41] 121851 argues that a material change occurred on May 11, 2010, when Thera received the FDA briefing materials, which included a Background Introductory Memorandum asking the Advisory Committee to comment on "the findings of glucose intolerance and development of diabetes associated with Egrifta [tesamorelin] therapy and its impact on longterm cardiovascular risk." This information was made public on May 25, 2010, when the FDA posted the memorandum, alongside all the briefing materials it had generated on tesamorelin, on its website.

[42] In my view, however, 121851 has not pointed to any evidence that could qualify as a material change in Thera's operations, capital or business as described in s. 5.3 of the *Securities Act*. And without some evidence of a material change that corresponds to the statutory requirements, 121851's action cannot reasonably hope to succeed.

[43] Tesamorelin operates by activating a growth hormone, which, in other contexts, has been associated with an increased risk of diabetes. Thera's phase-three clinical trials measured the blood sugar levels of participating patients to evaluate the risk associated with this potential side effect. The trials compared five glycemic parameters recognized by the scientific community and the American Diabetes Association in patients taking tesamorelin and patients taking a placebo, and revealed that tesamorelin did not have a clinically significant effect on the glucose levels of patients.

[44] The results of the clinical trials were disclosed to shareholders as they became available. In its November 2008 Annual Notice, for example, Thera summarized its clinical results to date and noted that

> the administration of [the hormone] is not indicated for glucose-intolerant patients, a condition often observed in these patients. Consequently, Theratechnologies decided to study the effect of tesamorelin in the treatment of this condition. Highlights of the study included a good safety profile, a clear effect on body composition and a clinically relevant reduction in visceral fat while subcutaneous fat was preserved.

[45] On November 11, 2009, Thera, in collaboration with two external experts, presented the combined results of its two phase-three clinical trials at the 12th European AIDS Conference. The fact of this presentation and its content were disclosed to investors via a press release, which stated that "[n]o clinically important changes in glucose parameters were observed after treatment with tesamorelin…"

[46] On March 1, 2010, Thera issued a press release announcing the publication of a study detailing its combined clinical results in the publicly available *Journal of Acquired Immune Deficiency Syndromes*. The press release provided a link to the study, which included an abstract highlighting the clinical results and concluding that the potential side effects of tesamorelin were not significant:

> Tesamorelin reduces visceral fat by approximately 18% and improves body image distress in HIV-infected patients with central fat accumulation. These changes are achieved without significant side effects or perturbation of glucose. [p. 311]

[47] Through these press releases, Thera disclosed to its shareholders that it was monitoring tesamorelin's side effects, including on patients' blood sugar levels. It provided both summaries and full studies detailing the results of its clinical trials. There is no allegation that any of these reports were either false or misleading. A reasonable investor who read Thera's news releases would have known that blood sugar issues and diabetes were potential side effects of the drug, and that Thera's clinical trials had found they were not clinically significant.

[48] As a result, this case can be distinguished from *Pezim v. British Columbia (Superintendent of Brokers)*, [1994] 2 S.C.R. 557, in which the Court held that information contained in drilling results regarding a mining company's exploration site could constitute a material change in the "business, operations, assets or ownership of the issuer," since they could reasonably be expected to significantly affect the company's assets. Unlike the drilling results at issue in *Pezim*, the potential side effects of tesamorelin had already been disclosed to shareholders well before the FDA published its questions and the rest of its briefing materials. There was no new information about the side effects of tesamorelin that required timely disclosure as of May 11, 2010.

[49] 121851's argument is more analogous to the claim in *Kerr v. Danier Leather Inc.*, 2007 SCC 44, [2007] 3 S.C.R. 331. The company, which was making an initial public offering (IPO) of its shares, had issued preliminary prospectuses which included a sales forecast for the fourth quarter of the fiscal year to its potential investors. Unseasonably warm weather, however, knocked the company's sales forecasts off track as the quarter progressed. After its IPO had closed, the company disclosed its intra-quarterly results in a press release, triggering a sharp drop in its share value. Although the company ultimately realized its initial sales forecasts, the claimants launched a class action, alleging that the company had withheld the intra-quarterly results to ensure the success of its IPO.

[50] This Court held that the intra-quarterly results did not constitute a material change to the business, operations or capital of the company because the warm weather that triggered the drop in sales was external to the company and its business:

> … a change in intra-quarterly results is not itself a change in the issuer's business, operations or capital and, for that matter, does not necessarily signal that a material change has occurred. Sales often fluctuate (as here) in response to factors that are external to the issuer.
>
> It almost goes without saying that poor intra-quarterly results may *reflect* a material change in business operations. A company that has, for example, restructured its operations may experience poor intra-quarterly results because of this restructuring, but it is the restructuring and not the results themselves that would amount to a material change and thus trigger the disclosure obligation. Additionally, poor intra-quarterly results may motivate a company to implement a change in its business, operations or capital in an effort to improve performance. Again, though, the disclosure obligation would be triggered by the change in the business, operations or capital, and not by the results themselves. [Emphasis in original; paras. 46-47.]

[51] The same is true in this case. 121851 argues that the FDA's preoccupation with the side effects represents a material change in Thera's operations, business or capital. But it

has not pointed to any evidence to suggest that the questions the FDA posed to its Advisory Committee about these side effects, or the contents of its Briefing Package more generally, departed in any way from the regular and routine process through which the FDA assesses whether a drug should be approved. Nor is there any evidence that the questions reflected new and undisclosed information about tesamorelin. In fact, the evidence on the record suggests the opposite. It is FDA policy to prepare briefing materials for an Advisory Committee, including information compiled by both the FDA and the sponsoring company, and to post those materials two days before an Advisory Committee meeting. Questions from the FDA to its expert Advisory Committee about the side effects of a drug do not constitute a departure from the normal FDA process, or, necessarily an indication of whether the drug will be approved. Rather, they are a routine step in the FDA's work to determine whether a drug's benefits outweigh its risks. As such, it is difficult to characterize these questions as any kind of change to Thera's business, operations, or capital requiring a reassuring public response from Thera.

[52] 121851 argues that the market's reaction demonstrates that the FDA's concerns about side effects constitute a material change. It points out that the Canadian Securities Administrators' "National Policy 51-201 Disclosure Standards" includes among its list of potentially "material" information "any development that affects the company's resources, technology, products or markets": Article 4.3. Because this example falls under the subheading of "changes in business and operations," 121851 submits that the FDA's questions are a development that could be considered a material change.

[53] This section of the policy, however, deals with the market impact of events, not whether they are best characterized as material facts or material changes. To adopt this list as dispositive of whether there was a change in the business, operations or capital of a reporting issuer would collapse the distinction between material facts and material changes, significantly expanding timely disclosure obligations beyond what is required by statute. This would, in effect, allow the Canadian Securities Administrators' policy to amend Quebec's securities legislation, contrary to this Court's ruling in *Pezim*.

[54] It is true that Thera had sometimes disclosed routine aspects of the FDA process in press releases to its shareholders in the months leading up to the Advisory Committee meeting, but this does not bring the FDA's questions to its Advisory Committee within the statutory definition of a material change. Thera had a statutory duty to disclose material changes in its operations, capital or business in a timely manner, not to reassure its investors at every stage of the FDA approval process.

[55] Finally, even if Thera had issued a press release on May 11, 2010 after it received the FDA's briefing materials, it is not clear what reassurance Thera could have provided at this stage, given that the outcome of the FDA process, as every reasonable investor would have known and as Thera repeatedly made clear, is always uncertain. As the U.S. Supreme Court acknowledged *in TSC Industries, Inc. v. Northway, Inc.*, 426 U.S. 438 (1976), there are risks of excessive disclosure, which could "simply … bury the shareholders in an avalanche of trivial information—a result that is hardly conducive to informed decisionmaking": pp. 448-49, cited in *Cornish*, at para. 41.

[56] Because the evidence does not credibly point to a material change that could have triggered timely disclosure obligations, there is no reasonable possibility that 121851's action under s. 73 of the *Securities Act* could succeed. I would allow the appeal with costs.

In 2015, Belobabba J (speaking for the Ontario Superior Court of Justice) adopted the reasonable possibility standard in *Theratechnologies* in *Coffin v Atlantic Power Corp*, 2015 ONSC 3686 (footnotes omitted):

> [18] In *Theratechnologies*, the Supreme Court provided a much-needed clarification of the "reasonable possibility" standard. The Court made clear that the leave threshold was more than a "speed bump" and that judges should undertake "a reasoned consideration of the evidence to ensure that the action has some merit." The "reasonable possibility" threshold, said the Court, requires that there be a "reasonable or realistic chance that the action will succeed."

VI. CHAPTER SUMMARY

The statutory regime relating to misrepresentations in an issuer's disclosure documents is complex, containing a number of defences for directors, professionals, and others who may otherwise be liable for a misrepresentation or omission in the disclosure. Case law, in particular the *Danier* case, is an important aspect of the contemporary legal regime, and students must read and be aware of this case in order to understand the liability regime as a whole. Finally, the statutory regime has been extended to include liability for misrepresentations contained in secondary market continuous disclosure documents. As the *IMAX* proceedings demonstrate, Ontario courts have only just begun to tackle issues like class certification and the increasing complexity of secondary market liability. *Theratechnologies* has since established a threshold requirement for bringing an action under secondary market liability provisions: there must be a "reasonable possibility" that the plaintiff's action—brought in good faith—"will succeed."

CHAPTER ELEVEN

Enforcement

I. INTRODUCTION

In recent years the adequacy of the enforcement of securities law has become a hot-button issue, largely because of a variety of securities market scandals involving allegations of misrepresentation and manipulation of financial reports, both in Canada and the United States. Rigorous enforcement has been construed as an essential element of restoring investor confidence in securities markets damaged by the bursting of the dot-com bubble (see (2001) 30:4 Economy & Soc'y); the Enron debacle (Peter Fusaro, *What Went Wrong at Enron: Everyone's Guide to the Largest Bankruptcy in US History* (Hoboken, NJ: Wiley, 2002)); and, more recently, the global financial crisis. For example, the ABCP crisis in Canada has produced calls for more vigorous enforcement. As we shall see later in this chapter, enforcement issues were identified both by the report of the Wise Persons' Committee (WPC) (Wise Persons' Committee to Review the Structure of Securities Regulation in Canada, *It's Time* (Ottawa: Department of Finance, 2003)) and by the Expert Panel on Securities Regulation in 2009 as a significant element of the justification for harmonizing the structure and substance of securities regulation across Canada. Meanwhile, the role of regulatory agencies in the enforcement of securities law has been cast in a negative light by academics who subscribe to the law and economics intellectual framework. According to this view, enforcement of appropriate practices in securities markets should be the province of investors who have been damaged, rather than within the ambit of regulators exercising discretionary powers (Jeffrey G MacIntosh, "Lessons of Bre-X (?): Some Comments" (1999) 32 Can Bus LJ 223-40; Rafael La Porta, Florencio Lopez-de-Silanes & Andrei Shleifer, "What Works in Securities Laws?" (2006) 61 J Fin 1. For an alternative view about the role of regulatory enforcement, see John C Coffee, "Law and the Market: The Impact of Enforcement" (2007) 156:2 U Pa L Rev 229); Richard A Posner, *A Failure of Capitalism: The Crisis of '08 and the Descent into Depression* (Cambridge, Mass: Harvard University Press, 2009); and Anat Admati & Martin Hellwig, *The Bankers' New Clothes: What's Wrong with Banking and What to Do About It* (Princeton, NJ: Princeton University Press, 2013) ch 13.

Most treatments of securities regulatory enforcement powers in Canada distinguish between criminal, administrative, and civil enforcement powers. Discussion of criminal enforcement in the securities context is further divided between relevant provisions of the *Criminal Code*, RSC 1985, c C-46 and quasi-criminal powers provided by securities legislation. We adopt this traditional distinction of enforcement powers in this chapter but, given the intense interest in this topic at the present time, also want to give an overview of the various reform efforts underway in this area of securities law. Only the administrative form of enforcement power provides for the provincial regulator to be the decision-maker at first instance. Determinations about breaches of the *Criminal Code* or the criminal offence provisions of securities law are made by provincial courts. Later in this chapter we will canvass the scope of the sanctioning powers provided to a securities regulatory tribunal under securities law; for now, it is sufficient to note that they range from the application of a power to require respondents to cease trading in securities to the levying of an administrative financial penalty for failures to comply with regulatory requirements. It should also be remembered that, as we saw in Chapter 2, the question of the precise structure of the adjudication arm of regulation is currently a contested one in a number of provinces. It is clear that regulators have a high degree of control over the enforcement process in the sense that regulatory enforcement staff is responsible for most investigation of potential infractions. This may change in the future, however, as criminal investigation authorities devote more resources to the securities area (Insider Trading Task Force, *Report—Illegal Insider Trading in Canada: Recommendations on Prevention, Detection and Deterrence* (November 2003)). One example of the effort to rationalize enforcement resources in this area has been the creation by the federal government of integrated market enforcement teams (IMETS). These teams involve the RCMP devoting resources to investigating fraud-related activities in the securities markets and, in doing so, working closely with provincial securities regulators and self-regulatory organizations (See The Hon Peter de C Cory & Marilyn L Pilkington, "Critical Issues in Enforcement," research study commissioned by the Task Force to Modernize Securities Legislation in Canada (September 2006), online: <http://www.tfmsl.ca/docs/V6(4)%20CoryPilkington.pdf>). More recently, the OSC participated in the establishment of the Joint Serious Offences Team (JSOT). This is a partnership between the OSC, the RCMP Financial Crime Program, and the

Ontario Provincial Police (OPP) Anti-Rackets Branch. JSOT is described on the OSC's website as combining "law enforcement policing skills with the OSC's expertise in forensic accounting and capital markets to investigate and prosecute serious violations of the law using provisions of the *Securities Act* … and *Criminal Code*." Between its inception in May 2013 and the end of 2014, the JSOT "investigated 22 matters, executed more than 80 search warrants, brought five cases before the courts on criminal matters and another nine on quasi-criminal proceedings." See <http://www.osc.gov.on.ca/en/NewsEvents_nr_20150302_enforcement-activity-2014.htm>.

On the other hand, we should not forget about the enforcement role of self-regulatory organizations (SROs) such as the Mutual Fund Dealers Association and the new Investment Industry Regulatory Organization of Canada (IIROC). (See Charles River Associates, "Securities Enforcement in Canada: The Effect of Multiple Regulators" in A Douglas Harris, ed, *WPC—Committee to Review the Structure of Securities Regulation in Canada: Research Studies* (Ottawa: Department of Finance, 2003), online: <http://www.wise-averties.ca/report_en.html>.) Since enforcement cases typically begin with the opening of an investigative file, let us start, therefore, with a brief discussion of the investigation powers provided for in securities legislation.

II. INVESTIGATION POWERS UNDER SECURITIES LAW

A. Scope of Investigation and Examination Powers

Provincial securities statutes in Canada typically provide regulators with a range of powers of investigation and examination. In Ontario, these provisions are located in Part VI of the Ontario *Securities Act*, RSO 1990, c S.5 (OSA) (see also part 17 of the British Columbia *Securities Act*, RSBC 1996, c 418 (BCSA), and title IX of the Québec *Securities Act*, CQLR c V-1.1 (QSA)). Section 11 of the OSA provides that the commission may order such investigation as it considers expedient for the administration of Ontario securities law or to "assist in the due administration of the securities or derivatives laws or the regulation of the capital markets in another jurisdiction." The Supreme Court's discussion of a similar provision in the BC *Securities Act* in the *Global Securities* decision is excerpted in Chapter 2. The scope of an investigation order that may be made by the Ontario Securities Commission (OSC) under s 11, typically on application by enforcement staff, is quite broad. It encompasses the following possibilities:

Scope of Investigation

(3) For the purposes of an investigation under this section, a person appointed to make the investigation may investigate and inquire into,

(a) the affairs of the person or company in respect of which the investigation is being made, including any trades, communications, negotiations, transactions, investigations, loans, borrowings or payments to, by, on behalf of, or in relation to or connected with the person or company and any property, assets or things owned, acquired or alienated in whole or in part by the person or company or by any other person or company acting on behalf of or as agent for the person or company; and

(b) the assets at any time held, the liabilities, debts, undertakings and obligations at any time existing, the financial or other conditions at any time prevailing in or in relation to or in connection with the person or company, and any relationship that may at any time exist or have existed between the person or company and any other person or company by reason of investments, commissions promised, secured or paid, interests held or acquired, the loaning or borrowing of money, stock or other property, the transfer, negotiation or holding of stock, interlocking directorates, common control, undue influence or control or any other relationship.

Right to Examine

(4) For the purposes of an investigation under this section, a person appointed to make the investigation may examine any documents or other things, whether they are in the possession or control of the person or company in respect of which the investigation is ordered or of any other person or company.

In addition, s 12 of the OSA allows the commission to order an examination of the financial affairs of a market participant. It is notable that these sections do not require evidence of any threshold level of suspicion on the part of enforcement staff in order to ground the request for the order. Once the commission grants a s 11 or s 12 order, s 13 provides that investigators have the same powers to summon attendance or compel testimony or the production of documents as do the courts for the trial of civil actions. This section also grants a search power, subject to the authorization of a provincial court judge. The power does not extend to the search of private residences (OSA, s 13(9)). See ss 142-144 of the BCSA and Alberta *Securities Act*, RSA 2000, c S-4 (ASA), ss 41 and 42 for similar provisions.

B. Safeguards for Subjects of Regulatory Investigation

These investigation and examination powers are, in principle, quite sweeping. Several other sections of this part of the OSA attempt to provide some boundaries to the use of the powers. For example, s 16(2) provides that testimony, documents, or reports provided under an investigation or examination order are for the exclusive use of the OSC or of "such other regulator as the Commission may specify in the order" and should not be disclosed or produced in any other proceeding "except as permitted under section 17." Meanwhile, this section provides that the commission may authorize disclosure of these materials to any person or company if it considers it would be in the public interest. While s 17(2) had provided that such disclosure could not be ordered unless the commission had "where practicable, given reasonable notice and an opportunity to be heard" to those providing testimony or other named persons or companies, a recent amendment to s 17 provides the commission with the power to make such an order without notice and without giving an opportunity to be heard if it considers it to be in the public interest (s 17(2.1)).

The following Supreme Court of Canada case discusses the OSC's role in disclosing compelled testimony to defendants in an OSA, s 127 proceeding.

Deloitte & Touche LLP v Ontario (Securities Commission)
2003 SCC 61, [2003] 2 SCR 713

IACOBUCCI J:

...

[3] Philip Services Corporation ("Philip") made a public offering of common shares in November 1997. Shortly thereafter, Philip made the first of a number of revelations of serious financial problems that had not been reflected in the material filed with the OSC, which included a prospectus, audited financial statements for the years 1995 and 1996,

and unaudited financial statements for the first nine months of 1997. All of the financial statements were prepared by the appellant, Deloitte & Touche LLP ("Deloitte").

[4] The revelations of Philip significantly reduced its earnings as set out in its 1995 and 1996 financial statements and substantially altered its 1999 financial outlook. The price of Philip shares dropped dramatically and it subsequently was delisted and sought bankruptcy protection.

[5] In May 1998, OSC Staff started an investigation into the adequacy of financial disclosures made by Philip with respect to its public offering. The OSC Staff were concerned that Philip was aware of the negative financial information in November 1997 but chose not to disclose that until after completion of the public offering.

[6] Staff investigators compelled information and testimony of individuals from Philip and Deloitte pursuant to s. 13 and s. 11 of the Ontario *Securities Act*, RSO 1990, c. S.5 (the "Act"). The power to compel documents and evidence under oath is subject to s. 16 of the Act, which prohibits disclosure of any of the compelled material. However, the OSC can under s. 17(1) of the Act order disclosure of the compelled material if the OSC concludes that disclosure is "in the public interest."

[7] Deloitte assembled some 324 files in response to the OSC summons and it was agreed to keep these in a separate secure location to which Staff would have access. Staff examined some but not all of the files and made copies of some of the documents. In addition, six Deloitte partners were examined under oath, with this testimony and the files forming part of what Doherty JA described as the "compelled material" ((2002), 159 OAC 257, at para. 2), a term that I will also use herein.

[8] Staff initiated proceedings under s. 127 of the Act against Philip and several officers of Philip in August 2000 and in support thereof issued a Statement of Allegations by Staff.

[9] The Statement of Allegations is some 36 pages in length consisting of detailed factual background and a series of allegations relating to Philip and the officers that in turn relate to various financial transactions and documents. Many matters are covered in the allegations but it is obvious that the financial statements prepared by Deloitte and financial transactions of Philip and the officers are important parts of the Statement. Suffice it to say that I agree with counsel for the OSC that the nature of the allegations is such that both the substance of the Deloitte audit as well as the process of auditing are issues in the s. 127 hearing. Or as the Court of Appeal and the OSC put it, what Deloitte knew (the substance) and when it knew (the process) will be central to the determination of the issues before the OSC.

[10] Pursuant to Rule 3.3(2) of the OSC Rules of Practice ((1997), 20 OSCB 1947), Staff is required to disclose to Philip and the officers all "relevant" material in its possession. Staff decided that all of the compelled material obtained from Deloitte was relevant to the s. 127 proceedings and should be disclosed to Philip and the officers. Consequently, Staff sought an order from the OSC to disclose under s. 17(1) and Deloitte opposed disclosure unless and until Staff could demonstrate the relevance of any document or testimonial transcript.

[11] The OSC determined it was in the public interest to disclose and Deloitte appealed to the Ontario Divisional Court. A majority of that court allowed the appeal and the Court of Appeal for Ontario overturned that decision and restored the disclosure order of the OSC.

. . .

[20] The principal issue in this appeal is whether the OSC acted unlawfully in finding it in the public interest to order disclosure of the compelled material to Philip and the officers. This raises the standard of review applicable to the OSC's impugned decisions and the factors that should be examined in making the determination.

[21] Deloitte acknowledged the wide discretion of the OSC to determine what is in the public interest. But Deloitte argued that burden was on the OSC to demonstrate that it is in the public interest to order disclosure even accepting that the Stinchcombe standard of relevance could be applied by the OSC. Deloitte argued that the OSC never examined all of the documents in question to determine relevance and thereby failed to protect Deloitte's privacy interests in the material obtained confidentially. Deloitte asserted that it had no obligation to point to any prejudice which would result from the improper disclosure of information since it was the duty of the OSC to order disclosure of only that information that was connected with the allegations. In oral argument, Deloitte recognized that if, in the hearing under s. 127, issues moved to the audit, the OSC could then decide whether disclosure could be made in the public interest. As the OSC did not agree with the approach argued by Deloitte, the OSC's decision was flawed and should be set aside.

[22] I agree with Doherty JA that the decision of the OSC to order disclosure in the public interest attracts a standard of review of reasonableness in accordance with the applicable jurisprudence, including the recent cases of *Dr. Q v. College of Physicians and Surgeons of British Columbia*, [2003] 1 SCR 226, 2003 SCC 19, and *Law Society of New Brunswick v. Ryan*, [2003] 1 SCR 247, 2003 SCC 20, which were decided after Doherty JA's reasons in the instant appeal. More specifically, the issue under appeal is whether the decision of the OSC to order disclosure of the compelled material, including documents that neither the investigators nor the OSC reviewed, was reasonable. Like Doherty JA, I find the decision of the OSC to be reasonable.

[23] The OSC acknowledged that the Staff had a disclosure obligation to Philip and its officers and defined the nature and scope of that obligation in terms of the "relevance" standard developed in Stinchcombe, supra, and its progeny. The Court of Appeal fully examined the factors applied by the OSC in determining whether the compelled material reached the relevance threshold and found the analysis and determination of the OSC to be reasonable.

[24] In particular, the OSC considered: the nature of the allegations against Philip and the officers; that the files in issue had been produced by Deloitte in response to a summons arising out of an investigation into the adequacy of the financial disclosure in the prospectus and related financial statements; the indices provided by Deloitte describing the files; the representations by Staff to the OSC that at least two of the Philip respondents had gone on record as intending to challenge the credibility of the Deloitte auditors in the s. 127 proceedings, and that some of the compelled material would be relied on by Staff in presenting its case.

...

[26] The use of the Stinchcombe relevance standard and its application in this case by the OSC were both reasonable decisions. The OSC reasonably rejected Deloitte's argument that the Staff could not establish relevance with respect to any documents it had not examined on the basis that, given the nature of the allegations made in the s. 127 proceedings and defences, the relevancy of the compelled material was to be determined as a whole. In other words, as the OSC observed, documents which might appear irrelevant to the OSC Staff might have considerable relevance to the defence of Philip and the officers,

and documents in isolation may not have relevance but might well have considerable relevance when studied in light of other information possessed by Philip or the officers. This approach also answers the argument of Deloitte for "disclosure by installment"; surely it is reasonable to disclose all the material at once so Philip and the officers can effectively plan and construct their response.

[27] In short, like the Court of Appeal, I find that the decision of the OSC was reasonable and soundly based with respect to the disclosure of all the compelled material to Philip and the officers to allow them in the circumstances to mount a full answer and defence. Also like the Court of Appeal, I agree that the relationship between Deloitte and Philip with respect to financial disclosure in the 1995, 1996 and 1997 audits will be central to the s. 127 proceedings. There is a reasonable possibility that all of the compelled material relating to Deloitte's audit of Philip will be relevant to the allegations against Philip and the officers. Consequently, the application by the OSC of the relevance standard from Stinchcombe was reasonable in all the circumstances. …

[28] It should be noted that the OSC, in cases like this, is in an awkward position. A proceeding has been ordered against respondents who are entitled to disclosure of information involving a third party. The OSC must search for an approach that provides fair consideration for the respondents in jeopardy and enables them to meet the case against them yet also is sensitive to the third party's privacy interests and expectations. In that respect, I agree with Doherty JA that Deloitte could have identified its concerns with some of the compelled material being disclosed. If Deloitte established that there was not a reasonable possibility that a particular document was relevant to the allegations, it would have been improper for the OSC to order disclosure.

[29] The OSC admittedly has a discretion owing to its expertise to order disclosure of the compelled information if found to be in the public interest. Like Doherty JA, I believe the OSC properly balanced the interests of disclosure to Philip and the officers along with the protection of the confidentiality expectations and interest of Deloitte. In this respect, I am of the view that in making a disclosure order in the public interest under s. 17, the OSC has a duty to parties like Deloitte to protect its privacy interests and confidences. That is to say that OSC is obligated to order disclosure only to the extent necessary to carry out its mandate under the Act. In this case, the OSC properly weighed the necessary disclosure and the interests of Deloitte.

Disclosure of testimony to criminal law enforcers requires the written consent of the person from whom it was obtained. However, by OSA, s 17(5), a court hearing a prosecution by the OSC is enabled to compel production of any of these materials and order their release to the defendant. Importantly, s 18 provides that testimony given under s 13 "shall not be admitted in evidence against the person from whom the testimony was obtained in a prosecution for an offence under section 122 or in any other prosecution governed by the *Provincial Offences Act*." It is clear that this requires strategic decisions to be made by enforcement staff at a relatively early stage in an investigation concerning whether the investigation is likely to lead to a s 122 prosecution or a s 127 enforcement action where the same strictures would not apply. See *R v Jarvis*, 2002 SCC 73, [2002] 3 SCR 757, excerpted below.

The OSC also introduced a controversial "credit for cooperation" policy in April 2002 by way of OSC Staff Notice 15-702 (2002), 25 OSCB 3949. This says that if potential respondents "act in a responsible manner during the course of an investigation and have self-policed, self-reported, and self-corrected the matters under investigation," regulatory staff may recommend that the matter not proceed by way of an OSA s 122 prosecution or may narrow the scope of allegations or recommend reduced sanctions in a s 127 matter, among other things. This policy was revised in March 2014 to allow the çommission to approve settlements of enforcement matters between enforcement staff of the OSC and respondents on the basis of no formal admissions of misconduct by the respondent(s). The policy sets out a number of criteria in order for respondents to qualify for a no-contest settlement, including prompt and full self-reporting by the relevant respondents.

For empirical analysis of settlements in the securities regulation context, see Anita Anand & Andrew Green, "Settlements in Securities Regulation: Empirical Evidence from Ontario" (July 2016) unpublished paper, on file with authors.

In Chapter 2, we discussed some of the issues that arise concerning whether provisions of the *Canadian Charter of Rights and Freedoms*, Part I of the *Constitution Act, 1982*, being Schedule B to the *Canada Act 1982* (UK), 1982, c 11, such as s 7 or s 8, offer any protections to defendants in these situations. We saw that the SCC's decision in *Branch*, [1995] 2 SCR 3, suggested that persons involved in securities trading did not have a high expectation of privacy in relation to their activities in a heavily regulated industry. Significant weight in the decision was placed on the fact that the evidence was not being compelled for the purpose of proving criminal charges. More recently, however, there have been suggestions that the Charter may apply "with full force to persons under investigation for 'regulatory crimes' from the point at which the authority has as its predominant purpose penal remedies" (James A Riley & Cathy Singer, "Process & Accountability for the OSC Enforcement Branch," paper presented to the Queen's Business Law Symposium, October 2004) (unpublished) at 27). The issue of the constitutional protections available to the targets of investigations, which may lead either to a regulatory hearing or a criminal prosecution, was addressed in the *Jarvis* case, in the context of violations of the *Income Tax Act*.

R v Jarvis

2002 SCC 73, [2002] 3 SCR 757

[The case involved a taxpayer who did not report sales of his deceased wife's art in his tax returns for 1990 and 1991. A Revenue Canada auditor wrote to the taxpayer requesting certain information, which was provided, and met with him to pursue the investigation. Following the collection of this information, the auditor referred her file to the Special Investigations Section of Revenue Canada, which embarked on another investigation to determine if a prosecution for tax evasion was warranted. Following the issuance of a search warrant and the collection of information from third parties, the taxpayer was charged with tax evasion.]

IACOBUCCI and MAJOR JJ (for the Court):

[1] Is there a distinction between the Canada Customs and Revenue Agency's ("CCRA") audit and investigative functions under the *Income Tax Act*, R.S.C. 1985 c. 1 (5th Supp.) ("ITA")? If it is indeed correct to draw such a distinction, when does the CCRA exercise its audit function and when does it exercise its investigative function? Finally, what are the legal consequences for the taxpayer when the CCRA exercises its investigative function?

[2] Ultimately, we conclude that compliance audits and tax evasion investigations must be treated differently. While taxpayers are statutorily bound to co-operate with CCRA auditors for tax assessment purposes (which may result in the application of regulatory penalties), there is an adversarial relationship that crystallizes between the taxpayer and the tax officials when the predominant purpose of an official's inquiry is the determination of penal liability. When the officials exercise this authority, constitutional protections against self-incrimination prohibit CCRA officials who are investigating ITA offences from having recourse to the powerful inspection and requirement tools in ss. 231.1(1) and 231.2(1). Rather, CCRA officials who exercise the authority to conduct such investigations must seek search warrants in furtherance of their investigation.

[3] Here, the material that the trial judge excluded from the Information to Obtain A Search Warrant owing to a *Charter* violation was in fact validly gathered pursuant to the auditor's inspection and requirement powers. Accordingly, the searches ultimately carried out were authorized by warrant, and no s. 8 violation occurred. Therefore, we would dismiss the appeal and confirm the Court of Appeal of Alberta's order of a new trial.

...

[65] It is worth repeating that the appellant does not attack the constitutionality of ss. 231.1(1) and 231.2(1). Rather, his argument is that the *admission into evidence* in tax evasion proceedings of statements and documents that were compelled by Revenue Canada officials under these sections was a violation of his rights under ss. 7 and 8 of the *Charter*. He thus argues that the evidence should be excluded under s. 24(2) of the *Charter*.

...

[67] It is beyond doubt that the appellant's s. 7 liberty interest is engaged by the introduction of statutorily compelled information at his trial for the s. 239 offences, owing to the threat of imprisonment on conviction: see *Re B.C. Motor Vehicle Act*, [1985] 2 S.C.R. 486, at p. 515, *per* Lamer J. (as he then was); *Reference re ss. 193 & 195.1(1)(c) of the Criminal Code (Canada)*, [1990] 1 S.C.R. 1123. The relevant principle of fundamental justice in the present case is the principle against self-incrimination, an elemental canon of the Canadian criminal justice system, standing for the notion that individuals should not be conscripted by the state to promote a self-defeating purpose: *R. v. S. (R.J.)*, [1995] 1 S.C.R. 451, at para. 81, *per* Iacobucci J. This Court has clearly established that the principle against self-incrimination finds residual expression under s. 7 … .

[68] In giving expression to this principle, however, s. 7 does not envelop an abstract and absolute rule that would prevent the use of information in all contexts in which it is statutorily compelled: *Jones*, *supra*, at p. 257; *S. (R.J.)*, *supra*, at paras. 96-100; *Fitzpatrick*, *supra*, at paras. 21 and 24; *White*, *supra*, at para. 45. A court must begin "on the ground," with a concrete and contextual analysis of all the circumstances, in order to determine whether or not the principle against self-incrimination is actually engaged: *Fitzpatrick*, at para. 25; White, at para. 46. This analysis necessarily involves a balancing of principles. One must, in assessing the limits on compellability demanded by the principle against self-incrimination, consider the opposing principle of fundamental justice suggesting that relevant evidence should be available to the trier of fact in a search for truth: *S. (R.J.)*, at para. 108, *per* Iacobucci J. These competing interests will often be brought to the foreground in regulatory contexts, where the procedures being challenged have generally been designed (and are employed) as part of an administrative scheme in the public interest … .

...

[71] The context-specific approach to s. 8 inevitably means, as Wilson J. noted in *Thomson Newspapers*, *supra*, at p. 495, that "[a]t some point the individual's interest in privacy must give way to the broader state interest in having the information or document disclosed." Naturally, if a person has but a minimal expectation with respect to informational privacy, this may tip the balance in the favour of the state interest: *Plant*, *supra*; *Smith v. Canada (Attorney General)*, 2001 SCC 88, [2001] 3 S.C.R. 902.

[72] Generally, an individual has a diminished expectation of privacy in respect of records and documents that he or she produces during the ordinary course of regulated activities: see, e.g., *Thomson Newspapers*, *supra*, at p. 507, *per* La Forest J.; *143471 Canada*, *supra*, at p. 378, *per* Cory J.; *Comité paritaire*, *supra*, at pp. 420-21; *Fitzpatrick*, *supra*, at para. 49. In the particular context of the self-assessment and self-reporting income tax regime, a taxpayer's privacy interest in records that may be relevant to the filing of his or her tax return is relatively low: *McKinlay Transport*, *supra*, at pp. 649-50.

...

[88] In our view, where the predominant purpose of a particular inquiry is the determination of penal liability, CCRA officials must relinquish the authority to use the inspection and requirement powers under ss. 231.1(1) and 231.2(1). In essence, officials "cross the Rubicon" when the inquiry in question engages the adversarial relationship between the taxpayer and the state. There is no clear formula that can answer whether or not this is the case. Rather, to determine whether the predominant purpose of the inquiry in question is the determination of penal liability, one must look to all factors that bear upon the nature of that inquiry.

[89] To begin with, the mere existence of reasonable grounds that an offence may have occurred is by itself insufficient to support the conclusion that the predominant purpose of an inquiry is the determination of penal liability. Even where reasonable grounds to suspect an offence exist, it will not always be true that the predominant purpose of an inquiry is the determination of penal liability. In this regard, courts must guard against creating procedural shackles on regulatory officials; it would be undesirable to "force the regulatory hand" by removing the possibility of seeking the lesser administrative penalties on every occasion in which reasonable grounds existed of more culpable conduct. This point was clearly stated in *McKinlay Transport*, *supra*, at p. 648, where Wilson J. wrote: "The Minister must be capable of exercising these [broad supervisory] powers whether or not he has reasonable grounds for believing that a particular taxpayer has breached the Act." While reasonable grounds indeed constitute a necessary condition for the issuance of a search warrant to further a criminal investigation (s. 231.3 of the ITA; *Criminal Code*, s. 487), and might in certain cases serve to indicate that the audit powers were misused, their existence is not a sufficient indicator that the CCRA is conducting a *de facto* investigation. In most cases, if all ingredients of an offence are reasonably thought to have occurred, it is likely that the investigation function is triggered.

[90] All the more, the test cannot be set at the level of mere suspicion that an offence has occurred. Auditors may, during the course of their inspections, suspect all manner of taxpayer wrongdoing, but it certainly cannot be the case that, from the moment such suspicion is formed, an investigation has begun. On what evidence could investigators ever obtain a search warrant if the whiff of suspicion were enough to freeze auditorial fact-finding? The state interest in prosecuting those who wilfully evade their taxes is of

great importance, and we should be careful to avoid rendering nugatory the state's ability to investigate and obtain evidence of these offences.

[91] The other pole of the continuum is no more attractive. It would be a fiction to say that the adversarial relationship only comes into being when charges are laid. Logically, this will only happen once the investigators believe that they have obtained evidence that indicates wrongdoing. Because the s. 239 offences contain an element of mental culpability, the state will, one must presume, usually have some evidence that the accused satisfied the *mens rea* requirements before laying an information or preferring an indictment. The active collection of such evidence indicates that the adversarial relationship has been engaged, since it is irrelevant to the determination of tax liability. Moreover, although there are judicial controls on the unauthorized exercise of power (*Roncarelli v. Duplessis*, [1959] S.C.R. 121; *Babcock v. Canada (Attorney General)*, 2002 SCC 57, [2002] 3 S.C.R. 3, at para. 25), we believe that allowing CCRA officials to employ ss. 231.1(1) and 231.2(1) until the point where charges are laid, might promote bad faith on the part of the prosecutors. Quite conceivably, situations may arise in which charges are delayed in order to compel the taxpayer to provide evidence against himself or herself for the purposes of a s. 239 prosecution. Although the respondent argued that such situations could be remedied by the courts, we view it as preferable that such situations be avoided rather than remedied. It is for this reason that the test is as set out above.

[92] Whether a matter has been sent to the investigations section is another factor in determining whether the adversarial relationship exists. Again, though, this, by itself, is not determinative. An auditor's recommendation that investigators look at a file might result in nothing in the way of a criminal investigation since there is always the possibility that the file will be sent back. Still, if, in an auditor's judgment, a matter should be sent to the investigators, a court must examine the following behaviour very closely. If the file is sent back, does it appear that the investigators have actually declined to take up the case and have returned the matter so that the audit can be completed? Or, does it appear, rather, that they have sent the file back as a matter of expediency, so that the auditor may use ss. 231.1(1) and 231.2(1) to obtain evidence for a prosecution (as was found to be the case in *Norway Insulation*, *supra*).

[93] To reiterate, the determination of when the relationship between the state and the individual has reached the point where it is effectively adversarial is a contextual one, which takes account of all relevant factors. In our opinion, the following list of factors will assist in ascertaining whether the predominant purpose of an inquiry is the determination of penal liability. Apart from a clear decision to pursue a criminal investigation, no one factor is necessarily determinative in and of itself, but courts must assess the totality of the circumstances, and make a determination as to whether the inquiry or question in issue engages the adversarial relationship between the state and the individual.

[94] In this connection, the trial judge will look at all factors, including but not limited to such questions as:

(a) Did the authorities have reasonable grounds to lay charges? Does it appear from the record that a decision to proceed with a criminal investigation *could have* been made?

(b) Was the general conduct of the authorities such that it was consistent with the pursuit of a criminal investigation?

(c) Had the auditor transferred his or her files and materials to the investigators?
(d) Was the conduct of the auditor such that he or she was effectively acting as an agent for the investigators?
(e) Does it appear that the investigators intended to use the auditor as their agent in the collection of evidence?
(f) Is the evidence sought relevant to taxpayer liability generally? Or, as is the case with evidence as to the taxpayer's *mens rea*, is the evidence relevant only to the taxpayer's penal liability?
(g) Are there any other circumstances or factors that can lead the trial judge to the conclusion that the compliance audit had in reality become a criminal investigation?

It should also be noted that in this case we are dealing with the CCRA. However, there may well be other provincial or federal governmental departments or agencies that have different organizational settings which in turn may mean that the above factors, as well as others, will have to be applied in those particular contexts.

E. Charter Consequences

[95] With respect to the consequences related to s. 8 of the *Charter*, *McKinlay Transport*, *supra*, makes it clear that taxpayers have very little privacy interest in the materials and records that they are obliged to keep under the ITA, and that they are obliged to produce during an audit. Moreover, once an auditor has inspected or required a given document under ss. 231.1(1) and 231.2(1), the taxpayer cannot truly be said to have a reasonable expectation that the auditor will guard its confidentiality. It is well known, as Laskin C.J. stated in *Smerchanski*, *supra*, at p. 32, that "[t]he threat of prosecution underlies every tax return if a false statement is knowingly made in it." It follows that there is nothing preventing auditors from passing to investigators their files containing validly obtained audit materials. That is, there is no principle of use immunity that prevents the investigators, in the exercise of their investigative function, from making use of evidence obtained through the proper exercise of the CCRA's audit function. Nor, in respect of validly obtained audit information, is there any principle of derivative use immunity that would require the trial judge to apply the "but for" test from *S. (R.J.)*, *supra*. If a particular piece of evidence comes to light as a result of the information validly contained in the auditor's file, then investigators may make use of it.

[96] On the other hand, with respect to s. 7 of the *Charter*, when the predominant purpose of a question or inquiry is the determination of penal liability, the "full panoply" of *Charter* rights are engaged for the taxpayer's protection. There are a number of consequences that flow from this. First, no further statements may be compelled from the taxpayer by way of s. 231.1(1)(d) for the purpose of advancing the criminal investigation. Likewise, no written documents may be inspected or examined, except by way of judicial warrant under s. 231.3 of the ITA or s. 487 of the *Criminal Code*, and no documents may be required, from the taxpayer or any third party for the purpose of advancing the criminal investigation. CCRA officials conducting inquiries, the predominant purpose of which is the determination of penal liability, do not have the benefit of the ss. 231.1(1) and 231.2(1) requirement powers.

[97] The predominant purpose test does not thereby prevent the CCRA from conducting parallel criminal investigations and administrative audits. The fact that the CCRA is investigating a taxpayer's penal liability, does not preclude the possibility of a simultaneous investigation, the predominant purpose of which is a determination of the same taxpayer's tax liability. However, if an investigation into penal liability is subsequently commenced, the investigators can avail themselves of that information obtained pursuant to the audit powers prior to the commencement of the criminal investigation, but not with respect to information obtained pursuant to such powers subsequent to the commencement of the investigation into penal liability. This is no less true where the investigations into penal liability and tax liability are in respect of the same tax period. So long as the predominant purpose of the parallel investigation actually is the determination of tax liability, the auditors may continue to resort to ss. 231.1(1) and 231.2(1). It may well be that there will be circumstances in which the CCRA officials conducting the tax liability inquiry will desire to inform the taxpayer that a criminal investigation also is under way and that the taxpayer is not obliged to comply with the requirement powers of ss. 231.1(1) and 231.2(1) for the purposes of the criminal investigation. On the other hand, the authorities may wish to avail themselves of the search warrant procedures under ss. 231.3 of the ITA or 487 of the *Criminal Code* to access the documents necessary to advance the criminal investigation. Put another way, the requirement powers of ss. 231.1(1) and 231.2(1) cannot be used to compel oral statements or written production for the purpose of advancing the criminal investigation.

[98] In summary, wherever the predominant purpose of an inquiry or question is the determination of penal liability, criminal investigatory techniques must be used. As a corollary, all *Charter* protections that are relevant in the criminal context must apply.

F. *Summary*

[99] By way of summary, the following points emerge:

1. Although the ITA is a regulatory statute, a distinction can be drawn between the audit and investigative powers that it grants to the Minister.
2. When, in light of all relevant circumstances, it is apparent that CCRA officials are not engaged in the verification of tax liability, but are engaged in the determination of penal liability under s. 239, the adversarial relationship between the state and the individual exists. As a result, *Charter* protections are engaged.
3. When this is the case, investigators must provide the taxpayer with a proper warning. The powers of compulsion in ss. 231.1(1) and 231.2(1) are not available, and search warrants are required in order to further the investigation.

For an analysis of the application of the principles in the *Jarvis* case to the securities regulatory context, see Glen Jennings, "Regulatory Investigations: Applying Jarvis in the Securities Context" (16 July 2012), online: <http://www.mondaq.com/canada/x/187068/Securities/Regulatory+Investigations+Applying+Jarvis+In+The+Securities+Context>.

A final recent innovation in Ontario in the investigative context is the introduction of a whistleblower program, which provides financial incentives for whistleblowers to come forward to report securities-related misconduct. There are many interesting features of this new program, only one of which is the fact that payment to whistleblowers will occur only if sanctions are imposed by the tribunal in an administrative enforcement context. See OSC Policy 15-601, *Whistleblower Program* (14 July 2016).

III. CRIMINAL CODE

Prosecution under *Criminal Code* provisions has not historically been a prominent feature of the enforcement of securities law in Canada. However, it is important to remember that there are a number of provisions therein dealing with securities law infractions, including a more recent prohibition against insider trading. Sections 380-384 as well as s 400 of the Code are relevant in this context. For example, s 380(1) makes it an indictable offence to "by deceit, falsehood or other fraudulent means" defraud the public or any person of "property, money, or valuable security or any service" where the subject matter exceeds five thousand dollars. Section 380(2) creates the offence of affecting the public market price of "stocks, shares, merchandise or anything that is offered for sale to the public" with intent to defraud. Section 382 makes it an offence to fraudulently manipulate stock exchange transactions by engaging in various strategies, such as matched orders and wash trading to "create a false or misleading appearance of active public trading." Meanwhile s 400 indicates that anyone who "makes, circulates or publishes a prospectus … that he knows is false in a material particular, with intent" to induce someone to become a shareholder or partner, or to deceive or defraud members, shareholders, or creditors of a company is guilty of an indictable offence. As discussed in Chapter 8, insider trading has recently been established as a *Criminal Code* offence. Section 382.1(1) makes it an indictable offence to directly or indirectly buy or sell a security "knowingly using inside information" that the accused possesses by virtue of various relationships to the issuer. Section 382.1(2) creates the *Criminal Code* offence of tipping.

It is also notable that Bill C-13 (*An Act to Amend the Criminal Code (Capital Markets Fraud and Evidence-Gathering)*, SC 2004, c 3), proclaimed into force in September 2004, increased the maximum term of imprisonment for those convicted of some of these indictable offences from 10 to 14 years. The same revisions also enumerated a set of "aggravating circumstances" that may be considered in imposing a sentence. These include the considerations that (1) the value of the fraud exceeded $1 million, (2) "the offence adversely affected, or had the potential to adversely affect, the stability of the Canadian economy or financial system or any financial market in Canada or investor confidence in such a market," (3) the offence involved a large number of victims, and (4) in committing the offence, the offender took advantage of the high regard in which the offender was held in the community. The enumeration of these aggravating circumstances clearly reflect the genesis of the *Criminal Code* revisions in the perceived crisis of investor confidence in North American capital markets after the tumultuous events involving companies such as Enron, Tyco, WorldCom, and Adelphia. In 2011, the federal government passed Bill C-21, titled *Standing up for Victims of White Collar Crime Act*, which, among other things, imposes a minimum prison sentence of two years for fraud-related offences whose value is in excess of one million dollars.

If the past is any guide, however, there appear to have been few prosecutions under the longer-standing *Criminal Code* provisions. For example, one of the rare prosecutions involving a false prospectus was *R v Hawrish* (1991), 95 Sask R 100 (QB), aff'd (1993), 113 Sask R 214

(CA). See also *R v Fast*, 2014 SKQB 84, aff'd 2015 SKCA 86. However, a recent example of the use of the *Criminal Code* to prosecute a securities-related matter was the *Drabinsky* case, excerpted below.

R v Drabinsky

2009 CanLII 12802 (Ont Sup Ct J) (footnotes omitted)

BENOTTO J:

[1] Garth Drabinsky was described as a creative genius. With his long time partner Myron Gottlieb, he built a live entertainment empire that spanned North America and was expanding to England and Australia. "Livent" was a leading producer of musicals, plays and concerts. By early 1998 it had launched 15 productions, won 14 prestigious Tony awards, and been nominated for dozens more. …

[2] Livent, through its founders, made important contributions to the entertainment industry, to tourism and to the lives of many who are involved in or who enjoy live theatre. Mr. Drabinsky was admired as "one of the most innovative forces in the theatre." Together with Mr. Gottlieb, he ran the company.

[3] On April 13, 1998, Mr. Drabinsky announced a change in management of Livent that would allow him to devote his time exclusively to the artistic and creative work of the company. It was part of a deal that included Michael Ovitz, who was well known in Hollywood and who had worked with the Walt Disney Corporation. Investors were putting over $30 million into the company. Mr. Drabinsky would become Vice-Chairman and Chief Creative Director. Mr. Gottlieb would become Executive Vice-President, Canadian Administration. The day-to-day accounting would be done by new management. There was a sense of excitement and enthusiasm. …

• • •

[5] The Ovitz deal closed in June 1998. The shares of Livent were trading at $11.40. Two months later, Mr. Drabinsky and Mr. Gottlieb were locked out of their offices. Five months later, the Toronto Stock Exchange suspended trading of Livent shares and the company declared bankruptcy in the United States and Canada. A year after that the shares were de-listed from the Toronto Stock Exchange.

[6] Mr. Drabinsky and Mr. Gottlieb are charged with two counts of fraud and one count of forgery. It is alleged that they directed a large scale accounting fraud by misstating the financial information in the books of Livent and its predecessor MyGar.

[7] The Crown relies on the testimony of former employees, the testimony of suppliers and the financial records of the corporation.

[8] The Defence submits that the evidence cannot be relied upon. The employees have conspired to implicate Mr. Drabinsky and Mr. Gottlieb in order to minimize their exposure to more serious consequences resulting from their participation in the fraud. The financial records do not establish that Mr. Drabinsky and Mr. Gottlieb knew about the accounting manipulations. Thus, according to the Defence, the Crown has not proved beyond a reasonable doubt that Mr. Drabinsky and Mr. Gottlieb had knowledge that there was anything improper in the accounting practices at MyGar or at Livent.

• • •

[15] The Crown alleges that Mr. Drabinsky and Mr. Gottlieb operated a kick-back scheme at MyGar which resulted in false information being included in the Initial Public Offering (IPO). Once the company went public, the Crown says that they directed an accounting fraud in order to artificially inflate the income of Livent and thereby keep investor funds flowing to it. The false financial statements were then filed publicly with the knowledge of Mr. Drabinsky and Mr. Gottlieb.

[16] While the evidence relating to each of the two fraud counts is different, the Crown alleges that both involve the essence of fraudulent conduct: intentional dishonest acts by the accused that put others at risk of economic deprivation. The forgery count arises out of the same conduct that gave rise to the second count of fraud: the intentional misstatement of the company's true financial situation in documents intended to be relied upon by the public to its prejudice.

. . .

[23] There was a loan agreement between LECC and the Royal Bank that limited the distribution to the partners to $75,000 per month. Cash flow was reported to the bank.

[24] The accounting at MyGar was straightforward. The partnership was tax driven to keep earnings as minimal as possible. One of the ways this was achieved was through the "cost recovery" method of amortizing preproduction costs. All the costs were capitalized to the opening of a production. No profit was recognized until the preproduction costs were recovered.

[25] Sometime in 1991 Mr. Eckstein became aware of large payments being made by MyGar to a company called Kofman Engineering on the basis of cheque requisitions rather than invoices. There was no back up for the cheques.

. . .

[28] … Kofman Engineering paid each of Mr. Drabinsky and Mr. Gottlieb $75,000 for a total of $150,000. On November 21, 1990 Kofman issued an invoice back to them for $175,000. This was to recoup the $150,000 paid to them personally plus $25,000 in legitimate work done. Kofman got a cheque back for $175,000 signed by Mr. Drabinsky and Mr. Gottlieb. This exchange of invoices and cheques would be repeated. Mr. Kofman testified that these invoices were false. Mr. Drabinsky and Mr. Gottlieb had never made any business introductions for Mr. Kofman even though the payment by Mr. Kofman to them was ostensibly for this service.

. . .

[37] The result of this accounting was to overstate the assets of MyGar in the financial statements. At the end of 1992, just before the Initial Public Offering, the assets of MyGar were approximately $97 million. Mr. Coort testified that about $6.8 million of the assets on the balance sheet were attributable to the invoice scheme. Of that amount, $4.2 million was in preproduction costs and $2.6 million was in fixed assets.

[38] Mr. Eckstein testified that he told Mr. Drabinsky and Mr. Gottlieb before the company went public that there were $4-6 million in assets on the books that had no real value. He suggested a write-off so that the public company could be started with a "clean set of books." … Mr. Drabinsky and Mr. Gottlieb told Mr. Eckstein that there was "no way we can write that off"; it would have "looked terrible." It ended up showing as assets of MyGar and these assets were part of the prospectus signed by Mr. Drabinsky and Mr. Gottlieb. When the company went public, the assets of MyGar were rolled into the public company.

[39] The Crown alleges that the motive for this scheme was to conceal partnership draws from the bank. The fraud alleged is not the scheme itself but the way the false invoices were booked. It was dishonest to show them as assets of MyGar. This formed part of the prospectus, the public was misled and its funds put at risk. Moreover, the inflation of assets in MyGar's books was carried into Livent and had a permanent effect with a continual carry-forward.

[40] Seven former employees of Livent testified. Their evidence, if believed, told the tale of an accounting system designed to minimize expenses and maximize profits. Adjustments and manipulations were routinely made to the financial statements on an arbitrary basis in order to keep the expenses as close to budget as possible. As a result, the financial statements did not represent the true financial state of the company.

[41] Two of the employees, Gordon Eckstein and Maria Messina testified that they witnessed Mr. Drabinsky and Mr. Gottlieb directing and discussing these manipulations. A third employee, Christopher Craib, testified that he saw Mr. Drabinsky directing them on one occasion. Other employees who took their instructions only from Mr. Eckstein spoke of the widespread system at Livent of improperly moving numbers that was so time consuming that one employee's full-time job was entering adjustments.

. . .

[43] The evidence tracked in detail the accounting methods employed at Livent to manipulate the income reported on the financial statements. The methods included:

- Expense rolls: arbitrarily moving operating expenses from one period to another.
- Amortization rolls: failing to subtract expenses that were supposed to be amortized by moving them to other periods.
- Show-to-show transfers: applying the expenses of one show to another.
- Transfers to fixed assets: allocating operating and preproduction costs to fixed assets accounts related to theatres and buildings under construction.
- Ticket purchases: allocating a portion of tickets purchased on Livent's behalf by suppliers to asset accounts.

[44] The Crown relies on the witnesses and the documents to establish the charges in Count 2 and Count 3.

. . .

[46] Much evidence in the Crown's case focused on the production of the quarterly financial statements and the executive meetings in connection with them. …

[47] The quarterly executive meetings generally followed a pattern. Mr. Eckstein said he would take management through the statements to compare the actual to the budget figures. The actual income was always lower than what had been projected. Not long after the company went public it was short of cash. Although about $28 million had been raised through the IPO, and more money was brought in through a Special Warrant Placement a few months later in September 1993, Livent was short of cash. The overspending was largely, but not exclusively in advertising. Mr. Drabinsky chaired the weekly advertising meetings. Mr. Eckstein said that the company was always overspending.

[48] The executive meetings, usually in Mr. Drabinsky's office, were raucous. There were loud arguments. Mr. Drabinsky would yell. He did not believe the expenses were so high. The executive would then discuss how to make the statements more closely match the budget. This was important because projections had been made to the financial analysts

who study corporations for brokerage houses and make recommendations about trading. It was usually Mr. Gottlieb who dealt with the analysts so he would make comments in this regard. Mr. Eckstein would then be instructed by Mr. Drabinsky, Mr. Gottlieb and Mr. Topol to make changes to the financial statements to get them closer to budget.

. . .

[55] The Audit Committee was an operating committee of the Board of Directors. It was charged with the oversight of financial reporting and disclosure. The committee reviewed all the quarterly statements. The final financial statements were presented to the Board of Directors. Members of the Audit Committee and the Board did not know about the adjustments.

[56] Deloitte & Touche were the external auditors. They also did not know about the adjustments. In fact, there was a concerted effort to hide the adjustments from them. A variety of methods were used including:

- Asking suppliers to verify false invoices;
- Failing to record some expenses;
- Moving expenses to fixed assets thereby "capitalizing" them;
- Manipulating the computer software to eliminate the trail of changes;
- Rolling forward expenses from one period to the next;
- Show-to-show transfers of expenses.

. . .

[58] Financial records were kept for each show that Livent produced. The show-to-show transfer of expenses made a particular production look as though it was doing better than it was. For example, *Kiss of the Spider Woman* in Boston actually lost money. …

. . .

[59] The movement of expenses to fixed assets was another useful tool used to reduce expenses. Preproduction costs were normally amortized over the potential life of a show which could be two years or less. Fixed assets could be amortized over 40 years.

[60] The sorts of adjustment just referred to accumulated quarter by quarter, year by year, so that by January 1998 the fixed assets were overstated by $20-25 million.

. . .

[79] On October 16, 1997 a $125 million U.S. bond offering closed. Meanwhile, the accounting staff was preparing the Q3/97 statements. A first set of statements printed from the Lawson General Ledger System showed a loss of over $20 million. Gordon Eckstein called Maria Messina, Diane Winkfein and Grant Malcolm into his office and directed them to manipulate the statements. He told them to take money in large lump sums out of certain accounts. …

[80] After that, Gordon Eckstein gave direction for additional documents to be prepared for the meeting with management. He asked Maria Messina to prepare a set of statements based on the actual numbers and then a set based on the manipulated numbers. … This was the first time Ms. Messina saw Mr. Drabinsky and Mr. Gottlieb discussing manipulations.

. . .

[88] Preparations of the booklet for the Audit Committee were underway. The most important document in the package was the schedule of preproduction costs which was done on a show-by-show basis. At the direction of Gordon Eckstein, amounts were moved from one show to another. There was no change in the balance just the movement from

show to show. It was done to be consistent with the previous quarter and to avoid any red flags for the committee.

. . .

[90] Still immobilized by fear, Maria Messina did nothing about the fraud. She said:

> … I can't believe that it happened to me … , I did not have the strength or the courage to disclose it … there was no way I was going to go up against Mr. Gottlieb and Mr. Drabinsky. They were men of money, power and influence and I was a nobody. …

. . .

[113] The following night, April 24, 1998 Christopher Craib called her at home at about 9:30 p.m. He said he had met that afternoon with Garth Drabinsky and learned that the Q1/98 statements were going to be manipulated by $20 million. There would be rolls and transfers and millions deleted from accounts payable and millions capitalized to fixed assets. As would become clear from the evidence, Mr. Drabinsky was not in Toronto as stated by Mr. Craib. He was in Washington D.C. at a luncheon hosted by President Clinton.

. . .

[115] The next day, Saturday April 25, Myron Gottlieb called her at home to request a certain schedule. She went to the office and got the schedule for him. He gave her a document relating to the due diligence request from KPMG. He wanted her to deal with the due diligence. She spoke to him about the proposed manipulations. She said she urged Mr. Gottlieb to speak to Mr. Drabinsky and reconsider making manipulations to Q1/98. Mr. Gottlieb replied that this was just income smoothing and there was nothing wrong with it. She also said he told her Q1 is our quarter, not "theirs," referring to new management.

. . .

[127] The meeting with new management went ahead. Ms. Messina said that the first thing she told them was that she disagreed with the loss figure and it was in fact closer to $13-14 million. She said the changes were a result of the meeting she had with Mr. Drabinsky. They told her to present financial information only to them, not to Mr. Drabinsky.

[128] As a result of the meeting, she prepared a document which showed her version of the loss for Mr. Webster and Mr. Maisel and possibly Mr. Furman. She prepared a reconciliation of how they got from a $19.4 million loss to a $230,000 loss by highlighting what she regarded as the accounts where there might be some "softness." She did not say fraud.

. . .

[131] On the morning of August 6, 1998, Mr. Webster asked her a question about the Chicago construction account. In response, Ms. Messina asked Tony Fiorino to prepare a schedule of the Chicago account for Mr. Webster. She felt that she had the option of either hiding the fraud or of telling the whole story. She chose the latter. …

. . .

[137] Mr. Drabinsky and Mr. Gottlieb were locked out as of Monday August 10, 1998.

. . .

[211] The Crown filed thousands of pages of documents. They include financial statements, quarterly financial statements, draft statements, back up documentation, summary documents, memos, working papers, handwritten notes, minutes of the Board meetings, corporate history documents and a forensic report.

[212] The Crown relies on the documents to corroborate the witness testimony. The Crown also submits that even if the witness testimony is disbelieved, the documents stand on their own and establish beyond a reasonable doubt the knowledge and participation of Mr. Drabinsky and Mr. Gottlieb in the accounting manipulations. Some of the documents contain handwriting identified by Ms. Messina and Mr. Eckstein to be that of Mr. Drabinsky. One document contains handwriting admitted to be that of Mr. Gottlieb.

[213] The Crown says that the documentation establishes beyond a reasonable doubt that there were fraudulent accounting practices at Livent. …

• • •

[251] The Defence submits that the Crown has not proved beyond a reasonable doubt that Mr. Drabinsky and Mr. Gottlieb knew about the accounting practises at either MyGar or at Livent.

[252] It is argued that the evidence of the Crown witnesses is untrue. They conspired to place the blame on Mr. Drabinsky and Mr. Gottlieb in order to avoid responsibility for their actions. Their evidence was tainted by the KPMG investigation which made it clear that they would be rewarded if they implicated Mr. Drabinsky and Mr. Gottlieb. Thus, the Crown evidence cannot be relied upon. The documents do not stand alone. They cannot be understood without the evidence of the witnesses who cannot be believed.

• • •

[335] The evidence establishes beyond a reasonable doubt that the system of accounting at Livent was fraudulent. The financial statements were manipulated. The object was to keep income as close to budget as possible. This was done by moving expenses from one period to another, by amortization rolls, by applying the expenses of one show to another and by allocating operating costs to fixed asset accounts.

[336] Has the Crown proved beyond a reasonable doubt that Mr. Drabinsky and Mr. Gottlieb knew about this?

Employees' Evidence

[337] Mr. Eckstein and Ms. Messina are the two witnesses who say they saw Mr. Drabinsky and Mr. Gottlieb participate in the fraud. Mr. Eckstein and Ms. Messina are co-conspirators in the fraud. They also have an interest in the outcome of the case.

[338] *Vetrovec v. The Queen* highlighted the need to give jurors clear and sharp warnings of the risk of adopting the evidence of such witnesses. While the trier of fact is entitled to convict on the basis of the unsavoury witness testimony if it is believed, comfort should be sought in the form of confirmatory evidence. Corroboration should come from an independent source. The defence position is that all the witnesses are part of the conspiracy to commit fraud and then blame Mr. Drabinsky and Mr. Gottlieb for it. They thus lack the necessary level of independence to corroborate each other. This was recently confirmed by the Supreme Court of Canada: "Where evidence is 'tainted' by connection to the *Vetrovec* witness, it cannot serve to confirm his or her testimony."

[339] These principles guide the credibility analysis of the witnesses.

• • •

[343] There is not only Mr. Eckstein's conduct which is problematic. There is also his credibility. Some of his testimony was exaggerated. Some of it was overstated. Some of it

was changed when successfully challenged. The defence has highlighted many examples of this.

[344] Mr. Eckstein is an unsavoury witness. He is also the perfect fall guy.

• • •

[356] Mr. Eckstein had been hired by Mr. Drabinsky and Mr. Gottlieb. He was the one that they put in charge of their accounting department. It was very much their company. Between the two of them, they were involved in all aspects of the company. They were sophisticated business people and had a comprehensive and extensive knowledge of finances of the business. Mr. Gottlieb dealt with financing and the analysts. Mr. Drabinsky approved everything. They went through the financial statements in detail during meetings that lasted hours. It is inconsistent with the way they operated the company that Mr. Eckstein would have had the inclination or the ability to institute the accounting procedures without their knowledge. It is inconsistent with the way they reviewed the finances that he would have continued without their knowledge.

[357] Mr. Drabinsky and Mr. Gottlieb may have had different areas of expertise within the company. Between them, they covered it all. ...

• • •

[360] I believe that Mr. Eckstein gave the management summaries to Mr. Drabinsky and Mr. Gottlieb and discussed the documents with them at management meetings. The documents were discussed in detail and, as time went on the nature of the directions to Mr. Eckstein evolved. It started with specifics and then became a direction to simply come up with the numbers that would match budget.

[361] Mr. Drabinsky and Mr. Gottlieb were part of the decision and the direction to Mr. Eckstein that began this accounting system, the object of which was to get the numbers close to budget. As time went on and the company grew, they may not have been aware of every detail. They may not have been aware of the mechanisms by which the staff was implementing the adjustments. They may not have known about the computer programme change. They did not even know how to work a computer. However, they knew that improper adjustments were being made. They needed to have the adjustment made in order to have the income meet projections.

• • •

[373] The defence would argue that her testimony in its entirety was part of this same talent for self-preservation. They say that she implicated Mr. Drabinsky and Mr. Gottlieb in order to reduce the consequences for herself.

[374] I do not agree.

[375] Ms. Messina failed miserably in her role as officer of a public company. To participate in a fraud violated her duty. She could have stopped it and did not. Her conduct was inexcusable.

[376] That said, I believe her evidence as to Mr. Drabinsky and Mr. Gottlieb's role in the fraud. In particular, I believe her evidence about the executive meetings in October 1997 and February 1998. Her evidence about the preparations for the meetings was consistent with the evidence of the other witnesses as to the way the statements were prepared. Her evidence was consistent with the documents that were prepared for the executive meetings. Her evidence about Mr. Drabinsky and Mr. Gottlieb being at the table where the documents were being discussed and the manipulations directed is consistent with

that of Mr. Eckstein. Ms. Messina may have got the dates wrong for the October meetings, but I believe the meetings did take place.

[377] Her evidence and that of Mr. Eckstein is also confirmed by the reality of Livent. It was created by Mr. Drabinsky and Mr. Gottlieb. It was their vision. …

[378] Ms. Messina's evidence that in October 1997 Mr. Drabinsky pushed aside the document containing the "real" numbers to focus on the manipulated is consistent with Mr. Eckstein's reasons for wanting the real and manipulated figures to be on one document for the year-end.

. . .

[411] The documents are significant in several respects:

- The fact that the documents exist confirms the testimony of the employee witnesses that reports and summaries were made. In this respect they stand on their own and do not require testimony to explain them.
- The documents impart information that does not require explanation. The listing of adjustments and comparison of actual versus reported income is clear on the face of the documents. In this respect also, they stand on their own.
- The evidence of the employees, which I believe, amplifies their significance. In this respect, I am mindful of the defence submission that a document created by a *Vetrovec* witness should not depend upon the same witness to explain it. However, the evidence taken as a whole supports the explanations given by the witnesses.
- When viewed in the context of the way Livent was run, the documents have an even greater significance. They were being discussed in detail by the creators of the company who were sophisticated, accomplished business people. They knew the business. They would have known and understood its financial statements.

[412] Grant Malcolm, Diane Winkfein, Tony Fiorino and Christopher Craib testified about the number and types of documents prepared for management. The documents corroborate the evidence that detailed summaries were prepared. …

. . .

[434] Counsel for Mr. Drabinsky raised several "pillars" of reasonable doubt. They all point to a lack of knowledge on the part of both Mr. Drabinsky and Mr. Gottlieb. They are:

1. Their conduct during the KMPG due diligence leading up to the Ovitz deal;
2. Mr. Eckstein's instructions to Mr. Fiorino;
3. The hiring of Maria Messina;
4. The firing of Mr. Topol.

The Due Diligence

[435] The defence points out that neither Mr. Drabinsky nor Mr. Gottlieb directed anyone as to what to do or what to say during the KPMG due diligence process. They were not panicked. Others were. Had they known about the fraud they would not have behaved this way.

[436] The conduct of Mr. Drabinsky and Mr. Gottlieb is not consistent only with lack of knowledge. It is also consistent with a confidence that nothing would be discovered. The accounting practices at Livent had gone on for a long time. They were entrenched. The

financial statements had been audited and presented to the Board of Directors and the Audit Committee. Deloitte & Touche had gone along with them. The practices had become a way of life and no one had detected them. The confidence could easily have been the result of having fooled the auditors for many years. Deloitte & Touche did not know about the fraud in the accounting system. This confidence seems to have been justified for KPMG did not detect the accounting irregularities either.

[437] The conduct of Mr. Drabinsky and Mr. Gottlieb in connection with the due diligence leading up to the Ovitz transaction does not, in the entire context of the facts I believe, raise a reasonable doubt.

. . .

The Law: Counts 1 and 2

[465] Commercial affairs are to be conducted honestly. This is the single precept that anchors the offence of fraud.

[466] The offence is set out in the *Criminal Code*, R.S.C. 1985, c. C-46, section 380. During the time frame of the indictment it was amended to increase the subject matter of the offence from $1000 to $5000. It now reads:

> 380.(1) Every one who, by deceit, falsehood or other fraudulent means, whether or not it is a false pretence within the meaning of this Act, defrauds the public or any person, whether ascertained or not, of any property, money or valuable security,
>
> (a) is guilty of an indictable offence and liable to a term of imprisonment not exceeding ten years, where the subject-matter of the offence is a testamentary instrument or where the value of the subject-matter of the offence exceeds five thousand dollars;

[467] In *R. v. Olan* the Supreme Court of Canada broadened the law of fraud by including the general concept of dishonesty in the prohibited acts and by making it clear that actual economic loss was not essential to the offence. This "expansive interpretation" of the law established fraud as an offence "capable of encompassing a wide range of commercial dealings" and "broad enough in scope to encompass the entire panoply of dishonest commercial dealings."

[468] The *actus reus* of the offence will be established by proof of:

1. the prohibited act and
2. deprivation.

[469] The prohibited act includes deceit, falsehood or other fraudulent means. "Other fraudulent means" includes acts which are not in the nature of falsehood or deceit but which "can be properly stigmatized as dishonest."

[470] The deprivation may consist of actual loss or the placing of the victim's pecuniary interest at risk.

[471] The *mens rea* of the offence is established by proof of:

1. subjective knowledge of the prohibited act and
2. subjective knowledge that the prohibited act could have, as a consequence, the deprivation of another's pecuniary interest or could put the pecuniary interest of another at risk.

[472] The question is whether the accused subjectively appreciated that certain consequences would follow from his act, not whether he believed they were moral: "… the defrauder will not be acquitted because he believed what he was doing was honest."

[473] The fact that the accused may have hoped deprivation would not occur or may have thought what he was doing was not wrong is no defense. Where the accused knowingly undertook the acts in question aware that deprivation or risk of deprivation could follow, the accused is guilty. This is so whether he actually intended the consequences or was reckless as to whether they would occur. In other words a "sanguine belief that all will come out right in the end" is not a defense. "Many frauds" are perpetrated by people who think there is nothing wrong with what they are doing or who think it will turn out alright in the end.

…

> … [T]his inquiry has nothing to do with the accused's system of values. A person is not saved from conviction because he or she believes there is nothing wrong with what he or she is doing. The question is whether the accused subjectively appreciated that certain consequences would follow from his or her acts, not whether the accused believed the acts or their consequences to be moral.

[475] It is essential that dishonest commercial practices which put the pecuniary interest of others at risk be visited with criminal sanctions.

…

Verdict: Count 1

[486] The first count on the indictment reads:

> Garth Howard Drabinsky and Myron Irwin Gottlieb stand charged that, between the 1st day of December 1989 and the 31st day of May 1993, in the City of Toronto and elsewhere in the Province of Ontario and elsewhere in Canada, unlawfully did by deceit, falsehood or other fraudulent means defraud the public of property, money or valuable security having a value in excess of $5,000 through the company's initial pubic offering on the Toronto Stock Exchange, by making false representations as to the financial position and assets of MyGar Partnership which then became the assets of Live Entertainment of Canada Inc., contrary to Section 380(1)(a) of the *Criminal Code of Canada.*

[487] I believe that Mr. Drabinsky and Mr. Gottlieb directed that the Kofman/Execway invoices be booked to fixed assets and preproduction costs. They had devised all aspects of this kick-back scheme themselves. Mr. Kofman, Mr. Wayment and the documents establish this. Mr. Eckstein only found out about the scheme when he saw large invoices which had no real backup. It makes perfect sense that Mr. Eckstein would ask what they were and how to book them. I accept his evidence that he was directed by Mr. Gottlieb and Mr. Drabinsky to book them to fixed assets and preproduction costs. Whether the instructions came on a sheet or sheets of paper, I accept that they came to him as instructions. By allocating the expenses in this way, the assets of MyGar were inflated. I accept Mr. Eckstein's evidence that he suggested a write down but this was refused by Mr. Gottlieb and Mr. Drabinsky. The assets of MyGar thus included invoices that were part of a kick-back scheme and so the statements were false.

[488] The secondary argument of the defence is that there is no proof of detriment or potential detriment caused by the misallocation. The company was in fact undervalued and there is no evidence as to how much of the misallocation remained on the books at the time of the IPO.

[489] *Olan* made it clear that economic loss is not essential to the offence of fraud. The imperiling of an economic interest of another is sufficient even if there was no loss in fact. Since actual detriment does not need to be proved, the question is: was there proof of potential detriment or risk of pecuniary loss?

[490] The very nature of the IPO is that the public is being asked to invest its money in the company. The public is entitled to rely on all the financial statements in determining whether to risk funds. Principals of a company putting forward financial statements as part of the IPO package know this. Where the statements include a falsehood, the investor is at risk.

[491] Indeed here, the falsehoods were deliberately left in the income statement to attract (or to avoid deterring) investors. It was thought that a write off would have looked terrible. It follows that the true state of affairs would have been less attractive to investors. It follows that the lie was meant to induce investors.

[492] The inclusion of a balance sheet that is false is an act of deceit, falsehood and dishonesty. Since members of the public are entitled to rely on these statements before risking their funds, there is potential risk to the public.

[493] If the balance sheet is false, it is no answer to say that the investors would only look to the income statement. One cannot pick and choose sections that may be more or less important to a potential investor. The reasons for investing may be as diverse as the number of investors.

[494] That the accused did not profit from the falsehood is irrelevant to the charge. That the public did not suffer is irrelevant to the charge.

[495] The inclusion of the false statements in the IPO was an act of deceit, falsehood and dishonesty which put the pecuniary interests of the public at risk.

[496] Mr. Drabinsky and Mr. Gottlieb are guilty of count 1.

Verdict: Count 2

[497] The second count on the indictment reads:

> Garth Howard Drabinsky and Myron Irwin Gottlieb stand charged that, between May 10, 1993, and August 10, 1998, both dates inclusive, in the City of Toronto and elsewhere in the Province of Ontario and elsewhere in Canada, and elsewhere in the United States of America, unlawfully did by deceit, falsehood or other fraudulent means defraud the public or property, money, or valuable security having a value in excess of $5,000, by making false representations as to the financial position of Live Entertainment of Canada Inc. and Livent Inc., contrary to Section 380(1)(a) of the *Criminal Code of Canada*.

[498] Mr. Drabinsky and Mr. Gottlieb founded Livent. They started with one production and one theatre. Between them they knew all aspects of the company's finances. They knew what money was coming in. They knew what the expenses were. They received and reviewed in detail the voluminous reports and summaries from the accounting staff. They went on "road shows" to promote the company. Their presentation notes show they both

spoke at a detailed, sophisticated level about matters including EBITA, cash flow, preproduction costs, and earnings per share. They knew how to raise money and how important the financial statements were in that regard.

[499] They knew and directed the accounting practices in order to keep the investment funds coming in.

[500] Mr. Drabinsky and Mr. Gottlieb were clearly dedicated to Livent. It is clear from enormous work they put into the company and the spectacular results they achieved on the creative front. It is also evident in Mr. Gottlieb's confidential memo to Mr. Drabinsky of March 4, 1998. There he spoke of the need to enter the Ovitz transaction with "eyes open." He articulated his concern that the commitment of Mr. Ovitz to Livent would not be "his first priority." He wanted assurances that the involvement would be a full-time effort. He went on to say:

> In the absence of a high degree of comfort in this area, I would rather retain independence and use the internally generated cash flow during the next two-three year period as a means of accomplishing a slow privatization that will allow us to better reflect real values.

[501] The founders were dedicated to the continuation of the company. It may be that all would have worked out in the end if Mr. Webster had not asked about the theatre account. It may be that shareholder value would have been enhanced, as planned, under new management. That does not matter. What matters is that there was deceit in the financial statements which put the property of others at risk.

[502] Mr. Drabinsky and Mr. Gottlieb were so devoted to the continuation of Livent that they directed the falsification of the financial statements in order to continue the flow of money to the company.

[503] I am satisfied beyond a reasonable doubt that Mr. Drabinsky and Mr. Gottlieb initiated the improper accounting system and knew of its continuation throughout the years 1994-1998. The actions of Mr. Drabinsky and Mr. Gottlieb satisfy all three of the ways a prohibited act can be conducted: they were deceitful, they perpetrated a falsehood and reasonable people would consider them dishonest.

[504] The company experienced exponential growth in a very short time. The exponential growth of the company was analogous to an athlete taking a performance enhancing drug. The result may be spectacular but the means involve cheating.

[505] Mr. Drabinsky and Mr. Gottlieb are guilty of count 2.

. . .

[511] Mr. Drabinsky and Mr. Gottlieb are guilty of count 3.

[512] For these reasons there will be guilty verdicts on all three counts on the indictment.

An appeal to the Ontario Court of Appeal from these convictions was unsuccessful, though the court reduced the sentences imposed by the trial judge. See *R v Drabinsky*, 2011 ONCA 582, leave to appeal to SCC refused.

A more recent case that illustrates the complexities of prosecuting financial crimes is the ultimately unsuccessful prosecution of several senior executives of Nortel Networks Corporation (one of Canada's oldest and best known corporations) for fraudulently misrepresenting the financial results of the company over a period of time in the early 2000s. The trial did not take place until 2012, with the lengthy trial judgment, which canvassed complicated evidence in great detail, ultimately being issued very early in 2013. The essence of the Crown's case against the Nortel senior executives was that they manipulated "accrued liability balances" on Nortel's financial statements in order to produce more positive financial results than was in fact the case.

R v Dunn
2013 ONSC 137

MARROCCO J:

[1] The defendants are charged with two counts of fraud.

[2] The first count alleges that, between January 1, 2000 and April 28, 2004, the three accused did, by deceit falsehood or other fraudulent means, defraud the public by deliberately misrepresenting the financial results of Nortel Networks Corporation.

[3] The second alleges that, between January 1, 2000 and April 28, 2004, the three accused did, by deceit falsehood or other fraudulent means, defraud Nortel Networks Corporation by deliberately misrepresenting the financial results of Nortel Networks Corporation.

[4] In both counts, it is alleged that the extent of the fraud exceeded $5,000.

. . .

[8] Nortel Networks Corporation ("Nortel") was in the business of providing data, wireless and optical networking products and services to telecommunications carriers and enterprise customers around the world. Between 1998 and 2001, Nortel Networks Corporation and its predecessor, Nortel Networks Limited, undertook a total of twenty-two acquisitions for an aggregate purchase price of $29 billion. These acquisitions were undertaken during a period of both strong economic growth in 1999 and 2000 and rapid infrastructure build-out by the telecommunications industry.

[9] By 2001, the telecommunications industry began to experience a slowdown attributed to excess capacity created as a result of the build-out, the consolidation of service providers within the industry and lower capital spending by industry participants. As a result, there was a dramatic and significant reduction in the demand for Nortel's products and services.

[10] In response to the industry and economic downturn in 2001, Nortel attempted to streamline its operations. Nortel reduced its overall workforce from approximately 94,002 to approximately 52,000 and incurred severance and termination charges in excess of $3.3 billion. Nortel discontinued aspects of its operations and divested itself of investments. Nortel recorded a write down of $12.4 billion for goodwill and other intangible assets in the quarter ending June 30, 2001.

[11] In 2002, Nortel reduced its workforce to 37,000 as at December 31, 2002. Nortel experienced a write down of its goodwill in its Optical business of approximately $595 million and, on December 13, 2002, Nortel pledged substantially all of its assets in favor of certain lenders.

[12] Nortel experienced net income losses of $197 million in 1999, $2.9 billion in 2000, $27.4 billion in 2001 and $3.6 billion in 2002.

[13] The equity of Nortel's shareholders shrank from $28.7 billion in 2000 to $1.9 billion in 2002.

[14] The circumstances had become so dire at Nortel that, when a quarterly result was announced, the auditors had to take a view of the next twelve months from the date of the quarterly report and opine on the likelihood of Nortel continuing as a going concern.

...

[26] Mr. Richmond indicated that the free-fall that Nortel was experiencing resulted in a situation where Nortel could be comfortable with the value of an asset on one day and next day be convinced that the asset was severely diminished in value.

...

[29] Nortel's first re-statement re-stated more than $900 million in excess accrued liabilities into previously-published Nortel financial statements. I am satisfied that one of the underlying reasons for the presence of these excess accrued liability balances was the determination of Nortel's Audit Committee, auditors, senior management and field staff to provide for every risk and, thereby, avoid unpleasant surprises.

...

[48] … In this case, the defendants are, in count one, facing a charge of defrauding the public by deliberately misrepresenting the financial results of Nortel Networks Corporation. Accordingly, if one applies the same conclusion that the Court of Appeal expressed in *R. v. Drabinsky, supra*, the conclusion in this case must be that the Crown has to prove that the accused knew that Nortel's financial statements contained misrepresentations that were material to the decision of a member of the investing public to buy, hold or sell Nortel publicly-traded securities.

[49] With respect to count two, the essence of the matter seems to be that the misrepresentation of Nortel's financial results created the economic risk that Nortel Networks Corporation would pay money to the defendants that ought not to be paid to them.

...

[59] Count number one alleges a fraud upon the public. Nortel was publicly-traded. I am satisfied that the public in this case includes the investing public. Persons who own publicly-traded Nortel securities are included in the term "public." Persons who are thinking of purchasing publicly-traded Nortel securities are included in the term "public." I accept and intend to apply the notion of materiality that is described in Mr. Chambers' report. A misrepresented financial result is material if, in light of the surrounding circumstances, the magnitude of the item is such that it is probable that the judgment of a reasonable member of the investing public would have been changed or influenced by the correction of the item. The omission of a financial result is material if, in light of the surrounding circumstances, the magnitude of the item is such that it is probable that the judgment of a reasonable member of the investing public would have been changed or influenced by the disclosure of the item.

...

[63] Mr. Dunn was Nortel's CEO during the time with which we are concerned. Prior to that, he was Nortel's CFO and, prior to that, he was Nortel's Corporate Controller.

[64] Mr. Dunn, Mr. Beatty and Mr. Gollogly were senior officers of a corporation publicly-traded on the New York Stock Exchange with annual revenues of approximately $10 billion per year during the time frame of the indictment.

[65] I am satisfied that Mr. Dunn, Mr. Beatty and Mr. Gollogly were aware of the specifics of SAB 99, the importance of determining whether items of financial information

were materially important and, finally, the importance of making the appropriate disclosure to the public.

. . .

[75] The Crown submits that there was a long-standing culture of Conservatism at Nortel and many of the witnesses who are chartered accountants or certified management accountants had to know that accrued liability balances therefore existed and were being used to meet earnings targets. The Crown submits that compliant employees assisted the accused in misrepresenting the financial results of Nortel Networks Corporation.

[76] I am satisfied that, during the time-frame of the indictment, there was at Nortel a culture of Conservatism, in the accounting sense of that term. I am satisfied that this culture existed for in excess of twenty years. It has to be remembered, however, that, until 1999, the SEC and the Ontario Securities Commission had not prohibited the practice of releasing accrued liability balances to bridge the gap between a company's actual performance and a previously announced financial target. Coincidentally, it was in the same year, 1999, that Nortel began experiencing significant losses.

. . .

[97] A general principle underlying US GAAP is that expenses are to be matched with revenues as long as it is reasonable to do so. When work or a product makes its contribution to revenue, expenses associated with that work or product are recognized even if those expenses cannot be known with precision. This matching principle is applied through accrual accounting. In such a situation, the accrued expenses are estimated.

[98] An accrued expense is an expense that has been incurred but not yet paid. An accrued liability is an obligation disclosed on the balance sheet that is not yet payable.

[99] Recording an accrued expense reduces income on the profit and loss statement and, simultaneously, results in the recording of an accrued liability on the balance sheet.

[100] Once the accrued liability is recorded on the balance sheet of a publicly-traded corporation like Nortel, the corporation is required to assess that accrued liability balance at the end of each financial quarter to determine whether something has occurred within that quarter which requires a change (*i.e.*, an increase or decrease) in the estimate of the liability.

[101] If an event has occurred within that quarter which requires a change in the estimate of the accrued liability balance, then the accrued liability balance should be either increased or decreased in that quarter. This is sometimes referred to as a "change in estimate."

[102] If an accrued liability balance is increased as a result of the change in estimate, earnings are negatively affected.

[103] If an accrued liability balance is decreased as a result of a change in estimate, earnings are positively affected.

. . .

[105] When the accrued expense becomes certain and is paid, the earnings of the corporation can be favorably affected. The following example, borrowed and slightly-amended from the Crown's expert evidence, illustrates this.

[106] Assume that, as a result of a contract into which it has entered, a publicly-traded corporation is involved in litigation at the close of its fiscal year ending December 31, 2002 and assume that an unfavorable outcome is probable. Management does not know

the exact amount it will have to pay, but its reasonable estimate is that the judgment against it will be for not less than $3 million and not more than $9 million. If no amount within that range appears to be a better estimate than any other, Financial Accounting Standards No. 5 ("FAS 5") requires that an expense of $3 million be recorded at December 31, 2002, *i.e.*, the expense estimate at the lowest end of the estimated range of appropriate exposures.

[107] Recording this expense on the profit and loss statement will have a $3 million negative impact on earnings for the period ending December 31, 2002. Recording this accrued expense also results in an accrued liability of $3 million being recorded on the balance sheet.

[108] In the example above, if the company thought that $4 million was the best estimate of its liability, then it would record $4 million as an expense/liability despite the fact that it was not at the lowest end of the range of appropriate liabilities. It is only when no amount within the acceptable range is a better estimate than any other that the lowest amount in the range must be chosen.

[109] Assume, for simplicity's sake, that the company settles the litigation for $2 million in the third quarter of 2003 and pays the plaintiff in that quarter. At the end of the third quarter of 2003, the company should eliminate the accrued liability of $3 million. $2 million of the liability was used to pay the plaintiff so the remaining balance is $1 million. This remaining $1 million excess is removed from the balance sheet and $1 million is recorded on the profit and loss statement as a positive impact on earnings. This is sometimes referred to as a "releasing" the accrued liability balance to the profit and loss statement or "releasing the accrual" or a "releasing the $1 million." Sometimes it is referred to as "reversing the accrual."

[110] In some of the documentation received in evidence, accrued liabilities were referred to as "provisions." Setting up accrued expense/liability was sometimes referred to as "provisioning."

...

[113] An accrued liability can be falsely stated on the balance sheet if any one of three things happens:

- first, if, contrary to US GAAP, the liability is fictitious;
- second, if, contrary to US GAAP, an artificially-high number is used to estimate the liability when it is first set up;
- third, if an event occurs within a quarter which calls for a change (*i.e.*, an increase or decrease) in the estimate of the accrued liability and, contrary to US GAAP, a change in estimate does not occur. From that point on, accrued liabilities will be either overstated or understated on the balance sheet.

[114] When there are excess accrued liability balances on the balance sheet, an opportunity is created to tailor earnings by arbitrarily "releasing the accrual" to positively impact earnings in the quarter where you want to increase earnings. The motive for tailoring earnings is often to meet a previously-publicized financial target. Such behavior is contrary to US GAAP. The financial results in the tailored quarter are misrepresented. Whether the misrepresentation is material is a separate consideration.

...

[170] Mr. Richmond testified that Nortel operated in at least sixty countries in the world. He stated that the organizational chart included dozens of separate entities operating in geographies all over the world. He pointed out that, every time you had a subsidiary Nortel Corporation, generally speaking, you had to conduct an audit.

[171] Mr. Richmond described Nortel as a large, complex organization with a large and complex audit-processing team. He estimated that there were hundreds of people involved in Nortel auditing.

[172] This fact is important because it means that the financial information which the Regions were forwarding to corporate headquarters each quarter was financial information which had been produced by entities which, themselves, had been audited.

. . .

[184] Ms. Helen Verity, the Director of Consolidations, indicated that the Consolidation Close meant that Nortel consolidated its results.

. . .

[192] The evidence established that there were up to twenty draft financial statements produced over the close. Each draft statement was numbered.

. . .

[197] Ms. Verity testified that she was responsible for managing the time-lines associated with the close process. Ms. Verity testified that there was a well-established close schedule. It was distributed by e-mail prior to the close and one of her responsibilities was to hold people accountable to that schedule. It was her responsibility to work with Nortel people to resolve timing issues.

. . .

[203] There was a Frank Dunn binder which was prepared for the purpose of giving Mr. Dunn a summary of the close. Douglas Beatty and Michael Gollogly and the Assistant Controller and several others received copies of this binder.

. . .

[207] Nortel had a long-standing corporate policy concerning estimates of liabilities. Nortel Corporate Policy 300.33 provided that any anticipated decline in the value of Nortel assets and any anticipated liabilities must be provided for in accordance with the accounting concept of Conservatism.

. . .

[210] The accounting concept of Conservatism is a characteristic of financial accounting. It is referenced in paragraph 17 of Accounting Principles Board Statement No. 4, as follows: "Conservatism. Frequently assets and liabilities are measured in the context of significant uncertainties historically; managers, investors, and accountants have generally preferred that possible errors in measurement be in the direction of understatement rather than overstatement of net income and net assets. This has led to the convention of Conservatism …"

. . .

[215] Mr. Richmond elaborated that, when an organization is experiencing the "free fall" that Nortel was experiencing, a customer that one day might appear sound may very well be in financial peril the next day. As a result, Mr. Richmond stated that it was his experience at Nortel that, in preparing Nortel's financial statements, there was an overarching desire by the directors and the executive management team to ensure that they

did the best job possible to prepare the financial statements to adequately account for risks.

[216] Mr. Richmond testified that Nortel was operating in an atmosphere of doubt about the value of its assets and the operative principle was "if in doubt provide for it."

[217] It struck Mr. Richmond as reasonable and unsurprising that Nortel employees and Deloitte professional staff defaulted to a position that was at the conservative end of the range when recording an accrued expense and liability estimating a particular risk. Mr. Richmond testified that this was something he personally embraced and that it was appropriate in Nortel's set of circumstances "to provide at the reasonably hard end of that conservative range." He also testified that the identification of the range involved considerable judgment.

...

[229] During the time period described in the indictment, Nortel lost billions. I do not find it unusual that sensible people confronted with that reality would think that the worst-case scenario was the best estimate of the risks to Nortel's assets. I also do not find it unusual that sensible people confronted with Nortel's reality would be slow to decrease accrued liabilities already on the balance sheet.

[230] I am satisfied that throughout the time period described in the indictment accrued liabilities at Nortel were estimated at the high-end of the range of estimates and sometimes on a worst-case scenario basis. According to the evidence a risk can be provided for on a worst-case scenario basis provided that it is the judgment of the person estimating the risk that the worst-case scenario is the best estimate of that risk.

...

[236] I am satisfied beyond a reasonable doubt that they knew that the policy of Conservatism had created excess accrued liabilities and, therefore, they knew that these excess liabilities could be released to assist in meeting financial targets.

[237] I also find that the enormous losses suffered by Nortel in these years created a situation in which senior management, Nortel's Board of directors and Nortel's auditors were quite reasonably concentrating on doing all things necessary to make sure that Nortel had sufficient cash reserves to survive and continue in business. I am satisfied that non cash impacting excess accrued liabilities on the balance sheet were not a priority.

...

[239] The evidence persuades me that accruals were present on Nortel's consolidated balance sheet which could not be supported by documentation. However, I decline to draw the inference that these accruals never existed. It seems more logical to me that the downsizing of Nortel, which involved the closing of offices, the selling of real estate and, undoubtedly, the storage of documents, created a situation in which supporting documentation for some of Nortel's accrued liability balances could not be located. Further, the loss of employees (two out of every three worldwide) created a situation in which the institutional memory concerning the unsupported accruals no longer existed within the company. I am satisfied that these were the reasons why unsupported accrued liabilities were present on Nortel's consolidated balance sheet.

[240] Also, the evidence does establish and, I so find, that excessive accrued liabilities existed because accrued liabilities were not released when they should have been and because accrued liabilities were not adjusted when they should have been.

...

[252] Mr. Cleghorn testified that, in the summer of 2002, Nortel employees were being approached by the competition. By this time, many employees at Nortel had been laid off or fired, sales were declining and the auditors considered Nortel to be a high-risk audit. Employees with stock options found that the options were worthless. In an effort to prevent valuable employees from leaving the company, Mr. Cleghorn testified that the Board adopted a Return to Profitability Bonus Plan.

[253] The Return to Profitability Bonus Plan was announced in November 2002. It provided eligible employees with a special bonus if Nortel achieved profitability for any quarter in the period from Q4 2002 through to and including Q4 2003.

[254] Profitability for the purpose of this bonus plan was based on pro forma earnings from continuing operations; it also included an accrual for the cost of the bonus in such period. In other words, there had to be sufficient pro forma earnings before taxes from operations to pay for the bonus. Senior executives would be paid in three tranches.

. . .

[265] Nortel's first decision to restate financial statements for 2000, 2001, 2002, Q1 2003 and Q2 2003 was announced on October 23, 2003.

[266] This restatement essentially restated excessive accrued balances on Nortel's balance sheet back to the quarters when they should have been released to the profit and loss statement.

. . .

[270] Mr. Richmond described the situation at Nortel when consideration was being given for the first time to restating financial statements from earlier periods. The immediate cause of this discussion was the release to the profit and loss statement in Q2 03 (the second quarter of 2003) of approximately $142 million in accrued liabilities which could no longer be supported. The release of this $142 million would have had a positive effect on earnings. These balances had been released during preparation of one of the preliminary drafts of Nortel's Q2 03 financial statements during the Q2 03 close process described earlier.

. . .

[273] It was Mr. Richmond's evidence that Mr. Dunn maintained that the $142 million was the total number of unsupported liabilities on Nortel's consolidated balance sheet. It was Mr. Dunn's view that the $142 million should remain released to the profit and loss statement of Q2 03 and that there should be appropriate disclosure of this fact in the press release publishing Nortel's Q2 03 financial results. Mr. Dunn maintained that his view should be respected because not only was he the CEO, but he had been, prior to that, Nortel's CFO and Corporate Controller.

[274] This is perhaps an appropriate time to observe the obvious. Mr. Dunn was spectacularly wrong; the first restatement identified in excess of $900 million of accrued liabilities that could no longer remain on Nortel's consolidated balance sheet.

. . .

[286] It was Ms. Sledge's evidence that, at some point during the Balance Sheet Review process, those involved realized that there would need to be a restatement of prior years' financial results. Her evidence in this regard is also consistent with Mr. Richmond's evidence that, as the Comprehensive Balance Sheet Review progressed, the quantum of excess accrued liabilities increased. Mr. Richmond indicated that, as a practical matter, the error with respect to accrued liabilities was so large that a Restatement was inevitable.

[287] I accept this aspect of Ms. Sledge's evidence.

. . .

[307] Mr. Wilson, whose evidence I accept, testified that the impact of the restatement of $900 million in accrued liability balances identified during the Comprehensive Balance Sheet Review was favorable to shareholders. The $900 million represented expenses on the balance sheet that did not have to be recognized. Shareholders' equity was increased by $900 million.

. . .

[319] I am not persuaded that any or all of the three accused insisted upon an unreasonably short timeline in an effort to make certain that the first restatement failed to uncover the true extent of the accrued liability problem on Nortel's balance sheet.

. . .

[324] I am not satisfied beyond a reasonable doubt that Nortel's original financial statements for 2000, 2001, 2002, Q1 03 and Q2 03 were materially misstated. I am not satisfied that Nortel's original financial statements for those fiscal years materially misrepresented Nortel's financial results. I am not satisfied beyond a reasonable doubt that Nortel's financial statements published after the first restatement materially misrepresented Nortel's financial results.

[325] I am satisfied that Nortel's original financial statements for the years 2000, 2001, 2002, Q1 03 and Q2 03 properly reflected Nortel's financial reality.

. . .

[348] The Second Restatement of Nortel's previously-published financial results was released January 11, 2005.

[349] A press release, dated January 11, 2005, announced the restatement of Nortel's consolidated financial results for the fiscal years ended December 31, 2001 and 2002. It also released a revision of Nortel's previously-announced results for the 2003 fiscal year.

. . .

[361] During Q1 03, Nortel's financial results were affected by the release of $361 million in accrued liability balances to income. These releases affected Nortel's balance sheet and profit and loss statement for Q1 03. The first restatement restated $111 million of these balances. The second restatement restated a further $106 million of these balances.

[362] During Q2 03, Nortel's financial results were affected by the release of $372 million in accrued liability balances to income. These releases affected Nortel's balance sheet and profit and loss statement for Q2 03. The first restatement restated $105 million of these balances. The second restatement restated a further $105 million of these balances.

[363] The Crown submits that this indicates that the original Q1 03 and Q2 03 releases were not in the "normal course" and that, therefore, Nortel's financial results were misrepresented in the original financial statements and the first restatement of those financial statements. The Crown argued that the effect of the two restatements was to demonstrate that approximately 2/3 of the accrued liability balances released during Q1 03 and Q2 03 were wrongly released in those periods. The Crown submits that this supports its argument that the Comprehensive Balance Sheet Review was misrepresented as comprehensive and that the resulting financial statements misrepresented Nortel's financial results.

. . .

[400] It is not contrary to the criminal law to attempt to manage the affairs of a corporation to achieve a financial target. The question is whether, in attempting to achieve

the targeted result, those responsible for preparation of the corporation's financial results cause the financial statements to misrepresent the corporation's financial results.

[401] Accordingly, the question becomes did the late entry accrued expenses/liabilities cause a misrepresentation of Nortel's financial results?

. . .

[491] It would be wrong to conclude in a criminal case such as this that the $319 million reduction in revenue means that Nortel's original financial statements misstated its revenue in 2001 in 2002 by $319 million. Describing the original JDS entries as false or wrong inaccurately characterizes what occurred and could easily lead to the false conclusion that something inappropriate happened when the original accounting was done. A consideration of the details of this transaction illustrates why it is impossible to draw the inference which the Crown urges from the fact that accounting entries are restated. The accounting for this transaction was changed because Deloitte changed its mind. A consideration of the specifics of this restatement of the JDS Uniphase transaction makes it clear that it is dangerous to generalize about items that are restated.

[492] When the facts of this specific restatement are known, it is clear that the accused could not have known that the original treatment of the $500 million purchase price discount was an error or wrong or false. Such words are not appropriate when describing the fact that Deloitte changed its mind.

. . .

[506] Mr. Kinney explained the difficulty he faced trying to clean up the Wireless balance sheet. Whether liabilities remained on the balance sheet came down to a judgment call based on the representation of the individual who was responsible for the specific accrued liability balances on the Wireless balance sheet. The tricky part, according to Mr. Kinney, arose because many of the liabilities had to do with liquidated damages or potential customer claims. These items were, therefore, self-determined. Within the sales organization, the decision was dependent upon internal representation that there was a liability and that the liability needed to remain on the balance sheet.

[507] Mr. Kinney said that he viewed the passage of time as the failsafe mechanism. The longer something was on the balance sheet without a claim the more confident he became that it could be taken off the balance sheet. Mr. Kinney said that, in his judgment, an accrued liability balance could be released to the profit and loss statement if there was a high degree of certainty, if not virtual certainty, that the liability no longer existed. Mr. Kinney said he followed the practice of allowing a cooling-off period when he thought an accrued liability balance could be released to the profit and loss statement. Specifically, he waited one extra quarter to make sure that an unexpected exposure did not present itself.

. . .

[524] The largest late entry accrued expense/liability in Q4 02 was $50 million. This accrual was in relation to 360 Networks litigation. This entry was reviewed during the second restatement. Deloitte's conclusion was "accrual was appropriate based primarily on in-house legal representation." Accordingly, this entry was never restated.

. . .

[543] Susan Shaw prepared a compilation dealing with accrued liabilities and presented it to Mr. Gollogly in Q4 02. Her compilation indicated that $303 million in accrued liabilities were no longer required and available for release.

. . .

[599] When I consider all the evidence, including the evidence to which I have made specific reference, I am not satisfied beyond a reasonable doubt that the accruals solicited by Mr. Harrison and recorded in Q4 02 resulted in a misrepresentation of Nortel's US GAAP financial results for Q4 02 or fiscal 2002.

[600] I am not satisfied that Nortel's financial results for Q4 02 were misrepresented due to the solicitation of late entry accrued liability expenses/balances.

[601] I am satisfied that $222 million of the $303 million identified by Ms. Shaw in 2002 as provisions no longer required and available for release were, in fact, released in Q3 02 and Q4 02. I am also satisfied that a portion of the $57 million identified as unreleased was so noted because it could not be identified and, therefore it cannot be determined whether those unsupported provisions were released or not in 2002 or 2003.

[602] I am not persuaded that the release of these accrued liability balances in Q3 02 and Q4 02 materially misrepresented Nortel's financial results in those periods or for the fiscal year 2002.

[603] The circumstances surrounding the $10 million released in Q1 2003 and the $14 million, released in Q2 2003 were not disclosed in the evidence. I am not satisfied that those releases misrepresented Nortel's financial results in Q1 03 or Q2 03.

[604] I am not satisfied beyond a reasonable doubt that the manner in which Nortel dealt with the $303 million in accrued liability balances identified by Susan Shaw as no longer required and available for release in her October 2002 compilation misrepresented Nortel's financial results in Q4 02, fiscal 2002, Q1 03 or Q2 03.

Q1 03 & Q2 03

The release of $361 million in Q1 03 and $372 million in Q2 03

[605] Quantitatively, Nortel released $361 million in accrued liability balances to its profit and loss statement in Q1 03. The Crown contends that, in its original filings, the accused, on behalf of Nortel, falsely represented that these accruals were in the normal course.

[606] Included in the $361 million and accrued liability balance releases were $80 million in accrued liability balance releases relating to Non-op. The Crown contends this $80 million was improperly released and, further, that the motive for the improper $80 million release was the desire on the part of the accused to qualify for a bonus and to meet previously-published financial targets.

. . .

[613] The Crown's expert did not express an opinion consistent with the Crown's contention.

. . .

[641] This is another accrued liability that was originally released in Q1 03. It was part of the $361 million in total releases for that quarter. It was not restated during the first restatement.

[642] It was also identified by Wilmer Cutler Pickering as a release which should be reviewed and, as such, was subject to "cradle-to-grave" reconsideration.

[643] Some context is helpful in considering this accrued liability balance.

[644] Nortel had several claims against Genuity, totaling approximately $156 million. Genuity alleged that Nortel was liable for substantial claims arising out of their business

relationship. Specifically, Genuity alleged that Nortel had supplied defective equipment, had resiled from a guarantee and, finally, that Nortel was liable to Genuity for contributions to a joint development and marketing fund.

[645] Genuity filed a petition for re-organization under the US Bankruptcy Code in November 2002. At the same time, Genuity proposed to sell all of its assets free and clear of pre-existing claims to an arm's length third-party purchaser.

[646] The arm's length purchaser received permission to purchase Genuity's assets in Q1 03 and the $19 million accrued liability balance was released to Nortel's profit and loss statement.

[647] Nortel's counsel advised that part of Genuity's claim was well-founded in its opinion. Nortel and Genuity reached a settlement at the end of Q2 03. Nortel's counsel was of the view that the settlement would not be approved by the Bankruptcy Court because they believed it would be opposed by others interested in Genuity's bankruptcy. However, there was no opposition to the settlement and the Bankruptcy Court approved the settlement in Q3 03.

[648] During the second restatement, the release was reviewed. The opinion of the Deloitte reviewers was that the Q1 03 release was appropriate. However, the U.S. National Office of Deloitte & Touche overruled the Deloitte reviewers and required that this conclusion be changed. Deloitte's U.S. national office required that the $23 million release in Q1 03 be classified as an error on the basis that the release should have occurred in Q2 03 instead of Q1 03.

[649] This release also undermines the position taken by the Crown with respect to the Q1 03 and Q2 03 releases. The Genuity release reveals that the $23 million released in Q1 03 was restated *into* Q2 03. The Crown's submission is undermined because it only takes into account releases that were restated out of Q2 03; it ignores the releases that were restated into Q2 03. This same observation applies to Q1 03. The Crown's submission does not take into account those releases restated into Q1 03.

[650] Finally, the specifics of this accrued liability balance indicate that it was restated because Deloitte, in essence, disagreed with itself.

[651] There is no evidence that would permit me to conclude that any or all of the accused were responsible for this error or for the failure to restate it in the first restatement.

...

[662] The specific releases to which I have referred demonstrate that the decision to restate on account of an error can be the same thing as saying that there was a decision to restate on account of a difference of opinion. Clearly new information can affect the decision to restate. Arguably hindsight can be a factor in the decision to restate.

[663] I agree with the Crown that the fact that accrued liability balances were restated is capable of supporting an inference that financial results were misrepresented, but I am not persuaded by the evidence which I have heard that I should draw such an inference in this case.

[664] As a result, I cannot give effect to the Crown's submissions concerning the inferences I should draw from the fact that original Q1 03 and Q2 03 accrued liability balance releases were restated.

[665] I am not satisfied beyond a reasonable doubt that the three accused misrepresented Nortel's Q1 03 and Q2 03 financial results by releasing to income $361 million and $372 million respectively in accrued liability balances. Further I am not satisfied that the

original release to income of $361 million and $372 million misrepresented Nortel's financial results.

. . .

[666] There was no triggering event in Q1 03 that would have justified the release of this $80 million in accrued liability balances to Nortel's profit and loss statements for Q1 03. This fact was well-known to everyone.

[667] The Crown alleges that the release of this $80 million in Non-Op accrued liabilities to the profit and loss statement in Q1 03 had the effect of changing pro forma losses in Q1 into a profit which resulted in substantial Return to Profitability and Restricted Stock Unit bonuses being paid to all three defendants in May 2003.

. . .

[676] I have no difficulty in accepting the fact that all three accused knew what targets had to be hit before they were entitled to the Return to Profitability Bonus and the Restricted Stock Unit Bonus. I attach no significance to that fact; it is simply rational economic behavior. The inference is easily drawn from the access that all three accused had access to Outlooks (forecasts), as well as their positions in the company. The evidence was, for example, that Mr. Dunn played a role in deciding the milestones for the Return to Profitability Bonus.

. . .

[714] I am satisfied that the Return to Profitability Bonus was payable in Q1 2003 with or without the release of $80 million in Non-op accrued liability balances. I am satisfied that the Success Plan Bonus was payable with or without the release of $80 million in Non-Op accrued liability balances. The Restricted Stock Unit Bonus Plan was not an issue in Q1 03.

[715] I am satisfied that Nortel achieved net US GAAP income in Q1 03 with or without the $80 million.

[716] I am satisfied that Mr. Hathway was not misled when he was told by either Mr. Beatty or Mr. Gollogly that the Return to Profitability Bonus would have been paid with or without the release of the $80 million in Non-op accrued liability balances.

[717] I am not satisfied that the accused used Non-op "cookie jar" accrued liability balances to manage earnings and permit the payment of a bonus in Q1 03.

[718] I am not satisfied that the inclusion of the $80 million with which we are concerned in Nortel's profit and loss statement for Q1 03 misrepresented Nortel's financial results.

. . .

[959] The Crown suggested that the way in which the Siemens accrued liability balance was manipulated illustrated the management of earnings to achieve a bonus target. The Siemens $4 million dollar release occurred originally in Q2 03. This is an appropriate place to examine that release in detail.

[960] In connection with the January 28, 2000 acquisition of a company called Qtera, that company and two of its employees were named as defendants in a lawsuit filed by Siemens ICN in Palm Beach County Florida. The lawsuit (*Siemens v. Qtera, Diner & Cao*) alleged, among other things, misappropriation of trade secrets.

[961] An accrued liability balance was set up to allow for the fact that Nortel might be unsuccessful in defending the lawsuit. The original accrued liability balance was in the amount of $36 million; it was part of a larger entry involving various Qtera balances.

[962] The original accrued liability balance was set up in Q3 01. In Q4 01, a portion of this balance, namely $32 million, was internally re-classified from Corporate to the United States where the litigation was taking place. This left the $4 million balance in Corporate on account of the Siemens litigation.

[963] Mr. Beatty was Nortel's Controller at this time and responsible for Corporate accrued liability balances.

[964] Nortel entered into a settlement agreement with Siemens on September 17, 2001. Nortel's first payment to Siemens on account of the settlement in the amount of $20 million occurred on October 25, 2001. A final payment of $12 million due in October 2002 remained.

[965] Mr. Beatty was required, as the CFO, to authorize the final $12 million payment. Upon being requested to authorize this payment, Mr. Beatty asked Mr. Gollogly, the Controller in October 2002, to look into the matter and advise him about it. Mr. Beatty was later told that the proposed final payment amount was correct and the final payment was made in October 2002. Accordingly, as of October 2002, approximately $32 million of the original $36 million accrued liability balance had been used. The accrued liability balance in the amount of $4 million remained with Corporate.

• • •

[992] I am not satisfied beyond a reasonable doubt that the three accused used the $4 million Siemens accrued liability balance to falsely represent to Nortel's Audit Committee, JLRC committee and board of directors that Nortel had achieved the financial results of meeting the Restricted Stock Unit Bonus Plan milestone of –6.5%.

[993] I am not satisfied that the restatement of this accrued liability balance to Q4 01 proves anything. Mr. Hathway thought that the accrued liability balance should have been released in Q4 02 when the final settlement payment was made. This seems to be a reasonable conclusion. It apparently was not correct according to Deloitte's opinion in the first restatement. The difference of opinion demonstrates that one should be careful before drawing an inculpatory inference based, in part, on the fact that an accrued liability balance was restated. The circumstances surrounding the restatement of an item are significant.

[994] Finally, I am not satisfied beyond a reasonable doubt that any or all of the three accused knew that the $4 million Siemens' accrued liability balance should have been released in Q4 01.

• • •

[1067] Minutes of the Audit Committee for July 24, 2003 indicate that Mr. John Cawthorne made a presentation dealing specifically with an analysis of Nortel's balance sheet. In his presentation, he pointed out that certain balance sheet accruals and provisions were established by management in prior periods dating back to 1999 and earlier. He indicated that these accruals and provisions were recorded by the company during periods when the balance sheet and income statement were much larger. Mr. Cawthorne indicated that these accruals and provisions were receiving greater scrutiny due to the shrinking size of Nortel's overall balance sheet and their materiality to the income statement. His presentation points out that there is a lack of documentation about certain accruals and that, as a result of that and the passage of time and the turnover of personnel, it is unclear what adjustments should have been made be made to these provisions in prior years. As a result, management has a project underway to gather support and determine the proper resolution of these questionable balances.

• • •

[1129] I am satisfied beyond a reasonable doubt that all three accused, by virtue of their long experience with Nortel and their positions of responsibility, well-understood how the men and women in the field were implementing Nortel's policy of Conservatism.

[1130] I am satisfied beyond a reasonable doubt that they knew that the policy of Conservatism and its implementation had created excess accrued liabilities which could be released to assist in meeting financial targets. Liabilities were very often estimated by men and women in the field on a worst-case scenario basis. As well, in order to avoid exposing Nortel to risks that were not provided for, there was a reluctance to reduce accrued liability balances in the appropriate quarter in response to a triggering event. The result was the presence of excess accrued liabilities on Nortel's balance sheet.

[1131] The evidence does establish, and I so find, that excessive accrued liabilities existed because genuine accrued liabilities were not released when they should have been and because genuine accrued liabilities were not adjusted when they should have been. I am not satisfied that any or all of the accused understood the extent of the excess accrued liabilities on Nortel's balance sheet.

[1132] I am satisfied that, in addition to excess accrued liabilities, there were accrued liabilities on Nortel's balance sheet which could not be supported.

[1133] The evidence persuades me that accruals were present on Nortel's consolidated balance sheet which could not be supported by documentation. I am satisfied that the downsizing of Nortel, which involved the closing of offices, the selling of real estate and, undoubtedly, the storage of documents, created a situation in which supporting documentation for some of existing accrued liability balances could not be located. Further, the loss of employees (two out of every three worldwide) created a situation in which the institutional memory concerning the unsupported accruals no longer existed within the company.

[1134] I am satisfied beyond a reasonable doubt that all 3 accused knew that there were unsupported accrued liabilities on Nortel's balance sheet. I am not satisfied that any or all of the accused understood the extent of the unsupported accrued liabilities on Nortel's balance sheet.

[1135] I am satisfied that neither the unsupported nor the excess accrued liabilities were fictitious. This finding does not mean that the release of accrued liabilities could not be used to manage earnings or achieve a pre-published financial target. It simply means that both the unsupported and the excessive liability balances originated from real risks.

[1136] I am satisfied, on the evidence, that Mr. Gollogly, virtually from the time he took over as Corporate Controller, turned his attention to Nortel's balance sheet.

[1137] I am satisfied that the enormous losses suffered by Nortel in fiscal 2000 and 2001 created a situation in which senior management, Nortel's Board of Directors and Nortel's auditors were concentrating their efforts and energy on doing what was necessary to make sure that Nortel had sufficient cash reserves to survive.

• • •

[1179] It would be imprecise and dangerous to conclude, without knowing the specifics of the transactions, that Nortel's prior published financial results were false because transactions such as these were restated. The more accurate statement is that Deloitte changed its mind about the accounting treatment for these transactions and, as a result, previously-published financial statements had to be changed. Once the specifics of the transaction are known, it is clear that the three accused could not have known about these so-called errors.

[1180] It would be wrong to infer that the three accused knew that an accrued liability balance that was restated was false in the absence of evidence concerning the specifics of the balance.

[1181] When I consider all of the evidence, it is my conclusion that the second restatement produced different results than the first restatement because the thresholds of the second restatement were different, because the second restatement concentrated on revenue recognition, as well as excessive accrued liability balances, and because Deloitte changed its mind about the accounting for specific transactions. Sometimes, as the specifics of the Genuity accrued liability balance demonstrate, Deloitte disagreed with itself. With respect to that release, the U.S. National Office of Deloitte & Touche disagreed with the Deloitte reviewers at Nortel and overruled them.

[1182] I am not satisfied by the evidence in this case, including the fact that the second restatement resulted in financial statements which were different than Nortel's previously-published and restated financial statements, proves that the previously-published and restated financial statements misrepresented Nortel's financial results. For example, in the period Q4 02, which occupied a considerable amount of the court's time, Nortel's original published financial statements reported a US GAAP loss of $248 million and revenue of $2.5 billion. After two restatements, Nortel reported a US GAAP loss of $294 million and revenue of $2.6 billion.

The Q1 & Q2 03 accrued liability balance releases

[1183] I am not satisfied beyond a reasonable doubt that the three accused deliberately misrepresented Nortel's original Q1 03 and Q2 03 published financial results by releasing $361 million and $372 million, respectively, to Nortel's Q1 03 and Q2 03 profit and loss statements.

[1184] The restated releases referred to in the evidence lead me to the conclusion that the decision to restate on account of an error can be the same thing as saying that there was a decision to restate on account of a difference of opinion. The difference of opinion can occur with the benefit of hindsight. The difference of opinion can be influenced by new information. As indicated earlier, when deciding to restate an accrued liability balance, sometimes Deloitte disagreed with itself. The specifics of each restated item are a story, the details of which cannot be inferred from the ending.

[1185] In the abstract, it is true that the fact that accrued liability balances in Nortel's balance sheet were restated is capable of supporting an inference that, in their original form, the financial statements misrepresented Nortel's financial results. Based on the evidence that I have heard, it is my conclusion that I should not draw such an inference in this case.

[1186] When I consider the evidence generally, including the evidence to which I have referred, I come to the conclusion that I am not satisfied by the evidence that, apart from the $80 million in Non-op releases, the Q1 03 and Q2 03 accrued liability releases were outside the normal course of business.

[1187] As a result, I cannot give effect to the Crown submissions concerning the inferences I ought to draw from the fact that the original Q1 03 and Q2 03 accrued liability balances were restated.

Verdict

[1188] For the reasons that I have set out and having regard to all the evidence, I am not satisfied beyond a reasonable doubt that Frank A. Dunn, Douglas C. Beatty and Michael J. Gollogly deliberately misrepresented the financial results of Nortel Networks Corporation and, therefore, I find each of them not guilty of counts one and two in this indictment.

QUESTIONS

1. What policy purposes are being served by the *Criminal Code* offence of insider trading? Are they necessary?
2. Compare and contrast the *Drabinsky* and *Dunn* cases. Identify the main factors that contributed to the opposite results in these two matters. Are there lessons to be drawn from this comparison about the usefulness of dealing with financial misconduct by way of criminal prosecution?

IV. QUASI-CRIMINAL OFFENCES

A. General Offence Provisions

Most provincial securities statutes contain one or more provisions creating quasi-criminal offences for specific or general breaches of securities law. Thus, for example, failure to file documents required by securities law, such as a prospectus, could render a person or company subject to fines and/or imprisonment under securities legislation (ASA, s 194; BCSA, ss 155, 155.1; OSA, s 122; QSA, ss 195(3), 202). So could the making of any misrepresentation in such a document. Indeed, one of the criticisms made by reporting issuers of rules introduced by provincial regulators requiring certification of financial statements or the establishment of procedures for the operation of audit committees, as discussed in Chapters 6 and 7, is that breaches of these rules could expose officers of reporting issuers to enhanced sanctions. Thus, for example, part 18 of the Companion Policy 52-109 to National Instrument 52-109, *Certification of Disclosure in Issuers' Annual and Interim Filings* (2008), 31 OSCB 10456, indicates that "[a] certifying officer providing a certificate containing a misrepresentation potentially could be subject to quasi-criminal, administrative or civil proceedings under securities law."

There are differences across provincial and territorial securities statutes in terms of how broadly or narrowly cast the offence provisions are. Compare, for example, OSA, s 122 with BCSA, s 155. The OSA specifies:

Offences, General

122(1) Every person or company that,

(a) makes a statement in any material, evidence or information submitted to the Commission, a Director, any person acting under the authority of the Commission or the Executive Director or any person appointed to make an investigation or examination under this Act that, in a material respect and at the time and in the light of the circumstances under which it is made, is misleading or untrue or does not state a fact that is required to be stated or that is necessary to make the statement not misleading;

(b) makes a statement in any application, release, report, preliminary prospectus, prospectus, return, financial statement, information circular, take-over bid circular, issuer bid circular or other document required to be filed or furnished under Ontario securities law that, in a material respect and at the time and in the light of the circumstances under which it is made, is misleading or untrue or does not state a fact that is required to be stated or that is necessary to make the statement not misleading; or

(c) contravenes Ontario securities law,

is guilty of an offence and on conviction is liable to a fine of not more than $5 million or to imprisonment for a term of not more than five years less a day, or to both.

BCSA, s 155 provides:

Offences

155(1) A person who does any of the following commits an offence:

(a) fails to file, provide, deliver or send a record that

(i) is required to be filed, provided, delivered or sent under this Act, or

(ii) is required to be filed, provided, delivered or sent under this Act within the time required under this Act;

(b) contravenes any of section 34, 49 to 57, 57.2, 57.3, 57.5, 57.6, 58, 59, 61, 85(b), 87, 121, 122, 124, 125, 148 or 168.1(1) of this Act;

(c) fails to comply with a decision made under this Act;

(d) contravenes any of the provisions of the regulations that are specified by regulation for the purpose of this paragraph;

(e) contravenes any of the provisions of the commission rules that are specified by regulation for the purpose of this paragraph.

(2) A person that commits an offence under this Act is liable to a fine of not more than $3 million, or to imprisonment for not more than 3 years, or both.

(3) [Repealed 1999-20-27.]

(4) If a person, other than an individual, commits an offence under subsection (1), an employee, officer, director or agent of that person who authorizes, permits or acquiesces in the offence commits the same offence whether or not that person is convicted of the offence.

(4.1) If an investment fund commits an offence under subsection (1), the investment fund manager commits the same offence whether or not the investment fund is convicted of the offence.

(5) Despite subsection (2), if a person has contravened section 57, 57.2 or 57.3, the fine to which the person is liable is

(a) not less than any profit made by all persons because of the contravention of section 57, 57.2 or 57.3, and

(b) not more than the greater of

(i) $3 million, and

(ii) an amount equal to triple any profit made by all persons because of the contravention of section 57, 57.2 or 57.3.

(6) and (7) [Repealed 2007-37-29.]

The offence provision in the BC legislation identifies a somewhat larger, more specific, number of substantive infractions than does the Ontario equivalent, which refers to misrepresentations made to the regulators or in filed documents along with the catch-all offence of "breach of Ontario securities law." However, it should also be noted that additions to the OSA proposed in 2002, creating the offences of engaging in fraud or market manipulation or making misleading or untrue statements, were proclaimed in December 2005 (OSA, ss 126.1, 126.2). There is also some inconsistency across provinces in terms of the maximum sanctions that can be applied following a conviction under these quasi-criminal provisions. In Ontario, for example, the maximum penalties under s 122 are a fine of "not more than $5 million or to imprisonment for a term of not more than five years less a day, or to both." Section 122(3) specifies that similar penalties may be applied to a director or officer who "authorizes, permits or acquiesces in the commission of an offence under subsection (1)" whether or not the person or company itself has been charged or convicted. Meanwhile BCSA, s 155 provides that a person committing an offence under the Act is liable to a fine of "not more than $3 million, or to imprisonment for not more than 3 years, or both." OSA, s 122(2) provides a due diligence defence with respect to the offences in ss 122(1)(a) and (b) only.

Clearly these provisions are intended to operate as a deterrent to breaching the substantive requirements of securities law (see Poonam Puri, "Sentencing the Criminal Corporation" (2002) 39:2-3 Osgoode Hall LJ 611, but see also Mary G Condon, "Rethinking Enforcement and Litigation in Ontario Securities Regulation" (2006) 32:1 Queen's LJ 1). Many provincial securities regulators have tended not to use prosecution under the offence provisions as an enforcement tool, preferring to make use of their administrative powers instead. There are presumably strategic reasons for this concerning the criminal burden of proof to be sustained in a quasi-criminal proceeding and the greater procedural and evidentiary protections accorded to accuseds in these situations. However, as noted above, this approach has been changing in recent years. For example, the Québec Financial Markets Authority has indicated that it would focus its enforcement efforts on prosecuting offences (*The Globe and Mail* (17 May 2004) B1). The AMF's most recent Enforcement report indicates that criminal prosecution is still an important priority, with 632 charges having been laid for offences under the *Securities Act* and the *Derivatives Act*. See <http://www.lautorite.qc.ca/en/press-releases-2015-conso.html_2015_amf-enforcement.html>.

An example of the use of quasi-criminal proceedings in a misrepresentation matter is the case of *R v Zelitt*. The Alberta Provincial Court found that the CEO of a company engaged in 11 counts of misrepresentation, failing to disclose material facts and changes, and providing false or misleading information, contrary to the ASA (*R v Zelitt*, [2003] AJ No 42 (QL) (Prov Ct) and *R v Zelitt*, [2002] AJ No 1394 (QL) (Prov Ct)). The company had falsely claimed to have developed new 3D imaging technology through its press releases, prospectus, annual information forms (AIFs), and material change reports. The market price of the shares fell from $4 to 10 cents when information that the technology did not exist was disclosed.

At trial, Zelitt was sentenced to four years in prison, a fine of $1.85 million, and prohibited from trading in securities or serving as director or officer of an issuer for 25 years (*R v Zelitt*, [2003] AJ No 59 (QL) (Prov Ct)). In determining the sentence, the court considered deterrence, denunciation, and protection of the public, finding that his behaviour over a period of time, the breach of trust, and the magnitude and impact of the violations were all contributing factors. In an appeal to the Alberta Court of Queen's Bench in 2006, the court upheld the original four-year term of imprisonment imposed on Zelitt at trial. It also reduced the $1.85 million fine imposed to the $1 million fine sought by the Crown at trial and eliminated an additional four-year term of imprisonment imposed in default of payment of the fines (*R v Zelitt*, [2006] AJ No 1338 (QL) (QB)).

B. Offence Provisions Dealing with Insider Trading

In many provincial and territorial statutes, the offence of insider trading is singled out for special attention. Thus, OSA, s 122(4) provides for the possibility of additional penalties on conviction for insider trading under s 76. The specific wording of this provision, which refers to an accused being "liable to a minimum fine equal to the profit made or the loss avoided by the person or company by reason of the contravention" on conviction, was the subject of an appeal in the *Harper* case, discussed in Chapter 8. The Ontario Court of Appeal disagreed with the interpretation of this wording made by the summary conviction appeal judge, which was itself an appeal from the trial judge's initial decision.

R v Harper

2003 CanLII 28110 (Ont CA)

BLAIR RSJ (ad hoc) (McMurtry CJO and Armstrong JA concurring): ...

"By Reason of the Contravention"

[19] The summary conviction appeal judge found no error in the trial judge's calculation of the amount of the fine in accordance with the formula set out in the *Securities Act*. He concluded, however, that a condition precedent to the utilization of subsection 122(4) had not been met and that the trial judge had therefore erred in applying the profit made/loss avoided formula rather than reverting back to the general penalty provisions of subsection 122(1).

[20] The condition precedent the appeal judge read into the section, on his analysis of the words "by reason of the contravention," was the requirement that there be evidence of the effect of the suppression of the material facts on the market. He held it is not enough that the contravention *contribute* to the profit made or loss avoided. Rather, there must be *a direct causal linkage* between the material non-disclosure and those results. The appeal judge pointed to the penal effects of subsection 122(4) as the rationale for this interpretation. The relevant portions of his decision in this regard are the following:

> In his Reasons for Sentence, the learned trial judge does not address the question of "by reason of the contravention." In my view it is necessary to do so before applying the provisions of section 122(4) of the *Securities Act*.
>
> In order to analyze what "by reason of the contravention" means in the section, the court must read subsection (5) of the section 122. "If it is not possible to determine the profit made or loss avoided by the person or company by reason of the contravention, subsection (4) does not apply but subsection (1) continues to apply."
>
> It is clear from this wording that the legislature intended that the crown must prove more than the simple profit or loss incurred in the prohibited trades. *The contravention is not simply the result of trades carried out, but is linked to the material facts withheld. There must be evidence of the effect of such suppression of material facts on the market.* This is so because of the stringent and onerous results of section 122(4).
>
> In many cases, the crown will have to rely on the general provisions of section 122(1)(c), which provides for a maximum fine of $1,000,000 on each count.
>
> In the case before me on appeal, I accept the submissions of counsel for the appellant that there was not sufficient evidence before the learned trial judge for him to come to the conclusion that the cause of the fluctuation in the market was "by reason of the contravention." The contravention being the trade by Mr. Harper while suppressing material information.

> The evidence disclosed for example, that at the same time this trading was going on, the infamous Bre-X scam was greatly affecting the market price of gold exploration mines such as Golden Rule. In addition, there were during the relevant times a number of press releases made by the independent Ghanaian Commission, which were negative. At least two of those being released on May 15, 1997 and July 15, 1997. There was certainly evidence before the court of other factors affecting stock prices at this time. This was a speculative gold stock in the early stages of exploration. No drill holes had been sunk or assayed prior to those referred to in the July, 1997 report of the Ghanaian Commission. Such stocks are notoriously volatile.
>
> In my view, on the evidence before the court it was not possible to conclude that profits made or loss avoided by Mr. Harper were "by reason of the contravention." *It is not sufficient to say that the contravention contributed to such profits or loss avoidances and in my view, the condition precedent to the imposition of a fine pursuant to section 122(4) has not been met.* That would, therefore, bring into play the provisions of section 122(5) which refer the sentencing court back to the general provisions for sentencing found in section 122(1) "… and on conviction is liable to a fine of not more than $1,000,000 or imprisonment for a term of not more than two years or to both."

(underlining in original; italics added [from the printed version of the case])

[21] Respectfully, in my opinion, the learned summary conviction appeal judge erred in his analysis and interpretation of the words "by reason of the contravention" in subsection 122(4), which he appears to have concluded meant "by reason of *the effect of the material non-disclosure on the market price* of the shares." That is not what the provision says, however. It says "by reason of *the contravention*."

[22] The "contravention," as the summary conviction appeal judge noted, is "the trade by Mr. Harper while suppressing material information." Put another way, the contravention is the trading with knowledge of undisclosed material facts while an insider in relation to the shares being traded. When this concept is imported into the language of subsection 122(4), the pertinent provision becomes "profit made or loss avoided by reason of the trading with knowledge of undisclosed material facts while an insider." This is not the language of cause and effect.

[23] In my view the phrase "by reason of the contravention" means "by virtue of the insider having engaged in the impugned trading." Mr. Harper traded in the Golden Rule shares when he had knowledge of material facts that had not been disclosed to the market. By doing so he avoided a loss. The loss was avoided "by reason of the contravention."

[24] It is a basic principle of statutory interpretation that the words of an Act are to be read in their entire context, and in their grammatical and ordinary sense, harmoniously with the scheme of the Act, the object of the Act, and the intention of the Legislature: *Rizzo & Rizzo Shoes Ltd. (Re)*, [1998] 1 S.C.R. 27, per Iacobucci J. at paragraph 21. It is also a principle of statutory interpretation that where the liberty of the subject is affected and there are two reasonable statutory interpretations available, the interpretation favouring the accused should be adopted: see *R. v. McIntosh*, [1995] 1 S.C.R. 686, per Lamer C.J., at paragraph 29. In my view, however, the language of subsection 122(4) is not open to two reasonable interpretations.

[25] The interpretation advanced here is consistent with the language of subsection 122(4). Reading the words "by reason of the contravention" to mean "by virtue of the insider having engaged in the impugned trading" fits with the ordinary and grammatical sense of the words, having regard to what constitutes "the contravention." Reading the

words as having cause and effect meaning in relation to the effect of the material non-disclosure on market price, does not.

[26] The interpretation advanced here is also consistent with the scheme and object of the Act, which is to recapture profits made or losses avoided by insiders trading in contravention of Ontario securities law. The interpretation advanced by the Respondent [Harper] makes it practically impossible to affect that purpose. The overall object of this aspect of the *Securities Act* is to police trading to ensure fairness in the securities market-place and to sanction contraventions. The clear legislative intent reflected in the language of the subsection is to provide a simple formula by which to quantify the extent of the loss which the Respondent avoided by reason of having contravened the law. As the Appellant puts it, in its factum, "any 'amount' which the Respondent received by illegally selling the securities of Golden Rule which exceeded what he would have received had he waited until he was legally entitled to sell those securities is a loss which the Respondent avoided 'by reason of the contravention.'"

[27] This interpretation enhances the purposes and objects of the Act, whereas the narrow interpretation advanced by the Respondent and adopted by the appeal judge undermines those goals, in my opinion. Indeed, the interpretation adopted by the appeal judge renders the provisions of subsection 122(4) pointless or futile, in practical terms. Rare would it be that the Crown could show a direct and sole causal connection between the failure to disclose the material facts and the profit made or loss avoided. There are a myriad of factors that routinely affect the price of publicly traded securities at any given time—particularly the market in junior gold mining stocks. These include such things as fluctuation in interest rates, the price of gold, world developments, announcements by other companies, and rumours. It would seldom, if ever, be possible for the Crown to isolate, and quantify, the effect of the suppression of the material facts on market price and to exclude from the subsection 122(4) calculation the effect that those other factors had on the average trading price and, therefore, on the loss avoided.

[28] Moreover, as the Appellant submits, the interpretation adopted by the appeal judge could well undermine the objective of regulating insider trading, namely to foster the disclosure of material information and to prevent unfair gains by those "in the know." That interpretation could operate as a disincentive to disclosure, because the longer the insider suppresses the material facts the greater the likelihood of the "other factors" impacting on the stock price.

[29] Some meaning must be given to the insertion of subsections (4) and (6) in section 122. The Legislature could not have intended to put in the statute a provision that is ineffective in practical terms and operates as a disincentive to disclosure. Were that the intention, the Legislature might as well have left the section with nothing more than the general fine and imprisonment mandate of subsection 122(1). It did not do so.

[30] I would therefore give effect to the Appellant's argument on this point and allow the appeal in that regard.

If the additional fines applicable for insider trading in provincial and territorial securities statutes are to have the deterrent effect sought by legislatures, evidence of prosecutorial effort in this regard is presumably necessary. However, we have seen in the excerpts in Chapter 8 from the Insider Trading Task Force and the research conducted by McNally &

Smith that there have been only a handful of criminal prosecutions for insider trading over the past 15 years, in the face of suggestions of significant lack of compliance with both the insider reporting requirements and the prohibition on illegal insider trading. An interesting recent insider trading case in Ontario was *Landen*.

R v Landen
2008 ONCJ 561

SHAMAI J:

[1] Barry Landen and Stephen Diamond face charges of insider trading, under s. 76(1)(a) of the *Ontario Securities Act* (the Act). In addition, Mr. Landen is charged with the offence under Section 76(2) of the Act known as tipping. The information alleges as follows:

Barry Landen:

1. In or about the months of September and October of 2003, at the City of Toronto and elsewhere in the Province of Ontario, being a person in a special relationship with Agnico-Eagle Mines Limited ("Agnico-Eagle"), did inform, other than in the necessary course of business, Stephen Diamond of a material fact or material change with respect to Agnico-Eagle before the material fact or material change had been generally disclosed, contrary to subsections 76(2) and 122(1)(c) of the *Securities Act*, RSO 1990, c. S.5, as amended (the "Act").
2. On or about October 10, 2003 and October 24, 2003, at the City of Toronto and elsewhere in the Province of Ontario, being a person in a special relationship with Agnico-Eagle, did sell securities of Agnico-Eagle with the knowledge of a material fact or material change with respect to Agnico-Eagle that had not been generally disclosed, contrary to subsections 76(1) and 122(1)(c) of the Act.

Stephen Diamond:

3. On or about October 23 and October 24, 2003, at the City of Toronto and elsewhere in the Province of Ontario, being a person in a special relationship with Agnico-Eagle, did purchase securities of Agnico-Eagle with knowledge of a material fact or material change with respect to Agnico-Eagle that had not been generally disclosed, contrary to subsections 76(1) and 122(1)(c) of the Act.

[2] Following an order I made on March 22, 2007, the Ontario Securities Commission (OSC) particularised the allegations as to material facts or material changes by providing the following ten particulars:

We allege that [the defendants] knew one or more of the following material facts or material changes during the material time frame set out in the information:

1. That Agnico-Eagle was experiencing persistent production difficulties that would likely not be resolved by the end of the third quarter of 2003;
2. That Agnico-Eagle would likely not meet its gold production forecast for the third quarter of 2003;

3. That Agnico-Eagle would likely not meet its gold production forecast for 2003;
4. That Agnico-Eagle would likely be reducing its long-term production forecast;
5. That Agnico-Eagle would likely have a net loss for the third quarter of 2003;
6. That Agnico-Eagle was experiencing financial problems or mine production problems in the third quarter of 2003 that would likely negatively affect the share price of Agnico-Eagle, including but not limited to a problem with reconciliation (as amended on July 7, 2008);
7. That Landen or parties related to Landen had sold shares or intended to sell shares in Agnico-Eagle prior to the public disclosure of information set out in 1-6 above;
8. That Landen or parties related to Landen had bought put options or intended to buy put options in Agnico-Eagle prior to the public disclosure of information set out in 1-6 above;
9. That Diamond should sell shares or buy put options in Agnico-Eagle prior to the public disclosure of information set out in 1-6 above; or
10. That the senior management of Agnico-Eagle was considering reducing its long-term gold production forecast including but not limited [sic] its forecast for 2004 (as added on July 7, 2008).

[3] OSC takes the position in this prosecution that regardless of whether any of the information set out particulars 1-6 was communicated to Stephen Diamond, knowledge of particulars 7 and 8 constitutes a material fact or material change, as it affects the prosecution against Stephen Diamond.

[4] I have concluded that the Ontario Securities Commission has proved its case on Count Two against Mr. Landen beyond reasonable doubt, but that the first and third counts have not been proved, and so I will dismiss them. …

• • •

[14] The evidence on this trial was lengthy and somewhat complex. To give the briefest of overview, it suffices to say that Barry Landen was a vice president at Agnico-Eagle (AE), a Canadian gold mining enterprise, which operates as a public company and is subject to regulation by the Ontario Securities Commission. Stephen Diamond is a long-time friend of his, working in unrelated business as a chartered accountant in Toronto. The press release of October 29, 2003 for Agnico-Eagle announced a net loss for the third quarter, a reduction in the annual forecast of gold production, and a reduction in the forecast of gold production for 2004. The impact of the announcement was a drop in share price the next day of 22%. The Ontario Securities Commission alleges that trades in Agnico-Eagle shares by Barry Landen through a holding company he controlled, Jakmin Investments, on October 10 and October 24, were made while he was in possession of material facts about Agnico-Eagle which to the time of the trades were undisclosed to the public. They allege that the trades realised a profit of $115,176 compared to the value of the shares after the third quarter press release. Ontario Securities Commission alleges that Mr. Landen communicated information about material facts or changes prior to its public disclosure to Mr. Diamond, thereby putting him in a special relationship in the terms of the Act, and making him an insider, subject to the rules under section 76(1). Mr. Diamond purchased a series of put options on Agnico-Eagle securities, prior to the third quarter announcement, and realised a profit of $201,955 by selling the options on October 30, 2003. Ontario Securities Commission relies principally on Mr. Landen's attendance at two meetings of

Agnico-Eagle management in October to put him in possession of the material facts or changes, at the time undisclosed to the public. With respect to Mr. Diamond, circumstantial evidence of possession of insider information is argued on the basis of his long friendship with Mr. Landen, a joint trading account they owned, and a transfer of funds from Mr. Landen to Mr. Diamond on October 20, 2003, days before Mr. Diamond's purchases of put options in Agnico-Eagle. These facts are uncontroverted, but whether they support the Ontario Securities Commission contention that Mr. Landen communicated insider information to Mr. Diamond during the months of September and October is the key issue in Mr. Diamond's case.

[15] Mr. Diamond testified in his own defence, and asserted an innocent explanation for the funds he received from Mr. Landen, and that his purchase of put options on October 23 and 24 was made on the basis of his own analysis of the market, not by reason of information he received from Mr. Landen. He denies receiving insider information from Mr. Landen at any time. There is no issue that he purchased securities of Agnico-Eagle on certain dates. That is, in the framework of his defence, however, not unlawful, as he claims he was not in a special relationship with Mr. Landen, as defined by the Act, thus not transgressing ss. 76(1).

[16] Mr. Landen rests his defence substantially on the position that the OSC has failed to prove the particularised material changes or material facts. He disputes that the information was not generally disclosed. To state it differently, he says that information as described in the particulars, if proved to be factual, was in any event generally disclosed. He advances the position as well that he has demonstrated due diligence in ascertaining this status.

...

[27] The OSC case with regard to all three counts depends on findings that its particulars amounted to material information in possession of the defendants, as demonstrated beyond reasonable doubt by the evidence, and not generally disclosed at the time of the impugned trades. A series of background factual matters assists in understanding both materiality and disclosure issues. Considerable evidence was led in the course of the trial about the technology of mining and the process which creates gold bars ("doribars") or gold concentrate out of raw ore. The business of gold mining, the raising of capital through the publicly traded company, and mining promotion was the subject of evidence, by way of testimony and exhibits. The reports of analysts in the financial sector with focus in this field, and the opinions of a well-known expert in the field, John Embry, were received, to assist the Court both on issues of materiality and on the question of what had been generally disclosed prior to the release of third quarter results on October 29, 2003.

...

Project Circle

[49] The late summer of 2003 brought another troubling issue, from the business perspective of Agnico-Eagle. As another gold company had apparently acquired an interest amounting to nearly 5% of Agnico-Eagle's outstanding shares, concern had been mounting that a hostile takeover bid was shaping up. In order to defend against such an eventuality, and to advise their investors on the valuation of the company, a consultation, dubbed "Project Circle" was called. Advisors from Scotia Capital and Merrill Lynch were

retained for the purpose of advising on valuation of the company, and how to defend against such a bid. …

[50] The October 1 meeting included Agnico-Eagle senior management: Sean Boyd, Ebe Scherkus, David Garofalo, Barry Landen and others; counsel to Agnico-Eagle Ms. Olasker, a communications consultant John Lute, and advisors from Scotia Capital and Merrill Lynch. The purpose of the meeting was to receive the advisors' preliminary advice and to discuss information required for purposes of preparing a financial model, in the context of an unsolicited tender offer. A review of analysts' reports was undertaken among other things.

[51] During the meeting a number of items relating to the state of the company's progress were discussed. Mr. Boyd said that in beginning the meeting, he provided information from the market, and indicated that production numbers were not as good as hoped for. The numbers were not specified. He spoke as well in the strategy part of the meeting of the possibility of rebuilding production targets for the upcoming quarter and as well for the next year, in order to position the company going forward. He talked about a strategy which would reverse the credibility issue the company was developing, by lowering the forecast then outperforming it.

. . .

[54] In the view of Ms. Olasker, the discussion at this meeting of "possibly lowering the bar," by revising downward the projected long term gold projection, itself amounted to a material fact. She commented in cross-examination:

> Certainly the sense in the room that day was that we had been apprised of a material fact … Looking back to the October 1 meeting where Sean made the point of, you know, "may make a lower the bar announcement" and then he actually comments on what he thinks the impact on the stock price will be … I think everyone in the room concluded from that that we were looking at something that was more likely than not.

. . .

[56] She characterised the poor third quarter results as a material fact as it would be market sensitive information. While the discussion about reducing long-term production was a material fact in her view, once the decision was taken to lower the 2004 projection, that would be material change.

. . .

[59] Yet another issue emerged in the management meeting of October 9, which was not previously known, and which appeared to have considerable potential significance.

Reconciliation Issue

[60] The poor third quarter results were exacerbated by the information obtained by Mr. Scherkus when he visited the mine on October 2 and 3 2003. He learned of a reconciliation problem: the amount of gold being produced after the milling process was far from expectation based on the quantity of ore extracted for milling. The problem was significant: there was a discrepancy of 6000 ounces of gold, or 16.5%. Previously the greatest discrepancy amounted to 2000 ounces. The analytical options were either that the mine was of much lesser quality than previously assessed, hence producing less gold; or that there was a problem in the process and reporting at the mill. The former would

represent a more serious issue than the latter, as it would reflect on the ore reserve; whereas the latter option meant there was an operational issue, which could be repaired.

[61] This issue was discussed at the October 9 management meeting. Present at the October 9 meeting were the Agnico-Eagle senior management. Mr. Landen was present. Mr. Scherkus had gone to the mine between the October 1 and October 9 meetings, as he customarily did at the end of each quarter. He had final corrected mill sheets for September. Production appeared to be at an unanticipated low, at 51,000 ounces for the quarter. With the significant reconciliation discrepancy, a broad reaching audit was planned. Mr. Boyd testified about the difficulties, which confronted management at the October 9 meeting. There was the issue of accessing the ore given technical problems earlier in the year. There was the continuing impact on production. Now there was the reconciliation issue. Gold production was "well short for the quarter and so for the year." Mr. Boyd said he was getting frustrated at having to go into the market and explain to investors and shareholders the pattern of not reaching projected production. He said he wanted a cushion in the projections, a lower target so that it could be fulfilled. Otherwise the credibility problem that he felt arose from continued missed projections would give rise to a confidence issue for the company, which would have a lasting negative impact. It was plain in that meeting that Agnico-Eagle was not meeting its Q3 target of 75,000 ounces of gold, and that even the lowered expectation of Mr. Boyd, that the production would be in the "low 60's" was significantly off, with production reported at 51,000 ounces.

[62] … This resulted in mine visits by Mr. Boyd and Mr. Scherkus on October 20-22 2003, though Mr. Scherkus and been there since October 14. Upon their return to Toronto, intensive preparation ensued, to finalise the press release and webcast scheduled for October 29. That press release had been announced on October 2, but the content of the announcement was not finalised until October 24.

[63] Although a final determination of the sampling process, challenging the erstwhile estimation of the mine's reserve was not yet concluded, it was determined by the end of senior management's mine visit that the reconciliation issue could be attributed to a production issue in the mill. Thus although the re-assessment of the reserve would be completed, there was no real concern that the mine did not hold the previously assessed quantity of ore. However, a decision was made to lower production projections. The decision to lower long range production was made on October 22. The record does not show any way in which Mr. Landen was privy to that information until some time between 3 and 4 pm on October 24, when he received the briefing book for the October 29 press release and associated webcast.

The Impugned Trades by Barry Landen

[64] During this period of time, Mr. Landen sold all the holdings of Jakmin Investments in AE. On October 10 he sold 10,000 shares, and on October 24, he sold the remaining 22,237 shares. There is significance in the time of the trade: the internal investigation determined he made the trade prior to knowing about the decision to lower the 2003 guidance and 2004 projection. The internal investigation determined that the trade was transacted at 11:52 a.m. and this was confirmed in the testimony of OSC investigator Lori Toledano. He did not receive the briefing book with the decisions in it, until sometime between 3 and 4 pm on October 24.

[65] Mr. Landen had sole authority to deal with the assets of Jakmin Investments. The trading tickets in relation to these transactions showed Mr. Landen to be an insider to AE. Mr. Landen had as recently as June and July 2003 filed 42 insider trading reports as required by securities regulation about his trading in AE securities. No such report was filed for these transactions.

The Impugned Trades by Stephen Diamond

[66] Mr. Diamond purchased put options on AE stock, of a value of $20,350 on October 23, and a further purchase of such options for $48,800 on October 24, 2003. He had received a cheque from Mr. Landen in the amount of $100,000 on October 20.

...

[76] ... [Ms. Olasker] maintained that although nothing showed that Mr. Landen knew of the Board's decision to reduce its 2004 production forecast prior to October 24 afternoon, Mr. Kraft's investigation, the Board and she believed that Mr. Landen was aware of the significance of the discussion to "lower the bar" for 2004, which took place at the October 1 meeting. This was notwithstanding Mr. Landen's statement to the Board of Directors on December 1, 2004 that he was not aware of the 2004 forecast issue until he received the briefing book on October 24, 2003.

...

[83] ... In sum, [Mr. Embry] expressed the view that whatever bad news was out there, it would not have justified a short sale, or a trade as risky as the options purchase by Mr. Diamond. He did acknowledge that his own approach to the market was as an investor and not a trader, which was clearly Mr. Diamond's approach. The latter was intent on short term forays in the market place, in hopes of profit on each play, rather than the slow and steady appreciation of a portfolio, which an investor seeks.

...

[86] Considerable discussion in the cross-examination dealt with which factor impacted the fall in stock price most significantly. I do not see the value of an analysis of relative impact of material information, so long as the impact is proved to be significant. In the case of the particulars which I find to be proved by the OSC, there is no issue that the record allows me to find their impact would be significant.

[87] Magnitude does matter in the determination of materiality of a contingent or speculative factor however. The test used by the Ontario Securities Commission, adopted from American jurisprudence defines materiality of such facts as a balancing of these two factors in light of the totality of the company activity. There is significance in the magnitude of the impact, when measured against the probability that the long term production forecast would be reduced. The assessment of materiality of the discussion of reducing long term production at the October 1 meeting must be framed in these terms. The test for determining materiality of contingent or speculative facts is discussed at length in the case of *Re Donnini*, 25 OSCB 6225, a decision of the Ontario Securities Commission:

> Materiality is reached when some unspecified minimum threshold of both probability and magnitude is reached. Only where there is some probability of the event's occurrence [e.g. the reduction in the long term production forecast] and some magnitude to the event can it be expected that a reasonable investor would consider the disclosure a factor in making an investment decision. Materiality is indicated when there are high probabilities the event will

> occur and the high magnitudes of the event's impact on the registrant .... Instead of balancing the two against each other, the materiality analyst will weigh both of them separately and then discount the potential magnitude by the probability of non-occurrence. ...

[88] Of note, the OSC refers to the decision of the United States Court of Appeals for the Second Circuit in the case of *Texas Gulf Sulphur*, as follows:

> [M]aterial facts include not only information in respect of earnings and distributions, but also facts which affect the probably future of the company and those which may affect the desire of investors to buy, sell or hold the company's securities.

Analysis: Are the Particulars Proven Material Facts or Changes?

[89] For reasons, which I will attempt to elucidate, I have concluded that the OSC has proved Particulars 6 and 10 to be material facts not disclosed to the general public at the time in question. The other particulars, for various reasons, have not been proved beyond reasonable doubt.

[90] Particulars one, two and three refer to information which on the evidence, was within the purview of the general public. I will deal only briefly with the issue of materiality on these points.

[91] Particular One, that AE was experiencing persistent production difficulties that would not likely be resolved by the end of third quarter of 2003, is a factor which appears in various forms in the discussion of analysts. ... The conference call on July 31, 2003 gave a clear indication of the continuing production issues faced by the company, and delineated the impact on production into August. ... Thus, while persistent production problems clearly amounted to a material fact over the period of the third quarter, and there was no reasonable showing on the evidence that they were resolving by the end of the third quarter, the issues were being aired among those knowledgeable investors and analysts, whom Mr. Embry called "opinion shapers."

[92] Particular Two, that AE would likely not meet its gold production forecast for the third quarter of 2003, is a factor whose significance was contextual. The market impact of meeting a gold forecast within a given quarter may, as an isolated factor, not be that great. Share prices may not be affected, all other things equal. Much of the evidence of Mr. Embry focussed on this, and his opinion in captured in the earlier quote of his testimony. However, in the context of a trend of missed forecasts, the significance was magnified. As well, this was the third quarter, and while a production forecast for the year was not predicated on each quarter being equally weighted, the evidence was that with the first two quarters severely underweighted, the significance from a market perspective of missing the third quarter forecast was magnified. This likelihood of missing third quarter production forecast was discussed in the analysts' reports, and as such was within the public discourse. ... No doubt it was material information, but it was generally disclosed to the public. It cannot be relied upon by the OSC as a result.

[93] Particular 3, that AE would likely not meet its gold production forecast for 2003, is subject to analysis as for Particular 2 .... .

[94] Although it is my view that the OSC cannot succeed on these particulars, as they were generally disclosed to a knowledgeable public, I would comment that had they been undisclosed, Mr. Embry's testimony was that the likelihood of not meeting the gold

production forecast for Q3 2003, and likely not meeting the gold production forecast for 2003 would have a significant impact on the market. He said, with regard to the quarter's results, that first, missing the third quarter target would make it impossible to make the year's production guidance, and second, that it would increase the uncertainty about just what the mine could produce. He stated that credibility issues of that sort are hated by the market.

[95] Particular 4 asserts the *likelihood* of AE *reducing* its long-term production forecast. This is close to, but significantly different from the assertion of Particular 10, that senior management of AE was *considering reducing* its long-term gold production forecast including but not limited to its forecast for 2004. The evidence has made it clear that while consideration of AE reducing its long term production forecast was expressed in the October 1, 2003 meeting for Project Circle, it did not move into the realm of likelihood until some time closer to October 22, when the decision was in fact taken. The evidence does not assist the Court in making a determination of when the reduction of long term gold production forecast resided in the terrain of likelihood, somewhere between the status of a significant item under consideration, or a decision. Nor is the simple term "long term" anywhere defined. The 2004 forecast has been referred to as long term, and indeed, in the terms of Particular 10, the 2004 forecast appears to be a subset of "long term" forecast. Again the record is barren in proving a basis for determining an indefinite long term forecast. I cannot find, apart from issues more properly dealt with under Particular 10, that there is a fact, far less a material fact, disclosed or undisclosed in the terms of Particular 4.

[96] I move now to Particular 5, the question of whether AE likely having a net loss for the third quarter of 2003 would have a significant impact on share price. I am not satisfied that the evidence provides clear and sufficient evidence of this assertion. I view this assertion as distinct from the production issues. The record does not provide a basis to conclude that if proved, the likelihood of a net loss in the quarter would be material information in and of itself. I will not rely on Particular 5 as part of the OSC case.

[97] Particulars 7, 8 and 9 relate only to Mr. Diamond. They propose a scenario wherein material information, as they particularise, has been communicated to Mr. Diamond, but not to the general public. These particulars enunciate a series of factors, which in my view do not amount to material facts or changes, regardless of whether they can be proved in the instant case. I find, for reasons I will expand upon shortly, that the OSC has not proved the transmittal of this information to Mr. Diamond by Mr. Landen. As to whether they would amount to material information if they had been communicated, I am sceptical, and would not draw such a conclusion. The particulars in numbers 7 and 8 assert that the fact that an insider, Mr. Landen, or parties related to him, have sold shares or bought put options prior to the public disclosure of the information set out in Particulars 1-6, would have a significant impact on the share price. Particular 9 is a more specific restatement of the proposition contained in 7 and 8. These assertions depend on the proof of Particulars 1-6, although, the OSC refined its position in relation to these particulars on May 11, 2007, saying that each of particulars 7 to 9 does not require *knowledge* of at least one of particulars 1-6, and knowledge effectively of Landen's market activity (or that of a party related to him) amounts to material fact or change regardless of whether particulars 1-6 or 10 was communicated to Mr. Diamond. There is nothing in the record to suggest that this information was capable of having a significant impact on market value of the

securities. In any event, I adopt the position expressed on behalf of Mr. Diamond, that the opinion of the Ontario Securities Commission, in its decision *Re: ATI Technologies* 29 OSCB 8558, has some application, even if it does not directly dispose of the point raised by particular 9. The hearing panel in *ATI* considered whether a woman, married to the CEO of a company, traded that company's shares "on the advice of her husband." The issue before the panel was whether such advice put the woman in a "special relationship" within the meaning of the Act. The relevant section of the Act is Section 76(5)(e). It defines a person as an insider to include one who "learns of a material fact or material change with respect to the issuer … ." The hearing panel in *ATI* stated that "That definition does not include a person who has received advice from an insider to trade shares … ." By implication, the advice from an insider to trade shares is not material information. By further extension, short of advice to sell securities, the mere information that an insider, Mr. Landen or parties related to him in this case, had sold or bought securities prior to public disclosure of certain information would not amount to a material fact, by application of the Commission ruling in *ATI*. Certainly nothing in the record of evidence supports the position that these particulars amount to material information. I conclude therefore that Particulars 7, 8, 9 do not amount to material information.

[98] Particular 6 raises the question of whether the financial problems or mine production problems of the third quarter, including but not limited to a reconciliation problem, would likely negatively impact the share price of AE. It is fair to say that many mine production problems were in the public discourse, as indicated earlier. It is unclear just what is intended in the allegation of financial problems. However, in specifying the reconciliation problem, this particular advances a basis for consideration as material fact. Mr. Landen is reported as commenting in the course of the internal investigation that there were always reconciliation issues under discussion. However, Mr. Scherkus and Mr. Boyd testified that at the October 9, 2003 meeting, the reconciliation issue was vastly more significant than in any other monthly report. There was a discrepancy of 16.5%: 6000 ounces difference between the projected gold output and the actual output. The highest previous discrepancy was 2000 ounces. This reconciliation issue was in the context of a production total of 51,000 ounces for the quarter, a number which made the achievement of the Q3 projections and consequently the year's production an virtual impossibility. The significance was magnified. While Mr. Scherkus did not think it reasonable that the discrepancy would be attributed to a miscalculation of the mine's reserve of gold, the possibility was one of only two. It had grave implications not only for that quarter and that month, but for the entire enterprise at LaRonde, then the only producing asset of AE. A plan was immediately put in place, to conduct labour intensive tests of the ore as it came out of the ground and as well to audit the mill. Clearly, there was great significance of this reconciliation discrepancy for senior management at AE. It had to be understood forthwith. If it was a matter of the reserve of the mine, it had significance, no doubt a material change which would require immediate public disclosure. If it was a "run of the mill" reconciliation issue, as Mr. Landen said arose regularly, it could be dealt with internally. Either way, it could significantly impact share value as of October 9.

[99] Mr. Embry confirmed the obvious: that a 6000 ounce variance in one month would have a negative impact on an investor, more or less depending on the experience of the investor. The fact that the extraction was from a new zone in the mine added significance to the already challenging news, as "till you put ore through the mill you're

always a little uncomfortable about what you get." As well, coming on the heels of previous poor performance, as Mr. Embry saw it, the discrepancy would amplify the market concerns. Mr. Embry said that even with optimism that it was a mill issue and not a mine issue, until it was explained it would be a significant piece of information.

[100] In the result, I view the reconciliation issue as a material fact. There is no evidence to suggest that anyone, but those present at the October 9 meeting, including Mr. Landen, and the pertinent staff, was aware of the reconciliation issue. Unlike production and mine issues which had been the subject of previous press releases, public discussions, and analyst opinions, the reconciliation issue was not disclosed to the general public. Thus, although the evidence showed mine production problems in the third quarter of 2003 which had been generally disclosed, that would likely negatively affect the share price of AE, the reconciliation issue was different to the extent that it had not been generally disclosed. The OSC has proved Particular 6 to be a material fact, not generally disclosed.

[101] Finally I consider Particular 10. As noted earlier, Particular 10 is a refinement of Particular 4 as alleged. It steps down the assertion of likelihood, to an assertion that senior management was *considering* reducing long-term gold production forecast; and it gives partial definition to the notion of long-term, by saying it is "including but not limited to its forecast for 2004." This Particular triggers the application of the test for material information which is contingent or speculative. The fact asserted is not the actual reduction of long term gold production, nor is it even its likelihood. It is the *consideration* of that reduction.

[102] This Particular refers to the discussion at the October 1 Project Circle meeting, of a reduction in the 2004 forecast. Mr. Gupta used the word "musings" to characterise Mr. Boyd's comments in this regard. Ms. Olasker, who had been counsel to the company for years, and had worked with Mr. Boyd for years as well, refers to the impact which his words had: "… those who were in attendance at that October 1 meeting thought everyone there was aware of the fact that the bar may be lowered." She was rigorously cross examined as to whether this reference could amount to a material fact. Against that prospect were offered the fact that it was not disclosed, although company policy and the TSX rules required timely disclosure not only of material change but also material fact. …

[103] In assessing whether Mr. Boyd's reference to the possibility of reducing 2004 production, in the course of the October 1, 2003 Project Circle meeting, I am mindful that it was a speculative event. The court must assess it in the terms adopted from the American jurisprudence by the Ontario Securities Commission in *Re Sheridan* [16 OSCB 6345], and again in *Re Donnini*, referred to earlier. In particular I take on the role of the materiality analyst described thus:

> Materiality is indicated when there are high probabilities the event will occur and the high magnitudes of the event's impact on the registrant … . Instead of balancing the two against each other, the materiality analyst will weigh both of them separately and then discount the potential magnitude by the probability of non-occurrence.

[104] It does not appear that the reduction of 2004 production guideline was at that point more than a possibility. However, the significance of it was considerable. In fact when interviewed by the OSC in November 2004, Mr. Boyd described the critical factor in the impact which the October 2003 quarterly report had on the market as the perception that LaRonde was a 300,000 ounces mine, not a 400,000 ounce mine, in terms of

annual production. It appeared to John Embry as well that the significance of long term production was paramount, to market assessment of the stock's worth. The magnitude of this assertion, to use the language of the jurisprudence on contingent or speculative facts, was considerable. The impact which a reduction in production might would, by all measures, be significant. The fact that it did not, in Ms. Olasker's, estimation rise beyond a possibility at the October 1 meeting, does not move the characterisation of this from being a material fact. The magnitude was so great that it outweighed the lesser degree of probability. In any event, the possibility was significant, as Ms. Olasker saw it. Her experienced assessment of capturing materiality is of great assistance to this court. In the context of a company whose credibility was suffering, to the knowledge of management, because of repeated production forecasts which could not be met, and which was about to announce a significant shortfall in quarterly production, based even on preliminary numbers, the possibility was real. In measuring magnitude and probability separately then "discounting the potential magnitude by the probability of non-occurrence," the "unspecified minimum threshold of materiality" is met. I must conclude that Mr. Boyd's reference to "lowering the bar" at the October 1, 2006 meeting amounted to a material fact.

• • •

[113] Mr. Landen was at the Project Circle meeting of October 1, 2003. There is nothing to contradict the obvious conclusion, that he was aware of the proceedings of the meeting. Indeed, as the employee of the company of longest standing (according to Ms. Olasker), I attribute to him considerable sensitivity to the significance of Mr. Boyd's statements in that meeting about reducing the 2004 production levels. Similarly, while he may in reference to the October 9 discussion of the reconciliation, best described in Mr. Scherkus' testimony, as an item which routinely came before the senior management in its analysis of monthly production numbers, the magnitude of the reconciliation cannot have escaped him: it was three times the size of any previous reconciliation discrepancy. … The immediate series of steps for audit, put in place by senior management, bespoke the significance of the reconciliation discrepancy for AE. A determination of the cause of the discrepancy had to made, in order to know whether a change, material by any definition, in the mine's reserve had to be announced, or whether an issue in mill procedures needed to be addressed. I am entitled to take the ordinary inference from the facts: that Mr. Landen was aware of the exceptional nature of the reconciliation issue and the steps taken to address it post haste as it was put to the meeting of October 9. To suggest that the non-disclosure of that information at the time he sold the securities, the following day or on October 24, when the results of the investigation of the reconciliation were apparently not known to him, does not amount to a defence. It neither raises a reasonable doubt as to materiality nor does it provide a basis for a defence of due diligence.

[114] Not only is his possession of that information the natural inference from his attendance at the meetings, there are a number of circumstances which shade his actions with consciousness of guilt. Mr. Landen did not comply with the internal company policies and Code of Business Conduct and Ethics. He did not comply with reporting obligations under the *Ontario Securities Act*, requirements he was well aware of, considering numerous and recent filings of that sort. The statement he made in the presence of his own counsel, to the Board of Directors on December 1, 2004, in the context of an internal investigation into a possible breach of his employment contract, that he did not consider his status as

an insider affecting the sale of Jakmin shares, is not credible. Mr. Landen was a long-time officer of AE, trained in accountancy. He had sole trading responsibility for all the securities held by the company which survived the founder of the company he worked for. He enjoyed an exceptional level of trust, given that portfolio. He decided to liquidate the entirety of the holdings in the company which the creator of the holding company had founded. Although it is hardly necessary, given the simple fact of his attendance at the meetings where these items were discussed, the dubious and shady way Mr. Landen dealt with these transactions adds to the atmosphere of suspicion attendant upon them.

[115] I find that Mr. Landen made the trades in the Jakmin shares on October 10 and 24 while in possession of material facts not generally disclosed, namely, as stated in Particulars 6 and 10. In the result, I find beyond reasonable doubt that:

- Mr. Landen was in a special relationship with Agnico-Eagle, being an officer;
- that he sold securities of Agnico-Eagle;
- that he knowledge of material information about that public company, as stipulated in Particulars 6 and 10;
- and that the material information had not been generally disclosed.

[116] Therefore I find that he is guilty on Count 2.

. . .

Evidence About Stephen Diamond

[118] Stephen Diamond, a long-time friend of Barry Landen's, shared a trading account and a bank account with Mr. Landen. Information about Mr. Diamond's options trades in AE, just prior to the October 29 announcement triggering a 22% fall in the share price, gave rise to an investigation, as the Canadian options exchange, Bourse de Montreal, showed an unusual volume of put options in AE, traded close to the time of this bad news announcement for AE. The investigation showed transfers of funds between Mr. Diamond and Mr. Landen. Mr. Landen wrote a cheque to Mr. Diamond for $100,000 on October 20, 2003. It was transferred to Mr. Diamond's brokerage account, from which the options were purchased. Mr. Diamond purchased put options on October 23 and 24 2003. He sold them on October 30, 2003, realising a profit of approximately $200,000. Subsequently he wrote a series of cheques to Mr. Landen: $50,000 on November 2, 2003; $25,000 on December 1, 2003 and $75,000 on December 16, 2003.

[119] As described in the evidence, options are high risk investments, which only sophisticated investors may make. A put option is profitable only when the purchaser of the put sells it when the share price is lower than the "strike" price of the option. The option may be purchased by someone regardless of whether the purchase owns shares in the company. If no shares are owned by the purchaser of the option, it is known as a "naked" put. Mr. Diamond did not own any shares in AE at the time he purchased these options. Mr. Embry described options trading like gambling.

[120] Mr. Diamond's purchases of these options accounted for the vast majority of total put options traded in Canada and the U.S. on the days in question. In fact, his purchases were of a volume unmatched in any previous trade on either the Canadian or American exchange.

. . .

[133] Only months later, in the fall of 1997, Mr. Diamond separated from his wife. He consulted his friend Barry Landen about opening a joint account for the purpose of trading securities. He was concerned that his wife could freeze his assets, or prevent him from trading. He took the view, without consulting a legal opinion, that by opening an account with Mr. Landen, he might "stop it or slow her down, or impede her ability to stop me because we're separated at this point." Apart from his name being on the account, Mr. Landen had nothing to do with the account. Mr. Diamond wasn't sure that Mr. Landen even had the information necessary to access the account, as it was online. He never put money into the investments, nor did he benefit from trades through the account, nor was Mr. Landen's authority required to deal with the account in any way. The account documentation does show that Mr. Landen was an insider of AE. At this point, Mr. Diamond expressed his investment goals as 65% high risk, and 35% medium risk. The form describes him as a sophisticated investor with goals of 50% short term gain and 50% long term.

[134] Mr. Diamond testified in detail about his trading history, with short sales, and some options trading. He said he was able to tolerate losses—to be wrong—and to make money on his trades from time to time. He said he felt he made money on balance, but that reviewing his losses "still hurt." He noted that his status as a trader was upgraded at a certain point due to the volume of transactions he entered into. He describes himself as a trader, not an investor, as his interest was taking short term positions that he could get into and out of quickly, perhaps in the same day. His definition of a trader as someone who "rather than going for that long-term investment … will flip stocks, will trade actively, will get in and out of a position in a much shorter period of time than somebody with a long-term investment strategy." This conforms to the definition provided by Mr. Embry. By the fall of 2003, Mr. Diamond had purchased some options, in companies other than AE. They were in no way as significant as his purchase of put options in AE. It appeared that so far as the online accounts were concerned, Mr. Diamond used the account in his and Mr. Landen's name. However, for the trades in AE securities, Mr. Diamond used the one in his name alone. He explained it this way:

> … [I]f I had done those trades in the Diamond-Landen account, then it would've put some, I thought, some sort of an obligation on Landen as an officer and a director of this particular company, he would've been put in a position of some sort of reporting on something he had no knowledge of (testimony, July 7, 2008).

[135] In cross-examination Mr. Diamond acknowledged that he traded in Agnico-Eagle stock in April 2003, but that he traded through the account he held jointly with Mr. Landen. He says that he realized that was the "wrong account," again on the basis that Mr. Landen was an insider, and so he "got in and got out as soon as I realized I was in the wrong account; I got out and lost sixty bucks in commission." He did tell Mr. Landen he had made a mistake in this regard, at the time.

[136] Mr. Diamond described receiving the money from Mr. Landen, on October 20, 2003. The loan was intended to assist with the renovation of his home, but he used approximately $70,000 of it for the purchase of a series of put options on AE on October 23 and 24. He described his ongoing overview of the stock, knowing that its third quarter results would be released on October 29. He testified that he moved funds from the joint account he had with Mr. Landen to his own trading account, because he believed, as evidence by

his action in April in relation to a trade in AE securities, that he might prejudice Mr. Landen by trading in AE securities through an account on which an insider was listed.

[137] He was cross-examined about his history of investment, and his base of information for making the purchases of put options in AE. He stated his assumptions in this way:

> I believed if there was a five percent drop in the stock, which on this particular stock could easily happen, with news that wasn't necessarily negative but didn't meet the expectation of others in the marketplace, so if there was a five percent drop in the stock, to my way of thinking, that may have translated into a twenty or twenty-five thousand dollar gain on these puts.

[138] Mr. Diamond gave detail of the renovation costs, which he anticipated, and acknowledged that he didn't think he had told his wife that he was using some of the funds he borrowed for the renovation to make a speculative investment. Some receipts were tendered in re-examination for identification by Mr. Diamond, and for his comment. As some of the renovation costs were paid in cash, there were not receipts for all the costs incurred. This was the case for the biggest single aspect of the renovation, which ended up costing around $70,000 for the entrance work. However, it was clear that the series of estimates and invoices and receipts supported Mr. Diamond's testimony about renovations and upgrading costs to his home during the period of October 2003. As well, a reporting letter from the lawyer, Mr. Diamond's father-in-law, who handled the purchase and sale of matrimonial home transaction, supported Mr. Diamond's testimony about the timing and expenses related to his new home.

[139] Mr. Diamond admitted that it was the purchases of AE options was a significantly larger play in options than he previously had made, but that it was not out of line with other trades he had committed to. He had previously traded in options, though only recently. He had entered into many short sale transactions. He had entered into one transaction which through leveraging and margin, represented a trade valued at more than his net worth. He stated that he was a somewhat sophisticated investor.

[140] Mr. Diamond was cross-examined about his awareness of the volume in trading in options in AE securities. He stated he was unaware of this data. The OSC rests its case on a few factors, which it argues cannot be explained by anything other than Mr. Diamond's receiving insider information from Mr. Landen. One such factor is the significant proportion of the volume in trade in AE put options by Mr. Diamond. He stated that he was entirely unaware of the volume of trades, that it was not a factor, which would have assisted his decision to buy, or not. Nothing in the record suggests that volume of trading in the form of security assists in decision making, and common sense does not further my understanding of the value of such information.

. . .

[143] Mr. Diamond stated that when he discovered the drop in share price was well beyond his expectation, his response went "from shock to glee."

[144] In cross-examination, on the issue of any communication he may have had with Mr. Landen about the trades, Mr. Diamond denies communication ahead of time. However, as he began repaying the loans which Mr. Landen had made him as detailed above, since 2000, he did tell him that he had made money on options on Agnico-Eagle, effectively betting against his company. Mr. Diamond testified that he did not recall Mr. Landen's reaction, and that the conversation did not stand out in his mind.

[145] Mr. Diamond said that the cheques he issued to Mr. Landen in November and December were by way of repayment of previous loans.

[146] Clearly, Mr. Diamond is a man whose willingness to engage in risky activity and be guided by his own counsel is reflected from the start of his career as an accountant—he went into his own practice rather than stay in big firm security. His history of risky though legal trading strategies tracks well before the impugned purchase of AE securities. Mr. Diamond's testimony about his involvement in the market shows a keen awareness of his past forays into the stock market, and though he acknowledges it as painful, the losses he incurred did not deter him from further trading. In assessing his credibility, I note that none of the obvious markers of dubious credibility are present: he has no criminal record, and although he has engaged in high risk stock market activity, there is no suggestion of any illegal or improper activity, prior to the trades in question. He was uncontradicted in his evidence to this Court. The inability to recall Mr. Landen's reaction, when told of Mr. Diamond's windfall in the put options, is least credible aspect of his testimony. However, in applying the law to Mr. Diamond's testimony, I cannot reject it on the basis of that one point alone. I find his testimony presents a consistent portrait of a man, who faced greater financial challenges than his income permitted him to afford, but who was willing to take chances in his self-reliant forays into high-risk stock market trades. The pattern of increased risk is supported by the evidence. His characterisation of AE's market status was consistent with the opinions of professional market analysts in the sector. The challenges of his new home transaction are at least partly supported by estimates and receipts presented to the court, and to the extent that it was not neatly and fully documented, it was not inconsistent with the profile which emerged of Mr. Diamond (though it might challenge stereotypes of chartered accountants).

[147] The prosecution relies on circumstances to show that Mr. Diamond received insider information from Mr. Landen, as it has particularised. The OSC contends that the coincidence of circumstances lead the Court to no other conclusion concerning Mr. Diamond than his guilt beyond reasonable doubt. The long-standing friendship between the men, the shared bank account and trading account, the transfer by Mr. Landen of $100,000 to Mr. Diamond days before Mr. Diamond invests $70,000 in a risky options trade: these are the key features of the case on the tipping count and the insider trading count against Mr. Diamond. Together with Mr. Landen's insider status at AE and his own trades during that time period, which effectively emptied the holding company of the founder of AE of all its stock in AE, the court is asked to find that no other conclusion can be drawn but that Mr. Landen shared insider information about AE with Mr. Diamond, and that Mr. Diamond was thereby in a special relationship with him as defined by the Act, and traded in securities while in possession of material information not generally disclosed about the company. The law is clear with regard to proof of criminal charges based on circumstantial evidence:

> A finding of guilt [could] only be made where there [was] no other rational explanation for the circumstantial evidence but that the defendant committed the crime (*Charemski* [[1998] 1 SCR 679], cited at para. 24, *R. v. Robert* [2000] OJ No. 688).

[148] In asking the Court to draw an inference, and the sole inference on the evidence, that Mr. Landen tipped Mr. Diamond, I take into account all of the evidence. The theory of the prosecution is attractive, given the confluence of circumstances featuring Mr. Landen

> and Mr. Diamond's long association, and the high risk investment made by Mr. Diamond just after receiving money from Mr. Landen, which rewarded his risk with a return of almost 300% in seven days. I have Mr. Landen's denial of giving information to Mr. Diamond, through an out-of-court statement. I have Mr. Diamond's denial, and a credible account of the circumstances of his personal life and his history as a trader which supported an innocent explanation. Though some parts of what Mr. Diamond says defy belief, notably that he does not recall Mr. Landen's response when he told him of his windfall by betting against Mr. Landen's company that is not sufficient to exclude the possibility that what he says is true. It forecloses the conclusion, on the requisite standard, that Mr. Diamond was an insider to Agnico-Eagle. It certainly leaves this court with a reasonable doubt about the OSC allegation of possession of insider information, and tipping. Both counts must fall as a result, and I am dismissing counts 1 and 3.

V. CIVIL ENFORCEMENT POWERS

Provincial regulatory power to seek civil remedies from a court for securities law infractions will not detain us long, not because they are not theoretically important, but because they have rarely been exercised by provincial commissions. This is in contrast to developments in the United States, where civil penalties have been a high-profile component of the regulatory landscape. See David Zaring, "Enforcement Discretion at the SEC" (2016) 94:6 Tex L Rev 1155. By way of example, s 128 allows the OSC to apply to the Ontario Superior Court of Justice for a "declaration that a person or company has not complied with or is not complying with Ontario securities law." If the court makes such a declaration, there is a wide variety of orders the court may make, including orders to comply with Ontario securities law, rescinding transactions, requiring compensation or restitution, payment of damages, disgorgement, and the rectification of past non-compliance. These remedies are available in addition to penalties imposed under OSA, s 122 or 127. Indeed, it is conceivable for a regulator like the OSC to take action in the same matter under all of ss 122, 127, and 128. An example of the use of OSA, s 128 was the *Ochnik* case (*Ochnik v Ontario Securities Commission*, [2007] OJ No 2171 (QL) (Sup Ct J)). See also, more recently, *Ontario Securities Commission v Robinson* (2009), 99 OR (3d) 739, 183 ACWS (3d) 1154 (Sup Ct J).

QUESTION

Why do you think provincial regulators do not use their civil enforcement role?

VI. ADMINISTRATIVE ENFORCEMENT POWERS

A. Introduction

A major component in the enforcement arsenal of provincial securities regulators is the power to make orders of various kinds that impose sanctions on market participants. The significance of these orders is that they may be made by the regulators following a hearing, thus obviating the need to prepare a criminal prosecution or an application for civil penalties to be heard by a court. (Note that in Québec it is possible for regulators to make a cease-trading order without a hearing.) Regulators may make the orders identified in their governing statutes if it is in "the public interest" to make them. It is in the discretion of the regulator to interpret the public interest in accordance with its statutory mandate. As we shall see, making orders in the public interest does not require a breach of securities law. It is also possible to make a public interest order in circumstances where there is, or has been, a quasi-criminal action in respect of the same matter without infringing on protections against double jeopardy for an accused. Thus, for example, the OSC made an order under s 127 of the OSA against Glen Harvey Harper, whose prosecution for insider trading under s 122 of the OSA was discussed in Chapter 8. The order prohibited Harper for 15 years from becoming or acting as an officer or director of any reporting issuer, and, subject to some exceptions, required him to cease trading in any securities for 15 years. In reaching its decision, the OSC noted that it had a "complete and independent jurisdiction under s. 127" that was applicable even where action had been taken under other legal provisions. See *In the Matter of Glen Harvey Harper* (2004), 27 OSCB 3937. It should also be noted that the conduct of hearings by provincial regulators is typically governed by provincial statutory powers and procedures legislation, or more detailed rules of practice made pursuant to such legislation.

More detail about the kinds of orders that may be made, ranging from cease-trading orders to reprimands to administrative fines in some provinces, will be provided below. Let us first consider the types of circumstances in which regulators in Canada have typically made public-interest enforcement orders.

B. The Substance of Public-Interest Enforcement Powers

1. Variation in the Subject Matter of Orders

In a research study prepared for the Wise Persons' Committee in 2003, Professor Mary Condon found significant variation in the kinds of matters that became the subject of administrative enforcement action across Canadian provinces. The executive summary of the study is reproduced below.

Mary Condon, "The Use of Public Interest Enforcement Orders by Securities Regulators in Canada" in A Douglas Harris, ed, *WPC—Committee to Review the Structure of Securities Regulation in Canada: Research Studies*
(Ottawa: Department of Finance, 2003), online:
<http://www.wise-averties.ca/report_en.html>

The purpose of this study is to examine the use of discretionary enforcement powers by securities regulators in Canada, in order to assess the implications of multiple regulators for the enforcement of securities law.

Regulatory enforcement decisions for the last three (and in some provinces, five) years were reviewed along the following parameters:

- nature of infraction;
- whether the respondent was previously known to enforcement personnel;
- connection between public interest analysis and goals of securities regulation;
- use of extra-provincial regulatory precedents in decision;

- articulation of distinct provincial interest in sanctioning respondent;
- nature of sanction imposed;
- use of regulatory precedents to structure discretion; and
- use of aggravating/mitigating factors to structure outcome.

The findings of the study are that:

- There was significant variation in emphasis across the provinces in relation to infractions pursued to an enforcement hearing. Some provinces focussed, for example, on illegal distributions of securities and others on acting as a broker or advisor without registration. There was more than a trivial number of instances where respondents had been the subject of enforcement proceedings in the past. Local regulators appear to play a significant role in the setting of enforcement priorities.
- There was notable consistency across the provinces in the articulation of the public interest that was the basis for making orders. It tended to be linked more to goals of maintaining public confidence in, and integrity of, capital markets than to those of market efficiency. There was almost no expression of unique provincial objectives in making public interest orders, suggesting a high degree of consistency in the philosophical underpinnings of regulatory intervention.
- On the other hand, there was some unevenness in the application of contextual sanctioning factors to individual respondents, in order to justify specific types and quantum of penalties. Some consistency did result from reliance on two regulatory precedents—one each from BC and Ontario—enumerating factors relevant to the individual sanctioning decision. The bigger provinces tended to make use of the multiple sanctions at their disposal in sanctioning respondents.

These findings suggest that:

- The status quo would be enhanced by additional transparency about the setting of provincial enforcement priorities and coordination among the provinces with respect to the mitigating/aggravating factors that structure sanctioning discretion.
- Similar attempts at coordination would be beneficial in relation to a passport system, which envisages a continued role for local enforcement, based on the jurisdiction of the investor making a complaint. If this model is adopted, care should be taken not to lose the benefit of local provincial knowledge about dubious market participants.
- Under a single regulator, a decentralized enforcement model—allowing for local enforcement offices across the country—would be preferable to a more centralized enforcement model. Local input into the setting of national enforcement priorities and the development of a consistent approach to dealing with the factors influencing the quantum and type of penalty should be preserved.

Professors Condon and Sarra have also found that the most frequent type of infraction pursued to a hearing by provincial securities commissions between 2004 and 2007 involved allegations of illegal distributions—that is, distributions of securities without a prospectus receipt in a context in which prospectus exemptions were not available. (See M Condon &

J Sarra, "Provincial Enforcement of Securities Regulation: Data and Debates" (2008) [unpublished, on file with authors]). Since Condon's research for the Wise Person's Committee in 2003, quantitative reporting about enforcement results sorted by category of infraction (illegal distribution, insider trading, etc) has now become a standard practice used by the CSA in its annual enforcement reports. See e.g. "CSA 2015 Enforcement Report," online: <https://www.securities-administrators.ca/uploadedFiles/CSA_ER2015_En.pdf>. For over a decade, there has been remarkable consistency in the outcome that illegal distributions are the most common securities infraction pursued to a tribunal hearing.

2. *Some Examples of Circumstances in Which Enforcement Orders Are Made*

Interspersed throughout this book are examples of the use of public-interest enforcement powers to deal with infractions of securities law. Thus, for example, *YBM*, *Coventree*, and *Azeff* dealing with inadequacies in prospectuses, continuous disclosure, and insider trading, respectively, are regulatory decisions made under the auspices of OSA, s 127. Recent decisions from other provinces include those of *Thow (Re)*, 2007 BCSECCOM 758 (20 December 2007) (order varied on appeal, [2009] BCJ No 211 (QL) (CA)) from British Columbia, and *Sea Sun Capital Corporation, Re*, 2009 ABASC 256 (28 May 2009) and 2009 ABASC 407 (13 August 2009) as well as *Arbour Energy Inc, Re*, 2012 ABASC 131 from Alberta.

In other instances, companies have been found to be trading without a prospectus because they improperly used the exemption for seed capital, when they should have registered and filed a prospectus (see e.g. *R v Boyle*, 2001 ABPC 152; *American Gold Mining Corporations*, 2003 BCSECCOM 330 (16 May 2003); *Re Dual Capital Management Ltd et al*, settlement order, Ontario Securities Commission (27 June 2003); *Re DJL Capital Corporation et al*, settlement order, Ontario Securities Commission (20 March 2003); and *De Bianco et al and Equal Rights Legal Defence Alliance Inc*, 2003 ABSECCOM 968904). The matter of *Re Limelight Entertainment Inc*, 2008 LNONOSC 78, 31 OSCB 1727 involved allegations of the sale of Limelight shares in circumstances in which prospectus and registration exemptions were unavailable. The Alberta Securities Commission came to a similar conclusion in this matter in 2007. Meanwhile, in *Conseillers de placement TIP Ltée (Re)*, 2004 CanLII 57094 (Qc CVM), the Commission des valeurs mobilières du Québec (CVMQ) found that the issuer failed to file documents in accordance with continuous disclosure requirements and found that the company and its principal had failed to respect important requirements of securities legislation designed for the protection of investors. Two recent market manipulation cases from British Columbia are *Re Sungro*, 2015 BCSECCOM 281 and *Poonian (Re)*, 2015 BCSECCOM 96.

3. *Enforcement Action Against Lawyers*

Most provincial and territorial regulators, such as those in British Columbia, Saskatchewan, Ontario, Québec, and Newfoundland have the power to reprimand market participants. Thus, one of the orders the OSC can make under OSA, s 127 is to reprimand "a person or company." We have already mentioned regulatory enforcement action taken against officers and directors of YBM. In 1999, the OSC sought to reprimand a lawyer who represented YBM because of his actions in connection with representing that issuer, and specifically because of allegedly misleading statements he made to the regulators to the effect that YBM had obtained a "series of favourable due diligence results" about its operations conducted by independent parties. Wilder brought an application for judicial review on the grounds that such an order against him was beyond the OSC's jurisdiction.

Wilder v Ontario Securities Commission
(2000), 47 OR (3d) 361 (Sup Ct J (Div Ct))

SWINTON J:

[1] This is an application for judicial review seeking an order in the nature of prohibition to prevent the respondent, the Ontario Securities Commission, from continuing proceedings commenced by Notice of Hearing pursuant to s. 127 of the *Securities Act*, RSO 1990, c. S.5, as amended, against the applicant, Lawrence D. Wilder, and for an order in the nature of certiorari quashing the Notice of Hearing as against him.

...

[4] On November 1, 1999 a Notice of Hearing was issued by the Ontario Securities Commission pursuant to its public interest jurisdiction in s. 127(1) of the *Securities Act*. Mr. Wilder was named as one of the respondents, along with YBM Magnex International Inc., various officers and directors of YBM, and its underwriters. With respect to Mr. Wilder, it was stated that the Commission would hold a hearing to consider whether, in the opinion of the Commission, it was in the public interest to make an order pursuant to s. 127(1)6 of the Act to reprimand him, as well as a number of other persons. The Notice went on to state that if the Commission determined that any of the named parties, including Mr. Wilder, had not complied with Ontario securities law, staff will request the Commission to consider whether an application should be made to the Superior Court pursuant to s. 128 of the Act.

[5] The Notice made reference to the Statement of Allegations by staff of the Commission, also dated November 1, 1999. That document sets out a detailed set of allegations in 24 pages. The key allegation against Mr. Wilder is found in a section entitled "Conduct Contrary to the Public Interest," paragraph 57:

> (f) that Wilder made statements in a letter dated July 4, 1997 to Staff of the Commission that in a material respect, and at the time and in light of the circumstances under which the statements were made, were misleading or untrue or did not state a fact that was required to be stated or that was necessary to make the statements not misleading; specifically, statements concerning the results of due diligence conducted in respect of YBM. In so doing, Wilder acted in a manner contrary to the public interest.

...

[7] The Statement of Allegations sets out a summary of information not disclosed by Mr. Wilder. Essentially, it is alleged by OSC staff that the letter contains a misleading misstatement of material facts, in that Mr. Wilder knew that YBM had not been the subject of a "series of favourable due diligence results pertaining to the business of YBM conducted by independent parties."

The Commission's Jurisdiction

[8] The issue on this application for judicial review is not whether the allegations of OSC staff that Mr. Wilder misled them are well-founded or not. The issue is whether the

Commission has jurisdiction to commence and continue these proceedings against Mr. Wilder pursuant to s. 127(1) of the *Securities Act*. In determining that issue, the Court has proceeded on the basis that the allegations in the Statement of Allegations are capable of proof.

. . .

The Interpretation of Section 127(1) of the Act

[12] The applicants and the intervenor argue that s. 127(1) should be interpreted so as not to apply to lawyers while acting in their professional capacity. In the alternative, they argue that if the section does apply in these circumstances, it is unconstitutional and should be read down.

[13] The purpose of the *Securities Act* is to provide protection to investors from unfair, improper or fraudulent practices, and to foster fair and efficient capital markets and confidence in those markets (s. 1.1). It is the responsibility of the Commission to carry out those objectives in exercising the powers conferred on it by the Act.

[14] There is nothing in the wording of s. 127(1)6 which would indicate that it does not apply to lawyers. Indeed, the term "person" is used here, in contrast to terms such as "market participant" in other clauses. Moreover, the applicants concede that lawyers are subject to the other enforcement provisions of the Act found in ss. 122 and 128, arguing that this creates no problem because the sections are enforced through the courts.

[15] Normally, words in a statute would be interpreted as having the same meaning throughout, leading one to conclude that "person" in s. 127(1)6 is meant to include lawyers acting in their professional capacity, just as the other sections do. However, the applicants argue that the background and purpose of s. 127(1)6 is inconsistent with a grant to the Commission of a power to discipline lawyers for professional misconduct, which is how the Commission's proceedings here are characterized. Support for this proposition was found in earlier proposals to amend the securities legislation put forth in 1990, which sought an express power for the Commission to discipline professionals ("Proposals for Amendments to the Securities Act in the Areas of Investigations, Enforcement and Remedies" (1990), 13 OSCB 405). These proposals generated opposition from various law firms, as well as the Law Society of Upper Canada, which expressed concern about the impact on the independence of the bar and the regulatory role of the Law Society. Further proposals were then forthcoming from the Commission relating to professionals, which were more circumscribed than those proposed initially ("Proposals to Amend the Enforcement Provisions of the Securities Act" (1991), 14 OSCB 1907). These were never enacted, and from this, the applicants ask this Court to infer that there is no power to discipline lawyers acting in their professional capacity under s. 127(1) in its current form.

[16] In my view, this conclusion does not follow. When the *Securities Act* was amended in 1994, it gave the Commission a general power, in s. 127(1), to reprimand a person or company, along with other powers, such as the power to order a market participant to submit to a review or to require reports, prospectuses and releases to be provided, withheld, or amended. The predecessor to s. 127(1), found in s. 27 of the Act prior to the amendments, permitted the Commission to reprimand only a registrant. Thus, it appears that with the enactment of s. 127(1) in its current form, the Legislature intended to

broaden the powers of the Commission to make orders in the public interest and chose words which do not preclude their application to lawyers.

[17] The applicants and intervenor nevertheless argue that the Law Society Act, RSO 1990, c. L.8 evidences an intention to leave the governance of the legal profession in Ontario to the Law Society. Indeed, in its factum, the Law Society submitted that it had exclusive and exhaustive powers over the regulation of professional conduct of lawyers.

[18] Moreover, it was argued that it would be contrary to the public interest to interpret the *Securities Act* as giving the Commission the power to discipline lawyers, since this would have a chilling effect on the ability of members of the public to obtain independent legal representation. Reference was made by the applicants and intervenor to the experience of lawyers before the United States Securities and Exchange Commission ("SEC") in support of the argument that the threat of proceedings by an administrative tribunal before which a lawyer practises will undermine clients' confidence in the lawyer's independence and will threaten solicitor–client confidentiality. The SEC, pursuant to Rule 2(e) (17 CFR s. 201.102(e)(1)), can deny the privilege of appearing before it to a person found to have engaged in "unethical or improper professional conduct," as well as one who has engaged in a wilful violation of federal securities law.

[19] There is nothing inconsistent between the Law Society's role in regulating the legal profession and the Ontario Securities Commission's proposed exercise of jurisdiction in the circumstances of this case. The Law Society and the Ontario Securities Commission both exercise public interest functions, but the public interests which they seek to protect are not the same. The Law Society has an important role to govern the legal profession in the public interest, and to ensure that members of the profession do not engage in professional misconduct or conduct unbecoming a barrister and solicitor. In carrying out its role, it has been given extensive disciplinary powers pursuant to s. 35(1) of the Act, as well as the power to order a member to institute new systems or procedures, to obtain or continue treatment or counselling or to participate in professional education (see, for example, ss. 40 and 44).

[20] The Ontario Securities Commission also has an important public interest role, that of protecting investors and the proper functioning of Ontario's capital markets. Ensuring proper disclosure and maintaining the integrity of its processes are an important part of this role. Here, it is alleged that Mr. Wilder intentionally misled Commission staff during the course of a prospectus review by writing the letter quoted earlier. Nothing in the Law Society Act indicates that a lawyer should be immune from proceedings by the Ontario Securities Commission under s. 127(1)6 where others would not be immune, solely because he is acting in a professional capacity. In proceedings such as these, the Commission is not usurping the role of the Law Society, as its objective is not to discipline the lawyer for professional misconduct; rather, its concern is to remedy a breach of its own Act which violates the public interest in fair and efficient capital markets, and to control its own processes.

[21] While the applicants and intervenor made reference to the chilling effect on the independence of counsel appearing before the SEC, it is important to recognize that the OSC is not claiming powers here like those possessed by the SEC. The OSC is not seeking to control access to practise before it, as can the SEC under Rule 2(e); rather, it purports to exercise its public interest jurisdiction to determine whether an individual should be

reprimanded because of alleged misconduct. As a matter of statutory interpretation, s. 127(1)6 can apply to a lawyer acting in a professional capacity.

The Constitutional Issue

[22] The applicants and intervenor rely, in the alternative, on a constitutional argument. They argue that the Rule of Law is a fundamental principle of the Canadian constitution. One of the primary ways in which the Rule of Law is protected is through the independence of the judiciary, and they argue that an independent bar, subject only to self-regulation or judicial oversight, is integral to the independence of the judiciary. Thus, they argue that the Ontario Securities Commission can not exercise disciplinary power over lawyers as a matter of constitutional law, and, therefore, s. 127(1)6 should be read down so as not to apply to lawyers acting in a professional capacity.

[23] The preamble to the Constitution Act, 1982 provides that "Canada is founded upon principles that recognize the supremacy of God and the rule of law." The Supreme Court of Canada has also recognized the fundamental importance of the rule of law in the Canadian constitutional order. For example, in *Reference re Secession of Québec* (1998), 161 DLR (4th) 385 (SCC) at 417, the Court states that:

> The principles of constitutional law and the rule of law lie at the root of our system of government. The rule of law, as observed in *Roncarelli v. Duplessis*, [1959] SCR 121 at p. 142, 16 DLR (2d) 689, is "a fundamental postulate of our constitutional structure." … At its most basic level, the rule of law vouchsafes to the citizens and residents of the country a stable, predictable and ordered society in which to conduct their own affairs. It provides a shield for individuals from arbitrary state action.

In an earlier passage, the Court noted that the principles are not made explicitly a part of the written constitution, but they assist in the interpretation of its text (at 410).

[24] The proposed proceeding against Mr. Wilder does not represent an encroachment on the independence of the bar. It is noteworthy that the applicants and the intervenor take the position that the allegation against Mr. Wilder could properly be before the courts—for example, through invoking the procedures in ss. 122 and 128 of the Act. They argue that the OSC, in contrast, is insufficiently independent to hear Mr. Wilder's case. This argument ignores the fact that the OSC acts as a quasi-judicial tribunal in conducting its enforcement proceedings. Such proceedings do not constitute state interference in the independence of the bar "in the political sense," as suggested by the applicants and intervenor. All that the Commission seeks to do here is to ensure that lawyers, among others, do not mislead the Commission, in the way that Mr. Wilder is alleged to have done. This exercise of jurisdiction by the Commission will not interfere with the ability of lawyers who practise securities law to continue to provide excellent and vigorous representation to their clients.

[25] Thus, the Commission's proposed proceeding does not interfere with the independence of the bar, nor can it be said to undermine the rule of law. Therefore, there is no reason to interpret s. 127 so as not to apply to lawyers acting in their professional capacity, and the application for judicial review is dismissed.

This power residing in securities regulators to reprimand lawyers acting on behalf of clients is likely to remain controversial as securities regulators in the United States enforce "up-the-ladder" reporting requirements against lawyers in the post-*Sarbanes-Oxley* environment. (See Sandra Rubin, "The Failed Gatekeeper," *Financial Post* (20 October 2004) FP3.) See also, more recently, *Re AiT Advanced Information Technologies Corp*, 2008 LNONOSC 22, 31 OSCB 712.

4. The Use of the Public-Interest Power in the Absence of a Breach of the Statute or Regulations/Rules

Possibly even more controversial than the use of public-interest orders against lawyers acting on behalf of clients has been the proposition that securities regulators have jurisdiction to make enforcement orders where there has been no breach of securities law. It is clear that the terms of most of the relevant statutory provisions in Canada granting such enforcement powers do not suggest that the granting of an order necessitates finding a breach of positive securities law. On the other hand, the argument is that sanctioning market participants and others because a transaction or conduct has been "abusive" but without a finding that they have breached the law imports a great deal of uncertainty for market participants as to how they should conduct themselves in securities markets. The OSC decision that is the high-water mark of this understanding of the role of public-interest enforcement powers is *Canadian Tire*, excerpted below. Since that decision was rendered by the OSC, subsequent appellate court assessments of the role of provisions like OSA, s 127 (formerly s 123) have established additional parameters for the use of such orders, in terms of the regulatory objectives that should be achieved by them. See *Asbestos*, below. It should also be noted that the application of an administrative penalty or an order requiring disgorgement of profits typically requires a finding of contravention of the law.

Re Canadian Tire Corp
(1987), 10 OSCB 857

REASONS: On December 9, 1986, CTC Dealer Holdings Limited ("Dealers") made an offer (the "Offer") to purchase 49% of the outstanding common shares of Canadian Tire Corporation, Limited ("Tire") at a price of $160.24 per common share. The Offer revealed that Alfred W. Billes ("Fred"), David G. Billes ("David") (collectively, the "Brothers") and Martha Gardiner-Billes ("Martha") (collectively, the "Billeses") had, pursuant to agreements entered into with Dealers, agreed irrevocably to deposit their total holdings of 2,101,150 common shares of Tire pursuant to the terms of the Offer and not to withdraw such shares. The Billeses' common shares amounted to 60.9% of the outstanding common shares of Tire.

As Dealers was the owner of approximately 17.4% of the outstanding common shares of Tire at the time of the bid, the bid for 49% guaranteed it control of Tire if its Offer were successful.

The sole registered shareholder of Dealers is the Canadian Tire Dealers' Association (the "Association"), an Ontario non-share corporation whose members are 361 Tire dealers.

On December 10, 1986, the Ontario Securities Commission (the "Commission") issued a Notice of Hearing pursuant to section 123(1) [now s 127] of the *Securities Act*, RSO 1980, c. 466, as amended (the "Act"), to consider whether it was in the public interest to impose a cease trading order on the Offer and on the common shares held by the Billeses.

Paragraph 14 of the Notice of Hearing alleged that the Offer was contrary to the public interest and therefore ought to be restrained on the following five grounds:

i) the making of the Bid and/or the tendering thereto of the Billes' common shares is in breach of the duties owed by CTC Dealer Holdings and/or the, Billeses to the Class A shareholders of Canadian Tire;
ii) the holders of the Class A shares have been misled as to the efficiency of the coattail;
iii) the Bid is, in substance, a purchase of all of the common shares of Canadian Tire but has been structured as a purchase of only 49% of the common shares, to circumvent the operation of the coattail;
iv) the Bid as structured may contravene s. 91 [now s 92] of the Act and is, in any event, inconsistent with the principles which underlie the provisions of section 91 and Commission Policy 1.3; and
v) if the Bid is successful, the principal customers of Canadian Tire will have acquired control of the company through the acquisition of only approximately 2% of the participating shares. The Dealers will thereby have created a fundamental conflict of interest which is contrary to the interests of the holders of the Class A shares and the public at large.

Following a nine day hearing (the "Hearing") which was held in conjunction with the Commission des valeurs mobilières du Québec pursuant to authority granted under s. 2(4) of the Act, the Commission announced on January 14, 1987 that it had issued a cease trade order against the Offer and against the common shares held by the Billeses. …

. . .

The four parties who requested standing were, collectively, holders of some 30,000,000 Class A shares.

The argument of the applicants for standing was put on the basis that they had a direct financial interest in the outcome of the proceeding and their rights would be directly affected. The Offer is for the voting shares only and is structured in such a way that it would not trigger the takeover protection provision attaching to the Class A shares (the "coattail"). The coattail would have the effect of converting the Class A shares to voting shares if a majority of the common shares then issued and outstanding were tendered and taken up pursuant to a takeover bid.

. . .

In order for the Billeses, as controlling shareholders, to be able to sell their shares to the public without filing a prospectus [in 1983], they required an exemption order from the Commission pursuant to section 73 of the Act. Counsel for the Billeses met with Salter, the then Director of the Commission, and Harry Malcolmson ("Malcolmson"), Associate Director, to discuss the reorganization and the proposed sale of the Class A shares. A memorandum by William Sheridan ("Sheridan"), counsel for David, of the meeting contains the following sentences:

> We also stressed that the Class A shareholders would, as a separate group, vote on the proposal. This aspect, as well as the insertion of the anti take-over bid provisions, both were very warmly received and it was my distinct impression that without them, we would have met with much greater resistance.

In the result, staff recommended the granting of a section 73 [now s 74] order. The Commission granted the application and, as noted, some 5 million Class A non-voting shares held by the Billeses as a result of the reorganization were sold to the public. The proceeds were used to pay down the financing obtained to purchase the common shares held by J.W.'s estate.

...

On December 9, 1986, Dealers made their Offer for 49% of the outstanding common shares of Tire at $160.24 per common share. It is clear that the price of $160.24 was set on the assumption that all holders of common shares (other than Dealers) would tender all their shares to the Offer. That is the only reasonable assumption, given the fact that the price being paid under the Offer for the common shares was some 400% greater than the price the common shares were trading at just prior to the announcement that the Dealers would make a takeover bid. The assumption is also reasonable on the basis that the Lock-up agreements, which were disclosed in the Offering Circular, assured the success of the Offer through the tendering of the Billeses' 60.9% control block.

...

The essential argument of Commission staff was that the Offer, when seen in light of the Billeses' desire to sell their control block from the late spring of 1986 onwards, and in the context of the share capital reorganization of Tire in 1983, and the reasons for providing takeover bid protection to the Class A shareholders, was contrary to the public interest as that term is used in section 123 of the Act. Counsel submitted that the Commission has jurisdiction under section 123, notwithstanding that there has not been a specific breach of the Act, the regulations or a policy statement, and that the nature of this transaction is contrary to the public interest. The jurisdiction of the Commission to act in this case was said to be based on the principles set out by the Commission in its decision in *Cablecasting Limited*, [1978] OSCB 37.

As to the transaction itself, it was argued that the Offer, and the Billeses' agreement to tender to it pursuant to the Lock-up agreements, was clearly abusive of the public trading markets and ought to be restrained. Counsel put the proposition that the agreements between the Billeses and Dealers under which the Dealers would bid $160.24 per share for 49% of the common shares, constituted an artificial transaction cleverly constructed to circumvent the takeover protection granted to the Class A shareholders in 1983.

...

VI. Reasons for Decision

...

A. The Basis for a Section 123 Order

It was argued by counsel for the Billeses and for the Dealers, that the power to issue a cease trade order under section 123 ought not to be made unless a breach of the Act, the regulations or a policy statement clearly has been demonstrated. We do not agree. Section

123, in its terms, is not so limited. Moreover, in past decisions, particularly in Cablecasting, the Commission has indicated that it would be prepared to use its power under section 123 to deal with situations that are inconsistent with the best interests of investors or where a transaction constitutes a flagrant abuse of the marketplace.

The point raised by counsel with respect to demonstrating a breach of the Act, regulations or a policy statement was specifically raised in *Cablecasting*. In that case, the Commission noted that under section 123, as well as a number of other sections, the Commission is vested with discretion that must be exercised in the public interest. For the most part, the Commission attempts to publish policy statements indicating the circumstances in which discretion will be exercised. But such policy statements cannot possibly cover every situation that can arise in a dynamic public market. In rejecting counsel's contention that an actual breach of a policy statement had to be demonstrated, the Commission made the following comment:

> The obvious conclusion, that the individual with an imagination sufficiently fertile to invent an unethical scheme which skirts the words of all published pronouncements may carry out that scheme with impunity, demonstrates the difficulties of the position.

We would adopt that holding of *Cablecasting* in this case. The Legislature deliberately has given the Commission a broad and unfettered power to move quickly to intervene in the capital markets to stop a trade or a transaction which it deems to be contrary to the public interest. The ambit of the Commission's power under section 123 is not hedged or confined by particular examples or by particular criteria, as is true elsewhere in the Act. Rather, the Legislature has vested in the Commission the power to intervene where it has been demonstrated that such intervention is necessary to fulfil the Commission's mandate to regulate the capital markets in the public interest.

To accede to counsel's contention that a specific breach of the legislation or of a policy statement must be shown before section 123 can be invoked would not only be contrary to the plain wording of section 123, but also would be a failure by the Commission to exercise the mandate vested in it by the Legislature. There are few areas in our public life that are as dynamic and as innovative as our capital markets. For the most part, that dynamism and innovation endure to the benefit of the economy at large and individual investors in particular. But that same dynamism and innovation can, and does, lead to abuse. A regulatory agency charged with oversight of the capital markets must have the capacity to move quickly to stop transactions which it considers to be injurious to the capital markets. Regardless of its rate of production, the Commission cannot possibly issue policy statements that cover, much less keep up with, the types of transactions that are conceived in the marketplace. It is in that sense that we adopt and reaffirm the statement quoted above from Cablecasting.

. . .

That the Commission is well aware of the necessity to proceed with caution where a breach of the Act or a policy statement has not been shown, is evidenced by the fact that this is only the second case since 1978 under section 123 where the Commission has had to deal with this particular point.

. . .

B. The Evidence

A review of the evidence in this case demonstrates why the public interest required that the offer and the tendering to it of their common shares by the Billeses required to be cease traded. The Billeses acquired control by buying J.W.'s shares from his estate in 1983 for some $73 million. To pay for those shares, they proposed a reorganization that would allow for a five for one split of the Class A shares and a split of the common shares into one common and four Class A shares. The Billeses would then sell the majority of their resultant Class A shares to the public to pay for their purchase of the estate's common shares.

Senior executives of Tire realized that a reorganization would be forthcoming to pay for the Billeses' purchase of control. Accordingly, they were concerned to ensure three objectives: first, a reasonable share split ratio; second, an independent board of directors; third, takeover protection for the Class A shareholders. …

As to the form of the takeover protection, the concern of the Billeses was that they not lose their long desired and hard won control position through any accidental circumstance. Accordingly, what was considered a simply worded, relatively straightforward clause that required a majority of the shares to be tendered and taken up before the Class A coattail would be triggered, was adopted. This was acceptable to everyone concerned, the Billeses, Tire's senior management, Tire's counsel, the Billeses' counsel, and their fiscal agents, for the simple reason that the Billeses constituted a 60% control block and had no intention of selling. If they were to sell their control position, then the coattail would be triggered, as a majority of the shares would be tendered to any bid. The coattail would also be triggered if the Billeses decided to sell through a private agreement at a premium greater than 15%, which agreement would require a follow-up bid under the terms of the Act.

The evidence of all the parties is clear that the Billeses' control was equated with the term "majority." The understanding among the parties most closely involved was that the protection given to the Class A shareholders was exactly the protection required in the circumstances; the Billeses had control and if they sold that control, a majority of the shares would pass and the coattail would be triggered. …

Consequent upon the reorganization, the Billeses sold to the public 5 million Class A shares for a total consideration of some $58 million. In short, the Billeses had purchased control of Tire and the public had largely paid for it through its purchase of their Class A shares. At the same time, Tire privately placed some 4.5 million Class A shares to institutional investors to raise some $50 million.

In late 1985, family disagreements made Fred realize that they could no longer act as a control group.

• • •

[T]he Billeses consulted an investment dealer, Merrill, to discuss the value of their shares and prospective purchasers. From the very first meeting that Fred had with Merrill, … the talk was of maximizing the value to the Billeses and the 49% premium price scenario was one of the scenarios that was on the table throughout.

As for a consideration of the Class A shareholders and the equity of passing control and obtaining the desired consideration without triggering the coattail, the only matter discussed was that such a transaction would be controversial. The position of the Class A shareholders was recognized through such terms as "skimming the value from the Class A's" and similar expressions. At no time did any one of the Billeses, as far as the documentary and oral evidence before this hearing indicated, express any concern for the position of the Class A shareholders or for the equity of the type of transaction that was being proposed. The sole concern of all those involved, the Billeses and their professional advisors, was to structure a transaction that would maximize the return to the Billeses without triggering the coattail.

...

Counsel for the Billeses argued that there is nothing artificial about bidding $160.24 for 49% of the outstanding common shares of Tire. The offer is at a fixed price for a maximum number of shares. It in no way depends on a formula. There is real value of $160.24 for the shares that will be tendered and taken up under the offer, and an assumed value, according to the best advice of the Billeses' financial advisors, of $12.00 for their remaining common shares. Those are both real economic values, and there is no artificiality in the transaction.

...

The evidence, and it is clearly the reality, is irrefutable that the transaction was structured to accommodate the desire of the Billeses to sell their entire control position without triggering the coattail. The Offer is so structured to accomplish that and, in that sense, may fairly be characterized as artificial, in that it appears on its face to be a bid for only 49% of the outstanding common shares at a fixed price. That is simply not the reality of the situation, and the Billeses recognized it, their professional advisors recognized it, their fiscal gents recognized it, the Dealers recognized it, their professional advisors recognized it, and their fiscal agents recognized it. And perhaps most importantly, the marketplace recognized it and hence, the intervention of the Class A shareholders in this case.

C. The Public Interest

In these circumstances, we have no hesitation in saying that this transaction is contrary to the public interest, as that term is used in section 123 of the Act. When the public market is sold some $100 million of Class A non-voting shares consequent upon a reorganization that, among other things, provides takeover protection to those shares and the controlling shareholders, some three years later, devise a scheme in conjunction with those who wish to obtain control of the Corporation, to circumvent the coattail while, in effect, receiving the full price for their shares, regulatory intervention to stop an abusive transaction is called for. A transaction such as is proposed here is bound to have an effect on public confidence in the integrity of our capital markets and on public confidence in those who are the controllers of our major corporations. If abusive transactions such as the one in issue here, and this is as grossly abusive a transaction as the Commission has had before it in recent years, are allowed to proceed, confidence in our capital markets will inevitably suffer and individuals will be less willing to place funds in the equity markets. That can only have a deleterious effect on our capital markets and, in that sense, it is in the public interest that this Offer be cease traded along with the Billeses' tendering of their common shares to the Offer.

D. The Integrity of Documents

Counsel for the Billeses and the Dealers raised the matter of the uncertainty that would be created in the capital markets if a cease trade order were issued in this case. The point was that actors in the capital markets must be able to rely on the clear words of documents—in this case, share attributes. The coattail here refers to a "majority" of the common shares being tendered and taken up and that has not happened. The transaction is legal, breaches no provision of the Act, and is structured with the clear wording of the Class A share attributes in mind. What message would the Commission be sending to the capital markets if it were to intervene in this case? How would actors know when their transactions which, on their face, appear to be within the terms of corporate documents, would be subject to challenge by the Commission? The capital markets cannot operate in that atmosphere, it was argued, and for that reason alone, the Commission ought not to interfere in this case. If it wishes to send a message to the marketplace with respect to non-voting shares or with respect to coattails and their operation, it should do so through the tried and tested medium of a draft policy statement or an interim policy statement that has immediate effect, if the Commission considers that it is necessary to act immediately.

...

There is unquestioned force in the point. Participants in the capital markets must be able to rely on the terms of the documents that form the basis of daily transactions. And it would wreak havoc in the capital markets if the Commission took to itself a jurisdiction to interfere in a wide range of transactions on the basis of its view of fairness through the use of the cease trade power under section 123. That, however, is not what we purport to do in this case, nor is it the stated basis upon which the Commission will exercise its section 123 jurisdiction, as indicated in its decisions in *Cablecasting* and *Lindzon*. The Commission's mandate under section 123 is not to interfere in market transactions under some presumed rubric of insuring fairness.

The Commission was cautious in its wording in *Cablecasting* and we repeat that caution here. To invoke the public interest test of section 123, particularly in the absence of a demonstrated breach of the Act, the regulations or a policy statement, the conduct or transaction must clearly be demonstrated to be abusive of shareholders in particular, and of the capital markets in general. A showing of abuse is something different from, and goes beyond, a complaint of unfairness. A complaint of unfairness may well be involved in a transaction that is said to be abusive, but they are different tests. Moreover, the abuse must be such that it can be shown to the Commission's satisfaction that a question of the public interest is involved. That almost invariably will mean some showing of a broader impact on the capital markets and their operation.

The facts of this case demonstrate the line that moves a transaction into the public interest category. Tire is one of Canada's best known public corporations and is the leader in its field. There are some 83 million Class A shares outstanding and they are widely held by both large institutional investors and small shareholders. The severe skew between the percentage of equity that controlled the Company—4%—and the 92% of the equity that had no say in management was well known. Accordingly, the takeover bid protection accorded to the A's at the time of the reorganization in 1983 was well known and an important factor in marketing the Class A shares. A transaction that is so patently designed to avoid the rights granted to holders of the Class A shares is, in the circumstances and for the reasons noted, so abusive of the Class A shareholders in particular, and of the capital markets in general, that the public interest test of section 123 is properly invoked.

With respect to the argument of certainty and that the Billeses and the Dealers are entitled to take the documents as written and insist on their legal rights, an analogue to the jurisdiction that the Commission is asserting under section 123 here, albeit in the completely different circumstances of a private company, is the judgment of Lord Wilberforce in the seminal case of *Ebrahimi v. Westbourne Galleries Ltd.*, [1973] AC 360 (HL). …

> … The "just and equitable" provision does not, as the respondents suggest, entitle one party to disregard the obligation he assumes by entering a company, nor the court to dispense him from it. It does, as equity always does, enable the court to subject the exercise of legal rights to equitable considerations; considerations, that is, of a personal character arising between one individual and other, which may make it unjust, or inequitable, to insist on legal rights, or to exercise them in a particular way.

In exercising our jurisdiction under section 123 in this case, we are, in one sense, subjecting "the exercise of legal rights to equitable considerations." Of course, the consideration here is the "public interest" of section 123 and the Commission is mandated by law to exercise that jurisdiction. For the Commission to act, there must be a clear showing that the interests of the public marketplace are involved. But allowing for that, the thought and the spirit behind Lord Wilberforce's statement is important. Whether it is a court of equity, or the Commission exercising its regulatory jurisdiction pursuant to the legal authority vested in it, there always will be occasions where the exercise of private legal rights must give way to broader considerations—in this case, considerations of the equitable operation of this Province's capital markets.

E. The Proper Forum

Counsel for the Billeses and the Dealers also argued that the Commission is not the proper forum for this case. The contention was that this is a private matter between the Class A shareholders and the controlling shareholders. Accordingly, the Class A shareholders should pursue their remedies in the courts where the issues can more properly be sorted out through the trial process. This contention is supported by the fact that the Notice of Hearing in paragraph 14 alleges breaches of fiduciary duty, and such breaches are properly matters to be tried in the courts, either under the oppression remedy or in a derivative action.

The contention that the issue here is a private one between two classes of shareholders is far wide of the mark. A purported sale of control in the circumstances set out above, where the rights of the holders of some 83 million Class A shares are concerned, is not a private matter, although individual rights in terms of a particular shareholding are involved. This is demonstrably a public matter involving a major public company and one that concerns and impacts on the public marketplace. In the sense in which counsel were using the idea of a private lis, any takeover bid would, according to their analysis, be a private matter between shareholders. Yet it is well known that takeover bids, the rules applying to them and how they are conducted, are very much a public matter in the sense of their concern to, and impact on the marketplace and its perceived integrity. The Commission, accordingly, has always played a major role in overseeing such transactions.

Moreover, the argument that this matter more properly belongs before the courts, mistakes the respective roles of the courts and the Commission in overseeing the management and actions of public companies and protecting shareholders' interests. The Commission is vested with the power to regulate the capital markets in the public interest and is given broad powers to do so. The power to intervene includes the power to cease trade and to do so, at least initially, without a public hearing if satisfied of the necessity. In carrying out its regulatory function, the Commission necessarily impacts on the rights and obligations of companies, directors and shareholders. But it does so from the perspective of the regulation of the public markets and their fair and efficient operation. The subjecting of takeover bids to an elaborate code of rules and regulations, backed by the power to issue a cease trade order, if conduct during the course of a bid calls for it, is perhaps the best known example of this regulatory function.

The courts, on the other hand, adjudicate rights between shareholders and their companies. In so doing, the judicial process has the advantage of the refinement of issues provided by pleadings, examinations for discovery and the trial process. Moreover, the courts are able to provide remedies appropriate to the individual case. What the courts are not structured to do, is to move quickly to regulate public markets through regulating shareholder and/or corporate conduct. To be sure, the injunction remedy is available in the proper case, but it is not a remedy designed to be used as a regulatory tool.

The line between when Commission action or judicial process is appropriate in shareholder and corporate matters is, of course, not so clearly marked as the foregoing comments would indicate. There is bound to be overlap as there is no clear line between securities and corporate matters and many issues before the Commission involve the conduct of fiduciaries. But the role of the Commission is not to determine breaches of fiduciary duty, or to deal with a breach of a corporate statute, in order to provide a private remedy. Rather, it is to regulate shareholder and corporate conduct in the context of, and for the purpose of, regulating the public securities markets. Again, the line will not always be clear as intervention in matters that from one aspect are of a private nature will, from another aspect, be seen to have public market implications. If the Commission should mistake its role in a particular case, or act beyond the jurisdiction granted, the courts can rectify the matter and set out a new balance through the appeal procedure granted under section 9 of the Act.

F. Breach of Fiduciary Duty

As to the allegations of breach of fiduciary duty here, we agree that in most cases, that is a matter best left to the courts to determine. Indeed, we declined to hear evidence on the allegation in paragraph 14(v) of the Notice of Hearing on just that basis. Our decision to impose a cease trading order does not depend on a finding of breach of fiduciary duty. However, an allegation of breach of fiduciary duty, and evidence which clearly concerns the conduct of those who are fiduciaries, can be important in supporting facts which otherwise would support a section 123 order. That is the case here. The Billeses are in a fiduciary position in at least two categories: as directors of Tire and as Tire's controlling shareholders.

. . .

Here, the relationship of the Billeses as controlling shareholders to the minority is clear. And it is equally clear that their conduct, particularly seen in light of the events of 1983, in seeking now to avoid the takeover bid protection that was inserted for the protection of the Class A shareholders is a failure on their part to act fairly and honestly. In that sense, their conduct supports the facts here which otherwise call for the invocation of a cease trade under section 123.

G. The Dealers

As to the Dealers, it was argued that they in no way acted in concert with or colluded with the Billeses in the sale of the Billeses' shares. They, for their own sound economic reasons, were desirous of purchasing the Billeses' shares. Indeed, that was not even their primary goal at the time they began discussions with the Billeses' representatives in October, 1986.

. . .

The evidence is clear that the Dealers and their advisors were well aware of the controversial nature of the transaction in that it was structured to avoid the triggering mechanism. In those circumstances, the Dealers cannot separate themselves from the Billeses. They are the group that wants control, it is their Offer and it is structured to suit their purposes as well as those of the Billeses. It is their Offer that gives life to the conception of this abusive transaction. Accordingly, it is appropriate that the Offer be cease traded.

A more recent example of the scenario represented by the *Canadian Tire* case, where a panel sanctioned respondents in the absence of a finding of a breach of a substantive provision of the *Securities Act* is the *Donald* decision of the OSC. We reviewed the *Donald* case in Chapter 8, where it was noted that the panel found that Donald had not breached the prohibition on insider trading in the OSA. This was because he was not in a special relationship with the relevant issuer when he purchased the issuer's shares, because RIM was not at the relevant time "proposing to make a takeover bid" for that issuer. This finding did not, however, end the matter for the panel. It went on to find that Donald's purchases of shares constituted conduct contrary to the public interest, even though it did not breach the prohibition under OSA, s 76. The panel found as follows:

> [314] Donald was an officer of RIM at the time he learned from Wormald, another RIM Vice President who, to his knowledge, was responsible for assessing possible acquisitions by RIM, of RIM's interest in acquiring Certicom and the other elements of the Three Facts. In our view, Donald had to have known that (i) the information he received from Wormald was confidential and had not been made public; (ii) if the information had been generally disclosed, it would have had a significant effect on the market price or value of Certicom shares; and (iii) the information was provided to him on a confidential basis in the expectation that he would not use the information for personal gain.
>
> [315] The 2008 RIM Golf Event was a private event attended only by RIM officers. Donald's discussion with Wormald about Certicom that evening was clearly about RIM's business, was clearly about information that had not been generally disclosed and that information was clearly confidential. We do not agree with Donald's assertion that Wormald should have informed him that the discussion concerning Certicom should be treated as confidential.
>
> [316] We should note that our conclusion that Donald did not breach subsection 76(1) of the Act is based on our determination that, on August 21, 2008, RIM had not yet reached the stage of proposing to acquire Certicom. RIM was, however, actively considering a potential transaction and that consideration gave rise to a proposal a relatively short time after Donald's purchases.
>
> [317] The facts of this matter are very unusual. We concluded that RIM was not, on the day following the 2008 RIM Golf Event, proposing to make a take-over bid or other business combination or arrangement involving Certicom, however, RIM, and more specifically, the Strategic Alliances Group, was in possession of information about Certicom only acquired by RIM through

its due diligence activities relating to Certicom. We heard evidence that RIM determined it should not purchase Certicom shares, both before and after the expiry of the 2007 NDA (along with the standstill provision contained therein). Wormald testified in this respect:

> … my recollection is there was a discussion with securities lawyers, and I don't remember who and which, there was a discussion with securities lawyers back in, you know, I'll call it March, April, May-type time frame about accumulating shares that, you know, where we were given the advice that the standstill that was in place at the time prevented us from effectively doing that.
>
> I recall a conversation after that standstill-based NDA expired with some securities lawyers, it may not have been all of them, it might have been a subset of them, that, you know, explored the issue a little bit more and left us with the conclusion that it just wouldn't really be very workable.

(Hearing Transcript, March 22, 2011 at page 122, line 22 to page 123, line 11)

[318] Donald, who was an officer and employee of RIM, learned of material facts about Certicom in the context of a confidential discussion with another RIM Vice President. Not only did Donald learn the Three Facts on August 20, 2008, but he learned of them directly from Wormald, the RIM officer who was the head of the Strategic Alliances Group. Donald was an experienced investor who had sophisticated knowledge of the wireless industry.

[319] Market participants and the officers of public companies, such as Donald, are expected to adhere to a high standard of behaviour. In our view, by purchasing securities with knowledge of material facts which had not been generally disclosed, Donald clearly failed to meet that standard and did so in a manner that impugns the integrity of Ontario's capital markets.

[320] We share the view of the Alberta Securities Commission expressed in *Seto* that the failure of the Commission to address trades that are based on information obtained as a result of a person's position or relationship that has not been made available to the market calls into question the very integrity of our capital markets.

[321] The Commission stated in *Donnini* [(2002), 25 OSCB 6225] that:

> … we did not need to find that Donnini used undisclosed material facts, or that he benefited personally from the misuse of inside information. We needed only to find that he traded while in possession of undisclosed material facts.

(*Donnini, supra* at para. 113)

[322] In this case, Donald had knowledge of confidential material facts about Certicom that were communicated to him as an officer of RIM when he purchased Certicom shares. Donald benefited personally from these purchases of Certicom shares, receiving proceeds of $600,000 from RIM when RIM acquired all of the shares of Certicom in March 2009. His gross profit was $295,000.

[323] Although we do not find any technical breach of subsection 76(1) of the Act, we find that Donald's purchases of Certicom shares directly engage the fundamental principles of securities regulation and the purposes of the Act. The unusual circumstances of this matter warrant a finding that Donald's conduct was contrary to the public interest.

[324] We find that Donald's purchases of Certicom shares in August and September 2008, while he was in possession of undisclosed material facts regarding RIM's interest in Certicom, constituted conduct contrary to the public interest. We find that Donald's conduct was abusive of the capital markets and to confidence in the capital markets.

VIII. Conclusion

[325] For the reasons set out above, we find that Donald did not breach subsection 76(1) of the Act but that his conduct was contrary to the public interest.

[326] We have also issued an order dated August 1, 2012 which sets down the date for the hearing with respect to sanctions and costs in this matter.

For further analysis of the history of and rationale underlying the public-interest power in securities regulatory enforcement, see Anita Anand, "Carving the Public Interest Jurisdiction in Securities Regulation: Contributions of Justice Iacobucci" (2007) 57:2 UTLJ 293.

C. Sanctions Available in Connection with Public-Interest Orders

1. *Philosophies of Sanctioning*

As indicated above, there has recently been some appellate court guidance provided to regulators as to the philosophy that should guide them in making orders in the public interest. The *Asbestos* decision, discussed in Chapter 2 and further excerpted below, makes clear that regulators are required to keep in mind both the purposes of their governing statutes and where they are enumerated. In addition, they are required to act in accordance with the philosophy underlying regulatory legislation in general, which is that it should protect societal interests rather than punish individual faults—that is, it should be protective and preventive rather than punitive.

As the facts recounted by Iacobucci J in his decision make clear, the *Asbestos* decision of the Supreme Court was the culmination of a lengthy and protracted dispute involving the minority shareholders of a Québec company called Asbestos Corp, the Québec government, and the OSC. In brief, certain minority shareholders of Asbestos Corp wanted the OSC to use its OSA s 127 power to intervene in a transaction whereby the Québec government would obtain control over Asbestos Corp by dealing only with the majority shareholder of the company. The OSC concluded that the use of its public-interest power under s 127 was not warranted in this instance. It should be noted that the concept, discussed in the decision, of a "follow-up offer" in the context of a takeover is no longer relevant under the OSA. In an earlier version of what is now s 93 of the OSA, a follow-up offer to minority shareholders was required in certain circumstances where a bidder made inappropriate use of the private agreement exemption from the takeover bid rules.

Committee for the Equal Treatment of Asbestos Minority Shareholders v Ontario (Securities Commission)
2001 SCC 37, [2001] 2 SCR 132

IACOBUCCI J: …

[2] The basic question raised by this appeal is whether the Court should intervene in the refusal of the Ontario Securities Commission ("OSC") to grant a remedy to the aggrieved minority shareholders through the exercise of its jurisdiction to act in the public interest under s. 127(1) of the Act.

. . .

[7] On October 22, 1977, Premier Lévesque announced the Québec Government's intention to take control of Asbestos. He was quoted in the press as saying that other shareholders would be "uncomfortable" if they were minority shareholders while the Government held control as the Québec Government must take positions and achieve

objectives that are not always those of ordinary shareholders. At the same time, the press quoted Québec's Finance Minister, Mr. Parizeau, as saying, "we will in any case make a bid for all public shares" and that a public offer for Asbestos Corp. shares would be at "an equivalent price" to that paid for the General Dynamics block.

[8] In May 1978, Québec incorporated the SNA as a vehicle to take control of Asbestos. All of SNA's shares were allotted to Québec's Minister of Finance.

[9] In September 1979, SNA made its first bid to acquire control of Asbestos. SNA offered to purchase all of GD Canada's shares in Asbestos for $42 per share. The offer stated that, once it acquired the shares held by GD Canada, the Québec Government would offer to purchase the remaining Asbestos shares at the same price. This offer was rejected by GD US, as parent of GD Canada. Their valuation came in at $99 per share. The difference in share price arose from the parties' projections for the future asbestos market.

[10] In June 1979, SNA's incorporating statute was amended to permit Québec to expropriate the assets of Asbestos. However, in the debates concerning this amendment, both Premier Lévesque and Finance Minister Parizeau emphasized their preference to acquire control of Asbestos by agreement with GD US and their intention to expropriate only if negotiations failed.

[11] Negotiations ceased while Asbestos challenged the constitutionality of the legislation permitting Québec to expropriate its assets. In the spring of 1981, the Québec Court of Appeal rejected the constitutional challenge ([1981] CA 43, aff'g [1980] CS 331) and this Court denied leave to appeal, … Québec then imposed a November 30, 1981 deadline for a negotiated agreement with GD US, failing which it would expropriate.

[12] On November 9, 1981, Québec and GD US reached an agreement pursuant to which SNA would acquire voting control of GD Canada and, therefore, indirect control of Asbestos. Under that agreement, SNA acquired control over GD Canada; however, SNA's payment for GD Canada was deferred through the operation of a "put and call" agreement. This form of the transaction was designed to benefit the tax position of GD US, and to provide GD US with a means to acquire the benefits of any subsequent improvement in the asbestos market.

[13] The 1981 transaction differed materially from the offer rejected by GD US in 1979. Under the 1981 transaction, SNA purchased GD Canada shares rather than Asbestos shares as it would have under the 1979 offer. Furthermore, the 1981 transaction was not accompanied by an undertaking to the minority shareholders of Asbestos to purchase their shares. On November 11, 1981, two days after the agreement was reached, Québec announced that it did not intend to make a follow-up offer to the minority shareholders. Instead, the Finance Minister said in a press release, [TRANSLATION] "it will be up to GD Canada to evaluate over the course of the years the advantage of increasing eventually its interest in [Asbestos Corp.]." In response to that statement, the shares of Asbestos fell to a four-year low. Six days later the Finance Minister was quoted by the press as saying: "[b]ut at the present time, I'm not buying the shares of General Dynamics … but if I force them out … then obviously I should do something with the minority shareholders."

[14] On February 12, 1982, the agreement among Québec, SNA, and GD US was formalized. GD Canada's name was changed to Mines SNA Inc. and its registered office was moved from Ottawa, Ontario, to Thetford Mines, Québec. In November 1986, GD US exercised its put option and, on December 9, 1986, SNA purchased the remaining

common shares of GD Canada held by GD US. No follow-up offer was ever made to the minority shareholders of Asbestos.

[15] In April 1988, the OSC issued a notice of hearing to determine two questions: (i) whether the transaction amounted to a take-over bid in Ontario, requiring SNA to make a follow-up offer to the minority shareholders of Asbestos, and (ii) whether the OSC should exercise its public interest jurisdiction under s. 124(1) (now s. 127(1), para. 3) of the *Securities Act* and take away Québec's trading exemptions in the Ontario capital markets.

[16] In addition to the details of the negotiations and transaction, the evidence before the OSC included press reports of the statements made by members of the Québec Government, noted above, as well as other articles quoting analysts as recommending caution and warning against the speculative nature of an investment in Asbestos. The OSC also examined the market performance of Asbestos shares during the relevant period in light of all of the information about Asbestos and the change of control transaction that was available to the market during the material times. The OSC also considered the testimony of witnesses called by the appellant. The OSC concluded that the statements made by members of the Québec Government did not constitute a promise to make a follow-up offer, that the minority shareholders and market analysts were aware of the speculative nature of an investment in Asbestos, and that the market was not materially misled by Québec or SNA.

. . .

[38] There are three main issues in this appeal:

1. What is the nature and scope of s. 127 jurisdiction to intervene in the public interest?
2. What is the appropriate standard of review?
3. Did the OSC make a reviewable error?

IV. Analysis

1. What Is the Nature and Scope of Section 127 Jurisdiction to Intervene in the Public Interest?

[39] Section 127(1) of the Act provides the OSC with the jurisdiction to intervene in activities related to the Ontario capital markets when it is in the public interest to do so. The legislature clearly intended that the OSC have a very wide discretion in such matters. The permissive language of s. 127(1) expresses an intent to leave it for the OSC to determine whether and how to intervene in a particular case:

> 127(1) The Commission *may* make one or more of the following orders *if in its opinion* it is in the public interest to make the order or orders … . [Emphasis added.]

[40] The breadth of the OSC's discretion to act in the public interest is also evident in the range and potential seriousness of the sanctions it can impose under s. 127(1). Furthermore, pursuant to s. 127(2), the OSC has an unrestricted discretion to attach terms and conditions to any order made under s. 127(1):

> (2) An order under this section may be subject to such terms and conditions as the Commission may impose.

[41] However, the public interest jurisdiction of the OSC is not unlimited. Its precise nature and scope should be assessed by considering s. 127 in context. Two aspects of the public interest jurisdiction are of particular importance in this regard. First, it is important to keep in mind that the OSC's public interest jurisdiction is animated in part by both of the purposes of the Act described in s. 1.1, namely "to provide protection to investors from unfair, improper or fraudulent practices" and "to foster fair and efficient capital markets and confidence in capital markets." Therefore, in considering an order in the public interest, it is an error to focus only on the fair treatment of investors. The effect of an intervention in the public interest on capital market efficiencies and public confidence in the capital markets should also be considered.

[42] Second, it is important to recognize that s. 127 is a regulatory provision. In this regard, I agree with Laskin JA that "[t]he purpose of the Commission's public interest jurisdiction is neither remedial nor punitive; it is protective and preventive, intended to be exercised to prevent likely future harm to Ontario's capital markets" (p. 272). This interpretation of s. 127 powers is consistent with the previous jurisprudence of the OSC in cases such as *Canadian Tire, supra*, aff'd (1987), 59 OR (2d) 79 (Div. Ct.); leave to appeal to CA denied (1987), 35 BLR xx, in which it was held that no breach of the Act is required to trigger s. 127. It is also consistent with the objective of regulatory legislation in general. The focus of regulatory law is on the protection of societal interests, not punishment of an individual's moral faults: see *R. v. Wholesale Travel Group Inc.*, [1991] 3 SCR 154, at p. 219.

[43] Furthermore, the above interpretation is consistent with the scheme of enforcement in the Act. The enforcement techniques in the Act span a broad spectrum from purely regulatory or administrative sanctions to serious criminal penalties. The administrative sanctions are the most frequently used sanctions and are grouped together in s. 127 as "Orders in the public interest." Such orders are not punitive: *Re Albino* (1991), 14 OSCB 365. Rather, the purpose of an order under s. 127 is to restrain future conduct that is likely to be prejudicial to the public interest in fair and efficient capital markets. The role of the OSC under s. 127 is to protect the public interest by removing from the capital markets those whose past conduct is so abusive as to warrant apprehension of future conduct detrimental to the integrity of the capital markets: *Re Mithras Management Ltd.* (1990), 13 OSCB 1600. In contradistinction, it is for the courts to punish or remedy past conduct under ss. 122 and 128 of the Act respectively: see D. Johnston and K. Doyle Rockwell, *Canadian Securities Regulation* (2nd ed. 1998), at pp. 209-11.

[44] More specifically, s. 122 makes it an offence to contravene the Act and, though the OSC's consent is required before a proceeding under s. 122 can commence, the provision authorizes the courts to impose fines and terms of imprisonment. Under s. 128, the OSC may apply to the Ontario Court (General Division) for a declaratory order. In making such an order, the courts may resort to a wide range of remedial powers detailed in that section, including an order for compensation or restitution which would be aimed at providing a remedy for harm suffered by private parties or individuals. In addition, further remedial powers are available under Part XXIII of the Act which deals with civil liability for misrepresentation and tipping and creates rights of action for rescission and damages.

[45] In summary, pursuant to s. 127(1), the OSC has the jurisdiction and a broad discretion to intervene in Ontario capital markets if it is in the public interest to do so.

However, the discretion to act in the public interest is not unlimited. In exercising its discretion, the OSC should consider the protection of investors and the efficiency of, and public confidence in, capital markets generally. In addition, s. 127(1) is a regulatory provision. The sanctions under the section are preventive in nature and prospective in orientation. Therefore, s. 127 cannot be used merely to remedy *Securities Act* misconduct alleged to have caused harm or damages to private parties or individuals.

2. *What Is the Appropriate Standard of Review?*

[46] A determination of the appropriate standard of review calls for the application of the "pragmatic and functional" approach first adopted by this Court in *UES, Local 298 v. Bibeault*, [1988] 2 SCR 1048. That approach was further developed by this Court in cases such as *Pezim*, *supra*, and *Southam*, *supra*.

[47] The recent jurisprudence of this Court on standards of review was summarized by Bastarache J. in *Pushpanathan v. Canada (Minister of Citizenship and Immigration)*, [1998] 1 SCR 982. The focus of the inquiry is on the particular provision being interpreted by the tribunal, and the central question is: was the question that the provision raises one that was intended by the legislators to be left to the exclusive decision of the administrative tribunal? There are four factors that are used to determine the appropriate degree of curial deference: (i) privative clauses; (ii) relative expertise of the tribunal; (iii) the purpose of the Act as a whole and the provision in particular; and (iv) the nature of the problem: a question of law or fact? None of the four factors is alone dispositive. Each factor indicates a point falling on a spectrum of the proper level of deference to be shown to the decision in question.

. . .

[49] In this case, as in *Pezim*, it cannot be contested that the OSC is a specialized tribunal with a wide discretion to intervene in the public interest and that the protection of the public interest is a matter falling within the core of the OSC's expertise. Therefore, although there is no privative clause shielding the decisions of the OSC from review by the courts, that body's relative expertise in the regulation of the capital markets, the purpose of the Act as a whole and s. 127(1) in particular, and the nature of the problem before the OSC, all militate in favour of a high degree of curial deference. However, as there is a statutory right of appeal from the decision of the OSC to the courts, when this factor is considered with all the other factors, an intermediate standard of review is indicated. Accordingly, the standard of review in this case is one of reasonableness.

3. *Did the OSC Make a Reviewable Error?*

(a) *The Interpretation of the OSC Decision*

[50] The parties to this appeal offer two different interpretations of the OSC reasons for judgment. The proper interpretation depends on how one views the OSC's treatment of the issue of the transactional connection with Ontario and the motive for structuring the transaction as it was done in this case. The appellant argues that the OSC "adopted a transactional nexus as a jurisdictional precondition" and "imposed an alternative prerequisite" by requiring "proof of a conscious motive to evade regulation as a precondition to the exercise of its public interest jurisdiction." The appellant argues that by failing to

consider other factors affecting an assessment of the public interest the OSC "failed or refused to carry out the mandate vested in it by the Legislature." In contrast, the respondents argue that the OSC considered the transactional connection as one of many factors relevant to the exercise of its discretion, and that it was appropriate for the OSC to consider motive as a factor in deciding whether it would exercise its public interest jurisdiction in this case.

[51] I agree with Laskin JA that "the Commission did not set up any jurisdictional preconditions to the exercise of its discretion" (p. 273). In my view, the erection of such a jurisdictional barrier by the OSC is inconsistent with its having fought in the earlier proceedings for the recognition of its jurisdiction to hear this matter. Furthermore, in its reasons in the present case, the OSC clearly rejected the idea that the transactional connection factor could act as a jurisdictional barrier to the exercise of its public interest discretion. …

[52] Moreover, at para. 68 of its reasons, rather than raising "transactional connection" as a jurisdictional barrier, the OSC identified the transactional connection with Ontario as one of several relevant factors to be considered in determining whether to exercise its public interest discretion, including, *inter alia*, the motive behind the structure of the transaction at issue:

> Were the transactions before us "clearly abusive of investors and of the capital market," to quote *Canadian Tire*? Were they "clearly designed to avoid the animating principles behind [the takeover bid] legislation and rules," to quote the same decision? Were they "clearly abusive of the integrity of the capital markets, which have every right to expect that market participants … will adhere to both the letter and the spirit of the rules that are intended to guarantee equal treatment of offerees in the course of a take-over bid, no matter by whom the bid is made" and is the result "manifestly unfair to the public minority shareholders … who lose the opportunity to tender their shares … at a substantial premium" to quote *H.E.R.O.*? And finally, does "the transaction in question [have] a sufficient Ontario connection or 'nexus' to warrant intervention to protect the integrity of the capital markets in the province," to quote that decision?

[53] Although in its reasoning, the OSC placed significant weight on the transactional connection factor, it did not, as alleged by the appellant, stop the inquiry upon finding there was an insufficient transactional connection with Ontario. Furthermore, in this respect, it was appropriate for the OSC to consider, as a factor relevant to the determination of whether to exercise its public interest jurisdiction in this case, the presence or absence of a motivation to structure the transaction so as to make what was essentially an Ontario transaction appear to be a non-Ontario transaction. In effect, the OSC found that what could otherwise appear to be the absence of an Ontario connection might be overcome by a finding that a transaction was improperly and deliberately structured so as to give such an appearance.

[54] The Court of Appeal correctly confirmed that it was appropriate for the OSC to consider motive as a factor in deciding whether it would exercise its public interest jurisdiction (at p. 277):

> The Commission also reasonably considered whether Québec and SNA intended to avoid Ontario law as relevant to the exercise of its discretion under s. 127(1)3. As I have already said,

> the purpose of an order under that section is to protect the Ontario capital markets by removing a participant who, based on past misconduct, represents a continuing or future threat to the integrity of these markets. Therefore, the Commission could not focus only on the effect of the transaction. This transaction was lawful. The Commission had to consider whether the Québec Government deliberately attempted to avoid the requirements of the Act. …

Therefore, Quebec's intention was relevant.

[55] The OSC did not identify motive as a precondition to the exercise of its public interest jurisdiction. On the contrary, the OSC held that it could consider motive as a factor in deciding whether to exercise the jurisdiction that it clearly had. Indeed, the OSC saw motive as a factor that might prompt it to make an order that it may not otherwise have made. Rather than a limitation on jurisdiction, the OSC considered motive as enlarging the circumstances under which the public interest would warrant intervention.

[56] In summary, I agree with Laskin JA that "[the OSC] did not consider a transactional connection and an intention to avoid Ontario law to be, as the Divisional Court contended, jurisdictional barriers or preconditions to an order under s. 127(1)3 of the Act" (pp. 277-78). The OSC clearly and properly rejected the argument that its public interest jurisdiction was subject to an implicit precondition. In analyzing the appellant's application for a remedy under s. 127(1), para. 3, the OSC proceeded by identifying and considering several factors relevant to the exercise of its discretion under that provision. The transactional connection with Ontario and the motive behind the structure of the transaction were two of several factors considered. I also agree with Laskin JA that the OSC "took into account and indeed gave prominence to factors that were relevant to the exercise of its discretion. It weighed those factors and made findings of fact on them …" (p. 273). Therefore, properly interpreted, the OSC did not adopt any jurisdictional preconditions, but instead exercised the discretion that is incidental to its public interest jurisdiction.

(b) Was the OSC Decision Reasonable?

[57] The OSC was cautious in the application of its public interest jurisdiction in this case. This approach was informed by the OSC's previous jurisprudence and by four legitimate considerations inherent in s. 127 itself: (i) the seriousness and severity of the sanction applied for, (ii) the effect of imposing such a sanction on the efficiency of, and public confidence in Ontario capital markets, (iii) a reluctance to use the open-ended nature of the public interest jurisdiction to police out-of-province activities, and (iv) a recognition that s. 127 powers are preventive in nature, not remedial.

[58] As noted above, in reaching its decision in this case, the OSC relied on its previous jurisprudence in *Canadian Tire*, *supra*, and [*Re HERO Industries Ltd* (1990), 13 OSCB 3775] … to identify the relevant factors to be considered. The OSC found that "the actions of the Québec Government and SNA failed to comply with the spirit underlying the take-over bid rules of the Act …" (para. 71). … This finding of fact is reasonable and supported by the evidence.

[59] Granted, the OSC did find that "the actions of the Québec Government and SNA … were abusive of the minority shareholders of Asbestos and were manifestly unfair to them" (para. 71). However, whether a s. 127(1) sanction is warranted depends on a consideration of all of the relevant factors together. In this case, the OSC also found that

the capital markets in general, and the minority shareholders of Asbestos in particular, were not materially misled by the statements of Québec's Minister of Finance respecting the prospect of a follow-up offer. This finding is supported by the evidence, including the several published reports that recommended caution and characterized an investment in Asbestos as speculative. In this case, such a finding can and did properly inform the OSC's discretion under s. 127.

[60] In addition, consistent with the two purposes of the Act described in s. 1.1 and because s. 127(1) sanctions are preventive in nature, it was open to the OSC to give weight to the fact that there has been no abuse of investors or other misconduct by the province of Québec or SNA in the 13 years since the transaction at issue in this appeal. The OSC was also entitled to give weight to the fact that the removal of the province's exemptions is a very serious response that could have negative repercussions on other investors and the Ontario capital markets in general.

[61] Furthermore, the OSC did not find that there was no transactional connection with Ontario in this case, but that the transactional connection was insufficient to justify its intervening in the public interest. …

[62] It is true that the OSC placed significant emphasis on the transactional connection factor. However, it was entitled to do so in order to avoid using the open-ended nature of s. 127 powers as a means to police too broadly out-of-province transactions. Capital markets and securities transactions are becoming increasingly international: see *Global Securities Corp. v. British Columbia (Securities Commission)*, [2000] 1 SCR 494, 2000 SCC 21, at paras. 27-28. There are a myriad of overlapping regulatory jurisdictions governing securities transactions. Under s. 2.1, para. 5 of the Act, one of the fundamental principles that the OSC has to consider is that "[t]he integration of capital markets is supported and promoted by the sound and responsible harmonization and co-ordination of securities regulation regimes." A transaction that is contrary to the policy of the Ontario *Securities Act* may be acceptable under another regulatory regime. Thus, the OSC's insistence on a more clear and direct connection with Ontario in this case reflects a sound and responsible approach to long-arm regulation and the potential for conflict amongst the different regulatory regimes that govern the capital markets in the global economy.

[63] In summary, the reasons of the OSC in this case were informed by the legitimate and relevant considerations inherent in s. 127(1) and in the OSC's previous jurisprudence on public interest jurisdiction. The findings of fact made by the OSC were reasonable and supported by the evidence. I conclude that the decision of the OSC in this case was reasonable and therefore should not be disturbed.

[64] For the foregoing reasons, I would dismiss the appeal with costs.

More recently, further guidance has been provided by the Supreme Court on the issue of whether it is appropriate for regulators to consider deterrence as an objective they are seeking to achieve by the application of sanctions under public-interest enforcement provisions. As we saw in Chapter 3, the Supreme Court of Canada's decision in *Cartaway* acknowledged that general deterrence as a basis for making an order was in accordance with the "protective and preventive" orientation of securities regulatory enforcement.

The Supreme Court's decision in *Cartaway* originated in a hearing held by the BCSC into the activities of a number of brokers who became involved as controlling shareholders in the

Cartaway company. In the process, they arranged a fundamental change in the nature of Cartaway's business without disclosing this to regulators or investors, and also made inappropriate use of prospectus exemptions to distribute additional securities of the company. Other participants involved in these transactions reached settlements with the BCSC, but not the specific respondents involved in the decision, excerpted below. Following their hearing, the BCSC imposed the maximum administrative penalty available under s 162 of the BCSA on the respondents. The quantum of penalty imposed was reduced by the BC Court of Appeal.

Cartaway Resources Corp (Re)
2004 SCC 26, [2004] 1 SCR 672

LeBEL J (McLachlin CJ and Iacobucci, Major, Bastarache, Binnie, Arbour, Deschamps, and Fish JJ concurring): …

[13] … On May 8, 1996, Cartaway announced that it had found significant mineralization on the Voisey's Bay claims based on a visual inspection of drilling samples. The share price jumped dramatically to $23, but later fell below $1 when an analysis of the samples failed to confirm these findings. Hartvikson and Johnson reaped in total $5.1 million in profits by trading Cartaway shares.

[14] The proceedings against Hartvikson, Johnson, Disbrow, Savics, Lyall, Stuart and First Marathon were commenced on July 17, 1998 when a notice of hearing was issued against them with respect to their conduct in relation to Cartaway.

…

[18] By buying control of Cartaway and then continuing to act as brokers and principals in the sale of Cartaway's shares, they put themselves in a conflict of interest with their duties to their clients and Cartaway. Hartvikson and Johnson did nothing to resolve these conflicts. They acted in their own interests contrary to the interest of their clients and Cartaway. Further, by purchasing the shares in a private placement prior to the disclosure of the acquisition of mineral claims, and then selling the shares to their clients at a higher price after the announcement of the acquisition of the claims, they acted contrary to the interests of their clients. They ensured that the investors in the private placement, and not their clients, would earn a higher return on the investment in Cartaway. They took unfair advantage of their positions as registrants, and engaged in conduct that seriously undermined the public confidence in the fairness of the capital markets. Consequently, they acted contrary to the public interest.

[19] The Commission found that Hartvikson and Johnson were the driving force behind the reorganization of Cartaway. Consequently, as control persons, they were undisclosed promoters under s. 1(1) of the Act and acted as undisclosed de facto directors of Cartaway. The Commission held that they should have disclosed their status as directors in the June 23, 1995 offering memorandum and the November 3, 1995 prospectus.

…

C. *The Sanctions Imposed by the Commission*

[26] In imposing sanctions on Hartvikson and Johnson under ss. 161 and 162 of the Act, the Commission weighed several important factors, including general deterrence,

protecting the securities market, the settlement agreements and the circumstances of the case.

[27] On one hand, the Commission considered the need to send a clear message that would deter inappropriate conduct by other participants in British Columbia's capital markets. It took into account the settlement agreements reached in proceedings against other First Marathon brokers. But in doing so, it compared the role of those individuals against Hartvikson and Johnson's leadership in perpetrating the illegal transaction and their deceitful conduct. Although deceit was not explicitly alleged in the notice of appeal, the respondents' credibility and misleading conduct was the focus of the proceedings from the outset. The Commission also took note of the $5.1 million in trading profits earned by Hartvikson and Johnson.

[28] On the other hand, the Commission took into account Hartvikson and Johnson's previously untarnished records and their positive contribution to the capital markets. Moreover, both respondents voluntarily surrendered their licences as registered trading representatives in 1996, and repented their actions. The Commission accepted that Hartvikson and Johnson would continue to make a positive contribution to British Columbia's capital markets, if permitted to do so. It is also notable that both offered to pay $100,000 towards a university foundation or program about business ethics.

• • •

[39] The following issues are raised on this appeal:

1. Whether the Executive Director has standing to bring this appeal.
2. Whether the Commission may consider general deterrence when ordering sanctions under s. 162 of the Act.
3. Whether the Commission must consider settlement agreements entered into by the Executive Director in assessing sanctions under the Act.
4. Whether the Court of Appeal should have referred the question of appropriate sanctions back to the Commission under s. 167(3) of the Act.

VI. Analysis

• • •

B. Standard of Review

[45] … This Court recognized in *Pezim*, *supra*, at pp. 593-94, that the Commission has special expertise regarding securities matters. The core of this expertise lies in interpreting and applying the provisions of the Act, and in determining what orders are in the public interest with respect to capital markets. In this case, the question of whether general deterrence is an appropriate consideration in formulating a penalty in the public interest falls squarely within the expertise of the Commission.

[46] Although courts are regularly called on to interpret and apply general questions of law and engage in statutory interpretation, courts have less expertise relative to securities commissions in determining what is in the public interest in the regulation of financial markets. The courts also have less expertise than securities commissions in interpreting their constituent statutes given the broad policy context within which securities commissions operate: *National Corn Growers Assn. v. Canada (Import Tribunal)*, [1990] 2 SCR 1324, at p. 1336.

[47] … The adjudicative function of the Commission in enforcement proceedings under s. 162 would generally call for less deference. In the present case the Commission is called upon to adjudicate a bipolar dispute rather than exercise a pure policy decision. Nevertheless, the Commission also plays a principal role in policy development, in the management of a complex securities regulation scheme and in reconciling the interests of a number of different groups and in protecting the public: *Brosseau v. Alberta Securities Commission*, [1989] 1 SCR 301, at pp. 313-14. This calls for some deference by the reviewing court: *Pezim*, *supra*, at p. 591.

[48] The interpretation of s. 162 is a question of statutory construction of the Commission's enabling statute. As I stated above, the application of s. 162 requires the determination of when an order is in the public interest, and this calls for the Commission to apply its expertise. Although the Commission's interpretation of s. 162 is not binding on future Commission decisions, once the Commission finds that it can take general deterrence into account, it is unlikely to break from this practice in the future. It therefore has some precedential value. On the whole, the nature of the question militates in favour of deference.

[49] … Specifically, is it reasonable for the Commission to consider general deterrence in determining whether a sanction under s. 162 would be in the public interest? …

• • •

[51] In my view, the Commission's interpretation of s. 162 was reasonable.

C. *General Deterrence*

[52] Deterrent penalties work on two levels. They may target society generally, including potential wrongdoers, in an effort to demonstrate the negative consequences of wrongdoing. They may also target the individual wrongdoer in an attempt to show the unprofitability of repeated wrongdoing. The first is general deterrence; the second is specific or individual deterrence: see C.C. Ruby, *Sentencing* (5th ed. 1999). In both cases deterrence is prospective in orientation and aims at preventing future conduct.

[53] General deterrence as an aim of sentencing in criminal law is well established: see *R. v. M. (C.A.)*, [1996] 1 SCR 500, at para. 56; *R. v. Morrisey*, [2000] 2 SCR 90, 2000 SCC 39, at paras. 44 and 46. One of its earliest proponents was Jeremy Bentham. In his view, where the same result cannot be achieved through other modes of punishment and the net benefit to society outweighs the harm imposed on the offender, a deterrent penalty should be imposed and tailored in order to discourage others from committing the same offence. He assumes that citizens are rational actors, who will adjust their conduct according to the disincentives of deterrent penalties: A. Ashworth, *Sentencing and Criminal Justice* (3rd ed. 2000), at p. 64. Similarly, law and economic theorists such as R.A. Posner view deterrent penalties as a kind of pricing system: "An Economic Theory of the Criminal Law" (1985), 85 *Colum. L. Rev.* 1193.

[54] However, general deterrence is not without its critics. In the criminal context, commentators and courts have expressed doubts as to the effectiveness of imprisonment as a general deterrent: *R. v. Wismayer* (1997), 115 CCC (3d) 18 (Ont. CA), at p. 36; *Sentencing Reform: A Canadian Approach: Report of the Canadian Sentencing Commission* (1987) (Archambault Report), at pp. 136-37.

[55] In this appeal we are asked whether it is reasonable to decide that general deterrence has a role to play in the policing of capital markets. The conventional view is that participants in capital markets are rational actors. This is probably more true of market systems than it is of social behaviour. It is therefore reasonable to assume, particularly with reference to the expertise of the Commission in regulating capital markets, that general deterrence has a proper role to play in determining whether to make orders in the public interest and, if they choose to do so, the severity of those orders.

[56] This approach is consonant with United States securities jurisprudence, which accepts that general deterrence may be a consideration in imposing penalties for fraudulent behaviour. The rationale is that the public interest demands appropriate sanctions to secure compliance with the rules, regulations and policies of the Securities and Exchange Commission ("SEC"): see, e.g., *United States v. Matthews*, 787 F.2d 38 (2d Cir. 1986), at p. 47. Civil penalties are increasingly important to the SEC for a number of reasons, including general deterrence: see R.G. Ryan, "Securities Enforcement: Civil Penalties in SEC Enforcement Cases: A Rising Tide" (2003), 17 *Insights* 17.

[57] The Commission imposed the financial penalty on Hartvikson and Johnson under s. 162 of the Act, which provides that if the Commission finds after a hearing that a person has acted contrary to the Act, regulations or a decision of the Commission, and it is in the public interest to make such an order, it may impose a fine of no more than $100,000.

[58] "Public interest" is not defined in the Act. This Court considered the scope of a securities commission's public interest jurisdiction in *Asbestos*, *supra* … . It should be observed that our Court was not considering the function of general deterrence in the exercise of the jurisdiction of a securities commission to impose fines and administrative penalties nor denying that general deterrence might play a role in this respect.

[59] Braidwood JA understood *Asbestos*, *supra*, to foreclose the imposition of public interest penalties for the purpose of general deterrence. With respect, Braidwood JA's interpretation was mistaken.

[60] In my view, nothing inherent in the Commission's public interest jurisdiction, as it was considered by this Court in *Asbestos*, *supra*, prevents the Commission from considering general deterrence in making an order. To the contrary, it is reasonable to view general deterrence as an appropriate, and perhaps necessary, consideration in making orders that are both protective and preventative. Ryan JA recognized this in her dissent: "The notion of general deterrence is neither punitive nor remedial. A penalty that is meant to generally deter is a penalty designed to discourage or hinder like behaviour in others" (para. 125).

[61] The *Oxford English Dictionary* (2nd ed. 1989), Vol. XII, defines "preventive" as "[t]hat anticipates in order to ward against; precautionary; that keeps from coming or taking place; that acts as a hindrance or obstacle." A penalty that is meant to deter generally is a penalty that is designed to keep an occurrence from happening; it discourages similar wrongdoing in others. In a word, a general deterrent is preventative. It is therefore reasonable to consider general deterrence as a factor, albeit not the only one, in imposing a sanction under s. 162. The respective importance of general deterrence as a factor will vary according to the breach of the Act and the circumstances of the person charged with breaching the Act.

[62] It may well be that the regulation of market behaviour only works effectively when securities commissions impose ex post sanctions that deter forward-looking market participants from engaging in similar wrongdoing. That is a matter that falls squarely within the expertise of securities commissions, which have a special responsibility in protecting the public from being defrauded and preserving confidence in our capital markets.

D. The Commission's Order Was Reasonable

[63] Further, it was reasonable in all the circumstances for the Commission to conclude that general deterrence applies in respect of Hartvikson and Johnson's conduct. While a specific breach of the Act is required to trigger the application of s. 162, unlike s. 161, the penalty that the Commission ultimately imposes should take into account the entire context, as well as the preservation of the public interest. The public interest must be satisfied under both ss. 161 and 162, and is not restricted to situations where the Commission imposes a ban on market participation under s. 161. Where conduct could be addressed under the two sections, the Commission may use both provisions to craft the order that is most in the public interest.

[64] The weight given to general deterrence will vary from case to case and is a matter within the discretion of the Commission. Protecting the public interest will require a different remedial emphasis according to the circumstances. Courts should review the order globally to determine whether it is reasonable. No one factor should be considered in isolation because to do so would skew the textured and nuanced evaluation conducted by the Commission in crafting an order in the public interest. Nevertheless, unreasonable weight given to a particular factor, including general deterrence, will render the order itself unreasonable. Iacobucci J in *Pezim*, *supra*, at p. 607, suggested that an example of such unreasonableness would be the exercise of the Commission's discretion in a manner that was capricious or vexatious.

[65] In my opinion, increasing the amount of the fine is not "a vexatious and capricious exercise of the Commission's discretion" but sends a clear message to other actors in the British Columbia securities market that a breach of s. 61 will be dealt with severely, and it is rational to assume that this conduct will accordingly be deterred. The Commission stressed the seriousness of the respondents' conduct and the damage done to the integrity of the capital markets, and found that when making an order that is in the public interest, "[w]e are obliged to take whatever remedial steps we determine are appropriate to maintain the public's confidence in the fairness of our markets" (para. 14).

[66] The Commission's order was also a reasonable one globally. The Commission weighed the aggravating and mitigating factors and determined the appropriate penalty. Hartvikson and Johnson were the primary movers behind the control group's deceitful conduct. They were the leading players in breaching s. 61 of the Act. It does not appear on the face of the Commission's reasons for making the order under s. 162 that it gave unreasonable weight to general deterrence.

[67] The respondents argued that the Commission erred in not giving appropriate weight to the settlements reached by the other members of the control group. I disagree.

[68] In my view, settlement agreements arrived at by co-respondents and the Executive Director are not binding on the Commission in determining the appropriate penalty for

other co-respondents, although such settlements are among the relevant factors in assessing the appropriate penalty under s. 162. There is no support in the Act to find that settlements between a party against whom enforcement proceedings are brought and the Executive Director are binding as precedent upon the Commission. Indeed, such an approach would unduly fetter the Commission's mandate to make orders in the public interest. Nor, in light of the discount accorded settlements, do they necessarily reflect the appropriate penalty in all cases.

[69] Moreover, there appear to have been reasonable grounds for the Commission to impose a heavier penalty pursuant to s. 162 upon Hartvikson and Johnson than upon their co-respondents. The Commission's sanction of Hartvikson and Johnson appears to be reasonable in comparison to the settlement agreements in light of the finding by the Commission that Hartvikson and Johnson were the driving force responsible for the events described in the notice of hearing. Parity with the settlement agreements is not necessary because the Commission concluded that the respondents were more culpable than the other brokers.

[70] Accordingly, the Court of Appeal erred by disregarding the Commission's findings as well as the weight the Commission gave them. The weight that the Commission attributed to general deterrence and the settlement agreements is reasonable in all the circumstances and should not be disturbed by this Court.

...

VII. Disposition

[75] In the result, I would allow the appeal with costs, and reinstate the Commission's order.

2. *Convergence and Variation in Sanctioning Options*

One of the complexities in the enforcement area of securities law is that the sanctioning possibilities afforded under the public-interest jurisdiction are not completely consistent across the country. Most provinces have the power to order trading in specific securities to cease. On the other hand, where provinces have the power to levy administrative penalties, they may not all levy the same maximum amounts. Not all provincial or territorial regulators have the power to order profits to be disgorged, and only a few have the power to order restitution to investors. See Manitoba *Securities Act*, CCSM c S50, ss 148.2(1) to (10), New Brunswick *Securities Act*, SNB 2004, c S-5.5 (NBSA), s 188.1(3), and the Saskatchewan *Securities Act, 1988*, SS 1988-89, c S-42.2 (SSA), s 135.6(4). By way of example, the types of orders that can be made in Ontario are as follows:

Orders in the Public Interest

127(1) The Commission may make one or more of the following orders if in its opinion it is in the public interest to make the order or orders:

1. An order that the registration or recognition granted to a person or company under Ontario securities law be suspended or restricted for such period as is specified in the order or be terminated, or that terms and conditions be imposed on the registration or recognition.

2. An order that trading in any securities by or of a person or company or that trading in any derivatives by a person or company cease permanently or for such period as is specified in the order.

2.1 An order that acquisition of any securities by a particular person or company is prohibited, permanently or for the period specified in the order.

3. An order that any exemptions contained in Ontario securities law do not apply to a person or company permanently or for such period as is specified in the order.

4. An order that a market participant submit to a review of his, her or its practices and procedures and institute such changes as may be ordered by the Commission.

5. If the Commission is satisfied that Ontario securities law has not been complied with, an order that a release, report, preliminary prospectus, prospectus, return, financial statement, information circular, take-over bid circular, issuer bid circular, offering memorandum, proxy solicitation or any other document described in the order,
   i. be provided by a market participant to a person or company,
   ii. not be provided by a market participant to a person or company, or
   iii. be amended by a market participant to the extent that amendment is practicable.

6. An order that a person or company be reprimanded.

7. An order that a person resign one or more positions that the person holds as a director or officer of an issuer.

8. An order that a person is prohibited from becoming or acting as a director or officer of any issuer.

8.1 An order that a person resign one or more positions that the person holds as an officer or director of a registrant.

8.2 An order that a person is prohibited from becoming or acting as a director or officer of a registrant.

8.3 An order that a person resign one or more positions that the person holds as a director or officer of an investment fund manager.

8.4 An order that a person is prohibited from becoming or acting as a director or officer of an investment fund manager.

8.5 An order that a person or company is prohibited from becoming or acting as a registrant, as an investment fund manager or as a promoter.

9. If a person or company has not complied with Ontario securities law, an order requiring the person or company to pay an administrative penalty of not more than $1 million for each failure to comply.

10. If a person or company has not complied with Ontario securities law, an order requiring the person or company to disgorge to the Commission any amounts obtained as a result of the non-compliance.

. . .

Hearing Requirement

(4) No order shall be made under this section without a hearing, subject to section 4 of the *Statutory Powers Procedure Act*.

On the other hand, the equivalent provisions in the BCSA provide that:

Enforcement orders

161(1) If the commission or the executive director considers it to be in the public interest, the commission or the executive director, after a hearing, may order one or more of the following:

(a) that a person comply with or cease contravening, and that the directors and officers of the person cause the person to comply with or cease contravening,

(i) a provision of this Act or the regulations,

(ii) a decision, whether or not the decision has been filed under section 163, or

(iii) a bylaw, rule, or other regulatory instrument or policy or a direction, decision, order or ruling made under a bylaw, rule or other regulatory instrument or policy of a self regulatory body, exchange or quotation and trade reporting system, as the case may be, that has been recognized by the commission under section 24;

(b) that

(i) all persons,

(ii) the person or persons named in the order, or

(iii) one or more classes of persons

cease trading in, or be prohibited from purchasing, any securities or exchange contracts, a specified security or exchange contract or a specified class of securities or class of exchange contracts;

(c) that any or all of the exemptions set out in this Act, the regulations or a decision do not apply to a person;

(d) that a person

(i) resign any position that the person holds as a director or officer of an issuer or registrant,

(ii) is prohibited from becoming or acting as a director or officer of any issuer or registrant,

(iii) is prohibited from becoming or acting as a registrant or promoter,

(iv) is prohibited from acting in a management or consultative capacity in connection with activities in the securities market, or

(v) is prohibited from engaging in investor relations activities;

(e) that a registrant, issuer or person engaged in investor relations activities

(i) is prohibited from disseminating to the public, or authorizing the dissemination to the public, of any information or record of any kind that is described in the order,

(ii) is required to disseminate to the public, by the method described in the order, any information or record relating to the affairs of the registrant or issuer that the commission or the executive director considers must be disseminated, or

(iii) is required to amend, in the manner specified in the order, any information or record of any kind described in the order before disseminating the information or record to the public or authorizing its dissemination to the public;

(f) that a registration or recognition be suspended, cancelled or restricted or that conditions, restrictions or requirements be imposed on a registration or recognition;

(g) if a person has not complied with this Act, the regulations or a decision of the commission or the executive director, that the person pay to the commission any amount obtained, or payment or loss avoided, directly or indirectly, as a result of the failure to comply or the contravention;

(h) that a person referred to in subsection (7) submit to a review of its practices and procedures;

(i) that a person referred to in subsection (7) make changes to its practices and procedures;

(j) that a person be reprimanded.

(2) If the commission or the executive director considers that the length of time required to hold a hearing under subsection (1), other than under subsection (1)(e)(ii) or (iii), could be prejudicial to the public interest, the commission or the executive director may make a temporary order, without providing the opportunity to be heard, to have effect for not longer than 15 days after the date the temporary order is made.

(3) If the commission or the executive director considers it necessary and in the public interest, the commission or the executive director may, without providing an opportunity to be heard, make an order extending a temporary order until a hearing is held and a decision is rendered.

(4) The commission or the executive director, as the case may be, must send written notice of every order made under this section to any person that is directly affected by the order.

(5) If notice of a temporary order is sent under subsection (4), the notice must be accompanied by a notice of hearing.

(6) The commission or the executive director may, after providing an opportunity to be heard, make an order under subsection (1) in respect of a person if the person

(a) has been convicted in Canada or elsewhere of an offence

(i) arising from a transaction, business or course of conduct related to securities or exchange contracts, or

(ii) under the laws of the jurisdiction respecting trading in securities or exchange contracts,

(b) has been found by a court in Canada or elsewhere to have contravened the laws of the jurisdiction respecting trading in securities or exchange contracts,

(c) is subject to an order made by a securities regulatory authority, a self regulatory body or an exchange, in Canada or elsewhere, imposing sanctions, conditions, restrictions or requirements on the person, or

(d) has agreed with a securities regulatory authority, a self regulatory body or an exchange, in Canada or elsewhere, to be subject to sanctions, conditions, restrictions or requirements.

(7) An order under subsection (1)(h) or (i) may be made against

(a) an exchange or a quotation and trade reporting system,

(b) a self regulatory body,

(c) a clearing agency,

(c.1) a credit rating organization,

(d) a registrant,

(e) a partner, director, officer, insider or control person of a registrant,

(f) a person providing record keeping services to a registrant,

(g) a person that manages a compensation, contingency or similar fund formed to compensate clients of dealers or advisers,

(h) an issuer,

(i) a custodian of assets or securities of an investment fund,

(j) a transfer agent or registrar for securities of an issuer,

(k) a director, officer, insider or control person of an issuer,

(l) a general partner of a person referred to in this subsection, or

(m) a person that the commission has ordered is exempt from a provision of this Act or the regulations.

Administrative penalty

162. If the commission, after a hearing,

(a) determines that a person has contravened

(i) a provision of this Act or of the regulations, or

(ii) a decision, whether or not the decision has been filed under section 163, and

(b) considers it to be in the public interest to make the order,

the commission may order the person to pay the commission an administrative penalty of not more than $1 million for each contravention.

An optimist might point out that there is increasing convergence across the provinces as to the types of orders that can be made. For example, Ontario obtained the power to levy an administrative penalty partly in order to bring Ontario into conformity with British Columbia, which has had the power for a longer period. Yet, as the executive summary from Condon's study for the WPC points out, there has been significant variation across the country as to the mobilization of various mitigating and aggravating circumstances in order to make sanction determinations in specific cases. There is also a lively academic debate about what "works" best in terms of sanctioning options. We saw in Chapter 10 that some academics believe that civil remedies work better than regulatory enforcement as a strategy for promoting good conduct by market participants. Even among those who see an important role for regulatory sanctions, there is no consensus that financial penalties are more successful at preventing misconduct than other sanctioning options. Thus, for example, Armour et al argue that reputational sanctions (the effect of an announcement of a regulatory investigation) are much more consequential to a firm than financial penalties (See John Armour, Colin Mayer & Andrea Polo, "Regulatory Sanctions and Reputational Damage in Financial Markets" (24 March 2016), online: <http://voxeu.org/article/financial-market-wrongdoing-fines-vs-reputational-sanctions>.)

Finally, it should be noted that some provincial commissions have obtained explicit legislative power to make sanctioning orders where there have been corrections or regulatory orders made against persons or companies in other jurisdictions. See e.g. OSA, s 127(10). Meanwhile, Alberta has streamlined the process of making reciprocal orders significantly. In 2015, it became the first province to introduce automatic reciprocation of orders made by securities regulatory authorities in other provincial jurisdictions, without the need for a hearing to be held. This is one response to the criticism that the securities enforcement system in Canada is ineffective because of its provincial nature. See ASC Notice 15-701 (2 July 2015).

3. *Management Cease-Trading Orders*

It has been noted that the cease-trading order (CTO) is the predominant type of order available under provincial administrative enforcement powers. However, the use of this power to sanction reporting issuers for inadequacies of disclosure or other shortcomings in complying with securities law may also have the effect of immobilizing investors who have had no involvement in these failures to comply. As a result, in 2002, Canadian Securities Administrators (CSA) staff, following an initiative from Ontario, issued a staff notice identifying the circumstances in which a management-only CTO might be issued by the principal regulator, instead of a general cease-trading order, in cases where reporting issuers do not file their financial statements on time. The current version of this policy is National Policy 12-203, *Cease Trade Orders for Continuous Disclosure Defaults* (2008), 31 OSCB 8375 as amended 1 January 2011.

D. Judicial Review of Regulatory Decisions

Throughout this chapter we have seen a number of examples of appellate court consideration of enforcement decisions taken by securities regulators, as well as discussion of the appropriate standard of review to be visited on that decision-making. Important Supreme Court decisions here include *Asbestos* and *Cartaway*, as well, of course, as the *Pezim* case, excerpted in Chapter 6. One final example of judicial reconsideration of a regulatory enforcement decision is the appeal launched by Mr Donnini against the sanctions imposed on him for insider trading infractions by the OSC in a s 127 hearing. The OSC's decision here was excerpted in Chapter 8.

Donnini v Ontario Securities Commission
[2003] OJ No 3541 (QL) (Sup Ct J (Div Ct))

Penalties

[25] As mentioned above, the OSC imposed a penalty on Donnini by suspending his registration for a period of 15 years and directed that he cease trading in securities, with the exception of his personal accounts and those in his registered retirement savings plans. He was also required to resign as a director or officer of Yorkton and prohibited from acting in that capacity for any company that is an issuer, that is a registrant. It, in addition, ordered him to pay costs in the amount of $186,052.30.

[26] In December 2001, following an 18-month investigation into the affairs of Yorkton, five senior officials, including Donnini were charged with various offenses, including conflict of interest charges relating to personal and corporate trading.

[27] Paterson did reach a settlement agreement with the OSC by making a $1,000,000 "voluntary payment" and receiving a two-year ban from serving as a director, executive or owner in the securities business. The OSC is not empowered to impose fines.

[28] There were a number of factors involving the penalty imposed on Donnini, which have caused us to examine it particularly carefully. The first factor is that one member of the three-person panel, while agreeing with the summary of the evidence made by the chairman, did not feel that Donnini was guilty of insider trading, but felt that he should not have traded until he checked whether the information he had about the planned warrant issue was indeed material. His failure to do so was, in his view, against the public interest. This does suggest that to one member, at least, the offence committed by Donnini was less reprehensible than many and not deserving of a suspension for such an extended period of time.

[29] A second factor is the comment made by the chairman of the panel in his Reasons following the liability hearing, but before the penalty hearing was convened. Speaking about Donnini, he said, "He has been unrepentant and unwilling to acknowledge that his conduct was not becoming a registrant and contrary to the public interest." In our view, any person charged with a crime in the criminal courts or an offence before a tribunal, which has the power to impose penalties, is entitled to deny his guilt and call upon the prosecution to establish it. Criminal courts have always recognized, when imposing sentence, that consideration should be given to an accused who pleads guilty and expresses remorse. The reverse of this situation, however, is not appropriate. An accused not pleading guilty is not and should not be subject to increased penalties simply because he has chosen to defend himself.

[30] In the material filed by the counsel for the OSC, a newspaper article recounts that at the time other officials from Yorkton who were facing unrelated charges were making their settlements, Donnini was offered a penalty of a five-year trading ban, which he refused. This raises a third factor, mainly the difference between the penalty imposed by the OSC on Paterson of 2 years and the 15-year ban imposed on Donnini. Paterson, after all, was the person in charge of this entire deal and was responsible for ensuring that it went through. He was the one who gave instructions to Donnini even asking him, after telling him about the terms of the transaction, what Yorkton's short position was on KCA stock. He admitted to the OSC that he ought to have exercised a greater degree of

management and control of Donnini's activities, but it seems to us that he played a more significant role in all that took place in what was the subject matter of this particular part of the overall investigation. Whether or not it was the intention of the OSC to do so, it has generated a message, through its actions, that the OSC will agree to lesser sanctions when an accused person has the "good sense" to admit liability and make a substantial "voluntary payment." Donnini did neither of these. Given Donnini's present age, he, in reality, faces a lifetime ban from participating in the investment business. We are of the view that this is wrong in principle. Whether a person charged by the OSC settles or requires the hearing to take place, such person should be treated in an even manner. Donnini was entitled to defend himself.

[31] When discussing sanctions, the OSC in this case referred to the earlier case of *MCJC Holdings Inc. and Michael Cowpland* (2002), 25 OSCB 1133. In that case at page 1136, it states one of the factors which the OSC would take into account was "the size of any profit (or loss avoided) from the illegal conduct." The OSC refused to accept any assertion made by Donnini's counsel that Donnini and Yorkton did not benefit from the trading complained of. Certainly we were not referred to any evidence that suggested that Donnini was a recipient of any benefit. All trades were carried out in the name of Yorkton (with, of course, the exception of the jitney trades).

[32] Counsel for the OSC referred us to the case of *Woods (Re)* (1995), 18 OSCB 4625 (Farley J) as support for the 15-year suspension imposed upon Woods. It does not appear to be an apt comparison because there were repeated offenses for which Woods was ultimately charged criminally and convicted of. Of interest in that case is the reference to the argument by counsel for Woods that a 15-year suspension would mean a lifetime ban. The OSC on that occasion indicated that since Woods was a young man, he would be able to return to the business after the suspension had run its course. This indicates that they specifically wished to avoid imposing a permanent ban. However, when considering the same situation in Donnini's case, the OSC said, "Donnini's entire working experience has been in the securities industry. He is approximately half way through a typical 35-year working life in the securities industry. Securities trading by house professionals is becoming more and more a career for younger persons." This apparently was the OSC's way of suspending Donnini for life without actually doing do.

[33] In our view, there is an unreasonable disparity between the suspension meted out to Paterson by way of settlement and that meted out to Donnini, notwithstanding that Donnini did not make or was unable to make any sort of "voluntary payment" of the sort made by Paterson. As indicated earlier, we are conscious of the obligation of this Court to yield curial deference to the findings of an administrative tribunal, which has an acknowledged special expertise. This is particularly so where in addition it has a disciplinary function. This does not mean, however, that the Court must accept whatever the tribunal concludes. It ought not to disturb the penalty imposed and substitute its judgment for that of the panel unless there is an error in principle or as Robins JA said in *Takahashi v. College of Physicians and Surgeons* (1979), 26 OR (2d) 353 (Div. Ct.):

> Unless the punishment clearly does not fit the crime so to speak.

[34] The OSC has, in earlier decisions, indicated its espousal of the principle that there should be a reasonable balance between sanctions imposed on other participants in an

impugned action and those meted out subsequently. In *Belteco Holdings Inc. (Re)*, [2002] 21 OSCB 7743, the OSC reached a settlement with some of the participants which included certain sanctions. After setting out the terms of the resulting order in its Reasons dealing with the remaining participants, the OSC said at 7746:

> We set out the terms of that order here principally because we accept the agreement … that whatever sanctions are to be imposed should be fair and should be proportional to the sanctions imposed by the Commission on others who were participants in the scheme which is the subject of these proceedings. …

In the result, the OSC imposed sanctions on the remaining participants, which in their words "paralleled" those imposed earlier.

[35] While recognizing that the OSC is not bound strictly to follow its own precedents, we are of the view that its penalty decisions should generally adhere to some recognizable pattern. We adopt the view expressed by Braidwood JA in the British Columbia Court of Appeal case of *Cartaway Resources Corp. (Re)* [2002] BCJ no. 2115 (CA) at paragraphs 93 and 94:

> … Counsel for Hartvikson submits that this creates a sense that Hartvikson received a greater punishment because he chose to contest his innocence in a hearing.

Certainly, it is not appropriate that access to the Commission threaten to heighten a potential penalty so radically. While the Commission may not be bound by all of the technical rules of stare decisis to the same extent as the courts, I am in agreement with counsel for Hartvikson that fairness requires that it generally follow its past decisions in order to avoid the appearance of arbitrariness. No doubt the decision of parties to pursue their rights before the Commission, rather than enter into settlements, will be based in part on their assessment of precedents of the Commission and published settlements. If the Commission can issue penalties which do not correspond with its previous decisions, then those engaged in the Commission's disciplinary process will be unable to intelligently assess whether to settle or proceed to a hearing. This result is undesirable.

[36] We agree with Donnini's counsel that the penalty imposed on him does not stand up to a somewhat probing analysis.

[37] We are, of course, bound to acknowledge that Donnini has a record of prior trading violations of CDNX and TSC [*sic*] regulations and has received prior warnings from the market surveillance department of the TSC. He also had some internal discipline problems with Yorkton as well. However, taking all of these factors into consideration, we are of the opinion that the period of suspension should be reduced to four years effective September 12, 2002.

Costs

[38] Towards the end of the hearing itself, OSC counsel produced a bill of costs of OSC staff in a total amount of $186,052.30. The figures that go to make up this amount fill a total of only six lines on the page. Counsel for Donnini objected to the document indicating, among other things, that there were no particulars given and of course, no opportunity for him to examine any supporting material to verify the bald statements made in this very

brief synopsis. A subsequent document entitled "Submissions on Costs Staff of the Ontario Securities Commission" was then produced. The same abbreviated bill was produced, plus a two-page argument on the OSC's right to be paid costs. The main objection raised by Donnini's counsel concerning this approach is that he was denied the opportunity to review any back-up material to the bill and if necessary, cross-examine the bill's proposer. The panel simply said in that regard, "We do not believe it desirable in this case to examine dockets or a summary of dockets for staff." In our view, a claim for costs in this amount justifies a more intense and searching examination than the OSC is prepared to allow.

[39] We are of the view that the OSC erred in this regard. An order for costs is simply a fine by another name, unless it is a true reflection of the actual and reasonable costs of the nature specified as recoverable in section 127.2 of the Act. These are questions of fact and, like all such questions, must be resolved upon evidence, disclosure, documents and including cross-examination. Accordingly, we direct that the matter of costs be referred back to the OSC to conduct an inquiry into the extent of the bill and to make available for counsel for Donnini all dockets, time dockets, journal and/or diary entries and other back-up material in support of it, and to make available all of the participants whose names appear on it for cross-examination by counsel for Donnini at a mutually convenient time.

[40] In the result, therefore, the appeal from liability is dismissed, the appeal from the sanctions imposed by the OSC pursuant to that finding is allowed and the term of suspension is reduced to four years from September 12, 2002. Finally, on the appeal from the cost order, this matter is returned to the OSC to conduct a hearing for a purpose of reviewing the extent of the amount of costs imposed.

[41] So far as the costs of this application are concerned, we view success as being divided. Accordingly in the exercise in the discretion of this court, we rule that there be no costs.

In late 2004, the OSC appealed the decision of the Divisional Court in *Donnini*. Judgment was delivered by the Ontario Court of Appeal in January 2005. It restored the decision of the OSC on the sanctions to be applied to Donnini's conduct, finding that "[t]he Commission wrote careful and extensive reasons on the sanctions issue. The Commission considered the extent and seriousness of the unlawful conduct, Donnini's experience in the market, his position in the industry, his other violations of securities law and Yorkton's own internal rules and, of particular importance, general deterrence." However, the determination of costs against Donnini made by the OSC panel was described by the Court of Appeal as "cavalier." The court accordingly allowed the appeal on costs, "but only to the extent of returning the matter of costs to the panel for consideration in accordance with a procedure that meets its obligation of fairness and due process to the appellant." See *Donnini v Ontario Securities Commission* (2005), 76 OR (3d) 43 (CA).

On the issue of costs addressed in *Donnini*, it should be noted that some provincial regulators have the power to require respondents to pay the costs of investigations and hearings. For example, s 127.1(4) of the OSA provides that the OSC may order persons or companies to pay investigative or hearing costs, such as witness fees or legal services provided to the OSC, including those incurred by experts, investigators or financial examiners, and staff of the OSC. Costs are payable where there has been an adverse decision against the respondent. In her study of the use of public-interest powers across Canada, excerpted above, Professor Condon found that the quantum of costs typically assessed against respondents varied significantly across the country, with amounts levied in Ontario being highest.

QUESTIONS

1. What, in your view, would be the best way to improve on enforcement outcomes in the securities law area?
2. How much would it help enforcement objectives to have national regulation of securities markets?

VII. CHAPTER SUMMARY

The role of public enforcement of securities law—courts applying criminal or civil penalties or regulators making administrative sanctioning orders—is controversial among scholars, practitioners, and investors. Many scholars argue that discretionary enforcement of criminal or administrative penalties, other than perhaps an anti-fraud rule, is an inefficient way to run securities markets given the costs of uncertainty for market participants and the bureaucracies required to run such a system. From this point of view, it would be preferable to leave much of the enforcement of good behaviour by market participants to investors suing for compensation. It is clear, however, that this is not a tenable proposition from a public and political point of view, as evidenced by the reaction in both quarters to recent events. What appears to be the challenge in the absence of normative agreement about the role of enforcement in a well-functioning securities market is to accomplish effective and robust public enforcement of securities law in as efficient a manner as possible, as exhorted by Iacobucci J in the *Asbestos* decision. This is likely to involve a significant degree of interprovincial cooperation, as well as enhanced cooperation among law enforcement agencies such as securities regulators, self-regulatory organizations, and various police forces. Some steps have been taken in this regard with the introduction of integrated market enforcement teams (IMETS) and in Ontario, with the establishment of the Joint Serious Offences Team (JSOT). What will be of interest in the future, however, is how the ongoing balance among various available enforcement options will be achieved, especially given the concurrent cooperative market regulator initiative. Apart from the issue of whether enforcement is best achieved by the exercise of private or public power, we may also see a rethinking of the emphasis currently placed by public regulatory bodies on the role of administrative orders rather than quasi-criminal or criminal prosecutions in accomplishing orderly securities markets. Yet provinces are continuing to refine the enforcement tools they use in the administrative enforcement context. We noted above the introduction in Ontario of the so-called no-contest settlement as a means of resolving complex securities matters more expeditiously. We also noted the recent introduction of a whistleblower program at the OSC. Since whistleblowers will only be paid if sanctions are imposed by the tribunal, this suggests the continued relevance of administrative sanctioning in the overall constellation of enforcement efforts related to financial misconduct.

CHAPTER TWELVE

Financial Market Intermediaries

I. INTRODUCTION

In order to fulfill the overarching purposes of securities regulation, securities regulators focus primarily on the regulation of two key groups: issuers, and those engaged in the business of trading and advising in securities. The other parties to a securities transaction—the investors who are purchasers of securities or secondary market sellers of securities—are generally not regulated in their activities except in respect of the prohibitions relating to insider trading and market manipulation, and in some activities relating to takeover bids.

The foregoing chapters have dealt principally with the regulation of issuers, a body of regulation that is largely focused on the efficient prevention of fraud and mispricing. As we have seen, the primary tool used by regulators to accomplish this objective is disclosure. This chapter will address the other key focus of regulatory effort relating to investor protection, which involves the regulation of individuals and firms that serve as intermediaries between the issuer firm and the investor. Most of these individuals and firms are engaged in the business of trading and advising in securities.

There are a number of distinct categories of intermediary whose activities are governed by securities regulation:

- A "dealer" is a person or company that trades in securities either on their own account or as an agent for others. In some jurisdictions outside Canada, such as the United States, the term "dealer" is used to refer to those who trade on their own account, the term "broker" refers to those who trade on behalf of others, and the term "broker-dealer" is used for firms that engage in both types of activity.
- An "adviser" is a person or company that engages in, or holds out as engaging in, the business of advising another with respect to investment in or the purchase or sale of securities.
- A "portfolio manager" is an adviser who manages the investment portfolio of one or more clients through discretionary authority granted by the clients.
- An "investment fund manager" is a person who directs the business operations or affairs of an investment fund, such as a mutual fund or other type of pooled investment.

A. The Market for Financial Advice in Canada

Canada's system of regulation with respect to financial products, including securities, insurance, banking services, pension services, payday lending, mortgage brokerage services, and others, is highly decentralized. Each of these fields of financial service is regulated separately, some federally and some provincially.

What retail consumers typically consider "financial advice" can include interactions with advisers relating to banking products and services, estate planning, insurance products, retirement planning, and investments in securities. Many of these areas of advice are overseen by different regulators, and some are subject to no regulatory oversight. For example, banking products and services are regulated by the federal government under the *Bank Act*, while credit unions, trust companies, and *caisses populaires* are most commonly regulated by provincial statutes. The preparation of wills and powers of attorney is a service often provided by licensed lawyers, but general estate planning advice is also provided by non-lawyers. Insurance products, which include retirement saving and investment products known as segregated funds, are regulated under provincial insurance statutes. General "financial planning" advice can be provided by any person and is not a regulated activity, though some provinces are considering whether such activity should be regulated.

Securities regulators have the jurisdiction to regulate persons and companies in relation to securities transactions and markets. As described more precisely below, these regulated individuals and firms include investment dealers and advisers whose business involves serving as an intermediary in securities markets. Provincial and territorial securities regulators regulate some of these intermediaries directly and some indirectly through authority delegated to the national self-regulatory organizations (SROs)—Investment Industry Regulatory Organization of Canada (IIROC) and Mutual Fund Dealers Association of Canada (MFDA). As discussed in Chapter 3, IIROC and MFDA both maintain and enforce market conduct rules, policies, and regulations that govern the activities of their respective members.

B. Development of Intermediary Regulation

The regulation of those engaged in the business of trading and advising on the trading of securities dates back to the earliest days of securities regulation. In the United States, the very earliest blue-sky laws introduced in the early 1900s included prohibitions against fraudulent and manipulative sales practices and required adviser registration. In 1935, the newly formed Securities and Exchange Commission (SEC) was tasked with studying investment trusts by the *Public Utility Holding Company Act* of 1935. This study found evidence of abusive investment adviser behaviour, including what would now be considered market manipulation and unreasonable fees. These findings led to the development of the *Investment Company Act* of 1940 and the *Investment Advisers Act* of 1940, which are still in force, in an amended form, today.

In Canada, some provinces sought to protect investors by enacting blue-sky laws similar to those in the United States that required all companies offering shares to the public to be registered. Ontario developed a somewhat different model with the *Securities Frauds Prevention Act* of 1928, which focused on the registration of the trader rather than the issuer by prohibiting trading in securities unless the trader was duly registered. The stock market crash in 1929 that triggered the great depression, and the 1929 decision of the Privy Council in *A-G Manitoba v A-G Canada*, which prevented the application of provincial blue-sky laws to federally registered companies, quickly led all Canadian provinces to adopt the Ontario approach of protecting investors through the registration of brokers and traders, and this model has remained fundamentally in place in all provinces and territories since that time.

1. *Fair-Dealing Model*

In the latter part of the 20th century, calls for the modernization of regulation relating to securities intermediaries grew increasingly prominent and culminated in a 2004 publication by the Ontario Securities Commission of an influential concept paper that launched a project known as the "fair-dealing model."

Ontario Securities Commission, "The Fair Dealing Model"
Concept Paper of the Ontario Securities Commission (January 2004)

I. Introduction

Project Background and Objectives

The "Fair Dealing Model" is an Ontario Securities Commission proposal to significantly reform the way the retail investment industry is regulated. While the ideas could be applied to other sectors such as insurance, in developing the model we have not looked beyond activities within our existing jurisdiction.

We began this project as a result of two developments. In 1999, the Canadian Securities Administrators committee on financial planning proficiency standards identified conflicts of interest in financial planning advice as a more significant concern than representatives' proficiency. The CSA committee undertook to pursue this area as the second phase of the Financial Planning Project. Around the same time, OSC Chair David Brown determined that changes in the social and economic environment, and in the business structures and objectives of the securities industry, warranted a fundamental re-examination of the regulations governing the delivery of financial advice to retail investors. He recognized that our regulations are still product-based, as they have been for decades, even though the industry has moved to an advice-based business model. In early 2000, the OSC launched the committee that has led to this Concept Paper.

Under the Fair Dealing Model, we would begin to regulate on the basis of the relationships formed between investors and financial services providers, rather than on the basis of the products they buy and sell. The Model would impact a wide range of the day-to-day activities and procedures of market participants. Yet at the same time, it is specifically designed to reflect the way they do business already. It represents our attempt to modernize the regulatory framework to meet the challenges of today's investment industry marketplace.

We've already referred to two of the Fair Dealing Model's major goals: addressing the conflicts of interest that are inherent in many client relationships, and updating the regulations to reflect the business model. Another key objective is to encourage all market participants to adopt the industry's best practices. There are very few proposed requirements in this paper that have not already been implemented voluntarily by industry leaders who believed they made good business sense.

We hold high expectations for the outcomes of this project. We believe the Fair Dealing Model will promote healthy competition for investors' business, based on quality and value for services. It should strengthen and clarify the relationship between financial services providers and their clients, allowing them to better understand their mutual expectations, roles and responsibilities. From the investor's perspective, it should improve the quality of information and advice that clients receive, leading to more informed decisions, and an increased level of confidence in their financial services providers. Ultimately, it should reduce the number of disputes between clients and their financial services providers. In our view, outcomes like these are synonymous with the notion of "fair dealing."

The fair-dealing model concept paper included numerous recommendations, proceeding from the core principle that regulatory standards should be based on the relationships formed between people and firms, rather than products sold.

The model proposed three specific types of adviser–client relationship, to be established at the outset of any client relationship: (1) self-managed, in which the firm provides execution services only and does not provide any advice; (2) advisory, in which the investor makes their own decisions based on the expert, objective advice of the adviser; and (3) managed-for-you, in which the investor relies completely on the adviser, who makes all investment decisions.

The concept paper set out three fundamental principles of fair dealing: (1) there should be a clear and documented allocation of responsibilities between the investor, the adviser, and the firm; (2) all dealings with retail investors should be transparent and disclosed in a manner that is useful and understandable to investors; and (3) any conflicts of interest should be managed to avoid self-serving outcomes.

The fair-dealing model also set out the principle that a representative has a general duty to advise any person carefully, fully, honestly, and in good faith, and that in an advisory or managed-for-you relationship, compensation must not be the primary motivator for any advice, but that recommendations or discretionary decisions must be based on the representative's expert judgment and the agreed-on investment objectives.

With respect to adviser compensation, the model recommended that financial services providers be required to disclose the total incremental cost of each transaction to clients, including all amounts of compensation received, and specific information about the nature and amount of compensation the firm would receive from a transaction, including any benefits received from a third party, such as a mutual fund manufacturer.

The paper also set out the recommendation that financial services providers be required to disclose meaningful information about the riskiness of the security and how it would affect the investor's portfolio before any transaction was completed, and set out recommendations regarding the content of account statements.

The fair-dealing model strongly influenced subsequent reforms relating to the regulation of the adviser–client relationship in Canada and led directly to several reform projects subsequently undertaken by the Ontario Securities Commission (OSC), Canadian Securities Administrators (CSA), IIROC, and MFDA.

2. *CSA Registration Reform Project and National Registration Database*

In Canada, prior to 2009, each Canadian jurisdiction had different requirements relating to the registration of individuals and firms, and those seeking registration in multiple provinces were required to submit individual applications in each province where they intended to do business. This was criticized as administratively inefficient and as imposing too high a regulatory burden on intermediaries.

One of the projects initiated in response to this situation was the CSA Registration Reform Project of the early 2000s, which developed from the fair-dealing model proposal and resulted in the substantial harmonization of adviser and firm registration across Canada. The purpose of the Registration Reform Project was to harmonize, streamline, and modernize the system for registration in Canada. The project's objectives included developing nationwide registration categories as well as proficiency and conduct requirements for registrants and the implementation of the core principles of the fair-dealing model, which included clarity of the investor–adviser relationship, transparency of compensation to advisers, and advisers' conflict-management systems.

One component of the Registration Reform Project was the development of the National Registration Database (NRD), which is the database maintained by the CSA to facilitate the registration of investment advisers and firms across Canada. The NRD was introduced in 2005, and its requirements and procedures were originally set out in National Instrument 31-101, *National Registration System*, which has since been replaced by NI 31-102, *National Registration Database*, and the requirements for registration set out in NI 31-103.

The Registration Reform Project concluded in 2009 with the implementation of National Instrument 31-103, *Registration Requirements, Exemptions, and Ongoing Registrant Obligations* (NI 31-103).

3. *National Instrument 31-103*

NI 31-103 sets out the requirements that must be met by an individual or firm seeking registration, the conduct requirements that a registered individual or firm and individual must meet in the course of carrying on activities requiring registration, and exemptions from the registration requirement.

NI 31-103 consolidated and harmonized requirements and restrictions governing registration and registrants as well as registration exemptions for all CSA jurisdictions, which previously existed in a number of acts, regulations, rules, notices, administrative practices, and discretionary orders.

II. REGISTRATION REQUIREMENTS

The fundamental requirement to register is found in provincial securities statutes. For example, s 25(1) of the Ontario *Securities Act* (OSA) stipulates that no person or company shall engage in or hold himself, herself, or itself out as engaging in the business of trading in securities unless the person or company is registered in accordance with Ontario securities law as a dealer or as a dealing representative of a registered dealer and is acting on behalf of the registered dealer. Section 25 also sets out similar registration requirements for underwriters, advisers, and others.

Companion Policy 31-103, *Registration Requirements and Exemptions*
As amended 11 January 2015

Requirement to Register

The requirement to register is found in securities legislation. Firms must register if they are:

- in the business of trading
- in the business of advising
- holding themselves out as being in the business of trading or advising
- acting as an underwriter, or
- acting as an investment fund manager

Individuals must register if they trade, underwrite or advise on behalf of a registered dealer or adviser, or act as the ultimate designated person (UDP) or chief compliance officer (CCO) of a registered firm. Except for the UDP and the CCO, individuals who act on behalf of a registered investment fund manager do not have to register.

However, all permitted individuals of any registrant must file Form 33-109F4 *Registration of Individuals and Review of Permitted Individuals* (Form 33-109F4).

There is no renewal requirement for registration, but fees must be paid every year to maintain registration.

Multiple Categories

Registration in more than one category may be necessary. For example, an adviser that also manages an investment fund may have to register as a portfolio manager and an investment fund manager. An adviser that manages a portfolio and distributes units of an investment fund may have to register as a portfolio manager and as a dealer.

Registration Exemptions

NI 31-103 provides exemptions from the registration requirement. There may be additional exemptions in securities legislation. Some exemptions do not need to be applied for if the conditions of the exemption are met. In other cases, on receipt of an application, the regulator has discretion to grant exemptions for specified dealers, advisers or investment fund managers, or activities carried out by them if registration is required but specific circumstances indicate that it is not otherwise necessary for investor protection or market integrity.

• • •

Fitness for Registration

The regulator will only register an applicant if they appear to be fit for registration. Following registration, individuals and firms must maintain their fitness in order to remain registered. If the regulator determines that a registrant has become unfit for registration, the regulator may suspend or revoke the registration. See Part 6 of this Companion Policy for guidance on suspension and revocation of individual registration. See Part 10 of this Companion Policy for guidance on suspension and revocation of firm registration.

Terms and Conditions

The regulator may impose terms and conditions on a registration at the time of registration or at any time after registration. Terms and conditions imposed at the time of registration are generally permanent, for example, in the case of a restricted dealer who is limited to specific activities. Terms and conditions imposed after registration are generally temporary. For example, if a registrant does not maintain the required capital, it may have to file monthly financial statements and capital calculations until the regulator's concerns are addressed.

Opportunity to Be Heard

Applicants and registrants have an opportunity to be heard by the regulator before their application for registration is denied. They also have an opportunity to be heard before the regulator imposes terms and conditions on their registration if they disagree with the terms and conditions.

Assessing Fitness for Registration—Firms

We assess whether a firm is or remains fit for registration through the information it is required to provide on registration application forms and as a registrant, and through compliance reviews. Based on this information, we consider whether the firm is able to carry out its obligations under securities legislation. For example, registered firms must be financially viable. A firm that is insolvent or has a history of bankruptcy may not be fit for registration.

In addition, when determining whether a firm whose head office is outside Canada is, and remains, fit for registration, we will consider whether the firm maintains registration or regulatory organization membership in the foreign jurisdiction that is appropriate for the securities business it carries out there.

Assessing Fitness for Registration—Individuals

We use three fundamental criteria to assess whether an individual is or remains fit for registration:

- proficiency
- integrity, and
- solvency

(a) Proficiency

Individual applicants must meet the applicable education, training and experience requirements prescribed by securities legislation and demonstrate knowledge of securities legislation and the securities they recommend.

Registered individuals should continually update their knowledge and training to keep pace with new securities, services and developments in the industry that are relevant to their business. See Part 3 of this Companion Policy for more specific guidance on proficiency.

(b) Integrity

Registered individuals must conduct themselves with integrity and have an honest character. The regulator will assess the integrity of individuals through the information they are required to provide on registration application forms and as registrants, and through compliance reviews. For example, applicants are required to disclose information about conflicts of interest, such as other employment or partnerships, service as a member of a board of directors, or relationships with affiliates, and about any regulatory or legal actions against them.

(c) Solvency

The regulator will assess the overall financial condition of an individual applicant or registrant. An individual that is insolvent or has a history of bankruptcy may not be fit for registration. Depending on the circumstances, the regulator may consider the individual's

> contingent liabilities. The regulator may take into account an individual's bankruptcy or insolvency when assessing their continuing fitness for registration.

A. Business Trigger for Registration

Prior to the implementation of NI 33-103 in 2009, the activities that required or "triggered" registration varied among types of activity and among jurisdictions. At that time, all jurisdictions except Québec had a "trade trigger" for dealing in securities, but a "business trigger" for advising in securities. Québec had a business trigger for both dealing and advising in securities. The trade trigger was a system that required registration for every trade unless an exemption was available, and there were many broad categories of exemption aimed at focusing regulatory attention. The trade trigger was problematic because it relied on statutory exemptions for occasional trades and exemptive relief for business organizations. The business trigger is an alternative system that requires registration only for those engaged in a pattern of repetitive trading activity. Comparable countries, including the United States, the United Kingdom, Australia, Hong Kong, and Singapore, were all using a business trigger for registration.

A key initiative of NI 31-103 was to extend the business trigger to both dealing in securities and advising in securities across Canada. The result of this reform was to establish the current system whereby anyone who is "in the business" of dealing or advising in securities must register.

Some provincial securities acts retain the trade trigger references, such as that found in s 34 of the BC *Securities Act*, which states that a person must not trade in a security unless he or she is registered in accordance with the regulations. NI 31-103 deals with these provisions in s 8.4, which clarifies that in British Columbia, New Brunswick, and Manitoba (the provinces that retain the trade trigger in their legislation), a person or company is exempt from the registration requirement if they are not engaged in the business of trading in securities or exchange contracts as a principal or agent, and do not hold themselves out as engaging in such business.

1. *Meaning of "In the Business"*

NI 31-103 sets out a number of factors that the CSA considers when assessing whether an activity is conducted as a business. The companion policy provides context for these factors.

> **Companion Policy 31-103**
> As amended 11 January 2015
>
> *Business Trigger for Trading and Advising*
>
> We refer to trading or advising in securities for a business purpose as the "business trigger" for registration.
>
> We look at the type of activity and whether it is carried out for a business purpose to determine if an individual or firm must register. We consider the factors set out below, among others, to determine if the activity is for a business purpose. For the most part,

these factors are from case law and regulatory decisions that have interpreted the business purpose test for securities matters.

Factors in Determining Business Purpose

This section describes factors that we consider relevant in determining whether an individual or firm is trading or advising in securities for a business purpose and, therefore, subject to the dealer or adviser registration requirement.

This is not a complete list. We do not automatically assume that any one of these factors on its own will determine whether an individual or firm is in the business of trading or advising in securities.

(a) Engaging in Activities Similar to a Registrant

We usually consider an individual or firm engaging in activities similar to those of a registrant to be trading or advising for a business purpose. Examples include promoting securities or stating in any way that the individual or firm will buy or sell securities. If an individual or firm sets up a business to carry out any of these activities, we may consider them to be trading or advising for a business purpose.

(b) Intermediating Trades or Acting as a Market Maker

In general, we consider intermediating a trade between a seller and a buyer of securities to be trading for a business purpose. This typically takes the form of the business commonly referred to as a broker. Making a market in securities is also generally considered to be trading for a business purpose.

(c) Directly or Indirectly Carrying On the Activity with Repetition, Regularity or Continuity

Frequent or regular transactions are a common indicator that an individual or firm may be engaged in trading or advising for a business purpose. The activity does not have to be their sole or even primary endeavour for them to be in the business.

We consider regularly trading or advising in any way that produces, or is intended to produce, profits to be for a business purpose. We also consider any other sources of income and how much time an individual or firm spends on all activities associated with the trading or advising.

(d) Being, or Expecting to Be, Remunerated or Compensated

Receiving, or expecting to receive, any form of compensation for carrying on the activity, including whether the compensation is transaction or value based, indicates a business purpose. It does not matter if the individual or firm actually receives compensation or in what form. Having the capacity or the ability to carry on the activity to produce profit is also a relevant factor.

(e) Directly or Indirectly Soliciting

Contacting anyone to solicit securities transactions or to offer advice may reflect a business purpose. Solicitation includes contacting someone by any means, including advertising that proposes buying or selling securities or participating in a securities transaction, or that offers services or advice for these purposes.

Business Trigger Examples

This section explains how the business trigger might apply to some common situations.

(a) Securities Issuers

A securities issuer is an entity that issues or trades in its own securities. In general, securities issuers with an active non-securities business do not have to register as a dealer if they:

- do not hold themselves out as being in the business of trading in securities
- trade in securities infrequently
- are not, or do not expect to be, compensated for trading in securities
- do not act as intermediaries, and
- do not produce, or intend to produce, a profit from trading in securities

During the start-up stage, securities issuers may not yet be actively carrying on their intended business. We consider a start-up securities issuer to have an "active non-securities business" if the entity is raising capital to start a non-securities business. Although the entity does not need to be producing a product or delivering a service, we would expect it to have a bona fide business plan to do so, containing milestones and the time anticipated to reach those milestones. For example, technology companies may raise money with only a business plan for many years before they start producing a product or delivering a service. Similarly, junior exploration companies may raise money with only a business plan long before they find or extract any resources.

However, securities issuers may have to register as dealers if they are in the business of trading. Conduct that would indicate that security issuers are in the business includes frequently trading in securities. While frequent trading is a common indicator of being in the business of trading, we recognize that trading may be more frequent during the start-up stage, as an issuer needs to raise capital to launch and advance the business. If the trading is primarily for the purpose of advancing the issuer's business plan, then the frequency of the activities alone should not result in the issuer being in the business of trading in securities. If the capital raising and use of that capital are not advancing the business, the issuer may need to register as a dealer.

Securities issuers may also have to register as a dealer if they

- employ or contract individuals to perform activities on their behalf that are similar to those performed by a registrant (other than underwriting in the normal course of a distribution or trading for their own account)
- actively solicit investors, subject to the discussion below, or
- act as an intermediary by investing client money in securities

For example, an investment fund manager that carries on the activities described above may have to register as a dealer.

Many issuers actively solicit through officers, directors or other employees. If these individuals' activities are incidental to their primary roles with an issuer, they would likely not be in the business of trading. Factors that would suggest that the issuer and these individuals are in the business of trading are:

- the principal purpose of the individual's employment is raising capital through distributions of the issuer's securities;
- the individuals spend the majority of their time raising capital in this manner;
- the individuals' compensation or remuneration is based solely or primarily on the amount of capital they raise for the issuer.

Securities issuers that are distributing securities are subject to the prospectus requirements unless an exemption is available. Regulators have the discretionary authority to require an underwriter for a prospectus distribution.

2. *Meaning of "Advising"*

The BC Securities Commission considered the nature of advice and advising in the 1995 case excerpted below.

In the Matter of the *Securities Act*, SBC 1985, c 83 and in the Matter of Robert Anthony Donas
(4 April 1995), BC Securities Commission

The notice of hearing alleges that Robert A. Donas acted as an adviser without being registered, contrary to section 20 of the Act … .

. . .

The first issue to be determined is whether Donas was "engaging in, or holding himself out as engaging in, the business of advising another with respect to investment in or the purchase or sale of securities." The concise Oxford Dictionary of Current English (1990 ed.) defines "advice" as "words given or offered as an opinion or recommendation about future action or behavior … ."

It is because the very nature of advising involves the offering of an opinion or recommendation to others that the Act requires advisers to be registered and to meet certain conditions as to their education and experience. This requirement is intended to protect the public, as was acknowledged by L'Heureux-Dubé J. in *Brosseau v. Alberta Securities Commission* (SCC) 57 D.L.R. (4th) 458 at p. 467:

> Securities Acts in general can be said to be aimed at regulating the market and protecting the general public. This role was recognized by this court in *Gregory & Co. Inc. v. Quebec Securities Commission* (1961), 28 D.L.R. (2d) 721 at p. 725, [1961] S.C.R. 584, where Fauteux J. observed at p. 588:
>
>> The paramount object of the Act is to ensure that persons who, in the province, carry on the business of trading in securities or acting as investment counsel, shall be honest and of good repute and, in this way, to protect the public, in the province or elsewhere, from being defrauded as a result of certain activities initiated in the province by persons therein carrying on such a business.

As indicated by the definition of "advice," the nature of the information given or offered by a person is the key factor in determining whether that person is advising with respect to investment in or the purchase or sale of securities. A person who does nothing more than provide factual information about an issuer and its business activities is not advising in securities. A person who recommends an investment in an issuer or the purchase or sale of an issuer's securities, or who distributes or offers an opinion on the investment merits of an issuer or an issuer's securities, is advising in securities. If a person advising in securities is distributing or offering the advice in a manner that reflects a business purpose, the person is required to be registered under the Act.

A later decision considering this issue and providing some comment on the implications of electronic communication to the determination of "advising" was the 2004 decision of the OSC in *Friesner*, immediately below.

In the Matter of the *Securities Act*, RSO 1990, c S.5, as amended and in the Matter of First Federal Capital (Canada) Corporation and Monte Morris Friesner
(2004), 27 OSCB 1603

[28] In *Donas*, the British Columbia Securities Commission clarified that there are two aspects to the question of whether an individual or company is acting as an adviser. The first issue to consider is whether an opinion or recommendation is being offered:

> The nature of the information given or offered by a person is the key factor in determining whether that person is advising with respect to investment in or the purchase or sale of securities. A person who does nothing more than provide factual information about an issuer and its business activities is not advising in securities. A person who recommends an investment in an issuer or the purchase or sale of an issuer's securities, or who distributes or offers an opinion on the investment merits of an issuer or an issuer's securities, is advising in securities.

[29] The second issue to consider is whether the respondent offered the recommendation in a manner that reflected a business purpose, reference *Costello* and *Maguire*. Where a respondent expects to be remunerated in some respect with respect to his activities, a business purpose is reflected, reference *Hrappstead* and *Costello*. There is, however, no requirement that any investor actually follow the recommendation, pay a commission, or invest with the respondent, reference *Hrappstead* and *Re Etherington* (2002), 25 O.S.C.B. 5323.

. . .

[31] The use of a web site on the internet to solicit investors and to offer advice, in and of itself, may be suggestive of a business purpose.

[32] The distribution of a recommendation to a large number of potential investors, such as through the use of the Internet or other forms of advertisement, has also been held to be reflective of a business purpose, reference *Donas* and *Maguire*.

[33] The provision of recommendations and information formulated by others may, nevertheless, constitute advising on behalf of the person providing the information. As was stated by this Commission in *Dodsley* at page 1801:

> Counsel for Dodsley argued that the nature of the information provided by Dodsley was authored by third parties and Dodsley simply recommended or offered an opinion on the merits of investing in commodities generally and that each person is asked to exercise his or her own judgement as to the merits of an investment. We do not accept that position. While certain of the materials were authored by third parties, much was authored by Dodsley and that which was authored by third parties was sent in a package which contained handwritten notes of Dodsley and was sent in a manner in which he expressly or impliedly make recommendations as to investments.

A number of cases have considered the meaning of "advising" in the context of individuals who have published newsletters, hosted radio broadcasts, or organized seminars promoting particular securities. Such activity has at times been found to fall within the definition of advising in securities. An important exemption regarding the provision of such advice, however, is now found in securities legislation, such as s 34 of the OSA and NI 31-103, s 8.25(2), which specifically provide that the adviser registration requirement does not apply to a person or company that acts as an adviser if the advice the person or company provides does not purport to be tailored to the needs of the person or company receiving the advice and that the person providing the advice fully discloses any financial or other interests that they have in the securities that are the subject of the advice.

B. Categories of Registration

1. Firm Registrants

There are three broad categories for the registration of firms: dealers, advisers, and investment fund managers. Within these categories, there are subcategories based principally on the type of securities with which the firm deals.

Firms that take part in more than one type of activity requiring registration are required to register in each applicable category. A firm registered in multiple categories is required to comply with the requirements of all the categories in which it is registered, though capital and insurance requirements are not cumulative—only the most stringent apply (CSA, *Notice and Request for Comment, Proposed National Instrument 31-103, Registration Requirements* (23 February 2007)).

a. Firm Dealers

There are five dealer categories for firms established in NI 31-103:

1. *Investment dealer.* A firm registered as an investment dealer may act as a dealer or an underwriter in respect of any security (NI 31-103, s 7.1(2)(a)).
2. *Mutual fund dealer.* A firm registered as a mutual fund dealer may act as a dealer in respect of any security of a mutual fund or labour-sponsored investment fund (NI 31-103, s 7.1(2)(b)).
3. *Scholarship plan dealer.* A firm registered as a scholarship plan dealer may act as a dealer in respect of a security of a scholarship plan, an educational plan, or an educational trust. Scholarship plans are a form of investment that is used specifically to

save for post-secondary education, and they are eligible for registration with the Canada Revenue Agency (CRA) as registered education savings plans (RESPs). The government of Canada actively began encouraging saving for post-secondary education through the Canada education savings grant in 1998, and investment in scholarship plans has increased significantly since that time. As of December 2011, the aggregate value of assets held in scholarship plans was $9.1 billion, or approximately 28.9 percent of all the assets held in RESPs (CSA Notice—Implementation of a New Prospectus Form for Scholarship Plans 36(2)2013, 36 OSCB (10 January 2013)).

4. *Exempt market dealers.* NI 31-103 introduced the new exempt market dealer (EMD) registration category in 2009. Exempt market dealers are restricted to dealing in prospectus-exempt securities and with persons to whom prospectus-exempt distributions can be made. Prior to 2009, Ontario and Newfoundland and Labrador had a similar category, known as the limited market dealer. Originally, British Columbia considered not adopting the EMD category because it was concerned that requiring registration of persons in the business of dealing in the exempt market would have a negative impact on the venture capital raising in the province and they were not persuaded that there was a market problem that would be addressed by the registration requirement (CSA, *Notice and Request for Comment, Proposed National Instrument 31-103, Registration Requirements* (23 February 2007)).
5. *Restricted dealer.* The restricted dealer category was another new category of registration introduced with NI 31-103. This category is intended to accommodate firms with limited dealing activities that do not fall within the other firm categories. The restrictions and requirements that apply to an individual or firm registered in the category will vary depending on the activity being carried on and will be set out in terms and conditions attached to the registration.

b. Firm Advisers

There are two adviser categories established for firms under NI 31-103 and s 26(6) of the OSA: (1) portfolio manager, and (2) restricted portfolio manager. As described above, portfolio managers are advisers who are authorized by their clients to manage the clients' investment portfolios on a discretionary basis. A firm registered as a portfolio manager may act as an adviser in respect of any security, while a firm registered as a restricted portfolio manager may do so only in accordance with the terms, conditions, restrictions, or requirements that have been applied to its registration. Typically, restricted portfolio managers are restricted to specific securities, types, or classes of securities or specified industries. This registration category accommodates specialized advisers who do not require or meet the proficiency requirements of the full portfolio manager registration.

c. Investment Fund Managers

The final broad category for firm registration set out in NI 31-103 is investment fund manager, which was a new registration category established under NI 31-103. This registration requirement applies to managers of all investment funds (including domestic, foreign, reporting issuers, and non-reporting issuers) other than private investment clubs.

The CSA decided to implement IFM registration after identifying specific risks relating to IFMs, including the incorrect or untimely performance of a number of essential services—for example, calculation of net asset value, preparation of financial statements and reports, provisions of transfer agency, or record-keeping services—and conflicts of interest between the fund manager and the investors. The registration of IFMs was intended to allow regulators to directly regulate fund managers, impose minimum capital and competency requirements on IFMs, and to impose a framework for avoiding and managing conflicts for IFMs (CSA, *Notice and Request for Comment, Proposed National Instrument 31-103, Registration Requirements* (23 February 2007)).

2. Individual Registrants

Individual registrants are required to be sponsored by a firm that is registered in one of the firm categories described above, and all firms will sponsor at least one registered individual. Proficiency requirements are imposed by NI 31-103 for each role.

Individuals who carry on activities that require registration in multiple categories on behalf of a registered firm are required to register and meet the proficiency requirements of all applicable categories.

It is possible for an individual to register in both a firm and individual category. For example, a sole proprietor who is registered in the firm category of portfolio manager may also be required to register in the individual category of advising representative (NI 31-103CP, s 2.1).

There are five individual registration categories:

1. *Dealing representative.* A dealing representative is permitted to act as a dealer or an underwriter in respect of a security that the individual's sponsoring firm is permitted to trade or underwrite (NI 31-103, s 2.1(2)(a); OSA, ss 25(1), 25(2)).
2. *Advising representative.* An advising representative may act as an adviser in respect of a security about which the individual's sponsoring firm is permitted to advise (NI 31-103, s 2.1(2)(b); OSA, s 25(3)).
3. *Associate advising representative.* An associate advising representative may act as an adviser in respect of a security about which the individual's sponsoring firm is permitted to advise, but only if the advice they are giving has been approved by a registered advising representative designated by their firm to provide such supervision (OSA, s 25(3)(c); NI 31-103, s 4.2).
4. *Ultimate designated person.* NI 31-103 introduced the requirement for registration of an ultimate designated person for each registered firm. The ultimate designated person (UDP) is the senior officer responsible for the activity of the registered firm and is often the chief executive officer or president of the firm. The UDP is responsible for ensuring that policies and procedures are in place to ensure the registrant's securities law obligations are met (NI 31-103, s 2.1(2)(d), s 5.1; OSA, s 25(5)).
5. *Chief compliance officer.* NI 31-103 also introduced the requirement for registration of a chief compliance officer for each registered firm. A firm's chief compliance officer (CCO) is responsible for the day-to-day monitoring of the registrant's compliance with its policies, procedures, and securities law requirements. Detailed requirements for CCOs are set out in NI 31-103, s 5.2. In smaller firms, the CCO and the UDP may be the same person (NI 31-103, s 2.1(2)(e); OSA, s 25(6)).

The purpose of requiring each firm to have a UDP and a CCO is to encourage a culture of compliance in registered firms, to establish minimum competencies for those with compliance responsibilities, and to give regulators the ability to deal directly with individuals who lack such competencies or demonstrate incompetence.

3. Process for Registration in Multiple Jurisdictions

For firms and individuals seeking registration in multiple jurisdictions, NI 31-103 works in conjunction with the Passport System, described in Chapter 3, and the provisions of National Policy 11-204, *Process for Registration in Multiple Jurisdictions*.

The process established is similar to that for the receipting of prospectuses in that passport jurisdictions fully rely on the approval of the prospective registrant's principal regulator (including Ontario), while Ontario requires an application to be submitted to it separately if the firm or individual is seeking registration in Ontario and Ontario is not the principal regulator. Under NP 11-204, this is referred to as an interface registration. In an interface registration, the prospective registrant will generally deal with their principal regulator only, and Ontario will determine whether to opt in or opt out of the principal regulator's determination.

C. Exemptions from the Requirement to Register

A number of exemptions from the registration requirement are included in part 8 of NI 31-103 and part 12 of the OSA. These exemptions are generally based on the nature of the intermediary, the nature of the security, or the nature of the investor.

Some exemptions rely on the concept of the "permitted client." Permitted clients are defined in s 1.1 of NI 31-103, and include the following: Canadian financial institutions and their subsidiaries; registered advisers, investment dealers, mutual fund dealers, and exempt market dealers; pension funds; Canadian and foreign governments of various levels; Crown corporations; individuals who beneficially own financial assets that exceed $5 million in value; and persons or companies with net assets of at least $25 million.

1. Exemptions from Dealer and Underwriter Registration

Part 8 of NI 31-103 sets out a number of circumstances in which the dealer registration requirement does not apply—for example, in respect of trades that are made through a registered dealer or to a registered dealer, investment fund trades into managed accounts, investment fund reinvestment trades, trades of private investment clubs with fewer than 50 beneficial securityholders, pooled loan funds administered by a registered trust company, some trades relating to mortgages on real property, trades relating to debt secured in accordance with personal property security legislation, and trades in insurance contracts by insurance companies. Foreign registered dealers are also exempt from registration in respect of certain trades of foreign securities in Canada.

Generally, the dealer requirement does not apply in respect of trades in debt securities issued by the government of Canada or a Canadian province or municipality, or those involving debt securities issued by Canadian financial institutions and certain international banks (NI 31-103, s 8.21; OSA, s 35(1)).

2. *Exemptions from Adviser Registration*

To avoid overlap of regulation and the potential for inconsistent regulatory requirements for those subject to multiple regulatory regimes, the adviser registration requirement does not apply to registered dealers that do not exercise discretionary authority over client accounts (because they are already subject to regulation as registered dealers) or to IIROC members with discretionary authority (who are subject to IIROC regulation for this activity). There is also a specific exemption for persons or companies giving advice that does not purport to be tailored to the needs of the person or company receiving the advice as long as any conflicts of interest are disclosed (NI 31-103, ss 8.23-8.25; OSA, s 34).

The adviser registration requirement also does not apply to certain foreign advisers who act as advisers to permitted clients if the adviser does not advise that client on securities of Canadian issuers (NI 31-103, s 8.26).

3. *Exemptions from Investment Fund Manager Registration*

Persons or companies that organize private investment clubs are exempt from the investment fund manager registration requirement if the fund they are organizing has no more than 50 beneficial securityholders; does not seek and has never sought to borrow money from the public; does not distribute and has never distributed its securities to the public; does not pay or give any remuneration for investment management or administration advice in respect of trades in securities, except normal brokerage fees; and requires securityholders to make contributions in proportion to the value of the securities held by them (NI 31-103, s 8.27).

Plan sponsors and plan service providers for defined contribution pension plans, group registered retirement savings plans, and group registered education savings plans are also exempt from the investment fund manager registration requirements (NI 31-103, s 8.28).

4. *Client Mobility Exemption*

A person or company that is registered to act as a dealer, underwriter, or adviser in its principal jurisdiction in Canada is permitted to provide services to up to ten clients in another jurisdiction in Canada without triggering the dealer registration requirement or the adviser registration requirement in the other jurisdiction, provided that the person or company provides only those services it is permitted to in its principal jurisdiction according to its registration, and deals fairly, honestly, and in good faith in the course of its dealings with an eligible client (NI 31-103, s 8.30).

QUESTION

The exemptions detailed above are based variously on the nature of the intermediary, the nature of the security, or the nature of the client in the transaction. What do these various circumstances have in common that has led regulators to exempt them from the registration requirements?

III. ONGOING REGISTRANT OBLIGATIONS

In addition to setting out the activities that require registration and the pre-requisite proficiencies for registration, NI 31-103 sets out numerous ongoing requirements for registrants in all categories. These requirements relate to the minimum capital that a firm is required to maintain, the levels of insurance that registrants are required to maintain, obligations with respect to the filing of information, and requirements relating to financial reporting. NI 31-103 also sets out specific requirements relating to the relationship of the registrant to their clients.

A. Membership in a Self-Regulatory Organization

As discussed in Chapter 3, provincial and territorial securities regulators have delegated authority for the market conduct of some categories of registrants to the national self-regulatory organizations (SROs), the Investment Industry Regulatory Organization of Canada (IIROC), and the Mutual Fund Dealers Association of Canada (MFDA). IIROC and MFDA both maintain and enforce market conduct rules, policies, and regulations that govern the activities of their respective members.

NI 31-103 provides that all investment dealers are required to be "dealer members" of IIROC, and all mutual fund dealers are required to be members of the MFDA.

Firms that are members of IIROC are exempt from NI 31-103 requirements relating to minimum capital levels; dealer insurance; notifying the regulator of a change, claim, or cancellation; various financial reporting requirements; and various client relationship requirements, including know your client and suitability (NI 31-103, s 9.3). These exemptions are in place because IIROC's Dealer Member Rules impose similar requirements on its members, and the exemptions apply only to firms that are compliant with the corresponding IIROC provisions.

Firms that are members of the MFDA are exempt from a similar range of requirements under NI 31-103, provided they are complying with the relevant corresponding MFDA requirements, which are found in the MFDA Rules (NI 31-103, s 9.4).

B. Internal Controls and Financial Conditions

Under NI 31-103, registered firms are required to establish, maintain, and apply policies, procedures, control, and supervision systems sufficient to ensure that the firm and each individual acting on its behalf complies with securities legislation and that the risks associated with its business are prudently managed (s 11.1).

In order to ensure accountability, firms are required to designate an ultimate designated person and a chief compliance officer as discussed above. The ultimate designated person should be the chief executive officer of the firm if it has one, its sole proprietor, or the officer in charge of the division of the firm whose activities require the firm to be registered. The chief compliance officer of the firm is required to be an officer or partner of the firm or the sole proprietor of the firm. Both the ultimate designated person and the chief compliance officer must be permitted to directly access the firm's board of directors at such times as they consider necessary or advisable (NI 31-103, ss 11.2-11.4).

All registered firms are required to maintain records to accurately record their business activities, financial affairs and client transactions, and compliance with securities legislation. NI 31-103 contains detailed requirements for the content and maintenance of registered firms' records, including those relating to financial information, compliance with insurance and capital requirements, internal control procedures, transaction identification, audit trail, account activity, client account opening, complaint handling, and client correspondence (NI 31-103, s 11.5).

Part 12 of NI 31-103 sets out regulations relating to the financial condition that registrants are required to maintain. These regulations set out the minimum capital that registrants in each category are required to maintain and the minimum insurance that each category of registrant is required to maintain. IIROC and MFDA member firms are exempted from the minimum capital requirements of NI 31-103 if they comply with the relevant corresponding IIROC and MFDA requirements.

Registrants are required to deliver annual and interim financial statements to their regulator in accordance with the requirements of NI 31-103, s 12.10, and are required to direct their auditor to conduct any audit or review required by securities regulators.

C. Client Relationships

The nature of the relationship between registrants and their clients has been an important area of focus for securities regulators and has been a topic of continuous consultation, public discussion, and reform since the publication of the fair-dealing model proposal in 2004. As part of the second phase of the CSA Registration Reform Project in 2007, IIROC and MFDA both implemented the core client relationship principles relating to registrants' obligations to know their clients and products, ensure all advice and recommendations are suitable for each client, avoid conflicts of interest, and handle client complaints fairly, as discussed below. These principles were mandated for all registrants in 2009 in part 13 of NI 31-103.

1. *Standard of Conduct for Registrants*

Underlying the core client relationship principles mandated by securities regulators are the standards of conduct and duties imposed on securities markets intermediaries through statute, regulation, and the application of common law principles. These standards and duties were discussed by the CSA in their 2012 consultation paper examining the possible introduction of a fiduciary standard for financial advisers and dealers. This reform project is discussed more fully later in this chapter.

Canadian Securities Administrators Consultation Paper 33-403, *The Standard of Conduct for Advisers and Dealers: Exploring the Appropriateness of Introducing a Statutory Best Interest Duty When Advice Is Provided to Retail Clients*
(25 October 2012) (footnotes omitted)

Current Statutory Standard of Conduct Requirements

Duty to Act Fairly, Honestly and in Good Faith

Securities Legislation in Canada imposes a duty on registered advisers and dealers to deal fairly, honestly and in good faith with their clients. This duty applies to advisers and dealers broadly in all dealings with their clients.

A threshold question is whether the obligation to act fairly, honestly and in good faith creates, or is equivalent to, a best interest standard. Many commentators believe that it is not (by itself) equivalent to, and falls short of, a best interest standard. Others disagree. We are not aware of any court or regulatory decision that has concluded that this duty creates, or is equivalent to, a fiduciary duty.

Statutory Best Interest Standard for Investment Fund Managers

Investment fund managers (IFMs) are currently subject to a general *statutory* best interest standard of conduct. Every IFM must (i) exercise the powers and discharge the duties of their office honestly, in good faith and in the *best interests* of the investment fund, and (ii) exercise the degree of care, diligence and skill that a reasonably prudent person would exercise in the circumstances. The articulation of that duty is consistent with the duty imposed on directors under applicable corporate law.

Statutory Best Interest Standard for Advisers and Dealers in Four Provinces When Discretionary Authority Present

Four provinces (Alberta, Manitoba, Newfoundland and Labrador, and New Brunswick) have a statutory requirement that when advisers or dealers have discretionary authority over their clients' investments, the adviser or dealers must act in the clients' best interests. This is consistent with, as discussed above, the common law where an adviser or dealer that has discretionary authority over a client's assets virtually always owes the client a fiduciary duty.

Québec

In Québec, according to both the general civil law and the *Securities Act* (Québec), registered dealers and advisers are currently subject to a duty of loyalty and a duty of care and must act in the client's best interest.

The 1994 reform of the *Civil Code of Québec* (the Civil Code) led to the introduction of these standards for specific legal relationships, namely, the administration of the property of others, the contract for services and the mandate.

In addition to remaining subject to the general regime of contractual liability under the Civil Code, the relevant doctrine and jurisprudence indicate that a relationship between an adviser or a dealer and a client is governed by the rules underlying those legal relationships (the determination of the applicable rules depends on the nature and scope of the relationship).

In any case, a duty of loyalty and, at a minimum, a duty to act in the best interests of a client as well as a duty of care are provided for in sections 1309, 2100 and 2138, respectively, of the Civil Code:

> 1309. An administrator shall act with prudence and diligence.
>
> He shall also *act honestly and faithfully in the best interest* of the beneficiary or of the object pursued.
>
> 2100. The contractor and the provider of services are bound to act in the best interests of their client, with prudence and diligence.
>
> 2138. A mandatary is bound to fulfill the mandate he has accepted, and he shall act with prudence and diligence in performing it.
>
> He shall also act *honestly and faithfully* in the best interests of the mandator, and avoid placing himself in a position that puts his own interest in conflict with that of his mandator. (italics added)

It is worth noting that according to the authors Crête, Brisson, Naccarato and Létourneau, this obligation to act with loyalty (or "faithfully") is comparable to that of the common law fiduciary standard:

> As Professor Naccarato mentioned in his study on the legal nature of trust, the higher degree of trust in contractual relationships develops when a person entrusts (rooted in the word "trust") property or a portion of his or her estate to another person who will act in the name or on behalf of the client. Such a higher degree of trust is also reflected in the complexity of services offered that require specialized knowledge as well as specific skills and abilities. The greater the imbalance between the respective parties' degree of knowledge, the more the vulnerable party will rely on the competency and honesty of the co-contractor. Under the civil law of Québec, this type of relationship, characterized by the presence of this higher degree of trust, could underpin a contract of mandate or other form of administration of the property of others, while under common law, the contractual relationship could be described as a "fiduciary relationship" to which fiduciary duties are connected.

The extent of these obligations under the Civil Code varies depending on the legal context and nature of the investment advisory relationship (e.g. discretionary account or non-discretionary account, executing broker only), taking into account the degree of trust, dependence and vulnerability of the client. The Supreme Court of Canada has acknowledged the higher degree of these obligations in the case of a portfolio manager as well as the prevailing role of trust in the mandate regime:

> As in the case of any mandate, the mandate between a manager and his client is imbued with the concept of trust, since the client places his trust in the manager—the mandatary—to manage his affairs. … This spirit of trust is reflected in the weight of the obligations that rest on the manager, which will be heavier where the mandator is vulnerable, lacks specialized knowledge, is dependent on the mandatary, and where the mandate is important. The corresponding requirements of fair dealing, good faith and diligence on the part of the manager in relation to his client will thus be more stringent.

Most importantly and as mentioned previously, sections 160 and 160.1 of the *Securities Act* (Québec) also require that all registered dealers and advisers and their representatives "deal fairly, honestly, *loyally* and in good faith with their clients" (italics added) and "[i]n their dealings with clients and in the execution of the mandates entrusted to them by their clients, … act with all the care that may be expected of a knowledgeable professional acting in the same circumstances."

Common Law Fiduciary Duty in Some Cases

As discussed above, depending on the nature of the relationship between the client and their adviser or dealer, Canadian courts (except in Québec, where the common law does not exist in respect of private law matters) may find that an adviser or dealer stands in a common law fiduciary relationship to their clients. As we have seen, Canadian courts have identified five non-exclusive and interrelated factors to assist in this determination: vulnerability, trust, reliance, discretion (over the client's account or investments), and professional rules or codes of conduct (see "When does a fiduciary duty arise at common law?" in Part 3 above).

The fourth factor, discretion, is an especially important element in the context of an investment advisory relationship because the advisory industry generally distinguishes between clients based on whether they have discretionary accounts or non-discretionary accounts. A discretionary account (also known as a managed account) is a type of client account for which an adviser or dealer has the discretion to make investment decisions and transact in securities without the client's express consent to each transaction; in a non-discretionary account, the client must consent to each transaction.

Accordingly, a common law fiduciary duty will virtually always arise where the client has a discretionary account. A fiduciary duty may also arise where the client has a non-discretionary account depending on the actual power or influence that the adviser or dealer has over the client, and the extent to which the client relies on the adviser or dealer. On this point, the Supreme Court of Canada recently stated that:

> [t]he nature of this discretionary power to affect the beneficiary's legal or practical interests may, depending on the circumstances, *be quite broadly defined. It may arise from power conferred* by statute, agreement, perhaps from a unilateral undertaking or, in particular situations *by the beneficiary's entrusting the fiduciary with information or seeking advice in circumstances that confer a source of power* (italics added).

This statement builds on previous caselaw that suggested that with regard to unsophisticated clients especially, the court will find that a fiduciary relationship exists even if "the ultimate discretion or power in the disposition of funds remained with the beneficiary."

Canadian courts explain this approach by noting that advisers and dealers fall into a continuum in providing advice, with discount brokers at one end (who provide no advice but simply execute transactions on a client's express instructions and who therefore are not subject to a common law fiduciary duty standard) and advisers or dealers with clients in discretionary accounts at the other end (who have complete discretionary trading authority and who therefore would be subject to a common law fiduciary duty). Whether a common law fiduciary duty applies to a relationship that falls somewhere in between in this continuum is a question of fact to be determined based on the nature of the client relationship in all the circumstances.

2. *Know Your Client and Suitability*

All registrants, other than investment fund managers, are required to take reasonable steps to know their client and to ensure that every purchase or sale of a security is suitable for the client before making a recommendation to buy or sell a security, accepting an instruction to buy or sell a security, or making a purchase or sale of a security for a client's managed account.

Section 13.2 of the companion policy to NP 31-103 explains the rationale for the know your client regulations as follows:

> Registrants act as gatekeepers of the integrity of the capital markets. They should not, by act or omission, facilitate conduct that brings the market into disrepute. As part of their gatekeeper role, registrants are required to establish the identity of, and conduct due diligence on, their clients under the know your client (KYC) obligation in section 13.2. Complying with the KYC obligation can help ensure that trades are completed in accordance with securities laws.
>
> KYC information forms the basis for determining whether trades in securities are suitable for investors. This helps protect the client, the registrant and the integrity of the capital markets. The KYC obligation requires registrants to take reasonable steps to obtain and periodically update information about their clients.

Pursuant to NI 31-103, s 13.2, the know your client regulations require registrants to establish the identity of every client and, if the registrant has cause for concern, to make reasonable inquiries as to the reputation of the client. If the client is a corporation, partnership, or trust, the registrant must establish the nature of the client's business, the identity of any individual who is a beneficial owner of, or exercises direct or indirect control or direction over, more than 25 percent of the voting rights attached to the outstanding voting securities of the corporation or, in the case of a partnership or trust, exercises control over the affairs of the partnership or trust. Registrants are also expected to establish whether a client is an insider of a reporting issuer or any other issuer whose securities are publicly traded.

In order to properly meet their suitability requirements, registrants must ensure that they have sufficient information regarding each client's investment needs and objectives, financial circumstances, risk tolerance and creditworthiness to evaluate the suitability of any investment, and they are expected to take reasonable steps to keep this KYC information current. An exception exists for permitted clients who have waived the suitability requirements in writing.

Registrants are obliged to ensure that all recommendations and securities transactions are suitable for their clients. If a client instructs a registrant to buy, sell, or hold a security, and the registrant is of the reasonable opinion that following the instruction would not be suitable for the client, the registrant must inform the client of the registrant's opinion and must not buy or sell the security unless the client specifically instructs the registrant to proceed nonetheless (NI 31-103, s 13.3(2)).

3. *Know Your Product*

Giving suitable advice requires registrants to not only know their client but also to understand the products they are recommending or trading. Section 3.4 of NI 31-103 establishes the regulatory requirement that an individual registrant "must not perform an activity that requires registration unless the individual has the education, training and experience …

including understanding the structure, features and risks of each security the individual recommends." This aspect of the more general proficiency requirements, often referred to as "know your product," applies even in circumstances when there is an exemption from the suitability obligation, and applies to all registrants, including IIROC and MFDA members.

IIROC sets out similar know-your-product requirements for its members (IIROC Notice 12-0109; IIROC Guidance Note 09-0087, *Best Practices for Product Due Diligence*). The MFDA has published Staff Notice MSN-0048, *Know Your Product* (31 October 2005), which clarifies the obligations of MFDA members regarding the due diligence required of dealer members prior to product approvals.

Recommendations and transactions that involve clients borrowing to invest have attracted particular attention from regulators because of the unique risk of such strategies and the potential conflict of interest for dealers and advisers, who are often compensated on the basis of the total amount that clients invest. CSA staff have expressed the view that they expect registrants to specifically assess the suitability of leveraged trades or leveraging strategies for clients who borrow funds to trade in securities. MFDA KYC rules clarify the obligation of their dealer members to specifically assess the suitability of orders involving the use of borrowed funds (MFDA Rule 2.2.1 and Policy No 2). The rule clarifies that dealer members must assess leverage suitability with consideration given to each client's investment knowledge, risk tolerance, and investment objectives. The MFDA has also published a leveraging supervision guide, which provides further guidance to its dealer members (CSA Staff Notice 31-336, *Guidance for Portfolio Managers, Exempt Market Dealers and Other Registrants on the Know-Your-Client, Know-Your-Product and Suitability Obligations* (9 January 2014)). If a registrant recommends that a client should use borrowed money to finance any part of a purchase of a security, the registrant is required to provide the client with a written statement before the purchase that states: "Using borrowed money to finance the purchase of securities involves greater risk than a purchase using cash resources only. If you borrow money to purchase securities, your responsibility to repay the loan and pay interest as required by its terms remains the same even if the value of the securities purchased declines" (NI 31-103, s 13.12).

4. *Conflicts of Interest*

All registered firms are required to take reasonable steps to identify material conflicts of interest that exist or that might arise between the firm and each client, and must respond to existing or potential conflicts of interest. If a reasonable investor would expect to be informed of a conflict of interest, the registered firm must disclose the nature and extent of the conflict of interest to the client in a timely manner (NI 31-103, s 13.4).

NI 31-103 contains detailed disclosure and consent requirements for certain transactions involving securities and issuers in which the registrant has an interest, recommendations relating to securities issued by the registered firm or an affiliate of the registered firm, and referral arrangements (NI 31-103, ss 13.5-13.11). Registrants are also prohibited from lending money, extending credit, or providing margin to their clients. The CSA has summarized the principle-based guidance in NP 31-103 as follows:

- The registrant should *avoid* the conflict if it is sufficiently contrary to the interests of a client (or the integrity of the capital markets) that there can be no other reasonable response.

- The registrant should *control* the conflict if it can be effectively managed by internal controls such as organizational structures, lines of reporting and physical locations.
- The registrant should *disclose* the conflict to their clients if a reasonable investor would expect to be informed about it, in addition to any other methods the registered firm may use to control the conflict.

Although the general rule is that advisers and dealers are able to decide for themselves how to apply these principles, securities legislation also contains specific prohibitions and restrictions (Consultation Paper 33-403, *The Standard of Conduct for Advisers and Dealers: Exploring the Appropriateness of Introducing a Statutory Best Interest Duty When Advice Is Provided to Retail Clients* (25 October 2012)).

Registrant business models and compensation structures have been criticized as placing the interests of financial advisers and firms fundamentally in conflict with those of their clients, and, in 2016, the CSA published a request for comment on a number of sweeping regulatory reforms in this area. These proposals are dealt with in detail below.

5. Complaint Handling

Securities regulations also explicitly set out the obligations registered firms have when dealing with client complaints. The general obligation is that registered firms are required to document and respond to each complaint made about any product or service offered by the firm or a representative of the firm in a manner that a reasonable investor would consider fair and effective (NI 31-103, s 13.15). If a client remains unsatisfied after a firm has had the opportunity to address their complaint, the firm is required to provide access to an independent external complaint resolution service to their client. Since 2011, the dispute resolution service provider mandated by the CSA for all registrants other than those in Québec is the Ombudsman for Banking Services and Investments (OBSI). In order to use the OBSI service, the client must agree that OBSI's recommendation regarding the complaint will not exceed $350,000 (NI 31-103, s 13.16).

The regulations provide specifically that when a registered firm receives a complaint from a client, the firm is required to provide the client with a written acknowledgement of the complaint that includes a description of the firm's obligations and the services that will be made available through OBSI. If the firm decides to reject the complaint or to make an offer to resolve a complaint, the firm must provide the client with written notice of its decision and include the contact information for OBSI. A client is dissatisfied with the firm's decision has 180 days to commence a complaint with OBSI after receiving written notice of the firm's decision. If the firm has not made a decision to reject or offer resolution within 90 days of receipt of the complaint; the client can opt to file their complaint with OBSI for investigation and resolution (NI 31-103, s 13.16).

QUESTIONS

1. Why do securities regulators set minimum capital requirements and insurance requirements for registrants?
2. Why do securities regulators delegate oversight of large groups of registered firms and individuals to IIROC and the MFDA? What are some of the advantages of the SRO oversight system?

3. Why does the CSA require that an independent dispute resolution service be provided when a client has an unresolved dispute with a registered firm?

IV. ENFORCEMENT: TERMS AND CONDITIONS, SUSPENSION, AND REVOCATION OF REGISTRATION

Under provincial securities acts, the registration of a person or company can be suspended or can be made subject to terms and conditions at any time if it appears to the director that the person or company is not suitable for registration, has failed to comply with securities law, or that the registration is "otherwise objectionable" (see e.g. OSA, s 28.)

A person or company that is facing the imposition of terms and conditions, suspension, refusal of reinstatement, or revocation of their registration must be given an opportunity to be heard (OSA, s 31).

A. Terms and Conditions

Terms and conditions can be imposed on registration, or at any time while a person or company is registered or is having their registration reinstated. Such terms and condition often involve matters such as a limitation on the nature of the clients or products a registrant is permitted to deal with, a restriction on accepting new clients, a requirement to undertake more frequent reporting, or a requirement to perform some or all functions under the supervision of another registrant. Terms and conditions may be temporary or permanent.

B. Suspension

A registered firm's registration can be suspended automatically in accordance with the requirements of NI 31-103 or can be suspended by a securities regulator under provincial securities legislation. Automatic suspension occurs if a firm fails to pay its annual registration fees or if its membership in IIROC or the MFDA is suspended or revoked.

While a registration is suspended, the firm is prohibited from undertaking any of the activities for which the registration is required, but the firm otherwise remains a registrant and subject to the jurisdiction of the regulator (NP 31-103, part 10). Such suspensions will remain in place until the registration is either reinstated or revoked. Any representative's registration will be automatically suspended if their sponsoring adviser or dealer firm's registration is suspended or if their employment with the firm is terminated (NI 31-103, ss 10.1-10.3; OSA, s 29). Automatic suspensions do not entitle firms to an opportunity to be heard (NP 31-103, part 10).

Securities regulators can suspend a firm's registration in the public interest if it appears to the director that the person or company is not or is no longer suitable for registration (OSA, s 28). The regulator may do this if it has serious concerns about the firm or any of its registered individuals. For example, such a determination may be made if a firm or one or more of its registered individuals is charged with a crime, especially fraud or theft (CP 31-103).

Suspended registrations will result in automatic revocation on the second anniversary of the suspension if they have not been reinstated unless a proceeding regarding the suspension has been commenced (NI 31-103, ss 10.5-10.6).

C. Revocation of Registration

Revocation is a serious regulatory penalty because it permanently removes a firm or an individual from the securities industry in which they have, in many cases, built a substantial business or a long career. Decisions to revoke registration can be made by a hearing panel as part of the penalty following an enforcement hearing but are most commonly made by the Director of a securities regulator on the basis of public interest or fitness for registration following client complaints or a regulator's own compliance review of the registrant's business activities and records. Although registrants must be given an opportunity to be heard before a revocation determination is made by a Director, the proceeding is generally less formal than an enforcement hearing. Decisions of the Director in such cases can be appealed to a regulatory hearing panel, which was the context of the *Sterling Grace* decision below.

In the Matter of Sterling Grace & Co Ltd and Graziana Casale
(3 September 2014), Ontario Securities Commission

I. Overview

A. Introduction

[1] This is an application (the "Application") by Sterling Grace & Co ("Sterling") and Graziana (Grace) Casale ("Casale") (together, the "Applicants"), pursuant to subsection 8(2) of the *Securities Act*, R.S.O. 1990, c. S.5, as amended (the "Act"), for the Ontario Securities Commission (the "Commission") to review a decision of a Director of the Commission issued November 18, 2013 ((2013), 36 O.S.C.B. 11243 (the "Director's Decision")).

[2] The Director's Decision suspended Sterling's registration as an exempt market dealer ("EMD") and Casale's registration as dealing market representative, ultimate designated person ("UDP") and chief compliance officer ("CCO"). Deputy Director, Marrianne Bridge (the "Director"), found that the Applicants lacked the requisite integrity and proficiency to remain registrants.

...

B. The Applicants

[4] Sterling was registered with the Commission as a limited market dealer ("LMD") on December 7, 2006 and its registration was recategorized as an EMD on September 28, 2009. Sterling was also registered as an EMD with securities regulators in Alberta and British Columbia on February 2, 2012. Sterling has offered for sale securities of several issuers, including Genwealth Venture Limited Partnership ("Genwealth"), which is an investment fund, Redstone Investment Corporation ("Redstone"), a finance company that holds itself out as providing loans to small and medium sized businesses, and Gingko Mortgage Investment Corporation ("Gingko").

[5] Casale is registered with the Commission as UDP, CCO and dealing representative of Sterling. She is also a permitted individual, as defined is paragraph [288] below, and has been an officer, director and shareholder of Sterling since the firm's inception. Casale

is also registered in Alberta and British Columbia as Sterling's UDP, CCO, dealing representative and a permitted individual as of February 13, 2012.

C. *History of the Matter*

[6] Between November 2012 and July 2013, Staff of the Compliance and Registrant Regulation Branch of the Commission ("CRR") conducted a compliance review of Sterling, pursuant to section 20 of the Act, for the review period of December 1, 2011 to November 30, 2012 (the "Compliance Review"). As part of that review, Casale provided an interview under oath on April 16, 2013 (the "Casale Interview"). On July 3, 2013, Staff noted at least eleven deficiencies in a compliance report (the "Compliance Report") sent to the Applicants. On the same day, in light of certain classified "significant deficiencies," Staff advised the Applicants via letter that they had recommended that the registration of Sterling and its registered individuals be suspended and that certain conditions be placed upon reinstatement.

[7] The Applicants gave notice to the Commission that they wished to exercise their right for an Opportunity to be Heard, pursuant to section 31 of the Act ("OTBH"). On October 28, 2013, an OTBH was held for the Director to consider Staff's recommendations. On that day, the Director heard submissions on behalf of Staff and the Applicants.

[8] The Director issued a written decision and reasons accepting Staff's recommendations on November 18, 2013.

D. *The Director's Decision*

[9] As referenced above, the Director made the following decision:

(a) the registration of Sterling is suspended permanently;
(b) the registration of Casale as UDP and CCO is suspended permanently;
(c) the registration of Casale as a dealing representative be suspended, and that she not be permitted to apply for reinstatement for a period of two years;
(d) Casale successfully complete the Conduct and Practices Handbook Course before applying for reinstatement of registration;
(e) Casale be subject to one year of strict supervision in the event her registration is reinstated; and
(f) Casale shall not be a permitted individual of a registered firm for a period of five years.

(Director's Decision, *supra* at para. 1)

[10] The Director found that Staff proved its allegations with respect to issues of integrity. These allegations included the existence of conflicts of interest, unreported capital deficiency, misrepresentations to Staff and trading without registration. The Director concluded that both of the Applicants lack the requisite integrity to remain registrants (Director's Decision, *supra* at para. 42). The Director was not persuaded by the Applicants' submissions that certain issues should be considered as issues of proficiency, rather than integrity (Director's Decision, *supra* at para. 40).

[11] The Director also found that Staff proved its allegations with respect to issues of proficiency. These allegations included improper reliance on prospectus exemptions,

failure to discharge the Know Your Product ("KYP") obligation, failure to discharge the Know Your Client ("KYC") and suitability obligations. She concluded that both of the Applicants lack the requisite proficiency to remain registrants (Director's Decision, *supra* at para. 48). The Director noted that because each of the proficiency issues she found related directly to the proficiency of a dealing representative, they support the suspension of Casale's registration as a dealing representative (*Ibid.*).

...

F. *Application for Hearing and Review Pursuant to Subsection 8(2) of the Act*

...

[15] The Applicants argue that the Director erred by failing to consider or give sufficient weight to the evidence presented by the Applicants and made findings based on a mischaracterization of issues of "proficiency" and "integrity." Therefore, the Applicants submit that the Director imposed sanctions that are unwarranted and unnecessary to fulfill the regulatory objective that the Applicants operate in compliance with Ontario securities laws and in the best interests of clients.

[16] In the Application, the Applicants further submit that the Director's Decision fails to deliver adequate reasons for requiring suspensions that, in effect, put the Applicants out of business. ...

...

VI. Analysis

A. *Legal Framework for Registration*

1. *Public Interest Jurisdiction*

[140] In exercising its discretion to review the decision of a Director, the Commission must act in the public interest with regard to its mandate and purpose as articulated under section 1.1 of the Act:

> 1.1 Purposes—The purposes of this Act are,
>
> (a) to provide protection to investors from unfair, improper or fraudulent practices; and
>
> (b) to foster fair and efficient capital markets and confidence in capital markets.

> (See *Re Michalik* (2007), 30 O.S.C.B. 6717 ("*Michalik*") at para. 44; *Sawh* ... [*Re Sawh* (2012), 35 O.S.C.B. 7434] paras. 150-151)

[141] Section 2.1 of the Act provides fundamental principles for the Commission to consider in pursuing the purposes of the Act, including the primary means for achieving those purposes. These include "requirements for the maintenance of high standards of fitness and business conduct to ensure honest and responsible conduct by market participants" (subsection 2.1(2)(iii) of the Act). One of these requirements is to be found in section 2.1 of the OSC Rule 31-505, which provides that a registered dealer and its representatives "shall deal fairly, honestly and in good faith with its clients." It is in the public interest for the Commission to ensure that these overarching principles of registrant conduct are adhered to, given the important role of registrants in the capital markets.

[142] In [*Mithras Management Ltd* (1990), 13 OSCB 1600], the Commission acknowledged that its discretion in the public interest is to be exercised prospectively to protect the public and the integrity of the capital markets. The Commission stated that:

> ... the role of this Commission is to protect the public interest by removing from the capital markets—wholly or partially, permanently or temporarily, as the circumstances may warrant—those whose conduct in the past leads us to conclude that their conduct in the future may well be detrimental to the integrity of those capital markets. We are not here to punish past conduct; that is the role of the courts... We are here to restrain, as best we can, future conduct that is likely to be prejudicial to the public interest in having capital markets that are both fair and efficient. In so doing we must, of necessity, look to past conduct as a guide to what we believe a person's future conduct might reasonably be expected to be; we are not prescient, after all.
>
> (*Mithras, supra* at pp. 1610-1611)

[143] These principles are relevant to our consideration of the Applicants' requests for continued registration under the Act.

2. Registration Under the Act

[144] The registration requirement for an individual or firm seeking to act as a dealer or dealing representative is set out in subsection 25(1) of the Act ... .

[145] It is well established that registration is a privilege, not a right, that is granted to individuals and entities that have demonstrated their suitability for registration (see *Re Trend Capital Services Inc.* (1992), 15 O.S.C.B. 1711 at p. 1765 ("*Trend*"); *Istanbul* [*Re Istanbul* (2008), 31 OSCB 3799] ... at para. 60; *Sawh, supra* at para. 142).

[146] Section 28 of the Act permits the Director to revoke or suspend, or to impose terms and conditions upon, a registration under the Act, if certain considerations are met. ...

[147] On its face, section 28 of the Act provides three bases for determining whether revocation or suspension of registration or imposition of terms and conditions are appropriate. The first basis is a determination that the person or company is not suitable for registration. The second is a determination that the person or company failed to comply with Ontario securities law. The third and last ground is a determination that the registration is otherwise objectionable. These three tests, if met, are separate bases for a remedy. Thus, a finding that one of these bases has been met is sufficient grounds for revocation or suspension of registration or imposition of terms and conditions, though the decision is ultimately a discretionary one.

(a) Suitability for Continued Registration

[148] Section 28 of the Act does not define how a registrant could be determined to be "not suitable." Therefore, in determining whether an individual or company is unsuitable for registration pursuant to subsection 28(a) of the Act, we are guided by the terms of section 27 of the Act, which addresses the test to be applied to an application for registration. Section 27 of the Act states:

27(1) Registration, etc.—On receipt of an application by a person or company and all information, material and fees required by the Director and the regulations, the Director shall register the person or company, reinstate the registration of the person or company or amend the registration of the person or company, unless it appears to the Director,

(a) that, in the case of a person or company applying for registration, reinstatement of registration or an amendment to a registration, the person or company is *not suitable for registration* under this Act; or

(b) that the proposed registration, reinstatement of registration or amendment to registration is *otherwise objectionable.*

(2) Matters to be considered—In considering for the purposes of subsection (1) *whether a person or company is not suitable for registration, the Director shall consider,*

(a) whether the person or company has satisfied,

(i) the requirements prescribed in the regulations relating to *proficiency, solvency and integrity*, and

(ii) such other requirements for registration, reinstatement of registration or an amendment to a registration, as the case may be, as may be prescribed by the regulations; and

(b) such other factors as the Director considers relevant. …

[149] We accept that the three criteria of proficiency, solvency and integrity for determining whether a person or company is "not suitable" for registration, which have been codified in subsection 27(2) of the Act, have been applied by the Director in other cases when assessing suitability for continued registration under section 28 of the Act and are appropriately considered in this case to determine whether a registrant is not suitable for the purposes of revocation, suspension or the imposition of terms and conditions upon a registration (*Waterview*, … [*Re Waterview Capital Corp* (2011), 34 OSCB 5059] at paras. 18-20).

[150] Requirements of proficiency are prescribed in Part 3 of NI 31-103. Section 2.1 of the OSC Rule 31-505 provides that a registered dealer and its representatives "shall deal fairly, honestly and in good faith with its clients" and section 1.3 of 31-103CP provides further guidance with respect to integrity and solvency.

[151] Our analysis of the Applicants' suitability for registration begins at paragraph [157].

(b) Failure to Comply with Ontario Securities Law

[152] As noted above, section 28 of the Act permits the Director to revoke or suspend, or to impose terms and conditions upon a registration under the Act, if it appears to the Director that the registrant has failed to comply with Ontario securities law. Accordingly, if the Director finds non-compliance, a registration may be revoked or suspended or terms and conditions may be placed upon it. Whether the Applicants have failed to comply with Ontario securities law is determined by analysis of whether on a balance of probabilities, the conduct of the registrants was not in compliance with the provisions or orders falling within the scope of Ontario securities law.

[153] The definition of "Ontario securities law" in subsection 1(1) of the Act includes: (a) the Act, (b) regulations made under the Act, and (c) a decision of the Commission or

a Director to which a person or company is subject. We note that this definition on its face is not confined to the provisions of the Act governing registration. However, compliance with those provisions would be expected as an aspect of the obligations of registration.

[154] Our analysis of whether the Applicants failed to comply with Ontario securities law begins at paragraph [262].

(c) Whether Continued Registration Is Otherwise Objectionable

[155] Section 28 of the Act does not define the concept of "otherwise objectionable." We adopt the view from Sawh that a purposive approach should be taken to the analysis of whether registration would be "otherwise objectionable" in light of the Commission's mandate, as expressed in section 1.1 of the Act to: (a) provide protection to investors from unfair, improper or fraudulent practices; and (b) foster fair and efficient capital markets and confidence in capital markets (*Sawh, supra* at para. 289).

[156] We address whether the continued registration of the Applicants is otherwise objectionable at paragraph [277].

B. Are the Applicants Suitable for Continued Registration?

[157] The three criteria for determining suitability for registration for the purpose of section 28 of the Act are codified in subsection 27(2) of the Act. These are whether the person or company has satisfied the requirements prescribed in NI 31-103 and OSC Rule 31-505 relating to proficiency, solvency and integrity (Subsection 27(2)(a)(i) of the Act).

[158] Staff's submissions did not focus on whether the Applicants currently lack financial solvency. The analysis of whether the Applicants are suitable to continue being registered will therefore focus on the application of both the proficiency and integrity criteria, established by subsection 27(2) of the Act and interpreted by previous case law (see for example, *Istanbul, supra* at para. 65), to the Applicants.

[159] In determining whether the Applicants are suitable for continued registration, their past conduct is relevant because it assists in determining whether the Applicants are likely to meet the standards of suitability imposed by Ontario securities law now and in the future (*Mithras, supra* at pp. 1610-1611; *Sawh, supra* at para. 157). Accordingly, the past conduct of the Applicants will be assessed against the statutory requirements existing at the time of the conduct. This analysis of past conduct will form one of the bases for determining whether the Applicants are suitable for registration under the current regulatory regime. In addition, the Applicants' evidence tendered at the Hearing and Review provides us with additional grounds for making the determination as to the Applicants' continued suitability for registration.

1. Characterizing Issues of Proficiency and/or Integrity

[160] The Applicants urge the panel to consider this to be a case of proficiency only. Specifically, the Applicants submit that four of the seven alleged compliance deficiencies, those relating to conflicts of interest, failure to report capital deficiencies, misrepresentation and trading without registration, are matters of proficiency rather than integrity. Staff disagrees with the Applicants characterization of these four issues. Both sides agree that the remaining three of the alleged compliance deficiencies relate to proficiency.

[161] Based on our review of the conduct at issue, we disagree with the Applicants' view that matters of integrity are not implicated in this case. We also do not agree that Staff has incorrectly identified matters of proficiency as matters of integrity.

[162] Many of the compliance deficiencies raised by Staff in this case may be accurately characterized as matters involving both proficiency and integrity. The two criteria for determining suitability need not be mutually exclusive or considered strictly in watertight compartments.

[163] Certain fact situations engage considerations of both proficiency and integrity. For instance, the inability to identify a conflict of interest may be a proficiency issue because proper identification requires the application of judgment in relation to the potentially competing interests of dealers and clients. The ultimate handling of a conflict may reflect on both proficiency in the application of the registered firm's compliance policies and the integrity of the registrant in their dealings with clients and appropriately responding to conflicts. The choice not to disclose a conflict of interest, particularly once it has been brought to a registrant's attention, may raise questions about a registrant's integrity.

[164] Whether an issue is characterized as a matter of proficiency, of integrity or both, the Commission may consider the circumstances and issue an appropriate remedy. The Applicants take the position that only matters of integrity merit periods of suspension to serve purposes of general and specific deterrence (citing *Istanbul*, *supra* at paras. 72-73 and 79-80; *Obasi*, *supra* at paras. 1, 30-32; *DiPronio*, *supra*). The Applicants' submissions seem to imply that issues of proficiency can always be addressed with education and supervision and, therefore, should not trigger suspension of a registration. We do not agree with the submission that only matters of integrity merit periods of suspension. In appropriate circumstances, a lack of proficiency may require regulatory responses beyond that of education and supervision.

[165] We find that the Director accurately noted that in this case "many of the issues were both integrity and proficiency issues" (Director's decision, *supra* at para. 4). We will address the alleged compliance deficiencies in turn and, if necessary, expand further on the appropriate characterization of each in our analysis below.

2. *Legal Frameworks Relating to Integrity and Proficiency*

(a) Integrity

[166] The term integrity is not defined under the Act. It is not disputed that the Commission has adopted the view that analysis of the integrity requirement involves consideration of "the honesty and character of the applicant" (*Istanbul*, *supra* at para. 66, citing *Wall*, *supra* at para. 23). The Commission in Istanbul stated that an assessment of integrity should be "guided by the criteria set out in paragraph 2.1(1)(iii) [now 2.1(2)(iii)] of the Act" (*Istanbul*, *supra* at para. 68). Subsection 2.1(2)(iii) of the Act states that the Commission shall have regard to fundamental principles, including "the maintenance of high standards of fitness and business conduct to ensure honest and responsible conduct by market participants."

[167] OSC Rule 31-505 imposes a standard of integrity on registered dealers. Specifically, section 2.1 of OSC Rule 31-505 provides that:

> 2.1 General Duties—
>
> (1) A registered dealer or adviser shall deal fairly, honestly and in good faith with its clients.
>
> (2) A representative of a registered dealer or registered adviser shall deal fairly, honestly and in good faith with his or her clients.

[168] We agree with the Applicants that section 1.3 of 31-103CP provides guidance on the matter of integrity requirements for registrants. It states that:

...

> **(b) Integrity**
>
> Registered individuals must conduct themselves with integrity and have an honest character. The regulator will assess the integrity of individuals through the information they are required to provide on registration application forms and as registrants, and through compliance reviews. For example, applicants are required to disclose information about conflicts of interest, such as other employment or partnerships, service as a member of a board of directors, or relationships with affiliates, and about any regulatory or legal actions against them.

[169] In our view, the regulatory framework contemplates an assessment of whether or not a firm has acted with integrity (*Waterview*, *supra* at para. 22, citing *Re Carter Securities Inc.* (2010), 33 O.S.C.B. 8691 at para. 87 ("*Carter*")). Although a firm may show its integrity in different ways, it has the capacity to demonstrate its integrity through, among other things, its compliance with Ontario securities law, its internal policies, and the attributes of persons carrying out specific roles within the firm. Thus, it is appropriate to consider in this case whether Sterling has demonstrated an appropriate level of integrity to remain registered. For the purposes of this analysis, the actions of Casale are attributable to Sterling. Given Casale's positions as UDP, CCO, dealing representative, sole shareholder and directing mind of Sterling, we were unable to distinguish between the Applicants.

[170] In assessing the integrity of applicants for registration, the Commission has considered factors including, the person or company's dealings with clients, compliance with Ontario securities laws and the use of prudent business practices (*Wall*, *supra* at para. 23; cited in *Istanbul*, *supra* at para. 66 and *Sawh*, *supra* at para. 257). In our view, those considerations are equally applicable in matters of whether a registration should be suspended or revoked or whether it is appropriate to impose terms and conditions upon it. We agree that an individual's honesty and candour in their dealings with the Commission is also a relevant consideration with respect to integrity (*Pyasetsky Director's Decision*, *supra* at paras. 17-18).

[171] We agree with the finding of a director of the Alberta Securities Commission in *John Doe* that the concept of integrity invoked in the registration regime is broader than dishonesty. Rather, it encompasses a duty of care and while a registrant may not be dishonest, he or she may "be reckless or lackadaisical over whether one complies with the rules or requirements of one's industry" (*Re John Doe* (2010), 33 O.S.C.B. 1371 at para. 37, citing *Re Doe* (2007), ABASC 296).

(b) Proficiency

[172] Registrants have an important function in the capital markets and proficiency requirements are established to ensure that the public deals with qualified persons or companies (*Michalik, supra* at para. 48). Proficiency requirements also support, promote and enhance the purposes of the Act, which include protecting the investing public by maintaining high standards of fitness and business conduct (*Sawh, supra* at para. 158).

[173] Subsection 3.4(1) of NI 31-103 sets out the proficiency requirement that: "[a]n individual must not perform an activity that requires registration unless the individual has the education, training and experience that a reasonable person would consider necessary to perform the activity competently." In *Michalik*, the Commission noted in reference to section 1.5 of OSC Rule 31-505, the precursor to subsection 13.2(2) of NI 31-103, that registrants are required to apply the "know your client" and "suitability" standards in carrying out their functions and, therefore, that they must meet the proficiency requirements to apply these standards (*Michalik, supra* at para. 23).

[174] In their submissions, Staff does not contest that the Applicants have enough education or experience to be considered suitable for registration. However, the evidence presented at the Hearing and Review raises the issue of whether Staff has satisfied us that the Applicants are lacking proficiency in fulfilling the know-your-client, suitability or know-your-product obligations required of an EMD as well as appropriate reliance on permissible exemptions from prospectus requirements.

[175] Consistent with our analysis above at paragraph [169], for the purposes of our assessment of proficiency the actions of Casale are attributable to Sterling, as she is and was the directing mind of the firm. Our conclusions on proficiency below are applicable to Sterling as a registered firm and Casale as a dealing representative.

. . .

(e) Know-Your-Client and Suitability Obligations

[215] The Commission has repeatedly recognized that the know-your-client and suitability requirements are essential to the investor protection purpose of the Act and "a basic obligation of a registrant" (*Re Daubney* (2008), 31 O.S.C.B. 4817 ("*Daubney*") at para. 15, citing *Re E.A. Manning Ltd.* (1995), 18 O.S.C.B. 5317 at p. 5339). We note that in this section of our decision the term "suitability" refers to a registrant's assessment of whether an investment is suitable for a client and ought not be confused with the overall analysis of the Applicants' suitability for continued registration.

[216] In *Daubney*, the Commission recognized that "KYC" and "suitability" obligations are conceptually distinct, but so closely connected and interwoven that the terms are at times used interchangeably (*Daubney, supra* at para. 16 citing *Re Lamoureux* (2001), ABSECCOM 813127 at p. 10). In that matter, the Commission accepted the Alberta Securities Commission finding in *Lamoureux* that:

> The "know your client" obligation is the obligation to learn about the client, their personal financial situation, financial sophistication and investment experience, investment objectives and risk tolerance.
>
> The "suitability" obligation is the obligation of a registrant to determine whether an investment is appropriate for a particular client. Assessment of suitability requires both that

the registrant understands the investment product and knows enough about the client to assess whether the product and client are a match.

(*Ibid.*)

[217] The know-your-client requirements are found in subsection 13.2(2) of NI 31-103, which provides:

> 13.2 Know your client— …
> (2) A registrant must take reasonable steps to
> (a) establish the identity of a client and, if the registrant has cause for concern, make reasonable inquiries as to the reputation of the client,
> (b) establish whether the client is an insider of a reporting issuer or any other issuer whose securities are publicly traded,
> (c) ensure that it has sufficient information regarding all of the following to enable it to meet its obligations under section 13.3 or, if applicable, the suitability requirement imposed by an SRO:
> (i) the client's investment needs and objectives;
> (ii) the client's financial circumstances;
> (iii) the client's risk tolerance, and
> (d) establish the creditworthiness of the client if the registered firm is financing the client's acquisition of a security.

[218] The Companion Policy, 31-103CP, indicates that registrants act as gatekeepers of the integrity of the capital markets and are required to establish the identity of, and conduct due diligence on, their clients.

[219] Subsection 13.3(1) of NI 31-103 describes the suitability obligation as follows:

> 13.3 Suitability—
> (1) A registrant must take reasonable steps to ensure that, before it makes a recommendation to or accepts an instruction from a client to buy or sell a security, or makes a purchase or sale of a security for a client's managed account, the purchase or sale is suitable for the client.

[220] It is well established that the Commission has adopted a three-stage analysis of suitability, according to which a registrant is obliged to:

a) use due diligence to know the product and know the client;
b) apply sound professional judgement in establishing the suitability of the product for the client; and
c) disclose the negative as well as the positive aspects of the proposed investment.

(*Re Foresight Capital Corp.*, 2007 BCSECCOM 101 at para. 52; cited in *Daubney*, *supra* at para. 17, *Sawh*, *supra* at para. 165 and *North American*, *supra* at para. 274)

[221] It is worth noting that guidance in section 13.3 of 31-103CP expressly states that registrants may not "delegate their suitability obligations" or "satisfy the suitability obligation by simply disclosing the risks involved with a trade."

[222] The consequence of the requirements in subsection 13.3(1) of NI 31-103 is that a registrant cannot fulfill these obligations by conducting an assessment of suitability after the trade has occurred. Not only does section 13.3 of NI 31-103 expressly say this, but to assess suitability after the securities are sold would undermine the goal of the suitability

analysis because the registrant would not actually be matching the product to the client's circumstances, objectives and risk tolerance at the appropriate time. The obligation on the registrant is to make a suitability assessment. The approach employed by the Applicants prevents the application of appropriate judgment in matching a product to a client's circumstances when the investment decision is made.

. . .

4. Findings on the Continued Suitability of the Applicants

[259] We find that the Applicants' failure to appropriately identify and disclose the conflicts or potential conflicts of interest resulting from their relationships with issuers on whose behalf they sell or have sold securities does not meet the "high standards of fitness and business conduct to ensure honest and responsible conduct by market participants" (subsection 2.1(2)(iii) of the Act) and does not fulfill the requirement to deal fairly, honestly and in good faith with clients (section 2.1 of the OSC Rule 31-505). The Applicants' failure to report and be forthright with Staff about their working capital deficiencies demonstrates a lack of integrity. Furthermore, Casale impugned her integrity by making misrepresentations to Staff with respect to (i) Sterling's capital deficiencies in April and May 2012, as well as (ii) the Applicants' involvement in the Gingko distribution to the 22 Investors. Finally, the Applicants' lack of compliance with the requirement to be appropriately registered to engage in trading activities is a further example of a lack of responsible conduct, which contributes to our concerns about the Applicants' integrity. Taken as a whole, these issues cause us significant concern with regard to the Applicants' suitability for continued registration.

[260] The Applicants failed to demonstrate an adequate understanding of the proper fulfilment of KYC and suitability obligations or how to assess whether investors qualified for exemptions. As a result of the Applicants' failure to meet their know-your-client and suitability obligations and failure to properly apply the AI exemption, some of their clients invested in high risk exempt products that were either not suitable or for which the Applicants had insufficient information to determine suitability. We find that these failures were not isolated or purely administrative, but reflected a lack of comprehension about the purpose and objectives of the regulations and therefore a lack of proficiency. This concern is exacerbated by the willingness of Casale and Sterling to perform "dealer after the fact" roles, which amounts to an abdication of the investor protection objectives of Ontario securities law. We find that the Applicants do not have the proficiency to continue being registered.

[261] Viewed in its entirety, the evidence shows that the Applicants fell below the standards required of registrants. The testimony of M.B. and the investors' letters of risk acknowledgement reveal that Casale, on behalf of Sterling, had successfully developed professional relationships with a number of clients. Unfortunately, neither of the Applicants exercised the required level of judgment and responsibility to consistently uphold the regulatory requirements concerning the obligations of registrants to their clients. In sum, we find that the Applicants lack the integrity and proficiency to continue being registered.

D. Surrender of Registration

Registered persons or companies that wish to cease to be a registrant are required to make an application to their securities regulator for surrender of their registration. Such applications are included in the Passport System, so must be made in accordance with MI 11-102 to the firm's principal regulator, and to Ontario if the registrant is registered there and Ontario is not its non-principal jurisdiction. There is no prescribed form for an application to surrender, but the application must include sufficient evidence and supporting documentation to allow the regulators to properly assess whether the statutory requirements for surrender are met and that granting the application is in the public interest.

The application to surrender will be accepted if the regulator is satisfied that the person or company has met all financial obligations to his, her, or its clients, that any other requirements prescribed by the regulations have been or will be appropriately fulfilled and that the surrender of the registration is not prejudicial to the public interest. Regulators are not obliged to accept an application to surrender registration and may instead decide to reject such an application or to impose any terms and conditions that they consider appropriate in the circumstances (OSA, s 30; NP 31-103).

QUESTIONS

Why have provincial governments given regulators such discretion with respect to the imposition of terms and conditions, suspension, and revocation of registrants? What are the arguments against such discretion?

V. CRITIQUES OF THE CURRENT SYSTEM AND REFORM PROPOSALS

A. Fragmentation in the Oversight of the Financial Advice Market

As discussed in the introduction to this chapter, Canada's system of regulation with respect to financial products is highly decentralized, with several fields of financial service, including banking, securities, pensions, and insurance, all regulated separately, some federally and some provincially.

What individual investors would reasonably consider "financial advice" and "financial planning" can include interactions with advisers from a broad range of fields overseen by an equally broad range of regulators, while some people providing financial planning and advice are subject to no regulatory oversight. General "financial planning" advice can be provided by any person and is not a regulated activity. In 2013, the Ontario government launched an initiative to investigate whether individuals engaged in financial planning and giving financial advice should be subject to regulatory oversight. This initiative led to the appointment of an expert committee, mandated to provide advice and recommendations in a final report to the government in 2016. The expert committee undertook extensive public consultations and developed a number of policy recommendations, which were published in April 2016. Several of these are excerpted below.

Financial Advisory and Financial Planning Policy Alternatives: Preliminary Policy Recommendations of the Expert Committee to Consider Financial Advisory and Financial Planning Policy Alternatives
(5 April 2016) (footnotes omitted)

D. Our Preliminary Policy Recommendations

We have put forward eight preliminary policy recommendations for reform together with a list of issues for further consideration. In making these preliminary recommendations, we are guided by our core principles and the clearly articulated need for change. In determining these recommendations, we settled on broad definitions of key terms in order to preclude individuals or firms from evading consumer-focused regulatory protections by characterizing their services as falling outside the scope of our recommendations.

The following preliminary policy recommendations are presented with a view to inviting further public input. We will take into account input from the upcoming consultation process in preparing our final report for the Ontario government. This consultation process is outlined in Section E below.

1. Regulation of Financial Planning in Ontario

We recommend that Financial Planning in Ontario be regulated as follows:

a. Regulation should be required of any individual who or firm that provides Financial Planning services either expressly or implicitly through Holding Out by way of titles, described services or otherwise;
b. Individuals who and firms that provide Financial Planning and whose Financial Product Sales and Advice activities are regulated by the existing regulatory framework for securities, insurance and mortgage brokering should have any associated Financial Planning activities regulated by their existing regulator or regulators for those who have more than one licence; and
c. Individuals or firms performing Financial Planning activities outside the current regulatory framework should have their Financial Planning activities regulated by the proposed Financial Services Regulatory Authority (FSRA).

Rationale: In response to our initial consultation, multiple parties emphasized the need to leverage the existing regulatory framework and avoid regulatory duplication that could prove costly for businesses and, ultimately, consumers. As a committee, we were mindful of the core principles outlined in our Initial Consultation Document that include consideration for regulatory efficiency and sensitivity to existing policy initiatives. In our deliberations, we considered the possibility of recommending a new regulatory body to undertake the regulation of Financial Planning by individuals or firms not otherwise regulated. We believe that the number of individuals and firms that provide Financial Planning services on a stand-alone basis would be too small to warrant the costs associated with a new regulatory body. We believe that the better approach is to recommend regulation of Financial Planning as a discreet activity within the existing regulatory framework. In our view, an Ontario-based integrated regulator of financial services, such as the proposed FSRA, is well-suited to bring stand-alone providers of Financial Planning services into the regulatory fold and work with other Regulators to achieve the harmonization of standards outlined in the ensuing recommendation.

2. *Harmonization of Standards*

We recommend that the education, training, credentialing and licensing of individuals engaged in the provision of Financial Planning be harmonized and subject to one universal set of regulatory standards.

Rationale: A recurring theme raised by commenters was the broad spectrum of qualifications and expertise possessed by individuals currently offering Financial Planning services in Ontario. From the consumer's point of view, it is difficult to navigate through the various credentials to ascertain their Financial Planning services providers' qualifications. This dynamic is exacerbated in an environment where many consumers rely heavily on a Financial Planning services provider to guide their financial decisions in order to yield improved financial security. It is essential, therefore, that providers of Financial Planning services possess a minimum level of proficiency and expertise. Since Financial Planning encompasses various sectors, we recommend that Regulators work cooperatively to develop a harmonized set of regulatory standards (including, if necessary, approving appropriate credentials) that apply consistently to all providers of this activity.

3. *Statutory Best Interest Duty*

We recommend that a Statutory Best Interest Duty (SBID) be adopted and applied to all individuals who and firms that provide Financial Product Sales and Advice and/or Financial Planning in Ontario. This SBID should be based on a uniform and codified standard of care.

Rationale: Currently, in Ontario, providers of Financial Product Sales and Advice and/or Financial Planning services are not subject to an explicit statutory requirement to act in their client's best interest. While Financial Planning as an activity is not subject to a general regulatory framework, the provision of Financial Product Sales and Advice generally is subject to know-your-client and suitability requirements—these requirements vary across sectors. As noted by multiple commenters, the focus of the suitability standards is limited to the sale of a Financial Product. Yet consumers expect to receive financial advice from an individual who is acting in their best interest. Commenters highlighted, however, that this expectation exists in a commission-oriented sales environment that may give rise to a Conflict in the recommendations provided to consumers. Multiple submissions noted that advisors may recommend products which are not in fact in the best interest of clients and that product recommendations are influenced by commissions. We believe that consumers who receive Financial Product Sales and Advice and/or Financial Planning services should receive those services from individuals who and firms that have a statutory duty to act in the consumer's best interest. Applying a SBID would make clear the legal duty of care and significantly reduce, if not eliminate, confusion (for consumers as well as individuals and firms that provide Financial Product Sales and Advice and/or Financial Planning) about whether a duty to act in the best interest of the client applies in a given situation. It would also bring regulatory requirements in line with consumer expectations.

. . .

6. *Titles and Holding Out*

We recommend that the use of titles by individuals and firms engaged in the provision of Financial Product Sales and Advice and/or Financial Planning be prescribed in order to reduce consumer confusion. Specifically, we recommend that:

a. Regulators work together to develop a circumscribed list of approved titles that are descriptive of the regulated activities and that these are the only titles permitted to be used by individuals and firms in their Financial Product Sales and Advice and/or Financial Planning activities;
b. Use of the title "Financial Planner," whether explicitly or by Holding Out that this service is being provided, is circumscribed to individuals regulated as outlined in Recommendations 1 and 2 above;
c. Individual designations, qualifications, and credentials (other than professional, academic qualifications, and those approved by the Regulators) are not permitted; and
d. Those engaged in providing Financial Product Sales and Advice and/or Financial Planning are not permitted to use corporate positions or titles given the consumer confusion that results and can result from the use of such titles.

Rationale: A prevalent theme raised by a number of commenters was the multitude of titles used in Ontario's financial services industry and the resulting scope for consumer confusion. There are currently no uniform or universal regulatory standards regarding the use of titles and Holding Out. Rather, the use of titles and Holding Out are in the hands of the individuals or firms who provide Financial Product Sales and Advice and/or Financial Planning services which leads to confusion. Individuals refer to themselves by a range of different titles, such as "financial advisor," "wealth advisor," "retirement planner," "wealth coach" and employ other similar types of titles, none of which are currently subject to regulatory constraint or standardization. This practice benefits neither the financial services industry nor its consumers. Our recommendation is intended to mitigate the noise, allowing consumers an opportunity to more easily identify professionals who can help them meet their financial goals.

B. Standard of Conduct

In 2012, the CSA released a consultation paper examining whether regulators should impose a statutory duty on dealers and advisers to act in the best interests of their clients when providing advice to retail investors. Below is an excerpt from that consultation paper outlining the background and rationale for the proposed changes.

Canadian Securities Administrators Consultation Paper 33-403, *The Standard of Conduct for Advisers and Dealers: Exploring the Appropriateness of Introducing a Statutory Best Interest Duty When Advice Is Provided to Retail Clients*
(25 October 2012) (footnotes omitted)

2) Background

The 2008 global financial crisis and its aftermath have generated significant debate on the standard of conduct that advisers and dealers owe to their clients when they provide advice on investing in financial products. The principal question is whether advisers and dealers should have an obligation to act in the best interests of their clients when providing advice to them. Several related questions have featured prominently in this debate, including:

- What are the current obligations of an adviser/dealer when providing advice to a client?
- Do investors and advisers/dealers understand the nature of their relationship?
- Do investors believe (and expect) that their advisers and dealers act in their best interests?
- Would a best interest standard affect the different compensation structures of advisers and dealers?
- What problems would be solved by the introduction of a statutory best interest standard for advisers and dealers?
- If a best interest standard were imposed, in what circumstances should it apply?

Against this backdrop, several international securities regulators are reconsidering the relationship between clients and the advisors who provide them with advice on investing in securities. This has included an examination of the standard of conduct applicable to advisers and dealers and/or consideration of some of the core elements of this relationship, such as how conflicts of interest, compensation structures and proficiency should be addressed and whether a statutory fiduciary (or best interest) duty should be imposed. In this respect, the U.K. and E.U. already impose a qualified best interest standard on their advisors, Australia has passed legislation making such a standard mandatory by July 1, 2013, and in the U.S., staff of the U.S. Securities and Exchange Commission (SEC) has recommended such a uniform standard be introduced for broker-dealers and investment advisers although both a detailed SEC cost-benefit analysis and an SEC draft rule have yet to be completed.

The standard of conduct debate occurring in other international jurisdictions has also arisen in Canada. There have been several Canadian conferences on the topic of whether Canada should, or should not, impose a statutory fiduciary duty on advisers and dealers. At an early such conference hosted by Canadian Foundation for Advancement of Investor Rights (FAIR Canada) and the Hennick Centre for Business and Law (York University), there appeared to be a lack of consensus on many of the important issues surrounding the possible imposition of a fiduciary duty. For example, the panellists did not agree on what a fiduciary duty encompasses, when it should apply and whether the current regulatory regime for advisers and dealers is functionally equivalent to such a standard, in any event. Regardless, most of the experts agreed that if a fiduciary duty is imposed, it is important to clearly address the expectations around the standard of conduct expected of advisers and dealers in providing advice.

The fiduciary duty debate in Canada is an important one. The debate has highlighted the need to consider enhancements to investor protection where advice is being given to investors since it is the advice that will often determine a client's decision to invest.

. . .

For the purposes of this Consultation Paper, when we refer to a "statutory" fiduciary duty or best interest standard, we mean any such duty that may be imposed under the securities laws, regulations, instruments or rules of a jurisdiction of Canada (Securities Legislation).

3) Fiduciary Duty: What It Is and When It Arises at Common Law

Fiduciary Duty—An Overview

A fiduciary duty is a duty of a person to act in another person's *best interests.* For our purposes, a fiduciary duty applicable to an adviser or dealer means that the adviser or dealer (the fiduciary) would have to act in the best interests of her client. In general, acting in your client's best interest means that the fiduciary must ensure that:

- Client interests are paramount,
- Conflicts of interest are avoided,
- Clients are not exploited,
- Clients are provided with full disclosure, and
- Services are performed reasonably prudently.

. . .

When Does a Fiduciary Duty Arise at Common Law?

In addition to the content of a fiduciary duty, it is important to understand when a fiduciary duty arises at common law. To understand this, one must understand the underlying purpose of fiduciary law. Canadian courts have recognized that the underlying purpose of fiduciary law is to "maintain the integrity of socially and economically valuable or necessary relationships of high trust and confidence that are essential for the effective interdependent functioning of society."

In certain types of relationships (lawyer/client, doctor/patient, trustee/beneficiary), a fiduciary duty presumptively arises at common law (these are called *per se* fiduciary relationships). In all other kinds of relationships (including investor advisory relationships whether the relationship is fiduciary in nature depends on the nature of the relationship. Courts will determine whether a fiduciary relationship exists based on the factual circumstances of the relationship (these are called *ad hoc* fiduciary relationships).

Canadian courts have identified five interrelated factors to be considered when determining whether "financial advisors" stand in a fiduciary relationship to their clients:

1. *Vulnerability:* the degree of vulnerability of the client due to such things as age or lack of language skills, investment knowledge, education or experience in the stock market.

2. *Trust:* the degree of trust and confidence that a client reposes in the advisor and the extent to which the advisor accepts that trust.
3. *Reliance:* whether there is a history of relying on the advisor's judgment and advice and whether the advisor holds him or herself out as having special skills and knowledge upon which the client can rely.
4. *Discretion:* the extent to which the advisor has power or discretion over the client's account or investments.
5. *Professional Rules or Codes of Conduct:* such rules and codes help to establish the duties of the advisor and the standards to which the advisor will be held.

These five factors are not intended to be exhaustive and evidence relevant to one factor may be relevant to a consideration of one or more of the other factors.

Fiduciary Duty Created by Statute

. . .

We believe that a statutory fiduciary duty would likely support a private law cause of action for damages by a beneficiary against a fiduciary for breach of the duty, because it establishes the nature of the relationship and therefore eliminates the need to prove the existence of a fiduciary duty. For additional discussion on this, see the section entitled "Strengthens legal remedy to retail clients for breach of fiduciary duty" in Part 8 below.

Conclusion

We believe that imposing a statutory duty on an adviser or dealer to "act in the best interests" of clients constitutes imposing a fiduciary duty. It is a separate question whether certain of the elements of a fiduciary duty referred to above should be qualified to take into account the particular circumstances and business models of advisers and dealers. Any statutory best interest duty imposed under Securities Legislation should address such issues. For further discussion, see Part 8 below.

Because acting in a client's "best interests" is at the heart of a fiduciary duty, we will generally refer in this Consultation Paper to a fiduciary duty as a "best interest" standard or duty.

. . .

6) Key Investor Protection Concerns with the Current Standard of Conduct in Canada

CSA staff has identified the following five key investor protection concerns with the current standard of conduct applicable to advisers and dealers in Canada. The applicability and significance of each concern in each CSA jurisdiction likely depends on the existing standard of conduct existing in each CSA jurisdiction.

Concerns At-a-Glance

1) There may be an inadequate principled foundation for the standard of conduct owed to clients.

2) The current standard of conduct may not fully account for the information and financial literacy asymmetry between advisers and dealers and their retail clients.

3) There is an expectation gap because investors incorrectly assume that their adviser/dealer must always give advice that is in their best interests.

4) Advisers/dealers must recommend suitable investments but not necessarily investments that are in the client's best interests.

5) The application in practice of the current conflicts of interest rules might be less effective than intended.

These concerns are more fully discussed below.

Concern 1: Principled Foundation

This concern is whether the current standard of conduct of advisers and dealers in respect of their clients is based on the most principled foundation. Some commentators believe that the principle underlying the current statutory standard of conduct is that advisory services are just like any other business transaction or interaction where the principles of "buyer beware," supported by prescriptive prohibitions and key disclosure requirements, are sufficient.

However, advice for investing in securities is arguably not just like any other business transaction or interaction (certainly when advisers and dealers are advising retail investors) because:

- many investors place substantial trust, confidence and reliance on the financial advice they receive (see further discussion below on this point),
- there is often information and financial literacy asymmetry between advisers/dealers and their clients (see further discussion below on this point),
- these issues are compounded by the increasing complexity of financial products and the fact that many financial products must be "sold" to, not "bought" by, investors,
- adviser and dealer compensation arrangements can create a conflict of interest between the interests of advisers and dealers and their clients, and
- amounts invested often constitute a major portion of investors' wealth and responsibility for funding the costs of living during old age is shifting more to investors.

Concern 2: Information and Financial Literacy Asymmetry

Despite the CSA's new and proposed rules around disclosure to investors (such as the new "fund facts" disclosure document for mutual funds and, as part of CRM, the cost disclosure and performance reporting initiative, advisers and dealers usually have more knowledge and information about the financial products they recommend to their clients.

Furthermore, the latest research available suggests that the poor financial literacy of investors remains a stubborn problem in Canada even though investors themselves want to improve in this area. This concern is not unique to Canada; securities regulators in other jurisdictions have also noted similar concerns about the poor financial literacy or capabilities of their investors.

Although financial literacy is a problem in and of itself, it becomes of greater concern when combined with (i) the information asymmetry referred to above, (ii) a general conflict of interest regime that relies heavily on disclosure, (iii) tacit approval by investors of compensation practices based on disclosure, (iv) the explicit or implicit suggestion by some advisers and dealers that they act in their client's best interests when they may not have a legal obligation to do so, and (v) cognitive biases on the part of investors that impair rational decision making.

Concern 3: Standard of Conduct Expectation Gap

The Investor Education Fund (IEF) recently completed an extensive study of approximately 2,000 Canadian investors that receive investment advice in respect of a non-discretionary account from an adviser or dealer (the IEF Study). The IEF identified a number of issues that are important for understanding the expectations and needs of investors in an advisory relationship.

The IEF Study provides strong evidence that most investors already believe that their adviser or dealer is required to act in their best interests. In the IEF Study, 70% of investors surveyed indicated that they believed that their adviser or dealer has a legal duty to put the client's best interests ahead of their own. Further, 76% of investors surveyed stated that they can trust their adviser or dealer to give them the best possible advice they can, with most investors believing that their adviser or dealer would identify the investments that are best for them. Finally, 62% of investors surveyed believed that their adviser or dealer would recommend the product that is best for the investor even if it resulted in less compensation for the adviser or dealer.

These findings are of concern because, as discussed above, advisers and dealers are not always legally required to act in their clients' best interests. These results indicate a significant gap between the expectations of investors and the actual legal protection that exists. Further, these expectations of investors are often created and reinforced by the advertising and promotional statements made by some advisers and dealers.

Concern 4: Recommendation of Suitable Investments Versus Investments in the Client's Best Interests

As noted above, under the current securities regime, advisers and dealers must ensure that, when they advise their clients about investing in securities, the investments are suitable. This is a lower standard than having to ensure that a purchase or sale of securities is in the client's best interests.

In practice, an adviser or dealer can often reasonably conclude that a large number of investment products are suitable for her client. In the face of so many "suitable" options, the adviser or dealer may be tempted to select a "suitable" product that is not necessarily the best one for the client.

This may result in investors acquiring a "suitable" investment but at an inflated price. Even slightly higher fees can have a significant negative impact on the value of a client's investment portfolio over the long term. Similarly, a suitability standard could have the effect of the client acquiring an investment that may be suitable but in circumstances in which another investment at the same price may be a better investment for the investor.

Concern 5: The Application in Practice of the Current Conflicts of Interest Rules Might Be Less Effective Than Intended

The intention of Canadian securities regulators in adopting the current principle-based rules in NI 31-103 regarding conflicts of interest was to ensure that clients receive meaningful disclosure about conflicts of interest without imposing unnecessary regulatory burdens on registrants. CSA staff have the following concerns with the effect of these rules on retail investors in practice:

a) First, CSA staff in certain jurisdictions have identified (in normal course compliance reviews) certain concerns with how the conflict rules are interpreted by some advisers and dealers in practice. For example, some firms narrowly interpret the current principles-based regulatory approach for dealing with conflicts of interest such that they (i) fail to appropriately identify and respond to conflicts or (ii) rely too heavily on disclosure (especially where the disclosure may be meaningless for the client). Further, some firms take the position that once disclosure is provided, the adviser or dealer need not comply with the general standard of conduct that would otherwise apply. This in turn can lead to situations where the interests of advisers and dealers are not aligned with the interests of their clients.
b) Second, commissions paid by issuers (or their agents) to advisers and dealers for recommending the issuer's securities may constitute such a fundamental conflict of interest that regulators should consider how best to mitigate this risk (e.g. prohibiting some or all "embedded" commissions; requiring more effective disclosure). The UK and Australia have directly addressed this issue in their reforms described above. The CSA is currently considering fee arrangements in the mutual fund industry as a separate policy initiative.
c) Third, how advisers and dealers respond to conflicts of interest involving their recommendations to buy, hold or sell securities in related or connected issuers could be strengthened. For example, a common business model for exempt market dealers is that they exclusively distribute the securities of related or connected issuers. Another example is the common practice of advisers and dealers recommending the purchase of securities of mutual funds that are related or connected. While NI 31-103 does currently include rules in this regard, these rules only apply to clients in managed accounts and/or rely on disclosure to manage the conflict. Further consideration is required to determine whether a stronger, more prescriptive approach is appropriate.

. . .

7) Consultation on the Appropriateness of Introducing a Statutory Best Interest Duty When Advice Is Provided to Retail Clients

Why a Statutory Best Interest Standard?

Having considered all of the issues discussed above in this Consultation Paper, CSA staff has decided to undertake a formal consultation on the desirability and feasibility of imposing a statutory best interest standard on advisers and dealers that provide investment advice to retail investors.

Our rationale for considering the imposition of a fiduciary duty at this stage, rather than another policy tool, is that a statutory best interest standard may be the best way to address the five investor protection concerns identified in Part 6 above and appears to offer the benefits, and may be flexible enough to address most or all of the competing considerations, identified in Part 8 below.

We note that each of the foreign jurisdictions that we have reviewed (U.S., U.K., Australia and the E.U.) have identified similar policy concerns and have either adopted a qualified statutory best interest standard (i.e., in the U.K., E.U. and Australia) or are considering adopting one (i.e., in the U.S.). Further, international bodies such as the International Organization of Securities Commissions (IOSCO) and the Organisation for Economic Co-operation and Development (OECD) are clear that financial intermediaries, such as advisers and dealers providing advice, should act in their clients' best interest.{147} While these international developments should not determine Canada's policy direction in this matter, they do support the conclusion that it is time to revisit the standard of conduct framework currently in place for advisers and dealers providing advice to retail investors and determine whether changes are required.

Possible Statutory Best Interest Standard for Consultation Purposes

CSA staff is seeking comment on the desirability and feasibility of introducing a statutory best interest standard for advisers and dealers when providing investment advice to retail investors. For consultation purposes, one possible articulation of this standard would be as follows:

> Every adviser and dealer (and each of their representatives) that provides advice to a retail client with respect to investing in, buying or selling securities or derivatives shall, when providing such advice,
>
> (a) act in the best interests of the retail client, and
>
> (b) exercise the degree of care, diligence and skill that a reasonably prudent person or company would exercise in the circumstances.

Although other articulations of statutory "best interest" duties already exist in certain CSA jurisdictions, as in Québec, we are exploring the possibility of harmonizing the appropriate standard of conduct for advisers and dealers that should apply across Canada. Common law and civil law remain distinct legal regimes, but both cover the same advisory services provided by advisers and dealers to their clients. If such a new harmonized standard of conduct for advisers and dealers in Canada is identified by the CSA, further work would be required, as necessary, to reflect it appropriately in each CSA jurisdiction (including in Québec).

We note that while no decision has been made whether a statutory best interest standard should be adopted, whether another policy solution is preferable, or whether the current regulatory regime is adequate, we believe that a public consultation will be more productive if that consultation focuses on and addresses a specific articulation of a best interest standard. Accordingly, the balance of this Consultation Paper will address the implications of a best interest standard as described above.

General Scope

For the purpose of this Consultation Paper, we will assume that the best interest standard articulated above would have the following terms:

(i) a "retail client" would mean any person or company that is not a "permitted client" (as such term is defined in section 1.1 of NI 31-103). As a result, a "retail client" would include individuals that have net financial assets of $5 million or less and companies that have net assets of less than $25 million;

(ii) a retail client would retain complete discretion whether to follow any advice received; an adviser or dealer who disagrees with the investment decision of a retail client and who has so advised the client, would have no further obligation to dissuade the client or to refuse to facilitate an order;

(iii) the duty would apply only when an adviser or dealer gives advice to a retail investor with respect to investing in securities. Thus, for instance, the duty would not apply to discount brokers who act as mere order takers;

(iv) the duty would be an on-going duty in the case of advisers and dealers other than exempt market dealers and scholarship plan dealers. The duty would terminate only upon the termination of the client relationship;

(v) the best interest standard could not be waived by a retail client as a contractual matter if advice is given to that client;

(vi) a common law retail client would be entitled to enforce the best interest standard as a private law right of action;

(vii) a non retail client would still be entitled to pursue a private law right of action based on the common law (in all Canadian jurisdictions except Québec) and the Civil Code of Québec would not be amended to deprive non retail clients of a right of action; and

(viii) the existing suitability requirement would continue to apply to advisers and dealers (and their representatives).

In addition to publishing this consultation paper, CSA members conducted a number of public and industry consultation meetings. The CSA received 93 comment letters in response to the best-interests-standard consultation paper, from a broad range of stakeholders. In 2013, the CSA published a status report on the consultation, summarizing this stakeholder input.

The stakeholders who commented in support of the introduction of a statutory best-interest standard generally expressed the view that Canada's current regulatory system does not appropriately protect investors, particularly with respect to the adviser–client relationship. In their view, the increasing complexity of financial products and the increasing need for Canadians to manage their own retirement savings, combined with low levels of financial literacy and a general public expectation that financial advisers will act in their clients' interests, together require that a best-interests standard be introduced by regulators. They also observed that such a standard has recently been introduced in other comparable jurisdictions, such as Australia and the United Kingdom, and that Canada is now lagging behind global standards in investor protection. Some commenters also noted that disclosure is not an effective antidote for conflicts of interest, and that adviser titles can be confusing and even misleading. Some also commented that the nature of Canada's current regulatory framework leads to investors receiving overly narrow, transaction-based advice on securities products, rather than holistic financial-planning advice.

The stakeholders who were opposed to the introduction of a statutory best-interest standard argued that the current regulatory framework in Canada already offers a high level of investor protection, including the duty to deal fairly, honestly, and in good faith with clients; obligations regarding investment suitability; extensive licensing and disclosure obligations;

and a fiduciary duty in appropriate circumstances. These commenters also questioned the appropriateness of significant regulatory reform in the absence of clear evidence of investor harm, especially at a time when numerous investor protection reforms have recently been implemented and the outcomes of these reforms have not yet been fully evaluated. Some also expressed the view that the existing suitability standard and duty to act fairly, honestly, and in good faith for their clients, when considered together result in a standard that approximates a best-interest duty, and that a requirement to identify the "best" or "better" products for clients would be subjective and difficult to enforce.

For more detail about the nuances of these opposing positions, see CSA Staff Notice 33-316, Status Report on Consultation under CSA Consultation Paper 33-403, *The Standard of Conduct for Advisers and Dealers: Exploring the Appropriateness of Introducing a Statutory Best Interest Duty When Advice Is Provided to Retail Clients* (17 December 2013).

Ultimately, the 33-403 Status Report concluded that more work was needed to reach a final regulatory outcome with respect to the standard of conduct for dealers and advisers. The work conducted by the CSA included additional consultation and research studies examining various aspects of the relationship between clients and registrants. This led to the publication of Consultation Paper 33-404, *Proposals to Enhance the Obligations of Advisers, Dealers and Representatives Toward Their Clients* (28 April 2016), discussed below.

C. Reforms Proposals

In 2016, the CSA released a further consultation paper exploring a number of specific or targeted reforms relating to the client–registrant relationship as well as additional proposals relating to the introduction of a statutory best-interest standard. In the paper, all CSA jurisdictions expressed the view that significant issues had been identified in the client–registrant relationship that required enhancements of the existing regulatory framework and all jurisdictions put forward a range of targeted reforms designed to improve the existing framework. However, disagreement among the jurisdictions was expressed regarding whether a regulatory best-interest standard should be pursued as a regulatory option, and even whether consultation should be undertaken on the subject.

Canadian Securities Administrators Consultation Paper 33-404, *Proposals to Enhance the Obligations of Advisers, Dealers, and Representatives Toward Their Clients*
(28 April 2016)

Part 5 Key Investor Protection Concerns in Connection with the Client–Registrant Relationship

Based on the evidence gathered to date, we have identified the following key investor protection concerns in Canada:

- *Clients are not getting the value or returns they could reasonably expect from investing:* At least part of the reason for this is the wording of the existing suitability requirement. Failure of registrants to consider all relevant factors, including product costs and investment strategies (such as the use of leverage or choosing active over passive management of assets) in their suitability analysis may prevent clients from meeting the goals of their investment activity.

- *Expectations Gap:* Most investors incorrectly assume that their registrants must always provide advice that is in their best interest. As a result, clients have misplaced reliance or trust on their registrants, resulting in opportunities for some registrants to take advantage of their clients and creating an expectations gap between clients and registrants. Most investors place too much reliance on their registrants, which exacerbates the agency problem inherent in the client-registrant relationship and can result in sub-optimal investments.

  Clients need to understand the nature of the relationship, and what level of trust and reliance they should afford their registrant. The problem of misplaced reliance is exacerbated when registrants (1) use titles or designations that exaggerate their proficiency or the services they actually provide and (2) sell a limited or proprietary shelf of products.
- *Conflicts of Interest:* The application in practice of the current conflicts of interest rules is, in many instances, less effective than intended. Not only is the concern that disclosure may be ineffective in mitigating conflicts of interest, disclosure may have a counter-intuitive effect of increasing reliance on advice where the client is told such advice is, or potentially is, conflicted. Part of the challenge for regulators is identifying when disclosure of conflicts is effective, and when it may exacerbate the conflict situation or is ineffective.
- *Information Asymmetry:* The current regulatory framework is, in many instances, less effective than intended in mitigating the consequences of the information and financial literacy asymmetry between registrants and their retail clients. With the limited financial literacy of most investors, the increasing complexity of securities products and the limited effectiveness of initiatives to improve financial literacy, coupled with the challenge that most investors have in avoiding biases and applying their financial knowledge in their decision making, more onus for prioritizing the client's interest and ensuring that clients understand the information and advice they receive should shift onto registrants.
- *Clients are not getting outcomes that the regulatory system is designed to give them:* There are a number of potential causes of this concern, including opaqueness in the suitability assessment, existing requirements that require more clarity to assist in effective enforcement, barriers to obtaining redress for a registrant breach, and lack of effective compliance and enforcement in certain cases.

1. Targeted Reforms

Consultation Paper 33-404 went on to set out a number of proposed targeted reforms to NI 31-103. The CSA expressed the view that many of these reforms would be consistent with their expectations of registrant conduct under the existing regulatory framework, but that making such expectations explicit would enhance the clarity and enforceability of those expectations. All CSA jurisdictions participated in the consultations on these targeted reforms.

The proposed targeted reforms included:

- Explicit requirements where conflicts of interest have been identified, including a requirement that registrants prioritize the interests of their client ahead of their own interests when responding to material conflicts of interest.
- A requirement that conflict of interest disclosures to clients be "prominent, specific and clear" as well as sufficiently meaningful to the client, and that the client fully understands the conflict and its consequences. Registrants disclosing a conflict of interest must have a reasonable basis for concluding that a client fully understands the implications and consequences of the conflict.
- Increasing the specificity of the know your client requirements by prescribing the nature of the client information that registrants are required to gather in relation to clients' investment needs and objectives, financial circumstances, and risk profile as well as more detailed requirements relating to documentation and record-keeping practices for KYC information.
- Explicit requirements that registrants have sufficient product knowledge and KYC information to support a suitability analysis for every recommendation. Regulations would also describe the specific product features that a registrant must understand and take into consideration, including the product's structure, strategy, features, costs, and risks, as well as how it compares to other products on the firm's product list, and would require registrants to understand and consider the impact of fees and costs on the performance of the product.
- Providing greater specificity regarding the considerations relevant to a determination of suitability in relation to basic financial suitability, investment strategy suitability, and product selection suitability.
- The proposed targeted reforms distinguish between firms that offer proprietary or mixed/non-proprietary product lists. A "proprietary product list" would be defined as a product list that includes only products proprietary to the firm. A "mixed/non-proprietary product list" would be a product list that includes either both proprietary and non-proprietary products or only non-proprietary products. Firms would be required to clearly disclose to their clients at the time of account opening whether they offer proprietary products only or a mixed/non-proprietary list of products and the implications of this to the advice the clients can expect to receive. Firms that are mutual fund dealers, exempt market dealers, scholarship plan dealers, or restricted dealers/advisers would be required to make a similar disclosure to their clients that they offer, as a result of their registration category, only a limited range of products and the impact of this limitation on the suitability analysis conducted by the firm and its representatives.
- Firms that offer mixed/non-proprietary products would be required to offer a range of products that that are appropriately representative of the reasonable universe of products most likely to meet the investment needs and objectives of their clients, based on the products that the firm is registered to advise on or trade in.
- Increased proficiency requirements for registrants and the introduction of a continuing education requirement.
- Introduction of a new requirement to NI 31-103 that explicitly prescribes all client-facing business titles for representatives.
- The introduction of an explicit statutory fiduciary duty for registrants when they manage the investment portfolio of a client through discretionary authority granted by the client.

2. Statutory Best-Interest Duty

Consultation Paper 33-404 also included detailed proposals building on the CSA's earlier consultations on the statutory best-interest duty for advisers when dealing with retail clients. The paper summarized the research conducted and commissioned by a number of CSA jurisdictions and set out the following proposal for consultation.

Canadian Securities Administrators Consultation Paper 33-404, *Proposals to Enhance the Obligations of Advisers, Dealers and Representatives Toward Their Clients*
(28 April 2016) (footnotes omitted)

Part 8 Proposed Framework for a Regulatory Best Interest Standard

Reasons all jurisdictions (except the BCSC) are consulting on the potential introduction of a regulatory best interest standard

All the jurisdictions of the CSA (except the BCSC) (the BIS Consulting Jurisdictions) are also consulting on the potential addition of a regulatory best interest standard to the current standard of care for registrants, in addition to the proposed targeted reforms set out in Part 7.

A regulatory best interest standard would require that a registered dealer or registered adviser shall deal fairly, honestly and in good faith with its clients and act in its clients' best interests, and that a representative of a registered dealer or registered adviser shall deal fairly, honestly and in good faith with his or her clients and act in his or her clients' best interests. The conduct expected of a registrant in meeting her, his or its standard of care would be that of a prudent and unbiased firm or representative (as applicable), acting reasonably. In complying with the standard of care, registrants would be guided by the following principles:

1. Act in the best interests of the client
2. Avoid or control conflicts of interest in a manner that prioritizes the client's best interests
3. Provide full, clear, meaningful and timely disclosure
4. Interpret law and agreements with clients in a manner favourable to the client's interest where reasonably conflicting interpretations arise
5. Act with care

The BIS Consulting Jurisdictions have not made a final decision on the adoption of such a standard but have articulated potential guidance in the form provided in Appendix H.

Any best interest standard in the context of Canadian securities legislation would be formulated as a regulatory conduct standard and not as a restatement or formulation of a fiduciary duty. This approach is preferable since:

- the content of the regulatory best interest standard is more comprehensive and tailored to the client-registrant relationship than a statutory fiduciary duty would be;
- the fiduciary duty and its content have developed primarily through case law. Securities regulators can appropriately express a regulatory best interest standard,

where the regulator imposes the existence and content of the standard, separate from the process undertaken in particular cases by the courts;
- fiduciary duty remedies are potentially too harsh for all instances of registrant misconduct; and
- fiduciary duty, as a common law concept with a long history and application across various disciplines and situations, lacks the upfront clarity and specificity we require, and that registrants expect, regarding registrant conduct standards that apply on a day-to-day basis.

The BIS Consulting Jurisdictions have also considered whether the use of the phrase "best interest" in the formulation automatically establishes a fiduciary duty. Our view is that it does not, since our express intention is not to establish a statutory fiduciary duty for registrants, and although the phrase "best interest" has been interpreted in some contexts as a fiduciary duty, in others it has not. With respect to the experience in the U.K. and Australia, two other common law jurisdictions, we understand that the statutory "best interest" standard in those jurisdictions does not, by itself, establish a fiduciary duty.

The OSC and the FCNB are of the current view that the introduction of a regulatory best interest standard would materially enhance the effectiveness of the proposed targeted reforms and strengthen the principled foundation of the client-registrant relationship. The OSC and FCNB believe that such a standard, as a governing principle, would have a number of benefits, such as assisting in the interpretation of more specific requirements and acting as a guide for registrants to address situations that fall between specific rules or that are novel.

The AMF, the ASC, the MSC and the NSSC are consulting on the best interest standard; however, considering the current regulatory and business environment and the research conducted by the ASC and the BCSC, all four share strong reservations on the actual benefits of the introduction of such a standard over and above the proposed targeted reforms, and are concerned with the potential unintended outcomes of the codification of such an aspirational standard of conduct. See concerns in "Reasons certain CSA jurisdictions have concerns with the potential regulatory best interest standard" below.

The FCAA recognizes that the introduction of a regulatory best interest standard would be a significant regulatory change and is interested in receiving and reviewing all comments on the proposed regulatory best interest standard.

The BIS Consulting Jurisdictions understand that there are different views on the adoption of a best interest standard, and we welcome all views. Comments will help the jurisdictions considering the adoption of a best interest standard make a decision on this matter.

The OSC and FCNB are of the view that the introduction of a regulatory best interest standard on the terms set out above would have the benefits identified below; the other BIS Consulting Jurisdictions are of the view that the regulatory best interest standard may have the identified benefits.

- *Governing principle.* A regulatory best interest standard would constitute a governing principle that would:
  - govern the interpretation of more specific regulatory requirements (e.g., those obligations related to KYC, KYP, conflicts of interest and suitability) as a result

of ambiguity, new developments or other changes in the investment environment, and
  - act as a guide for registrants and securities regulators to address situations arising in the client-registrant relationship that fall outside specific rules.
- *Closes the expectations gap.* A regulatory best interest standard, over and above the proposed targeted reforms, would help close the expectations gap between the standard of care that clients believe they are receiving from registrants and the standard of care that registrants are subject to under securities legislation. Clients would have the confidence that their relationship with a registrant is governed by a standard of care that prioritizes their interests and that this will govern the interpretation of specific rules as well as situations not presently covered by the rules. A statutory best interest standard would also align with the standard of conduct that representatives who seek to follow high standards of integrity themselves feel they already provide to their clients. In this sense, it would close this gap as well.
- *More objective, client-centered standard of care.* A regulatory best interest standard would be a more objective, client-centered standard of care than the current standard of care (i.e., dealing fairly, honestly and in good faith). At the heart of the regulatory best interest standard is a clear expectation that when registrants are faced with competing interests, their clients' interests are paramount. This would provide a more concrete, intuitive and actionable standard of care for registrants than the current standard of care.
- *Appropriate tone from the top.* The regulatory best interest standard would codify what we currently expect as a sound "tone from the top" at registrants, but now given the strength of a regulatory requirement. This would better enable management of firms to assert that the development of a strong compliance culture within the firm is the right thing to do and is a necessary risk management principle. This standard would strengthen the role of CCOs who, with their firms' knowledge, could implement the best practices to be adopted rather than accept minimum standards set out in prescriptive rules.
- *A principle-based approach allows greater flexibility for registrants.* Framing the regulatory best interest standard as a principle would allow the concept of the client's best interest to be the guiding principle that serves as guide to regulators' expectations and would allow registrants to take a flexible, tailored and contextual approach when dealing with (i) the varied conduct situations that can arise in respect of their clients, and (ii) the rapid pace of change within Canada's capital markets generally. In addition, the requirement for registrants to act in the best interest of clients and the focus on client outcomes are important elements of the proposed regulatory best interest standard that would support a principle-based approach, rather than a more prescriptive, process-based approach.
- *Investors responsible for investing to fund their retirement.* The savings landscape has changed—amounts invested by investors often constitute a major portion of their wealth and responsibility for funding the costs of living during old age is shifting more to investors. There are various causes for this change, including the shift away from defined benefit retirement plans in Canada. A regulatory best interest standard would acknowledge the critical importance of advice in savings,

including retirement, and the enormous financial stakes involved for Canadian investors.

- *Mitigates client-registrant information gap and validates clients' significant trust in registrants.* The adoption of a regulatory best interest standard may help to further mitigate concerns with the lower financial literacy of many investors by ensuring that the registrant has the clients' interests top of mind, rather than requiring clients (who may not be equipped to do so) to attempt to determine whether a particular course of action is in their best interests or not. This would place an appropriate obligation on the party to the relationship who is most often the most knowledgeable and financially literate, namely the adviser or dealer and their representatives. This aligns with what we know about clients' actual ability and/or confidence to manage their own financial affairs. It would also clarify that the registrant would be expected to objectively help formulate the client's best interests, providing a service that is necessary and appropriate for most clients. Since clients already believe that registrants must act in their best interest and place significant trust in registrants, this should not result in investors becoming less engaged in the relationship with their registrant but rather having the confidence to engage in a dialogue with a professional who is required to be unquestionably in the "client's corner."
- *Immediate impact.* The key investor protection concerns identified are so substantial that solutions could not await an iterative process of regulatory amendments if the concerns are not mitigated by such amendments or other initiatives, such as CRM2 and Point of Sale. The regulatory best interest standard would be an over-arching principle that would allow swifter regulatory action in the interests of investors where required and where registrants do not live up to the spirit of the proposed targeted reforms. While the CRM2 and the Point of Sale initiatives are important enhancements to our regime, their fundamental focus on disclosure is unlikely to sufficiently address the concerns we have identified in Part 5.
- *Assists in professionalization of advisers, dealers and representatives.* The best interest standard would assist in the progress toward the professionalization of the advisory role in Canada similar to other important services that require practitioners to comply with professional standards of conduct. Similarly, it would support and align with the evolution in organizational culture that regulators, and many registrants, have been encouraging for some time.
- *Aligns with conduct expectations of key international and domestic standard setters.* International bodies such as the International Organization of Securities Commissions (IOSCO), the Group of Twenty (G20) and the Organisation for Economic Co-operation and Development (OECD) are clear that, in the wake of the financial crisis, financial intermediaries, such as advisers and dealers, should act in their clients' best interest. International and domestic standard setters have also identified the over-arching obligation to act in the client's best interest, or to place the client's interest first, as a key component of the conduct expectation for their members.
- *Fosters confidence and trust in capital markets and strengthens investor protection.* The introduction of a regulatory best interest standard would increase confidence

and trust by investors in Canadian capital markets and would strengthen the protection for such investors. This may have the effect of encouraging investors (i) that are not currently invested in securities products to begin investing in securities products and (ii) that are currently invested in securities products to invest more of their overall financial assets in securities products.

For greater certainty, the proposed regulatory best interest standard is not intended to:

- interfere with the registration categories under Canadian securities legislation or the scope of application of those categories;
- prohibit firms from charging clients for their services;
- prohibit the offering of proprietary products by firms;
- guarantee that clients' securities investments never lose value, result in the "best" or "highest" returns for the client, or result in the lowest risk;
- always result in the lowest cost product on the firm's shelf being recommended to clients since the lowest cost product may not, based on an analysis of a client's investment needs and objectives, always be in the client's best interest; or
- interfere with the ability of courts to apply common law doctrines relating to, for example, fiduciary duty, negligence or contract law principles, to the client-registrant relationship.

The consultation paper also discussed the reasons for the lack of consensus among CSA jurisdictions as to whether the statutory best-interests standard should be introduced or should be the subject of consultation. Securities regulators from Ontario and New Brunswick both expressed the view that the proposed statutory best-interest standard would improve investor protection in Canada. Several other jurisdictions expressed significant reservations, however, stating:

> Staff of the BCSC, the AMF, the ASC, the MSC, and the NSSC (the Jurisdictions with Concerns about a BIS) have concerns with the proposed best interest standard, as follows:
>
> - The proposed best interest standard may exacerbate the expectations gap between clients and registrants because of the existing restricted registration categories and proprietary business models permitted in Canada. Clients may expect that all registrants have an unqualified duty to act in their best interests, not understanding that some conflicts would still be permitted.

The BCSC expressed similar concerns, which led them to decline to participate in the consultation altogether. One of the key reasons given for this position was that, in their view:

> The adoption of a broad, sweeping and vague best interest standard will create uncertainty for registrants and may be unworkable in the current regulatory and business environment. Introducing an over-arching duty called a best interest standard while continuing to permit certain fundamental conflicts to exist between registrants and their clients is not in the public interest. Doing so may exacerbate one of the issues we identified; the expectations gap between clients and registrants and may raise clients' expectations about investor protection that may not be realized under a best interest standard.

The current Canadian regulatory and business environment for registrants allows for a wide range of business models and registration categories. These range, on one end, from salespeople dedicated to selling only proprietary products to, on the other end, portfolio managers with fiduciary obligations over fully managed accounts. There are a host of business models between these two extremes.

For those business models that are closer to the "salesperson" end of the spectrum, it would be impossible to impose a regulatory standard on these registrants that is truly a "best interest" standard. That has been borne out through the collective experience in other jurisdictions around the world that have wrestled with fiduciary or regulatory best interest standards. It is simply not possible to require a salesperson of proprietary products only to act in a manner that is truly in an investor's best interest.

All of this is evident in the best interest standard proposed in this Consultation Paper. The proposed standard will not prohibit certain fundamental conflicts between registrants and their clients. Registrants will continue to be able to:

- sell a limited range or type of investment products (these registrants have the clear limitation that there may be nothing in the limited range of products they offer that is actually in the investor's "best interest" to buy);
- be owned by, or affiliated with, businesses that create the investment products they sell; and
- be compensated by investment product manufacturers rather than the clients they are meant to serve.

These arrangements are not consistent with what a client would expect from a standard that purportedly requires registrants to act in their "best interest."

3. *Mutual Fund Fees and Embedded Commissions*

Mutual fund fees and the manner in which intermediary advisers and firms are compensated by mutual fund manufacturers have been a focal point for critique, debate, and reform proposals in Canada and elsewhere for many years. The 2004 fair-dealing model proposal paper from the Ontario Securities Commission, discussed above, recommended enhanced disclosure to investors regarding adviser and firm compensation. Amendments in 2013 to NI 31-103, implementing what was known as "phase 2" of the client relationship model also focused on providing enhanced and simplified information to investors regarding the fees paid to investment advisers and mutual fund salespeople. These changes came into full effect for client reporting commencing in 2016.

Questions have been raised, however, about the effectiveness of disclosure as a mechanism for mitigating the conflicts of interest that may be created or exacerbated by certain adviser compensation models. Numerous factors, including low levels of financial literacy in the general public and common psychological biases, have been shown to affect how investors, advisers, and firms respond to various compensation models and have caused some to question whether compensation models that are common in the mutual fund industry, such as embedded fees, should be restricted or eliminated by regulation. In 2016, the CSA provided the following summary of research it has commissioned and considered to date on this subject.

Canadian Securities Administrators Consultation Paper 33-404, *Proposals to Enhance the Obligations of Advisers, Dealers, and Representatives Toward Their Clients*
(28 April 2016) (footnotes omitted)

National Smarter Investor Study

The National Smarter Investor Study, which was published on November 3, 2015 by the BCSC, examined client-registrant relationships in Canada. The study found that, among other things, 90% of respondents described their existing level of trust in their investment representative as strong or very strong. This trust led some clients to ask fewer questions about how their representatives were compensated and to place less importance on reading their account statements because they were confident that their representative was taking care of their money.

Fee-Based Versus Commission-Based Literature Review: The Brondesbury Report

On June 11, 2015, the CSA published a report prepared by The Brondesbury Group entitled *Mutual Fund Fee Research*. The Brondesbury Group conducted a literature review to assess the extent to which the use of fee-based versus commission-based compensation changes the nature of advice and impacts investment outcomes over the long term. The Brondesbury Group found that there is conclusive evidence that commission-based compensation creates problems that must be addressed. More specifically, the research found that:

- funds that pay a commission (sales loads and trailer fees) underperform those that do not, whether looking at raw, risk-adjusted or after-fee returns;
- representatives tend to push investors into riskier funds;
- investors cannot easily assess what form of compensation is best for them and readily make sub-optimal choices;
- representative recommendations are sometimes biased in favour of alternatives that generate more commission for the representative;
- compensation affects the effort made by representatives to overcome investor behavioural biases that may lead to sub-optimal returns; and
- while commission-based compensation is problematic, there are other conflicts that would likely persist under a fee-based model and that would affect the representative's conduct (e.g. advancement, recognition, affiliation between the investment fund manager and a dealer firm).

Fund Flows Research: The Cumming Report

On October 22, 2015, the CSA published a research paper prepared by a team led by Professor Douglas Cumming entitled *A Dissection of Mutual Fund Fees, Flows and Performance*. The paper found that conflicts of interest, specifically sales commissions and trailing commissions paid by fund companies (embedded registrant compensation), dealer affiliation and the use of deferred sales charge arrangements materially affect representative/dealer behaviour to the detriment of investor outcomes and market efficiency.

While generally, mutual fund flows should (and do) bear a relationship to the fund's past performance, the research found that:

- the payment of embedded registrant compensation and the use of deferred sales charge arrangements materially reduce the sensitivity of fund flows to past performance and increase the level of fund flows that have no relationship to performance;
- the converse is also true: fund flows for mutual fund series that do not pay embedded registrant compensation (fee-based series) are more sensitive to past performance;
- as embedded registrant compensation increases there is an associated reduction in future outperformance before fees; and
- fund flows from affiliated dealers of the investment fund manager show little to no sensitivity to past performance, and this lack of sensitivity is also associated with reduced future outperformance before fees.

. . .

Third-Party Research

In addition to the work performed or commissioned by the CSA, there is a variety of third-party research that identifies areas of concern with the client-registrant relationship, both domestically and internationally. The following sets out a short list of certain key third-party research findings.

Foerster Research

In 2014, a team of academics led by Professor Stephen Foerster published a paper entitled Retail *Financial Advice: Does One Size Fit All?* The paper focused on costs, benefits and customization of mutual fund advice and found that registrants influence investors' trading choices but that their advice materially underperforms passive investment benchmarks. Specifically, the research showed that, among other things:

- representatives induce their clients to take more risk, thereby raising clients' expected investment returns. However, they do not generally customize portfolios to their clients' attributes, but instead build very similar portfolios for all of their clients. Given the lack of customization, a question arises about why the advice is not cheaper. The paper finds that investors pay on average 2.5% of assets per year for advice. It states "if the equity premium is 6 percent, the 40-percentage point increase in risky share caused by [representatives] translates into 0.40 × 6% = 2.4% higher expected return … . But for the average investor, it is the [representative] who captures all of these additional returns";
- "[t]here is little evidence of [representatives] adding value through superior performance. The performance lag is largely due to the fees the investors pay, not due to the poor performance of the underlying assets." The significance of these negative net alphas is non-trivial (−2.91%). "Because investors could earn a net alpha of 0% by investing in the passive benchmarks, this estimate implies that the investors hand over a steady stream of potential savings year after year"; and

- "the typical investor who begins saving for retirement with a [representative] hands over a quarter of the present value of his or her retirement savings on day one."

Other Research

The findings from the Cumming Research are consistent with the findings of a research paper based on an analysis of United States (U.S.) data. Between 1993 and 2009, among U.S. mutual funds with loads or revenue sharing, higher payments to registrants led to higher inflows, suggesting that registrants' recommendations are biased by the payments they receive. Net returns are approximately 50 basis points lower for every 100 basis points of loads that are shared with registrants. This suggests biased advice, lower returns, and higher fees.

In the U.S., one study found that "[c]onflicted advice leads to lower investment returns. Savers receiving conflicted advice earn returns roughly 1 percentage point lower each year (for example, conflicted advice reduces what would be a 6 percent return to a 5 percent return)."

Another U.S. study found that "[registrants] fail to de-bias their clients and often reinforce biases that are in their interests. [Registrants] encourage returns-chasing behavior and push for actively managed funds that have higher fees, even if the client starts with a well-diversified, low-fee portfolio."

Several U.S. studies have found that conflicts of interest affect financial representatives' behavior and that registrants often act opportunistically because of payments they receive from product providers.

The current suitability process places too little emphasis on product cost despite a number of studies supporting the general position that "in virtually every single time period and data point tested, low-cost funds beat high-cost funds and costs are still the most dependable predictor of performance."

Canadian mutual fund investors are more highly invested in actively managed funds relative to fund investors in other jurisdictions. At June 2015, index-tracking funds comprised only 1.5% of the Canadian mutual fund market (excluding exchange traded funds) compared to 15.3% of the U.S. market and 11.2% of the United Kingdom (U.K.) market.

Finally, conflict disclosure, by itself, is generally an ineffective conflict mitigation strategy and may have counter-intuitive results, such as increasing reliance on conflicted advice, which results in sub-optimal outcomes for investors.

The CSA has pursued its examination of mutual fund fees in parallel with its consultation on the targeted reforms and best interest duty described above. In June 2016, the CSA published Staff Notice 81-327, *Next Steps in the CSA's Examination of Mutual Fund Fees*, which provided notice to stakeholders of securities regulators' preliminary views and upcoming consultations. The notice stated that after examining the available evidence, "the CSA find that the prevailing practice of remunerating dealers and their representatives for mutual fund sales through commissions, including sales and trailing commissions, paid by investment fund managers (embedded commissions) raises a number of investor protection and market efficiency issues that suggest a need to consider change. We believe there is considerable scope for better aligning the interests of investment fund managers and dealers/representatives with those of the investors they serve."

In Staff Notice 81-327, the CSA acknowledged that a regulatory measure such as the prohibition of embedded commissions would represent a significant change for the Canadian mutual fund industry and committed to undertaking more extensive consultation with market participants and investors before pursing such a rule change. Regulators expressed their intention to assess the consequences of eliminating embedded commissions on market participants and different types of investors in Canada, including how such a change might affect the market structure and business models for advisers and firms as well as access to advice for investors.

QUESTIONS

1. In your view, is the rationale for a statutory best-interest standard compelling? Can such a standard be practically imposed, given the current regulatory environment in Canada?
2. Should regulators continue to rely on investor education and disclosure as the principal means of mitigating the conflicts of interest that have been observed in the embedded mutual fund compensation models? What are the benefits of doing so?

VI. CHAPTER SUMMARY

This chapter has examined the regulatory environment for the intermediaries whose services are necessary for the smooth functioning of Canada's capital markets. We have considered the recent development of intermediary regulation, the current tests to determine who must be registered and the implications of registration, and the tools available to securities regulators to enforce compliance with the registration rules. We have also examined the critiques of the current system and reform proposals relating to fragmentation in the oversight of the financial advice market in Canada, the standard of conduct to which registrants are held, and the conflicts and behavioural influences presented by the fee models used to compensate those who sell securities products.

Financial market intermediaries have faced unprecedented change in their business environment over the past two decades, with significant innovation occurring on a technological level, challenges presented as a result of the economic downturn and the global financial crisis, and increasing regulatory involvement and reform. Securities regulators have always been concerned with the proficiency, solvency, and conduct of financial market intermediaries, but in recent years have become increasingly willing to engage in significant reform. Significant research is also being undertaken in relation to the impact of adviser conduct and market structure on investors, influenced strongly by the insights of behavioural economics regarding the way human decisions are influenced, often in counterintuitive ways, by external circumstances and internal biases. It remains to be seen precisely how regulators will balance the imperatives of investor protection and the promotion of efficient capital markets in light of these developments, but significant reform in this area appears inevitable.